BRITISH
COMPANY CASES
1994

CCH EDITIONS LIMITED
TAX, BUSINESS AND LAW PUBLISHERS
TELFORD ROAD, BICESTER
OXFORDSHIRE OX6 0XD
Telephone: Bicester (01869) 253300
Facsimile: Bicester (01869) 245814
DX: 83750 Bicester 2

ABOUT THE PUBLISHER

CCH Editions Limited is the UK and European affiliate of CCH Incorporated, which publishes leading tax and business law reporting services in the US.

Other CCH affiliates in Australia, Canada, New Zealand, Asia and Japan provide similar authoritative services in those countries.

A highly qualified editorial staff and many years of experience stand behind all CCH publications.

Disclaimer

This publication is intended to provide accurate information in regard to the subject matter covered. Readers entering into transactions on the basis of such information should seek the services of a competent professional adviser as this publication is sold on the understanding that the publisher is not engaged in rendering legal or accounting advice or other professional services. The publisher, reporters and editors expressly disclaim all and any liability and responsibility to any person, whether a purchaser or reader of this publication or not, in respect of anything and of the consequences of anything, done or omitted to be done by any such person in reliance, whether wholly or partially, upon the whole or any part of the contents of this publication.

Ownership of Trade Mark

The trade mark is the property of

Commerce Clearing House Incorporated, Riverwoods, Illinois, USA.
(**CCH** INCORPORATED)

ISBN 0 86325 393 8
ISSN 0269–0535

FOREWORD

British Company Cases 1994 reproduces the full text of British company law cases heard in the High Court, Court of Appeal, House of Lords, Judicial Committee of the Privy Council, Scottish Court of Session, Northern Ireland High Court, and reported during the year. Each case has a headnote outlining the facts, the decision and the reasons for the decision.

The decisions reproduced are listed alphabetically by name in the Cases Reported list. Cases and legislation referred to in the judgments are included in the Cases Cited list and the Legislation Finding List. The decisions are indexed by subject matter in the Topical Index.

Cases in this volume of *British Company Cases* should be cited as follows: [1994] BCC page. Thus the case of Nisbet v Shepherd which appears at page 91 would be cited –

Nisbet v Shepherd [1994] BCC 91.

The cases in this volume were reported by DSP Barbour, Barrister and E O'Grady, Barrister.

bcp94 prelims Mp   3

TABLE OF CONTENTS

CASES REPORTED IN 1994

This table lists all cases reported in British Company Cases 1994.
References are to pages.

Cases Reported in 1994

Cases Reported in 1994

COURTS

The following is a list of members of the judiciary in order of seniority as at 31 December 1994

Appellate Courts

House of Lords

The Lord High Chancellor: Lord Mackay of Clashfern

Lords of Appeal in Ordinary

Lord Keith of Kinkel
Lord Goff of Chieveley
Lord Jauncey of Tullichettle
Lord Browne-Wilkinson
Lord Mustill
Lord Slynn of Hadley

Lord Woolf
Lord Lloyd of Berwick
Lord Nolan
Lord Nicholls of Birkenhead
Lord Steyn

Court of Appeal

The Lord High Chancellor: Lord Mackay of Clashfern
The Lord Chief Justice of England: Lord Taylor of Gosforth
The Master of the Rolls: Sir Thomas Henry Bingham
The President of the Family Division: Sir Stephen Brown
The Vice-Chancellor: Sir Richard Rashleigh Folliott Scott

Lords Justices of Appeal

Sir Brian Thomas Neill
Sir Martin Charles Nourse
Sir Iain Derek Laing Glidewell
Sir Alfred John Balcombe
Sir Thomas Patrick Russell
Dame Ann Elizabeth Oldfield
    Butler-Sloss
Sir Murray Stuart-Smith
Sir Christopher Stephen Thomas
    Jonathan Thayer Staughton
Sir Michael Mann
Sir Donald Henry Farquharson
Sir Anthony James Denys McCowan
Sir Alexander Roy Asplan Beldam
Sir Andrew Peter Leggatt
Sir Paul Joseph Morrow Kennedy

Sir David Cozens-Hardy Hirst
Sir Simon Denis Brown
Sir Anthony Howell Meurig Evans
Sir Christopher Dudley Roger Rose
Sir Leonard Hubert Hoffmann
Sir John Douglas Waite
Sir John Ormond Roch
Sir Peter Leslie Gibson
Sir John Stewart Hobhouse
Sir Denis Robert Maurice Henry
Sir Mark Oliver Saville
Sir Peter Julian Millett
Sir Swinton Barclay Thomas
Sir Robert Andrew Morritt
Sir Philip Howard Otton

High Court of Justice
Chancery Division
The Vice-Chancellor: Sir Richard Rashleigh Folliott Scott

Sir Jeremiah LeRoy Harman
Sir John Leonard Knox
Sir William Aldous
Sir Donald Keith Rattee
Sir John Frank Mummery
Sir Francis Mursell Ferris
Sir John Murray Chadwick
Sir Jonathan Frederic Parker
Sir John Edmund Fredric Lindsay

Dame Mary Howarth Arden
Sir Edward Christopher
  Evans-Lombe
Sir Robert Raphael Hayim Jacob
Sir William Anthony Blackburne
Sir Gavin Anthony Lightman
Sir Robert Walker
Sir Robert John Anderson Carnwath
Sir Colin Percy Farquharson Rimer

Queen's Bench Division
The Lord Chief Justice of England: Lord Taylor of Gosforth

Sir Ronald Gough Waterhouse
Sir Frederick Maurice Drake
Sir Christopher James Saunders French
Sir Iain Charles Robert McCullough
Sir Oliver Bury Popplewell
Sir William Alan Macpherson of Cluny
Sir Michael Hutchison
Sir Richard Howard Tucker
Sir Robert Alexander Gatehouse
Sir Patrick Neville Garland
Sir Michael John Turner
Sir John Downes Alliott
Sir Harry Henry Ognall
Sir Konrad Hermann Theodor
  Schiemann
Sir John Arthur Dalziel Owen
Sir Francis Humphrey Potts
Sir Richard George Rougier
Sir Ian Alexander Kennedy
Sir Nicholas Addison Phillips
Sir Robin Ernest Auld
Sir Malcolm Thomas Pill
Sir Stuart Neil McKinnon
Sir Mark Howard Potter
Sir Henry Brooke
Sir Thomas Scott Gillespie Baker
Sir Igor Judge
Sir Edwin Frank Jowitt
Sir Michael Morland
Sir George Mark Waller
Sir Roger John Buckley
Sir Anthony Brian Hidden

Sir John Michael Wright
Sir Charles Barrie Knight Mantell
Sir John Christopher Calthorpe Blofeld
Sir Peter John Cresswell
Sir Anthony Tristram Kenneth May
Sir John Grant McKenzie Laws
Dame Ann Marian Ebsworth
Sir Simon Lane Tuckey
Sir David Nicholas Ramsay Latham
Sir Christopher John Holland
Sir John William Kay
Sir Richard Herbert Curtis
Sir Stephen John Sedley
Dame Janet Hilary Smith
Sir Anthony David Colman
Sir Anthony Peter Clarke
Sir John Anthony Dyson
Sir Thayne John Forbes
Sir Michael Alexander Geddes Sachs
Sir Stephen George Mitchell
Sir Rodger Bell
Sir Michael Guy Vicat Harrison
Sir Bernard Anthony Rix
Dame Anne Heather Steel
Sir William Marcus Gage
Sir Jonathan Hugh Mance
Sir Andrew Centlivres Longmore
Sir Thomas Richard Atkin Morison
Sir Richard Joseph Buxton
Sir David Wolfe Keene
Sir Andrew David Collins

Court of Session

The Court of Session, which is the highest civil tribunal in Scotland, consists of twenty-five judges four of whom, the Lord President and three judges, sit in the First Division, and the Lord Justice-Clerk and three other judges sit in the Second Division, the two Divisions together comprising the Inner House; the remaining judges officiate in the Outer House as Lords Ordinary.

Inner House Judges

First Division

Lord Hope (The Rt Hon J A D Hope PC), Lord President
Lord Allanbridge (W I Stewart)
Lord Mayfield (I MacDonald)
Lord Sutherland (R I Sutherland)

Second Division

Lord Ross (The Rt Hon D M Ross), Lord Justice-Clerk
Lord Murray (The Rt Hon R King Murray)
Lord Davidson (C K Davidson)
   (*seconded to the Scottish Law Commission*)
Lord McCluskey (The Rt Hon Lord McCluskey)
Lord Morison (A M Morison)

Outer House Judges

Lord Weir (D B Weir)
Lord Clyde (J J Clyde)
Lord Cullen (W D Cullen)
Lord Prosser (W D Prosser)
Lord Kirkwood (I C Kirkwood)
Lord Coulsfield (J T Cameron)
Lord Milligan (J G Milligan)
Lord Morton of Shuna (The Rt Hon the Lord of Morton of Shuna)
Lord Caplan (P I Caplan)
Lord Cameron of Lochbroom (The Rt Hon the Lord Cameron of Lochbroom)
Lord Marnoch (M S R Bruce)
Lord MacLean (R N M MacLean)
Lord Penrose (G W Penrose)
Lord Osborne (K H Osborne)
Lord Abernethy (J A Cameron)
Lord Johnston (ACM Johnston)
Lord Gill (B Gill)

ABBREVIATIONS

AC	Law Reports, Appeal Cases, 1891–current
ACLC	Australian Company Law Cases, 1982–current (CCH)
ACT	Advance corporation tax
A & E	Admiralty and Ecclesiastical Cases, 1865–1875
Ad & E	Adolphus & Ellis's Reports, King's Bench, 1834–1840
A-G	Attorney-General
ALJR	Australian Law Journal Reports, 1958–current
All ER	All England Law Reports, 1936–current
App Cas	Law Reports, Appeal Cases, 1875–1890
Atk	Atkyn's Reports, Chancery, 1736–1755
B & CR	Bankruptcy and Companies Winding up Cases, 1915–1942
BCC	British Company Cases, 1983–current (CCH)
BCLC	Butterworths Company Law Cases
Beav	Beavan's Reports, Rolls Court, 1838–1866
Bligh	Bligh's Reports, House of Lords, 1818–1821
BR	Bankruptcy Reports (US)
B & S	Best & Smith's Reports, Queen's Bench, 1861–1870
BTC	British Tax Cases, 1982–current (CCH)
CA 1948	Companies Act 1948 (repealed)
CA 1985	Companies Act 1985
CA 1989	Companies Act 1989
CA	Court of Appeal
CB	Common Bench Reports, 1845–1856
CCC	cwmni cyfyngedig cyhoeddus (public limited company); Cox's Criminal Cases, 1843–1941
CC(CP)A 1985	Companies Consolidation (Consequential Provisions) Act 1985
CCH	CCH Editions Limited
CEC	European Community Cases, 1989–current (CCH)
cf.	(*confer*) compare
ch. (Ch.)	chapter, Chapter (of Act)
Ch	Law Reports, Chancery Division, 1891–current
Ch App	Law Reports, Chancery Appeals, 1865–1875
ChD	Law Reports, Chancery Division, 1875–1890
CJ	Chief Justice
Cl & Fin	Clark and Finnelly's Reports, House of Lords, 1831–1846
CLC	Company Law Cases (Australia), 1971–1981 (CCH)
CLR	Commonwealth Law Reports, 1903–current (Australia)
Cmd, Cmnd, Cm	Command Paper
CMLR	Common Market Law Reports, 1962–current
Cr App R	Criminal Appeal Reports, 1908–current
Cr App R (S)	Criminal Appeal Reports (Sentencing), 1979–current
Crim LR	Criminal Law Review, 1954–current
CS(ID)A 1985	Company Securities (Insider Dealing) Act 1985

Ct Sess	Court of Session (Scotland)
cyf	cyfyngedig (limited)
D	Dunlop (Session Cases, 2nd Series) (Scotland), 1838–1862
De G M & G	De Gex, Macnaghten & Gordon's Reports, Chancery, 1851–1857
DLR; (2d); (3d); (4th)	Dominion Law Reports (Canada), 1912–1922; (Second Series), 1923–1968; (Third Series), 1969–1984; (Fourth Series), 1984–current
DTI	Department of Trade and Industry
E & B	Ellis & Blackburn's Reports, Queen's Bench, 1851–1858
ECR	European Court Reports, 1954–current
EEC	European Economic Community
EG	Estates Gazette, 1858–current
Eq	Equity Reports, 1853–1855; Equity Cases, 1866–1875
ER	English Reports, 1220–1865
ExD	Law Reports, Exchequer Division, 1875–1880
F	Federal Reporter (US); Fraser (Session Cases, 5th Series) (Scotland), 1898–1906
Fam	Law Reports, Family Division, 1972–current
F2d	Federal Reporter (Second Series) (US)
ff.	following
FLR	Family Law Reports, 1980–current; Federal Law Reports (Australia), 1956–current
FSR	Fleet Street Reports, 1963–current
F Supp	Federal Reporter Supplement (US)
FTLR	Financial Times Law Reports, 1986–1988
Hare	Hare's Reports, 1841–1853
HC	High Court
HL	House of Lords
HLCas	House of Lords Cases, 1846–1866
HMIT	Her Majesty's Inspector of Taxes
ICR	Industrial Cases Reports, 1972–current
IH	Inner House (Court of Session, Scotland)
IR	Irish Reports, 1894–current
IR 1986	Insolvency Rules 1986
J	Mr Justice
JBL	Journal of Business Law
JC	Justiciary Cases (Scotland)
KB	Law Reports, King's Bench Division, 1900–1952
LC	Lord Chancellor
LCJ	Lord Chief Justice
LJ	Lord Justice of Appeal; Law Journal Reports, New Series, 1831–1949

LJ (OS)	Law Journal Reports, Old Series, 1822–1831
Ll Rep	Lloyd's Reports, 1951–current
LR	Law Reports, from 1865
LT	Law Times Reports, 1859–1947
LTJo	Law Times Newspaper, 1843–1964
Law Soc Gazette	Law Society's Gazette
Ltd	Limited
M	Macpherson (Session Cases, 3rd Series) (Scotland), 1862–1873
Macq	Macqueen's Reports (Scotland), House of Lords, 1851–1865
Mer	Merivale's Reports, Chancery, 1815–1817
Moore Ind App	Moore's Indian Appeals, Privy Council, 1836–1872
Mor	Morison's Decisions, 1540–1808
MR	Master of the Rolls
M & S	Maule and Selwyn's Reports, King's Bench, 1813–1817
M & W	Meeson & Welsby's Reports, Exchequer, 1836–1847
My & Cr	Mylne & Craig's Reports, Chancery, 1835–1841
Myl & K	Mylne & Keen's Reports, Chancery, 1832–1835
n.b.	(nota bene) note well
ND	North Dakota
NI	Northern Ireland
	Northern Ireland Law Reports, 1925–current
NLJ	New Law Journal, 1965–current
NSWLR	New South Wales Law Reports, 1880–1900; 1971–current
NSWR	New South Wales Reports, 1960–1970
NW	North Western Reporter (US)
NZLR	New Zealand Law Reports, 1883–current
O.	Order
P	Law Reports, Probate, Divorce and Admiralty Division, 1891–1971
PC	Privy Council
P & CR	Property and Compensation Reports, 1950–current
PD	Law Reports, Probate Division, 1875–1890
plc	public limited company
PLR	Pension Law Reports, 1989–current
Price	Price's Reports, Exchequer, 1814–1824
Pt.	Part
Pty	Proprietary
P Wms	Peere Williams' Reports, Chancery and King's Bench, 1695–1735
QB	Law Reports, Queen's Bench Division, 1891–1900; 1952–current
QBD	Law Reports, Queen's Bench Division, 1875–1890
QC	Queen's Counsel
R	(regina) queen; (rex) king; Rettie (Session Cases, 4th Series) (Scotland), 1873–1898
RSC	Rules of the Supreme Court

S	Shaw (Session Cases, 1st Series) (Scotland), 1821–1838
SA	South African Law Reports, 1948–current
SALR	South Australian Law Reports, 1866–1892, 1899–1920
SASR	South Australian State Reports, 1921–current
SC	Court of Session Cases (Scotland), 1906–current
Sch.	Schedule
Sel Cas t King	Selected Chancery Cases, 1724–1733
SI	Statutory Instrument
SIB	Securities and Investments Board
Sim	Simons' Reports, Chancery, 1826–1852
SJ	Solicitors' Journal, 1857–current
SLT	Scots Law Times, 1893–current
SRO	Self-regulating Organisation
SR & O	Statutory Rules and Orders
SSAP	Statement of Standard Accounting Practice
Swan	Swanston's Chancery Reports, 1818–1819
TC	Tax Cases, 1875–current
TLR	The Times Law Reports, 1884–1952
TMA	Taxes Management Act (1970)
TPD	Transvaal Provincial Division Reports, 1902–1946
UK	United Kingdom
US	United States of America;
	United States Reports
USM	Unlisted Securities Market
v	versus
VAT	value added tax
V-C	Vice-Chancellor
Vern	Vernon's Reports, Chancery, 1680–1719
Ves Jun	Vesey junior's Chancery Reports, 1789–1817
VLR	Victorian Law Reports, 1875–1956
VR	Victorian Reports, 1870–1872; 1957–current
WLR	Weekly Law Reports, 1953–current
WN	Law Reports, Weekly Notes, 1866–1952
WN (NSW)	Weekly Notes, New South Wales, 1884–1970
¶	Paragraph

FOREIGN WORDS AND PHRASES

The following is a list of Latin and other words and phrases frequently found in decisions of the courts.

ab initio	from the beginning
ad hoc	arranged for this purpose
ad infinitum	to infinity
ad litem	for the law-suit
ad valorem	according to value
a fortiori	with stronger reason
alio intuitu	with a motive other than the ostensible and proper one
aliter	otherwise
a priori	deductively
bona fide	in good faith
caveat	warning, proviso
cadit quaestio	admitting of no further argument
certiorari	a writ, replaced by judicial review
cestui que trust	a person for whom another is trustee
contra	against
coram	before, in the presence of
corpus	the capital of a fund, as contrasted with the income
ejusdem generis	of the same kind
et al.	and others
et seq. (et sequens)	and the following
ex abundanti cautela	from excess of caution
ex debito justitiae	a remedy applicable as of right
ex gratia	as a favour
ex parte	an application in a judicial hearing made by one party in the absence of the other
hic	this, here
ibidem (ibid.)	in the same place
infra	below
in limine	at the outset
in loco parentis	in the position of parent
in re	in the matter of
in situ	in place
in specie	in its actual state, in kind
inter alia	among other things
inter partes	between or among the parties
inter se	among themselves
inter vivos	during lifetime
in toto	entirely
intra vires	within the powers of, e.g. a company
lis	legal action
locum tenens	a substitute
mandamus	a writ
modus operandi	a plan of working

bcp94 prelims Mp   18

mutatis mutandis	in the same manner with appropriate changes for the context
nisi	unless
nisi prius	unless before
obiter dictum	a judicial expression of opinion on a matter, not essential to the decision, and therefore not a binding authority
pari passu	rateable
passim	in various places
per alium	by means of another
per curiam	by the court
per diem	daily
per se	by itself, taken alone
prima facie	at first sight
pro rata	in proportion
quantum	a concrete quantity
quantum meruit	as much as he deserved
quid pro quo	consideration
re	in the matter of
res judicata	an issue already decided judicially
semble	it appears
sc. (scilicet)	namely, understand
sic	thus
simpliciter	without addition or qualification
sine qua non	an indispensable condition
stricto sensu	in its strict meaning
sub judice	in course of trial
sub nom	under the name of
sub voce	under a specified word
supra	above
ultra vires	beyond the powers, e.g. of (the directors of) a company
vide	see
viz. (videlicet)	in other words, namely

1994

BRITISH COMPANY CASES

Cited [1994] BCC

Re Unisoft Group Ltd.
Saunderson Holdings Ltd v Unisoft Group Ltd & Ors.

Court of Appeal (Civil Division).
Parker and Scott L JJ and Sir Michael Kerr.
Judgment delivered 11 June 1992.

Security for costs – Unfair prejudice petition – Whether court could order limited company presenting unfair prejudice petition to give security for costs – Companies Act 1985, s. 459, 726(1).

The Court of Appeal upheld the judgment of Morritt J [1992] BCC 494 that a limited company which presented a petition under s. 459 of the Companies Act 1985 was a 'plaintiff in an action or other legal proceeding' within the meaning of s. 726(1) of the 1985 Act and could be ordered to give security for costs.

The following cases were referred to in the judgment of Scott LJ:

Buckley v Bennell Design and Construction Pty Ltd (1974) 1 ACLR 301.
Crystal Theatres Ltd v Fuss (1940) 57 WN (NSW) 107.
Jamieson (J & W) Construction Ltd v Christchurch City Council [1986] 3 NZCLC 99,611.

Terence Cullen QC and Anthony Trace (instructed by Pothecary & Barratt) for the petitioner.

Robin Potts QC and Catherine Roberts (instructed by Mishcon de Reya) for the respondents.

JUDGMENT

Scott LJ: This appeal, from the judgment of Morritt J given on 12 March 1992 [1992] BCC 494, raises a short question of law. The question is whether the court has power under s. 726 of the *Companies Act* 1985 to order a petitioner under a s. 459 petition to give security for the costs of the petition. Section 726(1) is in these terms:

'Where in England and Wales a limited company is plaintiff in an action or other legal proceeding, the court having jurisdiction in the matter may, if it appears by credible testimony that there is reason to believe that the company will be unable to pay the defendant's costs if successful in his defence, require sufficient security to be given for those costs, and may stay all proceedings until the security is given.'

Subsection (2) introduces a like provision for Scotland.

A provision in substantially the same terms as the terms of s. 726 was introduced in the *Companies Act* 1862 and has formed part of companies legislation ever since. But it appears that the question whether the reference in s. 726, and its statutory predecessors, to 'plaintiff in an action or other legal proceeding' is to be narrowly construed or includes a petitioner under a petition has never previously been before the courts for decision.

The argument addressed to Morritt J was that 'plaintiff' meant plaintiff strictly so-called and could not be read so as to include a petitioner under a petition. Morritt J did not accept that submission. He held, first, that the reference in s. 726(1) to 'or other legal proceeding' would include originating summonses, originating notices of motion and also petitions. It was, I think, accepted before him by counsel then appearing for the appellant, Mr Trace, who is junior counsel before us, that the phrase was apt to include an originating summons or an originating notice of motion. But it was argued before the judge that it did not cover a petition. The judge concluded that there was no reason for limiting the scope of the reference and that the expression 'other legal proceeding' covered any other legal proceedings, whether petitions or any other form of originating process. The judge then turned to consider the meaning to be given to the word 'plaintiff' and concluded, consistently with what he had held was the meaning of 'other legal proceeding', that the word covered the person however called who originated the originating process in question. He said at p. 496C:

> 'It seems to me that "plaintiff" is used, in the context of both "action" or "other legal proceeding", not as indicating a person conventionally described as a plaintiff alone but as pointing to the person who has invoked the jurisdiction of the court by whichever form of originating process he has chosen, resulting in either an "action" or "other legal proceeding". It seems to me that that must have been the view of Parliament over the successive re-enactments of the Companies Act ever since 1862 because there cannot, as I see it, be any logic in a system whereby there is jurisdiction to order security for costs against a limited company which is a plaintiff strictly so-called in a writ action or in certain types of originating summons or originating notice of motion but not in other types of originating summons, originating notice of motion and not in petitions at all.'

Mr Cullen before us has advanced the argument for the appellant on a broader and rather different front. Mr Cullen has accepted that the jurisdiction under s. 726(1) to order security for costs would apply to petitions and, indeed, I think all forms of originating process, whether commenced by writ, originating summons, originating notice of motion, or petition. But he contends that the jurisdiction does not permit security for costs to be ordered in respect of any proceedings commenced under the *Companies Act* 1985. Under the *Companies Act* 1985, as originally enacted, not only petitions under s. 459 were provided for, but also ordinary winding-up petitions. Winding-up petitions are now provided for under s. 124 of the *Insolvency Act* 1986, but Mr Cullen's submission would cover those petitions as well as having been originally catered for in the *Companies Act* 1985.

The point argued by Mr Cullen before us was not argued before the judge, so we do not have his comments on it. It requires s. 726(1) to be read with the addition of some such words as 'other than any proceedings under this Act'.

In considering the weight to be given to Mr Cullen's submissions there are other statutory provisions to which reference can conveniently be made.

Order 23 of the Rules of the Supreme Court deals with security for costs in certain specified circumstances. It represents a codification of the rules which had previously been formulated for enabling, in certain circumstances, orders for security for costs to be made. The circumstances do not include impecuniosity or poverty. Order 23, r. 1(1) gives the court power 'on the application of a defendant to an action or other proceeding in the High Court' to order 'the plaintiff' to give security for 'the defendant's costs of the action'. This power in O. 23 is additional to the power conferred by s. 726 of the *Companies Act* 1985. The O. 23 power is not confined to corporate plaintiffs. Order 23, r. 1(3) provides that:

A

'references . . . to a plaintiff and a defendant shall be construed as references to the person (howsoever described on the record) who is in the position of plaintiff or defendant, as the case may be, in the proceeding in question . . .'

That definition of 'plaintiff' makes it clear that the expression is apt to cover the person howsoever called who commenced any originating process in the High Court.

B

A petition, whether a winding-up petition under s. 124 of the *Insolvency Act* 1986 or a petition under s. 459 of the *Companies Act* 1985, is plainly, in my opinion, an 'other proceeding' for the purposes of O. 23. Order 23, r. 1(3) requires references to a plaintiff to include the petitioner under a s. 459 petition. I can see no reason why s. 726 should be given a narrower scope, so far as the meaning of 'plaintiff' is concerned, than O. 23. The expression 'other legal proceeding' in s. 726 is, as a matter of ordinary language, apt to include a petition. There is no reasonable construction which would permit the exclusion of proceedings brought under the provisions of the *Companies Act* 1985. Simply reading s. 726 in its context, and notwithstanding the absence of any definition of what is meant by the expression 'plaintiff', the expression should in my opinion, consistently with that formed by Morritt J, be construed so as to include the person who is in the position of plaintiff in the legal proceeding in question. It seems to me that Mr Cullen's arguments, in distinction to those advanced by Mr Trace below, accept that, in general, this is so. Mr Cullen accepted that 'plaintiff' in s. 726 would cover, for example, a petitioner under a petition made under the Patents Acts, and would cover an applicant, so described, in an originating summons. He was thereby accepting that the expression 'plaintiff' should be given the sensible, broad meaning that was favoured by the judge below and that I myself would adopt.

C

D

It is interesting to notice also that in s. 225 of the *Supreme Court of Judicature (Consolidation) Act* 1925, the expression 'plaintiff' was defined as including:

E

'every person asking any relief . . . against any other person by any form of proceeding, whether the proceeding is by action, suit, petition, motion, summons or otherwise . . .'

That definition was not repeated in the *Supreme Court Act* 1981, which repealed the *Supreme Court of Judicature (Consolidation) Act* 1925, but the reason for that was not any legislative dissatisfaction with the definition, but was because there was no longer any need for the definition. In my opinion that broad definition of 'plaintiff' colours all references to 'plaintiff' in the rules and colours the references to 'plaintiff' in the successive Companies Acts.

F

In the appellant's skeleton argument various reasons are put forward for suggesting that a narrower meaning should be given to the expression 'plaintiff' in s. 726. One point relied on was s. 12(6) of the *Arbitration Act* 1950 whereby, under para. (a), the High Court was given the same power to make orders for security for costs of an arbitration 'as it has for the purpose of and in relation to an action or matter in the High Court'. This statutory provision, it was suggested in the skeleton argument, indicated that s. 726 would not by itself have enabled security for costs of an arbitration to be ordered. It seems to me, however, that s. 12(6) of the *Arbitration Act* 1950 was, so far as security for costs is concerned, directed to O. 23 of the Rules of the Supreme Court rather than to s. 726 of the *Companies Act* 1985. Order 23 would not by itself have applied to an arbitration. An arbitration could not be described as an action or other proceeding in the High Court. So s. 12(6) of the *Arbitration Act* 1950 was necessary to extend to arbitrations the O. 23 power to make orders for security for costs. Moreover, s. 726 draws no distinction between and applies equally to proceedings in the High Court and proceedings in the county court. Section 12(6) of the *Arbitration Act* 1950 is concerned only with High Court powers. It seems to me that s. 12(6) is no indication that a restrictive construction of 'plaintiff' in s. 726 should be adopted.

G

H

It was suggested also in the skeleton argument that Parliament, in providing by s. 459   A
a special right for minority shareholders or aggrieved shareholders to petition the court
on grounds of unfair prejudice, was unlikely to have intended that that right should be
cut down by being made subject to the provision in s. 726 for security for costs. But an
order for security for costs is always discretionary and an order for security for costs will
not be made if the court concludes that it would be unfair to make it. For my part I think
it would be much more unlikely that Parliament intended that insolvent limited liability
companies should be permitted to petition under s. 459 without any risk of having to give   B
security for costs under s. 726.

It was pointed out also that, if s. 726 applies to a petition under s. 459, it must by the
same reasoning apply to winding-up petitions now under s. 124 of the *Insolvency Act*
1986. I think the logic of this is sound, but I do not agree that the result would be to
impede the workings of the Companies Court as is suggested in the skeleton argument. I
do not think it likely that there would be a spate of applications for security for costs. If   C
a winding-up petition is based upon an undisputed debt, the applicant is entitled, *ex*
debito justitiae as it is sometimes put, to a winding-up order. It would make no difference
whether or not the applicant were an impecunious company. On the other hand, if there
were a genuine dispute about the debt on which the winding-up petition was based, the
petition would be dismissed, or at best stayed, whether or not the corporate petitioner
were impecunious. The proposition that dire consequences damaging to the efficient
functioning of the Companies Court would follow if s. 726 applies to petitions is, in my   D
opinion, fanciful.

It is interesting to notice, as is pointed out in the skeleton argument submitted on
behalf of the respondents, who we have not called upon, that similar legislation in
Australia and New Zealand has been given the wide construction that s. 726 was given
by Morritt J. There was reference to *Crystal Theatres Ltd v Fuss* (1940) 57 WN(NSW)
107, *Buckley v Bennell Design and Construction Pty Ltd* (1974) 1 ACLR 301 and *J & W*   E
Jamieson Construction Ltd v Christchurch City Council [1986] 3 NZCLC 99,611.

Returning to the particular point argued before this court by Mr Cullen, there is, in
my judgment, no justification whatever for reading into s. 726 some such words as would
be apt to exclude any proceedings brought under the *Companies Act* 1985 or other
companies legislation. In my judgment Morritt J was quite right in the view that he took
about the scope of s. 726 and I would dismiss this appeal.   F

Sir Michael Kerr: I agree and there is nothing I wish to add.

Parker LJ: I agree. It is accepted that the appeal must be dismissed unless this court is
prepared to read into s. 726 some such word as 'other than proceedings under this Act'
or 'other than proceedings in the Companies Court'. The suggestion that it is open to this
court and that this court should produce such wording is, in my judgment, without
foundation. When this Act was drafted, the legislators were well aware that the Act was   G
providing for a number of proceedings under the Act. The notion that Parliament
intended that there should be excluded all proceedings in the Companies Court, without
any mention having been made of that matter, appears to me to be an argument which
cannot possibly succeed and I, too, would dismiss this appeal.

(*Appeal dismissed with costs to be taxed and paid forthwith. Leave to appeal to the House*
of Lords refused)   H

Re Polly Peck International plc, ex parte the joint administrators.

Chancery Division (Companies Court).

Vinelott J.

Judgment delivered 28 January 1993.

Insolvency – Private examination – Director disqualification – Secretary of State sought disclosure of transcripts of interviews and documents obtained under threat of private examination powers – Whether disclosure would be for purposes of the administration – Insolvency Act 1986, s. 236; Company Directors Disqualification Act 1986, s. 7.

Administrators could disclose to the Secretary of State for the purpose of director disqualification proceedings the transcripts of interviews conducted, and documents provided, pursuant to powers in s. 236 of the Insolvency Act 1986, because such disclosure would be for the purposes of the administration.

Leslie Kosmin (instructed by Alsop Wilkinson) for the administrators.

AWH Charles (instructed by the Treasury Solicitor) for the Secretary of State.

JUDGMENT

Vinelott J: I had thought I should defer giving judgment in order to give a considered judgment in open court because the point is one I think likely to arise in the future. I have come to the conclusion that speed is of greater importance and that I should not delay in stating my conclusion which, as I have said, is a clear one.

I am concerned with a group of people who have been interviewed by one or other of the sets of administrators, for the most part by the team headed by Mr Morris. They are mostly persons who were under a duty under s. 235 of the *Insolvency Act* 1986 to give information and attend on the office-holder. Some were not, but they fell within s. 236 and in their case interviews were conducted and documents were provided under the threat that otherwise an order would be sought under s. 236.

In all these cases assurances were given, which although given in varying terms, can be expressed by saying that information given in the course of an interview and documents provided would not be disclosed by the office-holder, but would be used only for the purposes of the administration. The question is whether disclosing transcripts of the interviews and copies of the documents to the Secretary of State would or would not be for the purposes of the administration? If I felt any doubt about the answer to this question I would, of course, require that those persons be given notice before any such disclosure was made because it would be unfair, if there were doubt, that the office-holder should be put in a position where he might on one view be thought to have broken his assurance or undertaking. As I have said, I do not myself feel that any doubt can be entertained.

Under the *Company Directors Disqualification Act* 1986, s. 7(1), the Secretary of State, if it appears to him that it is expedient in the public interest that a disqualification order should be made, can make an application. He has a very limited period within which to make the application. He has power under subs. (4) to require an office-holder:

'(a) to furnish him with such information with respect to any person's conduct as a director of the company, and

(b) to produce and permit inspection of such books, papers and other records relative to that person's conduct as such a director,

as the Secretary of State or the official receiver may reasonably require for the purpose of determining whether to exercise, or of exercising, any function of his under this section.'

To my mind it is quite clear that the purposes of the administration must include the   A
gathering of information as to the conduct of the affairs of the company and those
responsible for it by an administrator in order that he can report to the Secretary of State
as he is required to do. He must do so in order that the Secretary of State can perform
his duty, which is the important one of taking proceedings if it appears that a
disqualification order should be made.

The importance of the prompt getting together of this information and of the report   B
of the Secretary of State is apparent, as I have said, from the very brief timetable in
subs. (3) as interpreted by the courts. Indeed, in this case the period had elapsed before a
full report could be made and an application had to be made for leave to make the
application out of time. That application is pending until such time as the Secretary of
State is prepared with an affidavit founded in turn upon a full report and on a disclosure
of all relevant information, and of course the court will not give leave unless the affidavit
detailing the grounds on which the order is sought can be served with the application.   C

In my judgment there is in this context no balancing of public interest or, to put it
another way, the public interest is itself identified and given priority by imposing these
duties. Some reliance was placed on Pt. 9 of the Insolvency Rules. That group of rules
deals with examination of persons concerned in company insolvency. Under r. 9.5(1) the
record of an examination is not to be filed unless the court otherwise directs. If it is filed
it is not open to inspection without the leave of the court by any person other than an   D
applicant under an applicable section or person who could have applied for the order in
respect of the same insolvency.

In my judgment that rule has nothing whatever to do with this case. It is dealing with
the way in which the record is dealt with by the court, whether it is to be filed and, if filed,
with the inspection of it. I am concerned with the anterior question whether the Secretary
of State has the right to require the administrator to furnish him with copies of any   E
examination or documents provided in pursuance of the duties I have described. He does
not and does not need to seek the leave of the court to inspect matters on the court file.
That I think is all I need say about the important category of those to whom assurances
or undertakings were given in the terms I have mentioned.

There are two interviewees whose position is at first sight nearer the borderline,
Mr Ellis and Mr Sizco (who has since died). I take the view, looking at the affidavit of
Mr Coleman and the exhibited correspondence, that it is quite clear that no assurance   F
or undertaking was given or is represented as having been given by the administrators
before Mr Ellis' interview. What he says in his letter of 4 March is that he entered into
the interview in good faith and on that basis expected and understood that it would not
be disclosed and had no reason to doubt the good faith of the administrators. If he
formed a false impression as to the scope of the administrator's duties and of the use
which he was required by statute to make of information which he obtained, that is his   G
own fault. Mr Sizco is perhaps nearer the borderline because Mr Coleman says that he
has been advised by the person who conducted the interview that it was on the basis of 'a
request for strict confidentiality' and that there should be no note taken. Again, it seems
to me that confidentiality is not really in issue where documents are disclosed to the
Secretary of State who has power to require them to be furnished in order that he may
consider taking proceedings under the Company Directors Disqualification Act. I accept
that there is perhaps an area of doubt and if Mr Sizco were living I think I would be   H
inclined as a precaution to require that he be notified before the record of the interview is
handed over. However, he is dead and it seems to me it would be going altogether too far
to require his personal representatives or anybody else to be notified.

There are two minor matters. It is clear that as regards documents provided with the
aid of the Swiss courts further guidance will have to be sought from those courts. As

A   regards the undertaking given in the course of proceedings started by Polly Peck against Mr Nadir and others on 6 February 1992, I propose to express no opinion whether disclosure of information furnished for the purposes of the administration is or is not within the terms of the undertaking. The matter has been debated in argument and Mr Kosmin will no doubt consider the matter further. If necessary an application will have to be made to Knox J to modify the undertaking.

B

(*Order accordingly*)

C

D

E

F

G

H

Stroud Architectural Systems Ltd v John Laing Construction Ltd.

A

Official Referees' Business.
His Honour Judge John Newey QC.
Judgment delivered 2 February 1993.

*Conversion – Retention of title – Preliminary issue – Whether supplier of goods
to insolvent company could maintain action in conversion – Whether retention of
title clause created charge – Whether charge was created by buyer – Whether
transfer of title and grant-back of security occurred simultaneously.*

B

This was a preliminary issue in an action by the plaintiffs, manufacturers and suppliers of
glazing, against defendant building contractors, claiming in conversion the return of certain
glazing units for which they had not been paid or their value. The plaintiffs had supplied the
units to glazing fixers ('TCCI') employed by the defendants as subcontractors to supply and
fix glazing on a building. The preliminary issue was whether upon a true construction of the
contract under which the plaintiffs supplied glazing to TCCI they retained title to it and
whether they had sufficient interest in the glazing and right to its possession to succeed
against the defendants in conversion.

C

Held, ruling accordingly:

1. Legal title passed to TCCI, the retention of title clause created a charge and not a
simple trust, the chargor was TCCI and not the plaintiffs, and the charge was a floating
charge and should have been registered. (Re Bond Worth Ltd [1980] Ch 228 followed.)

D

2. The transfer of title and grant-back of security occurred completely simultaneously.
(Abbey National Building Society v Cann & Anor [1991] 1 AC 56 applied.)

3. The plaintiffs' unregistered floating charge was valid against the defendants. An
equitable interest in goods coupled with a right to possess them was sufficient to enable a
valid claim to be made in conversion. (International Factors Ltd v Rodriguez [1979] QB 351
applied.)

E

4. However, even if the plaintiffs' equitable interest was sufficient (although void against
the receiver and creditors of TCCI), unless the charge had ceased to float and become
specific the plaintiffs did not have a right to possession.

The following cases were referred to in the judgment:

F

Abbey National Building Society v Cann & Anor [1991] 1 AC 56.
Aluminium Industrie Vaassen BV v Romalpa Aluminium Ltd [1976] 1 WLR 676.
Andrabell Ltd, Re [1984] 3 All ER 407.
Bond Worth Ltd, Re [1980] Ch 228.
Clough Mill Ltd v Martin [1985] 1 WLR 111.
Hendy Lennox (Industrial Engines) Ltd v Grahame Puttick Ltd [1984] 1 WLR 485.
Illingworth v Houldsworth & Anor [1904] AC 355.
International Factors Ltd v Rodriguez [1979] QB 351.

G

D J Pearce-Higgins (instructed by Church & Church) for the plaintiff.

Charles Cory-Wright (instructed by the solicitor for John Laing Construction plc) for
the defendant.

H

JUDGMENT

His Honour Judge John Newey QC: In this case the plaintiffs, Stroud Architectural
Systems Ltd, manufacturers and suppliers of glazing, have brought an action against the
defendants, John Laing Construction plc, building contractors, claiming in conversion
the return of certain glazing units for which they have not been paid or their value. The

A   plaintiffs had supplied the units to TCC International ('TCCI'), glazing fixers, who had been employed by the defendants as subcontractors to supply and fix glazing on a building, which the defendants were erecting for Janssens Pharmaceutical in Wantage, Berkshire. The defendants deny liability to the plaintiffs, asserting among other things that TCCI as a buyer in possession of the glazing sold it to them and that they thereby acquired a good title to them.

B   The parties have agreed that I should try preliminary issues in the case, which in substance are whether upon a true construction of the contract under which the plaintiffs supplied glazing to TCCI they retained title to it and whether they now have sufficient interest in the glazing and right to its possession to succeed against the defendants in conversion.

The contract for the supply of glazing between the plaintiffs and TCCI was concluded
C   in January 1992, and was on the basis of the plaintiffs' standard terms and conditions of business, which included the following:

'8. PROPERTY AND RISK. Ownership.

The equitable and beneficial ownership in all or any goods supplied or procured by (the plaintiffs) shall remain with (the plaintiffs) until payment in cash or cleared funds has been received in respect of all and any sums owed howsoever by the
D   buyer to (the plaintiffs) in respect of goods supplied.

In the event of any prior resale (the plaintiffs') beneficial entitlement shall attach to the proceeds of resale or to any claim for such proceeds.

In the event that (the plaintiffs) consider that the buyer is insolvent or about to become so (the plaintiffs) its authorised agents and representatives are hereby granted the right by the buyer of right of access to or egress from the property of
E   the buyer in order to identify and recover therefrom any (plaintiffs') goods in the possession of or any otherwise under the control of the buyer for which (the plaintiffs) have not been paid in full. Prior notice shall not be required but any such visits will only be made within reasonable business hours unless the prevailing circumstances render this impracticable.

The risk in the goods shall pass to the buyer on delivery to the buyer or the buyer's
F   carrier or when payment in full is made by the buyer, whichever is earlier.

16. TERMINATION ON THE BUYER'S BANKRUPTCY.

If the buyer commits any act of bankruptcy or makes any arrangement with his creditors or being a company enters into liquidation whether compulsory or voluntary . . . or have any receiver or administrator appointed or suffers any
G   execution whether legal or equitable to be levied upon his property or obtained against him then (the plaintiffs) may without prejudice to any other rights or remedies available to (them) by written notice forthwith determine the contract whereupon (the plaintiffs) shall have the right to recover any amount otherwise due together with the amount of damage suffered and/or loss and expense incurred (by the plaintiffs) by reason of the determination of this contract under this clause (the plaintiffs) shall additionally be entitled to enter upon any premises owned by
H   the buyer or at which the buyer was working to detach, recover and repossess all goods, materials, equipment or otherwise as may have been supplied by or on behalf of (the plaintiffs).

17.3 HEADINGS

Paragraph headings are for ease of reference and shall not affect interpretation.

17.4 COMPLETE AGREEMENT

These terms and conditions constitute the entire contract between (the plaintiffs) and the buyer . . .'

Between February and April the plaintiffs delivered the glazing to site; at the beginning of April TCCI informed them that they were no longer able to meet their obligations; on 3 April they wrote to the defendants claiming retention of title to materials supplied; and on 6 April TCCI went into administrative receivership. No charge had been registered in favour of the plaintiffs under s. 395 of the *Companies Act* 1985.

On 7 April the plaintiffs' solicitors sent a fax to TCCI's solicitors asserting that the plaintiffs were entitled to recover the glazing because of the retention of title clause. TCCI's solicitors replied immediately asking for an assurance that the plaintiffs would not enter on to 'any of the sites with a view to retrieving their items until after the administrative receivers had had an opportunity of considering (their) reservation of title claims'. On 15 April the plaintiffs' solicitors faxed and wrote asserting title to TCCI's solicitors with copies to the defendants and others. There followed letters between solicitors, in none of which was it asserted or admitted that the contract between the plaintiffs and TCCI had been terminated.

Both Mr Pearce-Higgins, who appeared for the plaintiffs, and Mr Cory-Wright, who appeared for the defendants, have cited numbers of cases and textbooks to me. I have considered them all, but I will refer specifically only to four cases which seem to me to be the most important.

In *Re Bond Worth Ltd* [1980] Ch 228, sellers sold man-made fibres to carpet manufacturers under the terms of contracts which provided that from 1 July 1976 (see pp. 235–236):

'(a) . . . equitable and beneficial ownership shall remain with (the sellers) until full payment has been received or until prior resale, in which case (the sellers') beneficial entitlement shall attach to the proceeds of resale or to the claim for such proceeds.

(b) Should the goods become constituents of or be converted into other products while subject to our equitable and beneficial ownership we shall have the equitable and beneficial ownership in such other products as if they were solely and simply the goods . . .'

In August 1977, the buyers went into receivership, whereupon the sellers claimed title to goods for which they had not been paid, except for those which had been resold in respect of whose proceeds of sale they claimed an interest.

Slade J held at pp. 245–247 that on delivery of the goods legal title to them passed to the buyers, who could sell them or use them for purposes of manufacture and who did not become bailees of the goods for the sellers. The judge said at p. 248E that the court was bound to look at the substance of the transaction and that:

'any contract which, by way of security for the payment of a debt, confers an interest in property defeasible or destructible upon payment of such debt . . . must necessarily be regarded as creating a mortgage or charge . . .'

He said that three features of a charge, namely chargor's right to redeem, chargee's obligation to account to chargor for any surplus realised on sale of subject-matter and chargor's obligation if sale produced less than amount of debt to pay the difference, were all present. At p. 249 the judge said that the language and stipulations of the contracts deprived the phrase 'equitable and beneficial ownership' of its primary meaning, which could have created a trust under which the seller was sole beneficiary, but gave rise to charges in favour of the seller.

A   Slade J went on to consider whether the charges were created by the sellers or by the buyers. He said at p. 253E:

B
> 'no authority has been cited which satisfies me that on the transfer of the legal property in land or chattels, it is competent to a vendor expressly to except from the grant in favour of himself an equitable . . . charge thereon to secure the unpaid purchase price . . . in such manner that the exception will take effect without any express or implied grant back of a . . . charge . . . In the case of either land or personal property, an express or implied grant back in favour of the original grantor is in my judgment required to create such . . . charge. If the court is satisfied that both parties to a transaction of sale have contracted that the vendor shall have defined rights by way of . . . charge over the subject matter of the sale, no doubt it will be prepared to imply the necessary grant back of such rights by the purchaser . . . This does not, however, remove the theoretical necessity of a grant back.'

C   At p. 256B Slade J gave his conclusion:

> '. . . that the proper manner of construing the retention of title clause, together with all the other relevant provisions of the contracts of sale read as a whole, is to regard them as effecting a sale in which the entire property in the (goods) passes to (the buyer) followed by a security, eo instanti, given back by (the buyer) to the vendor . . . In my judgment, therefore, (the buyer) rather than (the seller) must be regarded as creator of the relevant charge . . .'

D
Slade J next considered whether one of the three 'certainties' required for the existence of a valid trust was absent, namely certainty of subject-matter, because of the buyer's rights to sell the goods or incorporate them in other goods. At p. 266B the judge said:

E
> 'Does the authority and freedom of (the buyer), to which I have last referred, by itself negative the existence of a valid trust by way of equitable charge? In my judgment, in so far as it might be suggested that the clause operated to create in this manner an immediate *specific* charge, the answer to this question must be "yes". It is in my judgment quite incompatible with the existence of an effective trust by way of specific charge in equity over specific assets that the alleged trustee should be free to use them as he pleases for his own benefit in the course of his own business.'

F   The judge then mentioned 'floating charges' which can be granted by companies and as to the distinction between them and specific charges quoted from the description of them by Lord Macnaghten in *Illingworth v Houldsworth* [1904] AC 355 at p. 358:

> 'A specific charge, I think, is one that without more fastens on ascertained and definite property or property capable of being ascertained and defined; a floating charge, on the other hand, is ambulatory and shifting in its nature, hovering over and so to speak floating with the property which it is intended to affect until some event occurs or some act is done which causes it to settle and fasten on the subject matter of the charge within its reach and grasp.'

G
Slade J decided that the charges, which he had already held had been granted by the buyers were floating and, therefore, valid. Unfortunately, however, for the sellers, s. 95(1) of the *Companies Act* 1948 (substantially the same as s. 395 of the Act of 1985) provided that floating charges should be void against a liquidator or creditor of a company unless registered and the charges had not been registered.

H   In *Clough Mill Ltd v Martin* [1985] 1 WLR 111, *Bond Worth*'s case was considered. In *Clough Mill* sellers had sold yarn to buyers for resale or use in manufacturing fabric. The contract between them had among other things provided that the ownership of the material should remain with the sellers until they were paid or until the buyers sold the material to customers. On the appointment of a receiver to the buyers the sellers asserted title to the yarn and on the receiver permitting the buyers to continue manufacturing with it, brought an action in conversion against him. The judge at first instance dismissed the action holding that the retention of title clause created a charge on the yarn and that the charge was void for non-registration. The Court of Appeal allowed the appeal because the sellers had retained legal title to the yarn, the buyer could not create a charge on it and the sellers were entitled to recover it.

Goff LJ said at p. 116G:

> 'I for my part can see nothing objectionable in an agreement between parties under which A, the owner of goods gives possession of those goods to B, at the same time conferring upon B a power of sale and a power to consume the goods in manufacture, though A will remain the owner of the goods until they are either sold or consumed. I do not see why the relationship between A and B, pending sale or consumption, should not be the relationship of bailor and bailee, even though A has no right to trace the property in the goods into the proceeds of sale.'

On counsel for the receiver praying in aid Slade J's words at p. 248 in *Bond Worth*, which I have set out above, to the effect that conferring an interest defeasible on payment creates a mortgage or charge. Goff LJ said (at p. 119C):

> 'I see no difficulty in distinguishing the present case from that envisaged by Slade J. Under the . . . condition, the buyer does not, by way of security, *confer* on (the seller) an interest in property defeasible upon the payment of the debt so secured. On the contrary, the (seller) *retains* the legal property in the material.'

Oliver LJ and Sir John Donaldson MR agreed with Goff LJ. The Master of the Rolls said at p. 125D:

> '. . . it is possible to achieve security for an unpaid purchase price in different ways, with different legal consequences. The parties have chosen not to use the charging method . . .'

In *Abbey National Building Society v Cann* [1991] 1 AC 56 a son, who had previously received assistance from his mother in buying a house and had promised that she would always have a roof over her head, bought a house for occupation by her and a man whom she subsequently married. He bought the house with money obtained by means of mortgage and when he subsequently defaulted in payments under it the building society sought possession of the house. The mother and her husband claimed an equitable interest in the house, which by virtue of the mother's actual occupation of it when the mortgage was created they asserted had priority over the mortgage. The House of Lords held that when the son bought with the aid of a mortgage, the acquiring of the legal estate and the granting of the mortgage were one indivisible transaction, there was no *scintilla temporis* during which he held the legal estate free of the charge and during which his mother could have been in occupation. Lord Oliver of Aylmerton said at p. 92:

> '. . . as a matter of legal theory, a person cannot charge a legal estate that he does not have . . . Nevertheless, I cannot help feeling that it flies in the face of reality. The reality is that, in the vast majority of cases, the acquisition of the legal estate and the charge are not only precisely simultaneous but indissolubly bound together. The reality is that the purchaser of land who relies upon a building society or bank loan for the completion of his purchase never in fact acquires anything but an equity of redemption, for the land is, from the very inception, charged with the amount of the loan without which it could never have been transferred at all and it was never intended that it should be otherwise.'

In *International Factors Ltd v Rodriguez* [1979] QB 351, the plaintiffs by a factoring agreement purchased debts owing to a company of which the defendant was a director. The agreement provided that in the event of assigned debts being paid to the company, it would hold them in trust for the plaintiffs and immediately hand them over to them. In breach of the agreement four cheques sent to the company in respect of assigned debts were paid into the company's bank account on instructions from the defendant. At first instance I held that the defendant was liable in conversion. The Court of Appeal upheld me: Sir David Cairns, with whom Bridge LJ agreed, because the plaintiffs had an equitable title to the goods and an immediate right to possession; and Buckley LJ on the grounds that they had contractual rights which were sufficient.

To return to the plaintiffs' standard terms and conditions, cl. 8 did not attempt to clothe the plaintiffs with legal rights, but only equitable ones. It authorised the plaintiffs if they considered (presumably on reasonable grounds) that TCCI were insolvent to recover goods from their property without prior notice. Since TCCI informed the plaintiffs that they could no longer meet their obligations, the plaintiffs would have been fully justified in entering on TCCI's premises, but none of the glazing was there.

Clause 16 provided that in the event of TCCI having inter alia a receiver appointed to them the plaintiffs could by written notice determine the contract and would then be entitled to recover amounts due to them and damages in, it would seem, much the same way as normally applies in the case of lawful repudiation. 'Additionally', however, the plaintiffs were to be entitled to enter upon any premises at which TCCI had been working, which would include Janssens', and remove goods from them. Since this very valuable right was stated to be additional to the plaintiffs' more ordinary ones, it could not I think be exercised without a repudiation notice having been given. In my opinion none of the letters to which I have been referred constitutes such a notice of determination, but there may be others which I have not seen, so I am not able to decide whether a notice was given. Unless notice of termination was given any floating charge over TCCI's assets would no doubt remain 'ambulatory' and not settle so as to fasten on any specific assets.

The retention of title clauses and facts in this case are very similar to those in *Bond Worth*, so that Slade J's reasoning can be readily applied to it, namely that legal title passed to TCCI, that cl. 8 created a charge and not a simple trust, that the chargors were TCCI and not the plaintiffs, that TCCI's rights to deal with the goods were so extensive as to prevent their being sufficient certainty for a specific charge but not so as to exclude a floating charge and that any floating charge granted by TCCI should have been registered.

Mr Pearce-Higgins said that the Court of Appeal in *Clough Mill* had cast doubt upon the correctness of Slade J's judgment in *Bond Worth*, but I do not so read it. I think that the words of Goff LJ which I have quoted and his judgment as a whole assume or impliedly approve Slade J's judgment. Under the retention clause in *Clough Mill* the legal title to the goods remained with the sellers as in the forerunner of all title retention cases, *Aluminium Industrie Vaassen BV v Romalpa Aluminium* [1976] 1 WLR 676 and in *Hendy Lennox (Industrial Engines) Ltd v Grahame Puttick Ltd* [1984] 1 WLR 485 and *Re Andrabell Ltd* [1984] 3 All ER 407.

Mr Pearce-Higgins submitted that in view of the speeches in the House of Lords in the *Abbey National* case that there is no *scintilla temporis* when a purchaser is buying with the assistance of a mortgage, Slade J must have been wrong in holding that in *Bond Worth* there was a sale to the buyer followed by a charge granted by them to the sellers. I do not agree. Slade J did speak of the sale being 'followed' by the giving back of security, but he described both events as occurring *eo instanti*. I think that the House of Lords and Slade J each envisaged transfers of title and grants of security occurring completely simultaneously.

I must follow *Bond Worth* and decide that the plaintiffs' interest in the goods amounted only to a floating charge, with the result that since it was not registered under the 1985

A

Act it was as provided by s. 395 'void against the liquidator or administrator and any creditor of the company . . .' Since, however, the defendants were not apparently creditors of TCCI, but possibly even debtors to them, the unregistered floating charge was presumably valid against them, but not, of course, against the receiver. I have not heard any submissions as to the practical results of this legal position.

In the light of Sir David Cairns' and Bridge LJ's judgments in *International Factors* I think that an equitable interest in goods coupled with a right to possess them is sufficient to enable a valid claim to be made in conversion. I do not think, however, that the plaintiffs could succeed against the defendants upon that basis for, even if their equitable interest be sufficient, although void against the receiver and creditors of TCCI, unless the charge has ceased to float and become specific they cannot have a right to possession.

B

(*Order accordingly*)

C

D

E

F

G

H

A
McMullen & Sons Ltd v Cerrone.

Chancery Division (Luton County Court).
Roger Kaye QC (sitting as a deputy High Court judge).
Judgment delivered 28 May 1993.

Bankruptcy – Interim order – Moratorium for insolvent debtor – Whether distress
B *for rent was prohibited by interim order – Insolvency Act 1986, s. 252(2)(b).*

The self-help remedy of distress for arrears of rent was not 'other legal process' within s. 252(2)(b) of the Insolvency Act 1986. 'Legal process' meant process of a judicial or adjudicative or quasi-adjudicative nature and not rights which might be enforced without recourse to such process. (Exchange Travel Agency Ltd v Triton Property Trust plc [1991] BCC 341 not followed; Re Olympia & York Canary Wharf Ltd [1993] BCC 154 followed.)

C **Per curiam: When a comparison was made with s. 11(3) of the Insolvency Act 1986 it was noteworthy that Parliament sought fit expressly to include provision for distress in that section. No good reason for the distinction between the scheme applicable to companies under the Act and that applicable to individuals could be discerned. The court hoped that, at some stage, Parliament would recognise the anomaly of including express provision for distress in s. 11 but not in s. 252.**

D The following cases were referred to in the judgment:

Bellaglade Ltd, Re [1977] 1 All ER 319.
Berry (Herbert) Associates Ltd v IR Commrs [1977] 1 WLR 1437.
Birmingham and Staffordshire Gas Light Co, Ex parte (1871) LR 11 Eq 615.
Bishopsgate Investment Management Ltd, Re [1992] BCC 222; [1993] Ch 1.
Debtor (No. 1 of 1987), Re a [1989] 1 WLR 271.
E *Exchange Travel Agency Ltd v Triton Property Trust plc* [1991] BCC 341.
Exhall Coal Mining Co Ltd, Re (1864) 4 De G J & S 377, 46 ER 964.
International Tin Council, Re (1987) 3 BCC 103; [1987] Ch 419.
Lancashire Cotton Spinning Co, Re (1897) 35 ChD 656.
Memco (Engineering) Ltd, Re (1985) 1 BCC 99,460; [1986] Ch 86.
Naeem (a bankrupt), Re [1990] 1 WLR 48.
Olympia & York Canary Wharf Ltd, Re [1993] BCC 154.
F *Paramount Airways Ltd, Re. Bristol Airport plc v Powdrill* [1990] BCC 130; [1990] Ch 744.
Roundwood Colliery Co, Re [1897] Ch 373.
Seagull Manufacturing Co Ltd, Re [1993] BCC 241; [1993] Ch 345.
Smith (a bankrupt) v Braintree District Council [1990] 2 AC 215.
Winterbottom (G) (Leeds) Ltd, Re [1937] 2 All ER 232.

G Nicholas Peacock (instructed by McLellans, Hertford) for the applicant landlords.

Martin Collier (instructed by Pellys, Bishop's Stortford) for the respondents.

JUDGMENT

Roger Kaye QC: The matter before me raises a question of the true construction of the provisions of s. 252(2) of the *Insolvency Act* 1986. The question, which can be shortly
H stated, is can a landlord exercise the ancient self-help remedy of distress for arrears of rent when an interim order is in force under that section?

Section 252 provides as follows:

'(1) In the circumstances specified below [that is a reference to s. 253], the court may in the case of a debtor (being an individual) make an interim order under this section.

A

(2) An interim order has the effect that, during the period for which it is in force–

(a) no bankruptcy petition relating to the debtor may be presented or proceeded with, and

(b) no other proceedings, and no execution or other legal process, may be commenced or continued against the debtor or his property except with the leave of the court.'

B

The facts giving rise to this question are not in dispute.

The applicants are the freehold owners and landlords of retail premises at 36 Bucklersbury, Hitchin. They demised those premises to the respondents, Mr and Mrs Cerrone, under a lease dated 27 November 1981 and a supplemental lease dated 15 November 1985. The current passing annual rent under both leases is £15,000. The premises were used by Mr and Mrs Cerrone for the purposes of running a jewellery business trading as 'Hamilton Cerrone'.

C

The business, although initially successful, did not prosper. It declined through 1990 and 1991 and by November 1992 Mr and Mrs Cerrone found themselves in real financial difficulties. They proposed an individual voluntary arrangement under the provisions of Pt. VIII of the *Insolvency Act* 1986. On 26 November 1992 the Luton County Court made an interim order under s. 252(1) of that Act. That, of course, would have lasted only 14 days (see s. 255(6)), but the order was subsequently extended to 14 January 1993 and on that date extended still further (no doubt under s. 256(4) or 256(5)). There seems some doubt as to the exact date to which it was ultimately extended and, moreover, it seems now to have expired without being further extended, but it is common ground that at all material dates for the purposes of the matter before me the order was in force. Moreover what was the fate of the proposed voluntary arrangement itself is unclear.

D

By the end of November 1992 the arrears of rent owing by Mr and Mrs Cerrone to their landlords had risen to £16,500-odd. At that stage the landlords appear to have been ignorant of the interim order. In view of the size of the amount owing they resolved to distrain for the arrears by seizing goods on the demised premises. On 30 November bailiffs were instructed and they visited the premises on 4 December 1992. During that visit they discovered the existence of the interim order but in view of certain proposals made by Mr and Mrs Cerrone for payment of the current rent over the Christmas period the landlords instructed the bailiffs to withdraw. Following that withdrawal the landlords received a cheque from Mr and Mrs Cerrone for some £1,600-odd which they appropriated in reduction of the arrears leaving some £15,000-odd still owing.

E

F

Unfortunately the Christmas period did not prove to be profitable for Mr and Mrs Cerrone. On 8 January 1993 the nominee under the proposed voluntary arrangement wrote to the landlords' solicitors informing them that the business had not done as well as expected and that it was proposed to close down the business on 16 January and sell the stock.

G

The landlords thereupon decided to act quickly and to distrain for the arrears. On 13 January they reinstructed the bailiffs to distrain for the arrears of £15,000. On 14 January the bailiffs entered the demised premises and took possession of a quantity of jewellery.

Mr and Mrs Cerrone immediately protested about the distress in view of the interim order. The landlords disagreed, taking the view that notwithstanding the order they were entitled to act as they did. They made plans to sell the goods at auction on 21 January 1993. Mr and Mrs Cerrone accordingly attended before the district judge on 20 January and obtained an order restraining the continuation or completion of the distress and an order that the goods be restored to them. The district judge granted liberty to apply but directed that any application should be made to a judge of the High Court. It is not

H

A   entirely clear to me what jurisdiction he had to direct that, unless it be under the provisions of s. 42(2) or (3) of the *County Courts Act* 1984.

On 21 January 1993 the landlords applied to Ferris J to suspend the order of the district judge. On the landlords' giving undertakings in damages, to keep the seized goods in safe custody and not to dispose of them, the judge suspended the district judge's order until 28 January. On that day those undertakings were continued before Mummery J

B   pending the effective hearing of the landlords' motion to discharge the order of the district judge. It is that motion which is now before me.

I now turn to the consideration of s. 252. The starting point is the nature of the court's approach to construction of the *Insolvency Act* 1986. There are three general points to make at the outset.

First, the *Insolvency Act* 1986 is a consolidating Act. It consolidated the reforms of the

C   law of both individual and company insolvency reflected in the *Insolvency Act* 1985. It also consolidated, in the same Act, the retained provisions relating to company insolvency found in the *Companies Act* 1985. It thus includes in one single Act the principal statutory provisions relating both to individual as well as company insolvency. It is well known that many of the reforms in the 1985 Act were passed in the light of the *Report of the Review Committee on Insolvency Law and Practice* (1982, Cmnd 8558), under the chairmanship of Sir Kenneth Cork ('the Cork Report'). It is, however, also

D   well known that not all the recommendations of that report were accepted by Parliament. Two of the reforms recommended were that both a company and an individual should be able to promote a voluntary arrangement with their respective creditors under the supervision of a provisional trustee (see ch. 7 of the Cork Report). Here, again, much of the substance of the proposal, but not all the detail, was accepted by Parliament. The reforms, as enacted by Parliament, permit both companies and individuals to propose a

E   voluntary arrangement with their respective creditors under the supervision of a suitably qualified insolvency practitioner called a supervisor. The scheme or code applicable to company voluntary arrangements is to be found in Pt. I of the 1986 Act. That applicable to individual voluntary arrangements is in Pt. VIII. There are many common features to both codes: both involve supervision of the arrangement by a supervisor, both require the convening of a statutory meeting of creditors, both bind the creditors and the company to the arrangement (with or without modifications) if approved by the creditors

F   at the statutory meeting, both entitle a challenge to be made if the arrangement is unfairly prejudicial to the creditors or if there is some material irregularity at the meeting, and both entitle applications to be made to the court for directions in certain cases.

The section that falls for construction in this case, s. 252 falls within Pt. VIII of the 1986 Act. Part VIII was first enacted in Ch. I of Pt. III of the 1985 Act. It is thus part of the new provisions and does not derive from any previous legislation even if the language

G   of certain of the sections including s. 252 echoes words or phrases featuring in earlier insolvency legislation. Accordingly, in my judgment, the task of the court must be to approach the construction of the section afresh, unfettered by previous legislation or decisions under earlier Acts. I am fortified in the view that this is the correct approach in that this has been held to be the correct approach on previous occasions in the construction of different parts of the 1986 Act, different that is to Pt. VIII: see, for example, *Re a Debtor (No. 1 of 1987)* [1989] 1 WLR 271 (CA) at p. 276G–H;

H   *Re Bishopsgate Investment Management Ltd* [1992] BCC 222 (CA) at p. 229F–H; and *Smith (a bankrupt) v Braintree District Council* [1990] 2 AC 215 (HL).

Secondly, it is apparent from the Act itself that the intention of Parliament was, so far as possible, to harmonise the two systems of company and individual insolvency: see, in this respect, *Bishopsgate Investment Management Ltd* [1992] BCC 222 at p. 230A and *Re Seagull Manufacturing Co Ltd* [1993] BCC 241 (CA) at p. 242H. That, however, must

A

not be taken too far, for the statutory provisions may indicate from their very nature that Parliament intended that the two systems, although to be similar in many respects, should differ in some material respects. In the field of voluntary arrangements one noticeable difference is the scope for interim orders. An interim order may be obtained in connection with an individual voluntary arrangement, but not in the case of a company. In the latter case a company voluntary arrangement may be entered into where a winding-up order has been made or where an administration order is in force: see s. 1(3). But it may also be entered into outside these circumstances: see s. 1(1). Where a winding-up petition has been presented the court has power to stay pending actions or proceedings: see s. 126(1). After the winding-up order no action or proceeding can be commenced or proceeded with against the company without leave: s. 130(2), (3). In the case where an administration order is in force the Act contains wide provisions inhibiting the rights of creditors against the company: see s. 11(3). But outside these circumstances and in the absence of any agreement binding the creditors to the voluntary arrangement, no power is conferred by the *Insolvency Act* 1986 on the court to prohibit creditors from enforcing their rights in whatever manner they may legitimately do so against the company or its property. In the case of a proposal for an individual voluntary arrangement the position is different. Here the court has power, pending approval or rejection of the proposal, to make an interim order under s. 252 prohibiting creditors from acting in the manner prescribed by the section. Thus the two systems of company and individual voluntary arrangements, whilst adopting a common form or approach are not entirely uniform.

B

C

D

Thirdly, it is axiomatic that in construing an Act of Parliament regard must he had to the scope and purpose of the Act and of the Part of the Act within which the provision in question falls.

With these preliminary points in mind I must now deal with Pt. VIII of the 1986 Act. The scheme is clear. An individual who is a debtor may, as an alternative to bankruptcy, propose an arrangement with his creditors. If he does, he may seek and obtain an interim order under s. 252: see s. 253(1) and 255. Even before obtaining that order he may, so long as he has applied for an interim order, seek interlocutory relief, whereupon the court 'may stay any action, execution or other legal process against the property or person of the debtor': see s. 254. The interim order, once obtained, lasts for 14 days: s. 255(6). The court may only grant the order if it thinks that it is appropriate for the purpose of facilitating the consideration and implementation of the debtor's proposals: s. 255(2). The 14-day period is to enable the nominee, the qualified insolvency practitioner, to consider the proposal and prepare an independent report to the court stating whether or not the prescribed statutory meeting of creditors should be convened to consider it: s. 256. If the nominee requires more time, the court may extend the 14-day period: s. 256(4). If the nominee recommends a meeting be convened, the court is to extend the interim order to enable that to happen: see s. 256(5), 257. If the debtor shows no real intention of carrying through with his proposal, or if the nominee does not recommend a meeting, the interim order may be discharged: s. 256(6). Once the meeting has been held, the chairman of the meeting (usually the nominee) must report the result to the court: s. 259(1). If the meeting approves the proposal, it becomes binding on the creditors and the debtor (s. 260(1), (2)), and the interim order ceases to have effect on the expiration of a 28-day period running from the date the chairman presents his report to the court: s. 260(4). If the meeting does not approve the arrangement, the interim order may be discharged immediately: s. 259(2). The approved arrangement, of course, binds only those creditors who, in accordance with the rules (that is the *Insolvency Rules* 1986) had notice of and were entitled to vote at the meeting: s. 260(2)(b). Other creditors are unaffected and can, subject to the limits of s. 252 whilst any interim order is in force, enforce their rights.

E

F

G

H

A   It is thus clear that the purpose of the interim order is to protect and preserve the debtor's estate from claims of creditors for a relatively short period of time to enable the creditors to consider the debtor's proposals. Once they have had that opportunity, if they approve the proposal there is no longer any need for the interim order, for they will be bound by the arrangement and will all share in the arrangement in a just and fair manner (or at least in manner which is not unfairly prejudicial: see s. 262(1)(a)). In such circumstances no creditor could present a bankruptcy petition in respect of any existing

B   debt, i.e. one which is subject to the terms of the arrangement. If, on the other hand, the creditors decline to approve the arrangement, then there is likewise no need for the order to continue, for the creditors, in those circumstances, should be, and are, left free to pursue whatever remedy each considers appropriate, including the presentation of a bankruptcy petition. Thus the voluntary arrangement is a true alternative to bankruptcy.

      That being so, it is, I think, legitimate to see how the 1986 Act deals with the rights of

C   creditors in the interim period between presentation and disposal of the bankruptcy petition which is, I think, the closest analogy to the period between the initiation of the proposed voluntary arrangement and its disposal by the creditors' meeting. In this connection s. 285(1) and 285(2) are relevant. The remaining provisions of s. 285 are not relevant for these purposes because they deal solely with the situation after a bankruptcy order has been made.

D   The relevant parts of s. 285 provide as follows:

      '(1) At any time when proceedings on a bankruptcy petition are pending . . . the court may *stay any action, execution or other legal process against the property or person of the debtor. . .*

      (2) Any court in which *proceedings* are pending against any individual may, on proof that a bankruptcy petition has been presented in respect of that individual

E   . . . either *stay the proceedings* or allow them to continue on such terms as it thinks fit.' (emphasis added)

      Thus an application can either be made to the bankruptcy court to stay *any* action, execution or other legal process or to any court in which proceedings are pending to stay *those proceedings*. Again, however, what is contemplated by the legislation, at least in the usual case, is that for the relatively short period between presentation and hearing, the

F   rights of creditors should be restricted. This is obvious for the scheme is again to protect and preserve the estate for the benefit of all creditors should a bankruptcy order be made: see, for example, s. 284 restricting the debtor's right to dispose of his estate during the period between the presentation of the petition and the vesting of the estate in a trustee in bankruptcy.

      Now it is true that the wording of s. 285 differs slightly from s. 252. The former refers to action in subs. (1), whereas in s. 252(2)(b) this word is avoided, preferring instead the

G   wider expression 'other proceedings'. In the latter case there can, I think, be no doubt to what 'other proceedings' refer. The word 'other' must be read in conjunction with what has immediately preceded it, namely the reference to 'bankruptcy petition' in s. 252(2)(a). In my judgment, therefore, the words 'other proceedings' in s. 252(2)(b) are intended to relate solely to proceedings before a court, i.e. of a judicial or adjudicative nature. They are not apt to cover the ancient self-help remedy of distress for rent. This is entirely

H   consistent with s. 285(2) which plainly refers only to such proceedings.

      The words 'execution or other legal process' appear in both s. 252 and 285. The word 'execution' is, I think, a term of art, meaning execution or enforcement of some judicial process. It, too, is not apt to describe the process of distress.

      I thus turn to the crucial words in this case: 'or other legal process'. In both sections what must be considered is 'other legal process' 'against the property or person of the

debtor' (s. 285(1)) or 'against the debtor or his property' (s. 252(2)), which is the same   A
thing. A 'process' can be described as some course of action, but it must be 'legal'. That I
do not think for one moment is to be used in contradistinction to the word 'illegal' or
criminal for it is self-evident that criminal acts could not be contemplated on any footing.
Additionally, some regard must be had to the word 'other' before the words 'legal
process'. I therefore reach the conclusion that it was plainly intended that the word 'legal'
in the context of para. (b) of s. 252(2) was intended to colour the word 'process' and that
the word 'other' was intended to tie it to 'proceedings' and 'execution' giving the whole   B
of the paragraph a distinct flavour of judicial or enforcement proceedings or process. I
do not think that the word 'legal' is to be construed as widely as contended on behalf of
Mr and Mrs Cerrone, namely as meaning any lawful process or any process recognised
by the law or having a legal consequence. That, in my judgment, is not justified and goes
too far.

In my judgment, therefore, s. 252(2)(b) was intended to restrict only those rights which   C
a creditor could enforce by 'legal process' against the debtor or his property, that is
process of a judicial or adjudicative or quasi-adjudicative nature and not rights which
might be enforced without recourse to such process, i.e. the distress in this case. Some
support for this comes from the language of s. 254, dealing with the court's powers to
make an interlocutory order on a pending application for an interim order, where the
wording is clearly very similar to s. 285(1), (2) but, at the same time, intended to   D
complement s. 252 since it deals with what is to happen up to the effective hearing of the
application for an interim order. It would be surprising if the jurisdiction under one
section (s. 252) was very different from the other (s. 254).

I must now consider whether this view is affected by other analogous provisions or
decided cases to which I have been most helpfully referred by the researches of counsel.

I must start, I think, with *Smith (a bankrupt) v Braintree District Council* [1990] 2 AC   E
215 (HL) for that was a decision on s. 285(1). There the House of Lords held that the
words 'or other legal process' in s. 285(1) were apt to cover the process in Pt. VI of the
General Rate Act 1967 for the recovery of rates, including proceedings for committal
under that Act. Under s. 96(1) of that Act the payment of unpaid rates may be enforced
by distress and sale under warrant issued by the magistrates' court. If there is insufficient
distress the individual ratepayer may be liable to imprisonment. Section 102 enables the
court to issue a warrant for commitment where the distress is insufficient. At p. 230F–G   F
Lord Jauncey of Tullichettle (with whom the rest of the House agreed) said:

'My Lords, the words "or other legal process" must be construed in the context of
the underlying purpose of section 285, namely, the protection of the bankrupt's
estate for all his creditors. It follows that proceedings by one creditor to enforce
payment to himself are the sort of proceedings contemplated by the section. It
cannot be in doubt that the issue of a warrant of distress would fall within the   G
description "or other legal process". It would he both strange and illogical if the
bankruptcy court could stay such proceedings but had no power to stay the next
stage of the proceedings when distress had not been wholly successful. In my view,
as a matter of pure construction, the words "or other legal process" in section
285(1) are quite wide enough to comprehend all the machinery provided by Pt. VI
of the Act of 1967 for the recovery of unpaid rates, including proceedings for the
issue of a warrant of commitment.'   H

Mr Collier, who appeared for Mr and Mrs Cerrone, relied heavily on that passage. He
submits that that is apt to describe the warrant, or authority, the landlords issued to the
bailiffs authorising them to enter the demised premises to carry out the distress. But, as
was pointed out by Mr Peacock for the applicant landlords, in that passage Lord Jauncey
is referring to a warrant for distress issued under s. 96. The 'next stage' to which he is

A referring is likewise the process of application to a judicial tribunal for a warrant of commitment. In my view, therefore, this passage does not assist Mr and Mrs Cerrone.

In *Ex parte Birmingham and Staffordshire Gas Light Co* (1871) LR 11 Eq 615, Sir James Bacon CJ had to consider the words 'execution or other legal process' in s. 13(1) of the *Bankruptcy Act* 1869. That section and its successor, s. 9(1) of the *Bankruptcy Act* 1914, were in some respects the precursors to s. 285(1) of the 1986 Act. The question was

B whether the gas company could distrain for rent under special powers conferred on them by the relevant Act of Parliament enabling them to recover arrears for gas 'by the same means as landlords may recover rent in arrear'. The judge held (at p. 618):

> 'I think it quite plain that a distress for rent cannot be considered to be included in the expression "legal process", in as much as no legal process whatever is necessary; and the landlord may, if he thinks proper, distrain with his own hands. As little

C > can it be called an execution, for an execution is the result of a judgment which has been recovered in some Court of Law, but to a distress no legal proceedings whatever are necessary.'

Now that decision is not, of course, binding on me since, as I have previously mentioned, the provisions in the 1986 Act are to be construed afresh. It does not, however, assist Mr Collier.

D Finally, in the realm of individual insolvency, Mr Collier relied on a decision of Hoffmann J in *Re Naeem (a bankrupt)* [1990] 1 WLR 48. In that case Hoffmann J allowed an appeal against the decision of the registrar to revoke an individual voluntary arrangement entered into by a bankrupt. The landlord had sought to revoke the arrangement on the basis that it was unfairly prejudiced in that it could not forfeit the lease for arrears of rent. It was held the arrangement did not interfere with its proprietary

E right to forfeit but that it could only forfeit for the amount due to it under the arrangement. At p. 50D–H the judge said:

> 'Of course the effect of the interim order was to hold up the landlord's right to forfeit, but under section 260(4) of the Act of 1986 the interim order ceases to have effect 28 days after the date on which the report of the outcome of the creditors' meeting has been given to the court under section 259. Accordingly the interim

F > order no longer applies and the landlord is free to commence such proceedings for forfeiture as it may be advised.'

That the interim order held up the landlord's right to forfeit seems to have been an assumption of the judge and formed no part of the ratio of his decision. Moreover it is not entirely clear from the report precisely what type of forfeiture was contemplated, by proceedings in court or by exercising a right of re-entry without recourse to legal

G proceedings. If anything, the last sentence of the passage quoted points to the former rather than the latter. If so, then the passage quoted is entirely consistent with my construction of the section. But, if I am right in my construction of s. 252 so far, it is also right to point out, as does Mr Collier, that this produces something of an anomaly in that a landlord could not enforce his right to forfeit by court action where an interim order is in force under s. 252 but could by right of re-entry. But I see nothing in the judgment of Hoffmann J compelling me to reach a different conclusion to that reached

H so far.

I must now consider the provisions applicable to the scheme of company insolvency. I have already pointed out that there is no directly comparable provision in this sphere for obtaining an interim order. But, again, as I have already pointed out, a company voluntary arrangement may be proposed where an administration order is in force. In such case s. 11(3) of the *Insolvency Act* 1986 applies. This subsection provides as follows:

'During the period for which an administration order is in force–

(a) no resolution may be passed or order made for the winding up of the company;

(b) no administrative receiver of the company may be appointed;

(c) no other steps may be taken to enforce any security over the company's property, or to repossess goods in the company's possession under any hire-purchase agreement, except with the consent of the administrator or the leave of the court and subject (where the court gives leave) to such terms as the court may impose; and

(d) no other proceedings and no execution or other legal process may be commenced or continued, and no distress may be levied, against the company or its property except with the consent of the administrator or the leave of the court and subject (where the court gives leave) to such terms as aforesaid.'

It is to be noted that that subsection is in much wider terms than s. 252. I must also refer here to s. 126 of the Act which I mentioned above. That section derived from s. 521 of the *Companies Act* 1985 and in turn from s. 226 of the *Companies Act* 1948 and from earlier legislation. In many decisions under that section (and under the predecessor to s. 130(2) of the 1986 Act) it has been held that where a landlord has commenced his distress before winding up, but not by the time of the order completed the distress by sale, the court may restrain completion of the sale as a 'proceeding'. It is clear, however, from those decisions that this construction reached in the course of the last century has not been greeted with judicial favour but has, until the 1986 Act at least, been followed in view of the passage of time that the construction stood: see *Re Exhall Coal Mining Co Ltd* (1864) 4 De G J & S 377, 46 ER 964; *Re Lancashire Cotton Spinning Co* (1897) 35 ChD 656; *Re Roundwood Colliery Co* [1897] Ch 373; *Re G Winterbottom (Leeds) Ltd* [1937] 2 All ER 232; *Re Bellaglade Ltd* [1977] 1 All ER 319; *Herbert Berry Associates Ltd v IR Commrs* [1977] 1 WLR 1437 (HL) and *Re Memco (Engineering) Ltd* (1985) 1 BCC 99,460. Thus, as it seems to me, the intention of Parliament was quite plainly to leave no doubt, at least in relation to administration orders (and, thereby, where relevant, any period prior to approval of a proposal for a voluntary arrangement where an administration order is in force), that distress was intended to be covered also in s. 11(3)(d). Nevertheless I was urged to follow this line of cases.

But they do not, I think, assist Mr Collier. I have already considered that the word 'proceedings' in s. 252(2)(b) does not cover distress and I see nothing in these cases that affects that view. If anything it tends to show that Parliament was alive to the point and intended, at least so far as companies were concerned, specifically to deal with a point that had previously given rise to judicial disfavour by express words. Since the opening words of s. 11(3)(d) so closely resemble that of s. 252(2) it would have been a relatively simple matter to have included in s. 252(2) the words 'and no distress may be levied'. It is to be noted, too, that nothing resembling s. 11(3)(c) is to be found in s. 252.

I was referred to three cases on s. 11(3)(d). The first is *Re Paramount Airways Ltd. Bristol Airport plc v Powdrill* [1990] BCC 130. There the Court of Appeal held that the detention of an aircraft under the provisions of the *Civil Aviation Act* 1982 was caught by s. 11(3)(c). Sir Nicolas Browne-Wilkinson V-C added that he did not consider the right of retention fell within the concept of distress in s. 11(3)(d) nor did it fall within the words 'other proceedings' which he considered referred to judicial proceedings: see pp. 152–153.

Next I was referred to *Exchange Travel Agency Ltd v Triton Property Trust plc* [1991] BCC 341 where Harman J, obiter, decided that a landlord's right of re-entry could be covered by the words 'other legal process' in s. 11(3)(d). At p. 345G he said:

A
'It is clear that the s. 130 provision, which I have already referred to as providing for "proceedings . . . against the company or its property", covers the exercise of a peaceable right of re-entry pursuant to a proviso for re-entry in the lease, and it seems to me astonishing if "other legal process" here would not also cover that step. It seems to me that "legal process" is exactly how one would describe the exercise of a right by a person not in a contractual relationship with his tenant but holding a relationship by privity of estate between them. In my judgment it is a

B
correct use of words to describe a landlord who has legal rights, arising out of the privity of estate, which he exercises by the process of peaceable re-entry as exercising "legal process". It seems to me therefore that if this exercise of the right of re-entry be not a security, it is quite certainly the commencement of another legal process, and as I see it that must have been one of the purposes for which Parliament plainly intended the Act to operate.

C
It would be astonishing, in my mind, if Parliament has plainly prevented a landlord from issuing a writ for forfeiture or taking steps in the courts to effect a forfeiture and a re-entry, but has left entirely open and untouched the right to effect a peaceable re-entry.'

On that passage, too, Mr Collier relied. He argues, with some force, that the landlord's right of distress may be regarded in the same light. It would be anomalous, he submits,

D
for a landlord enforcing a right of re-entry by action to be restrained, but one enforcing a right by re-entry not to be. So, he argues, by parity of reasoning, a landlord exercising his self-help remedy of distress. He relies on the plain purpose of Pt. VIII of the 1986 Act which is to effect a complete moratorium on the rights of creditors pending the outcome of the proposal whilst an interim order is in force.

This passage of Harman J's judgment has, however, been subjected to judicial scrutiny

E
in *Re Olympia & York Canary Wharf Ltd* [1993] BCC 154. There the question arose whether the existence of an administration order and the operation of s. 11(3)(d) of the 1986 Act in particular, prevented the service by the applicant upon the respondent company (which was in administration) of a notice to complete making time of the essence, or prevented the applicant accepting a repudiatory breach of contract. Millett J held that the section did not. Millett J entirely agreed with Harman J's actual decision (that the right of re-entry was covered by s. 11(3)(c)) but disagreed with his approach on

F
s. 11(3)(d). After referring to s. 9(1) of the *Bankruptcy Act* 1914 (which, it will be remembered, is the precursor to s. 285(1),(2) and resembles the language of s. 254) he said at pp. 156–157:

'In s. 10 and s. 11 of the 1986 Act, Parliament has effected certain modifications to s. 9 of the *Bankruptcy Act* 1914. The word "action" has been replaced by the more compendious expression "proceedings" which is apt to denote any legal or quasi-

G
legal proceedings whether commenced by writ or otherwise; and a prohibition on the levying of distress has been expressly included, thereby dealing with a question which had previously caused difficulty.

In *Stroud's Judicial Dictionary* (5th edn, 1986) it is said that the word "process" is:

"the doing of something in a proceeding in a civil or criminal court, and that which may be done without the aid of a court is not a 'process'."

H
Therefore a distraint, whether for rent or any other payment, and whether the right of distress be given by common law, statute or, as it should seem, by any other authority was not a "process" nor was it an "execution, or other legal process" within the *Bankruptcy Act* 1869.'

Then, after quoting the passage in *Ex parte Birmingham and Staffordshire Gas Light Co* (1871) LR 11 Eq 615 I have set out above, he continued:

A

'The presence of the word "stay" in s. 9 of the *Bankruptcy Act* 1914, and the insertion of the word "legal" before "process" in s. 11(3)(d) of the 1986 Act support the impressions that the word "process" in each of the Acts means a process which requires the assistance of the court, and does not extend to the service of a contractual notice, whether or not the service of such a notice is a precondition to the bringing of legal proceedings.'

B

He also referred to his own judgment in *Re International Tin Council* (1987) 3 BCC 103 at pp. 116–117 where he had to consider the meaning of the phrase 'immunity from suit and legal process' and considered 'suit' extended to all forms of the adjudicative jurisdiction and the phrase 'legal process' as apt to describe all forms of the enforcement jurisdiction.

With this reasoning I respectfully agree. It seems to me that the cases on the construction of the language used in s. 252, particularly on the phrase 'other legal process', if anything, support the view that I have taken as to the true construction of s. 252(2). I must regretfully decline to adopt Harman J's approach. I can find, in particular, no good reason for distinguishing the approach under s. 285 from that under s. 252. When a comparison is made with s. 11(3) it is noteworthy that Parliament sought fit expressly to include provision for distress. Like both counsel before me, however, I can discern no good reason for this distinction between the scheme applicable to companies under the Act and that applicable to individuals. Given, however, there is an express distinction on the wording and despite the clear legislative purpose I have considered above I do not feel able to decide that the words in s. 252(2)(b) are apt to cover the common law remedy of distress. That this produces anomalies I have no doubt but to yield to the temptation to include distress within the embrace of s. 252 would, I think, create greater uncertainties for there would then, I anticipate, be great difficulty in drawing the line as to what was or was not included within the phrase 'legal process'. I can only express the hope that, at some stage, Parliament recognises the anomaly of including express provision for distress in s. 11 but not in s. 252. There seems no good reason why it should not be expressly included in the latter.

C

D

E

I would finally add that I have not found much assistance from the words 'commenced or continued'. Those words were thought to be of some influence in both *Paramount Airways (Bristol Airport plc v Powdrill)* [1990] BCC 130 and in *Re Olympia & York Canary Wharf Ltd* [1993] BCC 154, as being indicative of the adjudicative process. That I accept, but they are not entirely inapt to describe the commencement of the process of distress (e.g. by entry) and its continuation (e.g. by making arrangements for the sale of the goods seized).

F

In the result, therefore, the judicial and legislative authorities cited to me have not caused me to depart from my initial view that the distress was not prevented by s. 252, rather they have tended to reinforce this view. I therefore accede to the application of the landlords.

G

(*Order accordingly*)

H

A **Practice Note (Administration order applications: content of independent reports)**

Chancery Division.
17 January 1994.

B Administration orders under Pt. II of the *Insolvency Act* 1986 are intended primarily to facilitate the rescue and rehabilitation of insolvent but potentially viable businesses. It is of the greatest importance that this aim should not be frustrated by expense, and that the costs of obtaining an administration order should not operate as a disincentive or put the process out of the reach of smaller companies.

Rule 2.2 of the Insolvency Rules provides that an application for an administration order may be supported by a report by an independent person to the effect that the appointment of an administrator for the company is expedient. It is the experience of the
C court that the contents of the r. 2.2 report are sometimes unnecessarily elaborate and detailed. Because a report of this character is thought to be necessary, the preliminary investigation will often have been unduly protracted and extensive and, hence, expensive.

The extent of the necessary investigation and the amount of material to be provided to the court must be a matter for the judgment of the person who prepares the report and will vary from case to case. However, in the normal case, what the court needs is a concise
D assessment of the company's situation and of the prospects of an administration order achieving one or more of the statutory purposes. The latter will normally include an explanation of the availability of any finance required during the administration.

Every endeavour should be made to avoid disproportionate investigation and expense. In some cases a brief investigation and report will be all that is required. Where the court has insufficient material on which to base its decision, but the proposed
E administrator is in court, he may offer to supplement the material by giving oral evidence. In such a case he should subsequently provide a supplemental report covering the matters on which oral evidence was given so that this can be placed on the court file.

In suitable cases the court may appoint an administrator but require him to report back to the court within a short period so that the court can consider whether to allow the administration to continue or to discharge the order. In some cases the court may
F require the administrator to hold a meeting of creditors before reporting back to the court, both within a relatively short period.

It is the experience of the judges who sit in the Companies Court that, in general, a r. 2.2 report is valuable as a safeguard in assisting the court to see whether the application has a sound basis. However, there may be straightforward cases in which such a report is not necessary because it would provide little assistance. Practitioners are reminded that the rules do not require that a r. 2.2 report must be provided in every case.
G This statement is made after consultation with the other judges of the Chancery Division.

Sir Donald Nicholls V-C.

H

Re New Bullas Trading Ltd.

Court of Appeal (Civil Division).
Nourse and Russell L JJ and Scott Baker J.
Judgment delivered 15 December 1993.

Receivership – Debenture – Debenture attempted to create fixed charge over book debts and floating charge over proceeds – Whether charge created over book debts was a fixed charge – Insolvency Act 1986, s. 40.

This was an appeal by a debenture holder from a judgment of Knox J [1993] BCC 251 that a charge over the company's book debts contained in the debenture was a floating charge.

The debenture was expressed to create a fixed charge over the book and other debts owing to the company. It provided for the company to pay the proceeds of book and other debts into a designated account and to deal with such moneys in accordance with any directions from time to time given in writing by the debenture holder, and, in the absence of any directions by the debenture holder, for such moneys to be released from the fixed charge on the debts and to become subject to a floating charge created by the debenture. No directions were given by the debenture holder.

Administrative receivers of the company were appointed and under s. 40 of the Insolvency Act 1986 if the charge over book debts was created as a floating charge, the preferential debts would absorb all the proceeds and nothing would be left for the debenture holder. Conversely, if it was created as a fixed charge, the debenture holder would be paid in full and the amount available for preferential creditors would be reduced accordingly. On neither footing would anything be left for unsecured creditors whose debts were not preferential.

The judge (following Re Brightlife Ltd (1986) 2 BCC 99,359) held that, notwithstanding the parties' expressed intention to create a fixed charge, the extent to which the company was left free to deal with the book debts and the proceeds if and when collected compelled the court to conclude that there was a floating charge. The debenture holder appealed.

In the Court of Appeal it was common ground that the question depended on the intention of the parties, to be ascertained from the terms of the debenture; that there were no considerations of public policy, legal impossibility apart, which prevented them from making whatever contract they chose; that it was possible for them to create a fixed equitable charge over future as well as present book debts; that their declared intention was to create such a charge; but that that intention was nevertheless defeated if the other provisions of the debenture were inconsistent with it.

The debenture holder submitted, first, that the charge created by the debenture over book debts was, as it was expressed to be, a fixed charge; secondly and in the alternative, that the debenture created a fixed charge over book debts while they were uncollected and a floating charge over their proceeds, there being no legal objection to their being treated in that fashion. The preferential creditors argued that the distinction between book debts before collection and after realisation was unrealistic and artificial, and that it was of the essence of a fixed charge that the asset appropriated to the charge could not be released from it at the will of the mortgagor and without the consent of the chargee.

Held, allowing the debenture holder's appeal:

1. Knox J decided the case by rejecting the debenture holder's first submission. No trace of the second submission could be found in his judgment. Logically, the second submission, which was hardly, if at all, advanced before the judge, deserved to be considered first.

2. The book debts did not cease to be subject to the fixed charge at the will of the company. They ceased to be such because both parties, not the company alone, had determined that if the proceeds of a book debt were paid into the specified account at a time

A

when no directions had been given it should thereupon be released. The matter was governed by a clear agreement of the parties. Unless there was some authority or principle of law which prevented them from agreeing what they had agreed, their agreement must prevail.

3. Just as it was open to contracting parties to provide for a fixed charge on future book debts, so it was open to them to provide that they should be subject to a fixed charge while they were uncollected and a floating charge on realisation. No authority to the contrary had been cited and, the principle being as spacious as it had been expressed to be, no objection was on that account sustainable. The charge over book debts of the company, as created by the debenture, was, unless and until their proceeds were paid into the specified account, a valid fixed charge.

The following cases were referred to in the judgment:

Brightlife Ltd, Re (1986) 2 BCC 99,359; [1987] Ch 200.
Evans v Rival Granite Quarries Ltd [1910] 2 K B 979.
Siebe Gorman & Co Ltd v Barclays Bank Ltd [1979] 2 Ll Rep 142.
Tailby v Official Receiver (1888) 13 App Cas 523.
Yorkshire Woolcombers Association Ltd, Re [1903] 2 Ch 284 (CA); [1904] AC 355 (HL).

Jonathan Sumption QC and David Chivers (instructed by Lawrence Graham) for the appellant.

Mark Arnold (instructed by Clifford Chance) for the administrative receivers.

Martin Pascoe QC and Launcelot Henderson (instructed by the solicitor for the Inland Revenue) for the representative creditor.

JUDGMENT

Nourse LJ: He who lends money to a trading company neither wishes nor expects it to become insolvent. Its prosperous trading is the best assurance of the return of his money with interest. But against an evil day he wants the best security the company can give him consistently with its ability to trade meanwhile. Hence the modern form of debenture, which, broadly speaking, gives the lender a fixed charge over assets that the company does not need to deal with in the ordinary course of its business and a floating charge over those that it does.

An asset peculiarly problematical in this context is a book debt of the company. There being usually no need to deal with it before collection, it is at that stage a natural subject of the fixed charge. But once collected, the proceeds being needed for the conduct of the business, it becomes a natural subject of the floating charge. While the company is a going concern, it is no less an advantage to the lender that the debt should be collected and the proceeds used in the business. But on insolvency, a crystallised floating charge on proceeds, which, in the event supposed, are all the more likely to have been dissipated, may be worthless; whereas a fixed charge enabling the lender to intercept payment to the company may be of real value.

Previous authorities, starting with the decision of this court in *Re Yorkshire Woolcombers Association Ltd* [1903] 2 Ch 284, show that the attempts of draftsmen to achieve the twin objectives of freedom in trading and servitude on insolvency (a metaphor suggested by Fletcher Moulton LJ in *Evans v Rival Granite Quarries Ltd* [1910] 2 K B 979 at p. 998) have not always been successful. Charges described and intended to take effect as fixed charges on book debts have sometimes been held to take effect as floating charges. Of the modern English authorities, *Re Brightlife Ltd* (1986) 2 BCC 99,359 is a striking example of such a case. *Siebe Gorman & Co Ltd v Barclays Bank Ltd* [1979] 2 Lloyd's Rep 142 was a decision which went the other way.

In each of the previous authorities the draftsman treated book debts indivisibly, the question being to which form of charge they had, as such, been subjected. Here, for the

first time in a reported case, the draftsman has deliberately and conscientiously set out to   A
subject them to a fixed charge while they are uncollected and a floating charge on
realisation. The essential question, as it has emerged in this court, is whether the law
allows them to be treated in that fashion.

On 18 July 1989, New Bullas Trading Ltd ('the company'), under its then name of
Cetime Ltd, executed two debentures, one in favour of Lloyds Bank plc ('the bank') and
the other in favour of 3i plc ('3i'). The bank and 3i had previously agreed that in respect   B
of all assets of the company other than plant, machinery and equipment and goodwill
the bank's securities should rank in priority to those of 3i up to a maximum principal
sum of £1.55m plus interest, commission, costs, charges and expenses. It is unnecessary
to refer to the provisions of the bank's debenture, except to say that it included a charge
on all book debts, both present and future, due or owing to the company, which was
expressed to take effect as a first fixed mortgage by assignment; in other words, as a fixed
charge.   C

The material provisions of 3i's debenture, to which I will refer simply as 'the
debenture', are as follows. Clause 1 contains a covenant by the company to pay or
discharge to 3i all moneys and liabilities at any time or times due or owing or incurred by
the company to 3i. Clause 2 provides that their repayment or discharge shall be made on
demand unless otherwise agreed in writing. Clause 3 contains a charge by the company
of seven different categories of asset with the payment and discharge to 3i of all moneys   D
and liabilities thereby covenanted to be paid and discharged and all other sums intended
to be thereby secured. The assets charged include:

> 'FIFTH–THE book debts and other debts due or owing to the company both
> present and future:'

Clause 4 provides:

> 'THE charges on the property and assets FIRST SECOND THIRD FOURTH   E
> and FIFTH described are created as fixed charges . . .'

Clause 6 provides:

> 'THIS debenture is issued subject to and with the benefit of the conditions set out
> in the first schedule hereto . . . The bank specified in the fifth schedule hereto (or
> such other bank as 3i may agree to in writing) is therein referred to as "the bank".'

The bank so specified is the bank at its Wolverhampton Road, Dudley branch.   F

Of the conditions set out in the first schedule to the debenture, the following are
material. Condition 8 (to which the marginal note is 'Crystallisation of security subject
to demand for repayment') specifies the various events on the happening of which the
company is entitled to demand payment. Condition 9 (to which the marginal note is
'Crystallisation of security without demand') specifies the various events on the
happening of which the moneys secured become immediately payable without demand.   G
They include the appointment of a receiver (including an administrative receiver).

The condition on which the outcome of this case mainly depends is condition 12, to
which the marginal note is 'Book debts'. I set it out in full, adding numbers for the three
parts into which para. (A) is divided:

> 'During the continuance of this security the company shall:
>
> (A) [(i)] pay into a current account or a separate designated account (as 3i may   H
> require) of the company with the bank all moneys which it may receive in respect
> of the book debts and other debts hereby charged and (subject to any rights of the
> bank in respect thereof) pay or otherwise deal with such moneys standing in such
> account in accordance with any directions from time to time given in writing by 3i;
> [(ii)] prior to any demand being made under condition 8 hereof or to the provisions

A
of condition 9 hereof becoming operative in the absence of any directions from 3i any moneys received by the company and paid into such account in respect of the book debts and other debts hereby charged shall upon such payment in stand released from the fixed charge on such debts hereinbefore by this debenture created and shall stand subject to the floating charge hereinbefore by this debenture created over the other property and assets of the company; [(iii)] any such release shall in no respects derogate from the subsistence and continuance of the said fixed charge
B
on all other book and other debts of the company for the time being outstanding:

(B) if called upon to do so by 3i execute a legal assignment of such book debts and other debts to 3i in such terms as 3i may require and give notice thereof to the debtors from whom the debts are owing or incurred and take such other steps as 3i may require to perfect such legal assignment:

C
(C) deal with such book debts and other debts in accordance with any directions from time to time given in writing by 3i (subject to any rights of the bank in respect thereof) and in default of and subject to any such directions deal with the same only in the ordinary course of getting in and realising the same (but not sell assign factor or discount the same in any way):

(D) permit the bank to furnish directly to 3i from time to time upon request full statements and particulars of all the company's accounts with the bank and such
D
other financial statements and information respecting the assets and liabilities of the company as are from time to time available to the bank.'

The references in para. (A)(i) and (C) to the rights of the bank are evidently references to its rights under its own debenture.

The principal activities of the company were to act as agents for commissioning and consultant engineers to major oil companies and the supply of personnel to carry out
E
non-destructive testing services. No directions were ever given by 3i pursuant to either of para. (A)(i) or (C) of condition 12. On 6 November 1991 the applicants, Mr Roger Murray Griffiths and Mr Andrew George Pearce, two partners in Ernst & Young, were appointed by the bank to be joint administrative receivers of the company. On 12 November 1991, pursuant to powers contained in the debenture, they were appointed by 3i to act in the like capacity. Those appointments brought into play s. 40 of the
F
Insolvency Act 1986 which, so far as material, provides:

'(1) The following applies, in the case of a company, where a receiver is appointed on behalf of the holders of any debentures of the company secured by a charge which, as created, was a floating charge.

(2) If the company is not at the time in course of being wound up, its preferential debts . . . shall be paid out of the assets coming to the hands of the receiver in priority to any claims for principal or interest in respect of the debentures.'
G
The company went into creditors' voluntary liquidation on 28 September 1992, but that was after the provisions of s. 40 had taken effect. It appears that the major category of asset available for realisation by the administrative receivers was the company's book debts, to which s. 40(2) applies if the charge over them was, as created by the debenture, a floating, and not a fixed, charge. If it was a floating charge, the company's preferential debts are payable in priority to the claims of the debenture holders. If it was a fixed
H
charge, the claims of the debenture holders take priority over the preferential debts.

When the administrative receivers were appointed, the amounts owing by the company to debenture holders were £1.136m to the bank, £100,000 to 3i and £37,500 to some former minority shareholders of the company, who, on 18 July 1989, had agreed to postpone their securities to those of the bank and 3i. Realisations of book debts have proved very successful. As at 20 January 1993, the debt owed to the bank had been

discharged (save for a nominal amount of £37) and about £114,000 was owed to 3i. At A
that date the proceeds of realisations of book debts remaining in the administrative
receivers' hands amounted to approximately £459,714 with some £104,000 (estimated to
produce £26,000) remaining to be collected. The preferential debts had previously been
estimated at £608,500, consisting of £253,000 owed to the Inland Revenue and the
Department of Health and Social Security in respect of PAYE and National Insurance
contributions, £339,000 owed to the Customs and Excise in respect of VAT, £8,000 owed
to the Department of Employment and £8,500 to 33 employees. B

On these figures, it is clear that if the charge over book debts was created as a floating
charge, the preferential debts will absorb all their proceeds and nothing will be left for 3i.
Conversely, if it was created as a fixed charge, 3i will be paid in full and the amount
available for the preferential creditors will be reduced accordingly. On neither footing
will anything be left for unsecured creditors whose debts are not preferential. C

Doubts having arisen as to whether the charge over book debts was, as created, a fixed
or a floating charge, on 28 October 1992 the administrative receivers issued an originating
application in the Companies Court for the determination of that question. The
respondents were 3i, the Inland Revenue, the Customs and Excise and the Departments
of Employment and Social Security. By an order of the registrar, the Inland Revenue
were appointed to represent the interests of the respondents other than 3i. He also
directed that no notice of the application need be given to any other preferential creditors, D
i.e. the employees. The application came before Knox J who, on 11 February 1993, held
that the charge was a floating charge. 3i now appeals to this court.

Knox J's judgment is reported at [1993] BCC 251. Having considered the provisions of
the debenture and several of the previous authorities, including *Re Yorkshire
Woolcombers Association Ltd*, *Siebe Gorman & Co Ltd v Barclays Bank Ltd* and *Re
Brightlife Ltd*, the judge reached the conclusion that the case fell on the floating charge E
side of the line, in that the company's ability to deal with book debts was, at the creation
of the charge, not subject to any greater fetters than Hoffmann J had held to be
inadequate in *Re Brightlife Ltd*. He continued, at p. 265F:

'Absent a direction from 3i there was a freedom of action conferred upon the
company which was in my judgment inconsistent with the existence of a specific
charge.' F

In this court there has been much common ground. It is agreed that the question
depends on the intention of the parties, to be ascertained from the terms of the debenture;
legal impossibility apart, that there are no considerations of public policy which
prevented them from making whatever contract they chose; that it was possible for them
to create a fixed equitable charge over future as well as present book debts; that their
declared intention was to create such a charge; but that that intention was nevertheless G
defeated if the other provisions of the debenture are inconsistent with it.

Mr Sumption QC, for 3i, has made two main submissions, whose import can be
summarised as follows: first, on the footing that condition 12 treated, or must be taken
to have treated, book debts indivisibly, the charge created over them by the debenture
was, as it was expressed to be, a fixed charge; secondly and in the alternative, the effect
of condition 12 was to create a fixed charge over book debts while they were uncollected
and a floating charge over their proceeds, there being no legal objection to their being H
treated in that fashion. It seems that in the court below it was the first of these submissions
that was primarily, if not exclusively, relied on. Certainly it was by Knox J's rejection of
it that the case was decided as it was. No trace of the second submission can be found in
the judge's careful judgment. In this court it has assumed great prominence. Logically, as
it seems to me, it deserves to be considered first.

A   The question depends in the first instance on the true construction of condition 12. In order to trace the fate, actual or potential, of one of the company's book debts, it is necessary to start with condition 12(C), whose effect, in the absence of any written directions by 3i, is to require the company to get in the debt in the ordinary course by demanding payment from the debtor in full. On payment being made, condition 12(A)(i) requires it to be paid into a specified account of the company with the bank, where it must be paid or otherwise dealt with in accordance with any written directions given by

B   3i. Condition 12(A)(ii), which is in substance, though not in form, a proviso to condition 12(A)(i), then provides that, prior to crystallisation of the security under either of conditions 8 and 9 and in the absence of any written directions by 3i, the sum paid in shall be released from the fixed charge and become subject to the floating charge. Condition 12(A)(iii), in substance a further proviso, provides that the release of the sum paid in from the fixed charge shall not derogate from its continuation in relation to all

C   other outstanding book debts of the company.

     The judge held, and the parties are agreed, that when condition 12(A)(i) and (ii) are read together, it is seen that any directions given by 3i cannot have retrospective effect on any sums paid into the account beforehand. With that point out of the way, it is very clear, as Mr Henderson, for the Inland Revenue, accepts, that the parties intended to create a fixed charge over book debts while they were uncollected (and also, if there was any interval between collection and payment in, over the proceeds) and a floating charge

D   over the proceeds once they had been paid into the specified account. So the decisive question is whether the law allowed the parties to make an agreement to that effect.

     Mr Henderson has submitted that the distinction drawn between the book debts before collection and after realisation is unrealistic and artificial because a debt is worth nothing unless and until it is turned into money. He says that it is of the essence of a fixed charge that the asset is appropriated to the charge from the beginning and that it cannot be

E   released from it without the consent of the chargee. He relies strongly on a passage in the judgment of Vaughan Williams LJ in *Re Yorkshire Woolcombers Association Ltd* [1903] 2 Ch at p. 294, where he said:

> '. . . what you do require to make a specific security is that the security whenever it has once come into existence, and been identified or appropriated as a security, shall never thereafter at the will of the mortgagor cease to be a security.'

F   The short answer to these submissions is that here the asset does not cease to be subject to the fixed charge at the will of the company. It ceases to be such because both parties, not the company alone, have determined that if the proceeds of a book debt are paid into the specified account at a time when no directions have been given it shall thereupon be released. The matter is governed by a clear agreement of the parties. Unless there is some authority or principle of law which prevented them from agreeing what they have agreed, their agreement must prevail.

G   An equitable assignment, whether it takes effect as an out-and-out assignment or, as here, by way of charge, is a creature of exceptional versatility, malleable to the intention of its creators, adaptable to the subject-matter assigned. Provided it is in writing, made for value and the intention is clear, it requires no formalities of expression; it may take effect over property real or personal, and over estates or interests legal or equitable, vested or contingent or, as in the case of future book debts, mere expectancies.

H   In *Tailby v Official Receiver* (1888) 13 App Cas 523, the case in which it was decided by the House of Lords that an equitable charge over future book debts could validly be created, Lord Macnaghten said at p. 543:

> 'It has long been settled that future property, possibilities and expectancies are assignable in equity for value. The mode or form of assignment is absolutely immaterial provided the intention of the parties is clear. To effectuate the intention

A

an assignment for value, in terms present and immediate, has always been regarded in equity as a contract binding on the conscience of the assignor and so binding the subject-matter of the contract when it comes into existence, if it is of such a nature and so described as to be capable of being ascertained and identified.'

Having referred to the proposition that an assignment of future book debts not limited to a specified business was too vague to have any effect, and having found that it was unsupported by authority, Lord Macnaghten dealt with it as a matter of principle. At p. 545, he said:

B

'It was admitted by the learned counsel for the respondent, that a trader may assign his future book debts in a specified business. Why should the line be drawn there? Between men of full age and competent understanding ought there to be any limit to the freedom of contract but that imposed by positive law or dictated by considerations of morality or public policy? The limit proposed is purely arbitrary, and I think meaningless and unreasonable.'

C

These observations support the view that, just as it is open to contracting parties to provide for a fixed charge on future book debts, so it is open to them to provide that they shall be subject to a fixed charge while they are uncollected and a floating charge on realisation. No authority to the contrary has been cited and, the principle being as spacious as it has been expressed to be, no objection is on that account sustainable. For these reasons, I would accept Mr Sumption's second main submission and hold that the charge over book debts of the company, as created by the debenture, was, unless and until their proceeds were paid into the specified account, a valid fixed charge.

D

On the terms of condition 12(A) as I have construed and would implement them, Mr Sumption's first main submission and the ground on which the case was decided by Knox J do not arise for consideration. While repeating my belief that it was hardly, if at all, advanced before the judge, I would allow the appeal and make whatever declaration is appropriate to reflect the ground of decision indicated.

E

Russell LJ: I agree.

Scott Baker J: I also agree.

(*Appeal allowed*)

F

G

H

A Jenice Ltd & Ors v Dan.

Queen's Bench Division.
R Titheridge QC (sitting as a deputy High Court judge).
Judgment delivered 3 June 1992.

B
*Company identification – Company's name to appear in its correspondence etc. –
Company's name misspelled on cheques by omission of letter – Whether director
personally liable – Companies Act 1985, s. 349.*

**Where a company's cheques bore the name 'Primkeen Limited' when its name was
Primekeen Limited, the defendant director who signed the cheques was not personally liable
on them under s. 349(4) of the Companies Act 1985: the company's name was mentioned on
the cheques within the meaning of s. 349(1) despite the spelling or typographical error. A
misspelling by the omission of a letter in the middle of a word was distinguishable from the**
C **omission of a whole word (Hendon v Adelman (1973) 117 SJ 631), the transposition of
words (Atkin v Wardle & Ors (1889) 61 LT 23; (1889) 5 TLR 734 (CA)) or an unacceptable
abbreviation (Durham Fancy Goods Ltd v Michael Jackson (Fancy Goods) Ltd & Anor
[1968] 2 QB 839).**

The following cases were referred to in the judgment:

Atkin v Wardle & Ors (1889) 61 LT 23; (1889) 5 TLR 734 (CA).
D *Bocking v Roberts* [1974] QB 307.
Bondina Ltd v Rollaway Shower Blinds Ltd & Ors (1985) 1 BCC 99,590; [1986] 1 WLR
517.
Durham Fancy Goods Ltd v Michael Jackson (Fancy Goods) Ltd & Anor [1968] 2 QB
839.
Hendon v Adelman & Ors (1973) 117 SJ 631.
E *Penrose v Martyr* (1858) EB & E 499; 120 ER 595.
Wilkes (John) (Footwear) Ltd v Lee International (Footwear) Ltd & Ors (1985)
1 BCC 99,452.

Paul Staddon (instructed by Mackrell Turner Garrett) for the plaintiffs.

Marcia Shekerdemian (instructed by Landau & Co, Edgware) for the defendant.

F ### JUDGMENT

R Titheridge QC: This matter raises an interesting question. There are five actions
brought against the same defendant, Mr Joseph Saloman Dan, and they are all brought
in respect of cheques signed by the defendant, and clearly intended to be signed, on behalf
of a company of which he was a director called Primekeen Ltd.

All the plaintiffs in the five actions were manufacturers or suppliers of leather
G garments. The cheques were presented to the various plaintiffs in late 1990 or early 1991,
drawn on an account with the National Westminster Bank, Edgware branch. All the
cheques were dishonoured on presentation and were returned to the various plaintiffs
marked 'refer to drawer'. Soon thereafter the plaintiffs gave notice of dishonour. By
letter dated 11 February, the plaintiffs' then solicitors received notice under s. 98 of the
Insolvency Act 1986 concerning a proposed creditors' voluntary liquidation. Each of the
cheques bore the name 'Primkeen Limited' printed upon them, in the ordinary way in
H which cheques now have the account holder's name printed by the bank and, as I have
made clear already, the registered name of the company was in fact Primekeen, with an
'e' in the middle.

Those are agreed facts for the purpose of the matter before me, and having issued their
writs with the statement of claim endorsed thereon, the plaintiffs all applied for summary
judgment under O. 14. The application was resisted by the defendant, who said quite

shortly and simply and exhibited the relevant documents, 'Well, it's not my fault. I gave   A
the correct company name to the bank. It's all the fault of the bank, who have printed
the cheques, and I didn't know, I didn't appreciate, that the name had been misspelt'. In
those O. 14 proceedings, the defendant indicated his intention of joining the bank as a
third party, claiming against them that they owed him a duty to ensure that the relevant
statutory provision was complied with and not to do anything that would adversely affect
his position, as it would be adversely affected if he were personally liable on the cheques
because, as he put it, of an error on the part of the bank.   B

Master Turner ordered that the following issue should be determined in accordance
with the provisions of O. 14A:

> 'Whether the defendant is personally liable to the plaintiff in the circumstances set
> out in para. 8 of the statement of claim.'

And para. 8 of the statement of claim in each case reads as follows: C

> 'By virtue of s. 349(4) of the *Companies Act* 1985, the defendant is personally liable
> . . .',   .

and then it gives the total amount of the cheques in the particular action,

> '*Particulars:*

> The said cheques bear the incorrect name "Primkeen Limited" while the correct
> registered name of the company is "Primekeen Limited". The defendant is a   D
> director of Primekeen Limited and as such signed or authorised the signing of the
> said cheques.'

When I started to consider this matter, I wondered whether this was a matter properly
to be decided under the provisions of O. 14A, and I observed that the court could then
determine any question of law, or construction of any document, where it appeared to
the court that such a question is suitable for determination without a full trial of the   E
action, and that such determination will finally determine the entire cause or matter, or
any claim or issue therein, and my concern arose from the fact that the third party
proceedings were intended. My fear was increased when I learned that the third party
proceedings have now been issued and that the defence of the third party, as I understand
it in every action, is that no admission is made as to the defendant's liability to the
plaintiff under s. 349 of the Companies Act, and that the defence of the third party in
para. 7 alleges that 'the defendant deliberately used the cheque book knowing of the   F
discrepancy' as it is there described. And it occurred to me that it might at least be
arguable that the factual situation, whether the defendant did know of the error, or did
appreciate it, or even should have appreciated it, might have some bearing on the matter
and, more importantly, it occurred to me that the third party might wish to be heard. I
was fearful that if this matter were decided on this application between the plaintiff and
the defendant, the proceedings might be delayed by an appeal, with ultimately, in third   G
party proceedings (if the plaintiff were to succeed, those third party proceedings would
be simply between the third party and the defendant), matters of fact might be found by
the court that would bear upon this matter. However, I was told that the third party, the
bank, had been notified of the situation and had indicated no wish to be heard, but
having seen the terms of the recent correspondence with the third party, I thought it
prudent to accept the offer by counsel in this case, to make a further enquiry of the third
party to confirm that they had no wish to be heard on this particular issue and were   H
content that the matter should be decided as the master ordered that it should be decided.
And I am grateful to them for making that enquiry, which resulted in the answer that
they did understand the situation and were content that the matter should proceed today.

I am also extremely indebted to both counsel – on each side – for an able and concise
argument in a field which I am bound to say I do not find altogether easy; that may be

A because, instinctively, I shy away from questions of semantics and adopt what I myself would regard as a broad common sense approach to matters of this sort, looking very much at the purpose of relevant legislation and seeking a common sense solution.

The facts, as I have indicated, for the purpose of this hearing are agreed.

Let me now turn to the relevant statutory provisions. That is now s. 349 of the *Companies Act* 1985 and it provides as follows:

B '(1) Every company shall have its name mentioned in legible characters',

and then it sets out all the documents on which the name in legible characters should be mentioned – business letters, notices and so on, including in (c) bills of exchange and cheques and, I observe, orders for money or goods. Subsection (4) provides as follows:

C 'If an officer of a company or a person on its behalf signs or authorises to be signed on behalf of the company any bill of exchange, promissory note, endorsement, cheque or order for money or goods in which the company's name is not mentioned as required by subsection (1), he is liable to a fine; and he is further personally liable to the holder of a bill of exchange, promissory note, cheque or order for money or goods for the amount of it (unless it is duly paid by the company).'

On behalf of the plaintiff, counsel for the plaintiff submits that the matter is very simple and is in effect decided by well established and binding authority. He says that D none of these cheques bore the name of the company – that, I interpret, in the words of the statute, none of these cheques had the company name mentioned on the cheques, and the authorities upon which he relies I shall come to in a moment.

On behalf of the defendant, the submission is again that the case is simple, but not surprisingly for a very different reason. It is simple because the name of the company is mentioned, it is simply misspelt. And such error as there is, the error caused by the E misspelling or possibly a typographical error, is de minimis, and if one looks at the purpose of the legislation, the purpose is clearly to ensure that people dealing with companies know both that they are dealing with a limited company and know the identity of the particular limited company with which they are dealing. In effect, the object of the legislation is to avoid confusion and in this case there is no confusion at all, there is simply a misspelling based on a typographical error.

F Free of authority, I do not hesitate to say that I find the arguments for the defendant the more cogent and the more attractive. There is, in my judgment, in principle, a distinction to be drawn between a misdescription which may mislead (although authority clearly shows that it does not have to) and a spelling or typographical error which in the circumstances of a particular case cannot possibly mislead. In the course of argument, I reminded counsel of the words of Thomas Hobbes in *The Leviathan*:

G 'Words are the counters of wise men, they do but reckon by them, but they are the money of fools'

and, as I think I have already indicated, I am not over attracted in principle by matters of semantics. But I must consider, and carefully consider, the submissions of Mr Staddon, on behalf of the plaintiffs, that I am bound by authority.

So let me turn, and in the order in which he dealt with them in his submissions, to the H cases. First of all, he invited my attention to the case of *Atkin v Wardle & Ors* (1889) 5 TLR 734 though, as I observed at the end of argument, in the course of the typing of his skeleton argument, the name 'Atkin' appears with an extra 's' showing how easy it is to make errors of this sort. That was a case where, according to the skeleton argument, the South Shields Salt Water Baths Company Limited, was misdescribed in a bill as the 'Salt Water Baths Company Limited, South Shields', so that all the appropriate words were there, they were simply in the wrong order. The defendant directors accepted the bill as

directors of the 'South Shields Salt Water Baths Company' – that is putting most of the　A
words in the correct order but leaving out the word 'Limited'. It was held that the bill
was drawn and intended to be drawn upon the company, and accepted by the directors
on behalf of the company, so that it came precisely within the words of what was then
s. 42 of the *Companies Act* 1862, but that the real name of the company did not appear
upon the bill before it was accepted. And paraphrasing from the report of the judgment
of Lord Esher MR, when the directors accepted the bill they did not put the real name of
the company upon it, because they omitted the word 'Limited':　　　　　　　　　　　B

> 'Therefore, the name of the company did not appear upon the bill. It was said that
> by adding the two together, or by taking a piece from each and adding those pieces
> together they would get the right name of the company. That, however, would not
> do. It was said that the misdescription must be a material one, but the section
> contained no such qualification. The defendants had accepted a bill without the
> name of the company being on it, and they were personally liable.'　　　　　　　　C

Lindley LJ in his judgment (shortly summarised), said that s. 41 and 42 of the 1862 Act
were two of the most important sections and the court must take care not to relax them.

I was also given, most helpfully, the report in the Law Times (and it is a full report,
(1889) 61 LT 23) of the judgment in that case of Denman J, and it is rather surprising to
learn that, having reported Denman J's judgment in full, the Law Times did not report
the Court of Appeal decision. It is interesting to note that at least before Denman J the　D
case of *Penrose v Martyr* (1858) EB & E 499, to which I have been referred, was cited
and that the judge indicated that he had considerable doubt about the matter, saying (at
p. 26):

> 'On the whole, though not without considerable doubt, I am of opinion that the
> two variations from the proper designation of the company are sufficient to bring
> the defendants within the provisions of sec. 42, and that the intention of the Act
> was to ensure extreme strictness in all the transactions on behalf of limited　　E
> companies as regards the use of the registered name of the company, not only in
> enforcing the use of the word "limited", but in all other respects. Cases may easily
> be conceived in which a very slight variation from the registered name might lead
> a person to believe that he was taking a bill of a totally different kind of company
> from that to which the directors signing the bill really belonged, and it may well be
> conceived that sects. 41 and 42 were inserted, or rather re-enacted, by the　　　F
> Legislature, as they were after the decision of *Penrose v Martyr* with the intention
> of ensuring the strictest accuracy in this respect for the protection of the public.'

The next case upon which the plaintiffs rely is a case decided by Donaldson J in 1968.
That is the case of *Durham Fancy Goods Ltd v Michael Jackson (Fancy Goods) Ltd* [1968]
2 QB 839. There, the correct name of the company was Michael Jackson (Fancy Goods)
Ltd, but the bill was drawn addressed to 'M. Jackson (Fancy Goods) Ltd' and inscribed
with the words of acceptance:　　　　　　　　　　　　　　　　　　　　　　　　　G

> 'Accepted payable . . . For and on behalf of M. Jackson (Fancy Goods) Ltd,
> Manchester'.

Donaldson J held that 'M' was not an acceptable abbreviation for 'Michael', and that,
accordingly, the second defendant to the action, who was the director and secretary of
the company, had committed a criminal offence under what was then s. 108 of the
Companies Act 1948, but that that liability could not be enforced because of estoppel.　H
The judge said at p. 845F:

> 'Mr. Rokison for Mr. Jackson submits that there was sufficient compliance with
> the section in the present case because (a) the bill made it clear that the acceptors
> were a limited company and (b) there was no confusion as to their identity. In
> support of the first of these submissions he relied upon *Penrose* v. *Martyr* in which
> Crompton J. stated that the purpose of the corresponding statutory provision

A "was to prevent persons from being deceived into the belief that they had a security with the unlimited liability of common law, when they had but the security of a company limited"

and upon the judgment of Scrutton J. in *F. Stacey & Co. Ltd.* v. *Wallis* affirming this view and deciding that "Ltd." was an acceptable abbreviation for "Limited". Unfortunately for Mr. Jackson, the second submission is unsupported by

B authority. Indeed it is contrary to the tenor of the decision of Denman J. and of the Court of Appeal in *Atkins* v. *Wardle.*' – Interestingly, *Atkins* with an 's', another example of misspelling. – 'There the drawer of the bill was a shareholder in the "South Shields Salt Water Baths Company (Limited)" but he drew on "Salt Water Baths Company (Limited), South Shields" and the directors accepted on behalf of "South Shields Salt Water Bath Company" which was equally incorrect. No question of confusion as to identity or as to the status of the drawers as a

C limited liability company could have arisen. Nevertheless the directors were held to be personally liable, Lord Esher M.R. pointing out that the statute did not require the misdescription to be material.'

Stopping there it is clear to me that I am bound by the authority of *Atkin v Wardle*, reinforced as it is by the decision of Donaldson J, that the fact that the misdescription is not material is of no importance at all, and that I entirely accept. However, just looking

D at the case of *Durham Fancy Goods Ltd v Michael Jackson (Fancy Goods) Ltd*, I can and do distinguish it from the present case. There, as Donaldson J held, 'M' was not an acceptable abbreviation of 'Michael', and what in my judgment would be a comparable case to the present, would be a case where, as I put to Mr Staddon in the course of his interesting argument, the word 'Michael' was there but had been misspelt Micheal instead of Michael; or, for the sake of illustration, a case where the name was there, but instead

E of two of the letters being placed in the wrong order, one of them had been omitted. To that Mr Staddon said, 'Well, that's right. In the plaintiff's submission, that would not be compliance with the Act but in any case I distinguish it'. Myself, I find that situation indistinguishable, and it is a different situation, in my judgment, from the situation that in fact arose in that case.

Looking at the matter in principle, if Mr Staddon's submission is right, it means this; that if, perhaps because of pressure of time, a company director of a company like

F Michael Jackson (Fancy Goods) Ltd, writes out an order misspelling the name of the company in one of the ways I have indicated, he is, in the absence of payment for the goods by the company, personally liable for the order and has committed a criminal offence. And I look again at the words of the Act, and I ask: in those circumstances, is that a case – where an error of that sort is made, a misspelling, which not only causes no confusion but is incapable of causing confusion – where it can properly be said that the

G company's name is not mentioned? And for these purposes I shall assume that in the illustrations I have given, legible characters are used. But that poses another and perhaps interesting academic question: suppose the error is not in fact a misspelling at all, but in writing the word 'Michael', the 'a' or the 'e' (or perhaps both of them) become illegible or subject to confusion, is that a breach of the Act? I shall leave that interesting question, but I shall simply observe that this is a section which imposes a criminal liability. True,

H there is a great deal of difference between a criminal offence committed by inadvertence, which may be an offence of strict liability, and a criminal offence committed deliberately and perhaps with some fraudulent intent, and there are all sorts of variations between, but sitting in a criminal court I should find it extremely difficult to say that somebody responsible for an understandable and simple and common spelling error, were guilty of a criminal offence on the basis that, because of the spelling error, the court could be satisfied so that it was sure, that the company name was not mentioned in the document.

In my judgment I can also distinguish the *Atkin* case, because that was not a case of a   A
misspelling, that also was a case of the omission of a word or words or, as to the original
addressee, the wrong order of words. I derive support for my view upon the words of
Denman J in that case and, more importantly, to the case to which I have already referred
several times, and to which I shall come, *Penrose v Martyr*. But at all events, I have
reached the stage now when I can and do distinguish both the *Atkin* case and the *Durham
Fancy Goods* case.
                                                                                                B
I come now to the next case upon which the plaintiffs rely, which is the case of *Hendon
v Adelman* (1973) 117 SJ 631. There, the name of the company was 'L. & R. Agencies
Limited' and the director signed a cheque for the company, writing the name
'LR Agencies Limited', missing out the ampersand. This is the case of the missing 'e' that
I am now considering, that was the case of the missing ampersand. That was decided by
MacKenna J and it is interesting to note that the cheque had the printed words put there
by the bank, in accordance with what by then had become standard practice. And the   C
bank had not copied the company's name correctly and, as the judge observed, had
omitted the ampersand which connected the 'L' and 'R'. MacKenna J said that it would
not be consistent with earlier authorities if he were to hold that a description was
sufficient which totally omitted a connecting ampersand; 'LR Agencies' was not the same
thing as 'L. & R. Agencies'. The omission of a word seemed a worse defect than its
transposition or abbreviation, and 'transposition' I take to be a reference to the *Atkin*
case and 'abbreviation' to the *Durham Fancy Goods* case. The report of the judge's   D
judgment goes on:

> 'Section 108(1)(c) of the Companies Act 1948, which required that every company
> "shall have its name mentioned in legible characters" in cheques purported to be
> signed by or on behalf of the company, had not been complied with and, as the
> cheque had not been duly paid, each of the defendants was liable to the plaintiff.'

It is perfectly clear that the judgment of MacKenna J proceeded on analogy with the   E
Atkin and the *Durham Fancy Goods* case and related to the omission of a word, and
although at first sight it might appear that there is little difference between the error in
that case and the error in the present case, I find that there is a difference, and in my
judgment a misspelling, by the omission of a letter in the middle of a word, is not to be
equated with the omission of a whole word.

I entirely accept, on authority which is binding upon me, that a strict construction has   F
to be given to the statutory provision, but a strict construction does not require any court
to reach a nonsensical conclusion, and in my judgment the conclusion that the plaintiffs
invite me to reach is nonsensical. For, in truth, no ordinary person, looking at what has
happened in this case, would say, in the words of the section, that the company's name is
not mentioned. It is mentioned and it is misspelt and, as I have observed, in circumstances
that do not lead to any of the vices against which the statutory provisions were directed.
                                                                                                G
I do not in those circumstances propose to deal in full with the argument presented on
behalf of the defendant. There is a most helpful case summary setting out the cases that
have been decided and drawing attention to the particular relevant facts of each case.

I have been helpfully referred both to the current edition of *Palmer's Company Law*,
and to the twenty-fourth edition of *Palmer* where there is a passage at p. 85, under para.
7-04 indicating the view of the editor that what is now s. 349(4) was interpreted too
strictly in some of the cases. And the submission is made in the previous edition that   H
where there is no danger of confusion and a variation from the registered name of the
company is only trivial, the officer who signed on behalf of the company should not be
held personally liable. And it goes on, as it seems to me in principle is right:

> 'But it should not be misunderstood.' – having referred to recent cases of *Bondina
> Ltd v Rollaway Shower Blinds Ltd & Ors* (1985) 1 BCC 99,590 and *John Wilkes*

A *(Footwear) Ltd v Lee International (Footwear) Ltd & Ors* (1985) 1 BCC 99,452 – 'Only if the reference to the company is *unambiguous*, will the courts adopt a more liberal attitude to the interpretation of section 349(4).'

I am not myself convinced that the reference to a liberal interpretation of a penal statute is right. The principles applicable to the interpretation of a penal statute I regard as clear. However, I accept entirely the view of the author of the penultimate edition as to the

B principles to be applied and in my judgment the case of *Penrose v Martyr*, and I have a copy of the English Report, decided in the middle of the last century is of interest ((1858) 120 ER 595). The bill there was addressed to the 'Saltash Watermen's Steam Packet Company, Saltash', the word 'Limited' was in fact omitted. It was accepted by the secretary of the company, John Martyr, in these terms:

'Accepted, payable at Messrs Barclay & Co., Bankers, London.

C John Martyr, Secretary to the said Company.'

Coleridge J is reported as having said (at p. 502; 597):

'The object of the Legislature obviously was to force notice of the limited liability on those dealing with the Company; and the clause is in one sense penal, in another remedial. I cannot doubt that this is within the enactment.'

D Crompton J said:

'I think that the intention of the enactment plainly was to prevent persons from being deceived into the belief that they had a security with the unlimited liability of common law, when they had but the security of a Company limited; and that, if they were so deceived, they should have the personal security of the officer. Therefore I think we must see that the acceptance is one which, if the name had been right, would have bound the Company.'

E In the light of what is said about that case in subsequent authorities, it is my conclusion that the right approach, and the approach that authority shows is the right approach, is that the enactment should be construed strictly and that the court should be concerned, bearing well in mind that whether or not there has been any actual confusion is immaterial, should bear very much in mind the purpose of the legislation, but as I have indicated, there is a great deal of difference between the cases that have been decided and

F the present case, and there is a line to be drawn in the manner that I have indicated.

Support is also urged upon me on the defendant's side from the sixth edition of *Pennington's Company Law*, but although, broadly, I agree with the reason given in that work for the statutory provision, I do not regard it as other than a support, or a good source for the view I have already come to on the authorities.

G I should say one word about the de minimis principle. On behalf of the plaintiffs it is urged that de minimis has no application and I am invited to consider by analogy the dangerous drugs case of *Bocking v Roberts* [1974] QB 307. I do not myself regard that as being a helpful case for the purposes of deciding the present case.

On behalf of the defendants it is strongly urged that the de minimis principle should apply. That may be right, but I am not going to base my judgment on the application of

H the de minimis principle, although, as I make clear, I think that the argument has some force. What is important – and it does not seem to me that it matters whether one says that the de minimis principle is being applied or not – is to have regard to the actual words of the Act. Putting the matter in its simplest possible terms, as I have indicated, the question is: In the circumstances of this particular case, has the company, Primekeen, had its name mentioned in legible characters on these cheques? And in my judgment it has, despite a spelling or typographical error.

A

It follows that upon this issue I give judgment for the defendant, and I think it must follow that in those circumstances that disposes of all these actions, subject to appeal, between the plaintiffs and the defendant.

(*Order accordingly*)

B

C

D

E

F

G

H

A
Re Whitchurch Insurance Consultants Ltd.

Chancery Division (Companies Court).
Harman J.
Judgment delivered 2 November 1992.

B
Company meetings – Quorum – Power of court to order meeting – Whether it was impracticable to call or conduct meeting in deadlocked company – Materiality of pending unfair prejudice petition – Companies Act 1985, s. 371, 459.

This was an originating summons seeking an order pursuant to s. 371 of the Companies Act 1985 for an extraordinary general meeting of the company to be convened to remove the minority shareholder as a director.

C
The applicant held 666 of the 1,000 shares in the company and the respondent held the other 334. They were both directors and the only directors of the company. The business relationship between them broke down and meetings of the board and the company could not be held because the respondent failed to attend. On the working day before hearing of the s. 371 application, the respondent presented a s. 459 petition. The petition gave no substantial grounds for alleging oppression or prejudice save the attempt to remove the respondent at the intended meeting.

D
Held, making the order sought under s. 371:

1. The existence of a s. 459 petition at the date of hearing of the s. 371 application was a matter which bore upon the discretion of the court, but it did not prevent the court exercising its powers under s. 371. (Re Sticky Fingers Restaurant Ltd [1991] BCC 754 distinguished.)

2. In respect of this company on these facts it was right to exercise the discretion under s. 371. It was impracticable to hold a meeting and it was plainly right and desirable to get a proper board into the company by allowing the meeting to be held for the purpose of dealing with the present inquorate state, both of board meetings and general meetings. (Re Opera Photographic Ltd (1989) 5 BCC 601 followed.)

E

The following cases were referred to in the judgment:

El Sombrero Ltd, Re [1958] Ch 900.
Opera Photographic Ltd, Re (1989) 5 BCC 601; [1989] 1 WLR 634.
Paragon Group Ltd v Burnell & Ors [1991] Ch 498.
Sticky Fingers Restaurant Ltd, Re [1991] BCC 754.

F

Catherine Roberts (instructed by B P Collins & Co) for the applicant.

Richard King (instructed by David Lewis & Co) for the respondent.

JUDGMENT

G
Harman J: This is an originating summons issued on 18 September 1992 seeking an order pursuant to s. 371 of the Companies Act 1985, that an extraordinary general meeting of the company be convened by the court for the purpose of considering and, if thought fit, passing, the resolution in the schedule to the originating summons and for directions as to the manner in which the meeting should be called.

H
The case arises out of unhappy differences between Mr Ian Rudd ('Mr Rudd') and Rosalind Rudd ('Mrs Rudd') who is not Mr Rudd's wife or sister. She and Mr Rudd lived together as man and wife for something like ten years between 1981 and 1991. Unhappily, as in so many relationships, that personal relationship broke down and the parties have not lived together since October 1991. Mr Rudd and Mrs Rudd both held shares in the company. The division was 666 held by Mr Rudd and 334 held by Mrs Rudd. They were both directors and the only directors of the company. Not

surprisingly, the personal relationship having broken down, the business relationship   A
also became difficult.

In the result, in June 1992, in fact on 24 June, Mr Rudd wrote a formal letter to the directors seeking the convening of an extraordinary general meeting of the company to pass an ordinary resolution removing Rosalind Rudd from office as a director. The board of the company was unable to act upon that requisition because Mrs Rudd absented herself and the board was thus, as the jargon goes, inquorate. In the result,   B
Mr Rudd himself, as he was entitled to do, pursuant to s. 368(4) of the Companies Act 1985, gave formal notice convening an extraordinary general meeting to be held on Monday, 17 August at 9 am. That notice was given on 21 July 1992. Mrs Rudd made it clear, through a man calling himself a commercial counsellor, that that date was inconvenient to her but that expressly 25 August would be a convenient date for the holding of the meeting. By agreement the EGM was rescheduled for 25 August but 25 August came and Mrs Rudd did not attend. No effective extraordinary general meeting   C
could be held because one shareholder alone is not a quorum pursuant to the relevant provisions of the statute. There, therefore, followed this originating summons.

The originating summons came before the registrar, who would of course normally deal with such matters, on 23 October and, despite the evidence in support of the originating summons having been in Mrs Rudd's solicitor's hands since 2 October, no affidavit in answer had been filed or produced. Religious holidays running to six working   D
days in the month of October were alleged to have prevented the drafting of an affidavit. I find the excuse mere prevarication. On the morning of 23 October a handwritten affidavit sworn by Mrs Rudd was handed over saying that the contents were true and that the share register of the company, which shows the shares held as I have recited them, does not reflect the true position of the parties. In para. 3 Mrs Rudd swore:

> 'There was a specific understanding between Mr Rudd and myself there would remain a parity of shares between us at all times.'   E

That statement is now withdrawn as being not relied upon. That can only really mean that Mrs Rudd now admits that her affidavit was not true.

The registrar, faced on 23 October with that affidavit, said that the only thing to do was to adjourn the matter to the judge, which he did for today, 2 November, and ordered the parties to attend for cross-examination upon this stark issue of fact which apparently existed. However, Mr Rudd having filed an affidavit totally denying that there was any   F
question of parity of shareholdings, on 28 October, that is to say Wednesday of last week, Mrs Rudd swore a further affidavit saying that she withdrew the first affidavit, thereby removing the alleged issue of fact, and conceding that Mr Rudd is, indeed, a two-thirds beneficial owner of the shares in the company and she is a one-third holder of the shares in the company.

Mrs Rudd, however, having made various statements about the extent of religious   G
holidays that have occurred, now says that she is intending to present a petition under s. 459. Indeed, on Friday, 30 October, that is to say on the working day immediately before today, she did present a s. 459 petition. That petition does not contain the proper terms pursuant to the practice direction, which it is well known the companies judges regard as important, because there was joined with the claim to relief under s. 461 a plea for a winding up upon the just and equitable ground, but no statement about the applicability of s. 127 relief was included. No proper explanation has been given to me   H
how that happened. It is, of course, an error and quite a bad error.

Further, the petition as presented on Friday is in the form of the draft petition as it was when the affidavit was sworn. No substantial grounds for alleging oppression or prejudice are given save the attempt to remove Mrs Rudd at the intended meeting to be held pursuant to the court's summons under s. 371. That is to say, the petition alleges a

A   future exclusion from management not an exclusion existing at the date of presentation of the petition. Further, the petition makes in para. 13 two rather, as it seems to me, perfunctory allegations of mismanagement by Mr Rudd. Upon the evidence available to me it appears that Mrs Rudd is well up to managing the computer on which the company operates its affairs. It is said that she changes the passwords upon it, whatever that exactly means. But at present Mrs Rudd's claim that she had no means of knowledge or understanding of the conduct of the company's business for the periods which she alleges

B   in para. 13(a) and (b) of her present petition under s. 459, seems to me very doubtful.

The argument for Mr Rudd presented to me is that under s. 371 all the court has to consider is:

> 'Is it impracticable to call a meeting of the company or alternatively to conduct the meeting of the company in the manner prescribed by the Act?'

C   If the court is satisfied of either of those factual situations then the court 'may', plainly conferring a discretion, order a meeting to be held, called or conducted in the manner the court thinks fit, and the court may give ancillary or consequential directions upon such order being made.

In support of that argument Miss Roberts referred to the decision of Wynn Parry J, a very experienced company judge, in *Re El Sombrero Ltd* [1958] Ch 900, which decision I

D   followed and applied recently in a decision upon a different but comparable provision under O. 65, r. 4 of the Rules of the Supreme Court, called *Paragon Group Ltd v Burnell & Ors* [1991] Ch 498 which decision was upheld by the Court of Appeal. From those decisions, it is submitted, it is clear that the question for the court under s. 371 (as is the question for the court under O. 65, r. 4) is: does the evidence show that it is impracticable to conduct a meeting in the one case, alternatively, it is impracticable to serve a document in the other case, and the only questions are, what do the facts show about the difficulty

E   or not of doing either of those particular things.

The decision of Morritt J in *Re Opera Photographic Ltd* (1989) 5 BCC 601 is to much the same effect. In that case the shareholders held 51 per cent and 49 per cent of the share capital in contrast to the 66 per cent/34 per cent imbalance here. But the principal holding was that Morritt J did not accept that the existence of s. 459 prevented a shareholder asking the court in its discretion to convene a meeting under s. 371 in order to pass a

F   resolution under s. 303 of the *Companies Act* 1985.

I was referred to the decision of Mervyn Davies J in *Re Sticky Fingers Restaurant Ltd* [1991] BCC 754 where he had rather different facts before him. In his case a s. 459 petition had been presented on 8 March 1991 and a s. 371 application was issued on 23 May 1991, plainly as a step in the light of the extant s. 459 petition. The facts were totally different to those before me. Counsel before me said that he would not support the proposition of Mervyn Davies J at p. 757F in the report where that judge said:

G

> 'The difficulty, as I see it, arises from the fact that (1) it may be proper to use s. 371 to overcome the difficulty of achieving a quorum, but (2) it is not a proper use of s. 371 to use it indirectly to secure the removal of a director while a s. 459 petition is pending.'

Counsel observed by reference to the facts in this case where the s. 371 application was on the very verge of coming on for hearing today, Monday 2 November, when on Friday

H   30 October the s. 459 petition was presented, that he was not prepared to argue that in every case where a s. 459 petition is presented apparently with a view, at least in part, of frustrating an already pending s. 371 application there should be a bar to the exercise of the discretion given by s. 371. That concession by counsel seems to me to be right. With the greatest possible respect to Mervyn Davies J, whose views on the Companies Act I would always follow if possible, I cannot think that the mere existence of a s. 459 petition

at the date of hearing of the s. 371 application is inevitably a bar. It may be a bar. It is   A
obviously a matter which bears upon the discretion of the court, but it is not something
which prevents the court exercising its powers.

I am left with the question whether in respect of this company on these facts it is right
to exercise the court's discretion. I am wholly satisfied that it is impracticable to hold a
meeting within the meaning of that word and, in my view, it is plainly right and desirable
to get a proper board into this company by allowing the meeting to be held for the   B
purpose of dealing with the present inquorate state, both of board meetings and general
meetings.

In those circumstances, it seems to me, I can and should properly distinguish the
decision in *Re Sticky Fingers Restaurant*, follow the decision of Morritt J in *Opera
Photographic* and make the order which Miss Roberts seeks.

(Order accordingly)   C

D

E

F

G

H

A Re a Debtor (No. 64 of 1992).
Bradford & Bingley Building Society v a Debtor.

Chancery Division (Bankruptcy).
Colin Rimer QC (sitting as a deputy judge of the Chancery Division).
Judgment delivered 5 November 1993.

B *Bankruptcy – Individual voluntary arrangement – Statutory demand – Debtor sought to set aside statutory demand – Whether debt was 'a liquidated sum' – Whether creditor was bound by voluntary arrangement – Whether creditor had notice of meeting – Whether creditor could have 'constructive notice' of meeting – Insolvency Act 1986, s. 257(2), 260(2), 267(2), 268; Insolvency Rules 1986, r. 6.1(5), 12.16.*

C This was an appeal by a building society against a district judge's order setting aside a statutory demand which had been served by the society on the debtor. The demand alleged that the debtor owed the society the sum of £411,501.18 and that such sum was payable immediately and was unsecured.

The district judge accepted two arguments advanced by the debtor. The first was to the effect that the sum claimed in the demand was not 'a liquidated sum' within s. 267(2)(b) of the Insolvency Act 1986, and that therefore it was not competent for the society to base a statutory demand on it. The debtor argued that although the demand stated the amount of D the original loan to the debtor and her husband, it did not state either the amount of the total debt due at the date of the demand or the value which the society put upon the security (as required by r. 6.1(5) of the Insolvency Rules 1986).

The second argument was that the debtor was subject to a voluntary arrangement pursuant to Pt. VIII of the 1986 Act. The debtor asserted that the society was bound by such arrangement (under s. 260 of the 1986 Act) and that, in consequence, it ought not to E have served the statutory demand. The debtor's evidence was that the notice pursuant to s. 257 of the 1986 Act convening the meeting of creditors to approve the arrangement had been sent to the society. The society's evidence was that the notice had never been received (because it was sent to the wrong address of the society). The district judge held that although the society did not have actual notice of the meeting, nevertheless it did have 'constructive' notice of it, because notice of the meeting had been posted to it, albeit not F received (r. 12.16 of the 1986 rules) and it was therefore bound by the voluntary arrangement and precluded from serving the statutory demand.

Held, allowing the society's appeal:

1. Rule 6.1(5) recognised that it was competent for a secured creditor to put a value on its security and to serve a statutory demand for the amount of the total debt less such value. If the net figure resulting was not 'a liquidated sum' for the purposes of s. 267(2)(b), a G demand prepared in purported compliance with r. 6.1(5) could never be a valid demand.

2. If the value which the creditor put on his security was a value with which the debtor disagreed there would be a difference as to the correct amount of the sum due to the creditor, but that difference could not by itself result in the sum claimed in the demand ceasing to be 'a liquidated sum' and becoming an 'unliquidated' sum.

3. Although the society did not specify in the demand the two figures, for the indebtedness H and the value of the security, which it had used to arrive at the sum claimed to be due, that sum did represent the society's calculation of the debt less the value put by it on the security. Accordingly, the sum so arrived at was no less 'a liquidated sum' than it would have been if the society had correctly complied with r. 6.1(5) and had duly specified both the figures.

4. In specifying whether or not a creditor was bound by the arrangement, s. 260(2)(b) focused on whether or not he 'had notice of' the meeting, meaning had received notice of it.

By contrast, the presumed validation of a meeting under r. 12.16 depended essentially on   A
whether or not the notice was duly sent, whether or not actually received. Further, the only
presumption that r. 12.16 in terms raised was as to the validity of the summoning and
holding of the meeting: it did not purport also to raise a presumption that a creditor had
notice of the meeting when in fact he had none.

5. Accordingly, even though a s. 257 meeting might be presumed by r. 12.16 to have been
duly summoned and held, nevertheless a creditor who had no actual notice of it would not be   B
bound by any arrangement which was approved at it. The reason why he was not so bound
was that s. 260(2)(b) provided that the arrangement bound only those persons who (inter
alia) had notice of the meeting, whereas such creditor had none.

6. A creditor who did not receive, and remained in ignorance of, the notice of a meeting
which was sent to him could not be said to have 'constructive notice' of such meeting:
r. 12.16 did not deem the creditor to have had notice of the meeting, it merely provided (in
effect) that the non-receipt by him of a notice duly sent would not by itself be sufficient to   C
enable him to say that the meeting had not been duly summoned and held.

7. The society had no notice of the s. 257 meeting. Section 260(2)(b) therefore showed
that it was not one of the debtor's creditors which was bound by the voluntary arrangement.
It was therefore entitled to serve a statutory demand on the debtor with a view, if the same
was not complied with, to the subsequent presentation of a bankruptcy petition.

The following cases were referred to in the judgment: D

Debtor (No. 1 of 1987), Re a [1989] 1 WLR 271.
Debtor (No. 106 of 1992), Re a The Independent, 20 April 1992, Evans-Lombe QC.
McKeen, Re (unreported, 1 April 1992, Morritt J).

James Barker (instructed by Hammond Suddards, Manchester) for Bradford &
Bingley Building Society.   E

Jill Johnston (instructed by Tringhams) for the debtor.

JUDGMENT

Colin Rimer QC: This is an appeal by Bradford & Bingley Building Society ('the
society') against an order of District Judge Willers made on 18 February 1993 at the
Hertford County Court. By that order the district judge set aside a statutory demand
which had been served by the society on Mrs G ('the debtor') and ordered the society to   F
pay the debtor's costs of her successful application. The outline facts are as follows.

On 9 October 1992 the society served on the debtor a statutory demand under
s. 268(1)(a) of the *Insolvency Act* 1986. The demand alleged that the debtor owed the
society the sum of £411,501.18 and that such sum was payable immediately and was
unsecured. In view of one of the issues which I have to decide it is necessary to set out the
particulars in full. They read: G

'By a mortgage dated 27 November 1989 the debtor, together with [her husband]
covenanted to pay to Leamington Spa Building Society (the lender) the sum of
£675,250.00 together with interest thereon, costs and expenses. The debt was
secured on a [described property].

By cl. 5 of the said mortgage it is a term of the loan that if the borrower shall make
default in payment of any monthly instalment then in such case the mortgage debt   H
shall become immediately due and payment on 21 May 1991. [sic]

On 21 May 1991 the society obtained an order for possession of the property in
the High Court Chancery Division.

The society's anticipated loss based upon professional advice from independent
valuers is £411,501.18.

A   By an instrument of transfer of engagements dated 19 March 1991, Leamington Spa Building Society transferred all its property assets and liabilities to [the society] who are now entitled to the moneys demanded hereunder.'

On 23 October 1992 the debtor issued her application to have the demand set aside. It was supported by two affidavits sworn by her husband and herself. Those affidavits raised two arguments as to why the demand should be set aside.

B   The first argument was to the effect that the sum claimed in the demand was not 'a liquidated sum', and that therefore it was not competent for the society to base a statutory demand on it. It was asserted that the demand was instead for what was described as 'an inchoate anticipated loss' based on an undisclosed valuation. It was pointed out that, although the demand stated the amount of the original loan to the debtor and her husband, it did not state either the amount of the total debt due at the date of the demand or the value which the society put upon the security. It was said that what the society had done was to claim a sum equal to its estimate of the likely shortfall that it would suffer in the event of a sale of the security, and that its estimate was made on the basis of an unidentified valuation.

The second argument was that the debtor was subject to a voluntary arrangement made pursuant to Pt. VIII of the 1986 Act. The debtor asserted that the society was bound by such arrangement and that, in consequence, it ought not to have served the statutory demand.

The district judge accepted both arguments and set the demand aside. For the society, Mr Barker submitted that the district judge was in error on both grounds. For the debtor, Miss Johnston sought to uphold the district judge's judgment on both grounds. I will deal with each ground in turn.

(1) The 'no debt for a liquidated sum' point

In at least two respects the particulars of the debt set out in the statutory demand are unhappily formulated. First, something has obviously gone wrong with the drafting of the latter part of the second paragraph.

Secondly, although the society held a security for its debt, the demand failed to specify either the full amount of the debt at the date of the demand or the value which the society had put on its security at such date. The demand thus failed to comply with r. 6.1(5) of the *Insolvency Rules* 1986, which provides that:

'(5) If the creditor holds any security in respect of the debt, the full amount of the debt shall be specified, but–

    (a) there shall in the demand be specified the nature of the security, and the value which the creditor puts upon it as at the date of the demand, and

    (b) the amount of which payment is claimed by the demand shall be the full amount of the debt, less the amount specified as the value of the security.'

Rule 6.1(5) is in apparently mandatory terms; and r. 6.5(4) provides that the court may grant an application to set aside a statutory demand if (inter alia):

'(c) it appears that the creditor holds some security in respect of the debt claimed by the demand, and either Rule 6.1(5) is not complied with in respect of it, or the court is satisfied that the value of the security equals or exceeds the full amount of the debt;'

In view of r. 6.5(4)(c), it might perhaps be thought that the society's non-compliance with r. 6.1(5) might justify the setting aside of the statutory demand. However, Miss Johnston, who also appeared before the district judge, made clear that an argument along

those lines formed no part of the debtor's case, and, if I may say so, I consider that the   A
debtor was probably right in not so arguing. I should, however, explain why.

In this connection I was referred to *Re a Debtor (No. 1 of 1987)* [1989] 1 WLR 271, a
decision of the Court of Appeal. It is unnecessary to refer to the case in any detail, but
the principle of its decision is that deficiencies in the form and contents of a statutory
demand, even including errors involving the overstatement of the debtor's indebtedness
to the creditor, will not automatically entitle the debtor to have the demand set aside.   B
The question in every case is whether, on the facts, injustice would be caused to the
debtor by allowing the particular demand to stand. See, in particular, the judgment of
Nicholls LJ at pp. 276B–F and 279C–G.

In this case the debtor does not claim that the form of the statutory demand has
confused or perplexed her. She understood the route taken by the society in arriving at
the sum claimed of £411,501.18, namely that it had deducted an unspecified valuation of
the property from the (also unspecified) total debt due. It may be that both figures used   C
by the society in its calculation are disputed by the debtor. However, she does not contend
that the value of the security at the date of the demand either equalled or exceeded the
full amount of the debt. She recognises that her indebtedness to the society at that date
exceeded the amount of the security by a substantial margin, being probably well into six
figures, and that the excess remains unpaid.

With regard to the last point, various valuations obtained by the debtor and her   D
husband were put in evidence, suggesting that the security was worth (in May 1992)
between £600,000 and £700,000 and (in August 1992) from £550,000–£600,000. There
was also exhibited a letter of 4 September 1992 from the society stating that the society's
valuations of the property showed it to be worth only about £400,000–£450,000.
However, as against this range of valuations, the unchallenged evidence from the society
is that as at 30 September 1992 the total debt due to it was £942,758.66, with interest
accruing at a daily rate of £279.13. I add that I was told by Mr Barker that the property   E
was eventually sold in May 1993 for £500,000, but nothing turns on that for present
purposes.

In these circumstances, even though it may be that the debtor regards the statutory
demand as overstating her indebtedness (after giving credit for the value of the security),
she does not claim that the deficiencies in the form of the demand are, by themselves,
such as to merit its being set aside. In particular, she does not suggest that the non-   F
compliance with r. 6.1(5) was fatal to the demand. On this particular point I was referred
to a summary, reported in The Independent on 20 April 1992, of the decision in *Re
a Debtor (No. 106 of 1992)* of Mr Evans-Lombe QC, sitting as a deputy judge of the
Chancery Division. The summary is very brief, but is to the effect that it was not fatal to
the statutory demand that it did not refer to the security held by the creditor or specify
the value which the creditor put upon it, the debtor not having been prejudiced by such   G
defects.

The point which the debtor does take, and which the district judge accepted, is this. It
is that a bankruptcy petition can only be founded on a debt which is for 'a liquidated
sum' payable to the creditor and that therefore it follows that the sum demanded by a
statutory demand must also be for such a sum. The debtor's contention is that the sum
demanded by the statutory demand in the present case is not such 'a liquidated sum'.

The requirement for a debt founding a bankruptcy petition to be 'a liquidated sum' is   H
contained in s. 267(2)(b) of the 1986 Act. The material parts of s. 267(1) and (2) read:

'267 *Grounds of creditor's petition*

(1) A creditor's petition must be in respect of one or more debts owed by the
debtor, and the petitioning creditor or each of the petitioning creditors must be a
person to whom the debt or (as the case may be) at least one of the debts is owed.

(2) Subject to the next three sections, a creditor's petition may be presented to the court in respect of a debt or debts only if, at the time the petition is presented–

    (a) the amount of the debt, or the aggregate amount of the debts, is equal to or exceeds the bankruptcy level,

    (b) the debt, or each of the debts, is for a liquidated sum payable to the petitioning creditor, or one or more of the petitioning creditors, either immediately or at some certain, future time, and is unsecured,

. . .'

Mr Barker did not dispute, and I accept, that those provisions show that the society's demand can only have been a valid one if (inter alia) the £411,501.18 claimed can correctly be characterised as 'a liquidated sum'. Is it such a sum?

In support of the appeal Mr Barker submitted that it is. He referred me to the notes against RSC, O. 6, r. 2 at 6/2/4 in vol. 1 of the *Supreme Court Practice 1993*, which read as follows (at p. 34):

' *"Debt or liquidated demand"* – A liquidated demand is in the nature of a debt, *i.e.* a specific sum of money due and payable under or by virtue of a contract. Its amount must either be already ascertained or capable of being ascertained as a mere matter of arithmetic. If the ascertainment of a sum of money, even though it be specified or named as a definite figure, requires investigation beyond mere calculation, then the sum is not a "debt or liquidated demand", but constitutes "damages". '

He submitted that that provides a sufficient guide as to the indebtedness which will qualify as 'a liquidated sum' for the purposes of s. 267(2)(b); and that the amount of £411,501.18 claimed by the society duly qualified as such a sum. It was not in dispute that the society had arrived at the sum by deducting an unspecified valuation of the security ('£X') from the (also unspecified) total debt ('£Y'). If, as it should have done, the society had disclosed on the face of the demand both the £X and £Y figures, so that it could be seen how it had arrived at the debt claimed, then it could not be argued that the resulting figure was not 'a liquidated sum' for the purposes of s. 267(2)(b), since that is the very exercise which r. 6.1(5) required the society to perform. It can therefore make no difference that the society has taken a short cut, and merely asserted that the debtor is indebted to it in a particular sum, without also specifying the two figures, £X and £Y, which it has used to arrive at such sum.

Miss Johnston did not question that the passage cited from the *Supreme Court Practice* provided a sufficient guide as to the meaning of 'a liquidated sum' for the purposes of s. 267(2)(b). But she submitted that the identification of the sum said to be due from the debtor to the society for the purposes of supporting a statutory demand involved not just a mere matter of arithmetical calculation, but also the investigation of the two unspecified figures, £X and £Y, which it was essential to know before the sum said to be due to the society could be arrived at. Therefore the sum claimed was not 'a liquidated sum'.

Miss Johnston advanced a similar argument to the district judge, who accepted it. The relevant part of the notes of the district judge's judgment read:

'The arguments put forward by [the society] that where part of the debt is disputed and the balance is not paid the demand can still be relied upon, can only arise where the debt in which part is disputed is a liquidated sum.

It is evident from [the society's] evidence on valuation and from [the debtor's] evidence on valuation, that there is enormous discrepancy between the parameters. On the one hand [the society] contends £450,000 at the most and on the other hand [the debtor] contends that the most which would be realised is £650,000. That is a discrepancy between £200,000–£250,000 and even on the basis of what is outstanding to the society in September 1992 is potentially a quarter of the whole indebtedness.

I have to accept the argument and do, that that renders the figure so uncertain to fail to bring it within the concept of a liquidated sum.

The failure to recite the effects of the security is to render the claim one for an unliquidated sum.

In accordance with the rules and the Act, a bankruptcy petition could not be founded on the debt claimed in this demand and therefore the demand should not succeed and in this form should never have been served. The application should succeed on that ground.'

With all respect to her, I do not agree with the district judge's reasoning.

First, r. 6.1(5) recognises that it is competent for a secured creditor to put a value on its security and to serve a statutory demand for the amount of the total debt less such value. It appears to me therefore that the net figure resulting from that exercise must be in the nature of 'a liquidated sum' for the purposes of s. 267(2)(b): if it is not, I do not see how a demand prepared in purported compliance with r. 6.1(5) could ever be a valid demand.

Secondly, it appears to me to be within the obvious contemplation of r. 6.1(5) that the value which the creditor puts on his security will be a value with which the debtor may disagree. The range of disagreement may be wide or narrow, but its consequence in either case will be that there will in turn be a difference as to the correct amount of the 'liquidated sum' due to the creditor after deduction from the full amount of the debt of the value attributed to the security.

Thirdly, in my view the emergence of any such disagreement cannot by itself, and without more, provide a basis for a challenge to the validity of the statutory demand. In particular, it cannot by itself result in the sum claimed in the demand ceasing to be a demand for 'a liquidated sum' and becoming one for an 'unliquidated' sum. Further, the mere fact that there is a wide range between the competing valuations cannot in principle make any difference: the 'liquidated sum' does not become an 'unliquidated sum' merely because the parties are far apart as to whether or not it represents the true amount of the debtor's unsecured indebtedness.

Fourthly, one circumstance in which any such disagreement might be of important significance, and might even justify the setting aside of the demand, would be where the debtor was able to claim by credible evidence that the creditor had undervalued the security and that its true value either equalled or exceeded the full amount of the debt. This is the type of case to which r. 6.5(4)(c) is directed. However, in such a case the demand would be set aside, not because the debt claimed was not for 'a liquidated sum', but because there was a real issue as to whether, after giving proper credit for the value of the security, the debtor was indebted to the creditor at all.

Fifthly, although the society did not specify in the demand the two figures, £X and £Y, which it used in order to arrive at the sum claimed to be due, the debtor does not question that that sum does represent the society's calculation of the debt less the value put by it on the security. Accordingly, I cannot see how the sum so arrived at can be any less 'a liquidated sum' than it would have been if the society had correctly complied with r. 6.1(5) and had duly specified both the £X and £Y figures.

In the result, I have concluded that the sum claimed in the statutory demand is 'a liquidated sum' and that the first ground upon which the debtor relied in support of her application to set aside the demand is not well founded. In my judgment the district judge was in error in accepting the argument.

A   **(2) The debtor's voluntary arrangement**

The evidence relating to this aspect of the matter is as follows. In her affidavit in support of her application to set aside the statutory demand the debtor deposed that she was subject to a voluntary arrangement which was approved by a meeting of creditors held on 8 June 1992 and that it was still in force. In answer to that, Heather Wolstenholme, a partner in the society's former solicitors, deposed that the society had not been given notice of the proposed voluntary arrangement and that therefore it did not attend the meeting of creditors. Miss Wolstenholme went on to make the point that in these circumstances the society was not bound by the arrangement.

The debtor put in some evidence in reply, including an affidavit sworn by Angela Quait. Miss Quait deposed that she was employed by a firm called Sorskys Specialised Financial Services ('Sorskys') as an 'individual voluntary arrangement supervisor'. She said that the debtor attended Sorskys' offices on about 18 April 1992 when she was advised by Mr H J Sorsky, a partner, that she should enter into a voluntary arrangement. In response, the debtor provided Sorskys with a list of her creditors, including the society, and on 21 April 1992 Mr Sorsky was appointed her 'nominee' (i.e. pursuant to s. 253(2) of the 1986 Act).

Miss Quait deposes that on 18 May 1992 Mr Sorsky instructed her to notify all the debtor's known creditors of a proposed meeting (i.e. the s. 257 meeting) and that on the same day she sent a notification to each creditor convening it. She exhibited copies of the documents sent to each creditor, and says that the copy bundle sent to the society:

> 'was sent to its head office situate at Bradford & Bingley Building Society, PO Box 88, Crossflats, Bingley, West Yorkshire BD16 2UA, and has not been returned to me or my employers by the Post Office undelivered.'

The documents said to have been sent to each creditor included (inter alia):

(1)   a notice pursuant to s. 257 of the 1986 Act convening a meeting of creditors on 8 June 1992 for the purpose of considering and, if thought fit, passing the resolution that the debtor's proposed voluntary arrangement be approved and that Mr Sorsky be appointed its supervisor;

(2)   the debtor's statement of affairs: that disclosed that she had an interest in three properties (including the society's security), but that each was fully mortgaged, that there was no equity in any of them, and that she had no other assets. The society's debt was shown as £871,570 and its security was shown as being subject also to a second charge in favour of Barclays Bank plc for £68,430. The statement showed that there was a deficiency as regards unsecured creditors of £125,063. That sum represented the total indebtedness due to 13 specified creditors, described as 'non-preferential creditors', not including the society; and

(3)   a proposed scheme of arrangement under which the debtor would pay the supervisor £25,000 for the benefit of her creditors over a period of five years, at the rate of £5,000 a year. The source of these moneys was the fee income (forecast at £20,000 a year) expected to be earned by the debtor as a director of a company which she and her husband had formed in 1991.

The meeting of creditors took place on 8 June 1992, when the debtor's voluntary arrangement was approved, although Mr Wessley of Cape & Dalgliesh was appointed supervisor, not Mr Sorsky.

The society's evidence does not in terms challenge Miss Quait's evidence, but is to the effect that it did not receive the notice which Miss Quait says she posted to it and that it was thus ignorant that the s. 257 meeting had been convened. Of particular significance for the purposes of Mr Barker's argument before me is the evidence of Mr Andrew Hiller on behalf of the society. He deposes that the Crossflats address (to which Miss Quait says she posted the documents) was not the society's head office until 1 June 1992. Those premises were new premises, which were constructed for the society, and from which it was not fully operational until that date. He also says that the society's mortgage and administration department has never operated from the Crossflats premises, and that until 1 June 1992 the society's head office was at PO Box 2, Main Street, Bingley. He says that at all times, and as known by the debtor, the administration of the relevant mortgage account had been handled by the society's office at PO Box 1, Leamington House, Milverton Hill, Leamington Spa. He adds that had any correspondence relating to a mortgage been received at the Crossflats address, it would have been sent immediately to the head office at Main Street, Bingley. However, he says that this did not happen in this case, and that the inquiries he has made indicate that no notice of the s. 257 meeting was received by the society.

There was no cross-examination of the deponents before the district judge, and the position on the affidavit evidence is that there is in fact no factual conflict between the witnesses: in particular, there is no necessary inconsistency between Miss Quait's evidence that she posted the relevant documentation to the society and the society's evidence that it did not receive it. I understand the district judge to have approached the evidence on the basis that each deponent's evidence must be regarded as correct, and in my view that was the right approach. In the light of that evidence, and for reasons which I shall detail later, the district judge held that the society was bound by the voluntary arrangement which was approved on 8 June 1992 and that it was in consequence precluded from serving the statutory demand.

Mr Barker's submissions in support of this aspect of the society's appeal were as follows.

He referred first to r. 5.13 of the 1986 rules, which relates to the convening of the meeting of creditors to consider a proposed voluntary arrangement. Rule 5.13(2) provides that:

'(2) Notices calling the meeting shall be sent by the nominee, at least 14 days before the day fixed for it to be held, to all the creditors specified in the debtor's statement of affairs, and any other creditor of whom the nominee is otherwise aware.'

Mr Barker submitted, and it was not disputed, that notice of the meeting was thus required to be given to the society. In this respect the subrule essentially mirrors the requirement of s. 257(2) of the Act, which provides that:

'(2) The persons to be summoned to the meeting are every creditor of the debtor of whose claim and address the person summoning the meeting is aware.'

Mr Barker referred next to r. 12.4(1), to the effect that (subject to immaterial exceptions) notice of the meeting was required to be given in writing; and to r. 12.11(1), which provides that:

'(1) Subject to Rule 12.10 and as follows, Order 65 of the Rules of the Supreme Court applies as regards any matter relating to the service of documents and the giving of notice in insolvency proceedings.'

In this case, as to the 'as follows', the remaining provisions of r. 12.11 are not material. Mr Barker submitted that nor was r. 12.10; and that there had been a non-compliance with the service requirements of RSC, O. 65.

Taking RSC, O. 65 first, the relevant rule is r. 5. The material parts of it provide as follows:

'5(1) Service of any document, not being a document which by virtue of any provision of these rules is required to be served personally or a document to which Order 10, rule 1, applies, may be effected–

A
    (a)   by leaving the document at the proper address of the person to be served, or

    (b)   by post, or

   . . .

(2) For the purposes of this rule . . . the proper address of any person on whom a document is to be served in accordance with this rule shall be the address for service of that person, but if at the time when service is effected that person has no
B
address for service his proper address for the purposes aforesaid shall be–

   . . .

    (d)   in the case of a body corporate, the registered or principal office of the body.'

Mr Barker submitted that this was a case where proper service could only be effected by posting the notice to, or leaving it at, either the registered or principal office of the
C
society. However, the evidence was to the effect that the Crossflats address to which Miss Quait posted the documents was neither the registered nor the principal office of the society at the time of posting. Therefore, he said, proper notice of the proposed meeting was not sent to the society in accordance with r. 12.11 (incorporating RSC, O. 65). He further submitted that r. 12.10 does not assist the debtor. That deals with the manner in which postal service can be effected, and with when (unless the contrary is shown) a posted document is to be treated as being served. Its only provision of possible relevance
D
for present purposes is subr. (1A), which reads:

'(1A) A document to be served by post may be sent to the last known address of the person to be served.'

As to that, Mr Barker submitted that, even assuming that the subrule is capable of applying to postal service on a body corporate such as the society, nevertheless, in the
E
light of Mr Hiller's evidence, the Crossflats address to which the documents were posted cannot then have been regarded as the society's 'last known address'.

Thus, submitted Mr Barker, not only is the evidence to the effect that the society did not receive notice of the s. 257 meeting, it also shows that the manner in which notice was purportedly given to it did not comply with the requirements of the Insolvency Rules. In these circumstances he submitted further that (save perhaps to the limited extent to which I shall refer in a moment) the society is not bound by the voluntary arrangement
F
and was accordingly at liberty to serve a statutory demand on the debtor with a view to the subsequent presentation of a bankruptcy petition against her. He relied on the provisions of s. 260 of the 1986 Act, in particular subs. (2)(b). Section 260(1) and (2) provide:

'260   *Effect of approval*

G
(1) This section has effect where the meeting summoned under section 257 approves the proposed voluntary arrangement (with or without modifications).

(2) The approved arrangement–

    (a)   takes effect as if made by the debtor at the meeting, and

    (b)   binds every person who in accordance with the rules had notice of, and was entitled to vote at, the meeting (whether or not he was present or represented
H
at it) as if he were a party to the arrangement.'

Mr Barker submitted that the society did not have notice of the meeting, either 'in accordance with the rules' or at all. Therefore it is not one of the persons who, under s. 260(2)(b), are bound by the arrangement 'as if he were a party to' it; and it is accordingly entitled to serve a statutory demand and pursue bankruptcy proceedings against the debtor.

If Mr Barker is right thus far in his submissions, then in my view this is as far as he   A
needed to go in order to succeed on this aspect of the appeal. If the society is not bound
by the arrangement, then in principle I consider that it must be at liberty to serve a
statutory demand with a view, if it is not complied with, to the subsequent presentation
of a bankruptcy petition. I did not understand Miss Johnston to dispute this.

However, Mr Barker also submitted that a course which might also have been, or
might perhaps still be, open to the society would be to seek an extension of time for   B
applying to the court for the purposes of challenging the voluntary arrangement (see
s. 262 and 376 of the 1986 Act); but that, absent any successful such challenge, the society
either would or might be bound by the voluntary arrangement at least to the extent (1)
that it could not question that it was a valid arrangement at any rate as between the
debtor and those creditors who were bound by it under s. 260(2)(b) as if they were parties
to it; and (2) that any assets of the debtor which fell to be administered in accordance   C
with the arrangement would, or might, not be assets which would be available to be
distributed in a bankruptcy between those creditors (including the society) who were not
so bound by the arrangement. In short, he submitted that the assets subject to the
voluntary arrangement would, or might, only vest in any trustee in bankruptcy subject
to such arrangement.

In support of, in particular, points (1) and (2) above he referred me to the unreported   D
decision of Morritt J in *Re McKeen* (1 April 1992). That case is distinguishable on its
facts from the present one, in that (inter alia) there the creditor on whose petition a
bankruptcy order was made was not a creditor at the date when notice of the s. 257
meeting was given, but only became such subsequently (in this respect the summary of
the case in *Muir Hunter on Personal Insolvency* at p. 3024 (para. 3-040) appears to me to
be inaccurate). However, Mr Barker submitted that that distinction did not affect the
points of principle to be found in *Re McKeen* relevant to his submissions.   E

These last submissions of Mr Barker appeared to me to lead to potentially difficult
territory; in particular, they raised questions of an essentially future nature, and also
having a potential impact on persons not before the court. In view of this, and having
regard also to the relatively narrow front on which Miss Johnston argued this aspect of
the appeal, I have concluded that it is both unnecessary and inappropriate for me to
express any view on these particular submissions. In so concluding I make clear that I   F
intend no discourtesy to Mr Barker, and I am grateful to him for his arguments.

Turning now to the submissions in support of the district judge's judgment, Miss
Johnston did not join issue with most of the steps in Mr Barker's argument. In particular,
she did not seek to argue that, on the evidence, I should conclude that proper notice of
the s. 257 meeting was given to the society in accordance with the *Insolvency Rules* 1986,
although she made no express admission that it was not. In this connection, I should   G
perhaps comment that, whilst there is evidence as to where the society's head office was
at the material times, there is, I think, no evidence as to where (if different) its registered
office was at such times. Thus, there is no evidence that the Crossflats address (to which
Miss Quait posted the documentation) was not in fact the society's registered office at the
time of posting. However, the argument proceeded before me on the silent assumption
that it was not. I add that it would in my view in any event have been for the debtor to   H
show the contrary, whereas no attempt to do so appears to have been made.

Miss Johnston's principal point was instead that, even though the society had no actual
notice of the s. 257 meeting, it nevertheless had constructive notice of it; it was therefore
bound in all respects by the voluntary arrangement as if it were a party to it; and it was
therefore precluded from serving the statutory demand, since to do so would be to flout

A the arrangement by which it was so bound: there was no evidence of any default in connection with the voluntary arrangement and therefore no basis for the making of a bankruptcy order against the debtor (see s. 264(1)(c) and 276(1) of the Act). Her argument was, in its essentials, a repeat of the argument which had found favour with the district judge. The notes of the relevant part of the district judge's judgment are as follows:

B '[The debtor] also brings the application on the basis that she is protected by a voluntary arrangement. [The society] argues that it did not receive notice of the creditors' meeting. There is no doubt that for a creditor to be bound by a voluntary arrangement there must have been notice given. I have to accept that the postal rule on service must be relevant. It is not an absolute protection as unless one is satisfactorily satisfied otherwise, service is deemed to have taken place. Postal service has never allowed the person claiming the benefit to rely upon the same
C when there is proof to the contrary.

  This does not entirely help [the society] because there is also the principle of constructive notice and in this regard I rely upon the observations contained in *Muir Hunter* at p. 3024, namely,

   "Furthermore, if that creditor had received 'constructive notice' of the summoning of the meeting of creditors, in other words, if the notice was sent to
D   him, although he did not receive it, it is submitted that in accordance with this section [i.e. s. 260 of the 1986 Act] and r. 12.16, *post*, not only would the meeting have been duly summoned and held, but the creditor concerned would be bound by the meeting's decision."

  I cannot find any observation which causes me to doubt that it is right. To disregard the principle of postal service and the concept of constructive notice would then be to place on the rules and on the Act an unworkable interpretation.
E It would enable potentially an unscrupulous creditor, and I do not intend for a moment to impute that to [the society], as Miss Johnston puts it "to throw over the democratic process".

  There must be provision to contend with that and there is so within the concept of constructive notice.

F [The society] would have failed on the second ground – I find on the basis of the situation as it presents itself that the voluntary arrangement binds the creditor.'

  As I understand it, the reasoning adopted by the district judge was therefore as follows: (1) the society had rebutted any presumption which might otherwise have arisen that it had received notice of the convening of the s. 257 meeting in the ordinary course of the post; (2) therefore it did not have actual notice of the meeting; (3) nevertheless, it did have constructive notice of it, because notice of the meeting had been posted to it, albeit
G not received; (4) therefore it was bound by the voluntary arrangement as if it were a party to it and was thus precluded from serving the statutory demand.

  As to step (4), the district judge did not in terms state that, in holding the society to be bound by the arrangement, she regarded the society as being bound by it as if it were a party to the arrangement (cf. s. 260(2)(b)). However, if she was not holding the society to be bound in this manner, I find it difficult to see why she should have regarded the society as prevented from serving a statutory demand. Further, Miss Johnston's argument was
H to the effect that the society was bound in this manner, and I understood her to be doing no more than seeking to uphold the district judge's reasoning. The question for me, therefore, is: was this reasoning correct?

  One of the material considerations which apparently formed part of the district judge's reasoning leading to step (3) above was r. 12.16 of the 1986 rules, which provides:

'12.16 *Non-receipt of notice of meeting*

Where in accordance with the Act or the Rules a meeting of creditors or other persons is summoned by notice, the meeting is presumed to have been duly summoned and held, notwithstanding that not all those to whom the notice is to be given have received it.'

I comment first that, in my view, for the presumption under that rule to apply, it is a necessary precondition that those convening the meeting should have taken proper steps to summon it in accordance with the Act and the rules. Thus, in the present case, the nominee's duty pursuant to r. 5.13(2) was to give or send notice to each creditor referred to in the statement of affairs, or otherwise known to him, and to do so in compliance with the provisions of r. 12.11. The giving of such notice did not have to be by way of personal service, but could be by post. However, provided that notice was duly sent or given to all creditors entitled to receive it, then, even if any creditor did not actually receive it, r. 12.16 raises a presumption that the meeting has nevertheless been 'duly summoned and held'.

I shall assume first, without deciding, that in the circumstances of the present case, the meeting of 8 June 1992 would be presumed by r. 12.16 to have been duly summoned and held, an assumption which is the most favourable to the debtor for present purposes. On this assumption, but accepting (as is admitted) that the society had no actual notice of the meeting, is it nevertheless open to the society to deny that it is one of the persons whom s. 260(2)(b) provides are bound by the arrangement approved at the meeting?

The district judge appears to have answered 'no' to this question. However, I respectfully disagree. I draw attention to the fact that, in specifying whether or not a creditor is bound by the arrangement, s. 260(2)(b) focuses on whether or not he 'had notice of' the meeting (i.e., in my view, had received notice of it). By contrast, the presumed validation of a meeting under r. 12.16 depends essentially on whether or not the notice was duly sent, whether or not actually received. Further, the only presumption that r. 12.16 in terms raises is as to the validity of the summoning and holding of the meeting: it does not purport also to raise a presumption that a creditor had notice of the meeting when in fact he had none.

In my judgment, these considerations point to the conclusion that, even though a s. 257 meeting may be presumed by r. 12.16 to have been duly summoned and held, nevertheless a creditor who had no actual notice of it will not be bound by any arrangement which was approved at it. The reason why he is not so bound is that s. 260(2)(b) provides that the arrangement binds those persons (and, in my view, only those persons) who (inter alia) had 'notice' of the meeting, whereas such creditor had none.

In coming to a different view the district judge appears to have been much influenced by the sentence which she quoted from *Muir Hunter*, a sentence which was also central to Miss Johnston's argument. Counsel were not agreed as to the nature of the point which was being made in that sentence. In my view, in order to understand the sentence, it is necessary to read it in its context, and so I shall set out the whole of the main part of the commentary (on s. 260 of the Act) in which it appears. The relevant passages are as follows, starting at p. 3024:

'*Clause (b)*

Persons bound by the decision

Every person who had notice of the meeting, and was entitled to vote at it (whether or not he was present or represented there) is bound by the approved arrangement, as if he were himself a party to it. It appears therefore to be of the utmost importance to the debtor, and to his nominee and to their respective advisers, to

A   ensure that all persons entitled (under the Rules) to receive such notice, so that they may attend and vote, do receive such notice. If one or more of them do not receive such a notice, then in the absence of any Rule introducing some form of "constructive notice", a "creditor" (within the very wide definition referred to in s. 257(3), *ante*) who did not receive such notice, would not be bound; but *vide infra*
. . .

B   *Consequences of failure to bind a creditor by the arrangement*

The question arises, what will be the consequences of the failure, through lack of, or defective, notice, to bind a creditor, and whether this may expose the arrangement to a destructive "challenge" (whether or not in the s. 262 sense), so as to deprive the debtor, and the assenting creditors, of the security they did not enjoy under the Deeds of Arrangement Act 1914, this was the protection which was the principal objective of the enactment of the voluntary arrangements procedure. It

C   may well be the case that the debtor will be exposed to the risk of a bankruptcy petition at the suit of the "non-bound" creditor; but it does not follow that any such bankruptcy proceedings could invalidate the arrangement, so far as concerns the creditors' interest therein, and profit therefrom. Any such bankruptcy petition by a non-bound creditor with a suitable provable debt will no longer (as it would have done under the Act of 1914, *ipso facto*) upset the arrangement as constituting

D   an act of bankruptcy; for in view of the elimination of the acts of bankruptcy doctrine, the arrangement, once approved, will have become complete without the participation of that creditor. There seems to be no machinery to set aside the approved proposal constituting the arrangement, in so far as it effects a disposition of the debtor's property. Furthermore, if that creditor had received "constructive notice" of the summoning of the meeting of creditors, in other words, if the notice was sent to him, although he did not receive it, it is submitted that in accordance

E   with this section and r. 12.16, *post*, not only would the meeting have been duly summoned and held, but the creditor concerned would be bound by the meeting's decision.'

If the last sentence, the one relied on by the district judge, is taken in isolation, and out of context, then its natural interpretation is that, provided notice of a s. 257 meeting has been duly sent in accordance with the rules, a creditor to whom notice was so sent will be

F   bound by the voluntary arrangement approved at the meeting as if he were a party to it, even though he did not actually receive such notice, and therefore had no actual notice of the meeting. Miss Johnston submitted that this is what the sentence means, and that in this respect it is correct as a matter of law. It appears to me that the district judge also interpreted the sentence in this sense.

Mr Barker submitted that the sentence ought not to be interpreted in this way, and

G   drew attention to the fact that it appears in a passage under the subheading 'Consequences of failure to bind a creditor by the arrangement' and that (but subject, as it seems to me, to the effect of the 'vide infra') the authors had expressed a view to the contrary effect in the preceding passage under the heading 'Persons bound by the decision'. He submitted that the intended sense of the sentence in the context in which it appears is that, where an arrangement has been approved at a meeting which is presumed by r. 12.16 to have been duly summoned and held, a creditor who had no actual notice

H   of the meeting may nevertheless be bound by it at any rate to the extent that he may not be able to set the decision of the meeting aside: but that it is not also intended to mean that such creditor will be bound by the arrangement in the further sense that he is to be treated as a party to it.

I do not propose to express a view on these rival submissions as to the intended meaning of the sentence. If, however, it is intended to bear the wider meaning which the

district judge appears to have attached to it, then I would respectfully disagree with it. I
in any event respectfully disagree with the suggestion in it that a creditor who does not
receive, and remains in ignorance of, the notice of a meeting which is sent to him can (in
the bare circumstances apparently envisaged by Muir Hunter) nevertheless still have
'constructive notice' of such meeting. A person ordinarily only has 'constructive notice'
of a fact when he is put on notice of matters whose investigation would lead him to
discover it, an investigation which he abstains from making; or where he anyway
deliberately or carelessly fails to make inquiries which a prudent person in his position
ought to have made and which, if made, would have led him to discovery of the fact.
However, a creditor, such as the society, which never received a notice of a meeting which
is said to have been sent to it, cannot in my view, and without more, be said to have
'constructive notice' of the convening of the meeting. In particular, and as I have earlier
pointed out, r. 12.16 does not deem the creditor to have had notice of the meeting: it
merely provides (in effect) that the non-receipt by him of a notice duly sent will not by
itself be sufficient to enable him to say that the meeting had not been duly summoned
and held.

In the result I conclude that the district judge misdirected herself as to the law with
regard to this limb of the debtor's application. In my judgment she should instead have
concluded that the society had no notice of the s. 257 meeting; that s. 260(2)(b) therefore
showed that it was not one of the debtor's creditors which was bound by the voluntary
arrangement; and that it was entitled to serve a statutory demand on the debtor with a
view, if the same was not complied with, to the subsequent presentation of a bankruptcy
petition.

Having reached this conclusion, it is not necessary for me to express any view on
whether, on the facts which emerge from the evidence before the court, the s. 257 meeting
held on 8 June 1992 would in fact be presumed by r. 12.16 to have been duly summoned
and held. Whether or not it would is a matter which may have consequences affecting
other creditors who are not before the court and therefore I regard it as inappropriate to
say any more about it.

Conclusion

I have therefore come to the conclusion that the district judge was in error on both the
grounds on which she acceded to the debtor's application. I allow the society's appeal.

(*Order accordingly*)

A
Calor Gas Ltd v Piercy & Ors.

Chancery Division.
His Honour Judge Paul Baker QC (sitting as a High Court judge).
Judgment delivered 9 November 1993.

> *Bankruptcy – Individual voluntary arrangements – Voting rights – Requisite majorities – Votes to be left out of account; secured creditor – Whether vote of partly secured creditor was to be left out of account in its entirety – Charging orders – Whether charging order nisi should be made absolute – Charging Orders Act 1979, s. 1(5); Insolvency Act 1986, Pt. VIII; Insolvency Rules 1986, r. 5.17, 5.18.*

This was an appeal by a creditor against a district judge's decision holding that the chairman of a meeting summoned to approve individual voluntary arrangements was entitled to leave entirely out of account the appellant's vote on the basis that the appellant's claim was in part secured.

The appellant creditor was the landlord of premises in which the three debtors who were brothers were carrying on business in partnership. The creditor obtained judgment for over £17,000 for arrears of rent and a charging order nisi over the beneficial interest of one of the brothers in a house.

Individual voluntary arrangements were proposed for the brothers. At the meeting to approve the proposals the creditor's vote against approval was cast but the whole vote was left out of account by the chairman under r. 5.18(3)(b) on the ground that the creditor was partly secured by virtue of the charging order. On that basis the arrangements were approved. The creditor appealed.

There was also an appeal by the debtor against the master's decision ordering the charging order nisi in favour of the creditor to be made absolute.

Held, declaring that the claim of the appellant in so far as it was not secured should have been taken into account in calculating the vote for the purposes of r. 5.18, with the consequence that the resolutions to approve the proposals would have been rejected; and refusing to discharge the charging order absolute:

1. Rule 5.18(3)(b) did not read 'There is to be left out of account a creditor's vote in respect of any claim where the claim or part is secured', but provided that, '. . . there is to be left out of account a creditor's vote in respect of any claim or part of a claim . . . where the claim or part is secured.' The interpretation accepted by the chairman of the meeting and the district judge rendered the words 'or part of a claim' otiose. The words admitted of an alternative interpretation that where part of a claim was secured that part only was to be discounted, and that was the true construction of the rule.

2. The personal circumstances of the debtor were very straitened, and that was a strong factor pointing towards discharging the order. In all the circumstances it was difficult to say that the other creditors would be unduly prejudiced by the making of the order. There were special circumstances which pointed in favour of the master's decision to make the order absolute. The deprivation of the creditor of its statutory rights not to lose its security without consenting to it and to have its vote counted in so far as the debt was unsecured outweighed the other considerations (under the Charging Orders Act 1979, s. 1(5)).

The following cases were referred to in the judgment:

Naeem, Re [1990] 1 WLR 48.
Roberts Petroleum Ltd v Bernard Kenny Ltd [1983] 2 AC 192.

Clare Hoffmann (instructed by Fladgate Fielder) for the creditor.

Peter Castle (instructed by Aaron & Partners, Chester) for the debtors.

JUDGMENT

A

His Honour Judge Paul Baker QC: I have before me a number of appeals and cross-appeals arising out of the insolvency of three brothers who were trading in partnership as retailers of leather clothing. The principal question is one of some general importance. It is whether and to what extent the chairman of a meeting called to consider a resolution proposing an individual voluntary arrangement is entitled to leave out of the computation of the appropriate majority the vote of a partially secured creditor. It involves the correct interpretation of the *Insolvency Rules* 1986, particularly r. 5.18.

B

The appellants in the main appeals are Calor Gas Ltd. They are the landlords of the premises in which the debtors carried on the business. On 28 August 1992 they obtained judgment by consent in the Queen's Bench Division for £15,956 in respect of arrears of rent, together with £837.47 interest and £967 costs making a total of £17,760.55 of which £16,260.55 remained due and unpaid on 5 February 1993 when a charging order nisi under the *Charging Orders Act* 1979 was obtained in the Queen's Bench Division. That charging order nisi was over the beneficial interest of one of the brothers, Victor Bruce Piercy, in a house. It is his matrimonial home. It is subject to a first mortgage in favour of the Halifax Building Society in the sum of £37,000 approximately. It is common ground that the debtor and his wife are entitled equally to the beneficial interest. The value of the debtor's half share is some £3,300.

C

About a month before the charging order nisi was made, the debtors had consulted an insolvency practitioner, Mr Simon Edwards. He is a solicitor in the firm of Aaron and Partners of Chester.

D

After taking instructions from the debtors, Mr Edwards prepared proposals for individual voluntary arrangements. The proposals are in identical terms mutatis mutandis. Interim orders freezing the position were obtained under s. 252 of the *Insolvency Act* 1986 and later continued, the effect of which was to inhibit the presentation of a bankruptcy petition by the debtors or by any creditor, or the continuation of the execution process against the house without the leave of the court. That is the normal procedure following the presentation of such a proposal for an arrangement.

E

At this point I can refer to the material parts of the proposals which were put forward as a better alternative to the brothers becoming bankrupt. The partnership debts amounted to £34,852. Individual debts of the individual brothers I think are insignificant save for the liability of Victor Piercy under the first mortgage secured on his home. In para. 6 of the proposals it is stated:

F

'The major partnership creditors are Calor Gas Ltd, £16,260 and HM Customs and Excise for VAT which the brothers estimate at approximately £10,600.'

Then it annexes a list of creditors. The only secured one listed there is the Halifax Building Society. There are a number of further unsecured creditors, most with debts of a few hundred pounds: I think one goes over a thousand.

G

Paragraph 8 of the proposals states:

'The only substantial asset available to any of the brothers is the freehold property owned by VBP and his wife. This is worth approximately £45,000 and is subject to a mortgage of approximately £37,000 in favour of Halifax Building Society. There is a charging order nisi in favour of Calor Gas Ltd.'

H

Then in para. 11:

'Part 1 of the estimated statement of affairs shows the approximate equity available in the property owned by VBP and his wife. If VBP goes into bankruptcy it is likely there will not be any material payment except to the Halifax Building Society

A as mortgagee of the property. VBP's share of the equity will be exhausted in paying the fees and costs of the bankruptcy.'

Paragraph 12:

'Part 2 of the estimated statement of affairs shows the likely position if a voluntary arrangement is approved. It shows a deficit for unsecured creditors of approximately £36,790 and a likely payment to unsecured creditors of approximately 20.7 per cent of the amount owed to them.'

B

At para. 13 are set out the reasons for the proposal:

'The brothers are concerned that VBP and his wife should not lose their home as a result of the partnership debts and therefore DRP and APP [the other two brothers] are prepared to enter into voluntary arrangements rather than petition for their own bankruptcy which would be the easier option, for DRP and APP have no assets. It is therefore proposed that the creditors should enter into the voluntary arrangements to avoid the need for any of the brothers, particular VBP, to go into bankruptcy.'

C

Then we come in para. 14 to the proposal itself.

'It is proposed that the brothers will make an initial payment of £1,250 to a fund to be available for the voluntary arrangement.'

D Paragraph 15:

'Subsequently, commencing the first day of the month following the date the voluntary arrangements are approved, the brothers will undertake to be jointly and severally liable to pay the sum of £260 per month into the above fund for the period of three years. These monthly payments would amount to £9,360.'

Then the proposals deal with what the brothers are now doing. It is obviously a very modest level of employment that they are engaged in. Then it is said that if during the course of the arrangements VBP and his wife are unable to meet their mortgage repayments and their house is repossessed, any equity then available to VBP on the sale of the house will be made available to the fund for the benefit of all creditors, and similarly any increase in the house price will benefit the creditors.

E

Then para. 19:

'Provided the level of debts have been established, the supervisor may at his discretion make an interim payment of creditors after 19 months from the date of approval of the arrangements. A final distribution will be made three years after the date of approval of the arrangements. Unsecured creditors will be treated equally on a percentage basis. In return for receipt of the appropriate part of the fund, the creditors waive all claims against the brothers. The proposals deal with the costs and include a number of matters as required by the Insolvency Rules.'

F

G

Then passing to the reason why the creditors should approve the arrangement, para. 29 says this:

'It is not suggested that this proposal represents a good return to creditors. It is, however, better than the only available alternative which is bankruptcy for the brothers. It is likely that on a bankruptcy the only creditor to receive any payment would be the Halifax Building Society.'

H

Then it points out what funds the brothers would be contributing and how the costs would be considerably less than those on a bankruptcy, and that the fund will in the meantime bear interest in the solicitor's client account.

In the schedules I think I should notice that the property, 93 Whipcord Lane, is valued at £45,000 and less the costs of the sale and paying off the first mortgagees would leave £6,600, making £3,300 each for Mr and Mrs Victor Piercy.

A meeting of creditors was held on 23 March 1993 to consider the proposal. Before I deal with what happened there, I should read the following from the affidavit of Mr Calpin, Mr Edwards' assistant:

'Prior to the meeting of creditors held on 23 March to consider the proposals for individual voluntary arrangements in respect of each of the defendants in this matter, Mr Edwards advised them that if the proposals were rejected they should immediately present to the court petitions for their own bankruptcy. I prepared and gave to the defendants a bundle of blank forms which they would require to petition for their own bankruptcies. I explained to each of them how these forms should be completed and I advised them that there would be a fee payable to the court. I further explained to the defendants that should the proposals be rejected, if they presented themselves to the Chester County Court at 10 am the day after the meeting with the completed forms they would be adjudged bankrupt on that day.'

I can now go to the report of Mr Edwards as chairman of the meeting – this again is an important document. He records that:

'2. The arrangement was approved, subject to the following modifications:

2.1 that no creditor is to take any enforcement action or to seek or take or perfect any security;

2.2 that Mr Piercy shall have the right to withdraw from the voluntary arrangement if the charging order obtained by Calor Gas Ltd on the beneficial interest of Victor Brett Piercy in the property 93 Whipcord Lane, Chester, is not discharged. If Mr Piercy withdraws, then both Mr Piercy and creditors will be discharged from all obligations and restrictions arising under the IVA.

3. The only resolutions which were taken at the meeting were for the above two amendments and the vote on the IVA itself. Each of the resolutions was approved.

4. The creditors who were present in person or by proxy were as follows,'

and then he sets them out. There were eight creditors voting for the arrangements and the resolutions. There were two creditors voting against. One was a creditor with a relatively small debt called Knight Security; they were in for £411.30. The other was Calor Gas.

Then there is this important paragraph in the report:

'5. The vote of Calor Gas Ltd was cast in accordance with r. 5.17 but excluded from account in determining the requisite majority under r. 5.18(3)(b) as they hold a charging order nisi on the property of Victor Brett Piercy. As chairman of the meeting I took the view that the whole of the vote should be excluded from being taken into account. Accordingly, the majority in favour of the proposal was in excess of three-quarters of the value of those present and voting.'

It is clear if the only vote counted against was Knights Security for £411, the other eight were well above the required majority.

Then Mr Edwards ends his report by saying:

'6. Calor Gas Ltd have indicated an intention to apply to the court under s. 262 for a ruling (1) that the whole of their debt should have been taken into account for voting purposes as they do not consider a charging order nisi to constitute security, and (2) if the charging order does constitute security, then the extent of their votes above the security should have been taken into account. However, in the meantime the proposal stands approved.'

A   At some stage during the course of these proceedings, the point was taken that the charging order nisi did not constitute security but it is not a point that has been taken here. Calor Gas have taken their stand in this court on the second of those points mentioned in the report, that on the basis that the charging order does constitute a security, then the extent of their votes above the security should have been taken into account. As we have seen, the charging order is over an asset of £3,300 but the debt is £16,000-odd and therefore, even if one deducts the £3,300, there is still a very substantial

B   debt, reckoned to be between 60 and 65 per cent of those present and voting.

Those I think are sufficient of the facts for the moment to enable me to come to the first question to be considered which is whether the chairman was right to exclude the vote of Calor Gas Ltd in its entirety. Individual voluntary arrangements are covered by Pt. VIII of the *Insolvency Act* 1986 (s. 252–263 inclusive) and by Pt. 5 of the *Insolvency Rules* 1986. The latter is divided into three sections of which the first two are respectively

C   'The debtor's proposal' and 'Action on the proposal; creditors' meeting'. At this point I must refer to some of the rules.

In the former part, that is to say 'The debtor's proposal' I should call attention to the following. Rule 5.3 sets out the information which the proposal should contain. I think I need only notice here that r. 5.3(2) reads, so far as is material, as follows:

'The following matters shall be stated or otherwise dealt with, in the proposal—

D   (a) the following matters, so far as within the debtor's immediate knowledge—

               (i) his assets, with an estimate of their respective values,

               (ii) the extent (if any) to which the assets are charged in favour of creditors,

               (iii) the extent (if any) to which particular assets are to be excluded from the voluntary arrangement;'

E   Paragraph 8 of the proposal says:

'The only substantial asset available to any of the brothers is the freehold property owned by VBP and his wife. This is worth approximately £45,000 and is subject to a mortgage of approximately £37,000 in favour of the Halifax Building Society. There is a charging order nisi in favour of Calor Gas Ltd.'

F   This is supplemented by the estimated statement of affairs which shows VBP's share to be worth £3,300. So that property and the extent to which it is charged is indicated in the proposal when read with the statement of affairs.

Now I can go to the section of the rules which deals with the creditors' meeting. We come to r. 5.15 headed 'The chairman at the meeting':

(1) Subject as follows, the nominee shall be chairman of the creditors' meeting.

G   (2) If for any reason the nominee is unable to attend, he may nominate another person to act as chairman in his place; but the person so nominated must be either—

           (a) a person qualified to act as an insolvency practitioner in relation to the debtor, or

           (b) an employee of the nominee or his firm who is experienced in insolvency matters.'

H   In all ordinary cases the insolvency practitioner who has assisted in drawing up the proposal (the nominee) will chair the meeting and that indeed happened in this case, but there is a possibility of someone less well acquainted with the details of the proposal chairing the meeting in the absence of the nominee.

Now we come to the two important rules dealing with the voting rights which I shall have to read out.

'5.17(1) Subject as follows, every creditor who was given notice of the creditors' A
meeting is entitled to vote at the meeting or any adjournment of it.

(2) In Case 1, votes are calculated according to the amount of the creditor's debt
as at the date of the bankruptcy order, and in Case 2 according to the amount of
the debt as at the date of the meeting.'

Case 2 is the relevant case because there is no bankruptcy here.

'5.17(3) A creditor shall not vote in respect of a debt for an unliquidated amount, B
or any debt whose value is not ascertained, except where the chairman agrees to
put upon the debt an estimated minimum value for the purpose of entitlement to
vote.

(4) The chairman has power to admit or reject a creditor's claim for the purpose
of his entitlement to vote, and the power is exercisable with respect to the whole or
any part of the claim. C

(5) The chairman's decision on entitlement to vote is subject to appeal to the court
by any creditor, or by the debtor.

(6) If the chairman is in doubt whether a claim should be admitted or rejected, he
shall mark it as objected to and allow the creditor to vote, subject to his vote being
subsequently declared invalid if the objection to the claim is sustained.

(7) If on an appeal the chairman's decision is reversed or varied, or a creditor's D
vote is declared invalid, the court may order another meeting to be summoned, or
make such other order as it thinks just.
The court's power to make an order under this paragraph is exercisable only if it
considers that the matter is such as to give rise to unfair prejudice or a material
irregularity.

(8) An application to the court by way of appeal under this Rule against the E
chairman's decision shall not be made after the end of the period of 28 days
beginning with the day on which the chairman's report to the court is made under
section 259.

(9) The chairman is not personally liable for any costs incurred by any person in
respect of an appeal under this Rule.'

Now we come to the requisite majorities in r. 5.18 and this is the crucial rule: F

'(1) Subject as follows, at the creditors' meeting for any resolution to pass
approving any proposal or modification there must be a majority in excess of
three-quarters in value of the creditors present in person or by proxy and voting
on the resolution.

(2) The same applies in respect of any other resolution proposed at the meeting,
but substituting one-half for three-quarters. G

(3) In the following cases there is to be left out of account a creditor's vote in
respect of any claim or part of a claim–

(a) where written notice of the claim was not given, either at the meeting or
before it, to the chairman or the nominee;

(b) where the claim or part is secured;

(c) where the claim is in respect of a debt wholly or partly on, or secured by, a H
current bill of exchange or promissory note, unless the creditor is willing–

(i) to treat the liability to him on the bill or note of every person who is
liable on it antecedently to the debtor, and against whom a
bankruptcy order has not been made (or, in the case of a company,
which has not gone into liquidation), as a security in his hands, and

A
        (ii) to estimate the value of the security and (for the purpose of entitlement to vote, but not of any distribution under the arrangement) to deduct it from his claim.'

Those are the really critical paragraphs for this case but I should go on with the rest of the rule.

B
        '(4) Any resolution is invalid if those voting against it include more than half in value of the creditors, counting in these later only those–

        (a) to whom notice of the meeting was sent;

        (b) whose votes are not to be left out of account under paragraph (3); and

        (c) who are not, to the best of the chairman's belief, associates of the debtor.

        (5) It is for the chairman of the meeting to decide whether under this Rule–

C
        (a) a vote is left out of account in accordance with paragraph (3), or

        (b) a person is an associate of the debtor for the purposes of paragraph (4)(c);

and in relation to the second of these two cases the chairman is entitled to rely on the information provided by the debtor's statement of affairs or otherwise in accordance with this Part of the Rules.

D
        (6) If the chairman uses a proxy contrary to Rule 5.16, his vote with that proxy does not count towards any majority under this Rule.'

That is not a material provision in the context of this case. Finally:

        '(7) Paragraphs (5) to (9) of Rule 5.17 apply as regards an appeal against the decision of the chairman under this Rule.'

E
I have already read out, when dealing with the chairman's report, what the chairman did in relation to Calor Gas's vote and why, that is to say:

        'The vote . . . was cast in accordance with r. 5.17 but excluded from account in determining the requisite majority under r. 5.18(3)(b) as they hold a charging order . . . I took the view that the whole of the vote should be excluded from being taken into account.'

F
In an affidavit which was put before me this morning he explains further his reasoning. He had warning that Calor Gas were going to vote against; he explains that and says:

        'I thought I had better examine carefully the relevant provisions of r. 5.17 and 5.18. I would have been wrong to stop Calor Gas voting at all in respect of the secured element of their debt. When I read r. 5.17 it made clear that a secured creditor is entitled to vote for the whole of the amount that is due to him. When I read on, r. 5.18 seemed to me to say that although a secured creditor is entitled to cast his vote, it was not to be taken into account in determining whether the 75 per cent majority has been achieved. It seemed to me that the vote was to be treated as
G
an indivisible whole, and in the absence of any power on the part of the chairman to divide the vote into two or otherwise apportion it, it seemed to me that the only power I had was to determine whether Calor Gas was a secured creditor. I thought they were and thereafter left their vote out of account in accordance with the rule.'

H
If that be the correct construction of the rule, it does seem to yield an unfair result especially with regard to a creditor who contracted without security and who has become partly secured only in the course of enforcing a judgment. The fairer solution for all creditors would seem to require that the unsecured part of the debt should count in calculating the majority.

The argument against rests on what is claimed to be the clear and unambiguous wording of the rule. It is not suggested that this leads to a fairer result. The most that can

be said in its favour on the merits was that it led to a simple and quick solution which
placed no undue burden of examining the facts upon the chairman of the meeting who
would not necessarily be the nominee.

The argument based on strict construction found favour with Judge Woolley in the
court below. At this point I can look at his judgment with which the court has been
supplied. He set out the rule and dealt with certain academic discussions of this problem
which he thought were flawed, but then he goes on:

> 'The wording of r. 5.18(3)(b) is clear and unambiguous. It provides for the
> creditor's vote in respect of any claim or part of a claim where the claim or part is
> secured, to be left out of account. In other words, a creditor in that position is
> clearly entitled to vote but his vote is to be left out of account for the purpose of
> calculating the requisite majority.

> Contrast the position of a creditor whose claim is secured or partly secured by a
> bill of exchange or promissory note. Such a creditor is entitled to vote to the extent
> that he is willing to value his security and deduct it from his claim. There is no
> comparable provision in the case of a creditor secured in part on property. Rule
> 5.18(3)(c) specifically provides for a creditor whose claim is partly secured on a bill
> of exchange or promissory note; had it been intended to make a similar rule in
> respect of a partly secured creditor whose debt was secured on property, such a
> rule could so easily have been framed. The omission, in my judgment, is significant
> and aids the construction of r. 5.18(3)(b) as meaning precisely what it so clearly
> and unambiguously in my judgment provides.

> The provisions of r. 6.93(4) are also relevant. This rule relates to the entitlement of
> creditors to vote at a meeting called in a bankruptcy. The provisions of r. 6.93(4)
> enable the creditor in such a case to vote in respect of the balance of his debt after
> deducting the value of his security. Rule 5.18 which applies to voluntary
> arrangements could so easily have contained a similar provision but does not.

> It is interesting to note that the rule in bankruptcy makes a similar provision for a
> creditor who is partly secured by a bill of exchange or promissory note as in
> r. 5.18. What r. 6.93 provides for in a bankruptcy but r. 5.18 does not provide for
> in the case of voluntary arrangements is the right of a creditor partly secured on
> property to be taken into account in respect of the unsecured balance of his claim.
> Rule 5.18 could so easily have provided, as rule 6.93(4) provides in the case of a
> bankruptcy. So the rules clearly contrast a bankruptcy situation with a situation in
> which a creditors' meeting has been called to approve a voluntary arrangement.

> The deliberate omission in r. 5.18 supports the view that there is to be left out of
> account a creditor's vote in respect of any balance of the debt which is unsecured.
> Indeed, the wording of r. 5.18(3)(b) makes it, in my judgment, so obviously clear.'

Perhaps before going on I should just refer to the text of the rule that the judge relies
on, r. 6.93(4). This is the applicable rule following an actual bankruptcy. It starts off:

> '6.93(1) Subject as follows, at a meeting of creditors a person is entitled to vote as
> a creditor only if–'

and there are forms about that, and then coming to r. 6.93(4):

> 'A secured creditor is entitled to vote only in respect of the balance (if any) of his
> debt after deducting the value of his security as estimated by him.'

With the greatest respect I am unable to accept the judge's reasoning. In the first place,
I do not regard the terms of r. 5.18(3)(b) as unambiguous. The rule does not read:

> 'There is to be left out of account a creditor's vote in respect of any claim where
> the claim or part is secured.'

A   What it does provide is that:

> '. . . there is to be left out of account a creditor's vote in respect of any claim or part of a claim . . . where the claim or part is secured.'

The interpretation put forward by the chairman, which has found favour, renders the words 'or part of a claim' otiose, as I see it. To my mind, those words admit of an alternative interpretation that where part of a claim is secured that part only is to be

B   discounted. Simply as a matter of language I find the rule ambiguous on this and that opens up other interpretations.

Secondly, I do not find persuasive the argument based on the omission in r. 5.18(3)(b) of the corresponding provision in r. 6.93(4) relating to the creditors' meeting in bankruptcy which I have just read out. The reason for its omission to my mind is that it would have been inappropriate to have included it. Indeed, I go so far as to say I would

C   have been surprised to find it in, even though the rule-makers desired that only part of the claim should be discounted. In the case of an individual voluntary arrangement before one reaches the creditors' meeting to consider a proposal for an IVA, the proposal itself has to contain particulars of the extent to which the assets are charged; the proposal has to be reported on by the nominee and sent to the creditors. Hence in the normal case the creditor will not need to estimate his security. If he disagrees with a statement in the proposal he could put forward what he claims to be the true position in the written notice

D   of his claim which he has to give at or before the meeting if his claim is to be taken into account at all.

Accordingly, I see no great difficulty for the chairman at the meeting in determining the value of partly held security under r. 5.18(5). In the present case, for example, the proposal showed £3,300 as the secured part of the debt. Accordingly, those arguments addressed to me that without the comparable provisions in r. 6.93 the valuation of

E   securities is unworkable and, in my judgment, wide of the mark.

The reason for the inclusion of the provision regarding a bill of exchange or promissory note is to my mind equally obvious. Let us suppose that the debtor is holding a bill of exchange drawn by him and accepted by a customer, or a promissory note given by a customer and has negotiated the bill or note to the creditor. In these circumstances the primary liability to pay the bill or note on maturity is that of the acceptor or promissory. The debtor will only be secondarily liable. Accordingly, the bill or note is to be left out of

F   account unless the creditor can show that its value is less than its face value and then the machinery comes into play to show that. Those are matters which will not necessarily be known to the debtor when he comes to formulate the proposal.

I do not see that the inclusion of this provision provides any assistance in the construction of para. (3)(b).

G   As an alternative argument Miss Hoffmann suggested that the words 'In the following cases' in r. 5.18(3) showed that these provisions were only applicable to later provisions, i.e. the case in para. (4), counting up those opposed to the resolution, and not to the preceding provision in para. (1), the requisite majority to pass the proposal. I do not accept this alternative way of putting it. I put it on the basis I have already mentioned. It would appear to go too far for it would lead to the inclusion of creditors present and voting who had not presented a claim as well as the secured creditors.

H   In my view the following cases are simply the three that follow within para. (3) itself, and the exclusions are equally applicable in computations under para. (1) as they are in computations under para. (4). Put simply, one leaves out of account the para. (3) creditors on both sides of the equation, out of the computation of the majority for the proposal and out of the computation of those voting against. It is a shorthand way of putting that. The substantive difference between the two statements, apart of course from the majority

being less under (4) than (1) is the exclusion of associates in computing under para. (4)   A
whereas one does not exclude them in computing under para. (1). There is no question of
associates in this case and therefore I need not pursue that particular point further.

Holding the opinion I do of the true construction of this rule, I have to allow the
appeal against the decision of Judge Woolley in so far as he held that the chairman of the
meeting was entitled to leave entirely out of account the vote of the appellant on the basis
that the claim of the appellant was in part secured, and declare that the claim of the   B
appellant in so far as it was not secured should have been taken into account in
calculating the vote for the purposes of r. 5.18(1). The consequence is that the chairman
should have declared that the resolutions to approve the proposals had been rejected.

In those circumstances the cross-appeals become academic. Mr Castle agrees that they
should be dismissed, which leaves the debtors, if so advised, free to take the matter
further.   C

Charging orders appeal

The other substantive appeal is that of the debtors against the decision of Master Eyre
ordering that the charging order of 8 February 1993 be made absolute and refusing to
order that it be discharged. I have already mentioned the charging order nisi but now I
must look at it a little more closely. I should say the appeal is against two orders both   D
made on 22 June 1993 being an order dismissing the application to set the charging order
nisi aside and another order granting a charging order absolute. They were made at a
time when there were in place interim orders under s. 252 of the *Insolvency Act* 1986
pending the outcome of Calor Gas's application to the county court to revoke the
individual voluntary arrangements.

The application to the master to discharge the charging order nisi was made on   E
22 April 1993. It simply asks that the order made on 8 February by Master Creightmore
charging the beneficial interest of the defendant Victor Brett Piercy be discharged. The
grounds for the application were that they were insolvent. As to that, the master ordered,
by noting on a summons, which is a common practice in chambers, that the applications
were dismissed, then the costs, and the formal order which was subsequently drawn up,
dated 22 June and issued out of the court office a few days later.

The other application is Calor Gas's application for an order absolute. The master's   F
annotation on it reads: 'Order absolute 22:vi:93 (leave having been given per IA 86,
s. 252(2)(b).' For the formal order one has to go to the charging order absolute. That
omits to record the granting of leave. Those are the details of the orders that were made,
which orders the debtor Victor Brett Piercy here has appealed against.

Mr Castle challenged the grant of leave on the ground that leave should have been   G
applied for in the Chester County Court which alone had jurisdiction to give leave under
s. 252 as being seised with these bankruptcy proceedings. That is the first point I have to
deal with and I have to say I am unable to accept that submission. For this I must go to
the *Insolvency Act* 1986. Section 252 is the first of the sections in the group of Parts
dealing with the insolvency of individuals. The first part in this group is Pt. VIII dealing
with individual voluntary arrangements. Section 252 commences:

    H

'(1) In the circumstances specified below, the court may in the case of a debtor
(being an individual) make an interim order under this section.

(2) An interim order has the effect that, during the period for which it is in force–

    (a) no bankruptcy petition relating to the debtor may be presented or proceeded
       with, and

A (b) no other proceedings, and no execution or other legal process, may be commenced or continued against the debtor or his property except with the leave of the court.'

The court having jurisdiction in relation to insolvent individuals is defined in s. 373 of the Act:

B '(1) The High Court and the county courts have jurisdiction throughout England and Wales for the purposes of the Parts in this Group.

(2) For the purposes of those Parts, a county court has, in addition to its ordinary jurisdiction, all the powers and jurisdiction of the High Court; and the orders of the court may be enforced accordingly in the prescribed manner.'

Mr Castle places particular reliance on the next subsection.

C '(3) Jurisdiction for the purposes of those Parts is exercised–

(a) by the High Court in relation to the proceedings which, in accordance with the rules, are allocated to the London insolvency district, and

(b) by each county court in relation to the proceedings which are so allocated to the insolvency district of that court.'

D There is no doubt that the relevant county court for the purposes of these proceedings is the Chester County Court. But then there is the following subsection:

'(4) Subsection (3) is without prejudice to the transfer of proceedings from one court to another in the manner prescribed by the rules; and nothing in that subsection invalidates any proceedings on the grounds that they were initiated or continued in the wrong court.'

E In my judgment the master, who of course is part of the High Court, did have jurisdiction and I think it would be too restrictive to say that because one bankruptcy court has made an interim order or any other order, that precludes any other court from giving leave under s. 252. It may be that in any particular case the court to which application for leave is made should decline to exercise its jurisdiction and transfer the proceedings to another court, as indeed happened subsequently when the proceedings before the Queen's Bench Division were transferred into this division. I do not read

F subs. (3) as cutting down the wide terms of subs. (1). That subsection does not say 'Subject as hereinafter follows' or something like that. What it says is the High Court and the county courts have jurisdiction throughout England and Wales for the purposes of the Parts in this Group.

In my judgment Master Eyre had jurisdiction to give leave for the proceedings to be brought and so I cannot allow the appeal on that ground but I must examine the merits of it. It is agreed in considering this appeal that I have to look at the matter afresh. It is not like the appeal that I have just been dealing with; that was a true appeal against an

G order of a lower court.

The case to which I have been rightly referred and which deals with the sort of question that we have here, the interaction of charging orders and bankruptcy, is a decision of the House of Lords in *Roberts Petroleum Ltd v Bernard Kenny Ltd* [1983] 2 AC 192. I should say that though the final appeal was not heard until 1983, the case concerned a

H bankruptcy and orders made before the coming into force of the *Charging Orders Act* 1979. However, the previous legislation, s. 35 of the *Administration of Justice Act* 1956, did not differ markedly from the *Charging Orders Act* 1979.

On 23 March 1979 there was an order nisi charging some land of a company. On 2 April there was a resolution to wind up, thereby setting in train a creditors' voluntary liquidation. Two days later the order nisi was made absolute so that one sees an

important factual difference between that case and the present one here. The liquidation A
had started before the order was made absolute.

This was dealt with at four levels. It started before the district registrar who made an
order absolute; that was discharged by the judge in chambers, restored in the Court of
Appeal and ultimately discharged in the House of Lords. I need only look at the final
holding. I refer to the final holding in the headnote at p. 193 of the report.

> '. . . while each case was a matter for the individual judgment of the court in the B
> circumstances of that particular case, the compulsory winding up of a company,
> or a resolution of a company in general meeting for voluntary winding up, which
> brought into operation a statutory scheme for dealing with the assets of the
> company, was, without more, a "sufficient cause" for not making a charging order
> nisi over such assets absolute; and that, accordingly, Bristow J. had been correct in
> holding that the liquidation of the defendants was a sufficient cause for not C
> converting the charging order nisi obtained by the plaintiffs into an order absolute
> and the order absolute should be discharged . . .'

Those were the facts and the ultimate holding and now I must look at one or two
passages in the speech and it was the only reasoned speech, I think, on this aspect of the
case before their lordships. It was given by Lord Brightman. He says at p. 209A:

> 'The main thrust of Roberts's [the creditor's] argument is that the order nisi D
> imposes an immediate charge, which is correct, and that therefore at the date of
> the commencement of the liquidation the assets were already outside the statutory
> scheme. That proposition, by reference to that date, is also correct. The liquidator
> was unable, at that date, to collect those assets by going into possession, because
> the receiver was already in possession. But the weakness of the argument to my
> mind is that Roberts had no more than a defeasible charge at the date of the
> commencement of the liquidation, so that the right of the receiver to retain the E
> asset as against the liquidator was only a defeasible right. Neither the precarious
> existence of the charge nor the precarious possession of the receiver seems to me to
> afford a convincing reason for consolidating the position of the judgment creditor
> vis-à-vis the general body of unsecured creditors and thereby defeat quoad that
> asset the statutory scheme which was already in full force and effect. So, unless
> there is convincing authority pointing to a different conclusion, I would regard the
> intervention of the statutory scheme as a sufficient and indeed decisive "cause to F
> the contrary". I can see no logic in an additional requirement "such as a scheme of
> arrangement, formal or informal, agreed or being negotiated amongst the
> creditors" . . .'

That looked to an argument which had found favour in the Court of Appeal.

Then I think I should look at p. 211H: G

> 'No doubt there are differences between winding up procedures and bankruptcy
> procedures, but I doubt whether it is possible to decide this case in favour of Kenny
> without disapproving *Burston* [*Burston Finance Ltd v Godfrey* [1976] 1 WLR 719].
> Admittedly each case is a matter for individual judgment in the circumstances of
> that particular case; for the question is whether it appears to the court or to the
> judge that sufficient cause is shown against making the order absolute. There are
> no facts relied upon by Kenny in the instant case except its insolvency plus H
> intervening liquidation; and if they are "sufficient cause" in the instance case,
> similar circumstances ought to have been "sufficient cause" in *Burston*.'

I take that still to be the law, despite the changes in statute law since that time. Notably,
the *Charging Orders Act* 1979 has come into force and brought about certain changes
and relaxations in the Companies Act and Insolvency Act. Shortly, I do not accept, as

A   has been submitted to me, that this decision has been overtaken in some way by the Charging Orders Act so that now there would be a completed execution simply by the making of a charging order nisi.

The way the law has been relaxed is this. Previously, before a charging order nisi could be regarded as completed it had to be accompanied by the appointment of a receiver, and there was such a receiver in the *Roberts* case. All that the Charging Orders Act does is

B   that it ensures that an order without a receiver is completion of the execution but – and this is where the case comes in – the initial order nisi is still defeasible in the sense as it was used by Lord Brightman in the *Roberts* case.

The situation we have here is that the order nisi was obtained when there had been no bankruptcy order, and no independent voluntary arrangements or proposals for independent voluntary arrangements had been set on foot by means of obtaining an interim order.

C   I must now look at the *Charging Orders Act* 1979 itself before going on. I can start with s. 1(1). There is not a great deal of this that I need to refer to.

> 'Where, under a judgment or order of the High Court or a county court, a person (the "debtor") is required to pay a sum of money to another person (the "creditor") then, for the purpose of enforcing that judgment or order, the appropriate court may make an order in accordance with the provisions of this Act imposing on any
D   such property of the debtor as may be specified in the order a charge for securing the payment of any money due or to become due under the judgment or order.'

There is no suggestion that the order of Master Creightmore back in February was not a proper order under this subsection.

Now I think we go to s. 1(5):

> 'In deciding whether to make a charging order the court shall consider all the
E   circumstances of the case and, in particular, any evidence before it as to–
>
> (a) the personal circumstances of the debtor, and
>
> (b) whether any other creditor of the debtor would be likely to be unduly prejudiced by the making of the order.'

I think the only other section I need refer to is s. 3(1) dealing with conditional orders.

F   'A charging order may be made either absolutely or subject to conditions as to notifying the debtor or as to the time when the charge is to become enforceable, or as to other matters.'

The order is made ex parte in the first instance on the strength of an affidavit by the creditor, and then it comes before the court to determine whether it should stand and be made absolute or whether it should be discharged. In making that decision as to whether it should stand or be discharged, then the court has to take into account the matters in

G   s. 1(5).

Just before I examine those, we have in this case the order nisi and the order absolute. No bankruptcy has yet commenced, if it ever does. Nevertheless, there is this, which has been rightly stressed by Mr Castle, that while the interim orders are in place, no one – either the debtors themselves or another creditor – can present a petition for bankruptcy save with the leave of the court. That, I think, is the position now and I bear in mind that

H   as well as the terms of s. 1(5).

As I read *Roberts Petroleum Ltd v Bernard Kenny Ltd*, in considering whether an order should be made absolute after bankruptcy or liquidation almost as a matter of course the order will be discharged. Yet where there is no supervening bankruptcy the court has a wider discretion than where there had already been a bankruptcy. Even in the latter case where there had already been a bankruptcy, the court is not deprived of all discretion in

the matter and I take that from the passage of Lord Brightman's speech at p. 211 to   A
which I referred.

The first matter which the court particularly has to bear in mind is the personal
circumstances of the debtor. They are very straitened, and it would look as if he will have
to go bankrupt if the scheme is not accepted. That is a strong factor in pointing towards
discharging the order.

The next matter that has to be considered is whether any other creditor of the debtor   B
would be likely to be unduly prejudiced by the making of the order. This is more difficult.
Prima facie they would do better if the order were discharged and the assets sold for the
benefit of all the creditors, than retained for the largest. That follows logically. Or they
would be better if the scheme were reinstated. That appears clearly from the figures and
from the contents of Mr Edwards' affidavit. But one must look at that in a practical way.
Most of the other creditors are for relatively small sums. Hence, when it comes to   C
assessing what they are likely to get out of it, following the administration in bankruptcy
and sale of the assets by the trustee, each creditor is likely to receive a very small sum. In
such circumstances it is difficult to say that they would be unduly prejudiced by the
making of the order. Under the scheme they may get more but it is still small and they
have to wait three years before the matter is finally settled.

As against that I have to find that there are special circumstances which point in favour
of the master's decision to make the order absolute. Under the scheme it was sought to   D
impose the scheme on Calor Gas against its known opposition by discounting its vote on
the basis that it was a secured creditor.

Having come into the scheme on those terms, the scheme deprived Calor Gas of its
security. That was its avowed purpose. Calor Gas lost its security and became locked
into a scheme of which it disapproved. By those means the appellant in my judgment was
deprived of two important statutory rights. The first is to be found in s. 258(4) of the   E
Insolvency Act 1986. In relation to a creditors' meeting to consider proposed voluntary
arrangements it provides:

> 'The meeting shall not approve any proposal or modification which affects the
> right of a secured creditor of the debtor to enforce his security, except with the
> concurrence of the creditor concerned.'

It was sought to be argued on the basis of the case of *Re Mohammed Naeem (a*   F
Bankrupt) [1990] 1 WLR 48 that all that had happened was that the claim was modified.
The result of that case was that a landlord retained his right of forfeiture though over a
modified debt because the effect of the bankruptcy was to reduce the claim. That is not
to my mind a true analogy because here if the charging order is discharged then the
security itself has gone. If it is discharged by the court or by the scheme, the security has
disappeared. It does not survive as a security over a lesser amount or anything of that   G
sort.

It was the purpose of the scheme that the house should not be available for creditors.
Accordingly, if the scheme is binding, then the creditor has lost his security without
consenting to it.

The other statutory right is the right in r. 5.18(1) to have his vote counted in so far as
his debt is unsecured in the computation of a majority.   H

The attitude of Mr Edwards over this matter is that anyway they will do much better
under the scheme than they will do by having the benefit of their security; and I can see
the force of it. I look at his affidavit where he is describing discussions with the solicitors
acting for Calor Gas, and with the company secretary of Calor Gas. They culminated in
a telephone conversation on 19 March:

A '. . . when I tried again to get Miss Chambers to change her mind, and because I *still* had not been told any good reason for turning down the arrangement. Miss Chambers' file note is not an accurate record of the conversation. I was not panicking about not being paid for the good reason I had already been paid in full.'

He has explained about his fee and I see no reason not to accept what Mr Edwards says about that aspect of the matter. He continues:

B 'I simply would not let Miss Chambers off the hook until she explained a good reason for rejecting the proposal which seemed to me so obviously in the interests of all creditors including Calor Gas . . .

Miss Chambers has implied that the whole object of the scheme was to deprive Calor Gas of its charging order and that accordingly things were done in bad faith. The scheme was formulated some weeks before Calor Gas obtained their charging

C order and the only reason why the application to the court was delayed was that I would not do any material amount of work until I had been paid. It was crucial to the whole VA that Victor's house should be ransomed and clearly this could not be done if the charging order stayed in place. That was the reason for the amendment, that any of the brothers was free to pull out of the voluntary arrangement if the charging order could not be discharged. Having regard to the interests of the creditors as a whole, I have no doubt that it was better to have the

D security discharged so that a much greater benefit could accrue to creditors generally. Calor's share of this was worth more than the value of their security and therefore Calor Gas should have been better off under the scheme. The proposal and my involvement in it was a bona fide proposal designed to make a better return to creditors as a whole than on bankruptcy with some benefit to the debtor.'

For my part, I can accept that statement, that his proposal was a bona fide proposal

E designed to make a better return to creditors, but it does not meet the objection which I do find a formidable one, that Calor Gas were, even if they were cutting off their nose to spite their face, entitled under the rules to have a vote and to take their own decision. Although Mr Edwards has argued cogently there in the affidavit as to his reasons, nevertheless one can see respectable reasons for not going along with it. It involves three years' wait. Calor Gas are entitled to say 'We don't want to be bothered with this further; we want to take what we can get from it and we would prefer to submit to the statutory

F scheme for distribution on bankruptcy'. This is a voluntary arrangement put forward avowedly to benefit the debtor, to enable the debtor to retain the home. I have a lot of sympathy with the position that Mr Edwards and the debtors found themselves in but that is not the purpose of voluntary arrangements nor of the statutory scheme. Their purpose should be to pay off the creditors.

To my mind, the deprivation of Calor Gas of its statutory rights in that way and in the circumstances I have outlined outweighs the considerations I have to have regard to

G under s. 1(5) in relation to the debtor and the other creditors. If it had been appreciated in March that the scheme could not go forward without the consent of Calor Gas and accordingly the debtors had presented petitions as they were proposing to do, I can see that the order would most probably not have been made absolute but would have had to be discharged, I can only regard that as hypothetical but I can see very strong grounds for saying that the order then would be discharged.

H As it is, Calor Gas have had to incur a lot of additional expense and have been greatly delayed, and that seems to me to tip the balance the other way. In those circumstances I find that the order absolute should stand. There are special circumstances in this case so that that appeal is dismissed.

(Order accordingly)

Re Forte's (Manufacturing) Ltd.
Stanhope Pension Trust Ltd & Anor v Registrar of Companies & Anor.

Court of Appeal (Civil Division).
Sir Thomas Bingham MR, Hoffmann and Henry L JJ.
Judgment delivered 17 December 1993.

Power of court to declare dissolution of company void – Landlord applied to have dissolution of original tenant avoided after tenant became insolvent – Original tenant would have claim against solvent assignees of underlease – Whether assignees should be joined as parties – Whether dissolution should be declared void – Companies Act 1985, s. 651; Rules of the Supreme Court, O. 15, r. 6(2)(b).

This was an appeal by landlords against the refusal of an application to declare the dissolution of a company void under s. 651 of the Companies Act 1985 (see [1993] BCC 603).

The company went into members' voluntary liquidation in 1988 and was dissolved in 1992. It was previously the tenant of premises which were assigned ultimately to BCCI which was wound up insolvent in 1992. The landlords looked to the original tenant for the rent and applied for an order under s. 651 declaring the company's dissolution to have been void. The landlord's case was that in respect of the rent the company would have a right of indemnity against subsequent assignees which were solvent. The intermediate assignees applied to be joined (under RSC, O. 15, r. 6(2)(b)) to argue that their liabilities under the indemnities had been irrevocably discharged by the dissolution of the company. The registrar refused joinder and restored the company to the register. The judge allowed the assignees to be joined and reversed the registrar's order declaring the company's dissolution void. The landlords appealed.

Held, allowing the appeal and restoring the company to the register:

1. The judge had refused restoration on the basis that the jurisdiction should not be exercised to put the applicant in a better position than he would have been in, but that principle could not be extracted from the case relied on. The whole point of an application was to improve the applicant's position. (Re Servers of the Blind League [1960] 1 WLR 564 considered.)

2. A company was entitled to wind itself up notwithstanding that it would thereby become unable to fulfil contingent obligations. Contingent creditors had to prove for the value of their claims at the date of winding up. However, a creditor could amend his proof at any time. The rule that prior distributions could not be disturbed meant that it would usually not do him any good. Nevertheless a proof could be increased because a contingency had happened. (Re Northern Counties of England Fire Insurance Co Ltd. Macfarlane's Claim (1880) 17 ChD 337 considered.)

3. It was not necessary for the court to express any concluded view on whether the company would be entitled to recover under the indemnity. It was sufficient if the interest of an applicant under s. 651 was more than 'merely shadowy'. (Re Wood and Martin (Bricklaying Contractors) Ltd [1971] 1 WLR 293 considered.)

4. An order might be made under s. 651 to enable the company to meet a liability which would otherwise remain unpaid. That was a sufficient ground for exercising the discretion and the company would be restored to the register accordingly.

5. Usually the making of an order under s. 651 did not determine whether the applicant had a claim against the company or the company had a claim against a third party. In such cases a third party should not be entitled to intervene. However, in cases in which the order

A   would directly affect the rights of a third party, irrespective of whether the applicant had any claim against the company or the company had any claim against the third party, the third party was entitled to be joined.

The following cases were referred to in the judgment of Hoffmann LJ:

Bradley v Eagle Star Insurance Co Ltd [1989] AC 957.
Harrington Motor Co Ltd, Re [1928] 1 Ch 105.
B   *House Property and Investment Co Ltd, Re* [1954] Ch 576.
Macfarlane's Claim. Re Northern Counties of England Fire Insurance Co Ltd (1880) 17 ChD 337.
Northern Counties of England Fire Insurance Co Ltd, Re. Macfarlane's Claim (1880) 17 ChD 337.
Perkins, Re [1898] 2 Ch 182.
Portrafram Ltd, Re (1986) 2 BCC 99,160.
C   *Servers of the Blind League, Re* [1960] 1 WLR 564.
Spottiswoode, Dixon & Hunting Ltd, Re [1912] 1 Ch 410.
Wood and Martin (Bricklaying Contractors) Ltd, Re [1971] 1 WLR 293.

James Munby QC and Christopher Pymont (instructed by Jacques & Lewis) for the appellant landlords.

D   Terence Etherton QC and James Ayliffe (instructed by Paisner & Co) for the respondent companies.

JUDGMENT

Hoffmann LJ: A company is a legal person whose existence is bounded by events analogous to the birth and death of a natural person. It can come into existence by, among other things, registration under the *Companies Act* 1985. It will cease to exist
E   upon, among other things, dissolution after the winding up of its affairs under the *Insolvency Act* 1986. In the case of a company which has been voluntarily wound up, dissolution ordinarily occurs three months after the liquidator's final account and return has been registered (s. 201(2) of the *Insolvency Act* 1986).

Unlike a natural person, however, a company which has ceased to exist may be restored to life. In the case of a company dissolved after winding up, the court has power
F   under s. 651 of the *Companies Act* 1985 to declare the dissolution to have been void. This appeal concerns an application for such an order.

The company in question was a member of the Forte group called Forte's (Manufacturing) Ltd ('Forte'). On 27 October 1988, for the purposes of a reconstruction of various group companies and the directors having made a declaration of solvency, it passed a resolution for members' voluntary winding up. The liquidator advertised for claims in the normal way, paid the creditors and distributed the assets. His final account
G   and return were registered on 8 November 1991 and the company was therefore deemed to have been dissolved on 8 February 1992.

The applicants, whom I shall jointly call 'the landlord', are the lessors under two registered underleases granted in 1960 by which premises in Oxford Street were let to Forte for a term of 42 years. It covenanted, among other things, to pay the rent during the whole of the term. On 28 January 1964 Forte assigned the underleases to Post Inns
H   Ltd ('Post'), another company in the Forte group. On 29 September 1967 there was a further assignment within the Forte group to Forte Properties Ltd ('Properties'). On 9 February 1979 Properties assigned the underleases to BCCI.

In January 1992 BCCI was ordered to be wound up. It stopped paying rent and on 10 June 1992 the liquidators disclaimed the underleases. The landlord as usual looked to the original tenant for the rent. But the original tenant no longer existed. The landlord

therefore applied on 17 December 1992 for an order under s. 651 declaring the dissolution   A
of Forte to have been void.

There is usually little point in reviving a company to enable a new claim to be made because (as in this case) all its assets will have been distributed. It is a general principle of insolvency law that although a creditor can prove (or increase the amount of his proof) at any time during the liquidation, distributions which have already been properly made cannot be disturbed. But the landlord says that in this case its claim for rent will bring   B
into existence a new asset, namely, Forte's right of indemnity against Post under the covenant implied in the 1964 assignment by s. 24(1)(b) of the *Land Registration Act* 1925. This is a covenant:

> 'that during the residue of the term the transferee and the persons deriving title under him will pay, perform and observe the rent, covenants and conditions by and in the registered lease reserved and contained, and on the part of the lessee to   C
> be paid, performed and observed, and will keep the transferor and the persons deriving title under him indemnified against all actions, expenses, and claims on account of the non-payment of the said rent or any part thereof, or the breach of the said covenants or conditions, or any of them.'

Post is a solvent company and so the landlord says that the liquidator of Forte will be able to recover under the indemnity. Forte will be entitled to recover the full amount of the claim, even if the creditor is likely to be paid only a small dividend: see *Re Perkins*   D
[1898] 2 Ch 182. But in any case, the landlord in this case would receive substantially the whole of any payment under the indemnity. It is true that it will have no proprietary interest in the money. It will be an asset in the liquidation (*Re Harrington Motor Co Ltd* [1928] 1 Ch 105). But since the landlord will be the only outstanding creditor, this will make little practical difference. In fact the landlord says that if Forte is restored to the register, the liquidator is unlikely to want to be a regular quarterly conduit. He will   E
therefore be inclined to assign the right of indemnity to the landlord and drop out.

The registrar of companies and the former liquidator are normally the only respondents to an application under s. 651. But Post and Properties applied to be joined as defendants under RSC, O. 15, r. 6(2)(b) so that they could object to an order being made. The judge ([1993] BCC 603) said that their presence before the court was, in the words of r. 6(2)(b)(i), 'necessary to ensure that all matters in dispute in the cause or matter may be effectually and completely determined . . .' In this appeal, Mr Munby for   F
the landlord has challenged the decision and said that it was not a proper exercise of the judge's discretion. Since however Mr Etherton has appeared for Post and Properties both before the judge and in this court and the case has been fully argued, it will be more convenient to keep my comments on the question of joinder until after I have dealt with the merits of the application.

What are the principles upon which the power under s. 651 should be exercised? The   G
first two subsections read as follows:

> '(1) Where a company has been dissolved, the court may, on an application made for the purpose by the liquidator of the company or by any other person appearing to the court to be interested, make an order, on such terms as the court thinks fit, declaring the dissolution to have been void.
>
> (2) Thereupon such proceedings may be taken as might have been taken if the   H
> company had not been dissolved.'

Subsection (3) is immaterial and subs. (4)–(7) (which were introduced by amendment in 1989) provide that with the exception of applications made for the purpose of bringing proceedings against the company for personal injury or under the *Fatal Accidents Act* 1976, an application may not be made more than two years after the date of dissolution.

A   Subsection (1) thus confers a discretion in apparently unrestricted terms. But the judicial exercise of any statutory discretion is impliedly limited to the purposes for which it was conferred. What are the purposes of s. 651?

In *Re Servers of the Blind League* [1960] 1 WLR 564, Pennycuick J said (at p. 565):

> 'Generally speaking, the purpose of an order under section 651 is to enable distribution to be made of an asset which belonged to the company before
B   dissolution but which, for some reason, was overlooked and has vested in the Crown as bona vacantia . . .'

But the section can also be used to enable a new or increased claim to be made by a creditor. For example, in recent years, particularly since the section was amended in 1989, it has become fairly common for dissolutions to be declared void to enable a former employee of the company to make a claim for personal injury (for example, negligence in allowing him to contract an insidious industrial disease) which was not or could not have
C   been made at the time of the company's liquidation. The purpose of such applications is to obtain a judgment against the company which can be enforced against its insurer under the *Third Parties (Rights Against Insurers) Act* 1930. This Act provides that a right to indemnity under a contract of insurance vests in the claimant on the date of the winding up and does not become an asset in the liquidation. The applicant will therefore not have to prove as a creditor. He will need to revive the company only to obtain the
D   judgment which establishes the company's right to indemnity: *Bradley v Eagle Star Insurance Co Ltd* [1989] AC 957.

I think it would therefore be nowadays more accurate to say that ordinarily the purposes of s. 651 are either to enable the liquidator to distribute an overlooked asset or a creditor to make a claim which he has not previously made. *Re Servers of the Blind League*, from which I have cited above, is an example of an unsuccessful attempt to use
E   the section for an altogether different purpose. A charitable company had gone into voluntary liquidation. Dissolution took place on 6 June 1958. On 5 January 1959 occurred the death of Mrs Petrie, who bequeathed the company a quarter of her residuary estate. The effect of the company having ceased to exist was that, as in the case of the predecease of a natural legatee, the gift lapsed and accrued to the other residuary beneficiaries. The liquidator applied for an order declaring the dissolution void in order retrospectively to validate the legacy. Pennycuick J refused the order, saying that 'without
F   seeking to lay down any rule of universal application' he did not think that an order which would 'dispossess other persons who obtained a vested interest in the asset under a title not derived from the company' was properly within the intended purpose of the section.

This seems to me, if I may respectfully say so, quite right. The application had nothing to do with the distribution of assets or the making of claims in the liquidation. It was
G   simply an attempt to play ontological ducks and drakes with the law relating to legacies. But the judge in this case extracted from it a far wider principle. He said (at p. 607E) it showed that the jurisdiction under s. 651:

> 'ought not to be exercised to put the applicant for an order in a better position than he would have been in if the liquidation had been properly conducted and so to deprive third parties of benefits which have accrued to them during the course of the liquidation or thereafter.'

H   I have an initial difficulty in understanding what the principle means. 'If the liquidation had been properly conducted' suggests that the liquidation has not been properly conducted. But in this case it has. No one says that it has not. I suspect that what the judge meant was that the applicant should not be put in a better position unless the liquidation has not been properly conducted. But better than what? Presumably better than if he had proved in the liquidation. The only other possibility is that he should not

be in a better position than he is. But this makes no sense because the whole point of the   A
application is to improve the applicant's position.

Mr Etherton's submission is that if the landlord had proved in the liquidation, it could
only have claimed as a contingent creditor. BCCI was still trading and there had been no
default in any payment of rent. The value of its contingent claim would have been the
difference between the respective values of its reversion with and without Forte's
covenant (*Re House Property and Investment Co Ltd* [1954] Ch 576). At the time, this   B
would not have been a great deal. Nor, he said, would such a claim have given rise to any
liability on the part of Post under s. 24(1)(b) of the *Land Registration Act* 1925. The
implied covenant is to indemnify Forte against liability arising out of non-payment of
rent, not against liability to pay a notional difference in reversionary values at a time
when no failure to pay rent has yet occurred.

Mr Etherton is certainly right in saying that the landlord's claim will be greater now   C
than it would have been in 1988. He may well also be right in saying that a contingent
claim does not give rise to a right of indemnity under s. 24(1)(b). But why should that be
a reason for refusing an order under s. 651? The principle formulated by the judge cannot
be derived from *Re Servers of the Blind League*, for which I have already suggested a
much simpler explanation. Nor is it consistent with the purpose of the 1989 amendment,
which, as I have mentioned, was to extend indefinitely the time for reviving the company
so as to allow former employees to make claims alleging that they had contracted diseases   D
which had not yet manifested themselves at the time when the company was dissolved.
The applicants would often have been able to prove for little or nothing at the time of the
liquidation (if it had occurred to them to do so) and the revival of the company is
intended to put them in a better position and to deprive a third party, namely the
insurance company, of the immunity which, as the House of Lords demonstrated in
Bradley v Eagle Star Insurance Co Ltd, it would otherwise have enjoyed. Mr Etherton   E
says that the personal injury cases are distinguishable because the applicant, even if he
did not know it, had a vested claim at the time of the liquidation. But this technical
distinction is not reflected in the way the judge formulated his principle and would in any
case be highly artificial.

The exception for cases in which the liquidation was not properly conducted is intended
to accommodate *Re Spottiswoode, Dixon & Hunting Ltd* [1912] 1 Ch 410 in which Neville   F
J revived a company to enable a creditor to make a claim which was only contingent at
the time of the liquidation. The facts were that company A, which held partly paid shares
in company B, was wound up for the purposes of reconstruction. The potential liability
for calls was thus a contingent debt. The liquidator of company A transferred all its other
assets to company C, leaving company A with the shares but nothing to pay any calls
which might be made. After company A had been dissolved, company B made a call. It
applied for the restoration of company A to enable it to make a claim.   G

Neville J clearly thought that the directors of company A had not behaved very
honourably in using a reconstruction to remove the assets of the company and leave a
contingent creditor to whistle for his debt. But he did not suggest that there was anything
improper in the way the liquidation had been conducted. Due notice had been given and
the necessary resolutions properly passed. Neville J was glad that the then equivalent of
s. 651 gave him power to prevent company A from avoiding its plain liability. But the
same can be said in other cases, including this one, and has nothing to do with the way   H
the liquidation has been conducted. In my view *Re Spottiswoode, Dixon & Hunting Ltd*
contradicts the judge's principle and does not fall within the exception.

Mr Etherton said that an English company has an inalienable right to wind itself up
and dissolve, whatever might be its outstanding liabilities. It is entitled to have its assets
distributed to creditors and shareholders in accordance with the rules of liquidation,

A   paying contingent creditors the value of their claims at the date of liquidation and no more. Furthermore, there is a strong policy which required such distribution to be final and undisturbed.

In my judgment there are elements of truth in each of Mr Etherton's propositions, but they are qualified in various ways which do not allow such broad brush strokes to present an adequate picture of the law. A company is certainly entitled to initiate and complete

B   the process of winding up notwithstanding that it will thereby become unable to fulfil future or contingent obligations. Contingent creditors become entitled to prove for the value of their claims at the date of winding up, but the company cannot be required to set aside a fund against the possibility that the contingency may happen. The liquidator is entitled to distribute the assets in accordance with the rules and such distributions cannot afterwards be disturbed. *Re House Property and Investment Co Ltd*, in which a landlord tried unsuccessfully to require the liquidator of its original tenant company to

C   set aside a fund to pay the rent if the assignee should default, illustrates all these principles very well.

On the other hand, it is also a rule of winding up that a creditor may submit a proof or amend an existing proof at any time during the liquidation. The rule that prior distributions cannot be disturbed means that it may not do him much good, but in principle he is entitled to make his claim. Another principle of liquidation is that

D   contingent claims are valued in the light of subsequent events, so that a proof may be increased because the contingency has happened: see *Macfarlane's Claim* (1880) 17 ChD 337. Furthermore, it is possible that a creditor may be entitled to prove for an accrued debt when the contingency has occurred after the winding up. I express no opinion on this point, but whatever the form of the proof, there is no principle which excludes new or increased claims.

E   I also accept that the liquidator is entitled to complete the winding up and file his final accounts and report, with the consequence that the company is thereafter dissolved. But the finality of the dissolution is qualified by the express provisions of s. 651. While the power under that section remains exercisable, the dissolution is not final. The company may be revived, the liquidation reopened and new or increased claims made.

In my judgment, therefore, the judge was wrong in law to hold that he ought not as a matter of principle to make an order under s. 651. It was open to him to do so and it is

F   therefore open to this court to exercise its own discretion.

Mr Etherton's alternative submission, to which I have already alluded, is that the order would not serve any purpose because Post is not liable to indemnify Forte under s. 24(1)(b) of the *Land Registration Act* 1925 and there is no other potential source of funds to discharge Forte's liability. As I have said, I am willing for the purposes of argument to accept that no liability could have arisen under s. 24(1)(b) before actual

G   default occurred in payment of the rent. I am not persuaded that this remains true once the tenant has actually defaulted, even though this did not happen until after the date of the winding up. Nor do I think it necessarily matters for this purpose whether the default enables the landlord to prove for an accrued debt or to revalue a contingent one. Mr Etherton said that even if Post was liable on the indemnity, it could be only for the unpaid rent accrued to date. That again may well be true, but the court has power under s. 201(3) of the *Insolvency Act* 1986 to defer the date of dissolution of the company for

H   such time as the court thinks fit. The registrar or judge of the Companies Court might think it right to exercise this power to enable Forte to claim under the indemnity for each quarter's rent as it fell due. Mr Munby plausibly submits that if the court took this course, the liquidator would soon enough extricate himself from the chain of liability by assigning the benefit of the indemnity to the landlord. Mr Etherton once more appealed to be principle of finality as an objection to using s. 201(3) to prolong Forte's life until

the lease comes to an end in nine years' time. Once more I give the same answer: the   A
principle is subject to express statutory qualifications.

It is not however necessary for us to express any concluded view on whether or
how much or for how long Forte will be entitled to recover under the indemnity. As
Megarry J said in *Re Wood and Martin (Bricklaying Contractors) Ltd* [1971] 1 WLR 293
at p. 297, the interest of an applicant under s. 651 in having the company revived does
not have to be firmly established or highly likely to prevail. It is sufficient that it is not   B
'merely shadowy' and I think that the possibility that assets may become available under
the indemnity is far from shadowy.

It follows that an order under s. 651 may enable the company to meet a liability which
would otherwise remain unpaid. This seems to me a sufficient ground for exercising the
discretion and I would do so.

That leaves the now academic question of whether the judge should have allowed Post   C
and Properties to be joined in the proceedings. As Harman J remarked in *Re Portrafram
Ltd* (1986) 2 BCC 99,160 such applications are usually to all intents and purposes ex
parte. The registrar of companies, who appears by counsel instructed by the Treasury
Solicitor, will assist the court on whether the requirements of the section have been
satisfied but has no interest except in securing the registrar's costs. The making of the
order does not determine whether the applicant has a claim against the company or the
company has a claim against a third party. As I have already said, all that is required is   D
that the claim should not be 'merely shadowy'. It therefore seems to me that a third party
who merely wants to say that the applicant has no claim against the company or that the
proceedings which the revived company proposes to bring against him have no prospect
of success should not be entitled to intervene in the application.

There are however some cases in which an order will directly affect the rights of a third
party, irrespective of whether the applicant has any claim against the company or the   E
company has any claim against the third party. *Re Servers of the Blind League* was such
a case. The residuary legatees had a right (which in the event was adequately safeguarded
by Pennycuick J without their appearance) to their bequests under the will which would
have been divested if the judge had made the order. In those circumstances I think that
they were entitled to be joined in order to argue that such an order should not be made.

In this case it seems to me that Post and Properties were wanting to argue that in   F
principle their potential liabilities under their indemnities had been irrevocably
discharged by the dissolution of Forte. As I have said in the first part of this judgment, I
think that the alleged principle is fallacious. But it was sufficiently arguable to have
persuaded the judge and I think that Post and Properties were entitled to be joined in
order to argue it. I would nevertheless allow the appeal and restore Forte to the register.

Henry LJ: I agree.

Sir Thomas Bingham MR: I also agree on both points.   G

(Appeal allowed with costs. Leave to appeal to the House of Lords refused)

  H

A
Nisbet v Shepherd.

Court of Appeal (Civil Division).
Balcombe, Leggatt and Hoffmann L JJ.
Judgment delivered 28 June 1993.

Share transfer – Whether share transfer was 'proper instrument of transfer' –
B *Companies Act 1948, s. 75 (Companies Act 1985, s. 183).*

This was an appeal by a shareholder against a declaration that he was liable jointly and severally with the company for the company's debts under s. 24 of the Companies Act 1985 [before amendment by SI 1992/1699].

There were two members of the company before 1983. In that year the other member sold his shares to the appellant. To escape liability under s. 24, in the company's liquidation, the
C appellant argued that the transfer of the other member's shares to him was ineffective because there was no proper instrument of transfer within s. 75 of the Companies Act 1948.

The relevant stock transfer form was a conventional one, but it omitted some of the particulars for which the form made provision, in particular, it did not state the consideration money and was not stamped. The judge held that that was a mere irregularity and did not render the instrument not a proper instrument of transfer for the purpose of s. 75.

D *Held*, dismissing the appeal:

Particulars were required to be given of the consideration by s. 5 of the Stamp Act 1891. The phrase 'a proper instrument' did not mean an instrument complying in all respects with statutory requirements. In the context, 'proper' meant no more than 'appropriate' or 'suitable'. What it had to be suitable for was stamping. Because the document sufficiently recorded the transaction, the defects in the form were mere irregularities. It was an
E instrument chargeable with stamp duty. It was, therefore, a proper instrument, and the registration of the transfer was not invalid.

The following case was referred to in the judgment of Leggatt LJ:

Paradise Motor Co Ltd, Re [1968] 1 WLR 1125.

James H Allen (instructed by R C Moorhouse & Co, Leeds) for the liquidator.

F Aubrey Craig (instructed by G F Lodder & Sons, Stratford upon Avon) for the shareholder.

JUDGMENT

Leggatt LJ: This case constitutes a useful reminder to those in small businesses who want to limit their liability by trading through a company, that they will not succeed in
G doing so if they fail to ensure that no more than six months goes by without there being at least one other member of the company.

The question in this appeal is whether the appellant, Kenneth Eric Shepherd, was inadvertently successful in achieving that end, by accepting himself the transfer of another member's shares by means of a defective stock transfer form; by purporting to register the transfer; and by failing to present the form for stamping. He appeals against the
H judgment of Judge Maddocks, dated 9 March 1992, whereby it was declared that:

'Mr Shepherd is personally liable jointly and severally with Keith Moulton & Co Ltd' – which I shall call 'the company' – 'for the payment of each and all unsatisfied debts of the company contracted after 22 October 1983.'

The provision rendering him jointly and severally liable in that fashion is s. 24 of the *Companies Act* 1985. That section states that:

'If a company carries on business without having at least two members and does   A
so for more than 6 months, a person who, for the whole or any part of the period
that it so carries on business after those 6 months–

(a) is a member of the company, and

(b) knows that it is carrying on business with only one member,

is liable (jointly and severally with the company) for the payment of the company's   B
debts contracted during the period or, as the case may be, that part of it.'

The judge concluded that the omission from the relevant stock transfer form of the
consideration, the date of execution, the addresses of the transferor and the transferee,
and stamp duty were mere irregularities and were not such as to render the instrument
not a proper instrument of transfer for the purpose of s. 75 of the *Companies Act* 1948.
He also held that the registration by the company pursuant to the instrument of the   C
transfer was a lawful registration, and that the transferor of the shares ceased to be a
member of the company when the transaction was effected. In those respects the
appellant contends that the judge was wrong.

The facts of the matter can be shortly stated. Until 22 April 1983, Robert Walter
Trevor Moulton and Mr Shepherd were the only members of the company. Each of them
held 918 of the total of 1,836 issued shares. On that day, Mr Moulton transferred his
shares to Mr Shepherd for £20,000. He also resigned as a director of the company, and   D
ceased to have anything more to do with it. That transfer of Mr Moulton's shares is
recorded in the company's register of transfers. In the company's register of members,
there is shown an entry against Mr Moulton, recording a transfer of his shares. Against
Mr Shepherd there is a corresponding entry, showing his acquisition on the same day of
the same number of shares. The company's register of director's interest in shares of the
company also has entries which show the purchase on 22 April 1983 by Mr Shepherd of   E
918 shares from Mr Moulton.

When Mr Moulton resigned as a director, Mr Shepherd's wife was appointed a director
and secretary of the company. No transfer of shares of the company was made after
22 April 1983, until that date in 1990 on which Mr Shepherd transferred one share to
his wife so that the resolution might be passed for the winding up of the company.

The annual return of the company, made up to 14 September 1983, and filed with the   F
companies registration office, was certified by Mr Shepherd and his wife. It recorded the
transfer by Mr Moulton to him of the relevant number of shares on 22 April 1983. This
resulted in Mr Shepherd being the holder of all 1,836 issued shares. Each of the
company's annual returns between then and 1989 was certified by Mr Shepherd as
director and his wife as secretary, and showed Mr Shepherd as the sole member of the
company, holding all 1,836 issued shares.   G

The transfer by which Mr Moulton transferred his shares to Mr Shepherd was effected
by a stock transfer form. It was delivered by him to Mr Shepherd together with his share
certificate, and at the same time he paid Mr Moulton the agreed consideration of £20,000.
The stock transfer form was a conventional one, but it omitted some of the particulars
for which the form makes provision. It was, as Mr Craig on behalf of Mr Shepherd has
submitted, defective in that it was undated, it did not state the consideration money, it   H
contained no address of transferor or transferee, it was not signed by the transferee, and
in those circumstances, not surprisingly, it was not stamped. But Mr Craig acknowledges
that of those deficiencies by far the most important was the failure to state the
consideration money. He also accepts that if he is not successful in pointing to that
deficiency as affecting the instrument sufficiently for his purposes, none of the other
defects will.

A   Section 75 of the *Companies Act* 1948 provided, so far as material, that it is not lawful for a company to register a transfer of shares in or debentures of the company, unless a proper instrument of transfer has been delivered to it. Mr Craig argues that any purported registration in reliance upon an instrument of transfer which is not a proper instrument of transfer is by virtue of that provision a nullity and ineffective. He contends that if the purported registration by the company of the transfer from Mr Moulton to Mr Shepherd was a nullity, then Mr Moulton remains the legal owner of the shares, and

B   only the beneficial title passed to Mr Shepherd. He supports that submission by contending that where a member of a company transfers his shares to another person, he does not cease to be a member of the company, unless and until the transferee is registered.

     The case from which most assistance can be derived, and which has been cited before us by Mr Craig, is *Re Paradise Motor Co Ltd* [1968] 1 WLR 1125. That was a case

C   involving a gift of shares which took place unbeknown to the donee. Where relevant, therefore, his signature was forged. In that case the company's articles contained a requirement that the transfer of a share shall be in writing signed by both the transferor and the transferee. It should be said that in the present case also there was a similar requirement, by virtue of the incorporation of reg. 17 of Table A into the company's articles. Delivering the judgment of the court, Danckwerts LJ said, at p. 1140C, after

D   reciting the relevant part of s. 75 of the *Companies Act* 1948:

     'The transfer in the present case is certainly an instrument, and it appears that the section was passed to make sure that there was an instrument which could be stamped with stamp duty. The question is whether, in the present case, it is a proper instrument of transfer so as to satisfy the section, and whether the absence of the transferee's signature makes the transfer a nullity.'

E   At letter H on the same page, Danckwerts LJ continued:

     'The judge considered that the transfer was a nullity for lack of the transferee's signature, but, as indicated, these being fully paid shares, we consider that this may be regarded as an irregularity. The judge also considered that the transfer was not a "proper instrument" for the purposes of section 75, and that, therefore, the registration was illegal, and, consequently, void. We do not, however, consider

F   that a "proper instrument" necessarily means an instrument complying with the formalities prescribed by the articles; indeed, the section itself includes a case in which the articles may not provide for any transfer by instrument. Having regard to the purpose of the section, we would construe the phrase as meaning an instrument such as will attract stamp duty under the relevant fiscal legislation.'

     It was the case for the liquidator that the non-execution of the stock transfer form by Mr Shepherd is in this case similarly a mere irregularity which does not render the transfer

G   invalid or a nullity. In his skeleton argument on the liquidator's behalf, Mr Allen pointed out that, as the transferee of the shares, it was Mr Shepherd's responsibility to present the stock transfer form to the Stamp Office for assessment and payment, and that as he chose not to do so, he should not be permitted to avoid liability under s. 24 of the *Companies Act* 1985, by relying upon his own omission.

     It is Mr Craig's argument that, whereas in the *Paradise Motor* case there was a mere

H   failure to comply with the articles, here the stock transfer form was more defective in that, in particular, it failed to refer to the consideration supporting the transaction. That failure constituted a transgression of s. 5 of the *Stamp Act* 1891, which provides, so far as material, that:

     'All the facts and circumstances affecting the liability of any instrument to duty, or the amount of the duty with which any instrument is chargeable, are to be fully

and truly set forth in the instrument; and every person who, with intent to defraud   A
Her Majesty,

    (a) executes any instruments in which all the said facts and circumstances are
           not fully and truly set forth . . .

shall incur a fine of ten pounds.'

Mr Craig argues that the purpose of that provision manifestly is to make sure that all
such formalities are complied with. It is, in short, a provision designed to save the   B
Revenue trouble. He contends that the failure to recite the amount of the consideration
in the stock transfer forms, with which we are concerned, constituted a manifest breach
of s. 5 of the *Stamp Act* 1891, and that that should procure the result that the transfer
was a nullity.

For my part, I have difficulty in seeing why the failure to comply with s. 5 of the *Stamp
Act* 1891 in that respect should result in the instrument not being a proper instrument,   C
especially since it is acknowledged that, even if the consideration had been stated, the
Revenue could have gone behind it should they have wished to question the amount set
forth in the document.

Mr Craig admits that Mr Moulton did all that he could to divest himself of his interests
in the shares. But he maintains that what was done was only effective to convey the
beneficial title to Mr Shepherd unless and until the transfer was lawfully registered, and   D
that, because no such registration took place, Mr Moulton never ceased to be a member,
and at the date of the company's liquidation, both Mr Moulton and Mr Shepherd
remained members of the company.

In the light, in particular, of the decision in *Paradise Motor Co Ltd*, from which he
made an extensive citation, the judge concluded:

    'Applying the principles in *Re Paradise Motor Co* the position was as plain as can   E
    be that the legal holder was Mr Shepherd. The non-execution by the transferee was
    an irregularity only and did not render the registration void. The failure to state
    the consideration and the failure to have the instrument stamped did not result in
    the transfer not being one which would have attracted stamp duty. It was still an
    instrument which transferred the shares and did so for a consideration and was
    accordingly liable for ad valorem duty. That satisfies the requirements as expressed
    in *Re Paradise Motor Co*, and on the basis of the judgment of Danckwerts LJ the   F
    consequence of the failure to state the consideration would not, therefore, render
    the transfer and the registration void.

    A final consideration is that the registration has been acted upon over the years by
    Mr Shepherd being treated for all purposes as the registered holder.'

In this case, the articles required the transfer to be executed by the transferee, but, as I
have indicated, Mr Craig accepts that he is precluded by authority from relying upon   G
that defect. As it was put in a passage from *Buckley on the Companies Acts*, also cited in
the judgment in *Re Paradise Motor Co Ltd*, the lapse of time coupled with recognition of
the transferee as a shareholder may render the transfer incapable of being impeached.

The stock transfer form was delivered to and accepted by the company, which acted
on it by registering Mr Shepherd as transferee of Mr Moulton's shares, so recognising
him as the sole shareholder. Thereafter, at least seven years went by, in each of which Mr   H
Shepherd was content to record himself in the annual return as the sole shareholder. It
is, therefore, too late to impeach the transfer, unless it is invalidated by statute.
Particulars were required to be given of the consideration by s. 5 of the *Stamp Act* 1891.
The question is whether that omission in particular prevented the stock transfer form
from constituting a proper instrument. In my judgment, the phrase does not mean an
instrument complying in all respects with statutory requirements. In this context, 'proper'

A means no more than 'appropriate' or 'suitable'. What it had to be suitable for was stamping.

It was, incidentally, Mr Shepherd's duty to see that it was stamped. That would no doubt have required the addition to the document of the amount of the consideration, so that the stamp duty might be ascertained, but because the document sufficiently recorded the transaction, the defects in the form were mere irregularities. It was an instrument

B chargeable with stamp duty. It was, therefore, a proper instrument, and the registration of the transfer was not invalid. Mr Shepherd was at all material times the sole shareholder and that rendered inescapable the order that the judge made. I would accordingly dismiss the appeal.

Hoffmann LJ: I have considerable sympathy with the appellant, who has fallen into a trap created by an ancient and obsolete rule. Section 24 of the *Companies Act* 1985 requires that a company should have at least two members. In default of compliance it

C strips the remaining member of the protection of limited liability. The rule goes back to s. 48 of the *Companies Act* 1862 when the minimum number of members was seven. This reflects the evolution of company law from partnership, but the reason why it has survived through successive Companies Acts is obscure. It seems to serve no purpose in protecting the public or anyone else. It is not necessary that the second member should hold his share or shares beneficially. The appellant could have satisfied the requirements

D of the Act by transferring a single share to his wife, lawyer or accountant to hold in trust for himself. But he did none of these things. For the reasons given by Leggatt LJ I therefore agree that, since 1983, the appellant has been the sole member and is liable accordingly.

Balcombe LJ: I agree that this appeal should be dismissed for the reasons given by Leggatt and Hoffmann L JJ.

E *(Order accordingly)*

F

G

H

Ian Chisholm Textiles Ltd v Griffiths & Ors.

Chancery Division.
David Neuberger QC (sitting as a deputy Chancery Division judge).
Judgment delivered 17 September 1993.

Retention of title – Plaintiff supplier sought title to cloth which had been worked on – Which terms of trade covered transactions – Whether plaintiff's evidence sufficiently established that particular cloth had not been paid for – Whether retention of title clause created charge over cloth which had been worked on – Whether such charge required registration – Priority between charge and debenture – Companies Act 1985, s. 395.

This was a retention of title claim by the plaintiff supplier. The plaintiff was a supplier of cloth. The defendants were the receivers of various companies in a group which designed, manufactured and distributed ladies' clothes.

A retention of title clause was introduced into the trading relationship between the parties in 1990. That clause was allegedly superseded by a second set of terms of trade in May 1991.

At the time of the appointment of the receivers in September 1991, the debenture holder was owed over £6m and the plaintiff over £1.8m. The parties had reached agreement over cloth supplied by the plaintiff which was uncut and cloth which had been cut but not subject to any work or other processing. The plaintiff claimed that 42,000 'items' consisting of cloth which had been cut and had been the subject of some work or processing, with a view to being manufactured into dresses, were the property of the plaintiff.

The court considered the following issues: (1) whether the second set of terms was in substitution for or in addition to the first set of terms; (2) whether the plaintiff had established its case on the facts; (3) whether the effect of the retention of title agreement in relation to the items was to create a charge requiring registration pursuant to s. 395 of the Companies Act 1985; and (4) the priority between such a charge and the debenture.

Held, giving judgment for the receivers:

1. The second set of terms replaced the first set.

2. On the evidence, the court could not be satisfied that all the cloth comprised in the items had not been paid for, and while it was likely that at least some of it had not been paid for, it was impossible to decide how much.

3. There was no provision in the agreement dealing with the rights of the parties once the cloth was incorporated in an article with other goods. It seemed difficult to impute to the parties an intention that goods other than the cloth, which were never vested in the plaintiff, and which the parties must have anticipated would be combined with the cloth by the company at its own expense when the dresses were being manufactured, should nonetheless be transferred, and not merely transferred as security but transferred absolutely beneficially, to the plaintiff.

4. The court concluded that once the cloth supplied by the plaintiff was combined to any significant extent by the company with goods owned by the company or by a third party the plaintiff's beneficial ownership, if any, of the cloth was converted into the interest of a chargee over the dress in the process of manufacture or over the completed dress. In that sense title did remain with the plaintiff, albeit that the nature of the title was converted from that of beneficial owner to that of chargee.

5. The charge was registrable.

6. If it were necessary to decide the issue, the court would hold that, in so far as any charge granted to the plaintiff post-dated the debenture, the bank had priority under the debenture.

A   The following cases were referred to in the judgment:

Atlantic Computer Systems plc, Re [1990] BCC 859; [1992] Ch 505.
Borden (UK) Ltd v Scottish Timber Products Ltd & Anor [1981] Ch 25.
Clough Mill Ltd v Martin [1985] 1 WLR 111.
Hamilton, Young & Co, Re. Ex parte Carter [1905] 2 KB 772.
Jones v Smith (1843) 1 Ph 244; 41 ER 624.
B   *Modelboard Ltd v Outer Box Ltd* [1992] BCC 945.
Peachdart Ltd, Re (1983) 1 BCC 98,920; [1984] Ch 131.
Young, Hamilton & Co, Re. Ex parte Carter [1905] 2 KB 381; [1905] 2 KB 772 (CA).

Roger Bartlett (instructed by Shah & Burke) for the plaintiffs.

Nicholas Le Poidevin (instructed by Wilde Sapte) for the defendants.

JUDGMENT

C
David Neuberger QC: The facts

Ramar Dresses Ltd ('Ramar') is part of the Ramar group of companies ('the group') whose business is and was the design manufacture and distribution of ladies' clothes. The plaintiff supplies cloth to manufacturers of garments and Ramar became a customer of the plaintiffs in about 1982. From 1982–1989, the plaintiffs supplied cloth to Ramar and was paid promptly.

D   However, by early 1990, Ramar was in difficulties, and was not paying the plaintiff promptly for cloth. Accordingly, on 12 February 1990, the plaintiff and Ramar agreed that title to any cloth supplied would remain vested in the plaintiff until payment. The precise basis of that arrangement was agreed in writing in February 1990 in a letter from the plaintiff to Ramar, and countersigned by Ramar, dated 12 February 1990 in the following terms ('the first set of terms'):

E   'Herewith are our trading terms and conditions:

The property in goods sold shall be and remain in the company until the company has received payment in full for them, together with payment in full for any other goods supplied by the company to the customer the price for which is overdue for payment. This will include finished garments which have been made up from fabric purchased from our company, and we will be entitled to recover garments made F   up in our cloth, or fabric which has been made up and not paid for.'

Thereafter, the plaintiff continued to supply cloth to Ramar. However, the financial position of Ramar continued to deteriorate, and a director of the plaintiff became involved in finding a new director for the group and arranging for additional finance for the group. At the same time, the plaintiff, while anxious to continue its trading relationship with Ramar, was also concerned to ensure that its position was as fully protected as possible so far as unpaid cloth was concerned. The plaintiff and Ramar G   accordingly instructed solicitors to prepare a fuller form of retention of title agreement. On 29 May 1991, the plaintiff wrote to Ramar in the following terms:

'Please note that all transactions between us will be made subject to the attached retention of title and risk clause.'

The enclosed agreement ('the second set of terms'), which was signed and returned on behalf of Ramar, was headed 'Title and Risk', and it is necessary to set out much of its H   contents. So far as relevant, it provided as follows:

'1. Risk in goods shall pass to the buyer on delivery and the buyer shall insure the goods for their full value from that time.

2. Notwithstanding cl. 1, legal and beneficial ownership of the goods shall remain with the company until unconditional payment in full has been received by the company for the goods.

3. Until property in the goods passes to the buyer under cl. 2 the buyer shall A

   3.1 be bailee of the goods

   3.2 keep the goods separately and readily identifiable as the property of the company.

4. Notwithstanding cl. 2 the buyer may as principal in the ordinary course of its business sell the goods by bona fide sale at full market value.

   . . . B

6. Any resale by the buyer of the goods in which property is not passed to the buyer shall (as between the company and the buyer only) be treated as if made by the buyer as agent for the company.

7. The proceeds of sale of the goods shall be held by the buyer in trust for the company to the extent of all sums recoverable by the company under cl. 2. C

8. The buyer shall keep any proceeds of sale as referred to in cl. 7 in a separate account but in any event the company shall have the right to trace such proceeds (according to the principles in *Re Hallett's Estate* (1880) 13 ChD 696).

9. The buyer assigns to the company all rights and claims that the buyer may have against its own customers and others in respect of the goods specified in cl. 6, and proceeds of sale specified in cl. 7. D

10. At any time prior to property and goods passing to the buyer (whether or not any payment to the company is then overdue or the buyer is otherwise in breach of any obligation to the company) the company may (without prejudice to any other of its rights)

   10.1 retake possession of all or any part of the goods and enter any premises for that purpose . . . E

   10.2 require delivery up to it of all or any part of the goods

   10.3 terminate the buyer's authority to resell or use the goods forthwith by written notice to the buyer which authority shall automatically terminate . . . upon any insolvency of the buyer or its going into liquidation . . . or its having a receiver appointed . . .

11. The company may at any time appropriate to such indebtedness as it thinks fit F
sums received from the buyer notwithstanding any purported appropriation by the buyer.'

References to clauses hereafter in this judgment are to clauses in the second set of terms.

Thereafter, the plaintiff continued supplying substantial amounts of cloth to Ramar. However, by late summer 1991, it appeared that the financial position of the group and of Ramar was such that the proposed refinancing was not feasible, and, on 12 September G
1991, pursuant to the terms of a debenture of 10 October 1990 ('the debenture') granted to National Westminster Bank plc ('the bank') the defendants were appointed receivers of the various companies in the group, including Ramar.

At the time of the appointment of the receivers, Ramar was indebted to the bank in a sum of £6,541,234. The evidence before me is unclear as to the precise extent of Ramar's indebtedness to the plaintiff, but it is common ground that it is, and has been since the date of the appointment of the defendants as receivers, in excess of £1.8m. H

At the date of the receivership of Ramar, the cloth supplied by the plaintiff and still in the possession of Ramar can usefully be divided into three categories. First, uncut cloth. Second, cloth which had been cut, but not subject to any work or other processing. Third, cloth which had not only been cut, but which had been the subject of some work or processing, with a view to being manufactured into dresses. There were 42,000 items ('the

A   items') in the third category which could well have included, and probably did include, cloth which had been fully converted into dresses and upon which no further work needed to be done.

The plaintiff and the defendants have reached agreement over cloth in the first and second categories. However, the parties were, and indeed are, unable to agree the position with regard to cloth which falls into the third category, namely the items. The plaintiff's
B   case was that the items, at whatever stage of manufacture or completion as dresses, were the property of the plaintiff. The parties agreed that the defendants could continue to manufacture, where necessary, the items, and would sell the items when completed in the ordinary course of Ramar's business, and would pay 'such part of the proceeds of sale as relate to the invoice price of [the plaintiff's] cloth comprised in such finished goods' into a special bank account to await the outcome of the court's decision.

In reply to the plaintiff's claim that the items were at and immediately following the
C   date of the appointment of the defendants as receivers, the plaintiff's, the defendants' reply is that the second set of terms were in substitution for, and not in addition to, the first set of terms, and that, first, the plaintiff has failed to make out its case on the facts; secondly, that the effect of the first and of the second set of terms is not to retain title in the items or in the cloth comprised in the items in the plaintiff, but merely to give the plaintiff a charge over the items, and that charge is ineffective as against the receivers
D   because it was not registered under s. 395 of the *Companies Act* 1985, and, even if that is not right, it does not have priority as against the bank by virtue of the terms of the debenture; there is also an issue about air freight charges. In these circumstances, it seems to me that I have to consider the following issues:

(1)   Were the second set of terms in substitution for or in addition to the first set of terms?

E   (2)   Has the plaintiff established its case on the facts?

(3)   What is the effect of the retention of title agreement in relation to the items?

(4)   If the effect is to create a charge, did the charge require to be registered pursuant to s. 395?

(5)   If the charge did not require to be registered, does the debenture nonetheless have priority to it?

F   (6)   The air freight charges.

(1)   Was the second set of terms in substitution for, or in addition to, the first set of terms?

I consider that the second set of terms replaced the first set of terms. The first reason for this conclusion depends on comparing the closing words of the first sentence of the first set of terms with the provisions of cl. 2. The former provision involved the plaintiff
G   retaining title in goods not merely until those goods are paid for, but also so long as any other sum was 'overdue' from Ramar to the plaintiff. The latter, on the other hand, involved title to goods only being retained until full payment was received by the plaintiff for those goods. The natural inference of the latter provision must be that, once goods are paid for, title passes from the plaintiff to Ramar. That is inconsistent with the first set of terms. In addition, if the first set of terms survived, part of cl. 2 is otiose, in that it would have been unnecessary for the parties to provide for title being retained to goods
H   which had not been paid for.

Secondly, I refer to the terms of the plaintiff's letters of 12 February 1990, which enclosed the first set of terms, and 29 May 1991, which enclosed the second set of terms. The terms of the earlier letter simply referred to 'our trading terms and conditions', which suggests terms for the time being; the second letter, referring as it does to 'all transactions' being made subject to the second set of terms, suggests that that set of terms was intended

to replace the first set. Thirdly, comparison of the two sets of terms, the first being short   A
and contained in a letter, whereas the second were detailed and in a separate document
and, to both parties' knowledge, prepared by solicitors, seems to me to lead to the
inference that the second set of terms was intended to replace the first set.

There is obvious commercial force in the contrary argument based on the contention
that, given that the second set of terms arose from the financial position of Ramar
deteriorating, one would expect the second set of terms to confer more, rather than less,   B
protection on the plaintiff. However, the first set of terms did not contain provisions such
as cl. 10, and it could well be that the parties considered that the second set of terms were
so much more beneficial to the plaintiff in other respects that it was appropriate to cut
down the effect of the first set of terms in this particular respect.

(2) Has the plaintiff established its case on the facts?

   C

As a result of my conclusion that the second set of terms replaced the first set of terms,
it seems to me that the plaintiff can only establish that it has retained title to the cloth in
all the items in the third category if it can prove that:

(1)   none of the cloth from which the goods were made was ordered before 14 February
1990 (because, if it was, then title would already have passed to Ramar, there being
no retention of title agreement before 14 February 1990);

   D

(2)   in so far as any cloth was ordered between 14 February 1990 and 29 May 1991,
the batch of cloth remains unpaid for and/or at all times since delivery payment
was continuously overdue on some other goods;

(3)   in so far as any cloth was ordered since 29 May 1991, the batch of fabric remains
unpaid for.

The plaintiff has adduced no express direct evidence on those points, it merely being   E
stated in the affidavit sworn on the plaintiff's behalf that, after 29 May 1991, the plaintiff
supplied 'large quantities of fabric' to Ramar, and that Ramar owed it around £2m.

The defendants take the point that the plaintiff has not adduced evidence to establish
the necessary factual basis for its claim that it has retained title to the cloth in all the
items. This point was taken on behalf of the defendants in the third defendant's affidavit
which was sworn and served more than a year before this matter came on for hearing,   F
and the plaintiff did not seek to put in further evidence on the point. However, it is fair
to the plaintiff to mention that, immediately after this point is made in the third
defendant's affidavit, he goes on to say:

> 'Secondly, whilst Ramar itself is undoubtedly liable for the price of the 42,000
> items the defendants have not made themselves so liable . . .'

In the context of an affidavit whose immediately preceding sentence takes the very point   G
that the plaintiff has not established its claim, I do not read that as a concession, but it is
conceivable that might have been read by the plaintiff's advisers as a concession.

The plaintiff invites me to infer that the cloth comprised in the items has not been paid
for by virtue of the size of Ramar's debt to the plaintiff and Ramar's substantial
difficulties during the last year or so before the defendants were appointed receivers, as
well as from the partnership between the parties.

   H

I would be surprised if it transpired that the plaintiff was unable to establish that at
least a substantial portion of the cloth in the items had not been paid for. However, on
the evidence currently available, I cannot say that I am satisfied that all the cloth
comprised in the items has not been paid for, and while it is likely that at least some of it
has not been paid for, it is impossible for me to decide how much. In particular I do not
have any evidence as to the scale of the business between the parties so I am unable to

A draw any inferences from the amount owing to the plaintiff. In the circumstances, I am reluctantly drawn to the conclusion that the plaintiff has indeed failed to make out its case in this respect.

However, I propose to go on to consider the other issues for two reasons. First, they have been fully argued before me, and, for all I know, this case may go further. Secondly, as I indicated during the course of the hearing, I would be very reluctant indeed to deprive the plaintiff of any relief to which it would otherwise be entitled simply because

B it had failed on this part of the case. Not having heard the defendants on the point, I can only say at the present juncture that I would in principle be sympathetic to an application by the plaintiff for leave to adduce further evidence, subject to the defendants being appropriately protected, for instance with regard to costs.

(3) The effect of the retention of title agreement

C It may be that some of the cloth fabric comprised in the 42,000 items was supplied under the first set of terms and some of the cloth under the second set of terms. Accordingly, although it was really implicit in the submissions on behalf of the plaintiff that the 42,000 items were made out of cloth supplied after the second set of terms was effective, it is nonetheless necessary for me to consider the proper effect of both sets of terms.

D In principle, once goods supplied by a supplier have been worked on by a purchaser and incorporated with other goods to produce an article there are a number of possible consequences of a retention of title agreement where the goods concerned have not yet been paid for:

(1)   the retention of title agreement no longer applies;

(2)   the retention of title agreement applies to the extent that the purchaser retains
E   ownership of the supplied goods (in this case the cloth) but the other goods (in this case the thread, zips, buttons and other material) incorporated in the manufactured article (in this case the dress) remains the property of the manufacturer (or, if there is an effective retention of title agreement in relation to those other goods, with the supplier of the other goods);

(3)   title to the manufactured article remains in (so far as the supplied goods are
F   concerned) or is effectively transferred to (so far as any other goods are concerned) the supplier until payment; or

(4)   what was originally the supplier's unqualified beneficial ownership of the supplied goods becomes at some point transformed to a charge on the manufactured article (and title to which passes to the purchaser) to the extent of the value of the supplied goods.

G This case has been argued on the common assumption that, in relation to the items, neither possibility (1) or (2) apply. The plaintiff contends for (3), and the defendants for (4).

While the rights of the parties under a retention of title agreement, just as under any other agreement, must depend upon the proper construction of the agreement concerned, it seems to me that there must be a strong presumption, essentially based on commercial common sense, to the effect that, in the absence of very clear words, the parties would
H not have intended the result for which the plaintiff contends. In *Clough Mill Ltd v Martin* [1985] 1 WLR 111, Robert Goff LJ said (at p. 120C–D) that the difficulty of construing a particular provision:

'as simply giving rise to a retention by the plaintiff of title to the new goods is that it would lead to the result that, upon the determination of the contract under which the original material was sold to the buyer, the ownership of the plaintiff in the

new goods would be retained by the plaintiff, uninhibited by any terms of the   A
contract which had then ceased to apply; and I find it impossible to believe that it
was the intention of the parties that the plaintiff would thereby gain the windfall
of the full value of the new product, deriving as it may well do not merely from the
labour of the buyer but also from materials that were the buyer's, without any
duty to account to the buyer for any surplus of the proceeds of sale above the
outstanding balance of the price due by the buyer to the plaintiff.'
                                                                                 B
He therefore concluded that the relevant provision 'must be read as creating either a trust
or a charge'. In agreement, Oliver LJ said at p. 124C that:

'one is almost driven to the conclusion that the intention of (the relevant) part of
the clause was the creation of a charge on the newly manufactured article as and
when it comes into being, for it is difficult to see how, in practice, this provision
could otherwise be given a sensible operation, particularly where the manufactured
article incorporates also material supplied by other manufacturers which may have   C
been supplied on similar terms.'

To the same effect are the observations of Sir John Donaldson MR at p. 125E–F:

'If the incorporation of the yarn in, or its use as material for, other goods leaves
the yarn in a separate identifiable state, I see no reason why the plaintiff should
not retain property in it . . . However, in that situation, I should have thought that
the buyer was clearly purporting to create a charge on the "other goods" which   D
would never have been the plaintiff's goods. I say "purporting", because those
goods might themselves remain the property of another supplier . . . If, on the
other hand, the incorporation of the yarn created a situation in which it ceased to
be identifiable and the new product was created consisting of the yarn and the
other material, it would be necessary to determine who owned that product. If,
and to the extent that, the answer was the buyer, it seems to me that the fourth   E
sentence would create a charge.'

Observations to the same effect are also to be found in the judgment of Vinelott J in
Re Peachdart Ltd (1983) 1 BCC 98,920 especially at p. 98,926. The approach adopted by
Vinelott J in that case, which involved the conclusion that once the goods supplied
(leather) to the manufacturer had started to be incorporated in the manufactured articles
(handbags) the property in the leather passed to the manufacturer, and the purported   F
retention of title gave the supplier only a charge. His conclusion, which he accepted
involved doing 'some violence' to the wording of the clause was based, as I read it, upon
the strong presumption which I have described, and seems to have been approved, albeit
in general terms, in the judgment of Goff LJ in *Clough Mill* (at p. 120F).

I do not read these cases as laying down as a matter of law that the construction for
which the plaintiff contends is impossible. However, it does seem to me that those cases
confirm that if the retention of title agreement is to be given the effect that the supplier is   G
not merely to retain title to the supplied goods, but is also to have title transferred to him
in respect of other goods, so that the beneficial interest in the manufactured articles is
vested in the supplier, very clear words must be used.

In this case, the central provision with regard to title in the second set of conditions is
cl. 2, which states that 'ownership of the goods shall *remain* with the company' (emphasis
added). It seems to me that it is a little difficult in those circumstances to impute to the   H
parties an intention that goods other than the cloth, which were never vested in the
plaintiff, and which the parties clearly must have anticipated would be combined with
the cloth by Ramar at its own expense when the dresses were being manufactured, should
nonetheless be transferred and, be it noted, not merely transferred as security but
transferred absolutely beneficially, to the plaintiff. I have no evidence as to the extent to
which other goods would have been added to the cloth in order to make the dresses, or

A   what the plaintiff and Ramar would have anticipated to be the case in 1990 or 1991. It may be the case that the extra items would not be of great value, but that would not ultimately detract from the force of the point, especially in view of the added value to the cloth which Ramar's design and workmanship and other treatment must have involved.

However, the word 'remain' in cl. 2 might also be said to be inconsistent with the defendant's contention. However, in light of the fact that this was the particular difficulty
B   which faced the construction favoured by Vinelott J in *Peachdart*, that appears to me to be a point of less force. The provisions of the second set of terms appear to me to be in many ways similar to those in *Peachdart*, and it does not seem to me to be fanciful to take into account the fact that the parties would have been aware of the fact that, in connection with not dissimilar provisions designed to have similar effect, a judge was prepared to hold that a provision that title should 'remain' with a supplier was insufficient to rebut the presumption that the supplier would have no more than a charge once the
C   goods were combined with other goods. Secondly, the plaintiff's beneficial ownership of the cloth, once the cloth was combined with other goods to make a manufactured article, being converted into a charge over the dress could be said to be consistent with the literal reading of cl. 2, in the sense that title does 'remain' with the plaintiff, albeit that the nature of the title is converted from that of beneficial owner to that of chargee. In this connection, it will be remembered that before the 1925 legislation, mortgages of land
D   were effected by the mortgagor transferring the legal and beneficial interest in the land to the mortgagee (see Megarry & Wade *The Law of Real Property* (5th edn.) pp. 915–916).

It appears to me that the provisions of cl. 7 are more consistent with the defendant's contention that the second set of terms creates no more than a charge once the cloth which has been incorporated with other goods than with the plaintiff's contention that the beneficial ownership in respect of the whole of the combined article is vested in the
E   plaintiff. Clause 7 can only apply to manufactured dresses, because it only arises when Ramar effects a sale, and cl. 4 only permits a sale in the ordinary course of Ramar's business. Properly construed, it seems to me that if and when Ramar sells any completed dresses, the plaintiff has a charge on the proceeds of sale to the extent of what is due to it in respect of the batch of cloth from which the dress is made. It seems somewhat inconsistent with the plaintiff's contention that it has unqualified beneficial ownership in the dress if such ownership is converted into a mere charge over the proceeds of sale of
F   the same dress. It is fair to say that in one sense cl. 7 supports the plaintiff's case to the extent that it can be said that when the parties wish to create a charge in the second set of terms they say so. However, that does not seem to me to be a particularly strong point in view of the way in which cl. 7 is expressed.

So far as the other provisions of the second set of terms are concerned, I do not think that they greatly assist in resolving the dispute between the plaintiff and the defendants.
G   When one considers provisions such as cl. 3.2 and 10, it seems hard to argue against the contention that reference to 'goods' is something of a fluctuating concept, beginning with the cloth delivered by the plaintiff but developing as the cloth is worked on, so that 'the goods' eventually become transformed into dresses. However, that of itself does not advance the argument of either side, because the issue is not what is meant by 'the goods', but whether the nature of the plaintiff's interest in 'the goods' varies from that of beneficial owner until the goods are combined with other goods when it becomes that of
H   chargee, as the defendants contend, or whether, as the plaintiff contends, it remains that of beneficial owner throughout.

Perhaps the greatest problem facing the defendants' construction is that it involves reading cl. 2 as having two effects: the first is that of retaining beneficial title in the supplied goods absolutely in the plaintiff, until these goods are in some way incorporated in articles with other goods; the second is that of transferring the property in the supplied

goods to Ramar with a charge back over the article in the course of manufacture and   A
when completed in favour of the plaintiff. In the instant case, there is simply no provision
in the agreement dealing with the rights of the parties once the cloth is incorporated in
an article with other goods. In *Peachdart* and in *Clough Mill* there were in each case
specific provisions dealing with such a situation, and while those provisions presented
difficulties of construction, Vinelott J in *Peachdart* and the Court of Appeal in *Clough
Mill* felt able, for the reasons I have attempted to summarise, to construe those provisions   B
as effectively changing the nature of the supplier's rights over the goods supplied from
that of unencumbered owner to that of chargee.

The distinction between those cases and this case is highlighted by the decision and
reasoning of Mr Michael Hart QC in *Modelboard Ltd v Outer Box Ltd* [1992] BCC 945.
The retention of title clause in that case contained an express provision, cl. 11.8, dealing
with the circumstance of the 'goods the property of the company [being] admixed with
goods the property of the purchaser' (see at p. 948D). Mr Hart said at p. 953B–C: C

> 'In the present case, the key to the true construction of the contract lies, in my
> judgment, in the distinction apparent in the contract itself between the position in
> relation to the original board and the position in relation to the processed product
> ... The question is whether the plaintiff's rights in the finished product are the
> result of its having *retained* its title to the original board, or the result of its
> acquiring those rights under the express provisions of cl. 11.8. In my judgment, the   D
> contract is quite consistent with the conception that at some point in the process
> the plaintiff's retained property in the original board effectively disappears, and is
> replaced by a title, expressly conferred by cl. 11.8 in the finished product.'

Although that point undoubtedly has force, it is insufficient, in my judgment, to
establish the plaintiff's construction as the correct one. First, it appears to me that the
defendants' construction has a certain symmetry and, indeed, consistency in that the   E
changing nature of the 'ownership' vested in the plaintiff by cl. 2 mirrors the changing
identity of 'the goods' as that expression is used in the second set of terms. As 'the goods'
ceased to be purely the cloth, but started to incorporate buttons, thread, zips, and other
material, so did the nature of the 'ownership' referred to in cl. 2 change from that of
beneficial ownership to that of chargee. Secondly, the mere fact that in the three cases to
which I have referred the parties gave their minds to what should happen if the supplied
goods were incorporated with other goods does not mean that where the parties have   F
not, at least expressly, dealt with that situation, one should attribute to them an intention
to achieve such an unlikely result as that for which the plaintiff contends.

In these circumstances, I reach the conclusion that, in so far as the second set of terms
are concerned, once the cloth supplied by the plaintiff is combined to any significant
extent by Ramar with goods owned by Ramar or by a third party the plaintiff's beneficial
ownership, if any, of the cloth is converted into the interest of a chargee over the dress in   G
the process of manufacture or, as the case may be, over the completed dress.

Much of the reasoning which has led me to this conclusion in relation to the second set
of terms applies equally to the first set of terms. In view of the fact that the first set of
terms are far simpler than the second set, the analysis is correspondingly simpler. For
effectively the same reasons which lead me to the conclusion that the second set of terms
create a charge once the cloth supplied by the plaintiff is combined with other goods, I   H
reach the same conclusion in relation to the first set of terms.

(4) Is the plaintiff's charge void as against the defendants for non-registration?

On the basis that the plaintiff's interest is that of chargee, it is said to be void as against
the defendants because, as is common ground, no charge was registered by the plaintiff
pursuant to s. 395. The contest on this issue is whether the plaintiff is right in its

A   contention that no registration is needed. It is said that registration is required on the grounds that the charge falls within one or both of two categories of charge which are required to be registered, and fall within s. 396(1), namely:

> '(c) a charge created or evidenced by an instrument which, if executed by an individual, would require registration as a bill of sale,
>
> . . .

B

> (f) a floating charge on the company's undertaking or property . . .'

So far as s. 396(1)(c) is concerned, it is accepted by the plaintiff that the plaintiff's charge is within the definition of 'bill of sale' within s. 4 of the *Bills of Sale Act* 1878 unless it is within one of two exceptions, namely:

> '. . . transfers of goods in the ordinary course of business of any trade or calling . . . or any other documents used in the ordinary course of business as proof of the possession of control of goods . . .'

C

In my judgment, the plaintiff has failed to establish that the charge created by the first or second set of terms is 'in the ordinary course of business' of Ramar's trade. If the plaintiff wishes to rely upon this exception, it seems to me that the onus of proof is on the plaintiff to establish it. On behalf of the plaintiff, it is contended that the sheer volume of cases on retention of title agreement should be enough to discharge the onus of proof. I reject that

D   contention, not least because, with the possible exception of *Clough Mill*, none of the cases cited appear to me to involve materials similar to the cloth in the instant case. Quite apart from that, I think it would require a very exceptional case before the court was prepared to conclude merely on the basis that the volume of reported cases on a particular topic that something was 'in the ordinary course of business of any trade'. Furthermore, the evidence in this case is contrary to the plaintiff's contention. The inference I draw

E   from the evidence put before me on behalf of the plaintiff is that the plaintiff did not normally deal with its customers, who presumably were mostly in the same sort of business as Ramar, on the basis of retention of title arrangements, and it is certainly clear that from 1982 to 1990 the plaintiff traded in a substantial way with Ramar without such an arrangement, and only entered into a retention of title agreement when Ramar's financial circumstances became parlous.

F   I must also reject the alternative contention that the retention of title agreements are 'any other documents used in the ordinary course of business as proof of possession or control of goods'. This exception has, in my judgment, to be read in the context of the preceding words, namely 'bills of lading, India warrants, warehouse-keepers' certificates, warrants or orders for the delivery of goods'. I think it unlikely that either set of conditions would have been 'used in the ordinary course of business as proof of the possession of control of goods'. In any event, once again it seems to me that the onus of

G   establishing that either set of conditions fall within this exception is on the plaintiff, and there is simply no evidence to support such a contention. I was referred to the decision in *Re Young, Hamilton & Co. Ex parte Carter* [1905] 2 KB 381, affirmed [1905] 2 KB 772, but that in no way alters my conclusion on this aspect. It appears to me that it is essentially a matter of fact in each case as to whether the person who alleges that what is prima facie a bill of sale is excluded from that expression by one of the exceptions in s. 4 of the 1878 Act, and this the plaintiff has failed to do in the instant case.

H   Furthermore I consider that any charges which were created were floating charges within s. 396(1)(f). The authorities show that it is difficult to define with precision what amounts to a floating charge, and a number of definitions have been offered. At least for the purposes of the present case, I find the most convenient discussion to be that of Nicholls V-C in *Re Atlantic Computer Systems plc* [1990] BCC 859 at p. 872H–873E. It is clear from that passage and from the judgments and speech cited therein that the precise

definition of 'floating charge' presents some difficulty. However, where, as here, the   A
charge is over a floating body of goods whose identity, quantity, and nature is capable of
changing literally every minute, it appears to me that the charge must be a floating charge
rather than a fixed one.

Finally, on this aspect of the case, I draw comfort, but no more, from the fact that in
Peachdart, *Clough Mill* and *Modelboard* it was conceded in each case by the supplier that
if a charge was created then it was void for non-registration pursuant to s. 395 or its   B
statutory predecessor (in each case with the implied or express approval by the court of
such concession). It is also right to refer to *Borden (UK) Ltd v Scottish Timber Products
Ltd & Anor* [1981] Ch 25 where, albeit that they apparently disagreed as to whether the
arrangement constituted a floating charge, both Buckley and Templeman L JJ (at
pp. 46H–47C and pp. 44H–45D respectively) thought that the charge created by a
retention of title agreement would have been void for non-registration.

   C

(5) Do the plaintiff's charges created after the date of the debenture rank in priority to the debenture?

The debenture is a floating charge, and, accordingly, in the absence of any special
provisions to the contrary, the mere fact that it was registered does not give it priority.
However, by cl. 6(i)(a) of the debenture, Ramar covenanted with the bank:

> 'With reference to the property assets and rights subject to the floating charge . . .   D
> [Ramar] shall not be at liberty without the consent in writing of the bank
> to . . . create any mortgage or charge ranking in priority or pari passu with that
> charge . . .'

It is clear from the evidence that the plaintiff knew of the creation of the debenture at the
time it was granted by Ramar to the bank. In these circumstances, it is argued on behalf
of the defendants that the plaintiff must be deemed to have had notice not merely of the   E
existence of the debenture but also of the specific provisions thereof, and in particular cl.
6(i). On that basis, therefore, it is contended, the plaintiff being deemed to have had
notice of the terms of the debenture, and in particular cl. 6(i)(a) thereof, it cannot claim
that any charge granted to it after 10 October 1990 has priority over the debenture.

In view of my conclusion that the plaintiff's interest in the items is that of chargee and
that any such charge is void for want of registration, this issue does not need to be   F
decided. It raises a difficult point upon which there is an apparent conflict between two
leading textbooks, and accordingly I shall deal with the point shortly.

As I understand it, the only point in that argument which is contested by the plaintiff
is the contention that the plaintiff should be treated as having had notice of cl. 6(i)(a) of
the debenture simply because it had notice of the creation of the debenture. I was only
addressed very shortly on that issue. In favour of the proposition notice of the existence
of an agreement should be deemed to be notice of its terms are passages in *Snell's Equity*   G
(29th edn) at pp. 51–52 where one finds the following:

> 'The general principle is that a purchaser will be treated as having constructive
> notice of all that a reasonably prudent purchaser, acting on skilled advice, would
> have discovered. [W]here the purchaser had actual notice that the property was in
> some way encumbered . . . he will be held to have constructive notice of all that he
> would have discovered if he had investigated the encumbrance . . . [Thus] a   H
> purchaser with notice of a mortgage will have constructive notice of any other
> encumbrances referred to in the mortgage deed.'

On the other hand, in *Palmer's Company Law* (vol. 2, release 49) at para. 13.127 the
following is stated in relation to a prohibition in a floating charge against the grant of
subsequent legal charges:

A
'. . . a later legal mortgagee would be protected by invoking the familiar rule that a *bona fide* purchaser for value without notice of the legal estate takes free of prior equitable interests.

The practice has been adopted by banks and others of inserting details of such restrictive clauses in the registered particulars of charge. It is sometimes stated that this gives rise to constructive notice. This is not so since the details are not required in the form currently prescribed in England and Wales.'

B
If it were necessary to do so, I would follow the approach in *Snell's Equity*, and hold that, in so far as any charge granted to the plaintiff post-dated the debenture, the bank has priority under the debenture. First, the passage in *Snell* is supported by high authority, namely the judgment of the Lord Chancellor in *Jones v Smith* (1843) 1 Ph 244; 41 ER 624 at pp. 253–254; 628. Secondly, it seems to me that the passage in *Palmer* is directed towards a slightly different point, namely where a subsequent chargee is deemed

C
to have notice of the existence of the prior charge by virtue of the registration of the prior charge under s. 395, and not to the situation, as is the case here, where the subsequent chargee, that is the plaintiff, had actual notice of the existence of the prior charge, that is the debenture. However, as I have not heard full argument on the subject, and it is not necessary for my decision, this should be taken as no more than a tentative view.

D
(6) Air freight charges

This is a short point which does not strictly arise in view of the conclusions I have reached. It is whether the terms of the retention of title agreement and of the agreement reached in correspondence between the plaintiff and the defendants, after the appointment of the defendants as receivers, apply to air freight charges included in many of the invoices relating to the cloth supplied by the plaintiff to Ramar.

E
The prices quoted and charged for cloth by the plaintiff to Ramar were inclusive of sea freight charges. However, Ramar frequently wanted to have at least some of the cloth in any particular batch delivered urgently. This involved the cloth being despatched by air, and accordingly an extra charge was levied in respect of the cloth delivered by air. The invoices prepared by the plaintiff in these circumstances would set out a brief description of the material, its quantity, its price per meter, and the net amount. The invoice would then have another net amount which related to 'air charge' (where the whole batch went

F
by air) or a 'sea/air charge' (where only some of the batch went by air). This would be charged at a rate (normally less than £1) per metre.

The defendants' case is that the air charge or sea/air charge is not within 'payment in full . . . for the goods' within either the first or the second set of terms, but that, even if it is, the matter has been overtaken by the subsequent agreement between the plaintiff and the defendants, in which case the extra air charges are not within the 'price of [the plaintiff's] cloth', the expression used in the agreement reached in correspondence

G
between the plaintiff and the defendants following the defendants' appointment as receivers.

I reject the second part of that argument. It seems to me sensible to impute to the plaintiff and the defendants an intention that the money referred to in the agreement they reached was different from money governed by the retention of title agreements, which were the very basis for the agreement later reached in correspondence. Furthermore, the

H
expression 'invoice price' would seem to be quite capable of covering the air freight charges if they were indeed covered by the retention of title agreements, because, as I have mentioned, the air freight charges were included in the invoices.

On the other hand, while it is a more difficult point, I consider that the defendants' contention that what amounts to an agreed surcharge for air freight is not within the normal meaning of 'payment in full . . . for the goods'. The concept of 'payment for the goods' is, as it seems to me, different from the concept of 'payment for the transport of the goods'. It is fair to say that the plaintiff's case is, at least conceptually, somewhat strengthened by the fact that the price of the goods, without any additional charge, includes the cost of transport by sea: in other words, it would appear that the price quoted and charged for the goods was on a c.i.f. basis. In the end, however, I do not think that point is enough to vitiate the conclusion I have reached. It could, if anything, be said to support it, in the sense that it makes it all the more significant that the parties decided that the price agreed for the goods should not be increased to take into account air freight, but that air freight charges should be included as a separate item.

Conclusion

In these circumstances, I must dismiss the plaintiff's originating summons.

(Order accordingly)

A   # Thorne v Silverleaf.

Court of Appeal (Civil Division).
Ralph Gibson and Peter Gibson L JJ.
Judgment delivered 5 November 1993.

B
*Restriction on re-use of name of insolvent company – Personal liability for debts
of company following contravention of restriction on re-use of name – Plaintiff
was investor in company which went into insolvent liquidation – Company was
third with similar name to go into insolvent liquidation – Defendant was director
of all three companies – Whether plaintiff entitled to summary judgment on claim
that defendant was jointly liable for company's debts – Whether plaintiff could
not recover because he had aided and abetted offence of contravening prohibition
– Whether plaintiff had waived or was estopped from asserting any right to recover
C   – Whether there were issues to be tried on quantum – Insolvency Act 1986, s. 216,
217.*

This was an appeal by 'T' from a summary judgment for some £135,000 in favour of the
plaintiff, 'S', pursuant to s. 217 of the Insolvency Act 1986 (personal liability for debts
following contravention of s. 216 restriction on re-use of company name).

T had been the director of three companies each of which had the name 'Mike Spence' as
D   part of its name and each of which had gone into insolvent liquidation. S was an investor in
the last company. When that company went into liquidation S alleged that the conditions of
s. 216 and 217 of the 1986 Act were satisfied in relation to T as a director of the company,
and that he was personally liable jointly and severally with the company in respect of the
sum of £133,338 owed by the company to S.

T contended that he should have unconditional leave to defend because S aided and
abetted T in committing the criminal offence specified in s. 216 and thereby himself
E   committed a crime such that he could not be allowed to profit from his crime by recovering
the sum claimed; or S had waived or was estopped from asserting any right to recover the
sum claimed; alternatively there were issues to be tried on the amount of the claim which
was disputed by T.

Held, dismissing the appeal:

F   1. The fact that for the purpose of a criminal trial S as an aider and abettor would be
liable to be tried, indicted and punished as a principal offender did not make T's crime S's
crime for the purpose of the public policy rule. The moneys claimed by S were not something
to which but for the crime of aiding and abetting he would have no right or title. S did not
plead or rely on any illegality in what he himself did. The transactions under which moneys
went from him to the company and were recoverable by him from it were not illegal
transactions. He did plead an illegality, but that was the contravention by T of s. 216
G   through being a director of the company using a prohibited name, and that was not an
offence committed by S or the company.

2. Although T made S aware of his financial difficulties as well as of all the facts
constituting the offence under s. 216 and hence of the circumstances which led to liability
under s. 217, there was nothing which constituted a waiver by S of the right to recover from
T or a representation or promise by S not to seek recovery or any reliance by T on some
H   relevant conduct by S.

3. There was no case to go to trial on the quantum of the sum claimed by S.

The following cases were referred to in the judgments:

Ferguson v Weaving [1951] 1 KB 814.
Gray & Anor v Barr [1971] 2 QB 554.
Johnson v Youden & Ors [1950] 1 KB 544.

R v Chief National Insurance Commissioner, ex parte Connor [1981] QB 758.   A
St John Shipping Corp v Joseph Rank Ltd [1957] 1 QB 267.
Tinsley v Milligan [1993] 3 WLR 126.

Ian Mayes QC and Michael Duggan (instructed by Heath & Co) for the appellant.

Richard de Lacy (instructed by Sprecher Grier) for the respondent.

JUDGMENT   B

Peter Gibson LJ: This is an appeal by the first defendant, Richard Thorne, from part
of the order made on 20 November 1992 by His Honour Judge Micklem sitting as a
judge of the High Court. The judge gave judgment under O. 14 for the plaintiff, Michael
Silverleaf, for £133,338.22 together with interest in the sum of £2,849.60. He also granted
certain injunctions and he made a compulsory winding-up order against the second
defendant, Mike Spence Classic Cars Ltd ('the company'). Mr Thorne appeals against   C
the money judgment, contending that he should have been granted unconditional leave
to defend.

Mr Thorne has been the director of three companies each of which had the name 'Mike
Spence' as part of its name and each of which has gone into insolvent liquidation. The
first company was incorporated on 14 August 1968 and took the name Mike Spence
(Reading) Ltd on 14 September 1973. On Friday, 8 February 1990 it went into creditors'
voluntary liquidation. The second was incorporated on 6 March 1986 and took the name   D
Mike Spence (Motorsport) Ltd on 29 May 1986. On 20 October 1989 it went into
creditors' voluntary liquidation. Mr Thorne was a director of those two companies,
which I shall call 'Reading' and 'Motorsport' respectively, throughout the 12 months
prior to each going into liquidation. On 19 January 1990, the company was incorporated
and started to trade the next month. On 25 August 1992, Mr Silverleaf presented a
creditor's petition for the winding up of the company and it was on that petition that the   E
judge made the winding-up order on 20 November 1992.

Mr Silverleaf first met Mr Thorne in December 1987. Mr Silverleaf was looking for a
car to purchase and approached Reading which had a Lancia dealership. He bought a
car from Reading early in 1988 and became friendly with Mr Thorne through a shared
interest in racing historic Lancia cars. The company was set up by Mr Thorne specifically
to restore and deal in cars primarily for historic motor sport.   F

In October 1989, Mr Silverleaf bought a car from the company. In about July 1990
Mr Thorne told Mr Silverleaf of his financial difficulties following the liquidation of
Reading and Motorsport, the debts of which to their bankers he had personally
guaranteed. He said that he was very short of working capital and could not buy cars for
stock to deal in, which made it difficult to run the company's business. Mr Thorne was
aware that Mr Silverleaf had moneys available for investment, and a discussion followed
on the way in which Mr Silverleaf might invest money in relation to the company. It was   G
orally agreed that the company would purchase cars with Mr Silverleaf's money as his
agent and when a car was sold, he would be repaid the original purchase price plus 25
per cent of the net profit. The result therefore was a form of joint venture between Mr
Silverleaf and the company. Mr Silverleaf by that time also used the company to support
him in motor racing, both he and Mr Thorne at one time sharing the same racing car.
From time to time Mr Silverleaf provided the company with substantial sums of money   H
pursuant to the agreement reached with Mr Thorne. He took a closer interest in the
company's affairs and on his own account, which in this respect is not challenged, he
attended nine or ten monthly meetings, at which Mr Thorne discussed with the
management of the company the company's affairs. Mr Silverleaf initially took the
minutes of the meetings. In August 1991 such was the company's poor financial position
that Mr Silverleaf lent it £25,000 to protect his ability to race for the following season. In

A   November 1991, Mr Thorne told Mr Silverleaf that the company needed further moneys to meet wages and a further £17,000 was lent. Early in 1993 Mr Silverleaf's father started to help out at the company's premises and Mr Silverleaf received further information about the company's finances from his father. By mid-June 1992 relations between Mr Silverleaf and Mr Thorne were at breaking point. On 17 June Mr Silverleaf wrote to Mr Thorne, complaining that his cars had been sold without the company returning to him his capital investment in them, making clear that he would not provide any further

B   financial support until certain conditions (including the provision of information which he requested and the entry by him and Mr and Mrs Thorne into a written agreement providing security) were satisfied and saying:

> 'Put bluntly, I do not consider that you are fit to have the stewardship of the business . . . For the foreseeable future I perceive no role for you except in sales and purchasing . . . You cannot retain either the title or function of managing

C   > director . . . Unless you have provided all the required information within seven days and have made substantial progress towards the required formal agreement, I shall require you to repay to me forthwith all moneys I have advanced to you for use by [the company] . . .'

On 30 July 1992 the company instructed chartered accountants, Pannell Kerr Forster, to advise it and on 5 August 1992 they produced a report addressed to the company for

D   Mr Thorne's attention. This included an estimated statement of affairs as at 31 July 1992 using the latest management information available down to 30 June 1992. This showed an estimated deficiency for unsecured creditors in excess of £200,000 even on a going-concern basis. The debt owed by the company to Mr Silverleaf was put at £134,600. In the light of that report Mr Thorne agreed to place the company in creditors' voluntary liquidation. But then he changed his mind. Mr Silverleaf sought to recover the cars bought by the company as his agent but that was refused by Mr Thorne. On 18 September

E   1992, Mr Silverleaf commenced proceedings, initially against Mr Thorne alone, but later adding the company as a defendant. By the statement of claim it is alleged that the company owed to Mr Silverleaf £133,338.22 'being money lent by [Mr Silverleaf] to it on various occasions and/or in the alternative money had and received by it to the use of [Mr Silverleaf]'. It is also alleged that the conditions of s. 216 and 217 of the *Insolvency Act* 1986 are satisfied in relation to Mr Thorne as a director of the company, and that he is personally liable jointly and severally with the company in respect of the sum owed by

F   the company to Mr Silverleaf.

Before the judge, Mr de Lacy on behalf of Mr Silverleaf was able to prove that the moneys claimed were owed by the company. The figures were based on the company's own computerised records, a print-out of which had been provided by the company's bookkeeper, and the figure of what was owed by the company to Mr Silverleaf appearing in the Pannell Kerr Forster report was accepted by the judge as 'a comparatively recent

G   check by an independent person broadly confirming Mr Silverleaf's claim'. The judge rejected an argument by Mr Duggan on behalf of Mr Thorne based on Mr Thorne asserting in his affidavit evidence that he disputed the claim by Mr Silverleaf. The judge further accepted that s. 216 and 217 applied in the present case and rejected arguments by Mr Duggan to the effect that the court had a discretion in the matter.

It is convenient now to refer to the applicable statutory provisions. The marginal note

H   to s. 216 is misleadingly 'Restriction on re-use of company names', the restriction in fact being on directors of certain companies. By subs. (1):

> '(1) This section applies to a person where a company ("the liquidating company") has gone into insolvent liquidation on or after the appointed day and he was a director or a shadow director of the company at any time in the period of 12 months ending with the day before it went into liquidation.'

Each of Reading and Motorsport was for the purposes of this section the liquidating   A
company and Mr Thorne was a director of each in the 12 months before it went into
insolvent liquidation.

By subs. (2):

> 'For the purposes of this section, a name is a prohibited name in relation to such
> person if–
>
>   B
>
> (a) it is a name by which the liquidating company was known at any time in
> that period of 12 months, or
>
> (b) it is a name which is so similar to a name falling within paragraph (a) as to
> suggest an association with that company.'

The name of the company, using as it did 'Mike Spence' as part of that name, was so
similar to the name of Reading and of Motorsport as to suggest an association with those   C
companies. Accordingly the name was a prohibited name in relation to Mr Thorne.

Subsections (3) and (4) so far as material read as follows:

> '(3) Except with the leave of the court or in such circumstances as may be
> prescribed, a person to whom this section applies shall not at any time in the period
> of 5 years beginning with the day on which the liquidating company went into
> liquidation–   D
>
> (a) . . .
>
> (b) in any way, whether directly or indirectly, be concerned or take part in the
> promotion, formation or management of any such company, or
>
> (c) . . .
>
> (4) If a person acts in contravention of this section, he is liable to imprisonment or   E
> a fine, or both.'

Thus the effect of Mr Thorne acting in contravention of the section is to render him
liable to criminal sanctions.

As contemplated by subs. (3), circumstances have been prescribed which constitute
exceptions to the prohibitions in that subsection. Those exceptions are contained in the   F
Insolvency Rules 1986 (see r. 4.228–4.230). It is common ground that none applies to Mr
Thorne, who never sought the leave of the court, no doubt because he was unaware of
the statutory provisions.

Section 217 imposes, as its marginal note accurately states, a personal liability for debts
following a contravention of s. 216. Subsections (1)–(5) read as follows:

> '(1) A person is personally responsible for all the relevant debts of a company if at   G
> any time–
>
> (a) in contravention of section 216, he is involved in the management of the
> company, or
>
> (b) as a person who is involved in the management of the company, he acts or
> is willing to act on instructions given (without the leave of the court) by a
> person whom he knows at that time to be in contravention in relation to the   H
> company of section 216.
>
> (2) Where a person is personally responsible under this section for the relevant
> debts of a company, he is jointly and severally liable in respect of those debts with
> the company and any other person who, whether under this section or otherwise,
> is so liable.

A   (3) For the purposes of this section the relevant debts of a company are–

        (a) in relation to a person who is personally responsible under paragraph (a) of subsection (1), such debts and other liabilities of the company as are incurred at any time when that person was involved in the management of the company, and

B   (b) in relation to a person who is personally responsible under paragraph (b) of that subsection, such debts and other liabilities of the company as are incurred at a time when that person was acting or was willing to act on instructions given as mentioned in that paragraph.

    (4) For the purposes of this section, a person is involved in the management of a company if he is a director of the company or if he is concerned, whether directly or indirectly, or takes part, in the management of the company.

C   (5) For the purposes of this section a person who, as a person involved in the management of a company, has at any time acted on instructions given (without the leave of the court) by a person who he knew at that time to be in contravention in relation to the company of section 216 is presumed, unless the contrary is shown, to have been willing at any time thereafter to act on any instructions given by that person.'

D   When one applies those provisions to Mr Thorne, he was a person involved in the management of the company as director (as well as being concerned and taking part in the management of the company, though these latter facts are not relied on in the statement of claim), and that was in contravention of s. 216. Accordingly he is a person responsible for all the debts and other liabilities of the company incurred at a time when he was involved in the management of the company and that, subject to the question of quantum, includes the moneys claimed by Mr Silverleaf to be owed to him by the
E company.

    That the sections should apply to impose both a criminal liability on someone in Mr Thorne's position is somewhat surprising, if, as is commonly thought, the mischief aimed at by the sections is the eradication of the 'phoenix syndrome' (see, for example, *Gore-Browne on Companies* (44th edn, para. 35.5). In the Cork Committee's report on *Insolvency Law and Practice* (1982, Cmnd 8558), attention was drawn to the widespread
F dissatisfaction at the ease with which a person trading through the medium of one or more companies with limited liability can allow such a company to become insolvent, form a new company, and then carry on trading much as before, leaving behind him a trail of unpaid creditors, and it was pointed out that the dissatisfaction was greatest where the director of an insolvent company has set up business again using a similar name for the new company, and trades with assets purchased at a discount from the liquidator of the old company (see para. 1813 ibid.). But it is clear that the sections as
G enacted apply to a wider set of circumstances than the case of a person attempting to exploit the goodwill of a previous insolvent company. However in the absence of an application under s. 216(3) for leave, the court is left with no discretion on the application of the sections, and so long as the statutory provisions remain unaltered a creditor of a company is entitled to take advantage of them, if they can be shown to be applicable.

    Mr Mayes QC, who now appears with Mr Duggan for Mr Thorne, submits that
H unconditional leave to defend should be given on one or more of the following grounds:

    (1) on liability, there are issues of fact and law to be tried, viz. whether by his conduct Mr Silverleaf:

        (a) aided and abetted Mr Thorne in committing the criminal offence specified in s. 216 and thereby himself committed a crime such that he cannot be allowed to profit from his crime by recovering the sum claimed, or (b)　waived or is estopped from asserting any right to recover the sum claimed;　　A

(2)　on quantum, there are issues of fact to be tried, the sum claimed being disputed by Mr Thorne.

I shall consider them in turn. The first ground is one which was not advanced before the judge, though Mr de Lacy very properly did not seek to prevent it being argued before us.

Mr Mayes relied on the test of aiding and abetting as propounded by Lord Goddard　　B CJ in *Ferguson v Weaving* [1951] 1 KB 814 at pp. 818–819:

'It is well known that the words "aid and abet" are apt to describe the action of a person who is present at the time of the commission of an offence and takes some part therein.'

He also referred us to the earlier words of the Lord Chief Justice in *Johnson v Youden* [1950] 1 KB 544 at p. 546:　　　　　　　　　　　　　　　　　　　　　　　C

'Before a person can be convicted of aiding and abetting the commission of an offence he must at least know the essential matters which constitute that offence. He need not actually know that an offence has been committed, because he may not know that the facts constitute an offence and ignorance of the law is not a defence. If a person knows all the facts and is assisting another person to do certain things, and it turns out that the doing of those things constitutes an offence, the　D person who is assisting is guilty of aiding and abetting that offence, because to allow him to say, "I knew of all those facts but I did not know that an offence was committed", would be allowing him to set up ignorance of the law as a defence.'

The complexity of the present law on aiding and abetting has been recently demonstrated by the Law Commission in its consultation paper on *Assisting and Encouraging Crime* (1993, LCCP No. 131), but let me accept that the essential elements of the crime are contained in the two quotations of Lord Goddard.　　　　　　　E

Mr Mayes said that these elements were satisfied by Mr Silverleaf attending and participating in so many management or board meetings as well as by his provision of moneys that enabled the company to carry on business, and by his knowledge of the circumstances of the offence under s. 216, whether or not he actually knew that a crime was being committed by Mr Thorne. Mr Mayes relied on s. 8 of the *Accessories and Abettors Act* 1861 (as amended) which provides:　　　　　　　　　　　　　　F

'Whosoever shall aid, abet, counsel, or procure the commission of [any indictable offence], whether the same be [an offence] at common law or by virtue of any Act passed or to be passed, shall be liable to be tried, indicted, and punished as a principal offender.'

He submitted that this had the effect that Mr Thorne's crime became Mr Silverleaf's crime for the purpose of the application of the rule of public policy that no person is　G permitted to found rights upon his deliberate commission of a crime. He contended that Parliament could not have intended that an aider and abettor of a person committing an offence under s. 216 would be able to recover under s. 217. It is not disputed that the public policy rule applies to rights conferred by statute (see *R v Chief National Insurance Commissioner, ex parte Connor* [1981] QB 758). Accordingly Mr Mayes submitted that Mr Silverleaf's conduct should be examined at the trial and that on this ground he had a good arguable case on liability.　　　　　　　　　　　　　　　　　　　H

I cannot accept this. The public policy rule prevents the enforcement of rights directly resulting from the crime of the plaintiff. As Devlin J said in *St John Shipping Corp v Joseph Rank Ltd* [1957] 1 QB 267 at p. 292:

'the property or money must be identifiable as something to which, but for the crime, the plaintiff would have had no right or title.'

A The crime in question is that said to have been committed by Mr Silverleaf, viz. that of aiding and abetting, not the committing of an offence under s. 216 by Mr Thorne. The fact that for the purpose of a criminal trial Mr Silverleaf as an aider and abettor would be liable to be tried, indicted and punished as a principal offender does not make Mr Thorne's crime his crime for the purpose of the public policy rule. The moneys claimed by Mr Silverleaf are not something to which but for the crime of aiding and abetting he would have no right or title.

B The matter can be further tested by reference by analogy to the test held to be relevant to the applicability of the maxim *ex turpi causa non oritur actio*, a maxim that is closely akin to the public policy rule. In *Tinsley v Milligan* [1993] 3 WLR 126 Lord Browne-Wilkinson, with whom Lord Jauncey and Lord Lowry agreed, said at p. 153:

C 'In my judgment the time has come to decide clearly that the rule is the same whether a plaintiff founds himself on a legal or equitable title: he is entitled to recover if he is not forced to plead or rely on the illegality, even if it emerges that the title on which he relied was acquired in the course of carrying through an illegal transaction.'

In the present case, Mr Silverleaf does not plead or rely on any illegality in what he himself did. The transactions under which moneys went from him to the company and are recoverable by him from it were not illegal transactions. He does plead an illegality,
D but that is the contravention by Mr Thorne of s. 216 through being a director of the company using a prohibited name, and that is not an offence committed by him or the company. As Mr de Lacy pointed out, the cause of the liability under s. 217, viz. Mr Thorne's directorship coupled with the use of the company's name, did not lie with Mr Silverleaf at all. He did not appoint and had no power to remove Mr Thorne from his directorship.

E That is sufficient to dispose of this ground of appeal, but I would add the following further observations.

(1) If, contrary to my opinion expressed above, it is relevant to the rule of public policy whether a plaintiff has been an aider and abettor of the defendant director in respect of an offence under s. 216 by reason of a circumstance other than that relied on by the plaintiff, so that in the present case it becomes material to consider whether Mr Silverleaf aided and abetted Mr Thorne in the latter being concerned or taking part in
F the management of the company, I am far from satisfied on the evidence that it has been shown that there is a triable issue as to whether Mr Silverleaf did aid and abet that offence. He certainly did not cause that offence, and there is no evidence that Mr Thorne would have ceased his conduct if Mr Silverleaf had not behaved as he did. He assisted in that conduct only indirectly in that he was the provider of finance, but it was common ground that that was not enough. Other than by writing the minutes of meetings, which
G in my judgment is not material, I do not see that Mr Silverleaf did more than many an institutional lender does regularly in the course of monitoring his loan and, when dissatisfied, indicating the terms on which support will continue.

(2) Even if that were wrong and there is sufficient evidence to allow the matter to go to trial at which Mr Silverleaf might be shown to have been an aider and abettor of an offence under s. 216, it does not follow that he would be precluded from exercising the remedy afforded by s. 217. I say that for two reasons. First, s. 217(1) has itself expressly
H extended civil liability beyond those who as persons involved in the management of a company commit an offence under s. 216 to what might be described as a limited class of aiders and abettors, viz. those described in s. 217(1)(b). They are persons who are involved in the management of the company and act or are willing to act on instructions given by a person whom they know to be in contravention of s. 216. Mr de Lacy laid emphasis on the fact that the relevant knowledge is not merely that sufficient for the

purposes of the crime of aiding and abetting, that is to say knowledge of the facts A
constituting the crime even if without knowledge that it is a crime. In s. 217(1)(b)
knowledge that it is a crime is required. It would be surprising in those circumstances if
Parliament contemplated that aiders and abettors in general were precluded, even
without express wording, from taking advantage of the section. Second, it is now well-
established that the rule of public policy does not apply automatically to every crime. In
R v Chief National Insurance Commissioner [1981] QB 758, Lord Lane CJ at p. 765 said:
B
'in each case it is not the label which the law applies to the crime which has been
committed but the nature of the crime itself which in the end will dictate whether
public policy demands the court to drive the applicant from the seat of justice.'

I cannot see that Mr Silverleaf's conduct could be said to be such as to drive him from
the seat of justice.

I turn next to waiver and estoppel. Mr Mayes made it clear that this was only a second C
line of defence and I can deal with this point quite shortly. He relies on the fact that, as
the evidence shows, Mr Thorne made Mr Silverleaf well aware of his financial difficulties
as well as of all the facts constituting the offence under s. 216 and hence of the
circumstances which led to liability under s. 217. Nevertheless I cannot see anything that
would arguably constitute a waiver by Mr Silverleaf of the right to recover from Mr
Thorne or a representation or promise by Mr Silverleaf not to seek recovery or any
reliance by Mr Thorne on some relevant conduct by Mr Silverleaf. I reject this ground D
too.

Finally I come to the argument on quantum. As already stated, Mr Silverleaf's claim
was quantified by reference to the company's own computerised records and a printout
produced by the company's bookkeeper. Full details of that quantification were put in
evidence. The figure was corroborated, as the judge found, by the figure in the Pannell
Kerr Forster report. Mr Thorne in his evidence says that he disputes both that figure and E
that in the accountants' report, but he is wholly unspecific as to precisely what it is that
he disputes. He says that he cannot obtain access to the company's books, now with the
liquidator, but I find it hard to believe that he, as a director, has been denied even the
opportunity of looking at the books. As for the accountants' report, the author of the
report has said that the figures are taken from the company's management accounts as
explained by Mr Thorne to him. I can see no reason to interfere with the judge's
conclusion that there is no case to go for trial on the quantum of the sum claimed by F
Mr Silverleaf.

I would dismiss this appeal.

Ralph Gibson LJ: I agree that this appeal must be dismissed for the reasons given by
Peter Gibson LJ.

It appeared to Parliament that the mischief, at which s. 216 of the *Insolvency Act* 1986 G
is directed, was of such gravity that a person acting in contravention of that section
should not only be subjected to criminal sanctions by s. 216(3), of which the severity
would depend upon the discretion of the court; but that such person should also thereby
be made personally responsible by s. 217(1)(a) for all debts of the company incurred at a
time when that person was involved in the management of the company. It must have
been supposed that such a person would, in the ordinary course of things, learn of this
provision of the law or that directors of companies which go into insolvent liquidation H
should be left to inform themselves of the consequences in law of acting in contravention
of s. 216.

That burden of responsibility for the debts was also imposed upon a further category
of persons by s. 217(1)(b), namely any person who is involved in the management of the
company and who acts or is willing to act on instructions given (without the leave of the

court) by a person whom he knows to be in contravention in relation to the company of s. 216; but such a person is not by the words of s. 216 caused himself to be in contravention of s. 216 and therefore guilty of the offence created by s. 216(3).

No express limitation is placed upon the right of any creditor of the company to enforce the personal liability so created of a person acting in contravention of s. 216, or caught by s. 217(1)(b), for example so as to exclude a claim either by a creditor who was, at the date at which the debt arose, aware of the facts which gave rise to contravention of s. 216 or by a creditor who was at such date aware both of the facts and that they constituted such contravention.

The mere fact that no specific mention is made in the Act of disentitlement of any such creditor to enforce the personal liability of a person acting in contravention of s. 216 does not exclude the operation of any rule of the common law which would have that effect because the enactment may be taken to have been made, in the absence of any indication to the contrary, 'against the background of the law as it stood at the time': see per Lord Lane CJ in *R v Chief National Insurance Commissioner, ex parte Connor* [1981] QB 758 at p. 765B.

Lord Lane continued:

'. . . It is not every type of crime which operates so as to cause public policy to make the courts reject a claim.'

He noted that in *Gray v Barr* [1971] 2 QB 554, Salmon LJ, in a passage which Lord Lane expressly approved, said (at p. 581):

'In particular, I am not deciding that a man who has committed manslaughter would, in any circumstances, be prevented from enforcing a contract of indemnity in respect of any liability he may have incurred for causing death or from inheriting under a will or upon the intestacy of anyone whom he has killed.

Manslaughter is a crime which varies infinitely in its seriousness. It may come very near to murder or amount to little more than inadvertence, although in the latter class of case the jury only rarely convicts.'

Salmon LJ in that passage was referring to the offence of manslaughter, for example arising from negligence in the use of a motor car, which amounts to more than, but little more than, inadvertence. There was, of course, nothing inadvertent in what Mr Silverleaf did in his dealings with the company, Mike Spence Classic Cars Ltd. His inadvertence was in not being aware of the consequences in law of the conduct of Mr Thorne. If Mr Silverleaf's actions in his dealing with the company did constitute a crime under the statute, I would hold that they are not such as to require the court to deprive him of the right which Parliament provided by s. 217 that he should have.

It is, I acknowledge, at first look surprising that Mr Silverleaf should, in these circumstances, acquire a right to recover from Mr Thorne the amount of loans made by Mr Silverleaf to the company. Mr Silverleaf could have insisted upon making the loans to Mr Thorn personally, or he could have required a personal guarantee. He did not do so. It seems that neither of them was aware of s. 217 or of its effect. I also have in mind that the creation of the personal liability of Mr Thorne to Mr Silverleaf reduces the ability of Mr Thorne, if in fact it existed, to pay other debts, for example such debts of the company as were in fact guaranteed by him. Further, there is no more conscious wrongdoing in what was done by Mr Thorne than in what was done by Mr Silverleaf. The essential difference, however, between the two of them is that Parliament, in effect, placed upon a director in the position of Mr Thorne the obligation to avoid acting in contravention of s. 216 or pay the consequences. The enactment of the provisions for personal liability in the terms contained in s. 217 was, I think, clearly intended to provide a more effective deterrent than would be achieved by criminal sanctions. I can see no

A

reason to suppose that Parliament intended the provision of the personal liability of a
director under s. 217 not to be applicable in the circumstances of this case, and the
common law does not, in my judgment, require the court to deprive Mr Silverleaf of the
right arising under those provisions.

(*Appeal dismissed with costs, to include costs reserved by Morritt J. Costs, after being
taxed and agreed, to be paid out of the security paid into court*)

B

C

D

E

F

G

H

A ## Menzies v National Bank of Kuwait SAK.

Court of Appeal (Civil Division).
Balcombe and Butler-Sloss L JJ and Sir Christopher Slade.
Judgment delivered 9 November 1993.

Transactions defrauding creditors – Whether transaction was at undervalue –
B *Insolvency Act 1986, s. 423(1)(c).*

This was an appeal by a bank against a judge's refusal to strike out a claim by a creditor of a company in liquidation for leave to bring proceedings under s. 423 of the Insolvency Act 1986 as a victim of an alleged transaction at an undervalue between the company and the bank.

The company in 1985 entered into a contract with the Kuwait Ministry of Public Works
C for the fitting out and furnishing of the Kuwaiti Conference Centre. The company employed a Kuwaiti company, 'AJ', as its local agent. AJ arranged the financing of the contract through the National Bank of Kuwait. The bank required the company to execute an assignment of all moneys to become due to the company from the ministry under the contract and a recourse agreement under which those moneys would be paid direct by the ministry to the company's account with the bank. In 1987, after the contract was substantially completed, the company gave a letter of instructions to the bank to allocate moneys received
D under the contract first to AJ, then to pay off the company's overdraft to the bank, then any further moneys to AJ. The company was then in financial difficulties. The bank applied moneys received by it from the ministry in respect of the contract in accordance with the letter of instructions.

A substantial UK creditor of the company, 'M', attempted to challenge payments of KD 381,266 (about £840,000) under s. 423 of the Insolvency Act 1986. Although there was
E an argument that if AJ had no entitlement to the moneys concerned the payments themselves could be 'transactions' challengeable under s. 423, the court proceeded on the basis that it was the giving of the letter of instructions which was under attack as the relevant transaction for the purpose of s. 423. It was common ground that M could properly be regarded as a victim of the relevant transaction within the definition in s. 423(5).

Held, allowing the bank's appeal, striking out M's application and points of claim, and
F refusing leave to bring or continue proceedings for an order against the bank under s. 423 of the 1986 Act:

There was no realistic prospect of M satisfying the court under s. 423(1) that the transaction was 'entered into at an undervalue'. For the purposes of s. 423(1)(c), the company did not provide any consideration in giving the letter of instructions. The letter did not create any security. AJ and the bank were already secured. The letter simply gave effect to an agreement providing for the future allocation, as between AJ and the bank, of sums to
G which they were already entitled as secured creditors. There was thus no basis on which M could persuade the court that the consideration obtained by the company was 'significantly less than the value, in money or money's worth, of the consideration provided by' the company, since the company provided no consideration whatever in money or money's worth for the transaction. M's proposed application under s. 423 failed in limine because this primary requirement of s. 423(1) could not be satisfied.

H The following cases were referred to in the judgments:

Ashmore v British Coal Corporation [1990] 2 QB 338.
M C Bacon Ltd, Re [1990] BCC 78.

Richard Hacker (instructed by Simmons & Simmons) for the appellant.

The respondent appeared in person.

JUDGMENT   A

Sir Christopher Slade: This is an appeal by the National Bank of Kuwait ('the bank'), brought with the leave of Dillon LJ given on 15 January 1993, from part of an order made by Chadwick J on 9 October 1992. The respondent to the appeal is Mr Rowan Menzies who is a substantial creditor in the liquidation of Ayala Holdings Ltd ('Ayala') and has appeared in person before this court. I can take the factual background largely from the summary contained in the judge's careful judgment.   B

Ayala was incorporated in this country in 1976. It was engaged in the business of fitting out and furnishing substantial and prestigious buildings outside the UK, and in particular in the Middle East. In December 1985 it entered into a contract with the Kuwait Ministry of Public Works ('the ministry') for the fitting out and furnishing of the Kuwaiti Conference Centre. The value of the contract was about KD 4.8m (approximately £11m at the rates of exchange then prevailing).   C

Ayala employed a Kuwaiti company, Al Julaiah Trading and Contracting Co ('Al Julaiah'), as its local agent or sponsor in connection with the contract. Al Julaiah, on behalf of Ayala arranged the financing of the contract through the bank, which was its own banker, but thus became also the banker to Ayala.

The bank provided, among other facilities, the issue of a performance bond guaranteed by Al Julaiah, an advance payment guarantee, a facility letter and the opening of letters of credit for the benefit of Ayala's suppliers. As a condition of so doing, the bank required and Ayala executed an assignment of all moneys to become due to Ayala from the ministry under the contract and a recourse agreement under which those moneys would be paid direct by the ministry to Ayala's account with the bank.   D

By or before April 1987 the work under the contract had been substantially completed, but moneys remained due from the ministry, and Ayala had a residual liability in respect of defects during a maintenance period. Settlement of the final account was held up pending the snagging work which had to be done in respect of defects. Ayala was in financial difficulties and indeed Mr Menzies contends that it had already become insolvent. The judge found it reasonably clear that some arrangements had to be made in Kuwait to ensure that, notwithstanding these difficulties, the snagging works were done, so that settlement and final payment under the contract could be achieved.   E

In July 1987 Mr Mark Maley, the managing director of Ayala, visited the bank in Kuwait. He was accompanied by the managing partner of Al Julaiah, Mr Hijazi. Following that visit – and, Mr Menzies alleges, as a result of it – Ayala, by a telex letter of 19 August 1987 sent by Mr Maley, gave instructions to the bank (expressed to be irrevocable) in the following form: F

'Further to our recent telephone call and telex. As previously advised you Mr Hijazi and Al Julaiah are giving assistance in finalising outstanding matters on this   G contract. In return for their assistance I would like to confirm and extend our instructions to you, that is that the allocation of funds received by National Bank of Kuwait for our work under the above contract should be allocated as follows:

1. The first KD 300,000 should be credited to the account of Al Julaiah at National Bank with the exception of KD 5,000 which can be deducted from the next payment to be received and applied to our No. 1 account with you   H to cover interest to the end of June 1987.

2. Thereafter further funds should be applied to our No. 1 account at your bank until such time as the overdraft is closed.

3. Thereafter all further income from this source should be transmitted on receipt to the account of Al Julaiah.

A   Please note this is an irrevocable instruction for which we would be grateful for your acceptance and I now hope that settlement of all our affairs on this contract will be sorted out in the near future.'

Pursuant to this letter of 19 August 1987 (which I will call 'the 1987 letter of instructions') the bank paid to Al Julaiah KD 191,000 in February 1988 and a further KD 80,000 in February 1989.

B   Meantime on 19 January 1988, a petition had been presented for the winding up of Ayala. The petition was strenuously opposed during 1988 and for the greater part of 1989, Mr Menzies himself being an opposing creditor. As the judge observed, it may well be that if a final settlement of the account in respect of the Kuwaiti contract could have been achieved and payment were made by the ministry, Ayala would have had sufficient funds to pay its debts in full.

C   In June 1989, however, a final settlement of the dispute between Ayala and the ministry was agreed in Kuwait. Under it a sum of KD 450,525 or thereabouts was to be paid by the ministry. Mr Menzies, on learning that this sum was to be paid in Kuwait to Kuwaiti creditors, thereby excluding English creditors from any benefit, applied to the English court and on 24 July 1989 obtained an undertaking restraining Ayala from signing the settlement agreement. On 13 September 1989 Millett J made an order by consent which released Ayala from that undertaking and directed that it should not make payments to

D   Al Julaiah unless certain conditions were satisfied.

Ayala's solicitors duly gave the bank the instructions required by Millett J's order. By a letter dated 27 September 1989, however, the bank expressed the view that it was bound by the law of Kuwait to give effect to the 1987 letter of instructions unless restrained by an order of the court. As a result Mr Menzies learned of the existence of that letter.

E   This disclosure to Mr Menzies seems to have caused a fundamental change in his attitude to the winding up of Ayala. He no longer opposed the petition but became a supporting creditor. He himself applied for the appointment of a provisional liquidator in respect of Ayala, who was on 2 November 1989 duly appointed. On 21 November 1989 a compulsory winding-up order was made.

Nevertheless on 26 December 1989, pursuant to the 1987 letter of instructions, the bank applied moneys recovered by it from the ministry in respect of the Kuwaiti contract in transferring a sum of KD 110,266 to the account of Al Julaiah with the bank and in

F   discharging Ayala's liability on its current account with the bank in the amount of KD 277,967.

Section 168(3) of the *Insolvency Act* 1986 ('the 1986 Act') confers on the liquidator of a company which is being wound up by the court in England and Wales the right to apply to the court for directions in relation to any particular matter arising in the winding up. As the judge observed (particularly having regard to the provisions of s. 127 and 129

G   of the 1986 Act, relating to dispositions of a company's property after the commencement of its winding up), one would normally have expected the right of the bank to retain moneys and its obligations to make payments out of the proceeds of the Kuwaiti contract received by it from the ministry after the commencement of Ayala's winding up in January 1988 to have been investigated by the liquidator and if necessary resolved by the court on an application by the liquidator under s. 168 or in other proceedings brought by him in Ayala's name for that purpose. It appears, however, that the liquidator has

H   never been in funds sufficient to enable him to take any such action.

Against this background Mr Menzies, as a substantial unpaid creditor of Ayala, has himself sought to pursue a number of remedies. He issued an application under s. 212 of the 1986 Act against Mr Maley, the former managing director of Ayala. After a hearing of more than three weeks, the application was dismissed by His Honour Judge Baker QC by a judgment of 13 November 1991, to which I will revert.

Following that dismissal Mr Menzies on 27 November 1991 issued an application for   A
relief against the bank, by which he sought in effect (inter alia):

(1)   a declaration that the failure to register the bank's security under the *Companies Act* 1985 made the security void against the liquidator under s. 395 of that Act;

(2)   an order that the bank pay the liquidator the sterling equivalent of the sums of KD 191,000, KD 80,000, KD 110,226 and KD 277,967 respectively mentioned above which had been paid or retained by it after the commencement of the winding up.   B

On 5 March 1992 Mr Menzies, with the leave of the registrar, amended the application to include relief set out in a document entitled 'Pleadings of the applicant', which Mr Menzies had delivered to the bank on or about 18 February 1992 and which was ordered to stand as his points of claim.

By notice dated 25 March 1992 the bank applied to strike out that application and the points of claim.   C

As the judge pointed out, prima facie the proper plaintiff in proceedings to recover property or obtain reimbursement for the benefit of a company in liquidation is the company itself acting through its liquidator; the circumstances in which such proceedings can properly be brought in a winding up by a person other than the company or its liquidator are to be regarded as exceptions to the general statutory principle. The judge, in my view rightly, considered that he had to approach the bank's striking out application   D on the basis that the application of March 1992 made by Mr Menzies as a creditor, and which purported to be made under the 1986 Act and Pt. 7 of the Insolvency Rules, could not be allowed to proceed unless he could bring himself within one or more identifiable provision or provisions in the 1986 Act or the rules which confer upon a creditor the right to proceed by way of application in the winding up.

The judge decided that there was nothing in the 1986 Act which enabled Mr Menzies as a creditor to seek in proceedings in this liquidation a declaration against the bank as   E chargee to the effect that a charge was void against the liquidator by reason of s. 395 of the *Companies Act* 1985. He accordingly struck out that part of Mr Menzies' application which sought a declaration to this effect. There is no cross-appeal from this part of his order.

In the court below the payments of KD 277,967 and KD 110,266 referred to above were challenged by Mr Menzies both under s. 212 and under s. 423 of the 1986 Act. For   F the reasons given in his judgment (essentially on the grounds that the bank was not a person falling within s. 212(1)), the judge struck out the claim based on s. 212 of the 1986 Act. There is again no cross-appeal from this part of his order.

However the payments of KD 191,000, KD 80,000 and KD 110,266 referred to above were further challenged under s. 423 of the 1986 Act, which so far as material provides:

'(1) This section relates to transactions entered into at an undervalue; and a person   G enters into such a transaction with another person if–

(a)   he makes a gift to the other person or he otherwise enters into a transaction with the other on terms that provide for him to receive no consideration;

(b)   . . . or

(c)   he enters into a transaction with the other for a consideration the value of which, in money or money's worth, is significantly less than the value, in   H money or money's worth, of the consideration provided by himself.

(2) Where a person has entered into such a transaction, the court may, if satisfied under the next subsection, make such order as it thinks fit for–

(a)   restoring the position to what it would have been if the transaction had not been entered into, and

(b) protecting the interests of persons who are victims of the transaction.

(3) In the case of a person entering into such a transaction, an order shall only be made if the court is satisfied that it was entered into by him for the purpose–

    (a) of putting assets beyond the reach of a person who is making, or may at some time make, a claim against him, or

    (b) of otherwise prejudicing the interests of such a person in relation to the claim which he is making or may make.

. . .

(5) In relation to a transaction at an undervalue, references here and below to a victim of the transaction are to a person who is, or is capable of being, prejudiced by it; and in the following two sections the person entering into the transaction is referred to as "the debtor".'

Section 424 of the 1986 Act specifies the persons who may apply for an order under s. 423. So far as material it provides:

'(1) An application for an order made under section 423 shall not be made in relation to a transaction except–

    (a) in a case where the debtor . . . is a body corporate which is being wound up . . . by the official receiver . . . or the liquidator . . . of the body corporate or (with the leave of the court) by a victim of the transaction . . .

(2) An application made under any of the paragraphs of subsection (1) is to be treated as made on behalf of every victim of the transaction.'

Section 425(2) of the 1986 Act provides:

'(2) An order under section 423 may affect the property of, or impose any obligation on, any person whether or not he is the person with whom the debtor entered into the transaction . . .'

In substance, though not in form, Mr Menzies' claim seeks reimbursement by the bank of the three sums last referred to above, totalling KD 381,266 (about £840,000 at current exchange rates).

In the court below and in this court, it was and is common ground that Mr Menzies could properly be regarded as a victim of the relevant transaction within the definition contained in s. 423(5). Section 424(1), however, authorises a victim of a transaction at an undervalue to make an application under s. 423 only with the leave of the court, and Mr Menzies had obtained no such leave when he made his application of 27 November 1991. Nevertheless in the court below, the bank was sensibly content that the judge should deal with the matter as though an application for such leave was before him. Logically the question of leave or no leave must come first, because if leave were refused, questions of striking out the s. 423 claim would not arise.

In considering an application or proposed application under s. 423 of the 1986 Act, the first task of the court is to identify the relevant 'transaction' which is under attack. In the course of argument in the court below, it emerged that if the application proceeded, Mr Menzies would seek to allege that the moneys which were paid by the bank to Al Julaiah pursuant to the 1987 letter of instructions were moneys to which Al Julaiah had *no entitlement whatever*. On the basis of such an allegation, he might have been able to contend that the payments themselves were relevant 'transactions' for the purpose of s. 423. However, his full and lengthy points of claim had contained no such allegation. Paragraph 11(iii) of that pleading, for example, had referred merely to payments made by the bank 'in respect against [Ayala] of which [Al Julaiah] was unsecured'. In these circumstances, in my view clearly rightly, the judge declined to consider the proposed s. 423 application either on the basis that the moneys paid by the bank to Al Julaiah

pursuant to the 1987 letter of instructions were moneys to which Al Julaiah had no
entitlement or that the payments of such moneys were themselves relevant transactions.
As he put it:

'If that is the case which Mr Menzies wishes to make then it needs to be spelt out
unambiguously and with particularity in his pleading. For the purpose of the
application before me, I shall proceed on the basis that it is the letter of instruction
alone which is said to be a transaction at an undervalue for the purposes of s. 423.'

In this court Mr Menzies sought to repeat the assertion that the moneys paid by the
bank to Al Julaiah pursuant to the 1987 letter of instructions were moneys which were
not owed to Al Julaiah. Since, however, he had lodged no respondent's notice nor given
the bank any notice of his intention to resurrect this assertion (which could have given
rise to important questions of evidence) nor produced any proposed amendment of his
points of claim, we did not think it right to permit him to pursue it. We must proceed, as
did the judge, on the basis that it is solely the giving of the 1987 letter of instructions
which is under attack as the relevant 'transaction' for the purpose of s. 423 and that, as
at that date, Al Julaiah was a creditor of Ayala in a sum of at least KD 295,000 (i.e. KD
300,000 less KD 5,000). (I note from Judge Baker's judgment in the Maley proceedings
that Mr Menzies had originally made the same allegation that Al Julaiah were not entitled
to the KD 300,000 but had later withdrawn it, reducing it to an allegation that they were
not secured creditors in respect of this sum.)

Having thus identified the 1987 letter of instructions as the relevant 'transaction', the
next question for the court was and is whether that was a transaction 'entered into at an
undervalue' within the meaning of s. 423(1). This, as the judge described it, is a primary
requirement of s. 423. If this requirement is not satisfied, an application made under the
section must inevitably fail in limine on that ground if no other.

The judge took the view that, in relation to the relevant transaction in the present case,

'the allegations in para. 16, and also in para. 18 of the points of claim, if established
at a trial, would or might enable the court to reach the conclusion that the primary
requirement of s. 423 was satisfied.'

I think I should quote the most material passages in para. 16 and 18 of the pleading,
because they contain the substance of Mr Menzies' crucially important assertion that, by
giving the instructions to the bank in the 1987 letter, Ayala entered into a 'transaction at
an undervalue'. These passages read as follows:

'16. *The attempts by NBK and AJ to become secured in the summer of 1987*

Maley stated in his evidence [in the Maley proceedings] that he visited the NBK
[the bank] with Hijazi in July 1987 . . . and that . . . both NBK and AJ [Al Julaiah]
at that time considered both NBK and AJ to be exposed and competing creditors
for scarce funds. Therefore (according to Maley), he was persuaded by AJ and
NBK to attempt to extend AJ's security – and this led to AH's [Ayala's] fax
containing the "irrevocable instruction" sent on 19 August 1987, purporting to
give AJ further security against AH's creditors in the sum of KD 300,000. The
purported consideration for this instruction was that AJ was making certain small
payments to complete essential work in Kuwait, i.e. agreeing to fund the remedial
work required on the contract and also to further fund the preparation of the final
claim, and for doing all this AJ required further security.

The applicant contends that the reasons given by AH for this further additional
security and the purported consideration for it were bogus in that AJ had only
paid some KD 3,000 to advance the claim and pay creditors, and had paid nothing
towards the remedial work all of which was carried out by a new company named
Ayala Abbott & Butters Ltd.

A   Accordingly the applicant contends that the giving of the irrevocable instruction of 19 August 1984 [sic] was a transaction at an undervalue (IA 1986, s. 423) and he seeks leave of the court (s. 424) to set this transaction aside as he is the victim of it. NBK subsequently acted in accordance with the irrevocable instruction and paid AJ on final settlement to the detriment of the applicant and other creditors, who received nothing.'

B   The most material parts of para. 18 of the points of claim read as follows:

'18. . . .

The applicant contends that the purported irrevocable instruction given on 19 August 1987 by AH to NBK authorising irrevocable payment of KD 300,000 from future contract receipts to AJ is voidable at the instance of the liquidator or creditors in that it was given for bogus or inadequate consideration at a time when AH was insolvent. The reason given in respect of the essential maintenance

C   payments to be made by AJ was false. AJ paid nothing and had never agreed to pay anything. All the maintenance was carried out by Ayala Abbott & Butters ("AAB") and invoiced to Ayala Design & Build, another member of the Ayala group.

The reason given for the need to fund preparation of the claim was also false. Safco and Integrated Surveys had agreed to progress the claim for a contingency fee of

D   five per cent of the final settlement award.'

On analysis, the allegations made in para. 16 and 18 as to the circumstances in which the irrevocable instructions came to be given on 19 August 1987 accordingly amount to this. As at that date, the bank and Al Julaiah considered themselves to be exposed and competing creditors of Ayala for scarce funds. The purpose or a purpose of the giving of these instructions was therefore to grant Al Julaiah additional security as against Ayala's

E   creditors in a sum of KD 300,000. The consideration purportedly given by Al Julaiah to Ayala for the grant of this additional security was (it is said): (1) the making of certain small payments by Al Julaiah to complete essential work in Kuwait and (2) the further funding of the preparation of Alaya's final claim under its contract with the ministry. In truth it is alleged, as to (1), Al Julaiah neither had agreed to pay nor paid anything to complete the work in Kuwait, but all the maintenance was carried out by Ayala Abbott and Butters and invoiced to Ayala Design & Build, another member of the Ayala group;

F   as to (2), save for a sum of about KD 3,000 paid by Al Julaiah to advance the claim against the ministry and pay creditors, it was not Al Julaiah, but a company called Safco and Integrated Surveys which had agreed to advance the claim (for a contingency fee and a share of the final settlement award).

Assuming in favour of Mr Menzies that the last-mentioned payment of KD 3,000 was the only consideration received by Ayala for the giving of the 1987 letter of instructions,

G   that payment would still have prevented the relevant transaction from falling within s. 423(1)(a) of the 1986 Act. To satisfy the primary requirement of the section on an application made thereunder, Mr Menzies would therefore have to persuade the court that the transaction fell within 423(1)(c). To do so, he would have to establish that the consideration for which Ayala gave the 1987 letter of instructions was 'significantly less than the value, in money or money's worth, of the consideration provided by' Ayala.

H   I see no realistic prospect of Mr Menzies establishing that, in giving the 1987 letter of instructions, Ayala provided any consideration, even on the basis of the allegations made in his points of claim. In my judgment the facts set out in para. 6 of his pleading (which is headed 'Financing of contract SPF 85/8', coupled with the correspondence relating to financing which is contained in document 12 of his 'Bundle of documents in opposition to strike-out application of respondent', make it reasonably plain that as at 19 August 1987 Al Julaiah and the bank were already secured. The letter of that date did not create any security. Its purpose was simply to give effect to an agreement providing for the future allocation, as between Al Julaiah and the bank, of sums to which they were already entitled as secured creditors.

The conclusion set out in the immediately preceding paragraph entirely accords with a finding of fact reached by Judge Baker in the Maley proceedings. We were told that Mr Menzies has made three unsuccessful applications for a retrial of the claim against Mr Maley and that an appeal against Judge Baker's judgment was dismissed on 6 January 1993 because of Mr Menzies' failure to comply with an order for security of costs (though we were also told that an appeal against the order for security was pending). It is clear that before Judge Baker the question whether or not, as at 19 August 1987, Al Julaiah was a secured creditor was a very live issue. In the course of a very full and careful judgment he concluded:

> 'I read these [instructions] simply as making an agreement between two parties – the debtor on the one hand and the creditors on the other as to priorities . . . It did not either lessen or add to the security which Al Julaiah already had.'

Mr Hacker, on behalf of the bank, has submitted that in view of this finding, reached after a long trial with full evidence, it would be an abuse of the process of the court if Mr Menzies were to seek to relitigate this matter of fact on an application under s. 423. In this context he referred us to (inter alia) the recent decision of this court in *Ashmore v British Coal Corporation* [1990] 2 QB 338. I, for my part, do not find it necessary to rely on this line of authority. It will suffice to say that nothing in Mr Menzies' submissions or in the documentation before us has come near to persuading me that Judge Baker reached the wrong conclusion on this point. Mr Menzies referred us in this context to the provisions of s. 395 of the *Companies Act* 1985 (referred to above), but I cannot see how those provisions can lend any support to his submission that Al Julaiah or the bank were not already secured creditors at the time when the 1987 letter of instructions was given.

Accordingly in my judgment we must approach this appeal on the basis that the 1987 letter of instructions conferred on Al Julaiah or the bank no rights by way of security beyond those which they already possessed; it merely regulated the priorities as between the two creditors concerned. I therefore see no basis on which Mr Menzies could hope to persuade the court that the consideration obtained by Ayala was 'significantly less than the value, in money or money's worth, of the consideration provided by' Ayala, so as to bring the case within s. 423(1)(c). For, in my judgment, so far as his pleadings and the evidence show, *Ayala provided no consideration whatever in money or money's worth for the transaction.* It follows that in my judgment Mr Menzies' proposed application under s. 423 would fail in limine because the primary requirement of subs. (1) could not be satisfied.

Even if Mr Menzies could satisfy that primary requirement, he would still have to surmount further hurdles, some statutory and others relating to the exercise of the court's discretion, if he was to persuade the court that he should be given the leave sought. In the course of his judgment, the judge considered a number of such further hurdles and decided that none of them precluded the grant of leave sought by Mr Menzies. I do not think it necessary or helpful to express any view on these further matters, save to the extent below.

It must be noted that s. 423(3) of the Act imposes a second mandatory requirement which an applicant under the section must satisfy if he is to obtain relief. It precludes the court from making an order 'in the case of a person entering into such a transaction' unless it is satisfied that it was entered into by him for one or other of the purposes set out in subpara. (a) and (b). As to this subsection, the judge expressed the view that the words which I have last quoted,

A   'may have the effect of limiting the restriction in that subsection to cases where the order is made against the debtor as defined in subs. (5).'

He pointed out that s. 423 can be invoked in cases in which the debtor is not the subject of bankruptcy or winding-up proceedings. He observed:

'If the opening words of s. 423(3) do not have that effect, then it is difficult to see what purpose they do serve.'

B   I respectfully disagree with the judge on this point. Section 423(3), as drafted, would not have made sense if the opening words, 'In the case of a person entering into such a transaction' had been omitted. They were, I think, clearly inserted by the draftsman for the simple, but necessary, purpose of defining the word 'him' in the subsequent phrase 'entered into by him'. Furthermore the construction placed by the judge on the subsection seems to me to ignore the mischief which s. 423 was intended to remedy, as explained in

C   the *Report of the Review Committee on Insolvency Law and Practice* (Cmnd 8558) para. 1210 et seq. In my judgment therefore it would have been a further necessary condition precedent to a successful s. 423 application by Mr Menzies against the bank that he should establish that Ayala gave the 1987 letter of instructions for one or other of the purposes mentioned in s. 423(3). The judge thought it arguable that the allegations in para. 16 of the points of claim, to the effect that Ayala's purpose in giving that letter was to give Al Julaiah a security against the interests of other creditors, would, if established,

D   suffice to satisfy this second requirement which is imposed by s. 423(3), relating to the purpose of the person entering into the transaction. I do not think it necessary to decide whether the judge's opinion on this point was correct. However this point does prompt me to make some more general observations.

As Mr Menzies' argument proceeded, it became increasingly clear that the real substance of his complaint in regard to the 1987 letter of instructions is that it constituted and was intended as a *preference* of Al Julaiah and the bank. Indeed he frequently used

E   the phrase 'fraudulent preference' in the course of his submissions. Following the recommendations of the Cork Report (Cmnd 8558), the 1986 Act does not refer to a 'fraudulent' preference. It does however, contain a separate section (s. 239) which gives 'the office-holder' the right to apply to the court for an order restoring the position to what it would have been if the company concerned had not at a 'relevant time' given a 'preference' as therein defined. For the purposes of that section (see subs. (4)) a company

F   gives a preference to a person if:

'(a) that person is one of the company's creditors . . . and

(b) the company does anything . . . which . . . has the effect of putting that person into a position which, in the event of the company going into insolvent liquidation, will be better than the position he would have been in if that thing had not been done.'

G   Section 239(5) precludes the court from making an order under the section:

'unless the company which gave the preference was influenced in deciding to give it by a desire to produce in relation to that person the effect mentioned in subsection (4)(b).'

Whether or not Ayala was so influenced, it may well be that the 1987 letter of instructions at least constituted a 'preference', since it could be said that its practical

H   effect was, in the event, to leave Al Julaiah and the bank more or less fully protected as creditors of Ayala, while its other creditors, of whom Mr Menzies is by far the most substantial, are receiving nothing in the liquidation. On this account, Mr Menzies and the other creditors of Ayala deserve sympathy.

The liquidator of Ayala, as 'office-holder', would have the right to bring proceedings under s. 239, but as I have already explained, it appears that he is more or less without

funds with which to conduct litigation. By a deed of assignment dated 10 February 1993　A
he assigned to Mr Menzies 'all rights to and choses in action relating to or in any way
arising out of or in connection' with the proceedings. The deed recited that it was intended
that the liquidator be joined as a party to the proceedings but he has taken no part in
them and an order dated 20 May 1993 (from which I understand there has been no
appeal) Knox J held that the assignment did not assign to Mr Menzies any rights to bring
any proceedings, claims or causes of action which the liquidator and/or Ayala may be
entitled to bring or assert against the bank.　B

Mr Menzies therefore has no right to make any claim against the bank based on s. 239
and for present purposes the possibility of the liquidator having any such claim has to be
disregarded. It must be stressed that the claim which is under consideration on this appeal
is a claim not under s. 239 but under s. 423, which is concerned not with wrongful
preference as such but with transactions 'entered into at an undervalue'. For the reasons
given above, I have come to the clear conclusion that Mr Menzies has shown no realistic　C
prospect of establishing that the 1987 letter of instructions constituted a transaction
'entered into at an undervalue' in the relevant sense; his s. 423 claim would therefore be
bound to fail in limine.

I suspect that Chadwick J, who had many issues to consider, did not have the benefit
of so full an argument on this point as we have had in this court from the helpful
submissions both of Mr Hacker for the bank and Mr Menzies (who told us that he is a　D
member of the bar). On the short grounds which I have stated I would: (1) allow this
appeal; (2) strike out the whole of Mr Menzies' notice of application dated 27 November
1991 as amended; (3) strike out the whole of the document described as 'Pleadings of the
applicant' served on the bank and ordered by the registrar to stand as points of claim;
and (4) refuse leave to Mr Menzies to bring or continue proceedings for an order against
the bank under s. 423 of the 1986 Act.

Since preparing this judgment, I have seen and considered a copy of a letter dated 25　E
October 1993 written by Mr Menzies to the clerk to Balcombe LJ in which he submits
(rightly or wrongly) that the effect of Chadwick J's order dated 9 October 1992, as varied
by an order made by him dated 30 October 1992, taken together with (1) para. 4 of an
order made by him dated 15 January 1993, (2) para. 2(c) of an order made by Sir Mervyn
Davies dated 3 March 1993; and (3) para. 1 of the order made by Knox J dated 20 May
1993, is that Mr Menzies has been granted leave to amend his points of claim so as to
contend that 'Al Julaiah is not a creditor at all', though 'currently such leave to amend is　F
stayed'. He states that 'should the liquidator withdraw from the proceedings', he has
every intention of amending his points of claim.

As already stated, however when this appeal came on for hearing, Mr Menzies had
lodged no respondent's notice, nor given any notice of his intention to resurrect the
assertion that Al Julaiah was not a creditor, nor produced any proposed amendment of
his points of claim. Furthermore we have been referred to no evidence, beyond his bare　G
assertion, that the allegation has any foundation. In these circumstances I would not for
my part think it right to include the grant or confirmation of any leave to amend Mr
Menzies' points of claim in the order which this court makes on this appeal, so as to save
the remaining parts of that pleading from being struck out.

Balcombe LJ: I have had the advantage of reading in draft the judgment of Sir
Christopher Slade. I would allow this appeal for the reasons which he gives; I also agree　H
with the order he proposes. I add a few words of my own only because we are differing
from the judgment of Chadwick J on the limited issues to which this appeal relates.

The principal issue on this appeal is whether the 1987 letter of instructions was a
transaction entered into by Ayala at an undervalue within the meaning of s. 423(1) of the
Insolvency Act 1986. The definition of a 'transaction at an undervalue' in s. 423(1) is in

A   all relevant respects the same as the definition in s. 238(4) of the same Act. In *M C Bacon Ltd* [1990] BCC 78, Millett J had to consider (inter alia) whether the granting of a debenture by a company was a transaction entered into by the company at an undervalue within s. 238(4)(b) (which corresponds to s. 423(1)(c)). He said (at p. 92C):

'To come within that paragraph the transaction must be:

(1) entered into by the company;

B   (2) for a consideration;

(3) the value of which measured in money or money's worth;

(4) is significantly less than the value;

(5) also measured in money or money's worth;

(6) of the consideration provided by the company.

C   It requires a comparison to be made between the value obtained by the company for the transaction and the value of consideration provided by the company. Both values must be measurable in money or money's worth and both must be considered from the company's point of view.

In my judgment, the applicant's claim to characterise the granting of the bank's debenture as a transaction at an undervalue is misconceived. The mere creation of a security over a company's assets does not deplete them and does not come within

D   the paragraph. By charging its assets the company appropriates them to meet the liabilities due to the secured creditor and adversely affects the rights of other creditors in the event of insolvency. But it does not deplete its assets or diminish their value. It retains the right to redeem and the right to sell or remortgage the charged assets. All it loses is the ability to apply the proceeds otherwise than in satisfaction of the secured debt. That is not something capable of valuation in

E   monetary terms and is not customarily disposed of for value.

In the present case the company did not suffer that loss by reason of the grant of the debenture. Once the bank had demanded a debenture the company could not have sold or charged its assets without applying the proceeds in reduction of the overdraft; had it attempted to do so, the bank would at once have called in the overdraft. By granting the debenture the company parted with nothing of value,

F   and the value of the consideration which it received in return was incapable of being measured in money or money's worth.

Mr Vos submitted that the consideration which the company received was, with hindsight, of no value. It merely gained time and with it the opportunity to lose more money. But he could not and did not claim that the company ought to have received a fee or other capital sum in return for the debenture. That gives the game away. The applicant's real complaint is not that the company entered into the

G   transaction at an undervalue but that it entered into it at all.'

In my judgment the reasoning of Millett J applies, mutatis mutandis, to the 1987 letter of instructions. It is unfortunate that Chadwick J was not referred to this case.

I add that I also agree with Sir Christopher Slade on the construction of s. 423(3), that the sole purpose of the words 'In the case of a person entering into such a transaction' is to identify the 'him' in the succeeding phrase 'entered into by him'.

H   Mr Menzies' real complaint is that the 1987 letter of instructions constituted a preference of Al Julaiah and the bank. His difficulty is that this can only be attacked by the liquidator of Ayala and Mr Menzies is either unable or unwilling to put the liquidator in funds for that purpose.

I add, finally, that I am in complete agreement with Sir Christopher Slade where he says, at the end of his judgment, that it is now far too late for Mr Menzies to seek to

A

make a case before us, not based solely on the 1987 letter of instructions, but on the basis, which Chadwick J clearly rejected, that the payments by the bank to Al Julaiah pursuant to the 1987 letter of instructions were of moneys to which Al Julaiah had no title, and accordingly that the payments were themselves transactions entered into at an undervalue.

Butler-Sloss LJ: I agree.

B

(*Appeal allowed. Plaintiff's notice of motion struck out. Leave for the plaintiff to bring or continue proceedings against the bank refused. Leave to appeal to the House of Lords refused. Mr Menzies to pay the costs of the appeal, to include those reserved on 11 November 1993, and the costs of the application, to be taxed and paid forthwith*)

C

D

E

F

G

H

A

R v Brockley.

Court of Appeal (Criminal Division).
Henry LJ and Otton and Garland JJ.
Judgment delivered 12 November 1993.

B
Director disqualification – Undischarged bankrupt acting as director – Whether offence of strict liability – Company Directors Disqualification Act 1986, s. 11, 13.

The offence of acting as a director while an undischarged bankrupt under s. 11(1) of the Company Directors Disqualification Act 1986 was an absolute offence and there was no requirement of mens rea, and accordingly the appellant was rightly convicted even though he was unaware that he had not been discharged from his bankruptcy.

C
The following cases were referred to in the judgment of the court:

Gammon (Hong Kong) Ltd & Ors v A-G of Hong Kong [1985] AC 1.
Sweet v Parsley [1970] AC 132.
R v Sheppard & Anor [1981] AC 394.

Frank Phillips (Registrar of Criminal Appeals) for the appellant.

D
Kevin Riordan (Department of Trade and Industry solicitor) for the Crown.

JUDGMENT OF THE COURT
(Delivered by Henry LJ)

Mr Brockley appeals against his conviction in the Crown Court at Swansea (before His Honour Judge Lewis Bowen) of acting as a director of a company being an
E undischarged bankrupt, contrary to sec. 13 of the *Company Directors Disqualification Act* 1986. The particulars of offence read as follows:

'Frank Brockley, between 1 October 1988 and 29 December 1989, being an undischarged bankrupt, acted as a director of a company known as Rouxfort Ltd without leave of the court by which he was adjudged bankrupt.'

The undisputed facts were these. On 18 March 1976 Mr Brockley had been adjudicated
F bankrupt. Under sec. 8(2) of the *Insolvency Act* 1976 the official receiver in 1981 made an application to the court in respect of the adjudication (as he was bound to do). Mr Brockley could not be found to be served with notice of this application. On 4 June 1981 the court considered the discharge of Mr Brockley under that section and that discharge was refused. He was ultimately discharged from bankruptcy on 29 December 1989 under the provisions of the *Insolvency Act* 1986.

G
Meanwhile, he had, without leave of the court, carried on the business of the named company (a hotel) from 1 October 1988.

Mr Brockley originally pleaded not guilty to this indictment. His defence was that he genuinely believed that he had been discharged from his bankruptcy before 1 October 1988. The grounds for this belief were as follows. In the summer of 1988 Mr Brockley was involved in litigation in which he had counsel and solicitors acting for him. One of
H those in the employ of his then solicitors was Mr England, a paralegal. Mr England advised Mr Brockley that he would by that time have been automatically discharged under the provisions of the *Insolvency Act* 1986. Inquiry of the official receiver would have shown that he was not discharged, but Mr Brockley made no such inquiry.

The prosecution made a formal admission to the court that Mr Brockley was unaware that he was *not* discharged from his bankruptcy.

The question that the court had to consider was whether on those facts Mr Brockley   A
had a defence to the charge in law.

Section 11(1) of the *Company Directors Disqualification Act* 1986 provides:

'It is an offence for a person who is an undischarged bankrupt to act as director
of, or directly or indirectly to take part in or be concerned in the promotion,
formation or management of, a company, except with the leave of the court.'
B
The sole question was whether this constituted an absolute offence or whether mens
rea should be imported into it, in which case he had a defence, namely that he did not
know that he was an undischarged bankrupt.

This issue was argued as a preliminary point before the judge. He found in a reasoned
judgment that it was an absolute offence. Thereupon, the appellant changed his plea to
one of guilty and was sentenced to a six-month term of imprisonment suspended for two
years. He now applies to this court for leave to appeal against conviction, the registrar   C
having referred the matter directly to the full court. We treat this application as the
hearing of the appeal.

Both we and the court at first instance were referred to the familiar line of authorities.
Sweet v Parsley [1970] AC 132, *R v Sheppard* [1981] AC 394, and finally *Gammon (Hong
Kong) Ltd & Ors v A-G of Hong Kong* [1985] AC 1. We consider that we, as the trial
judge did, can go straight to Lord *Scarman*'s distillation of the law to be found in   D
Gammon at p. 14B:

'. . . the law relevant to this appeal may be stated in the following propositions . . .

  (1) there is a presumption of law that mens rea is required before a person can
      be held guilty of a criminal offence;

  (2) the presumption is particularly strong where the offence is "truly criminal"   E
      in character;

  (3) the presumption applies to statutory offences, and can be displaced only if
      this is clearly or by necessary implication the effect of the statute;

  (4) the only situation in which the presumption can be displaced is where the
      statute is concerned with an issue of social concern . . .

  (5) even where a statute is concerned with such an issue, the presumption of   F
      mens rea stands unless it can also be shown that the creation of strict liability
      will be effective to promote the objects of the statute by encouraging greater
      vigilance to prevent the commission of the prohibited act.'

In this case the court is concerned with (4) and (5).

The mischief the section is aimed at is clear, and is set out in the note to the section in
Halsbury's Statutes, vol. 8 (4th edn, 1991 reissue), p. 791:
G
'This section prevents an undischarged bankrupt from escaping the consequences
of his disabilities by "turning himself into a company" . . .'

That mischief is clearly an issue of social concern, as the trial judge rightly found. This
then takes us to Lord *Scarman*'s fifth proposition – will the creation of strict liability be
effective to promote the objects of the statute by encouraging greater vigilance to prevent
the commission of the prohibited act? The answer to this question is clear. Strict liability   H
will oblige those who have been adjudicated bankrupt to ensure that their bankruptcy
has, in fact, been discharged before they engage in any of the forbidden activities in
relation to a company. If mens rea were required, then a bankrupt who lay low, buried
his head in the sand, and took part in the prohibited activities, would have a defence and
an advantage not available to the responsible bankrupt who took steps to establish his

A   position before taking part in such activities. Such a conclusion would be contrary to the clear legislative intention and unacceptable.

Therefore, in our opinion, the judge was right for the right reasons. In those circumstances this appeal must be dismissed.

(*Appeal dismissed*)

B

C

D

E

F

G

H

Chohan v Saggar & Ors.   A

Court of Appeal (Civil Division).
Nourse, Balcombe and Waite L JJ.
Judgment delivered 17 November 1993.

Transactions defrauding creditors – Court order restoring position to what it
would have been – Order not to prejudice accrued rights of innocent third parties   B
– Whether power to restore and protect as far as practicable – Materiality of
value of asset(s) lost to debtor – Insolvency Act 1986, s. 423, 425.

This was an appeal by the plaintiff from a judge's order reversing a transaction defrauding
creditors under s. 423 of the Insolvency Act 1986.

In 1987 the second defendant, 'B', was the registered proprietor with title absolute of a
freehold property in Hillingdon, subject to a legal charge in favour of Anglia Building   C
Society. B then executed a transfer of the property, expressed to be made in consideration
of the sum of £50,000, to the first defendant, 'S'. On the same day the legal charge was
discharged and S executed a fresh legal charge in favour of Chelsea Building Society to
secure a loan of £25,000. About a month later S executed a trust deed, by which she declared
that she held the property in trust for 'M', a business associate of B.

On the application of the plaintiff who was a judgment creditor of B, the judge found (see   D
[1992] BCC 306) that before the transfer S was a protected tenant of the whole of the
property. On the basis of its agreed vacant possession value at that time (£75,000), the
intention of B was that it should appear to be sold to S as a sitting tenant, whereas it was in
fact to be sold to M at a reduced sum of £50,000. The judge held that B made the transfer
with the dominant purpose of removing assets from the reach of actual or potential claimants
or creditors and that the requirements of s. 423(1)(c) and (3)(a) had been satisfied. It was
accepted that the plaintiff was a victim of the transaction within s. 423(1)(c) and that S was   E
not. In a further judgment (see [1992] BCC 750) the judge set aside the trust deed but not
the transfer. He identified a potential conflict between the provisions of s. 423(2)(a) and
425(2)(a) – the building society being within the protection conferred by the latter provision
– and held that s. 423(2)(a) had to be construed so as to provide for the restoration of the
antecedent position 'as far as possible'. S should be compensated for the loss of her protected
tenancy because she could not be restored to that position. The judge declared that Chelsea
Building Society was entitled to be registered as first legal chargee of the property and that   F
the equity of redemption was held upon trust for S as to 56/75ths and B (effectively for his
creditors) as to 19/75ths.

On appeal the plaintiff argued that the judge was wrong to find that S was a protected
tenant; secondly, that the judge should have set aside the transfer (which would necessarily
have carried the trust deed with it) and that it was not open to him merely to set aside the
trust deed; thirdly, that if it was open to him not to set aside the transfer, the proportions of   G
the beneficial interest in the equity of redemption assigned to S and B respectively were
wrong and should be adjusted more favourably to B.

Held, allowing the appeal to the extent of varying the interests of B and S in the property:

1. The judge was right on the tenancy question.

2. It was open to the judge to set aside the trust deed but not the transfer. The judge   H
recognised, correctly, that his power under s. 423(2) to make an order restoring the position
and protecting the interests of the victims of the transaction was constricted by s. 425(2)(a),
which made it necessary that the order should not prejudice the interest of Chelsea Building
Society. The inevitable result, as the judge held, was that the power under s. 423(2) was a
power to restore and protect so far as practicable. Moreover, it was not expressed as a
power to set aside the transaction. Provided that it was exercised in order to restore the

A position and protect the interests of the victims of the transaction so far as practicable, the whole or any part of the transaction might be set aside.

3. The object of s. 423–425 being to remedy the avoidance of debts, the 'and' between para. (a) and (b) of s. 423(2) had to be read conjunctively and not disjunctively. Any order made under that subsection must seek, so far as practicable, both to restore the position to what it would have been if the transaction had not been entered into and to protect the interests of the victims of it. It was not a power to restore the position generally, but in such a way as to protect the victims' interests; in other words, by restoring assets to the debtor, to make them available for execution by the victims. So the first question the judge had to ask was what assets had been lost to the debtor. B's interest in the property at the time of the transfer was worth £19,000.

4. On the basis of the agreed vacant possession value of £75,000, the judge awarded B and S shares of 19/75ths and 56/75ths respectively. He was right to work on that value, not on the tenanted value of £50,000, and also to award B a share which, had the property been unencumbered, would have been worth £19,000. But he was wrong, as between B and S, to apply that share to the equity of redemption in the property. On the footing that the property was sold with vacant possession for £75,000 and that the amount outstanding under the legal charge in favour of Chelsea Building Society was £25,000, the judge's order would produce for B, not £19,000, but £12,666. It would not restore the asset lost. The judge's order not having achieved what it could and ought to have achieved under s. 423(2), he erred in principle and the court ought to vary his order by providing that as between B and S the amount owing under the legal charge in favour of Chelsea Building Society should be debited wholly against S's 56/75 share of the beneficial interest in the property.

The following cases were referred to in the judgment of Nourse LJ:

Arbuthnot Leasing International Ltd v Havelet Leasing Ltd & Ors (No. 2) [1990] BCC 636.

Street v Mountford [1985] AC 809.

Sir William Goodhart QC and David Parry (instructed by Singh & Choudry) for the appellant.

Peter Ralls (instructed by Lass Salt & Garvin) for the first respondent.

The second respondent did not appear and was not represented.

Richard Ritchie (instructed by Kenwright & Cox) for the third respondent.

JUDGMENT

Nourse LJ: This appeal arises mainly under s. 423–425 of the *Insolvency Act* 1986 (provisions against debt avoidance). The particular provision to which attention must be paid is s. 423(2).

Immediately prior to 17 November 1987 the second defendant, Ajit Singh Sat Bhambra, was the registered proprietor with title absolute of the freehold property known as 27 Denziloe Avenue, Hillingdon, Middlesex ('the property'), subject to a legal charge in favour of Anglia Building Society. On that date Mr Sat Bhambra executed a transfer of the property, expressed to be made in consideration of the sum of £50,000, to the first defendant, Aruna Saggar. On the same day the legal charge was discharged and Mrs Saggar executed a fresh legal charge in favour of Chelsea Building Society to secure a loan of £25,000. About a month later she executed a trust deed, by which she declared that she held the property in trust for a Mr John Mallard, a business associate of Mr Sat Bhambra who has since died.

By an order made on 20 July 1992 under s. 423(2) of the 1986 Act, Mr Edward Evans-Lombe QC, sitting as a deputy judge of the Chancery Division, ordered the trust deed to

be set aside and declared that, subject to the legal charge in favour of Chelsea Building   A
Society, Mrs Saggar held the property upon trust as to 19/75 parts for Mr Sat Bhambra
(effectively for his creditors) and as to 56/75 parts for herself. The deputy judge gave two
judgments, the first on 8 October 1991 ([1992] BCC 306) and the second on 20 July 1992
([1992] BCC 750). In the first he had to set out the material facts, which he described as
somewhat complicated, at considerable length. Because it is no longer in issue that the
requirements of s. 423(1)(c) and (3)(a) were satisfied, they can now be stated
comparatively briefly, mainly in the judge's own words.   B

Mr Sat Bhambra is a Sikh, who until about 1985 was the editor of a newspaper
circulating amongst Sikhs in this country. In 1973 Mrs Saggar, who had come to London
from Kenya in 1971, started working for Mr Sat Bhambra in a travel agency run by him.
In May or June 1975 she began a close relationship with Mr Sat Bhambra, which resulted
in the birth of a daughter to them in February 1976. In 1977 their relationship ended,
although it appears that they remained in close touch. Mr Sat Bhambra bought the   C
property in early 1983, his title thereto being registered on 1 March 1983. He bought it
with the assistance of a loan from Anglia Building Society of £30,108. Mrs Saggar and
Mr Gleeson, a man much older than her whom the judge described as having become a
sort of unofficial parent for her, moved into occupation of part of the property. The
judge found that Mrs Saggar in due course became a protected tenant of the whole of the
property. I will refer to that matter in greater detail later.   D

In 1984 and 1985 Mr Sat Bhambra became embroiled with the police as a result of
allegations that he had been concerned in the illegal importation of drugs into this
country. On 5 July 1984 there was published in Mr Sat Bhambra's newspaper an article
concerning the plaintiff in this action, Jagjit Singh Chohan, another Sikh, whom the
judge described as a leading light in the Sikh community and in particular a leading light
in the Sikh Separatist Movement. Dr Chohan claimed that the article was defamatory of
him and on 10 September 1984 he issued a writ in the Queen's Bench Division claiming   E
damages for libel. On 4 March 1985 Mr Sat Bhambra was arrested and charged with the
illegal importation of drugs. After remaining in custody for some weeks, he was released
on bail. However, on 21 March 1985, while he was in custody, judgment was entered
against him in the libel action in default of defence, with damages to be assessed. On
2 April 1985 Dr Chohan obtained a Mareva injunction restraining the disposition of
Mr Sat Bhambra's assets. Thereafter Dr Chohan indicated through his solicitors that   F
he would accept a sum of £20,000 plus costs in settlement of his claim. In February 1988
the damages were assessed at £40,000.

By the beginning of 1985 Mr Sat Bhambra had got into arrears with his mortgage
repayments to Anglia Building Society and in May 1985 proceedings for possession of
the property were commenced. In October 1986 a further writ for libel was issued against
Mr Sat Bhambra by Mr Bedi. Again judgment in default was obtained, with damages to   G
be assessed. Ultimately the damages were assessed at £100,000, although Mr Evans-
Lombe pointed out that there was no evidence before him to the effect that prior to 17
November 1987 Mr Sat Bhambra was aware of the scale of the likely damages under that
claim. On 31 October 1986 he was convicted of illegally importing drugs and was
sentenced to nine years' imprisonment. He was still in prison at the date of the trial. On
19 December 1986 he suffered a further judgment at the suit of the Punjab and Sind
Bank in the sum of £28,422.   H

It is clear that by 17 November 1987, when the transfer of the property in favour of
Mrs Saggar was executed, Mr Sat Bhambra was deeply in debt. Although the
consideration was expressed to be £50,000, the amount actually paid by Mrs Saggar on
the transfer was rather more than £31,000, being the amount required to discharge the
Anglia Building Society mortgage. £25,000 came from the advance by Chelsea Building

A   Society and the remaining £6,000 from a sum provided by Mrs Saggar's father. The judge found that the trust deed, which is undated, was brought into existence approximately a month after the execution of the transfer. It was executed both by Mrs Saggar and by Mr Mallard. It recited that it was supplemental to the transfer and that the sum of £50,000 'was in fact provided as to £19,000 by [Mr Mallard] out of his own equity', as to £6,000 by Mrs Saggar's father and as to the balance of £25,000 by a mortgage advance to Mrs Saggar from Chelsea Building Society 'the principal interest secured thereunder to be repaid by' Mr Mallard. As I have said, Mrs Saggar declared that she held the property in trust for Mr Mallard, to whom Mr Sat Bhambra owed an uncertain amount which the judge said could not be put higher than £11,000. It was probably nearer £7,000.

Because of these proceedings Mrs Saggar has not been registered as the proprietor of the property, nor has the legal charge in favour of Chelsea Building Society been entered in the charges register. The writ was issued on 22 June 1988. By his amended statement of claim Dr Chohan, having referred to the default judgment in the libel action of 21 March 1985, alleged, first, that at that date Mr Sat Bhambra did not have money with which to pay the damages when assessed; secondly, that in the knowledge that he was liable to pay damages to Dr Chohan Mr Sat Bhambra transferred the property to Mrs Saggar; and, thirdly:

> 'The transfer aforesaid was made with intent to defeat the claims or in the alternative of putting the said property beyond the reach or in the further alternative of otherwise prejudicing the interests of the plaintiff against the second defendant as a judgment creditor and fraudulently.'

Dr Chohan claimed a declaration accordingly and orders that the property be sold and that Mrs Saggar should give vacant possession thereof.

In his first judgment the deputy judge found, first, that immediately prior to 17 November 1987 Mrs Saggar was a protected tenant of the whole of the property; secondly and on the basis of its agreed vacant possession value at that time (£75,000), that the intention of Mr Sat Bhambra was that it should appear to be sold to Mrs Saggar as a sitting tenant, whereas it was in fact to be sold to Mr Mallard at a reduced sum of £50,000; thirdly, that Mr Sat Bhambra was at the time under great pressure from his creditors; fourthly, that Mr Sat Bhambra made the transfer with the dominant purpose of removing assets from the reach of actual or potential claimants or creditors. On those findings he held that the requirements of s. 423(1)(c) and (3)(a) had been satisfied. Except for the finding as to Mrs Saggar's protected tenancy, none of those findings and holdings is questioned by Dr Chohan, the only party who has appealed to this court. Indeed, except for that one finding, he maintains that thus far the judge had been right at every point.

At the end of his first judgment the judge expressed the view that the transfer should be set aside. But he did not feel able to decide on the appropriate form of an order under s. 423(2) without hearing submissions on behalf of Chelsea Building Society. Having expressed some preliminary views, he therefore adjourned the hearing, so that if the form of order could not be agreed the matter could come back for further argument. No agreement having been reached, the matter was restored accordingly.

At this point it is convenient to refer to the material provisions of s. 423–425 of the 1986 Act. So far as material s. 423 provides:

> '(1) This section relates to transactions entered into at an undervalue; and a person enters into such a transaction with another person if. . .
>
> (c) he enters into a transaction with the other for a consideration the value of which, in money or money's worth, is significantly less than the value, in money or money's worth, of the consideration provided by himself.

(2) Where a person has entered into such a transaction, the court may, if satisfied   A
under the next subsection, make such order as it thinks fit for–

    (a) restoring the position to what it would have been if the transaction had not
       been entered into, and

    (b) protecting the interests of persons who are victims of the transaction.

(3) In the case of a person entering into such a transaction, an order shall only be
made if the court is satisfied that it was entered into by him for the purpose–   B

    (a) of putting assets beyond the reach of a person who is making, or may at
       some time make, a claim against him, or

    (b) of otherwise prejudicing the interests of such a person in relation to the claim
       which he is making or may make.

   . . .

                                                                          C

(5) In relation to a transaction at an undervalue, references here and below to a
victim of the transaction are to a person who is, or is capable of being, prejudiced
by it; and in the following two sections the person entering into the transaction is
referred to as "the debtor".'

Section 424 makes provision for those who may apply for an order under s. 423. It has
been accepted throughout that Dr Chohan is entitled to apply as 'a victim of the
transaction', within S. 424(1)(c). Subsection (2) provides that an application made under   D
any of the paragraphs of subs. (1) is to be treated as made on behalf of every victim of
the transaction. It must be emphasised that Mrs Saggar was not a victim of the
transaction.

Section 425(1) provides that, without prejudice to the generality of s. 423, an order
made under that section with respect to a transaction may have the specific effect or
effects which are then set out in the six following paragraphs. Section 425(2) provides: E

'An order under section 423 may affect the property of, or impose any obligation
on, any person whether or not he is the person with whom the debtor entered into
the transaction; but such an order–

    (a) shall not prejudice any interest in property which was acquired from a
       person other than the debtor and was acquired in good faith, for value and
       without notice of the relevant circumstances, or prejudice any interest   F
       deriving from such an interest, and

    (b) shall not require a person who received a benefit from the transaction in
       good faith, for value and without notice of the relevant circumstances to pay
       any sum unless he was a party to the transaction.'

By s. 425(3) 'the relevant circumstances' are defined as the circumstances by virtue of
which an order under s. 423 may be made in respect of the transaction.   G

In his second judgment, the judge started by rejecting a submission made on behalf of
Mrs Saggar that, since the court was not bound to make an order under s. 423(2), no
order should here be made. That point has not been revived in this court. Having then
identified a potential conflict between the provisions of s. 423(2)(a) and 425(2)(a), the
judge held that s. 423(2)(a) must be construed so as to provide for the restoration of the
antecedent position 'as far as possible'. Next he held that Chelsea Building Society was   H
an equitable mortgagee of the property from Mrs Saggar and was thus within the
protection conferred by s. 425(2)(a). Turning to Mrs Saggar, he decided, with some
hesitation, that he should seek by his order to give her some compensation for the loss of
her protected tenancy, since he did not find it possible to restore her to that position. He
concluded that he should make an order of the same kind as that made by Scott J in
Arbuthnot Leasing International Ltd v Havelet Leasing Ltd (No. 2) [1990] BCC 636.

A   Having declared that Mrs Saggar was a protected tenant of the property prior to her purchase, the judge's order dated 20 July 1992 contains a declaration that Chelsea Building Society is entitled to be registered as first legal chargee of the property and that the equity of redemption is held upon trust for Mrs Saggar and Mr Sat Bhambra in the shares mentioned at the beginning of this judgment. It then contains an order that the trust deed (but not the transfer) should be set aside, together with various ancillary orders.

B   As to that order, Dr Chohan says, first, that Mrs Saggar was a licensee and not a tenant of the property; secondly, that the judge's initial intention to set aside the transfer (which would necessarily have carried the trust deed with it) was correct and that it was not open to him merely to set aside the trust deed; thirdly, that if it was open to him not to set aside the transfer, the proportions of the beneficial interest in the equity of redemption assigned to Mrs Saggar and Mr Sat Bhambra respectively were wrong and

C   should be adjusted more favourably to Mr Sat Bhambra. Although he contended to the contrary by his notice of appeal, Dr Chohan now accepts that Chelsea Building Society is entitled to be registered as first legal chargee.

     I will deal first with the tenancy question, for which purpose some further recital of the facts is necessary, again for the most part in the judge's own words.

D   Mrs Saggar and Mr Gleeson moved into the property in January 1983. She occupied one bedroom with her young daughter and paid Mr Sat Bhambra a rent of some £25 per week. He maintained a rent book, in which the payments of rent were recorded and signed off by him. The other principal bedroom was kept by Mr Sat Bhambra for use by him as an office; initially it was kept locked. Mr Gleeson occupied a relatively minor bedroom, referred to as a box-room. Mr Gleeson and Mrs Saggar shared the use of the remaining rooms in the house, such as the bathroom, kitchen and sitting-room. Mr Sat

E   Bhambra came to the house from time to time and occasionally slept in it. There also appears to have been an occasion when guests of his slept there. But his visits were mainly for the purpose of collecting rent from the tenants and the occasions when he stayed overnight were very few.

     In July 1986, Mr Sat Bhambra apparently having no further use for the other principal bedroom, Mrs Saggar took over that room and used it as a bedroom for her daughter, paying an additional rent of £25 per week. In about August or September of the same

F   year Mr Gleeson moved out of the property, which was thereafter occupied only by Mrs Saggar and her daughter, although it appears that at infrequent intervals Mr Sat Bhambra did come there for his own purposes. However, those visits must have ended when he was sent to prison on 31 October 1986.

     On those facts, the judge decided that Mrs Saggar had become a tenant (necessarily a protected tenant) of the whole of the property before the freehold was transferred to her

G   on 17 November 1987. In spite of the submissions of Sir William Goodhart QC, for Dr Chohan, to the contrary, I think that the judge's decision was correct. Mr Sat Bhambra's giving up of the second principal bedroom, coupled with the payment of an additional weekly rent of £25 and the departure of Mr Gleeson very shortly afterwards, points unequivocally to the view that Mrs Saggar thereafter had exclusive possession (and therefore a tenancy – see *Street v Mountford* [1985] AC 809) of the whole of the property. That view of the matter is not at all invalidated by Mr Sat Bhambra's having made

H   infrequent visits for his own purposes between July and October 1986. The natural inference must be that once he had ceased to occupy the other principal bedroom and Mrs Saggar had started to pay an additional rent for it, his visits were not made pursuant to any enforceable legal right. Even if they were, I do not see how the reservation of some such minimal right could have reduced Mrs Saggar's status to that of a licensee. For these reasons, I would affirm the judge's decision on the tenancy question.

The next question is whether it was open to the judge to set aside the trust deed but   A
not the transfer. Here the judge recognised, correctly, that his power under s. 423(2) to
make an order restoring the position and protecting the interests of the victims of the
transaction was constricted by s. 425(2)(a), which made it necessary that the order should
not prejudice the interest of Chelsea Building Society, being an interest acquired from a
person (Mrs Saggar) other than the debtor in good faith, for value and without notice of
the relevant circumstances. The inevitable result, as the judge held, is that the power
under s. 423(2) is a power to restore and protect so far as is practicable. Moreover, it is   B
important to note that it is not expressed as a power to set aside the transaction. Provided
that it is exercised in order to restore the position and protect the interests of the victims
of the transaction so far as is practicable (see below), the whole or any part of the
transaction may be set aside. Thus, for example, where the transaction is made up of
more than one component the power may be exercised by setting aside one component
and not the other or others of them. Any lingering doubt on this question is dispelled by   C
a consideration of the wide range of possible orders specified in s. 425(1). It is clear that
Parliament intended the court to have much fuller powers than were previously available
under s. 172 of the *Law of Property Act* 1925. I therefore reject Sir William Goodhart's
submission that it was not open to the judge to set aside the trust deed but not the
transfer.

That brings me to the third and most difficult question we have to decide. The power   D
under s. 423(2) being one to make such order as the court thinks fit, did the judge, in
making a declaration that the equity of redemption in the property was held by Mrs
Saggar upon trust as to 19/75 parts for Mr Sat Bhambra and as to the remaining 56/75
parts for herself, err in principle?

It is accepted on all sides that the judge could not make an order restoring Mrs Saggar's
protected tenancy in the property, because that would have prejudiced the interest of
Chelsea Building Society. For the same reason he could not make an order restoring the   E
freehold to Mr Sat Bhambra. The course he adopted was to make an order giving Mr
Sat Bhambra and Mrs Saggar fractions of the beneficial interest in the equity of
redemption. In his second judgment [1992] BCC 750, the judge explained the fractions he
proposed to award as follows (at p. 755E):

> 'In my [first] judgment I found that a sale of the property, subject to Mrs Saggar's
> protected tenancy, to her for £50,000 would not, if completed, by payment by the   F
> purchaser of £50,000, be a sale at an undervalue. It was that part of the transaction
> which resulted from the declaration of trust and in particular the declaration in
> favour of Mr Mallard, whose role in the transaction was never clarified and who
> may or may not have been a simple nominee for Mr Bhambra, which led to my
> conclusion that this was a transaction at an undervalue. The plaintiff did not seek
> to contend that at the time of the transaction the property was not worth   G
> approximately £75,000 and that a discount of £25,000 on that price was not
> justified if Mrs Saggar was indeed, as I found, a protected tenant. The amount of
> the undervalue can, in my judgment, be reasonably assessed, as of 1987, as being
> that part of the purchase price shown on the declaration of trust as notionally
> being paid by Mr Mallard, namely £19,000. Given that it seems reasonable to
> assume that the property was then worth £75,000 it represented then 19/75ths of
> what the property might then be assumed to have realised if sold with vacant   H
> possession.'

Sir William Goodhart's initial attack on the judge's fractions was based on the
proposition that they wrongly assigned the whole of the 'marriage value' (i.e. the £25,000
difference between the value with vacant possession and the value subject to the tenancy)
to Mrs Saggar. He said that where landlord and tenant combined to make a sale with

A　vacant possession it was the invariable practice to divide the marriage value between them. However, Mr Ralls, for Mrs Saggar, objected that that was a new point on which evidence could have been led below; it could not therefore be taken for the first time in this court. In his reply Sir William, in my view correctly, recognised the force of that objection and the point was not pressed. But he still maintained that the judge's fractions were too favourable to Mrs Saggar. He said that the beneficial interest should be divided

B　in proportions corresponding to the actual or notional contributions of Mrs Saggar and Mr Sat Bhambra to the purchase price of £50,000, that is to say 31/50 to Mrs Saggar and 19/50 to Mr Sat Bhambra. He added that since Chelsea Building Society's charge had been incurred solely in order to assist Mrs Saggar in acquiring her interest in the property, the amount owing under it should be discharged wholly out of her share.

　　The object of s. 423–425 being to remedy the avoidance of debts, the 'and' between para. (a) and (b) of s. 423(2) must be read conjunctively and not disjunctively. Any order

C　made under that subsection must seek, so far as practicable, both to restore the position to what it would have been if the transaction had not been entered into and to protect the interests of the victims of it. It is not a power to restore the position generally, but in such a way as to protect the victims' interests; in other words, by restoring assets to the debtor to make them available for execution by the victims. So the first question the judge must ask himself is what assets have been lost to the debtor. His order should, so

D　far as practicable, restore that loss. A similar approach was adopted by Scott J in *Arbuthnot Leasing International Ltd v Havelet Leasing Ltd (No. 2)* [1990] BCC 636 at p. 645A, where in reference to s. 423(2)(a) he said:

　　'There is an element of discretion involved here implicit in the use of the word "may". But in my judgment the courts must set their faces against transactions which are designed to prevent plaintiffs in proceedings, creditors with unimpeachable debts, from obtaining the remedies by way of execution that the

E　law would normally allow them.'

　　Here, immediately before 17 November 1987, Mr Sat Bhambra was entitled to the property subject to the legal charge for £31,000-odd in favour of Anglia Building Society and subject also to Mrs Saggar's protected tenancy. If he had disposed of his interest in the open market on that date, he would, on the basis of the agreed tenanted value of £50,000, have received £19,000. Instead of that, the transaction into which he entered

F　brought him, or must be taken to have brought him, nothing. So the asset lost was an interest in the property worth £19,000.

　　How should that loss be restored? One possibility would have been to create a charge on the property for £19,000. An order of that kind is not sought by Dr Chohan. He seeks a share of the beneficial interest in the property and there can be no doubt that it was open to the judge to make an order in that form. Indeed, it is more in keeping with

G　s. 423(2) to replace one interest in the property with another. The question is whether it was open to the judge to make a disposition of the beneficial interest in the particular way that he did.

　　On the basis of the agreed vacant possession value of £75,000, the judge awarded Mr Sat Bhambra and Mrs Saggar shares of 19/75ths and 56/75ths respectively. In my view he was clearly right to work on that value, not on the tenanted value of £50,000, and also

H　to award Mr Sat Bhambra a share which, had the property been unencumbered, would have been worth £19,000. But I respectfully think that he was wrong, as between Mr Sat Bhambra and Mrs Saggar, to apply that share to the equity of redemption in the property. On the footing that the property was sold with vacant possession for £75,000 and that the amount outstanding under the legal charge in favour of Chelsea Building Society was £25,000 (the present amount of the debt), the judge's order would produce for Mr Sat Bhambra, not £19,000, but £12,666. It would not restore the asset lost.

The judge's order not having achieved what it could and ought to have achieved under s. 423(2), I am of the opinion that he erred in principle and that we in this court ought to vary his order by providing that as between Mr Sat Bhambra and Mrs Saggar the amount owing under the legal charge in favour of Chelsea Building Society should be debited wholly against her 56/75 share of the beneficial interest in the property. To that extent, and to that extent only, I would allow the appeal. This result, although more favourable to Dr Chohan and the other victims of the transaction than that which would be produced by the judge's order, is less favourable to them than the result for which Sir William Goodhart contended. On his approach and on the like footing as above, a sale would have produced for Mr Sat Bhambra, not £19,000, but £28,500. That would go further than is necessary to restore the asset lost.

Mr Ralls expressed concern at the prospect of the amount owing to Chelsea Building Society being debited wholly against Mrs Saggar's share. He assumed that that amount would include the society's costs of the proceedings both here and below, which have since been estimated by its solicitors at some £24,000. That may or may not prove to be the case, depending on what orders as to costs are made after judgment in this court. But if it is the case, the result, although regrettable, is inevitable. Mrs Saggar not having herself been a victim of the transaction, the practical effect of s. 423(2) and 425(2)(a) is to put Chelsea Building Society first, Dr Chohan and the other victims second and Mrs Saggar third.

Balcombe LJ: I agree.

Waite LJ: I also agree.

(*Order for costs below to remain. The Chelsea Building Society to be at liberty to add its costs of the appeal to its security. The plaintiff to pay Chelsea Building Society's costs of the appeal. Order not to be enforced in respect of costs incurred on or after 19 September 1992 without the leave of the court. If and so far as those costs had been added to the building society's security, the plaintiff to pay any amount owing under the order to Mrs Saggar. Full minute to be agreed by counsel. Apart from these orders, no order as to costs of the appeal except Legal Aid taxation of the costs of the plaintiff and Mrs Saggar*)

A

El Ajou v Dollar Land Holdings plc & Anor.

Court of Appeal (Civil Division).
Nourse, Rose and Hoffmann L JJ.
Judgment delivered 2 December 1993.

B
Knowing receipt of trust funds – Knowledge of company – Plaintiff victim of fraud sought to trace proceeds to company – Whether plaintiff could trace proceeds – Whether knowledge of director was attributable to company.

This was an appeal by the plaintiff from a judgment of Millett J [1993] BCC 698, raising the question whether, for the purposes of establishing a company's liability under the 'knowing receipt' head of constructive trust, the knowledge of one of its directors could be treated as the knowledge of the company.

C
The plaintiff was one of many victims of a massive share fraud carried out in Amsterdam by three Canadians between 1984 and 1985. He claimed to be able to trace some of the proceeds of the fraud from Amsterdam through intermediate resting places in Geneva, Gibraltar, Panama and Geneva (again) to London, where they were invested in a joint venture to carry out a property development project in Battersea in conjunction with the first defendant, Dollar Land Holdings plc ('DLH'). The plaintiff sought to recover from DLH, alleging that DLH's chairman, 'F', possessed the necessary knowledge attributable to DLH that the funds represented the proceeds of fraud.

D

On the question of F's knowledge the judge held that F's position as chairman and non-executive director of DLH was insufficient by itself to constitute his knowledge ipso facto the knowledge of DLH. He further held that F did not act as the agent of DLH in obtaining the money from the Canadians: F discovered that the Canadians were fraudsters and that their money had been obtained by fraud at a time when he was acting in his own interest and as a director of another company, and not as a director of DLH. In seeking finance on ordinary commercial terms, and in the absence of anything to put it on inquiry, DLH was not bound to inquire as to the source of the money it was offered; and, that being so, F was under no obligation to tell DLH what he knew. The judge also held that at the time of the relevant transaction (in March 1988) F had ceased to be a director of DLH for nine months, and he had nothing at all to do with the transaction: even if F's knowledge could have been attributed to DLH in 1986, it was wrong to treat DLH as still possessing that knowledge in 1988.

E

F

By a respondent's notice, DLH challenged the judge's finding that the plaintiff had established that the money in an account in Geneva, used to secure an advance to finance the project, represented the proceeds of the fraud, which had been remitted from Gibraltar to Panama.

G
The issues on the appeal were: the source of the money in the Geneva account; the identity of the assets received by DLH and the dates when it received them; and whether the admitted knowledge of the frauds on the part of F could be imputed to the company.

Held, allowing the appeal:

1. The judge's conclusions on the assets received by DLH were correct, as was his finding that the money could be traced to the proceeds of fraud by the Canadians.

H
2. The transactions to be considered were those by which DLH received assets representing the moneys fraudulently misapplied. The responsibility for the management and control of those transactions was not to be determined by identifying those who were responsible for deciding that DLH would participate in the project and the nature and extent of that participation, far less by identifying those who were responsible for business decisions generally. Millett J's unchallenged conclusion that the 'moving force' behind the company's

activities was 'S', although neither a director nor an employee, did not preclude a finding   A
that F was the company's directing mind and will in relation to some activities.

3. In relation to the relevant transactions, F as an individual exercised powers on behalf
of the company which identified him as the company's directing mind and will. So far as the
constitution of DLH was concerned, he committed the company to the transaction as an
autonomous act which the company adopted by performing the agreement.

4. It did not matter that by the time of the relevant transaction F had ceased to be a   B
director. Once his knowledge was treated as being the knowledge of the company in relation
to a given transaction, the company continued to be affected with that knowledge for any
subsequent stages of the same transaction.

5. F acquired his knowledge of the fraudulent misapplication as a director of another
company. As agent, he was under no obligation to disclose his knowledge to DLH, there
being no duty on DLH to enquire as to the source of the offered money. (*Re David Payne &*   C
Co Ltd [1904] 2 Ch 608 applied.)

The following cases were referred to in the judgments:

Baldwin v Casella (1872) LR 7 Ex 325.
Blackburn, Low & Co v Thomas Vigors (1887) 12 App Cas 531.
Blackley v National Mutual Life Association of Australasia Ltd [1972] NZLR 1038.
Carew's Estate Act, Re (No. 2) (1862) 31 Beav 39; 54 ER 1051.   D
Dresser v Norwood & Anor (1864) 17 CB(NS) 466; 144 ER 188.
Fenwick, Stobart & Co Ltd, Re [1902] 1 Ch 507.
Gladstone & Anor v King (1813) 1 M & S 35; 105 ER 13.
Hampshire Land Co, Re [1896] 2 Ch 743.
Kelly v Cooper & Anor [1993] AC 205.
Lennard's Carrying Co Ltd v Asiatic Petroleum Co Ltd [1915] AC 705.
Payne (David) & Co Ltd, Re [1904] 2 Ch 608.   E
Powles v Page (1846) 3 CB 16; 136 ER 7.
R v Andrews-Weatherfoil Ltd [1972] 1 WLR 118.
Regina Fur Co Ltd v Bossom [1957] 2 Ll Rep 466.
Tanham v Nicholson (1872) LR 5 HL 561.
Tesco Supermarkets Ltd v Nattrass [1972] AC 153.
Turton v London and North-Western Railway Co (1850) 15 LT(OS) 92.

   F

Michael Beloff QC, Roger Ellis and Sarah Moore (instructed by Bower Cotton &
Bower) for the appellant.

Romie Tager (instructed by Kaufman Kramer Shebson) for the respondents.

JUDGMENT

Nourse LJ: Introduction

   G

Of the questions that remain in dispute in this case, the most important is whether, for
the purposes of establishing a company's liability under the 'knowing receipt' head of
constructive trust, the knowledge of one of its directors can be treated as having been the
knowledge of the company. That is essentially a question of company law. There are or
have been other questions on tracing and constructive trust.

The company is the first defendant, Dollar Land Holdings plc ('DLH'). The director is   H
Mr Sylvain Ferdman, who was the chairman and one of the three directors of DLH
between June 1985 and June 1987. The party who seeks to recover against DLH in
constructive trust is the plaintiff, Abdul Ghani El Ajou. He has put his claim at £1.3m.
On 12 June 1992, after a trial extending over some 11 days, Millett J delivered a reserved
judgment dismissing the plaintiff's action [1993] BCC 698. He held that the plaintiff had
an equitable right to trace the money into the hands of DLH, but that Mr Ferdman's

A knowledge of their fraudulent misapplication could not be treated as having been the knowledge of DLH, either on the ground of his having been its directing mind and will or on the ground of his having been its agent in the transaction. The judge found that another person closely concerned with the affairs of DLH, Mr William Stern, did not have the requisite knowledge of the misapplication. The plaintiff now appeals to this court. He does not seek to upset the judge's finding in regard to Mr Stern. DLH has put in a respondent's notice whose primary purpose is to impugn the judge's finding as to one part of the tracing exercise.

B

Millett J's judgment is reported at [1993] BCC 698. Because the report sets out in full the judge's clear and necessarily lengthy statement of the facts and because the issues have narrowed in this court, the facts can now be stated relatively briefly. I will state them mainly in the judge's own words.

C   The facts

The plaintiff is a wealthy Arab businessman resident in Riyadh. He was the largest single victim, though only one of many victims, of a massive share fraud carried out in Amsterdam between 1984 and 1985 by three Canadians, Allan Lindzon (or Levinson), Lloyd Caplan and Harry Roth ('the Canadians'). Some of the proceeds of the fraud were passed from Amsterdam through intermediate resting places in Geneva, Gibraltar, Panama and Geneva (again) to London, where in 1986 they were invested in a joint

D venture to carry out a property development project at Nine Elms in Battersea in conjunction with DLH. The interest of the Canadians in the joint venture was bought out by DLH in 1988, which is a public limited company incorporated in England but resident for tax purposes in Switzerland. It is a holding company. Its principal activities, carried on through its subsidiaries, are property dealing and investment. At the material time it was in a substantial way of business. It denies that in 1986 it had any knowledge

E that the money which the Canadians invested in the project represented the proceeds of fraud. Moreover, in buying out their interest in 1988 it claims to have been a bona fide purchaser for value without notice of the fraud.

Mr Ferdman is a Swiss national, resident in Geneva. He worked for many years for the Bank of International Credit in Geneva. In 1972 he left the bank and set up his own company, Société d'Administration et de Financement SA ('SAFI'), through which he acted as a fiduciary agent. SAFI was originally owned jointly by Mr Ferdman and an

F old-established Swiss cantonal bank of good reputation, but in 1982 Mr Ferdman became its sole proprietor. SAFI acted as a fiduciary agent for clients who did not wish their identities to be disclosed. Two of its clients were Mr Singer and Mr Goldhar, who were associates of the Canadians. Mr Ferdman was accustomed to accept funds from clients without questioning their origin, and to act for clients who were anxious to conceal their identity. He regarded the need to preserve his clients' anonymity as paramount – without

G it he would have had no business – and to this end he was willing on occasion to present himself or SAFI as a beneficial owner and to make false statements to that effect. The judge found that it must have been plain to Mr Ferdman by the end of October 1985 that Singer and Goldhar were implicated in a fraud. Moreover, Mr Ferdman admitted to the judge at the trial that he knew perfectly well that the Canadians were involved with Singer and Goldhar in the fraud and were not just behind them. The Canadians also had a fiduciary agent resident in Geneva who acted for them. He was Mr David D'Albis, an

H American citizen.

DLH is an English company which was formerly listed on the London Stock Exchange. In June 1985 its entire issued share capital was acquired by Keristal Investments and Trading SA ('Keristal'), a Panamanian company beneficially owned by a Liechtenstein foundation. In the annual reports of DLH Mr Ferdman described himself as the beneficial owner of Keristal, but that was not the case. He was simply preserving

the anonymity of his principals, the founders and beneficiaries of the Liechtenstein   A
foundation, who were two US citizens resident in New York ('the Americans'). The judge
recorded that the plaintiff was satisfied that the Americans had no connection of any
kind with the Canadians or their associates or any of the other persons involved in the
fraud.

DLH was acquired as a vehicle for the Americans' property dealings in the United
Kingdom. Its business activities were under the direction of Mr William Stern, described   B
by the judge as a property dealer who suffered a spectacular and well-publicised
bankruptcy as a result of the 1974 property crash. He was engaged in the business of
identifying opportunities for property investment and introducing them to investors
willing to pay him a fee or a share in the eventual profits. Mr Stern had lived in Geneva
as a boy and was acquainted with Mr Ferdman. They became friends, though they lost
contact with each other for some years. Mr Stern knew that he was a fiduciary agent and   C
had established SAFI, which he believed still to be jointly owned by Mr Ferdman and a
reputable cantonal bank. From time to time he suggested deals to Mr Ferdman and
enquired of him whether he had any suitable investors among his clients.

Mr Ferdman introduced the Americans to Mr Stern, who was able to recommend a
successful investment in a UK property. The Americans were willing to make further
investments in the UK, and Mr Stern suggested that he should look for a suitable English
vehicle, if possible a quoted company, which they could acquire and use as a medium for   D
further investment. Mr Stern found DLH and Keristal acquired it as a pure cash shell in
June 1985. Mr Ferdman and Mr Favre and Mr Jaton, two fellow directors of SAFI, were
appointed to be the directors of DLH and Mr Ferdman its chairman. The judge described
the three of them as nominee directors representing the interests of the beneficial owners.
They played no part in the conduct of DLH's business which was carried on by Mr Stern
in consultation with the Americans. Mr Stern was not a director of DLH, but he was   E
appointed managing director of Dollar Land Management Ltd, one of its subsidiaries.
DLH was in a substantial way of business and was able to raise very large sums on the
security of its assets. At the end of 1986 it had secured bank loans and other mortgage
creditors of more than £10m. By the end of 1987 that figure had risen to more than £30m.

Mr Stern asked Mr Ferdman if he could find an investor willing to put up equity
finance for the Nine Elms project. Mr Ferdman, who was to receive from DLH an   F
introductory commission of five per cent of the funds obtained, brought one of the
Canadians, Roth, to London in March 1986 and introduced him to Mr Stern, who
provided him with a detailed investment proposal which included a profit forecast. All
negotiations were conducted between Roth and Mr Stern. Mr Ferdman played no part.
By a letter dated 20 March 1986 and addressed to Roth, care of SAFI in Geneva, the
terms which had been agreed between him and Mr Stern were set out. Although that
letter was signed by Mr Ferdman, it was composed entirely by Mr Stern. I will return to   G
it later in this judgment.

On 25 March Mr Ferdman copied the letter of 20 March (with two variations which
the judge inferred were made at the request of the Canadians) by telex to Mr D'Albis,
who gave instructions on the same day for £270,000 to be transferred from Geneva to
the Royal Bank of Scotland in London for the account of DLH's solicitors,
Grangewoods. The judge found that that sum represented proceeds of the fraud and that   H
finding has not been questioned in this court. Subsequently, Mr Ferdman despatched a
duplicate of the telex in the form of a letter on DLH's headed paper, and over his own
signature, to Yulara Realty Ltd ('Yulara') in Panama. That letter was dated 7 April.
Again, I will return to it later. Yulara was a Panamanian company owned by the
Canadians, which Mr Ferdman knew was a vehicle for their investment in the Nine Elms

A project. Mr Ferdman retained on his own files a copy of the letter countersigned by a Panamanian lawyer on behalf of Yulara by way of acceptance.

Contracts for the purchase of the Nine Elms site were exchanged on 26 March. The purchaser was a subsidiary of DLH, Dollar Land (London) Ltd ('DLH London'). The £270,000 which Grangewoods had received on the previous day was used to pay the deposit. On 11 June 1986 DLH London assigned the benefit of the contract to DLH for £100,000 and on the same day DLH entered into a contract for the sale of the site to

B Regalian Properties (Northern) Ltd ('Regalian'). Completion took place on the same day at a price of £2.7m, £1m of which was recorded as being paid by DLH.

The further funding of the project was complex. Reduced to its essentials, the method adopted was as follows. On 6 May 1986 Keristal (expressed to be represented by Mr Ferdman) and Yulara (expressed to be represented by the Panamanian lawyer) entered

C into a written loan agreement which was signed by them on behalf of Keristal and Yulara respectively. The agreement recited that Keristal was the holding company of DLH and that Yulara and DLH had entered into an agreement as per the letter dated 7 April. Article 1 was in substance a further recital to the effect that Yulara was making available or had given to Keristal (it is not clear which) the amount of up to $2.5m for as long as the agreement as per the letter of 7 April would be in force. By art. 2 Keristal accepted that amount on terms that it undertook to use the funds (a) 'in order to make a joint

D venture in a certain real estate investment in London' in accordance with the terms contained in the letter dated 7 April and (b) 'in order to [obtain] a bank guarantee of £1,300,000 to be issued in favour of [DLH London] or another company owned by [DLH]'.

On 12 and 16 May respectively two sums of $1,541,432 and $1,143,000, making a total of $2,684,432, were credited to an account of Keristal ('the Keristal No. 2 account') at

E Banque Scandinave in Geneva. The account was operated by SAFI and was used exclusively for the purpose of funding the Nine Elms project. The bank statement for the account shows that the first sum came from the Bank of America; the source of the second is not shown. The judge found that both sums were traceable to Panama as proceeds of the fraud. That is the finding which the respondent's notice seeks to impugn. I will return to it shortly.

F Pursuant to arrangements made by Mr Ferdman, Scandinavian Bank Group plc in London then agreed to advance £1.3m to Factotum NV ('Factotum'), a shelf company previously incorporated by Mr Ferdman in the Netherland Antilles, which he decided to make use of as a convenient vehicle for channelling the money to DLH. (Factotum is the second defendant in the action, but it has no assets and has never been served.) The advance was supported by a guarantee given by Banque Scandinave secured on the

G moneys in the Keristal No. 2 account. The whole of the loan from Scandinavian Bank in London to Factotum was drawn down and £1,030,000 was paid into Grangewoods' client account on 29 May. Of those moneys £745,598.60 were used to discharge the amount due from DLH on completion of the purchase of the site on 11 June. The balance was used to discharge obligations of DLH and to make various other payments at the direction of DLH, including payment to Mr Ferdman of his introductory commission of £65,000.

H It is clear from the foregoing that the £1,030,000 paid to Grangewoods represented moneys that had been credited to the Keristal No. 2 account. It is also clear that the moneys so credited belonged to the Canadians. What is in dispute is the judge's finding that they represented moneys which Mr D'Albis had sent to Panama from Gibraltar on 30 March and 1 April 1986, a fact that had to be established in order that they could be treated as proceeds of the fraud. It is convenient to deal with that question now.

Tracing through Panama

The question was dealt with by the judge between pp. 713 and 715. He said that the plaintiff was unable, by direct evidence, to identify the moneys in the Keristal No. 2 account with the money which Mr D'Albis had sent to Panama only a few weeks before. However, he thought that there was sufficient, though only just, to enable him to draw the necessary inference. At p. 713G, he continued:

> 'One of the two sums received in the Keristal No. 2 account was $1,541,432
> received on 12 May 1986 from Bank of America. That corresponds closely with the sum of $1,600,000 transferred to Bank of America, Panama on 1 April 1986. In relation to the later transaction, Bank of America may, of course, merely have been acting as a correspondent bank in New York and not as the paying bank; and the closeness of the figures could be a coincidence. It is not much, but it is something; and there is nothing in the opposite scale. The source of the other money received in the Keristal No. 2 account is not known, but from the way in which the Canadians appear to have dealt with their affairs, if one sum came from Panama, then the other probably did so too.'

At p. 714C, after considering other points on each side, the judge said that the fact remained that there was no evidence that the Canadians had any substantial funds available to them which did not represent proceeds of the fraud. At p. 715A, he concluded:

> 'In my judgment, there is some evidence to support an inference that the money which reached the Keristal No. 2 account represented part of the moneys which had been transmitted to Panama by the second tier Panamanian companies some six weeks previously, and the suggestion that it was derived from any other source is pure speculation.'

Mr Tager, for DLH, submitted that neither of the routes followed by the judge led to the conclusion that he reached. He took us carefully through the bank statement for the Keristal No. 2 account. He relied on the fact that there were two separate credits to it of very precise amounts, the second having been made four working days after the first. It had been impossible to identify the source of the second credit. All this suggested that the two credits had come from different sources. There was no necessary connection between the first and the sum of $1.6m that had been sent from Gibraltar to the Bank of America in Panama on 1 April. Mr Tager argued that there were other very substantial funds available to the Canadians. He disputed the judge's view that there was no evidence that they had any substantial funds available to them that did not represent proceeds of the fraud. He submitted that the plaintiff had not discharged the evidential burden of establishing the necessary link.

Having carefully considered these and other arguments of Mr Tager, I remain unconvinced that the judge drew the wrong inference. I well appreciate both that the question is of critical importance to the plaintiff's case and that, since it depends almost entirely, if not exclusively, on documentary evidence and undisputed events, we in this court are, in theory at any rate, in as good a position to draw an inference as the judge himself. In practice, however, the judge, after an 11 day trial, was in a much better position than we are. From all that I have seen and heard of the case, I would feel no confidence at all in saying that the judge had drawn the wrong inference.

The assets received by DLH

On the footing that the moneys credited to the Keristal No. 2 account were proceeds of the fraud, it becomes necessary to identify the assets received by DLH and the dates when it received them. The plaintiff's position is a simple one. He says that DLH received £270,000 on 25 March 1986 and a further £1,030,000 in June 1986 (though logically he

A ought to say on 29 May 1986, when the latter sum was paid into Grangewoods' client account; see further below). The judge considered these questions at pp. 716–717. He thought that the position was somewhat more complicated than the plaintiff would have had it.

As to the £270,000, the judge said, at p. 716G:

B 'The sum of £270,000 was never received by DLH. It was paid into Grangewoods' client account, and their client at the time must be taken to have been DLH London. DLH London was not a nominee or agent for DLH. As had previously been agreed between Roth and Mr Stern, it was the intended contractual purchaser of the site, and the money was to be used exclusively for the payment of the deposit on exchange of contracts. In my judgment, DLH did not receive the money at all, and DLH London did not receive it beneficially but upon trust to apply it for a specific purpose. DLH London used the money, as it was bound to do, to pay the

C deposit on the site, and thereby acquired for its own benefit a corresponding interest in the site which it subsequently sold and transferred to DLH. The plaintiff can follow his money through these various transactions, but the relevant asset capable of being identified as having been received by DLH is an interest in the site corresponding to the payment of the deposit.'

This question depends on the true construction and effect of the letter of 20 March

D 1986. Both Mr Beloff QC, for the plaintiff, and Mr Tager referred to its terms at some length in order to determine whether DLH London had acted as principal or as agent for DLH. Although he was not greatly concerned either way, Mr Beloff submitted that DLH London had acted as agent and that the £270,000 was accordingly received by DLH on 25 March. But in my view the judge was right, as a matter of construction, to conclude that DLH London, and not DLH itself, was the principal, so that it was that company that was Grangewoods' client when the money was received. I therefore agree with the

E judge that DLH did not receive anything on 25 March, but that on the assignment of the benefit of the contract to it on 11 June it received an interest in the site corresponding to the payment of the deposit.

As to the balance of £1,030,000, the judge said, at p. 717A:

'The sum of £1,030,000 was also paid into Grangewoods' client account, but by then their client had become DLH. The money was disbursed on the instructions

F and for the benefit of DLH. Only £745,598.60 was used to pay the money due to the vendor on completion, but this was the result of the arrangements which DLH had made with Regalian. So far as Yulara is concerned, the whole £1.3m must be taken to have been disbursed as agreed between them on the acquisition of a 40 per cent interest in the project. Moreover, in my judgment, on a proper analysis of the transaction between Yulara and DLH, Yulara's money should be treated as having been invested in its share of the project, and not in or towards the

G acquisition of DLH's share.

The investment proved highly successful. In itself it was not a breach of trust and caused the plaintiff no loss. Had he been able to intervene before the Canadians were bought out, he could have claimed the whole of Yulara's interest in the project; but whatever the extent of DLH's knowledge of the source of Yulara's funds, his claim would have been confined to Yulara's interest in exoneration of

H that of DLH. In the events which have happened, the plaintiff is in my judgment bound to treat his money as represented by Yulara's interest in the project, and must rely exclusively on the transaction on 16 March 1988 when Yulara's interest was bought out by DLH.'

For a reason which will become clear when I deal with the question whether Mr Ferdman was the directing mind and will of DLH, Mr Beloff expressed greater concern

at the judge's decision of this question. However, subject to one point, I feel unable to   A
differ from his reasoning on it.

I am puzzled by the judge's suggestion that by the time the £1,030,000 was paid into
Grangewoods' client account their client had become DLH. At p. 709F he had found
that that payment was made on 29 May, before the assignment of the benefit of the
contract by DLH London to DLH on 11 June. However, this point (which was not
addressed in argument), though it may be of importance in relation to the date at which
DLH must be treated as having had knowledge of the fraud (see below), does not affect   B
the judge's view of the asset received by DLH in respect of the £1,030,000 and the date
when it received it.

Knowledge

It having been established that DLH received assets representing proceeds of the fraud,
I come to the question of knowledge. By the end of the hearing there could have been no   C
doubt that Mr Ferdman himself had the requisite knowledge. At p. 718H, the judge said
of him:

> 'He freely admitted that he knew that the persons who were providing the money
> for the Nine Elms project were the persons who had been behind the fraud in
> Amsterdam; and that by 7 April 1986, when he signed the letter to Yulara, he knew
> (or assumed) that the money which he would be receiving into the Keristal No. 2   D
> account was part of the proceeds of the fraud.'

Thus arises the most important question remaining in dispute, which is whether Mr
Ferdman's knowledge can be treated as having been the knowledge of DLH. The plaintiff
contends that it can and ought to be, first, on the ground that Mr Ferdman was, in
relation to DLH's receipt of the assets representing the moneys fraudulently misapplied,
its directing mind and will; secondly and alternatively, on the ground that he was its
agent in the transaction. Because a company's directing mind and will are often the mind   E
and will of one or more of its directors and because a director is for many purposes an
agent of the company, there is a danger of confusion between the two grounds on which
the plaintiff relies. But they are, as the judge made clear, quite separate. The plaintiff can
succeed on either. The convenient course is to deal with the law and the facts in regard to
each of them in turn.

Directing mind and will

This doctrine, sometimes known as the alter ego doctrine, has been developed, with no
divergence of approach, in both criminal and civil jurisdictions, the authorities in each
being cited indifferently in the other. A company having no mind or will of its own, the
need for it arises because the criminal law often requires mens rea as a constituent of the
crime, and the civil law intention or knowledge as an ingredient of the cause of action or
defence. In the oft-quoted words of Viscount Haldane LC in *Lennard's Carrying Co Ltd*   G
v Asiatic Petroleum Co Ltd [1915] AC 705 at p. 713:

> 'My Lords, a corporation is an abstraction. It has no mind of its own any more
> than it has a body of its own; its active and directing will must consequently be
> sought in the person of somebody who for some purposes may be called an agent,
> but who is really the directing mind and will of the corporation, the very ego and
> centre of the personality of the corporation.'   H

The doctrine attributes to the company the mind and will of the natural person or
persons who manage and control its actions. At that point, in the words of Millett J at
p. 719B:

> 'Their minds are its mind; their intention its intention; their knowledge its
> knowledge.'

A It is important to emphasise that management and control is not something to be considered generally or in the round. It is necessary to identify the natural person or persons having management and control in relation to the act or omission in point. This was well put by Eveleigh J in delivering the judgment of the Criminal Division of this court in *R v Andrews-Weatherfoil Ltd* [1972] 1 WLR 118 at p. 124C:

B 'It is necessary to establish whether the natural person or persons in question have the status and authority which in law makes their acts in the matter under consideration the acts of the company so that the natural person is to be treated as the company itself.'

Decided cases show that, in regard to the requisite status and authority, the formal position, as regulated by the company's articles of association, service contracts and so forth, though highly relevant, may not be decisive. Here Millett J adopted a pragmatic approach. In my view he was right to do so, although it has led me, with diffidence, to a conclusion different from his own.

C DLH contends that its directing mind and will in relation to its receipt of the assets representing the moneys fraudulently misapplied were either the mind and will of Mr Stern alone or of Mr Stern and the Americans together. They were not the mind and will of Mr Ferdman. The judge's acceptance of this contention is expressed at p. 719D:

D 'In 1986 [DLH's] directors were all officers of SAFI, but they were merely nominee directors representing the interests of the Americans. Mr Ferdman was a non-executive director. His only executive responsibilities were to act as a fiduciary agent, represent the interests of the Americans, and ensure that the necessary corporate documentation was in order. The witnesses agreed that, in the early days of DLH, Mr Ferdman played a bigger role than he did [later]; but I do not think that that was due to any change in his role. He was always responsible for the formal paper work, but not for the business. As the business expanded, so his relative importance diminished. Even in 1986, he played no part in business decisions. These were taken by Mr Stern in consultation with the Americans. In my judgment, Mr Ferdman's position as chairman and non-executive director of DLH was insufficient by itself to constitute his knowledge ipso facto the knowledge of DLH.

F It has not been alleged, still less established, that the other two officers of SAFI, who with Mr Ferdman constituted the board of DLH in 1986, shared Mr Ferdman's knowledge of the source of the Canadians' money, but in my judgment it would make no difference if they did. Like Mr Ferdman, they were merely nominee directors with non-executive responsibility. They had no authority to take business decisions. In relation to its business affairs in 1986, neither Mr Ferdman alone nor the board as a whole can realistically be regarded as the directing mind

G and will of DLH.'

In disagreeing with the judge on this question, I start from the position that the transactions to be considered are those by which DLH received assets representing the moneys fraudulently misapplied. The responsibility for the management and control of those transactions is not to be determined by identifying those who were responsible for deciding that DLH would participate in the Nine Elms project and the nature and extent of that participation, far less by identifying those who were responsible for business

H decisions generally. Neither Mr Stern nor the Americans made any of the arrangements for the receipt or disbursement of the moneys by Grangewoods. Nor did they commit DLH to the obligations correlative to their receipt. None of them had the authority to do so. That was the responsibility of Mr Ferdman. The crucial considerations are that Mr Ferdman made all the arrangements for the receipt and disbursement of the £270,000 and the £1,030,000; that it was he who signed the letter of 20 March to Roth; that it was

he who, on 25 March, copied that letter to Mr D'Albis; that it was he who signed and   A
despatched the letter of 7 April to Yulara; that it was he who, on 6 May, signed the
agreement with Yulara; and that it was those steps that caused DLH to become involved
in the project and enabled it later to acquire the assets representing the moneys
fraudulently misapplied.

Each of the steps taken by Mr Ferdman was taken without the authority of a resolution
of the board of DLH. That demonstrates that as between Mr Ferdman on the one hand
and Mr Favre and Mr Jaton on the other it was Mr Ferdman who had the de facto   B
management and control of the transactions. It may be that that state of affairs involved
some breach of the directors' duties to DLH. But that would not enable DLH to say that
Mr Favre and Mr Jaton were parties to its directing mind and will in any relevant respect.
Mr Tager sought to show that they did perform duties as directors of DLH. No doubt
they did. But there is no real evidence that they had any responsibility for the transactions
in question. In my view the directing mind and will of DLH in relation to the relevant   C
transactions between March and June 1986 were the mind and will of Mr Ferdman and
none other. That means that DLH had the requisite knowledge at that time.

Next, I must consider whether the plaintiff's right to recover is affected by Mr
Ferdman's having ceased to be a director of DLH in June 1987. This question is of
significance only in relation to the £1,030,000. It has no bearing on the £270,000. At p.
721B, Millett J, having repeated his view that, in regard to the £1,030,000, the relevant   D
transaction was the acquisition by DLH of Yulara's interest in the joint venture on 16
March 1988, continued:

> 'By then Mr Ferdman had ceased to be a director of DLH for nine months, and he
> had nothing at all to do with the transaction. Even if, contrary to my judgment,
> Mr Ferdman's knowledge should be attributed to DLH in 1986, it would be quite
> wrong to treat DLH as still possessing that knowledge in 1988. As Megarry V-C
> pointed out in *Re Montagu's Settlement Trust* [1987] Ch 264 at p. 284, a natural   E
> person should not be said to have knowledge of a fact that he once knew if at the
> time in question he has genuinely forgotten all about it. In my judgment, where the
> knowledge of a director is attributed to a company, but is not actually imparted to
> it, the company should not be treated as continuing to possess that knowledge
> after the director in question has died or left its service. In such circumstances, the
> company can properly be said to have "lost its memory".'
                                                                                            F
While I might agree with the judge that the knowledge of a director, who had known
of a misapplication of trust moneys at the time of their misapplication but had genuinely
forgotten all about it by the time that they were received by the company, could not be
attributed to the company, I am unable to see how that can assist DLH here. The steps
that caused DLH to become involved in the project and enabled it later to acquire the
asset representing the £1,030,000 were all taken between March and June 1986.
Moreover, although the judge held that the plaintiff was bound to treat the £1,030,000 as   G
represented by Yulara's interest in the project, he found, at p. 709F, that that sum had
been paid into Grangewoods' client account on 29 May 1986 and had thereafter been
wholly disbursed as directed by DLH, £745,000 approximately in satisfaction of the
purchase price. In the circumstances, DLH having had the requisite knowledge at the
time that it became involved in the project and when the £1,030,000 was disbursed as it
directed, it would in my view be unrealistic to hold that it ceased to have that knowledge
simply because the mind and will that had been the source of it played no part in the   H
receipt of the asset itself. I am therefore of the opinion that DLH is on this ground liable
to the plaintiff in constructive trust.

Agency

Although the views so far expressed are enough to dispose of the appeal in favour of
the plaintiff, I turn briefly to the alternative question whether Mr Ferdman's knowledge

A   ought to be imputed to DLH, on the ground that he acted as DLH's agent in the transaction.

Millett J thought that it was not accurate to describe Mr Ferdman as having acted as the agent of DLH in obtaining money from the Canadians. I am not sure that I would agree with him on that question. The real question is whether Mr Ferdman acted as the agent of DLH in the transactions by which it received assets representing the moneys fraudulently misapplied. I find it unnecessary to answer either question. That is because

B   I agree with the judge that, even if Mr Ferdman was DLH's agent, his knowledge could not, as a matter of law, be imputed to it.

It is established on the authorities that the knowledge of a person who acquires it as a director of one company will not be imputed to another company of which he is also a director, unless he owes, not only a duty to the second company to receive it, but also a duty to the first to communicate it: see *Re Hampshire Land Co* [1896] 2 Ch 743 and *Re*

C   *Fenwick, Stobart & Co Ltd* [1902] 1 Ch 507.

Mr Ferdman acquired his knowledge of the fraudulent misapplication as a director of SAFI. I do not doubt that he owed a duty to DLH to receive it. But I agree with the judge that he owed no duty to SAFI to communicate it. I also agree with him that the facts of this case are indistinguishable in any material respect from those in *Re David Payne & Co Ltd* [1904] 2 Ch 608.

D

Conclusion

I would allow the appeal. On that footing, it becomes necessary to consider the relief to which the plaintiff is entitled, a consideration so far made unnecessary by the judge's dismissal of the action. Although it would be possible for this court to deal with that question itself, I think it preferable to remit it for consideration by the judge.

E   **Rose LJ:** I gratefully adopt the recital of facts in the judgment of Nourse LJ. For the reasons which he gives, I agree that the appellant's submissions with regard to the payment of the deposit and the balance of the money fail. The judge's conclusions, namely that the deposit was paid to Dollar Land Holdings London beneficially and that the balance was received by DLH on trust to invest on behalf of Yulara pursuant to a joint venture agreement, were, on the evidence before him, correct. Equally, the judge's

F   finding, which DLH seek to challenge, that the money can be traced to the proceeds of fraud by the Canadians, is, in my view, unimpeachable.

The submissions with regard to the role of Ferdman and whether his knowledge of the fraudulent origin of the invested funds should be attributed to DLH raise considerations of more general importance. In English law the concept of a company's directing mind and will has its origins in the speech of Viscount Haldane LC in *Lennard's Carrying Co Ltd v Asiatic Petroleum Co Ltd* [1915] AC 705 at p. 713. In *Tesco Supermarkets Ltd v*

G   *Nattrass* [1972] AC 153, Lord Diplock at p. 200A identified those who are to be treated in law as being the company as:

> 'those natural persons who by the memorandum and articles of association or as a result of action taken by the directors, or by the company in general meeting pursuant to the articles, are entrusted with the exercise of the powers of the company.'

H   Lord Reid at p. 171F said:

> 'Normally the board of directors, the managing director and perhaps other superior officers of a company carry out the functions of management and speak and act as the company . . . But the board of directors may delegate some part of their functions of management giving to their delegate full discretion to act independently of instructions from them.'

At p. 190G Lord Pearson said: A

'There are some officers of a company who may for some purposes be identified
with it, as being or having its directing mind and will, its centre and ego, and its
brains . . . The reference in section 20 of the Trades Descriptions Act 1968 to "any
director, manager, secretary or other similar officer of the body corporate" affords
a useful indication of the grades of officers who may for some purposes be
identifiable with the company . . .'   B

There are, it seems to me, two points implicit, if not explicit, in each of these passages.
First, the directors of a company are, prima facie, likely to be regarded as its directing
mind and will whereas particular circumstances may confer that status on non-directors.
Secondly, a company's directing mind and will may be found in different persons for
different activities of the company.

It follows that Millett J's unchallenged conclusion that Stern, although neither a   C
director nor an employee, was the 'moving force' behind the company's activities does
not preclude a finding that Ferdman was the company's directing mind and will in
relation to some activities.

In the present case, the company's activity to which Ferdman's knowledge was
potentially pertinent was the receipt of over £1m for investment. Ferdman had been
appointed by the Americans for two reasons in particular: first, as a Swiss resident
operating the formal aspects of the company he was able to confer the tax advantages of D
non-resident status on DLH on the basis that its 'central management and control' was
in Switzerland not England; and secondly because the Americans did not want Stern to
be seen to have any official role in the company. Ferdman was a director and chairman
of the board and his services were charged for at a higher rate than that for other
directors. He instructed accountants and solicitors. He convened meetings. He claimed
in the company's accounts to be its ultimate beneficiary. He was a necessary signatory of E
legal documents and signed the Yulara agreement without needing the authority of a
board resolution to do so: by so doing he committed the company to that agreement.

Having regard to these matters, it seems to me to be plain that, for the limited purposes
here relevant, i.e. the receipt of money and the execution of the Yulara agreement, he was
the directing mind and will of the company. In consequence, his knowledge of the fraud
was DLH's knowledge and, in this respect, I differ from Millett J. It is immaterial that
by March 1988, when DLH acquired Yulara's interest, Ferdman had ceased to be a   F
director. That cessation did not deprive DLH of its continuing knowledge in relation to
the transaction, which embraced both the initial receipt of the money in May 1986 and
the ultimate acquisition of Yulara's interest.

If the appellant does not succeed on this point, Mr Beloff's alternative submission
based on agency is, in my view, doomed to fail. This court is, in my judgment, bound to
hold, on the authority of *Re David Payne* [1904] 2 Ch 608 that, qua agent, Ferdman was   G
under no obligation to disclose his knowledge to DLH, there being no duty on DLH to
enquire as to the source of the offered money. I agree with Hoffmann LJ's analysis of the
three categories of agency cases to which he refers and with his conclusion that they have
no application in the present circumstances. To the extent indicated I would allow this
appeal.

Hoffmann LJ: This is a claim to enforce a constructive trust on the basis of knowing
receipt. For this purpose the plaintiff must show, first, a disposal of his assets in breach   H
of fiduciary duty; secondly, the beneficial receipt by the defendant of assets which are
traceable as representing the assets of the plaintiff; and thirdly, knowledge on the part of
the defendant that the assets he received are traceable to a breach of fiduciary duty.

There is no dispute that the first requirement is satisfied. The Canadians bribed the
plaintiff's fiduciary agent to give them over US $10m of his money in return for worthless

A   shares. The argument in this appeal has been over, first, which assets were received beneficially by DLH; secondly, whether they are traceable as representing the plaintiff's money; and thirdly, whether the admitted knowledge of the frauds on the part of Mr Ferdman, chairman of DLH, can be imputed to the company.

(1) Identifying the assets beneficially received

B   The judge has found as a fact that certain assets received by DLH, namely the benefit of the deposit paid under the contract for the purchase of the Nine Elms site and Yulara's interest in the development, were traceable in equity as proceeds of fraud. Both sides have challenged certain aspects of this finding.

(a) *The deposit*

C   The plaintiff says that the asset received by DLH was not the benefit of the deposit but the money used to pay it. This had been sent on 25 March 1986 to DLH's subsidiary DLH London, which entered into the contract to buy the site and afterwards assigned that contract (with the benefit of the deposit) to DLH. The plaintiff says that DLH London received the money as agent for DLH. The only evidence for this claim is that it was paid pursuant to an agreement between Roth and DLH. But that in my judgment is no reason why DLH London should not have received the money beneficially and this
D   would be consistent with its having been the contracting party and subsequently assigning that contract for a substantial consideration to DLH.

(b) *The main investment*

The plaintiff says that the other asset received by DLH was not Yulara's interest in the project, which it acquired on 16 March 1988, but the £1,030,000 invested by Yulara on 29 May 1986. In my judgment the judge was right in holding that money was not received
E   by DLH beneficially but on trust to invest on behalf of Yulara. DLH and Yulara were joint venturers. Yulara was making an equity investment by which it acquired a proprietary interest in half the share of profits due to DLH under its arrangements with Regalian and the benefit of a guarantee by DLH that its capital would be repaid. DLH received no part of this investment beneficially until it bought out Yulara's interest.

F   (2) Tracing

DLH challenges the judge's finding that the money can be traced to the proceeds of fraud which the Canadians had remitted to Panama. In my view, this was a finding which the judge was entitled to make. Mr Tager says that it might have been the proceeds of frauds on other people or even the money realised by the Canadians when they sold the business. It might have been, but as against the plaintiff I do not think that the Canadians would have been entitled to say so. Nor is DLH. The mixed fund was impressed with an
G   equitable charge in favour of the plaintiff which was enforceable against the Canadians and persons claiming under them.

(3) Knowledge

The judge correctly analysed the various capacities in which Mr Ferdman was involved in the transaction between DLH and the Canadians. First, he acted as a broker,
H   introducing the Canadians to DLH in return for a five per cent commission. In this capacity he was not acting as agent for DLH but as an independent contractor performing a service for a fee. Secondly, he was authorised agent of DLH to sign the agreement with Yulara. Thirdly, he was at all material times a director and chairman of the board of DLH. There are two ways in which Mr Ferdman's knowledge can be attributed to DLH. The first is that as agent of DLH his knowledge can be imputed to

the company. The second is that for this purpose he *was* DLH and his knowledge was its   A
knowledge. The judge rejected both.

(a) *The agency theory*

The circumstances in which the knowledge of an agent is imputed to the principal can
vary a great deal and care is needed in analysing the cases. They fall into a number of
categories which are not always sufficiently clearly distinguished. I shall mention three
such categories because they each include cases on which Mr Beloff placed   B
undifferentiated reliance. In fact, however, they depend upon distinct principles which
have no application in this case.

(i) Agent's knowledge affecting performance or terms of authorised contract

First, there are cases in which an agent is authorised to enter into a transaction in
which his own knowledge is material. So for example, an insurance policy may be avoided   C
on account of the broker's failure to disclose material facts within his knowledge, even
though he did not obtain that knowledge in his capacity as agent for the insured. As Lord
Macnaghten said in *Blackburn, Low & Co v Vigors* (1887) 12 App Cas 531 at p. 542:

> 'But that is not because the knowledge of the agent is to be imputed to the principal
> but because the agent of the assured is bound as the principal is bound to
> communicate to the underwriters all material facts within his knowledge.'

   D

In this category fall two of the cases upon which Mr Beloff QC relied, namely *Turton
v London and North-Western Railway Co* (1850) 15 LT(OS) 92 and *Dresser v Norwood*
(1864) 17 CB(NS) 466. In the former case the agent was authorised to conclude a contract
of carriage on behalf of the principal. The agent's knowledge of the carrier's standard
terms of business was held sufficient to enable those terms to be treated as included in the
contract. The agent, said Pollock CB, 'made the same contract in this case as if he had
made it for himself'. In the latter case, the agent was authorised to enter into a contract   E
for the purchase of wood. His knowledge that the vendor was a factor dealing for a
principal was held sufficient to enable the contract to be treated as made with the
principal and so preclude the purchaser from relying on a set-off against the factor.
Neither are cases of imputation of knowledge. Rather, the agent's knowledge affects the
terms or performance of the contract which he concludes on behalf of his principal.

These principles have no application in this case. We are not concerned with the   F
contractual terms upon which DLH received the traceable assets but whether it had the
knowledge which would impose a constructive trust. In other words, real imputation of
knowledge is required.

(ii) Principal's duty to investigate or make disclosure

Secondly, there are cases in which the principal has a duty to investigate or to make
disclosure. The duty to investigate may arise in many circumstances, ranging from an   G
owner's duty to inquire about the vicious tendencies of his dog (*Baldwin v Casella* (1872)
LR 7 Ex 325) to the duty of a purchaser of land to investigate the title. Or there may be
something about a transaction by which the principal is 'put on inquiry'. If the principal
employs an agent to discharge such a duty, the knowledge of the agent will be imputed
to him. (There is an exception, the scope of which it is unnecessary to discuss, in cases in
which the agent commits a fraud against the principal.) Likewise in cases in which the   H
principal is under a duty to make disclosure (for example, to an insurer) he may have to
disclose not only facts of which he knows but also material facts of which he could expect
to have been told by his agents. So in *Gladstone v King* (1813) 1 M & S 35; 105 ER 13 a
marine insurance policy was avoided because the master of the ship knew that it had
suffered damage, even though he had not in fact communicated this information to the
owner. The case of *Regina Fur Co Ltd v Bossom* [1957] 2 Ll Rep 466 upon which

A Mr Beloff strongly relied, also concerned the duty to make disclosure under an insurance policy and therefore falls within the same category.

None of these cases are relevant because in receiving the traceable assets, DLH had no duty to investigate or make disclosure. There was nothing to put it on inquiry.

(iii) Agent authorised to receive communications

B Thirdly, there are cases in which the agent has actual or ostensible authority to receive communications, whether informative (such as the state of health of an insured: *Blackley v National Mutual Life Association* [1972] NZLR 1038) or performative (such as a notice to quit: *Tanham v Nicholson* (1872) LR 5 HL 561) on behalf of the principal. In such cases, communication to the agent is communication to the principal. These cases also have no application here. Mr Ferdman did not receive information about the frauds in his capacity as agent for DLH. He found it out while acting for the Canadians.

C

(iv) Agent's duty to principal irrelevant

What it therefore comes to is that Mr Ferdman, an agent of DLH, had private knowledge of facts into which DLH had no duty to inquire. Mr Beloff said that Mr Ferdman nevertheless owed DLH a duty to disclose those facts. He then submits that because he had such a duty, DLH must be treated as if he had discharged it.

D I am inclined to agree that Mr Ferdman did owe a duty, both as broker employed by DLH to find an investor and as chairman of the board, to inform DLH that the Yulara money was the proceeds of fraud. I reject Mr Tager's submission, based on *Kelly v Cooper* [1993] AC 205, that no term can be implied in a contract with a Swiss fiduciary agent which requires him to disclose that the money for which he is being paid a five per cent procurement commission has been stolen. There is no evidence that Switzerland will enforce a confidence in iniquity any more than this country.

E But Mr Beloff's submission that DLH must be treated as if the duty had been discharged raises an important point of principle. In my judgment the submission is wrong. The fact that an agent owed a duty to his principal to communicate information may permit a court to infer as a fact that he actually did so. But this is a rebuttable inference of fact and in the present case the judge found that Mr Ferdman did not disclose what he knew to anyone else acting on behalf of DLH. In some of the cases in F the third of the categories I have mentioned, the fact that an agent with authority to receive a communication had a duty to pass the communication on to his principal is mentioned as a reason why the principal should be treated as having received it. I think, however, that the true basis of these cases is that communication to the agent is treated, by reason of his authority to receive it, as communication to the principal. I know of no authority for the proposition that in the absence of any duty on the part of the principal G to investigate, information which was received by an agent otherwise than as agent can be imputed to the principal simply on the ground that the agent owed to his principal a duty to disclose it.

On the contrary, I agree with the judge that *David Payne & Co Ltd* [1904] 2 Ch 608 at p. 611 is authority against such a proposition. In that case the Exploring Land and Minerals Co Ltd lent £6,000 to David Payne & Co Ltd for 30 days on the security of a debenture. One Kolckmann, a stockbroker who was concerned in an ambitious and H somewhat dubious scheme of flotation involving David Payne & Co Ltd, was also a director of the Exploring Land Co. In his capacity as stockbroker he knew that the money would not be applied to any authorised purpose of the company but diverted to the use of its controlling shareholder. He actually signed the cheque by which the money was advanced. David Payne & Co Ltd went into liquidation and the liquidator challenged the validity of the debenture on the ground that Kolckmann's knowledge of the ultra

vires purposes for which the money would be used should be imputed to the Exploring   A
Land Co.

Buckley J appears to have assumed that, as a director of the Exploring Land Co,
Kolckmann owed a duty to disclose what he knew about the real purposes for which the
money would be used. But he regarded this as insufficient to enable that knowledge to be
imputed to the company. He said at p. 611 (emphasis added):

> 'I understand the law to be this: that if a communication be made to his agent   B
> *which it would be his duty to hand on to his principals . . .* and if the agent has an
> interest which would lead him not to disclose to his principals the information that
> he has thus obtained, and in point of fact he does not communicate it, you are not
> to impute to his principals knowledge by reason of the fact that their agent knew
> something which it was not in his interest to disclose and which he did not disclose.'

It is true that in the Court of Appeal, both Vaughan-Williams LJ and Romer LJ said   C
that Kolckmann owed no duty to impart his knowledge to the Exploring Land Co. Thus
Romer LJ said at p. 619:

> 'I take it that in such a transaction the lending company was not bound to inquire
> as to the application of the money at all by the borrowing company. That being
> so, it appears to me that knowledge independently acquired by a director in his
> personal capacity in respect to a matter which was irrelevant so far as concerned   D
> the lending company is knowledge which cannot be imputed to the company, for
> it was knowledge of something which did not really concern the lending company
> as a matter of law. Therefore, you cannot imply a duty on the part of the director
> to have told these facts to the lending company, or a duty on the part of the lending
> company to have inquired into that question . . .'

It is however clear from the process of reasoning that what Romer LJ means is that in
the absence of a duty to inquire, there was no duty of disclosure on the part of the   E
director on which an outsider could rely for the purpose of imputing his knowledge to
the company. I do not think that it would have affected his conclusion if the director had
for some other reason (e.g. some internal company rule) owed a duty of disclosure with
which he did not in fact comply. I agree with Buckley J that this would have been
irrelevant.

It follows that in my judgment Millett J was right to hold that Mr Ferdman's position   F
as agent or broker does not enable his knowledge to be imputed to DLH.

(b) *The 'directing mind and will' theory*

The phrase 'directing mind and will' comes from a well-known passage in the judgment
of Viscount Haldane LC in *Lennard's Carrying Co Ltd v Asiatic Petroleum Co Ltd* [1915]
AC 705 which distinguishes between someone who is 'merely a servant or agent' and   G
someone whose action (or knowledge) is that of the company itself. Despite their
familiarity, it is worth quoting the terms in which Viscount Haldane said that the
directing mind could be identified (at p. 713):

> 'That person may be under the direction of the shareholders in general meeting;
> that person may be the board of directors itself, or it may be, and in some
> companies it is so, that that person has an authority co-ordinate with the board of   H
> directors given to him under the articles of association, and is appointed by the
> general meeting of the company, and can only be removed by the general meeting
> of the company. My Lords, whatever is not known about Mr Lennard's position,
> this is known for certain, Mr Lennard took the active part in the management of
> this ship on behalf of the owners, and Mr Lennard, as I have said, was registered
> as the person designated for this purpose in the ship's register.'

A   Viscount Haldane therefore regarded the identification of the directing mind as primarily a constitutional question, depending in the first instance upon the powers entrusted to a person by the articles of association. The last sentence about Mr Lennard's position shows that the position as reflected in the articles may have to be supplemented by looking at the actual exercise of the company's powers. A person held out by the company as having plenary authority or in whose exercise of such authority the company acquiesces, may be treated as its directing mind.

B   It is well known that Viscount Haldane derived the concept of the 'directing mind' from German law (see *Gower's Principles of Modern Company Law* (5th edn, 1992) p. 194, note 36) which distinguishes between the agents and organs of the company. A German company with limited liability (GmbH) is required by law to appoint one or more directors (*Geschäftsführer*). They are the company's organs and for legal purposes represent the company. The knowledge of any one director, however obtained, is the

C   knowledge of the company (Scholz, *Commentary on the GmbH Law* (7th edn, 1986), section 35). English law has never taken the view that the knowledge of a director ipso facto imputed to the company: *Powles v Page* (1846) 3 CB 16; 136 ER 7; *Re Carew's Estate Act (No. 2)* (1862) 31 Beav 39; 54 ER 1051. Unlike the German *Geschäftsführer*, an English director may as an individual have no powers whatever. But English law shares the view of German law that whether a person is an organ or not depends upon the extent of the powers which in law he has express or implied authority to exercise on

D   behalf of the company.

    Millett J did not accept that Mr Ferdman was the directing mind and will of DLH because he exercised no independent judgment. As a fiduciary he acted entirely upon the directions of the American beneficial owners and their consultant Mr Stern. All that he did was to sign the necessary documents and ensure that the company's paper work was in order. This involved seeing that decisions which had really been taken by the

E   Americans and Mr Stern were duly minuted as decisions of the board made in Switzerland.

    But neither the Americans nor Mr Stern held any position under the constitution of the company. Nor were they held out as doing so. They signed no documents on behalf of the company and carried on no business in its name. As a holding company, DLH had no independent business of its own. It entered into various transactions and on those

F   occasions the persons who acted on its behalf were the board or one or more of the directors.

    It seems to me that if the criterion is whether the candidate for being the 'directing mind and will' was exercising independent judgment, as opposed to acting upon off-stage instructions, not even the board of directors acting collectively would in this case have qualified. It also did what it was told. But Mr Tager was inclined to concede that the

G   board, acting as a board, could properly be regarded as the directing mind and will. It was certainly held out in certain quarters as such. DLH claimed non-resident status from the Inland Revenue on the ground that its 'central management and control' was situated in Switzerland.

    The authorities show clearly that different persons may for different purposes satisfy the requirements of being the company's directing mind and will. Therefore the question

H   in my judgment is whether in relation to the Yulara transaction, Mr Ferdman as an individual exercised powers on behalf of the company which so identified him. It seems to me that Mr Ferdman was clearly regarded as being in a different position from the other directors. They were associates of his who came and went. SAFI charged for their services at a substantially lower rate. It was Mr Ferdman who claimed in the published accounts of DLH to be its ultimate beneficial owner. In my view, however, the most significant fact is that Mr Ferdman signed the agreement with Yulara on behalf of DLH.

There was no board resolution authorising him to do so. Of course we know that in fact
he signed at the request of Mr Stern, whom he knew to be clothed with authority from
the Americans. But so far as the constitution of DLH was concerned, he committed the
company to the transaction as an autonomous act which the company adopted by
performing the agreement. I would therefore hold, respectfully differing from the judge,
that this was sufficient to justify Mr Ferdman being treated, in relation to the Yulara
transaction, as the company's directing mind and will. Nor do I think it matters that by
the time DLH acquired Yulara's interest in the Nine Elms project on 16 March 1988, Mr
Ferdman had ceased to be a director. Once his knowledge is treated as being the
knowledge of the company in relation to a given transaction, I think that the company
continues to be affected with that knowledge for any subsequent stages of the same
transaction. So, for example, if (contrary to the judge's finding) the £1,030,000 sent by
Yulara on 29 May 1986 had been received beneficially by DLH as a loan, but Mr
Ferdman had resigned or died a week earlier, I do not think that the DLH could have
said that it received the money without imputed knowledge of the fraud. And in my
judgment the subsequent acquisition of Yulara's interest was sufficiently connected with
the original investment to be affected by the same knowledge.

I would therefore allow the appeal. I do not regard this as an unsatisfactory outcome.
If the persons beneficially interested in a company prefer for tax or other reasons to allow
that company to be for all legal purposes run by off-shore fiduciaries, they must accept
that it may incur liabilities by reason of the acts or knowledge of those fiduciaries.

(*Order accordingly*)

A

Re Hydrodan (Corby) Ltd.

Chancery Division.
Millett J.
Judgment delivered 17 December 1993.

Wrongful trading – Shadow director – De facto director – Whether terms de facto and shadow directors overlapped – Whether directors of parent company were shadow directors of subsidiary of which parent was a shadow director – Insolvency Act 1986, s. 214.

1. The liability for wrongful trading imposed by s. 214 of the Insolvency Act 1986 extended to de facto directors as well as to de jure and shadow directors.

2. An allegation that a defendant acted as de facto or shadow director, without distinguishing between the two, was embarrassing. It suggested that de facto and shadow directors were very similar, that their roles overlapped, and that it might not be possible to determine in any given case whether a particular person was a de facto or a shadow director. The terms did not overlap. They were alternatives, and in most and perhaps all cases were mutually exclusive.

3. The directors of a parent company which was alleged to be a shadow director of a subsidiary, would not ipso facto themselves be shadow directors of the subsidiary. If (which was not alleged) the directors of the parent as a collective body gave directions to the directors of the subsidiary (which were Channel Island companies) and the directors were accustomed to act in accordance with such directions, the result would be to constitute the parent, but not its directors, a shadow director of the company.

A G Boyle QC (instructed by Dibb Lupton Bromhead) for the eighth defendant.

A G Bompas (instructed Paisner & Co) for the fifth defendant.

Gregory Hill (instructed by Emsley Collins, Leeds) for the liquidator.

JUDGMENT

Millett J: These are appeals by the fifth and eighth defendants respectively from an order made on 4 August 1993 by District Judge Whitehurst in the Northampton County Court dismissing their applications to strike out proceedings which had been brought against them.

The proceedings arise in the liquidation of Hydrodan (Corby) Ltd ('the company'), a wholly-owned indirect subsidiary of Eagle Trust plc ('Eagle Trust'). The company was ordered to be compulsorily wound up by the Northampton County Court on 13 December 1988 on a creditors' petition which had been presented on 17 October 1988.

On 18 February 1993 the liquidator made an application in the Northampton County Court against fourteen defendants alleging that they had been guilty of wrongful trading and seeking orders against them under s. 214 of the *Insolvency Act* 1986. The defendants included Eagle Trust itself, one of its subsidiaries and all its directors. The liquidator supported his application by an affidavit setting out the evidence upon which he relied.

On 19 April 1993 the fifth defendant, Mr Thomas, applied to strike out the liquidator's application against him. He supported his application by a short affidavit. On 5 May 1993 the eighth defendant, Dr Hardwick, made a similar application. The two defendants' applications were heard by the District Judge on 18 May 1993. He gave judgment on 4 August 1993 and dismissed both applications, but very sensibly ordered the liquidator to serve points of claim. Mr Thomas and Dr Hardwick now appeal to this court.

Meanwhile, on 5 October 1993, the liquidator duly served points of claim against all the defendants. Mr Hill, who appears before me for the liquidator, concedes that the points of claim truly represent the liquidator's case as supported by the evidence filed by

him, and there is no further evidence available to him which would support any other or   A
further pleadings.

Accordingly, counsel have agreed before me that the issue is exactly the same as that
which would have arisen had the points of claim been before the District Judge and the
question is whether they should be struck out as disclosing no reasonable cause of action
against Mr Thomas and Dr Hardwick. The company or the group structure is not entirely
clear, but for the purpose of present appeals I must take the structure to be that alleged   B
by the liquidator. Eagle Trust had a wholly-owned subsidiary, Midland City Partnerships
Ltd ('MCP') which in turn had a wholly-owned subsidiary, Landsaver MCP Ltd (which
I will call 'Landsaver 19'). The liquidator alleges that the company is a wholly-owned
subsidiary of Landsaver 19 and thus a wholly-owned indirect subsidiary of Eagle Trust.
Eagle Trust had eight or nine directors, some of whom were executive directors and some
of whom were non-executive directors. As one would expect, the executive directors were   C
also directors of MCP and of Landsaver 19, the operating companies; but they were not
directors of the company. The titular and only directors of the company were two
Channel Island companies: Tuscan Investments Ltd and Ithaca Investments Ltd, which
were appointed directors of the company on 18 March 1986.

The liquidator alleges that the company was trading wrongfully from 24 April 1986
until 17 October 1988, the date on which the winding-up petition was presented. As
against Mr Thomas and Dr Hardwick, the liquidator alleges that they became responsible   D
for the wrongful trading of the company as from 15 April 1987, the date on which they
were appointed to be directors of Eagle Trust.

Liability for wrongful trading is imposed by s. 214 of the *Insolvency Act* 1986. The
statutory liability is imposed exclusively upon persons who are or were at the material
time directors of the company in liquidation. But s. 214(7) provides that in the section
'director' includes a shadow director. A shadow director is defined in s. 251 of the   E
Insolvency Act 1986 in these terms:

' "Shadow director", in relation to a company, means a person in accordance with
whose directions or instructions the directors of the company are accustomed to
act . . .'

I need not recite the proviso to that definition.

Directors may be of three kinds: de jure directors, that is to say, those who have been   F
validly appointed to the office; de facto directors, that is to say, directors who assume to
act as directors without having been appointed validly or at all; and shadow directors
who are persons falling within the definition which I have read.

The defendants accept, though for the purpose of these appeals only, that the liability
imposed by s. 214 extends to de facto directors as well as to de jure and shadow directors.
It appears to me that that concession is plainly correct. Liability for wrongful trading is   G
imposed by the Act on those persons who are responsible for it, that is to say, who were
in a position to prevent damage to creditors by taking proper steps to protect their
interests. Liability cannot sensibly depend upon the validity of the defendant's
appointment. Those who assume to act as directors and who thereby exercise the powers
and discharge the functions of a director, whether validly appointed or not, must accept
the responsibilities which are attached to the office. Nevertheless, the statutory liability is   H
imposed exclusively upon directors of one or other of the three kinds that I have
mentioned. Accordingly, the liquidator must plead and prove against each defendant
separately that he or it was a director of the company.

Mr Thomas and Dr Hardwick were never appointed directors of the company. It is
submitted on their behalf that the liquidator has neither pleaded the necessary facts nor
put forward the necessary evidence to establish that either of them was a de facto or

A   shadow director of the company. In para. 1.7 of the points of claim under the heading 'Summary', the liquidator has pleaded the substance of his case as follows:

> 'The individual respondents also personally acted as de facto or shadow directors of the company as hereinafter pleaded in relation to them respectively.'

This makes it necessary to examine the later allegations in the pleadings in order to discover what the facts are relied upon to support the allegation that Mr Thomas and Dr

B   Hardwick were de facto or shadow directors of the company.

I would interpose at this point by observing that in my judgment an allegation that a defendant acted as de facto or shadow director, without distinguishing between the two, is embarrassing. It suggests – and counsel's submissions to me support the inference – that the liquidator takes the view that de facto or shadow directors are very similar, that their roles overlap, and that it may not be possible to determine in any given case whether

C   a particular person was a de facto or a shadow director. I do not accept that at all. The terms do not overlap. They are alternatives, and in most and perhaps all cases are mutually exclusive.

A de facto director is a person who assumes to act as a director. He is held out as a director by the company, and claims and purports to be a director, although never actually or validly appointed as such. To establish that a person was a de facto director of a company it is necessary to plead and prove that he undertook functions in relation

D   to the company which could properly be discharged only by a director. It is not sufficient to show that he was concerned in the management of the company's affairs or undertook tasks in relation to its business which can properly be performed by a manager below board level.

A de facto director, I repeat, is one who claims to act and purports to act as a director, although not validly appointed as such. A shadow director, by contrast, does not claim or purport to act as a director. On the contrary, he claims not to be a director. He lurks

E   in the shadows, sheltering behind others who, he claims, are the only directors of the company to the exclusion of himself. He is not held out as a director by the company. To establish that a defendant is a shadow director of a company it is necessary to allege and prove: (1) who are the directors of the company, whether de facto or de jure; (2) that the defendant directed those directors how to act in relation to the company or that he was one of the persons who did so; (3) that those directors acted in accordance with such

F   directions; and (4) that they were accustomed so to act. What is needed is, first, a board of directors claiming and purporting to act as such; and, secondly, a pattern of behaviour in which the board did not exercise any discretion or judgment of its own, but acted in accordance with the directions of others.

In the present case, there were titular directors of the company. They were Channel Island companies. That fact alone may be sufficient to justify an inference that they were

G   accustomed to act in accordance with the directions of others; in which case there were shadow directors of the company. But there is nothing pleaded in the points of claim to suggest that there were, in addition to the titular directors, any other persons who claimed to be directors of the company at all.

Counsel have argued the case before me on the footing that sufficient facts are pleaded to justify the inference that Eagle Trust, and possibly MCP as well, acted as a shadow director of the company. I shall assume that that is so. Against Dr Hardwick – I take

H   him first as the simpler of the two – what is alleged is pleaded under the heading of 'The respondents' respective involvement' and is contained in para. 23 of the points of claim, as follows:

> 'Dr Hardwick, as a director of Eagle Trust, is, with the other directors thereof, collectively responsible for the conduct of that company [i.e. Eagle Trust] . . . in relation to the company.'

It is therefore the liquidator's case that Eagle Trust was a director of the company A
(presumably a shadow director); and Dr Hardwick's liability is based exclusively upon
the fact, being the only fact alleged against him, that he was one of the directors of Eagle
Trust. As one of the directors of a shadow director, it is alleged, he was one of those
collectively responsible for Eagle Trust's conduct; and was accordingly a shadow director
of the company. In my judgment the conclusion does not follow from the premise.

The liquidator submitted that where a body corporate is a director of a company, B
whether it be a de jure, de facto or shadow director, its own directors must ipso facto be
shadow directors of the company. In my judgment that simply does not follow.
Attendance of board meetings and voting, with others, may in certain limited
circumstances expose a director to personal liability to the company of which he is a
director or its creditors. But it does not, without more, constitute him a director of any
company of which his company is a director.

It is not alleged against Dr Hardwick that he did anything at all in relation to the C
affairs of the company, not even that he voted as a director of Eagle Trust in respect of
any matter in relation to the affairs of the company.

In my judgment the mere fact that Dr Hardwick was a director of Eagle Trust does
not establish that he was either a shadow director or a de facto director of the company.
The expression 'collectively responsible' obscures the relevant legal relationship. By
reason of his appointment as a director of Eagle Trust, Dr Hardwick owed fiduciary D
duties and a duty of care to Eagle Trust, but it does not follow that he ever gave
instructions to the directors of the company or that the directors of the company were
accustomed to act on his instructions. Nor does it follow that he ever acted as a director
of the company.

It is possible (although it is not so alleged) that the directors of Eagle Trust as a
collective body gave directions to the directors of the company and that the directors of E
the company were accustomed to act in accordance with such directions. But if they did
give such directions as directors of Eagle Trust, acting as the board of Eagle Trust, they
did so as agents for Eagle Trust (or more accurately as the appropriate organ of Eagle
Trust) and the result is to constitute Eagle Trust, but not themselves, shadow directors of
the company.

In practice, in a case of the present kind, it is much more likely that it will be found F
that the executive directors of the ultimate parent company (or some of them) have from
time to time individually and personally given directions to the directors of the subsidiary
and thereby rendered themselves personally liable as shadow directors of the subsidiary.
But if all they have done is to act in their capacity as directors of the ultimate holding
company, in passing resolutions at board meetings, then in my judgment the holding
company is the shadow director of the subsidiary, and they are not. G

Against Mr Thomas, the liquidator has pleaded rather more. He has pleaded as
follows:

'1. [Mr Thomas] participated in the decision to sanction the disposal of Landsaver
19's assets to another company, Company 22, and Company 22 to Central Pacific
Securities and to [two named gentlemen], which disposals had the effect of
impeding the identification of the company's assets and of increasing the costs of H
the liquidation.'

Then follows the same allegation as that against Dr Hardwick:

'2. Generally as a director of Eagle Trust [he] is, with the other directors thereof,
collectively responsible for the conduct of that company in relation to the
company.'

A   The first of those pleadings does not allege anything in relation to the affairs of the company. It does not in terms allege that Mr Thomas gave any directions to the directors of the company or that he acted in any way in relation to the company's affairs. On the contrary, all that he appears to have done is to have participated in a decision – I take it a decision of Eagle Trust – to sanction, that is, to approve or authorise, certain disposals not by the company, but by another company, Landsaver 19.

B   I find it difficult to extract from that pleading any relevant relationship between Mr Thomas and the company. But assuming that such a connection can be extracted, the most that is alleged against Mr Thomas is that as one of the directors of Eagle Trust, he was party to a decision by Eagle Trust to authorise or approve of a disposal of its assets by a wholly-owned subsidiary. That allegation in my judgment is not even sufficient to constitute Eagle Trust a shadow director of the company. It is a commonplace that the disposal of a subsidiary or a subsidiary's business by its directors would require the

C   sanction or approval of the parent company, acting in this instance as the shareholder. Provided that the decision is made by the directors of the subsidiary, exercising their own independent discretion and judgment whether or not to dispose of the assets in question, and that the parent company only approves or authorises the decision, then in my judgment there is nothing which exposes the parent company to liability for the decision or which constitutes it a shadow director of the subsidiary.

D   In my judgment therefore the liquidator has neither pleaded nor adduced any evidence to support any allegation that either Mr Thomas or Dr Hardwick is or was at any material time a director of the company. Accordingly the proceedings against those two defendants must fail and ought now to be struck out. I allow the appeals accordingly.

(Order accordingly)

E

F

G

H

Re Leyland DAF Ltd.
Talbot & Anor v Edcrest Ltd.

Court of Appeal (Civil Division).
Nourse and Henry L JJ and Sir Roger Parker.
Judgment delivered 21 December 1993.

Administrative receivership – Receivers of manufacturer sought repossession of vehicles from delivery company – Delivery company was creditor and refused to release vehicles – Whether there was agreement giving exclusive jurisdiction to Dutch courts – Whether appointment of receivers affected jurisdiction agreement – Materiality of proceeding under summary remedy for getting in company's property – Civil Jurisdiction and Judgments Act 1982, Sch. 1 (Brussels Convention on jurisdiction and enforcement of judgments), art. 17; Insolvency Act 1986, s. 234.

This was an appeal by the administrative receivers of Leyland DAF Ltd ('Leyland') from an order of Nicholls V-C staying proceedings by the receivers in favour of proceedings in the Dutch court (see [1993] BCC 626).

The receivers had applied for an order under s. 234 of the Insolvency Act 1986 requiring the respondent, Edcrest Ltd, to permit the receivers to enter Edcrest's premises and take back Leyland's vehicles, which were stored there pending delivery to customers. Edcrest was owed substantial sums of money by Leyland. Edcrest claimed that the arrangements between the parties were governed by Dutch law, by virtue of a term, complying with art. 17 of the Brussels Convention, in a contract between Leyland and Edcrest's parent company ('the frame agreement'). Edcrest argued that under Dutch law it was not obliged to hand over the vehicles until it was paid, having, in effect, a lien.

The judge held that since Edcrest had signed the frame agreement document in approval of its terms, there was an agreement between Leyland and Edcrest satisfying the requirements of art. 17 and conferring exclusive jurisdiction on the Dutch courts. The judge further held that the use of the s. 234 procedure did not put the receivers in a better position than the company as far as the jurisdiction agreement was concerned. The receivers appealed.

Held, dismissing the appeal:

1. Edcrest was a party to the frame agreement and Leyland and Edcrest thereby agreed for the purposes of art. 17 that any dispute between them as to Edcrest's right to retain vehicles thereunder should be referred to and resolved by the Dutch court.

2. Unless and until the Dutch court had determined that Edcrest had no right of retention under Dutch law, it could not be said that Leyland appeared to be entitled to the vehicles which it sought to recover and no relief could be granted to the receivers under s. 234(2).

3. The debenture holder and receivers had no superior right to reject the exclusive jurisdiction clause. The receivers were as much bound by the exclusive jurisdiction clause as was Leyland.

The following case was referred to in the judgment of Nourse LJ:

London Iron & Steel Co Ltd, Re [1990] BCC 159.

Anthony Mann QC and Peter Arden (instructed by Wilde Sapte) for the appellants.

Mark Barnes QC and Fay Stockton (instructed by Barlow Lyde & Gilbert) for the respondent.

JUDGMENT

Nourse LJ: On 28 May 1993 the Vice-Chancellor made an order staying all further proceedings in an application by the joint administrative receivers ('the receivers') of

A Leyland DAF Ltd ('Leyland') against Edcrest Ltd in favour of proceedings in the Netherlands (see [1993] BCC 626). The basis of the Vice-Chancellor's decision was that Leyland and Edcrest were parties to an agreement containing an exclusive jurisdiction clause within art. 17 of the Brussels Convention and that the receivers were bound by it no less than Leyland. In reaching that conclusion the Vice-Chancellor decided a number of questions, including two on the construction of the agreement and one on s. 234(2) of the Insolvency Act 1986. The nearly two days of argument we heard last week, mostly on

B behalf of the appellant receivers, having failed to persuade us either that the questions were not entirely straightforward or that the Vice-Chancellor's decision was not entirely correct, we have taken a little time to be sure of expressing our own views with a brevity that is appropriate.

The facts are fully stated in the judgment of the Vice-Chancellor and need not be repeated. Leyland's ultimate parent is a Dutch company called Van Doorne's

C Bedrijfswagenfabriek DAF BV ('DAF'). On 11 October 1991 DAF, Leyland and another Dutch company called GM de Rooy & Zonen Internationaal Transport Bedrijf Eindhoven BV ('de Rooy') became parties to a written agreement in English headed 'Operations agreement', which has been referred to in the proceedings as 'the frame agreement'.

The first question is whether, as the Vice-Chancellor held, Edcrest, which is a wholly-

D owned subsidiary of de Rooy, also became a party to the frame agreement.

It starts by stating that it is made between (1) DAF, (2) Leyland, those 'parties' being thereinafter jointly and severally called the 'company', and (3) de Rooy, thereinafter called the 'haulier'. There are two recitals, the first stating the business of the company and the second being in these terms:

E
> 'The parties hereto wish to enter into a frame agreement regarding transportation by transporter and/or storage of certain vehicles produced by the company, hereinafter called the "vehicles", such transportation/storage to be performed by the haulier and/or its subsidiaries.'

All that is on p. 1. The operative provisions (annexes apart) run from pp. 2 to 19. Clause 1, headed 'Subsidiaries', is in two parts. The first sentence of the first part is in these terms:

F
> 'Where [in] the following provisions of this agreement the term "haulier", "party" or "parties" is used, such term shall – unless the context otherwise requires – be deemed to include subsidiaries of the haulier or as the case may be shall mean the subsidiary concerned of the haulier.'

The first sentence of the second part is in these terms:

> 'The haulier guarantees the strict and due performance by (any of) its subsidiaries

G of the obligations arising out of this agreement and/or related documents.'

The second sentence of the second part provides that the haulier shall indemnify the company in case of failure by any of the subsidiaries 'to comply with any such obligation'.

I gratefully adopt the Vice-Chancellor's summary of cl. 2–21 (at p. 628E):

> 'Clause 2 provided for the company to give written instructions to the haulier,
H which the haulier would accept, for the storage of vehicles or the transport of them by transporter. The agreement was to apply to every such instruction. The company was to pay the haulier for the services provided, at specified rates. The haulier was obliged to inspect the vehicles, to store them in good condition and provide adequate security pending receipt of delivery instructions, to carry out stock care procedures, to provide sufficient vehicles and equipment to fulfil its obligations under the agreement, and so forth. The agreement was to continue for

five years from 1 January 1991. The haulier was not permitted to subcontract   A
performance of its obligations without consent.'

The last of the operative provisions (annexes apart) is contained in cl. 22, headed
'Governing law':

'This agreement shall be governed by and construed in accordance with the laws
of the Netherlands. All disputes and differences between the parties arising out of
or in connection with this agreement shall ultimately be referred to and resolved   B
by the court of justice of 's Hertogenbosch, the Netherlands.'

On p. 19 we find this:

'THUS made up in triplicate at Eindhoven on 11-10-1991'.

Underneath there are signatures on behalf of DAF and Leyland and the signature of Mr
de Rooy on behalf of de Rooy. He also signed on behalf of Edcrest under the words 'For
approval'.   C

The receivers say that Mr de Rooy's signing of the frame agreement 'for approval' on
behalf of Edcrest did not make Edcrest a party to it. They have sought, but have failed,
to enlighten us as to what other purpose there could have been in it. They simply say that
when you look at the terms as a whole you have to conclude that Edcrest was not
intended to be a party. For my part, I think that they point to exactly the opposite
conclusion.   D

The second recital contemplates that transportation or storage may be performed not
by de Rooy itself but by one or more of its subsidiaries. The first part of cl. 1 provides
that in the provisions following not only the term 'haulier', but also the terms 'party' or
'parties' shall, unless the context otherwise requires, be deemed to include subsidiaries
generally or 'the subsidiary concerned'. The receivers say that the last two of those
definitions, expressed as they are to apply only to the provisions following, confirm that   E
the parties, expressed as they are in p. 1, do not and cannot include subsidiaries.

I disagree. I think that the provisions as a whole contemplate that a subsidiary may be
or become a party. That appears most clearly from the second part of cl. 1, which, in
referring to 'obligations', can only mean the obligations of subsidiaries. They are
envisaged as 'arising out of this agreement and/or related documents', for example out of
a written instruction by the company to a subsidiary of de Rooy to perform   F
transportation or storage on the terms of the frame agreement, being an instruction
accepted by the subsidiary in writing. While it is true that an obligation thus assumed by
a subsidiary would normally arise not under the frame agreement, but under a separate
agreement between it and the company, it could arise alternatively from a joinder of the
subsidiary as a party to the frame agreement. Moreover, and this is the important point
for present purposes, the inclusion of such a provision in an agreement signed at its
inception by a subsidiary 'for approval' shows clearly that the subsidiary was intended to   G
be a party to it. I see no conflict between this view of Edcrest's status as a party to the
frame agreement and the terms in which p. 1 of it is expressed. Indeed there is a harmony
between them. In my view the structure of the frame agreement is consistent with an
intention that DAF, Leyland and de Rooy should be the principal parties to it and the
'parties' for the purposes, for example, of cl. 13 (duration) and cl. 14 (termination). Those
are matters in which a subsidiary of de Rooy could not have been intended to have a say,
the clauses being provisions where 'the context otherwise requires' for the purposes of   H
the definitions in the first part of cl. 1. In cl. 22, on the other hand, the context does not
require that the 'parties' shall not include a subsidiary, i.e. Edcrest, which is already a
party to the frame agreement.

For these reasons, like the Vice-Chancellor, I hold that Edcrest was a party to the
frame agreement and that Leyland and Edcrest thereby agreed that any dispute between

A   them as to Edcrest's right to retain vehicles thereunder should be referred to and resolved by the court at 's Hertogenbosch, being an agreement within art. 17 of the Brussels Convention on jurisdiction and enforcement of judgments in civil and commercial matters, which was incorporated into English law by s. 2 of the *Civil Jurisdiction and Judgments Act* 1982.

So far as material, art. 17 provides:

B   'If the parties, one or more of whom is domiciled in a Contracting State, have agreed that a court or the courts of a Contracting State are to have jurisdiction to settle any disputes which have arisen or which may arise in connection with a particular legal relationship, that court or those courts shall have exclusive jurisdiction. Such an agreement conferring jurisdiction shall be either–

(a) in writing or evidenced in writing . . .'

C   So the question now is whether the receivers are in some way able to say that, unlike Leyland, they are not bound by cl. 22 of the frame agreement. If they are so bound, their application for delivery up of the vehicles retained by Edcrest is as much liable to be stayed under art. 17 as an application by Leyland itself.

The question depends, at any rate in the first instance, on s. 234 of the *Insolvency Act* 1986, to which the marginal note is 'Getting in the company's property'. Subsections (1) and (2) provide:

D   '(1) This section applies in the case of a company where–

(a) an administration order is made in relation to the company, or

(b) an administrative receiver is appointed, or

(c) the company goes into liquidation, or

(d) a provisional liquidator is appointed;

E   and "the office-holder" means the administrator, the administrative receiver, the liquidator or the provisional liquidator, as the case may be.

(2) Where any person has in his possession or control any property, books, papers or records to which the company appears to be entitled, the court may require that person forthwith (or within such period as the court may direct) to pay, deliver, convey, surrender or transfer the property, books, papers or records to the office-

F   holder.'

It is an apparent oddity of s. 234 that it nowhere states on whose application an order made by the court under subs. (2) may be made. That does not matter here, because it is obvious that an application may be made by the office-holder, in this case the receivers. On their behalf it was submitted that a receiver may apply in the interests of the debenture holder who appointed him as much as in the interests of the company. Assuming that

G   that distinction could have practical consequences of some kind, I nevertheless regard the submission as being entirely beside the point. Either way, the property recoverable under s. 234(2) is confined to property 'to which the company appears to be entitled'.

Although in *Re London Iron & Steel Co Ltd* [1990] BCC 159 it was held by Warner J that the court has power under the subsection to determine whether the company is entitled to the property or not, it can have no such power where, as here, that question has been referred to the decision of a foreign court. In the present case, unless and until

H   the Dutch court has determined that Edcrest has no right of retention under Dutch law, it cannot be said that Leyland appears to be entitled to the vehicles which it is sought to recover. At present, no relief can be granted to the receivers under s. 234(2). The receivers having elected to proceed under s. 234(2), it would seem that that ought to be an end of their resistance to Edcrest's application for a stay in favour of proceedings in the Dutch court. However, assuming that it was not, we listened to much learned argument and

citation of authority on their behalf in support of the proposition that the debenture   A
holder, although taking subject to any right of retention enjoyed by Edcrest under Dutch
law, nonetheless had a superior right to reject the exclusive jurisdiction clause, albeit that
that clause was part and parcel of the agreement under which the right of retention arose
and was, in the words of the Vice-Chancellor (at p. 632B), 'another of the terms governing
Edcrest's possession and retention of the vehicles'. That proposition, being unsupported
by any authority cited and contrary to principle and common sense, is one which I wholly
reject. Like the Vice-Chancellor, I therefore hold that the receivers are as much bound by   B
the exclusive jurisdiction clause as is Leyland.

The only other question is whether the frame agreement applies to spare parts as well
as to vehicles. In answering that question in the affirmative, I gratefully adopt what was
said about it by the Vice-Chancellor (at p. 632F):

'The operative clauses of the frame agreement make no reference to the carriage of   C
spare parts. The recitals and the operative clauses are concerned with vehicles. In
fact, in addition to vehicles, de Rooy and Edcrest were already transporting spare
parts for Leyland when the frame agreement was made. On 16 April 1991, some
months before the agreement was signed, Mr van der Tempel, on behalf of
Leyland, and Mr de Rooy had signed a document headed "Overview of prices
transports de Rooy/Edcrest UK". The document set out the rates, as from
1 January 1991, payable for transporting spare parts. The document also made   D
provision for the amount of compensation payable to Edcrest consequential upon
use of Edcrest's vehicles for five days per week rather than six days as envisaged
when the rates were calculated. That document was included as one of the
documents forming annex 3, headed "charges", to the frame agreement. The frame
agreement provided that the annexes should form an integral part of the
agreement.

In my view the proper inference to be drawn from the inclusion of this document   E
as part of annex 3 is that the parties intended that, so far as applicable, the terms
of the frame agreement should apply to the transport of spare parts as well as the
transport of vehicles. That is hardly surprising. The only other explanation for the
inclusion of this document in the annex is a mistake. I see no reason to think there
was a mistake. The oral evidence I heard from those with first-hand knowledge of
the contractual negotiations confirms this.'   F

It follows that in granting a stay of the receivers' application the Vice-Chancellor was
right to make no distinction between vehicles and spare parts.

I would dismiss this appeal.

Henry LJ: I agree. It is a useful working hypothesis, these days perhaps too often
ignored, that good law is both simple and produces a result that is sensible, predictable   G
and readily intelligible. The appellant's submissions on each of the three points they
raised satisfied neither test.

First, at the time of the negotiations of the frame agreement, Edcrest were already
doing and were intended to continue to do the UK haulage and deliveries for Leyland.
That agreement detailed the terms on which they were to continue to perform those tasks
and required their approval of those terms by signature. That agreement included them   H
in the definition of 'parties' (except where the context otherwise required) and had an
exclusive jurisdiction clause for the resolution of disputes between the parties (clearly in
context including disputes between Edcrest and Leyland). It would be both curious and
disturbing if against that background arcane forensic subtlety made them mere
subcontractors and freed Leyland from the exclusive jurisdiction clause. But the law is
not so foolish.

A   Similarly if the debenture holder's administrative receiver took free from Edcrest's right of retention and the concomitant exclusive jurisdiction clause otherwise binding on Leyland simply by what was described in submissions to us as 'a change of hat', I agree with my Lord that both legal principle and common sense would be affronted.

     Lastly, Edcrest were carrying Leyland's spares and annex 3 to the agreement detailed the pricing formulae under which they were to continue to do this. Spares were not mentioned in the body of the agreement, and that is the high point of the appellant's submissions. Either the omission of any mention of spares from the body of the agreement or the inclusion of the annex with its detailed prices for the carriage of spares was perhaps a mistake. The factual matrix made it quite clear that the mistake was the omission of specific mention of the spares from the body of the agreement. No other construction would have made sense, but sense made no boundary to the appellant's submissions on this point.

     I too would dismiss this appeal.

     Sir Roger Parker: I agree with both judgments and I can find nothing which I can usefully add.

     (*Appeal dismissed with costs to be taxed and paid forthwith, to include costs for and occasioned by the amendment of the notice of appeal. Leave to appeal to the House of Lords refused*)

Powdrill & Anor v Watson & Anor.
Re Paramount Airways Ltd (No. 3).

A

Court of Appeal (Civil Division).
Dillon, Leggatt and Henry L JJ.
Judgment delivered 22 February 1994.

Administration orders – Whether administrators had 'adopted' contracts of employment – Appeal – Administrators dismissed employees – Whether claims of employees under employment contracts were secured on company's assets in priority to administrators' remuneration – Whether claims carried interest – Whether administrators had offered employees new contracts – Whether administrators could contract out of adoption – Insolvency Act 1986, s. 19(5).

B

This was an appeal by the joint administrators of Paramount Airways Ltd ('Paramount') from a judgment of Evans-Lombe J [1993] BCC 662 that the contracts of employment of former employees of the company had been adopted by the administrators within the meaning of s. 19(5) of the Insolvency Act 1986. The judge then decided whether certain sums claimed by the employees resulting from their dismissals took priority under s. 19(5).

C

The administrators were appointed on 7 August 1989. They caused Paramount to continue trading with a view to seeking a buyer for its business as a going concern. On 14 August, the administrators wrote to the employees stating that they did not and would 'not at any future time adopt or assume personal liability in respect of your contracts of employment'. Attempts to find a buyer failed and the employees were dismissed at the end of November.

D

Two employees petitioned under s. 27 of the 1986 Act claiming that various sums including pay in lieu of notice, unpaid holiday pay, so-called loyalty bonuses agreed with the administrators and pension contributions, were payable under s. 19(5). The petitioners were made respondents to an application by the administrators for directions as to how they should deal with the claims being advanced by the respondents as a result of their dismissal.

E

The judge held that an administrator could contract out of the adoption of contracts of employment, but that the administrators' letter of 14 August was ineffective to exclude adoption of the contracts which the administrators had procured Paramount to continue to perform. Accordingly liabilities incurred under those contracts of employment while the joint administrators were in office were charged on the assets of the company under s. 19(5) in priority to the administrators' remuneration and expenses. Such liabilities included payments in lieu of notice, holiday pay and pension contributions. The agreement to pay bonuses was a separate agreement and claims under it and claims for compensation for unfair dismissal did not attract the protection of s. 19(5) because they did not arise under the relevant contract of employment. The administrators appealed. The respondents cross-appealed in relation to the bonus payments.

F

G

Held, dismissing the appeal and cross-appeal:

1. If administrators continued, after the 14-day period mentioned in s. 19(5), to employ staff and pay them in accordance with their previous contracts, they would be held impliedly to have adopted those contracts of employment. The word 'adopted' in s. 19(5) connoted, in relation to contracts of employment, 'the continuance of which is expressly or impliedly accepted'.

H

2. If administrators wanted to use existing staff they had either to adopt the existing contracts or negotiate new contracts. But if they negotiated new contracts they must not be sham.

3. The judge held that the letter of 14 August was far too obscure to be construed as an offer to employees of employment on terms other than of their previous contractual

A   entitlement. He was plainly right. The letter pointed out that the administrators would not be personally liable to the employees for their salaries and so forth. Apart from that, it conveyed the intention that they would continue to be employed under their previous contracts. It pointed in favour of adoption rather than against it, despite the phrase at the end about the administrators not adopting, and not at any future time adopting contracts of employment. The mere assertion by an administrator or receiver that he was not adopting the contract was mere wind with no legal effect, because adoption was a matter not merely

B   of words but of fact. Here all the facts pointed to the administrators having adopted the contracts.

4. It was not necessary to consider what might or might not be permissible to include in a contract of employment in lieu of the contract which was subsisting at the time of the appointment of the administrators in other cases.

5. Subject to the ordinary principles of mitigation of damages, the employees were

C   entitled to two months' pay in lieu of notice. That was payable out of the property of the company in the custody or under the control of the administrator. The same applied in relation to pension contributions and holiday pay. Although strictly sums payable under s. 19(5) were only payable when the administrator vacated office, it was well understood that administrators would, in the ordinary way, pay expenses of the administration including the salaries and other payments to employees as they arose during the continuance of the

D   administration.

6. The employees were entitled to interest because the administrators had had money invested and earning interest while being held until the questions were resolved, and it was right that the administrators as officers of the court should pay interest at the rate they had earned and pay the moneys to the respondents in respect of their entitlement. (*Ex parte James* (1874) LR 9 Ch App 609 applied.)

E   7. The bonus agreement was a separate contract and not covered by s. 19(5) as a contract of employment adopted by the administrators.

The following cases were referred to in the judgment of Dillon LJ:

Guardians of the Poor of Salford Union v Dewhurst [1926] AC 619.
James, Ex parte (1874) LR 9 Ch App 609.
Specialised Mouldings Ltd, Re (unreported, 13 February 1987, Harman J).

F   Michael Crystal QC and Mark Phillips (instructed by Wilde Sapte) for the administrators.

Robin Potts QC and Richard Snowden (instructed by Burrough & Co, Cardiff) for the respondents.

JUDGMENT

G   **Dillon LJ:** This is an appeal by Mr Powdrill and Mr Atkinson, who are the joint administrators of a company called Paramount Airways Ltd, against an order made by Evans-Lombe J in the Companies Court on 27 July 1993 (see [1993] BCC 662). The respondents are two former employees of the company, Captain Watson and Captain Unwin. There is a further point taken, in effect by cross-appeal by a respondent's notice to which I shall have to come.

H   The general question arises in the field relating to the continued employment by the company, after the appointment of the administrators, of staff previously in the company's employment and the extent of the benefits which the staff so employed are entitled to claim as administration expenses within the meaning of s. 19(5) of the *Insolvency Act* 1986.

The basic facts are that the company operated a charter airline from Bristol Airport and certain other airports in the UK. The administrators were appointed by Warner J by an order of 7 August 1989. The administrators sent a letter to all employees on 14 August 1989 as follows:

'I write to advise you that we were appointed joint administrators of the above company by an order of the High Court dated 7 August 1989. Under the provisions of the *Insolvency Act* 1986 the joint administrators act as agents of the company.

We are currently investigating the company's position but as yet we are uncertain as to the true contractual position between yourself and the company.

Nothing in this letter is to be taken to affect the true identity of your employer, however, we should like to take this opportunity of reassuring you that the company will continue to pay your monthly salary during the interim period, including that payable on 31 August 1989, together with any other sums which you are contractually entitled to pursuant to the terms and conditions of your contract of employment. We hope that we may have your co-operation during this period.

We wish to make it clear that the joint administrators act at all times as agents of the company and without personal liability. The administrators are not and will not at any future time adopt or assume personal liability in respect of your contracts of employment.

signed

R A Powdrill in his capacity as joint administrator of Paramount Airways Ltd acting as its agent and without personal liability.'

Following that, a question arose in relation to keeping the airline captains and first officers in the employment of the company while it was in administration and it was hoped that it might be able to arrange to sell the business as a going concern. In those circumstances the administrators, in September 1989, wrote a further letter to all captains and first officers as follows:

'Further to our meeting on 21 September 1989 and following representations from Mr W B Morgan, we would propose making the following additional payments to captains and first officers.

These payments will be made to all captains and first officers remaining in employment and working for Paramount Airways Ltd as at 31 October 1989, or as at the date of a sale of the business if earlier; and who have not tendered their resignation by such time.

Payments will be made for the period commencing 1 September 1989 and will be apportioned if foreshortened by a sale.

If the administrators remain in office after 31 October 1989, this arrangement will continue on a monthly basis until further notice with each month end date being relevant for not having tendered resignations.

The following payments are proposed:

CAPTAINS

For September – £300
For October and each subsequent months – £400

FIRST OFFICERS

For September – £250
For October and each subsequent months – £300

The first payment will be made with the October salary and will include September payments.

A   This arrangement will not be binding upon the company following the administrators' resignation.

The administrators are not adopting any or all terms of any contracts of employment or service you have and act only as agents of Paramount Airways Ltd and without personal liability.'

On 3 November 1989 the statutory creditors' meeting was held in accordance with the

B   scheme of the Act and it passed a resolution approving that the administrators should seek to sell the company as a going concern. From their appointment until, at any rate, the end of September, the administrators had been concerned not only to work out what could be put to the creditors at the creditors' meeting but to keep the charter airline business operating through the peak holiday season of that year. Despite the approval of the meeting of 3 November, by 30 November the administrators found that they had been unable to find any buyer and, apart from a 'wet lease' of a single plane, which for

C   present purposes is immaterial, the operations of the company had been suspended. Accordingly, on 30 November a meeting was held when the employees were told that that was the state of affairs. On 5 December 1989 letters of dismissal were sent to all staff, except possibly the few required for the wet lease arrangement, terminating their contracts of employment summarily, and indeed retrospectively, namely as from 30 November.

D   In September 1991 each of the respondents, Captain Watson and Captain Unwin, issued a petition under s. 27 of the Insolvency Act claiming what they said to be their entitlement as a result of their dismissals. The very proper reaction of the administrators to that was that they issued a summons on 31 October, seeking the directions of the Companies Court on these matters and they joined the respondents as parties to the summons.

E   The system of administration is a new system recommended by the Cork Committee which is introduced in the *Insolvency Act* 1986. The scheme is, under s. 8:

'(1) . . . if the court—

     (a) is satisfied that a company is or is likely to become unable to pay its debts (within the meaning given to that expression by section 123 of this Act), and

     (b) considers that the making of an order under this section would be likely to

F   achieve one or more of the purposes mentioned below,

the court may make an administration order in relation to the company.

(2) An administration order is an order directing that, during the period for which the order is in force, the affairs, business and property of the company shall be managed by a person ("the administrator") appointed for the purpose by the court.'

G   The purposes for whose achievement an administration order may be made include, under s. 8(3), (a) the survival of the company and the whole or any part of its undertaking as a going concern, and (d) a more advantageous realisation of the company's assets than would be effected on a winding up.

I need not go, in great detail, into the scheme of the Act, but it is pertinent to note that under s. 11 the effect of the making of an administration order is that any petition for the

H   winding up of the company shall be dismissed and any administrative receiver of the company shall vacate office.

It is further provided by s. 11(3) that:

'During the period for which an administration order is in force—

     (a) no resolution may be passed or order made for the winding up of the company;

(b) no administrative receiver of the company may be appointed;   A

(c) no other steps may be taken to enforce any security over the company's property, or to repossess goods in the company's possession under any hire-purchase agreement, except with the consent of the administrator or the leave of the court and subject (where the court gives leave) to such terms as the court may impose; and

(d) no other proceedings and no execution or other legal process may be   B commenced or continued, and no distress may be levied, against the company or its property except with the consent of the administrator or the leave of the court and subject (where the court gives leave) to such terms as aforesaid.'

Section 14(1) provides:

'The administrator of a company–   C

(a) may do all such things as may be necessary for the management of the affairs, business and property of the company, and

(b) without prejudice to the generality of paragraph (a), has the powers specified in Schedule 1 to this Act . . .'

He is further given power under subs. (2) to remove any director of the company and   D appoint any person to be a director of it whether to fill a vacancy or otherwise and under subs. (3) to apply to the court for directions in relation to any particular matter arising in connection with the carrying out of his functions.

It is also provided by s. 14(5) that, in exercising his powers, the administrator is deemed to act as the company's agent. He is not, therefore, personally liable under contracts he makes or contracts which he adopts.

Section 15(1) provides that: E

'The administrator of a company may dispose of or otherwise exercise his powers in relation to any property of the company which is subject to a security to which this subsection applies as if the property were not subject to the security.'

Section 15(3) provides that:

'Subsection (1) applies to any security which, as created, was a floating charge . . .'   F

Section 18 provides for the discharge of an administration order and of the administrator at the discretion of the administrator and mandatorily if it appears to the administrator that the purpose or each of the purposes specified in the order has been achieved or is incapable of achievement, or he is required to do so by meeting of the company's creditors.

Section 19 is concerned with the vacation of office by an administrator. Subsection (2)   G provides by alternative (b) that the administrator shall vacate office if the administration order is discharged. Subsections (3), (4) and (5) then provide as follows:

'(3) Where at any time a person ceases to be administrator, the next two subsections apply.

(4) His remuneration and any expenses properly incurred by him shall be charged on and paid out of any property of the company which is in his custody or under   H his control at that time in priority to any security to which section 15(1) then applies.

(5) Any sums payable in respect of debts or liabilities incurred, while he was administrator, under contracts entered into or contracts of employment adopted by him or a predecessor of his in the carrying out of his or the predecessor's

A functions shall be charged on and paid out of any such property as is mentioned in subsection (4) in priority to any charge arising under that subsection.

For this purpose, the administrator is not to be taken to have adopted a contract of employment by reason of anything done or omitted to be done within 14 days after his appointment.'

B So far as subs. (4) is concerned, the remuneration of the administrator and his expenses properly incurred are to be charged out of any property of the company which is in his custody or under his control at the time of his ceasing to be administrator and if that property was subject to a security to which s. 15(1) applies, that is to say, a security which was initially a floating charge, it is to be paid in priority to that charge.

We are not concerned with specific charges. In addition, we have the provision that the administrator is not to be taken to have adopted a contract of employment by reason of
C anything done or omitted to be done within 14 days after his appointment. That gives him a time of 14 days to endeavour to take stock, and what has been done in that period cannot be relied on as showing that he has adopted a contract of employment. After the 14 days it becomes a question whether he has or has not adopted a contract of employment by reason of anything done or omitted after the 14 days.

I should next pass, to complete the summary of the facts, to the terms of the contract
D of employment of the respondents which appears to have been in the company's standard form. We have a form for Captain Watson which tells us that the date of commencement is as appendix 1, but does not include appendix 1. Nothing, however, turns on that. It is relevant to notice certain clauses, because of the issues which are raised. One is cl. 8 which is concerned with holidays and is relevant because one of the matters in issue is the entitlement of the respondents to holiday pay. Clause 8 provides:

E '(a) The company's holiday year begins on 1 April and ends on 31 March.'

The relevant year, therefore, in the present case, is the year that began on 1 April 1989. It is expressly provided by subcl. (e):

'Except as otherwise agreed in writing . . . holiday entitlement expires on 31 March annually and may not be carried forward to the next holiday year.'

Subpara. (c) provides:
F
'Your holiday entitlement is 28 days plus eight associated days off per annum or, in year of joining, pro rata from your date of commencement until 31 March next following.'

Then it is said, and it is understandable from the nature of the business:

'Except as agreed in writing with the company's director of flight operations no
G holiday may normally be taken between 1 May and 30 September each year . . .'

Finally, and this is where holiday pay comes in, subpara. (f) provides:

'On termination of employment other than for misconduct your holiday entitlement will be paid on the basis of one-twelfth of the annual entitlement for each full calendar month's service from the previous 1 April or, if you commenced employment after such date, then your date of commencement, less any leave
H taken.'

Clause 10 is concerned with contracting out which means, in relation to the staff pensions, the company's pension scheme:

'You may, if you wish, join Holdings' pension scheme on the applicable terms and conditions . . . whereupon you will become contracted out of the State Earnings Related Pension Scheme.'

The pension scheme was contributory by the employees and also by company
contributions.

There is cl. 12 which deals with notice of termination of employment:

> 'Notice of termination of employment to be given either by yourself or the
> company . . . shall be in writing and as follows:
>
> (a) During a probationary period comprising the first six months of your
> employment hereunder: two weeks
>
> (b) Thereafter: two months . . .'

There is a minor point, which is not in issue on this appeal, that there was doubt at one
stage whether the employing company of Captain Watson and Captain Unwin at the
crucial time was the company Paramount Airways Ltd or its parent company Paramount
Holdings Ltd, but the conclusion which is not challenged is that though there was talk of
the holding company becoming the employer, the employment continued as employment
by Paramount Airways Ltd. In the letter of 14 August the passage saying, 'Nothing in
this letter is to be taken to affect the true identity of your employer . . .' was merely
preserving at that stage whether the employer was Paramount Airways or the holding
company.

It is accepted by the administrators that during the time from their appointment on
7 August until 30 November they were bound to pay to each of the employees, whose
services were used by them, his salary and to pay for him the contributions to the pension
fund according to the rates appropriate under his service agreement which had been in
force before the appointment of the administrators, subject to an addition in relation to
bonus payments under the bonus payment scheme, which is the subject of the cross-
appeal by respondent's notice, which I lay on one side for the moment. It is also accepted
that they would be entitled to a portion of holiday pay in respect of that year. But it is
asserted for the administrators that they did not ever adopt the previous contracts
because they said in the letter to each employee of 14 August 1989, apart from making it
clear that they as joint administrators at all times acted as agents of the company and
worked without personal liability, that they were not and would not at any future time
adopt or assume personal liability in respect of the employees' contracts of employment.

In the letter of September 1989 to the captains and first officers there is a ritual
incantation in the last paragraph:

> 'The administrators are not adopting any or all terms of any contracts of
> employment or service you have and act only as agents of Paramount Airways Ltd
> and without personal liability.'

That is said, notwithstanding that by September the administrators had been making
payments to the employees, and in the September letter where the additional payments
were provided for, the additional payments were said to be being made to all captains
and first officers remaining in 'employment' and working for Paramount Airways Ltd as
at 31 October 1989 etc.

One wonders how, if they had not adopted the contracts, these employees, and
particularly the captains and first officers, came to be in their employment at all.

It is submitted, however, that to adopt a contract of employment the administrators
must do something positive. It is said that here, by the original August letter, they said
that they would not. As I see it, that does not do. If they continue substantially after the
14 days to employ staff and pay them in accordance with their previous contracts, they
will be held impliedly to have adopted those contracts of employment.

The whole function of administration will normally require that the administrators
carry on the business of the company concerned, with a view either, with the benefit of

A   the moratorium, to trade out of difficulties into profit so that the directors can take over and the company can carry on as a going concern after the administrators have been discharged or, at any rate, to have time to find a buyer for the business as a going concern. They will, therefore, want employees. But if they want to use the existing staff they must, as I see it, either adopt the existing contracts or negotiate new contracts. But if they are going to negotiate new contracts they must not be sham.

B   In the present case it is suggested that by the letter of 14 August they have offered the employees new contracts on the basis that the employees will work as required and will be paid their monthly salary and the pension provisions together with any other sums to which the employees were contractually entitled, pursuant to the terms and conditions of the previous contracts of employment, but without adopting the contract of employment and, in particular, without adopting the terms of the contract of employment which would require the employee to be given notice of termination of his contract or paid two

C   months' salary with other benefits in lieu of notice, and without adopting any term of the contract of employment which might require the administrators to pay at any future time any sum calculated by reference to pact service of the employee, such as holiday pay, in respect of the period from 1 April 1989 to the appointment of the administrators on 7 August.

The judge held that the letter in question was far too obscure to be construed as an

D   offer to employees of employment on terms other than of their previous contractual entitlement. In my judgment, he was plainly right. The letter is, understandably, pointing out that the administrators will not be personally liable to the employees for the employees' salaries and so forth. Apart from that, it is conveying the intention that they will continue to be employed under their previous contracts. It points in favour of adoption rather than against it, despite the phrase at the end about the administrators not adopting, and not at any future time adopting contracts of employment.

E   That phrase seems to have become, as I have said, a ritual incantation as a result of a case of Harman J called *Re Specialised Mouldings Ltd*, decided apparently on 13 February 1987. The case is summarised in a textbook of Gordon Stewart called *Administrative Receivers and Administrators* (1987). That reference has been picked up by professor Goode in his book *Principles of Corporate Insolvency Law* at p. 101–102. In that passage Professor Goode says this:

F   'If the above interpretation of "adopted" be correct,'

and, in my view, it is, and he is talking about an administrative receiver, not an administrator,

      'the receiver who allows a contract of employment to continue does not escape liability merely because in doing so he makes it clear that the company remains the employer and that he, the receiver, is not adopting the contract. However, in *Re*

G   *Specialised Mouldings Ltd*, Harman J. held, on an application for directions under section 35 of the Insolvency Act, that a receiver can avoid adopting an employment contract by stipulating expressly that he does not do so. In reliance on this decision it has become common practice for a receiver to write to all employees after his appointment to say that their contracts with the company will be continued on the same basis as previously, that the receiver is not adopting the contract, and that he assumes no personal liability in relation to the employee's employment. The

H   authority of the decision is somewhat weakened by the fact that the learned judge did not reduce his judgment to writing, and it is submitted that it is wrong. Adoption is not merely a matter of words but of fact. It is difficult to see how a receiver can claim not to have adopted a contract of employment if he allows the contract to remain in force and continues to make use of the employee's services. Such an interpretation drives a coach and horses through section 44(2)'

I interject, that is of the Insolvency Act relating to administrative receivers,   A

'and deprives it of any significant meaning.'

With all respect to Harman J, a decision that he has given where there is no report, transcript or note of the reasons by which he reached his conclusion and no indication of what the facts were, cannot rank as a helpful authority. No doubt, he did not particularly intend something so denuded of judgment to be an authority in future times, but it does not help at all. And the mere assertion by an administrator or receiver that he is not   B
adopting the contract is mere wind with no legal effect, because adoption is a matter not merely of words but of fact. Here all the facts point to the administrators having adopted the contracts.

We were asked to consider further whether the administrators could, if they made fresh contracts with employees, exclude some matter which would be their liabilities it they adopted the existing contracts. We were referred, in respect of that, by Mr Potts to the   C
decision of the House of Lords in *Guardians of the Poor of Salford Union v Dewhurst* [1926] AC 619, which held that where Parliament had said that poor law officers were to have pensions, the guardians could not, and the poor law officers could not, contract out of a mandatory requirement by agreeing that the poor law officers should not have pensions. That is an important principle in relation to statutory construction and application, but I do not find it necessary to consider its application in the present case. I   D
have expressed my clear view on adoption, as it is in this case and in any circumstances where the administrators take advantage of the services of an employee. I do not find it necessary to go further and consider what might or might not be permissible to include in a contract of employment in lieu of the contract which was subsisting at the time of the appointment of the administrators in other cases and in other facts, for instance, where there might be a contract with a managing director whose contract with the company contained 'golden handshake' provisions and so forth.   E

As the contract had been adopted, the first question we have to consider is whether the employees whose contracts were thus adopted are entitled to notice in accordance with the contractual terms or payment of salary in lieu of notice. We consider this as a general question. It may, of course, be that on the ordinary principles of mitigation of damages, an employee will have taken other employment during what would otherwise have been his notice period, and what they earn in the other employment must of course be set   F
against anything to which they may claim to be entitled under s. 19(5).

The crucial words in s. 19(5) are:

'... sums payable in respect of debts or liabilities incurred, while he was administrator, under contracts ... of employment adopted by him or a predecessor of his ...'

Although strictly sums payable are, under s. 19(5), only payable when the   G
administrator vacates office, it is well understood that administrators will, in the ordinary way, pay expenses of the administration including the salaries and other payments to employees as they arise during the continuance of the administration. There is no need to wait until the end, and it would be impossible as a practical matter to do that. What is picked up at the end are those matters which fall within the phrase, but have not been paid.   H

As I see it, the liability to pay wages in lieu of notice arose when the employee was dismissed at 30 November, or a few days later when the notices were sent out. The administrator was still the administrator then. He had not vacated the office, and it was he who terminated the contracts. He still had not vacated the office because, as a practical matter, apparently, of the need to have these issues decided. It has been felt that the company which is no longer carrying on any business should remain strictly in

A administration until these proceedings have been disposed of, before being put into liquidation on a petition by the administrators in the usual way where administration does not lead to the sale of the business as a going concern or to trading into profit or achieving any of the other objects under s. 8(3).

As I see it, one looks at the contract which is the contract that has been adopted and which was a continuing contract before that. One sees what notice was required to terminate it. The administrator could give that notice and pay the salary under the terms

B of the contract during the continuance of the notice or he can give, as he did in this case, summary notice of termination, in which event a liability or debt is incurred to the employee of the amount of the salary in lieu of notice which he should have received. That arises under the contract under which he was employed which had been adopted.

In my judgment, the salary for the two months is covered by that clause and the employee is entitled to have it paid out of any property of the company which is in the

C custody or under the control of the administrator now. The same goes, as is conceded, if that result is right in respect of salary, to payments in respect of the employee's membership of the pension scheme.

I then come to holiday pay. It must follow, in my judgment, that the holiday pay is likewise to be calculated for the two month period of the notice that should have been given; the same wording applies.

D The question is then in respect of the holiday pay back to 1 April 1989 in the case of those employees who had not taken their full holiday allowance during the holiday year that then began. They must give credit for such holidays as they have had. But, again, in my judgment, the holiday pay is covered by the same words:

'. . . sums payable in respect of debts or liabilities incurred . . .'

Holiday pay is not payable until the employee's employment has been terminated; that

E flows from the wording of the contract. It is not right, although it is a contingent potential liability in one sense, to say that at 1 April the company incurred a contingent liability for holiday pay for the whole of the year in respect of each of its employees which would be gradually reduced as they took their holidays during the year, and finally reduced yet further if the year expired without their having terminated their employment. The natural reading, in my judgment, is that the liability for holiday pay was incurred when the

F administrators terminated the employment and the whole liability in respect of the whole period from 1 April was incurred from that date and not earlier. It is also incurred under the contract of employment which had been adopted by the administrators because it is the very contract which provides for what the holiday pay is and when it is to be paid.

There is then a question on the appeal as to interest. Should the sums which the employees are entitled to, carry interest? The judge, in his order, directed that:

G 'The applicants' – that is the administrators – 'should pay the respondents interest on any sums falling to be paid as debts and liabilities incurred under their contracts of employment . . . from 30 June 1990 until payment at the rate of interest which the applicants have received on the funds in their hands since that date, and, in any event, at the rate at which interest would have been payable had the funds been paid into the Insolvency Services Account on 30 June 1990.'

That was in a supplemental judgment following discussion after delivery of the main

H judgment.

What the judge said after deciding that interest should be paid in principle, was that, since the insolvency estate is bound to pay those moneys into the insolvency estate's account, the appropriate rate of interest is the interest that would have been on that account. The judge is, in referring to the insolvency estate's account, referring, I think, to the Insolvency Services Account mentioned in the order, but it appears that

administrators are not required to pay the funds they hold into that account; they are
entitled to leave surplus moneys on deposit in bank accounts and that is what these
administrators have done. Therefore, the words in the judge's order:

'. . . and, in any event, at the rate at which interest would have been payable had
the fund been paid into the Insolvency Services Account on 30 June 1990.'

are inappropriate and should be deleted.

The judge dealt with the matter of principle, as to whether interest should be payable,
by saying in very general terms, it seems to me, that there is no reason in principle why,
where sums become due in the course of administration as an expense of that
administration and they are not paid and they are ultimately held to be payable, those
entitled to receive payment should not receive interest. I would not wish to support as
wide a declaration as that because the circumstances in which sums may not be paid
initially as they are incurred and may come to be paid much later on may vary very
considerably. There may be cases of debt or damages which the administrators are liable
to pay, not personally liable for, but liable to pay out of the assets in their hands under
s. 19(5) where the course of events may lead to an award of interest under the Supreme
Court Act. There may be other circumstances where interest may be payable under
another heading and I do not see that it is necessary to consider in this case whether the
full width of the judge's pronouncement is justified. I guard myself in that respect.

In the present case the administrators have very properly made this application to the
court by summons for directions in October 1991. We are now heading for two-and-a-
half years later. The application was itself prompted by the respondents' s. 27 applications
made in September 1991. In those circumstances, as the administrators have had money
invested and earning interest while being held until the question is resolved, it is right,
and in accordance with the principle in *Ex parte James* (1874) LR 9 Ch App 609, that the
administrators should pay interest at the rate they have earned and pay the moneys to
the respondents in respect of their entitlement. Accordingly, I would accept that basis for
the order, which Mr Potts says was the basis on which the claim was put to the judge in
the court below.

I see no reason, therefore, to differ from the date, 30 June 1990, which was the date the
judge in his discretion selected as the date from which interest should run. It is the date
from which claims were made on behalf of some former employees to interest on their
benefits as well as to the benefits themselves. There has been no argument about date in
this court. It is said, however, that the court should not allow the benefit of this decision
as to interest to inure to other employees than those who have specifically claimed
interest. But we are dealing with this matter on the basis that the administrators are
officers of the court and they have applied to the court for directions. In my judgment, it
would not be right that the benefits of the respondents' success should not extend to all
employees who have also been deprived of their benefits.

Finally, there is the point taken by way of respondent's notice in respect of the bonuses
which were paid under the letter set out at the beginning of this judgment, of September
1989, to the captains and first officers, Mr Potts submits that these bonus payments,
referred to as loyalty bonus payments, for those who remained in the employment of and
working for Paramount Airways Ltd as at 31 October 1989, and who had not tendered
their resignations by that time, and as at the ends of each subsequent month if the
arrangement had gone on for longer, were really a concealed pay rise and what is being
done is to try and contract out of the benefits of giving a pay rise. The question, as I see
it, depends entirely on the construction of this letter, and what strikes me about it is that
it makes provision for the administrators remaining in office after 31 October 1989 and
says that, on that basis, this arrangement will continue on a monthly basis until further
notice, with each month and date being relevant for not having tendered resignations. I

A   regard this as a genuine letter, save for the final paragraph, and not a sham for a pay rise and I do not see, taken as a genuine letter, that the bonus arrangement is made necessarily coterminous with the employment.

Of course, if the employment is terminated and they cease working for Paramount Airways, the bonus will also cease. But the bonus could be terminated at the end of a month without terminating the underlying contract of employment. The additional payment would then cease but the basic salary would continue to be payable. In these

B   circumstances, I regard this as a separate contract and not covered by the words in s. 19(5) as a contract of employment adopted by the administrator.

It follows, save in respect of the minor alteration, cutting out a few words about the rate of interest, that I agree with the judge on all points and, largely, for the reasons he gave, save that I do not put the right to interest so wide or go so far as he did into the question of contracting out.

C   I would, therefore, dismiss the appeal and the cross-appeal by respondent's notice.

Leggatt LJ: Nothing has persuaded me that, as used in s. 19(5) of the *Insolvency Act* 1986, the word 'adopted' connotes, in relation to contracts of employment, anything other than 'the continuance of which is expressly or impliedly accepted'. That is what the administrators unequivocally did by their letter of 14 August 1989 without confining the

D   contracts of employment to rights arising after the administration order was made.

Whatever the consequences for insolvency law which Mr Michael Crystal QC may apprehend, the point is in my judgment too plain for argument. The essential question is whether the relevant debts or liabilities were incurred while administrators were acting as such. I was at first attracted by Mr Crystal's argument that the right to holiday pay constituted a contingent liability which was incurred from time to time before the administration order was made, the contingency being the termination of the contract of

E   employment without all the holiday earned during the current year having been taken. But cl. 8(f) of the contract of employment provides:

> 'On termination of employment, other than for misconduct, your entitlement will be paid . . .'

It follows that not until termination, and so during the period of administration, will that debt have been incurred. Since s. 19(5) applies to debts or liabilities, debts in respect of

F   holiday pay have to be paid out of property of the company in the hands of the administrators in accordance with that provision. Since the rights to contractual notice and to pension contributions during the period of notice arose out of contracts of employment which the administrators adopted, the sums due in respect of those rights following dismissal must be similarly dealt with for the reasons explained by Dillon LJ.

I say nothing about contracting out since it does not arise in this case. The bonus

G   payments that the respondents also claim were made under new contracts which were to continue on a monthly basis until further notice, but made no provision for any periods of notice. There is no warrant for regarding the contracts as coterminous with contracts of employment. The contracts for bonus payment in this case were brought to an end by dismissal. About interest, I do not wish to add anything to what Dillon LJ has said. It follows that I agree that the order should go which he has proposed.

H   **Henry LJ:** I agree with the judgments given and do not wish to add anything to them.

(*Appeal and cross-appeal dismissed. Taxation of the costs if not agreed including cost of respondent's notice on the indemnity basis. Leave to appeal to House of Lords refused*)

AIB Finance Ltd v Bank of Scotland.   A

Court of Session (Inner House).
Lord Justice-Clerk Ross, Lord Murray and Lord McCluskey.
Judgment delivered 14 July 1993.

Ranking of floating charges in Scotland – Deeds creating standard security and
floating charge executed on same day – Floating charge contained 'negative   B
pledge' clause – Whether clause regulated ranking – Whether standard security
'created' after floating charge – Whether standard security created by grantor –
Companies Act 1985, s. 410(5), 464(1)–(4).

This was a special case raising the issues (1) whether a standard security was created
subsequent to the date of execution of a floating charge, and (2) whether the order of ranking
of the securities was regulated by a provision in the floating charge.   C

The standard security and the floating charge were granted by Lothian Cars Ltd. Both
deeds were executed on 19 December 1986; the standard security (in favour of the first
party) was recorded in the register of sasines on 30 December 1986, and the floating charge
(in favour of the second parties) was registered in the register of charges on 30 December
1986. The standard security was registered in the register of charges on 9 January 1987.
On 14 March 1991 the third parties were appointed as joint receivers of the whole property   D
and undertaking of Lothian Cars Ltd.

The floating charge in favour of the second parties included a 'restrictive clause'
prohibiting the creation, subsequent to the date of the charge, of any fixed security or any
other floating charge having priority over or ranking pari passu with the floating charge,
excepting a fixed security in favour of the bank (the second parties) which would have
priority over the floating charge.   E

The first party argued that the restrictive clause was a 'negative pledge' within s. 464(1)(a)
of the Companies Act 1985 and not a ranking clause within s. 464(1)(b). Thus the ranking
of the securities was not regulated within the meaning of s. 464(3) and the standard security
had priority under s. 464(4)(a). The second and third parties argued that the floating charge
ranked in priority to the standard security. A negative pledge could be effective to alter the
order of ranking laid down in s. 464(4), albeit that negative pledges achieved ranking in a   F
negative manner. Under the restrictive clause, the standard security was created subsequent
to the floating charge. Having regard to the terms of s. 410(5) of the 1985 Act, the floating
charge was created on the date upon which it was executed namely 19 December 1986. The
standard security on the other hand was created on the date on which the creditor's right
became a real right, namely, 30 December 1986. The first party submitted that the standard
security was not created after the floating charge for the purposes of the restrictive clause,
despite the wording of s. 410(5)(b) of the 1985 Act. Furthermore, the standard security was   G
not 'created' by Lothian Cars Ltd, because the standard security was not recorded by the
act of Lothian Cars Ltd since it was the first party and not Lothian Cars Ltd which recorded
the standard security and thus brought the real right into existence.

Held, by a majority, that the floating charge ranked in priority over the standard security:

1. (Per Lord Justice-Clerk Ross and Lord McCluskey) The order of ranking of the
floating charge and the standard security was regulated by provisions contained in the   H
floating charge within the meaning of s. 464(3). The restrictive clause was effective to alter
the order of ranking otherwise laid down in s. 464(4). The order of ranking in s. 464(4) could
be displaced by either a negative pledge (s. 464(1)(a)) or by a ranking clause (s. 464(1)(b)).
In any event a negative pledge of the kind described in s. 464(1)(a) would be effective to
displace the normal order of ranking without relying on s. 464(3).

A   2. (Per Lord Justice-Clerk Ross and Lord McCluskey) 'Create' in s. 464 meant the same thing as in s. 410 and in the restrictive clause. The date of recording the security in the register of sasines was the date of creation of the charge.

    3. (Per Lord Justice-Clerk Ross and Lord McCluskey) The standard security could properly be described as created by Lothian Cars Ltd although it was recorded in the general register of sasines by the first party. A charge was created by the grantor of the security.

B   3. (Per Lord Murray dissenting) The floating charge clause's prohibition against 'creating' subsequent securities was to be read as a prohibition against granting them subsequently. On that basis the standard security was not subsequent to the date of the floating charge. It followed that ranking priority between them was not regulated by the clause.

C   The following case was referred to in the opinions:

Pepper v Hart [1992] BTC 591; [1993] AC 593.

J E Drummond Young QC (instructed by Drummond Miller WS) for the first party.

GNH Emslie QC (instructed by Steedman Ramage WS) for the second and third parties.

D   OPINIONS

Lord Justice-Clerk Ross: The special case has been presented because of a dispute which has arisen as to the priority of ranking between a standard security and a floating charge. Both the standard security and the floating charge were granted by Lothian Cars Ltd. Both deeds were executed on 19 December 1986; the standard security which was granted in favour of the first party was recorded in the division of the general register of sasines for the county of West Lothian on 30 December 1986, and the floating charge

E which was granted in favour of the second parties was registered in the register of charges on 30 December 1986. The standard security was registered in the register of charges on 9 January 1987. On 14 March 1991 the third parties were appointed as joint receivers of the whole property and undertaking of Lothian Cars Ltd.

The floating charge in favour of the second parties includes inter alia the following provision (which is hereinafter referred to as 'the restrictive clause'):

F   '. . . we (Lothian Cars Ltd) are hereby and shall be prohibited from creating subsequent to the date hereof any fixed security or any other floating charge as defined by the *Companies Act* 1985 or any statutory modification or re-enactment thereof for the time being in force having priority over or ranking pari passu with the floating charge hereby created excepting any fixed security which may subsequent to the date of these presents be granted by us in favour of the bank (the second parties) which shall have priority over the floating charge hereby created.'

G As is made clear in the special case the issues for determination are (1) whether the standard security was created subsequent to the date of execution of the floating charge for the purposes of the provisions in the floating charge above referred to, and (2) whether the order of ranking of these deeds inter se is regulated by the said provisions in the floating charge for the purposes of s. 464(3) of the *Companies Act* 1985.

The contentions of the parties are set forth in the special case. On behalf of the first

H party Mr Drummond Young began his submissions by referring to the relevant statutory provisions in relation to floating charges which are to be found in the *Companies Act* 1985.

In terms of s. 462, it is competent for a company to create in favour of the creditor in a debt or obligation a floating charge. Ranking of floating charges is dealt with in s. 464, which provides inter alia as follows:

'(1) Subject to subsection (2), the instrument creating a floating charge over all or any part of the company's property under section 462 may contain–

    (a) provisions prohibiting or restricting the creation of any fixed security or any other floating charge having priority over, or ranking pari passu with, the floating charge; or

    (b) provisions regulating the order in which the floating charge shall rank with any other subsisting or future floating charges or fixed securities over that property or any part of it.

(2) Where all or any part of the property of a company is subject both to a floating charge and to a fixed security arising by operation of law, the fixed security has priority over the floating charge.

(3) Where the order of ranking of the floating charge with any other subsisting or future floating charges or fixed securities over all or any part of the company's property is not regulated by provisions contained in the instrument creating the floating charge, the order of ranking is determined in accordance with the following provisions of this section.

(4) Subject to the provisions of this section–

    (a) a fixed security, the right to which has been constituted as a real right before a floating charge has attached to all or any part of the property of the company, has priority of ranking over the floating charge;

    (b) floating charges rank with one another according to the time of registration in accordance with Chapter II of Part XII;

    (c) floating charges which have been received by the registrar for registration by the same postal delivery rank with one another equally.

    . . .'

Section 410 deals with registration of charges. It provides inter alia as follows:

'(1) The following provisions of this Chapter have effect for the purpose of securing the registration in Scotland of charges created by companies.

(2) Every charge created by a company, being a charge to which this section applies, is, so far as any security on the company's property or any part of it is conferred by the charge, void against the liquidator or administrator and any creditor of the company unless the prescribed particulars of the charge, together with a copy (certified in the prescribed manner to be a correct copy) of the instrument (if any) by which the charge is created or evidenced, are delivered to or received by the registrar of companies for registration in the manner required by this Chapter within 21 days after the date of the creation of the charge.

(3) Subsection (2) is without prejudice to any contract or obligation for repayment of the money secured by the charge; and when a charge becomes void under this section the money secured by it immediately becomes payable.

(4) This section applies to the following charges–

    (a) a charge on land wherever situated, or any interest in such land (not including a charge for any rent, ground annual or other periodical sum payable in respect of the land, but including a charge created by a heritable security within the meaning of section 9(8) of the Conveyancing and Feudal Reform (Scotland) Act 1970),

    . . .

    (e) a floating charge.

A (5) In this Chapter "company" (except in section 424) means an incorporated company registered in Scotland; "registrar of companies" means the registrar or other officer performing under this Act the duty of registration of companies in Scotland; and references to the date of creation of a charge are–

    (a) in the case of a floating charge, the date on which the instrument creating the floating charge was executed by the company creating the charge, and

B   (b) in any other case, the date on which the right of the person entitled to the benefit of the charge was constituted as a real right.'

Section 415 deals with the duty of a company to register charges created by it. Section 415 is in the following terms:

'(1) It is a company's duty to send to the registrar of companies for registration the particulars of every charge created by the company and of the issues of
C debentures of a series requiring registration under sections 410 to 414; but registration of any such charge may be effected on the application of any person interested in it.

(2) Where registration is effected on the application of some person other than the company, that person is entitled to recover from the company the amount of any fees properly paid by him to the registrar on the registration.

D (3) If a company makes default in sending to the registrar for registration the particulars of any charge created by the company or of the issues of debentures of a series requiring registration as above mentioned, then, unless the registration has been effected on the application of some other person, the company and every officer of it who is in default is liable to a fine and, for continued contravention, to a daily default fine.'

E Section 417 deals with the register of charges to be kept by the registrar of companies. Section 417 is in the following terms:

'(1) The registrar of companies shall keep, with respect to each company, a register in the prescribed form of all the charges requiring registration under this Chapter, and shall enter in the register with respect to such charges the particulars specified below.

F   . . .

(3) In the case of any other charge, there shall be entered–

    (a) if it is a charge created by the company, the date of its creation, and if it was a charge existing on property acquired by the company, the date of the acquisition of the property,

    (b) the amount secured by the charge,

G   (c) short particulars of the property charge,

    (d) the persons entitled to the charge, and

    (e) in the case of a floating charge, a statement of any of the provisions of the charge and of any instrument relating to it which prohibit or restrict or regulate the company's power to grant further securities ranking in priority to, or pari passu with, the floating charge, or which vary or otherwise
H regulate the order of ranking of the floating charge in relation to subsisting securities.

(4) The register kept in pursuance of this section shall be open to inspection by any person.'

At the heart of Mr Drummond Young's submission lay the proposition that in the Act of 1985 Parliament drew a distinction between provisions prohibiting or restricting the

creation of fixed securities or other floating charges – commonly called a negative pledge
on the one hand and ranking clauses on the other hand. Putting the matter shortly his
submission was that the restrictive clause in this case was a negative pledge and not a
ranking clause at all. Mr Drummond Young also contended that it was necessary to
determine when the standard security in this case had been created for the purpose of the
restrictive clause; he submitted that the standard security was created on the date when it
was executed by the grantor. All that the grantor had to do in relation to the standard
security was to execute and deliver it. Before the creditor in the standard security could
acquire a real right the standard security required to be recorded (s. 11(1) of the
Conveyancing and Feudal Reform (Scotland) Act 1970), but it was the creditor and not
the grantor who required to effect registration in the general register of sasines. Mr
Drummond Young further maintained that unless that was so, serious practical
difficulties might occur. For example, a debtor might grant a standard security, but time
would necessarily elapse before it could be registered in the general register of sasines.
Before it was registered and the creditor obtained a real right, the debtor might grant a
floating charge with a negative pledge. If the argument put forward on behalf of the
second and third parties was correct, the negative pledge granted after the date of the
standard security would strike at the standard security even though the negative pledge
did not exist when the standard security was executed and delivered, and even though the
creditor under the standard security could not have had notice of it.

Mr Drummond Young recognised that s. 410(5) defines 'the date of creation of a
charge' but he maintained that that definition was for the purposes of Ch. II of Pt. XII
of the statute and was of relevance when considering whether there had been timeous
registration of a charge created by a company. This was because s. 410(2) provides for
registration within 21 days after 'the date of the creation of the charge'. He accordingly
submitted that the definition in s. 410(5) had no bearing on the construction to be placed
on the restrictive clause in the floating charge. In these circumstances Mr Drummond
Young contended that the standard security was not created subsequent to the date of
execution of the floating charge since both had been executed on the same date.

Mr Drummond Young also developed further his argument to the effect that the
provisions in the restrictive clause of the floating charge did not regulate the order of
ranking between the floating charge and the standard security for the purpose of s. 464(3)
of the *Companies Act* 1985. His submission was that s. 464(3) refers only to ranking
clauses and not to negative pledges. He emphasised that it was important to keep a
distinction between ranking clauses and negative pledges, and he maintained that his
submission to that effect was strengthened by a consideration of s. 140 of the *Companies
Act* 1989. Although this section had not yet been brought into force, he maintained that
the proper inference to draw from the alteration which was proposed to be made to
s. 464(3) of the Act of 1985 was that at present the subsection did not refer to negative
pledges but referred to ranking clauses only. In the circumstances, he submitted that the
restrictive clause did not serve to regulate the order of ranking, and that accordingly
s. 464(4)(a) applied. The standard security was recorded on 30 December, 1986, and a
real right then came into being (s. 11(1) of the *Conveyancing and Feudal Reform
(Scotland) Act* 1970); the third parties were appointed joint receivers on 14 March 1991,
and the floating charge then attached the property of the company subject to the charge.
He accordingly submitted that the standard security had priority of ranking over the
floating charge. Mr Drummond Young therefore invited the court to answer the three
questions in the case in the negative.

Mr Emslie for the second and third parties invited the court to answer the three
questions in the case in the affirmative upon the basis that the floating charge ranked in
priority to the standard security. He stressed that what the court had to do was to
construe the restrictive clause. He submitted that a negative pledge could be effective to

A alter the order of ranking laid down in s. 464(4). He stated that at first sight when one
looked at s. 464(3), the impression might be gained that there was identity between it and
s. 464(1)(b) and not with s. 464(1)(a). However he maintained that negative pledges
achieved ranking in a negative manner. Accordingly he contended that on a true
construction of s. 464(3) the subsection was intended to apply both to clauses under
s. 464(1)(a) and under s. 464(1)(b).

B Mr Emslie further submitted that even if that were not so, the negative pledge as
described in s. 464(1)(a) standing alone was fully effective to displace the normal ranking
laid down in s. 464(4). Mr Emslie also submitted that the date of registration of the
floating charge did not enter into the consideration for present purposes. No question
arose as to prior notice or prior registration of the floating charge as a requirement for
effective ranking.

C Both counsel were agreed that there was no judicial authority on the subject of ranking.
Mr Emslie referred to the history of floating charges in Scotland. That history reveals
that the concept of a floating charge was repugnant to the principles of Scots law, and
was not recognised under the common law. Floating charges were introduced into the
law of Scotland by the *Companies (Floating Charges) (Scotland) Act* 1961. Section 5 of
the Act of 1961 dealt with the ranking of floating charges, and Mr Emslie pointed out
that s. 5(2)(c) referred to a negative pledge. He accordingly submitted that in the Act of
D 1961 negative pledge was seen as affecting ranking. He next referred to the *Companies
(Floating Charges and Receivers) (Scotland) Act* 1972. Mr Emslie submitted that this
Act had made changes to the ranking of floating charges. Section 5 of the Act of 1972
deals with the ranking of floating charges. Section 5 of the Act of 1972 is in substantially
the same form as s. 464 of the Act of 1985. Mr Emslie pointed out that in the Act of 1972
the law relating to the ranking of floating charges had been altered in two principal
respects. First, whereas s. 5 of the Act of 1961 was concerned with a provision prohibiting
E the company from subsequently creating any fixed security having priority over the
floating charge, in s. 5 of the Act of 1972 the reference was to provisions prohibiting or
restricting the creation of any fixed security or any other floating charge having priority
over the floating charge. Secondly, s. 5(3) of the Act of 1972 made it plain that the order
of ranking of the floating charge with any other subsisting or future floating charges or
fixed securities may be regulated by provisions contained in the floating charge in
F question.

Mr Emslie next referred to a number of textbooks and reports which he maintained
demonstrated that s. 464(3) was not intended to apply to provisions as described in
s. 464(1)(b) only but was also intended to apply to negative pledges as described
in s. 464(1)(a). In this connection he referred to the report of the Scottish Law
Commission (No. 14 of 1970, Cmnd 4336); *Palmer's Company Law* (25th edn), vol. II,
para. 13.216; Halliday, *Conveyancing Law and Practice*, vol. III, para. 41-22 and 41-25;
G McDonald's *Conveyancing Manual*, para. 23.6; *Gloag and Henderson's Introduction to
the Law of Scotland* (9th edn), para. 25.27; and *Stair Memorial Encyclopaedia of the Laws
of Scotland*, vol. 4, para. 664.

It is unnecessary to examine these books in any detail. I accept that in all these works
when ranking of floating charges is being dealt with, reference is made to inter alia
provisions in the nature of negative pledge. The textbook writers appear to me to do little
H more than paraphrase the language used in s. 464, and there can be no doubt that s. 464
is dealing with the ranking of floating charges and that it includes a reference to negative
pledges. Likewise in the Scottish Law Commission Report, under the heading of
'Conventional ranking clauses' reference is made to what is in effect a negative pledge.

Under reference to *Pepper v Hart* [1993] AC 593, Mr Emslie invited us to consider the
Hansard report of proceedings in the House of Lords when the bill which became the

Act of 1972 was introduced. I am doubtful whether in this instance it is legitimate to consult the Hansard report because I do not accept that there is ambiguity or obscurity in the statute. In any event, the report does no more than to show that when the subject of ranking of floating charges was being described, reference was made to inter alia what is in effect a negative pledge.

Mr Emslie further submitted that on any view it was clear that the negative pledge was intended to affect ranking. Mr Emslie maintained that the practical difficulty which Mr Drummond Young had apprehended when considering the terms of s. 410 did not really exist. He maintained that when Mr Drummond Young referred to difficulties which would arise where the creditor of a standard security had no notice that a floating charge had been created with a negative pledge, what he was really saying is that there ought to have been a provision in s. 464 dealing with notice. Mr Emslie also contended that the court should not look at the provisions of s. 140 of the Act of 1989 which had not yet been brought into force, for the purpose of construing the provisions of the earlier Act of 1985. Under reference to *Craies on Statute Law* (7th edn), p. 148 he submitted that the rule was that resort to a later Act for the interpretation of an earlier Act could rarely be justified. In any event, he submitted that s. 140 of the Act of 1989 merely clarified what was plain from the Act of 1985. His submission at the end of the day was that a negative pledge was capable of affecting the order of ranking.

On the subject of whether the standard security in this case was created subsequent to the floating charge, he submitted that it clearly was. He founded on the provisions of s. 410(5) of the Act of 1985 for the purpose of showing what was meant by creation. He contended that the definition in that subsection was not confined to the part of the Act where it appeared. He pointed out that the reference to 'In this Chapter' in s. 410(5) did not exclude the definition for present purposes. He further maintained that there was nothing to indicate that 'creation' in s. 464 had a different meaning from s. 410. He stressed that in s. 464(4)(b) and in s. 464(5) express reference is made to Ch. II of Pt. XII where s. 410 appears. He accordingly contended that the clear implication was that Parliament intended that the definition should be applied in s. 464 when reference was made to 'creating a floating charge'.

Mr Emslie maintained that having regard to the terms of s. 410(5) the floating charge was created on the date upon which it was executed namely 19 December 1986. The standard security on the other hand was created on the date on which the creditor's right became a real right, namely, 30 December 1986.

The question remains as to whether the standard security had been created by Lothian Cars Ltd. Mr Drummond Young had maintained that registration was the responsibility of the creditor, and accordingly could not be regarded as a step taken by Lothian Cars Ltd. Mr Emslie maintained that that was not so and that all steps in the creation of the charge must be taken as the acts of the creator. He pointed to s. 410(2), s. 410(5), s. 415 and s. 417(3)(a) in all of which reference is made to the creation of a charge by a company. He submitted that both execution and recording are to be treated as emanating from the grantor. In this connection he founded on the provisions of s. 415(1) which place upon the company a duty to send to the registrar of companies for registration the particulars of 'every charge created by the company'. In terms of s. 410(5) in the case of a standard security, the charge would not be created by the company until it was recorded, and he maintained that this showed that recording should properly be regarded as an act of the company even though it was effected by the creditor.

Finally he contended that the prohibition in the restrictive clause was against creating any subsequent fixed security or any other floating charge. The restrictive clause also provided for an exception in respect of a subsequent fixed security granted by Lothian Cars Ltd in favour of the bank. He maintained that the use of the word 'creating' in the

A main part of the clause and the use of the word 'granted' in the exception clearly showed that 'creation' involved something more than mere granting. Mr Emslie accordingly invited us to answer the three questions in the case in the affirmative.

The questions which arise in this case require the court to construe the provisions of the restrictive clause, and the court can only do that against the background of the relevant statutory provisions. Although there is obvious attraction in Mr Drummond Young's emphasis upon the distinction in s. 464(1) between (a) negative pledges and (b)
B ranking clauses, I have come to be of opinion that both negative pledges and ranking clauses can affect the ranking of floating charges. It is clear that from the Act of 1961 onwards negative pledges have been included under the general description of the ranking of floating charges. In my opinion Mr Emslie is well-founded in his assertion that a negative pledge does achieve ranking albeit in a negative manner.

C I am accordingly satisfied that the present case is one where the order of ranking of the floating charge and the standard security is regulated by provisions contained in the floating charge. The restrictive clause is effective to alter the order of ranking otherwise laid down in s. 464(4). On a proper construction of s. 464(3) I am satisfied that the order of ranking in s. 464(4) can be displaced by either a negative pledge (s. 464(1)(a)) or by a ranking clause (s. 464(1)(b)). I agree with Mr Emslie that the legislation since 1961 dealing with the ranking of floating charges has made it clear that a negative pledge is recognised
D as affecting ranking.

In any event, even if that were not so, I would still hold that without relying on s. 464(3) at all a negative pledge of the kind described in s. 464(1)(a) would be effective to displace the normal order of ranking. The ordinary order of ranking is laid down in s. 464(4). That subsection begins with the words 'Subject to the provisions of this section'. That accordingly means that s. 464(4)(a) is subject to inter alia s. 464(1)(a) and s. 464(2).
E Section 464(1) is stated to be 'Subject to subsection (2)'. Accordingly what s. 464(1) is providing is that subject to s. 464(2) there can be a negative pledge, and that shows that a negative pledge can have an effect upon ranking (except for a fixed security arising by operation of law). I also agree with Mr Emslie that what s. 464(3) refers to is the provisions of the deed creating the floating charge, and it is unnecessary to consider when notice was given or what the state of knowledge of the parties was. Mr. Drummond
F Young in the course of his argument referred to the matter of notice, but nothing is said about notice in the statement of facts in this case, and accordingly it does not require to be considered so far as this special case is concerned.

As already observed, in the course of his argument Mr Drummond Young sought to rely upon the provisions of s. 140 of the *Companies Act* 1989 which amends s. 464. That section, however, is not yet in force, and in my opinion it has no bearing on the present case. I am not persuaded that it is legitimate in the present case to consider the terms of
G the Act of 1989 when endeavouring to interpret the provisions of the Act of 1985. What one requires to do so far as the Act of 1985 is concerned is to ascertain Parliament's intention at the time when that legislation was enacted.

When one has regard to the terms of the restrictive clause the critical question is whether the standard security was created subsequent to the floating charge. This raises the question of what is meant by 'creating' in the restrictive clause. I appreciate that
H s. 410(5) opens with the words 'In this Chapter'. However, various tenses of the verb 'create' are used in the earlier subsections of s. 410 and in various other sections of the Act of 1985 including s. 462 and s. 464. In my opinion there is no reason to think that the verb 'create' in s. 464 should have any different meaning from the meaning which it has in s. 410. It is also significant that in s. 464(4)(b) and s. 464(5) there is express reference to Ch. II of Pt. XII of the Act of 1985. I am also of opinion that in the restrictive

clause when the word 'creating' is used, it must be used in the same sense in which that A
word is used in s. 410 and 464 of the *Companies Act* 1985.

A question then arises as to whether the standard security was created by Lothian Cars
Ltd, and if so whether it was subsequent to the floating charge. As I understood it, Mr
Drummond Young's contention was that the real right under the standard security which
came into being when the standard security was recorded could not be regarded as the
act of Lothian Cars Ltd since it was the first party and not Lothian Cars Ltd who B
recorded the standard security and thus brought the real right into existence. I am not
persuaded that this is so. Even though it was the first party who recorded the standard
security, the language used in the *Companies Act* 1985 makes it clear that a charge such
as a standard security is regarded as having been created by the grantor. Thus in s. 410(2)
which is dealing with registration of charges, the charge is described as 'created by a
company'. That must mean created by the grantor of the security. The same is true of
s. 415 and 417. C

In my opinion in the present case the standard security can properly be described as
created by Lothian Cars Ltd although it was recorded in the general register of sasines
by the first party and it is the date of such recording which is the date of creation of the
charge in terms of s. 410(5)(b). Section 417 deals with registration of charges, and
s. 417(3)(a) shows that what requires to be entered in the register is the date of the
creation of the charge if it is a charge created by the company. This makes it perfectly D
clear that even though the date of creation may depend, in the case of a standard security,
upon the date upon which the standard security was recorded in the general register of
sasines, the charge is still to be regarded as having been created by the company. I am
confirmed in this conclusion by reference to the later provisions of the restrictive clause
which contain an exception in favour of any fixed security subsequently granted by
Lothian Cars Ltd in favour of the second parties. The use of the verb 'granted' shows
that something different from creation was intended. This is consistent with creating a E
security being something more than merely granting the deed.

I am accordingly satisfied that Lothian Cars Ltd did not merely grant the standard
security; they also created it. In terms of s. 410(5)(b), the date of creation of the standard
security is the date when the creditor recorded the standard security and thus obtained a
real right. That was 30 December 1986. In terms of s. 410(5)(a), the floating charge was
created on the date it was executed, namely, 19 December 1986. It follows that the F
floating charge ranks in priority over the standard security.

In general I am of opinion that the approach of Mr Emslie is to be preferred. I would
accordingly move your Lordships to answer all three questions in the case in the
affirmative.

Lord Murray: The substance of this special case for the opinion of the Court of Session
is to determine which of two charge-holders on the property of a company in receivership G
is entitled to prior ranking of their respective charges. The first party is AIB Finance Ltd
('AIB'). The second parties are the governor and company of the bank of Scotland
('BOS'). The third parties are the joint receivers of Lothian Cars Ltd ('LC').

The agreed facts are that on 19 December 1986 in respect of a loan from AIB, LC
granted a standard security to AIB over heritable property belonging to them. On the
same date LC granted a bond and floating charge to BOS. On 30 December 1986 the
standard security was recorded by AIB in the register of sasines. On the same date BOS H
recorded their floating charge in the register of charges kept by the registrar of companies.
On 9 January 1987 AIB recorded their standard security in the register of charges. On 14
March 1991 joint receivers were appointed to LC's whole property and undertaking.

It was further not disputed that a floating charge comes into existence when it is
executed and that it is held, under s. 410(5)(a) of the *Companies Act* 1985 to have been

A created, for purposes of registration as a charge, on that date; that, for purposes of registration as a charge, a standard security is held to be created when the right of the charge-holder is constituted as a right in rem; and that BOS's floating charge did not attach to LC's property until 14 March 1991.

The issues between the parties are centred on the following clause in the instrument creating the floating charge in favour of BOS:

B '. . . we (Lothian Cars Ltd) are hereby and shall be prohibited from creating subsequent to the date hereof any fixed security or other floating charge as defined by the *Companies Act* 1985 or any statutory modification or re-enactment thereof for the time being in force having priority over or ranking pari passu with the floating charge hereby created excepting any fixed security which may subsequent to the date of these presents be granted by us in favour of the bank (the second parties) which shall have priority over the floating charge hereby created.'

C AIB and BOS construe this clause differently in the context of the relevant statutory provisions. The third parties take their stand with BOS and were represented by the same solicitors and counsel.

For AIB it is contended that the clause does not provide for regulation of ranking of charges nor does it regulate ranking as between itself and AIB's standard security. Further the standard security was not created by LC after the floating charge; for LC granted it on the same date and played no further part in bringing it into force as a registrable charge. That was done by AIB recording it in the general register of sasines on 30 December 1986. By s. 11(1) of the *Conveyancing and Feudal Reform (Scotland) Act* 1970 a right in rem thereby vested in AIB as grantee.

For BOS it is contended that the standard security could not be said to have been created until after the floating charge was created on 19 December 1986. For while under E s. 410(5)(a) reference to the date of creation of a floating charge was to the date on which the instrument creating the floating charge was executed, namely 19 December 1986, under (b) in any other case it was the date on which the right of the charge-holder was constituted as a real right, which was 30 December 1986 for AIB's standard security.

The parties are divided essentially about the construction to be put on the foregoing clause of the instrument creating the floating charge in the context of s. 464 of the F *Companies Act* 1985. The material subsections of that section are as follows:

'(1) . . . the instrument creating a floating charge . . . may contain–

(a) provisions prohibiting or restricting the creation of any fixed security or any other floating charge . . . or

(b) provisions regulating the order in which the floating charge shall rank with any other subsisting or future floating charges or fixed securities . . .

G (2) . . .

(3) Where the order of ranking of the floating charge with any other subsisting or future floating charges or fixed securities . . . is not regulated by provisions contained in the instrument . . . the order of ranking is determined in accordance with the following . . .

H (4) . . .

(a) a fixed security, the right to which has been constituted as a real right before a floating charge has attached . . . has priority of ranking over the floating charge . . .'

The questions of law are in substance:

(1)   Was the standard security created after the creation of the floating charge?

(2)   Does the clause of the floating charge instrument regulate the order of ranking of   A
the floating charge and the standard security?

(3)   Does the floating charge have priority?

Counsel for AIB argued with great cogency and persuasive force that the prohibition
of LC from creating any fixed security or floating charge subsequent to 19 December
1986 must be read as being a prohibition from granting any such deed. The word 'create'
in this context did not have the technical meaning it had in relation to s. 410 of the 1985   B
Act. In the latter's sense of creation, the standard security was not fully in existence until
the grantee had registered it in the general register of sasines. As regards s. 464(1)(a) and
(b), (a) covered negative pledges and did not deal with regulation of ranking at all.
Only (b) dealt with regulation. The clause under consideration dealt in terms with (a)
and not (b).

Counsel for BOS argued with equal cogency and persuasiveness that the word 'create'   C
could not have one meaning in s. 410, dealing with registration of charges, and a different
meaning in s. 464, dealing with ranking of charges. As the standard security had been
created, in the sense of the 1985 Act, after 19 December 1986, it was struck at by the
floating charge clause. In any event that clause regulated the order of ranking of the
floating charge and the standard security, since its prohibition and restriction affected
ranking. Section 417(3)(e) equiparated the contents of s. 464(1)(a) and (b) as both
involving regulation. The clause was sufficient to exclude operation of the provisions of   D
subs. (4)(a). Without the latter the standard security enjoyed no priority.

Counsel for AIB invited the court to answer all three questions of law in the negative.
Counsel for BOS invited the court to answer all three questions in the affirmative.

As regards the issue raised by the first question of law, I have come to the conclusion,
not without difficulty, that the interpretation of the floating charge clause for which AIB
contend is to be preferred. On the argument for BOS if the standard security had been   E
granted by LC on 18 December 1986, the day before the floating charge was created, it
would not have pre-dated the floating charge, which appears rather a startling assertion.
similarly if it had been granted two months before 19 December 1986, but had not yet
been registered, it would still not have pre-dated the floating charge. This anomaly and
associated anomalies are avoided by AIB's interpretation, which proceeds on the view
that 'creation' in s. 410(5) means becoming a registrable charge. It is intelligible to say   F
that a standard security is made by the grantor executing it and is created a registrable
charge when recorded (normally, as here, by the grantee) in the register of sasines. There
must already be a right in terms of s. 410(5)(b) for it to be constituted later as a real right.
The date which the deed bears has then some meaning and effect instead of no meaning
or effect. The floating charge clause's prohibition against 'creating' subsequent securities
is therefore to be read as a prohibition against granting them subsequently. It cannot
forbid what LC have already done or what they cannot prevent. I therefore answer the   G
first question in the negative.

In respect of the second question, neither of the contending versions of the meaning of
s. 464 is wholly satisfactory. It is not surprising then that material amendments to the
section have been enacted by s. 140 of the *Companies Act* 1989. But these have not yet
been brought into force by statutory instrument. I do not think that s. 140 can properly
be used as an aid to interpretation of the original section, if only because the amendments   H
may never be implemented. Prima facie s. 464(1)(b) appears to contemplate provisions
regulating the ranking of all charges and securities, not just some of them; and (a) appears
limited to provisions excluding or restricting the granting of subsequent ones. Counsel
for BOS strongly urged that a para. (a) provision would affect ranking and so would
regulate it, particularly when regard was had to the change between the 1961 Act version
and that of 1972 when power of restriction was added to power of prohibition. I find that

A view persuasive, particularly having regard to the provisions of s. 417(3)(e), but the difficulty for this argument is the wording of subs. (3) of s. 464, to the effect that the (4)(a) priority will prevail where the order of ranking 'is not regulated' by provisions in the floating charge instrument. As this floating charge clause is silent about other than subsequent fixed securities, and I have already reached the view that AIB's standard security was not subsequent to the date of the floating charge, it follows that ranking priority between them is not in fact regulated by this clause. Accordingly I would answer

B the second question in the negative. It follows then that question 3 would also be answered in the negative.

Lord McCluskey: The issues in this special case, as formulated in the statements of facts, issues and contentions and also in the questions of law, arise from the terms of the bond and floating charge granted on 19 December 1986 by Lothian Cars Ltd in favour of the second parties (referred to as 'the floating charge') and from s. 464(3) of the

C *Companies Act* 1985. The researches of counsel discovered no case law that assists greatly in resolving the issues; and although we were referred to various texts by living authors concerning the general effect of the relevant statutory provisions, I agree with your lordship in the chair that none of them seems to be consciously and expressly addressing any point of statutory construction that we may have to decide. Nonetheless I have found it valuable to adopt the approach suggested by Mr Emslie, for the second and third

D parties, and to consider the legislative history which led to the enactment of s. 464 of the *Companies Act* 1985. This appears to me to be clearly the correct course as the floating charge is a pure statutory creature in Scotland and of fairly recent origin.

We are concerned here with two concepts which occur in that section or in the floating charge and have an important bearing upon the correct understanding of the provisions which the floating charge contains. There is the concept of the 'creation of' or 'creating'

E a fixed security; and there is the concept of 'regulating' the order of ranking among securities. So I propose in examining the terms of the earlier legislation to pay particular attention to any light that may be shed thereby upon these two concepts.

The power to create a floating charge in Scotland was introduced by the *Companies (Floating Charges) (Scotland) Act* 1961. Section 1(1) made it competent for an incorporated company to:

F   'create in favour of the creditor a charge, in this Act referred to as a floating charge, over all or any of the property, heritable and moveable, which may from time to time be comprised in its property and undertaking.'

The floating charge was to take effect on the commencement of the winding up of the company by attaching to the company's property, but subject inter alia to the rights of any person then holding a fixed security over any part of the property and ranking in

G priority to the floating charge. Section 8(1) defined 'fixed security' as meaning:

       'any security, other than a floating charge or a charge having the nature of a floating charge, which on the winding-up of the company in Scotland would be treated as an effective security over that property . . .'

Clearly when Pt. II of the *Conveyancing and Feudal Reform (Scotland) Act* 1970 came into force and allowed the creation of a standard security, that definition would have

H been apt to include a standard security of the kind granted by Lothian Cars Ltd on 19 December and recorded on 30 December 1986. Section 2 of the 1961 Act enacted that a floating charge might be:

       'created . . . only by the execution, under the seal of the company, of an instrument of charge as nearly as practicable in the form set forth in the First Schedule to this Act . . .'

–or by certain other types of written instrument. It is abundantly plain from the whole   A
provisions of s. 2 that it was to be the execution of the appropriate instrument that was
to 'create' the floating charge. Section 3 declared that a floating charge was to have effect
'notwithstanding that it is not recorded in the Register of Sasines' in relation to any
heritable property in Scotland. Section 5 of the 1961 Act was the first precursor of s. 464
of the 1985 Act. It contained provisions about ranking: a fixed security arising by
operation of law was to have priority over any floating charge (subs. (1)). Subsection (2)
contained provisions about the priorities as between a floating charge and a fixed security   B
not arising by operation of law. Again, the fixed security was to have priority unless three
conditions were fulfilled. They included:

'(b) the floating charge was registered before the right of the creditor in the fixed
security was constituted as a real right, and

(c) the instrument creating the floating charge prohibited the company from
subsequently creating any fixed security having priority over, or ranking equally   C
with, the floating charge.'

Subsection (3) contained further provisions which regulated ranking as between several
floating charges: they were to rank according to the time of their registration; this
provision, including the proviso, further illustrates that, in the case of a floating charge,
creation preceded registration. Section 6 provided for registration with the registrar of
companies. There is, in my opinion, no room for doubt that the provisions in s. 5 of the   D
1961 Act were provisions designed to enable the grantor of the instrument creating the
floating charge to regulate the ranking inter se of the floating charge and any fixed
security to which subs. (2) applied. Condition (c) of s. 5(2) allowed the instrument creating
the floating charge to contain a prohibition on the subsequent creating by the company
of any fixed security having priority over or ranking equally with the floating charge;
accordingly, if such a provision was included in the instrument, the effect (provided the
other conditions were also met) was to reverse the ranking as between any fixed security   E
and any floating charge affected. The *Companies (Floating Charges and Receivers)
(Scotland) Act* 1972 effectively re-enacted most of these provisions. Section 3 of that Act
was new. It read:

'For the avoidance of doubt, it is hereby declared that a floating charge shall,
subject to the Act of 1948, have effect in accordance with this Act in relation to
any heritable property in Scotland to which it relates, notwithstanding that the   F
instrument creating it is not recorded in the Register of Sasines.'

Section 5, like its predecessor, s. 5 of the 1961 Act, dealt with ranking of floating charges
both in competition with fixed securities and with other floating charges. It reiterated the
notion of creating a fixed charge by written instrument and, along with s. 7, envisaged
and sanctioned an instrument of alteration. Section 5(1) enabled either such instrument
to contain: G

'(a) provisions prohibiting or restricting the creation of any fixed security or any
other floating charge have priority over, or ranking pari passu with, the floating
charge [which was the subject of the instrument]; or

(b) provisions regulating the order in which the floating charge shall rank with
any other subsisting or future floating charges or fixed securities over that property
or any part of it.'   H

Section 7 allowed a company to execute an instrument of alteration; and subs. (3) thereof
applied the registration provisions in the amended 1948 Act to any such instrument
which:

'(a) prohibits or restricts the creation of any fixed security or any other floating
charge having priority over, or ranking pari passu with, the floating charge; or

A   (b) varies, or otherwise regulates the order of, the ranking of the floating charge in relation to fixed securities or to other floating charges . . .'

Thus these provisions made it clear that a company could restrict as well as totally prohibit the creation of any fixed security which might compete with the floating charge created. It is, in my opinion, clear that s. 5 of the 1972 Act re-enacted the provisions in s. 5 of the 1961 Act which I have earlier characterised as 'provisions designed to enable

B   the grantor of the instrument creating the floating charge to regulate the ranking inter se of the floating charge and any fixed security'. In the 1972 Act, the provisions about prohibition and restriction in s. 5 and 7 were provisions which enabled the grantor of the instrument to determine which should rank first, the floating charge created (or altered) by the instrument, or any future fixed security. Indeed as the power to *restrict* was expressly conferred it appears to me that an instrument under that Act could contain quite a complicated regulation of the competitive ranking as between a floating charge

C   and some future fixed security. Provisions in an instrument which derived from these sections of the 1972 Act would in the ordinary use of language be fairly described as provisions 'regulating' the order of ranking of the floating charge with any other fixed security. The ordinary meaning of 'regulates' in these sections is well illustrated by s. 7(3)(b) which referred to an instrument of alteration which 'varies, or otherwise regulates the order of, the ranking . . .': the use of the word 'varies' as a synonym for

D   'regulates' makes it clear that 'regulates' was being used in one of its ordinary senses as meaning controlling things by placing them in some relative order. I now come to s. 5(3) of the 1972 Act. It read:

    'Where the order of ranking of the floating charge with any other subsisting or future floating charges or fixed securities over all or any part of the company's property is not regulated by provisions contained in the instrument creating the

E   floating charge or in any instrument of alteration, the order of ranking shall be determined in accordance with the following provisions of this section.'

Subsection (4) then laid down the rules as to the order of ranking being rules which were to apply unless the grantor chose to exercise his right to regulate the order. As he could influence, vary or determine the order by various methods, including the use of 'prohibiting or restricting' provisions of the kind specified in s. 5(1)(a) it would, in my

F   opinion, be entirely proper and sensible to speak of an instrument containing such provisions as one where the order of ranking was regulated by provisions contained in it. Subsections (1) and (3) of s. 464 of the *Companies Act* 1985 are in virtually the same terms as s. 5(1) and (3) of the 1972 Act, though without any reference to instruments of alteration. Accordingly, I consider that s. 464(3) also treats prohibiting or restricting provisions in an instrument (s. 464(1)(a)) as provisions which regulate the order of ranking. These considerations would lead me to answer the second question in the

G   affirmative purely on the basis of what I considered to be the clear meaning of s. 464(3) of the *Companies Act* 1985. In so doing I seek no help from the proceedings in Parliament to which we were referred. I doubt if they provide any real help anyway; but on the view I have formed of the meaning of s. 464 from its terms alone, in the light of the legislative history, I do not think that the conditions necessary for resort to such methods (as summarised by Lord Browne-Wilkinson at pp. 634–635 in *Pepper v Hart* [1993] AC 593)

H   obtain. I do not consider it legitimate to look at the terms of s. 140 of the 1989 Act (not yet in force) to determine the meaning of differently worded provisions in the 1985 Act or indeed of the similar provisions in the 1972 Act which I consider were effectively re-enacted in 1985.

    I can deal more briefly with the first question and the 'creation' issue it raises. The expression in the floating charge quoted in art. 3 is:

'. . . creating subsequent to the date hereof any fixed security or any other floating   A
charge having priority over or ranking pari passu with the floating charge hereby
created excepting any fixed security which may subsequent to the date of these
presents be granted by us in favour of the bank . . .'

Much of the language here echoes the statutory language. That is hardly surprising given
the statutory origin of floating charges and of all the rules governing their relationship
with fixed securities. The idea of 'creating' a floating charge is statutory and, in the light   B
of the statutory provisions the only possible date of creation for such an entity is the date
of execution of the instrument containing it. However, the word 'creation' fits less well
with a standard security, especially in a context such as this when the authors were plainly
dealing with and seeking to regulate competitive ranking. So the floating charge itself
uses the term 'granted' and the original Act (1961) used, in its ranking provisions, the
phrase 'before the right of the creditor in the fixed security is *constituted* as a real right'.
It appears to me, given the terms of Pt. II of the *Conveyancing and Feudal Reform*   C
(Scotland) Act 1970, that, for ranking purposes, the creation process of a standard
security is not complete until the standard security has been recorded. Thus s. 9(2) uses
the phrase 'grant and record'; this follows s. 9(1) which enables a standard security to be
'created'; and the effect of these provisions is to say that, in this context, a standard
security may be created by being granted and recorded. Accordingly, on the agreed dates
here, the standard security was created subsequent to the date of the floating charge. On
that basis it would follow that question 1 must be answered in the affirmative.   D

I am conscious that in my reasoning I have not dealt seriatim with all the submissions
advanced by counsel in relation to these matters. But that is because your lordship in the
chair has done so comprehensively and I agree with your lordship's conclusions on each
of them. Nor have I anything to add regarding the issue as to whether or not it was
Lothian Cars Ltd that created the standard security in this case; I agree with your
lordship's reasoning on that issue as well.   E

In the circumstances, I agree with your lordship in the chair that all three questions fall
to be answered in the affirmative.

(Order accordingly)

F

G

H

A
Re W & A Glaser Ltd.

Chancery Division (Companies Court).
Harman J.
Judgment delivered 13 and 14 October 1993.

B
Liquidation – Liquidation committee – Liquidation committee's inspection of liquidator's records – Members of liquidation committee obtained order to inspect 'books, papers and documents of the company and of the liquidation' – Whether order made without jurisdiction – Whether applicants were members of liquidation committee – Whether liquidation committee properly constituted – Insolvency Rules 1986 (SI 1986/1925), Pt. 4, Ch. 12; Insolvency Regulations 1986 (SI 1986/ 1994), reg. 8, 26, 27.

C
1. Documents passing between a liquidator as office-holder and the Department of Trade and Industry concerning possible disqualification of directors were not documents which were within any of the statutory rights of the liquidation committee to inspect, or in respect of which the liquidation committee could properly put questions to the liquidator and ask him to report to them. Nor could such documents possibly be described as documents of the company, nor did they record any step in the liquidation or deal with any assets in the liquidation which might concern a creditor.

D
2. In any event, the conclusion from the evidence and from the rules was that no liquidation committee was properly constituted in the liquidation of the company, despite the certificate given by the liquidator in July 1991. The applicants were not qualified to be members of the liquidation committee because they were not creditors.

The following cases were referred to in the judgment:

E
Arrows Ltd, Re (No. 4) [1993] BCC 473; [1993] Ch 452.
Barlow Clowes (Gilt Managers) Ltd, Re [1991] BCC 608; [1992] Ch 208.
Marcel & Ors v Commissioner of Police of the Metropolis & Ors [1992] Ch 225.
Morris & Ors v Director of the Serious Fraud Office & Ors [1992] BCC 934; [1993] Ch 372.
Movitex Ltd, Re [1990] BCC 491, [1992] BCC 101 (CA); [1992] 1 WLR 303.

F
Philip Jones (instructed by Judge Sykes & Harrison) for the liquidator.

Paul Girolami (instructed by the Treasury Solicitor) for the Department of Trade and Industry.

Mr Joseph and Mr Messon appeared in person.

JUDGMENT
G
(Delivered 13 October 1993)

Harman J: This is a case, to use an inaccurate word, bedevilled by procedural irregularity. There are technically, I think, five applications or purported applications before the court, using the word application in its general and not its technical sense.

The first in time is a document which is in the form of an ordinary application, using that word in its technical sense, under the *Insolvency Rules* 1986 (SI 1986/1925), headed
H
in respect of matter 003692 of 1992, in the matter of W & A Glaser Ltd and of the Insolvency Act. It describes the applicants as Graham Joseph, member of the liquidation committee and William Messon, also a member of the liquidation committee, and the respondent as Melvyn Samuel Langley, liquidator. It says:

'Take notice we intend to apply to the judge at 10.30 am on 30 March for various relief.'

The document is undated but the original was stamped on 26 March with the ordinary   A
application fee. It plainly was not treated as a normal ordinary application since under
the Insolvency Rules 14 days' notice of any such application is required.

The second application under the same heading purports to be a notice of motion to
be moved before Morritt J on 26 April by a notice dated 21 April. That notice of motion
was for the committal of Mr Langley for disobeying an order of Mummery J on 30
March and the order was purportedly amended by adding some words into the second   B
page.

The third matter is a purported notice of motion with the same heading issued on
4 May returnable on Monday, 10 May by Mr Langley as liquidator of the company
for directions for the further conduct of the liquidation.

There was then a notice of an ordinary application with the same number and basic
heading in which the Department of Trade and Industry was named as the applicant and   C
Mr Joseph, Mr Messon and Mr Langley were listed as respondents. That application
was issued on 9 July and returnable on 19 July. That sought, first, an order under O. 15,
r. 6 of the Rules of the Supreme Court, to add the DTI as a respondent to the motion in
this matter for the committal of Mr Langley by the notice of motion which I mentioned;
secondly, an order for directions on that hearing, an order that the order of Mummery J
of 30 March be varied pursuant to r. 7.47 of the Insolvency Rules and consequential
relief.   D

Finally, there is a motion by notice dated 15 September on behalf of Mr Langley for
directions, that being in the substance by way of amendment to his original application
for directions, this time seeking specific directions in considerable detail to take up the
points raised by the DTI in their application.

The difficulties have arisen because the original applicants, Mr Joseph and Mr Messon,
have throughout acted in person and have perhaps naturally proceeded upon such   E
informal guidance as they have received from clerks in the office of the Companies Court
and consequently have issued the first application as an ordinary application and, second,
consequentially upon that have contained no reference to the statute or the rules, or other
foundation for jurisdiction for the orders they seek.

The matters came before me on 26 July when I made a series of directions and in the
result the matter then came on for hearing before me yesterday. It was by common   F
consent of all, including Mr Joseph and Mr Messon expressly, that the first of the various
applications, using that word in a general and not the technical sense, to be taken was
the DTI's application either to have a determination as to the meaning of Mummery J's
order on 30 March and if the meaning was not as Mr Messon and Mr Joseph said it was
then for the exercise of the court's powers under r. 7.47 to vary that order.

The order itself made on 30 March recites that the applicants were heard in person and   G
counsel was heard for Mr Langley. That was Mr Jones of counsel, whom I have had the
advantage of having before me and who can therefore as counsel report to me the
procedure which was applied on Tuesday, 30 March.

The order made was, first, that the application be adjourned to 26 April; secondly, that
time be given to Mr Langley to file evidence in answer; thirdly, that Mr Langley be
restrained from putting to an annual meeting of creditors a resolution for the election of
further members of the creditors' committee and from putting to that meeting the   H
resolutions in a particular proxy form which counsel observed to me was in fact an
unnecessary restriction, based upon an inappropriate proxy form having been sent out
by error; fourthly, and here the difficulties begin to arise, that all the books, papers and
documents of the company and of the liquidation, not 'of the liquidator's' notice, be put
into the hands of the respondent's solicitors, that is Mr Langley's solicitors, for

A   safekeeping within 48 hours; fifthly, that the members of the liquidation committee are to be at liberty to inspect and take copies of the books, papers and documents of the company and of the liquidation at the office of the said solicitors on 72 hours' notice.

     I am told by Mr Jones, and it was expressly accepted by Mr Joseph in his observations to me, that no specific mention was made to Mummery J of any documents, or other records, concerning a report made by Mr Langley to the DTI in accordance with his duty

B   as an office-holder under the *Company Directors Disqualification Act* 1986. However, it was pointed out to me by Mr Joseph, and is undoubtedly correct, that his affidavit sworn on 26 March in support of the original application contains at para. 12 a very substantial and long paragraph running over two pages, a reference at the end of it to the content of the 'unfit conduct report' and supporting papers which have not been made available for inspection.

C   Mr Messon also swore an affidavit which is, I think, *ipsissima verba* in identical terms and the point of which I confess I entirely fail to understand. I wonder indeed whether the costs of that pointless affidavit are proper costs to be allowed. One of the exhibits, as Mr Joseph pointed out to me, to his affidavit was a letter which Mr Langley had produced. The letter is dated 4 February 1992 and is to Mr Langley from the Insolvency Service, signed on behalf of the chief examiner. It refers to the company, and to the unfit conduct report 'submitted in the above matter and received in the unit'. The letter states

D   that it appears that while the conduct of the directors is properly identified, it is not of sufficient seriousness to merit an application for disqualification, and says that the volume of cases is such that no detailed explanation can be given in ordinary cases.

     It is clear that no reference was made before Mummery J to any relevant section of the Act or to any of the Insolvency Rules. The application by the DTI is based upon the proposition that under the statutory scheme relating to the disqualification of directors,

E   the duty imposed on the office-holder by s. 7 of that Act is entirely separate from the specific duties of a liquidator to conduct a liquidation. The duty is imposed under s. 7(3) on office-holders to report to the Secretary of State if it appears to the office-holder that the conditions in s. 6(1) of the *Company Directors Disqualification Act* 1986 have been satisfied and gives a power in subs. (4) to the Secretary of State to require the liquidator, or administrative receiver, administrator, or former persons holding that office, to furnish information as the Secretary of State may reasonably require.

F   That is effected by the *Insolvent Companies (Reports on Conduct of Directors) No. 2 Rules* 1986 (SI 1986/2134) which were made on 4 December 1986 and came into force on 29 December 1986. Those rules require reports, by r. 3(2), to be in specific forms which are set out. The factors which Mr Girolami called to my attention are that a person required to report under the sections need not be in office at the relevant date. Rule 4(5) shows that is so, and the obvious example is of an administrator whose administration has come to an end, for example because the company has gone into liquidation, and the

G   administration order having been discharged there is no longer any administration nor any office of administrator, but nonetheless there is plainly an obligation to discharge. Similar conclusions would follow when a liquidator had retired or been removed from office.

     The result is that there may be a different office-holder in the place of the office-holder called on to report. It follows, Mr Girolami submitted, that the ordinary words 'books

H   and records of the company' cannot really apply to reports by office-holders who may have ceased to be in office at all and are not concerned any further with the company's affairs. Further, the question arises as to by what right do these applicants apply to see these documents. Mr Girolami suggested that there were three possible foundations for the right. Before I turn to consider those three I should make this observation. Companies are artificial creatures. They are creatures of statute or occasionally of the royal

prerogative under charter. The statute may be a specific Act of Parliament or it may be   A
one of the enabling Companies Acts since 1862 but by whatever machinery a company is
brought into existence they are all artificial bodies, artificially created by an Act in the
law. The rights and powers of the court to deal with such artificial bodies are prescribed
by the sections of statute, the provisions which may be applicable to the prerogative and
the rules which have been made as subordinate legislation by the relevant rules
committee.

The Companies Court, whose jurisdiction was invoked by this application and which   B
I now seek to exercise, is not a court possessing inherent jurisdiction of its own to make
any orders it thinks fit against persons interested in companies. On all occasions in
dealing with companies one must find statutory rule or authority showing what
application may be made. Upon that basis, Mr Girolami suggested there might be three
routes by which Mr Joseph and Mr Messon could have sought the order from Mummery
J for production of documents and restraint upon holding of meetings.   C

So far as documents were concerned, the first possibility was s. 112(1) of the *Insolvency
Act* 1986. That provides:

> 'The liquidator or any contributory or creditor may apply to the court to determine
> any question arising in the winding up of a company, or to exercise, as respects the
> enforcing of calls or any other matter, all or any of the powers which the court
> might exercise if the company were being wound up by the court.'   D

It is clear, therefore, that the only persons who are given rights to apply under that
section are the liquidator, and it was not the liquidator's application, or a contributory
or creditor. Neither of these applicants made any reference either in their application or
in their affidavit in support to their own status save to describe themselves as members
of the committee of inspection. But this section gives no powers of any sort to the court
to make orders on the application of members of the committee of inspection by virtue   E
of their holding that position.

I have been told, although it is not in any way clearly established in evidence, that Mr
Messon is not in any sense a creditor of the company. He has no claims of his own
against the company at all. He, therefore, plainly cannot be within s. 112. Mr Joseph
claims that the evidence is not before me to prove it but that he is a creditor by assignment
post liquidation of a small debt, I think a sum of £16.75 (if that is not precisely the   F
amount it is very much of that order and the precise amount down to the pence cannot
matter). He therefore has a tiny interest in this company whose deficiency as regards
unsecured creditors is something approaching £1m. There are no assets available which
are likely to produce any dividend to unsecured creditors.

Bearing that in mind, the court should read s. 112(2):

> 'The court, if satisfied that the determination of the question or the required   G
> exercise of power will be just and beneficial, may accede wholly or partially to the
> application on such terms and conditions as it thinks fit . . .'

Prima facie, it would be surprising if upon an application by a post liquidation creditor
by assignment, in respect of a sum which would not have given that creditor any locus to
apply, for example, for the winding up of the company (his debt being far below the
minimum of £750), the court would think it just and beneficial in a case where there is a   H
deficiency of a million-odd pounds, or just under, and no assets at all, to exercise its
powers. It seems most likely that such exercises would be a total *brutum fulmen*.

These considerations would have been relevant to the judge had he had his attention
called to s. 112. The power of the court which would have been perhaps sought to be
exercised, Mr Girolami suggests would have been the power under s. 155 of the Act. That

A   section applies to creditors' voluntary windings up although it is expressed in terms of compulsory windings up. Section 155(1) provides:

> 'The court may, [the power is obviously discretionary] at any time after making a winding-up order, make such order for inspection of the company's books and papers by creditors and contributories as the court thinks just . . .'

First, of course, that again is only a power to make an order in favour of creditors and
B   contributories and Mr Messon is not such so he could not come within that power. Secondly, the inspection is only of the company's books and papers and prima facie that must be books and papers down to the date of the commencement of the winding up.

The power conferred by s. 155 was not referred to specifically before Mummery J and the order made purports to be in much wider terms, including as it does words taken, regrettably, from the terms of the application which the litigant in person had drafted.
C   The words refer not only to the books and papers of the company but the books, papers *and documents* (my emphasis) of the company, an addition of words which probably adds little if anything, but if the words do add something then the section does not warrant the addition. If the words add nothing then they are unsuitable, because mere tautology, to be included in the order. It is difficult to think of a document which is neither a book nor a paper. If there be any such documents, it is a very small extra word but the phrase 'and documents' nowhere appears in the statute or the rule.

D   The order goes on, using the words of Mr Joseph's own application, 'and of the liquidation' not, notice, 'of the liquidator'. The phrase 'books, papers and documents of the liquidation' is wholly unknown at any point in the rules and the statute affecting insolvent companies. The judge plainly did not have in mind these sections when making this order.

Mr Girolami then suggested that the application might be based on the right of
E   members of the liquidation committee to enforce Mr Langley's obligation to permit inspection of the records. Prima facie that would seem the most likely foundation for this order since the application is expressed to be by Mr Messon and Mr Joseph as members of the liquidation committee not as creditors at any point. This is therefore the only apparently apt basis for the order. That arises under the *Insolvency Regulations* 1986 (SI 1986/1994). Those regulations were made on 20 November 1986 and came into force
F   on 29 December 1986. They provide by reg. 8:

> 'The responsible insolvency practitioner [here the liquidator] shall prepare and keep administrative records in relation to each separate insolvent containing–
>
> (a) the minutes of the proceedings at any meeting of creditors and contributories including a record of every resolution passed at the meeting;
>
> (b) the minutes of the proceedings at any meeting of the creditors' committee
G   and the liquidation committee;
>
> (c) the record of every resolution passed at any meeting of the creditors' committee and the liquidation committee;
>
> (d) a copy of every resolution passed under Rules 4.167 and 6.162 (resolutions by post) and a note that the concurrence of the relevant committee was obtained; and
>
H   (e) any other matters that may be necessary to give an accurate record of his administration.'

Those records are described in the rules as administrative records and are plainly much narrower than books, papers and documents of the liquidation.

Regulation 26 provides that reg. 8 applies in a creditors' voluntary winding up and reg. 27(2) provides that the liquidator shall submit the records required to be kept

under reg. 27(1) to the liquidation committee when required for inspection. Regulation   A
27(1) provides that the liquidator shall prepare and keep (a) separate financial records in
respect of each company, and (b) such other financial records as are required to explain
the receipts and payments entered under subpara. (a) and as to trading accounts enter
receipts of payments. Thus there is an obligation under reg. 27(2) on the liquidator to
submit the records to the liquidation committee but only the records under reg. 27(1).

The result is that the liquidation committee plainly has a right and they must be   B
entitled to apply to the court for enforcement of that right to have inspection of those
particular records but that is not all 'the books, papers and documents of the liquidation',
quite plainly.

Mr Girolami for the DTI was particularly concerned with what were described in
argument as director disqualification documents. That would include the letter of
4 February 1992 which was exhibited to Mr Joseph's affidavit as I have already
mentioned, the report referred to in Mr Joseph's affidavit as an unfit conduct report   C
adopting, very naturally, the words of the letter from the Insolvency Service. Neither of
those documents could conceivably fall within the records required to be kept under reg.
27(1). Thus there is no method of argument relying upon this right of inspection under
these regulations which could lead to the judge having any jurisdiction to order
production of or the committee having any right to see the documents.

It is patently obvious when one reads reg. 8, which also applies to a creditors' voluntary   D
winding up, that nothing there can possibly be described as apt to cover the
disqualification of director documents, whether by correspondence, the report in the
statutory form, or any other document passing between the office-holder and the DTI.

It follows that reg. 27 has, as Mr Girolami submitted, no possible application as a
justification for this order.

I have also considered the Insolvency Rules themselves. Rule 4.155(1) provides: E

'Subject as follows, it is the duty of the liquidator to report to the members of the
liquidation committee all such matters as appear to him to be, or as they have
indicated to him as being, of concern to them with respect to the winding up.'

Rule 4.155(2) allows the liquidator to refuse to comply if the request is frivolous or the
cost would be excessive or there are not sufficient assets to enable him to reply. There are
then references to the summary report on a late liquidator, which include a reference to   F
his answering questions the committee may put to him as regards his conduct of the
winding up. Plainly no questions could be put in respect of the obligations to report to
the DTI under the separate and different Act relating to the disqualification of directors
which are not, in my view, part of the conduct of the winding up as that phrase is used in
r. 4.155(3) of the Insolvency Rules.

Further, it is quite clear, in my view, that r. 4.155(1) requiring a report must require a   G
statement by the liquidator either on paper or orally, it does not matter which, which he
must make to the committee. The requirement of this rule has nothing to do with the
primary papers, books and records of the liquidation which the liquidator is otherwise
obliged to keep and allow inspection of. The rule imposes a completely separate
obligation to report requiring a summary to be made, I suppose, by the liquidator dealing
with the matter.

Further, it is to be noticed that the Insolvency Rules themselves contain in r. 12.13 an   H
obligation of confidentiality. That provides that where in insolvency proceedings the
insolvency practitioner considers in the case of a document forming part of the records
of the insolvency that it should be treated as confidential, or it is otherwise thought to be
kept private, he may decline to allow it to be inspected by a person who would otherwise
be entitled to inspect it. Persons who would be entitled to inspect documents may include

A the members of a liquidation committee. There is a right of appeal to the court under r. 12.13(3) but such an appeal plainly is not a proceeding which has been taken in this case at all.

It is, in my view, clear enough that the documents passing between the liquidator as office-holder and the DTI concerning possible disqualification of directors are not in any sort of sense documents which are within any of the statutory rights of the liquidation
B committee to inspect, or in respect of which the liquidation committee could properly put questions to the liquidator and ask him to report to them. Nor could such documents possibly be described as documents of the company, nor do they record any step in the liquidation or deal with any assets in the liquidation which might concern a creditor.

It follows, in my view, that prima facie, if the order of 30 March does cover these documents, there was probably no jurisdiction in the judge so to order and certainly
C without careful consideration of the rules and duties of liquidators to report there could have been no proper order made. I was told by Mr Jones, and I entirely accept and understand, that the matter came before Mummery J on a Tuesday in the ordinary Companies Court list. Anyone who has exercised that jurisdiction over recent years is well aware that the Monday list will have been extremely heavy and crowded and a great many matters will have been stood over to the Tuesday as taking longer than a few minutes to dispose of, which is all that can be done on the Monday, and in the
D circumstances there is enormous pressure on the judge to dispose of matters.

This matter was brought before Mummery J for the first time on the Tuesday morning by two litigants in person. I say that with no disrespect to them. Mr Joseph has addressed me courteously and fairly and done his best to help and be clear. Nonetheless, he will be the first, I think, to accept that these technical powers and provisions are not matters with which he is fully familiar, or should be fully familiar; it is not his job to be fully
E familiar with these regulations and rules nor the statutory sections.

Consequently, he was not and would not be expected to be in a position to help the judge by showing him what the statutory powers and jurisdiction were. Mr Jones of counsel is, of course, a person skilled in the law and familiar with company liquidations. He would have been able, had he been invited, to take the judge through the matters but his client had, as Mr Jones told me at this hearing and as he apparently informed
F Mummery J at the time, no objection to the documents referred to being inspected by the liquidation committee. He had no particular difficulty in acceding to that request without considering whether in fact it was an enforceable request and one which Mr Joseph and Mr Messon (1) had any locus standi to demand, (2) had any position under the rules or statute to require him. Thus counsel did not attend at all to that question. He was simply perfectly prepared on his client's instructions to concede it and the matter went through without any reference to any of these sections which I have recited, and on which I have
G been enormously helped by the extremely lucid and well presented argument from Mr Girolami for the DTI.

In consequence, it seems to me, it is quite clear that the judge never considered these questions at all and his order which is in wide, vague, and non-statutory nor rule-provided form, was one which had he considered it he would never have made. The words are, however, extremely wide given the fact that Mr Joseph's affidavit specifically
H referred to the 'unfit conduct report', although I suspect the judge never noticed in the hurry on a Tuesday morning the details of what was being mentioned. There could hardly be time for him to absorb all that detail; it has taken me two days, I think, or a day and a half at least to reach the point when I am delivering this judgment. Nonetheless, the point was specifically there before the judge. The letter from the Insolvency Service which is part of the documents conveniently described by Mr Girolami as the director

disqualification documents, was in fact before the judge and the words in para. 4 of the   A
order are of the widest and most general sort.

I therefore conclude with some regret that I think the words do, as drawn, cover the
director disqualification documents, so to describe them, although I am convinced that
that was in a sense per incuriam in that the judge's mind did not go with the wide effect
of the terms of his order. Nonetheless, I must hold that the documents are covered by the
terms used.   B

I then have to consider the unusual jurisdiction under r. 7.47 of the Insolvency Rules
(inherited from the old Bankruptcy Act and going back certainly to the 1914 Act, and I
think well before) which provides in subr. (1):

> 'Every court having jurisdiction under the Act to wind up companies [and the
> Companies Court as part of the Chancery Division of the High Court is a fortiori
> that court] may review, rescind or vary any order made by it in the exercise of that   C
> jurisdiction.'

Thus, most unusually a puisne judge may sit to review, rescind or vary, an order made
by the Companies Court or any judge of it. It is quite clear the words 'the court' in this
subrule mean exactly what they say and they do not mean the judge of that court who
made the order.

Mr Girolami submitted that I ought to review and rescind or vary the order of 30   D
March because, as he said, the obligations arising were confidential matters between the
office-holder and the DTI. He referred particularly to *Re Movitex Ltd* both at first
instance, [1990] BCC 491 at pp. 496F–498G, and on appeal [1992] BCC 101 in Scott LJ's
judgment at p. 103H and especially at p. 105H and on to the end.

Mr Girolami pointed out that there is no attempt in *Re Movitex* to consider the
position of third parties to whom obligations of confidence are owed. All the documents
being considered were documents which related to the particular parties before the court   E
and did not affect the third parties. The court, he submitted, would not make an order
affecting a third party without considering the position of that third party if there was a
duty of confidence owed to a third party. He cited in that respect *Marcel v Commissioner
of Police of the Metropolis* [1992] Ch 225 and the application of that decision in *Morris v
Director of the SFO* [1992] BCC 934.

Mr Girolami also called my attention to the words of Millett J in *Re Barlow Clowes*   F
(Gilt Managers) Ltd [1991] BCC 608 at pp. 613H–614H, and the Court of Appeal
decision in *Re Arrows Ltd (No. 4)* [1993] BCC 473.

The particular observations are very clear in those cases that the court has to consider,
when an obligation of confidence is owed to a third party, whether that obligation of
confidence should be overridden. When the obligation arises out of statutory provisions
compelling a person to act, there is plainly a strong public interest in restraining the use   G
of the documents for any purpose other than the purpose which the statute has created.
The obligations here of the office-holder to the DTI plainly are compulsory. There are
powers to proceed against the office-holder for default which plainly give the DTI a
special position and special rights of confidentiality. It may be of great importance to
preserve that.

As against that, one has to consider the interests of Mr Joseph and Mr Messon who   H
have but the slightest interest in the report and the other director disqualification
documents. Mr Joseph may or may not have a legitimate interest as a post liquidation
creditor by assignment for the small debt which he claims, to find out what are the
underlying facts as to the conduct of the directors, or possibly as to the conduct of the
liquidator in the liquidation. Those facts are not the matters with which the report is
concerned. The report is secondary evidence of the facts, a report of events which had

A   happened earlier, and will contain reflections by the liquidator of his conclusions drawn from those facts. Nothing in that report can affect a creditor's right nor can it affect the member of a liquidation committee at all.

In my view, when one comes to it, there is really nothing in the way of substantial interest on the side of these applicants to set against, as I see it, the undoubted fact, first, that there are no statutory powers or jurisdiction to have these documents produced at all and, secondly, that had there been, there was a serious obligation of confidence in
B   favour of the DTI and no substantial interest to put into the scale upon the other side of the balance.

I therefore conclude that I ought, unusually, to review Mummery J's order in this case and that I should vary it by substituting words which make it quite clear that the phrase 'books, papers and documents of the company' is to be deleted, but that the books and papers of the company and the records of the liquidator within the obligation imposed
C   under reg. 27 and reg. 8 of the Insolvency Regulations are covered but no other or wider documents. On that basis I shall determine the first direction given and thereby vary that order.

(Order accordingly)

JUDGMENT
D   (Delivered 14 October 1993)

Harman J: I delivered a judgment on part of these proceedings yesterday and observed that they were, unfortunately, bedevilled by technical and procedural defects upon every side. I then, having dealt with the application of the Department of Trade and Industry, or rather more accurately the arguments of the Department of Trade and Industry on the liquidator's application for directions before me to which the department was made
E   a respondent, construed the order of Mummery J made on 30 March 1993. Paragraph 4 of that order, referring to 'books, papers and documents of the company and of the liquidation' was in such wide, general and vague words that in my judgment that paragraph could have encompassed documents which were referred to during argument for brevity as 'the director disqualification documents'. Those were documents passing between Mr Langley as the voluntary liquidator and the Department of Trade and Industry or the Insolvency Service on behalf of the department concerning possible
F   disqualification of directors of this company. In my judgment, those documents were not documents that should have been included in the order, although the documents might be within the wide words in which the order was drawn.

At that point, counsel for the department withdrew and the matter proceeded with the further hearing of the ordinary application by Mr Joseph and Mr Messon originally presented to the court on 26 March. That ordinary application came on for its first hearing on 30 March before Mummery J when the aforementioned order was made.
G   Further parts of that application stood adjourned first to 26 April, then further adjourned and eventually adjourned to come on before me yesterday and today.

Mr Joseph had been reading his evidence and the exhibits in support of his application yesterday afternoon. This morning when the court sat Mr Jones for the liquidator rose to call to the court's attention a point which Mr Jones frankly and helpfully said to me ought to have been noticed earlier but had not been. If correct the point had substantial
H   consequences upon this application.

The point is as follows: the ordinary application of 26 March was made by Mr Joseph and Mr Messon as members of the liquidation committee of this company, W & A Glaser Ltd. The evidence in support was primarily, indeed I think entirely, about their position as members of the liquidation committee. Further evidence since filed seems to establish, although I would not wish to find this as a positive finding of fact, that the probable fact

is, and it is not asserted to the contrary, that Mr Messon has no personal claim against   A
the company. He is not a creditor of this company at all. Mr Joseph, it is admitted by the
voluntary liquidator in his affidavit of 21 April 1993, three weeks after the order of
Mummery J, is now a creditor. There is in evidence an assignment made 19 June 1992,
that is about a year into this liquidation, between a company called Eagle Couriers
(Scotland) Ltd incorporated in Edinburgh and Mr Joseph whereby £16.44 (I think
yesterday I referred to it as £16.75 erroneously but I cannot think that makes any
difference to anybody), being the debt due to the Scottish company, was assigned to Mr   B
Joseph in consideration of the payment by Mr Joseph of that sum, £16.44.

Upon that footing, Mr Jones for the liquidator drew my attention to the probability
that neither Mr Joseph nor Mr Messon were, properly speaking, members of the
liquidation committee and that in all probability there is no proper liquidation
committee, no liquidation committee of this company at all. Mr Jones's submissions in
the outline terms he made them to me were (1) that only members or creditors of a   C
company are qualified to be members of a liquidation committee, (2) a corporate body
can be a member of a liquidation committee, but (3) a corporate creditor elected as a
member or appointed as a member of a liquidation committee can only transact the
business of the committee by appointing a representative.

It appears to me in fact that the power to appoint representatives is wider than simply
giving powers to corporate members. It appears to me that any creditor appointed or   D
elected to a liquidation committee, whether a natural person or a corporate member, can
appoint a representative and the representative is to attend, vote, and so on, at the
meetings of the committee. Nonetheless, the representative remains a representative. His
term of office as a representative must be a matter between him and the creditor member
of the liquidation committee by which the individual is appointed to represent the
creditor. A representative may be appointed to attend one meeting of the liquidation
committee only or may be appointed for a term. The representative may be a   E
professional, a lawyer, an accountant or anybody else, and may, unless the terms of
appointment prohibit it, be removed by the creditor member of the liquidation committee
at any time and may have limited or unlimited powers to act on behalf of that creditor
member.

Mr Jones justified his submission by reference to Ch. 12 of Pt. 4 of the *Insolvency Rules*
1986 (SI 1986/1925). These start at r. 4.151, which refers to companies being wound up   F
on the grounds that they are unable to pay their debts as insolvent windings up and
solvent windings up where that is not the ground.

Rule 4.152 provides:

'Subject to Rule 4.154 below, the liquidation committee shall consist as follows–

     (a) in any case of at least 3, and not more than 5, creditors of the company,
         elected by the meeting of creditors held under section 141 of the Act, and   G

     (b) also, in the case of a solvent winding up . . . of up to 3 contributories . . .'

I can ignore (b); this is not a solvent winding up. It follows that a liquidation committee
is to be composed of creditors of the company.

Subrule (2) provides that the committee must have at least three members before it can
be established, and subr. (3)–(5) provide: H

'(3) Any creditor of the company (other than one whose debt is fully secured) is
eligible to be a member of the committee, so long as–

     (a) he has lodged a proof of his debt, and

     (b) his proof has neither been wholly disallowed . . . nor . . . rejected . . .

(4) No person can be a member as both a creditor and a contributory.

A   (5) A body corporate may be a member of the committee, but it cannot act as such otherwise by a representative appointed under Rule 4.159.'

That acknowledges the long standing Chancery tag that a company has neither soul to be damned nor body to be kicked nor, of course, a person to sit at the board of the liquidation committee other than a representative, and this requires the representative to be appointed under r. 4.159.

B   Members of the committee elected or appointed to represent the creditors are called creditor members. Those elected or appointed to represent contributories are called contributory members. That provision of subr. (6) caused some hesitation in reading because it appears to refer to representatives. I do not believe that it does so refer. Mr Jones helpfully emphasised that the words are 'Members of the committee elected or appointed to represent the creditors' not 'a creditor'. The difference between the definite and indefinite article in that phrase is significant because one can see that the members of

C the committee are there to look after the interests of all creditors, not simply the interests of themselves. Subr. (6) is not directed when it uses the words 'appointed to represent', to representatives of a corporate or individual creditor. Subrule 7 is irrelevant.

Rule 4.153(1) provides:

> 'The liquidation committee does not come into being . . . until the liquidator has issued a certificate of its constitution.'

D The provisions under the rest of 4.153 are plainly not of any significance.

Rule 4.154 is inapt for this case and need not be considered. Rule 4.155 I had to consider in detail yesterday and, as Mr Girolami observed to me this morning, the difficulties which appeared about the duties of a liquidator and the enforcement of such duties are entirely resolved once one appreciates that members of the committee must be persons who are creditors of the company. Such persons would have rights, by virtue of

E their status or locus as creditors of the company, to make applications to the court under all the relevant provisions of the act and the other provisions of the rules. That also, of course, applies to the Insolvency Regulations, as well as the Insolvency Rules, which might otherwise have given rise to difficulties as to how duties owed by the liquidator to members of the committee were to be enforced. All those difficulties disappear once one sees that a member of the committee must be a creditor.

F   The details of r. 4.155 therefore have been considered and that creates a duty upon the liquidator to report to the members of the liquidation committee and such persons must be creditors even though those actually attending the committee are representatives of creditors. Meetings are to be held under r. 4.156 as called by the liquidator and the duty under r. 4.156(2) emphasises the difference between a creditor member of the committee and his representative. In r. 4.156(3) notice has to be given to every member of the committee, or his representative if designated for that purpose, but that maintains the

G distinction between membership of the committee and the person acting for the member of the committee as representative of that member.

Rule 4.158 (the quorum) refers to the meeting being constituted of at least two creditor members present thereby emphasising the fact that members must be creditors, even though their presence is by a representative. Rule 4.159 refers to creditors having representatives and r. 4.159 simply authorises any member, a natural person or a

H corporation, to be represented by another person duly authorised by him for that purpose. The representative must under r. 4.159(2) hold a letter of authority entitling him to act generally or specially, which letter must be signed by or on behalf of the committee member, with a specific incorporation of an implied authority from a proxy.

The right of the chairman at any meeting of the liquidation committee to require production of the letter of authority and for exclusion of the claiming representative if it

appears that his authority is deficient, is set out in r. 4.159(3). Rule 4.159(4) excludes the   A
spectral presence of bodies corporate sitting in some curious manner at the committee
table; that is impossible; it also excludes bankrupts. Rule 4.159 also prevents a person
being a representative of more than one creditor or being both a member and a
representative of another member of the committee. Thus any creditor member of the
committee may have one representative authorised in writing but every member can only
act at a meeting if the member is either present or separately represented.

  B

Resignation is dealt with in r. 4.160 and termination (r. 4.161) refers to the person's
membership of the liquidation committee being terminated, which obviously is different
from the termination of the representative's capacity. If a representative of a creditor is
unfortunately run over by a bus while approaching the committee, the membership of
the committee does not change; the creditor remains a member of the committee but no
one is physically present to represent him at the meeting because of the representative's
unfortunate demise. Equally, the removal of a representative by a creditor member who   C
is dissatisfied with his representative's conduct would not alter the composition of the
committee.

It is clear that the termination provisions in r. 4.161 are about the committee members'
position. There are provisions for the filling of creditors' membership under r. 4.163, with
a power in the liquidator to fill a vacancy, or for creditors to fill a vacancy, by
appointment curiously rather than by election, but by a majority of creditors. The   D
provisions for voting are very clear; that each member present himself or by his
representative has one vote (that is r. 4.165(1)) and similarly the expenses of members in
r. 4.169 are prescribed as expenses directly incurred by members of the liquidation
committee or by their representatives attendant or otherwise on the committee business.
Rule 4.170 makes it very clear that there are what one might loosely call insider dealing
rules which apply both under r. 4.170(1)(a) to the member of the liquidation committee
itself, and separately and independently under r. 4.170(1)(b) to representatives and their   E
associates.

Thus the whole of the chapter clearly emphasises the distinction between the members
of the committee, who must be creditors of the company, and the representatives of
creditor members, whom creditors may resolve to appoint as they think fit, which is
nothing to do with the liquidator.

In this case the original return to the registrar of companies made on 10 July 1991, a   F
date long before Mr Joseph had become an assignee in June 1992 of the debt of £16.44,
is signed by Mr Langley and contains a certificate that a liquidation committee has been
duly constituted and the membership is as follows:

(1)   Mr Messon (his professional address given) representing Emile (Leicester) Ltd.
That must be erroneous. It should have been, I suppose, Emile (Leicester) Ltd and
its address, it being, as I understand it, a creditor of the company. That company   G
being a creditor member of the committee could then appoint Mr Messon to
represent it entirely easily but that appointment of a representative should not
appear on this certificate. It has nothing to do with the constitution of the
committee itself. No appointment of Mr Messon as a representative of that creditor
appears to exist.

(2)   Mr Saunders, who may or may not have some position as creditor; it is unclear.

  H

(3)   Mr Joseph, his address given as 'of Express Technical' but designated as if he
himself is to be the member of the committee with no tag such as appears against
Mr Messon's name as representing a company. Express Technical Ltd was, I think,
a creditor of the company and could have been appointed as a corporate member
of the committee of inspection. If so appointed that company could then have
perfectly validly appointed Mr Joseph to represent them if they so wished. But

A   there was no way on this date that Mr Joseph, who was clearly not then a creditor of any sort, could possibly be properly a member of the liquidation committee.

The certificate given by Mr Langley, which noticed that he is a licensed insolvency practitioner who should know the rules and apply them, is entirely inappropriate under the rules. In my judgment the conclusion from the evidence and from the rules is that no liquidation committee was properly constituted, despite the certificate given by Mr

B   Langley on 10 July 1991, and certainly Mr Messon is not, nor was Mr Joseph at any time down to June 1992, qualified to be a member of the liquidation committee. Mr Joseph has never been appointed or elected since June 1992 and indeed, as I have said, in my view there is no liquidation committee properly constituted of this company.

The result must be that there can be no obligations from the liquidator owed to the non-existent liquidation committee and the result further must be that the application

C   made on 26 March, which came before Mummery J on 30 March, was entirely misconceived and made by persons having no locus standi at that time to apply to the court at all. It must be emphasised, however, that neither Mr Joseph nor Mr Messon is in any way to blame for this unfortunate muddle. They had been certified, they had been treated as members of the liquidation committee and they had every reason to accept the way the licensed insolvency practitioner had designated them. He was quite wrong. They had in fact no status, but it is not a matter which should be charged as blameworthy to

D   them as they believed bona fide on reasonable grounds that they were members of the liquidation committee.

The result is that, in my view, there could not have been any proper basis for making an injunction restraining Mr Langley from holding further meetings of creditors before making a report to the liquidation committee because there was no liquidation committee to which to report. There can have been no proper basis for requirements for inspection

E   of documents by these gentlemen as members of the liquidation committee because they were not members of the liquidation committee, there being no such committee and they not being qualified at that time to be such. There is a possible question that Mr Joseph might in March 1993 have been eligible for membership of a liquidation committee but quite certainly he was not qualified by election or appointment at March 1993.

It follows, in my view, that the power under r. 7.47 which I invoked yesterday to

F   modify the order of Mummery J ought, in my view, to have been invoked upon a wider basis. There is a power expressly given by r. 7.47 to rescind an order made by the court and in my view that is the order which I should now make, it now appearing that there never were any properly constituted proceedings before the court at the time of making the order of 30 March at all. That does not mean that the order was not valid while it stood but the question of contempt of it I have already dealt with on a separate motion and held that the applicants could not proceed upon the contempt within the rules. It

G   seems to me, however, that the right thing to do now is to rescind the whole of Mummery J's order on the ground that the application was not properly before the court and there is no liquidation committee of this company at all.

I shall therefore proceed to refuse Mr Messon's and Mr Joseph's application and dismiss it. The order which has been continued from time to time restraining various acts by Mr Langley expires, as I understand it, today being the final hearing of this adjourned

H   application. If I dismiss the application, no restraint can remain in force after today and nothing will be extant of this order which can after today have any effect at all. That, therefore, is the decision to which I come on Mr Joseph and Mr Messon's application. It leaves standing, and I shall deal with later, the liquidator's application for directions. That, of course, is a regular and a proper application well within the rules upon which some steps must be taken.

A

As I have said, it seems to me that Mr Messon and Mr Joseph were misled by the licensed insolvency practitioner into believing they had locus standi to make this application. I do not think in these circumstances that any order should be made against them in respect of costs. On the other hand, I do not think any order should be made in their favour in respect of costs because it seems to me it may well be that upon examination, if they had locus standi, I should not have afforded them any further relief. The right order, therefore, seems to me to be that the costs of each party to that application should lie where they fall and there should be no order as between the parties.

B

(Order accordingly)

C

D

E

F

G

H

A
Re Packaging Direct Ltd.
Jones & Anor v Secretary of State for Trade and Industry.
Chancery Division (Companies Court).
Jacob J.
Judgment delivered 2 November 1993.

B
Disqualifying unfit directors of insolvent companies – Two-year time-limit for disqualification application – Whether leave properly granted for application out of time – Whether there was substantial unexplained delay – Assessing strength of case against director – Company Directors Disqualification Act 1986, s. 6, 7(2).

These were two appeals from the district registrar's decision in the county court giving the Secretary of State leave to take disqualification proceedings out of time.

C
Held, setting aside the leave granted:

1. The district judge had erred in principle in relation to delay. He ought to have held that there was both substantial and excessive delay. For instance, notice of intention to apply was given to the appellants nine months before the two-year period expired, but the application for leave was nine weeks after the period expired. The reasons given for the delay were inadequate.

D
2. The court had to guard against virtually trying the case instead of merely allowing it to go forward for trial. If there was a conflict of evidence the court had to be guided, normally, by the evidence in support in judging the strength of the case. If there was no conflict then the respondents' evidence could simply be added to the evidence in support to enable the court to decide whether there was a sufficiently strong case of unfitness.

E
3. The district registrar erred in concluding that the case against one of the appellants should go forward because a particular point deserved to be properly argued. That was an error, because the registrar should have been considering whether there was a sufficiently strong case. The second reason was that cross-examination might change the court's view of the assertions contained in the affidavits. That was an error because the strength of the case had to be assessed on the basis of the uncontested affidavit evidence. The case against that director was weak and certainly did not amount to a good reason for allowing the application to proceed outside the two-year period.

F
4. There might have been a case for disqualification against the other appellant, but it simply was not shown to be a strong one, one strong enough to provide a good reason why it should be brought out of time.

The following cases were referred to in the judgment:

G
American Cyanamid Co v Ethicon Ltd [1975] AC 396.
Cedac Ltd, Re [1991] BCC 148; [1991] Ch 402.
Copecrest Ltd, Re [1993] BCC 844.
Porzelack KG v Porzelack (UK) Ltd [1987] 1 WLR 420.
Probe Data Systems Ltd, Re (No. 3) [1992] BCC 110.
Sevenoaks Stationers (Retail) Ltd, Re [1990] BCC 765; [1991] Ch 164.

Bridget Lucas (instructed by Eatons) for the appellants.

H
Stephen Moverley Smith (instructed by the Treasury Solicitor) for the Secretary of State for Trade and Industry.

JUDGMENT

Jacob J: I have before me two appeals, by Mr Jones and Mr Cass, from the decision of the district registrar for the Ipswich County Court. Messrs Jones and Cass were two directors of a company called Packaging Direct Ltd. The company went into creditors' voluntary liquidation on 26 November 1990.   A

The company was insolvent and the Secretary of State (via the official receiver) wishes to apply to the court for a disqualification order under the *Company Directors Disqualification Act* 1986. This he can do under s. 7(1) where it appears to him 'that it is expedient in the public interest' that such an order should be made.

Such an application is subject to s. 7(2). This provides that: B

'Except with the leave of the court, an application for the making under that section (i.e. s. 6) of a disqualification order against any person shall not be made after the end of the period of 2 years beginning with the day on which the company of which that person is or has been a director become insolvent.'

In this case the two-year period expired on 25 November 1992, by which time the Secretary of State had not made any application. So he had to make his application to   C the court for leave to apply out of time. This he did, it is agreed, on 27 January 1993. He was some nine weeks out.

Applicable principles

1. The principles for the grant of leave out of time are, it was common ground between the parties, those set forth by Scott LJ in *Re Probe Data Systems Ltd (No. 3)* [1992] BCC   D 110 at p. 118G:

'In considering an application under s. 7(2) for leave to commence disqualification proceedings out of time the court should, in my opinion, take into account the following matters: (1) the length of delay; (2) the reasons for the delay; (3) the strength of the case against the director; and (4) the degree of prejudice caused to the director by the delay . . .'

These four factors must be balanced against each other, and in the end the court must   E come to the conclusion that there is shown a 'good reason for the extension' per Hoffmann LJ in *Re Copecrest Ltd* [1993] BCC 844 at p. 852A.

There are two competing public interests at stake. First that 'unfit' directors should be disqualified, and second that a person charged with being 'unfit' should know what the charge is, and should have it actually commenced within the period specified by Parliament so as not to have it hanging over him. The scheme under the Act envisages,   F as Hoffmann LJ said in *Copecrest* at p. 850D, that:

'. . . the Secretary of State will ordinarily have at least 18 months in which to consider the information about the director's conduct, ask for any further information which he needs, decide whether to bring proceedings, and to prepare the necessary application and supporting evidence.'

2. The legal test for disqualification is that contained in s. 6(1), namely, whether a   G person's conduct as a director 'makes him unfit to be concerned in the management of a company'. Section 9(1), via Sch. 1, identifies certain matters to which the court should have regard, but those matters are in no way limiting. As was made clear in *Re Sevenoaks Stationers (Retail) Ltd* [1990] BCC 765 at p. 773C per Dillon LJ:

'These are ordinary words of the English language and they should be simple to apply in most cases. It is important to hold to those words in each case.'   H

Dillon LJ went on to say at p. 773F:

'. . . the true question to be tried is a question of fact – what used to be pejoratively described in the Chancery Division as a "jury question".'

By that I understand the Lord Justice to mean that the question of unfitness is to be decided on the totality of the evidence before the court – a value judgment taking into

A   account the conduct of the person in question in the management of the company (or companies). It follows that even where a director accepts or does not dispute an allegation made against him (e.g. failure to file statutory accounts) he can deal with the matter another way, in particular by providing a reasonable explanation by way of mitigation.

3. In looking at the delay and the reasons for it, the court must look at the whole period from the liquidation to the application for leave out of time, not merely the period

B   after the two years have expired: *Re Probe Data Systems Ltd (No. 3)* at p. 119B. Delay which the directors themselves have caused, or contributed to, will not normally be treated as of significance, see *Re Copecrest Ltd*.

4. An appeal from the district registrar is a true appeal from an exercise of judicial discretion: *Re Probe Data Systems Ltd (No. 3)*. So what must be considered is whether the exercise of discretion by the district registrar was a proper exercise of discretion. In

C   other words the court on appeal can only interfere with his decision on the familiar principles upon which a higher court disturbs the discretion exercised by a lower court. The appellant must show that no reasonable district registrar could have arrived at the decision reached or that the district registrar took into account matters he should not have done or that he failed to take into account matters which he ought to have done, or that he erred in law. If the appeal court comes to such a conclusion then it must exercise its own discretion. Otherwise it should not interfere.

D

5. The Act by s. 16(1) requires that a person intending to apply for the making of a disqualification order by the court shall give not less than ten days' notice of his intention to the person against whom the order is sought (the so-called 'ten-day letter' provision). The requirement to give such a letter is directory not mandatory: *Re Cedac Ltd* [1991] BCC 148.

E   6. None of the above principles were in dispute. But there was a dispute as to how the court should approach an application for leave, in relation to Scott LJ's third point, namely the 'strength of the case'. For the Secretary of State it was contended that the court should primarily look at the evidence in support of the application for disqualification – the 'charge' so to speak. Then unless the reply evidence showed an obvious flaw in the charge, the court should form its view as to strength on that charge.

F   Both appellants contended that this approach is wrong and that the court should look at the evidence on both sides in making this judgment. So, for instance, in the case of Mr Cass, whilst the 'charge' contained in the liquidator's (Mr Conquest's) affidavit made his conduct look serious, his explanation rendered the case against him weak.

There are obvious procedural dangers in the appellants' approach, if taken to the extreme. For if the court investigates the strength of the case in too fine a detail, then it will be virtually trying the case instead of merely allowing it to go forward for trial.

G   Moreover it would be doing so without the benefit of cross-examination or, perhaps, further witnesses. Much the same sort of problem arises in relation to other interlocutory procedures of the court (e.g. the grant of an interlocutory injunction or security for costs, or leave to serve out of the jurisdiction). In such cases the court has to consider the ultimate merits of a case on incomplete evidence. In some cases (e.g. an interlocutory injunction application) it may be able to avoid considering the strength of the case beyond the threshold of 'a serious question to be tried': *American Cyanamid Co v Ethicon Ltd*

H   [1975] AC 396. But in others, e.g. security for costs, the court must necessarily look at the merits, which it does without going into fine detail, taking a broad brush approach. The warning given by Sir Nicolas Browne-Wilkinson V-C in *Porzelack KG v Porzelack (UK) Ltd* [1987] 1 WLR 420 is as apposite to an application for leave under s. 7(2) of the *Company Directors Disqualification Act* 1986 as it is for an application for security. He said at p. 423E:

> 'A detailed examination of the possibilities of success or failure merely blows the case up into a large interlocutory hearing involving great expenditure of both money and time.'

A

In the end the question is one of degree. At one extreme there will be a serious charge, perhaps involving allegations of dishonesty, all hotly denied. At the other there will be a charge, but the evidence in reply will either refute the charge altogether or will admit and mitigate. If there is a conflict of evidence then the court ought normally to act on the evidence in support in judging the strength of the case. But if there is no conflict, then, provided the case is not blown up out of proportion, the respondents' evidence can simply be added to the evidence in chief. The court can then take the lot into consideration in forming the overall 'jury' view as to whether there is a sufficiently strong case of unfitness to weigh down considerations of delay.

B

The facts

C

I therefore turn to consider the facts. The company was small and the appellants were the only directors (from September 1988) and shareholders. Mr Cass held 29,775 shares and Mr Jones 13,225. I think it material to note that one Bronwen Howley was company secretary, for she was and is the wife of a chartered accountant who, it is manifest from the evidence, assisted her husband, Peter Howley. He has made an affidavit in support of the directors. It is a feature of the district registrar's decision that, although the affidavit is mentioned, none of its contents are specifically addressed.

D

The business of the company was ultimately sold by the liquidator as a going concern. There were unsecured creditors in the sum of £345,000 who in the end were to receive a payment of 13p in the pound. These figures appear not from the statement of affairs originally prepared by Mr Conquest on 24 November 1990, but from his letter of 3 February 1993 apparently circulated to members and creditors, though Mr Jones said he did not receive a copy directly. The statement of affairs in this case presents a slightly blacker picture. Mr Laskey's affidavit, sworn after that letter, does not mention it – as was, in principle, desirable. There is not much difference in this case (the statement of affairs suggested 10p in the pound). But in my view it is important that upon an application for leave the court is given the latest information available concerning the progress of a liquidation. Otherwise an unfair picture of the strength of the case could be given.

E

F

Factor (1): The delay

The district registrar was not particularly clear in his findings concerning the delay. He said (under the heading 'Delay'):

> 'There were a number of periods which were not readily understandable despite the explanations given by Mr Laskey';

G

and (under the heading 'Reasons for the delay'):

> 'It is difficult to avoid the impression that too little was being done over too long a period of time';

and (under the heading 'My conclusion'):

> 'Whilst something was being done at intervals over the two-year period, I do not find that the Department of Trade kept up momentum as they should have done. There are patent shufflings in Mr Laskey's affidavit ... where there is no convincing explanation for the delay. I do not think it is anything for those concerned to be proud of and I hope it will not happen again.'

H

Miss Lucas submitted on the basis of dates set forth in the district registrar's decision that the delay was ten out of 12 months (September 1991 to September 1992) and 12

A   out of 14 months (September 1991 to November 1992). Moreover, even though Mr Conquest's affidavit in support of the application was on 26 November 1992 (one day late), the application itself was not made until late January 1993.

There is also this further fact. On 17 February 1992, ten-day letters were sent to the respondents. By that date the decision to proceed had actually been made. There were still some nine months to go. Both respondents naturally reacted. Mr Jones did so by

B   telephone at some unspecified date and was told he need do nothing until the papers were served. He says as the weeks and months passed he believed that the proceedings would not be commenced. Mr Cass's solicitors sent a 'what is going on?' letter on 25 June 1992. They said:

> 'We should be pleased to receive the application and evidence in support. From information we have we are quite surprised that this step is being taken. Therefore

C   we would like an opportunity to investigate the matter as soon as possible.'

That letter never even received the courtesy of an acknowledgment. Nor was it put in evidence by the Secretary of State.

The district registrar did not mention either the telephone conversation or the letter in his decision. I think he erred here, for in my judgment, these make the delay even more culpable. The official receiver was in effect challenged to bring the proceedings on soon –

D   in the vernacular, 'put up or shut up'.

In my judgment therefore the district registrar did err in principle in relation to delay. He ought to have held that the delay was both very substantial and excessive.

Factor (2): Reasons for the delay

E   The timetable is given by Mr Laskey. There is less explanation of it. I have to say that I find the reasons given for the delay inadequate. This was not a large company. Both directors were co-operative – the suggestion in Mr Conquest's evidence that Mr Cass failed to answer his questionnaire is explained by Mr Cass who says he expressly spoke to one Suzanne Prior at Grant Thornton (Mr Conquest's firm) and volunteered to attend an interview. It is not necessary to go into the details of the explanation beyond identifying three matters illustrating its inadequacy:

F   (a)   There is no mention of Mr Cass's solicitors' letter. Was it read and deliberately ignored or had the case gone completely to sleep?

(b)   Mr Laskey says that during the period 10 October 1992 to 26 November 1992, after it had been decided that an allegation as to accounting records should not be proceeded with, Mr Conquest's affidavit was re-engrossed and sent to him for swearing. The date when this happened is not given. Mr Laskey goes on to say:

G

> 'Unfortunately, despite a number of reminders, the liquidator failed to get round to swearing the affidavit until 26 November 1992, by which time it was too late to make the application.'

The very language chosen indicates a lack of urgency, even though the two-year period was about to expire.

H   (c)   The period after the affidavit was sworn again shows a relaxed approach. Some of it (though by no means all) was apparently for the purpose of obtaining counsel's advice. Yet the material was available earlier and counsel's advice could have been obtained earlier.

So I conclude, as I think did the district registrar (though he did not say so in so many words) that the delay is by no means properly accounted.

Factor (3): The strength of the case

A

I begin with the case against Mr Cass. He was only involved with the company for about one day a week and was not responsible for its day-to-day management. Indeed he was not based at the company's premises. He had specifically retained Mr Howley, a chartered accountant, to prepare all accounts (including management accounts) and to report to him. The district registrar said:

> 'As a consequence Mr Cass had no direct knowledge of some of the matters mentioned in Mr Conquest's affidavit, and Mr Cass maintains, it is difficult to see how he can be thought to be unfit to be a company director when he employed at his own expense a suitably qualified person to oversee the company finances. That is a strong argument, and it is tempting to say that the case against Mr Cass is on the weak side.'

B

The district registrar then gives two reasons why, even though he has nearly concluded that the case against Mr Cass is weak, he thinks the case should go forward. First he suggests that the legal question of:

C

> 'whether a director can escape disqualification ... because he had appointed suitably qualified staff is one that deserves to be properly argued.'

As to that, whilst there may be something in it, I do not see it making a 'strong' case, which is what the district registrar should have been considering. That was an error of principle. The second reason he gave was that:

D

> 'it may be that examination and cross-examination would change one's view of the assertions contained in the affidavits.'

I do not think that will do in the circumstances of this case. There is nothing to suggest that Mr Cass's account of events, corroborated by the accountant Mr Howley, is likely to look different upon a full hearing. Again I think there was an error of principle. The strength of the case must be assessed here on the basis of the uncontested affidavit evidence. I think the district registrar should have acceded to what he himself called the 'tempting' conclusion. He ought to have found the case against Mr Cass weak, and certainly not enough to amount to a 'good reason' for allowing the application to proceed outside the normal two-year period set by Parliament, all the more especially when one adds substantial, excessive and unexplained delay.

E

It is not necessary to consider Scott LJ's fourth factor ('prejudice') though if necessary I would have found the district registrar faultless in his consideration of this factor.

F

I turn to Mr Jones. He was the man in day-to-day charge of the company. He therefore knew or ought to have known what was going on. As I have said his evidence is not challenged. So the right course must be to look at the charges contained in Mr Conquest's affidavit and see what Mr Jones has to say about them.

First it should be noted that none of the charges are of dishonesty, such as false accounting or the like. They are the sort of charges which might have been levelled at the directors of many failed companies in the early 1990's when bank interest rates were so high. I propose to summarise each charge, and Mr Jones' answer, and in the end to see whether the whole amounts to a strong case. I do not see that the district registrar did that, as I think he should have done. All he said was:

G

> 'The affidavit of Mr Jones does not, in my judgment, contain a refutation of each of the matters mentioned by Mr Conquest. Rather he seeks to explain why certain things happened. It may be that the court will accept Mr Jones' explanations, and it could be that it would then decide the case against him had not been made out.'

H

That seems to be no more than an 'arguable case' type of test, rather than an assessment of its strength. And it takes no account of the fact that Mr Jones' evidence is not

A   challenged. So I think the district registrar did err in principle and I must consider the matter myself.

There were six charges: first there was an admitted failure to prepare and file accounts as required by s. 242. What both Mr Jones and Mr Cass say, corroborated by the accountant Mr Howley, is that the job had been given to the company secretary, Mrs Howley, and that it was Mr Howley who was expressly given the duty actually to do

B   it. He was at fault, as he admits. Whilst Mr Jones therefore properly acknowledges that he had a duty which was not fulfilled, he has provided good unchallenged evidence in mitigation.

Secondly Mr Conquest says the directors failed to give sufficient attention to the company's financial affairs and points particularly to a failure to produce monthly management accounts. In his affidavit at para. 20, he says he asked Mr Jones for copies of these 'which he has so far failed to do'. I find that allegation most surprising. Firstly

C   Mr Laskey says in his affidavit that it was decided not to proceed with the allegation of accounting records (and gives that as a reason for part of the delay caused by necessary redrafting of the affidavit). And secondly Mr Jones has produced a copy of a letter dated as early as 5 November 1991 which he sent to Mr Conquest in response to the latter's request for such accounts. It informs him in plain terms that the accounts were prepared by Mr Howley and asks Mr Conquest to write to Mr Howley direct. Apparently

D   Mr Conquest never did so, and the management accounts only emerged in the course of this application. Mr Conquest's para. 20 was plainly unfair in the circumstances.

Mr Moverley Smith could not avoid this point. Ingeniously he then said, 'Well, the fact that they had management accounts makes things worse – they ought to have known all the more that the company was in real difficulty'. In other words he adds this to Mr Conquest's next charge, namely that the company was knowingly continued in business beyond a date when there was no reasonable prospect of all creditors being paid.

E   This charge is supplemented by two further charges, namely financing the business with Crown revenues and operating a bank account by issuing cheques which were dishonoured.

If not dealt with these charges would, I think, amount to a strong case. After all it would be difficult to conclude that a man should have the privilege of trading with limited liability if he was prepared willy-nilly to let the company carry on despite bouncing

F   cheques and the tax man beating at the door. But Mr Jones and Mr Howley do provide important mitigating evidence. They convincingly show that they were trying to sell the company as a going concern (indeed the liquidator did eventually sell the assets to one of the parties with whom the directors had been in negotiation), that the creditors were kept informed of the position (indeed the largest creditor, for nearly half the company's debts, was a prospective purchaser) and that both the Inland Revenue and Commissioners of

G   Customs and Excise were kept informed on a continuous basis. Mr Jones sent a letter to Mr Conquest as early as 1 August 1991 where he dealt with a number of the matters concerning creditors and attempts to sell the business and courteously offered further assistance. As to the cheques, Mr Jones attributes part of the problem to late payment of money by a factoring company into the bank account and, on one occasion, early presentation of a large cheque contrary to an express agreement. The cheques were honoured on representation.

H   Finally there is an allegation of undue remuneration of directors having regard to the profitability and turnover of the company. It appears that Mr Jones was working much more than ordinary hours for the company and took about £20,000 per annum. That does not seem an unreasonable amount and I note that is what he is receiving now as a consultant to the packaging industry (where he has a number of respectable clients). It is fair to say that Mr Moverley Smith did not press this point.

Overall I do not gain the impression that there is a pressing need to have Mr Jones disqualified. There may have been a case for disqualification, but it simply was not shown to be a strong one, one strong enough to provide a good reason why it should be brought out of time, particularly having regard to the large and largely unexplained delay.

Again I do not find it necessary to consider the question of prejudice to Mr Jones. In the result I allow both appeals and will set aside the leave granted.

(*Order accordingly*)

Re Wisepark Ltd.

Chancery Division (Companies Court).
Evans-Lombe J.
Judgment delivered 5 November 1993.

Voluntary arrangement – Whether claim for costs was debt within voluntary arrangement – Insolvency Act 1986, s. 382, 383; Insolvency Rules 1986 (SI 1986/1925), Pt. 6, Ch. 8.

A claim for costs was not a contingent liability within s. 382 of the Insolvency Act 1986 but was only a claim which came into existence when the court made an order for costs, and accordingly a claim for costs was not a claim which could properly be made in a voluntary arrangement. If such a claim were within the voluntary arrangement procedure, it would fall to be adjudicated upon by the supervisor upon proof in the absence of agreement and upon the supervisor would fall the duty to assess whether there was a liability. That would involve the supervisor in effectively making an order for costs in a High Court proceeding which he was not entitled to do by force of s. 51 of the Supreme Court Act. Such a claim therefore survived the voluntary arrangement and could be pursued against the debtor (if made good).

Jane Giret (instructed by Herbert Smith) for the applicants.

Isaac Jacob (instructed by Ralph Haring & Co) for the respondents.

JUDGMENT

Evans-Lombe J: This case raises what is, I find, an extremely difficult point. I have before me an application in the winding up of Wisepark Ltd by the two Messrs Chatwani for an order that Mr Bimji, not a party to the proceedings in the winding up, pay certain costs personally incurred by the company in defending the proceedings to wind it up. There is clear jurisdiction for the court to make such an order in the normal case.

The problem arises in the following circumstances. The winding up itself arises from complicated litigation between the Chatwani family and the Bimji family. In their case, the Chatwanis (and this may be a great over-simplification, but I think to over-simplify is justified) obtained an order for costs against Mr Bimji and the company (Wisepark Ltd) which has been taxed. Also in those proceedings, the Bimjis and the company obtained an order for costs against the Chatwanis which has not been taxed, but in respect of which it is said that the ultimate order when taxed will come out at a larger sum than the order for costs that the Chatwanis have obtained.

On 10 September 1992 the Chatwanis presented a petition to wind up the company, of which the hearing date was to be 25 November. On 17 September an application was made on behalf of the company to stay the petition and restrain its advertisement. That application was stood over twice.

On 21 September the application to stay came before Chadwick J ex parte on notice. The judge commented that in the absence of evidence contradicting the allegation that the company was insolvent, the application to stay and restrain advertisement would, if it was brought back before him, receive little sympathy. He, however, thereafter stood over the application to come on as an application as a motion by order.

That motion came on before Lindsay J on 8 and 9 October. He gave judgment on 12 October dismissing the application. Lindsay J said in his judgment:

'Would creditors generally be harmed by such a stay and restraint? I must consider the company's trading and insolvency. As for its trading, I have met with some degree of equivocation in seeking to find whether or not the company is actually trading. A chartered accountant instructed by the company says in his affidavit that the company has been trading. One director of the company concerned says,

rather ambiguously, that the company is a trading company. He says it continues   A
to buy and sell gold, but another director is setting up further activities in that field
and that he, the first director, believes that it will trade more fully in the future.
Against that I am told that Chadwick J was informed that the company was not
trading and three further indications support what he was told.'

Then he goes on to consider those three indications and says:

> 'However, even looking at the company as merely a property holding company   B
> with creditors having that future protection under s. 127, the company is, of course,
> capable of losing money in the interim. I have not seen any trading or profit and
> loss account for any period of the company, nor am I given evidence that the
> company is or is not losing money. There is evidence that the company has
> indicated that it is unable to pay the interest on one of its loans.'

Then the judge says: C

> 'As for the company's solvency, notwithstanding Chadwick J's comment and my
> own dissatisfaction expressed at the end of the first day, the evidence of the
> company's solvency in terms of its having assets exceeding its liabilities is far from
> satisfactory. Given that the heavily qualified September 1991 accounts for the
> company reveal an asset deficiency of more than a million pounds, the company
> was plainly in the position in which a full and substantial explanation of its   D
> financial position was going to be necessary. An accountant in very late evidence
> deposes that it is solvent, though his conclusion depends on unsupported property
> valuations and on directors' valuations as to stock, tools and machinery. The
> directors on whom he has relied for that information do not include the one with
> the most complete knowledge . . .
>
> The statement of affairs, Mr Jacob tells me, are mixed debts owing to and from   E
> related and associated companies. The accountant swears . . .'

I do not think I need read the rest of the judgment, but the passage goes on until the
judge deals with the evidence that was before him as to the company's solvency.

It is said that because of statements subsequently made after the winding up had taken
place and which are quite inconsistent with the evidence that was put in at the hearing of
the winding up before Lindsay J, the evidence described by him in his judgment, primarily   F
that from an accountant instructed by directors, including the respondent to this
application, it can be demonstrated that that evidence was wilfully false and exposed
those who procured it to be made subject to an order for costs, being the costs incurred
in the two-day hearing before Lindsay J because they procured the company to defend
the proceedings on unjustifiable grounds.

Continuing with the history of the case, the petition came to be heard on 25 November
1992 when it was stood over; it was again stood over on 7 December. By a letter of 23   G
January 1993 the company's solicitors wrote to a creditor who was by then considering
being substituted as petitioner in respect of the petition, namely, the Guardian Royal
Exchange, to the effect that the company had no assets. It is that letter which is
inconsistent with the evidence which had been filed before Lindsay J.

On 1 March 1993 an order substituting the Guardian Royal Exchange to the petition,
or giving them carriage of the petition, was made and when the petition finally came to   H
be heard on 22 March 1993 Mummery J made a winding-up order.

The application that Mr Bimji pay the costs incurred before Lindsay J was filed in
April 1993 and that was supported by an affidavit, namely, the fifth affidavit of
Mr Bushell in the proceedings. That application was on 21 May adjourned to come on
as a motion by order. Meanwhile on 11 May Mr A P Bimji, the respondent to these

A proceedings, together with three other of the Bimji family (I assume them to be his brothers) put forward an application for a voluntary arrangement.

On 11 June solicitors for the Chatwanis submitted proofs of debt in that voluntary arrangement. One of those proofs was for a sum of £15,148 identified as being their claim for costs incurred before Lindsay J, because the proof describes the particulars of the claim by reference to the fifth affidavit of Mr Bushell.

B On 12 July that voluntary arrangement as modified was approved by the creditors by a majority of £8.8m to £1.02m. It appears that the debt or the claim for £15,000-odd in respect of the costs formed part of a sum of £125,000 voted against approval by the Chatwanis. In the course of the meeting at which the resolution approving the voluntary arrangement was passed, the claim of a company (Bedford Corner Hotel Ltd) for £5.9m was scaled down by the nominee who chaired the meeting to some £626,000 and that amount was voted against approval, but was, of course, insufficient to carry the day.

C In due course an application has been made inter alia by the Bedford Corner Hotel under s. 262 to set aside the approval by the creditors on the grounds that its debt should not have been reduced in the manner I have just described and if it had not been so reduced, the resolution would not have obtained the necessary three-quarters majority. That application has not been heard and is pending.

I conclude my account of the facts by saying that, as I understand it, Mr A P Bimji is D legally aided before this court.

The effect of an approval of a scheme of arrangement by creditors in the normal case is effectively to subsume the claims of creditors in the arrangement where there is a contractual release of those claims against provisions in the scheme to pay a dividend on those claims from assets which have been placed in the scheme. The release takes effect by force of the Act from the date of approval (see s. 260 of the Insolvency Act). There is E no provision (I notice this in passing) for suspending the release pending a challenge to the approval under s. 262. However, if that challenge is successful the court may, amongst the other orders that it can make, annul the approval and upon such an annulment taking place the creditors and the debtor are restored to the position which they were in prior to the approval, namely, their claims are revived.

Under the scheme in question by para. 1.8 the scheme imports the provisions of the Insolvency Rules (bankruptcy), r. 6.96 to 6.114. Those are the provisions of the rules F empowering a trustee in bankruptcy to deal with the admission or rejection of proofs of debt. It contains a scheme for him to rule on such proofs and for appeal against any such ruling.

The problem in the present case arises in this way: my attention has been drawn to s. 51 of the Supreme Court Act as reconstituted by the *Courts and Legal Services Act* 1990, s. 4. It is apparent that by this section (which is that which deals with the award of G costs) the only entity entitled to make orders in respect of costs incurred in proceedings is the court. That is true of the Court of Appeal, the High Court and any county court.

The problem that is revealed is this: if the claims which the Chatwanis have in the matter before me are to be treated as debts in the voluntary arrangement and so subject to the statutory release, first, the liability (which is not admitted by Mr Bimji) to pay the claim (which is a claim for costs) and the extent of that claim would, without s. 51, fall to be determined by the supervisor appointed in respect of the voluntary arrangement under H the imported bankruptcy rules, r. 6.96 to 6.114. Plainly, that cannot be done because the power to award costs in default of agreement between the parties is, by s. 51, vested in the court.

The problem is illustrated when one looks at the way the matter is dealt with in this scheme of arrangement. The contractual release is contained at para. 20 which provides as follows:

'The creditors shall not upon the proposals being accepted by them in accordance   A
with the Act, commence or continue any steps, action, proceedings, execution or
other legal process and no distress may be levied against me for recovery or
payment of any debts or liabilities owed to them at the date of the meeting of
creditors and shall only be entitled to receive such dividends as may be distributed
by the supervisor in accordance with these proposals.'

The creditors are defined by para. 1.2:   B

'Creditor and security, etc., and related expressions are to be construed in
accordance with s.383 [of the Insolvency Act].'

If one goes to s. 383(1)(a):

' "Creditor"–

(a) in relation to a bankrupt, means a person to whom any of the bankruptcy   C
debt is owed [then there is an immaterial provision], and

(b) in relation to an individual to whom a bankruptcy petition relates, means a
person who would be a creditor in the bankruptcy if a bankruptcy order
were made on that petition.'

So the material words are:

' "Creditor" . . . in relation to a bankrupt, means a person to whom any of the   D
bankruptcy debt is owed . . .'

For 'bankruptcy debt' we look back to s. 382 and bankruptcy debt in relation to a
bankrupt means any of the following:

'(b) any debt or liability to which he may become subject after the commencement
of the bankruptcy (including after his discharge from bankruptcy) by reason of
any obligation incurred before the commencement of the bankruptcy . . .'   E

Then subs. (3):

'For the purposes of references in this Group of Parts to a debt or liability, it is
immaterial whether the debt or liability is present or future, whether it is certain or
contingent or whether its amount is fixed or liquidated, or is capable of being
ascertained by fixed rules or as a matter of opinion; and references in this Group
of Parts to owing a debt are to be read accordingly.'   F

In the course of arguments I suggested that a liability for costs is a contingent claim in
which the claim comes into existence at the time when acts are done which expose the
party to an order for costs: if he is a party to the action, the incurring of costs in the
action; if he is a non-party when he does things which may give rise to the jurisdiction of
the courts to award costs against the non-party.

If that is so, then the result, it seems to me, is deadlock because a debt so defined would   G
clearly fall within the provisions of subs. (3) of s. 382 or, rather, would clearly fall within
subs. (1)(b) of s. 382 as qualified by subs. (3) of that section. One would therefore have
produced a situation in which there was a debt released by cl. 20 of the voluntary
arrangement which restrains the creditor from taking any legal process for the recovery
of any debt. It would then follow that the debt would fall to be adjudicated upon by the
supervisor upon proof in the absence of agreement and upon the supervisor would fall
the duty to assess whether there was a liability. This in turn would involve the supervisor   H
in effectively making an order for costs in a High Court proceeding which he is not
entitled to do by force of s. 51.

It seems to me that the only way out of this difficulty is the conclusion to which I have
been driven, that a claim for costs is not a truly contingent claim and that it is a claim
which comes into existence when the court makes its order for costs. If that is the case,

A   the effect on the present proceedings is that this claim for costs was not in fact a claim which could properly have been made in this voluntary arrangement.

I therefore have to consider whether the fact that it was made in the voluntary arrangement and that its amount was voted in the resolution which resulted in the approval of the voluntary arrangement, estops the claimant from contending the contrary. It seems to me that no such estoppel has arisen, even though the debt was

B   proved, and voted. It was voted against the resolution that was ultimately passed, so I cannot see anything in the nature of detriment such as would make good an estoppel against the claimant.

It seems to me, therefore, and in my judgment this is my conclusion, that the claim for costs with which I am confronted is not a claim which ought properly to have formed part of the voluntary arrangement. It did not form part of it and the release contained in that voluntary arrangement did not have the effect of releasing it. It will be a claim, it

C   seems to me, which survives that voluntary arrangement and can be pursued against Mr Bimji (if made good) hereafter.

It follows from that that the second stage of the matter which is before me is reached, which is to determine whether or not Mr Bimji ought properly to pay or make a payment in respect of the costs incurred before Lindsay J. By Mr Jacob I have been shown authorities which I need not cite, but which are plainly to the effect that save in

D   exceptional circumstances the proper court to determine such an issue, namely, the issue whether a non-party should pay the costs of any individual proceedings, is the judge who heard those proceedings. I can see nothing that is exceptional in the present case or in the nature of the present case (which was a winding-up petition) in respect of which an application was made on sworn evidence for a stay, both of the petition, or, alternatively, advertisement of the petition. There is nothing exceptional in those circumstances which should make me accept the task of concluding whether such an order for costs should be

E   made.

I have, because the matter was brought on before me and because I was urged to deal with the issue with which I have just dealt in a way as a preliminary point, dealt with that point, but it seems to me that the application should now be stood out from my list and should come on before Lindsay J when he is available to deal with it. I am told that at some stage later this month it is possible that the matter could be dealt with by him. It

F   would clearly be appropriate (if possible) that the matter be dealt with as quickly as can be. His recollection of the proceedings must inevitably be becoming somewhat blurred by the passage of time. The object of the rule, as I understand it, is that the judge who dealt with the matter who was familiar with it should deal with any such application for costs.

Accordingly, on my order, having ruled as I have on what I may describe as a

G   jurisdictional point, I stand over the balance of the application so the matter can be brought on at the earliest possible time before Lindsay J.

(*Order accordingly*)

H

Re Circle Holidays International plc.
Secretary of State for Trade and Industry v Smith & Ors.

Birmingham County Court.

His Honour Judge Micklem.

Judgment delivered 11 November 1993.

> *Disqualifying unfit directors of insolvent companies – Respondent director applied to strike out evidence as hearsay – Whether Insolvency Rules about affidavits applied to disqualification proceedings in county court – Court's approach to evidence of insolvency practitioner in disqualification proceedings.*

This was an application by the second respondent to director disqualification proceedings by the Secretary of State, seeking to strike out substantial parts of the main affidavit filed on behalf of the Secretary of State and many of the exhibits thereto.

It was the broad submission of the second respondent that hearsay evidence was not admissible in support of an application under the Disqualification Act.

Two questions in particular were argued: whether the provisions of the Insolvency Rules 1986 with regard to affidavits applied to disqualification proceedings in the county court; and whether the court should approach in some special way the evidence of the insolvency practitioner (in this case administrator) in proceedings brought under the Disqualification Act by the Secretary of State based broadly on the administrator's report as office-holder under s. 7(3) of the Act.

Held, dismissing the respondent's application:

1. Rule 2 of the Insolvent Companies (Disqualification of Unfit Directors) Proceedings Rules 1987 required the court to apply the County Court Rules as to affidavits and r. 7.57 of the Insolvency Rules had no application to disqualification proceedings in the county court.

2. The affidavit of the administrator was admissible though it contained hearsay matter. (Re Rex Williams Leisure plc [1993] BCC 79 followed.)

3. In so far as the exhibits to the administrator's affidavit consisted of documents from the company's records, including draft documents, the Secretary of State was entitled to put them in evidence for what they were worth.

4. The company, acting by its directors, having placed a r. 2.2 report with all its appendices before the court and invited the court to act on it on the hearing of the company's application for an administration order, no director could be heard to say that the court could not look at that report in subsequent proceedings arising as a consequence of the making of the administration order.

5. The court considered first whether the material was hearsay, and if it was, next considered whether it came within O. 20, r. 10 of the County Court Rules. In view of the possibility that those rules did not apply, the court considered whether the material was saved because the administrator's affidavit fell into a special category. If there was no such special category, the court still declined as a matter of discretion to strike out any part of the administrator's affidavit.

The following cases were referred to in the judgment:

Dobson & Anor v Hastings & Ors [1992] Ch 394.
Koscot Interplanetary (UK) Ltd, Re [1972] 3 All ER 829.
Langley Marketing Services Ltd, Re [1992] BCC 585.
Probe Data Systems Ltd, Re (No. 3) [1992] BCC 110.
Savings & Investment Bank Ltd v Gasco Investments (Netherlands) BV & Ors [1984] 1 WLR 271.

A
Tasbian Ltd, Re (No. 2) [1990] BCC 322.
Williams (Rex) Leisure plc, Re [1993] BCC 79; [1994] Ch 1.

Malcolm Davis-White (instructed by the Treasury Solicitor) for the Secretary of State for Trade and Industry.

Rex Tedd QC (instructed by Hatlem-Olsen, Market Harborough) for the respondents.

B
JUDGMENT

His Honour Judge Micklem: Circle Holidays International plc ('Circle') became insolvent and on 21 June 1990 an administration order was made in the Birmingham County Court, under the terms of which two partners in KPMG Peat Marwick, Mr Philip Ramsbottom and Mr AAE Benzie, were appointed administrators of Circle.

C
In due course in 1992 the Secretary of State for Trade and Industry issued an originating application in the same court under s. 6 of the *Company Directors Disqualification Act* 1986 (the 'Disqualification Act') against the five directors of Circle.

The managing director of Circle, Mr Matias Valiente Umpierrez ('Mr Valiente'), who is the second respondent to the Secretary of State's application, has issued an application seeking to strike out substantial parts of the main affidavit filed on behalf of the Secretary of State and many of the exhibits thereto and, by the second paragraph, to strike out the whole originating application. Mr Valiente's application is now before me. Submissions

D
on para. 2 of the application have by agreement been deferred until after delivery of this judgment on the issue of striking out evidence.

It is the broad submission of counsel for Mr Valiente that hearsay evidence is not admissible in support of an application under the Disqualification Act. Counsel for Mr Valiente accepted in opening that if the result of his present application were to be that substantial parts of the affidavit of the administrator were struck out, the Secretary of

E
State should have an opportunity of putting in detailed evidence, not being objectionable as hearsay, in support of his case.

Counsel for Mr Valiente stated on instructions that Mr Valiente intended to defend the application for disqualification, to put in substantial evidence and to seek a direction for cross-examination of the Secretary of State's witnesses. But he submitted that Mr Valiente needed to know – and was entitled to know – precisely what case and what witnesses he had to meet. He needed to know, as he put it, the chapter and verse of, for

F
example, conversations on which reliance as placed.

Two questions of some general interest, on which there appears to be no authority, have among others been argued before me, namely:

(1)   do the provisions of the *Insolvency Rules* 1986 with regard to affidavits apply to disqualification proceedings launched in the county court? and

G
(2)   ought the court to approach in some special way an application to strike out the evidence of the insolvency practitioner who has been appointed administrator in proceedings brought under the Disqualification Act by the Secretary of State based broadly on his report under s. 6 of the Act?

Do the Insolvency Rules apply?

H
In support of his main submission counsel for Mr Valiente relies on r. 3 of the *Insolvent Companies (Disqualification of Unfit Directors) Proceedings Rules* 1987 (SI 1987/2023: 'the 1987 rules') which is headed: 'The case against the respondent' and provides:

'(1) There shall, at the time when the summons is issued, be filed in court evidence in support of the application for a disqualification order; and copies of the evidence shall be served with the summons on the respondent.'

(2) The evidence shall be by one or more affidavits, except where the applicant is the official receiver, in which case it may be in the form of a written report (with or without affidavits by other persons) which shall be treated as if it had been verified by affidavit by him and shall be prima facie evidence of any matter contained in it.'

(3) There shall in the affidavit or affidavits or (as the case may be) the official receiver's report be included a statement of the matters by reference to which the respondent is alleged to be unfit to be concerned in the management of a company.'

Next counsel relies on s. 21 of the Disqualification Act, which provides that s. 6–10 amongst others of that Act are deemed to be included in Pt. I–VII of the *Insolvency Act* 1986 for the purpose inter alia of s. 411 of that Act which gives power to make insolvency rules. Next counsel submits that the power has been exercised by the inclusion in the Insolvency Rules of r. 7.7 as to the use of affidavit evidence, r. 7.8 as to the filing and service of affidavits and, of crucial importance to his case, r. 7.57 which provides under the heading 'Affidavits', so far as material for present purposes:

'(1) Subject as follows, the rules and practice obtaining in the High Court with regard to affidavits, their form and contents, and the procedure governing their use, are to be taken as applicable in all insolvency proceedings in any court.

(2) In applying RSC Order 41 (which relates to affidavits generally), there are to be disregarded provisions which are inconsistent with, or necessarily excluded by, the following paragraph of this rule.'

The Rules of the Supreme Court, O. 41, r. 5(1) provides 'subject to' specific rules, of which the relevant one for the purposes of the present dispute is (e) 'any Order made under Order 38, rule 3', an affidavit 'may contain only such facts as the deponent is able of his own knowledge to prove.'

Lastly, on this aspect of the case, counsel for Mr Valiente relies on the decision of the Court of Appeal in *Re Tasbian Ltd (No. 2)* [1990] BCC 322 confirmed in *Re Probe Data Systems Ltd (No. 3)* [1993] BCC 110, the principles of which, he submits, are not confined to appeals.

The question of whether the Insolvency Rules apply is of significance, because O. 20, r. 10 of the County Court Rules 1981 provides:

'(4) Unless the court otherwise orders an affidavit may be used notwithstanding that it contains statements of information or belief.

(5) Every affidavit shall state which of the facts deposed to are within the deponent's knowledge and which are based on information or belief and shall be given, in the former case his means of knowledge and, in the latter case, the sources and grounds of the information and belief.'

Thus put broadly, the County Court Rules apply the rule as to hearsay evidence applicable in the High Court only to interlocutory proceedings, to all proceedings in the county court.

Counsel for the Secretary of State accepted that it could not be said that the affidavit of the administrator complied with the more relaxed county court rule in O. 20 r. 10 in every respect, because he could not submit that the administrator had sufficiently identified the source of his information in respect of each of the facts deposed to which were not within his personal knowledge.

Faced with the apparent difficulty that in contending for the application of the County Court Rules to disqualification proceedings in the county court, he was contending for a rule more favourable in one court than in another for which there could be no obvious reason in the context of a jurisdiction to disqualify directors, counsel for the Secretary of

A State was at pains to point to the substantial discretion given to the courts under the Civil Evidence Act, the Rules of the Supreme Court and the County Court Rules as to the admission of evidence. He submitted that at the hearing of the application for disqualification, it was likely that the same ruling as to admissibility on any particular piece of evidence, could and would be arrived at whether the hearing was proceeding in the one court or the other.

B I need not deploy the arguments in detail. It is sufficient to say that I accept the broad thrust of that argument and do not regard the apparent advantage to the Secretary of State in launching proceedings in the county court, if the County Court Rules apply, as of great significance. My decision proceeds on other grounds.

Unhappily, such authority as there is on the application of the Insolvency Rules to disqualification proceedings does not all point one way. The foundation of the Secretary of State's case is to be found in the 1987 rules themselves. Under the heading 'Form of
C application' r. 2 provides:

'An application to which these Rules apply shall be made–

(a) in the High Court, by originating summons (Form 10 in Appendix A to the Rules of the Supreme Court, with such adaptation as may be appropriate), and

D (b) in a county court, by originating application, such an application being nevertheless referred to in these Rules as a summons;

and the Rules of the Supreme Court 1965 or (as the case may be) the County Court Rules 1981 apply accordingly, except where these Rules make provision to inconsistent effect.'

It is not suggested that with regard to affidavits the 1987 rules themselves make provision to inconsistent effect. I observe at this stage that there is no hint in the 1987
E rules themselves that the Insolvency Rules have any bearing on the subject matter of r. 2. Although the heading to r. 2 relates only to the form of the application, that matter is dealt with in para. (a) and (b), and the reference to the County Court Rules applying '*accordingly*' is naturally read both as applying to something other than the form of the application and as importing generally that applications in the form prescribed are to be governed in the county court by the County Court Rules.

F The Vice-Chancellor had to consider r. 2 of the 1987 rules in the context of a dispute in the High Court as to whether the Rules of the Supreme Court or the Insolvency Rules governed the filing of affidavits and inspection of the file in disqualification proceedings in the High Court in *Dobson v Hastings* [1992] Ch 394. The 1987 rules made no express provision for these matters. But the Vice-Chancellor held that there was no difficulty or lacuna because the Rules of the Supreme Court were applied to disqualification proceedings in the High Court by r. 2 of the 1987 rules.

G Rules 7.30(1) and 7.31 of the Insolvency Rules make specific provision for these matters in relation to 'all' (r. 7.30(1)) and 'any' (r. 7.31) 'insolvency proceedings'. The Vice-Chancellor held at p. 401A:

'In my view it is clear that rules 7.30 and 7.31 of the Insolvency Rules have no application to disqualification proceedings brought in accordance with the Disqualification Rules. The opening words of r. 7.30 and 7.31 provide expressly
H that those rules apply to "insolvency proceedings". "Insolvency proceedings" are defined in rule 13.7, read with rule 0.2, as any proceedings under the Insolvency Act 1986 or the Insolvency Rules 1986. But the originating summons issued against Mr. Dobson and Mr. Woodward is not a proceeding under that Act or those rules. It is a proceeding under section 7(1) of the Disqualification Act and under the Disqualification Rules.

In submitting to the contrary Mr. Gray placed reliance on section 21 of the
Disqualification Act. In my view that reliance was misconceived. Section 21(2)
provides that certain sections of the Disqualification Act, including section 7, are
deemed included in Parts 1 to 7 of the Insolvency Act 1986, but that is only for the
purpose of certain sections of the latter Act. One of the specified sections is the
rule-making section, section 411. Section 411 provides that rules may be made "for
the purpose of giving effect to Parts 1 to 7 of this Act". Thus, section 21 enables
rules to be made regarding disqualification proceedings as though the relevant
sections of the Disqualification Act had been included in Parts 1 to 7 of the
Insolvency Act. Section 21, so far as material in the present case, does no more
than that.

The upshot of all this is that the relevant rules regarding inspection of the court file
in the present case are the Rules of the Supreme Court.'

That decision was naturally relied on by counsel for the Secretary of State, but he very
properly drew the attention of the court to the fact that, as appears from the report, the
decision of the Court of Appeal in *Re Tasbian (No. 2)* [1990] BCC 322, on which counsel
for Mr Valiente relies, was not drawn to the attention of the Vice-Chancellor.

In *Re Tasbian Ltd (No 2)* the Court of Appeal, in the context of a dispute as to
whether the Insolvency Rules as to appeals applied to proceedings under the
Disqualification Act or not, held that the Insolvency Rules did apply. Dillon LJ, who
gave what was, in effect, the judgment of the court arrived at that conclusion by
identifying the court to which applications under the Disqualification Act were to be
made – that is, the court having jurisdiction under the Insolvency Act to wind up the
company.

The Insolvency Rules provide for appeals in Pt. 7, Ch. 8, which is headed 'Appeals in
insolvency proceedings'. The first rule in that chapter is r. 7.47, which provides so far as
material:

'(1) Every court having jurisdiction under the Act to wind up companies may
review, rescind or vary any order made by it in the exercise of that jurisdiction.

(2) An appeal from a decision made in the exercise of that jurisdiction by a county
court or by a registrar of the High Court lies to a single judge of the High Court
. . .'

Giving judgment in *Re Tasbian Ltd (No. 2)*, Dillon LJ set out s. 6, 8 and 10 of the
Disqualification Act and continued at p. 326F:

'Section 25 provides that the Act would come into force simultaneously with the
Insolvency Act 1986. That Act now contains the statutory provisions relating to
the winding up of companies.

Section 21 provides by subs. (2) that s. 6–10, and certain other sections that I need
not mention, of the Disqualification Act are deemed included in Pt. I–VII of the
Insolvency Act 1986 for the purpose of certain specified sections of that Act,
including s. 411, which confers powers to make insolvency rules.

Section 411 provides by subs. 1:

"Rules may be made–

(a) in relation to England and Wales, by the Lord Chancellor with the
concurrence of the Secretary of State, or

(b) in relation to Scotland [. . .]'

There are various detailed procedure provisions which I need not read.

A   Pursuant to that power, two sets of rules have been made. One is the *Insolvency Rules* 1986; the other is the *Insolvent Companies (Disqualification of Unfit Directors) Proceedings Rules* 1987 . . . These latter are said to have been made by the Lord Chancellor under s. 411 and 413 of the *Insolvency Act* 1986 and s. 21 of the *Company Directors Disqualification Act* 1986.

B   They refer to the Companies Act and to the Disqualification Act. They define "registrar" as having the same meaning as in para. (4) and (5) of r. 13.2 of the *Insolvency Rules* 1986. That in effect brings in the gentleman conveniently referred to as "the registrar" in the Companies Court. They then deal with the form of application, the form of summons and the endorsements on it and the filing of evidence. The only important rule is r. 7, which is concerned with the hearing of the application.'

C   Then Dillon LJ sets out that rule and refers to the practice which has grown up of what is, in effect, a pre-trial review. He continues at p. 328B of the report:

'Apart from the *Insolvent Companies (Disqualification of Unfit Directors) Proceedings Rules* 1987, which I have mentioned and which replaced an earlier set of rules under the Disqualification Act, there are the Insolvency Rules under the *Insolvency Act* 1986, s. 411. They include in Ch. 8, r. 7.47 the heading of which is "Appeals and reviews of court orders (winding up)". Rule 7.47 provides:'

D   –and he sets out that rule. He continues at p. 328D:

'In r. 7.47(2) the reference to "a decision made in the exercise of that jurisdiction by a . . . registrar" must, in my judgment, be a reference to the jurisdiction under the Act to wind up companies referred to in r. 7.47(1). However it is plain that that is not limited to the mere making of winding-up orders. It is a conventional formula of long-standing under successive Companies Acts and it is the formula which

E   underlay the point mentioned by Wynn-Parry J in the passage which I have read, cited from him by Megarry J in *Re Rolls Razor Ltd (No. 2)*' [[1970] Ch 576 at p. 588].

The Insolvency Act contains in Pt. I–VII many provisions conferring this, that or the other power on "the court". For instance, under Pt. II it is "the court" which has the power to make an administration order. It is "the court" which has power

F   in a voluntary winding up to determine on the application of the liquidator or any creditor or contributory any question arising in the winding up, or to exercise all or any of the powers which the court might exercise if the company were being wound up by the court. It is "the court" likewise, which has power to decide all issues arising in a compulsory winding up, including matters such as proof of debt and misfeasance proceedings, and any of the numerous other proceedings which can arise. "The court" is defined in s. 744 of the *Companies Act* 1985 as being in

G   relation to a company, the court having jurisdiction to wind up the company. That definition in the Companies Act is imported into the Insolvency Act by the final words of s. 251 of the Insolvency Act, where it says that:

"any expression for whose interpretation provision is made by Part XXVI of the Companies Act, other than an expression defined above in this section, is to be construed in accordance with that provision."

H   Consequently it follows, in relation to r. 7.47(2) of the Insolvency Rules, that any decision made by a registrar of the High Court, in the exercise of the jurisdiction of the Chancery Division as the court having jurisdiction to wind up companies, is subject to appeal to a single judge of the High Court and not to this court.

What then is the position – is it indeed different? – in relation to appeals under the Disqualification Act?"

Then, omitting two sentences, Dillon LJ continues (at p. 329A):   A

'When one turns to s. 6(3)(b) of the Disqualification Act, however, one finds, in
the case of a company which is being wound up voluntarily, that the court having
jurisdiction in the case of an application to disqualify a director of such a company,
is to be "any court having jurisdiction to wind up the company". To my mind that
necessarily means "the court" in relation to that company, which is referred to in
r. 7.47(1) and if the registrar exercises jurisdiction conferred on that court in such   B
a case directly by s. 6(3)(b) of the Disqualification Act, an appeal will, in my
judgment, plainly lie to a single judge of the High Court rather than to this court.
In the same way, in the case of a person who is or has been a director of a company
in relation to which an administration order is in force, "the court", under s. 6(3)(c)
of the Act, is to be the court by which that order was made. One finds that, via
Pt. II of the Insolvency Act 1986 and s. 251 importing s. 744 of the *Companies Act*
1985, that is to be the court having jurisdiction to wind up the company, and any   C
order made by the registrar is, again, an order made by him as a part of the court
having jurisdiction to wind up the company in question. So again the appeal would,
in my judgment, lie to a single judge of the High Court.'

Hoffmann J had to consider the ambit of r. 2 of the 1987 rules in the context of an
appeal from an order made by a judge in the county court in *Re Langley Marketing
Services Ltd* [1992] BCC 585. The first point taken was that there was no proper order to   D
be appealed, as the order of the county court judge had been made without jurisdiction
on a purported appeal from the district judge which the county court judge had had no
jurisdiction to entertain.

Hoffmann J applied *Re Tasbian Ltd (No. 2)* and held that the county court judge had
had no jurisdiction. Having quoted r. 2 of the 1987 rules, he dealt at p. 586E with the
submission made to him as to its effect in this way: E

'It is, of course, true that the 1987 rules postdate the general Insolvency Rules, but
if one accepts that the scheme of the Insolvency Rules, in dealing with the right of
appeal, is to produce a single system for appeals against orders made in the
winding-up jurisdiction and that orders under the Disqualification Act are treated
in accordance with the *Tasbian* decision as having been made in the exercise of that
jurisdiction, it would seem to me rather curious that a further stage of appeal
within the county court should have been introduced for orders under the   F
Disqualification Act by the very general provision of r. 2 of the 1987 rules. That
rule, as I have said, is headed "Form of application", and its main purpose is to
characterise the proceedings in the county court as having been made by
originating application and to go on to say that the County Court Rules shall
apply "accordingly". The thrust of the rule, therefore, is to apply the appropriate
county court procedure for dealing with originating applications, rather than other   G
forms of county court process. I do not think that the rule was intended to disturb
the system of appeals laid down for winding-up proceedings generally by the
provisions of the Insolvency Rules.'

Counsel for Mr Valiente accordingly submits, first, that there is a single system of
appeals under the Insolvency Rules against orders made in the winding-up jurisdiction,
that orders made under the Disqualification Act are treated as having been made in the   H
exercise of that jurisdiction, and that there is by virtue of the decision of Hoffmann J a
limitation on the apparently wide ambit of r. 2 of the 1987 rules. That I accept. He goes
on to submit that there is a further limitation in relation to affidavits on the ambit of r. 2
if the 1987 rules are read as they must be in the context of the Insolvency Rules. Rule
7.57 of the Insolvency Rules, which deals with affidavits and on which counsel for Mr
Valiente relies, is contained in Ch. 9 of Pt. 7 of the Insolvency Rules, which deals with

A   court procedure and practice. Chapter 9 is headed 'General'. The first rule in that chapter is r. 7.51, which is headed: 'Principal court rules and practice to apply'. Rule 7.51 of the Insolvency Rules provides:

> 'Except so far as inconsistent with the Insolvency Rules, the Rules of the Supreme Court and the practice of the High Court apply to insolvency proceedings in the High Court, and the County Court Rules and the practice of the county court apply to insolvency proceedings in a county court, in either case with any necessary modifications.'

Rule 7.52 deals with rights of audience, r. 7.53 with rights of attendance in company insolvency proceedings, r. 7.54 with attendances by an insolvency practitioner, r. 7.55 with formal defects and r. 7.56 with restrictions on concurrent proceedings. Then follows r. 7.57 as to affidavits with its express application to 'all insolvency proceedings in any court'. The expression 'insolvency proceedings' is defined for the purposes of the Insolvency Rules by r. 13.7 as 'any proceedings under the Act or the Rules'. The Act is defined by r. 0.2 for the purposes of the rules as the *Insolvency Act* 1986, and the rules are defined by the same rule as the *Insolvency Rules* 1986.

On these rules I observe, first, that as a matter of definition of the ambit of the Insolvency Rules in the Insolvency Rules themselves, r. 7.57 does not apply to proceedings under the Disqualification Act; secondly, that there would have been no difficulty in principle in making the Insolvency Rules apply generally to proceedings under the Disqualification Act, since the Disqualification Act received the royal assent on the same day as the Insolvency Act; thirdly, that that course was not adopted; and fourthly, that the 1987 rules were later made without the inclusion amongst *them* of any general rule applying the Insolvency Rules to disqualification proceedings. On the contrary, the 1987 rules contain r. 2, couched in the most general terms applying the County Court Rules to disqualification proceedings in the county court, save only where the 1987 rules themselves make provision to inconsistent effect.

It is, I think, of some significance that in the Insolvency Rules, which in general apply the rules and practice of the particular forum in which the application is proceeding under r. 7.51, save in so far as inconsistent with those rules themselves, an express inconsistent provision is inserted applying the High Court rules and practice as to affidavits across the board by r. 7.57. But it does not necessarily follow that because that measure of uniformity of practice was thought to be appropriate in the context of insolvency proceedings, it must be inferred to have been thought appropriate in the different context of disqualification proceedings.

On the contrary, it would, I think, be proper to draw the opposite inference from the two sets of rules when read together. For each contain a provision applying the Rules of the Supreme Court and the High Court practice to applications launched in the High Court, and the County Court Rules and the county court practice to applications launched in the county court, subject in each case to there being no inconsistent provision in the respective rules themselves, and in one case there is and in the other case there is not just such an inconsistent provision as to affidavits for use in proceedings in the county court. Moreover, the possibility of including just such a provision in the 1987 rules can hardly have escaped the draftsman in the light of the existence of r. 7.57 in the Insolvency Rules.

I have considered the wording of the two sets of rules first without regard to authority, but counsel for Mr Valiente did not I think in his submissions suggest that there must be some necessary implication from the circumstances of the making of the rules and their respective terms that r. 7.47 of the Insolvency Rules is imported into the 1987 rules, but rather that the decision in *Re Tasbian Ltd (No. 2)* necessarily leads to the conclusion.

In these circumstances, I must return to *Tasbian Ltd (No. 2)*. Here the question to be   A
answered seems to me to be this. Given that for the purposes of appeals, applications
under the Disqualification Act are to be treated in the same way as insolvency
proceedings and come with an Insolvency Rule set out under that rubric, has the decision
of the Court of Appeal, either expressly or by implication, made proceedings under the
Disqualification Act 'insolvency proceedings', within the meaning of that expression in
the Insolvency Rules, either for all purposes, or for the more limited purpose of displacing
the prima facie meaning of r. 2 of the 1987 rules? I am unable to see that it has.   B

First, Dillon LJ does not anywhere in *Tasbian Ltd (No. 2)* say in general terms that
disqualification proceedings are insolvency proceedings. Secondly, I have the advantage
of knowing what the Court of Appeal itself thinks was expressly decided in *Tasbian Ltd
(No. 2)* because of the challenge launched against that decision in *Probe Data Systems
Ltd (No. 3)* [1992] BCC 110 in which Scott LJ gave what was, in effect, the judgment of
the court. Having set out the relevant Acts and rules and noting at p. 112G that the 1987   C
rules contain no reference to appeals and do not purport to regulate the procedure for
appeals, Scott LJ had to consider a submission that there were very strong reasons for
treating *Tasbian Ltd (No. 2)* as not binding.

In rejecting that submission, Scott LJ said at p. 117E:

> 'If the decision [in *Tasbian Ltd (No. 2)*] and its ratio decidendi remain binding
> what will be the consequences?   D

> The first and obvious consequence is that all appeals from orders made under the
> Disqualification Act 1986 in cases where the orders were made pursuant to a
> jurisdiction conferred on "the court having jurisdiction to wind up the company",
> will be subject to r. 7.47 and 7.49 of the Insolvency Rules. So appeals will lie in the
> first instance to the single judge and, thence, with leave, to the Court of Appeal.

> The second consequence is a mirror of the first. Mr McDonnell has satisfied me   E
> that, if r. 7.47 and 7.49 do not apply, the consequence would not be that appeals
> would lie direct from registrars to the Court of Appeal. Instead the *Re Rolls Razor
> (No. 2)* procedure would apply in the High Court. An application would have to
> be made to a Chancery judge to discharge the registrar's order, with an appeal
> from the judge to the Court of Appeal. In the county court an appeal to the county
> court judge from the decision of the registrar would, in accordance with the County
> Court Rules, be the first step, with an appeal from the county court judge to the   F
> Court of Appeal as the second step. The decision in *Re Tasbian Ltd (No. 2)* has
> deprived the parties of these procedures and substituted in their place the r. 7.47
> and 7.49 procedures.'

Thirdly, the line of reasoning on which Dillon LJ's judgment is based – namely, the
definition of 'the court' as the court having jurisdiction to wind up the company in
question – has not in my judgment any direct bearing on other aspects of procedure in   G
the relevant courts than that of appeals from them which were directly in issue in that
case. The line of reasoning is clearly not one which leads directly to the conclusion that
disqualification proceedings are 'insolvency proceedings' *tout court*. Nor does it lead
directly to *any* conclusion as to what the practice of the court as to affidavits in
disqualification proceedings should be.

Fourthly, Dillon LJ at p. 327A of the report made it clear that he was *not* considering   H
r. 2 of the 1987 rules as of any significance to the matter before him, where, in setting out
the parts of the rules relevant to the decision of the case before him, he says, after citing
and commenting on the definition of 'the registrar' in r. 1(2)(c):

> 'They then deal with the form of the application, the form of summons and the
> endorsements on it and the filing of evidence. *The only important rule is r. 7*. . .'
> (emphasis added)

A   Fifthly, I note that in *Langley Marketing Services Ltd*, Hoffmann J in placing a limit
on the ambit of r. 2 of the 1987 rules which, if I may respectfully say so, was necessarily
implied in the decision of the Court of Appeal in *Tasbian Ltd (No. 2)*, clearly regarded
r. 2 of the 1987 rules as effectively applying the general county court procedure as to
originating applications to applications under the Disqualification Act, and the
application of that procedure would involve abiding by the County Court Rules as to
affidavits.

B   Sixthly, counsel for Mr Valiente, whilst submitting that the rule as to affidavits set out
in the Insolvency Rules was to be imported into the 1987 rules by virtue of the decision
of *Tasbian Ltd (No. 2)* and relying on *Langley Marketing Services Ltd* as placing a limit
on the effect of r. 2 as regards appeals, felt himself unable to draw a line to show what
other limits there were. If one thinks in terms of time, there is a limitation on appeals at
the end of the county court procedure, but it is in my judgment difficult not to draw the

C   conclusion that the draftsman of the 1987 rules intended the County Court Rules to
apply at the beginning of the procedure, to the initial affidavit – which by r. 3 is to be
filed in court at the time when the originating application, which is the very subject matter
of r. 2, is issued – when he wrote 'and . . . the County Court Rules 1981 shall apply
accordingly'.

Bearing in mind all the considerations set out above, I have come to the conclusion

D   that r. 2 of the 1987 rules requires me to apply the County Court Rules as to affidavits
and that r. 7.57 of the Insolvency Rules has no application to these proceedings in the
county court.

Double hearsay

I am satisfied that the County Court Rules, O. 20, r. 10 permits an affidavit to include
secondhand or double hearsay of the type, 'I am informed by A and verily believe that

E   he has been informed by B, and verily believe that . . .'

The power to strike out

Order 20, r. 10(1) of the County Court Rules provides, so far as relevant:

'Subject to the following paragraph of this rule, the provisions of the RSC with
respect to–

F   (d) the striking out of any matter which is scandalous, irrelevant or otherwise
oppressive . . .

shall apply in relation to an affidavit for use in a county court as they apply to an
affidavit in relation for use in the High Court.'

The wording of RSC, O. 41, r. 6 is permissive: 'The court may order to be struck out . . .'

G   The wording is disjunctive, so that a court may strike out on any one of the three grounds
(see *Savings & Investment Bank Ltd v Gasco Investments (Netherlands) BV* [1984]
1 WLR 271).

The context of the rules in which the power to strike out has to be exercised

I have already set out r. 3 of the 1987 rules which requires evidence to be by way of
affidavit and further requires that the affidavit shall include a statement of the matters by

H   reference to which the respondent is alleged to be unfit to be concerned in the
management of a company. The affidavit, or one of the affidavits, in support of an
application has of necessity, therefore, something of the character of a pleading and is to
that extent unlike an ordinary affidavit filed in county court proceedings.

Rule 6 provides for the filing of evidence by the respondent and of further evidence by
the applicant, and by virtue of r. 7, the district judge has power to regulate the filing of

evidence and give directions on such other matters as he thinks necessary or expedient with a view to the expeditious disposal of the application, which must, in my judgment enable him, for example, to direct the attendance of witnesses for cross-examination.

The official receiver

Rule 3 makes an exception for the official receiver and enables him to put in his evidence by way of written report, which is given a special evidential status and constitutes an exception to the hearsay rule.

Inspectors' reports

A further exception to the hearsay rule has grown up in relation to the reports of inspectors appointed by the Department of Trade and Industry under s. 431 of the *Companies Act* 1985 in the context of petitions to wind up companies.

I have been taken through the cases but rather than attempt my own summary gratefully adopt that of the Vice-Chancellor in *Re Rex Williams Leisure plc* [1993] BCC 79 at p. 84G. Where he says:

'I was referred to several authorities: *Re ABC Coupler and Engineering Co Ltd (No. 2)* [1962] 1 WLR 1236; *Re Travel & Holiday Clubs Ltd* [1967] 1 WLR 711; *Re SBA Properties Ltd* [1967] 1 WLR 799; *Re Allied Produce Co Ltd* [1967] 1 WLR 1469; *Re Koscot Interplanetary (UK) Ltd* [1972] 3 All ER 829; and *Re Armvent Ltd* [1975] 1 WLR 1679. These decisions establish that the contents of inspectors' reports may properly be taken into account by the court when considering a petition for the winding up of a company brought by the Secretary of State in exercise of his powers under what is now s. 124A of the 1986 Act. The rationale of this principle is that an inspector's report is not ordinary hearsay evidence because inspectors act in a statutory fact-finding capacity. Further, it would be nonsensical if the court could not take the report into consideration in deciding whether it was just and equitable to wind up the company when the statute envisages that it is from the report itself that the Secretary of State will reach his conclusion on whether or not it is expedient in the public interest that the company should be wound up and a petition should be presented accordingly. Dillon J observed in *Re St Piran Ltd* [1981] 1 WLR 1300 at p. 1306D:

"It would be strange . . . if Parliament had intended that the Secretary of State should have to rely on entirely fresh evidence and should not be able to present the report to the court and rely on the findings of the inspectors."

In the *St Piran* case, Dillon J went further and applied the same approach to a petition presented by a contributory. He held (at p. 1306G):

"If inspectors are appointed because there is ground for suspecting that material information has been withheld from shareholders in a company and the inspectors by questioning the directors and examining documents not available to the general body of shareholders establish that this is so and report accordingly, there may well be little public interest involved to make it expedient for the Secretary of State to present a petition. A minority shareholder aggrieved by consistent withholding of material information might, nonetheless, wish to petition, and it would to a considerable extent, as it seems to me, defeat the object of having the inspectors' inquiry if the aggrieved shareholder could not rely on their report.

Accordingly, I see no valid reason why the inspectors' report cannot be used to support a contributory's petition to the same extent that it can be used to support a petition by the Secretary of State." '

A

Books and papers orders under s. 447 of the Companies Act 1985

In *Re Rex Williams*, the Vice-Chancellor was dealing with an application to strike out material put forward on behalf of the Secretary of State in a disqualification application in the High Court made under both s. 6 and s. 8 of the Disqualification Act. I shall have to make extensive quotations from his judgment both on this point, on which counsel for the Secretary of State relies by analogy, and on other matters. I understand that the Vice-

B   Chancellor's judgment is the subject of an appeal which is unlikely to be heard until next year. I do not know which aspects of the judgment are being appealed and of course the Vice-Chancellor's judgment is binding on me as it stands.

The Vice-Chancellor held at p. 85G that:

> '. . . the approach adopted by the court to the use of the contents of an inspectors' report on a winding-up petition is equally applicable on an application for a

C   > disqualification order founded on such a report.'

He expressed his reason for so doing in this way:

> 'That is so, because the rationale underlying the use of the contents of an inspectors' report on a winding-up petition is equally applicable to a disqualification application based on the contents of such a report. In the latter case as much as the former Parliament must have intended that the Secretary of

D   > State should be able to present a case to the court founded on the information gathered by the inspectors and set out in their report. Indeed, s. 441 of the *Companies Act* 1985 as amended now provides expressly that a copy of an inspectors' report is admissible on applications under s. 8 of the Disqualification Act as evidence of any fact stated therein.'

The Vice-Chancellor then went on to consider information garnered under s. 447 of the *Companies Act* 1985. Counsel for the Secretary of State submits that the reasons

E   which led the Vice-Chancellor to approach material garnered under an order under s. 447 in the same way as an inspector's report, should equally lead the court to approach the affidavit of an administrator in a disqualification application based on an administrator's 'D' report under the *Insolvent Companies (Reports on Conduct of Directors) No. 2 Rules* 1986 ('the Reports No. 2 Rules') in the same way.

I accept that submission and shall in a moment turn to the judgment of the Vice-

F   Chancellor once more, pausing to interject from time to time the words 'so here' to indicate by way of shorthand that I regard the point being made by the Vice-Chancellor as equally applicable to the affidavit of an administrator filed on an application under s. 6 of the Disqualification Act. But before doing so, it will be convenient to set out the statutory framework within which the Secretary of State's present application proceeds.

Section 6(1) of the Disqualification Act provides:

G   > 'The court shall make a disqualification order against a person in any case where, on an application under this section, it is satisfied–
>
> (a)   that he is or has been a director of a company which has at any time become insolvent (whether while he was a director or subsequently), and
>
> (b)   that his conduct as a director of that company (either taken alone or taken together with his conduct as a director of any other company or companies)

H   > makes him unfit to be concerned in the management of a company.'

Section 7(1) is headed 'Applications to court under section 6; reporting provisions' and provides:

> 'If it appears to the Secretary of State that it is expedient in the public interest that a disqualification order under section 6 should be made against any person, an application for the making of such an order against that person may be made–

(a) by the Secretary of State, or   A

(b) if the Secretary of State so directs in the case of a person who is or has been a director of a company which is being wound by the court in England and Wales, by the official receiver.'

Section 7(3) provides:

'If it appears to the office-holder responsible under this section, that is to say–

(c) in the case of a company in relation to which an administration order is in force, the administrator . . .   B

that the conditions mentioned in section 6(1) are satisfied as respects a person who is or has been a director of that company, the office-holder shall forthwith report the matter to the Secretary of State.'

Section 7(4) provides so far as material to this application:

'The Secretary of State . . . may require the . . . administrator . . .   C

(a) to furnish him with such information with respect to any person's conduct as a director of the company, and

(b) to produce and permit inspection of such books, papers and other records relevant to that person's conduct as such a director,

as the Secretary of State . . . may reasonably require for the purpose of determining   D
whether to exercise, or of exercising, any function of his under this section.'

The Reports No. 2 Rules provide by r. 3 that they apply to all reports made under s. 7(3) of the Disqualification Act and that the report shall be made in the form specified and 'in the manner and to the extent required by the applicable form', which in the case of an administrator is Form D6. The administrator is required in the body of Form D6 to identify each director whose conduct appears to him to fall within s. 6 and to give   E
details of that conduct, having particular regard to Sch. 1 of the Act. The particulars are to be given in part D6B of the form and immediately above the place for the administrator's signature at the end of part B of the form is the statement: 'The details given in Part D6(B) . . . are correct to the best of my knowledge, information and belief.'

I note the reference not only to the administrator's knowledge but also to his information and belief. I ask myself what sort of information the administrator is likely to have available to him. In general terms and without attempting an exhaustive list the   F
answer is a copy of the Insolvency Rules, r. 2.2 report, put before the court on the application for his appointment, information supplied by the directors orally or in writing, including a statement of affairs of the company, information supplied by other officers or employees of the company, information appearing in the books and papers of the company, information supplied by the auditors of the company and information supplied by creditors of the company. The draftsman of the rules must have had such   G
matters in mind at least. The Secretary of State has no independent knowledge of the company beyond what the administrator tells him on the basis of his knowledge, information and belief and such further information as the Secretary of State elicits in exercise of his powers under r. 7.4.

Form D6, and in particular part B, expressly contemplates that 'additional pages' may be necessary in which to set out the relevant particulars. It is, I think, possible to infer from that reference the sort of detail into which the administrator is expected to go at   H
that stage. Clearly he is not expected to identify the source of every item of information from which it appears to him that the director falls within s. 6.

If the Secretary of State needs more, it is anticipated that he will ask for it under r. 7.4. Though the administrator is not engaged in an investigation of the company's affairs *eo nomine* he has a duty to apprise himself of them and to protect the interests of the

A company's creditors. Moreover, as an office-holder he has under s. 234(2) of the Insolvency Act a power in a proper case to invite the court to order relevant papers to be delivered to him; a wide range of persons, including pre-eminently officers of the company, are required by s. 235 to co-operate with the administrator and under s. 236 of the Insolvency Act the administrator can invite the court in a proper case to order a wide class of person to appear before the court and supply information relating to the company's affairs.

B I return to the judgment of the Vice-Chancellor in *Re Rex Williams* at p. 86A where he says:

'What, then, of information garnered under s. 447? Section 447 is another power conferred upon the Secretary of State by the same Part, Pt. XIV, of the *Companies Act* 1985. The Secretary of State may at any time, if he thinks there is good reason to do so, authorise an officer of his or any other competent person to require a C company to produce to the officer or other person any documents which he, the officer or other person, may specify: see s. 447(3), as amended. This power includes authority, if the documents are produced, to require any person who is a present or past officer or employee of the company to provide an explanation of the documents (subs. (5)(a)(ii)). Failure to comply with a requirement to produce documents or provide an explanation is a criminal offence.

D One then asks oneself: what use is the Secretary of State intended to make of information so obtained? The answer is that Parliament envisaged that similar consequences should flow from information obtained by an authorised person under s. 447 as apply in the case of information obtained by inspectors and set out in their report. In the former case as well as in the latter, the Secretary of State may act on this information in deciding to present a winding-up petition on the ground E that it is just and equitable to wind up the company: see s. 124A(1)(a) of the *Insolvency Act* 1986. Likewise, as can be seen from s. 8(1) of the Disqualification Act quoted above, Parliament envisaged that information or documents obtained under s. 447 may form the basis for a decision by the Secretary of State to apply for a disqualification order on the ground that it appears to him expedient in the public interest that such an order should be made.'

F The analogy here is close. Although the wording of s. 7 of Disqualification Act is markedly different from that of s. 8, which uses the phrases 'from a report' and 'from information or documents', it is clear that Parliament envisaged that the report of the administrator may form the basis or, with his affidavit, one of the bases, for a decision by the Secretary of State to apply for a disqualification order, and in the great majority, if not all, cases as in this case, it does so. Moreover, under the Disqualification Act and ancillary rules, as under s. 447 of the *Companies Act* 1985, the relevant office-holder has G to carry out a fact-finding operation supported with statutory powers, though not an investigation *eo nomine* specifically directed towards the gathering of information with a view to the disqualification of directors.

I note that an inspectors' report under s. 447 is not given special evidential status under the Companies Act itself, though s. 441 of that Act does accord special status to reports under s. 431 or 432 of that Act. Thus the decision of the Vice-Chancellor in *Re Rex* H *Williams* as to a report under s. 447 is some indication that the principle *inclusio unius exclusio alterius* must be used with caution in this area of the law, and in the present case in particular in relation to the submission of counsel for Mr Valiente based on the wording of r. 3 of the 1987 rules, despite the apparently unqualified words of Megarry J in *Re Koscot Interplanetary (UK)* [1972] 3 All ER 829 on which counsel for Mr Valiente relied in this connection. It will be convenient to refer to this case in rather more detail hereafter in relation to the admissibility of exhibits.

The Vice-Chancellor continues:

'I appreciate that a s. 447 direction leads to a less formal and less elaborate investigation than the appointment of inspectors under s. 431. But under both sections the information is being sought and provided pursuant to statutory powers and obligations. The differences in the two procedures do not dictate that in the one case the court can take into account the information obtained and in the other case it cannot.'

So here, although there is no formal investigation at all. The difference in procedure does not dictate that in the one case the court can take into account the information so obtained and in the other it cannot.

I return to the judgment of the Vice-Chancellor at p. 86E where he says:

'Rather, in both cases the evidence is admissible but the court should take the differences into account when deciding, having regard to all the evidence and all the circumstances of the particular proceedings, how much importance or weight should be attached to the information in question.'

So here. I hold that the affidavit of the administrator is admissible though it contains hearsay matter. In some ways, the case for admitting the affidavit under this head may be stronger than the case for admitting material garnered pursuant to a s. 447 books and papers order, in as much as the administrator himself makes an affidavit as to what he has found.

The Vice-Chancellor continues:

'The court is well able to do this. The court will have due regard to the source and nature of the information and also the circumstances in which it was provided. The court will be astute to see that a company or a defendant is not prejudiced by the hearsay nature of the information. If the defendant's evidence raises an issue which needs to be tried, the court will take appropriate steps to ensure that the issue is justly and fairly resolved. Templeman J adverted to this in *Re Armvent Ltd* [1975] 1 WLR 1679 at p. 1685H, in the context of a winding-up petition:

"... even if the report of the inspectors is challenged nevertheless it ought to be treated as prima facie evidence and ... it ought to be left to a judge in any case having read the report and having seen the witnesses to make up his own mind whether it is just and equitable to wind up the company. The whole machinery of the inspectors' report was evolved to enable the Secretary of State to present a winding-up petition where the Secretary of State considers the public interest so demands. It would be unfortunate if once the Secretary of State has reached that conclusion on proper grounds based on the inspectors' detailed report, that the court should be right back to square one and start again as though the inspectors had never come on the scene at all. A great deal may depend on the contents of the report and the evidence set out in the report; but I would hope that a report of this nature would be accepted by the court as being prima facie evidence of the main conclusions drawn by the inspectors. Once evidence is sworn to the contrary then if the Secretary of State fails to support the report by direct evidence which removes any doubt cast on the validity of the inspectors' conclusions the court would not be slow to dismiss the petition."

So here. The Vice-Chancellor went on, in *Re Rex Williams* to say:

'I shall therefore not strike out those passages in the chief examiner's affidavit concerned with the s. 447 interviews.'

The exhibits to the administrator's report

These stand on a somewhat different footing. County Court Rule, O. 20, r. 10(4) does not in terms cover exhibits. As to authority, counsel for Mr Valiente relied on the

A   judgment of Megarry J in *Re Koscot Interplanetary (UK)* [1972] 3 All ER 829. In that case the Secretary of State was seeking to wind up two companies, one English and one Swiss, and wished to rely on two documents which were hearsay that had been exhibited to an affidavit of an officer of the Department of Trade and Industry. Megarry J said at p. 833D:

B   'It seems to me that the authorities establish that in relation to petitions such as those before me there are two special categories of material to which the court must give due consideration. First, by virtue of r. 30, the affidavit by the petitioner verifying the petition is admissible for the purpose of providing evidence of the truth of the statements in the petition, even though such evidence may be hearsay. Second, the inspectors' reports made under the *Companies Act* 1948, under the procedure obtaining before the *Companies Act* 1967 came into force, have a special status–

C   "not as evidence in the ordinary sense, but as material on which, if it is not challenged, the court can proceed to making a winding-up order on the ground that it is just and equitable so to do":

I borrow the language of Pennycuick J in the *SBA* case. But that is all. I can find nothing in the case that supports any contention that in this type of case there is any open licence to admit hearsay evidence generally. I can see neither that the authorities have established any such open licence, nor that it would be just to do

D   so. I do not see why the normal rules should not be applied to all hearsay evidence in such cases, save only as respects the affidavit verifying the inspectors' report, and anything else for which some statutory sanction may be found. None has been suggested for the documents here in question. *Expressio unius est exclusio alterius*: if statute makes certain special categories of evidence or material admissible, even though hearsay, that very particularity in making those categories admissible

E   leaves other categories of hearsay evidence in their outer darkness. Accordingly, the contention of counsel for the petitioner on the first point fails.'

That judgment was given at a time when the approach to inspectors' reports in winding-up cases had not been fully worked out, and it seems to me that the principle of *expressio unius est exclusio alterius* cannot at the present time be applied with its full rigour, both in the light of developments since that case was decided in the approach to

F   inspectors' reports in the exercise of the court's jurisdiction to wind up companies, and in approaching the exercise of the jurisdiction under the Disqualification Act in the light of *Rex Williams*.

However that may be, having regard to the express provision as to the statements by the official receiver in r. 3(2) of the 1987 rules, I must by analogy approach the present application, so far as it is an application to strike out exhibits, on the footing that there

G   is no wholesale licence to admit exhibits containing hearsay evidence generally in applications under the Disqualification Act.

Exhibits which are documents found in the company's records

With regard to this category of exhibits, I once again had the advantage of guidance from the Vice-Chancellor in *Re Rex Williams*. He said at p. 87D:

H   'A further aspect of the evidence challenged by the defendants concerns documents which have been found in the company's records or produced pursuant to s. 447. These have been exhibited to the affidavits. Some of the documents are, or may be, draft documents such as accounts or reports which were never finalised and approved or draft minutes of meetings which were never circulated or approved, or drafts of letters which were never sent. Here also I do not think I should strike out the criticised material. The Secretary of State must be entitled to put such

documents in evidence, for what they may be worth. At the hearing of the   A
summons there may be argument about their evidential significance or even their
relevance, but that does not mean they should be struck out from the affidavit
evidence at this stage as inadmissible. Those are matters to be looked into properly
at the hearing of the disqualification application. Meanwhile, if the accounts or
reports were never finalised or approved or the letters never advanced beyond the
stage of drafts, the defendants can say so in their evidence and explain the position.
This should not give rise to any embarrassment for them in this case. Nor is there   B
any question of this course being oppressive to them because of the volume of the
documentation or for any other reason.'

So here. Insofar as the exhibits to the administrator's affidavit consist of documents
which have been found in the company's records, including draft documents and
documents which may not have been executed in accordance with the relevant statutory
provisions, I do not think I ought to strike out the criticised material because in my   C
judgment, the Secretary of State must be entitled in an application of this nature to put
them in for what they are worth.

The exercise of the discretion to strike out – justice for the respondent

It was an important part of the case put forward on behalf of Mr Valiente that it would
be unjust to him to have to answer any hearsay evidence. On this aspect of the case also
I have the advantage of guidance from the Vice-Chancellor in *Re Rex Williams*. He said   D
at p. 87F:

'I appreciate that if affidavits containing hearsay evidence may be put before the
court in support of a disqualification application, one result is to place on a
defendant the onus of responding to hearsay evidence and showing cause why an
order should not be made. I do not find this altogether surprising. I am mindful of
the grave consequences a disqualification order can have. A disqualification order   E
is a serious interference with the freedom of an individual. I am also mindful that
the Secretary of State or the official receiver will not usually have first-hand
knowledge of the matters on which the disqualification application is founded but,
and this is important, a defendant to a disqualification application inevitably will
have such knowledge. Many disqualification applications are not defended. When
they are, the facts which are seriously in issue may be very limited. It would be   F
absurd, because it would be pointless, for the affidavit evidence in chief always to
consist exclusively of matters within the personal knowledge of the deponent.
Frequently disqualification applications are based on a defendant's conduct as a
director over many months or even years. There is a measure of practical good
sense in a procedure whereby the plaintiff has first to set out his case, with sufficient
clarity and identification of the evidence being relied on for the defendant to know
where he stands. Then the defendant puts in his evidence. The plaintiff can see   G
what factual issues there are, and he can then take steps and incur expense in
adducing where necessary first-hand evidence on these issues, before the hearing.
In this way the genuine issues can be resolved properly and fairly in the interests of
the defendant and in the public interest. This procedure does not prejudice a fair
and just trial of the issues.'

Once again, with all that I would respectfully agree. In the present case, under s. 6 of   H
the Act also, it would be absurd, because pointless, to limit the affidavit evidence-in-chief
of the administrator exclusively to matters within his personal knowledge.

The Civil Evidence Act

At the hearing of the application to disqualify Mr Valiente, it will be open to the
Secretary of State to put in material under the *Civil Evidence Act* 1968 which would, in

A   the absence of that Act, be inadmissible as hearsay evidence, provided that he complies with the relevant provisions of the Act as to notice.

    Counsel for the Secretary of State submits that relevant material which is capable of being made admissible under the Civil Evidence Act should not, in the absence of some special circumstance which makes its admission at this stage oppressive, be struck out of the Secretary of State's evidence, and that it would be absurd in the context of the statute

B   and rules governing applications under s. 6 of the Disqualification Act to require the Secretary of State to give appropriate notices under the Civil Evidence Act before or at the time of filing his initial evidence. I accept both those submissions.

Comment and submissions in the affidavit in support of the application

    The Vice-Chancellor dealt with this in *Re Rex Williams* at p. 87B:

C   'Nor shall I strike out the passages which consist of comments and submissions based on the exhibited interview notes. In a case such as this it can be helpful in practice for an affidavit to spell out, concisely and lucidly, the inferences and conclusions a party will ask the court to draw from the evidence. Indeed, the disqualification rules require that the plaintiff's affidavits or the official receiver's report are to include a statement of the matters by reference to which the defendant is alleged to be unfit to be concerned in the management of a company (r. 3(3)). So

D   the plaintiff's case must be stated clearly in the evidence. The defendant must know what case he has to meet. I do not see how the inclusion of this material in the plaintiff's evidence can prejudice the defendant. At the hearing the court will have no difficulty, when disputes of fact arise, in identifying which parts of the affidavits or the official receiver's report are comment as distinct from evidence of fact. That is so in the present case.'

E   Counsel for Mr Valiente did not seek to strike out matters of comment or submission in the present case.

The facts of the present case

    There are two affidavits filed in support of the Secretary of State's case on this application. There is a formal affidavit sworn on 18 June 1992 by Mr Patrick John Chillery, a principal examiner in the disqualification unit of the Department of Trade and Industry, stating that the Secretary of State has received information from Mr Philip

F   Ramsbottom (one of the joint administrators of Circle) from which it appeared to the Secretary of State expedient in the public interest that a disqualification order under the Disqualification Act should be made against each of the five directors of Circle who is a respondent to his application. By para. 6 of that affidavit, Mr Chillery deposes that:

    '. . . the matters by reference to which the respondents are in my opinion unfit to be concerned in the management of a company are set out in para. 18A, B and C

G   of the affidavit of Mr Philip Ramsbottom and filed herein.'

Secondly, an affidavit filed by Mr Philip Ramsbottom also on 18 June 1992.

    The business of Circle was that of a holding company for a group of companies owning, selling and managing timeshare properties in Lanzarote.

    The allegations made against the directors are serious. Paragraph 18 of Mr Ramsbottom's affidavit, to which Mr Chillery refers in his affidavit, is headed:

H   'Misfeasance'. There are three main heads: (A) Charging Spanish properties, (B) Sales of weeks without authorisation – that is, sales by the company of weeks for occupancy of apartments not owned by Circle, and (C) Unauthorised retention of deposits.

    The nature of the case which Mr Valiente and his co-directors have to meet is further clarified under four heads by Mr Ramsbottom in para. 21 of his affidavit, headed 'Matters determining unfitness', as follows:

'The conduct of the respondents as directors of Circle and of LC Sales in the case   A
of Mr Smith, Mr Matthews, Mr Murray and Mr Valiente are in my opinion such
as to justify the conclusion that the respondents are unfit to be concerned in the
management of a company.

(A) The respondents Mr Smith and Mr Valiente deliberately arranged for the
specific powers of attorney to be created empowering the respondent Mr
Smith to encumber the Spanish properties contrary to the intentions of the   B
timeshare structure. They abused the authority given under the powers
which they were aware would jeopardise the interests of the timeshare
purchasers. This was done by charging the trust properties to BCI in order
to obtain a loan of £4m to a business associate of the respondents and Circle,
when such properties were already held to the sole benefit of the timeshare
owners.

(B) The respondents sold timeshare property without having proper legal title.   C
This was at least to the detriment and at worst in fraud of the purchasers.

(C) The respondents took deposits of £14,840 against apartments to which
Circle or its subsidiaries did not have legal title, to the detriment of those
depositors.

(D) The respondents caused or allowed timeshares to be sold on the basis of   D
representations to potential purchasers that RBS (Royal Bank of Scotland)
was trustee of the relevant club when this was not the case. This was at best
grossly careless and at worst fraudulent.'

There have been three relevant reports on the affairs on Circle on which inter alia Mr
Ramsbottom has based his view that the directors are unfit. In order of preparation these
are:

(1) A letter dated 12 March 1990, addressed to Mr Valiente, marked: 'Personal and
confidential', running to seven pages and apparently signed by a Mr Thom G
Borgen (the Borgen report).

(2) A report dated 10 April 1990, prepared by KPMG on the instructions of the Royal
Bank of Scotland given by a letter dated 15 March 1990, the antepenultimate
para. of which letter states: F

'Your report should be made available to the group at the same as it is made
available to us.'

That has been called the Echo report. The Borgen report was clearly made
available to KPMG and it appears as an appendix to the Echo report.

The Echo report runs to some 140 pages, of which some 93 pages are appendices.

(3) The r. 2.2 report, dated 6 June 1990, prepared on the instructions of the company   G
to support its application to the court for an administration order and made by
KPMG. The Echo report is, in turn, appendix 1 to this report.

Approbation and reprobation

It seems to me to be a clear matter of principle, that the company acting by its directors   H
having placed the r. 2.2 report with all its appendices before the court and invited the
court to act on it on the hearing of the company's application for an administration
order, no director of the company can be heard now to say that the court cannot look at
that report with all its appendices in subsequent proceedings arising out of and as a
consequence of the making of the administration order and by virtue of the administrator
performing the public duty imposed on him by s. 7(3) of the Disqualification Act.

A   That being the principle is there anything special in the circumstances of Mr Valiente which should lead the court not to apply it in his case? I turn to Mr Valiente's personal position in relation to these reports. He was the addressee and recipient of the Borgen report.

Mr Valiente does not dispute that he was the managing director of Circle at the date of the administration order. It appears from the Borgen report that he became managing director and majority shareholder, through a company controlled by him known as
B   Stonegate Ltd, in about June 1989.

The Echo report states in para. 1.2, under the heading 'Basis of information':

'The information contained in this report is based on the following: discussions, principally with Mr Valiente, managing director and Mr N J Stern, financial controller of Circle and Mr T Borgen, adviser to the group; audited accounts for
C   the year ended 31 December 1988 for the group; management accounts for the year ended 31 December 1989; and a draft group balance sheet at 15 March 1990 prepared by Mr N Stern. A brief review of the books, records and accounting systems of the group. A review of the profit and cash-flow forecast of the group for the period ending 31 December 1990. Discussions with Stephenson Harwood, solicitors; discussions with Royal Bank of Scotland representatives of trustee division, consumer banking division, advances department and legal department.'

D   Paragraph 1.3 deals with the scope of the work done by KPMG at that time in these terms:

'The scope of this investigation was substantially less than an audit conducted in accordance with generally accepted auditing standards. We have relied upon explanations given to us by management, without seeking to verify these in detail against independent sources. We have, however, satisfied ourselves that such
E   explanations are consistent with such other information as was available to us.'

As to the r. 2.2 report, Mr Valiente was managing director of Circle both when KPMG were instructed to report and when the decision to seek an administration order was taken by the board of Circle. There is no possibility that an application of the general rule that a man cannot rely on a document at one moment and deny it the next will work any hardship on Mr Valiente; quite the reverse. It would, in my judgment, be contrary to
F   all common sense and sense of fairness if this material were not to be before the judge at trial. It will of course be for the judge to decide what weight to give to the various parts of the evidence at that time.

The matter can be tested in relation to the allegation in para. 18B of Mr Ramsbottom's affidavit that the directors of Circle were responsible for sales of weeks without authorisation. The allegation is that as a result of this wrongdoing of the directors some £2.5m had to be paid out to rectify the situation. The allegation is during the course of
G   trading, weeks of occupancy for apartments not owned by Circle or any of its subsidiaries were sold to the public.

There is now produced and shown to me a list of these apartments marked PR9. Exhibit PR9 records the numbers of 16 apartments at Club Calypso; 6 apartments at Lago Verde; 5 apartments at Las Calas II and 30 apartments at Las Calas III.

These matters are dealt with in the Borgen report under the heading 'Clubs/complexes
H   not in trust' in this way:

'There has also been sold a considerable amount of timeshare weeks relating to stock not being in trust; five apartments of Las Calas II (owning company?), 30 apartments of Las Calas III (Matias Valiente Umpierrez SA), 16 apartments of Calypso (owning company?) six apartments of Lago Verde (owning company?), 54 apartments of Valena (MVU SA). This company, MVU SA seems still to be the

owning company of 30 apartments of Club Las Calas III and of the whole of the   A
Club Valena. These are consequently not in trust. MVU SA also holds the title to
2,000 sq m of business premises of the business complex Las Calas III.

The background for this situation seems to be the following. Due to the aggressive
marketing and expansive business ambitions, the consortium had agreed to
purchase the said Valena and Las Calas III properties from a third property,
probably in late 1987 or during the early months of 1988. Although settled through   B
a so-called private agreement, the legally binding contract was not finalised in
accordance with Spanish law. At this time CH had completed a substantial number
of sales of this stock. Circle Holidays were faced with financial problems and could
not complete the purchase agreement formally. In order to avoid that Circle
Holidays was discredited/scandalised, it was agreed that Matias Valiente should
assist in securing the arrangement. His company MVU SA consequently bought
the properties for selling it on to Circle Holidays International plc. This latter   C
arrangement was legally formalised by a purchase contract in accordance with
Spanish law. The contract, being undated, was entered into in March 1988.'

Mr Borgen explains how he obtained the information on which the Borgen report is
made at p. 1 of the report, where he says to Mr Valiente:

'My findings are based upon interviews, research of file and documents made
available to me.'   D

As counsel for Mr Valiente points out here, Mr Borgen is not reporting from his own
personal knowledge. There is no indication of the precise source on which Mr Borgen is
relying for each item of information in the report, and his report itself comes into the
evidence as an appendix to a report which itself is appended to the r. 2.2 report, which is
not said formally to have been compiled by the deponent Mr Ramsbottom personally,
but which Mr Ramsbottom exhibits to his affidavit.   E

But what is the reality of the situation? Mr Valiente commissioned the Borgen report
and it was presented to him. Some at least of the relevant matter relates to his own
company and as to that, it can reasonably be inferred that he himself was the informant
of Mr Borgen. As to information of which he was not the source, Mr Valiente was
managing director of Circle when he received that report. He had a duty to inform
himself at once as to the matters of which he was formally ignorant but which were   F
revealed to him for the first time by the report. He cannot possibly be prejudiced by the
admission of this material.

Exhibit DR9 to Mr Ramsbottom's affidavit particularises the apartments said to have
been improperly dealt with, and Mr Valiente cannot be prejudiced by the continuance in
evidence of that exhibit, though the compiler of the exhibit is not identified, nor is the
source of the compiler's information. It would in my judgment be wrong to strike out
this material at this stage when the extent to which any of it is in dispute is not yet known.   G

As to the first matter of complaint against the directors in para. 18A of Mr
Ramsbottom's affidavit that they wrongly charged the Spanish properties, I note that at
p. 6 of his report Mr Borgen in his final remarks gave it as his opinion that priority
number one must be to,

'rectify the trust systems removing claims on the properties in order to avoid an
international scandal involving several thousands of innocent timeshare   H
purchasers.'

He expressed the opinion that only if that objective was met was there any future for
the company. The same considerations apply here as to the complaint about
unauthorised sales of weeks. It is not in my judgment prejudicial to Mr Valiente or
oppressive to leave this matter in evidence against him.

A   The Echo report does not stand on precisely the same footing. It was commissioned by a bank, although it was at once communicated to Mr Valiente and his co-directors. Counsel for Mr Valiente drew attention to three features of the report which he said were objectionable as follows:

(1)   It does not appear that the written statements were taken by KPMG from persons with first-hand knowledge. If notes of interviews were taken, there is no reference
B   to them in the report and the precise source of much of the factual content of the report is unidentifiable.

(2)   Though there clearly were discussions with Mr Valiente and what he said in such discussions would plainly be potentially admissible against him as admissions, there is no indication as to what he said or whether the conversations were directly with Mr Ramsbottom or someone else, nor as to the relevance of what he said to
C   the substance of this application.

(3)   There is an inextricable mixture of unattributed hearsay and comment.

I think the first two criticisms are fairly made out. As to the third criticism, I think there is a mixture, but the two strands are not inextricable. However, in my judgment it is not oppressive to Mr Valiente for this report to remain in evidence for broadly the same reasons as I have set out in relation to the Borgen report.

D   Counsel for Mr Valiente indicated in the course of the first day of the hearing that Mr Valiente was not, in fact, seeking to strike out all the material identified in his application. The particular passages to which objection was limited were agreed in correspondence before the second day of the hearing. They are identified in a letter dated 20 July 1993 from the Treasury solicitor to Mr Valiente's solicitors, Hatlem-Olsen of 43 High Street, Market Harborough. I need not repeat the list here. Objection is taken both to passages in Mr Ramsbottom's affidavit and to the inclusion of a number of exhibits to that
E   affidavit. I do not consider it right in the exercise of the court's discretion to strike out any of the material. I have set out my reasons in general terms above. Not every reason given applies to each passage sought, or to each exhibit sought, to be struck out, but often there are several relevant reasons. I do not propose to go through the passages one by one identifying in each case which reason or reasons apply, as I do not anticipate any difficulty arising in identifying which are applicable to each if the necessity or desirability
F   of doing so were to arise.

Where and in so far as Mr Valiente is not precluded from taking any objection to the material by the principle that one cannot approbate and reprobate with regard to a document, I have considered first whether the material is hearsay, and if it is, I have next considered whether it comes within the County Court Rules, O. 20, r. 10. But in view of the possibility that I am wrong as to the application of those rules, I have also considered whether it is saved because Mr Ramsbottom's affidavit falls into a special category. It
G   may be that some court whose decision is binding on me will in the near future decide that there is no such special category and I have, therefore, to face the possibility that nearly everything turns not on whether the particular evidence in question is presently admissible, but on whether as a matter of discretion it ought to be struck out now rather than left in on the footing that the trial judge can decide the matter easily enough when the issues have been identified.

H   A number of matters relevant to the exercise of that discretion have been identified earlier in this judgment, often by reference to passages in the judgment of the Vice-Chancellor in *Re Rex Williams*. I will not repeat them here. There are, however, further relevant considerations which I should mention.

Dealing first with the passages sought to be struck out of the affidavit of Mr Ramsbottom. None of them are scandalous. All of them appear to me to be relevant,

and having been taken through each passage in turn, I am not persuaded that it would
be oppressive if any of them were to remain in evidence. There really is no difficulty in
disentangling what is alleged to be fact from comment, and it would be a simple matter
for Mr Valiente to decide whether he accepts or denies any particular matter put forward
as fact.

As to the passages sought to be struck out of para. 18, it will be helpful to him to have
this statement of the ambit of the matters of which complaint is made. If the issue on
each passage turned on an exercise of discretion, I would still decline to strike out any
part of Mr Ramsbottom's affidavit.

Most of the passages now sought to be struck out are to be found in para. 18 of Mr
Valiente's affidavit, but the other three passages deserve separate mention. Of these the
first is para. 7. This is headed 'History' and is in these terms:

> 'The following information was obtained from the staff of Circle from the books
> and records of the company, much of which is contained in a report dated 6 June
> 1990 prepared under r. 2.2 of the *Insolvency Rules* 1986 to support the petition
> presented by Circle for the appointment of administrators. The report is now
> produced and shown to me marked PR3. It should be noted that the report and its
> appendices were prepared at a very early stage of the investigations and I should
> make it clear that it is now apparent that some of the detail is not perfectly accurate
> and our subsequent activities have rendered some of the information out of date.'

Naturally, counsel for Mr Valiente drew particular attention to the caveat as to the
information in the r. 2.2 report, and he suggested that Mr Valiente might be prejudiced
because he could not know precisely which of the facts in the report were now said to be
incorrect. It is manifest that the substantive objection to this paragraph is that it
introduces the r. 2.2 report. I have dealt with the considerations affecting that report
earlier in this judgment and it is sufficient to say here that it would in my judgment be
pointless to strike out this paragraph, taking the view I do of the admissibility of the r.
2.2 report.

The next paragraph sought to be struck out is para. 15. This paragraph sets out the
method adopted by Circle for holding the various apartments – a land-holding company,
the shares in which are transferred to a trustee; various companies are named. In the
remote event that Mr Valiente has any quarrel with the brief description of this method,
which must be apparent from the papers received by the administrator on his
appointment, he can say so. I would not strike out this paragraph.

The last paragraph which Mr Valiente seeks to have struck out of Mr Ramsbottom's
affidavit is para. 20. This paragraph begins with the words 'the above actions could have
affected' and is designed to draw attention to the potential seriousness of the faults
alleged. It continues with a brief explanation of how some of the most serious potential
consequences were in the event avoided. Mr Valiente is faced with no difficulty here. He
can easily decide which of the factual allegations he accepts and which he denies. In the
exercise of the court's discretion I would not strike this out.

The exhibits objected to are these:

(1)　　PR3, the r. 2.2 report, to which is appended the Echo report, to which in turn is
appended the Borgen report. I have dealt with these above. If an admission or
non-admission of this exhibit turned on an exercise of discretion alone, I would
still decline to exclude it at this stage.

(2)　　PR4, a copy of what appear to be typed but unsigned minutes of a board meeting
which come from the papers of the company. The Secretary of State must be
entitled to put these before the court for what they are worth, and I would not
exclude them now.

A   (3)   PR6, a copy of what appear to be minutes of a general meeting of the company not signed by the chairman but apparently 'certified' by a firm of solicitors. Again, the Secretary of State must be entitled to put these before the court for what they are worth, whichever rules of court apply to this application.

(4)   PR7, a list of certificates said by the administrator not to have been issued by Circle at the date of appointment of the administrators. This helps to particularise B   the allegation made against the directors and I would not strike it out.

(5)   PR8, a letter dated 5 October 1990 from Mr Holdsworth. This is hearsay evidence obtained from a third party, to which objection is taken (as with PR6) only if the County Court Rules do not apply. The letter is put in by Mr Ramsbottom as the only evidence in support of his belief stated in para. 18A(iv) that certain things were done to the knowledge of all the respondents. Even if the Rules of the Supreme Court applied I would not strike out that this exhibit. The directors had C   a duty to know these things.

(6)   PR9, which I have dealt with above in connection with the allegation that there must have been sales of weeks without authorisation.

(7)   PR10, a copy of further unsigned board minutes to which the same considerations apply as to PR4.

D   (8)   PR12, this appears to be a computer print out recording the contracts of sales and acceptance of deposits in relation to apartments in the complexes Las Calas II and Las Calas III, which has been annotated by an unknown person. It is relied upon by the Secretary of State in relation to the third allegation against Mr Valiente and his co-directors in para. 18C of Mr Ramsbottom's affidavit that Circle retained £14,840 of deposits taken on apartments not owned by Circle.

E   It seems to me that it is helpful to Mr Valiente to have these particulars of this allegation and I would not strike out this schedule. Mr Valiente can decide now how many of the instances cited, if any, he accepts and the Secretary of State will have an opportunity to review and supplement his evidence on the disputed items before the matter is tried.

(Summons dismissed. Second respondent to pay the Secretary of State's costs of the
F   *application in any event. Basis of costs reserved to judge hearing disqualification*
application)

G

H

Longden & Anor v Ferrari Ltd & Anor.

Employment Appeal Tribunal.
Mummery J, Ms Corby and Mr Thomas.
Judgment delivered 22 November 1993.

Administrative receivership – Transfer of undertakings regulations – Unfair dismissal – Whether appellants were unfairly dismissed by administrative receivers before business was sold – Whether transfer of undertaking effected by series of transactions – Whether transfer or reason connected with it was reason for dismissal.

This was an appeal from the industrial tribunal which decided that the two appellants were not unfairly dismissed by administrative receivers before a business was sold.

The company concerned went into administrative receivership on 6 March 1991 and the receivers attempted to sell the business as a going concern. The ultimate purchaser contacted the receivers on 14 March. On 27 March, before a sale was agreed, the purchaser paid the receivers some £4,000 to keep the business 'ticking over' and also indicated to the receivers the names of various individuals (not including the appellants) whom they thought it essential to retain in employment pending further negotiations. The appellants were dismissed on 28 March and the business sold on 10 April.

The industrial tribunal found that the appellants were not employed 'immediately before' the transfer of the undertaking within the meaning of reg. 5(3) of the Transfer of Undertakings (Protection of Employment) Regulations 1981. The transfer was effected by the agreement of 10 April 1991, and not by a series of two or more transactions ante-dating the dismissals of 28 March. Nor were the appellants unfairly dismissed before the relevant transfer, because neither the transfer nor a reason connected with it was the reason or principal reason for their dismissal within the meaning of reg. 8(1).

Held, dismissing the appeal by a majority:

1. The industrial tribunal was correct in law in holding that the appellants were not employed 'immediately before' the transfer of the company's undertaking. The transfer was effected by a single transfer on 10 April 1991, not by a series of two or more transactions dating from 26 or 27 March.

2. (By a majority) There was evidence before the tribunal on which it could reasonably come to the conclusion that financial constraints and pressure from the bank were the reasons for the dismissal of employees on 28 March and that neither the transfer on 10 April nor a reason connected with the transfer was the reason or principal reason for the dismissals.

3. It was a matter of concern that the representative of the applicants did not apparently seek to obtain documents from the receivers' files relevant to this issue or ask for any adjournment to do so. Although these matters gave cause for concern about the manner in which the applicants' case was conducted before the industrial tribunal, they were not (in the view of the majority) grounds for finding that the industrial tribunal reached a decision which was not, on the evidence before it, a permissible option.

4. The view of the minority was that the industrial tribunal erred in law because it conflated the context of the dismissals with the selection for dismissal. There was evidence that there were serious financial constraints, that the receivers had to cut costs and that they had to make some staff redundant. But the industrial tribunal should have considered whether the dismissals of the appellants as opposed to other staff whose names were indicated by the purchaser were for a reason connected with the transfer. The industrial tribunal should have made a finding of fact whether all those whose names were indicated were retained and whether all those whose names were not were dismissed.

A   5. In the view of the minority there was also a public policy point. The purpose of the regulations was to give protection to employees where there was a transfer. If receivers could successfully plead financial constraints, this opened up a potentially large loophole. The majority tried to block this potential loophole by calling for 'the best evidence' from receivers. But this of itself did not sit easily with the public policy behind the formation of industrial tribunals: there was no legal aid and the aim was to provide a cheap and informal remedy. If the view of the minority prevailed no such potential loophole would arise.

B   The following cases were referred to in the judgment:

Litster & Ors v Forth Dry Dock & Engineering Co Ltd & Anor [1989] ICR 341.
Wheeler v Patel & Anor [1987] ICR 631.

Richard Calland (instructed by T Owen, Calne) for the appellants.

Hugh Jackson (instructed by Clifton Ingram, Wokingham) for the second respondent.

C

JUDGMENT
(Delivered by Mummery J)

The main question raised by this appeal is whether, on the correct construction and application of the *Transfer of Undertakings (Protection of Employment) Regulations* 1981, the transfer of the undertaking of Ferrari Ltd (the first respondent), acting by

D   administrative receivers, to Kennedy International Ltd (the second respondent) in the spring of 1991 was 'effected by a series of two or more transactions' within the meaning of reg. 3(4) and 5(3).

The point is of general and practical importance for those employed by a transferor in an undertaking transferred; for a transferor and, in cases where a transferor has fallen into financial difficulties, the receivers and managers, administrative receivers,

E   administrators or liquidators appointed over the assets and undertaking of a transferor; and for a transferee of an undertaking.

The proceedings

The industrial tribunal, sitting at Bristol on 24 January and 27 May 1992, dismissed complaints of unfair dismissal brought by Mrs R E Longden and Mr J N Paisley against

F   Kennedy.

Both applicants had been employees of Ferrari in its Hermes Cifer division which operated from two different premises. The Hermes side of the undertaking was based in Southwark and was concerned with the development of computer software and some manufacturing work. The Cifer side was based in a large factory at Melksham, in Wiltshire, and was concerned with the development, manufacture, sale and maintenance of computer terminals, software and spares. Mrs Longden and Mr Paisley were based at

G   Melksham. Mrs Longden had worked for Ferrari since late September 1987. She was director and general manager of the Hermes Cifer division. Mr Paisley had worked for Ferrari since October 1977. He was an operations manager.

Unfortunately, in the spring of 1991 Ferrari fell into grave financial difficulties. On 7 March 1991 Mr Alan Lewis and Mr John Talbot, insolvency practitioners with Arthur Andersen & Co, were appointed joint administrative receivers of Ferrari by Lloyds Bank

H   plc pursuant to powers conferred by a debenture. The future of the Hermes Cifer division was, therefore, in serious doubt.

The complaints to the industrial tribunal arose out of the circumstances in which Mrs Longden and Mr Paisley were dismissed on 28 March 1991 and in which the receivers subsequently entered into a written receivership sale of assets agreement dated 10 April 1991 with Ferrari and Kennedy.

The industrial tribunal accepted the contention of the applicants that there was a A transfer of an undertaking from Ferrari to Kennedy and rejected Kennedy's contention that there was simply a transfer of assets. That point is not appealed. The tribunal held, however, that the claims for unfair dismissal failed for two reasons:

(1) Neither of the applicants was employed by Ferrari 'immediately before' the transfer of the undertaking. That transfer had been effected by the agreement of 10 April 1991. It was not effected by a series of two or more transactions ante-dating the dismissals of 28 March.

(2) Neither of the applicants should be treated as unfairly dismissed by Ferrari on 28 March 1991 before the relevant transfer, because neither the transfer nor a reason connected with it was the reason or principal reason for their dismissal within the meaning of reg. 8(1), as interpreted and applied to reg. 5 by the House of Lords in *Litster & Ors v Forth Dry Dock & Engineering Co Ltd & Anor* [1989] ICR 341.

The question on this appeal is whether the industrial tribunal erred in law on those two points.

The 1981 regulations

The legal significance of the primary facts found by the industrial tribunal about the circumstances in which the applicants were dismissed by Ferrari and the undertaking of Ferrari was transferred to Kennedy depends on the true construction of the relevant provisions of the 1981 regulations (before they were amended by the *Trade Union Reform and Employment Rights Act* 1993). The relevant regulations read as follows.

Regulation 3 deals with relevant transfers.

'(1) Subject to the provisions of these Regulations, these Regulations apply to a transfer from one person to another of an undertaking situated immediately before the transfer in the United Kingdom or a part of one which is so situated.

(2) Subject as aforesaid, these Regulations so apply whether the transfer is effected by sale or by some other disposition or by operation of law.

. . .

(4) It is hereby declared that a transfer of an undertaking or part of one may be effected by a series of two or more transactions between the same parties, but in determining whether or not such a series constitutes a single transfer regard shall be had to the extent to which the undertaking or part was controlled by the transferor and transferee respectively before the last transaction, to the lapse of time between each of the transactions, to the Intention of the parties and to all the other circumstances.'

Regulation 5 deals with the effect of a relevant transfer on contracts of employment.

'(1) A relevant transfer shall not operate so as to terminate the contract of employment of any person employed by the transferor in the undertaking or part transferred but any such contract which would otherwise have been terminated by the transfer shall have effect after the transfer as if originally made between the person so employed and the transferee.

(2) Without prejudice to paragraph (1) above, on the completion of a relevant transfer–

(a) all the transferor's rights, powers, duties and liabilities under or in connection with any such contract shall be transferred by virtue of this Regulation to the transferee; and

A (b) anything done before the transfer is completed by or in relation to the transferor in respect of that contract or a person employed in that undertaking or part shall be deemed to have been done by or in relation to the transferee.

(3) Any reference in paragraph (1) or (2) above to a person employed in an undertaking or part of one transferred by a relevant transfer is a reference to a
B person so employed *immediately before the transfer, including, where the transfer is effected by a series of two or more transactions, a person so employed immediately before any of those transactions.*'

Regulation 8 deals with dismissal of an employee because of a relevant transfer.

'(1) Where either before or after a relevant transfer, any employee of the transferor or transferee is dismissed, that employee shall be treated for the purposes of
C Part V of the 1978 Act and Articles 20 to 41 of the 1976 Order (unfair dismissal) as unfairly dismissed if the transfer or a reason connected with it is the reason or principal reason for his dismissal.'

Although not directly relevant to the issues raised on this appeal it should be noted that reg. 8(2) provides that:

'Where an economic, technical or organisational reason entailing changes in the
D workforce of either the transferor or the transferee before or after a relevant transfer is the reason or principal reason for dismissing an employee–

(a) paragraph (1) above shall not apply to his dismissal; but

(b) without prejudice to the application of section 57(3) of the 1978 Act or Article 22(10) of the 1976 Order (test of fair dismissal), the dismissal shall for the purpose of section 57(1)(b) of that Act and Article 22(1)(b) of that
E Order (substantial reason for dismissal) be regarded as having been for a substantial reason of a kind such as to justify the dismissal of an employee holding the position which that employee held.'

No submissions were made by either party on the provisions of reg. 8(2).

The arguments advanced on the appeal concentrated on the construction and application of reg. 3(4) and 5(3) to the facts of this case. There were, however, some areas
F of common ground which should be stated before the detailed legal arguments and the facts are considered.

(1) The 1981 regulations were designed to give effect to Council Directive 77/187 of 14 February 1977. The purpose of the directive was to provide, in the context of 'transfers of undertakings, businesses or parts of businesses to other employers as a result of legal transfers or mergers' . . . 'for the protection of employees in the event of a change of employer, in particular, to ensure that their rights are safeguarded.'
G
(2) Although the claims made by the applicants are based on the regulations and not on a claim of direct effect of any article in the directive, it is the duty of the court to give to the regulations a construction which accords with the decisions of the European Court of Justice upon the corresponding provisions of the directive, to which the regulations were intended by Parliament to give effect. The process of construction may extend to the implication in the regulations of words necessary to achieve that result. Thus, it was
H held by the House of Lords in the *Litster* case that reg. 5(3) should be read as if there were inserted after the words 'immediately before the transfer' the words 'or would have been so employed if he had not been unfairly dismissed in the circumstances described in regulation 8(1)': see [1989] ICR 341 at p. 371B–G.

There are no articles in the directive and there are no decisions of the European Court of Justice which directly deal with the main question in this case namely, in what

circumstances is the transfer of an undertaking effected by a series of two or more   A
transactions?

We wish to add some preliminary observations relevant to the construction of reg. 3(4)
and 5(3) which cannot be seriously disputed.

(1)   Those particular regulations have an evident anti-avoidance purpose. They should,
where the words allow, be construed in a purposive manner in order to defeat
ingenious devices and schemes designed to deprive employees in an undertaking of   B
the protection which it is intended they should have in the context of a transfer.

(2)   The obvious case at which reg. 3(4) and 5(3) are aimed is that of an attempt to
disguise the fact that there is a transfer of an undertaking within the meaning of
the regulations and the directive. The parties to the proposed transfer of an
undertaking may, with professional advice, arrange for the transfer to be effected
in a series of two or more transactions dealing with separate assets, none of which,   C
taken individually, could be regarded as the transfer of an undertaking. A
composite plan of sub-division or fragmentation of a transfer may be adopted for
no sensible commercial purpose, other than to avoid the consequence of the
application of regulations enacted for the protection of employees. These
regulations direct the tribunal to treat as a single transfer of an undertaking a
transfer which is effected by such a series of transactions. Although these
regulations do not define a transfer, they direct a tribunal to treat what might in   D
form be a series of separate transactions as, in substance, a single transfer. In
determining whether or not there is a single transfer the tribunal is directed by
reg. 3(4) to look at all the circumstances, including the extent to which the
undertaking or part was controlled by the transferor and transferee respectively
before the last transaction, to the lapse of time between the transactions and to the
intention of the parties. Those are matters expressly set out in reg. 3(4) as relevant   E
to the question whether or not such a series of transactions constitutes a single
transfer.

(3)   A similar approach is required in dealing with the related question in reg. 5(3)
whether a person is employed in an undertaking or part of one *immediately before*
the transfer. In such cases the tribunal must ask itself:

     (a)   Was the transfer effected by a series of two or more transactions? and, if so,   F

     (b)   Was the person employed in the undertaking *immediately before any* of those
transactions?

In order to decide whether the industrial tribunal erred in law in this case it is necessary
to summarise the facts found by it and the reasoning which led it to conclude that the
applicants' complaints should be dismissed.

   G

The facts

The relevant events took place in the period from 6 March 1991 to 10 April 1991,
i.e. between the appointment of the administrative receivers and the entering into the
receivership sale of assets agreement. It was during that period, on 28 March, that
Mrs Longden and Mr Paisley were dismissed by Ferrari without prior warning or
consultation.   H

The crucial question is whether anything happened during that period which the
industrial tribunal, on a correct appreciation of the law, should have held to be a series
of two or more transactions by which the transfer of the undertaking of Ferrari to
Kennedy was effected. If the industrial tribunal should have come to such a conclusion,
then it follows that it should also have asked itself whether Mrs Longden and Mr Paisley

A   were employed in the undertaking of Ferrari immediately before *any* of those transactions.

The industrial tribunal heard evidence from Mrs Longden and from Mr Welham, the managing director of Kennedy. For reasons which we shall explain later, it did not hear any oral evidence from the administrative receivers. There were also documents put before the tribunal arranged in an agreed bundle of 60 pages for use on this appeal. It

B   appears from the tribunal's decision and the documents placed before the tribunal that the relevant facts are as follows.

Kennedy is a subsidiary of the Shugart Corporation of the USA. That company manufactures computer equipment. Kennedy acts as its sales and service arm in the UK.

On 14 March 1991 Mr Welham contacted the receivers with a view to investigating a possible purchase of some or all of Ferrari's undertaking or its assets. He visited the

C   premises at Melksham, but not the premises in Southwark. The information he obtained was not enough to enable him to formulate a detailed proposal. After a visit to the US to report to his superiors Mr Welham again made contact with the receivers who were anxious to reach some conclusion about Ferrari's affairs. There had been negotiations with other possible purchasers.

On 22 March Kennedy made what was described as a 'budgetary offer', in US dollars

D   for the Hermes Cifer division. It does not appear from the industrial tribunal's decision or from the documents what is meant by a 'budgetary offer' or what was the amount of it. It is, however, clear that no agreement was made for the transfer of the undertaking at that stage.

On 26 March the receivers' solicitors (Cameron Markby Hewitt) faxed to Kennedy's solicitors a letter headed 'subject to contract' and attached a draft contract relating to the sale of certain assets of Ferrari.

E

On 27 March Mr Welham was telephoned by a representative of the receivers who informed him that Kennedy's offer had been accepted and that he should go to London that evening to sign the appropriate documentation. Mr Welham refused to do this. He pointed out that he had only made a 'budgetary offer' based on assumptions that the papers he had seen were accurate and he declined to sign anything. He did not have sufficient information about Ferrari's business to enable Kennedy to conclude a binding

F   agreement. The reaction of the receivers' representative was that, as the receivers were under pressure from the bank, they would 'pull the plug' by closing down the whole undertaking, auctioning off the assets and dismissing all the staff.

Mr Welham thought that it was crucial that Ferrari should continue to operate while further enquiries and negotiations were being conducted with the receivers with a view to eventual purchase. Kennedy therefore agreed to pay the receivers £4,000 to enable Ferrari

G   to keep 'ticking over' for another week.

Also on 27 March, Mr Welham faxed to the receivers a copy of a 'family tree' of Ferrari's management staff with which he had been supplied earlier. On that copy Mr Welham and Mr Greenfield, a representative of the parent company from the USA, ringed the names of various individuals whom they thought it was essential to retain in employment pending further negotiations. The names of Mrs Longden and Mr Paisley

H   were not ringed. On the following day the receivers gave them notice of termination of their employment. It is not clear from the tribunal's decision or from the documents put before the tribunal that the receivers dismissed on 28 March all those on the family tree whose names were not ringed or that there were retained all those whose names were ringed. An attempt was made to clarify the position during the hearing of the appeal. There were obvious difficulties in obtaining clear instructions at this late stage. It does, however, appear from a list in the agreed bundle of documents that the majority of the

49 employees in the Hermes Cifer division were dismissed on 28 March and the rest, with   A
the exception of Mr Wattam, on 10 April. Most of the latter group were re-engaged by
Kennedy with changed job descriptions.

The Easter weekend followed during which Kennedy made efforts to speak to various
members of Ferrari's staff. Negotiations continued. In particular, it appears from a letter
dated 5 April 1991 from Arthur Andersen & Co to Mr Greenfield of the Shugart
Corporation, that it was agreed that the receivers were prepared 'in consideration of the   B
payment in the sum of £20,000 to allow you exclusively a period ending at 5 pm on
Wednesday, 10 April 1991 to complete the sale to you of the Cifer/Hermes division on
the following conditions'. The conditions provided that the £20,000 would be
immediately transferred into the client account of the receivers' solicitors; that the deposit
would be non-refundable in the event that a binding contract for the sale of the Cifer/
Hermes business substantially in the form of the draft contract previously issued were
not completed by 5 pm on Wednesday, 10 April; that if the sale was completed before   C
that time the sum of £20,000 would be deducted from the purchase price and that
Mr Greenfield should confirm that he had received substantially all the information he
required in order to complete the proposed acquisition of the Cifer/Hermes division for
a total consideration of £172,000 plus VAT. The letter also confirmed that the receivers
had received the sum of £4,000 by way of contribution to payroll costs and it was
confirmed that that sum would be applied towards the purchase price if contracts were   D
completed between them.

That letter is not referred to in the decision of the industrial tribunal, but it was agreed
between counsel that that letter was before the tribunal.

The negotiations resulted in the receivership sale of assets agreement dated 10 April.
After completion of the agreement Kennedy removed all the plant and equipment from
the Hermes premises in London and Melksham. Stocks of components were taken to the   E
USA and quantities of equipment to Kennedy's own premises at Reading. The Melksham
factory was closed down. Some of Ferrari's staff, mainly consisting of those ringed by
Kennedy on the family tree on 27 March, were re-engaged by Kennedy.

The transfer point

Having concluded that there was a transfer of an undertaking, the industrial tribunal   F
considered the submission of the applicants, who were represented at the hearing, that,
although the agreement for the sale of Ferrari's undertaking was signed on 10 April, the
actual transfer was effected by a series of transactions, the first of which was the payment
by Kennedy of the sum of £4,000 on the evening of 27 March. The tribunal rejected that
submission stating that it was not satisfied that the payment of £4,000 by Kennedy was
intended to be a down-payment on account of a binding agreement to purchase the   G
undertaking. It accepted the evidence of Mr Welham that the payment was made to
induce the receivers to keep the Hermes/Cifer division going while negotiations were
being pursued. The tribunal thought that it was by no means clear when that money was
paid that a binding contract would necessarily follow. The tribunal commented that it
was obvious that a great deal of negotiation and re-negotiation took place between
27 March and 10 April when the agreement was signed in its final form.

It is clear from the tribunal's reasoning on this point and from its acceptance of the   H
arguments advanced on behalf of Kennedy that, in its view, the transfer was effected by
the agreement signed on 10 April and that the transfer was not effected by a series of two
or more transactions. In those circumstances it followed that, in the view of the industrial
tribunal, the applicants were not employed in the undertaking of Ferrari immediately
before the transfer of the undertaking.

A In the view of this tribunal, there was no error in law on the part of the industrial tribunal in its construction of the 1981 regulations or in its application of them to the facts of the case. Mr Calland, on behalf of the applicants, submitted that on a correct construction of the regulations, the tribunal should have held that the transfer was effected by a series of two or more transactions, the first of which was the sending out of the draft contract of sale on 26 March or the holding payment of £4,000 on 27 March. He submitted that by 27 March negotiations were well developed and that there had occurred at least two transactions by which the transfer of the undertaking was effected.

B The transfer took place over a period of time. The evidence showed that, during the period from 26 March onwards, control of the undertaking had to some extent passed from Ferrari to Kennedy by virtue of the £4,000 payment. It was intended by the receivers and by Kennedy that there should be a transfer and only a short period of time elapsed between the transactions starting with the issue of the draft contract of sale on 26 March.

C In those circumstances the tribunal should have held, applying the language of reg. 3(4) and 5(3), that this was a case of a single transfer effected by a series of two or more transactions and that both Mrs Longden and Mr Paisley were employed in the undertaking of Ferrari immediately before the transaction in the form of the issuing of the contract on 26 March or before the transaction in the form of the £4,000 payment on 27 March.

D This tribunal is unable to accept that submission as a correct construction of the regulations. For the purposes of this argument it may be assumed in the applicants' favour that the matters relied on on 26 and 27 March were a series of two transactions. The crucial question is whether the transfer of the undertaking was '*effected* by a series of two or more transactions'. The industrial tribunal was correct in holding that the transfer of Ferrari's undertaking was effected by the agreement of 10 April and that it was not effected by a series of two or more transactions dating from 26 or 27 March.

E What happened on 26 March and 27 March and other dates before the agreement of 10 April was a succession of events which can be loosely described as causally linked to one another and to the ultimate conclusion of the receivership sale of assets agreement. It is not, however, sufficient for the purposes of reg. 5(3) that there exists a series of two or more transactions linked in a chain of events. The language of the regulations requires that the transfer of the undertaking is '*effected*' *by* a series of two or more transactions. The transactions of 26 and 27 March did not have that effect. The transfer was not

F 'effected' by a series of two or more earlier transactions. It was effected by the single agreement of 10 April. This construction is consistent with the decision in *Wheeler v Patel* [1987] ICR 631 at p. 636G that 'where there is a contract for sale of a business followed some period later by completion of that contract, there is only one transaction'. The transfer took place on completion.

  The industrial tribunal was correct in law in holding that neither Mrs Longden nor
G Mr Paisley was employed by Ferrari 'immediately before' the transfer of Ferrari's undertaking to Kennedy. In brief, the transfer of Ferrari's undertaking to Kennedy was effected by a single transfer on 10 April 1991, not by a series of two or more transactions. Immediately before 10 April neither of the applicants was in the employment of Ferrari. They had been dismissed on 28 March.

Reason for dismissal point

H
  The second point on the appeal can be dealt with more briefly. It is common ground that the industrial tribunal, by reference to the provisions of reg. 8 and 5, as interpreted in the *Lister* case, correctly asked the question whether the applicants were dismissed because of the transfer or a reason connected with the transfer. The tribunal concluded that neither the transfer nor a reason connected with the transfer was the reason or principal reason for the applicants' dismissal on 28 March.

On this point the tribunal concluded, as a matter of fact, that the receivers dismissed   A
Ferrari's employees on 28 March because of financial constraints, and of pressure from
the bank which had appointed them, and not because they had received any request or
instruction from Kennedy. Although Kennedy had identified on 27 March on the marked
family tree those employees who it was essential to retain, the tribunal did not accept that
that request necessarily carried with it a request that the other employees should be
dismissed.

  B
On behalf of Mrs Longden and Mr Paisley, Mr Calland made a number of criticisms
of the way in which the industrial tribunal reached its decision on this point.

(1)   The tribunal erred in its application of the principle in the *Litster* case that an
employee is entitled to the protection of the regulations where he would have been
employed immediately before the transfer had he not been unfairly dismissed for a
reason connected with the transfer.

  C
(2)   The tribunal's decision on this point was perverse for a number of reasons.
Kennedy had made it plain to the receivers before dismissal which employees
Ferrari wanted to be retained in the undertaking. In the circumstances, this request
must have had some bearing on the decision of the receivers to dismiss
Mrs Longden and Mr Paisley, along with others whose names were not ringed on
the family tree. The tribunal wrongly approached the matter on the basis that there
had to be collusion between the transferor and the transferee. It did not follow   D
from the absence of collusion that the transfer had nothing to do with the dismissal
of the employees. Further, the tribunal's finding that the receivers dismissed the
employees because of financial constraints and pressures is not supported by
evidence. The day before the dismissal the receivers had obtained £4,000 from
Kennedy in order to keep the undertaking 'ticking over' for a further week while
negotiations continued between the receivers and Kennedy. No evidence was given   E
of pressure from the bank. The tribunal failed to consider the insignificance of the
savings that would be achieved by the dismissals in the context of the overall
financial position of the undertaking; it had also failed to take into account the
proximity of the dismissals to the completion of the transfer on 10 April. The
tribunal had failed to look at all the objective circumstances in which the dismissals
occurred.

(3)   The tribunal also erred in law in reaching its decision without hearing evidence   F
from the receivers. The decision on this point should be reversed or the case should
be remitted to the tribunal for further evidence.

The majority of this tribunal are unable to accept these submissions. The industrial
tribunal correctly addressed itself to the point for decision as formulated in the *Litster*
case. There was evidence before the tribunal on which it could reasonably come to the
conclusion that financial constraints and pressure from the bank were the reasons for the   G
dismissal of employees on 28 March and that neither the transfer on 10 April nor a
reason connected with the transfer was the reason or principal reason for the dismissals.

The majority of this tribunal agree that, if there were no countervailing evidence, the
events which occurred between 27 March and 10 April 1991 would strongly indicate that
the dismissals on 28 March were for a reason connected with the transfer. Kennedy is,
however, able to point to evidence on which the tribunal could make a finding that the   H
dismissals were not for a reason connected with the transfer. Mr Welham gave evidence
that he was unhappy at the dismissals on 28 March and had not wanted any dismissals
to occur. It is true that no oral evidence was given by the receivers themselves and no
sworn evidence was given by any employee of the receivers. It appears, however, from
the decision of the industrial tribunal and the documents included in the agreed bundle
that the representative of the applicants at the hearing agreed to the industrial tribunal

A   looking at documents on that point. The industrial tribunal states that its conclusions on
this point are derived from those documents. The documents in question include a report
by the official receiver containing a summary of the statement of affairs of Ferrari at
7 March 1991. It appears from that report that the cash in hand was only £4,671 and
that the estimated total deficiency of Ferrari exceeded £16.7m. According to para. 7 of
the report the receivers and managers appointed on 7 March 1991 continued trading only
for two weeks. There were before the industrial tribunal letters from the receivers'
B   representative who dealt with the matter, Mr Greg Robertson, while he was a manager
in the London office. At the time when Kennedy's solicitors were attempting to obtain
information in January 1992 Mr Robertson had gone to work in Sydney, Australia.
Letters were obtained from him in which it was stated that the receivers had retained the
services of all employees at Melksham initially in order to attempt to sell the business as
a going concern. The initial response was not encouraging for a going concern sale and
C   the receivers therefore found it necessary to rationalise costs in order to minimise the
receivers' trading loss. He stated that, as part of this strategy, a number of employees
were dismissed. He stated in another letter of 22 January, in response to further inquiries
from Kennedy's solicitors, that 'the employees were dismissed in order to cut costs and
minimise the receivers' trading loss'. The decision records that the industrial tribunal also
heard evidence from Mr Welham that he was told by the receivers' representative on
27 March that the receivers were under pressure from the bank to close down the whole
D   undertaking, auction off the assets and dismiss all the staff.

In the light of this evidence, it is not correct to submit, as the applicants do, that the
decision of the tribunal on this point was made without evidence and perversely.

We would add that it is, in general, desirable that in cases of this kind the best evidence
available is brought by the parties before the tribunal. It is a matter of concern that the
E   representative of the applicants did not apparently seek to obtain documents from the
receivers' files relevant to this issue or ask for any adjournment to do so, even though it
appeared from Mr Robertson's letter of 22 January that the information relevant to the
dismissal 'should be contained in the files at my London office'. Further, the
representative of the applicants agreed to the letters from Mr Robertson being put before
the tribunal without, it appears, seeking an adjournment to obtain further documents or
oral evidence. Although these matters give cause for concern about the manner in which
F   the applicants' case was conducted before the industrial tribunal, they are not, in the view
of the majority, grounds for finding that the industrial tribunal reached a decision which
was not, on the evidence before it, a permissible option.

The view of the minority is that it is not possible to support the decision of the tribunal
on this point. The view of the minority is that the industrial tribunal erred in law in its
application of the principle of *Litster* case for three reasons:

G   (1)   The industrial tribunal wrongly took into account an irrelevant consideration,
namely Mr Welham's feelings of unhappiness at the dismissals which took place.
In most cases of redundancy the employer is not happy about them and has not
wanted them to occur. But the correct test is objective, not subjective.

(2)   The industrial tribunal erroneously conflated the context of the dismissals with the
selection for dismissal. There was evidence that there were serious financial
H   constraints, that the receivers had to cut costs and that they had to make some
staff redundant. In the view of the minority the industrial tribunal should have
considered whether the dismissals of Mrs Longden and Mr Paisley, as opposed to
other staff whose names were ringed on the family tree, were for a reason connected
with the transfer. The industrial tribunal should have made a finding of fact
whether all those whose names were ringed on the family tree were retained and

A

whether all those whose names were not ringed were dismissed. It erred in not doing so.

(3) There is a public policy point. The purpose of the regulations is to give protection to employees where there is a transfer. If receivers could successfully plead financial constraints, this could open up a potentially large loophole. The majority try to block this potential loophole by calling for 'the best evidence' from receivers. But this of itself does not sit easily with the public policy behind the formation of industrial tribunals. At that level there is no legal aid and the aim is to provide a cheap and informal remedy. However, if the view of the minority is to prevail no such potential loophole would arise.

B

For the reasons given above by this tribunal, or the majority of it, the appeal is dismissed on both points.

(*Order accordingly*)

C

D

E

F

G

H

Re Philipp and Lion Ltd.

Chancery Division (Companies Court).
Arden J.
Judgment delivered 26 November 1993.

> *Disqualifying unfit directors of insolvent companies – Application to be made
> within two years of company becoming insolvent – Proceedings issued on first day
> court office was open after two-year period expired (on day when offices were
> closed) – Whether proceedings out of time – Company Directors Disqualification
> Act 1986, s. 7(2).*

**Director disqualification proceedings issued on the first day the court office was open
after the last day of the two-year period mentioned in s. 7(2) of the Company Directors
Disqualification Act 1986 were not out of time. That was because there was a general rule**
**that if the last day prescribed for the doing of an act, for which it was necessary that the
court office should be open, fell on a day when the court office was closed, time was extended
to the next day when the court office was open. (Pritam Kaur v S Russell & Sons Ltd [1973]
QB 336 applied.)**

The following cases were referred to in the judgment:

Director of Public Prosecutions v Ottewell [1970] AC 642.
Pritam Kaur v S Russell & Sons Ltd [1973] QB 336.
R v Greville [1929] Crim App R 719.
R v Middlesex Justices (1843) 2 Dowl NS 719.
Trow v Ind Coope (West Midlands) Ltd & Anor [1967] 2 QB 899.

Mark Cunningham (instructed by the Treasury Solicitor) for the Secretary of State for
Trade and Industry.
Leolin Price QC (instructed by Gouldens) for the applicant.

JUDGMENT

Arden J: This is the application of the third respondent, Mr Monaghan, to strike out
the originating summons in these proceedings, and the only question is, is the two-year
period in s. 7(2) of the *Company Directors Disqualification Act* 1986 (the 1986 Act) to be
extended if the day on which the period expires is one on which the court offices are
closed?

Section 7(2) provides:

> 'Except with the leave of the court, an application for the making under that
> section [s. 6] of a disqualification order against any person shall not be made after
> the end of the period of 2 years beginning with the day on which the company of
> which that person is or has been a director became insolvent.'

It is common ground:

(1)   that Philipp and Lion Ltd became insolvent for the purposes of s. 7(2) of the 1986
Act on 3 May 1991, the date on which it entered creditors' voluntary liquidation;

(2)   that the last day of the two year period 'beginning with' that date was 2 May 1993;
and

(3)   that the offices of the court were closed on 1, 2 and 3 May 1993, being a weekend
and the May Day bank holiday.

The date in (2) above, 2 May 1993, was arrived at by including 3 May 1991 as the first
day of the period. Although I have not heard full argument on the point, this would seem
to follow from the decision of the Court of Appeal in *Trow v Ind Coope (West Midlands)
Ltd* [1967] 2 QB 899.

The proceedings under s. 6 in this case against Mr Monaghan were issued on 4 May   A
1993. I am not concerned with either the merits of the substantive application or the
reasons for the delay. Nor is there any application before me under s. 7(2) for leave to
make the application after the expiry of the two-year period. What Mr Monaghan
contends is that the application was not made in time and therefore ought to be struck
out.

The starting point in resolving the question set out above is the decision of the Court   B
of Appeal in *Pritam Kaur v S Russell & Sons Ltd* [1973] QB 336. That case concerned a
claim for damages under the Fatal Accidents Acts 1846 to 1959 and under the *Law
Reform (Miscellaneous Provisions) Act* 1934. The limitation period expired on a
Saturday. It was held that a writ issued on the following Monday was in time. The
members of the Court of Appeal were Lord Denning MR, Karminski LJ and Megarry J.
In his judgment, Lord Denning referred to the fact that if time expired on the Saturday,
the limitation period was effectively shortened by one day whereas if time expired on the   C
Monday it was effectively extended. Lord Denning continued (at p. 349C–F):

> 'Those arguments are so evenly balanced that we can come down either way. The
> important thing is to lay down a rule for the future so that people can know how
> they stand. In laying down a rule, we can look to parallel fields of law to see the
> rule there. The nearest parallel is the case where a time is prescribed by the Rules
> of Court for doing any act. The rule prescribed in both the county court and the   D
> High Court is this: If the time expires on a Sunday or any other day on which the
> court office is closed, the act is done in time if it is done on the next day on which
> the court office is open. I think we should apply a similar rule when the time is
> prescribed by statute. By so doing, we make the law consistent in itself: and we
> avoid confusion to practitioners. So I am prepared to hold that when a time is
> prescribed by statute for doing any act, and that act can only be done if the court
> office is open on the day when the time expires, then, if it turns out in any particular   E
> case that the day is a Sunday or other dies non, the time is extended until the next
> day on which the court office is open.
>
> In support of this conclusion, I would refer to *Hughes v Griffiths* (1862) 13 C.B.N.S.
> 324. It was on a different statute, but the principle was enunciated by Erle C.J., at
> p. 333:
>
>> ". . . Where the act is to be done by the court, and the court refuses to act on   F
>> that day, the intendment of the law is that the party shall have until the earliest
>> day on which the court will act." '

Karminski LJ agreed with Lord Denning. Megarry J in his judgment took the view
that the rule laid down by Lord Denning was only a prima facie rule. In so far as Megarry J
was differing from the view of Lord Denning and Karminski LJ, I am bound by their
view as the view of the majority.   G

The ratio of the case is in my judgment to be found in the final sentence of the first
paragraph in the passage that I have quoted from Lord Denning's judgment. The ground
of the decision was thus that there was a general rule that if the last day prescribed for
the doing of an act, for which it was necessary that the court office should be open, fell
on a day when the court office was closed, time was extended to the next day when the
court office was open.   H

Mr Price submitted that the decision could not be applied to statutes imposing liability
which is penal in character because there was, in the absence of a specific statutory
provision dealing with the situation, a doubt as to what Parliament intended which ought
to be resolved in favour of the person subject to the liability. On this point Mr Price
referred me to the passage headed 'Principle against penalisation under a doubtful law'
in Bennion on *Statutory Interpretation* (2nd edn) at pp. 571–574. As Mr Cunningham

A   submitted, the 1986 Act is at most penal in character only in a qualified sense. Assuming, however, that it is a statute to which the canon of construction on which Mr Price relies is applicable, I take the view that there is no doubt for this purpose. Parliament must be taken to have been aware of the decision in *Pritam Kaur* and, by making no contrary provision, to have intended it to apply. Being so satisfied, I am not prevented from giving effect to that conclusion by the principle to which Mr Price refers (see *DPP v Ottewell* [1970] AC 642 at p. 649D–E).

B   The rule laid down in *Pritam Kaur* applies only where an act is required to be done at the court office. Thus the decision in *R v Middlesex Justices* (1843) 2 Dowl NS 719, cited by Mr Price, where it was held that a notice of appeal had to be served on a Sunday, is not in my judgment in point in this case. In *R v Greville* [1929] Crim App R 719 it was held that time for leave to appeal expired on a Sunday. The reason given was that Sunday for this purpose was not a dies non. The report does not disclose whether anything had

C   to be filed with the court office on that day, and so it is not clear what was decided. Be that as it may, I hold that I am bound by *Pritam Kaur*.

   Mr Price submitted that the fact that s. 7(2) permits an extension of time with leave of the court implicitly excludes the rule in *Pritam Kaur*. Assuming, as I do, that the rule may be excluded expressly or by implication by the terms of the enactment in question, I take the view that the provision for leave is not a provision which achieves this effect. The

D   provision for leave in s. 7(2) and the rule in *Pritam Kaur* cover different situations. I see no reason why Parliament should be taken to have intended that an application for leave should be made simply because the court office was not open on the last day of the two-year period.

   Accordingly I propose to dismiss the summons dated 7 July 1993. I note that my decision accords with a previous decision of the registrar of the Companies Court in

E   another matter in chambers to which I was referred.

(Order accordingly)

F

G

H

Re Pamstock Ltd.

A

Chancery Division (Companies Court)
Vinelott J.
Judgment delivered 24 November 1993.

> *Disqualifying unfit directors of insolvent companies – Whether specialist*
> *in assisting small and newly formed companies by providing financial advice*
> *and obtaining outside finance was unfit – Company Directors Disqualification*
> *Act 1986, s. 6.*

B

1. The respondent's conduct as a director of Pamstock Ltd was such as to compel the court to make a disqualification order. Pamstock was inadequately capitalised and was reliant on borrowing from the participators and the bank, which put creditors at risk. Pamstock consistently made losses and by the end of September 1986 its current liabilities exceeded its current assets. Creditors were kept at bay by issuing cheques which the company was unable to meet. The debts due to the Crown increased year by year until at the end of its life the company was financed to a substantial extent by moneys due to the Crown much of which had accrued over a long period.

C

2. This was not the case of a director who had taken large remuneration or who had obtained other benefits from a company at the expense of creditors. The respondent suffered financially to a greater extent than the creditors taken as a whole. However the question was not whether there was culpable misconduct in the sense that he benefited himself at the expense of creditors. He failed to put into place an adequate system of management and allowed the company to trade beyond the point at which trading should have ceased. To that extent he fell short of the standard.

D

3. In this context the failure to file accounts and returns promptly was also a serious default. Creditors (including, in this case, the Crown) might be prejudiced if accounts which would have shown that a company's assets exceeded its liabilities and that it was continuing to trade at a loss and was dependent upon the continued support of its participators, were not filed.

E

4. The respondent had not been involved in the affairs of any company which had ended in an insolvent winding up since 1987–88. He made a practice of ensuring that a chartered accountant was appointed secretary of all companies with which he was concerned to ensure that annual accounts and returns were promptly filed. The past misconduct in the case of Pamstock could not be overlooked, but the order should be for the minimum period of two years. The mandatory terms of s. 6 compelled the court to disqualify a respondent even though the misconduct occurred some years before and the court was satisfied that he had since shown himself capable of behaving responsibly.

F

5. It seemed to have become the practice of the official receiver to include in his report every matter which could be the possible subject of a complaint. The result in this case was that the evidence had been overloaded with complaints relating to matters some of no substantial weight and going back over a very long period of time. It was right that the official receiver should conduct a search through the records and should put before the court details of all companies in which a respondent had been concerned and which had gone into insolvent liquidation and to draw attention to cases where the respondent had been a director or secretary of a company which had failed to file annual accounts or returns promptly. However, that could be done in a schedule or addendum without raising separate complaints except where there was a serious failure for which the respondent could be said to be responsible whether alone or with others.

G

H

The following cases were referred to in the judgment:

Sevenoaks Stationers (Retail) Ltd, Re [1990] BCC 765; [1991] Ch 164.
Swift 736 Ltd, Re [1993] BCC 312.

A   David Chivers (instructed by the Treasury Solicitor) for the official receiver.

Matthew Collings (instructed by Stephenson Harwood) for the respondent.

JUDGMENT

Vinelott J: This is an application by the official receiver acting at the direction of the Secretary of State for Trade and Industry pursuant to s.7(1)(b) of the *Company Directors*
B   *Disqualification Act* 1986. The official receiver seeks an order in the terms of s.1(1) disqualifying the respondent, Robert Edwin Glover Iggulden, for such period as the Court may think fit from being concerned in the management of a company.

The case is one that has given me considerable anxiety. The unusual feature of the case is that the respondent specialises in assisting small and in many cases newly formed companies by providing financial advice and obtaining outside finance. The companies he assists are frequently companies which invite subscription for shares in companies
C   formed under the Business Expansion Scheme. In this field, the provision of, in broad terms, venture capital, the respondent is often asked or required to accept a directorship. It is also a field in which there are inevitably a proportion of casualties – companies which are forced into insolvent liquidation not as a result of culpable misconduct or even a want of skill and care but because an expected market does not materialise or because of adverse circumstances which could not reasonably be foreseen.

D   The complaint made by the official receiver relates to the conduct of the respondent in relation to ten companies over a period of fifteen years. During that period he has also been associated with a large number of successful, some very successful, companies. Moreover, the consequences for the respondent of a disqualification order are bound to be exceptionally severe. In most cases which come before the courts the effect of a disqualification order is that the respondent is deprived of the privilege of carrying on
E   business through a company with the protection of limited liability unless the court is satisfied that a company of which he proposes to be appointed a director is on a sound financial footing and that the public dealing with it will not be put at risk. In the instant case the stigma of disqualification will make it difficult for the respondent to continue in his chosen field; moreover, it is likely to be impracticable for the respondent to apply to the court for leave to act as a director of every company which he may be asked to advise or for which he is instrumental in obtaining financial support from third parties and of
F   which he may be required to act as a director.

Before turning to examine the complaints made by the official receiver I should I think say more about the respondent's history.

The respondent

The respondent left school in 1959 when he was 18 and joined James Capel & Co. For
G   a time he worked on the Stock Exchange floor as a 'blue button'. While he was with James Capel he developed an interest in investment in small quoted companies. In 1965 with the support of friends he set up Dunbar Securities Ltd which carried on business as investment adviser investing in unquoted venture capital opportunities. In 1969 Dunbar Securities Ltd was split into two companies, one of which carried on the old business of investment adviser and the other, Dunbar & Co Ltd, business as a small merchant bank. The respondent at this time was the only executive director of both those companies.
H   Shortly thereafter as a result of disagreement with a group of outside investors the respondent and the other directors of the Dunbar companies resigned and sold their shares to the other shareholders. Dunbar & Co has since become part of Allied Dunbar plc.

While with Dunbar Securities the respondent had been instrumental in the formation of a company, Centredisc Ltd, of which he was a founder shareholder and the finance

director. Centredisc built up a very substantial international sound recording business. It A
was later floated on the Stock Exchange under the name Trilion plc. Another company
which the respondent advised was Goad Rigg & Co, a fur and hide broking company,
which was diversifying. With the assistance of the respondent, Goad Rigg & Co bought
a number of small laundries and later a block of shares in National Sunlight Laundries.
National Sunlight Laundries owned a 30 per cent stake in a laundry known as
Chippenham Sanitary Steam Laundry Ltd which plays an important part in the later
history. B

In 1978 the respondent joined a group of accountants who had started a company
specialising in advising institutions on the making and supervision of investment in
unquoted companies. He became a 25 per cent shareholder and a director of this
company which was known as Larpent Newton Ltd. He remained with Larpent Newton
Ltd for nine years and it was during this period that he was concerned with many of the
companies of which complaint is made by the official receiver. In 1987 the respondent C
joined a well known company, Johnson Fry Corporate Finance Ltd, a subsidiary of
Johnson Fry plc, which again specialises in providing financial advice and procuring
finance for small and medium-sized public and unquoted companies and in the
promotion of Business Expansion Schemes and investment in Enterprise Zone
businesses. This field of business contracted, largely as a result of fiscal changes after
1989, and in June 1990 the respondent left Johnson Fry. Since then he has carried on D
business also in the field of financing small companies through his own company, Open
View Ltd, and through another company which he owned, Management Options Ltd.
He also acts as non-executive director of a number of companies representing investors
and is on the non-executive directorship panel of substantial financial concerns including
Hill Samuel Venture Capital and Midland Montague Ventures.

The companies in relation to which complaints are made fall into three groups. There
is first, Pamstock Ltd ('Pamstock'), the company mentioned in the title to these E
proceedings. The charges in relation to Pamstock are first that the respondent allowed
Pamstock to trade while insolvent and known to be in financial difficulty at the expense
of creditors, secondly that he failed to give sufficient attention to Pamstock's financial
affairs, in particular by allowing the tendering of cheques without due regard to the
prospect of them being honoured, and thirdly that he failed to ensure that annual
accounts and returns were promptly filed. F

The second group comprises three companies, Kingsland Workshop Urethanes Ltd
('Kingsland'), Salop Realisations Ltd ('Salmet') and Leisure Newspapers Ltd ('Leisure
Newspapers') in relation to which the charge that is made is that the respondent allowed
them to trade while insolvent and known to be in difficulties at the expense of creditors.
In relation to Leisure Newspapers it is also said that he failed to ensure that annual
accounts and annual returns were promptly submitted. G

The third group comprises companies in relation to which the only charge that is made
is that he failed to ensure that annual accounts and annual returns were promptly filed.
The companies in relation to which this is the only charge are Livewire Audio and
Lighting Hire Ltd ('Livewire') (where the only charge relates to a failure to ensure that
annual accounts were promptly filed), Chippenham Sanitary Steam Laundry (later
known as Westwood Linen) which I have already mentioned, Farhana Design (UK) Ltd
('Farharna UK'), Farharna Designs Productions Ltd ('Farharna Productions'), Leisure H
Dimensions Ltd ('Leisure Dimensions'), and Management Options.

Chippenham Sanitary Steam Laundry and Pamstock

It will be convenient first to say something about the history of Chippenham Sanitary
Steam Laundry Ltd which was later renamed Westward Linen Ltd. Although the only

A charge made in relation to this company is that the respondent failed to ensure that annual accounts and returns were promptly filed it was the predecessor of Pamstock which took over part of its business.

Chippenham Sanitary Steam Laundry Ltd was an old established domestic laundry. The involvement of the respondent started in 1977 following the acquisition of an interest (later a controlling interest) in National Sunlight Laundries by Goad Rigg & Co.

B National Sunlight Laundries had a 30 per cent stake in Chippenham Sanitary Steam Laundry. The domestic laundry business has suffered a severe decline since the war in part because of the greatly increased cost of labour and fuel but more importantly as a result of the spread of domestic washing/drying machines and launderettes. The respondent's evidence was that in 1945 there were 1,000 small domestic laundries in the London area whereas there are now only about 100. To survive many laundries switched

C from domestic laundering to the provision of linen on hire in particular to hotels and restaurants; the laundry hires out its own linen freshly laundered and later collects it and replaces it with fresh laundry also on hire. Chippenham Sanitary Steam Laundry started to move in this direction shortly before 1977 when Goad Rigg acquired a stake in National Sunlight Laundries.

The respondent was offered the position of managing director at a salary of £5,000 per annum; the linen hire business requires large advance purchases of linen and the

D respondent was asked to assume office as managing director to assist with the consequent financial problems. The change was not a success. One reason is that the staff proved incapable of exercising proper control. In the linen hire business it is important that linen is carefully checked on return; linen is often misused by hirers who for instance may use table napkins as washcloths.

At first the business continued to make a modest profit. The audited accounts for the

E year to 30 September 1978 show a net profit after charging directors remuneration of £1,071 and in the following year £935. Disaster struck in the course of the following year. It was the delayed result of a substantial increase in oil prices. In the year to 30 September 1980 the company made a loss of £89,000 and in the following year a loss of £58,200. The London part of the business, which was the substantial part, was sold to National Sunlight Laundries in 1980 and the company ceased trading in May 1982. It went into

F voluntary liquidation with an estimated deficiency (disregarding share capital) of just under £140,000; of this something over £10,000 was owed to Management Options.

It is not suggested by the official receiver that the respondent was guilty of misconduct or indeed that the failure of the company could have been avoided by more careful management. The complaint made against the respondent is that accounts to the year 30 September 1978 and 1979 which were due on 30 July 1979 and 1980 respectively were not

G filed until 27 September 1980 and that the accounts for the year to 30 September 1980 were not filed at all. It is also said that the annual returns for the periods ending on 8 March 1977, 3 March 1978, 23 April 1979 and 30 May 1980 were filed between three and six months late and in the case of the annual return for 1981 was not filed at all. The respondent's explanation is that when he was first appointed managing director, an employee of the company's accountants was the secretary and responsible for producing the company's accounts and filing the accounts and annual returns. He ceased to be

H eligible as company secretary when the *Companies Act* 1976 came into force. The respondent became secretary on 30 June 1979. However, that was very shortly before the sale of the company's main business to National Sunlight Laundries and the subsequent cessation of business and again he relied upon the accountants to continue to file these returns as they had before. I shall return to these failures when I come to deal with this third category of companies.

I must now turn to Pamstock which is the company in relation to which the most   A
serious charges are made. Notwithstanding the failure of Chippenham Sanitary Steam
Laundry the respondent remained of the opinion that the linen hire business could be
profitably operated if confined within a limited geographical area and if the business
concentrated on the supply of linen to country house hotels and similar customers. He
thought that the West Country where there are a number of hotels of this kind within a
comparatively small area would be a profitable area in which to operate. The long-term
objective was to acquire a clientele of eight to twelve large country house hotels and to   B
supply all their requirements for linen. Pamstock was incorporated on 17 May 1982 and
commenced trading immediately. It acquired the remaining stock and equipment of
Chippenham Sanitary Steam Laundry and traded under that company's new name,
Westward Linen.

It is important to observe that it is not suggested that there was any impropriety in the
way in which the assets of Chippenham Sanitary Steam Laundry were acquired or in the   C
fact that the business was continued under its new name. The assets were acquired from
the liquidator, a qualified insolvency practitioner, at a price ascertained by independent
valuation.

However Pamstock was never properly capitalised. It had a paid up capital of £2 all of
which was beneficially owned by Open View. Finance for the purchase of the assets was
provided by the respondent, his wife, a company called Trolbourne Ltd, Management   D
Options, Open View and Pamstock's bankers. There were only two directors, the
respondent and Mr Ford who represented Trolbourne Ltd but who took no actual part
in the management of the business. The respondent was also appointed secretary.
Pamstock never traded at a profit. The audited accounts show that it made losses in every
year – £2,442 in the year to 30 September 1982 and in the following years, £11,960,
£8,126, £36,546 and finally in the year to 30 September 1986, £49,530. Working capital   E
was also provided by the respondent, his wife, Trolbourne Ltd, Management Options
and Pamstock's bankers. The auditor's report on the accounts for the year to 30
September 1984 was qualified by a note stating that the going concern basis on which the
accounts had been prepared might not be appropriate because the company had made a
trading loss of £8,811 and that although its current assets exceeded its current liabilities
it was dependent on the continued support of its parent company; the auditor's report on
the accounts for the following year contained a note that although it made a trading   F
profit of £1,030 its current assets exceeded its current liabilities and it was dependent on
'the renewal of long term loans of £89,804'; in the following year the auditor's report was
qualified by the statement that it had made a loss of £12,983, that its capital liabilities
exceeded its current assets by £121,762 and that the company was dependent on long
term loans from its parent company of £33,491.

The business was sold to a company called Guarantee Cleaners Ltd on 7 October 1988
for £85,000 of which £10,000 was paid to Open View, £10,000 to Guarantee Cleaners'   G
solicitors, who undertook to pay certain debts due to Pamstock's creditors, and £65,000
to Management Options in part settlement of a debt due to that company and secured
by a debenture. Guarantee Cleaners also collected book debts owed to Pamstock and,
under the terms of the sale, these moneys were used towards payment of Pamstock's
creditors. The respondent himself paid debts due to Pamstock's creditors amounting to
almost £106,597 including a debt of almost £69,000 due to Pamstock's bankers which   H
was guaranteed by the respondent. Although some creditors were not paid in full no steps
were taken to wind up the company compulsorily until 3 October 1989 when the
Commissioners of Inland Revenue presented a petition. The total indebtedness shown in
the statement of affairs amounted to £199,637 of which £19,292 was due to trade
creditors, £61,943 to the Crown in respect of PAYE, NIC and VAT, £106,597 to the
respondent and a further £11,805 to Management Options.

A   The respondent's explanation of the failure of Pamstock is shortly this. Pamstock started business with one customer, a London hotel which it inherited from Chippenham Sanitary Steam Laundry. That contract lasted only a short time. However, Pamstock succeeded in its original aim of obtaining contracts with some local hotels and restaurants. The business grew. The result was a considerable drain on the capital resources of the respondent and Open View who together produced the working capital needed by Pamstock by way of loan. The demand for working capital was considerable

B   because if a new contract is taken on linen has to be bought in advance – the cost is recouped over a period of some months. Also, as business is seasonal the cash flow is mostly during the summer months. It is said that the accounts give a misleading impression of the profitability of Pamstock in its early years in that linen is depreciated over 27 months, a period which is shorter than its expected life; kitchen items are charged against profit and loss account. The respondent's case is that if adjustments are made for

C   these items Pamstock's financial position was such as to give reasonable confidence that it would turn the corner and become a profitable company, at least so long as it could rely on continued financial support from Open View, Management Options and the respondent. Things started to go wrong in 1987. First, Pamstock lost the account of an hotel which was its main and most prestigious customer. Then one of the joint managers in charge of day to day business, Carol Kearton, became ill. Lastly, there was trouble with the boiler. When Pamstock acquired the assets of Chippenham Sanitary Steam

D   Laundry it had to buy a new boiler – Chippenham Sanitary Steam Laundry's boiler was being bought on hire purchase. There were complaints from neighbours of smuts emanating from the chimney. The boiler had to be switched to gas. That work was not efficiently carried out and there were delays and consequent interruptions to the cash flow. All this might have been surmounted if a further injection of capital or further loans had been forthcoming. However, it coincided with a period when there were other demands on his resources, in particular by a company I have already mentioned, Salmet.

E

    By June 1987 it was clear that Pamstock could not survive. The respondent none the less continued to trade while efforts were made to sell the business as a going concern. Negotiations were opened with two possible purchasers, Guarantee Cleaners and Regency Laundries Ltd. Agreement was ultimately reached for the sale of the business to Guarantee Cleaners although not until another year had passed. I have already set out

F   the way in which the proceeds of £85,000 paid by Guarantee Cleaners Ltd was dispersed. The £10,000 paid to Open View represented the premiums on an insurance policy on property owned by Open View and let to Pamstock. Pamstock sublet part of this property during the last year of its life and not only failed to pay rent due to Open View but failed to account for a proportion of the premiums paid by sub-tenants. The respondent took the view that Open View had a moral if not a legal claim to treat an equivalent sum as trust moneys and that Open View's claim ranked ahead of other creditors. The £65,000

G   paid to Management Options represented part of the debt due to Management Options which had taken a debenture to secure the money owed by Pamstock. Most of the creditors were paid though some were asked to accept a composition and a sum due to the contractors who had installed the new boiler or converted it to gas was not paid. The respondent took the view that the work had been incompetently done and had resulted in serious losses to Pamstock. The main debts which remained unpaid were those owed

H   in respect of VAT, PAYE and NIC. However, in October 1989 after the Revenue had presented a winding-up petition the respondent offered to pay the sum then claimed by the Revenue as to £10,000 by the end of December and as to the balance by instalments of £500 per month for three years. That offer was withdrawn when the Revenue persisted with the winding-up petition. The respondent and Management Options lost very considerable sums as a result of the failure of Pamstock. I have already mentioned the sum of just under £107,000 paid by the respondent personally to the creditors of

Pamstock or to Pamstock's bankers under his guarantee. Management Options were   A
owed a total of £90,000 though part of this (some £25,000) represented a repayment of
tax paid by Open View as a result of the surrender of tax losses of Pamstock and of
course £65,000 was repaid out of the proceeds of the sale to Guarantee Cleaners.

That is the respondent's explanation of the reasons for the failure of Pamstock. It is
not suggested by the official receiver that the venture was initially rash or imprudent or
that the respondent personally received benefits at the expense of the creditors or that   B
there was anything approaching dishonesty in the way in which the business was
conducted. The respondent in fact obtained no benefit. He was not paid a salary and the
only expenditure by Pamstock on his behalf was that it paid the rent, some £2,500 per
annum, on a small flat which he occupied when he visited the business. The criticisms
made on behalf of the official receiver fall under three heads.

(1) The first complaint is that the respondent, the sole working director, failed to give   C
sufficient attention to the financial affairs of Pamstock. The day to day management of
the company was in the hands of joint managers, Carol Kearton and Gerry Boyce.
However, they were not directors and, as I understand it, were offered and declined an
appointment as directors. The official receiver relies upon a statement in the respondent's
initial interview that he attended the premises infrequently 'probably every three months'.
I am satisfied having heard the respondent's evidence that this gives a misleading
impression of the respondent's involvement in the management of Pamstock. He was   D
sent monthly reports and accounts and spoke regularly to Carol Kearton on the
telephone. However, it is accepted by the respondent that he was not kept as fully
informed of the financial position of the company as he should have been. He was not
given full up to date details of the amount of linen purchased, the sums owing to the linen
suppliers and of moneys due in respect of work done to the plant and machinery. Carol
Kearton was overworked and even before her illness failed to keep herself or the   E
respondent fully informed as to the financial position of Pamstock at any given time. He
endeavoured to rectify the defect by finding a middle manager who would take part of
the burden from Carol Kearton and Gerry Boyce but although there were a number of
middle managers (nine over a period of six years) none of them stayed very long. The
specific criticism made is that Carol Kearton made a practice of issuing cheques which
she knew would not be met on presentation. Pamstock, in effect, got additional credit
during the period while the cheques were presented and returned unpaid. The respondent   F
knew of this practice – he referred to Carol Kearton as an expert 'juggler' of Pamstock's
resources. He tried, he says, to persuade her to cease this practise. In fact he failed to do
so and indeed the company's position was such that it could not always meet moneys due
to its creditors, in particular linen suppliers, without further injection of loans from him
or one of his companies. The official receiver has produced a list of cheques unpaid which
were presented sometimes more than once. The dishonoured cheques amount to a very
large total though, of course, many of them were ultimately met.   G

What is said on behalf of the official receiver is that a consistent practise of juggling
resources by issuing cheques in the knowledge that they will not be met on presentation
is commercially disreputable conduct. A creditor may be mislead into thinking that his
debt will be paid and may forebear from taking proceedings or even afford further credit
in the expectation that the cheque will be cleared. As the only managing director it was
the respondent's responsibility to ensure that this practice ceased – he cannot rely on   H
delegation to a manager once the conduct was known to him.

(2) The second complaint is that Pamstock continued to trade while insolvent. Even if
the depreciation charge is rewritten, as the respondent says it should be, Pamstock made
losses in every year with the possible exception of the year ending 30 September 1985. Of
course, a trading loss is to be expected during the early years of a new company and the

A   nature of Pamstock's business was such that the expansion of its business was matched initially by an increase in the loss shown in its profit and loss account. However, it was throughout dependent upon the financial support of the respondent and Management Options and as its trading difficulties increased and as the respondent and Management Options became less able to finance the business it could only survive by the adoption of the disreputable practice adopted by Carol Kearton.

B   The official receiver relies in particular on the steady increase in Pamstock's indebtedness for PAYE, NIC and VAT. The respondent's answer is that the Revenue were kept aware of the company's position and in effect acquiesced in the use of moneys owed to the Crown to finance the company's trade. I do not think that that contention is sustainable. Correspondence with the Revenue shows that as early as May 1985 when the Crown debts amounted in the aggregate to just over £10,000 post dated cheques were issued for payment by instalments and in the event they were not met. They were later

C   replaced with other cheques which were met. In November 1986 the total Crown debts amounted to over £30,000 and the respondent agreed that the arrears would be paid off at the rate of £3,000 per month the position being reviewed after three months. Two payments were made but on 17 February 1987 the respondent wrote asking that the sums paid to meet the arrears should be reduced to £1,500 per month. Proceedings for recovery were threatened but in May 1987 a further arrangement was made to clear PAYE and

D   NIC arrears (which went back as far as 1985–86). The arrangement was that current liabilities would be met on the twentieth of each month; £1,000 would be paid towards arrears on the fifteenth of each month and a further £2,500 on the twenty-fifth of each month. A cheque for £1,250 dated 10 July 1987 was returned unpaid and the Director of Taxes wrote in August to say that the matter had been referred to head office. The respondent replied that the company had faced unexpected difficulties as a result of bad weather and the switch from oil to gas and on 4 September he made further proposals

E   including payments of £8,000 in the near future and £8,000 by the end of September. In the event only £4,000 was paid of the second instalment and that not until 2 November. On 17 March 1988 the enforcement office of the Revenue wrote to say that the full amount of the arrears and instalments would have to be paid. By 24 May 1988 the amount demanded by the Revenue had increased to nearly £46,000. The respondent wrote to the enforcement office on 21 June 1988. His letter sounded an unduly optimistic note. Having referred to Carol Kearton's illness he said that his own review indicated

F   that the company had been returned to a position where it had a surplus cash flow and that the summer would be committed to making major repayments, £6,000 per month for four months, and thereafter when the summer season came to an end £3,000 per month. He added that the offer was made against 'the background of a company that had made consistent losses, had negative shareholder funds and was entirely supported by loans from the shareholders and its bankers'.

G   It seems to me that the picture which emerges is of the Revenue being fobbed off by promises and in some instances cheques which were not met while the company struggled on past the point at which the respondent knew that the only course left open to him was to sell the company as a going concern. When it was sold the revenue debt which had accrued over a long period remained unpaid. It was not until a winding-up petition was presented that the respondent offered to take responsibility for the debt, an offer which

H   was withdrawn when the Revenue persisted with the winding-up petition. The plain inference in my judgment is that the offer was made to avoid a compulsory winding-up order and the consequent risk of proceedings under the Directors Disqualification Act or possibly for wrongful trading.

    (3) The third complaint relates to the failure to file accounts and annual returns. Pamstock's audited accounts for the year to 30 September 1983 should have been filed by 30 July 1984. They were not filed until 8 May 1985. More importantly no accounts

were filed for any subsequent years. Annual returns for 1983 were due on 28 December   A
1984 and were filed on 8 May 1985; annual returns for 1984 were due on 11 February
1985 and were not filed until 6 June 1985. Again no annual returns were filed thereafter.
The failure to file accounts and returns is a serious matter in the case of a company like
Pamstock which was consistently making losses and was dependent on the financial
support of the respondent and his companies. In particular, as I have said, the reports of
the auditors for the years to 30 September 1984, 1985 and 1986 would have warned   B
creditors that the company was making losses, that in the year to 30 September 1986 its
current liabilities exceeded its current assets by a substantial margin and that throughout
this period the company was dependent on long term loans from its parent. The
respondent's answer to this last point was that the company's creditors were well aware
of the position of Pamstock and would not have learned anything new from the accounts
if they had been available for inspection. I do not think that is a sufficient answer. No
doubt there were creditors, in particular suppliers of linen, who knew that Pamstock was   C
struggling and knew the difficulties faced by companies which like Pamstock had to buy
linen to meet the demands of a new customer long before any return was obtained, I
accept the respondent's evidence that 'time critical' suppliers of fuel oil and the like were
paid promptly. However, if annual accounts are not filed creditors are deprived of a
means of informing themselves of the position of those to whom credit is afforded and
the Revenue in particular might have been less indulgent to Pamstock than they in fact
were if they had known that the company would be unable to meet its debts unless it   D
could be further financed by the respondent and his companies or by an outside investor
or by the sale of the business.

The question is whether these failings on the part of the respondent by themselves
justify the conclusion that his conduct shows that he is unfit to be a director of a limited
liability company. I shall have to come back to express my conclusions on this point at
the end of this judgment. I must first say something about the complaints made against   E
the respondent in relation to other companies, most of which went into insolvent
liquidation.

Trading while insolvent – other companies

(1) *Kingsland*

Kingsland Workshop Urethanes Ltd was a venture capital company formed on the   F
advice of Larpent Newton while the respondent was a director of that company. It was
formed to take over the assets and work in progress of a partnership, Kingsland
Workshops, carried on by Mr P W Kingsland and Mr D R Shawcross who became
respectively the director responsible for administration, purchasing and bookkeeping and
the director responsible for production and engineering. It was introduced to Larpent
Newton by a client, Minster Trust Ltd. The respondent became a non-executive director
representing in effect Minster Trust Ltd and Larpent Newton. His function was to   G
monitor the progress of the company on behalf of those two companies which had
together invested substantial moneys by way of preference and ordinary share capital. As
its name suggests its business was to be the manufacturer of polyurethane foam
mouldings. It had a brief life. It was incorporated on 17 March 1980, commenced trading
on 16 June 1980 and ceased trading on 6 February 1981. It went into voluntary
liquidation on 25 February 1981 and was wound up compulsory, on a trade creditor's   H
petition, on 1 May 1981. The company incurred substantial start up costs for the
purchase of machinery. However the machinery turned out to be badly designed and an
attempt to claim against the manufacturers was abandoned when it became clear that the
design had been approved by Kingsland. The statement of affairs shows that it had
insignificant assets and liabilities to creditors amounting to some £234,000. It is not
suggested by the official receiver that the respondent was responsible in any way for the

A   disaster which overtook Kingsland or that he obtained any undue benefit. Minster Trust
     and Larpent Newton lost considerable sums (approximately £125,000) which they had
     invested in Kingsland; the respondent did not himself obtain any benefit save that a
     modest fee was charged by Larpent Newton for his services as, in effect, a representative
     director.

         What is said is that the respondent as a director with experience in financial affairs
B   (though he was not, as the official receiver at first said, the finance director) was
     responsible for allowing Kingsland to build up arrears in respect of PAYE, NIC and
     VAT and in effect to use them as working capital. The total arrears due to preferential
     creditors which includes arrears of wages, holiday pay and rates as well as PAYE, NIC
     and VAT is just over £27,000 out of the total deficiency of £234,000. All the Crown debts
     are preferential and were thus incurred in a relatively short period before the demise of
     the company – indeed the company only traded for less than a year. In this context the
C   claim that the respondent must accept responsibility for the build up of these
     comparatively modest arrears of Crown debts is, in my view, exaggerated.

     (2) Salmet

         Salmet (which later became Salop Realisations Ltd) was another commercial disaster.
     It was incorporated in January 1985 and commenced trading in March of that year. It
     ceased trading on 6 February 1987 and went into receivership on 25 February 1987. A
D   winding-up petition was presented by a trade creditor on 11 February and the winding-
     up order was made on 13 April 1987. Salmet was heavily insolvent. The statement of
     affairs gives the value of the assets after deducting a debt due to a secured creditor as just
     over £207,000. There are debts due to preferential creditors for wages, holiday pay,
     PAYE and NIC of almost £133,000 leaving a surplus of approximately £75,000 for other
     unsecured creditors. Unsecured creditors and expenses (including moneys owed to
E   Salmet's bankers) and deposits from customers amount to £565,000. To this must be
     added a loan from a connected company, Salmet Holdings Ltd, of just under £90,000
     leaving a total deficiency of almost £580,000. The deputy official receiver, Mr Navier, in
     his report gives the likely deficiency (apart from sums due to the holders of ordinary and
     preference shares) as approximately £655,000.

         Salmet was another company which came to the respondent through Larpent Newton.
F   Larpent Newton were asked by the Greater Manchester Superannuation Fund to find
     suitable unquoted investments. The respondent introduced Salopian Industries (Metals)
     Ltd. That came to nothing when Salopian Industries (Metals) Ltd's bank refused to co-
     operate with a reorganisation and the company was put into receivership. That was
     followed by a management buy-out in which the respondent advised the management.
     The three members of the management team concerned were Mr A J Walters who became
     the managing director responsible for production and the finance of overseas contracts,
G   Mr J N West who became the commercial director responsible for the sales department
     and obtaining orders, and Mr R A Jones, an accountant who became the financial
     director and secretary. The respondent was appointed a non-executive director and
     chairman. His primary function was to act as chairman at weekly management meetings.
     But he kept in regular contact with Mr Walters.

         Salmet bought the stock, work in progress and current contracts, plant and machinery
     used in what was thought to be the viable part of the business of Salopian Industries
H   (Metals) Ltd at a cost of £100,000 which was funded by the directors including the
     respondent (who contributed £12,500). Payment for the stock and work in progress was
     deferred and was payable at the rate of £5,000 and £10,000 per month respectively. A
     further £45,000 was found by the sale and leaseback of the plant and machinery from a
     finance company. It also obtained a loan of £100,000 from its bankers as working capital.
     Salmet took over two large contracts, one with the Syrian Government which was

partially completed and expected to break even. In the event it proved unprofitable. The   A
company then diversified from its original business, the manufacture of poultry related
products, into industrial wire and related products which it sold through Salmet Holdings
Ltd. In October 1986 it entered into a contract for the supply of poultry cages to a Dutch
company which was expected to be profitable but for which ECGD cover was required.
There were delays in receiving cover from the ECGD and as a result of the delay and of
the withholding of the full amount due from the discounting bank the company ran out
of money.   B

The respondent originally invested £12,500 in Salmet. When the company reached its
overdraft limit he made loans to the company totalling £35,000. The loans were later
converted into preference shares. He also guaranteed Salmet's overdraft to a limit of
£75,000 and bought the freehold of the premises occupied by Salmet through one of his
companies which was then occupied by Salmet rent free. In consideration of the
investment he had made the other directors transferred the ordinary shares of the   C
company (the issued share capital consisted of 2 shares of £1 each) to the respondent for
a nominal consideration. The respondent thus lost a very considerable sum. It was this
loss which severely restricted his ability to assist Pamstock at a critical time in the life of
that company.

The other directors also lost their investment in the company. None of the directors
was paid a substantial salary, Mr. Jones was paid £16,000 later increased by 3.8 per cent
but still later, when the company was in difficulties, reduced to £15,000; Mr West received   D
the same salary and in addition a bonus of £4,000; Mr Walters was initially paid £16,000.
This was later increased to £20,000. The respondent was not paid a salary but Larpent
Newton was paid £1,000 per month for his services. For a time, when the company was
in difficulty, that fee was also waived. The respondent and I think the other directors
attribute the failure of the company to the delay on the part of the ECGD and the
withholding of moneys by the discounting bank.   E

Towards the end of the company's life the respondent appointed an outside managing
director, Mr B Croft, to make an appraisal whether the company was capable of being
saved if further finance could be found. On his advice the company ceased trading.

It is not suggested that the failure of the company was the result of any rash conduct
on the part of those who participated in the management buy-out. The complaint made
is that the directors 'made a decision' to pay only those creditors who pressed for payment   F
and continued to trade knowing that the company was unable to pay other creditors,
particularly the Crown. The respondent's evidence is that the financial director (who was
a chartered accountant) produced monthly statements which showed that receipts from
the discounting bank would suffice to pay trade creditors in full and that he was in close
contact with the Inland Revenue and in course of agreeing a schedule for the payment of
Crown debts by instalments at the moment when a decision was made to cease trading.
The official receiver relies primarily on the total amount of the Crown debts when Salmet   G
ceased trading. The debts in respect of PAYE and NIC amounted to approximately
£113,000. However, as the whole of this debt was preferential it must have been incurred
at the latest in the last year of Salmet's life. It must also be viewed in the in the context of
a total deficiency of something over half a million pounds. I do not think that on this
evidence I can properly conclude that the directors, including the respondent, deliberately
or negligently continued to trade at a time when they knew and ought to have known
that the company had no reasonable prospect of meeting the debts due to its creditors   H
and that they deliberately delayed payment of Crown debts and in effect used Crown
moneys as working capital.

(3) *Leisure Newspapers*

Leisure Newspapers was incorporated on 6 March 1985 and commenced trading in
April 1986. Administrative receivers were appointed on 11 January 1988. This company

A   was also heavily insolvent. The statement of affairs shows the value of the company's assets as expected to realise some £65,000 (of which £8,000 was specifically charged) and debts due to preferential creditors (PAYE, NIC and VAT wages and holiday pay) as a little over £89,000, leaving a deficiency in the amounts due to preferential creditors of just over £32,000. There was a balance of £187,000 due to the holder of a floating charge (ranking after the preferential creditors). Other unsecured debts amounted to £205,250 leaving a total deficiency in the amounts due to creditors of £424,000.

B   Leisure Newspapers was formed to produce a 'freebie' newspaper to be called Leisure Express. The title was acquired from a connected company Charmiso Ltd. Leisure Newspapers was a subsidiary of a substantial public company, Portsmouth and Sunderland Newspapers plc ('PSN') which acquired 51 per cent of its issued share capital of 890 shares of £1 each. PSN also provided a loan of £100,000 to be paid by instalments and secured by a floating charge. The revenue, of course, was to be derived from

C   advertisements. The project was a failure. Leisure Newspapers commenced trading in 1986. In December 1987 PSN demanded repayment of the loan stock and on 11 January 1988 appointed joint administrative receivers. There was a very large board, 12 in all, though two resigned, one in March 1986 and the other in December 1986. Sir Richard Storey, the chairman of PSN, was one of the directors. He introduced Peter Howcroft as the managing director. Mr Willmott was the director responsible for the production of the newspaper. It is not clear what role the other directors played. Only one of the

D   directors was paid more than £5,000 per year; he was paid between £5,000 and £10,000 in 1986 and between £15,000 and £20,000 in 1987. The respondent was a non-executive director and chairman. He received no remuneration but a fee of £8,000 was agreed to be paid to Larpent Newton. The respondent in his evidence is critical of the involvement of PSN which he said substantially controlled the company's cash flow. The management accounts were, he says, wildly inaccurate and the company was in effect dependent on

E   credit from PSN which did the printing. The respondent, as non-executive director and chairman, attended fortnightly management meetings and monthly board meetings.

Two complaints are made by the official receiver. The first is that the debts owed to preferential creditors include £23,000 due in respect of VAT (incurred between February 1987 and January 1988), £37,500 for PAYE (of which £13,700 accrued in 1986–87 and the balance in 1987–88), and £27,000 in respect of NIC (of which £4,200 accrued in 1986–87 and the balance in 1987–88). The Crown debts were for the most part preferential

F   though it is not clear from the evidence precisely how much was preferential since the preferential debts include unspecified sums for wages and holiday pay. The complaint made by the official receiver is that the inference from these facts is that the board of Leisure Newspapers including the respondent decided to pay only those creditors who pressed for payment and traded in effect at the expense of creditors, in particular the Crown, who did not press for payment and so used money due to the Crown as working

G   capital. No audited accounts were filed although accounts for the years to 31 August 1986 and 31 August 1987 were due on 3 January 1987 and 31 June 1987 respectively. The annual return due on 18 April 1986 was not filed until 31 December 1987 and the next annual return due on 17 January 1987 (six days after the administrative receiver was appointed) has never been filed. The claim made by the official receiver is that the respondent bears 'collective responsibility' for the late filing and failure to file accounts and returns.

H   I think these claims so far as directed to the respondent personally are misconceived. Leisure Newspapers was in substance run as a subsidiary of PSN in conjunction with others interested in the field of journalism and advertising. The chairman of PSN, Sir Richard Storey, was a director. PSN was responsible for the production of management accounts and PSN controlled the company in as much as they printed the newspaper and added the cost so far as not paid by Leisure Newspapers to the amounts secured by the

floating charge. There is no evidence that the respondent himself 'decided' to allow the   A
Crown debt to mount up unreasonably or that he knew of or should personally take
responsibility for the failure of the secretary to file accounts and returns. In the case of
Leisure Newspapers and of the other two companies in this category I think the
respondent is justified in feeling that he has alone been picked on and blamed for failures
which so far as not the unforeseen consequences of adverse trading conditions were
failures for which others, who have not been the subject of any application under the
Act, were primarily responsible.   B

Failure to file accounts and returns

(1) *Leisure Dimensions*

Leisure Dimensions was incorporated on 25 January 1972 and went into voluntary
liquidation on 26 August 1977. The statement of affairs shows gross assets (including a   C
sum due from Management Options) estimated to realise just under £18,000 and
liabilities to preferential creditors (VAT and PAYE) of £8,000 leaving a surplus for
unsecured creditors of just under £10,000. The debts of unsecured creditors are shown as
£63,500 including a sum of £21,500 due to Management Options. The estimated deficiency
is thus just under £54,000. The official receiver calculates the final deficiency as £58,000.
The respondent's contact with Leisure Dimensions arose from his time with Centredisc.
Leisure Dimensions which carried on business as wholesalers and manufacturers of   D
games, puzzles and toys supplied Centredisc with promotional gifts. At a time when it
was running into financial difficulties it asked the respondent as finance director of
Centredisc to pay in advance to fund the manufacture of these gifts. That was in July
1974. The respondent says he became a non-executive director at this time because of the
involvement of Centredisc. He had no executive role though he sometimes helped in the
work of assembling puzzles in his spare time when the company was busy. He also   E
became the company secretary. Management Options acquired 56 per cent of the issued
share capital of the company which amounted to 999 £1 shares. Leisure Dimensions did
not recover from its difficulties; both the principal director, Mr M J Ford, and the
respondent attribute its failure to the dramatic increases in interest rates between 1974
and 1976 and to the failure of the company's customers to pay promptly. It is not
suggested that there was any misconduct on the part of the management or that the
failure of the company was due to rash conduct on the part of the directors. The failure   F
on the face of it seems a typical failure of a small company at a time of financial
stringency.

The criticism made by the official receiver relates to failure to file returns and accounts
promptly and in some cases not at all. The accounts for 31 December 1973 were due on
31 October 1974 – about three months after the respondent became a director. They were
filed one day late. The accounts for the period to 31 September 1975 were due on 31 July   G
1976 and those for the following year on 31 July 1977. They were not filed. The annual
return for 1974 was due by 17 September 1974, two months after the respondent became
a director; it was not filed until 1 December 1976 on which date the annual return for
1975 which was due on 25 October 1975 was also filed. There was no annual general
meeting for 1976 and the annual return which became due on 15 December 1976, six
months before the voluntary winding up, has never been filed.

The respondent's explanation is that when he became a director the company was   H
having difficulties in obtaining accounts from its auditors. He introduced his own
accountants but they had difficulty in obtaining records from the previous accountants.
As a result no accounts were filed for the two years preceding the voluntary winding up
of the company. Annual returns although filed late (after the new auditors had been
appointed) were filed with the exception of the annual return for 1976 which was not filed

A before the voluntary liquidation. After then the respondent had no involvement with the affairs of this company.

The respondent, of course, became responsible on his appointment as company secretary and one of the directors for ensuring that accounts and returns were filed promptly. However having regard to the comparatively brief period of his association with the company, the size of the company and to the efforts he made to ensure that
B proper accounts were kept by the introduction of his own accountants, I do not think that these failures can be regarded as a matter of grave significance.

(2) *Livewire Audio and Lighting Hire Ltd ('Livewire')*

Livewire was incorporated on 10 December 1974 and went into voluntary liquidation on 28 April 1978. The statement of affairs shows assets estimated to realise £35,000, an
C amount of £18,000 due to secured creditors and a surplus after paying unsecured creditors of £7,000. Mr Navier in his report says that there were no realisations. He estimates the likely final deficiency as £28,000.

Livewire was originally a subsidiary of Centredisc. Centredisc planned to close it down. The respondent thought that the management of Live Wire could make a success of it and bought the company from Centredisc for some £10,000. He was the company
D secretary from the start and became a director on 1 April 1976 when the company was bought from Centredisc. There were a number of executive directors who were also appointed when Livewire was separated from Centredisc. Livewire moved to new premises, the lease of which was guaranteed by the respondent and he or one of his companies bought and leased to it the equipment it needed. He played no part in the day to day management. He was absent in India for a time in 1977 and when he returned he found that considerable arrears of rent and hire purchase instalments had accrued. He
E resigned in January or February 1978 though his resignation was not filed.

This is, I think, another typical example of an unsuccessful attempt by the managers of a part of a leisure business who faced the closing down of their branch and consequent redundancy and also acquired this business in the hope that with the assistance of the respondent they could save their jobs. There is no suggestion by the official receiver that there was any misconduct on the part of the directors or that the failure was due to
F imprudence.

The criticism of the official receiver relates again to the failure to file accounts (none were filed), the late filing of the annual return for 1976 (which was due on 22 July 1976 and was not filed until 9 December 1976) and the failure to file the annual return for 1977. The respondent's explanation is that he left it to Mr Richards, the managing director, to file accounts and returns. The official receiver relies on the 'collective
G responsibility' of the directors of whom there were two in addition to the respondent, Mr Richards and Mr Edmunds. The respondent, as the secretary of Livewire, should not have left these matters to Mr Richards even though Mr Richards was for most of the relevant period the only active director. However, having regard to the nature of the business, the modest size of the company and the respondent's brief association with it I do not think that the respondent's failure to ensure that accounts and returns were
H promptly filed is a matter to which I should attach very grave importance. There is no suggestion that creditors were misled or were likely to be misled by the failure to file accounts. It is apparent from the statement of affairs that the accounts would have shown a company with a surplus of assets over liabilities (I think it can be inferred that the assets would have been shown in the accounts at the amount at which they were estimated to realise in their statement of affairs), although in the event they realised nothing in the voluntary liquidation.

(3) *Farharna Design (UK) Ltd ('Farharna UK') and Farharna Designs Productions Ltd*   A
(*'Farharna Productions'*)

These two companies were the children of Ms Farharna Khan and her husband Peter
Coleman. She was a designer of greeting cards and giftware; Peter Coleman was the sales
end of the business which was initially carried on between them in partnership.

Farharna UK was incorporated on 20 December 1979 and went into voluntary
liquidation on 21 May 1985. The partners were the first directors; the respondent and   B
D G Clements were appointed directors on 6 October 1983. They both resigned shortly
before the company went into liquidation (Mr Clements at the end of December 1984
and the respondent on 24 April 1985). The statement of affairs shows stock in trade at
£24,000, a debt due from Farharna Productions of £8,500 and cash at bank £4,270, a
total of just under £37,000. Preferential creditors (PAYE, NIC and VAT) amount to just
over £12,000 leaving a surplus for other creditors of just under £25,000. The debts due to
unsecured creditors amount to £109,000 and include sums due in respect of PAYE, NIC   C
and VAT of just over £5,000 and a debt due to the previous partnership of just over
£47,000. The assets in fact realised only £13,350 and so only some £8,300 was available
for preferential creditors who received a dividend of 60p in the pound.

Farharna Productions was incorporated in May 1983 and commenced trading late in
1983. It ceased trading early in 1985 and went into voluntary liquidation in May 1985.
Ms Farharna Khan was a director from the incorporation of the company until it went   D
into voluntary winding up. The respondent was a director from November 1983 until
April 1985. The secretary was D G Clements who resigned on 31 December 1985; no
successor was appointed. The statement of affairs shows debts estimated to realise
£21,000, cash at bank and a VAT refund amounting together to £3,000, and unsecured
creditors with debts of £30,705. However the unsecured creditors comprise the
partnership Farharna Design and Farharna UK; the only other unsecured debt was a   E
sum of £100. There is no indebtedness in respect of any Crown debt.

The respondent's account of the history of these companies is that Farharna UK was
formed when Ms Farharna Khan received commissions from W H Smith and Marks &
Spencer. She decided to work in a flat she had in the Canary Islands. She was reluctant
to leave the conduct of the company's business to her principal salesman, Mr Clements,
who had been appointed director, unless the respondent was appointed as non-executive
chairman to supervise him. In the event Ms Farharna was attracted by an offer from a   F
company which wanted to secure her services as a designer and she decided to move to
New York. That was the end of Farharna UK. Farharna Productions was originally
formed to buy products from the partnership and later from Farharna UK and to resell
them. It never got off the ground.

The business of both these companies and indeed of the partnership was brought to an
end by Ms Farharna's decision to move to New York. It is not suggested by the official   G
receiver that the directors continued to trade after the point at which they should have
known the companies could not continue. The criticisms made relate to the failure to file
accounts and annual returns. The accounts of Farharna UK for the years to 31 March
1981, 1982 and 1983 were filed consistently late; they were due to be filed before 31
January 1982, 1983 and 1984 respectively; the accounts for the first two years were filed
together on 20 July 1983 and the accounts for the last period were filed on 17 October   H
1984. The accounts for the year to 31 March 1984 were due on 31 January 1985 and have
never been filed. The respondent, of course, ceased to be a director in April 1985. It is
said that the respondent bears a 'collective responsibility' for the directors' failure to file
the accounts for the year to 31 March 1983 (the first accounts due after he became a
director) and for the failure to file accounts for the year to 31 March 1984. Annual
returns were similarly filed consistently late. The annual returns for the period to

A   14 November 1983, that is the first annual return after the respondent became a director, should have been filed by 12 December 1983 but was not filed until 3 October 1984. The annual return for the period to 1984 should have been filed at latest on 11 February 1985 but has never been filed. However the respondent ceased to be a director in April 1985. In the case of Farharna Productions there is only one relevant year. The accounts for the year to 31 August 1984 should have been filed before 13 December 1984 and the last date for filing of the annual return for 1984 was 23 November 1984. Neither was filed.

B
     The respondent's explanation of the failures in respect of annual accounts is that there was difficulty in obtaining opening stock figures for the business taken over from the partnership. Moreover the two principal directors insisted in retaining a part-time bookkeeper who had acted for the partnership and who was not competent to draw company accounts. He arranged for Larpent Newton to provide an assistant but when Ms Farharna went to New York any attempt to bring the accounts into order and to file

C   accounts and the annual return was abandoned.

     Again although there was fault on the part of the respondent, in the context of this small and ephemeral company I do not think that the fault can be considered a serious one.

D   **Management Options**

     The respondent carried on his private business activities through two companies, Open View and Management Options. Open View was the principal company and owned the properties which he let to some of the companies which he financed – including Salmet, Livewire and Pamstock. It still owns these properties which it lets at a substantial profit. It is also a member of the British Venture Capital Association. Management Options was used primarily as a corporate body through which loans were made to the companies

E   which the respondent helped to finance. When he joined Johnson Fry in February 1987 he decided that he did not need two companies and Management Options ceased to carry on any business. The name Management Options has since been used by Open View as its trading name.

     Management Options was incorporated on 1 November 1971. Its registered address was the respondent's home. Although its business ceased in the year ending 30 September

F   1988 there was some delay in signing off the final accounts, due I understand to some difficulty in bringing the accounting period into line with that of Pamstock, and it was not dissolved until 30 June 1990. The respondent's evidence which I accept was that it had no outside creditors.

     The official receiver's complaints relate solely to the late filing of accounts and annual returns. Accounts for the years to 31 March 1985, 1986 and 1987 were regularly filed

G   though in the case of the accounts for the year to 31 March 1986 they were nine months late. The accounts for the year to 31 March 1988 and 31 March 1989 have not been filed. Annual returns for the periods to 6 February 1985 and 8 October 1987 were promptly filed but the return for the period to 6 May 1986 has never been filed. Annual returns for the years to 31 December 1988 and 1989 have never been filed. The respondent's explanation is that the company was inactive and in effect a bare shell after 31 March 1987. That of course does not excuse him from his or his wife's duty to file accounts and

H   annual returns, but in the context of a company like Management Options which was a conduit pipe through which loans were made to other companies and which had few outside creditors, I do not think that this can be regarded as a serious default.

     In *Re Swift 736 Ltd. Secretary of State v Ettinger* [1993] BCC 312, Sir Donald Nicholls V-C dealt fully with the responsibility of a director to ensure that a company files accounts and returns promptly; a director must (at p. 315F):

'fully and frankly disclose information about deficiencies in accordance with the　A
statutory provisions. Isolated lapses in filing documents are one thing and may be
excusable, but not so persistent lapses which show overall a blatant disregard for
this important aspect of accountability. Such lapses are serious and cannot be
condoned even though, and it is right to have this firmly in mind, they need not
involve any dishonest intent.'

Later in his judgment (at p. 315H) he observed that:　　　　　　　　　　　　　B

'It may be that, despite the disqualification provisions having been in operation for
some years, there is still a lingering feeling in some quarters that a failure to file
annual accounts and so forth is a venial sin. If this is still so, the sooner the attitude
is corrected the better it will be. Judicial observations to this effect have been made
before, but they bear repetition.'

Mr Chivers who appeared for the official receiver stressed that a director does not　C
discharge his responsibilities in this regard by leaving it to others and particular the
company accountants, even while they were permitted to act as the company secretary,
to do so.

At the hearing, Mr Chivers produced an elaborate and at first sight intimidating
schedule showing all instances where an account or a return was filed late or not at all.
However, I think Mr Collings, who appeared for the respondent, was justified in saying　D
that the schedule gives a misleading impression. In three of the cases mentioned the
complaint is that accounts were filed up to nine weeks and in a further three cases up to
six months late. A persistent failure to file accounts or returns promptly may in some
circumstances found the inference that a respondent whether wilfully or not acted in
disregard of his statutory obligation. I do not think that inference can properly be drawn
on the facts of this case. In many of the other cases the appointment of a receiver or
liquidator intervened before the date for filing an account or return had arrived. Strictly,　E
a director is not relieved by the appointment of a receiver or liquidator from his
obligation to see that annual returns and accounts which ought to have been filed before
the appointment are duly filed. However, it must frequently happen that directors assume
wrongly that the responsibility has passed to the receiver or liquidator. Further, Mr
Chivers' schedule covers a very long period; the first default relied on is a failure to file
accounts and returns in relation to Leisure Dimensions which was wound up as long ago
as 26 August 1977. In only a few cases was the respondent the company secretary or a　F
director who might be regarded as having a specific responsibility for the filing of
accounts and returns; the complaints relate for the most part to 'the collective
responsibility' of the board. The last and most important point is that it is not said by the
official receiver that in the case of any of these companies there was a failure to keep
proper books of account and records. In *Re Swift 736 Ltd* the Vice-Chancellor observed
(at p. 316A) that:　　　　　　　　　　　　　　　　　　　　　　　　　　　　G

'the evidence showed there were repeated failures in respect of company after
company, though not in every case, to keep proper accounting or other statutory
records . . .'

–as well as a failure to prepare and file annual accounts and returns. There was also:

'in case after case . . . a failure by (the director concerned) at the time to account
for the deficiencies or provide explanations of them.'　　　　　　　　　　　　H

Lastly, no steps seem to have been taken by the registrar of companies to call on the
companies concerned to deliver accounts and returns. It is, of course, open to the registrar
of companies in a serious case to institute proceedings before the magistrates for a fine.

Although these defaults, occurring over a long period and in relation to more than one
company, do show a failure by the respondent to recognise and discharge important

A duties which are imposed on the directors of companies, I do not think that these failures in themselves justify a conclusion that the respondent has been shown to be a person who is unfit to be concerned in the management of a company.

Conclusion

B In reaching this conclusion I have left out of account Pamstock to which I must now return. I have reached the conclusion after very anxious consideration that the respondent's conduct as a director of Pamstock is such as to compel me to make a disqualification order. Pamstock was throughout inadequately capitalised (its initial share capital was only £2) and was reliant on bank borrowing and borrowing from the participators to finance its trade. That no doubt is true of many newly formed companies but it does carry the inevitable consequence that creditors are put at risk unless the bank borrowing is fully secured by guarantees from the participators and the participators are

C in a position to continue to finance the trade and willing to provide any further finance necessary to meet any losses. Pamstock in fact consistently made losses. I accept the respondent's evidence that he thought he had found a niche in the market and that if he could provide adequate support during the early years Pamstock would earn a profit. However, by 1985 the company had moved into a position where it was dangerously exposed and by the end of September 1986 its current liabilities exceeded its current

D assets. Not only was it dependent on the support of the respondent and his companies but creditors were kept at bay by Ms Kearton's practice of 'juggling' with its resources by issuing cheques which the company was unable to meet thereby keeping creditors at bay. The creditors were dependent upon the respondent's willingness to fund the company and the risk to creditors was necessarily increased when a debenture was granted to Management Options. In the event the proceeds of sale were wholly absorbed by the debt due to Management Options and the two payments to Open View and to

E Guarantee Cleaners Ltd's solicitors, the last of which was made to ensure that the company did not default on debts due to 'time critical' creditors. Lastly the debts due to the Crown increased inexorably year by year until at the end of its life the company was financed to a substantial extent by moneys due to the Crown much of which had accrued over a long period. And the Crown was held off by promises which the respondent ought to have known the company was very unlikely to be able to honour.

F I accept that this is not the case of a director who has taken large remuneration or who has obtained other benefits from a company at the expense of creditors. The respondent obtained no benefit beyond the use of a flat for the purposes of the company's business and of course he suffered financially to a greater extent than the creditors even if taken as a whole. However the question is not whether there was culpable misconduct in the sense that he benefited himself at the expense of creditors. The failure of Pamstock with substantial debts which could only be met if and to the extent that the respondent

G personally honoured them came about in part because he failed to put into place an adequate system of management and, when the company was clearly running into difficulty, allowed it to continue to trade beyond the point at which trading should have ceased. To that extent the respondent in my judgment fell short of the standard of conduct which is today expected of a director of a company which enjoys the privilege of limited liability. In this context the failure to file accounts and returns promptly is also a serious default. Creditors (including, in this case, the Crown) may be prejudiced if

H accounts which would have shown that a company's assets exceed its liabilities and that it is continuing to trade at a loss and is dependent upon the continued support of its participators are not filed.

I reach this conclusion with regret. I have had the advantage of seeing the respondent give oral evidence when he was skilfully cross-examined by Mr Chivers. There is no evidence that the respondent has been involved in the affairs of any company which has

ended in an insolvent winding up since 1987–88. He told me and I accept that in recent   A
years he has made a practice of ensuring that a chartered accountant is appointed
secretary of all companies with which he is concerned and is instructed to ensure that
annual accounts and returns are promptly filed. The respondent seemed to me (so far as
I can judge from the evidence before me) to be a man who today is capable of discharging
his duties as a director, honestly and diligently. His failures in relation to Pamstock came
at a time when his time was fully occupied with the affairs of other companies and when   B
he was under considerable financial pressure. However, I cannot, I think, be sure that
these difficulties wholly excuse the respondent's serious misconduct in relation to
Pamstock.

Nor can it be said that his subsequent conduct justifies the conclusion that his past
misconduct should be overlooked upon the ground that there is no reason today for
saying that a disqualification order is needed for the protection of the public. A
disqualification order must to some extent express the view of the court as to the   C
seriousness of past misconduct. As I observed at the beginning of this judgment, a
disqualification order is likely to have a disproportionately severe effect on him. Apart
from the stigma of a disqualification order it will be difficult and may be impossible for
him to continue in his career as the provider of venture capital and as a professional non-
executive director if he must seek leave before accepting any appointment. However, as
Mr Collings expressed it, under the legislation as it now stands, I am required to have   D
tunnel vision and to consider whether in relation to Pamstock the respondent's conduct
fell short of the minimum standard which the court today requires to be observed by the
director of a company which enjoys the privilege of limited liability, and if it does, to
impose a disqualification order for a minimum of two years. I have reached the
conclusion after anxious consideration and some hesitation that in the circumstances I
am bound to make a disqualification order. In the circumstances of this case I think I am
justified for making the order for the minimum period of two years.   E

There are two matters to which I feel I should draw attention. In my judgment those
concerned with the operation of the 1986 Act, which I understand is now under review,
should consider whether it is necessary in a case which has been fully heard in the High
Court to require the court, if satisfied that a respondent has been a director of a company
which has been become insolvent and that his conduct as a director of that company
taken alone or in conjunction with his conduct as director of any other company makes   F
him unfit to be concerned with the management of a company, to disqualify him even
though the misconduct may have occurred some years ago and even though the court
may be satisfied that the respondent has since shown himself capable of behaving
responsibly. The mandatory terms of s. 6 are in marked distinction to the terms of s. 4
under which the court has a discretion to make a disqualification order if in the course of
the winding up of a company it appears to the court that he has been guilty of fraudulent
trading or of fraud.   G

Secondly, since the decision of the Court of Appeal in *Re Sevenoaks Stationers (Retail)
Ltd* [1990] BCC 765 it seems to have become the practice of the official receiver to include
in his report every matter which could be the possible subject of a complaint. The result
in this case is that the evidence has been overloaded with complaints relating to matters
some, in my judgment, of no substantial weight and going back over a very long period
of time. They include some insignificant delays in filing annual accounts and returns and   H
instances when as a non-executive director the respondent is said to bear a 'collective
responsibility' for the failure of the directors as a body to see that accounts and returns
are filed promptly. In the case of the three companies where it is said that they continued
to trade at a time when the directors ought to have known that they were insolvent – in
all of which cases the respondent was a non-executive director or in some instances a
non-executive director and chairman – the only ground for this complaint is the

A 'collective responsibility' of the board for an inferred intention on the part of the board to delay payment of Crown debts and to use moneys which ought to have been paid to the Crown as working capital. It is right that the official receiver should conduct a search through the records and should put before the court details of all companies in which a respondent has been concerned and which have gone into insolvent liquidation and to draw attention to cases where the respondent has been a director or secretary of a company which has failed to file annual accounts or returns promptly. However, that

B can be done in a schedule or addendum without raising separate complaints except where there is a serious failure for which the respondent can be said to be responsible whether alone or with others. In this case after examination of a very large body of evidence relating to no less than ten companies I have reached the conclusion that the only matter which requires serious investigation is the affairs of Pamstock. When counsel have had an opportunity of considering this judgment I shall want to hear further argument as to

C whether the respondent should be ordered to pay the whole of the official receiver's costs or whether any order for costs should be made upon an indemnity or a standard basis.

(*Order accordingly. The respondent to pay one-half of the costs. Leave to appeal on the question of costs*)

———————————

D

E

F

G

H

Re William Steward (Holdings) Ltd.

Court of Appeal (Civil Division).
Balcombe, Stuart-Smith and Peter Gibson L JJ.
Judgment delivered 3 December 1993.

Share transfer – Transmission on death – Whether directors could refuse to register transfer to deceased shareholder's widow – Companies Act 1948, Sch. 1, Table A, reg. 30, 31.

This was an application by executors seeking rectification of a company's register of members to replace the name of a deceased shareholder with that of his widow. The directors refused to register such transfer.

Article 5 of the company's articles of association permitted a member to transfer shares to a 'privileged relation' among others. The right to transfer shares, except in the case of a transfer expressly authorised by art. 5, was subject to restrictions in art. 6. The directors had the right under art. 6(G) to call upon personal representatives to give a transfer notice in respect of a holding registered in the name of a deceased member. Article 6(I) allowed an exception to the ordinary operation of a transfer notice required by the directors in respect of specified shares 'to the extent that a transfer of any such shares in favour of a person to whom they may be transferred pursuant to art. 5 shall have been lodged'. The directors served a notice under art. 6(G); the executors then lodged a transfer in favour of the widow.

The judge held that only a member and not his executors could take advantage of art. 5. The words at the end of reg. 30 of Table A giving the directors the same right to decline registration as they would have had in the case of a transfer before the member's death, did not extend the right of a member to his executors. Likewise the provisions of reg. 31 that a notice of election given by an executor should be treated as signed by the member as if the death had not occurred were 'simply supplementary' to reg. 30.

Held, allowing the appeal and ordering rectification of the register:

1. The articles, including the regulations of Table A incorporated in the articles, had to be construed together and effect given, so far as possible, to every provision; it was only if the express articles were inconsistent with the incorporated regulations of Table A that the former would override the latter.

2. In the first place, the transmission on death provisions of Table A governed the rights of the personal representatives of a deceased member in respect of his shares. The argument which found favour with the judge, that reg. 30 and 31 did no more than provide that the directors' power to refuse registration applied to personal representatives, failed to give effect to the words 'the same right' in reg. 30 and the final words of reg. 31 which deemed the deceased member to have signed the transfer. The judge erred in giving primacy to the wording of art. 5 and 6 without giving proper effect to the wording of reg. 30 and 31.

3. The hypothesis applicable by reason of reg. 30 and 31 where the personal representatives elected to have the shares registered in the name of another by executing a transfer to that other person, viz. that the transfer was made by the deceased member, meant that the personal representatives could come within the art. 6(I) exception by lodging timeously a transfer to a privileged relation of the deceased member. That was what occurred following service by the directors of the notice under art. 6(G), when the executors lodged the transfer in favour of the widow.

The following cases were referred to in the judgment of Peter Gibson LJ:

Greenhalgh v Mallard & Ors [1943] 2 All ER 234.
Moodie & Anor v W J Shepherd (Bookbinders) Ltd & Ors [1949] 2 All ER 1044.
North-West Transportation Co Ltd v Beatty (1887) 12 App Cas 589.

A   Philip Heslop QC and Malcolm Davis-White (instructed by Taylor Joynson Garrett) for the appellant.

Edward Bannister QC and Catherine Roberts (instructed by Bristows Cooke & Carpmael) for the respondent.

JUDGMENT

B

Peter Gibson LJ: The issue in this appeal is whether the articles of association of the respondent, William Steward (Holdings) Ltd ('the company'), on their true construction give to the personal representatives of a deceased shareholder the right to the transmission of his shares to his widow as provided for in his will or whether they give the directors the right to refuse registration of the transfer of those shares to her. His Honour Judge Paul Baker QC, sitting as a judge of the High Court, held that the latter

C   was the case. The applicants, Margaret Stothers and Nicholas Cooper, the executors of the will of the late Michael Stothers, had sought rectification of the company's register of members by striking out Mr Stothers' name and inserting in lieu thereof the name of his widow, Mrs Stothers, and they now appeal from the order of the judge dismissing their application.

The company is the holding company of a group of companies the business of which

D   is that of electrical engineers. It is a private company incorporated on 1 April 1935 under the *Companies Act* 1929. Mr. Stothers joined the company in 1963, buying a substantial holding of shares in the company. He was appointed a director and at the time of his death he was chairman and chief executive of the company and majority shareholder, holding 40,001 ordinary shares ('the holding') of the 80,000 issued ordinary shares. The remaining 39,999 shares are held by the other directors and their family trusts and the company's pension fund. Mr Stothers died on 22 April 1989. Probate of his will dated 25

E   July 1985 was granted on 18 May 1989. Under the will in the events that happened the holding is held for Mrs Stothers absolutely.

Since Mr Stothers' death there have been protracted negotiations between the board of the company and Mrs Stothers with a view to the holding being sold to the board but they reached an impasse. On 22 May 1989 there was a request that the shares be registered in the name of the executors and Mr Stothers' share certificates were sent to the company,

F   but when the negotiations for sale did not succeed, on 30 September 1991 the applicants asked that the holding be registered in Mrs Stothers' name. On 14 November 1991 a notice under art. 6(G) of the company's articles was served by the board on the applicants, requiring them to serve a transfer notice so as to set in train a procedure under the articles for the sale of the holding. But on 6 December 1991 a transfer signed by the applicants as executors and by Mrs Stothers as the proposed transferee was sent

G   to the company, and if the company was obliged to register that transfer, that would have had the effect of preventing the transfer notice procedure from operating further. On 10 December 1991 the company responded, reporting that the directors had met to consider the transfer and had resolved to refuse to register such transfer. The directors have since declined to give any reason for such refusal. These proceedings for rectification of the company's register of members under s. 359 of the *Companies Act* 1985 were commenced on 23 December 1991. The Judge dismissed the application on 15 May 1992.

H   The applicants have not sought to say in these proceedings that the directors' decision to refuse to register the transfer is tainted by any breach of duty. They say that they reserve their position on that point. The company has not sought to argue that there was any procedural defect in connection with the submission of the transfer. The issue before the judge turned, and before us turns, entirely on the true construction of the articles of the company.

A

The relevant articles were adopted on 30 March 1972. By art. 2, Pt. II of Table A (as set out in Sch. 1 to the *Companies Act* 1948) is expressed to apply except as thereinafter provided. By regulation 1 of Pt. II, the regulations contained in Pt. I of Table A are to apply with, so far as material, the exception of reg. 24. By reg. 2:

'The company is a private company and accordingly–

(a) the right to transfer shares is restricted in manner hereinafter prescribed . . .'

B

However, reg. 3 (by which it is provided: 'The directors may, in their absolute discretion and without assigning any reason therefor, decline to register any transfer of any share, whether or not it is a fully paid share') was expressly excluded by art. 3 of the company's articles. Under reg. 1 of Pt. I of Table A, unless the context otherwise requires, words or expressions in the regulations are to bear the same meaning as in the *Companies Act* 1948. By s. 26 of that Act the subscribers and every other person who agrees to become a member of a company and whose name is entered in its register of members are to be members of the company. In Pt. I of Table A the regulations relating to the transfer of shares are reg. 22–28 (save for reg. 24 excluded by Pt. II of Table A, as I have mentioned). Regulation 24 contained a provision similar to the excluded reg. 3 of Pt. II. Regulation 23 of Pt. I provides:

C

'Subject to such of the restrictions of these regulations as may be applicable, any member may transfer all or any of his shares by instrument in writing in any usual or common form or any other form which the directors may approve.'

D

Under Pt. I of Table A the regulations relating to the transmission of shares are reg. 29–32 which, so far as material, read as follows:

'29. In case of the death of a member the survivor or survivors where the deceased was a joint holder, and the legal personal representatives of the deceased where he was a sole holder, shall be the only persons recognised by the company as having any title to his interest in the shares; but nothing herein contained shall release the estate of a deceased joint holder from any liability in respect of any share which had been jointly held by him with other persons.

E

30. Any person becoming entitled to a share in consequence of the death or bankruptcy of a member may, upon such evidence being produced as may from time to time properly be required by the directors and subject as hereinafter provided, elect either to be registered himself as holder of the share or to have some person nominated by him registered as the transferee thereof, but the directors shall, in either case, have the same right to decline or suspend registration as they would have had in the case of a transfer of the share by that member before his death or bankruptcy, as the case may be.

F

31. If the person so becoming entitled shall elect to be registered himself, he shall deliver or send to the company a notice in writing signed by him stating that he so elects. If he shall elect to have another person registered he shall testify his election by executing to that person a transfer of the share. All the limitations, restrictions and provisions of these regulations relating to the right to transfer and the registration of transfers of shares shall be applicable to any such notice or transfer as aforesaid as if the death or bankruptcy of the member had not occurred and the notice or transfer were a transfer signed by that member.

G

32. A person becoming entitled to a share by reason of the death or bankruptcy of the holder shall be entitled to the same dividends and other advantages to which he would been entitled if he were the registered holder of the share, except that he shall not, before being registered as a member in respect of the share, be entitled in respect of it to exercise any right conferred by membership in relation to meetings of the company . . .'

H

A   Article 5 of the company's articles reads, so far as material, as follows:

'The directors may in their absolute discretion and without assigning any reason therefor refuse to register any transfer of any share (whether or not it is a fully paid share) not being a transfer made pursuant to the provisions of this article or of the next succeeding article.

B   (A) A member (hereinafter called 'the transferor') may at any time transfer all or any shares without restriction as to price or otherwise:

> (i) To any other member holding shares of the same class as the shares being transferred; or
>
> (ii) To a privileged relation (as hereinafter defined) of the transferor; or
>
> (iii) To trustees to be held upon family trusts (as hereinafter defined).

C   . . .

(B) For the purposes of this article:

> (i) "privileged relation" means the grandfather or grandmother of the transferor, any lineal descendant of such grandfather and grandmother, any person who is or has been married to any such grandfather or grandmother or to any such lineal descendant or any stepchild or adopted child of the transferor or of such grandfather or grandmother or of any such lineal descendant;
>
> (ii) "family trusts" means trusts under which no immediate beneficial interest in the shares in question is for the time being vested in any person other than the transferor or a privileged relation of the transferor.'

Article 6 provides that except in the case of a transfer of shares expressly authorised by art. 5, the right to transfer shares in the company is subject to the restrictions which are there set out. In short, para. (A)–(F) require that a proposing transferor should give a transfer notice to the company that he desires to transfer his shares, thereby constituting the company as his agent for the sale of the shares to any member or members of the company at a price to be certified by the company's auditors. If a purchaser member or purchaser members willing to purchase at that price can be found by the company within three months, the proposing transferor is bound on payment of the purchase price to transfer the shares to the purchaser or purchasers. If no purchaser can be found in that time, the proposing transferor then has six months in which he can transfer the shares to outside purchasers on a bona fide sale at not less than the certified price.

Paragraphs (G), (H) and (I) (so far as material) of art. 6 read as follows:

'(G) A person entitled to a share in consequence of the death or bankruptcy of a member shall be bound at any time, if and when called upon in writing by the directors so to do, to give a transfer notice in respect of all the shares then registered in the name of the deceased or bankrupt member.

(H) For the purpose of ensuring that a transfer of shares is duly authorised hereunder or that no circumstances have arisen whereby a transfer notice is required to be given hereunder the directors may from time to time require any member or the legal personal representatives of any deceased member or any person named as transferee in any transfer lodged for registration to furnish to the company such information and evidence as the directors may think fit regarding any matter which they may deem relevant to such purpose. Failing such information or evidence being furnished to the satisfaction of the directors within a reasonable time after request the directors shall be entitled to refuse to register the transfer in question or (in case no transfer is in question) to require by notice in writing that a transfer notice be given in respect of the shares concerned. If such

A

information or evidence discloses that a transfer notice ought to have been given in respect of any shares the directors may by notice in writing require that a transfer notice be given in respect of the shares concerned.

(I) In any case where under the provisions of these presents the directors have required a transfer notice to be given in respect of any shares and such transfer notice is not duly given within a period of one month, such transfer notice shall, except and to the extent that a transfer of any such shares in favour of a person to B whom they may be transferred pursuant to art. 5 shall have been lodged prior to the expiration of the said period, be deemed to have been given at the expiration of the said period and the provisions of these presents shall take effect accordingly.'

The approach of the judge was first to consider art. 5 and 6. He described them as being exhaustive in the sense that if a member wished to transfer his shares for any reason, he had to operate art. 6 unless he could bring himself within art. 5. Article 6, he C said, applied to persons who are not members but yet had the ability to transfer shares, but the discretion given by the beginning of art. 5 to the directors to decline to register a transfer covered the case where a transferor transferred shares in breach of art. 6 and a transfer was presented which did not comply with art. 5 and 6. After referring to the relevant articles he said:

'Going back to art. 5(A), the words there are that it applies to a member and only to a member. It is clear that a member, and only a member, can make a transfer D within art. 5(A) and so, to my mind, it would require express words in another article that the rights conferred by art. 5(A) to transfer without restriction were to extend to other classes of transferors.'

He then referred to the concluding words of reg. 30 and said:

'There is nothing in there which extends the rights of members under the articles E to embrace other persons who are not members but stand in the shoes of members, either by bankruptcy or by death. It simply reiterates or confirms the right of the directors to refuse in certain circumstances . . . [T]he concluding words of reg. 30 in the case of transmission "on bankruptcy or death" are simply to bring in by reference as it were, the restrictions on transfer which apply to inter vivos transfers.'

The judge then adverted to a more general consideration, saying:

F

'The articles are framed in such a way that the directors have a general discretion to refuse to register transfers but members have certain privileges and can execute transfers in favour of certain limited classes of transferees. If it were otherwise, if it was construed as the applicants would have it here, then in effect it would give a controlling shareholder a power to nominate a successor by will so long as the nominee was in the very wide class of privileged relations. During his lifetime a member, of course, could do that. He could transfer all his shares to somebody G else. In his lifetime he has obligations towards the company of which he is a director which are removed on death. In life, in practice, he would not transfer his interest to another person without regard to his own position and to that of the company.'

That, he said, reinforced the construction that he would get out of the words themselves.

He then turned to reg. 31. He said:

H

'Regulation 31 I would regard as simply supplementary to [reg. 30] and brings in, in the case of notices given by executors electing to be registered themselves, or transfers giving effect to an election to nominate another and so forth, the provisions in relation to the right to transfer and so forth, again by reference to what would have happened had the member been alive to make the transfer.

A   I can deal shortly with the judge's more general consideration which Mr Heslop QC, appearing for the applicants, criticised and Mr Bannister QC, appearing for the company, did not seek to defend. The construction of the articles must be the same in its application to a majority holding as it is to a minority holding, and a member may or may not be a director. A shareholder as such owes no duties to the company and can exercise his rights entirely as he pleases without regard to the position of the company (see, for example, *North-West Transportation Co Ltd v Beatty* (1887) 12 App Cas 589 at p. 593 in relation to voting rights). I do not think that the judge's more general consideration is one which carries or ought to carry any weight in the construction of the articles.

In approaching the question of construction I am guided by the following general considerations:

(1)   Shares, being personal property are prima facie transferable; if the right of transfer is to be taken away it must be done by language of sufficient clarity in the articles (see *Greenhalgh v Mallard* [1943] 2 All ER 234 at p. 237 per Lord Greene MR).

(2)   The articles, including the regulations of Table A incorporated in the articles, must be construed together and effect given, so far as possible, to every provision; it is only if the express articles are inconsistent with the incorporated regulations of Table A that the former will override the latter.

(3)   There is a distinction well recognised in company law between the transfer of shares and their transmission on death (*Moodie v W J Shepherd (Bookbinders) Ltd* [1949] 2 All ER 1044 at p. 1054 per Lord Reid).

If one asks what are the rights of the personal representatives of a deceased member in respect of his shares, one inevitably goes in the first place to the transmission on death provisions of Table A. There in reg. 30 one finds that the personal representatives are given the right to elect either to be registered themselves as holders of the deceased's shares or to have some person nominated by them registered as the transferee thereof, but the directors have 'the same right to decline registration as they would have had in the case of a transfer of the share by that member before his death'. The mechanics of that election are spelt out in reg. 31: the personal representatives must, if electing to be registered themselves, do so by a notice in writing, and, if electing to have another person registered, they must execute a transfer of the shares to that person, but:

> 'All the limitations, restrictions and provisions of [the] regulations relating to the right to transfer and the registration of transfers of shares shall be applicable to any such notice or transfer as aforesaid as if the death . . . of the member had not occurred and the notice or transfer was a transfer signed by that member.'

The words which I have cited from each of the two regulations emphasise that one is required to look at what the position would have been if the member himself had been transferring the shares to the personal representatives (if they elect to be registered themselves) or to the person nominated by them (if they elect to have that person registered).

The argument of Mr Bannister to the contrary which found favour with the judge, viz. that the cited words do no more than provide that the directors' power to refuse registration applies to personal representatives and trustees in bankruptcy, fails to give effect to the words 'the same right' in reg. 30 and the final 24 words of reg. 31 which deem the deceased or bankrupt member to have signed the transfer. Mr Bannister had to acknowledge that on his construction the directors had only a similar right to decline registration as they would have had on a transfer by the deceased member before his death. To discover what right the directors have to decline registration if the transfer was by the deceased member before his death and what restrictions under the regulations (including the articles) relating to the right to transfer and to the registration of transfers

if the deceased member signed the transfer, one goes to art. 5 and 6. By art. 5, Mr Stothers   A
had the right to transfer the holding to Mrs Stothers as being a privileged relation.
Accordingly the directors would not have had any right to decline registration, and the
opening words of art. 5 have no application.

The directors do have the right under art. 6(G) to call upon the personal representatives
to give a transfer notice in respect of the holding while registered in the name of the
deceased member. They also have the right under art. 6(H) to require the personal   B
representatives to furnish such information and evidence as the directors may think fit
regarding any matter which they may deem relevant to the purpose of ensuring that a
transfer of shares is duly authorised or that no circumstances have arisen whereby a
transfer notice is required to be given under the articles. Paragraphs (G) and (H) of art. 6
are described by the judge as 'the transmission provisions' of the articles and undoubtedly
para. (G) only applies whilst shares are still registered in the name of a deceased or
bankrupt member and para. (H) also applies (although not exclusively) to such a   C
situation. But they are only transmission provisions to the limited extent provided for in
those paragraphs and in my opinion they can operate satisfactorily alongside the express
transmission provisions of the regulations incorporated into the articles. Mr Bannister
submitted that art. 6(G) would be almost pointless if the articles were construed in the
way for which Mr Heslop contended. I cannot accept that. As is pointed out in *Buckley
on the Companies Acts* (14th edn, 1981) p. 941 the articles of a company sometimes   D
contain provisions which allow pressure to be put upon personal representatives to
transfer the shares of the deceased member. A provision like art. 6(G) is one such
provision.

Paragraph (I) allows an exception to the ordinary operation of a transfer notice
required by the directors in respect of specified shares 'to the extent that a transfer of any
such shares in favour of a person to whom they may be transferred pursuant to art. 5   E
shall have been lodged'. That wording prompts the enquiry to whom the shares might be
transferred pursuant to art. 5, and that presupposes that a member is transferring the
shares. But given the hypothesis applicable by reason of reg. 30 and 31 under which the
personal representatives can elect to have the shares registered in the name of another by
executing a transfer to that other person, viz. that the transfer is made by the deceased
member, in my judgment the personal representatives can come within the exception by
lodging timeously a transfer to a privileged relation of the deceased member. That is what   F
has occurred in the present case following the service on 14 November 1991 by the
directors of a notice under art. 6(G), when the applicants as executors lodged the transfer
in favour of Mrs Stothers on 6 December 1991. I would add that on Mr Bannister's
construction the exception to para. (I) would have no application at all to a case where
the directors have required under para. (G) that a transfer be given, because, he says,
only a member can transfer under art. 5 and he denies that it is necessary to consider to   G
whom the deceased member himself could have transferred shares pursuant to art. 5.
Accordingly, he would limit the operation of the exception to those cases where the
directors have required under para. (H) that a transfer notice be given by persons other
than the personal representatives. That result I find surprising.

It follows that I respectfully disagree with the judge in his construction of the articles.
He erred, in my judgment, in giving primacy to the wording of art. 5 and 6 without giving   H
proper effect to the wording of reg. 30 and 31. I am the happier to reach this conclusion
because it avoids what to my mind is the anomalous and irrational position that whereas
a shareholder is entirely free to transfer his shares to another member or to a privileged
relation or to trustees on trusts for privileged relations the moment before his death, yet
he is not able to procure that the shares go to such person or persons on his death unless
the directors choose to agree.

A   I would allow this appeal and make the order of rectification of the register of members of the company which was sought by the applicants in their notice of motion.

Balcombe LJ: I agree that this appeal should be allowed for the reasons given by Peter Gibson LJ and, although we are differing from the decision of the judge below, there is nothing I can usefully add.

Stuart-Smith LJ: I agree that this appeal should be allowed for the reasons given by

B   Peter Gibson LJ.

(Appeal allowed with costs in the Court of Appeal and below)

———————————

C

D

E

F

G

H

Re Leigh Estates (UK) Ltd.

Chancery Division (Companies Court).
Richard Sykes QC (sitting as a deputy High Court judge).
Judgment delivered 8 December 1993.

Winding up – Council sought winding up for unpaid rates of company in administrative receivership – Whether council sought 'class remedy' – Court to have regard to wishes of creditors – Insolvency Act 1986, s. 195.

This was a winding-up petition presented by a council based on a debt of £70,983.94 in respect of unpaid rates on an unoccupied property owned by the company which was in administrative receivership.

Joint administrative receivers of the company, a member of the Mountleigh group, were appointed by a syndicate of banks owed £386m by the company. The company had assets estimated at £56m including a property in London EC3. The Common Council of the City of London obtained a liability order from the City of London magistrates against the company in respect of unpaid rates and, after an unsuccessful attempt to levy distress, presented the petition. The council's view was that if a winding-up order were made then the receivers or possibly the banks would become liable for the rates on the premises. Any disbursement by them would be recoverable as an expense of the receivership or as part of the secured debt.

The petition was opposed by the company appearing by the administrative receivers, the syndicate of banks and other companies within the group (also in receivership) owed £152m. The debt owed to other unsecured creditors was less than £6m. The opposing creditors contended that a winding up would damage the process of realisation of the company's assets to the disadvantage of creditors generally.

Held, dismissing the petition:

1. The council's reason for seeking to wind up the company was not to swell the company's estate or otherwise improve the lot of the unsecured creditors but rather to gain for itself a preference over the secured and unsecured creditors alike. That was not in the interests of the class of unsecured creditors.

2. The banks' reasons for opposing the petition were precisely the same as would be advanced by entirely unsecured creditors opposing the petition, namely that a winding-up order was likely to cause the available assets to be reduced. Although the size of the assets might appear to be largely irrelevant to unsecured creditors because of the vast gap to be bridged before they got anything, that was not a reason for ignoring the opposing creditors' position. If, as in the present case, no complaint was made about the secured creditors' debt or security, there was no reason why the secured creditors should not be allowed to have as loud a voice as other unsecured creditors in respect of the unsecured portion of their debt: they had precisely the same interest in maximising the surplus (if any) available for unsecured creditors.

The following cases were referred to in the judgment:

Alabama, New Orleans, Texas & Pacific Junction Railway Co, Re [1891] 1 Ch 213.
Banister v Islington London Borough Council (1972) 71 LGR 239.
Crigglestone Coal Co Ltd, Re [1906] 2 Ch 327.
Holders Investment Trust Ltd, Re [1971] 1 WLR 583.
Ratford & Anor v Northavon District Council (1986) 2 BCC 99,242; [1987] QB 357.

Elizabeth Gloster QC and Richard Gillis (instructed by Clifford Chance) for the company and opposing creditors.

Lloyd Tamlyn (instructed by the Comptroller and City Solicitor) for the City of London.

A   JUDGMENT

Richard Sykes QC: I have before me a petition for the compulsory winding up of
Leigh Estates (UK) Ltd ('the company').

Background

The company is a member of the ill-fated Mountleigh group and the evidence before
B   me is that its liabilities amount to some £544m and its assets to some £56m. A large
proportion of the liabilities arise under guarantees of the debts of other members of the
group. Joint administrative receivers have been appointed in respect of the company by
a syndicate of banks who are creditors to the extent of some £386m. Amongst the
properties of which the company is either freeholder or lessee is 14 Lovat Lane, London
EC3R 8DT. It has remained unoccupied for a considerable period.

C   The petitioning creditor is the Common Council of the City of London ('the City
Council') and its petition is based on a debt of £70,983.94 in respect of rates levied on the
property at Lovat Lane. The rate was levied on the property as an unoccupied
hereditament; on 5 November 1992 the City Council obtained a liability order from the
City of London magistrates against the company in respect of the above-mentioned sum.

After an attempt to levy distress in respect of the unpaid rate which was completely
D   unsuccessful the City Council presented this petition on 19 March 1993.

Arrayed against the petition are the company itself, appearing by the administrative
receiver, Barclays Bank plc as security trustee for the bank syndicate of lenders with a
debt of some £386m, the banks which are members of the syndicate and various other
companies in the same group as the company with debts of some £152m. I should say at
once that the vast preponderance of the intercompany debt is owed to companies also in
receivership and under the control of the same receivers.

E   According to the evidence the remaining unsecured creditors of the company amount
to under £6m. No other creditor appears earlier to support or oppose the petition.

Barclays Bank plc is, as already mentioned, security trustee for the bank syndicate
lenders. It is not necessary for me to describe in detail the complicated cocktail of security
granted by the company to Barclays in respect of the banks' advances to the group. There
are two relevant points:

F   (1)   the only charges over the Lovat Lane property were floating charges, all of which
          have of course now crystallised;

(2)   on the unchallenged evidence there is a vast shortfall as respects security. The
          assets charged as security for the banks are thought by the receivers to have a value
          of some £56m, leaving the banks as unsecured creditors of some £330m.

G   **The position of the petitioner**

I can state this clearly by quoting para. 18 of the affidavit of Mr Malcolm Robertson,
a senior legal assistant in the office of the Comptroller and City Solicitor. He says:

'I humbly submit that this court should make the winding-up order for the
following reasons. At present, liability in respect of unpaid rates for the premises
falls upon the company itself. If the assets of the company are as set out in the
H   affidavit of Mr James, then the liability of the company is of no value to the
Council.

Therefore, so long as the receivership continues, the rates due in respect of the
premises will remain unpaid, increasing the burden resting with other ratepayers.
If a winding-up order is made in respect of the company, then the receivers or
possibly the banks will become liable for the rates charged on the premises. Thus

petitioning for the winding up of the company is the only way to help to ensure   A
that the council is paid rates accruing in respect of the premises.'

I should point out at this stage that, if it is correct that the receivers or the banks
become liable for rates charged on 'the premises' (the Lovat Lane property) following
the making of a winding-up order:

(1)   the amount disbursed will be recoverable by the payer either as receivers' costs or
as part of the secured debt and hence in priority to unsecured creditors;   B

(2)   recovery of the rates by the City Council will be at the expense of the secured
creditors and will cause any remote prospect of the unsecured creditors receiving
anything to disappear even further over the horizon; and

(3)   the City Council will, as the result of a winding-up order being made, achieve a
preferential status such as formerly attached to rates but which was removed by
the *Insolvency Act* 1986.   C

The position of the company and opposing creditors

Mr Stephen James, one of the administrative receivers, has given detailed evidence of
the financial disadvantages to the receivership and hence to the secured creditors and to
the remote prospect for unsecured creditors if a winding-up order is made. That evidence
is not admitted, but not challenged.   D

The company and the opposing creditors base their opposition on the damage to the
process of realisation of the company's assets likely to be inflicted by a winding up, and
accordingly the disadvantage to creditors generally. They argue than if the Common
Council is correct in its claim that a winding-up order will enable it to claim rates against
the receivers or the debenture-holders, that is a bad reason for making a winding-up
order since it gives the Common Council a preference to which it is not entitled by statute   E
and makes the position of other unsecured creditors even more hopeless.

Conclusion

The following matters are clear:

(1)   Although a petitioning creditor may, as between himself and the company, be   F
entitled to a winding-up order *ex debito justitiae*, his remedy is a 'class right', so
that, where creditors oppose the making of an order, the court must come to a
conclusion in its discretion after considering the arguments of the creditors in
support of and opposing the petition: see *Re Crigglestone Coal Company Ltd* [1906]
2 Ch 327, in particular the statements of principle of Buckley J at first instance,
and s. 195 of the *Insolvency Act* 1986.

(2)   The court is not entitled to refuse to make a winding-up order on the ground only   G
that the company's assets have been mortgaged to an amount equal to or in excess
of those assets: s. 125(1) of the *Insolvency Act* 1986.

(3)   The insolvency regime recognises the ability of creditors who are secured but whose
security is deficient to participate in the liquidation, in respect of the shortfall, as
unsecured creditors: *Insolvency Rules* 1986, r. 4.75(1)(g), 4.67(4), 4.88, 4.95–4.99.
   H

It is plain from the well-known authorities on the subject that, where there are some
creditors supporting and others opposing a winding-up petition it is for the court to
decide as a matter of judicial discretion, what weight to attribute to the voices on each
side of the contest. Surprisingly there appears to be no case in which there has been any
real discussion about the weight to be attributed to the unsecured portion of debts which,
as events have turned out, are not fully secured.

A   Looking at the matter as one of principle, I consider that if the court is satisfied that secured creditors have a shortfall as regards their security it should treat those creditors as falling within the class of unsecured creditors to the extent of the shortfall. It then becomes necessary to see why a winding-up order is sought and in particular whether it is sought in order to impugn the secured creditors' debt or security. If so, and if there appears to be some substance in the petitioner's claim, the court should put much less weight on the opposition of those whose debt or security is under attack.

B   If, as in the present case, no complaint is made about the secured creditors' debt or security I see no reason why the secured creditors should not be allowed to have, in respect of the unsecured portion of their debt, as loud a voice as other unsecured creditors; they have precisely the same interest in maximising the surplus (if any) available for unsecured creditors. The general rule must be subject to other exceptions, however: if the opposition is mounted in order to advance the secured creditors' position as such in a manner considered to be contrary to the interests of the unsecured creditors, the secured creditors should be ignored.

C   In the present case the likelihood of unsecured creditors having anything at all is remote in the extreme. Since parliament has ordained by s. 125(1) of the *Insolvency Act 1986* that this is not of itself a reason for refusing a winding-up order, I must, I think, proceed on the same basis as if there was to be a surplus for unsecured creditors. Certainly s. 125(1) does not require me to ignore the voices of those who oppose the petition.

D   The one voice to which weight is not normally attached in the case of a winding-up petition by a creditor is that of the company itself. I propose to attach no extra weight to that of the company, represented by the administrative receivers, in the present case.

    There are a number of cases in which the court has refused to give weight to the debts owed to other companies in the same group as the company itself. In the present case the likelihood is that the persons with an economic interest in the debts owed to other group companies are the banks which are of course direct creditors of the company for £386m. In the circumstances I do not regard their voice as being any louder if I add to that amount another £152m, in which they are interested through other companies.

E   If I assume that the Common Council are correct in their claim that, following a winding-up order, they are entitled to recover rates from the receivers or the debenture-holders I find that their reason for seeking to wind up the company is not to swell the estate of the company or otherwise to improve the lot of the unsecured creditors but rather to gain for themselves a preference over the secured and unsecured creditors alike. It might reasonably be said that this attitude is not acting in the interests of the class of unsecured creditors. It is clear that in other 'class' situations the voice of one who votes against the interests of the class is disregarded: see e.g. *Re Alabama, New Orleans, Texas & Pacific Junction Railway Co* [1891] 1 Ch 213, *Re Holders Investment Trust* [1971] 1 WLR 583. Similarly, it seems to me, I should disregard the voice of the Common Council.

F

G   On the other side, the banks' reasons for opposing the petition, as expressed in the evidence, are precisely the same as the reasons one would expect to be advanced by entirely unsecured creditors opposing the petition, namely that a winding-up order is likely to cause the available assets to be reduced. Although the size of the assets may appear to be largely irrelevant to unsecured creditors because of the vast gap to be bridged before they get anything, this does not appear to me to be a reason for ignoring the position adopted by the opposing creditors.

H   Accordingly even if the Common Council are correct in their view that following a winding-up order they will be entitled to recover rates in respect of the Lovat Lane property I intend to dismiss their petition.

    If, on the other hand, the Common Council are not correct, their expressed reason for desiring a winding-up order falls to the ground. They thus advance no reason for such an order whilst the opposing creditors have reasons which I feel bound to take into account. Accordingly in this event also I intend to dismiss the petition.

The rates question

In the case of non-domestic unoccupied property, such as the Lovat Lane property, s. 45 of the *Local Government Finance Act* 1988 provides for rates to be levied on the owner of the property. Section 65(1) of the same Act defines the owner as the 'person entitled to possession' of the relevant hereditament.

In a nutshell, the argument advanced by Mr Tamlyn, for the Common Council, is that a winding-up order would cause the administrative receivers to cease to be agents of the company and that they in a personal capacity, or perhaps the debenture holders, would accordingly become the persons entitled to possession of the Lovat Lane property and hence liable for rates thereon.

Miss Gloster QC, for the company and opposing creditors, argues that the agency of the administrative receiver is deemed to terminate on liquidation only for certain limited purposes and that in any event the company's possession of property would not cease on liquidation in the absence of positive steps by the administrative receivers to dispossess the company.

In the circumstances I have decided to express no opinion on this question, interesting as it is. This is because:

(1)   It makes no difference to my decision.

(2)   I see within the basic question a number of sub-questions where, at this level, I may be constrained by authority to a result which a higher court might refuse to accept.

(3)   In particular, there may be a conflict between the decision of the Divisional Court in *Banister v Islington London Borough Council* (1972) 71 LGR 239 and that of the Court of Appeal in *Ratford v Northavon District Council* (1986) 2 BCC 99,242.

(4)   Finally, it seems to me that the appropriate forum for a decision on this question is a court before whom it comes as the main question in issue.

For the reasons given earlier, I dismiss the petition.

(Order accordingly)

A
R v Institute of Chartered Accountants in England and Wales & Ors, ex parte Brindle & Ors.

Court of Appeal (Civil Division).
Nolan and Hirst L JJ and Sir Roger Parker.
Judgment delivered 21 December 1993.

B
Company auditors – Recognised supervisory bodies – Supervisory body placed auditors under enquiry – Whether enquiry should be adjourned pending outcome of litigation – Companies Act 1989, Pt. II.

This was an appeal by a firm of chartered accountants, Price Waterhouse, from a decision of the Divisional Court ([1993] BCC 736) refusing judicial review of a decision of the accountants' regulatory body, the Institute of Chartered Accountants in England and Wales,
C
to proceed with disciplinary proceedings against the firm in relation to the firm's actions as auditors of BCCI Holdings (Luxembourg) SA and its subsidiaries.

The applicants' case was that to proceed with the enquiry, and not to adjourn it, before the determination of various pieces of litigation which were extant or pending, was productive of unfairness. The respondents denied unfairness and argued that to accede to the applicants' arguments would effectively abdicate the Institute's function as the principal regulator of auditors and would fail to deal with public concern at the audit of BCCI. The
D
handbook of the Institute's investigation committee stated that disciplinary proceedings must be deferred if they were likely to interfere with the course of justice (para. 14.02), but also that even where there was a case for adjournment the investigation committee would press ahead with disciplinary proceedings where to fail to do so would be inconsistent or would appear to be inconsistent with its duties as a regulator or as a professional body, for example where the Institute was the prime regulator of the conduct in question (para. 14.07).

E
After the applicants had been placed under enquiry, the Institute adopted a new disciplinary scheme and the applicants sought to have the enquiry carried on under the new scheme, but were refused. The applicants challenged the decision not to agree to a transfer.

The Divisional Court held that there was no real risk of injustice which would entitle the court to intervene so as to prevent the Institute's performance in the public interest of an important investigative procedure which was part of a supervisory function underpinned by
F
statute, especially as the procedure was to be performed in regard to a uniquely spectacular and serious banking failure. The court also refused judicial review of the decision not to agree to transfer the enquiry to the new disciplinary scheme. The firm appealed. It was common ground that the decision not to adjourn was not to be judged by reference to the Wednesbury principle of irrationality, but by whether or not it was productive of a real risk of prejudice or injustice: R v Panel on Takeovers and Mergers, ex parte Fayed [1992] BCC 524 per Neill LJ at p. 531D.

G
Held, allowing the appeal, quashing the decision of the committee of inquiry to proceed immediately and prohibiting it from continuing the disciplinary proceedings until the trial of the liquidators' action against the appellants at first instance had been concluded (with liberty to the respondents to apply to vary or set aside the order for prohibition), and quashing the refusal to agree that the proceedings should be continued under the revised scheme:

H
1. In the light of all the considerations, the court was satisfied that the serious prejudice to Price Waterhouse, leading to a very great risk of injustice, outweighed the countervailing considerations.

2. (Per Hirst LJ and Sir Roger Parker) The decision not to transfer the enquiry to the new scheme was open to review and should be quashed. As the disciplinary proceedings were to be adjourned, the question of transfer did not arise. If and when the proceedings continued,

**Price Waterhouse would be able to make a further application to transfer in the light of the   A
circumstances then prevailing.**

The following cases were referred to in the judgments:

Air Canada & Ors v Secretary of State for Trade & Anor [1983] 2 AC 394.
Associated Provincial Picture Houses Ltd v Wednesbury Corporation [1948] 1 KB 223.
Conteh v Onslow-Fane (The Times, 26 June 1975, CA).
Conway v Rimmer & Anor [1968] AC 910.   B
Duncan & Anor v Cammell, Laird & Co Ltd [1942] AC 624.
Parry-Jones v Law Society & Ors [1969] 1 Ch 1.
Price Waterhouse v BCCI Holdings (Luxembourg) SA [1992] BCLC 583.
R v Panel on Takeovers and Mergers, ex parte Fayed [1992] BCC 524.
Tournier v National Provincial and Union Bank of England [1924] 1 KB 461.
W v Egdell [1990] Ch 359.   C

David Oliver QC and Nigel Giffin (instructed by Herbert Smith) for the appellants.

Robert Carnwath QC and John Howell QC (instructed by Bates Wells & Braithwaite) for the respondents.

JUDGMENT

Nolan LJ: The appellants are the partners in Price Waterhouse, the well known firm   D
of chartered accountants. They appeal against a decision of the Divisional Court (Mann LJ and Sedley J) refusing their application for judicial review in respect of decisions affecting the conduct of a disciplinary inquiry to which they are subject. The inquiry has been set up under the provisions of a joint disciplinary scheme operated by the first, second and third respondents. Its conduct has been entrusted to a committee of inquiry composed of Sir John Bailey, Mr Rawlinson and Mr Milne who are respectively the thirteenth, fourteenth and fifteenth respondents.   E

In June 1987 the appellants co-ordinated the world wide audits and reviewed the consolidation of the accounts of Bank of Credit and Commerce International Holdings (Luxembourg) SA and its subsidiaries, a group of companies to which I shall refer as 'BCCI'. The collapse of the BCCI group on 5 July 1991 led indirectly to the setting up of the disciplinary proceedings to which I have referred. It has also led to the commencement of civil proceedings against the appellants by the liquidators of BCCI and by or on behalf   F
of a number of BCCI's creditors. The appellants requested the committee of inquiry to suspend the operation of the disciplinary proceedings until at any rate the first stage of the civil litigation in this country had been completed, but the request was refused in a letter written by Sir John Bailey on behalf of the committee on 16 December 1992 and the refusal was confirmed at a meeting between the parties on 25 February 1993. This refusal by the committee is the first of the decisions with which we are concerned on the   G
appeal.

The appellants also requested that, if the disciplinary proceedings were to go ahead, they should be conducted under the provision of a new form of the joint disciplinary scheme which came into existence in January 1993. The request was refused by Mr Michael Chance, the sixteenth respondent, who had been appointed executive counsel to the revised scheme. This refusal constitutes the second decision with which the present appeal is concerned.   H

The judgment of Mann LJ ([1993] BCC 736) sets out, if I may say so, an admirable summary of the factual and statutory background to the case, the provisions of the joint disciplinary scheme in its original form and as applied to the appellants, and the main features of the revised scheme. The summary appears between pp. 727 and 743 of the judgment, and there would be no point in my repeating it in full. I must, however, refer

A to the main events which have led to the present state of affairs, and the particular factors upon which the appellants rely.

The first signs of trouble at BCCI seem to have appeared, at any rate so far as the appellants are concerned, in early 1990. The first affidavit of Mr Stacy who is one of the appellants, tells us that in 1990 a number of Price Waterhouse partners became members of a committee of investigation initially set up by the Abu Dhabi government (the majority shareholder of the BCCI parent company) to investigate certain aspects of
B BCCI's business. In the course of that investigation, personnel from Price Waterhouse interviewed the chief executive of BCCI and his senior staff, who confessed to substantial fraud. Subsequently Price Waterhouse were appointed by the Bank of England under s. 41 of the *Banking Act* 1987 as 'competent persons' to report to the bank upon the situation. The report in draft form (never apparently finalised) was delivered by Price Waterhouse to the bank shortly before 5 July 1991. It was followed by the withdrawal of
C the banking licences of the BCCI group on that date.

On 9 July 1991 the Chancellor of the Exchequer and the Governor of the Bank of England appointed Lord Justice Bingham:

> 'to enquire into the supervision of BCCI under the Banking Act; to consider whether the action taken by all the United Kingdom authorities was appropriate and timely; and to make recommendations.'

D The report was presented in July 1992 and in his covering letter Lord Justice Bingham made it clear that he had not attempted to evaluate the professional quality of the auditing of BCCI's accounts, or form a judgment whether irregularities should have been discovered by the auditors earlier, a point to which I shall return. He did, however, pay tribute to the very high level of the co-operation which he had received from, amongst others, the appellants. The appellants had submitted a 300-page memorandum, and the
E six members of the firm most closely connected with the affair had given oral evidence.

The appellants are on the statutory register of firms eligible for appointment as auditors under s. 35 of the *Companies Act* 1989. One of the qualifications for such registration is membership of a recognised supervisory body: see s. 25(1). The first three respondents are, of course, all recognised supervisory bodies, and the appellants are members of the first respondent, the Institute of Chartered Accountants in England and Wales. Part II of the *Companies Act* 1989 contains extensive provisions setting out the
F statutory duties of recognised supervisory bodies. The joint disciplinary scheme was set up in pursuance of these statutory provisions and of the institute's own objects as set out in its supplemental charter of 21 December 1948. Clause 1(a)(iv) of the charter declares that the principal objects of the institute include the maintenance of 'high standards of practice and professional conduct by all its members'; and subcl. (viiiA) contains specific provision for the institute to maintain, either alone or in conjunction with one or more
G other professional accountancy bodies (together called 'the participants'), a scheme for investigating and making findings as to the professional or business conduct, efficiency and competence of any member of any of the participants.

This was the genesis of the joint disciplinary scheme which was established by the first three respondents, approved by the Privy Council, and brought into effect on 31 December 1986. The scheme is administered by an executive committee which is appointed for this purpose by the councils of the three institutes (para. 5(a)). Paragraph
H 6(a) provides:

> "Whenever the executive committee receives a report from an investigation committee of any of the participants which concerns, or which in the opinion of the investigation committee may concern, the professional or business conduct, efficiency or competence of one or more members and/or member firms (whether or not referred to specifically in the report) and the investigation committee making

the report certifies that in its opinion the matter is one which gives rise to or   A
includes questions of public concern, the executive committee shall as soon as
practicable appoint a committee of inquiry to enquire into the matter and into
such facts and circumstances arising in the course of the enquiry into the matter as
the committee of inquiry considers appropriate.''

Paragraph 6(f) provides that a committee of inquiry:

'shall have power to reach a finding on the professional or business conduct,   B
efficiency or competence of every member under enquiry and of every member firm
under enquiry . . .'

On 19 March 1992 the investigation committee of the English and Welsh institute,
acting under para. 6(a), issued a certificate and reference in these terms:

'*Certificate and reference by the investigation committee*

1. The investigation committee has considered facts and matters laid before it   C
    on 19 March 1992 by the secretary relating to the actions of Price
    Waterhouse as auditors of BCCI Holdings (Luxembourg) SA and its
    subsidiary companies. They are contained in the following documents:

    (a) Price Waterhouse evidence to the Treasury and Civil Service
         Committee of the House of Commons, contained in a memorandum
         of 5 February 1992.   D

    (b) A confidential Price Waterhouse draft report, dated 22 June 1991,
         addressed to the Bank of England under s. 41 of the *Banking Act* 1987.

    (c) Press and television comment, in particular:

         i. a transcript of Channel 4 broadcast "Bandung File Special" on
             13 August 1991;   E

         ii. an extract from the Independent of 10 July 1991;

         iii. an extract from the Financial Times of 11 July 1991.

    (d) Price Waterhouse letters and reports:

         i. addressed to the directors of BCCI Holdings (Luxembourg) SA,
             dated 18 April 1990;   F

         ii. addressed to the audit committee of BCCI Holdings
              (Luxembourg) SA, dated 3 October 1990;

         disclosed to the institute in confidence by the Bank of England.

2. The investigation committee having considered these facts and matters
    hereby certifies that in its opinion they give rise to or include matters of
    public concern and that in all the circumstances they out to be referred to   G
    the executive committee to be dealt with in accordance with the joint
    disciplinary scheme.

3. The investigation committee therefore refers the above facts and matters to
    the executive committee to be dealt with in accordance with the joint
    disciplinary scheme.'

Before us, the appellants did not question the lawfulness of this decision. They accept   H
that the necessary procedural steps have been correctly followed by the English and
Welsh institute and by the executive committee. Their appeal to us is not therefore
directed against the appointment of the committee of inquiry, still less against its
membership. Sir John Bailey is a former Treasury Solicitor. Mr Rawlinson and Mr Milne
are distinguished members of the accountancy profession. The principal concern of the
appellants, as I have said, is that the committee should hold its hand until the trial at first

A   instance of the main proceedings brought in this country against the appellants has been concluded.

I pause at this stage to note that, despite specific requests by Herbert Smith on the appellants' behalf for particulars of the case against the appellants, the reference passed on by the executive committee to the committee of inquiry is couched in wide and general terms. Although, as we shall see, the principal areas of concern into which the committee
B   believes it should enquire are set out in their letter of 16 December 1992, the request for particulars of the case against the appellants remains unanswered to this day. What has been made clear, however, from an early stage is that the decision of the secretary to make a report to the investigation committee was not the result of an external complaint. The matter is dealt with in para. 2 of the institute's letter of 18 February 1992 to Herbert Smith which reads as follows:

C   'No external complaint has been made against your client in relation to this matter. Under bye-law 79(c) the term "complaint" refers to facts or matters coming to the attention of the secretary indicating that a member or student may have become liable to disciplinary action. The facts or matters in question are those contained in Price Waterhouse's report entitled "Report on Sandstorm SA under s. 41 of the *Banking Act* 1987" (draft: 22 June 1991) together with various press reports culled from the national and accountancy press.'

D   To return, however, to the narrative of events following the reference to the committee of inquiry, on 27 June 1992 Sir John Bailey wrote to Price Waterhouse enclosing the certificate and reference and saying amongst other things:

       'I should make it clear that my committee has not put your firm under enquiry and that we are at present only collecting information about the matter. Should your
E   firm subsequently be put under enquiry you will receive written notice to that effect in accordance with reg. 9(a).'

There then followed a further period of correspondence and meetings during which the parties (including BDO Binder Hamlyn, the investigating accountants appointed by the committee of inquiry) explored the question of how the committee might proceed, and during which the committee made approaches for information to other parties including
F   the Serious Fraud Office and the Bank of England.

BDO Binder Hamlyn made a number of enquiries of the appellants during the autumn of 1992. On 10 November 1992 they sent a list of no less than 23 topics upon which they wanted information. In their reply of 20 November the appellants expressed concern about the nature and quantity of the information sought, having regard to the fact that the appellants had been told that they were not under enquiry. In that letter the appellants also reiterated the concern which had been expressed by them and by Herbert Smith on
G   their behalf about the breaches of confidence which would be involved if the appellants answered all the questions put to them, and about the prejudicial effect which the information supplied might have upon the appellants' defence to the civil proceedings brought against them. In the meantime, Lord Justice Bingham's report had been published in part on 22 October 1992. In his prefatory letter Lord Justice Bingham, as I have mentioned, acknowledged with gratitude the help which he had received from the
H   appellants, amongst others. He said:

       'In deciding what was said and done during the 19 year history of BCCI, I have relied heavily on contemporary notes and minutes of meetings and conversations, particularly those made by the Bank of England and Price Waterhouse, believing these to be, on the whole, the most reliable guide to what was said and done at the time.'

He made it clear however that he had:

'. . . not attempted to evaluate the professional quality of the audits of BCCI's accounts conducted over the years, in London or the Caymans or elsewhere, or to form a judgment whether irregularities in its business should have been discovered by the auditors earlier.'

We now come to Sir John Bailey's letter of 16 December 1992. He referred to the issues which Lord Justice Bingham had not attempted to determine and said:

'They are, of course, issues which are apt for consideration by a disciplinary inquiry and which are covered by my committee's terms of reference.'

The letter continues:

'Accordingly after carefully considering your letter and discussing it with the committee's legal advisers, the committee have decided that it ought now to put the UK firm of Price Waterhouse formally under inquiry, and this letter is to give you notice to that effect in accordance with reg. 9(a).

The principal areas of concern into which the committee believes it should enquire are:

(i) Whether the extent of the pervasive fraud within BCCI should have been detected earlier by your firm's audit work;

(ii) Whether, in the light of the evidence of fraud which had already come to light by 30 April 1990 and the declared doubts which your firm had at that date concerning the authenticity and value of material assets stated in the balance sheet of BCCI at 31 December 1989, the form of your firm's audit report was adequate, notwithstanding the undertakings of support received from the principal shareholder;

(iii) Whether assisting the management of BCCI with restructuring its operations, as well as advising the majority shareholder, adversely affected or was compatible with your firm's role as auditors.'

He added that the committee was anxious for its investigating accountants to pursue their work with vigour immediately after the Christmas break.

In a long letter dated 21 December 1992 and at the meeting held with the members of the committee of inquiry on 25 February 1993, the appellants and their advisers tried to persuade the committee to change its mind, but to no avail. The appellants and their advisers also urged at that meeting that if the committee was determined to go ahead with the enquiry it should support a request by the appellants to the executive counsel appointed for the purposes of the revised joint disciplinary scheme to accept the appellants' request that the enquiry would be conducted under that scheme, but the committee decided on the contrary, to advise the executive counsel in the opposite sense. The appellants applied for judicial review of these decisions on 15 March 1993, and were granted leave to move by Tuckey J on 21 May 1993. They were subsequently granted leave to amend their application, so as to include within their targets the decision of the executive counsel taken on 17 June 1993, to refuse to agree to the transfer of the inquiry to the revised scheme.

There are three further matters of fact which I must set out before coming to the issues in the appeal. The first consists of the other proceedings in which the appellants are involved. In order of time of commencement, these begin with an action in the Queen's Bench Division by Mr and Mrs Khasruzzman who claim to be depositors of BCCI and who claim damages for deceit in the sum of US$600,000. The deceit is said to arise from the auditors' certificate given to the parent company's accounts for the year ending 31 December 1989.

A   The second is an action brought in the Chancery Division by the liquidators of the
BCCI companies which operated in this country. The defendants are the appellants and
also Ernst and Whinney who were BCCI's principal auditors until 1987. These
proceedings are based on alleged negligence and/or breach of duty and/or breach of
contract and/or breach of statutory duty in connection with work done in respect of the
audits of the BCCI companies for 1985 and other matters. The amount claimed in respect
of 1985 alone is in excess of $8 billion. The 1985 action has been consolidated with similar
B   actions in respect of the years 1986 and 1987. The statement of claim, as it stands at
present, runs to some 720 pages. It is estimated that the process of discovery will involve
many tens, if not hundreds, of thousands of the appellants' documents. One of the
liquidators has sworn an affidavit estimating that the number of BCCI documents in the
UK alone is upwards of 100m, situated in 40 locations.

        Thirdly, there are two sets of proceedings between the appellants and Ernst and
C   Whinney in which each effectively claims contribution from the other.

        Fourthly, there is a consolidated set of proceedings known as the Hamid action in
California. It is based upon the provisions of the US Racketeer-Influenced and Corrupt
Organisations Act, and claims on behalf of a world wide class of BCCI depositors
damages and interest including treble damages pursuant to the Act. The statement of
claim runs to some 500 pages with more than 1,500 pages of exhibited documents. At
D   present the action stands dismissed at first instance, but the dismissal decision is subject
to an appeal which is expected to take place in the summer of 1994. If the action goes
ahead, the plaintiffs will be entitled to a jury. There is also an action in Texas on the same
lines. The future of this action is expected to depend upon the result of the appeal in the
California proceedings.

        Actions against some of the appellants' partners have also been commenced by the
E   liquidators in the Cayman Islands and in Luxembourg. According to the second affidavit
of Mr Natali of Herbert Smith, the Cayman Islands action is likely to be most complex
and onerous for the appellants, and to compare in scale with the liquidators' action in
England.

        In addition to these proceedings and to others which may be added to the list, the
appellants are heavily engaged in the quite different role of assisting the Serious Fraud
Office and also the US regulatory authorities in their investigations. Over 100 notices
F   under s. 2 of the *Criminal Justice Act* 1987 have been served upon Price Waterhouse
partners and managers since July 1991, and it is anticipated that Price Waterhouse
personnel will be required to give evidence for the prosecution in criminal proceedings
brought against officers or employees or customers of BCCI. In para. 65 of his first
affidavit, Mr Stacy states that the difficulty which arises from the appellants' need to
comply with the demands made upon them in so many different contexts is that there is
G   only a limited number of partners and senior managers at Price Waterhouse who were
involved in dealing with the affairs of BCCI prior to its collapse. Mr Oliver QC,
representing the appellants, told us that effectively the number was confined to the six
individuals who gave evidence to Lord Justice Bingham.

        The second of the remaining matters of fact with which I must deal is the nature of the
proceedings under the original scheme and under the revised scheme respectively. The
original scheme is strictly inquisitorial in nature. Under para. 6(f) of the scheme, to which
H   I have already referred, the committee of inquiry has power to reach a finding on the
professional or business conduct, efficiency or competence of the member or member
firm under inquiry. Paragraph 6(g) provides that, before reaching an adverse finding, the
committee shall give the member or member firm concerned a reasonable opportunity of
making representations, and where representations are to be made orally, shall permit
the member or member firm to be represented. Under para. 6(j) if the finding reached

under para. 6(f) is adverse to the member firm, the committee may censure, reprimand, admonish or fine the firm or withdraw its registration as an auditor or its investment business certificate. Paragraph 8 gives a right of appeal to the executive committee.

Despite the draconian nature of its powers, the regulations governing the conduct of proceedings before the committee under the original scheme do not provide for the member or member firm concerned to be furnished with particulars of the complaint or complaints under inquiry, nor, as I have mentioned, have such particulars in fact been furnished to the appellants. Further, the rights of the member or member firm and their representative at the hearing are strictly limited and do not include a right of cross-examination. The regulations annexed to the scheme, so far as material, read as follows:

'13. If the committee of inquiry proposes to hear evidence of any witness it shall notify each member or member firm under inquiry of the witness, and when and where the evidence is to be heard. The committee of inquiry shall allow any member under inquiry and any partner in any member firm under inquiry who is designated under reg. 3 and/or a representative of any such member or member firm to be present while any witness is giving evidence.

14. At a hearing the committee of inquiry shall put such questions to the witness as the committee of inquiry considers appropriate in order to elucidate facts or clarify evidence.

15. At a hearing of evidence by a witness who is a member under inquiry or is a partner in a member firm under inquiry ... he may be accompanied by a representative. Any other witness may be accompanied by a solicitor or counsel. Subject to reg. 16, such representative, solicitor or counsel, is permitted to be present for the purpose only of advising the witness he is accompanying.

16. No person who attends a hearing under reg. ... 13 or accompanies a witness under reg. 15 shall be entitled to address the committee of inquiry or to ask questions of any witness save only that, after the committee of inquiry has questioned the member or designated partner in a member firm giving evidence, a representative or member firm may ask supplementary questions of the member designated partner.'

Mr Carnwath QC representing the respondents referred us to reg. 8 which provides for the conduct and proceedings of the inquiry to be determined by the chairman in consultation with the other members of the committee, and told us on instructions that Sir John Bailey had indicated his willingness to permit cross-examination even though the regulations gave no entitlement to it, and even though, as we were told, cross-examination has never been permitted by any previous committee of inquiry. It seems to me, however, with respect, that Sir John's proposal does not meet the point. The powers of the chairman under reg. 8 are expressed to be 'subject to the scheme and to these regulations'. While the appellants might welcome the rules thus being relaxed in their favour, the same could not be expected of a witness hostile to their cause. As Mr Oliver points out, many witnesses, even if not hostile, might be expected to protest forcefully and with justification if the committee sought to confer upon the appellants, at the expense of the witnesses, a right which was clearly excluded by reg. 15 and 16.

The corresponding provisions of the revised scheme are fundamentally different and may reasonably be supposed to have been inspired by dissatisfaction with the original scheme. The revised scheme is essentially of an adversarial character. It provides, as I have said, for the appointment of an executive counsel who must be legally qualified. It is to him that the executive committee now refers a recommendation of the investigation committee that a particular case should be dealt with under the scheme and it is he who decides, after inquiry, whether there are grounds upon which a joint disciplinary tribunal (rather than a committee of inquiry) could make an adverse finding concerning the

A professional or business conduct, efficiency, or competence of a member or member firm: see para. 6(f). If he reaches that decision, then under the same subparagraph he must request the executive committee to appoint such a tribunal and at the same time must deliver to the executive committee a formal complaint specifying the manner in which he alleges that the conduct or quality of the work of the member or member firm concerned fell below what was to be expected, and must set out particulars sufficient to enable it to be properly understood by the tribunal. Paragraph 6(h) provides that even before this

B stage is reached, the executive counsel must notify the member or member firm concerned of his proposed action, and must give the member or member firm an opportunity of making written representations to him. If, none the less, the executive counsel decides to proceed under para. 6(f), then by reg. 13 the formal complaint referred to in that subparagraph must be accompanied by a summary of the facts or matters which the executive counsel considers could result in an adverse finding, and a copy of the

C complaint must be sent to the member or member firm concerned. Regulations 18 and 19 provide for the exchange of lists of witnesses and summaries of evidence between the executive counsel and the member or member firm in advance of the hearing. At the hearing itself, under para. 6(d) of the scheme and reg. 23, the executive counsel acts as complainant and leads evidence against the member or member firm, and the latter have the full right of cross-examination and of leading their own evidence. The provisions for the imposition of penalties, and for an appeal to the executive committee, are on the

D same lines as those of the original scheme. Paragraph 3 of the scheme authorises the executive counsel to agree to the transfer to him of an existing inquiry by a committee of inquiry.

The last matter of fact which I should mention is the investigation of the appellants by the joint monitoring unit ('JMU'). The JMU is an agent of the English and Welsh and Scottish institutes, and its function is to investigate the competence of audit firms who

E are or wish to be registered under the 1989 Act. It operates under powers delegated to it by the audit registration committee of the English and Welsh institute.

On 10 August 1992 the practice regulation department of the English and Welsh institute wrote to the appellants referring to the collapse of BCCI and saying that the committee had a duty to satisfy itself in the public interest that the appellants' procedures applicable to the audits of regulated clients such as banks and investment businesses were

F adequate to ensure that such audits were carried out properly and with integrity and with a proper degree of independence. The letter went on to request information under six specified heads relating to the audits of regulated clients of the appellants, and added that the committee had instructed the JMU to review the information provided and to carry out a monitoring visit to the firm. In para. 21 of his affidavit, Mr Stacy states that after an examination lasting several weeks, the JMU's findings were positive. According to the information received by Mr Stacy, the JMU representatives commented that the firm's

G quality assurance procedures were of the highest order and made only a few very minor criticisms. After the conclusion of argument before us, the parties discovered that a news release had been issued by the audit registration committee on 2 August 1993 setting out the result of the JMU enquiry, and this was supplied to us. It said:

'The ARC announced today that an enquiry into aspects of the current audit procedures and controls within Price Waterhouse has been completed. The

H enquiries, which involved the JMU, were in response to the issue raised by the firm's audit of the Bank of Credit and Commerce International. No regulatory action has been proposed as a result of any of these enquiries.'

Thus it appears to be established to the satisfaction of the audit registration committee that there is no cause for public concern about Price Waterhouse retaining its registration under the Act.

I now turn to the decision of the committee refusing to adjourn its inquiry until the first stage of the pending litigation has been concluded. It has been common ground before us that the decision is not to be judged by reference to the Wednesbury principle of irrationality but by whether or not it is productive of a real risk of prejudice or injustice. Thus in *R v Panel on Takeovers and Mergers, ex parte Fayed* [1992] BCC 524, Neill LJ said at p. 531D:

> 'It is clear that the court has power to intervene to prevent injustice where the continuation of one set of proceedings may prejudice the fairness of the trial of other proceedings. The existence of this power has been recognised in a number of cases including *Jefferson Ltd v Bhetcha* [1979] 1 WLR 898; *R v British Broadcasting Corporation, ex parte Lavelle* [1983] ICR 99; and more recently in the unreported decision in *R v Solicitors Disciplinary Tribunal, ex parte Gallagher* (30 September 1991). But it is a power which has to be exercised with great care and only where there is a real risk of serious prejudice which may lead to injustice.'

These principles are broadly reflected in the handbook issued by the investigation committee. Paragraph 14.01 of the handbook states that in general disciplinary proceedings should not be postponed simply because of court proceedings, but para. 14.02 provides that:

> 'disciplinary proceedings must be deferred if they are likely to interfere with the course of justice.'

The note to para. 14.02 refers to civil cases tried by a jury as an area where any advance publicity directed to an issue that the jury will have to decide creates a clear possibility of prejudice, and the appellants point in this connection to the possibility – though at present it is unquantifiable – that the California proceedings will involve a trial by jury. Paragraph 14.07 states, however, that even where there is a case for adjournment under the preceding paragraphs the investigation committee will press ahead with disciplinary proceedings where to fail to do so would be inconsistent or would appear to be inconsistent with its duties as a regulator or as a professional body, for example where the institute is the prime regulator of the conduct in question. Mr Oliver does not dispute that the institute may be regarded as the prime regulator so far as the auditing activities of the appellants are concerned. He submits, however, that in the unique circumstances of the present case, a grave risk of serious injustice will exist if the committee proceeds immediately with its inquiry. He developed his submission both in general terms and under six specific heads, namely:

(1) *Confidentiality*

The appellants are concerned that they will not be able to defend themselves adequately before the committee of inquiry unless they are enabled to break confidence. The problem arises not so much in connection with BCCI itself, because it would be an implied term of the contract between the appellants and BCCI that the appellants were entitled to disclose confidential matters if this was necessary for their own protection. The position would be different, however, in relation to confidential documents or information which had come into the possession of the appellants and which related to customers of BCCI with whom the appellants have no contract. Proceedings have already been commenced, and orders obtained, by three BCCI customers or groups of customers with a view to preserving this confidentiality. In these and in any other case where the point might arise, submitted Mr Oliver, the appellants would need to apply to the court for orders releasing them from the obligation of confidentiality, and bearing in mind the nature of the case it was to be assumed there were many customers who for their own protection would strongly resist such applications. The appellants have already taken the initiative in proceedings against the holding company which are reported at [1992] BCLC 583, in

A order to obtain leave to disclose confidential information to Lord Justice Bingham's inquiry. Millett J granted the application, but it was plain that he found the case one of considerable difficulty. He was strongly influenced by the fact that the inquiry was set up to review the Bank of England's performance of its statutory functions, and that s. 39 of the *Banking Act* 1987 contained express provisions enabling the bank in appropriate cases to override not only banker's confidentiality but even legal professional privilege. The section would, of course, be of no relevance in the present case.

B As against that, submitted Mr Oliver, if the civil proceedings ran their course before the enquiry was continued, it was reasonable to assume that any relevant confidential information would have come into the open by way of discovery, against which confidentiality is no bar.

(2) *Disclosure of documents*

C The regulations governing the joint disciplinary scheme contain provisions designed to ensure that documents provided for the inquiry or created during it (such as transcripts of evidence) are only supplied to parties or witnesses on confidential terms. It is reasonable to assume, however, said Mr Oliver, that the liquidators of BCCI may very well be asked to give evidence to the inquiry and that in this capacity they will obtain information which may be of considerable interest to them in their proceedings against

D the appellants even if they are restricted as to its use.

(3) *Prejudice to the trial process*

The danger that any adverse findings that might be contained in the report of the committee would, when published, prove prejudicial in the eyes of a jury is at present confined to the possibility that the Californian and other US proceedings may be allowed to continue. This, as I have said, is an unquantifiable possibility. The appellants accept

E that it is an imponderable factor, but submit that this does not necessarily mean that it is without legal weight.

(4) *The generation of documents discoverable in litigation*

The particular concern of the appellants here is that submissions in documentary form, and transcripts of all the evidence would be discoverable in the civil proceedings. Sir John Bailey, conscious of this difficulty, has stated that the committee would claim public

F interest immunity for any documents not independently covered by legal professional privilege. The appellants submit, however, that the scope accorded by the courts to public interest immunity has tended to diminish in recent years. The respondents accept, as did the Divisional Court, that the outcome of a claim by the committee for such immunity cannot be anticipated, but submit that a real risk of injustice under this head is not established. The appellants point out, however, that public interest immunity, even if

G established in this country, would not be recognised abroad, and so might be circumvented.

(5) *Coincidence of issues*

Mr Oliver submits that the first two of the principal areas of concern specified in Sir John Bailey's letter of 16 December 1992 – namely whether the extent of the pervasive fraud within BCCI should have been detected earlier by the appellants' audit work, and

H whether the form of the appellants' audit report upon BCCI balance sheets at 31 December 1989 was adequate – fall squarely within the ambit of the allegations of negligence which are either expressly pleaded or bound to arise in the action by the liquidators. For the respondents, Mr Carnwath submits that there is an inevitable coincidence of issues when multiple proceedings have to be taken in relation to the same subject-matter, but it does not follow that prejudice or injustice thereby result.

(6) *Strain upon resources*   A

The appellants, while acknowledging that their resources are very substantial, point out that they are not unlimited. They say that the inevitably very large and irrecoverable costs incurred in responding to the inquiry represent a major burden to them, quite apart from the expenditure of time involved. I have already mentioned the difficulty and consequential delay arising from the fact that so few members of the firm were directly involved in the affairs of BCCI, and that these few have to bear the principal burden of responding to enquiries from whatever source.

Having reviewed these matters in the Divisional Court, Mann LJ said at [1993] BCC at p. 746G:

> 'I have discussed Mr Oliver's six heads separately if only because they cannot all be discussed at once. Mr Oliver submitted that it was the amalgam of heads rather than any individual one which was important. However, as I have concluded that none of the heads gives rise to a real risk of injustice an amalgam of the heads cannot produce a favourable result for the applicants.
>
> In summary I find no real risk of injustice which would entitle this court to intervene so as to prevent the performance in the public interest of an important investigative procedure which is part of a supervisory function underpinned by statute. The more especially as the procedure is to be performed in regard to a uniquely spectacular and serious banking failure.'

Mr Oliver, in his skeleton argument, submitted with appropriate deference that there was a logical fallacy in considering that, since none of the six heads gave rise to a real risk of injustice, an amalgam of them could not do so either. In my judgment there is no force in this submission. It seems to me that Mann LJ was simply saying, in effect, that nought plus nought equals nought, a proposition whose logic cannot be faulted.

Like Mann LJ, I am unimpressed by the consideration that the continuation of the inquiry at this stage would impose a great strain on the appellants' resources of time and money. The critical question as I see it is whether its continuation at this stage would delay, impede and prejudice the appellants in the conduct of their defence in civil proceedings to an extent which cannot be justified in the public interest.

Mr Carnwath accepts that difficulties may arise over the questions of confidentiality and disclosure to opposing parties, but he submits that the Divisional Court was justified in concluding that a real risk of substantial injustice is not demonstrated by the six factors whether taken individually or collectively. The main problem is, of course, that we are dealing with a question of risk and not with one of established fact. As the authorities demonstrate, the court should be slow to interfere with the assessment of risk carried out by a body such as the committee in the present case. But in the context of litigation on such a scale that, if only partly successful, it might well destroy the appellants' business, the risk of prejudice, even if this amounts to no more than forensic disadvantage, clearly demands careful appraisal.

To my mind the critical question is best approached by considering the individual and imponderable factors in the context of facts which are known or can be assumed with reasonable safety. The first of such facts is that, if the committee proceeds as planned, it will be considering matters of enormous complexity and (at present) undefined scope under a procedure which is, to say the least, unhelpful to the appellants. Secondly, this is not a case in which it can be expected that the inquiry can be completed fairly promptly, and without impinging upon the appellants' preparations for the civil proceedings. The committee cannot, of course, sit continuously, but only as and when its members and the parties are available. Mr Oliver suggested that the inquiry might well still be in progress when the liquidators' action comes on for trial in, he estimated, the year 2000, and while

A   this may be unduly pessimistic, it seems certain that if the inquiry proceeds, it must have a distracting and delaying effect upon the other proceedings in which the appellants are concerned, including prosecutions by the Serious Fraud Office which depend upon their evidence.

B   These considerations might count for little if the committee of inquiry had been set up to consider allegations of misconduct against the appellants or any of their staff, since the need to discover whether the allegations were well founded would, in the circumstances, plainly command a high degree of priority. If that were the case, the public interest would take precedence over the private concerns of the appellants, however pressing and numerous. As it is, however, there is no such allegation. On the contrary – and this is the third factor which weighs with me – the appellants have played a leading part in assisting the regulating authorities, here and abroad, and have evidently been accepted by them as reliable and responsible witnesses. The appellants are also

C   entitled in this connection to invoke the JMU report as evidence of their fitness to continue as registered auditors. So this is not a case in which disciplinary proceedings have to be pursued as a matter of urgency.

Fourthly, there seems to me to be a positive advantage in the committee having the benefit of findings of fact, arrived at by a judge in a fair trial after the issues with which the committee are principally concerned have been extensively canvassed, before they

D   proceed to a decision in the disciplinary inquiry. In this connection, it is to be borne in mind that the liquidation is being carried out by order of the court and that the liquidators are acting as officers of the court. It can safely be assumed that they will pursue their action against the appellants with all due diligence and zeal.

I take full account of the view expressed by Mr Harris, the director of the professional conduct department of the English and Welsh institute, in para. 13 of his affidavit where

E   he says:

> 'In order to maintain public confidence in the proper conduct of order 12, the institute needs to be able to demonstrate that it has acted swiftly to investigate the conduct of members in high profile cases where there has been public concern at the performance of the auditors.'

But it seems to me that this important point has been substantially met by the

F   commencement of the disciplinary proceedings. It is of course unsatisfactory that their completion should be deferred for what is likely to be a considerable number of years but, as I have said, the scope of the inquiry and the pace at which the committee is likely to be able to proceed would make that inevitable in any event. It is unsatisfactory from the point of view of the appellants, as well as that of the public, that a question mark should be left hanging over their observance of professional standards in their audit of the BCCI companies for so long. The interests of justice are, however, paramount, and it

G   seems to me for the reasons given, that these call for the granting of the adjournment which is sought.

Accordingly I would order that the decision of the committee of inquiry to proceed immediately with its work should be quashed, and that the committee should be prohibited from continuing the disciplinary proceedings until the trial of the liquidators' action against the appellants at first instance has been concluded. I would grant the

H   respondents liberty to apply to vary or set aside the order for prohibition, so as to cover the possibility of unforeseen developments in the proceedings, such as (though this seems highly unlikely) their settlement before the trial.

In the circumstances it becomes unnecessary at this stage to determine whether the decision of the executive counsel, refusing to agree that the proceedings should be continued under the revised scheme, was legally valid. The matter can be raised again

when the trial of the action by the liquidators has been concluded, and can be determined   A
in the light of the circumstances then prevailing.

I would therefore for my part allow the appeal to the extent indicated by what I have
said and no further. But Hirst LJ and Sir Roger Parker take the view that the decision of
the executive counsel can and should be quashed as well. Accordingly our order will so
provide.

Hirst LJ: I agree that this appeal should be allowed for the reasons given by Nolan   B
LJ. Since we are differing from the Divisional Court, I wish to add a judgment of my
own. I gratefully adopt Nolan LJ's exposition of the facts and of the old and new
disciplinary schemes of the accountancy profession.

The decision not to adjourn

It is not in dispute that the underlying principle is that upheld by the Divisional Court,
as laid down by the Court of Appeal in *R v Panel on Takeovers and Mergers, ex parte*   C
Fayed [1992] BCC 524 (per Neill LJ at p. 531):

> 'It is clear that the court has power to intervene to prevent injustice where the
> continuation of one set of proceedings may prejudice the fairness of the trial of
> other proceedings . . . But it is a power which has to be exercised with great care
> and only where there is a real risk of serious prejudice which may lead to injustice.'

I accept Mr Carnwath's submission, which is fully in line with the approach of the   D
Court of Appeal in the *Fayed* case, that the power to intervene should be most sparingly
exercised, and that it is only in exceptional cases that the disciplinary process (to which
the institute rightly attaches great importance in the public interest) should not be allowed
to go ahead unhindered.

However, it is clear that the adjudication which the court has to make is a balancing
exercise, and that, heavily though the scales will initially weigh in the institute's favour,   E
there may be cases where the considerations of serious prejudice to the member are so
strong that they will prevail.

When assessing the weight of the considerations on the institute's side of the scale, the
intrinsic importance of the disciplinary process is clearly a very significant but not an
overriding factor; it will also be necessary to evaluate the degree of public importance of
the case under consideration, the seriousness of the allegation of professional
incompetence and/or professional misconduct, and the urgency of their resolution in the   F
disciplinary context. Thus, for example, allegations of dishonesty or other professional
malpractice which, if proved, would be likely to lead to the striking off of a member,
must clearly weigh heavily or perhaps even overwhelmingly on the institute's side of the
scale.

In the course of his skeleton argument, Mr Carnwath submitted that:

> 'there is no reason to assume that private litigation in connection with auditors'   G
> activities should necessarily have priority over the statutory supervision in the
> public interest.'

I agree. But equally there is no reason (as Mr Carnwath seemed to suggest) that the
opposite assumption should be made. Each case must depend on its own facts and the
institute's own handbook, para. 14.02, rightly recognises that in some cases it will be
appropriate for the statutory supervision to give way ('Disciplinary proceedings must be   H
deferred if they are likely to interfere with the course of justice').

I now turn to the individual factors relied on by Mr Oliver on behalf of Price
Waterhouse.

(1) I am satisfied that the degree of overlap between the issues raised in the disciplinary
proceedings and those raised in the liquidators' action are so complete as to amount in

A Mr Oliver's words to virtual total eclipse. In both proceedings the same facts are in issue, and the basic professional standards invoked are identical and non-controversial; the fact that in the action some more controversial embellishments are added does not affect the comparison of the basic standards relied upon. This to my mind is a most important consideration, both because in my judgment it is inherently unfair that two tribunals should contemporaneously be considering the same issue (*Conteh v Onslow-Fane* The Times, 26 June 1975, CAT No. 291) and because it affects the evaluation of (2) below.

B In the *Conteh* case, the plaintiff, Mr Conteh, was a professional boxer and the defendant, Mr Onslow-Fane, represented the British Boxing Board of Control. There were pending a civil action brought by Mr Conteh for breach of contract against a boxing promoter and others; also disciplinary proceedings instituted by the board against Mr Conteh arising out of the same events.

C In the leading judgment in *Conteh's* case (with which Buckley and Stephenson L JJ agreed) Sir John Pennycuick stated:

'I think an obvious ground for the intervention of the court so as to restrain proceedings before a domestic tribunal is that there are pending in the High Court proceedings in which the same issue, or substantially the same issue, is raised and which the association concerned is not in a position to stay. The court will not as a rule allow the prosecution of the same issue in concurrent proceedings before
D different tribunals . . .

It follows that, although the parties to the domestic hearing are the board and Mr Conteh, while the parties to the High Court action are Mr Conteh and Messrs Prager, Duff, Francis and Levene, the two sets of proceedings turn upon an identical issue and that if the domestic hearing is allowed to continue there will be in substance a duplication of proceedings. Indeed, the board recognises that the
E determination before its committee can only be provisional and must yield to the decision in the action when it ultimately comes to be made. Given this state of affairs, the court has a judicial discretion to restrain the hearing before the committee on the ground of duplication of proceedings.'

I accept that in the *Conteh* case, as Mr Carnwath pointed out, the overlapping issue was of much narrower compass, but I do not think that affects the general principle laid down.
F It is also quite true, as the Divisional Court stressed, that in the present case 'the two proceedings are essentially different in nature', but I do not with respect agree with the Divisional Court that this affects the inherent unfairness any more than it did in the *Conteh* case.

(2) I for my part am satisfied that, if the disciplinary proceedings proceed in parallel with the other proceedings, the burden which will be placed upon Price Waterhouse, and
G in particular upon the six key personnel, has not been exaggerated. It is unnecessary for me to repeat the very powerful evidence presented by Price Waterhouse under this head, showing the vast volume of work in which they are already engaged, for the preparation of their case in the civil actions, and for their assistance to the SFO and the US authorities (itself a public duty). It will involve not only the marshalling of a huge number of documents (in itself a mammoth task), but also a multiplicity of explanatory papers and
H memoranda covering work in a large number of different countries affecting a large number of BCCI branches and/or subsidiaries. The burden of this exercise is truly daunting, possibly I dare say unprecedented, and on a scale which dwarfs the *Fayed* case, with which Mr Carnwath sought to draw a comparison. Bearing in mind the degree of overlap already demonstrated, I consider that to add to the existing tasks the conduct of a major campaign on yet another front is so onerous as to be oppressive, even allowing for the fact that Price Waterhouse is a very big firm with very large corporate resources.

In my judgment, contrary to the view of the Divisional Court, this consideration is so A
powerful as to give rise in itself to a real risk of injustice.

(3) On discovery of documents, Mr Oliver relies on two points which he suggests will
give the liquidator and/or other opponents in civil litigation unfair advantage: (a)
premature disclosure of existing discoverable documents; and (b) generation in the
enquiry of new documents.

Dealing with the latter point first, it seems to me inevitable that the enquiry will B
generate daily transcripts (which are mandatory under both the old and the new schemes)
and also extensive papers and/or memoranda emanating from both sides, which would
be discoverable in the civil litigation, and which would not have come into existence but
for the enquiry. If Price Waterhouse is required to produce these documents it goes
without saying that the liquidator and other opponents in civil litigation will gain a
substantial and to my mind unfair advantage. The answer given by Mr Carnwath is that C
Sir John Bailey would seek to protect these documents by claiming public interest
immunity, and the Divisional Court regarded this as removing any risk of injustice under
this head. While of course I accept that Sir John would make every effort to secure this
end, I for my part have very grave doubts whether he would be successful, seeing how
greatly the scope of such a claim has been circumscribed outside the realms of national
security since *Duncan v Cammell Laird* [1942] AC 624, notably as a result of the more
recent House of Lords decisions in *Conway v Rimmer* [1968] AC 910 and *Air Canada v* D
Secretary of State for Trade [1983] 2 AC 394. No authority was cited in which a
comparable claim to public interest immunity was upheld, and the situation in the present
case would seem not dissimilar to that of a claim by a local government authority, as to
which the following comment appears in *Cross on Evidence* (7th edn, 1990):

> 'It is however likely to be rare that a claim for public interest immunity, raised only
> by a local authority, and supported by affidavits not from ministers, but local E
> professional advisers will prevail against the public interest in the administration
> of justice . . .'

I therefore consider that this aspect counts as a significant prejudice.

By comparison premature disclosure is of small consequence, and although I accept it
does give a small advantage to Price Waterhouse's opponents in the civil litigation I
would not regard it as in itself significantly prejudicial. F

In my judgment these three factors of major prejudice taken in combination
demonstrate a very serious degree of prejudice to Price Waterhouse which is likely to lead
to injustice, without recourse to the other two factors with which I can deal more briefly.

So far as confidentiality is concerned, I accept Mr Carnwath's argument that, with two
possible exceptions, no serious problem would arise under this head because the
documents would be required as part of a statutory disciplinary process (*Parry Jones v* G
Law Society [1969] 1 Ch 1) or because of the principle laid down in *Tournier v National
Provincial and Union Bank of England* [1924] 1 KB 461 as to the contractual right of the
bank to use customers' documents, or because Price Waterhouse themselves would be
entitled to produce any such documents as were required to further their own defence
(*Tournier's* case). The only exceptions may be in relation to documents of BCCI's
customers and in relation to documents of BCCI's foreign subsidiaries, neither of which
would be covered by the *Tournier* principle, and for which it might be necessary to seek H
to invoke the general principle that the public interest in disclosure outweighed
confidentiality (*W v Egdell* [1990] Ch 359).

While these principles might not provide a complete answer to the problem of
confidentiality, the risk in my judgment is not so great as to amount in itself to a major
prejudice.

A So far as the prejudice in other trials is concerned, only jury trials would qualify. At present the prospect of such trials in California or Texas depends on the outcome of the Californian appeal. I accept that there is a contingent element of risk, but in the present state of uncertainty I would not rate that risk either as a major prejudice taken by itself.

However, these last two items taken together do add some additional degree of prejudice to the three major factors principally relied upon above, and I agree with

B Mr Oliver that the proper approach is to examine all the items in aggregate as well as individually.

It is now necessary to consider the countervailing factors relied upon by Mr Carnwath.

I accept without reservation that the intrinsic importance of the disciplinary procedure is a matter in itself of very considerable weight, and that it is (all other things being equal) desirable that the disciplinary enquiry should go ahead, to meet the obvious public

C concern that the accountancy aspects of the spectacular banking collapse of BCCI should be investigated, especially as they fell outside the scope of the Bingham enquiry. However it does not seem to me that there are here any special considerations either of seriousness or urgency.

The areas of enquiry foreshadowed in Sir John Bailey's letter (still not the subject of any specific charges) are as follows:

D '(i) Whether the extent of the pervasive fraud within BCCI should have been detected earlier by your firm's audit work.

(ii) Whether in the light of the evidence of fraud which has already come to light by 30 April 1990 and the declared doubts which your firm had at that date concerning the authenticity and value of material assets stated in the balance sheet of BCCI at 31 December 1989, the form of your firm's audit report was adequate,

E notwithstanding the undertakings of support received from the principal shareholder.

(iii) Whether assisting the management of BCCI with restructuring its operations, as well as advising the majority shareholder, adversely affected or was compatible with your firm's role as auditors.'

None of these matters affects the integrity of Price Waterhouse or of any of their partners or employees, let alone suggesting dishonesty or professional malpractice.

F Paragraphs (i) and (ii) are concerned with the competence of Price Waterhouse in relation to their auditing of BCCI. While no doubt important lessons can be learnt (see below), they do not affect the fitness or qualification of Price Waterhouse to continue to act as auditors of large public companies, in view of the clearance they have since received from the JMU.

G Paragraph (iii) raises the question of conflict of interest which, if the criticism is valid, would presumably apply generally in the accountancy field, and could appropriately be the subject-matter of a general ruling.

Moreover, in so far as there are lessons to be learnt (a point strongly emphasised by Mr Carnwath) it seems to me that they can equally well be learnt as a result of the civil action, and I respectfully disagree with the Divisional Court's view that the standard of appraisal will be 'quite different' in the two proceedings.

H Mr Carnwath submits that the committee are uniquely well fitted to evaluate such lessons in the light of Price Waterhouse's conduct of the audit, and of course I fully recognise their professional expertise, but I do not think they are necessarily better fitted than a High Court judge assisted by expert accountancy evidence from both sides.

I recognise that the delay which will ensue upon an adjournment will be very considerable in view of the time which will elapse before the completion of the civil trial, but at the end of the day it seems to me very likely that its outcome (if it proceeds to judgment) will radically affect, and probably greatly shorten the disciplinary proceedings, since the court's conclusion must inevitably be highly influential if not decisive in the minds of the committee. If on the other hand the civil action is settled, then the enquiry can proceed forthwith. Should the two sets of proceedings continue in parallel up to their conclusion, I am not persuaded that the enquiry (which must thoroughly cover the same huge volume of material) would be finished any earlier.

In the light of all these considerations, weighing the balance as best I can, I am satisfied that the serious prejudice to Price Waterhouse, leading to a very great risk of injustice, outweighs the countervailing considerations.

In consequence I would allow the appeal under this head.

The refusal to transfer

Nolan LJ has already set out the relevant provisions of the old and new disciplinary schemes. The new scheme was approved by the Privy Council with effect from 21 January 1993.

Under the new scheme it is provided that where enquiries were already in place on that date they should continue in accordance with the old scheme, but that if a member firm under enquiry and the executive counsel agree to a transfer then the enquiry can take place under the new scheme.

Not surprisingly Price Waterhouse applied through their solicitors Herbert Smith by letter dated 2 June 1993 on the grounds, obviously, that the procedure under the new scheme is much fairer.

By letter dated 17 June 1993 Mr Chance refused to agree, and wrote as follows:

'I do not consent to the inquiry being taken over by me under para. 3 of the revised scheme. I would not wish to take over the work of a committee of inquiry which was appointed some time ago and which has already set about its task unless that appeared to me to be justified. No reasons are given in your letter why I should agree to the proposed change of procedure. Having considered all the circumstances, however, I am not persuaded that my assumption of the inquiry is required for it to be fairly conducted and for it to reach proper conclusions on the basis of relevant material.

I have borne in mind Sir John Bailey's indication that any requests in relation to the procedures which might apply at the committee's hearings will be considered sympathetically. I have also had regard to the risk that material obtained from the Bank of England might not be available to me after the repeal of s. 85(1)(g) of the *Banking Act* 1987.

In all the circumstances, I am not willing to take over an inquiry for which a committee of inquiry was appointed over a year ago and which seems well equipped to discharge the task on which it has already embarked.'

This was supplemented by an affidavit sworn on 9 July 1993 in which he stated that, following his discussion with Sir John Bailey:

'whilst, without access to Price Waterhouse's files, it is inevitable that a great deal of work remains to be done, it is nevertheless the case that Sir John and his fellow members of the enquiry team have undertaken a very considerable amount of work. If I took over the enquiry I would have to duplicate much of that work.'

The reference in Mr Chance's letter to s. 85(1)(g) of the *Banking Act* 1987 concerns a number of confidential documents which were released by the Bank of England on 20 November 1992 for the purpose of the disciplinary proceedings under the provisions of

A　s. 85(1)(g) which forms part of Pt. V of the 1987 Act, headed 'Restriction on disclosure of information'. Section 82(1) provides:

'(1)　Except as provided by the subsequent provisions of the Part of this Act–

(a)　no person who under or for the purposes of this Act receives information relating to the business or other affairs of any person; and

B

(b)　no person who obtains any such information directly or indirectly from a person who has received it as aforesaid,

shall disclose the information without the consent of the person to whom it relates and (if different) the person from whom it was received as aforesaid.'

Section 85(1)(g) provides:

(1)　Section 82 above does not preclude the disclosure of information–

C

(g)　with a view to the institution of, or otherwise for the purposes of, any disciplinary proceedings relating to the exercise of his professional duties by an auditor of an authorised institution or former authorised institution or an accountant or other person nominated or approved for the purposes of section 39(1)(b) above or appointed under section 41 above . . .'

Section 85(1)(g) was repealed as from 31 December 1992 (*Banking Coordination*
D　*(Second Council Directive) Regulations* 1992 (SI 1992/3218), reg. 40(1)).

The perceived 'risk' referred to by Mr Chance, as explained by Mr Carnwath, is that the person identified under s. 82(1) might be either Sir John Bailey himself or the members of his committee, and that, once s. 85(1)(g) was repealed, it would be illegal for him or his committee to pass the documents on to the new committee. This doubt arose as a result of the letter from the Bank of England dated 4 December 1992, which also
E　expressed anxiety as to the dissemination of the information beyond the committee and its legal advisers.

In my judgment this objection (which it should be stressed is put forward only as a potential risk) is unsound, since I am satisfied that, on the proper construction of s. 82(1), the 'person' to whom the information was originally disclosed by the Bank of England was the institute, which is a corporate body apt to fall within the ambit of the word 'person'. The narrower construction would cause great practical difficulties, e.g. if the
F　chairman died, or was incapacitated, or retired, would his successor be debarred from receiving the information?

It follows that there can be no objection to the transfer of the Bank of England material between the old and the new disciplinary arms of the institute, and the position is unaffected by the repeal of s. 85(1)(g).

So far as the dissemination of information is concerned the new committee will be as
G　well able as the old to restrict its circulation to the committee members themselves and their legal advisers, no doubt in consultation with the Bank of England.

As to the other objections put forward by Mr Chance:

(1)　Sir John Bailey would, I feel sure, do his utmost to adapt the procedure in the manner sought by Price Waterhouse, but I am quite satisfied that, on the proper construction of r. 16, cross-examination is debarred, and that the only admissible
H　examination of a witness by Price Waterhouse's representative would be re-examination of their own witness. It follows that the proposed relaxation of the rule by Sir John Bailey could, and probably would, be met by a valid objection from the witness whose cross-examination was sought.

(2)　It is quite clear that a major part of the work already done under the old scheme is the investigation conducted by BDO Binder Hamlyn on behalf of the committee,

and there would not seem to be any reason why that work should not be made A
available to an inquiry under the new scheme. It is very unclear on the evidence set
out above how much, if any, extra work has been done by Sir John Bailey and the
committee themselves.

In my judgment, therefore, Mr Chance's reasons are legally flawed in relation to the
Banking Act and in relation to the proposed relaxation of the old procedure, and the
remaining reason is open to serious objection of unreasonableness. Perhaps even more B
important, he gives no weight at all to the comparative fairness of the two schemes, which
was plainly the basis for Herbert Smith's request for a transfer.

It follows that in my judgment Mr Chance's decision is open to review, and should be
quashed.

In my judgment the new scheme substitutes an essentially adversarial procedure for an
essentially inquisitorial procedure, ensuring precise notification of charges with full C
particulars, comprehensive exchange of witness statements in advance, and an inter
partes hearing with a legally qualified chairman and the executive counsel acting as in
effect the prosecutor, and with full scope for cross-examination and opening and closing
submissions on behalf of the member concerned. Consequently, I consider that the new
procedure is much fairer than the old, which is no doubt the reason why it has been
introduced. As a result, in my judgment, when the enquiry takes place I think there is a
very strong case that it should be conducted under the new scheme, though ultimately D
the decision will rest with Mr Chance.

I would therefore allow the appeal under this heading also.

Sir Roger Parker: I agree that this appeal should be allowed. I gratefully adopt the
accounts of the background facts which appear in the judgment of Mann LJ in the
Divisional Court and which have been given in the judgments of Nolan and Hirst L JJ.
I give a judgment of my own, partly because we are differing from the judgment of the E
Divisional Court, and partly because there are certain differences between the judgments
just delivered.

The first impugned decision: the principles

Although it is common ground that the approach should be that set out in the
judgment of Neill LJ in the *Fayed* case, it is in my view necessary to consider his statement F
closely. It contains two propositions: (1) there is power to intervene to prevent injustice
where the continuation of one set of proceedings may prejudice the fair trial of other
proceedings; (2) that power should only be exercised where there is a real risk of serious
prejudice which may lead to injustice.

That proposition clearly recognises that what has to be considered is the possibility of
injustice and that the power to intervene is not limited to cases where it is shown that
there will be injustice. There are two further points to be mentioned with regard to Neill G
LJ's propositions: first, although he refers to possible injustice in the fair trial of the other
proceedings, it is in my view also necessary to consider the fairness or otherwise of the
proceedings which it is sought to restrain. The power to intervene could in my view be
properly exercised in cases where the fair trial of such proceedings might itself be open to
criticism, and where it might be prejudiced by the continuation of both sets of
proceedings. This was indeed recognised by Neill LJ when he expressed his conclusion H
thus ([1992] BCC 524 at p. 531G):

'. . . I can see no arguable case that there is any real risk to the conduct of the 1987
action or to the fairness of the trial of this action.'

Secondly, Neill LJ gives us examples of the cases where the power to intervene could
be exercised: (1) where the publicity given to the result of a disciplinary hearing might

A have a possible influence on a jury in a criminal trial which is about to start; and (2) where publicity given to the evidence in one set of proceedings might lead to the fabrication of evidence in later proceedings. I venture to stress that these are no more than examples.

In particular, it should be noted that, as the law on contempt demonstrates, the effect of adverse publicity about a party may prejudice fair trial in that, without any question B of fabrication of evidence or of interference with witnesses, witnesses may be deterred from coming forward to give evidence.

The investigation committee's handbook

It was contended for the respondents that the provision in para. 14.02: 'Disciplinary proceedings must be deferred if they are likely to interfere with the course of justice' was C subject to the provisions in para. 14.07 which is in the following terms:

> 'Even where there is a case for adjournment under the preceding paragraphs, the investigation committee will press ahead with disciplinary proceedings where to fail to do so will be inconsistent, or would appear to be inconsistent, with its duties as a regulator or as a professional body, for example where the institute is the prime regulator of the conduct in question.'

D In my judgment, para. 14.07 has no application to a case which falls within para. 14.02. If that paragraph applies, there is not merely a case for adjournment, there is a mandatory requirement to adjourn. Paragraph 14.07 applies only to the intervening paragraphs. It would be strange, if not astonishing, were it otherwise. I cannot accept that the institute intended that, merely because it is the prime regulator, it should continue with proceedings which it had concluded were likely to interfere with the course of justice. It is I suppose conceivable that para. 14.02 might be overridden, not by para. 14.07, but by E some paramount public interest, but that is another matter.

The case for deferment

I agree with both judgments which have been delivered. I add however some observations on two matters. First I would for myself have no hesitation in holding that the continuation of both the High Court actions and the disciplinary proceedings together creates a real risk of serious prejudice which may lead to injustice and interfere F with the fairness of both sets of proceedings. The cost burden upon Price Waterhouse and the diversion of the skills and energies of their partners and staff from providing audit services to the public whilst they endeavour to deal with parallel investigations by different tribunals into immensely complicated facts and issues as to their conduct going as far back as 1985 and beyond, may not be of great importance. What appears to be plain however is that their ability to meet each set of proceedings will inevitably be G prejudiced by the necessity to deal at the same time with the other. This position is exacerbated by the fact that they will at the same time have to assist the Serious Fraud Office in preparation for, and trial of, various criminal proceedings. In this connection, Mr Carnwath has accepted that the stage might be reached where the last straw will break the camel's back. There can in my view be no doubt that the continuation of the disciplinary proceedings would amount to the last straw.

H Secondly, I respectfully disagree with Mann LJ when he said:

> 'As I have concluded that none of the heads gives rise to a real risk of injustice, an amalgam of the heads cannot produce a favourable result for the applicants.'

Nothing added to nothing of course equals nothing. But a number of real risks of prejudice, none of which alone might lead to injustice, could in my judgment, when added together, amount to a real risk of prejudice sufficiently serious to produce such a result.

A

The case for continuation

I can discern no public interest which, in this case, demands that the disciplinary proceedings continue. They are unlikely to be concluded any sooner than the High Court actions. Price Waterhouse's existing audit procedures and control have been found not to require any regulatory action by the JMU, and their past acts or omissions will be thoroughly and fairly investigated in the High Court actions under procedures which are fairer than those provided for by the old disciplinary scheme.

B

The second impugned decision

I agree that this decision should be set aside for the reasons given by Hirst LJ. I would, however, also set it aside on the further ground that it appears to me to be clear that Mr Chance failed to take into account certain relevant and important considerations, namely the existence and consequences of the pending actions in the High Court.

C

In the light of those actions, it appears to me that consideration should have been given to the desirability of pursuing a general unstructured enquiry at the same time as Price Waterhouse were facing specific allegations in the High Court actions, or whether justice did not demand that, if disciplinary proceedings were to be continued, Price Waterhouse should at least know what charges they were to face therein and have the better opportunity to meet it, which is provided by the new scheme. Furthermore it seems to me possible that had he accepted transfer, Mr Chance might well have concluded that he was unable to frame and particularise the charge until the High Court actions had been determined. This of course would mean a long delay, but the disciplinary proceedings would then be shorter. There might indeed be no proceedings at all, for it might be found that Price Waterhouse were, if liable, liable only on some basis that did not justify any disciplinary charge.

D

Mr Oliver urged us to recommend, in the event that we set aside the decision, to make it clear that we took the view that there should be a transfer. Even if we were presently of the view that disciplinary proceedings should continue and of the view that we would ourselves have transferred them, the decision is one for Mr Chance. As, however, the disciplinary proceedings are to be adjourned, the question cannot presently arise. If and when they continue, Price Waterhouse will be able to make a further application to transfer in the light of the circumstances then prevailing, and Mr Chance will have to consider such application also in the light of such circumstances. I would allow the appeal under both heads and set aside both decisions.

E

F

(Appeal allowed with costs (limited to the English proceedings by the liquidators, after the conclusion of the first instance). Leave to appeal to the House of Lords refused)

———————————

G

H

Galoo Ltd & Ors v Bright Grahame Murray.

Court of Appeal (Civil Division).
Glidewell, Evans and Waite L JJ.
Judgment delivered 21 December 1993.

Auditors – Negligence – Plaintiffs claimed that audited accounts contained inaccuracies – Plaintiffs alleged that defendant accountants were in breach of duties in contract and in tort to companies and purchaser – Whether acceptance of loans could constitute damage – Whether auditors' negligence caused or merely allowed companies to incur trading losses – Whether auditors knew that purchaser of company would rely on accounts and intended purchaser so to rely.

This was an appeal by the plaintiffs against an order striking out various of their claims and a cross-appeal by the defendants against the decision not to strike out all the plaintiffs' claims.

The plaintiffs were, first, 'Galoo', a company in liquidation, second, 'Gamine', which owned all the shares in Galoo, and third, 'Hillsdown', which acquired the shares in Gamine. The plaintiffs claimed that the audited accounts of Galoo and Gamine for the years 1985–1989 and the draft audited accounts for the year 1990 contained substantial inaccuracies, that in auditing the accounts without discovering or reporting such inaccuracies the defendant accountants, 'BGM', were negligent and in breach of duties owed in contract and tort to Galoo and Gamine and in tort to Hillsdown, and that as a result the plaintiffs had all suffered loss and damage.

It was accepted before the judge that the same principles applied to claims by Galoo and Gamine for damages for breach of contract or in tort. The facts which would establish a breach of contract by the defendants had been pleaded. The judge then considered whether the plaintiffs would be entitled to substantial damages. He held that neither Galoo nor Gamine could recover damages for incurring an obligation to repay sums advanced by Hillsdown, or for trading losses as a result of relying on the negligent auditing by the defendants and thus continuing to trade when they would otherwise not have done so. He therefore struck out those claims.

The judge held that Hillsdown's claim in tort for loss resulting from the original purchase by Hillsdown of the shares in Gamine did disclose a reasonable cause of action and he therefore declined to strike it out. This was the subject of the cross-appeal. The judge struck out Hillsdown's claims for loss resulting from making loans to Gamine and from the purchase of further shares in Gamine.

Held, dismissing the appeal and cross-appeal:

1. The acceptance of a loan could not of itself be described as a loss causing damage. If anything it was a benefit to the borrower. A loss might result from the use to which the loan moneys were put, but no such resultant loss was pleaded, and even if it were it might very well be difficult to attribute it to BGM.

2. The breach of duty by the defendants gave the opportunity to Galoo and Gamine to incur and to continue to incur trading losses; it did not cause those trading losses, in the sense in which the word 'cause' was used in law.

3. Hillsdown's claim in tort, for losses caused by reliance (as was alleged) upon representations made in or by reference to the completion accounts, at the time of the original purchase, should not be struck out. It was plain that the 1986 accounts were to be prepared not only for the purposes of the audit but also for the purpose of fixing the consideration under the purchase agreement. It was common ground that the defendants knew of the terms of that agreement and that the accounts which they were to submit to the purchasers were to be for the purposes of those provisions. The claim could not be struck

out on the ground that the accounts submitted to Hillsdown by BGM were expressed to be A
draft accounts, or on the ground that the acquisition agreement gave Hillsdown's
accountants access to the companies' books and the right to review the completion accounts.
Evidence was required on those issues. (**Caparo Industries plc v Dickman & Ors [1990] BCC
164 and Morgan Crucible Co plc v Hill Samuel & Co Ltd & Ors [1991] BCC 82 considered.**)

4. In relation to Hillsdown's claim for loss resulting from making loans to Gamine, the
statement of claim did not plead that BGM knew that Hillsdown would rely on the accounts B
approved by the auditors for the purpose of deciding whether to make the loans or increase
loans already made, and intended that Hillsdown should so rely. Likewise, in relation to
Hillsdown's claim for loss resulting from the purchase of further shares in Gamine (not
under the original acquisition agreement) it was not pleaded that BGM knew when auditing
the accounts or supplying them that Hillsdown would rely upon those accounts, nor that
BGM intended that they should so rely, for the purpose of calculating the purchase price
under the supplemental agreement. The pleaded facts did not establish a duty of care on C
BGM in relation to either issue. (**Caparo Industries plc v Dickman & Ors [1990] BCC 164
applied.**)

The following cases were referred to in the judgments:

Alexander & Ors v Cambridge Credit Corporation Ltd & Anor (1987) 5 ACLC 587.
Al-Nakib Investments (Jersey) Ltd & Anor v Longcroft & Ors [1990] BCC 517; [1990]
1 WLR 1390.   D
Al Saudi Banque & Ors v Clark Pixley (1989) 5 BCC 822; [1990] Ch 313.
Candler v Crane, Christmas & Co [1951] 2 KB 164.
Caparo Industries plc v Dickman & Ors [1990] BCC 164; [1990] 2 AC 605.
Hedley Byrne & Co Ltd v Heller & Partners Ltd [1964] AC 465.
March v E & M H Stramare Pty Ltd & Anor (1991) 171 CLR 506.
Monarch Steamship Co Ltd v Karlshamns Oljefabriker A B [1949] AC 196.   E
Morgan Crucible Co plc v Hill Samuel & Co Ltd & Ors [1991] BCC 82; [1991] Ch 295.
Quinn v Burch Bros (Builders) Ltd [1966] 2 QB 370.
Smith v Eric S Bush [1990] 1 AC 831.
Ultramares Corporation v Touche (1931) 174 NE 441.

Hugh Bennett QC and Jonathan Acton Davis (instructed by Biddle & Co) for the
plaintiffs.
Ian Hunter QC and Graham Dunning (instructed by Squire & Co) for the defendant.   F

JUDGMENT

Glidewell LJ: The first plaintiff, Galoo Ltd ('Galoo'), which is now in liquidation,
formerly traded in animal health products. The second plaintiff, Gamine Ltd ('Gamine'),
owned all the shares in Galoo. Both the first and second plaintiffs have changed their
names. Galoo was formerly Peter Hand (GB) Ltd, and Gamine was Peter Hand Holdings G
Ltd.

The defendants, Bright Grahame Murray ('BGM'), are a firm of chartered
accountants. From 1981 until 1991 they were the auditors of the accounts of Galoo, and
from 1984 until 1991 of the accounts of Gamine.

In 1987, the third plaintiff, Hillsdown Holdings plc ('Hillsdown'), purchased 51 per
cent of the shares in Gamine from the holders of those shares. Between March 1987 and H
January 1993 Hillsdown made loans to Galoo and Gamine which amounted in total to
over £30m. In May 1991 Hillsdown purchased a further 44.3 per cent of the shares in
Gamine.

By a specially indorsed writ issued on 6 October 1992, the plaintiffs claim that the
audited accounts of Galoo and Gamine for the years 1985 to 1989 and the draft audited

A   accounts for the year 1990 contained substantial inaccuracies, that in auditing the accounts without discovering or reporting such inaccuracies BGM were negligent and in breach of duties owed in contract and tort to Galoo and Gamine and in tort to Hillsdown, and that as a result the plaintiffs have all suffered loss and damage.

BGM applied to strike out the statement of claim indorsed on the writ on the ground that it disclosed no reasonable cause of action. We have not been supplied with a copy of the application but it seems that it was made under RSC, O. 18, r. 19(1)(a) and under the inherent jurisdiction of the court.

B

The application was heard by Mr Ronald Walker QC, who gave judgment on 17 May 1993. He ordered:

(1)   that the claims of the first and second plaintiffs should be struck out and that the action by them should be dismissed pursuant to O. 18, r. 19 of the RSC and/or the inherent jurisdiction of the court;

C

(2)   that part of the third plaintiff's claims should be struck out, as indicated in his judgment, and that the third plaintiff should amend its statement of claim so as to reflect the decision and to pursue only that part of the claim not struck out.

The deputy judge granted leave to all the plaintiffs to appeal against his order, and for the defendants to cross-appeal against his refusal to strike out the whole of the claims of the third plaintiffs.

D

The plaintiffs now appeal against the decision to strike out, and the defendants cross-appeal against the decision not to strike out part of the claim by Hillsdown.

The nature of these proceedings

E   Although the application was more widely framed, in this appeal it has properly been treated as an application under O. 18, r. 19(1)(a) only (with one exception to which I shall refer later). On such an application, no evidence is admissible by virtue of O. 18, r. 19(2). I therefore do not understand why the papers before the judge, and before this court, included and include a number of affidavits. As the deputy judge correctly said:

'For the purposes of the applications, all the allegations in the statement of claim must be assumed to be true.'

F

The issue for the court is therefore, making that assumption, is the plaintiffs' claim nevertheless bound to fail? Only if the answer in relation to any claim is 'Yes' should that claim be struck out. On the other hand I agree with the deputy judge that if the statement of claim does not disclose a reasonable cause of action on a particular claim, that claim should be struck out at this stage, thus saving an unnecessary trial, perhaps lengthy, on that claim. I also take the view that, since the court at this stage is concerned only with the allegations in the statement of claim and not with evidence, the court hearing the application was and is in as good a position to decide the issue now as it would have been at the conclusion of a trial.

G

Order 18, r. 19(1) expressly provides that the court, as an alternative to striking out a pleading, may order that it be amended. Obviously if, after an amendment properly made, the statement of claim does disclose a reasonable cause of action, it should not be struck out. So the deputy judge, without objection by Mr Hunter on behalf of the defendants, made his decision in relation to a draft amended statement of claim which was before him. With some further amendment to which reference was made in the hearing before the deputy judge, this document has been submitted to us. For the purposes of this appeal I shall treat the statement of claim so amended as the effective statement of claim. When I come to consider the claims in detail I shall do so by reference to the paragraph numbers in the draft amended statement of claim.

H

The issues and the judge's decision

A

(1) Claims by Galoo and Gamine for damages for breach of contract or in tort.

It was accepted before the judge that the same principles apply to damages under both heads. No different argument has been presented to us. The facts which would establish a breach of contract by the defendants have been pleaded. Thus these plaintiffs are entitled at least to nominal damages. The deputy judge however said in his judgment:

> 'I was not, however, invited to refuse to strike out the claims on the basis that they could properly proceed with a view to obtaining nominal damages, and it appears to have been accepted that even if RSC, O. 18, r. 19(1)(a) would not be satisfied in those circumstances, then the claim would be demurrable by reason of the further provisions of that subrule.'

B

I agree that this was a proper approach for the deputy judge to adopt.

The judge then considered whether the first and second plaintiffs would be entitled to substantial damages for the pleaded loss under two heads: (a) by incurring an obligation to repay the sums advanced by Hillsdown; and (b) by incurring trading losses as a result of relying on the negligent auditing by the defendants and thus continuing to trade.

C

The deputy judge decided that neither Galoo nor Gamine could recover damages under either head, and he therefore struck out their claims.

The claims by Hillsdown are all in tort. They are claims for damages under the following heads.

D

(2) For loss resulting from the original purchase by Hillsdown of the shares in Gamine. The deputy judge decided that the statement of claim did disclose a reasonable cause of action on this head and therefore declined to strike it out. This is the subject of the cross-appeal.

(3) For loss resulting from making the loans to Gamine. The deputy judge struck out this claim.

E

(4) For amounts paid under a supplementary agreement for the purchase of the further 44.3 per cent of the shares in Gamine, and for payments made to Mr Sanders at the same time for loss of office. These claims were also struck out.

I shall deal with each of these issues in turn, in that order. Before I do so, however, it is necessary to refer to the statement of claim in more detail.

F

Facts alleged common to all issues

I have already described the parties briefly. By para. 4 of the statement of claim, it is alleged that by a written agreement dated 25 February 1987 Hillsdown purchased 51 per cent of the issued £1 shares in the capital of Gamine. The vendors of the shares were Mr Michael Sanders, the chairman and managing director of both Galoo and Gamine, together with members of his immediate family, and also Mr Roger Tabakin, a partner in the defendant firm and trustee of the Sanders family settlement. This agreement is described as 'the acquisition agreement'.

G

Paragraph 10 sets out the method of calculation of the shares purchased under the acquisition agreement. It was to be 5.2 times the net profits of Gamine as set out in the completion accounts, which were defined as including the audited accounts of Galoo and Gamine for the year ending 31 December 1986. The agreement provided that the parties should jointly procure as soon as practicable and in any event within 90 days of the date of completion the preparation of the completion accounts, which 'shall be audited' by BGM. BGM were required to calculate the net profits from the completion accounts, and deliver to the vendors and to Hillsdown copies of the completion accounts and a statement setting out the net profits and the shareholders' funds.

H

A   Paragraph 11 sets out a further provision of the acquisition agreement, that, if the vendors so elected, Hillsdown would be required to purchase the remaining shares in Gamine in annual tranches, and that the price payable for each such tranche of shares should be calculated by reference to the pre-tax earnings of Gamine for the relevant year as shown by the accounts for that year, which were to be prepared and audited by BGM.

B   Paragraph 5 pleads that by a supplemental written agreement made between Hillsdown and the vendors dated 21 May 1991, Hillsdown purchased further shares in Gamine from the vendors for a sum of £967,000. Moreover, by an agreement made on the same day between Gamine and Mr Michael Sanders, Hillsdown made a termination payment of £30,000 to Mr Sanders as compensation for loss of office.

By para. 8:

C   'In the premises (BGM) owed duties to (Galoo and Gamine) as implied terms of each of the annual contracts under which they acted as auditors of (Galoo and Gamine) and also in tort:

> (i) To perform the functions prescribed by the relevant provisions of the Companies Act in force at the material time, which functions included a duty to report to the company's members on the annual accounts of the company and to state in each report whether in (BGM's) opinion the annual accounts had been properly prepared in accordance with the Companies Act;

D

> (ii) To do all such work and carry out all such investigations as would enable (BGM) properly to discharge the above functions; and

> (iii) In performing the above functions and work to comply with the requirements set out in the Auditing Standards and Guidelines of the Institute of Chartered Accountants in England and Wales and to exercise reasonable professional care and skill in performing the above functions and work.'

E

Paragraph 9 pleads that BGM owed duties in tort equivalent to those pleaded in para. 8 to Gamine as shareholders in Galoo in auditing the accounts of Galoo for each of the years 1981–1990 and to Hillsdown as shareholders of Gamine in auditing the accounts of Gamine for each of the years 1986–1990.

F   It is alleged that in respect of each of the years 1985–1990 Mr Sanders and/or the company secretary of Galoo falsely overstated the stock held by Galoo for the purpose of preparing the annual accounts of Galoo and Gamine. By the time the accounts for the year 1990 were drawn the value of the fictitious quantities of stock was approximately £15.3m. Further, the value of the stock of Galoo included in the accounts of Galoo and Gamine for the year 1990 included finished products to a value of £1,818,335 and work in progress totalling £1,391,000 neither of which ever existed. By reason of these matters, the audited accounts for each of the years 1985–1989 and the draft audited accounts for the year ended 31 December 1990 of Galoo and Gamine were materially misstated and not properly prepared in accordance with the Companies Acts. Particulars are given year by year of the estimated actual stock contrasted with the stock shown in the accounts for each year, which shows the estimating margin of falsity as £2.5m in the 1985 accounts, rising to £11.8m in the 1989 accounts and £15.361m in the 1990 accounts.

G

H

Allegations relevant to Galoo and to Gamine

Paragraph 19 alleges that in auditing the accounts of Galoo and Gamine for each of the years 1985–1990 BGM acted negligently and in breach of their duties in contract and in tort as set out earlier. Particulars of the alleged negligence and breach of duty are given.

Paragraph 20 pleads:

'If (BGM) had performed their duties properly and with reasonable professional care and skill the accounts of (Galoo and Gamine) for each of the years 1985–1990 and/or (BGM's) report on those accounts would have shown that those companies instead of being profitable and having substantial assets, were in fact unprofitable and worthless. In these circumstances:

> (i) the insolvency of (Galoo and Gamine) would have been revealed and those companies would have ceased to trade immediately;
>
> (ii) (a) (Galoo and Gamine) would not have accepted or continued to accept the advances or further advances from Hillsdown referred to in subpara. (iii) below and/or incurred any other liabilities.'

The advances referred to in (iii) are pleaded as advances by Hillsdown to Galoo and Gamine between March 1987 and January 1993 in the total amount of £30,649,943.

Paragraph 21 pleads that Galoo and Gamine have suffered loss and damage,

'As a result of continuing to trade after they would otherwise have done,'

–of which particulars would be provided in due course.

Such particulars have now been provided in the following form:

> 'The nature of the case is that had (BGM) detected the fraud during their audit of the 1985 accounts, the steps preliminary to liquidation of the companies would have been commenced in early 1986 leading to their liquidation in approximately mid-1986. In the case of (Galoo) the loss can be quantified as follows . . .'

The particulars then plead that in mid-1986 Galoo's net liabilities were approximately £2m. Galoo was put into liquidation upon discovery of the fraud. The current best estimate is that it has net liabilities of approximately £27m. The difference between these two estimates of net liabilities, i.e. £25m, was a loss caused by Galoo continuing to trade after mid-1986 and thus represents both its loss and a consequential fall in its net assets. Moreover, during 1988 Galoo made a dividend payment of £500,000 which would not have been made if BGM had detected the fraud.

Galoo was essentially the only subsidiary of Gamine, and thus the fall in the net asset value of Galoo had a direct affect on the net asset value of Gamine.

Further, Galoo and Gamine accepted the loans from Hillsdown in the total sum of £30,649,943 which 'were necessary only because of the stock overstatements and which masked the said overstatements'.

Issue 1: Claims by Galoo and Gamine for damages for breach of contract or in tort

As I have said, this claim is for damages which are pleaded under two heads, which it is necessary to consider separately.

The first part of this claim is for damages for the loss allegedly incurred by Galoo and Gamine as a result of accepting and continuing to accept the loans from Hillsdown totalling over £30m. This part of the claim is added by the amendment to the statement of claim.

The deputy judge dealt with this matter shortly but clearly. He said:

> 'As a matter of fact, I do not accept that accepting loans involving an obligation simpliciter to repay them can be described as damage. At the moment of accepting the loan, the company which accepts the loan has available that amount of money and the obligation to repay that amount of money, and I simply fail to see how that can amount to damage. If there is damage, it must consist of parting with those moneys in certain circumstances.'

A   I entirely agree with the deputy judge on this issue. Like him, I do not understand how the acceptance of a loan can, of itself, be described as a loss causing damage. If anything it is a benefit to the borrower. Of course, a loss may result from the use to which the loan moneys are put, but no such resultant loss is pleaded, and even if it were it might very well be difficult to attribute it to BGM. I therefore agree with the deputy judge on this issue.

B   The second head of damage claimed by Galoo and Gamine is that they incurred trading losses as a result of relying on the negligent auditing by BGM and thus continued to trade when they would otherwise not have done. The claim under this head is for damages for trading losses of approximately £25m incurred in and between 1986 and 1990 and for making a dividend payment of £500,000 in 1988, as set out in the particulars to which I have referred. This claim requires more detailed consideration.

C   It can be expressed as follows.

(a)   If they had not acted in breach of their duty in contract or tort, BGM would have detected the fraud during their audit of the 1985 accounts.

(b)   In that case, Galoo and Gamine would have been put into liquidation in mid-1986 and thus ceased to trade at that date.

(c)   If the companies had ceased to trade, they would neither have incurred any further
D   trading losses nor paid the dividend in 1988.

(d)   Therefore the trading losses and the loss caused by the dividend payment were caused by the breach of duty by BGM.

This argument depends upon the nature of the causation necessary to establish liability for breach of duty, whether in contract or in tort. There is no doubt that this is one of the most difficult areas of the law. Both counsel are agreed that, at least in the context of this
E   case, the principles applicable to liability in either contract or tort are the same.

Mr Hunter, for the defendants, submits that the plaintiff's case depends upon the adoption of the 'but for' test of causation which, at least in contract, is not the proper test in English law. This is causation of the kind which has sometimes been referred to as a 'causa sine qua non'.

In para. 1785 of the 25th edition of *Chitty on Contracts*, the editors say:

F   'The important issue in remoteness of damage in the law of contract is whether a particular loss was within the reasonable contemplation of the parties, but causation must also be proved; there must be a causal connection between the defendant's breach of contract and the plaintiff's loss. The courts have avoided laying down any formal tests for causation: they have relied on common sense to guide decisions as to whether a breach of contract is a sufficiently substantial cause
G   of the plaintiff's loss. (It need not be the sole cause.)'

For these propositions the editors quote three authorities, including the decision of the House of Lords in *Monarch Steamship Co Ltd v Karlshamns Oljefabriker AB* [1949] AC 196 and *Quinn v Burch Bros (Builders) Ltd* [1966] 2 QB 370.

In the *Monarch Steamship* case, the defendants' ship was chartered to carry a cargo from Manchuria to Sweden. The ship should have reached Sweden in July 1939 but the
H   boilers were defective, which resulted in the defendants breaking their contractual duty to provide a seaworthy ship. She was delayed and did not leave Port Said, at the north end of the Suez canal, until 24 September 1939. By that date the Second World War had broken out. The British Admiralty prohibited the ship from proceeding to Sweden and ordered her to proceed to, and discharge at, Glasgow. The cargo was eventually transshipped and delivered to Sweden at extra cost. The purchasers of the cargo sued the ship owners for damages. The ship owners by their defence claimed that the cause of the

additional expense was the order from the Admiralty, not their breach of contract in   A
failing to provide a seaworthy ship. The House of Lords rejected this argument, and held
that the damages were recoverable.

However, in the course of the speeches in the House of Lords, their Lordships
considered what test to apply in order to decide whether the defendants' breach of
contract was causative of the plaintiffs' loss. In particular Lord Porter at p. 212 said that
it had to be determined whether the breach of contract was 'the effective cause'. Lord   B
Wright at pp. 227–228 said:

> 'There is, however, in this case a contention of a more general nature, which is that
> the delay which resulted from the defective boilers did not in any legal sense cause
> the diversion of the vessel. It is said that the relation of cause and effect cannot be
> postulated here between the unseaworthiness and the restraints of princes or the
> delay. As to such a contention it may be said at once that all the judges below have   C
> rejected it . . . If a man is too late to catch a train, because his car broke down on
> the way to the station, we should all naturally say that he lost the train because of
> the car breaking down. We recognise that the two things or events are causally
> connected. Causation is a mental concept, generally based on inference or
> induction from uniformity of sequence as between two events that there is a causal
> connection between them. . . . The common law however is not concerned with
> philosophic speculation, but is only concerned with ordinary everyday life and   D
> thoughts and expressions, and would not hesitate to think and say that, because it
> caused the delay, unseaworthiness caused the Admiralty order diverting the vessel.
> I think the common law would be right in picking out unseaworthiness from the
> whole complex of circumstances as the dominant cause.'

In *Quinn v Burch Bros* the defendants were main contractors on a building project. The
plaintiff was an independent subcontractor carrying out plastering and similar work.   E
Under the contract between them, the defendants were to supply any equipment
reasonably necessary for the plaintiff's work. On the day in question, the plaintiff
required a step-ladder in order to carry out work to ceilings, but despite his request the
defendants did not supply one. The plaintiff found a folded trestle, which he propped
against the wall and used as if it were a ladder to allow him to reach the ceiling. While he
was standing on the trestle the foot of it slipped and he fell and broke his heel. He claimed
that his injuries and resultant loss were the result of the defendants' breach of contract.   F

Paull J held that the defendants were in breach of contract in failing to supply a step-
ladder, but that the breach did not cause the plaintiff's accident. This court unanimously
dismissed the plaintiff's appeal. Danckwerts LJ in a short judgment expressed his
reasoning in four propositions, of which the third and fourth were (at p. 391G):

> '(3) The cause of the plaintiff's accident was the choice by the plaintiff to use the
> unsuitable equipment. (4) The failure of the defendants to provide the equipment   G
> required may have been the occasion of the accident but was not the cause of the
> accident.'

Salmon LJ said at p. 394G:

> '. . . the defendants realised that, if there were a breach of contract on their part to
> supply the step-ladder, that breach would afford the plaintiff the opportunity of   H
> acting negligently, and that he might take it and thereby suffer injury. But it seems
> to me quite impossible to say that in reality the plaintiff's injury was caused by the
> breach of contract. The breach of contract merely gave the plaintiff the opportunity
> to injure himself and was the occasion of the injury. There is always a temptation
> to fall into the fallacy of post hoc ergo propter hoc; and that is no less a fallacy
> even if what happens afterwards could have been foreseen before it occurred.'

A   We have been referred by counsel to two Australian cases. *Alexander v Cambridge Credit Corporation* (1987) 5 ACLC 587 was a decision of the Court of Appeal of New South Wales. The facts were very similar to those of the present case. In 1971 the auditors of the Cambridge Credit Corporation, in their annual audit certificates, failed to note that the balance sheet and other accounts did not show provisions which should have been made. If the appropriate note had been made it was highly probable that a receiver would have been appointed. The company eventually was put into receivership in 1974.

B   The company claimed damages for negligent breach of contract against the auditors. The judge at first instance found that, but for the breach of contract by the auditors, the company would have gone into receivership in 1971, and it had suffered damage in the sum of $145m, the increase over the period 1971–1974 in the deficiency of the company's assets. By a majority, the Court of Appeal allowed the appeal, holding that there was no causal connection between the breach of contract and the damage. The judges expressed

C   their opinions as to the proper principle of causation in different language, although in the event the dissent by Glass JA was as to the application of the facts to the law rather than as to the principle, on which he was in a majority. He said at p. 591:

> '. . . the evidence here in my view supports the common sense conclusion that but for this company's continuance in trade in the same line of business, under the same management in breach of the same ratios it would not have run down its
> D   assets. Being in trade when it should have been in receivership was a cause of the $57m loss it suffered. If an unseaworthy vessel puts to sea because marine surveyors have negligently certified it, its loss will also be due to the marine hazards which cause it to founder. But it is equally true that its loss could not have occurred but for the fact that it put to sea as a result of a negligent survey.'

The fact that Glass JA did not agree with his colleagues in the result shows that, inevitably, not all judges regard common sense as driving them to the same conclusion.

E   In his judgment, Mahoney JA said at p. 604:

> 'In the broadest sense, that loss was a result of the defendants' breach. If a defendant promises to direct me where I should go and, at a cross-roads, directs me to the left road rather than the right road, what happens to me on the left road is, in a sense, the result of what the defendant has done. If I slip on that road, if it collapses under me, or if, because I am there, a car driving down that road and not
> F   down the right road strikes me, my loss is, in a sense, the result of the fact that I have been directed to the left road and not the right road.

> But, in my opinion, it is not everything which is a result in this broad sense which is accepted as a result for this purpose in the law. Thus, if, being on the left road, I slip and fall, the fact alone that it was the defendant's direction, in breach of contract, which put me there will not, without more, make the defendant liable for
> G   my broken leg. I say 'without more': if there be added to the breach the fact that, e.g., the left road was known to be dangerous in that respect he may, of course, be liable. But, in relation to losses of that kind, the fact that the breach has initiated one train of events rather than another is not, or at least may not be, sufficient in itself. It is necessary, to determine whether there is a causal relationship, to look more closely at the breach and what (to use a neutral term) flowed from it.

H   In the present case, the company's loss resulted from the defendants' breach in the sense that the course of events vis-à-vis the company would have gone in a different direction had it not been for that breach. But that, I think, is not, or is not necessarily, sufficient. Thus, the breach allowed the company to continue in business. If its net worth had fallen because, e.g., the main buildings it owned had been destroyed by an earthquake, I do not think that loss would have been causally related to the breach which let the company continue in business.

A

. . .

It may sometimes be argued that a breach exposes the plaintiff to particular dangers and that if what happens subsequent to the breach is loss from a danger of that kind, the loss may be seen as a result of the breach: see, e.g., the reference to arguments of this kind in the preface to the second edition of Hart & Honore at p. lviii. But, again, I do not think that this argument is open to the company. To allow the company to continue in existence is, in a sense, to expose it to all the dangers of being in existence. But allowing the company to remain in existence does not, without more, cause losses from anything which is, in that sense, a danger incident to existing. There are some dangers loss from which will raise causal considerations and some will not. But the company's case has been conducted on the basis that there is not to be – and there has in fact not been – a detailed examination of what particular things caused the fall in net value of the company between 1971 and 1974 and the nature for this purpose of them.

B

C

In the end, the company's case has been that the loss it claims was caused by the breach because, and because alone, the breach allowed the company to continue in existence. Some of the incidents flowing from its existence during 1971–74 may be the results of the breach; some, e.g., those flowing from earthquakes or the like, will not be. But the basis of the plaintiffs' claim has been such that no inquiry is to be or has been pursued, for this purpose, into what in fact happened, why and the relationship of what happened to the breach. I do not think that that is enough to establish a causal relationship.'

D

At p. 624, McHugh JA said:

'In the proved circumstances of this case, I do not think that the issue of the certificates by the auditors constituted a cause of Cambridge's loss of $145m. The existence of a company, as counsel for Cambridge conceded, cannot be a cause of its trading losses or profits. Yet that is what the case for Cambridge comes to. Except in the sense that the issue of the certificates induced the trustee not to take action against Cambridge and thereby permitted Cambridge to exist as a trader, the issuing of the certificates was not one of the conditions which were jointly necessary to produce the loss of $145m. To assert in these circumstances that the issue of the certificates was a cause of the loss in my opinion is to depart from the common sense notion of causation which the common law champions.'

E

F

It will be seen that all the judges considered that the 'but for' test was not enough, and that two of them expressly relied on the application of common sense.

The recent decision of the High Court of Australia in *March v Stramare* (1991) 171 CLR 506 was in an action in tort. The plaintiff claimed damages for injuries sustained when, driving his car at night, he ran into the back of a truck owned by the defendants which their driver had parked at a position where it straddled the centre line of a six-lane road. The defendants alleged that their driver's negligence did not cause the accident. A majority in the Supreme Court of South Australia had held that the defendants were not liable. The High Court allowed the appeal. Four of the five members of the Court took the view that the 'but for' test was not a definitive test of causation in tort.

G

In his judgment, Sir Anthony Mason CJ said at p. 515:

'The common law tradition is that what was the cause of a particular occurrence is a question of fact which 'must be determined by applying common sense to the facts of each particular case', in the words of Lord Reid: *Stapley* [1953] AC at 681.

H

. . .

It is beyond question that in many situations the question whether Y is a consequence of X is a question of fact. And, prior to the introduction of the

A   legislation providing for apportionment of liability, the need to identify what was the 'effective cause' of the relevant damage reinforced the notion that a question of causation was one of fact and, as such, to be resolved by the application of common sense.

B   Commentators subdivide the issue of causation in a given case into two questions: the question of causation in fact – to be determined by the application of the 'but for' test – and the further question whether a defendant is in law responsible for damage which his or her negligence has played some part in producing: see, e.g. Fleming, *Law of Torts*, 7th ed. (1987), pp 172–173; Hart and Honoré, *Causation in the Law*, 2nd ed. (1985), p 110. It is said that, in determining this second question, considerations of policy have a prominent part to play, as do accepted value judgments: see Fleming, p 173. However, this approach to the issue of causation (a) places rather too much weight on the 'but for' test to the exclusion of the 'common sense' approach which the common law has always favoured; and (b) implies, or seems to imply, that value judgment has, or should have, no part to play in resolving causation as an issue of fact. As Dixon CJ, Fullagar and Kitto JJ remarked in *Fitzgerald v Penn* . . . 'it is all ultimately a matter of common sense' and 'in truth the conception in question (i.e. causation) is not susceptible of reduction to a satisfactory formula.'

C

D   In the court below, only one authority was cited to the deputy judge on this issue, and that was more concerned with remoteness of damage than with causation. Without the benefit of reference to the authorities to which we have been referred, he concluded:

'Trading losses . . . are losses which by their nature do not flow from whatever statement appears in the accounts as to the state of the company's assets or profits; they flow from trading. If a company trades, it may suffer losses or it may enjoy profits, and those losses or gains depend upon a number of factors such as the prudence of the trading, market conditions, and so on. It does not seem to me that trading losses as such can possibly be attributed to statements as to the status of the company before that trading ever takes place.

E

. . .

It seems to me that, for the reasons I have given . . . trading losses as such cannot arguably be said to be damages which flow from the auditors' negligence.'

F   For those reasons he found for the defendants on this issue.

The passages which I have cited from the speeches in the *Monarch Steamship* case make it clear that if a breach of contract by a defendant is to be held to entitle the plaintiff to claim damages, it must first be held to have been an 'effective' or 'dominant' cause of his loss. The test in *Quinn v Burch Bros*, that it is necessary to distinguish between a breach of contract which causes a loss to the plaintiff and one which merely gives the opportunity for him to sustain the loss, is helpful but still leaves the question to be answered, 'How does the court decide whether the breach of duty was the cause of the loss or merely the occasion for the loss?'

G

The answer in my judgment is supplied by the Australian decisions to which I have referred, which I hold to represent the law of England as well as of Australia, in relation to a breach of a duty imposed on a defendant whether by contract or in tort in a situation analogous to breach of contract. The answer in the end is 'By the application of the court's common sense'.

H

Doing my best to apply this test, I have no doubt that the deputy judge arrived at a correct conclusion on this issue. The breach of duty by the defendants gave the opportunity to Galoo and Gamine to incur and to continue to incur trading losses; it did not cause those trading losses, in the sense in which the word 'cause' is used in law.

For these reasons I would dismiss the appeals by the first plaintiff, Galoo, and the second plaintiff, Gamine.

Facts alleged relevant to Hillsdown

I go on to consider the cross-appeal and the appeal by Hillsdown under the remaining heads. This requires further reference to the proposed amended statement of claim.

In para. 12 and 13, Hillsdown plead that the defendants sent a copy of the accounts of Gamine to Hillsdown accompanied by a letter dated 25 March 1987, which said, as did the audited accounts, that the net profits for the year ended 31 December 1988 were £650,944 and the shareholders' funds, £1,809,004. The shareholders' funds of Galoo at 31 December 1986 were said to be £3,486,518. It is then pleaded that at the time of making the representations in the letter and when they audited the accounts of Galoo and Gamine for the year ended 31 December 1986, BGM knew of the existence and terms of the acquisition agreement. They accordingly knew that the purchase price under that agreement was to be calculated by reference to the accounts of Galoo and Gamine for the year ended 31 December 1986 as a multiple of the net profits of Gamine for that year, and that if the shareholders' funds in Galoo were less than £2,150,000 the vendors would be in breach of warranty towards Hillsdown. The pleading alleges that BGM owed duties in tort to Hillsdown in making the representations referred to in the letter, and in auditing the accounts of Galoo and Gamine for the years 1986–1990, to exercise reasonable skill and care. It is further alleged that the defendants owed duties in tort to Hillsdown in auditing the accounts of Gamine for each of the years 1986–1990 as shareholders in Gamine, after Hillsdown acquired the 51 per cent shareholding.

Paragraph 9A of the draft amended statement of claim amplifies this last pleading as follows:

'Further (and in amplification of paragraph 9(ii) hereof) the defendants knew or ought to have known from the date of the acquisition agreement onwards that:

(i) The third plaintiffs were the owners of and the source of support for the first and second plaintiffs.

(ii) The third plaintiffs by virtue of the provisions of the shareholders' agreement made on 25 February 1987 could neither replace the defendants as auditors of the second plaintiffs nor sell the assets of the second plaintiffs other than at full market value nor wind up the second plaintiffs until after the acquisition by the third plaintiffs of the remainder of the shares in the second plaintiffs.

(iii) The third plaintiffs were obliged, at the option of the remaining shareholders in the second plaintiffs, to acquire their shares in the second plaintiffs at a price to be fixed by reference to accounts which could be audited only by the defendants.

(iv) That the third plaintiffs were year by year to the knowledge of the defendants advancing substantial sums to the second plaintiffs and supporting that company in reliance on the defendants' work . . . The third plaintiffs will say that such knowledge is shown by, inter alia,

(a) In each of the years 1987–1990 the defendants requested and obtained from the third plaintiffs letters of comfort in respect of the third plaintiffs' support of and continued lending to the second plaintiffs.

(b) The accounts packs for each of the years 1987–1990 contained details of the said support and lending which details were supplied by the defendants.

A   And in the premises that:

       (v) The third plaintiffs were using the defendants' accounts and audit work in their consideration of the existing lending to, and/or the making of, further advances to the first and second plaintiffs.'

There is a further alternative pleading that if the defendants were not in breach in relation to the auditing of the accounts when they sent the letter of 25 March 1987, they
B   were in breach after 6 August 1987 and 16 September 1987 when the accounts of Galoo and Gamine were respectively signed.

Paragraph 18 pleads that the representations made by BGM in their letter of 25 March 1987 were false in that Gamine made a net loss, not a net profit, in the year ended 31 December 1986, that at that date the shareholders' funds of Gamine were in deficit and that the shareholders' funds of Galoo were a mere £10,000, not the £3,486,518 shown in
C   the accounts and referred to in the letter.

Paragraph 19 gives particulars of the alleged negligence of BGM in auditing the accounts of Galoo and Gamine for each of the years 1985–1990.

Paragraph 20 reads:

       'If the defendants had performed their duties properly and with reasonable care and skill the accounts of the first and second plaintiffs for each of the years 1985–
D   1990 and/or the defendants' reports of those accounts would have shown that those companies, instead of being profitable and having substantial assets, were in fact unprofitable and worthless. In these circumstances:

       (i) The insolvency of the first and second plaintiffs would have been revealed and those companies would have ceased to trade immediately;

       (i) (a) . . .
E

       (ii) The third plaintiffs would not have entered into the acquisition agreement and/or would not have made any of the payments which they in fact made thereunder;

       (iii) The third plaintiffs would not have made or continued to make the advances to the first and second plaintiffs which they in fact made between March 1987 and January 1993 in the total amount of £30,649,943;
F

       (iv) The third plaintiffs would not have entered into the supplemental agreement and/or would not have paid the sum of £967,000 thereunder or any part thereof and would not have paid Michael Sanders the sum of £30,000.'

The loss and damage sustained by Hillsdown is alleged to be the total of:

(1)   the purchase consideration under the acquisition agreement, approx £1.726m;

G   (2)   advances made totalling £30,649,943, against which credit will be given for the price received on the sale of Gamine; and

(3)   the amounts paid under the supplemental agreement and to Mr Sanders, £997,000, of which £910,000 has been recovered, leaving a loss of £87,000.

Economic loss in tort

H
     Before turning to the issues raised in the appeal by Hillsdown and the cross-appeal by the defendants, it is necessary to consider the effect of recent authorities on the circumstances in which a plaintiff may recover damages for purely economic loss in tort. The two major decisions are those of the House of Lords in *Caparo Industries plc v Dickman* [1990] 2 AC 605; [1990] BCC 164 and of this court in *Morgan Crucible Co v Hill Samuel & Co* [1991] Ch 295; [1991] BCC 82.

In *Caparo Industries* the plaintiffs, who already owned some shares in another   A
company, Fidelity plc, bought further shares after the publication to them as
shareholders of, and in reliance upon, the audited accounts of Fidelity for the year ending
31 March 1984. The defendants had audited the accounts. The issue was whether the
defendants owed the plaintiffs a duty of care in tort the breach of which entitled the
plaintiffs to sue for damages. The Court of Appeal by a majority found in favour of the
plaintiffs, but the House of Lords unanimously allowed the defendants' appeal. Giving
the judgment of this court in *Morgan Crucible*, Slade LJ described the effect of the   B
decision in *Caparo Industries* in the following words (at p. 86D):

> 'The House of Lords reversed this decision, holding in effect that in certifying a
> company's accounts for the purpose of the *Companies Act* 1985, an auditor owes
> no duty of care to a potential takeover bidder, whether or not he is already a
> shareholder of the company. It was held that foreseeability, no matter how high,
> that a potential bidder might rely on the audited accounts did not suffice to found   C
> a duty of care, since there was no sufficient relationship of proximity between
> auditor and potential bidder.'

In his speech in *Caparo Industries*, Lord Bridge referred to *Candler v Crane, Christmas
& Co* [1951] 2 KB 164, *Hedley Byrne & Co Ltd v Heller* [1964] AC 465 in which Denning
LJ's dissenting judgment in *Candler v Crane, Christmas* was approved, and *Smith v Eric
S Bush* [1990] 1 AC 831. Lord Bridge continued at p. 171E: D

> 'The salient feature of all these cases is that the defendant giving advice or
> information was fully aware of the nature of the transaction which the plaintiff
> had in contemplation, knew that the advice or information would be
> communicated to him directly or indirectly and knew that it was very likely that
> the plaintiff would rely on that advice or information in deciding whether or not
> to engage in the transaction in contemplation. In these circumstances the defendant
> could clearly be expected, subject always to the effect of any disclaimer of   E
> responsibility, specifically to anticipate that the plaintiff would rely on the advice
> or information given by the defendant for the very purpose for which he did in the
> event rely on it. So also the plaintiff, subject again to the effect of any disclaimer,
> would in that situation reasonably suppose that he was entitled to rely on the
> advice or information communicated to him for the very purpose for which he
> required it. The situation is entirely different where a statement is put into more or   F
> less general circulation and may foreseeably be relied on by strangers to the maker
> of the statement for any one of a variety of different purposes which the maker of
> the statement has no specific reason to anticipate. To hold the maker of the
> statement to be under a duty of care in respect of the accuracy of the statement to
> all and sundry for any purpose for which they may choose to rely on it is not only
> to subject him, in the classic words of Cardozo CJ to 'liability in an indeterminate
> amount for an indeterminate time to an indeterminate class:' (*Ultramares*   G
> *Corporation v Touche* (1931) 174 NE 441 at p. 444); it is also to confer on the world
> at large a quite unwarranted entitlement to appropriate for their own purposes the
> benefit of the expert knowledge or professional expertise attributed to the maker
> of the statement. Hence, looking only at the circumstances of these decided cases
> where a duty of care in respect of negligent statements has been held to exist, I
> should expect to find that the 'limit or control mechanism . . . imposed upon the   H
> liability of a wrongdoer towards those who have suffered economic damage in
> consequence of his negligence', rested in the necessity to prove, in this category of
> the tort of negligence, as an essential ingredient of the 'proximity' between the
> plaintiff and the defendant, that the defendant knew that his statement would be
> communicated to the plaintiff, either as an individual or as a member of an
> identifiable class, specifically in connection with a particular transaction or

A transactions of a particular kind (e.g. in a prospectus inviting investment) and that the plaintiff would be very likely to rely on it for the purpose of deciding whether or not to enter upon that transaction or upon a transaction of that kind.'

Lord Bridge then quoted the passage from the dissenting judgment of Denning LJ in *Candler v Crane, Christmas & Co* [1951] 2 KB 164, starting at p. 179. I repeat this classic statement, familiar though it is.

B 'Let me now be constructive and suggest the circumstances in which I say that a duty to use care in statement does exist apart from a contract in that behalf. First, what persons are under such duty? My answer is those persons such as accountants, surveyors, valuers and analysts, whose profession and occupation it is to examine books, accounts, and other things, and to make reports on which other people – other than their clients – rely in the ordinary course of business.

C . . .

Secondly, to whom do these professional people owe this duty? I will take accountants, but the same reasoning applies to the others. They owe the duty, of course, to their employer or client; and also I think to any third person to whom they themselves show the accounts, or to whom they know their employer is going to show the accounts, so as to induce him to invest money or take some other action on them. But I do not think the duty can be extended still further so as to
D include strangers of whom they have heard nothing and to whom their employer without their knowledge may choose to show their accounts. Once the accountants have handed their accounts to their employer they are not, as a rule, responsible for what he does with them without their knowledge or consent.

. . .

The test of proximity in these cases is: did the accountants know that the accounts
E were required for submission to the plaintiff and use by him?

. . .

Thirdly, to what transactions does the duty of care extend? It extends, I think, only to those transactions for which the accountants knew their accounts were required. For instance, in the present case it extends to the original investment of £2,000 which the plaintiff made in reliance on the accounts, because the accountants knew
F that the accounts were required for his guidance in making that investment; but it does not extend to the subsequent £200 which he made after he had been two months with the company. This distinction, that the duty only extends to the very transaction in mind at the time, is implicit in the decided cases.

. . .

It will be noticed that I have confined the duty to cases where the accountant
G prepares his accounts and makes his report for the guidance of the very person in the very transaction in question. That is sufficient for the decision of this case. I can well understand that it would be going too far to make an accountant liable to any person in the land who chooses to rely on the accounts in matters of business, for that would expose him to 'liability in an indeterminate amount for an indeterminate time to an indeterminate class': see *Ultramares Corporation v Touche*
H per Cardozo CJ. Whether he would be liable if he prepared his accounts for the guidance of a specific class of persons in a specific class of transaction, I do not say. I should have thought he might be, just as the analyst and lift inspector would be liable in the instances I have given earlier. It is perhaps worth mentioning that Parliament has intervened to make the professional man liable for negligent reports given for the purposes of a prospectus: see ss. 40 and 43 of the Companies Act 1948. That is an instance of liability for reports made for the guidance of a specific

class of persons – investors, in a specific class of transactions – applying for shares.   A
That enactment does not help, one way or the other, to show what result the
common law would have reached in the absence of such provisions; but it does
show what result it ought to reach.

My conclusion is that a duty to use care in statement is recognised by English law,
and that its recognition does not create any dangerous precedent when it is
remembered that it is limited in respect of the persons by whom and to whom it is   B
owed and the transactions to which it applies.'

Lord Bridge commented:

'It seems to me that this masterly analysis, if I may say so with respect, requires
little, if any, amplification or modification in the light of later authority and is
particularly apt to point the way to the right conclusion in the present appeal.'

Lord Oliver said at p. 184H: C

'Furthermore, it is clear that "knowledge" on the part of the respondents embraced
not only actual knowledge but such knowledge as would be attributed to a
reasonable person placed as the respondents were placed. What can be deduced
from the *Hedley Byrne* case, therefore, is that the necessary relationship between
the maker of a statement or giver of advice ("the adviser") and the recipient who
acts in reliance upon it ("the advisee") may typically be held to exist where (1) the   D
advice is required for a purpose, whether particularly specified or generally
described, which is made known, either actually or inferentially, to the adviser at
the time when the advice is given; (2) the adviser knows, either actually or
inferentially, that his advice will be communicated to the advisee, either specifically
or as a member of an ascertainable class, in order that it should be used by the
advisee for that purpose; (3) it is known either actually or inferentially, that the
advice so communicated is likely to be acted upon by the advisee for that purpose   E
without independent inquiry, and (4) it is so acted upon by the advisee to his
detriment. That is not, of course, to suggest that these conditions are either
conclusive or exclusive, but merely that the actual decision in the case does not
warrant any broader propositions.'

Lord Jauncey said at p. 203H:

'If the statutory accounts are prepared and distributed for certain limited purposes,   F
can there nevertheless be imposed upon auditors an additional common law duty
to individual shareholders who choose to use them for another purpose without
the prior knowledge of the auditors? The answer must be no. Use for that other
purpose would no longer be use for the "very transaction" which Denning LJ in
the *Candler* case [1951] 2 KB 164 at p. 183 regarded as determinative of the scope
of any duty of care. Only where the auditor was aware that the individual   G
shareholder was likely to rely on the accounts for a particular purpose such as his
present or future investment in or lending to the company would a duty of care
arise. Such a situation does not obtain in the present case.'

A different conclusion was reached in *Morgan Crucible Co plc v Hill Samuel Co Ltd*
[1991] BCC 82.

The plaintiffs in that action made a bid for another company, 'FCE'. The initial bid   H
was made in reliance upon the accounts of FCE which had been audited by the second
defendant, Judkins. Further statements were made by FCE and its advisers in defence
documents seeking to defeat the plaintiffs' takeover bid. The plaintiffs increased their bid
and succeeded in purchasing FCE. Thereafter the plaintiffs began the action alleging that
the audited accounts and the post-bid statements which in part referred to those accounts
were all misleading, and that FCE was worth much less than they had paid for its shares.

A   Hoffmann J, following the decision in *Caparo Industries*, held that the claim, whether as originally pleaded or as proposed to be amended, was bound to fail. He therefore disallowed the amendment ([1990] BCC 686).

The Court of Appeal allowed the plaintiffs' appeal, so far as the post-bid statements were concerned. I quote three passages from the judgment of the court delivered by Slade LJ: at p. 90H:

B   'As we read the decision in *Caparo*, what their Lordships regarded as the crucial, fatal weakness in the plaintiff's case, which negatived the existence of a relationship of proximity, was the fact that the relevant statement by the auditors *had not been given for the purpose for which the plaintiff had relied on it.*'

At p. 92B, in a passage dealing with the case against FCE's directors, Slade LJ said:

C   'Their Lordships in *Caparo* regarded the purpose of the statutory requirement for an audit of public companies under the (Companies Act 1985) as the making of a report to enable shareholders to exercise their class rights in general meeting – not as extending to the provision of information to assist shareholders or others as to the making of decisions as to the future investment in the company. These, as we read the decision in *Caparo*, were the essential elements of its ratio by which the plaintiff's claim on the facts of that case were held to be untenable.

D   In these circumstances, we are of the opinion that it is at least arguable that the present case can be distinguished from *Caparo* on its assumed facts. On such facts, each of the directors, in making the relevant representations, was aware that Morgan Crucible would rely on them for the purpose of deciding whether or not to make an increased bid, *and intended that they should*; this was one of the purposes of the defence documents and the representations contained therein. Morgan Crucible duly did rely on them for this purpose. In these circumstances,

E   subject to questions of justice and reasonableness, we think it plainly arguable that there was a relationship of proximity between the directors and Morgan Crucible sufficient to give rise to a duty of care – particularly bearing in mind that, while Morgan Crucible had their own independent advisers, much of the information on which the accounts and profit forecast were based was presumably available to the defendants alone.'

F   –and at p. 96D, dealing with the case against Judkins, the auditors:

       'Once again, it may be of critical importance for the trial judge to consider in the context of duty of care and proximity whether Morgan Crucible could reasonably have regarded themselves as persons to whom the relevant representations were directly or indirectly addressed. For present purposes, however, we think it will suffice to say that in our judgment Morgan Crucible, on their proposed pleadings

G   and the assumed facts, have established an arguable case as to duty of care for the same reasons *mutatis mutandis* as those relating to the directors in the case of the financial statements and the same reasons *mutatis mutandis* as those relating to the directors and Hill Samuel in the case of the profit forecast.'

It follows from that decision that an accountant and auditor of a company may owe a duty of care to a takeover bidder if he approves a statement which confirms the accuracy of accounts which he has previously audited or which contains a forecast of future profits,

H   when he has expressly been informed that the bidder will rely on the accounts and forecast for the purpose of deciding whether to make an increased bid, and intends that the bidder should so rely.

We were also referred to decisions of Millett J in *Al Saudi Banque v Clark Pixley* [1990] Ch 313; (1989) 5 BCC 822 and of Mervyn Davies J in *Al-Nakib Investments (Jersey) Ltd v Longcroft* [1990] 1 WLR 1390; [1990] BCC 517.

In *Al Saudi Banque* the judgment was given on 28 July 1989, after the decision of this   A
court in *Caparo Industries* but more than six months before the House of Lords gave its
decision in that case. Al Saudi was one of ten banks which made loans to a company.
The defendants were the company's auditors, who had audited the annual accounts for
three years before the company was compulsorily wound-up, with an estimated deficiency
of £8.6m. The banks, in the action, alleged that the defendants ought reasonably to have
foreseen that the banks would rely on the accuracy of the auditors' reports in deciding
whether to continue, renew or increase their advances to the company, and thus that the   B
defendants owed the banks duties of care of which they were in breach. The breach was
that the reports did not give a full and accurate account of the company's affairs.

Millett J held that the banks were not in the position of shareholders, to whom the
auditors owed a statutory duty to report; and that since the auditors did not know that
the company intended to supply the audited accounts to the banks they were under no
such duty of care. Lord Bridge in *Caparo Industries* at p. 173E described Millett J's   C
rejection of the bank's claim as emphatic and convincing, Lord Oliver referred to Millett
J's judgment with approval and Lord Jauncey said he had no doubt it was correctly
decided.

Al-Nakib Investments, which was decided after the House of Lords had given the
decision in *Caparo Industries*, was an application of the principles derived from that
decision, and I therefore do not find it necessary to make more detailed reference to it.   D

The distinction between the set of facts which it was held in *Morgan Crucible* would
suffice to establish a duty of care owed by auditors from those facts which it was held in
Caparo Industries would not have this effect is inevitably a fine one. In my judgment that
distinction may be expressed as follows. A mere foreseeability that a potential bidder
may rely on the audited accounts does not impose on the auditor a duty of care to the
bidder, but if the auditor is expressly made aware that a particular identified bidder will
rely on the audited accounts or other statements approved by the auditor, and intends   E
that the bidder should so rely, the auditor will be under a duty of care to the bidder for
the breach of which he may be liable.

I therefore turn to apply these principles to the issues in Hillsdown's appeal and BGM's
cross-appeal.

Issue 2: Loss resulting from the original purchase by Hillsdown of the shares in Gamine   F

This is the subject of the defendants' cross-appeal.

In his judgment, the deputy judge referred to the terms of the acquisition agreement,
which was permissible even though he was not entitled to refer to evidence, because that
agreement was specifically referred to (though the whole of it was not included by
reference) in the statement of claim. The deputy judge also referred to, but apparently
did not rely upon, some correspondence. The statement of claim referred to (though did   G
not quote in full) all or almost all the relevant terms of the acquisition agreement.
Paragraph 10 summarised inter alia the following clauses in the agreement:

> '3.1 The purchase consideration . . . shall be such sum as equals 5.2 times the net
> profits of (Gamine) as reflected in the completion accounts, which term
> includes the audited accounts of Galoo and Gamine for the year ended 31
> December 1986.   H

> 4.1 The parties shall jointly procure as soon as practicable and in any event
> within 90 days of the date of completion the preparation of the completion
> accounts which shall be . . . audited by (BGM).

> 4.3 (BGM) shall circulate the net profits and the shareholders' funds from the
> completion accounts and shall deliver to the vendors and (Hillsdown) copies

A   of the completion accounts and a statement setting out the net profits and
         shareholders' funds.'

In addition the statement of claim set out the terms of a letter written by BGM to
Hillsdown dated 25 March 1987 which accompanied what were described as 'A copy of
the consolidated accounts of the above company for the year ended 31 December 1986'.
As I have already said, this was the letter in which BGM informed Hillsdown that the net
B   profits of Gamine for the year ended 31 December 1986 were £650,944 and the
shareholders' funds £1,809,004, and that the shareholders' funds of Galoo at the same
date were £3,486,518. It is clear that the letter constituted a representation that not merely
what was said in the letter itself but also the audited accounts gave an accurate account
of the state of the company's affairs.

Paragraph 13 of the statement of claim expressly pleads that:

C   'At the time of making the above representations and when they audited the
         accounts of (Galoo and Gamine) for the year ended 31 December 1986, the
         defendants knew of the existence and terms of the acquisition agreement. They
         accordingly knew that:

         (i) the amount of the purchase consideration payable by (Hillsdown) to the
             vendors under the acquisition agreement was to be calculated by reference
D   to the accounts of (Galoo and Gamine) for the year ended 31 December
             1986 and as a multiple of the net profits of (Gamine) for that year as
             calculated and stated by BGM; and

         (ii) if the net profits as shown by the completion accounts were less than
              £500,000 and/or if the shareholders' funds in (Galoo) were less
              than £2,150,000 and if the capital and reserves in Gamine were
E   less than £1,080,000 the vendors would be in breach of warranty towards
              Hillsdown.'

When dealing with this issue in his judgment, the deputy judge said:

         'It is therefore plain that the 1986 audited accounts were to be prepared not only
         for the purposes of the audit but also for the purpose of fixing the purchase
         consideration under this agreement. It is common ground that the defendants
F   knew of the terms of this agreement and that the accounts that they were to submit
         to the purchasers were to be for the purposes of those provisions.

         In those circumstances, the case is immediately, on its face, taken outside the
         Caparo principles by reason of those matters.'

In my view that reasoning is entirely correct.

G   However, two further arguments were advanced to the deputy judge and are now
advanced to us by Mr Hunter for BGM as to why nevertheless this part of the plaintiffs'
claim should also be struck out.

The first point made by Mr Hunter is that the accounts submitted to Hillsdown by
BGM with their letter of 25 March 1987 were no more than draft accounts. The final
accounts were not approved or signed on behalf of the respective companies until after
H   Hillsdown's purchase of the shares in Gamine had been completed. The deputy judge
said of this point:

         'True it is that they were or may have been draft accounts, but it is plain to me that
         they were being treated as the accounts submitted for the purposes of cl. 4 of the
         agreement . . . and it has not been suggested that any subsequent accounts were
         supplied for that purpose.

Therefore, to put it no higher, it is plainly arguable (and indeed it appears to me to   A
be the case as I have said) that those accounts were treated as completion accounts,
whether they were, in fact, draft accounts or not.'

I note that the statement of claim does not say that these accounts were draft accounts.
The letter of 25 March 1987 describes them as 'The consolidated accounts of the above
company for year ended 31 December 1986'. It would thus be necessary to introduce
evidence to show that they were draft accounts. But quite apart from that, it is to my   B
mind clearly arguable that the accounts submitted with the letter of 25 March 1987 were
intended to be the completion accounts upon which the calculation of the purchase price
of the shares then being purchased by Hillsdown was to be made. I entirely agree with
the deputy judge's conclusion on this issue.

The second point made by Mr Hunter is that cl. 4.1 of the acquisition agreement
specifically gave to Hillsdown's accountants the right to have full access to the books of
the companies and to receive full information, together with the right to review the   C
completion accounts within 28 days of their being delivered to Hillsdown. Moreover
cl. 4.6 provided a mechanism for resolving any dispute with respect to the completion
accounts or the statement referred to in cl. 4.3 by a nominated firm of chartered
accountants.

The statement of claim does not set out the full wording of these clauses of the
acquisition agreement, but clearly it would not be right to allow a pleading which had   D
not set out the full terms of a clause in an agreement to stand if, once the full terms were
taken into account, the pleading should be struck out.

In dealing with this submission, the deputy judge quoted the passage from the speech
of Lord Oliver in *Caparo Industries* which I have quoted above, in which Lord Oliver set
out the principles to be deduced from *Hedley Byrne*. To recapitulate, the third principle
Lord Oliver described as:

   E

'it is known either actually or inferentially that the advice so communicated
is likely to be acted upon by the advisee for that purpose *without independent
enquiry . . .*'

Mr Hunter relied on this passage for the proposition that the opportunity provided by
cl. 4.1 of the acquisition agreement for Hillsdown's accountants to make such
independent enquiry meant that there could be no duty of care on BGM.

   F

The deputy judge said of this submission:

'Although that may be right and may prove to be right, it seems to me that the
completion accounts were being prepared specifically for the purpose of
determining the amount of the purchase consideration. The function of the
purchasers' accountants was not necessarily precisely similar to that of the
defendants'. It may require evidence as to what was the contemplated function of
the purchasers' accountants and what the contemplated "review" would have   G
involved, but it seems to me, to put it no higher, well arguable that the review
which the purchasers' accountants were to carry out would not be the same exercise
as the preparation of the completion accounts which the defendants were to carry
out. Clearly the purchasers' accountants would not, for example, be in as good a
position as the defendants would have been to calculate the value of the stock as
at 31 December 1986, which date by then would, of course, necessarily have passed.
It may be that the evidence will reveal that matters which would or should have   H
been discovered by the defendants on an audit close to that date could not have
been apparent to the reviewing accountants some time later.

This is, I think, a matter which requires evidence and, in those circumstances, I am
not prepared to strike out the claims so far as they are based upon losses flowing
from the payment of the consideration under the acquisition agreement.'

A   I entirely agree with that reasoning. For those reasons I would dismiss the cross-appeal.

Issue 3: The loss to Hillsdown resulting from making the loans to Gamine

It will be remembered that para. 9A of the amended statement of claim specifically pleads that:

B   'The defendants knew or ought to have known from the date of the acquisition agreement onwards that . . .

   (iii) (Hillsdown) were obliged, at the option of the remaining shareholders in (Gamine) to acquire their shares in (Gamine) at a price to be fixed by reference to accounts which could be audited only by (BGM).

   . . .

C   (v) (Hillsdown) were using (BGM's) accounts and audit work in their consideration of the existing lending to and/or the making of further advances to (Galoo and Gamine).'

It will be seen that the statement of claim does not plead that BGM knew that Hillsdown would rely on the audited accounts for the purpose of making further loans, nor that BGM intended that Hillsdown should so rely.

The deputy judge said that in his view the situation pleaded was indistinguishable from D   that contemplated in *Caparo Industries* and which was before Millett J in *Al Saudi Banque*.

He set out the argument advanced to him by Mr Bennett, for the plaintiffs, that BGM knew that the purpose of the acquisition by Hillsdown of the first tranche of shares was the advancement of the business of Galoo and Gamine, that loans and advances were likely to be made, and that as auditors, they would know in any particular year that E   loans had been made in the preceding years. He therefore argued that one of the purposes of auditing the accounts was the vouching of the fact that the companies were solvent.

The deputy judge said of that argument:

'Those matters as it seems to me, go to foreseeability and only to foreseeability and they do not establish the degree of proximity that is, on the authorities, required. At the end of the day, it seems to me that it is not shown to be pleaded that any particular loan was made in reliance upon a particular set of accounts or that the F   defendants promulgated any set of accounts for the purpose of any specific loan or indeed for the purpose of loans at all, and the mere fact of the knowledge that loans would or might be made is not sufficient to create that degree of proximity. Accordingly, the cause of action in respect of the loans is in my judgment obviously unsustainable.'

On this issue also I agree with the deputy judge. As I have said, the statement of claim G   does not plead the facts which in *Morgan Crucible* were held to be those necessary in order to establish a duty of care, namely that the auditor knew that the intending lender would rely on the accounts approved by the auditors for the purpose of deciding whether to make the loans or increase loans already made, and intended that the intending lender should so rely. In other words I agree with the deputy judge that the statement of claim does not set out facts which establish a duty of care in this respect on the principles H   derived from *Caparo Industries*, *Morgan Crucible* and the earlier decision of Millett J in *Al Saudi Banque*.

Issue 4: The amounts paid under the supplemental agreement for the further 44.3 per cent of the shares in Gamine, and the £30,000 paid to Mr Sanders for loss of office

So far as is relevant to this claim, the statement of claim pleads in para. 9(ii) that BGM owed duties in tort to Hillsdown, as shareholders of Gamine, in auditing Gamine's

accounts for each of the years 1986–1990. The same duty of care is again pleaded in   A
para. 14. Paragraph 11 reads:

'The acquisition agreement further provided . . . that, if the vendors so elected,
(Hillsdown) would be required to purchase the remaining shares in (Gamine) in
annual tranches and that the price payable for each such tranche of shares was to
be calculated by reference to the pre-tax earnings of (Gamine) for the relevant year
as shown by the accounts in that year, which accounts were to be prepared and   B
audited by the defendants.'

The same point is made in para. 9A(iii) which I have set out above.

Finally, in para. 20(iv) it is pleaded that Hillsdown would not have entered into the
supplemental agreement and would not have paid the sum of £967,000 thereunder or any
part thereof and would not have paid Mr Michael Sanders the sum of £30,000 if BGM
had performed their duties properly and with reasonable professional care and skill.   C

It should be noted that the purchase by Hillsdown of 44.3 per cent of the shares in
Gamine under the supplemental agreement was a purchase under a new agreement, not
in accordance with the provision in the acquisition agreement under which Hillsdown
could be required to purchase the remaining shares in Gamine in annual tranches. If the
original terms of the acquisition agreement had been followed, the price for the annual
tranches would specifically have been calculated by reference to the earnings of Gamine
for relevant years, as shown by the audited accounts. If that had been the case, then the   D
purchase of the remaining shares would probably have been in precisely the same position
as the purchase of the original 51 per cent of the shares. In other words, it might then
well be arguable that the statement of claim did disclose a duty of care owed by BGM to
Hillsdown, which at least would be dependent upon the determination of facts. Thus had
the original agreement been followed, it would probably not have been right to strike out
this part of the claim.   E

But it is not pleaded that BGM knew when auditing the accounts or supplying them
that Hillsdown would rely upon those accounts, nor that BGM intended that they should
so rely, for the purpose of calculating the purchase price under the supplemental
agreement. Thus again in my view the pleaded facts do not establish a duty of care on
BGM in relation to this issue.

In his judgment on this issue, the deputy judge said: F

'Had further purchases of shares taken place in accordance with those provisions,
then it is clear to me that, subject to an argument which might flow from the fact
of the audit being carried out both by the company's accountants and the
purchasers' auditors, the same considerations as applied in the case of the original
acquisition would here obtain, because the defendants would be aware that the
accounts were being relied upon for the purpose of fixing the price of the shares   G
under this agreement; not, it should be said, for the purpose of determining the
wisdom of an acquisition of shares under this agreement, but simply for the
purpose of determining the price.

However, it is common ground, and it emerges from the pleadings, that the
subsequent purchase of shares which took place in 1991 was not a purchase in
accordance with the provisions of this agreement. What happened was that in 1991
there was a different agreement entered into in relation to the sale of 44.3 per cent   H
of the shares in the second plaintiff. The consideration for the sale of those shares
was, I was told, £967,000 and it is not alleged that that sum was fixed by reference
to any formula or by reference to any set of accounts.'

I agree with the deputy judge on this issue also, and for the reasons I have briefly
explained I would therefore uphold his judgment in relation to this issue.

A   **Conclusion**

In summary therefore I conclude that the deputy judge's decision on each of the issues before him was correct. I would therefore dismiss both the appeal and the cross-appeal.

Evans LJ: I agree entirely with the judgment of Glidewell LJ and that both the appeal and the cross-appeal should be dismissed.

B
With regard to the cross-appeal, I add my express agreement with the passage from the judgment of the deputy judge which Glidewell LJ has quoted, in which he stated his reasons for holding that the claim in tort, for losses caused by reliance (as is alleged) upon representations made in or by reference to the completion accounts, at the time of the original purchase, should not be struck out. What he emphasised, rightly in my view, is that this allegation is one which should proceed to trial. It cannot be said as a matter of law at this interlocutory stage that the pleaded facts are necessarily insufficient to give

C   rise to a cause of action. To this extent, the claim may be one which has more in common with the one which was allowed to proceed to trial in *Morgan Crucible Co plc v Hill Samuel & Co Ltd* [1991] BCC 82 than with the allegation of reliance on audited accounts, prepared by a company's statutory auditors and published by them to shareholders, which was struck out in *Caparo Industries plc v Dickman* [1990] BCC 164.

Permitting this allegation to proceed to trial does not mean that the duty of care, which

D   is alleged to have been broken, will necessarily be held to have arisen from whatever facts are established by evidence at the trial. A distinction between the *Morgan Crucible* and the *Caparo* situations has to be drawn, and the line of demarcation is unclear. Whether the claim succeeds or not will depend upon not only the plaintiff proving the facts which it alleged, but also the extent to which Hillsdown's right to review the completion accounts negatives the duty of care which they allege.

E
The plaintiffs do not refer to that aspect of the matter in the amended statement of claim, and rightly so. But if the evidence shows that this 'right of intermediate examination' excludes any duty of care which might otherwise arise, the claim will fail. That is why evidence is necessary. If it was necessary to decide this issue on the basis of the plaintiffs' pleaded facts, then I would be inclined to the view that Hillsdown, who were known to be advised by an international firm of accountants and auditors and who would have full access to the company's books, would not be likely to rely upon statutory

F   accounts, draft or otherwise, prepared by the defendants, when deciding whether or not to bid for the company, and if so at what price. But no conclusion can be reached without drawing inferences in the defendants' favour, and that in my judgment it would be wrong to do at this interlocutory stage.

It is tempting to distinguish between *Caparo* and *Morgan Crucible* on the basis that in the latter, though not the former case, the identity of a particular purchaser of shares in

G   the company was known to the defendants when they represented that the company's accounts which they had prepared were fair and true. This excludes individual members of the body of existing shareholders to whom the statutory accounts are published (*Caparo*), whilst including an identified takeover bidder, as in *Morgan Crucible*. But there could be intervening situations, for example, where an existing shareholder is known to be a potential purchaser of more shares, with a view to acquiring the whole or a majority of the shares. The identification test would not provide the answer in such a case. No

H   duty of care would be owed to such a person, in my judgment, on those facts alone, because the third of the four propositions listed by Lord Oliver in *Caparo* already quoted by Glidewell LJ, as it was by Slade LJ in *Morgan Crucible*, would not be satisfied:

> 'it is known either actually or inferentially that the advice so communicated is likely to be acted upon the advisee for that purpose without independent inquiry...'

and, vitally, it could not be said that the auditors in such a case 'intended that they   **A**
should' act upon it, for that purpose (per Slade LJ [1991] BCC at p. 92C).

If it is right to confine the duty of care, meaning, to restrict the class of persons who
can recover damages if the adviser/representer is negligent, to cases where the defendant
is shown not merely to have known that the individual plaintiff would or might rely upon
the representation but to have intended that it should be relied upon, by him and for the
particular purpose and without intermediate examination, then the resulting analysis   **B**
comes close to the 'voluntary assumption of responsibility' which has been referred to in
many of the authorities but which was discounted as a test of liability in *Smith v Eric S
Bush* [1990] 1 AC 831 per Lord Griffiths at p. 862B:

> '. . . I do not think that voluntary assumption of responsibility is a helpful or
> realistic test for liability. It is true that reference is made in a number of the speeches
> in *Hedley Byrne* to the assumption of responsibility as a test of liability but it must   **C**
> be remembered that those speeches were made in the context of a case in which the
> central issue was whether a duty of care could arise when there had been an express
> disclaimer of responsibility for the accuracy of the advice . . . The phrase
> "assumption of responsibility" can only have any real meaning if it is understood
> as referring to the circumstances in which the law will deem the maker of the
> statement to have assumed responsibility to the person who acts upon the advice.'

Lord Devlin referred in *Hedley Byrne* to 'a relationship equivalent to contract' ([1964]   **D**
AC 465 at p. 530) and it is clear from Lord Griffiths' speech that the contractual analogy
cannot serve as a definition of the cases where the duty of care may arise. But if the
statement is made to an identifiable person and the maker not only knows that it will or
is likely to be acted upon but also intended that it should be acted upon *for a particular
purpose*, then these may well exemplify 'circumstances in which the law will deem the
maker of the statement to have assumed responsibility' to the person who acts upon it   **E**
(per Lord Griffiths). The 'indeterminate class of persons' referred to by Cardozo CJ is
thus reduced to an interpersonal relationship where liability may be imposed, and it
would seem unreasonable and even unjust to do so, in my view, if the defendant could
not be said to have assumed responsibility towards the plaintiff, not necessarily as an
individual, in the circumstances of the case. It is sufficient for present purposes to note
that the relationship by definition must be 'voluntary' in the sense that no consideration
proceeds from the plaintiff for the defendant's advice.   **F**

Nor is it necessary to decide finally whether the facts alleged in the amended statement
of claim are sufficient of themselves to establish liability, because that will depend also
on the significance of the plaintiffs' right to review the completion accounts, which as
already stated in my judgment is an issue fit for trial.

Waite LJ: I agree that the appeal and the cross-appeal should be dismissed for the
reasons given in both judgments.   **G**

(*Defendant's costs of the first and second plaintiffs' appeals to be taxed and paid forthwith;
defendant to have its costs of the appeal against the third plaintiff. The third plaintiff to
have its costs of the cross-appeal. Leave to appeal to the House of Lords refused*)

  H

A

Re Kingscroft Insurance Co Ltd.

Chancery Division (Companies Court).

Harman J.

Judgment delivered 21 December 1993.

B

Insolvency – Inquiry into company's dealings, etc. – Private examination – Whether order for private examination survived discharge of office-holder – Insolvency Act 1986, s. 236.

An order for the production of books and documents and for private examination obtained by provisional liquidators under s. 236 of the Insolvency Act 1986 was spent when the winding-up petitions were dismissed and the provisional liquidators ceased to hold office. Once the office had come to an end, the office-holder's powers under s. 236 ceased to be applicable and an order rightly formerly made under s. 236 had to be discharged.

C

The following cases were referred to in the judgment:

Greys Brewery Co, Re (1883) 25 ChD 400.

Oriental Credit Ltd (Company No. 003318 of 1987), Re (1987) 3 BCC 564.

Silkstone and Dodworth Coal and Iron Co, Re (1881) 19 ChD 118.

Matthew Collings (instructed by Kingsley Napley) for the applicant.

D

Lloyd Tamlyn (instructed by Freshfields) for the former provisional liquidators.

JUDGMENT

Harman J: This is an ordinary application by notice issued on 10 December 1993 pursuant to an undertaking given to me on 8 December 1993 by counsel for the applicant who is a solicitor in private practice. In order to understand the matter it is necessary to

E
set out some of the history. In early 1991 four insurance companies called Kingscroft Insurance, El Paso Insurance, Lime Street Insurance and Mutual Reinsurance each presented their own petition for winding-up on the ground of insolvency, in that the companies were unable to pay their debts as they fell due. Very shortly after the presentation of the four petitions orders were made appointing Mr Bond and Mr Hughes provisional liquidators for each of the four companies. The winding-up petitions have come before the court on several occasions over 1991, 1992 and 1993. The petitions were

F
regularly adjourned upon the ground that the provisional liquidators, who were the same distinguished chartered accountants in each company, were trying to prepare a scheme of arrangement under s. 425 of the *Companies Act* 1985 and hoped to propose the scheme to creditors for approval.

The provisional liquidators have been very active over the last three years. There has been a variety of litigation both brought against the companies in liquidation by leave of

G
the court and brought by the companies under the control of the provisional liquidators. There have also been applications by the provisional liquidators for leave to take various steps, such as obtaining orders from the Federal Bankruptcy Court in New York, of an unusual kind. All four of the companies had had their underwriting business conducted by an underwriting agent called H S Weavers & Co. That company together with its parent company has been the subject of an inspection by inspectors appointed by the Department of Trade and Industry under s. 432 of the 1985 Act. The inspectors reported

H
to the department and their report was published in September 1993.

Meanwhile in May 1992 a petition was presented to wind up Walbrook Insurance ('Walbrook') by Transit Casualty Insurance Co on the ground that Walbrook was unable to pay its debts as they fell due. Walbrook had also been a company included in the 'Weavers stamp', that is to say its underwriting affairs had been conducted by H S Weavers & Co. In the circumstances an application was made to the court to appoint the

same distinguished chartered accountants as provisional liquidators of Walbrook and   A
Mr Bond and Mr Hughes were so appointed. The winding-up petition in respect of
Walbrook was also stood over from time to time since it was hoped by the petitioner,
and by the provisional liquidators, that Walbrook's affairs could be subject to the
proposed scheme of arrangement. Since May 1992 the five insurance companies the
subject of the pending petitions have been known to those dealing with their affairs, and
to the court, as the 'KWELM' companies, that word being an acronym of the five initial
letters of the companies' names.   B

The publication of the inspectors' report in September 1993 gave to the provisional
liquidators a great deal of information about dealings with the assets of the KWELM
companies by various individuals and entities which had been until then unknown. As a
result the provisional liquidators sought to obtain information and documents which
might assist them in recovering assets for the benefit of creditors of the KWELM
companies. One such step by the provisional liquidators was an application to the court   C
on 23 November 1993 pursuant to s. 236 of the *Insolvency Act* 1986. The application was
made, as is usual, to the registrar of the Companies Court in chambers. It was made, as
is usual, ex parte.

The registrar made an order in a fairly usual form requiring the applicant to this
application to produce books and documents held by the applicant relating to persons
and companies with whom the applicant had connections. The order also required the   D
applicant to attend before an officer of the court for oral examination. The time-limits
set by the order were extremely short requiring production of books and documents by
8 December and attendance for examination on 10 December. I think the order was
served on the applicant on Friday, 26 November and although he is a practising solicitor
he considered, perfectly sensibly, that he needed advice from another firm of solicitors
who naturally instructed specialist counsel.

The result was that counsel appeared before me ex parte in the Companies Court on   E
Wednesday, 8 December. Either counsel or solicitors had informed those acting for the
provisional liquidators that the ex parte application for extensions of time to comply
with the order of Mr Registrar Buckley was to be made and counsel for the provisional
liquidators was present in court when Mr Collings for the applicant made his ex parte
application to me. Naturally no papers had been prepared for that extremely urgent
application but Mr Collings undertook to cause to be filed an ordinary application setting   F
out the relief which the applicant would seek and to have sworn and filed an affidavit
setting out the facts. Those undertakings have been performed.

Counsel for the provisional liquidators suggested that little relief was needed by the
applicant. However on assurances of co-operation over producing papers I gave the
applicant further time but I refused to adjourn the oral examination fixed for Friday, 10
December. I then directed that the intended ordinary application be listed before me inter   G
partes on Tuesday, 21 December.

On the same day as the ex parte hearing, 8 December 1993, there came before me the
hearing of the petition for the sanction of a scheme of arrangement in respect of the
KWELM companies. Sir Thomas Stockdale of counsel appeared for the companies and
propounded the scheme of arrangement. Counsel for other interested parties, including
the Policy Holders Protection Board and for the Law Debenture Trust Corporation, also
appeared and invited me to sanction the scheme of arrangement. The scheme had been   H
approved by overwhelming majorities of the creditors of each of the KWELM
companies.

In due course I so ordered but the scheme also required, to be effective, the assistance
of orders from the US Federal Bankruptcy Court in New York. Without those orders
the scheme would have been unable, or at least very difficult, to be carried out.

A   Application to the New York court was expected to be made in the next few days and if that court made the orders the scheme as sanctioned could be put into effect. If the New York court declined to make orders as asked it would be necessary to reconsider the scheme and decide whether it should be varied, which might well require further meetings of creditors, or dropped, or whether it could be implemented notwithstanding the absence of the New York orders. In all the circumstances I was asked to and did direct that the order sanctioning the scheme of arrangement should not be drawn up until 15 December

B   1993, and then only upon the court being told that the scheme administrators desired to proceed. Thus the order pronounced on 8 December sanctioning the scheme was conditional and might never come into effect.

Following upon my sanction under s. 425(2) of the 1985 Act there were called on before me the five winding-up petitions in respect of the KWELM companies. The petitions had been listed in the daily cause list so that any person concerned could see the

C   pending matters and attend if desired. Counsel for the company as petitioner in four of the petitions and counsel for Transit Casualty Insurance Co as petitioner on the Walbrook petition appeared before me. Counsel in each petition asked me to dismiss the petition, as had been envisaged by the scheme of arrangement, but to direct that the orders dismissing the petitions should also not be drawn up until 15 December 1993. No one appeared to oppose. I made orders as asked.

D   With that statement of the background facts I now return to this application. It is made, naturally, in the winding-up proceedings under which Mr Registrar Buckley's orders pursuant to s. 236 of the 1986 Act had been made. The winding-up proceedings have, however, been dismissed and come to an end by virtue of my orders passed and entered on 15 December 1993. Thus although there were originating proceedings on foot when the ordinary application was issued there are no proceedings on foot today.

E   The ordinary application sets out as its principal relief various orders relaxing the requirements for production of books and documents. However it also contains the useful rubric 'Further or other relief' and it was under that part of the application that Mr Collings addressed me. He submitted that since the winding-up petitions had now been dismissed there were no proceedings in which orders under s. 236 of the 1986 Act could be made, or if made could be effective and continued, and there was no person qualified to make or continue applications under s. 236. In order to make that submission

F   good Mr Collings turned to the statute.

Section 236 appears in Pt. VI of the 1986 Act to which Part the title is 'Miscellaneous provisions applying to companies which are insolvent or in liquidation'. The first section in that Part is s. 230 with the cross-heading 'Office-holders'. Section 230 requires each of four such persons, an administrator, an administrative receiver, a liquidator, and a provisional liquidator to be 'qualified to act as an insolvency practitioner in relation to

G   the company'. One starts therefore with the stress upon office-holders as persons with special qualifications. Sections 233 and 234 both define office-holders in particular relationships and both include the four types of office which I have listed above, with the addition in s. 233 of the supervisor of a voluntary arrangement. Section 234 applies where a company has one of the four office-holders acting in respect of it. It imposes a duty on 'any person' who has any company property, books or paper, I paraphrase for simplicity, to deliver those things pursuant to a court order to the office-holder. Section 235 gives

H   powers to require persons connected with a company to give information to an office-holder and, in addition, to the official receiver.

Section 236 itself, pursuant to which the order of 23 November was made, starts with the words 'This section applies as does section 234' with an immaterial addition. By subs. (2) 'The court may, on the application of the office-holder, summon to appear before it' a list of persons who may have information concerning the affairs of the

company. By subs. (5) and (6) the court is given draconian powers to arrest and keep in   A
custody persons whom it considers are required for the purpose of assisting the court.
The section, which is frequently used and often produces most useful material for the
purpose of administering the affairs of an insolvent company, is thus one which the court
must be careful to see is used for the proper purposes for which such wide-reaching
powers are granted by Parliament.

These powers have had a substantial history going back to the original *Companies Act*   B
1862 where s. 115 was, I think, the governing section. In the *Companies Act* 1948 such
powers were given by s. 268 but in that section they were in a much wider form than they
are in s. 236 of the 1986 Act. Under s. 268 of the 1948 Act it was provided that the court
may at any time after the appointment of a provisional liquidator or the making of a
winding-up order summon before it any officer of the company or person known or
suspected of having in his possession property or any person whom the court deems
capable of giving information. Thus that section applied only to provisional liquidations   C
and compulsory liquidations. It did not apply to administrative receiverships and, of
course, the office of an administrator under an administration petition did not then exist.
But although the circumstances when the court could exercise that jurisdiction were
narrower, the persons upon whose application the powers could be exercised were much
wider because there was no restriction at all upon the person who could make the
application, whereas under the new legislation, the 1986 Act, an order can only be made   D
on the application of an office-holder.

It is notable that these sections have always been remarkable. As *Buckley on the
Companies Acts* (14th edn) points out the liquidator may apply ex parte, the object being
to keep the proceedings secret, a prima facie case is not necessary, suspicion may be
enough. *Buckley* adds that the court may make an order of its own motion, and referred
to a case in the Weekly Notes. It is, in my judgment, clear that under s. 236 of the 1986   E
Act Parliament has restricted the jurisdiction and required an application to be made by
an office-holder so that the court's power to make orders of its own motion has probably
gone. The principle upon which I say that is that where Parliament has legislated in a
particular field in a particular manner, the former prerogative rights, as they are
sometimes called, are curtailed and the court is limited to the powers and to the extent of
the powers given by Parliament.

An order under any of these far-reaching sections, from 1862 to today, has never been   F
a matter of right and the powers thereby given have been described as inquisitorial, unlike
almost all proceedings in these courts. They are powers which have been described in old
authority as 'remarkable and far-reaching'.

Mr Collings today does not argue that the order of 23 November 1993 was not made
upon a proper application nor that the order was not in its terms capable of being granted
in the correct exercise of the court's discretion. He does not impugn the exercise by   G
Mr Registrar Buckley of that discretion and does not submit that the order should be set
aside as one which should never have been made. That is not the nature of his case.

Mr Collings' submission is that since the order was made the circumstances have
completely changed in that there is now no office-holder, no office which could be filled
by an office-holder, there are no relevant originating proceedings on foot, and that, in
the circumstance, it is quite plain that nobody could now apply for orders under s. 236   H
affecting the gentleman who is his client. Further, Mr Collings observes that under s. 237
of the 1986 Act the powers of the court to enforce the order are plainly extremely limited.
That is because s. 237(1) provides, omitting immaterial parts, that:

> 'If it appears to the court, on consideration of any evidence obtained . . . that any
> person has in his possession any property of the company, the court may, on the

A   application of the office-holder, order that person to deliver the whole . . . to the
office-holder.'

and under subs. (2) again orders may be made on the application of the office-holder.
There being no office-holder, no application under s. 237 can be made and the powers to
enforce the s. 236 order must to that extent have fallen away. Mr Collings therefore
submits that there has been a fundamental change by the dismissal of the winding-up
petitions and the cessation of any office the holder of which could now enforce, or even

B   seek, such an order as this.

It seems to me that the whole purpose of this wide and inquisitorial power is
undoubtedly to assist the office-holder in the carrying out of his office. It seems to me to
follow inevitably that, when there is no office, there cannot be a purpose of assisting the
holder of that non-existent office. The office has ceased and the purpose of assisting
the performance of the functions of the person filling the office has gone. As it seems to

C   me, the result must be that today, there being no office, no office-holder, and no purpose
of assisting him to be fulfilled, the order has, in effect, become spent. Mr Collings did not
submit that the order, as it were, died of its own weight upon the cessation of the office
the holder of which had obtained it. He does not say that an order ceases to be an order
simply because of that event. His submission is that the order should now be discharged
as, in effect, spent since there is no purpose for which it should be maintained on foot. In

D   my view that is right. Nothing submitted to me by counsel for Mr Bond and Mr Hughes,
who obtained the order in their former capacity as provisional liquidators but who have
been discharged from that office which has ceased to exist in relation to the KWELM
companies and now fill a role which is not that of an office-holder, as administrators
under the scheme of arrangement, seems to me to come anywhere near the point.

I entirely accept Mr Tamlyn's submission that the examination under s. 236 is an
examination by the court. It is to be noted, however, that the Insolvency Rules, r. 9.4

E   provides for the method of the conduct of such examination by the court and it starts
plainly by providing in r. 9.4(2) that persons who could have applied for an order may,
with the leave of the court and if the applicant does not object, attend the examination
and put questions to the respondent but only through the applicant. That plainly shows
that other persons who did not themselves apply for or obtain an order under s. 236 may
be given leave to attend the examination, but such leave can only be given to persons

F   who themselves were office-holders and could have applied under s. 236 for an order.
Plainly Mr Bond and Mr Hughes in their capacity as the scheme administrators are not
persons who could have applied for an order and are not within r. 9.4(2).

Further it is to be noticed that questions may only be put through the applicant. The
applicant must mean the person who made the application and that was in this case the
provisional liquidators. As such, they no longer exist; there are no provisional liquidators
because there is no pending winding-up petition. Consequently, there is no person who

G   can properly be described as the applicant unless the word is merely historic, which I do
not believe it is.

Rule 9.4(4) provides further that:

'Where application has been made under the applicable section on information
provided by a creditor . . . that creditor may . . . attend the examination and put
questions . . . but only through the applicant . . .'

H   So the same point arises again: who is entitled to administer the questions under this
rule? The answer seems plain, only the applicant. The applicant can only mean, in my
view, not the individual person who was the office-holder when he made the application
but a person holding the relevant office. While the office continued those persons were,
in this case, the provisional liquidators. It seems to me that all of the material here points
to the whole order being dependent upon there being an office which entitles the holder

of that office to seek the order, to enforce the order, and to put questions in the course of   A
the examination under the order; and the fact that the examination is by the court, as is
undoubted, so that the witness is not the witness of the applicant at all but is a person
subject to an inquisitorial form of discovery, does not bear upon the question, in my
view.

The reference in the case of *Re Greys Brewery Co* (1883) 25 ChD 400 at pp. 407 and
408 where Chitty J refers to the discretion do not seem to me to come anywhere near the   B
point which I have to consider, nor do the observations of Sir George Jessel MR sitting
in the Court of Appeal in *Re Silkstone and Dodworth Coal and Iron Co* (1881) 19 ChD
118 where he refers at p. 120 to the importance of committing the matter to the official
liquidator but under the control of the court, seem to me to assist in this case. I observe
that the office-holders are persons who may or may not be officers of the court; many
office-holders are not officers of the court, e.g. administrative receivers appointed out of
court, but they are none the less office-holders. As it seems to me, the specific jurisdiction   C
confined to office-holders by s. 234 and 236 points to those persons being persons who
are given special statutory rank and in no way can trench upon the general proposition
that the order could not now be obtained and, therefore, should not any longer be
continued so as to be enforced.

I was referred to my own decision in *Re Oriental Credit* (1987) 3 BCC 564 where I
relied upon s. 37 for the power to grant injunctions, holding that that power could be   D
exercised in aid of a then extant and pending order under s. 236 although there was no
cause of action in the person making the application. I do not in the least repent of the
proposition I there laid down which has indeed been approved by the Court of Appeal,
but that does not seem to me to bear at all upon the continuation in force of an order
which could no longer be made and which, in large part, cannot now be enforced by
virtue of s. 237.

   E

In *Re Oriental Credit* the question, as I saw it, was, could the court act to assist in an
extremely active and continuing case of an examination under s. 236, with acting office-
holders. Nothing in my view in that case bears at all upon the situation which arises here
which is, so far as I am aware, novel. It seems to me that in principle it must be right that,
once the office has come to an end, the powers under s. 236 have themselves ceased to be
applicable and orders rightly formerly made should be discharged at this point in time.
I therefore will make the order sought by Mr Collings that the order should now   F
be discharged. That means the order both as made on 23 November and as varied on
16 December 1993. I have not entered upon the question whether the variation
of 16 December was, in the light of the dismissal of the winding-up petition and the
discharge of the provisional liquidators on 15 December, within the jurisdiction of the
registrar, that is if there was power to make that order at all. I suspect that in the
Insolvency Rules (of which I have cited r. 9.4) in fact there was no power to make such
an order as the registrar purported to make but that is not a point upon which I am   G
deciding the matter. I am deciding it upon the fundamental question of jurisdiction:
should this order be continued when the office which caused it to be made has ceased? In
my view it should not.

(Order accordingly)

―――――――――――――

   H

A # Re Selectmove Ltd.

Court of Appeal (Civil Division).
Balcombe, Stuart-Smith and Peter Gibson L JJ.
Judgment delivered 21 December 1993.

B *Winding up – Whether petition debt disputed on substantial grounds – Company alleged agreement with Revenue to pay arrears of tax in instalments – Whether there was agreement between company and Revenue – Whether agreement was supported by consideration – Whether Revenue estopped from asserting that debt was due.*

This was an appeal by the company against the making of a winding-up order on a petition by the Inland Revenue. The company argued that the debt to the Revenue was C disputed on the basis of an alleged agreement by the Revenue to accept payment of arrears of tax in instalments.

The issues on appeal were whether there was acceptance by the Revenue of the company's proposal to pay in instalments; if there was an agreement, whether it was supported by consideration moving to the Revenue; and whether, if there was no agreement, the Revenue was estopped from asserting that its debt was due.

D *Held*, dismissing the company's appeal:

1. The collector of taxes did not have actual authority to conclude the agreement or otherwise bind the Revenue, and there was no representation by the Revenue that he had the Revenue's authority to accept the offer or to convey the Revenue's acceptance. (Armagas Ltd v Mundogas SA (1986) 2 BCC 99,197 applied.)

E 2. An agreement between the company and the Inland Revenue to pay arrears of tax by instalments was unenforceable for want of consideration moving to the Revenue. (Foakes v Beer (1884) 9 App Cas 605 applied.)

3. As the collector had no actual or ostensible authority to make the agreement claimed by the company, he had no authority to make the promise said to found the estoppel against the Revenue. Further, because the company failed to honour its promise to pay the instalments, it was not inequitable or unfair for the Revenue to demand payment of the F arrears, nor to serve a statutory demand and present a winding-up petition to enforce the debt.

The following cases were referred to in the judgment of Peter Gibson LJ:

Allied Marine Transport Ltd v Vale do Rio Doce Navegacao SA [1985] 1 WLR 925.
Armagas Ltd v Mundogas SA (1986) 2 BCC 99,197; [1986] AC 717.
G *D & C Builders Ltd v Rees* [1966] 2 QB 617.
Foakes v Beer (1884) 9 App Cas 605.
Gebr van Weelde Scheepvaartkantor BV v Cia Naviera Sea Orient SA [1985] 2 Ll Rep 496.
Pinnel's Case (1602) 5 Co Rep 117a; 77 ER 237.
Stilk v Myrick (1809) 2 Camp 317; 170 ER 1168.
Stonegate Securities Ltd v Gregory [1980] Ch 576.
H *Vanbergen v St Edmunds Properties Ltd* [1933] 2 KB 223.
Williams v Roffey Bros & Nicholls (Contractors) Ltd [1991] 1 QB 1.

Christopher Nugee (instructed by Stockler Charity) for the appellant.

AWH Charles (instructed by the Inland Revenue solicitor's department) for the respondent.

JUDGMENT   A

Peter Gibson LJ: This is an appeal by Selectmove Ltd ('the company') from the order made on 19 January 1993 by His Honour Judge Moseley QC, sitting as a judge of the Companies Court, whereby on the petition of the Commissioners of Inland Revenue as creditors he compulsorily wound up the company.

The issue before us, as it was before the judge, is whether the debt of the company to the Revenue is disputed in good faith on substantial grounds.   B

There is no doubt as to the correct approach to that issue. The jurisdiction of the Companies Court to wind up companies is not for the purpose of deciding a factual dispute concerning a debt which is sought to be relied on to found a petition. Until the petitioner can establish that he is a creditor, he is not entitled to present a petition based on a claimed debt. Accordingly the practice of the Companies Court is to dismiss a creditor's petition based on a debt which is disputed by the company in good faith and   C on substantial grounds (see, for example, *Stonegate Securities Ltd v Gregory* [1980] Ch 576 at p. 580 per Buckley LJ).

In July 1991 the company owed the Revenue substantial amounts of tax ('PAYE') which it had deducted from the emoluments of its employees under the PAYE system and National Insurance contributions ('NIC'), the arrears going back to the previous fiscal year. On 15 July 1991 Mr ffooks, the managing director of the company, met Mr   D Polland, a Collector of Taxes, at the latter's office. Mr ffooks' account of what occurred is contained in a letter dated 11 October 1991 from him to the Revenue and is verified by his affidavit of 27 November 1992. In that letter he said that he explained to Mr Polland that the company was having cash flow problems, but that the company's bank was being supportive. He said that he suggested to Mr Polland that it could not be in anyone's interest for the company to be put into compulsory liquidation when the typesetting market in which the company was engaged usually picked up after the summer, and that   E the company had been trading 'marginally profitably' since the start of the financial year. Mr Polland, he said, asked him if he was in a position to put forward a proposal to pay back the arrears of PAYE and NIC and told him that any proposal should include the prompt payment of any future PAYE and NIC as they fell due. He further said that he told Mr Polland that because of the lengthy credit terms usual in the publishing industry, even if the company continued to trade at a profit, this would not be reflected in cash   F coming in to the company for four or five months. He continued:

> 'I therefore proposed that the company would pay any future PAYE and NIC liability as it fell due commencing with the liability for August (due September) and this has been done.
>
> I further proposed that the arrears of PAYE and NIC would be paid at a rate of £1,000 per month from 1 February 1992.   G
>
> Mr Polland said that such a proposal went further than he would have liked and that he would have to seek approval from his superiors to whom he would recommend it considering the support that both I and our bankers were giving the company. He said he would revert to me if it was unacceptable.
>
> To date I have not heard from him and as I have made the two payments which were due under the agreement it is clear that this agreement has come into   H existence.'

The Revenue dispute that Mr Polland made any agreement with Mr ffooks. However, it was accepted that for the purpose of the hearing before the judge the company's version of the facts of what occurred should be taken as correct, and the same assumption has been common ground on this appeal.

A   The company did not hear further from the Revenue until 9 October 1991. By then, on 19 August 1991, it had duly paid PAYE and NIC for August 1991 amounting to £2,309, but it had not paid PAYE and NIC for September 1991 although that had become due on 19 September 1991. On 9 October 1991 the Revenue wrote to the company, demanding payment of PAYE and NIC arrears totalling £24,650 and threatened a winding-up petition if payment was not made. It was to that letter that Mr ffooks was responding by his letter dated 11 October 1991 in which the agreement between
B   Mr ffooks and Mr Polland was alleged. On 11 October 1991 the company paid the September PAYE and NIC in the sum of £1,821. On 22 November 1991 a further payment of PAYE and NIC for October and November in the sum of £2,699 was made, again late. In 1992, seven cheques of £1,000 each were paid to the Revenue, the first two on 3 March 1992. Again there were failures by the company to honour what Mr ffooks said was agreed with Mr Polland, viz. the payment of £1,000 per month from 1 February
C   1992. On 18 October 1991 the employees of the company were given notice of dismissal and on 24 October 1991 the company sold all its work in progress to another company, the intention of the sale agreement being, according to the company's solicitor, Mr Stockler, to provide £1,000 per month to settle the Revenue's claim.

However the Revenue continued to press for payment and served a statutory demand for payment of £19,650.15. On 7 September 1992 the Revenue presented its winding-up
D   petition based on a claimed debt of £17,466.60.

On behalf of the company it was contended before the judge that it had an arguable case that the Revenue had accepted the proposal put by Mr ffooks to Mr Polland on 15 July 1991. The Revenue took two points on this contention, each of which was accepted by the judge. The first was that no agreement was concluded by the silence of the Revenue in response to Mr ffooks' proposal. The second was that if there was an agreement there was no consideration therefor.
E   The company also argued in the alternative that by reason of the agreement between Mr ffooks and Mr Polland the Revenue is estopped from relying on the debt as due. That argument too was rejected by the judge on the ground that there was no agreement or promise by the Revenue to give rise to any estoppel.

Similar contentions were advanced by Mr Nugee for the company before us, and I shall consider in turn the following issues:
F
(1)   Was there an acceptance by the Revenue of Mr ffooks' proposal?

(2)   If there was an agreement, was it supported by consideration moving to the Revenue?

(3)   If there was no agreement, is the Revenue estopped from asserting that its debt is due?
G

(1) Acceptance

The judge referred to the affidavit evidence of Mr ffooks in which he had stated what had occurred at the meeting with Mr Polland on 15 July 1991 and the absence of any communication from the Revenue at any time before 9 October and had asserted that the offer had been accepted. The judge said:
H
> 'It is not asserted . . . that Mr Polland said anything to the effect, "if you do not hear from me, take it that there is an agreement between us".'

But that seems to me to be what necessarily is the effect of Mr ffooks' assertion of the acceptance of the offer.

The question is whether an agent who makes clear to an offeror that he lacks the principal's authority to accept the offer can, by indicating that he would refer the offer to

his principal and that he would come back to the offeror only if the offer was not   A
acceptable, bind the principal to accept the offer by the agent's subsequent silence. Mr
Charles, for the Revenue, drew our attention to the general rule that silence will not
normally amount to acceptance of an offer since acceptance cannot be inferred from
silence alone 'save in the most exceptional circumstances' (*Allied Marine Transport Ltd v
Vale do Rio Doce Navegacao SA* [1985] 1 WLR 925 at p. 937 per Robert Goff LJ). But
the authorities that support the general rule are cases where an offeror sought to impose
on the offeree a term as to acceptance by silence. For my part, as at present advised, I   B
would accept the observation of Evans J in *Gebr van Weelde Scheepvaartkantor BV v Cia
Naviera Sea Orient SA* [1985] 2 Ll Rep 496 at p. 509:

> 'The significance of silence, as a matter of law, may also be different when there is
> an express undertaking or an implied obligation to speak, in the special
> circumstances of the particular case.'

Where the offeree himself indicates that an offer is to be taken as accepted if he does   C
not indicate to the contrary by an ascertainable time, he is undertaking to speak if he
does not want an agreement to be concluded. I see no reason in principle why that should
not be an exceptional circumstance such that the offer can be accepted by silence. But it
is unnecessary to express a concluded view on this point.

The more substantial objection taken by Mr Charles is as to the want of authority of
Mr Polland. That he had no authority to agree to the proposal, Mr Polland had made   D
clear to Mr ffooks. It is not suggested by Mr Nugee that Mr Polland had actual authority
to conclude the agreement or otherwise to bind the Revenue by his silence. He has to
assert that Mr Polland had ostensible authority and he submits that such authority
extended to conveying his principal's acceptance by his subsequent silence. The difficulty
that I have with this submission stems from the fact that it is trite law that ostensible
authority involves a representation by the principal as to the extent of the agent's
authority and no representation by the agent as to the extent of his authority can amount   E
to a holding out by his principal (see, for example, *Bowstead on Agency* (15th edn)
p. 286). In *Armagas Ltd v Mundogas SA* (1986) 2 BCC 99,197 the House of Lords
expressly approved (at p. 99,203) the following remarks by Robert Goff LJ ([1986] AC
717 at pp. 730–731):

> 'the effect of the judge's conclusion was that, although Mr Magelssen did not have
> ostensible authority to enter into the contract, he did have ostensible authority to   F
> tell Mr Jensen and Mr Dannesboe that he had obtained actual authority to do so.
> This is, on its face, a most surprising conclusion. It results in an extraordinary
> distinction between (1) a case where an agent, having no ostensible authority to
> enter into the relevant contract, wrongly asserts that he is invested with actual
> authority to do so, in which event the principal is not bound; and (2) a case where
> an agent, having no ostensible authority, wrongly asserts after negotiations that he
> has gone back to his principal and obtained actual authority, in which event the   G
> principal is bound. As a matter of common sense, this is most unlikely to be the
> law.'

In the present case I am not aware of any fact which would enable Mr ffooks
reasonably to believe that the superiors, to whom Mr Polland referred, were themselves
making a representation that Mr Polland had their authority to accept the offer or to
convey their acceptance by his silence. Accordingly, I would hold that the judge was right   H
to conclude that there was no acceptance, though my reasons differ from those of the
judge.

(2) Consideration

There are two elements to the consideration which the company claims was provided
by it to the Revenue. One is the promise to pay off its existing liability by instalments

A   from 1 February 1992. The other is the promise to pay future PAYE and NIC as they fell due. Mr Nugee suggested that implicit in the latter was the promise to continue trading. But that cannot be spelt out of Mr ffooks' evidence as to what he agreed with Mr Polland. Accordingly the second element is no more than a promise to pay that which it was bound to pay under the fiscal legislation at the date at which it was bound to make such payment. If the first element is not good consideration, I do not see why the second element should be either.

B

   The judge held that the case fell within the principle of *Foakes v Beer* (1884) 9 App Cas 605. In that case a judgment debtor and creditor agreed that in consideration of the debtor paying part of the judgment debt and costs immediately and the remainder by instalments the creditor would not take any proceedings on the judgment. The House of Lords held that the agreement was *nudum pactum*, being without consideration, and did not prevent the creditor, after payment of the whole debt and costs, from proceeding to

C   enforce payment of the interest on the judgment. Although their Lordships were unanimous in the result, that case is notable for the powerful speech of Lord Blackburn who made plain his disagreement with the course the law had taken in and since *Pinnel's Case* (1602) 5 Co Rep 117a and which the House of Lords in *Foakes v Beer* decided should not be reversed. Lord Blackburn (at p. 622) expressed his conviction that:

D   'all men of business, whether merchants or tradesmen, do every day recognise and act on the ground that prompt payment of a part of their demand may be more beneficial to them than it would be to insist on their rights and enforce payment of the whole.'

   Yet it is clear that the House of Lords decided that a practical benefit of that nature is not good consideration in law.

   Foakes v Beer has been followed and applied in numerous cases subsequently, of which

E   I shall mention two. In *Vanbergen v St Edmunds Properties Ltd* [1933] 2 KB 223 at p. 231 Lord Hanworth MR said:

       'It is a well established principle that a promise to pay a sum which the debtor is already bound by law to pay to the promisee does not afford any consideration to support the contract.'

   More recently in *D & C Builders Ltd v Rees* [1966] 2 QB 617 this court also applied

F   *Foakes v Beer*, Danckwerts LJ (at p. 626) saying that the case:

       'settled definitely the rule of law that payment of a lesser sum than the amount of a debt due cannot be a satisfaction of the debt, unless there is some benefit to the creditor added so that there is an accord and satisfaction.'

   Mr Nugee however submitted that an additional benefit to the Revenue was conferred by the agreement in that the Revenue stood to derive practical benefits therefrom: it was

G   likely to recover more from not enforcing its debt against the company, which was known to be in financial difficulties, than from putting the company into liquidation. He pointed to the fact that the company did in fact pay its further PAYE and NIC liabilities and £7,000 of its arrears. He relied on the decision of this court in *Williams v Roffey Bros & Nicholls (Contractors) Ltd* [1991] 1 QB 1 for the proposition that a promise to perform an existing obligation can amount to good consideration provided that there are practical benefits to the promisee.

H

   In that case the defendant, which had a building contract, subcontracted work to the plaintiff at a price which left him in financial difficulty and there was a risk that the work would not be completed by the plaintiff. The defendant agreed to make additional payments to the plaintiff in return for his promise to carry out his existing obligations. The plaintiff sued for payment under the original agreement and the further agreement. The defendant argued that its promise to make additional payments was unenforceable

and relied on *Stilk v Myrick* (1809) 2 Camp 317, in which Lord Ellenborough CJ held to   A
be unenforceable for want of consideration a promise by a ship's captain to seamen,
hired to crew the ship to and from the Baltic, of extra pay for working the ship back from
the Baltic after two men had deserted. This court rejected that argument without
overruling *Stilk v Myrick*. Glidewell LJ, with whom Purchas and Russell L JJ agreed,
expressed the law to be this (at pp. 15–16):

> '(i) if A has entered into a contract with B to do work for, or to supply goods or   B
> services to, B in return for payment by B; and (ii) at some stage before A has
> completely performed his obligations under the contract B has reason to doubt
> whether A will, or will be able to, complete his side of the bargain; and (iii) B
> thereupon promises A an additional payment in return for A's promise to perform
> his contractual obligations on time; and (iv) as a result of giving his promise, B
> obtains in practice a benefit, or obviates a disbenefit; and (v) B's promise is not
> given as a result of economic duress or fraud on the part of A; then (vi) the benefit   C
> to B is capable of being consideration for B's promise, so that the promise will be
> legally binding.'

Mr Nugee submitted that although Glidewell LJ in terms confined his remarks to a
case where B is to do the work for or supply goods or services to A, the same principle
must apply where B's obligation is to pay A, and he referred to an article by Adams and
Brownsword in (1990) 53 MLR 536 at pp. 539–540 which suggests that *Foakes v Beer*   D
might need reconsideration. I see the force of the argument, but the difficulty that I feel
with it is that if the principle of the *Williams* case is to be extended to an obligation to
make payment, it would in effect leave the principle in *Foakes v Beer* without any
application. When a creditor and a debtor who are at arm's length reach agreement on
the payment of the debt by instalments to accommodate the debtor, the creditor will no
doubt always see a practical benefit to himself in so doing. In the absence of authority
there would be much to be said for the enforceability of such a contract. But that was a   E
matter expressly considered in *Foakes v Beer* yet held not to constitute good consideration
in law. *Foakes v Beer* was not even referred to in the *Williams* case, and it is in my
judgment impossible, consistently with the doctrine of precedent, for this court to extend
the principle of the *Williams* case to any circumstances governed by the principle of
Foakes v Beer. If that extension is to be made, it must be by the House of Lords or,
perhaps even more appropriately, by Parliament after consideration by the Law   F
Commission.

In my judgment, the judge was right to hold that if there was an agreement between
the company and the Revenue it was unenforceable for want of consideration.

(3) Estoppel

Mr Nugee submitted that if the agreement was unenforceable for want of consideration   G
the Revenue is nevertheless estopped by the doctrine of promissory estoppel. As I
understood him, he was saying that the Revenue could not go back on its implied promise
not to enforce the debt, given as it was in return for the company's promise to pay the
future PAYE and NIC as they fell due and to pay the arrears by monthly instalments of
£1,000 from 1 February 1992. He said that the company had acted on the Revenue's
promise and it would be inequitable to allow the Revenue to renege on its promise.

Mr Charles did not accept that the Revenue could be estopped as a matter of private   H
law from performing its statutory duty, but he accepted that as a matter of public law the
Revenue could be prevented from acting unfairly. He did not suggest that an objection
of unfairness could not be taken in the present proceedings.

It is unnecessary to consider the rival arguments in further detail as in my opinion
Mr Nugee's submission cannot succeed for at least two reasons. First, as Mr Polland had

A   no actual or ostensible authority to make the agreement claimed by the company, he had no authority to make the promise said to found the estoppel against the Revenue. Second, because the company failed to honour its promise to pay the September PAYE and NIC as they fell due, it was not inequitable or unfair for the Revenue on 9 October 1991 to demand payment of all the arrears, nor, in the light of the further late payments of the October and November PAYE and NIC and of various of the monthly instalments of £1,000, was it unfair or inequitable to serve a statutory demand and present a winding-up petition to enforce the debt.

For these reasons despite the able and well-sustained arguments of Mr Nugee I would dismiss this appeal.

Stuart-Smith LJ: For the reasons given in the judgment of Peter Gibson LJ I agree that this appeal should be dismissed.

Balcombe LJ: I agree.

(*Appeal dismissed. Respondent's costs of the appeal to be costs in the liquidation. No order for appellant's costs. Leave to appeal to the House of Lords refused*)

Transag Haulage Ltd v Leyland DAF Finance plc & Anor.

A

Chancery Division.
Knox J.
Judgment delivered 13 January 1994.

Insolvency – Receivership – Relief against forfeiture – Hire-purchase agreements terminable on appointment of receivers – Owners entitled to repossession on termination – Whether provisions were a penalty – Whether hirer had forfeited a proprietary right – Whether court had discretion to grant relief against forfeiture – Whether court should exercise discretion.

B

This was a summons by a company in administrative receivership seeking an order relieving the company from the consequences under three hire-purchase agreements of the appointment of the receivers.

The company was a haulage company. The defendants were the owners of the vehicles which were the subject of the three hire-purchase agreements made in 1991. The vehicles were lorries which cost nearly £60,000 each. There was a down payment of £22,000 or £23,000 and 36 monthly instalments of £1,000. When the administrative receivers were appointed in November 1993 the lorries were together valued at between £65,000 and £72,500. The amount of remaining future instalments was then just over £14,000. Under cl. 13(f) of the agreements, they were terminable on appointment of the receivers and on termination by virtue of cl. 14 the owner could retake possession of the vehicles. Once the hirer had paid all the sums due under the agreement he could buy the lorry for £5 under cl. 24.

C

D

The receivers argued that the provisions of the agreements were such as to attract the equitable doctrine of relief from penalties or forfeiture.

Held, granting relief from forfeiture if the company paid to the second defendant a sum equal to the outstanding instalments within seven days:

E

1. The law relating to penalties did not apply because there was no recovery of a sum of money in respect of a breach of contract. The owners asserted a right to recover possession of the goods on the happening of an event which the commercial contracts constituted by the agreements provided should entitle the owners to effect that recovery. (Export Credits Guarantee Department v Universal Oil Products Co & Ors [1983] 1 WLR 399 applied.)

F

2. The balance of authority was in favour of the view that even a provision for payment of a sum on an event, such as a liquidation of the hirer under a hire-purchase agreement, was not a penalty. No authority was cited for the proposition that the right to retake possession of the goods subject to a hire-purchase agreement, as opposed to the right to demand payment of a sum of money on such an event, could constitute a penalty. (Re Apex Supply Company Ltd [1942] Ch 108 considered.)

G

3. The loss of the right to buy the goods for £5 under cl. 24, which was still contingent when the agreements were terminated consequent upon the appointment of the administrative receivers, could properly be described as forfeiture of a proprietary, and not merely a contractual, right. The court had jurisdiction to relieve against the forfeiture or loss of an otherwise existing contingent proprietary right in the shape of an option to buy. (BICC plc v Burndy Corporation & Anor [1985] Ch 232 applied.)

H

4. The court should not grant relief unless satisfied that the terms upon which it was granted would confer upon the owner at least as valuable rights as the owner would have enjoyed under the original agreements; and that failure to do so would confer a substantial windfall on the owner over and above what the original agreements provided for the owner to receive. Relief would not be granted if the conduct of the hirer had disentitled him to receive it.

A   The following cases were referred to in the judgment:

Apex Supply Co Ltd, Re [1942] Ch 108.
Barton Thompson & Co Ltd v Stapling Machines Co [1966] Ch 499.
BICC plc v Burndy Corporation & Anor [1985] Ch 232.
Export Credits Guarantee Department v Universal Oil Products Co & Ors [1983] 1 WLR 399.

B   *Goker v NWS Bank plc* The Times, 23 May 1990.
Piggin, Re; Dicker v Lombank Ltd (1962) 112 LJ 424.
Starside Properties Ltd v Mustapha [1974] 1 WLR 816.
Sterling Industrial Facilities Ltd v Lydiate Textiles Ltd & Anor (1962) 106 SJ 669.

Mrs H Galley (instructed by Jaques & Lewis) for the plaintiff.

Brian Doctor (instructed by Hammond Bale) for the defendants.

C

JUDGMENT

Knox J: The summons in these proceedings was issued on 17 December 1993. The plaintiff is Transag Haulage Ltd ('the company') which is in administrative receivership. The affidavit in support of the motion which is before me sworn by a Mr Mark Docherty describes the company's business as follows:

D   '5. Transag is a haulage company. It has four principal contracts for the transportation of goods over the Dartford Crossing. The contracts are expected to continue for the foreseeable future and comprise the principal business of Transag. Transag's book debt is currently in the order of £141,000. The receivers believe that the business is worth £300,000 and the freehold property referred to above is worth approximately £150,000.

E   6. There are 20 employees and a fleet of 12 vehicles, which operate from the freehold premises in Gravesend.

'7. Of the 12 vehicles, three are the subject of the proceedings. I will refer to those three vehicles as "the vehicles".'

I propose to call them by the same name.

The defendants in these proceedings are Leyland DAF Finance plc and Lease Plan
F   UK Ltd. Between them they are the owners of the vehicles which are the subject of three hire-purchase agreements, one for each of the vehicles. In my judgment it is not necessary for me to analyse the relationship between the two defendants for the purposes of these proceedings. The first defendant was the original owner and has made an assignment in favour of the second defendant. But there is no doubt that between the two of them they constitute the owner for the purposes of the three hire-purchase agreements, which I will
G   call 'the agreements'.

The first agreement was dated 4 January 1991. The price specified for the lorry in that case was £59,340. A down payment was made of £23,340, leaving £36,000 to be paid by instalments of £1,000 for each of the ensuing 36 months, i.e. over three years. The second agreement was dated 28 March 1991, the price £58,362 and the down payment £22,362, the instalments being the same as in the first agreement. The third agreement was dated 30 May 1991, the price in this case being £59,631, the down payment £23,631, and the
H   instalments again 36 times £1,000.

The evidence on both sides regarding their value at the date when the administrative receivers were appointed, which was 23 November 1993, is remarkably close, in the sense that the plaintiff's evidence is very similar to that of the defendants. The defendants' evidence on that score is that the first lorry is worth £19,000 or thereabouts, and the second and third £24,000 each making a total of £67,000 for the three. The plaintiff's

value for the three is £72,500 if sold as part of a going concern, and £65,000 on an   A
individual basis.

Again there is very little difference between the parties' evidence as to the amount that
was outstanding at the date of the appointment of the administrative receivers, 23
November 1993. On the plaintiff's evidence it is said that there was £14,015 outstanding.
On the defendants' evidence it is said that there was £14,388.97 outstanding. Those are
not arrears, of course; those are in respect of what was to come. The agreements in all   B
other respects were identically the same. That is to say, the only differences are in the
price and the down payments.

The provisions of cl. 3 were in common form providing for the payment of instalments
and it is not necessary to read the details of that.

Clause 13, headed 'Termination', provided as follows, so far as relevant:

'Upon the occurrence of any of the following ("events of default") . . .'   C

There is then a long list of events not all of which is it necessary for me to read in full:
(a) is default by the hirer in the payment of instalments or other sums; (b) is a failure by
the hirer to observe the terms and conditions of the agreement; (c) reads 'if any
representation made by the hirer shall be incorrect'; (d) deals with petitions or receiving
orders in bankruptcy being made or presented against the hirer – the form seems to be a
rather old-fashioned one; (e) relates to the making of a winding-up order other than for   D
the purpose of amalgamation or reconstruction or the making of any composition or
arrangement with creditors; (f) I should read in full, and it reads as follows:

'or . . . if a receiver shall be appointed of the hirer's assets or any part thereof or if
any distress execution distraint or other legal process shall be levied or threatened
on the goods or any part of the hirer's assets . . .'

'The goods', of course, are what I am calling the vehicles. Subclause (g) is judgments   E
remaining unsatisfied for more than seven days and (h) is the hirer abandoning the goods.
The clause finally provides that:

'Then and in that event this agreement shall be determinable forthwith and without
notice at the option of the owner.'

The next clause, cl. 14, headed 'Consequences of termination', reads as follows:

'Upon termination of this agreement under cl. 13 hereof–   F

(a) The hirer shall return the goods to the owner in good serviceable repair and
     condition (fair wear and tear excepted) . . .

(b) The owner may at its discretion retake possession of the goods and for that
     purpose shall be entitled to enter upon any land or building where the goods
     are or are thought to be situated.   G

(c) The goods shall no longer be in the possession of the hirer with the consent
     of the owner.

(d) Without prejudice to any pre-existing liability of the hirer in damages to the
     owner, the hirer shall pay to the owner:

     (i)   the amount of the arrears of the instalments due at the date of
           termination together with interest thereon payable under cl. 3(d)   H
           hereof;

     (ii) any damages which the hirer may be liable to pay to the owner for
           breach of the terms and conditions of the agreement;

     (iii) all costs and expenses incurred by the owner in recovering or
           attempting to recover the goods;

(iv) such sum as shall be equal to the aggregate of the instalments remaining unpaid less (in case of goods which are resold by the owner within three months of the termination of this agreement) a sum equal to the proceeds of sale or (in the case of goods which are not resold by the owner within three months of the termination of this agreement) such sum as in the opinion of the owner is equal to the realisable value of such goods at the date of repossession such sums to be certified by the owner to the hirer in accordance with cl. 22 hereof.'

Clause 16, headed 'Termination by the hirer', reads, so far as relevant:

'The hirer may at any time before the final instalment herein falls due determine this agreement by giving 14 days' notice in writing to the owner whereupon:

(a) cl. 15(b) will apply, and

(b) the hirer shall be liable to pay to the owner:

(i) such sum equal to the aggregate of the instalments remaining unpaid in respect of this agreement . . .

(ii) the amount of any arrears of the instalments due at the date of termination together with interest thereon . . .

(iii) any damages which the hirer may be liable to pay to the owner for breach of the terms and conditions of the agreement.'

Clause 22, headed 'Certification by the owner', reads:

'A certificate signed by the manager of the principal office or any branch office of the owner as to any amount due from or to the hirer under this agreement shall be prima facie evidence that the amount so certified was in fact due from or allowable to the hirer at the date of such certificate.

Finally, cl. 24, headed 'Transfer of ownership to the hirer', reads:

'If the hirer (having duly observed and performed all the terms and conditions of this agreement whether expressed or implied, and having paid all sums due under this agreement) shall pay to the owner the sum of £5 the hiring thereby constituted shall determine and the hirer shall become the absolute owner of the goods but until such time the goods shall remain the sole property of the owner and the hirer shall be a mere bailee thereof.'

There was in fact no failure to pay instalments by the company before 23 November 1993 when the administrative receivers were appointed. On 2 December 1993, on behalf of the second defendant, a letter was written to the company asserting that the agreements were terminated on 23 November 1993 as a result of the appointment of the administrative receivers describing that as a 'breach of the agreement' under cl. 13 thereof. The expression 'breach' is something of a misnomer but nothing, in my judgment, turns on that inaccuracy of description.

On the next day, 3 December 1993, proposals were made by the administrative receivers for the parties to give mutual undertakings for the second defendant not to seek to take possession of the vehicles and for the administrative receivers to continue to make payments under the agreements. Those proposals were not acceptable to the defendants, and in particular the second defendant.

On 6 December 1993 a cheque for £14,015 (which is the figure that the company in its evidence claims to be the outstanding figure as at 23 November 1993) was sent by one of the joint administrative receivers of the company in full and final settlement of all amounts due under the agreements. The cheque has not been either presented or returned to its sender.

On 14 December 1993 solicitors acting for the administrative receivers informed the   A
second defendant that the effect of the defendants' taking possession of the vehicles
would be to prevent the administrative receivers from carrying on and selling the current
business which was what they were at the time seeking to do. There ensued a debate by
correspondence whether or not the agreements had in fact been terminated and whether
the court could or would grant relief from forfeiture.

Evidence sworn on behalf of the company (to which I have already made one reference,   B
the affidavit of Mr Docherty), also includes the following:

'*Receivers' intentions with regard to the administrative receivership*

19. The receivers believe that the finance company, or alternatively Lease Plan
UK Ltd, intend to try and take possession of the vehicles. The vehicles are required
to carry on business as a haulage company. If Transag does not have a full fleet of
vehicles it will be unable to honour its existing contractual commitments.   C

20. Transag is currently trading at a marginal level of profit of approximately
£2,000 per week. If additional contracts are lost it will be uneconomic for the
business to continue to trade.

21. The receivers intend, if possible, to sell the business of Transag as a going
concern, the estimated realisation being in the order of between £300,000 and
£350,000 (excluding the freehold property). The receivers have contemplated the   D
possibility that no buyer will be found in the next seven days. However, the
receivers will be seeing a potential buyer today, who they believe is genuinely
interested in making the purchase and who has expressed that interest for some
time. The receivers also believe that the buyer will await the outcome of the action.
If no buyer is found it may be that the receivers will have to take the decision to
close the business down and to sell off the assets individually. However, there is
still a real possibility that a buyer will be found in the next seven days and the   E
receivers believe that a higher figure will be obtained if the business can be sold as
a going concern.'

The writ, as I have already mentioned, was issued on 17 December 1993 and on that
day, on an ex parte application, an injunction was granted restraining the defendants
from interfering with the company's possession or use of the vehicles. The motion that
has come before the court is an inter partes motion which was issued pursuant to an   F
undertaking in that behalf when the interlocutory ex parte order was made on 17
December 1993. The parties have, however, sensibly as it seems to me, agreed to treat
this motion as the trial of the action and the relief that is sought in the writ reads as
follows:

'An order that the defendants be relieved from the forfeiture of an agreement . . .'

The agreements are then set out, with their dates, the parties are stated and the   G
registration numbers of the vehicles are stated:

'upon such terms as the court shall think fit.'

That is fairly evidently a misprint for a claim that the plaintiff be relieved from the
forfeiture. Secondly, a declaration that cl. 13(f) of each of the agreements referred to in
para. 1 constitutes a penalty and is accordingly void. Thirdly, further or other relief and
costs.   H

There have been no further pleadings served on either side but the parties were agreed
before me that the issue that arose and which needed to be decided in the interests of all
parties as soon as possible was whether the court should relieve (whether it is called a
penalty or a forfeiture) the plaintiff company from the consequences under the
agreements of the appointment of the administrative receivers to its assets.

A

It was submitted for the administrative receivers that cl. 13(f), which I have read and need not repeat, did not apply to administrative receiverships but only to other receiverships. This submission was not pressed and in my judgment rightly so. I see no possible basis for excluding administrative receiverships from the expression used 'if a receiver shall be appointed of the hirer's assets or any part thereof'.

B

The expression 'administrative receiver' is a label given by statute, initially s. 45(2) of the *Insolvency Act* 1985, now s. 29(2) of the *Insolvency Act* 1986. It reads:

'In this chapter 'administrative receiver' means–

    (a) a receiver or manager of the whole (or substantially the whole) of a company's property appointed by or on behalf of the holders of any debentures of the company secured by a charge which, as created, was a floating charge or by such a charge and one or more other securities . . .'

C

The label is given to a particular category of receivers or receivers and managers. No reason was advanced for suggesting that those that came within that definition were not receivers appointed of the hirer's assets or any parts thereof. On the contrary, it is clear in my view that an appointment of such receivers would be an important, if not the principal, category of receivership which the parties to the agreements would have intended to include within para. 13(f).

D

I therefore conclude that an event making the agreements determinable forthwith without notice by the owner did in fact occur on 23 November 1993. It was not contended that, if the agreements were made thus determinable, they were not determined by the letter of 2 December 1993. What was contended was that, on the true construction of the agreements, and in particular the combined effect of cl. 14 and 22 thereof, if the agreements were determined, any excess in value of the vehicles, whether as a result of sale or certified valuation on behalf of the owner over the amount of outstanding instalments not yet due under the agreements, would be liable to be refunded by the owner to the company as hirer.

E

Clause 14 in terms only provides for payments by the hirer to the owner and not vice versa. What was relied on by Mrs Galley as justifying the implication of an obligation on the owner to make the claimed payment of surplus in value over the future instalments was the inclusion in cl. 22 of the reference to 'any amount due from or to the hirer'. That, it was said, expressly contemplated a payment being made to the hirer as well as a payment by the hirer and, therefore, cl. 14 should be read in a corresponding way so as to permit and require where there was such a surplus of value in the goods over the future instalments a payment to the hirer of that surplus. In my judgment that argument fails for two reasons. First, it does not take account of the full form of cl. 22, which is in my view a carefully drawn provision and states, as the result of the certificate when given, that it provides prima facie evidence that the amount certified is in fact due from or allowable to the hirer at the date of the certificate. The clause does not say 'payable to' but 'allowable to' the hirer, and that exactly fits the credit which the hirer is in terms given against the liability otherwise imposed upon the hirer by cl. 14 to pay the amount of future instalments. Far from there being an implication to be drawn from the terms of cl. 22 regarding the true construction of cl. 14, in my view, when cl. 22 is read as a whole, it shows that the reference at the outset of that clause to 'an amount due to the hirer' is intended to refer to a credit to which the hirer is entitled against a liability otherwise imposed upon the hirer, and this exactly fits the terms of cl. 14. No implication or modification of cl. 14 is, in my view, called for.

F

G

H

The second reason for rejecting the argument on construction that the hirer can be entitled to receive a payment under cl. 14 is quite simply that the language will not bear that construction, and there is nothing like the requisite context for implying such a term whether the officious bystander or business efficacy is relied upon.

Mrs Galley for the company submitted that if her argument on construction was   A
rejected, as I have rejected it, the provisions of the agreements were such as to attract the
equitable doctrine of relief from penalties or forfeiture. She referred to *Chitty on
Contracts* (26th edn), para. 3634 of which starts as follows:

> 'The view has been advanced that the court has power in equity to relieve the hirer
> from the forfeiture of instalments already paid.'

That has indeed excited a degree of academic comment but it deals with a different   B
question, namely whether past payments can be recovered. This is different from the case
raised before me where the question is whether relief can be granted from the provision
that the owner may retake the goods on the happening of an event such as the
appointment of a receiver of the hirer's assets. Recognising this distinction, Mrs Galley
said that she only relied upon the statement in *Chitty*, which I have read, as authority for
the proposition that the court has jurisdiction to grant relief from forfeiture in relation to
hire-purchase agreements. I accept that the opposite proposition, namely that the court   C
can never have jurisdiction to grant relief from forfeiture in relation to a hire-purchase
agreement, is far too widely stated. Thus, in *Barton Thompson & Co Ltd v Stapling
Machines Co* [1966] Ch 499, Pennycuick J said (at p. 509):

> 'I am not prepared to hold that it is plain and obvious as a matter of law that in
> the absence of unconscionable behaviour the court has in no circumstances power
> to relieve against forfeiture under any conceivable lease of a chattel. This is, I think,   D
> a point which the plaintiffs should be allowed to argue if their case is otherwise
> maintainable.'

The application there was one to strike out an application by a hirer for relief from
forfeiture where the hirer had fallen into arrears and the application to strike out in fact
succeeded, because of the absence of an averment of willingness by the hirer to pay all
arrears. The statement quoted above by Pennycuick J is strictly obiter, but it was relied   E
upon by Edmund Davies LJ in *Starside Properties Ltd v Mustapha* [1974] 1 WLR 816 at
p. 822.

The general position as to jurisdiction was summarised by Dillon LJ in *BICC plc v
Burndy Corporation* [1985] Ch 232 at p. 251F in the following terms:

> 'In *Shiloh Spinners Ltd. v. Harding* [1973] A.C. 691, the House of Lords held that
> the court had jurisdiction to grant relief against forfeiture of proprietary rights in
> circumstances outside the ordinary landlord and tenant relationship; but the case   F
> was concerned with a claim for relief against a right of re-entry on land, and the
> speeches do not cast light on the extent to which jurisdiction exists to grant relief
> against forfeiture of property other than an interest in land. In *Barton Thompson
> & Co. Ltd. v. Stapling Machines Co.* [1966] Ch. 499, 509, Pennycuick J. considered
> it to be arguable that relief could be granted against forfeiture of a lease of chattels.
> That view seems to have been approved by Edmund Davies L.J. in *Starside*   G
> *Properties Ltd. v. Mustapha* [1974] 1 W.L.R. 816, 822; and in *Stockloser v. Johnson*
> [1954] 1 Q.B. 476, 502, Romer L.J. apparently considered that the court would
> have power in an appropriate case to grant relief by way of extension of time to a
> purchaser of a diamond necklace who had failed to pay the final instalment of the
> price in due time.

> There is no clear authority, but for my part I find it difficult to see why the   H
> jurisdiction of equity to grant relief against forfeiture should only be available
> where what is liable to forfeiture is an interest in land and not an interest in
> personal property. Relief is only available where what is in question is forfeiture of
> proprietary or possessory rights, but I see no reason in principle for drawing a
> distinction as to the type of property in which the rights subsist. The fact that the
> right to forfeiture arises under a commercial agreement is highly relevant to the

A   question whether relief against forfeiture should be granted, but I do not see that it can preclude the existence of the jurisdiction to grant relief, if forfeiture of proprietary or possessory rights, as opposed to merely contractual rights, is in question.'

Mr Doctor for the defendants submitted that the provisions of cl. 13(f) of the agreements could not constitute a penalty from which a court of equity could grant relief

B   because it was a clause empowering the owner to terminate the agreement on the occurrence of an event and not on the non-performance of a contractual obligation and this, he submitted, could not constitute a penalty. He cited *Sterling Industrial Facilities Ltd v Lydiate Textiles Ltd* (1962) 106 SJ 669 in which Diplock LJ is reported in a somewhat condensed report as having said this:

> 'A penalty was a sum agreed to be paid in the event of non-performance of a
C   contractual obligation. Here there was no question of any breach of obligation but the defendants were sued in respect of sums payable in a specified eventuality. It had been conceded that there was no case in which it had been held that a payment to be made in a specified eventuality was a penalty or to be treated as such. His Lordship was not prepared to extend the definition of "penalty" and, save for certain passages in the speech of Lord Denning in *Bridge v. Campbell Discount Co. Ltd.* . . . there was no authority which suggested that it should be. This might have
D   been an improvident bargain, but the law did not relieve against improvident bargains where the parties were at arm's length, as they were here.'

He said he would dismiss the appeal.

Further authority for that proposition is to be found in *Export Credits Guarantee Department v Universal Oil Products Co* [1983] 1 WLR 399. The headnote reads as follows:

E   > 'In 1970 a number of agreements were concluded relating to the design, construction and installation by the defendants of an oil refinery for a group of companies in Newfoundland ("the Newfoundland companies"), and to the financing of the project. One such agreement was "the construction contract", made between the third defendants and one of the Newfoundland companies. The financing was effected by the issue by the Newfoundland companies of a series of promissory notes, in return for which a consortium of banks headed by K. Ltd.
F   provided funds to one of the companies. The plaintiffs by contracts with K. Ltd. guaranteed the promissory notes, and by clause 7(1) of an agreement ("the premium agreement") with the defendants, required the defendants, in the event of default in the performance of their obligations under other agreements, including the construction contract, to repay to the plaintiffs any sums paid by the plaintiffs under the contracts of guarantee. Some of the promissory notes were dishonoured by the Newfoundland companies, and the plaintiffs duly indemnified K. Ltd. in
G   accordance with the guarantee contracts. The plaintiffs alleged that the third defendants were in default under the construction contract, and claimed from the defendants, pursuant to clause 7(1) of the premium agreement, a sum equivalent to that paid to K. Ltd. On the trial of a preliminary issue, Staughton J. held that clause 7(1) did not operate as a penalty clause and was enforceable. The Court of Appeal dismissed an appeal by the defendants.

H   On appeal by the defendants:-

> *Held*, dismissing the appeal, that since clause 7(1) provided for the defendants to reimburse the plaintiffs in respect of actual loss suffered by the plaintiffs under the guarantee contracts, in the event of breach by the defendants of contractual duties owed by them to other parties, and not to the plaintiffs, the clause was not a penalty clause . . .'

Lord Roskill, at p. 403, said:

> 'My Lords, one purpose, perhaps the main purpose, of the law relating to penalty clauses is to prevent a plaintiff recovering a sum of money in respect of a breach of contract committed by a defendant which bears little or no relationship to the loss actually suffered by the plaintiff as a result of the breach by the defendant. But it is not and never has been for the courts to relieve a party from the consequences of what may in the event prove to be an onerous or possibly even a commercially imprudent bargain. The appellants could only secure the finance from Kleinworts if the respondents were prepared to give Kleinworts the guarantee which Kleinworts required. The respondents were only prepared to give their guarantee to Kleinworts upon the terms of the premium agreement which included the stringent right of recourse provided for in clause 7(1). The appellants accepted those terms which provided for the right of recourse to arise upon the happening of a specified event, and that specified event has now happened. But as my noble and learned friend, Lord Keith of Kinkel, observed during the argument, this is not a case where the respondents are seeking to recover more than their actual loss as compensation by way of damages for breach of the contract to which they were a party. They are seeking, and only seeking, to recover their actual loss, namely, the sums which they became legally obliged to pay and have paid to Kleinworts.'

I accept that the law relating to penalties does not apply in the present case where there is no recovery of a sum of money in respect of a breach of contract involved. What is involved is the assertion by the owners of a right to recover possession of the goods on the happening of an event which the commercial contracts constituted by the agreements provided should entitle the owners to effect that recovery. No monetary money claim is being made by the defendants nor indeed is any claim being advanced on behalf of the company for recovery of sums already paid by it.

The other general principle which I accept from the *Export Credits* case to which I have referred above is that I should not be disposed to extend the law by relieving against an obligation in a contract entered into between two parties, if the situation does not fall within well defined limits in which the court has in the past shown itself able to interfere. I interpret that attitude stated by Lord Roskill, in a passage which I have not quoted in terms, as being an indication that precedent is an important factor in assessing whether or not the court can and should exercise its relieving powers.

The balance of authority is, in my judgment, in favour of the view that even a provision for payment of a sum on an event, such as a liquidation of the hirer under a hire-purchase agreement, is not a penalty: *Re Apex Supply Co Ltd* [1942] Ch 108 is an example of such a conclusion. But whether this is so or not, no authority was cited to me for the proposition that the right to retake possession of the goods subject to a hire-purchase agreement as opposed to the right to demand payment of a sum of money on such an event could constitute a penalty, and I do not accept that it could. It is for that reason that I have concluded that no penalty is involved in this case.

Since no penalty is involved, the only head under which a claim to relief can in my view be advanced is under the jurisdiction to relieve against forfeiture. As to this, the following statement taken from *Snell's Principles of Equity* (29th edn), at p. 541, was quoted with approval in *Starsign Properties v Mustapha* by Edmund Davies LJ at p. 821. The passage in *Snell* reads as follows:

> *'Forfeitures*
>
> **1. Principles of relief.** The principle is that in appropriate and limited cases courts of equity will grant relief against forfeiture for breach of covenant or condition where the primary object of the bargain is to secure a stated result and the provision for forfeiture is added as security for the production of that result. In determining

A   whether a case is appropriate for relief, the court considers the conduct of the applicant for relief (and in particular whether his default was wilful), how grave the breaches were, and what disparity there is between the value of the property forfeited and the damage caused by the breach. In general, equity granted relief only where the forfeiture in substance was merely security for payment of a monetary sum, as where the contract for sale of land makes provision for payment of the price by instalments and confers on the vendor a right in the event of default

B   to rescind the contract and retain the moneys already paid; but the jurisdiction is not confined to such cases, and it applies, e.g. to a right of entry reserved on an assignment of leasehold premises in respect of the assignee's breaches of positive and restrictive covenants designed to protect the assignor's adjoining premises. The doctrine of relief against forfeiture is, however, restricted to contracts concerning the transfer of proprietary or possessory rights, whether in land or

C   other assets; it is thus inapplicable to the right of shipowners under a time charter to withdraw the vessel upon non-payment of hire, or to a provision for termination of an exclusive licence granted to the buyer of goods to use the plaintiff's trade names and trade marks.'

The only forfeiture that I can discern in the case before me where no claim is being made in respect of past payments by the company is the loss of the contingent right to buy the goods for £5 under cl. 24. That right is exercisable if the hirer has duly observed

D   and performed all the terms and conditions of the agreement and has paid all sums due under the agreement. That necessarily presupposes that the agreement has run its course, without being terminated before the end of the period during which instalments were payable, which is not what happened in relation to any of the three agreements before me when the administrative receivers were appointed in November last, although in fact the period under the first agreement has subsequently expired. So the right under cl. 24

E   was still contingent when the agreements were terminated consequent upon the appointment of the administrative receivers. In my view, although that right was then subject to that contingency, it can nevertheless be truthfully said that there was a forfeiture of proprietary or possessory rights and not merely contractual rights. Even a contingent right to exercise an option appears to me to be properly described as a 'proprietary right'.

F   It remains to examine how far the authorities establish that the court's jurisdiction to relieve can be invoked in circumstances such as the present. The only precedents found and cited by Mrs Galley do not extend to any case in which the court has in fact relieved against a provision in a hire-purchase agreement, allowing the owner to retake possession upon the appointment of a receiver of a hirer's assets. In addition to the cases already mentioned in this judgment, Mrs Galley cited *Re Piggin* (1962) 112 LJ 424, a decision of Judge Carey Evans in the Norwich County Court in which he held that a trustee in

G   bankruptcy of a hirer could recover from the owner of a van the subject of a hire-purchase agreement not only the surplus of the proceeds of the sale of the van over outstanding instalments at the date of the act of bankruptcy (this was an old bankruptcy) but also additional sums for which the van could have been sold had the official receiver co-operated with the bankrupt in the sale.

It is not easy to see the precise basis upon which the case was ultimately decided.

H   Disregarding an argument on reputed ownership which was rejected, two arguments were advanced on behalf of the trustee in bankruptcy. The first was that a clause giving a right to repossession on bankruptcy was void as against the trustee in bankruptcy as an attempt to deprive the creditors of an asset of the bankrupt. This argument was in terms accepted by Judge Carey Evans, who is reported as having laid down the very broad proposition that any provision whereby a bankrupt sought to deprive his trustee in bankruptcy of the contractual advantages he had acquired for valuable consideration was void as against the trustee. Whether that is sustainable as a matter of bankruptcy law I need not examine. But if the case was decided on that ground, it is of no assistance on the subject of relief against forfeiture where no bankruptcy is involved.

The other issue dealt with is reported in the following terms:

> 'The last point debated before him was whether equity could grant relief in hire-purchase cases and if so, ought it to do so in this case? He was not prepared to hold that the facts brought this case within the principle of equity intervening where the finance company's conduct was inexcusable. Here they were only seeking to rely upon what they conceived to be their legal rights to redress the losses on other transactions with the bankrupt. After considering the authorities His Honour came to the conclusion that equity might properly be invoked to prevent the hirer, or someone claiming through him, forfeiting the benefit of the agreement and losing all he had paid and the vehicle too when the owners were offered the full balance due to them. Such relief could be claimed here – the trustee undertook within hours to pay the balance. The trustee was entitled to recover the sum he had lost of £103 4s. 6d.'

That in fact was the figure the van could have been sold for with co-operation.

The basis upon which this last conclusion was reached is not entirely clear to me but it seems that the earlier specific finding that the clause in question was void as against the trustee in bankruptcy was at least a very important factor. Quite apart from the fact that *Re Piggin* is not a decision of the High Court, it is not in my view an authority which extends beyond the context in which it was decided, namely that of bankruptcy.

Finally, and perhaps most importantly, I was referred to *Goker v NWS Bank plc* which is only reported in *The Times* newspaper for 23 May 1990. In that case an injunction restraining a finance company, which had made a hire-purchase agreement over a car, from exercising its right to sell the car was discharged. Very experienced counsel for the finance company conceded that there was jurisdiction to grant relief from forfeiture of proprietary or possessory rights but submitted that it should be exercised only in exceptional circumstances. Sir Gervase Sheldon accepted that submission. He is reported as saying this:

> 'Sir Godfray [Le Quesne who appeared for the defendant finance company] had conceded that the court had a general jurisdiction in such cases to grant relief [against] forfeiture – a jurisdiction which extended beyond the statutory provisions and existed for the hirer's protection.
>
> On the other hand, his Lordship accepted it was a jurisdiction which was unlikely to be used save in exceptional circumstances in which the court was satisfied that no significant prejudice would result to the lender from the grant of relief.
>
> In the present case if relief were not granted the defendants stood to make an unexpected windfall of not less than about £10,000 if in addition to retaining the sums already paid and payable to them by the plaintiff they were able to dispose of the vehicle and keep the proceeds.
>
> Sir Godfray had submitted that where a hirer had shown himself to be a defaulter, to oblige the owner of the goods to forgo his contractual rights and to return the goods to the hirer would be to oblige the owner to accept a risk greater than that contemplated when the contract was made.
>
> It was a submission which, in his Lordship's judgment, had considerable force. That was a case in which it would not be appropriate to grant the plaintiff the relief for which he had asked.

A   The plaintiff's conduct had been particularly remiss. In another case, maybe, a hirer's failure to pay one or more instalments might be less serious and more easily excused and explained and one which did not cast doubts on his readiness and ability to maintain payments in the future.

Nevertheless, where such doubts did exist, as in this particular instance, his Lordship apprehended that a hirer who sought relief from forfeiture would be faced by an obstacle he would not easily be able to overcome.'

B

Although the recognition of the existence of the court's jurisdiction proceeded upon a concession, and was strictly obiter, it seems to me to fall within the principle stated by Dillon LJ in the passage which I have quoted from *BICC v Burndy Corporation* in that there was a forfeiture or loss of an otherwise existing contingent proprietary right in the shape of an option to buy. Although there is no conclusive precedent in favour of the existence of the court's jurisdiction, there is none against it either, and I propose to be guided by what I take to be the underlying principle stated in Dillon LJ's judgment.

C

The final question therefore, given that I hold that the jurisdiction does exist, is, should the jurisdiction be exercised? In general, I would not grant relief unless I was satisfied that the terms upon which it was granted would confer upon the owner at least as valuable rights as the owner would have enjoyed under the original agreements. In addition, I would not grant relief unless I was satisfied that failure to do so would confer a substantial windfall on the owner over and above what the original agreements provided for the owner to receive. Finally, I would not grant relief if I considered that the conduct of the hirer had disentitled it to receive it. In particular, I take the following factors to be relevant in the present case:

D

(1)   The determination of the agreements occurred close to the end of the three-year period for the payment of instalments. As regards the first of the agreements, there was only some six weeks out of three years to go and even in relation to the third there was only just over six months.

E

(2)   No breach of the agreements has been established in evidence before the termination took effect. In particular, all sums due were duly paid down to their date.

F

(3)   The appointment of a receiver of the assets of the hirer is an event which is likely to cause the owner considerable problems and against which it is in my view perfectly proper for an owner to seek to be protected. I do not regard the provisions of cl. 14 as intrinsically unconscionable and indeed such provisions are very common and are to be found notably in the *Encyclopaedia of Forms and Precedents*. I should add in passing under that head that it was common ground that these were hire-purchase agreements which were not governed by the *Consumer Credit Act* 1974.

G

(4)   The agreement is a commercial document entered into at arm's length between two significant commercial entities.

(5)   The termination of the agreements, if relief against forfeiture is not granted, will confer on the owner a windfall of the order of £53,000 in that it will be able to realise assets worth £65,000 or so and keep the proceeds instead of receiving either £14,015 or £14,388.97 over the ensuing six months. I note that the existence of a windfall of the order of £10,000 did not deter Sir Gervase Sheldon from discharging the injunction and refusing relief from forfeiture in the *Goker* case but the figures in the present case show that the owner's windfall is greater both in absolute and in proportionate terms in relation to the agreed price placed upon the goods.

H

In *Goker* the windfall was £10,000 on a price of just over £45,000, some 22 per cent. In the present case it is £53,000 or thereabouts on an aggregate price of £177,333, which is just under 30 per cent. But, far more importantly, in *Goker*'s case the hirer had been in repeated default and Sir Gervase Sheldon accepted that what was being asked for amounted to requiring the owner to accept a risk greater than that contemplated when the contract was made.

(6)   If the defendants receive forthwith all that they were due to receive by the end of next May, they will not suffer any detriment that I can see or run any risk in relation to the benefits reserved to them by the agreements. On the contrary, there will be a degree of acceleration of payments in their favour.

(7)   The refusal of relief from forfeiture may cause significant loss to the company.

Taking all those above considerations into account, I have reached the conclusion at the end of the day that this is indeed one of those rare cases where it would be right for the court to grant relief from forfeiture if the company pays to the second defendant a sum equal to the outstanding instalments as at 23 November 1993 within seven days from today's date. The amount involved should be susceptible of exact calculation. But, if it cannot be agreed, then I propose to direct that there should be a payment of £14,015, which both parties accept is outstanding, to the second defendant; and a payment of £373.97, which is the amount in dispute, into court or (if the parties so agree) into the joint names of their solicitors to abide the event of an inquiry what was the amount of such outstanding instalments as at 23 November 1993 and to direct such an inquiry with the costs thereof reserved.

(*Order accordingly*)

A

B

C

D

E

F

G

H

A
Re an Application pursuant to r. 7.28 of the Insolvency Rules 1986.

Chancery Division (in bankruptcy).
Millett J.
Judgment delivered 21 January 1994.

B
Insolvency – Court procedure and practice – Inspection of records of insolvency proceedings – Whether 'insolvency consultant' searching for customers was inspecting records for proper purpose – Insolvency Rules 1986 (SI 1986/1925), r. 7.28.

An 'insolvency consultant' searching the records of insolvency proceedings at the Bankruptcy Registry for the names and addresses of potential customers for his services,
C
was not inspecting the records for a proper purpose within the meaning of r. 7.28 of the Insolvency Rules 1986 and such inspection was refused.

The applicant appeared in person.

JUDGMENT

Millett J: This is an application under r. 7.28 of the *Insolvency Rules* 1986. Rule 7.28
D
provides as follows:

'(1) Subject as follows, the court's records of insolvency proceedings shall be open to inspection by any person.

(2) If in the case of a person applying to inspect the records the registrar is not satisfied as to the propriety of the purpose for which inspection is required, he may refuse to allow it. The person may then apply forthwith and ex parte to the judge,
E
who may refuse the inspection, or allow it on such terms as he thinks fit.

(3) The judge's decision under paragraph (2) is final.'

Mr Klibansky is an insolvency consultant who carries on the business of advising bankrupts and prospective bankrupts and persons seeking lawfully to avoid bankruptcy. He advises them of their rights and liabilities and the practical consequences of a bankruptcy order.
F

Until recently he or his representative were in the habit of attending the search room of the Bankruptcy Registry where they made multiple searches against the names of all individuals who had had a bankruptcy petition against them with a view to offering them their services.

Recently one of Mr Klibansky's representatives who was attending for this purpose
G
was questioned and asked the purpose for which he was making a search of the records. He explained that he was making a multiple search and was told that he could not do so but was obliged to search against named individuals. This was impractical, given the purpose for which the search was needed.

The registrar certified that he was not satisfied as to the propriety of the purpose for which inspection was required, and ruled that in future Mr Klibansky and his representatives could not inspect, or use the records, for the purposes which I have
H
described.

Mr Klibansky now appeals to me. He submits that the records of insolvency proceedings are public records open to members of the public, of which he is one, and that there is nothing intrinsically improper in the purpose for which he seeks to inspect them. Whatever views the registrar may hold of his touting for business, it cannot be said to be unlawful, immoral or improper.

In my judgment the word 'propriety' in r. 7.28(2) does not possess the meaning which   A
Mr Klibansky seeks to ascribe to it. Although the records of insolvency proceedings are
available for public inspection, the registrar must be satisfied that inspection is required
for a legitimate purpose, having regard to the purpose for which statute made the records
available for inspection. That purpose is to enable persons who have a legitimate interest
in a particular insolvency proceeding to discover what has taken place.

Creditors (though not only creditors) obviously have a legitimate purpose to inspect   B
the record of insolvency proceedings which relate to their debtor. In a case of wide public
interest the press may also have a legitimate interest in the proceedings. But I cannot
think that an insolvency consultant such as Mr Klibansky has a legitimate interest, within
the meaning of the Insolvency Rules, in the insolvency records in order to ascertain the
names and addresses of potential customers for his services.

Accordingly, in my judgment, the purpose for which Mr Klibansky has requested a   C
search is not a proper purpose within the meaning of r. 7.28(2). I dismiss the application.

(*Order accordingly*)

D

E

F

G

H

A
Re Dicetrade Ltd.
Secretary of State for Trade and Industry v Worth & Anor.
Court of Appeal (Civil Division).
Dillon, Leggatt and Henry L JJ.
Judgment delivered 21 February 1994.

B
Disqualifying unfit directors of insolvent companies – Costs – Director sought leave under disqualification order to act as director – Whether Secretary of State should have costs of application on indemnity basis – Company Directors Disqualification Act 1986, s. 6, 7, 17.

1. On an application under s. 6 and 7 of the Company Directors Disqualification Act 1986 the general rule was that the Secretary of State should have his costs on the standard basis and only in special circumstances on the indemnity basis.

C
2. An application by the director to be allowed to continue as a director of a particular company, dealt with as was desirable at the same time as the hearing for the disqualification order, was unlikely to take up a substantial part of the time of the total hearing if the Secretary of State merely put forward considerations for the court to consider. In those circumstances, it would be convenient not to make a separate order in respect of the costs of that application.

D
3. If a disqualified director made an application for leave sometime later arising out of fresh circumstances, that application would properly be regarded as free-standing. There was no general principle which would entitle the Secretary of State to be paid his costs of attending on the application automatically on the standard basis even if the Secretary of State, on consideration, did not oppose the application. There was no special position of the Secretary of State. No order for costs might be appropriate where the Secretary of State intimated to the applicant or the applicant's solicitors any particular points that were relied on so that they could be drawn to the attention of the court, but stated that he did not oppose the grant of the relief sought.

E

4. In the present case extra costs were incurred by the Secretary of State because the director was not ready with her application under s. 17 and that application had to be stood over. In those circumstances, the correct order was that she should pay the costs of the application, but on the standard basis only.

F
The following cases were referred to in the judgment of Dillon LJ:

Godwin Warren Control Systems plc, Re [1992] BCC 557.
Southbourne Sheet Metal Co Ltd, Re [1991] BCC 732; [1992] BCC 797, [1993] 1 WLR 244 (CA).
Wedgecraft Ltd & Ors, Re (unreported, 7 March 1986, Harman J).

Paul Girolami (instructed by the Treasury Solicitor) for the Secretary of State.

G
The respondent appeared in person.

JUDGMENT

Dillon LJ: This is an appeal, by leave granted by the judge, by the Secretary of State for Trade and Industry against an order made by Chadwick J on 9 September 1992 by which, having given leave to the respondent to this appeal, Miss Jackson, to act as a director of and be concerned and take part in the management of a company called B E Jackson of Croydon Ltd, he made no order as to the costs of the application by Miss Jackson of 8 July 1992 on which that leave was granted.

H

It is sought by the notice of appeal that Miss Jackson should be ordered to pay the costs of her application for leave to act as a director, notwithstanding disqualification, on the indemnity basis.

The position is that Miss Jackson had acted as a director of a company called Dicetrade   A
Ltd, which went into liquidation. In consequence of the matters that arose in relation to
Dicetrade the Secretary of State made an application under s. 6 and 7 of the *Company
Directors Disqualification Act* 1986 for Miss Jackson's disqualification.

That application came before Harman J on 22 July 1992. He made an order
disqualifying Miss Jackson from being a director of a company or in any way, directly or
indirectly, being concerned in the management of a company for a period of four years   B
commencing on that date.

Harman J found that the conduct of that company's affairs had been deplorable and
that Miss Jackson had shown herself unfit to be a director of a company, though he also
seems to have accepted, at the end of the argument, that her conduct had not in fact been
as serious as he had supposed at the outset of the hearing from what he had seen in the
papers.   C

Miss Jackson launched her application to be allowed to act as a director of B E
Jackson of Croydon Ltd in advance of the hearing before Harman J. It was a family
company. She had been concerned in the management and seems, at present, to be in
control of that company, but there do not appear to have been any complaints about the
way the business was managed.

At the time of the hearing before Harman J of the Secretary of State's disqualification   D
application, the material required for considering the application for leave under s. 17 of
the Disqualification Act for Miss Jackson to be a director of B E Jackson of Croydon
Ltd was not complete and her tackle was not in order. The application was therefore
adjourned to come on when ready. It came on before Chadwick J.

There are several points that I should mention. The first is that the costs that the
department seek are costs on the indemnity basis. We have been referred to a substantial   E
number of decisions in the Chancery Division which have been concerned not with costs
of applications under s. 17 by themselves but costs of disqualification applications under
s. 6 where a disqualification order is made. The beginning of that line of authority which
leads Mr Girolami to the submission that if costs are awarded on an indemnity basis on
applications for disqualification under s. 6 they should equally or a fortiori be awarded
on an indemnity basis where leave is granted under s. 17, is a view which seems to have
started with Harman J in a case, *Re Wedgecraft Ltd & Ors*, which he decided on 7 March   F
1986 (transcript p. 7B):

> '. . . the usual practice has been to say these are costs which fall upon the official
> receiver as representing the public wholly because of what has now been held to be
> misconduct of a serious sort . . . In the circumstances there does not seem any
> reason why the public should have to pay for this application which has been
> brought for their protection; and indemnity costs has been the usual order made.'   G

At least various judges at first instance have treated that as the usual order. Others
have not. In particular, in one case Chadwick J did not. He said:

> 'In my view the Crown should be treated in the same way as any other litigant in
> this regard and, accordingly, I propose to order costs on the standard basis.'

That was in *Re Godwin Warren Control Systems plc* [1992] BCC 557 at p. 570C.

   H

As to the general approach to the costs of the Crown of an application for a
disqualification order under the Disqualification Act, we now have the guidance of this
court in the case of *Re Southbourne Sheet Metal Co Ltd* [1992] BCC 797. That was a case
in which the Crown started disqualification proceedings against a company director but,
at a later stage, decided that the material was not sufficient to warrant that and
discontinued the proceedings.

A   The case came before Harman J, who granted the Secretary of State leave to discontinue the proceedings but declined to make any order that the Secretary of State should pay the director's costs of the proceedings ([1991] BCC 732). The judge made no order as to the costs of the proceedings. The judge's decision was put this way (at p. 733F):

B   'I think I can properly say that there has grown up something of a practice in this court not to visit upon the DTI costs incurred by a director who has been proceeded against in a case where there is cause to investigate . . . but, more than that, cause to believe that there is a prima facie case of unfitness to be a director, which prima facie case is then rebutted by the evidence that comes in.'

Nourse LJ said, at page 798C:

C   '. . . I am of a clear opinion that any such practice is contrary to principle and that (the director's) appeal must therefore be allowed . . .'

It follows from the discussion of the cases in Nourse LJ's judgment, and from the judgment of McCowan LJ, who agreed with him, also from the judgment of Beldam LJ, that there was no justification for a special costs rule in this type of litigation. It is not right to say that proceedings under the Disqualification Act being public interest proceedings are different to other civil proceedings when it comes to costs. The Secretary of State must take his chance in such litigation, just like any other litigant. Therefore the

D   Secretary of State had to pay the costs of the director against whom he decided to discontinue. Equally, there can be no general rule that on an application under s. 6 and 7 of the Disqualification Act the Secretary of State should prima facie have indemnity costs. The prima facie order should be that the Secretary of State has costs on the standard basis.

There may be cases in which indemnity costs are warranted by the circumstances of

E   the case, e.g. by the fact, in accordance with normal practice, that extravagant claims have been made by the director and a wholly false and futile defence has been put forward, or claims have been defended where there is no conceivable basis for the defence, as may have been the case in some of the cases at first instance to which we have been referred. But the general rule should be that the Secretary of State gets his costs on the standard basis, and only in special circumstances on the indemnity basis.

F   What, then, if there is an application by the director to be allowed to continue as a director of a particular company notwithstanding disqualification? It is in everyone's interests that if that is envisaged before the disqualification application comes on for hearing, and if the director has advice it will have been envisaged, then it should be heard at the same time because, from the point of view of the director, it is desirable that if he or she is going to be allowed to continue as director of that company there should be no time passing before the leave is granted.

G   If the application is dealt with at the same time as the hearing for the disqualification order and if, as one would expect, the Secretary of State merely puts forward the considerations that the court ought to consider, it is unlikely to take up a substantial part of the time of the total hearing. In those circumstances, if the amount of time taken up is relatively small it will no doubt be the convenient course not to make a separate order in respect of costs of that sort of application.

H   In the present case we have a situation in which it was not possible to deal with it at the same time, and the application had to be stood over. It came on at a later date.

The judge, in dealing with costs, said this:

'There is no lis between the applicant and the Secretary of State. The Secretary of State is not before the court either to support or oppose the application, but to call the court's attention to relevant matters. The applicant has no choice in whether or not the Secretary of State appears; neither does the Secretary of State. The provisions of s. 17(2) of the Act are mandatory. Whatever the result of the application it is impossible for it to be said in any true sense that the Secretary of State has either won or lost.'

Then he said:

'There is no "event" . . . and it would be impossible to identify any general principle which would require costs orders to be made for the payment of the Secretary of State's costs in the case of applications which do not succeed; but not paid in the case of those which do succeed.'

He said:

'The practice, if there be one, of requiring an applicant for leave to pay the Secretary of State's costs of attending on the application on an indemnity basis must lead to the imposition of an automatic financial burden on anyone who seeks to exercise the right to apply for leave which the statute undoubtedly gives him or her. I do not think it was the intention of the legislature to impose such a burden in every case.'

Then he concluded that it was not right as a matter of practice that the applicant should always be required to bear in addition to his or her own costs further costs over which he or she had no control.

I have dealt with the case where the application for leave under s. 17 is heard at the same time as the application for the disqualification order. If a disqualification order is made and there is an application for leave advanced some while later by the disqualified director arising out of fresh circumstances then, in my judgment, it would properly be regarded as free-standing and I do not believe that there is any general principle which would entitle the Secretary of State to be paid his costs of attending on the application automatically on the standard basis even if the Secretary of State, on consideration, did not oppose the application. There is no special position of the Secretary of State.

Moreover, the situation could be dealt with by the Secretary of State intimating to the applicant or the applicant's solicitors, as might be the case, any particular points that were relied on so that they could be drawn to the attention of the court, but stating that he did not oppose the grant of the relief sought. Such an application could then be dealt with most appropriately as a matter where no order as to costs was appropriate.

In the present case the matter that strikes me is that it was because Miss Jackson was not ready with her application under s. 17 that that application had to be stood over and could not be dealt with by Harman J. I regard that as a different circumstance because it has meant that extra costs were incurred by the Secretary of State because Miss Jackson did not have her tackle in order soon enough.

In these circumstances, in my view, the correct order in this case is that Miss Jackson should be ordered to pay the costs of her application, but on the standard basis only. Not the indemnity basis.

Leggatt LJ: I agree.

Henry LJ: I agree.

(Order accordingly. No order as to costs of the appeal)

A
Secretary of State for Trade and Industry v Sananes & Ors.
Nottingham County Court.
District Judge Cowling.
Judgment delivered 17 March 1993.

Disqualifying unfit directors of insolvent companies – Whether office-holder's
report to Secretary of State was privileged – Company Directors Disqualification
B *Act 1986, s. 7(4).*

The purpose of office-holders' making reports to the Secretary of State under s. 7(4) of
the Company Directors Disqualification Act 1986 was to assist the Secretary of State in
deciding whether to exercise his statutory powers under s. 7(1); the reports were part of the
information required by the Secretary of State in deciding whether to act and part of his
decision-making process: on that ground they were privileged.

C The following cases were referred to in the judgment:

Highgrade Traders Ltd, Re [1984] BCLC 151.
Waugh v British Railways Board [1980] AC 521.

Paul Girolami (instructed by Wragge & Co, Birmingham) for the applicant.

Nicholas Yell (instructed by Josiah Hincks, Son & Bullough, Leicester) for the
respondents.

D
JUDGMENT

District Judge Cowling: In this application within these proceedings the respondents
seek discovery of reports made by certain holders of office under s. 7(3) of the *Company*
Directors Disqualification Act 1986, namely, under para. (b) the liquidator, para. (d) the
administrative receiver and also the documents filed with the Secretary of State under
E s. 7(4) of that Act, under which the Secretary of State can require such office-holder to
furnish information to him as to a person's conduct as a director of a company and
produce documents relevant to that person's conduct as a director for the purpose of
determining whether to exercise any functions under s. 7, which is the function of deciding
whether to commence proceedings for disqualification order under s. 6.

It is said on behalf of the respondents that the Secretary of State has not stated what
documents were supplied under s. 7(4). The forms of report are specified in the *Insolvent*
F *Companies (Reports on Conduct of Directors) No. 2 Rules* 1986 (SI 1986/2134). Under
rule r. 4(7), penalties are imposed on office-holders for failing to make reports. There is
no specific statutory provision that the reports are privileged.

This application has been argued, quite rightly, under three main heads. The first is
relevance, the second is privilege and the third public interest immunity. I will deal first
with relevance.

G **Relevance**

The respondent says that these are quasi criminal proceedings. The applicant says no,
that they are quasi penal proceedings. The respondent says that if they are quasi criminal,
there is a duty, as on a prosecutor, to disclose all documents which could help the
respondents. The respondents want to see if the opinions expressed by the administrative
receiver and liquidator in the documents in question differ from those expressed in the
affidavits of Miss Lewis which were before the court to use as a basis for cross-
H examination.

Also, there may be references in those reports, say the respondents, to the degree of
cooperation by the respondents with the liquidator, their behaviour during the
liquidation and whether any assets of the company have disappeared. The highest point
which the respondents can put the case is that the documents may assist them and it is
for them to decide.

The applicant refers to the *County Court Rules* 1981, O. 14, r. 8. Are the documents A
needed to dispose fairly of the action or save costs? Are they necessary to dispose fairly
of the action? Is there a fatal flaw in the Secretary of State's decision to bring the
proceedings?

The applicant says this is a fishing expedition, which is not allowed and would not be
allowed in judicial review proceedings, where there is a wider than usual discovery. I have
been referred to a passage in the *Supreme Court Practice 1993*, p. 439 at 24/3/1 on that B
particular point. I do not think I need read it out again. Also, on p. 440. I will read out
that paragraph as far as it is relevant:

> 'As a general principle in judicial review discovery will be ordered where it is
> required in order that the justice of the case may be advanced and where it is,
> within the meaning of O. 24, r. 8, necessary for disposing fairly of the matter; the
> Court should not order discovery, however, where there is no material before it to C
> show that the reasoning of the respondent's decision-making process is defective
> or unreasonable or open to challenge, and where the purpose of the application is
> to study the respondent's documents to see if some flaw in the decision-making
> process can be established.'

The applicant says that the report under r. 4 of the 1986 rules will not help. They would
be bald, factual reports and the most the reports will disclose is a view of the
administrative receiver or of the liquidator and they will not take the matter any further, D
because the view or the opinion of the court is what is required ultimately and what will
count as to whether these respondents are disqualified.

The applicant says it will not be relevant to cross-examine Miss Lewis on the report of
the administrative receiver and his view. The receiver has no direct knowledge of the
underlying facts. It is not the primary document from which facts can be derived. The
report might be used to attack the credit of Miss Lewis and discovery on that ground E
should be refused. There is direct authority on that on p. 461 of the White Book under
24/8/2:

> 'As in the case of interrogatories . . . discovery solely for the purpose of impeaching
> the credit of the opposite party and giving him a bad name will not be ordered; it
> probably does not "relate to a matter in question," within r. 1 and in any event
> should be refused as a matter of discretion under this rule . . .' F

The respondents in reply say that the reports may include primary facts on which the
respondent can rely: as mentioned before, whether they have cooperated with the
liquidator, whether assets have gone missing and the opinion of the administrative
receiver would be of the utmost probative value to the respondents. They accept there
are problems so far as credibility of the applicants' witnesses are concerned. They deal
with motivation and say that the documents could be material to assist the court as to G
how to exercise its discretion. Any improper reason for bringing the case to court should
be brought out.

My finding on this aspect of the case is this. I have not seen the documents and
therefore cannot say that they do not contain factual information or inferences which
will not assist the court in coming to its decision. On that ground alone, they may be
relevant and ought to be disclosed. However, that is not an end of the matter, because H
there are two further facts to be considered.

Privilege

The next matter is, are the documents privileged? The respondent points out that the
reports were not to lawyers, but to the Secretary of State. I am referred to the White
Book at p. 445, the note to 24/5/9:

A

'The general principle is that the documents . . . are privileged if, and only if, coming into existence for the purpose of obtaining legal advice in existing or anticipated proceedings . . .'

There is the problem about documents which come into existence for more than one purpose, for example, accident reports. If the dominant purpose of the document is for existing or anticipated legal proceedings, they are privileged. That is a House of Lords decision in *Waugh v British Railways Board* [1980] AC 521. What is the dominant

B

purpose? It is not necessarily that in the mind of the maker of the document. One has to look at the purpose of the person under whose direction the document is produced, for example, employers or insurers. Where the dominant purpose of insurers in obtaining a report is for submission to their legal advisers for advice as to whether a claim on them should be paid or resisted, the document will be privileged.

I have been referred to the case of *Re Highgrade Traders Ltd* [1984] BCLC 151. I will

C

read para. (1) of the headnote of that report on p. 152:

'Documents brought into being with the dominant purpose of obtaining legal advice as to whether a legal claim should be made or resisted and which would lead to a decision whether or not to litigate were protected by legal professional privilege and it was not necessary that the documents be brought into existence for the dominant purpose of actually being used as evidence in anticipated litigation or only after a decision to make or resist a claim had been made.'

D

I need not go any further with that.

In this case the respondents say the reports were not made primarily for the purpose of litigation or to obtain legal advice, but to enable the Secretary of State to learn what is happening in company liquidations. They are required for the proper functioning of government. At most, they are required not for anticipated litigation, but for possible litigation. They are unsolicited advice received by the Secretary of State. There is no obligation on him to take any notice of the reports. He could simply file them.

E

The respondents' counsel, Mr Yell, distinguishes the *Re Highgrade Traders* decision, because in this case the fact-finding was not instigated by the Secretary of State. In *Highgrade* the reports were commissioned by the insurers to which they were made. The Secretary of State has not put the wheels in motion for the specific purpose of obtaining legal advice. The Secretary of State is under no duty to obtain legal advice before instigating proceedings such as these. However, I look first at s. 7(1) of the *Company Directors Disqualification Act* 1986: an application for an order under s. 6 may be made

F

by the Secretary of State in the circumstances there set out. That is a matter for his discretion. Then one looks at s. 7(3): if it appears to an office-holder as there defined that the conditions in s. 6(1) are satisfied, he shall report the matter to the Secretary of State. It is a duty on the office-holder. Under s. 7(4) the Secretary of State may call on the office-holder to furnish information and supply documents reasonably required for the purpose of determining whether to exercise any function under the section.

G

The purpose of making these reports is therefore very clear. It is to assist the Secretary of State in deciding whether to exercise his statutory powers under s. 7(1). The reports are part of the information required by the Secretary of State in deciding whether to act. They are part of his decision-making process. Mr Girolami says the Secretary of State will place these reports, and other evidence, before legal advisers before deciding whether to proceed.

The purpose of the reports and the documents which may have been supplied under

H

s. 7(4) seems to me to be perfectly clear. I am satisfied that all the documents sought by the respondents are privileged and on that ground I refuse an order for their production by the applicant. Having made that decision, I do not need to consider the thorny and third question of public interest immunity.

(Order accordingly)

Re RMCA Reinsurance Ltd & Anor.

Chancery Division (Companies Court).
Morritt J.
Judgment delivered 15 October 1993.

Scheme of arrangement – Whether court would direct meeting of class containing one member – Whether meeting had to be held in UK – Companies Act 1985, s. 425.

Where a scheme of arrangement was proposed under s. 425 of the Companies Act 1985 in relation to two reinsurance companies incorporated in the Republic of Singapore, the court would direct a class meeting to be held for the class of 'Singapore preferential creditor' even though there was only one person in that class (the appropriate officer of the Inland Revenue in Singapore); furthermore there was no territorial restriction on the place at which the meeting could be held pursuant to the directions of the court.

The following cases were referred to in the judgment:

East v Bennett Bros Ltd [1911] 1 Ch 163.
Hastings Deering Pty Ltd, Re (1985) 3 ACLC 474.

Gabriel Moss QC and Mark Arnold (instructed by Davies Arnold Cooper) for the applicants.

JUDGMENT

Morritt J: The summonses before me were issued by two reinsurance companies incorporated in the Republic of Singapore and seek orders for the convening of meetings pursuant to s. 425 of the *Companies Act* 1985 at which a proposed scheme of arrangement would be considered by the companies' various classes of creditors. The evidence in support of the application shows that this step is being taken on the advice of Cork Gully having considered all the possible alternatives given that, as advised by Coopers & Lybrand, both reinsurance companies are insolvent. On the merits of the matter there is an overwhelming case for granting the relief sought.

Two points have been raised during the course of the hearing for my consideration. The first arises from one class of creditor, which is described as Singapore preferential creditor. It is considered that there is only one person who falls within that class, namely, the appropriate officer of the Inland Revenue in Singapore. The question arises therefore whether the meeting at which that class is to consider the scheme can validly be held, or directed to be held, given that there could only be one person present.

Similar points appear to have arisen in the past. The first case brought to my attention is a decision of Warrington J in *East v Bennett Bros Ltd* [1911] 1 Ch 163. That concerned a passage in the company's memorandum and articles dealing with an increase in capital which required the sanction of preference shareholders by resolution at a separate meeting. There was at the time only one preference shareholder and the question arose whether his presence could constitute a meeting for the purposes of the articles. Warrington J held that it could because, although the primary meaning of the word 'meeting' is a meeting of more than one person, in the circumstances of that case it must have been in the mind of the draftsman that there might in certain circumstances be only one member of the class. At p. 168 he said:

'The question resolves itself into this. On the construction of this particular memorandum and the particular part of it, can there be such a thing as a meeting of one shareholder? It is not a question of there being several shareholders, and one shareholder only attending the so-called meeting, but where there is only one shareholder, so that a meeting in the sense of an assembly of persons is impossible.

A   The object of the provisions in the memorandum is quite plain. It is to obtain, before the issue of new shares, the assent in a binding and formal manner of the person or persons whose rights are affected.'

Then at p. 169 he said:

B   '. . . I am entitled to see what is the object of the provision in the memorandum of association. Plainly, as I have already said, that object is that before affecting the rights of the preference shareholders it shall be necessary to obtain and record in a formal manner the assent of the preference shareholders to that course. I think I may take it also that the persons who framed this document may have had, and must be taken to have had, in their minds the possibility at all events that this particular class of shares might fall into the hands of one person.'

Then the concluding paragraph at p. 170 reads:

C   'I think on the whole that I may give effect to obvious common sense by holding that in this particular case, where there is only one shareholder of the class, on the true construction of the memorandum, the expression "meeting" may be held to include that case.'

That decision was followed by the Supreme Court in New South Wales in *Re Hastings Deering Pty Ltd* (1985) 3 ACLC 474. I have been referred to the relevant statutory
D   provisions contained in s. 315 of the Companies (New South Wales) Code which for present purposes is in substantially the same terms as the provisions of s. 425 of the *Companies Act* 1985.

The decision of Kearney J was that he should conclude on substantially the same grounds as Warrington J in *East v Bennett Bros Ltd*, that the primary use of the word 'meeting' was displaced so that a meeting could consist of a single person. He said at
E   p. 475:

'The position under s. 315 creates, in my view, a clear context for treating the references therein to "a meeting" as including the artificial sense of a meeting constituted by a single individual.

One starts with the well accepted principle, as exemplified in the decision of Street J in *Montana Frocks Pty Ltd and Companies Act* (1967) 2 NSWR 584, that the
F   legislation creates as a condition precedent to the court's jurisdiction to approve a scheme of arrangement, the holding of the requisite meetings. The meetings called for in the present instance are meetings respectively of the members of the company and of the various classes of members, existing either because of difference in the nature of shareholdings or by difference in interests which exist between various groups of shareholders . . .

G   The terms of subs. (4) of s. 315 emphasise the mandatory requirement for such meetings to be held as an essential foundation to the scheme of arrangement taking effect so as to bind the members, classes of members and the company respectively.

In the present case, by reason of the difference in interests between the single individual shareholder and the general body of shareholders, such individual shareholder is, in my view, properly regarded as constituting a class of the members of the company. It follows that in order to fulfil the requirements of subs. (4) a
H   meeting of such a class must be convened.'

That decision is not technically binding on me but I certainly propose to follow and adopt it because of the reasoning and its innate common sense. It follows therefore that I conclude that there is jurisdiction to order a meeting under s. 425 even though there is only one person capable of falling within the class so that there cannot be more than one person present at the meeting.

The second point arises in relation to where the meeting may take place. In subs. (1),   A
the court is authorised to:

> '. . . order a meeting of the creditors or class of creditors, or of the members of the
> company or class of members (as the case may be), to be summoned in such
> manner as the court directs'.

The section is entirely silent as to the place where the meeting may take place but I can
see nothing in the nature of the section or in the context of the Companies Act as a whole   B
which would require it to be limited to a meeting to be held within any part of the UK.
Section 425 in terms applies to companies incorporated abroad and it is within the
experience of practitioners in the Companies Court that the court has on many previous
occasions directed meetings to be convened which are to be held abroad. There is, I am
told, no authority on the matter. In my judgment it is plain that there is no territorial
restriction on the place at which the meeting may be held pursuant to the directions of
the court.   C

I therefore decide both those points of principle in favour of the applicant and I will
make in each case an order in terms of the minute with the amendments which were
discussed with counsel during the course of the hearing.

(Order accordingly)

D

E

F

G

H

A
Re Barn Crown Ltd.

Chancery Division (Companies Court).
His Honour Judge Rich QC (sitting as a High Court judge).
Judgment delivered 24 January 1994.

B
Winding up – Avoidance of property dispositions – Whether payments into bank account were dispositions of company's property to bank – Insolvency Act 1986, s. 127.

Payments in the form of third-party cheques accepted by a bank, collected by it on the company's behalf and credited to the company's account in the winding up of the company, were not dispositions of the company's property within s. 127 of the Insolvency Act 1986. In
C
collecting payment upon a cheque, the bank credited the customer's account with the amount of the cheque. If the account was already in credit, no disposition of the property of the customer took place in favour of the bank. The amount standing to the credit of the customer's account was increased in return for the surrender of the cheque, which became a voucher for payment. It was the drawer of the cheque whose property was disposed of. All that happened between the customer and the banker was an adjustment of entries in the statement recording the accounts between them.

The following cases were referred to in the judgment:
D
Gray's Inn Construction Co Ltd, Re [1980] 1 WLR 711.
Leslie (J) Engineers Co Ltd, Re [1976] 1 WLR 292.
Loteka Pty Ltd, Re (1989) 7 ACLC 998.
Mal Bower's Macquarie Electrical Centre Pty Ltd, Re (1974) CLC ¶40-109; [1974] 1 NSWLR 254.
McGuinness Bros (UK) Ltd, Re (1987) 3 BCC 571.
E
Mersey Steel and Iron Co Ltd v Naylor, Benzon & Co (1884) 9 App Cas 434.
National Australia Bank Ltd v KDS Construction Services Pty Ltd (1988) 6 ACLC 28.

Andrew Feldman (instructed by Clifford Harris & Co) for the liquidator.

Thomas Lowe (instructed by Bazley White & Co) for the bank.

JUDGMENT

F
His Honour Judge Rich QC: The order to wind up this company was made on 19 February 1992 and the applicant was appointed liquidator. He applies by application dated 30 May 1993 for a declaration that the receipt of amounts totalling £37,134.30 by the respondent bank, between 23 October 1991 and 24 February 1992, constituted dispositions of the company's property, which were void pursuant to s. 127 of the *Insolvency Act* 1986.

G
The form of the application is in the winding-up proceedings. The Insolvency Rules provide for such applications 'under the Act or Rules'. Section 127 provides that:

'In a winding up by the court, any disposition of the company's property . . . made after the commencement of the winding up is, unless the court otherwise orders, void.'

It follows therefore that such an application and any application by a respondent for the validation of any disposition is an application under the Act
H
The application continues by seeking an order that the bank pay the liquidator the said sum of £37,000-odd. Although counsel could not point to the provisions of the rules which provide for the making of such order on such an application, I was referred to the decision of Harman J in *Re McGuinness Bros (UK) Ltd* (1987) 3 BCC 571 in which he assumes such jurisdiction and to *Re J Leslie Engineers Co Ltd* [1976] 1 WLR 292, where Oliver J made such an order on an application by summons. And I accept that where the

declaration is made under s. 127 upon an application to which the person who has the   A
benefit of the disposition is a party, it is appropriate to make an order for payment, but
as I think only in such cases.

The bank admits that such payments as are referred to in the application were made to
it after the commencement of the winding up by the presentation of the petition on
13 September 1991; 23 October 1991 is 14 days after the advertisement of that petition.
Payments in the form of third-party cheques were accepted by the bank, collected by it   B
on the company's behalf and credited to the company's account. After allowing for
£2,854.68, which stood to the company's credit at the date when the liquidator was
appointed, and has been paid to him, and £800 which was paid to the company in cash,
the sum of £37,134.30 claimed represented the total receipts into the company's account
over the period.

By affidavit dated 6 May 1993, the bank's solicitor had disputed whether the receipt   C
by the bank of these sums constituted dispositions of the company's property. Upon
opening on behalf of the liquidator Mr Feldman therefore sought leave to amend the
application to seek alternative relief, namely a declaration that payment out from the
company's account did constitute such dispositions and an order for payment of a like
sum.

Mr Lowe, who appeared for the bank, claimed that to allow such an amendment   D
nearly two years after the winding-up order had been made raised a possibility of
prejudice to the respondent because on the application as originally made it would not
have been necessary to investigate the reasons for the payments, whereas in order to
determine whether such dispositions as were involved in the making of payments should
be validated, it would be necessary to know whether, for example, they were made in
respect of debts incurred before or after the commencement of the winding up, and such
investigation, if not made promptly, would be difficult.   E

I am not certain that there really is such a distinction between the two claims, having
regard to the basis upon which the actual order for payment was arrived at by the Court
of Appeal in *Re Gray's Inn Construction* [1980] 1 WLR 711. The risk of such prejudice
was, however, in any event, sufficiently overcome by an agreement on the basis of which
the amendment was allowed. It was agreed on behalf of the liquidator to limit any claim
for repayment to £16,094.96 or such larger sum not exceeding £20,000 as might be proved   F
in the liquidation within six months of 20 January 1994. On that basis the bank, for itself,
agreed not to seek validation of any dispositions in excess of such sums. The amendment
was therefore allowed.

In the event, however, the amendment, except in so far as it limited the scope of any
order for payment which would result from a declaration on the application as originally
made, proved an unnecessary complication in the proceedings. Mr Lowe, on behalf of   G
the bank, did not dispute that the payments out of the account did constitute dispositions
of the company's property, but, as was accepted by Mr Feldman, they were not
dispositions of such property to the bank. Although Mr Feldman reserved the right to
claim payment of such sums from the bank on grounds other than mere restitution, he
accepted that any such claim ought to be pleaded in some way, and he therefore accepted
that it would not be appropriate for me to make an order for payment by the bank on
the present application unless I held that the receipts by the bank did constitute   H
dispositions of the company's property.

Mr Lowe accepted that if such receipts did constitute such dispositions, then it would
be appropriate to make an order upon the present application for payment in the agreed
form. Thus, the sole issue for my determination is whether receipts by the bank did
constitute dispositions of the company's property.

A
It was further agreed for the purposes of determining that issue, that the company's account with the bank should be treated as having been in credit at all material times. As a matter of fact this was not strictly accurate because for some three days the account was overdrawn because some cheques which had been paid into it had been dishonoured. The liquidator did not, however, seek to found any claim upon that fact, and I therefore, by agreement, treat the account as having been in credit at all material times.

B
The application, as originally made, relied upon some observations of Buckley LJ in *Re Gray's Inn Construction Ltd*. In that case the Court of Appeal reversed a decision of Templeman J where he held that payments of cheques to a bank in circumstances where the company was throughout running an overdraft, were not dispositions of property within the predecessor of s. 127. Buckley LJ said at p. 715H:

'The judge proceeded on the basis which he held to be the position in law, that payment of moneys to the credit of a company's account, whether it is in credit or not, do not constitute a disposition of the company's property. That is a view with which, with deference to the judge, I feel unable to agree. When a customer's account with his banker is overdrawn he is a debtor to his banker for the amount of his overdraft. When he pays a sum of money into the account, whether in cash or by payment in of a third party's cheque, he discharges his indebtedness to the bank pro tanto. There is clearly in these circumstances . . . a disposition by the company to the bank of the amount of the cash or of the cheque. It may well be the case, as Mr Heslop has submitted, that in clearing a third party's cheque and collecting the amount due upon it, the bank acts as the customer's agent, but as soon as it credits the amount collected in reduction of the customer's overdraft, as in the ordinary course of banking business it has authority to do in the absence of any contrary instruction from the customer, it makes a disposition on the customer's behalf in its own favour discharging pro tanto the customer's liability on the overdraft. Mr Heslop was constrained in the course of the argument to accept that this is so. In the present case the company's account with the bank was overdrawn, so I need not consider what the position would have been if any cheque had been paid in when the account was in credit, but I doubt whether even in those circumstances it could properly be said that the payment in did not constitute a disposition of the amount of the cheque in favour of the bank.'

F
Mr Feldman has shown me that the writers of various textbooks on company and on banking law have not challenged this dictum as to the position which did not arise in that case, namely a payment in when the account was in credit. Naturally such dictum, falling from Buckley LJ, although obiter, commands the greatest of respect. Harman J also made some observations in *Re McGuinness* which might be taken to support this dictum, although if it was so intended, it was also clearly obiter because *McGuinness* was also a case of an overdrawn account. I cite from his judgment at p. 574, where he says:

'However, the matter stands that in law all the dispositions of the company's property after the winding up are void. It is clear that payments out of or into the bank account are dispositions of property. That follows from *Gray's Inn Construction* and was indeed well-known long before that case was decided.'

The only reasoned explanation to which my attention has been drawn for reaching the same conclusion in respect of an account out of which the bank makes a disposition in its own favour, discharging, pro tanto, the customer's liability on the overdraft, to quote Buckley LJ's explanation of the position of the overdrawn account, and one which places the receipts of the cheques which it collects on the customer's behalf to the credit of the customer's account to be held to the customer's order, is found in a passage in Professor Goode's *Principles of Corporate Insolvency Law* at pp. 187–188 under the heading 'Payments into a bank account'. He there said:

'Where the company pays cash (as opposed to a cheque) into its account, the   A
payment constitutes a disposition of its property, whether or not the account is in
credit, for ownership of the cash passes to the bank. If the account is in credit the
company acquires a corresponding claim against the bank, which will be recorded
by a credit of the payment to its account, so that the net effect of the transaction is
simply to convert an asset of the company from one form, cash, into another, a
claim on the bank. Hence in terms of its effect the breach will usually be a merely
technical one, but the position would be otherwise if the bank were to become   B
insolvent before the company had withdrawn the amount credited.

The position is somewhat different in the case of a cheque. Deposit of the cheque
with the bank for the purpose of collection is not in itself a disposition within
section 127 where the company's account is in credit, for the bank collects purely
as agent and has no interest of its own in the cheque. The position is otherwise
where the company owes money to the bank, for it then acquires a lien on the   C
cheque and if the view above is correct this constitutes a disposition for the purpose
of section 127. When the bank collects the cheque for the company it receives the
payment initially as agent for the company but immediately borrows it back as
part of the banker-customer relationship and credits the borrowing to the
customer's account. The collection process itself involves the disposition of an asset
of the company, for the bank surrenders the customer's cheque, which represents   D
both a negotiable instrument and the embodiment of a claim against the drawer,
in exchange for payment, so that one form of property belonging to the company
is converted into another. Crediting of the proceeds of the cheque to an account
already in credit is a further, albeit technical, disposition of the company's
property, for its claim against the bank to money had and received in respect of
the proceeds collected is replaced by a new claim against the bank in its capacity
as borrower, as recorded by the credit to the account. Similarly, where the account   E
is overdrawn the effect of the bank's act in crediting the proceeds is to apply the
moneys collected on the company's behalf in discharge of the debt due to the bank
and thereby to extinguish pro tanto the company's claim against the bank in
respect of the sum collected. The original asset thus disappears in the same way as
where the proceeds are credited to an account not in overdraft, but with the very
different result that the bank obtains a preference over other creditors, so that the
breach of section 127 is no longer technical.'   F

Mr Feldman adopts this passage as his argument for the declaration originally sought,
and I certainly treat the views of Professor Goode with respect and do not differ from
them lightly. In this reasoning Professor Goode accepts that the deposit of the cheque by
the company with the bank does not involve a disposition because the bank is the
company's agent. Nevertheless he treats the conversion of the property in the cheque into
a debt from the bank to the company as a disposition of the company's property. To   G
equate such transformation with a disposition does not appear to me to accord with
ordinary English usage wherein a disposition connotes the transfer or alienation of an
asset, not its mere conversion into a different form which is nonetheless as much within
the control of the owner.

If Professor Goode's construction does not accord with ordinary usage I certainly see
no reason to give other than the natural meaning to a section which seeks to override
property rights, particularly when the avoidance of such transactions as Professor Goode   H
would bring within the definition does not appear to me to be necessary in order to avoid
the mischief of preference of creditors, at which he, as I think rightly, says that the section
is aimed.

Mr Feldman found himself constrained to accept that if this reasoning of Professor
Goode is right then the mere payment of a debt to the company by making out a cheque

A   which converts one chose in action into another (an action on the cheque) is also a disposition of the company's property. Indeed it appears that in the case of *Mersey Steel and Iron Co Ltd v Naylor, Benzon & Co* (1884) 9 App Cas 434 a debtor was advised that such was the effect of s. 153 of the *Companies Act* 1862, which was to the same effect as s. 127 of the present Act, the debtor therefore refused to pay such sums which became due in accordance with a contract with the company after the presentation of a petition to wind it up. The House of Lords held that because of such advice the debtor should not

B   be held to have repudiated the contract, but the Lord Chancellor made this comment on that advice at p. 441:

> 'On the 10th of February, which was before the winding-up order was made, and while that state of things still continued, the company by their secretary wrote to say that they thought (being so far correct and thinking rightly) that the objection was not well founded in law . . .'

C   I accept that parenthetic observation on the advice that led to the withholding of payment, and I think that it is not enough to constitute a disposition, that a transaction involves a conversion of a chose in action, or even the property in a negotiable instrument into a chose more nearly in possession.

In the Supreme Court of New South Wales, Street CJ in Eq, considered the meaning of the word 'disposition' in *Re Mal Bower's Macquarie Electrical Centre Pty Ltd* (1974)

D   CLC ¶40-109. He held (what Mr Lowe is not minded to support in this case) that a payment out of money by a bank is not a disposition; but in doing so he made some observations which I do find helpful in analysing the process of collection of a third party's cheques on behalf of a company against whom a petition had been presented. He said at p. 27,774:

> 'The phrase "disposition of the property" in s. 227 has a statutory origin in
E   > England well back in the last century. I have been unable to trace the phrase to its source, but it seems likely to have originated from the word "dispone", used in Scottish law as a word meaning "to transfer or alienate". The Oxford Dictionary includes as one of the meanings of "dispone" – "Sc[ots] Law. To make over or convey officially or in legal form (1555)". The same work includes, in the definition of "disposition", ". . . spec. in Law, the action of disponing". The word "disposition" in one or other of its forms, and in varying contexts, is a
F   > commonplace in revenue statutes. There is, however, little guidance to be had from examining such other contexts, apart from noting that the concept associated with the use of such word involves the presence of both a disponor and a disponee.

> There is in my view great force in Mr McLelland's argument that the paying by a bank of a company's cheque, presented by a stranger, does not involve the bank in a disposition of the property of the company so as to disentitle the bank to debit
G   > the amount of the cheque to the company's account. The word "disposition" connotes in my view both a disponor and a disponee. The section operates to render the disposition void so far as concerns the disponee. It does not operate to affect the agencies interposing between the company as disponor and the recipient of the property as disponee. As was put in the course of argument, if a company, after presentation of the petition, delivered goods to a carrier consigned to a
H   > purchaser, the purchaser would face the avoidance of the transaction under s. 227, but the carrier would not be placed in the position of a tortious handling of the goods. Again, if a company were to send its wages clerk up to the bank to cash the weekly wages cheque and bring back the proceeds for making out the pay packets, the payment of the cheque would involve no disposition of the company's property: the company's property belonged to it just as much when it was in the bank as when it was in the form of cash in the hands of the wages clerk. The element of

disposition only enters into the situation when something passes out from the   A
company to a disponee. It is the passing to the disponee which is the relevant
disposition avoided by s. 227. Taking further the example of a wages cheque, the
giving by a company to the employee of his wages out of the cash brought back by
the wages clerk would be disposition of property of the company to the employee.
Alternatively, if the company gave to the employee directly a cheque for him to
present to collect for himself, the handing over of that cheque would be a
conditional disposition within s. 227. The intermediary functions fulfilled by the   B
bank in respect of paying cheques drawn by a company in favour of and presented
on behalf of a third party do not implicate the bank in the consequences of the
statutory avoidance prescribed by s. 227.'

In *Re J Leslie Engineers Co Ltd* [1976] 1 WLR 292, Oliver J likewise identified the act
of disposition by reference to the receipt by the disponee. Two sums were in issue in that
case. One of £250 was paid to the respondent, Mr Greaves, by five money orders bought   C
by a director, Mr Hadrys, with the company's cash, drawn from the company's bank
account by a cheque for cash. The other was a sum of £800 paid to the respondent by a
cheque drawn on Mr Hadrys' personal account, but, unknown to Mr Greaves, backed,
when it had to be represented, by a company cheque in favour of Mr Hadrys paid into
Mr Hadrys' joint account with his wife at the same bank as the company's account to
enable the cheque given to Mr Greaves to be met. Oliver J dealt with the application to   D
treat the payment of the £250 as void as follows (p. 297F):

'It is submitted by Mr Potts, on behalf of the respondents, that the "dispositions"
which were avoided by section 227 do not include such dispositions as are
constituted by the payments to the respondents in this case; that "the dispositions"
at which the section is aimed are the initial dispositions only – that is to say the
encashments of the two cheques – and it is against Mr Hadrys alone that any claim
will lie. I cannot think that as a general proposition that can be right. It seems to   E
me to be wholly immaterial, so long as one is dealing with the company's property,
whether the purported disposition is made by the company or by a third party, or
whether it is made directly or indirectly.

I feel, therefore, no difficulty – and, I may add, no doubt – about the initial
payment of £250. The bank notes received from the bank was as much the
company's property, and identifiable as such, as were the moneys in the account,   F
and it seems to me to make not the slightest difference that Mr Hadrys took the
bank notes and converted them into money orders payable to Mr Greaves. There
was, throughout, a clearly identifiable property of the company which passed
directly from the company's hands (in the person of Mr Hadrys, its controlling
director) to those of the respondents: see for instance *Taylor* v. *Plumer* (1815) 3 M
& S 562. That disposition was, in my judgment, quite clearly invalidated by the   G
section unless and until this court otherwise orders.'

By contrast, the disposition of the company's property in the case of the £800 took place
when the cheque was paid to Mr Hadrys, not when Mr Hadrys' cheque to Mr Greaves
was met. Oliver J continues:

'The second payment, however, creates to my mind, very much greater difficulty.
The disposition which Mr Evans-Lombe, on behalf of the liquidator, attacks, is   H
not the drawing of the cheque to Mr Greaves or the sending to him of that cheque,
and it is not – or is it not alone – drawing by Mr Hadrys of the cheque on the
company's account. It is the application by the bank of the funds in the joint
account to meet Mr Greaves' cheque when it was re-presented. That, says
Mr Evans-Lombe, was the disposition of the company's property which is avoided
and which gives the liquidator the right to recover the sum claimed from the

A
respondents. Now it must be remembered that the invalidation of a disposition of the company's property and the recovery of the property disposed of, are two logically distinct matters. Section 227 says nothing about recovery; it merely avoids dispositions, and is in these terms . . .'

–which the judge sets out.

B
'What is the appropriate remedy in respect of the invalidated disposition is a matter not regulated by the statute and that has to be determined by the general law. In order to succeed against the respondents, the liquidator does not necessarily have to demonstrate a transaction invalidated by section 227 for there may be claims to recover moneys paid on other grounds. He does, however, have to show a right of recovery, and it is Mr Evans-Lombe's contention that he does that if he demonstrates that the transaction is one which is bitten by section 227 and persuades the court that it ought not to validate it. I think that I should say straight

C
away that although, as I have said, I cannot accept that the respondents were not aware that they were contracting with a limited company, I cannot on the evidence before me find any indication that when the £800 payment was made, or indeed at any material time, the respondents knew or had reason to suspect that the funds to meet it had been provided by the company. I cannot, therefore, treat the case as one of collusive payment and I think that I must accept that, so far as the

D
respondents were concerned, they thought that the moneys were being paid by Mr Hadrys or his wife out of their own resources.

Looking at the transaction in stages, there was clearly no disposition of any property of the company when the cheque in favour of the respondents was first sent and presented. When the cheque on the company's account was drawn and presented there quite clearly was a disposition of the company's property, and one which is, unless validated, avoided by section 227. But that cheque was paid in

E
with a number of other cheques and, after allowing for the overdraft, the moneys represented by the cheque became mixed with Mr Hadrys' own moneys throwing up a credit balance of some £950.'

I think I have to read on later in this judgment at p. 299D, where he makes this observation on the property of the company:

F
' "The property of the company" for the purposes of the section was, as it seems to me, not the credit balance in the account owed by the bank to Mr and Mrs Hadrys, but the sum total of the rights of the company created by the transactions leading up to the creation of that balance. I do not think that the meeting, out of the credit balance held by the bank to the order of Mr and Mrs Hadrys, of the re-presented cheque in favour of the respondents was a disposition of the property of the company simply because the company could, by appropriate proceedings, have

G
obtained a declaration of charge on that credit balance.'

This appears to me to be a more practical approach to the definition of the moment at which the company's property is disposed of than what appeared to me to be an over-technical analysis of the banking process in the passage which Mr Feldman adopted from Professor Goode as his argument. I derive assistance also in analysing the effect of banking transactions for the purposes of this section from another Australian case,

H
decided by McPherson J in the Queensland Supreme Court, *Re Loteka Pty Ltd* (1989) 7 ACLC 998. I should incidentally pay tribute to Mr Lowe's industry which has brought these and other Commonwealth authorities, not all of which is it necessary for me to cite, to the court's attention. In that case the liquidator sought, as the applicant before me does by the amended application, to recover from a bank, which did not freeze the operation of the account of a company against whom a petition for winding up had been presented (but which account remained in credit), sums paid out of such account. The

judge recounts the effect of depositing a cheque in an account which is in credit by citing   A
a passage from another case, *National Australia Bank Ltd v KDS Construction Services
Pty Ltd* (1988) 6 ACLC 28 at p. 31. His account is not, I think materially different from
Professor Goode's. It reads (at p. 1,003):

> 'The effect of the receipt by a bank of a cheque deposited by a customer to the
> credit of his current account turns upon the terms of the contract between the bank
> and its customer. In the ordinary course of business when a customer deposits a   B
> cheque to the credit of his account, the bank becomes his agent for collection of
> the cheque from the paying bank and, if the customer's account is in credit, the
> collecting bank borrows the proceeds from the customer when collected:
> *Joachimson v Swiss Bank Corporation* [1921] 3 KB 110 at p. 127; *A L Underwood
> Ltd v Bank of Liverpool* [1924] 1 KB 775 at p. 791. If the customer's account is in
> debit, the proceeds are applied in reduction of the overdraft. In either situation the
> collecting bank does not become a holder for value of the cheque at any time   C
> before it is cleared: *A L Underwood Ltd v Barclays Bank. . .* at pp. 804 and 805;
> *National Commercial Banking Corporation of Australia Ltd v Batty* (1986) 160
> CLR 251 at p. 273. In collecting the proceeds the collecting bank exhausts the
> operation of the cheque (*A L Underwood Ltd v Bank of Liverpool* at p. 791),
> notwithstanding that the paying bank holds it thereafter as a voucher on account
> of its customer the drawer: *Midland Bank Ltd v Reckitt* [1933] AC 1 at p. 14.'   D

The reference to the status of the paid cheque as a voucher prompts a question which
Professor Goode did not address: what is the effect of declaring the disposition of the
cheque void? If the drawer's bank is bound to return it as remaining the company's
property, is it to be treated on such return as still being a valuable instrument? Is, for
example, the fact that it is out of date to be disregarded? And if so, on what basis? Is the
fact that it has been paid to be disregarded, although there is no basis on which the   E
disposition to the company which is made by the payment of the cheque is to be avoided
by s. 127?

McPherson J was concerned with a claim to avoid not payments into the company's
account but payments out of it. He goes on from his description of the process of a
cheque to conclude that in the case of a payment out of the account there is of course a
disposition to the payee but that it takes place upon the delivery of the cheque. He deals,   F
however, with the effect of the presentation of a cheque as follows (at p. 1,004):

> 'In paying the customer's cheque, the bank debits the customer's account with the
> amount of the cheque drawn in favour of the stranger. In doing so, the bank, if the
> customer's account is overdrawn, lends its own money to the customer. That
> involves no disposition of the customer's property to the bank. Equally, if the
> account is sufficiently in credit to meet the cheque, no disposition of property of   G
> the customer takes place in favour of the bank. The amount standing to the credit
> of the customer's account is simply diminished thus reducing pro tanto the
> indebtedness of the bank to the customer. It is the payee of the cheque that receives
> the benefit of the proceeds of the cheque. All that happens between customer and
> banker is an adjustment of entries in the statement recording the accounts between
> them . . .'

I think that the collection of a cheque, which is what I am concerned with, can be   H
similarly analysed. In collecting payment upon a cheque the bank credits the customer's
account with the amount of the cheque. If the account is already in credit, no disposition
of the property of the customer takes place in favour of the bank. The amount standing
to the credit of a customer's account is increased in return for the surrender of the cheque,
which becomes a voucher for payment. It is the drawer of the cheque whose property is

A disposed of. All that happens between the customer and the banker is an adjustment of entries in the statement recording the accounts between them.

I would accordingly decide the sole issue left for my determination, after the various agreements and concessions to which I have referred, against the liquidator. I would therefore refuse the declaration sought and the application as originally made. On the amended application, it is conceded by the respondent that the payments were

B dispositions and since Mr Feldman has given the liquidator's undertaking not to seek repayment of any of these sums from the payees, who are of course not before the court, there does not appear to me to be any reason why I should not grant that declaration as against the bank.

For the reasons which I have already given, however, I would refuse an order for payment by the bank, leaving the liquidator to seek payment if he is so advised by proceedings in which his grounds for so claiming can be fully pleaded.

C

(Order accordingly)

D

E

F

G

H

Ridehalgh v Horsefield & Anor and related appeals including Philex plc v Golban (Company No. 0022 of 1993).

Court of Appeal (Civil Division).
Sir Thomas Bingham MR, Rose and Waite L JJ.
Judgment delivered 26 January 1994.

Costs – Wasted costs – Winding up – Restraining presentation of petition – Petition debt bona fide disputed – Whether costs of application to restrain presentation of petition were 'wasted costs' – Supreme Court Act 1981, s. 51(6), (7).

These were six appeals against 'wasted costs orders' including an appeal against an order made in the Companies Court against solicitors and in favour of Philex Ltd (see [1993] BCC 726). Philex obtained an injunction restraining the presentation of a winding-up petition, on the ground that the petition debt was bona fide disputed, and an order for costs against the prospective petitioner, 'G', on the indemnity basis. Philex then applied for G's solicitors to pay those costs personally as 'wasted costs' under s. 51(6) and (7) of the Supreme Court Act 1981, as amended by s. 4 of the Courts and Legal Services Act 1990. The judge made the order sought on the basis that the solicitors were parties to a negotiating offer which made unreasonable or improper use of the implied threat of a winding-up petition as an inducement to the company to compromise the claim. The solicitors appealed arguing that the relevant compromise was contained in a letter which made it quite clear that G accepted that there was a dispute making the continuance of winding-up proceedings inappropriate and confirmed that he did not intend to present a winding-up petition. In any event the letter had been approved by counsel on whose advice the solicitor was entitled to rely.

Held, allowing the appeal:

There could be circumstances in which a solicitor who advised his client to make use of a threat of proceedings that would (if brought) amount to an abuse of the process, might be found to have been guilty of improper or unreasonable conduct. However, there was no evidential basis for the judge's conclusion that misconduct of that sort had occurred in the present case. The solicitor was, moreover, entitled to rely upon the fact that he was acting on the advice of counsel, both generally in regard to the prosecution of G's claim and specifically in regard to the compromise proposal.

The following cases were referred to in the judgment of the court:

Barrister, Re a (wasted costs order) (No. 1 of 1991) [1993] QB 293.
Company No. 0012209 of 1991, Re a [1992] 1 WLR 351.
Currie & Co v The Law Society [1977] QB 990.
Davy-Chiesman v Davy-Chiesman & Anor [1984] Fam 48.
Edwards v Edwards [1958] P 235.
Filmlab Systems International Ltd & Anor v Pennington & Ors [1993] TLR 383.
Gupta v Comer [1991] 1 QB 629.
Holden & Co v Crown Prosecution Service [1990] 2 QB 261.
Locke v Camberwell Health Authority [1991] 2 Med LR 249.
Mauroux v Soc Com Abel Pereira da Fonseca SARL [1972] 1 WLR 962.
Myers v Elman [1940] AC 282.
Myers v Rothfield [1939] 1 KB 109.
Orchard v South Eastern Electricity Board [1987] QB 565.
Rondel v Worsley [1969] 1 AC 191.
Saif Ali & Anor v Sydney Mitchell & Co & Ors [1980] AC 198.
Sinclair-Jones v Kay [1989] 1 WLR 114.
Symphony Group plc v Hodgson [1994] QB 179.

A *Thew (R & T) Ltd v Reeves (No. 2)* [1982] QB 1283n.
Wilkinson v Wilkinson & Anor [1963] P 1.

Duncan Matheson QC and Guy Mansfield (instructed by Barlow Lyde & Gilbert) for the solicitors and the Law Society.

Timothy Otty (instructed by Iliffes) for Philex.

Rupert Jackson QC and David Hodge (instructed by Ms Janice Bye) for the Bar
B Council.

Ian Burnett and James Laughland (instructed by the Treasury Solicitor) as amici curiae.

JUDGMENT OF THE COURT
(Delivered by Bingham MR)

C This is the judgment of the court. Different sections of the judgment have been written by different members. Each of us concurs fully in all sections.

There are six appeals before the court. All of them (save one in which this issue has been compromised) raise the same question: in what circumstances should the court make a wasted costs order in favour of one party to litigation against the legal representative (counsel or solicitor) of the other? It is a question of great and growing
D significance. It is desirable that this court should give such guidance as it can.

Two of the cases before us come on appeal from the county court. Three come on appeal from the High Court, one from each division. In all of these cases wasted costs orders were made and the legal representatives who were the subject of the orders appeal. In the remaining case, the issue first arose in this court: on allowing an appeal against the decision of a county court, the court invited the solicitors who had acted for the parties in the court below to show cause why they should not be ordered personally to pay the
E costs thrown away. The solicitors have appeared by counsel in this court in response to that invitation.

Since the question raised by these appeals is of general concern to their members, both the Law Society and the General Council of the Bar sought and were granted leave to make submissions to the court. Since the question is also of concern to the public, we offered the Attorney-General a similar opportunity of which he took advantage, and
F counsel were accordingly instructed to represent the wider public interest. All the parties to the six appeals were also represented, save for one party in the compromised appeal. We gratefully acknowledge the help we have had from all solicitors and counsel involved in mounting and presenting these cases.

Our legal system, developed over many centuries, rests on the principle that the interests of justice are on the whole best served if parties in dispute, each represented by
G solicitors and counsel, take cases incapable of compromise to court for decision by an independent and neutral judge, before whom their relationship is essentially antagonistic: each is determined to win, and prepares and presents his case so as to defeat his opponent and achieve a favourable result. By the clash of competing evidence and argument, it is believed, the judge is best enabled to decide what happened, to formulate the relevant principles of law and to apply those principles to the facts of the case before him as he has found them.

H Experience has shown that certain safeguards are needed if this system is to function fairly and effectively in the interests of parties to litigation and of the public at large. None of these safeguards is entirely straightforward, and only some of them need be mentioned here:

(1) Parties must be free to unburden themselves to their legal advisers without fearing that what they say may provide ammunition for their opponent. To this end a

cloak of confidence is thrown over communications between client and lawyer,   A
usually removable only with the consent of the client.

(2)   The party who substantially loses the case is ordinarily obliged to pay the legal
      costs necessarily incurred by the winner. Thus hopeless claims and defences are
      discouraged, a willingness to compromise is induced and the winner keeps most of
      the fruits of victory. But the position is different where one or both parties to the
      case are legally aided: s. 17 of the *Legal Aid Act* 1988 and Pt. XIII of the *Civil*   B
      Legal Aid (General) Regulations 1989 restrict the liability of legally assisted parties
      to pay costs if they lose. And sometimes the losing party is impoverished and
      cannot pay.

(3)   The law imposes a duty on lawyers to exercise reasonable care and skill in
      conducting their clients' affairs. This is a duty owed to and enforceable by the
      client, to protect him against loss caused by his lawyer's default. But it is not an
      absolute duty. Considerations of public policy have been held to require, and   C
      statute now confirms, that in relation to proceedings in court and work closely
      related to proceedings in court advocates should be accorded immunity from
      claims for negligence by their clients: *Rondel v Worsley* [1969] 1 AC 191; *Saif Ali &*
      Anor v Sydney Mitchell & Co & Ors [1980] AC 198; *Courts and Legal Services Act*
      1990, s. 62.

(4)   If solicitors or barristers fail to observe the standards of conduct required by the   D
      Law Society or the General Council of the Bar (as the case may be) they become
      liable to disciplinary proceedings at the suit of their professional body and to a
      range of penalties which include fines, suspension from practice and expulsion
      from their profession. Procedures have changed over the years. The role of the
      courts (in the case of solicitors) and the Inns of Court (in the case of barristers) has
      in large measure been assumed by the professional bodies themselves. But the
      sanctions remain, not to compensate those who have suffered loss but to compel   E
      observance of prescribed standards of professional conduct. Additional powers
      exist to order barristers, solicitors and those in receipt of legal aid to forgo fees or
      remuneration otherwise earned.

(5)   Solicitors and barristers may in certain circumstances be ordered to compensate a
      party to litigation other than the client for whom they act for costs incurred by
      that party as a result of acts done or omitted by the solicitors or barristers in their   F
      conduct of the litigation.

It is the scope and effect of this last safeguard, and its relation with the others briefly
mentioned, which are in issue in these appeals. We shall hereafter refer to this jurisdiction,
not quite accurately, as 'the wasted costs jurisdiction' and to orders made under it as
'wasted costs orders'. These appeals are not concerned with the jurisdiction to order legal
representatives to compensate their own client. The questions raised are by no means   G
academic. Material has been placed before the court which shows that the number and
value of wasted costs orders applied for, and the costs of litigating them, have risen
sharply. We were told of one case in which the original hearing had lasted five days; the
wasted costs application had (when we were told of it) lasted seven days; it was estimated
to be about half-way through; at that stage one side had incurred costs of over £40,000.
It almost appears that a new branch of legal activity is emerging, calling to mind Dickens'
searing observation in *Bleak House*:   H

> 'The one great principle of English law is, to make business for itself . . . Viewed
> by this light it becomes a coherent scheme, and not the monstrous maze the laity
> are apt to think it.'

The argument we have heard discloses a tension between two important public
interests. One is that lawyers should not be deterred from pursuing their clients' interests

A   by fear of incurring a personal liability to their clients' opponents; that they should not be penalised by orders to pay costs without a fair opportunity to defend themselves; that wasted costs orders should not become a back-door means of recovering costs not otherwise recoverable against a legally aided or impoverished litigant; and that the remedy should not grow unchecked to become more damaging than the disease. The other public interest, recently and clearly affirmed by Act of Parliament, is that litigants should not be financially prejudiced by the unjustifiable conduct of litigation by their or

B   their opponents' lawyers. The reconciliation of these public interests is our task in these appeals. Full weight must be given to the first of these public interests, but the wasted costs jurisdiction must not be emasculated.

The wasted costs jurisdiction

The wasted costs jurisdiction of the court as applied to solicitors is of long standing,
C   but discussion of it can conveniently begin with the important and relatively recent case of *Myers v Elman* [1940] AC 282. At the end of a five-day hearing before a jury the plaintiff obtained judgment for damages for fraudulent conspiracy against five defendants, with costs. Nothing could be recovered from any of the defendants. Nor, perhaps, was any recovery expected, for at the end of the trial the plaintiff's counsel applied for an order that the costs of the action should be paid by the solicitors who had acted for the defendants.
D
Notice was duly given to the solicitors and a further five day hearing followed to decide whether the solicitors or any of them should make payment. In the case of one solicitor, Mr Elman, the trial judge (Singleton J) considered two complaints: that he had filed defences which he knew to be false; and that he had permitted the filing of an inadequate affidavit verifying his clients' list of documents. In considering these complaints the judge had before him a considerable correspondence between Mr Elman and his clients which
E   the plaintiff's advisers had (naturally) not seen before; the reports of the case do not disclose how it came about that the clients' privilege in that correspondence was waived.

Singleton J rejected the complaint relating to the defences but upheld that based on the defective affidavit of documents. Nothing, held the judge, should be said which might prevent, or tend to prevent, either solicitor or counsel from doing his best for his client so long as the duty to the court was borne in mind, but if he were asked or required by
F   the client to do something which was inconsistent with the duty to the court it was for him to point out that he could not do it and, if necessary, cease to act: see *Myers v Rothfield* [1939] 1 KB 109 at pp. 115, 117. The judge ordered Mr Elman to pay one-third of the taxed costs of the action and two-thirds of the costs of the application. Mr Elman appealed and the Court of Appeal by a majority reversed the decision of the judge. It appeared that the work in question had been very largely delegated to a well-qualified managing clerk and the conduct complained of had been his, not Mr Elman's. The
G   majority held that to make a wasted costs order the court must find professional misconduct established against the solicitor, and such a finding could not be made where the solicitor was not personally at fault.

On further appeal to the House of Lords, Lord Russell of Killowen dissented on the facts but the House was unanimous in rejecting the Court of Appeal's majority view. While their Lordships used different language, and may to some extent have seen the
H   issues somewhat differently, the case is authority for five fundamental propositions:

(1)   The court's jurisdiction to make a wasted costs order against a solicitor is quite distinct from the disciplinary jurisdiction exercised over solicitors.

(2)   Whereas a disciplinary order against a solicitor requires a finding that he has been personally guilty of serious professional misconduct the making of a wasted costs order does not.

(3)   The court's jurisdiction to make a wasted costs order against a solicitor is founded on breach of the duty owed by the solicitor to the court to perform his duty as an officer of the court in promoting within his own sphere the cause of justice.

(4)   To show a breach of that duty it is not necessary to establish dishonesty, criminal conduct, personal obliquity or behaviour such as would warrant striking a solicitor off the roll. While mere mistake or error of judgment would not justify an order, misconduct, default or even negligence is enough if the negligence is serious or gross.

(5)   The jurisdiction is compensatory and not merely punitive.

When *Myers v Elman* was decided, the court's wasted costs jurisdiction was not regulated by the Rules of the Supreme Court, although O. 65, r. 11 did provide for costs to be disallowed as between solicitor and client or paid by a solicitor to his client where such costs had been 'improperly or without any reasonable cause incurred' or where:

'by reason of any undue delay in proceeding under any judgment or order, or of any misconduct or default of the solicitor, any costs properly incurred have nevertheless proved fruitless to the person incurring the same'.

There was also provision in O. 65, r. 5 for a solicitor to pay costs to any or all parties if his failure to attend or deliver a document caused a delay in proceedings. But the rules reflected no general wasted costs jurisdiction. Following the decision, the rules were not amended to regulate the court's inherent wasted costs jurisdiction, but the jurisdiction itself was preserved by s. 50(2) of the *Solicitors Act* 1957. In 1960 a new rule (which later became O. 62, r. 8(1)) was introduced which did regulate, although not enlarge, this inherent jurisdiction. The new rule provided:

'Subject to the following provisions of this rule, where in any proceedings costs are incurred improperly or without reasonable cause or are wasted by undue delay or any other misconduct or default, the court may make against any solicitor whom it considers to be responsible (whether personally or through a servant or agent) an order–

(a)   disallowing the costs as between the solicitor and his client; and

(b)   directing the solicitor to repay to his client costs which the client has been ordered to pay to other parties to the proceedings; or

(c)   directing the solicitor personally to indemnify such other parties against costs payable by them.'

In (a) and (b) the effect of the old rule was reproduced. In (c) the effect of *Myers v Elman* was recognised. It is plain that expressions such as 'improperly', 'without reasonable cause' and 'misconduct' are to be understood in the sense given to them by their Lordships in that case.

Both before and after introduction of the new rule, contested applications for wasted costs orders against solicitors did come before the courts. *Edwards v Edwards* [1958] P 235, *Wilkinson v Wilkinson & Anor* [1963] P 1, *Mauroux v Soc Com Abel Pereira da Fonseca SARL* [1972] 1 WLR 962, *Currie & Co v The Law Society* [1977] QB 990 and *R & T Thew Ltd v Reeves (No. 2)* [1982] QB 1283n are examples. But we believe such applications to have been infrequent. In the course of their practices the three members of this court were personally involved in only one such application.

During the 1980s the tempo quickened. In *Davy-Chiesman v Davy-Chiesman & Anor* [1984] Fam 48 a legally aided husband made an application for ancillary relief against his wife. The judge who heard the application dismissed it, observing that it was without any merit, should not have been made and most certainly should not have been pursued to the end. The wife obtained the usual costs order against the husband, not to be enforced

A without leave of the court. She then sought costs against the legal aid fund. The Law Society, as administrator of the legal aid fund, applied that the husband's solicitor personally pay the costs of both husband and wife. The judge rejected that application and the Law Society appealed. The judgment of the Court of Appeal is authority for two propositions:

(1)   Subject to any express provision of the Legal Aid Act or regulations to the
B   contrary, the interrelationship of lay client, solicitor and counsel and the incidents of that relationship, for instance relating to privilege, are no different when the client is legally aided from when he is not.

(2)   Although a solicitor is in general entitled to rely on the advice of counsel properly instructed, he is not entitled to follow such advice blindly but is in the ordinary way obliged to apply his own expert professional mind to the substance of the
C   advice received.

On the facts, the Court of Appeal held that the solicitor should have appreciated the obvious unsoundness of the advice given by counsel after a certain date, and should have communicated his view to the Law Society. The court therefore allowed the appeal in part. The court plainly regarded counsel as substantially responsible, but there was at the time no jurisdiction to make an order against a barrister.

D   In *Orchard v South Eastern Electricity Board* [1987] QB 565 the plaintiff was again legally aided with a nil contribution. His claim failed. The usual order, not to be enforced without leave, was made in the defendants' favour. An application was made against the plaintiff's solicitors personally and this was dismissed both by the trial judge and on appeal. In the course of his judgment on appeal, Sir John Donaldson MR made certain observations about the position of the Bar, but it would seem that these were obiter since no claim was or could have been made against counsel for the plaintiff. The case is
E   notable first for the Master of the Rolls' ruling on the exercise of the jurisdiction under O. 62, r. 8 as it then stood. At p. 572D he said:

'That said, this is a jurisdiction which falls to be exercised with care and discretion and only in clear cases. In the context of a complaint that litigation was initiated or continued in circumstances in which to do so constituted serious misconduct, it must never be forgotten that it is not for solicitors or counsel to impose a pre-trial
F   screen through which a litigant must pass before he can put his complaint or defence before the court. On the other hand, no solicitor or counsel should lend his assistance to a litigant if he is satisfied that the initiation or further prosecution of a claim is mala fide or for an ulterior purpose or, to put it more broadly, if the proceedings would be, or have become, an abuse of the process of the court or unjustifiably oppressive.'

G   Secondly, the decision reaffirms that a solicitor against whom a claim is made must have a full opportunity of rebutting the complaint, but recognises that he may be hampered in doing so by his duty of confidentiality to the client 'from which he can only be released by his client or by overriding authority' (p. 572G). Thirdly, the judgments highlight the extreme undesirability of claims for wasted costs orders being used as a means of browbeating, bludgeoning or threatening the other side during the progress of the case (pp. 577G and 580E). Such a practice, it was pointed out, could gravely
H   undermine the ability of a solicitor, particularly a solicitor working for a legally aided client, to do so with the required objectivity and independence.

In 1986 the relevant Rules of the Supreme Court were amended. Order 62, r. 8 became O. 62, r. 11, but with some rewording. It now read:

'(1) Subject to the following provisions of this rule, where it appears to the court that costs have been incurred unreasonably or improperly in any proceedings or have been wasted by failure to conduct proceedings with reasonable competence and expedition, the court may–

    (a) order–

        (i) the solicitor whom it considers to be responsible (whether personally or through a servant or agent) to repay to his client costs which the client has been ordered to pay to any other party to the proceedings; or

        (ii) the solicitor personally to indemnify such other parties against costs payable by them; and

        (iii) the costs as between the solicitor and his client to be disallowed;

  or

    (b) direct a taxing officer to inquire into the matter and report to the court, and upon receiving such a report the court may make such order under sub-para. (a) as it thinks fit.'

It is noteworthy that the reference to 'misconduct' is omitted, as is the implication that any conduct must amount to misconduct if it is to found a wasted costs order. More importantly, reference to 'reasonable competence' is introduced, suggesting the ordinary standard of negligence and not a higher standard requiring proof of gross neglect or serious dereliction of duty.

The Court of Appeal had occasion to construe the new rule in *Sinclair-Jones v Kay* [1989] 1 WLR 114. In his judgment May LJ read the new rule as substantially different from the old (p. 121A), and as intended to widen the court's powers (p. 121F). It was no longer necessary to apply the test of gross misconduct laid down in the older authorities (p. 122A). The court regarded the new power as salutary, particularly as a means of penalising unreasonable delay (pp. 121H, 122A, C).

In *Holden & Co v Crown Prosecution Service* [1990] 2 QB 261, the court's decision in *Sinclair-Jones v Kay* was criticised and not followed, but the correctness of that judgment was affirmed in *Gupta v Comer* [1991] 1 QB 629, where O. 62, r. 11 as it then stood was again considered. Part of the court's reasoning in upholding the earlier decision cannot, it would seem, survive later authority, but there is no ground to question its conclusion that the new rule was intended to cut down limitations hitherto thought to restrict the court's jurisdiction to make wasted costs orders.

In his judgment in *Gupta v Comer*, Lord Donaldson of Lymington MR referred to legislative amendments to s. 51 of the *Supreme Court Act* 1981 which would enable new rules to be made 'imposing an even stricter standard than that which O. 62, r. 11 has been held to impose' (p. 635E). This was a reference to what became the *Courts and Legal Services Act* 1990. Section 4 of that Act substituted a new s. 51 in the *Supreme Court Act* 1981. Relevant for present purposes are the following subsections of the new section:

'51(1) Subject to the provisions of this or any other enactment and to rules of court, the costs of and incidental to all proceedings in–

    (a) the civil division of the Court of Appeal;

    (b) the High Court; and

    (c) any county court,

shall be in the discretion of the court.

. . .

(6) In any proceedings mentioned in subsection (1), the court may disallow, or (as the case may be) order the legal or other representative concerned to meet, the

A whole of any wasted costs or such part of them as may be determined in accordance with rules of court.

(7) In subsection (6), "wasted costs" means any costs incurred by a party–

  (a) as a result of any improper, unreasonable or negligent act or omission on the part of any legal or other representative or any employee of such a representative; or

B   (b) which, in the light of any such act or omission occurring after they were incurred, the court considers it is unreasonable to expect that party to pay.

. . .

(13) In this section "legal or other representative", in relation to a party to proceedings, means any person exercising a right of audience or right to conduct litigation on his behalf.'

C The new subs. (6) of s. 51 was extended to civil proceedings in the Crown Court. Section 111 made a similar amendment to the *Prosecution of Offences Act* 1985, applicable to criminal proceedings in the Court of Appeal, the Crown Court and the magistrates' court. Section 112 of the Act amended the *Magistrates' Courts Act* 1980 to similar effect. We should also draw attention to s. 62 of the Act, which was in these terms:

'62(1) A person–

D   (a) who is not a barrister; but

  (b) who lawfully provides any legal services in relation to any proceedings,

shall have the same immunity from liability for negligence in respect of his acts or omissions as he would have if he were a barrister lawfully providing those services.

(2) No act or omission on the part of any barrister or other person which is accorded immunity from liability for negligence shall give rise to an action for breach of any contract relating to the provision by him of the legal services in question.'

E

With effect from 1 October 1991, O. 62, r. 11 was amended to supplement the new s. 51 of the Supreme Court Act. It is enough to summarise the effect of the rule without reciting its full terms. Where the court makes a wasted costs order, it must specify in its order the costs which are to be paid. As under previous versions of the rule, the court F may direct a taxing officer to inquire into the matter and report back or it may refer the matter to a taxing officer. The court may not make an order under s. 51(6) unless it has given the legal representative a reasonable opportunity to appear and show cause why an order should not be made, although this obligation is qualified where the progress of proceedings is obstructed by a legal representative's failure to attend or deliver a document or proceed. The court may direct the Official Solicitor to attend and take such part in any proceedings or inquiry under the rule as the court may direct.

G Some aspects of this new wasted costs regime must be considered in more detail below. It should, however, be noted that the jurisdiction is for the first time extended to barristers. There can in our view be no room for doubt about the mischief against which these new provisions were aimed: this was the causing of loss and expense to litigants by the unjustifiable conduct of litigation by their or the other side's lawyers. Where such conduct is shown, Parliament clearly intended to arm the courts with an effective remedy H for the protection of those injured.

Since the Act there have been two cases which deserve mention. The first is *Re a Barrister (wasted costs order) (No. 1 of 1991)* [1993] QB 293. This arose out of an unhappy difference between counsel and a judge sitting in the Crown Court in a criminal case. It was held on appeal, in our view quite rightly, that courts should apply a three-stage test when a wasted costs order is contemplated:

(1)   Has the legal representative of whom complaint is made acted improperly,   A
unreasonably or negligently?

(2)   If so, did such conduct cause the applicant to incur unnecessary costs?

(3)   If so, is it in all the circumstances just to order the legal representative to
compensate the applicant for the whole or any part of the relevant costs? If so, the
costs to be met must be specified and, in a criminal case, the amount of the costs.

We have somewhat altered the wording of the court's ruling but not, we think, its effect.   B

The second case, *Symphony Group plc v Hodgson* [1994] QB 179, arose out of an
application for costs against a non-party and not out of a wasted costs order. An
observation of Balcombe LJ at p. 194B is however pertinent in this context also:

'The judge should be alert to the possibility that an application against a non-party
is motivated by resentment of an inability to obtain an effective order for costs
against a legally aided litigant. The courts are well aware of the financial difficulties   C
faced by parties who are facing legally aided litigants at first instance, where the
opportunity of a claim against the legal aid board under section 18 of the Legal
Aid Act 1988 is very limited. Nevertheless the Civil Legal Aid (General)
Regulations 1989 (S.I. 1989 No. 339), and in particular regulations 67, 69, and 70,
lay down conditions designed to ensure that there is no abuse of legal aid by a
legally assisted person and these are designed to protect the other party to the   D
litigation as well as the Legal Aid Fund. The court will be very reluctant to infer
that solicitors to a legally aided party have failed to discharge their duties under
the regulations – see *Orchard v South Eastern Electricity Board* [1987] QB 565 –
and in my judgment this principle extends to a reluctance to infer that any
maintenance by a non-party has occurred.'

'Improper, unreasonable or negligent'   E

A number of different submissions were made on the correct construction of these
crucial words in the new s. 51(7) of the *Supreme Court Act* 1981. In our view the meaning
of these expressions is not open to serious doubt.

'Improper' means what it has been understood to mean in this context for at least half
a century. The adjective covers, but is not confined to, conduct which would ordinarily
be held to justify disbarment, striking off, suspension from practice or other serious   F
professional penalty. It covers any significant breach of a substantial duty imposed by a
relevant code of professional conduct. But it is not in our judgment limited to that.
Conduct which would be regarded as improper according to the consensus of
professional (including judicial) opinion can be fairly stigmatised as such whether or not
it violates the letter of a professional code.

'Unreasonable' also means what it has been understood to mean in this context for at   G
least half a century. The expression aptly describes conduct which is vexatious, designed
to harass the other side rather than advance the resolution of the case, and it makes no
difference that the conduct is the product of excessive zeal and not improper motive. But
conduct cannot be described as unreasonable simply because it leads in the event to an
unsuccessful result or because other more cautious legal representatives would have acted
differently. The acid test is whether the conduct permits of a reasonable explanation. If
so, the course adopted may be regarded as optimistic and as reflecting on a practitioner's   H
judgment, but it is not unreasonable.

The term 'negligent' was the most controversial of the three. It was argued that the
1990 Act, in this context as in others, used 'negligent' as a term of art involving the well-
known ingredients of duty, breach, causation and damage. Therefore, it was said,
conduct cannot be regarded as negligent unless it involves an actionable breach of the

A   legal representative's duty to his own client, to whom alone a duty is owed. We reject this
    approach:

    (1)   As already noted, the predecessor of the present O. 62, r. 11 made reference to
           'reasonable competence'. That expression does not invoke technical concepts of
           the law of negligence. It seems to us inconceivable that by changing the language
           Parliament intended to make it harder, rather than easier, for courts to make
B   orders.

    (2)   Since the applicant's right to a wasted costs order against a legal representative
           depends on showing that the latter is in breach of his duty to the court it makes no
           sense to superimpose a requirement under this head (but not in the case of
           impropriety or unreasonableness) that he is also in breach of his duty to his client.

        We cannot regard this as, in practical terms, a very live issue, since it requires some
C   ingenuity to postulate a situation in which a legal representative causes the other side to
    incur unnecessary costs without at the same time running up unnecessary costs for his
    own side and so breaching the ordinary duty owed by a legal representative to his client.
    But for whatever importance it may have, we are clear that 'negligent' should be
    understood in an untechnical way to denote failure to act with the competence reasonably
    to be expected of ordinary members of the profession.

D   In adopting an untechnical approach to the meaning of negligence in this context, we
    would however wish firmly to discountenance any suggestion that an applicant for a
    wasted costs order under this head need prove anything less than he would have to prove
    in an action for negligence: 'advice, acts or omissions in the course of their professional
    work which no member of the profession who was reasonably well-informed and
    competent would have given or done or omitted to do'; an error 'such as no reasonably
    well-informed and competent member of that profession could have made' (*Saif Ali v
E   Sydney Mitchell & Co*, at pp. 218D, 220D, per Lord Diplock).

        We were invited to give the three adjectives (improper, unreasonable and negligent)
    specific, self-contained meanings, so as to avoid overlap between the three. We do not
    read these very familiar expressions in that way. Conduct which is unreasonable may
    also be improper, and conduct which is negligent will very frequently be (if it is not by
    definition) unreasonable. We do not think any sharp differentiation between these
F   expressions is useful or necessary or intended.

Pursuing a hopeless case

        A legal representative is not to be held to have acted improperly, unreasonably or
    negligently simply because he acts for a party who pursues a claim or a defence which is
    plainly doomed to fail. As Lord Pearce observed in *Rondel v Worsley* [1969] 1 AC 191 at
G   p. 275B,

           'It is easier, pleasanter and more advantageous professionally for barristers to
           advise, represent or defend those who are decent and reasonable and likely to
           succeed in their action or their defence than those who are unpleasant,
           unreasonable, disreputable, and have an apparently hopeless case. Yet it would be
           tragic if our legal system came to provide no reputable defenders, representatives
H   or advisers for the latter.'

    As is well known, barristers in independent practice are not permitted to pick and choose
    their clients. Paragraph 209 of their code of conduct provides:

           'A barrister in independent practice must comply with the "Cab-rank rule" and
           accordingly except only as otherwise provided in paragraphs 501 502 and 503 he
           must in any field in which he professes to practise in relation to work appropriate

to his experience and seniority and irrespective of whether his client is paying privately or is legally aided or otherwise publicly funded:

(a) accept any brief to appear before a court in which he professes to practise;

(b) accept any instructions;

(c) act for any person on whose behalf he is briefed or instructed;

and do so irrespective of (i) the party on whose behalf he is briefed or instructed (ii) the nature of the case and (iii) any belief or opinion which he may have formed as to the character reputation cause conduct guilt or innocence of that person.'

As is also well-known, solicitors are not subject to an equivalent cab-rank rule, but many solicitors would and do respect the public policy underlying it by affording representation to the unpopular and the unmeritorious. Legal representatives will, of course, whether barristers or solicitors, advise clients of the perceived weakness of their case and of the risk of failure. But clients are free to reject advice and insist that cases be litigated. It is rarely if ever safe for a court to assume that a hopeless case is being litigated on the advice of the lawyers involved. They are there to present the case; it is (as Samuel Johnson unforgettably pointed out) for the judge and not the lawyers to judge it.

It is, however, one thing for a legal representative to present, on instructions, a case which he regards as bound to fail; it is quite another to lend his assistance to proceedings which are an abuse of the process of the court. Whether instructed or not, a legal representative is not entitled to use litigious procedures for purposes for which they were not intended, as by issuing or pursuing proceedings for reasons unconnected with success in the litigation or pursuing a case known to be dishonest, nor is he entitled to evade rules intended to safeguard the interests of justice, as by knowingly failing to make full disclosure on ex parte application or knowingly conniving at incomplete disclosure of documents. It is not entirely easy to distinguish by definition between the hopeless case and the case which amounts to an abuse of the process, but in practice it is not hard to say which is which and if there is doubt the legal representative is entitled to the benefit of it.

Legal aid

Section 31(1) of the *Legal Aid Act* 1988 provides that receipt of legal aid shall not (save as expressly provided) affect the relationship between or rights of a legal representative and client or any privilege arising out of the relationship nor the rights or liabilities of other parties to the proceedings or the principles on which any discretion is exercised. (The protection given to a legally assisted party in relation to payment of costs is, of course, an obvious express exception.) This important principle has been recognised in the authorities. It is incumbent on courts to which applications for wasted costs orders are made to bear prominently in mind the peculiar vulnerability of legal representatives acting for assisted persons, to which Balcombe LJ adverted in *Symphony Group* and which recent experience abundantly confirms. It would subvert the benevolent purposes of this legislation if such representatives were subject to any unusual personal risk. They for their part must bear prominently in mind that their advice and their conduct should not be tempered by the knowledge that their client is not their paymaster and so not, in all probability, liable for the costs of the other side.

In *Rondel v Worsley* the House of Lords held that a barrister was immune from an action for negligence at the suit of a client in respect of his conduct and management of a case in court and the preliminary work in connection with it. A majority of the House held that this immunity extended to a solicitor while acting as an advocate. In *Saif Ali v Sydney Mitchell* a majority of the House further held that the immunity only covered pre-trial work intimately connected with the conduct of the case in court. These decisions

A   were based on powerfully argued considerations of public policy, which included: the requirement that advocates should be free to conduct cases in court fearlessly, independently and without looking over their shoulders; the need for finality, so that cases are not endlessly relitigated with the risk of inconsistent decisions; the advocate's duty to the court and to the administration of justice; the barrister's duty to act for a client, however unsavoury; the general immunity accorded to those taking part in court proceedings; the unique role of the advocate; and the subjection of advocates to the discipline of their professional bodies.

B

We were reminded of these matters when considering submissions on the interaction of s. 4, 111 and 112 of the Courts and Legal Services Act and s. 62 of the same Act. On one submission, s. 62 must be read subject to the other sections. On that view, if an advocate's conduct in court is improper, unreasonable or negligent he is liable to a wasted costs order. On a second submission, s. 4, 111 and 112 must be read subject to s. 62. On that view, a wasted costs order can only be based on improper, unreasonable or negligent conduct which does not take place in court and is not intimately connected with conduct of the case in court. On yet a third submission, s. 4, 111 and 112 should be read subject to s. 62 but in a more limited sense: improper or unreasonable conduct would found an order whether in court or out of it, but negligent conduct would not found an order unless it fell outside the ambit of the recognised immunity for work at the trial and before it.

C

D

In our judgment (and subject to the important qualification noted below) the first of these submissions is correct, and for a number of reasons:

(1)   There is nothing in s. 4, 111 and 112 to suggest that they take effect subject to the provisions of s. 62.

(2)   Part II of the 1990 Act, in which s. 62 (but not the other sections) appears, is directed to widening the categories of those by whom legal services are provided. It was therefore natural to enact that those providing services also or formerly provided by lawyers should enjoy the same immunity as lawyers. To the same end, s. 63 enacts that such persons should enjoy the same professional privilege as a solicitor. There is nothing in s. 62 to suggest that it is intended to qualify the apparently unqualified effect of the other sections, to which (in the scheme of the Act) it is in no way related.

E

F

(3)   Nothing in the Act warrants the drawing of any distinction between improper and unreasonable conduct on the one hand and negligent conduct on the other. Such a distinction is in any event unworkable if, as we have suggested, there is considerable overlap between these expressions.

(4)   If the conduct of cases in court, or work intimately connected with the conduct of cases in court, entitles a legal representative to immunity from the making of wasted costs orders, it is not obvious why s. 111 and 112 were applied to magistrates' courts, where no work would ordinarily be done which would not be covered by the immunity.

G

(5)   It was very odd draftsmanship to define a legal representative in s. 51(13) as a person exercising a right of audience if it was intended that anyone exercising a right of audience should be immune from the liability imposed by s. 51(6).

H

(6)   It would be anomalous to interpret an Act which extended the wasted costs jurisdiction over barristers for the first time as exempting them from liability in respect of their most characteristic activity, namely conducting cases in court and advising in relation to such cases. It would be scarcely less anomalous to interpret an Act making express reference to negligence for the first time as exempting advocates from liability for negligence.

(7)   It is one thing to say that an advocate shall be immune from claims in negligence   A
by an aggrieved and unsuccessful client. It is quite another for the court to take
steps to rectify, at the expense of the advocate, breaches by the advocate of the
duty he owed to the court to further the ends of justice.

(8)   It is our belief, which we cannot substantiate, that part of the reason underlying
the changes effected by the new s. 51 was judicial concern at the wholly
unacceptable manner in which a very small minority of barristers conducted cases   B
in court.

We referred above to an important qualification. It is this. Although we are satisfied
that the intention of this legislation is to encroach on the traditional immunity of the
advocate by subjecting him to the wasted costs jurisdiction if he causes a waste of costs
by improper, unreasonable or negligent conduct, it does not follow that we regard the
public interest considerations on which the immunity is founded as being irrelevant or
lacking weight in this context. Far from it. Any judge who is invited to make or   C
contemplates making an order arising out of an advocate's conduct of court proceedings
must make full allowance for the fact that an advocate in court, like a commander in
battle, often has to make decisions quickly and under pressure, in the fog of war and
ignorant of developments on the other side of the hill. Mistakes will inevitably be made,
things done which the outcome shows to have been unwise. But advocacy is more an art
than a science. It cannot be conducted according to formulae. Individuals differ in their   D
style and approach. It is only when, with all allowances made, an advocate's conduct of
court proceedings is quite plainly unjustifiable that it can be appropriate to make a
wasted costs order against him.

Privilege

Where an applicant seeks a wasted costs order against the lawyers on the other side,   E
legal professional privilege may be relevant both as between the applicant and his lawyers
and as between the respondent lawyers and their client. In either case it is the client's
privilege, which he alone can waive.

The first of these situations can cause little difficulty. If the applicant's privileged
communications are germane to an issue in the application, to show what he would or
would not have done had the other side not acted in the manner complained of, he can   F
waive his privilege; if he declines to do so adverse inferences can be drawn.

The respondent lawyers are in a different position. The privilege is not theirs to waive.
In the usual case where a waiver would not benefit their client they will be slow to advise
the client to waive his privilege, and they may well feel bound to advise that the client
should take independent advice before doing so. The client may be unwilling to do that,
and may be unwilling to waive if he does. So the respondent lawyers may find themselves
at a grave disadvantage in defending their conduct of proceedings, unable to reveal what   G
advice and warnings they gave, what instructions they received. In some cases this
potential source of injustice may be mitigated by reference to the taxing master, where
different rules apply, but only in a small minority of cases can this procedure be
appropriate. Judges who are invited to make or contemplate making a wasted costs order
must make full allowance for the inability of respondent lawyers to tell the whole story.
Where there is room for doubt, the respondent lawyers are entitled to the benefit of it. It
is again only when, with all allowances made, a lawyer's conduct of proceedings is quite   H
plainly unjustifiable that it can be appropriate to make a wasted costs order.

Causation

As emphasised in *Re a Barrister (wasted costs order) (No. 1 of 1991)*, the court has
jurisdiction to make a wasted costs order only where the improper, unreasonable or

A   negligent conduct complained of has caused a waste of costs and only to the extent of such wasted costs. Demonstration of a causal link is essential. Where the conduct is proved but no waste of costs is shown to have resulted, the case may be one to be referred to the appropriate disciplinary body or the legal aid authorities, but it is not one for exercise of the wasted costs jurisdiction.

Reliance on counsel

B

We endorse the guidance given on this subject in *Locke v Camberwell Health Authority* [1991] 2 Med LR 249. A solicitor does not abdicate his professional responsibility when he seeks the advice of counsel. He must apply his mind to the advice received. But the more specialist the nature of the advice, the more reasonable is it likely to be for a solicitor to accept it and act on it.

C   ### Threats to apply for wasted costs orders

We entirely agree with the view expressed by this court in *Orchard v South Eastern Electricity*, that the threat of proposed applications should not be used as a means of intimidation. On the other hand, if one side considers that the conduct of the other is improper, unreasonable or negligent and likely to cause a waste of costs we do not consider it objectionable to alert the other side to that view; the other side can then
D   consider its position and perhaps mend its ways. Drawing the distinction between unacceptable intimidation and acceptable notice must depend on the professional judgment of those involved.

The timing of the application

In *Filmlab Systems International Ltd v Pennington* [1993] TLR 383 Aldous J expressed
E   the opinion that wasted costs orders should not, save in exceptional circumstances, be sought until after trial. He highlighted a number of dangers if applications were made at an interlocutory stage, among them the risk that a party's advisers might feel they could no longer act, so that the party would in effect be deprived of the advisers of his choice. It is impossible to lay down rules of universal application, and sometimes an interlocutory battle resolves the real dispute between the parties. But speaking generally we agree that in the ordinary way applications for wasted costs are best left until after the end of the
F   trial.

The applicant

Under the rules, the court itself may initiate the enquiry whether a wasted costs order should be made. In straightforward cases (such as failure to appear, lateness, negligence leading to an otherwise avoidable adjournment, gross repetition or extreme slowness)
G   there is no reason why it should not do so. But save in the most obvious case, courts should in our view be slow to initiate the enquiry. If they do so in cases where the enquiry becomes complex and time-consuming, difficult and embarrassing issues on costs can arise: if a wasted costs order is not made, the costs of the enquiry will have to be borne by someone and it will not be the court; even if an order is made, the costs ordered to be paid may be small compared with the costs of the enquiry. In such cases courts will usually be well advised to leave an aggrieved party to make the application if so advised;
H   the costs will then, in the ordinary way, follow the event between the parties.

The procedure to be followed in determining applications for wasted costs must be laid down by courts so as to meet the requirements of the individual case before them. The overriding requirements are that any procedure must be fair and that it must be as simple and summary as fairness permits. Fairness requires that any respondent lawyer should be very clearly told what he is said to have done wrong and what is claimed. But the requirement of simplicity and summariness means that elaborate pleadings should in general be avoided. No formal process of discovery will be appropriate. We cannot imagine circumstances in which the applicant should be permitted to interrogate the respondent lawyer, or vice versa. Hearings should be measured in hours, and not in days or weeks. Judges must not reject a weapon which Parliament has intended to be used for the protection of those injured by the unjustifiable conduct of the other side's lawyers, but they must be astute to control what threatens to become a new and costly form of satellite litigation.

'Show cause'

Although O. 62, r. 11(4) in its present form requires that in the ordinary way the court should not make a wasted costs order without giving the legal representative 'a reasonable opportunity to appear and show cause why an order should not be made', this should not be understood to mean that the burden is on the legal representative to exculpate himself. A wasted costs order should not be made unless the applicant satisfies the court, or the court itself is satisfied, that an order should be made. The representative is not obliged to prove that it should not. But the rule clearly envisages that the representative will not be called on to reply unless an apparently strong prima facie case has been made against him and the language of the rule recognises a shift in the evidential burden.

Discretion

It was submitted, in our view correctly, that the jurisdiction to make a wasted costs order is dependent at two stages on the discretion of the court. The first is at the stage of initial application, when the court is invited to give the legal representative an opportunity to show cause. This is not something to be done automatically or without careful appraisal of the relevant circumstances. The costs of the enquiry as compared with the costs claimed will always be one relevant consideration. This is a discretion, like any other, to be exercised judicially, but judges may not infrequently decide that further proceedings are not likely to be justified. The second discretion arises at the final stage. Even if the court is satisfied that a legal representative has acted improperly, unreasonably or negligently and that such conduct has caused the other side to incur an identifiable sum of wasted costs, it is not bound to make an order, but in that situation it would of course have to give sustainable reasons for exercising its discretion against making an order.

Crime

Since the six cases before the court are all civil cases, our attention has naturally been directed towards the exercise of the wasted costs jurisdiction in the civil field. Attention has, however, been drawn in authorities such as *Holden v Crown Prosecution Service* and *Gupta v Comer*, above, to the undesirability of any divergence in the practice of the civil and criminal courts in this field, and Parliament has acted so as substantially (but not completely) to assimilate the practice in the two. We therefore hope that this judgment may give guidance which will be of value to criminal courts as to civil, but we fully appreciate that the conduct of criminal cases will often raise different questions and depend on different circumstances. The relevant discretions are vested in, and only in, the court conducting the relevant hearing. Our purpose is to guide, but not restrict, the exercise of these discretions.

Philex plc v Golban

The appellants in *Philex plc v S Golban (trading as Capital Estates)* are solicitors against whose firm a wasted costs order was made in the Companies Court (see [1993]

A   BCC 726). Their client had claimed to be a creditor of the company, which was solvent. The debt was disputed. The client had nevertheless made use of the statutory demand procedure as a means of pressure to force payment. The company applied for and obtained an injunction to restrain the issue of a winding-up petition, and an order for their costs of that application against the client on an indemnity basis. Having reason to doubt the solvency of the client, the company applied further that their costs should be made the subject of a wasted costs order against his solicitors. The judge made such an order, not upon the ground that the solicitors were open to any criticism for issuing the statutory demand in the first place, but because at a later stage (when the payment time allowed by the statutory demand had expired) they were parties to a negotiating offer which made unreasonable or improper use of the implied threat of a winding-up petition as an inducement to the company to compromise the claim.

B   The facts, which are helpfully set out in the full and careful judgment of Knox J, were these. On or about 18 December 1992 the alleged debtor company Philex plc ('Philex') completed the purchase of a property in north west London ('the property') for a price in the region of £370,000. The alleged creditor Mr S Golban claimed to be entitled to an introduction fee or commission on the purchase, in respect of which he invoiced Philex as follows on 22 December 1992:

C   'For introduction of the above property purchase from L & S Properties at purchase price £370,000 and completion taken place on 21 December 1992. Agreed commission of 3 per cent: £11,100.'

D   The claim was promptly denied on behalf of Philex, whose finance director, Mr Torbati, replied on 24 December:

   'We are in receipt of your invoice . . . which we do not understand. So far as we are aware we have no liabilities outstanding to yourselves.'

E   On that same day (24 December) the appellant firm (acting as solicitors for Mr Golban through a partner to whom it will be convenient to refer as 'the solicitor') served on Philex a statutory demand in the approved form, Form 4.1. That form has endorsed upon it in heavy black type the warning:

   'REMEMBER! The company has only 21 days after the date of service on it of this document before the creditor may present a winding-up petition.'

F   It was signed by Mr Golban, who designated the solicitor as the person to whom any communications were to be addressed. The demand reasserted the commission claim in the sum of £11,100 and alleged that Philex had refused to pay it. The letter from the solicitor's firm covering service of the statutory demand included a note that their offices would be closed from 1.30 pm that day (24 December) to 9.30 am on Monday, 4 January 1993.

G   On Thursday, 31 December 1992, Iliffes, solicitors acting for Philex, wrote to the solicitor's firm in response to the statutory demand. They disputed that Mr Golban had at any time acted for or been engaged for any purpose by Philex, which did not deny that he had been concerned in discussions with it about the purchase but contended that the company had been given to understand that he was acting exclusively on behalf of the vendors. The letter continued:

H   'Our client is a solvent company. The reason that our client refuses to pay your client the sum claimed or any other sum is that your client has no entitlement to be paid. The alleged debt is disputed by our client and your client's statutory demand is an abuse of the process of the Companies Court. Unless we receive your client's undertaking by 4 pm on Monday, 4 January 1993 [which was the first working day after the date of that letter and was also the day on which the solicitor's office was due to reopen] that he will take no further steps in relation to the statutory demand

and that he will not issue a winding-up petition in respect of it our client will make   A
an immediate application to the Companies Court to restrain your client from
presenting a petition and will apply for its costs on the indemnity basis in
accordance with the principles laid down in Re a Company. . .'

–a reference to Hoffmann J's reaffirmation in Re a Company No. 0012209 of 1991 [1992]
1 WLR 351 at p. 354 of the principle that it is an abuse of the process of the Companies
Court to present a winding-up petition to secure payment of a debt concerning which   B
there is a genuine dispute.

The solicitor duly found that letter of 31 December waiting for him when he returned
to his office on 4 January, and sent a copy of it (together with a copy of the law report of
Re a Company) to his client Mr Golban, whom he knew to be abroad and not due to
return until 5 or 6 January. He did not feel that he could give the required undertaking
without instructions from his client. The 4 pm deadline allowed by Iliffes' letter of 31
December accordingly passed, and on 5 January Iliffes issued an originating application   C
in the Companies Court returnable on 25 January and seeking an order for an injunction
restraining Mr Golban from presenting any petition to wind up Philex based upon the
statutory demand. That application was served on the solicitor's firm the same day (5
January) under cover of a letter which stated that the affidavit in support would be served
shortly.

This supporting affidavit was in fact served on the solicitor's firm on Friday, 8 January.   D
It was sworn by Mr Torbati, who stated Philex's general case as follows. Mr Golban had
indeed introduced the property to Philex's managing director (Mr Sabourian) and had
acted as an intermediary to convey to the vendors certain offers that were initially made
for it by Philex. Those offers did not, however, bear fruit. Philex thereafter entered into
direct negotiations with the vendors which led eventually to an agreement for sale in
which Mr Golban had played no part. Mr Torbati went on to describe Mr Sabourian as   E
having expressed the wish, nevertheless, to make some ex gratia payment to Mr Golban
for his introduction. He had suggested a figure of £2,000, which Mr Golban had rejected
as wholly inadequate.

The solicitor did not read this evidence on the Friday on which it was served, but
considered it on Monday, 11 January (having in the meantime sent a copy of it without
comment to Mr Golban). It should be noted that the judge had no criticism to make,
down to that point, of the solicitor's conduct in any respect whatsoever.   F

On that same day (Monday, 11 January) the solicitor wrote a letter to Iliffes which
contained no more than a simple acknowledgment of receipt of the affidavit. His client's
comments on that affidavit were received on 13 January: it may safely be assumed
(although privilege has not been waived) that those comments dissented strongly from
Mr Torbati's version of events.

Thursday, 14 January was the expiry date of the 21-day period allowed by the statutory   G
demand. On that day the solicitor was telephoned by Mr Evered of Iliffes, who asked
him whether Mr Golban was intending to resist the pending application for an injunction
against presentation of a petition (due to be heard on 25 January), pointing out at the
same time that it was now crystal clear that there was a genuine dispute about the claim
and that Mr Golban was at risk of having to pay costs on an indemnity basis if he
invoked the winding-up procedure. The solicitor replied that he had explained this to his   H
client, who was nevertheless adamant that he was owed the money and wanted to go
ahead. When Mr Evered asked him whether he intended to issue a petition, because (if
he did) Philex would apply immediately for an ex parte injunction to restrain its
advertisement, the solicitor replied that he would have to take instructions and would get
back to him on that point. After that conversation, the solicitor had to leave immediately
to attend a court engagement, and when he returned to his office he found a fax copy of

A   an ex parte injunction which had been obtained by Iliffes that day prohibiting the issue by Mr Golban of any petition to wind up Philex until the conclusion of the hearing due to take place on 25 January.

On Friday, 15 January at the latest (it was possible according to the finding of the judge that the relevant advice had been given two days earlier on 13 January) the solicitor advised Mr Golban specifically that in the current state of the evidence a genuine dispute B   existed as to the subject-matter of the statutory demand, and that it would be an abuse of the process of the court to present any petition founded upon it. Mr Golban accepted that advice, but at the same time gave the solicitor certain instructions, as to which there has, again, been no waiver of privilege, but it may safely be assumed from what followed that they included a request to see if something in the nature of a compromise could be salvaged from the existing situation. The solicitor accordingly that same day drafted a letter to Iliffes to which reference will be made shortly, but did not post it that day C   because he wanted to have it approved by counsel to whom he submitted the draft for consideration over the weekend.

On Monday, 18 January Iliffes faxed a letter to the solicitor seeking to substantiate a suggestion previously made that Mr Golban had become the subject of bankruptcy proceedings, and giving him notice that:

D   'unless terms can be agreed for the relief sought and payment of our client's costs prior to the hearing of the application on 25 January we shall seek that an order be made against your firm personally to pay our client's costs on the indemnity basis.'

On 19 January the solicitor sent to Iliffes the letter which had been submitted in draft to counsel. It included the following passages:

E   'It appears from your client's affidavit that he has offered payment of £2,000 to our client in satisfaction of the claim. Whilst our client wishes to reserve his rights to pursue the full claim he is nevertheless prepared to accept payment of £2,000 together with our reasonable costs if this can be agreed before 25 January. If not, our client intends to issue proceedings for the full amount of his claim and seeks your confirmation that the sum of £2,000 will be paid into court in such proceedings.

F   In spite of his reservations arising from the discrepancy between what you have stated on behalf of your client and what your client states in his affidavit our client accepts that the evidence contained in the affidavit establishes, prima facie, a dispute rendering inappropriate the continuation of the winding-up procedure and confirms that he does not intend to present a winding-up petition.

We note your comments regarding our position and the alleged bankruptcy of our G   client. He has, as you know, denied to us that he is bankrupt and in view of your persistence in asserting this we have made a search against our client which has disclosed that there are no subsisting entries. We are therefore unable to agree with your contention that we should be personally liable for costs and will certainly oppose any such application.'

The proposal in that letter for settlement of Mr Golban's claim for £2,000 and his costs H   was rejected by Iliffes on 21 January. No agreement was reached as to how matters should proceed at the hearing on 25 January. The upshot was that counsel attended that hearing, on the instructions of the solicitor on behalf of Mr Golban, and offered no resistance to an order for an injunction in the terms prayed by the originating application. An order was made that Mr Golban should pay Philex's costs of the application on an indemnity basis. An application intimated at that hearing for such costs to be paid by the solicitor's firm personally was adjourned to a later date, and was dealt with by Knox J

on 30 June 1993 when he made the wasted costs order now under appeal. This was an　　A
order that the solicitor's firm:

'do pay the wasted costs incurred by (Philex) after 13 January 1993 to be taxed if
not agreed but credit should be given for such costs as would have been incurred
in disposing of the (application) by consent.'

The judge's reasons for treating the costs incurred by Philex from and after 14 January
1993 as 'wasted' for the purposes of s. 51(6) and (7) were expressed in these terms (at　　B
p. 733E):

'I have come to the conclusion that it was unreasonable and indeed improper to
use proceedings which by 11 January 1993 (the solicitor) should have realised and
did realise amounted to an abuse of the process of the court as a vehicle to secure
a compromise on the basis of the £2,000 claim which at one stage was offered. (The
solicitor) did indeed, on his own evidence, advise his client Mr Golban not to　　C
proceed with the statutory demand on 15 January. He should, and indeed may,
have done so when Mr Golban gave (the solicitor), on or about 13 January, his
comments on Mr Torbati's affidavit. The fact that Mr Golban continued to believe
in the merits of his case for commission is not any justification for not accepting
that the winding-up procedure was inappropriate and should not be followed.'

This passage makes it clear that the conduct of the solicitor which the judge regarded　　D
as unreasonable or improper for the purposes of s. 51(7) consisted of his adoption on
Mr Golban's behalf from and after 14 January 1993 of the tactic of threatening the use of
a winding-up petition, presented in abuse of the process of the court, as a bargaining
counter to improve his client's prospects of persuading Philex to accept a compromise of
the claim at the suggested figure of £2,000 plus costs.

The appellant firm submits that this finding of misconduct was not open to the judge
on the evidence and can only have been founded on a misreading of the correspondence.　　E
It points out:

(1)　That the relevant compromise was proposed in the letter of 19 January, in which it
was quite clearly and unconditionally stated that Mr Golban accepted that the
evidence established a bona fide dispute making the continuance of the winding-
up procedure inappropriate, and confirmed that he did not intend to present a
winding-up petition. There was therefore no question of the solicitor using　　F
potentially abusive proceedings as 'a vehicle to secure a compromise'.

(2)　That the compromise proposal was in any event contained in a letter whose text
had been approved by counsel on whose advice the solicitor was entitled to rely.

With every respect to the views of a judge with wide experience in this field of the law
who had obviously given the case detailed and careful attention, these submissions are in
our judgment well founded. We do not suggest that there could never be circumstances　　G
in which a solicitor who advised his client to make use of a threat of proceedings that
would (if brought) amount to an abuse of the process might be found to have been guilty
of improper or unreasonable conduct. It is simply that we are unable to find any
evidential basis for the judge's conclusion that misconduct of that sort had occurred in
the present case. The solicitor was, moreover, entitled to rely upon the fact that from 15
January onwards he was acting on the advice of counsel, both generally in regard to the
prosecution of Mr Golban's claim to commission and specifically in regard to the　　H
compromise proposal, the terms of which (as proposed in the letter of 19 January) had
been approved by counsel.

Mr Otty, arguing in support of the notice to affirm which has been served in the appeal
by Philex, suggested that there was an alternative ground on which the judge could (and
in his submission should) have based a wasted costs order. From 14 January onwards

A   the solicitor had a client who was eligible in law (the 21 days of the statutory demand having expired) to present a winding-up petition, and who – although willing to acknowledge that the debt demanded was a disputed debt, and willing even to accept that to present a petition would involve abuse of the court process – was nevertheless not prepared to take the crucial step of instructing his solicitor to give a formal undertaking to the court that no petition would be presented. From that point, therefore, so Mr Otty argued, it became the solicitor's duty to stop acting altogether, and to tell Mr Golban

B   that he must either take different advice or act in person. Had the solicitor ceased to act from 14 January onwards, the wasted costs would, it is asserted, have been saved.

We are unable to accept that argument. The solicitor was not criticised by the judge for anything he did (or omitted to do) down to and including 13 January. It would involve setting an over-scrupulous standard for the solicitor, as well as running some risk of unfairness to the client, if the solicitor were to be expected to terminate his retainer

C   abruptly on 14 January, with the hearing only 11 days away, solely upon the ground that the client, although willing to give appropriate assurances, was unwilling to authorise the formal undertaking which would make any contest at that hearing unnecessary. Nor does it appear to us that the costs of a contested hearing on 25 January would necessarily have been saved by his ceasing to act. It is by no means unlikely that Mr Golban, deprived of his solicitor, would have insisted upon maintaining his opposition and would have resisted the application thereafter as a litigant in person. The same objection applies

D   to Mr Otty's alternative submission (to which it is unnecessary to refer in detail) that costs could have been avoided if advice that presentation of a petition would be abusive of the process had been given to Mr Golban by the solicitor on 13 January instead of 15 January 1993.

For these reasons the appeal will be allowed and the wasted costs order discharged.

(*Order accordingly*)

E

F

G

H

McIsaac & Anor, Petitioners (Joint liquidators of First Tokyo Index Trust Ltd).

Court of Session (Outer House).
Lord Cameron of Lochbroom.
Judgment delivered 13 and 27 January 1994.

Insolvency – Inquiry into company's dealings, etc. – Private examination – Liquidators sought production of documents from auditors and oral examination – Whether order could be made against former employee of auditors who resided out of jurisdiction – Whether orders sought were oppressive and unreasonably wide – Whether undertaking of confidentiality could be required from liquidators in relation to documents produced – Insolvency Act 1986, s. 236.

This was a petition for orders under s. 236, 237 and 426 of the Insolvency Act 1986 for production of documents by Coopers and Lybrand as auditors of First Tokyo Index Trust Ltd, the company of which the petitioners were joint liquidators, and for examination on oath of Coopers' personnel and, in furtherance thereof, for authorisation and approval of letters of request in respect of certain individuals for examination on oath in England and for another individual in New York.

The assets of First Tokyo had disappeared into other Maxwell group companies and it was the liquidators' case that in order to investigate what had happened it was essential for them to obtain from Coopers and the partners and employees (and former employees) of Coopers who were involved in dealing with First Tokyo, information in their possession relating to the business, dealings, affairs and property of First Tokyo. That information should also enable the petitioners to assess whether Coopers themselves bore any responsibility in connection with the loss of First Tokyo's assets, and whether the petitioners might have claims against other parties and the strength of those claims.

The respondents opposed the orders sought as both oppressive as to their purpose and unreasonable in their width.

A former employee of Coopers submitted that since he was not resident in the jurisdiction and was not served with the petition while within the jurisdiction, no order under s. 236 and 237 could be pronounced against him as he was not subject to the jurisdiction.

The respondents also submitted that an undertaking of confidentiality could be required from the liquidators in relation to documents produced.

Held, making orders for production:

1. It was competent for the court to make an order for production and examination against the respondent out of the jurisdiction, for the reason that there was provision for seeking the co-operation of the court in New York where he resided in executing orders made under s. 236 and 237 of the Insolvency Act 1986.

2. The petitioners had demonstrated prima facie grounds for consideration by the court of their application for the exercise of the extraordinary powers given to the court by s. 236 and 237. There were insufficient countervailing considerations which weighed against the making of such orders.

3. However discovery from the documents would be limited to the topics set out in specific heads. Moreover, at this stage it was unnecessary to pronounce any orders for production or oral examination against the individual respondents, without prejudice to the petitioners' right to seek such an order if co-operation was not forthcoming to any reasonably stated requirements.

4. The respondents were not entitled to an undertaking from the petitioners. The duties and obligations of a liquidator's office were such as to define and delimit to a sufficient

A extent the use to which a liquidator could put information obtained under s. 236 and neither statute nor principle required undertakings to be given as a consequence of and consequent upon the grant of an order under s. 236. A liquidator might within his discretion choose to give an undertaking, so long as he did not inhibit the full and proper discharge of the duties and obligations of his office, but he could not be required to do so.

5. A practice whereby those whom the liquidator, or anyone on his behalf, interviewed for the purposes of a liquidation, would be given copies of documents which the liquidator
B had obtained for the purposes of the liquidation, but to which the individual had been referred in the course of examination, fell outwith the proper exercise of his duties, since by that means the liquidator would enable such documents to go beyond the limits of the liquidation and possibly enter the public domain.

The following cases were referred to in the opinion:

C *Arrows Ltd, Re (No. 4)* [1993] BCC 473; [1993] Ch 452.
Barlow Clowes (Gilt Managers) Ltd, Re [1991] BCC 608; [1992] Ch 208.
British and Commonwealth Holdings plc, Re (No. 2) [1992] BCC 977; [1993] AC 426.
Cloverbay Ltd, Re (No. 2) [1990] BCC 414; [1991] Ch 90.
North Australian Territory Co, Re (1890) 45 ChD 87.
Norton Warburg Holdings Ltd, Re (1983) 1 BCC 98,907.
D *Paramount Airways Ltd, Re (No. 2)* [1992] BCC 416; [1993] Ch 223.
Rolls Razor Ltd, Re (No. 2) [1970] Ch 576.
Seagull Manufacturing Co Ltd, Re [1993] BCC 241; [1993] Ch 345.
Tucker (R C) (a bankrupt), Re, ex parte Tucker (K R) [1990] Ch 148.

R L Martin QC (instructed by Brodies) for the petitioners.

W A Nimmo Smith QC and A Murphy (instructed by Aitken Nairn) for the
E respondents.

OPINION
(Delivered 13 January 1994)

Lord Cameron of Lochbroom: The petitioners are the joint liquidators of First Tokyo Index Trust Ltd ('First Tokyo'). In the petition they set out the circumstances in which
F they came to be appointed. They also set out that notwithstanding that in July 1991 the net assets of First Tokyo including a very substantial portfolio of investments totalled over £53m, by reason of what can only have been improper and unauthorised dealings, the portfolio of investments was disposed of so that when the petitioners came to be appointed as joint liquidators upon a special resolution by First Tokyo to be wound up voluntarily on 10 December 1991, First Tokyo no longer had the said investments nor any other comparable assets.
G
In the petition the petitioners set out an account of events based upon evidence recovered by the petitioners through the investigations which they have carried out since their appointment. They say however that their understanding of events remains incomplete and may not be entirely accurate.

In para. 7 of the petition the petitioners explain that they have presented this petition to further their investigations, to advance their understanding of the business, dealings
H and affairs of First Tokyo prior to their appointment and to help them assess which persons may bear responsibility for the loss of First Tokyo's assets.

To this end the petitioners seek orders under s. 236, 237 and 426 of the *Insolvency Act* 1986 against each of the respondents apart from the Lord Advocate, firstly, for production of documents specified in the appendix to the petition and secondly, for examination on oath of the individual respondents and, in furtherance thereof, for

authorisation and approval of letters of request in respect of certain individuals for   A
examination on oath in England and for another individual in New York.

I deal at the outset with an issue of competency which arises in regard to the ninth
respondent who is a former employee of Coopers and Lybrand ('Coopers'), the seventh
respondents. Counsel submitted that since he was not resident in this jurisdiction and
was not served with the petition while within this jurisdiction, no order under s. 236 and
237 could be pronounced against him as he was not subject to the jurisdiction of this   B
court. Reference was made to the opinion of Dillon LJ in *Re Tucker* [1990] Ch 148 and
to a passage in a Scottish text book, St Clair and Drummond Young on the *Law of
Corporate Insolvency in Scotland* at p. 58 to this effect. It was also pointed out that the
provisions of Sch. 1 and 8 to the *Civil Jurisdiction and Judgments Act* 1982 did not apply
to proceedings relating to the winding up of a company.

In my opinion, these submissions are misconceived. I read the provisions of s. 236(2)
and (3) along with those of s. 237(3) as showing that the phrase 'any person' in s. 236(2)   C
is not confined to persons who are resident in this jurisdiction or who have been
personally served with the petition within the jurisdiction, but extends to any person
whether within the UK or not. The effectiveness of the court's powers to make an order,
and hence the propriety of making an order, in the event that the person is in a place
outside the UK, will then depend upon whether the court can use effectively the
provisions of s. 426. In the present case the US falls within the definition of a relevant   D
country or territory for the purposes of s. 426(5).

Counsel for the pursuers also referred me to two English cases which cast doubt upon
the ambit of the decision in *Re Tucker*, namely *Re Seagull Manufacturing Co Ltd* [1993]
BCC 241 and *Re Paramount Airways Ltd (No. 2)* [1992] BCC 416. These cases would
suggest that *Re Tucker* should be read in the context of the statutory provision there
under consideration, and did not extend to the provisions presently under consideration.   E
These cases are helpful but at the end of the day, in my opinion, the matter is one of
statutory construction. On that basis I have no hesitation therefore in rejecting the
submission for the ninth respondent that it is not competent for this court to make an
order for production and examination against him, for the reason that there is provision
for seeking the co-operation of the court in New York where he resides in executing any
orders that may be made under s. 236 and 237 of the *Insolvency Act* 1986 and further
that this can be achieved by making application to the machinery provided for by the   F
Evidence (Proceedings in Other Jurisdictions) Act 1975.

Some discussion took place before me as to whether the present were to be regarded as
summary proceedings or not. I do not consider that this is a helpful approach. The
present are proceedings which fall to be raised by way of petition in terms of r. 189(a)(v)
of the Rules of Court. The procedure is thus governed by the provisions of the Rules of
Court. To the extent that the court is likely to deal with the matter by way of a hearing   G
on the petition and any answers that may be lodged and upon ex parte statements, it can
be said that the procedure is summary. Moreover, in any urgent case, I have no doubt
that the court would be prepared to dispense with requirements of the rules and intervene
to secure that material documentary or oral evidence is not lost or destroyed. That is not
the present case.

The seventh respondents were appointed as auditors of First Tokyo in early 1989. It is   H
not in dispute that they acted as such thereafter until at least late 1991. Nor is it in dispute
that they provided company secretarial assistance to First Tokyo from February 1989 to
June 1990, that after June 1990 they provided a registered office to First Tokyo, initially
in Edinburgh and thereafter in Glasgow, and that between June and October 1990 one
of their members of staff took minutes of First Tokyo board meetings. It is also not in
dispute that Coopers' personnel attended certain board meetings of First Tokyo between

A 7 March 1989 and 10 June 1991. Additionally, there is no dispute that Coopers were instructed in early 1991 to advise on the tax consequences of a stock lending programme which had been undertaken for First Tokyo after March 1989 but which had extended beyond the limits authorised by First Tokyo, and its effect upon First Tokyo's investment trust status. This programme was terminated by resolution of the board of First Tokyo on 26 February 1991. However there remained a dispute between First Tokyo and London and Bishopsgate International Investment Management plc ('LBI') who had
B been authorised under a management agreement to undertake the stock lending programme, which dispute concerned the propriety of their actings. The independent directors of the First Tokyo board instructed Arthur Andersen to undertake a review of Coopers' audit papers for First Tokyo for the year ending 31 December 1990. Their report on their review was submitted on 28 June 1991. It identified from documentation available to them a number of deficiencies, as they saw it, in Coopers' conduct of First
C Tokyo's audits. In the meantime at a board meeting on 30 April 1991 when it was resolved that LBI be dismissed as managers of First Tokyo's portfolio, and prior to consideration of a resolution for the winding up of First Tokyo, Kevin Maxwell, a board member of First Tokyo and also a director of LBI, indicated that Headington Investment Ltd ('HIL'), which was one of a number of Maxwell companies which together held 24.9 per cent of the shares in First Tokyo and of which he was a director, would bid for the entire share capital of First Tokyo. Upon this indication the First Tokyo board decided
D to suspend the resolution dismissing LBI pending the outcome of the offer and further not to put forward a resolution for winding up while the offer remained current.

Subsequently it was decided that the bid on behalf of HIL would be made by a subsidiary, 'Adviser', formed for the purpose. The purchase was to be financed by a loan facility from Swiss Bank Corporation ('the bank') and was to be secured by a charge over the First Tokyo portfolio, which portfolio was to be delivered once the bid had been
E successful. The security could not however be delivered until First Tokyo had been re-registered as a private company and the directors of First Tokyo had made a statutory declaration stating that First Tokyo would be able to pay its debts as they fell due during the 12 months following the giving of assistance. Pending delivery, the loan was to be guaranteed by HIL and the First Tokyo portfolio was to be frozen. By letter dated 8 May 1991 the chairman of First Tokyo instructed LBI that no investment transactions should thenceforth be carried out by LBI on behalf of First Tokyo without specific
F approval from the chairman and two other named directors.

For the purpose of the offer bid a number of related agreements were entered into between the bank, HIL and Adviser, including a credit facility agreement dated 3 July 1991. This included provision that Adviser would procure that First Tokyo did not sell the portfolio shares without the prior consent of the bank. Under the bid for purchase of the whole shareholding of First Tokyo, the price to be paid by Adviser for each issued
G share was to be calculated in accordance with a formula calculated by LBI as specified in the offer which produced a formula asset value ('FAV'). The date for calculation was the day after the offer was declared unconditional, which in the event was 30 July 1991. At a meeting of the First Tokyo board on 2 July 1991, it was resolved that since the fixing of First Tokyo's portfolio at the date of the announcement of the offer was a principal condition of the loan financing to Adviser, no instruction should be given for the disposal or encumbrance of the portfolio shares until the later of two dates, namely seven days
H after the date that the FAV was announced (in the event 5 August 1991) or 21 days after the date that the bid was declared wholly unconditional (in the event 29 July 1991).

It is not disputed that in relation to the bid offer, Coopers' personnel worked on the proposed financial assistance package. They were also concerned in calculating both the estimated FAV as at 20 June 1991 and the actual FAV on 30 July 1991 on behalf of First Tokyo and further reviewed the calculations on behalf of HIL. Coopers' personnel also

prepared letters of comfort on 2 July 1991 and 2 August 1991, both for First Tokyo and   A
their financial advisers and for HIL and their financial advisers, to the effect that Coopers
saw no reason why they should be not be able to give the necessary report for the
production of which Coopers were responsible under s. 156(4) of the *Companies Act*
1985. This report related to the giving of financial assistance by First Tokyo in the
purchase of its own shares. Nor is it in dispute that while Coopers' personnel commenced
working on the report on three separate occasions, namely on about 3 September 1991,
24 October 1991 and 7 November 1991, on each occasion they were instructed by   B
Mr Jonathan Ford, the finance director of LBI, to put the report 'on hold'.

The petitioners aver that beginning on 31 July 1991 a series of instructions was given
by LBI to Morgan Stanley Trust Co ('MSTC'), who had had custody of the First Tokyo
portfolio since January 1989. These resulted in the disposal of all portfolio shares and
the payment away of the disposals to persons other than First Tokyo in contravention of
the board resolution of 2 July 1991 and the agreements with the bank, with the apparent   C
intention of alleviating financial difficulties of companies in the Maxwell group. The
petitioners also make averments regarding communications between Coopers and MSTC
and other parties between 29 July 1991 and 2 August 1991 from which, it is said, on 31
July Coopers learnt that the First Tokyo portfolio was no longer intact and that this was
not disclosed in letters written at that time to First Tokyo and to HIL and their respective
advisers concerning the FAV. It is further averred that by 2 August 1991, when Adviser   D
gave notice that they wished to borrow £56.8m under the credit facility agreement, which
sum was in fact advanced on 6 August 1991, First Tokyo securities to the value of £16.4m
had been sold and the proceeds paid over for the benefit of Maxwell Communication
Corporation plc and further securities to a value of £27m had been deposited with Credit
Suisse as collateral for a loan facility to Robert Maxwell Group plc, these last being sold
in the latter half of August 1991 and the proceeds paid to Credit Suisse and thence on to
other companies in the Maxwell group. It is further averred that of the remaining lines   E
of securities, all but five were disposed of before the death of Robert Maxwell on
5 November 1991.

The petitioners also aver that work on the report required by s. 156(4) of the *Companies
Act* 1985 would normally involve enquiries into the financial affairs of the company
concerned, including its assets, liabilities and financial projections. They also aver that an
internal Coopers' document shows that by 25 October 1991 two of the respondents,   F
namely the fifth and ninth respondents, were aware that a very large part of the First
Tokyo portfolio had been liquidated and most of the cash realised had been paid to other
Maxwell companies. In para. 41 of the petition it is said that:

'In order to carry out the duties of their office, the petitioners require to investigate
as fully as possible the conduct of the affairs of First Tokyo, the circumstances of
the sale or disposal of First Tokyo's assets and the disposal of the proceeds of sale,
with a view to recovering such moneys as may remain recoverable and otherwise   G
pursuing such remedies as may appear appropriate.'

In para. 42 of the petition it is said that:

'In order to carry out that investigation, it is essential for the petitioners to obtain
from Coopers and the partners and employees (and former employees) of Coopers
who were involved in dealing with First Tokyo, information in their possession
relating to the business, dealings, affairs and property of First Tokyo. That   H
information is likely to be highly important for the petitioners' understanding of
First Tokyo's affairs. Quite apart from enabling the petitioners to further their
understanding of First Tokyo's business, dealings and affairs, however, the
information should also enable the petitioners to assess whether Coopers
themselves bear any responsibility in connection with the loss of First Tokyo's

A   assets, and whether the petitioners may have claims against other parties and the
strength of those claims.'

In para. 43 of the petition the petitioners set out their understanding of the part played
by the individual respondents in the matters with which Coopers were concerned and as
appears from Answer 42, subject to the further explanation set out there in relation to
the fifth and sixth respondents, there is no substantial dispute on these matters between
B   parties.

These averments form the basis for counsel for the petitioners' submissions that the
orders sought, both as regards the production of documents and the oral examinations,
should be granted now. I should note at this stage that counsel for the respondents
accepted that in an appropriate case a liquidator was entitled, for the purposes of
liquidation, to investigate whether within the assets of the company there was a
prospective liability on the part of a third party to make reparation to the company for
C   loss arising to the company from a negligent act or breach of trust or the like on the part
of that third party, and further that for that purpose it was competent to seek orders in
terms of s. 236 and 237 of the 1986 Act.

Both counsel accepted that the proper framework for the determination of the issue
arising in this case was to be found in the first place in the speech of Lord Slynn of Hadley
in *Re British and Commonwealth Holdings plc (No. 2)* [1992] BCC 977. In particular at
D   p. 984D Lord Slynn said of the power of the court under s. 236 to make an order for the
production of documents that it was not limited to documents which could be said to
have been needed to reconstitute the state of the company's knowledge. He continued:

'At the same time it is plain that this is an extraordinary power and that the
discretion must be exercised after a careful balancing of the factors involved – on
the one hand the reasonable requirements of the administrator to carry out his
E   task, on the other the need to avoid making an order which is wholly unreasonable,
unnecessary or "oppressive" to the person concerned.'

Later on he says,

'The protection for the person called upon to produce documents lies, thus, not in
a limitation by category of documents ("reconstituting the company's state of
knowledge") but in the fact that the applicant must satisfy the court that, after
balancing all the relevant factors, there is a proper case for such an order to be
F   made. The proper case is one where the administrator reasonably requires to see
the documents to carry out his functions and the production does not impose an
unnecessary and unreasonable burden on the person required to produce them in
the light of the administrator's requirements. An application is not necessarily
unreasonable because it is inconvenient for the addressee of the application or
causes him a lot of work or may make him vulnerable to future claims, or is
G   addressed to a person who is not an officer or employee of or a contractor with the
company in administration, but all these will be relevant factors, together no doubt
with many others.'

It also is to be noted that at pp. 985–986 where Lord Slynn was considering the
criticisms of the order made in that case, he pointed out amongst other things that there
is no embargo in principle against ordering third parties to produce documents and
H   further that, while it is a fact that may be taken into account that papers may be produced
which could possibly lay the haver open to further claims, that is only one factor to be
balanced against the reasonable requirement of the office-holder seeking the order. He
also made reference to the size of the financial crash in that case where creditors and
investors stood to lose vast sums, as also the need in such a very complex situation to
check the accuracy of the various financial documents and to know not only what
representations were made but how accurate they were. Furthermore, at pp. 983–984 in

his speech Lord Slynn refers with approval to passages from earlier cases which relate to   A
the court's power to summon persons to appear who may be able to provide information
concerning the promotion, formation, business, dealings, affairs or property of the
company. In particular, the passages cited from *Re Rolls Razor Ltd (No. 2)* [1970] Ch
576 and from *Re North Australian Territory Co* (1890) 45 ChD 87 emphasised the
requirements to allow the liquidator to achieve full understanding of the affairs of the
company with which he is concerned by use of the machinery provided by s. 236 and 237
while at the same time guarding against its use or its being put into motion where   B
unnecessary mischief was going to be done or hardship inflicted upon a third person.

I was also referred to *Re Cloverbay Ltd (No. 2)* [1990] BCC 414. In that case Sir
Nicolas Browne-Wilkinson V-C observed that the case for making an order against
officers of the company was stronger than it would be against a third party and that an
order for oral examination was likely to be more oppressive than one for the production
of documents. Counsel for the defenders also referred me to the decision of Vinelott J in   C
Re Norton Warburg Holdings Ltd (1983) 1 BCC 98,907. In relation to application for
orders under s. 307(2) of the *Companies Act* 1948, it was there held that it was for the
court to determine in exercising its discretion how best the investigation of the company's
affairs might be carried out and that in doing this it had to balance the views of the
liquidator, which were entitled to great weight, with the requirement that the
investigation should not be carried out in a way which was oppressive or unfair to the   D
persons ordered to be examined.

Counsel also referred me to the substance of the correspondence which passed between
the petitioners or their solicitors on the one hand and individual respondents and their
solicitors on the other, between 20 December 1991 and 24 November 1993.

Reference is made to this correspondence in the petition and answers and it forms
productions lodged on behalf of the parties. From the discussion it is apparent that there   E
has already been production of documents from Coopers' files to the petitioners, and
further, that in April 1992 the petitioners were given access to Coopers' files relative to
FAV calculations, other work regarding the acquisition by Adviser and the work done
by way of financial assistance between September and November 1991. There were at the
same time interviews between the petitioners and the first, second and ninth respondents.
In the latter stages of the correspondence, in particular from 23 July 1993 onwards, it
appears that an impasse had been reached in relation to requests by the petitioners for   F
further disclosure of documents and information, including requests to interview the first,
second and ninth respondents. In their letter of 31 August 1993 the petitioners' solicitors
wrote setting out the reasons for their requests. By their reply of 10 September the
respondents' solicitors wrote to the effect that their clients must regretfully decline to
provide further assistance since they had not been provided with any information which
would enable them to form a view on whether the petitioners could satisfy a judge that   G
the request for assistance was reasonable. On 3 November 1993 the petitioners' solicitors
wrote to the respondents' solicitors that the petitioners' investigations had revealed 'the
involvement of further Coopers and Lybrand individuals/employees in the affairs of'
First Tokyo. These were the third, fourth, fifth, sixth and eighth respondents. Letters to
these individuals invited them to be interviewed on oath and to confirm whether they had
any documents or records relating to the company and that if they had, whether they
would supply them before the interview. On 5 November the respondents' solicitors   H
wrote to say that in relation to those individuals for whom they then acted and had
instructions, they were not willing to attend an interview without a further explanation
as to why their assistance was required. In their answers, the respondents say this:

'Despite repeated requests, (the petitioners' solicitors) have failed to specify why
they require further documentation and interviews. Explained and further averred

A   that Coopers have in excess of 50 files covering work on behalf of First Tokyo.
They have expended a considerable amount of firm time in assisting the petitioners
to date. It is believed that the petitioners' failure to fully appreciate the significance
of documents produced to them will result in Coopers' duplicating much work in
the form of assistance already given to the petitioners. Explained and further
averred that failure by the petitioners to adequately specify by reference to nature
and time those documents or events they wish to investigate presents Coopers with
B   an unspecified task. Such a task would involve large numbers of Coopers' staff
carrying out unspecified searches which would consequently prevent them from
performing their normal duties. Explained and further averred that the width of
the call for documents by the petitioners is unreasonable.'

Counsel for the respondents explained that his clients were willing to co-operate upon
a proper basis but that it was hazardous to expose individuals to a general examination
C   and that more particularly where the petitioners were apparently intent upon determining
whether there was ground for a potential claim against Coopers and indeed on clarifying
matters to see whether there was a defence. Before any order should be made the
petitioners should be more specific as to the nature of the information which was sought
or required. In relation to the documents sought to be recovered, counsel criticised as
oppressive the very general discovery sought and made particular criticisms of the
D   relevance of the calls under heads (1), (4), (5) and (11)–(14). As regards the remaining
heads he submitted that since the petitioners had already had access to Coopers' files in
April 1992, and furthermore information and documents had thereafter been made
available to them as was apparent from correspondence between March 1992 and
November 1992, the calls were unnecessary. Accordingly the orders sought on both
branches were both oppressive as to their purpose and unreasonable in their width.

I note at this point that in the course of his reply to these last submissions counsel for
E   the petitioners indicated that the petitioners were prepared to allow individuals a sight
beforehand of the files upon which they were to be examined. He also indicated that for
instance the working papers which were sought under the generality of the appendix
could provide a basis for examination of individuals as to their recollection of material
matters. In addition he submitted that there was warrant for suggesting that even if it
could be said that there was oppression arising from the threat of litigation, that threat
F   would only be relevant in relation to those who were partners of Coopers, and of course
Coopers itself, and could not be said to be of the same measure in relation to those who
were only employees, whether present or past.

Looking to the manifest enormity of the loss of assets suffered by First Tokyo between
the end of July 1991 and November 1991 and also the circumstances in which the
opportunity to deal with the investment portfolio of First Tokyo in and after July 1991
arose, against the background history of unauthorised transactions with that portfolio
G   through the agency of LBI, one of the Maxwell group of companies, and also having
regard to the petitioners' averments regarding the contemporary assurances and
representations received by or given to Coopers, firstly, relative to these various
transactions and again at the stages when the offer bid was made, when the FAV was
being calculated and when the report for the purposes of the Companies Act was being
prepared, together with the petitioners' concern that they do not yet have the fullest
H   information by way of documentary material or explanation from those in Coopers
concerned with these various transactions, notwithstanding the information that they
have already received, I am satisfied that the petitioners have demonstrated prima facie
grounds for consideration by the court of their application for the exercise of the
extraordinary powers given to the court by s. 236 and 237. I also bear in mind that the
position of Coopers as auditors and financial advisers to First Tokyo put them in a
special relationship to First Tokyo, notwithstanding that in some respects they and the

other respondents are to be regarded as third parties, being persons other than those   A
mentioned in s. 235 of the 1986 Act.

The question is whether there are countervailing considerations which weigh against
the making of such orders on either or both their branches. One factor is that a purpose
of the further investigation by the petitioners is to allow them to determine whether and,
if so, to what extent Coopers might bear any legal liability for the dissipation of First
Tokyo's assets. On the other hand these issues also bear upon the question of whether   B
others with whom Coopers were then dealing, may also bear legal liability having regard
to the nature of the transactions and the information tendered by those other individuals.
This is particularly pertinent in relation to the events at the end of July 1991. Another
factor is the degree to which to date Coopers and individual respondents have co-
operated with the petitioners in the production of documents and the giving of
information even in matters in which, at least potentially, it could be said that a claim   C
against Coopers could arise, and their willingness to continue such co-operation if made
aware of the specific areas in which information is being sought from each of them.

In carrying out the balancing exercise which is called for in such a case as the present,
I have been influenced particularly in the view which I have reached by the facts that
there has already been a demonstrably substantial amount of cooperation by Coopers
and certain individual respondents with the petitioners, that as I understand it all the
respondents are prepared to cooperate further in so far as clear indication is given as to   D
the topics upon which and the areas about which they would be examined and that
examinations to be worthwhile would require to await further discovery of documents. I
have also been influenced by the tenor of the authorities cited to me which suggest that
in general an order for production of documents, even against a third party, would be
regarded as less oppressive than an order for oral examination. I accept that there may
be burdens upon a haver in requiring to search through many files for documents, as is   E
suggested in this case on behalf of Coopers, though not on behalf of individual
respondents, but I consider that the present is just such an exceptional case as Lord Slynn
had in mind in *British and Commonwealth* as to outweigh any such objection.
Furthermore, I see no reason why by proper cooperation between solicitors and
accountants on both sides, any disruption cannot be kept to the minimum.

Against that background and also having in mind the fact that the petitioners are   F
obviously better placed now to be specific as to the areas which they wish to explore
further, having regard to the amount of information which they have already obtained
both from Coopers and certain of the respondents and from other sources, I do not
consider that it is reasonable or necessary for the order for production which I intend to
pronounce against Coopers, to be as general as the opening paragraph of the appendix
to the petition requires and I will limit discovery from the documents to the topics set out
in the specific heads. In this regard I am satisfied that these heads all bear upon matters   G
which the petitioners properly require to investigate in order to obtain as complete a
picture as they can of what passed concerning the business, dealings, and affairs of First
Tokyo, not only so far as it directly concerns Coopers' actings, understandings and
knowledge but those of all other parties with whom they or individual respondents dealt.
That is to say, it is required not only to seek understanding of what happened or who
said, or did not say, what and when, but to review any potential claims against any party
which may be available as an asset of First Tokyo.   H

In relation to the individual respondents against whom orders both for production and
for oral examination are sought, it was clear from submissions made to me that it is most
likely that Coopers hold all the relevant documentary material for which discovery is
sought. Moreover, at this stage it would appear unnecessary to pronounce any like orders
for production against the individual respondents since material for any oral examination

A   may only appear after the order for production against Coopers is satisfied. In reaching
this view I have in mind that it is the stated intention, as I understand it, of each
respondent to cooperate with the petitioner granted that they are advised of the area
upon which each is to be examined, so long as the court is satisfied that in general the
petitioners are entitled to make investigation into those areas which fall within the heads
for which production of documents is sought. I also have in mind that the petitioners
have stated that in advance of any examination, the individual respondent would be
B   given a sight of the documents upon which he was to be examined. There thus appears to
be an opportunity for the petitioners and their professional advisers on the one hand and
the individual respondents and their professional advisers on the other to reach an
accommodation on the matter of the provision of information. More particularly I have
in mind that it was stated at various times throughout counsel's submissions on behalf of
the respondents, that they had no wish to delay or embarrass any investigations which it
C   was considered proper and reasonable that the petitioners should now institute. *In hoc
statu* I will not make any order for production or examination against any individual
respondent, but this is without prejudice to the petitioners' right to seek such an order if
co-operation is not forthcoming to any reasonably stated requirements made by the
petitioners for information and for production of documents by individual respondents.

I have put the case out by order for the purpose of settling the terms of the introduction
to the calls in para. 1 of the appendix. At the same time consideration can be given to the
D   nature of any undertakings which may be required by Coopers of the petitioners in
relation to such further documents as may be produced in response to the court's order.

(Order accordingly)

OPINION
(Delivered 27 January 1994)
E
Lord Cameron of Lochbroom: At the by order roll hearing consequent upon my
opinion dated 13 January 1994, parties agreed that the matter be further continued to
allow them to consider their respective positions in the light of the views which I had
expressed. The case was therefore continued for two weeks. At the further hearing,
counsel intimated that while certain matters had been agreed, other outstanding matters
remained unresolved. These revolved about two issues. First was the wording of the
F   adjusted call for production of documents together with related amendments to the
prayer of the petition and the petition itself. Second was the propriety of the requirement
that the petitioner give an undertaking in relation to documents produced, similar in
content to that recorded in my opinion in the petition of the present petitioners against
Richard Gauld and others (30 September 1993, unreported).

I was invited by counsel for the respondents to make changes to the order for
G   production sought in the prayer of the petition by deleting reference to production 'to
the court' and by substituting reference to the place of production, namely the address of
the respondents' agents. I agree with counsel for the petitioners that this is otiose. It is
unnecessary to provide in such an order where sight of the documents is to be given
preparatory to production in terms of such an order. I have therefore refused to make
the alteration sought in the order to be granted.

H   Counsel for the respondents next invited me to incorporate in the amended preamble
to the calls in the appendix, an exclusion for documents 'otherwise subject to privilege or
confidentiality' in addition to the exclusion of documents passing between the
respondents and their legal advisers in contemplation of or for the purpose of litigation.
It was also submitted that the exclusion of any documents passing after 30 November
1991 might not be sufficiently wide since there might be such documents passing prior to
that date which ought to be covered by the exclusion. In recognition of this latter point,

the order that I have pronounced excludes such documents whether passing before or A
after 30 November 1991. As regards the former point, I agree with counsel for the
petitioners that the plea of privilege or confidentiality is always available in relation to
any specific document in a process such as the present, just as much as in an ordinary
action. Accordingly since no such plea can presently be taken in relation to the calls as
they are framed, the proper time at which the point can be taken is when production of
any particular document is objected to on that ground. In such an event the document
can be sealed up and brought before the court for the issue to be adjudicated upon in B
similar manner to the procedure where a commission and diligence is executed in an
ordinary action.

I now turn to the second issue. Counsel for the respondents sought support for his
submission that an undertaking could be required, by reference to the general purpose of
Pt. VI of the *Insolvency Act* 1986, namely that the powers of the liquidators were given
by statute for the purposes, and the purposes alone, of the liquidation. Concern was C
expressed that copies of the documents recovered by way of the order for production
could become available to third parties if such parties were to be examined by way of the
proof of witness procedure familiar to English practitioners. I understand that under that
procedure the witness would receive a copy of the signed witness statement together with
a copy of any document referred to in the statement. Reference was also made to the
control which the courts in England exercise by virtue of r. 9.5 of the *Insolvency Rules* D
1986, (which has no counterpart in the Scottish Rules) and to the opinions in *Re Arrows
Ltd (No. 4)* [1993] BCC 473.

There is no doubt that the liquidators are only entitled to use information,
documentary or otherwise, which they have obtained in the course of carrying out their
functions, in relation to the purposes of the liquidation, which will include the getting in
of any assets of the company available in the liquidation. The duties and obligations of a
liquidator's office are such as to define and delimit, in my opinion, to a sufficient extent E
the use to which a liquidator can put such information and neither statute nor principle
requires undertakings to be given as a consequence of and consequent upon the grant of
an order under s. 236 of the 1986 Act. I am fortified in this view by reference to an
opinion to the same effect by Millett J in *Re Barlow Clowes (Gilt Managers) Ltd* [1991]
BCC 608 at p. 614A. There he expressed the view that information obtained by the use
of the court's compulsory powers under s. 236 of the 1986 Act did not require that F
assurances of confidentiality be given by a liquidator as they would not have been
necessary, for disclosure would have been permitted only to the extent that such
disclosure was for the benefit of the liquidation. Again in *Arrows (No. 4)* Dillon LJ at
p. 483B pointed out that the purpose of r. 9.5 of the *Insolvency Rules* 1986 was to provide
some machinery as to how transcripts of examinations in the possession of the court were
to be kept. G

Earlier in his opinion at p. 480F, he pointed out that the confidentiality which attached
to such examinations was not for the protection of the person being examined but for the
protection of the office-holder. I do not consider that there is any difference in principle
between information obtained from documents produced by reference to the office-
holder's powers under s. 236 and that obtained by way of examination of individuals
under those powers, since the information in either case is to be devoted to the same
purposes, namely, those of the liquidation. H

I therefore reject counsel's submission that in principle the respondents are entitled to
demand an undertaking from the petitioners that they will only use the documents
produced in response to the court's order for the purposes of the liquidation and will not
disclose them to third parties except in pursuance to a court order. Obviously a liquidator
may within his discretion choose to give an undertaking, so long as he does not inhibit

A   the full and proper discharge of the duties and obligations of his office, but he cannot be required to do so. As at present advised, I would regard a practice whereby those whom he, or anyone on his behalf, interviewed as liquidator for the purposes of a liquidation, would be given copies of documents which the liquidator had obtained for the purposes of the liquidation, but to which the individual had been referred in the course of examination, as falling outwith the proper exercise of his duties, since by that means the liquidator would enable such documents to go beyond the limits of the liquidation and

B   possibly enter the public domain.

I would only add that at the end of the hearing I was invited to make an award of expenses not only in respect of the further hearing on the by order roll, but also of the original hearing. I decided to reserve the latter expenses to await the final determination of the petition having regard to the reservation of the petitioners' right to return to court to secure orders for examination and production of documents in respect of the

C   respondents other than Coopers and Lybrand. I did intimate that I noted the points made by counsel for the petitioners in respect to the petitioners' success in countering the plea to competency stated on behalf of the ninth respondents and the general plea to relevancy stated for all the respondents which last was based upon the submission that any order for production and examination was unnecessary. These points can however be considered further at the time that the final motion for expenses is considered.

D   (*Order accordingly*)

E

F

G

H

Allied Dunbar Assurance plc v Fowle & Ors.

Queen's Bench Division.
Garland J.
Judgment delivered 28 January 1994.

Striking defunct companies off register – Restoration to register – Property of dissolved company to be bona vacantia – Crown disclaimer of property vesting as bona vacantia – Effect of company's revival after dissolution – Company struck off as defunct and dissolved – Lease passed bona vacantia to Crown and was disclaimed – Company's name restored to register – Whether sureties for company's obligations under lease were released on company's dissolution – Whether sureties' liability revived on restoration – Whether disclaimer was disposition of bona vacantia property – Companies Act 1985, s. 653–657; Insolvency Act 1986, s. 178–182.

These were appeals by the sureties for a company's obligations under a lease. The company was the assignee of the lease from 'Pneumatic'. The company was dissolved in April 1992 having earlier been struck off the register, pursuant to s. 652(5) of the Companies Act 1985. The interest under the lease became vested in the Crown as bona vacantia pursuant to s. 654. In April 1993, the Crown disclaimed the lease, at the instance of the sureties, pursuant to s. 656. In September 1993, the company was ordered to be restored by the registrar, and on 30 September was restored pursuant to s. 653.

The issues in the appeals concerned the effect of the disclaimer and restoration on the liabilities of the sureties to the plaintiff lessor and to Pneumatic.

The sureties argued that they were discharged from liability by the disclaimer which was deemed to take effect from the moment that the leasehold interest was vested in the Crown as bona vacantia in April 1992 (s. 657(1)). Their liability did not revive in September 1993 because the disclaimer in April 1993 constituted a 'disposition' under s. 655 entitling the company to compensation under s. 655(2), and relieving them of their liabilities under their covenants both to the plaintiff and Pneumatic.

The plaintiff and Pneumatic submitted that since on disclaimer the property was deemed never to have vested in the Crown and on restoration to the register the company was deemed to have continued in existence as if its name had not been struck off, the rights and liabilities of the sureties were revived with retroactive effect. In any event the sureties' liability was not extinguished by the dissolution. The plaintiff further submitted that on the construction of the covenant between the sureties and the plaintiff it was possible to find an intention that the sureties should continue to be bound notwithstanding disclaimer.

Held, dismissing the appeals:

1. The sureties were released on the disclaimer. (Stacey v Hill [1901] 1 KB 660 applied.)

2. The sureties' liability revived retroactively when the company was restored to the register because the effect of s. 653(3) was that the company was deemed to have continued in existence as if its name had not been struck off. The lease therefore was deemed never to have vested in the Crown so that no question of bona vacantia or disclaimer ever arose. The Crown's disclaimer was not a disposition within s. 655.

The following cases were referred to in the judgment:

A E Realisations (1985) Ltd, Re (1987) 3 BCC 136.
British and Commonwealth Holdings plc v Quadrex Holdings Inc [1989] QB 842.
Carter (R G) Ltd v Clarke [1990] 1 WLR 578.
Dixon (C W) Ltd, Re [1947] Ch 251.
Finley, Re. Ex parte Clothworkers' Co (1888) 21 QBD 475.
Lister, Re. Ex parte Bradford Overseers and Bradford Corporation [1926] Ch 149.

A

Murphy v Sawyer-Hoare & Anor [1993] 27 EG 127.
Nottingham General Cemetery Co, Re [1955] Ch 683.
No. 1 London Ltd, Re [1991] BCC 118.
Paradise Motor Co Ltd, Re [1968] 1 WLR 1125.
Stacey v Hill [1901] 1 KB 660.
Stratton's Disclaimer, Re [1958] Ch 42.
Thompson & Riches Ltd, Re [1981] 1 WLR 682.

B

Tyman's Ltd v Craven [1952] 2 QB 100.
Warnford Investments Ltd v Duckworth & Ors [1979] Ch 127.
Yarmarine (IW) Ltd, Re [1992] BCC 28.

Timothy Fancourt (instructed by Nabarro Nathanson) for the plaintiff.

Gavin Lightman QC (instructed by Clifford Harris & Co) for the sureties (first and second defendants).

C

David Hodge (instructed by Reynolds Porter Chamberlain) for the third defendant.

JUDGMENT

Garland J: These are appeals by Mr Fowle and Mr Hicks to whom I shall refer as 'the sureties' against orders of District Judge Litchfield giving summary judgment in action 914 for the plaintiffs against the sureties and Chicago Pneumatic Tool Co Ltd to which I shall refer as 'Pneumatic', the third defendant, and for Pneumatic on its contribution

D

notice against the sureties. In action 2319, judgment was given for the plaintiffs against Pneumatic and for Pneumatic on its third party notice against the sureties. Since there were no issues of fact between the parties and the only matters to be determined were of law, I was invited by Mr Hodge for Pneumatic to decide all matters of law and give judgment in open court. Mr Lightman for the sureties submitted that I should not accept this invitation and should not give final judgment, but instead give leave to defend and

E

transfer the action to the Chancery Division so that the issues could be fully argued before being taken to the Court of Appeal as important matters of principle requiring determination by a higher court, the more so, if the applicability of *Stacey v Hill* [1901] 1 KB 660 to a Crown disclaimer is to be challenged.

I was referred to note 14/3-4/11 at p. 153 of the *Supreme Court Practice* and to the passages in *R G Carter Ltd v Clarke* [1990] 1 WLR 578 and *British and Commonwealth*

F

Holdings plc v Quadrex Holdings Inc [1989] QB 842. It is to be noted that both these cases were decided before O. 14A came into force but, with all due respect to Mr Lightman's submissions, I find myself in complete agreement with that part of the note which reads:

'Where the court is satisfied that there are no issues of fact between the parties, it would be pointless to give leave to defend on the basis that there is a triable issue of law, and this is so even if the issue of law is complex and highly arguable, but it is otherwise if the issue of law is not decisive of all the issues between the parties or

G

if the issue is of such a character as would not justify its being determined as a preliminary issue or if the answer to the question of law is in any way dependent on undecided issues of fact . . .'

The extent of the facts necessary to define the issues of law do not take up a very significant part of this judgment, and as has already been said, are not in dispute at all. The points of law are wholly determinative of the rights of the parties. I was told quite

H

frankly that these proceedings were merely a step on the way to the Court of Appeal and it would be quite wrong in my view to put the parties to the delay and expense of a further hearing in the High Court. I therefore propose to deal with the issues before me.

The genesis of the actions

By a lease dated 30 September 1977, Hambro Life Assurance Ltd granted a 20-year term of part of CP House, 97/107, Uxbridge Road, Ealing to Consolidated Pneumatic

A

Tool Co Ltd which subsequently changed its name to Chicago Pneumatic Holdings Ltd and to which I shall refer as 'Holdings'. On 26 August 1980, the lessor granted Holdings a licence to assign to the company which became Chicago Pneumatic Tool Co Ltd to which I have already referred as 'Pneumatic', the third defendant in action 914, and the sole defendant in action 2319. Pneumatic covenanted with the lessor to observe and perform the lessee's obligations under the lease and to assume liability for any existing breaches of covenant or condition. The assignment was executed on 1 September 1980.

B

On 22 December 1987, the lessor, which by then had become Allied Dunbar Assurance plc, the plaintiffs, granted Pneumatic a licence to assign to Millrow Ltd, which subsequently became KGP Technical Services Ltd and to which I shall refer as 'KGP'. The assignment was executed on the same day.

The sureties, Mr Fowle and Mr Hicks, were directors of KGP and covenanted by cl. 9 of the general conditions of the licence that the assignee, KGP, would comply with the lessee's covenants and conditions and that in default of compliance, notwithstanding any time or indulgence given to the defaulting person, the sureties would comply with those obligations. By the assignment, the sureties further covenanted with Pneumatic to procure and further guarantee to Pneumatic that at all times KGP would observe and perform the covenants under cl. 2 of the assignment [KGP's covenants to Pneumatic] and in the event of any default, the sureties would observe and perform the same and indemnify Pneumatic for any breach. The covenants in cl. 2 by KGP to Pneumatic were, in summary, to pay the rent, observe and perform the lessee's covenants and to indemnify Pneumatic against any claims on account of any omission to pay the rent or observe the covenants.

C

D

On 7 April 1992, KGP was dissolved having earlier been struck off the register, pursuant to s. 652(5) of the *Companies Act* 1985. The interest under the lease became vested in the Crown as bona vacantia pursuant to s. 654. On 22 April 1993, the Crown disclaimed the lease, at the instance of the sureties, pursuant to s. 656. On 10 September 1993, KGP was ordered to be restored by the registrar, and on 30 September was restored pursuant to s. 653. The issues in these appeals concern the effect of the disclaimer and restoration on the liabilities of the sureties to the plaintiffs and to Pneumatic, having particular regard to the effect of s. 655 and 657, and the application by subs. 2 of s. 657, of s. 178(4) and 179–182 of the *Insolvency Act* 1986.

E

The statutes

F

It is therefore necessary to turn to the statutes. Section 652 of the *Companies Act* 1985 empowers the registrar to strike off the register a company which he has reasonable cause to believe is not carrying on business or is not in operation. On publication of a notice of the striking off in the Gazette, the company is dissolved. On dissolution, property vested in the company immediately before its dissolution, including leasehold property, is deemed to be bona vacantia and to belong to the Crown. Section 656 allows the Crown to disclaim property vested in it by virtue of s. 654, subject to time-limits which are set out in subs. (3). On disclaimer, s. 657 provides by subs. (1):

G

'Where notice of disclaimer is executed under section 656 as respects any property, that property is deemed not to have vested in the Crown under section 654.'

Subsection (2) provides:

'As regards property in England and Wales, section 178(4) and sections 179 to 182 of the Insolvency Act shall apply as if the property had been disclaimed by the liquidator . . . immediately before the dissolution of the company.'

H

Section 653 permits the revival or reanimation of the company in the following terms:

'(1) The following applies if a company or any member or creditor of it feels aggrieved by the company having been struck off the register.

A

(2) The court, on an application by the company or the member or creditor made before the expiration of 20 years from publication in the Gazette of notice under section 652, may, if satisfied that the company was at the time of the striking off carrying on business or in operation, or otherwise that it is just that the company be restored to the register, order the company's name to be restored.

B

(3) On an office copy of the order being delivered to the registrar of companies for registration the company is deemed to have continued in existence as if its name had not been struck off; and the court may by the order give such directions and make such provisions as seem just for placing the company and all other persons in the same position (as nearly as may be) as if the company's name had not been struck off.'

Section 655 deals with the effect of such a revival on the vesting of property in the Crown under s. 654 as follows:

C

'(1) The person in whom any property or right is vested by section 654 may dispose of, or of an interest in, that property or right notwithstanding that an order may be made under section 651 or 653.

(2) Where such an order is made–

D

(a) it does not affect the disposition (but without prejudice to the order so far as it relates to any other property or right previously vested in or held on trust for the company), and

(b) the Crown, or as the case may be, the Duke of Cornwall shall pay to the company an amount equal to–

(i) the amount of any consideration received for the property or right, or interest therein, or

E

(ii) the value of any such consideration at the time of the disposition,

or, if no consideration was received, an amount equal to the value of the property, right or interest disposed of, as at the date of the disposition.'

Section 651 empowers the court to declare a dissolution of a company void:

'(1) Where a company has been dissolved, the court may, on application made for the purpose by the liquidator of the company or by any other person appearing to the court to be interested, make an order, on such terms as the court thinks fit, declaring the dissolution to have been void.

F

(2) Thereupon such proceedings may be taken as might have been taken if the company had not been dissolved.'

Although this section is prima facie concerned with companies in liquidation, it can provide an alternative route to reanimation or revival for a company struck off under

G

s. 652, see *Re Thompson & Riches Ltd* [1981] 1 WLR 682.

Finally, I turn to the *Insolvency Act* 1986 as applied by s. 657(2). Section 178 deals with a liquidator's power to disclaim onerous property. Subsection (4) reads as follows:

'A disclaimer under this section–

(a) operates so as to determine, as from the date of the disclaimer, the rights, interests and liabilities of the company in or in respect of the property

H

disclaimed; but

(b) does not, except so far as is necessary for the purpose of releasing the company from any liability, affect the rights or liabilities of any other person.'

Section 181 defines the court's powers to make orders in respect of disclaimed property: s. 179 and 182 deal specifically with leaseholds. In summary, any person claiming an

426 Allied Dunbar Assurance plc v Fowle **[1994] BCC**

(*Garland* J)

interest in a disclaimed leasehold or who is under any liability in respect of it other than A a liability discharged by the disclaimer, may apply to the court, which has very wide powers, for an order vesting the property in him. Section 181 provides as follows:

'(1) This section and the next apply where the liquidator has disclaimed property under section 178.

(2) An application under this section may be made to the court by–

B

(a) any person who claims an interest in the disclaimed property, or

(b) any person who is under any liability in respect of the disclaimed property, not being a liability discharged by the disclaimer.

(3) Subject as follows, the court may on the application make an order, on such terms as it thinks fit, for the vesting of the disclaimed property in, or for its delivery to–

C

(a) a person entitled to it or a trustee for such a person, or

(b) a person subject to such liability as is mentioned in subsection (2)(b) or a trustee for such a person.'

Reference should also be made to subs. (4) of s. 182 which provides:

'Where subsection (1) applies and a person claiming under the company as underlessee or mortgagee declines to accept an order under section 181, that person is excluded from all interest in the property.'

D

In the course of argument, counsel drew attention to differences between a Crown disclaimer and liquidator's disclaimer. First, a Crown disclaimer under s. 657(1) results in the property being deemed not to have vested in the Crown under s. 654 whereas a disclaimer under s. 178(4) operates as from the date of the disclaimer. The Crown's right to execute a notice of disclaimer may be waived by taking possession of the property (s. 656(2)) whereas a liquidator may disclaim notwithstanding that he has taken possession of the property, endeavoured to sell it or otherwise executed rights of ownership in relation to it (s. 178(2)).

E

Counsel examined the historical evolution of the present legislation both as a guide to construction and also to put in context authorities decided under, in particular, the *Bankruptcy Act* 1883 and the *Companies Act* 1948. It is necessary to refer briefly to the 1948 Act and to the *Companies Act* 1981. Sections 352–355 of the 1948 Act contain parallel provisions to s. 651–654, 656 and 657(1) of the 1985 Act but the equivalent of s. 655 was introduced by s. 108 of the Act of 1981; and as has already been noted, s. 657(2) was added, by amendment, by the *Insolvency Act* 1986. Accordingly, before the 1981 Act, the Crown could not safely dispose of bona vacantia, and before the 1986 Act, an interested party could not apply for a vesting order following a Crown disclaimer as he could in the case of liquidator's disclaimer. Subsections (2) and (3) of s. 178 of the Insolvency Act are in almost the same terms as s. 55(1) of the *Bankruptcy Act* 1883, subs. (4) as s. 55(2) and s. 181 and 182 as s. 55(6).

F

G

The actions

In action 914, the plaintiffs recovered judgment on 29 October 1993 against all three defendants in the principal sum of £158,999.51 together with interest, in respect of rent, service charges and insurance premiums due under the lease from 25 December 1991 to 26 December 1992. If this principal sum falls to be apportioned as at 7 April 1992, the amount due up to that date would be £63,898.79 and the amount due thereafter would be £95,100.72. Pneumatic were given judgment on their contribution notice against the sureties for the same principal sum.

H

© **1994 CCH Editions Limited**

bcp94 ftc Mp 426 —bcp159 100

A   In action 2319, judgment was given for the plaintiffs against Pneumatic in the principal sum of £59,214.04 and for Pneumatic against the sureties on the third party notice in the same amount. This represented rent, service charges and insurance falling due between 25 March and 30 June 1993, that is before KGP were restored to the register on 30 September. The sureties now appeal against the judgments based on liabilities said to have arisen between 7 April 1992 and 30 June 1993 both to Allied and Pneumatic.

B   **The issues**

These can be very simply stated. The sureties' argument is that:

(1)   They were discharged from liability by the disclaimer which is deemed to take effect from the moment that the leasehold interest was vested in the Crown as bona vacantia on 7 April 1992 (s. 657(1)).

C   (2)   Their liability did not revive on 30 September 1993 because the disclaimer on 22 April 1993 constituted a 'disposition' under s. 655 entitling KGP to compensation under subs. (2), and relieving them of their liabilities under their covenants both to Allied and Pneumatic.

Allied and Pneumatic submit that:

(1)   Since on disclaimer the property is deemed never to have vested in the Crown and on restoration to the register the company is deemed to have continued in existence as if its name had not been struck off, the rights and liabilities of the sureties are revived with retroactive effect.

D

(2)   In any event the sureties' liability was not extinguished by the dissolution. They concede that there is cogent authority against them but wish to keep the point open on the basis that there is a valid distinction to be drawn between the effect of a Crown disclaimer and that of a liquidator's disclaimer.

E   (3)   Mr Fancourt for the plaintiffs submitted that on the construction of the covenant between the sureties and the plaintiffs it was possible to find an intention that the sureties should continue to be bound notwithstanding disclaimer.

A number of subsidiary issues emerged, including arguments in terrorem based on the possible consequences of the acceptance of other parties' submissions.

F   **(1) Release of surety on disclaimer**

It is necessary to distinguish two situations: (1) the simple lease, with no underletting or assignment; and (2) where there is an underlease or assignment – see *Warnford Investments Ltd v Duckworth & Ors* [1979] Ch 127.

In the case of a simple lease, *Stacey v Hill* [1901] 1 KB 660 decided that s. 55(2) of the *Bankruptcy Act* 1883, which is not materially different from s. 178(4) of the *Insolvency Act* 1986, had the effect of determining the lease as between lessor and lessee from the date of the disclaimer so that the surety's liability for future arrears of rent was also determined. If it were not so, a surety liable to the lessor would be entitled to an indemnity from the lessee company and would require to be released under what is now subs. (4)(b) 'for the purpose of relieving the company'.

Mr Fancourt for the plaintiffs and Mr Hodge for Pneumatic submitted that in the second situation, where there had been an assignment or where there was a subsisting underlease, the lease continues in existence and the company, on disclaimer, is only relieved of its rights and liabilities under the lease so that the first reason for the decision in *Stacey v Hill* does not arise; nor does the second, because the company has ceased to exist and cannot be liable to indemnify the surety. There may well be considerable force in these arguments but the trend of authority is against them. In chronological order, the following decisions must be considered.

Re No. 1 London [1991] BCC 118 (Hoffmann J) – A company was dissolved under s.   A
652. The Crown disclaimed the lease guaranteed by the applicant who applied for a
vesting order under s. 181(2)(b) of the Insolvency Act as a person 'under any liability in
respect of the disclaimed property, not being a liability discharged by the disclaimer'. The
disclaimed property was, of course, the unexpired term and Hoffmann J said at p. 119F:

> 'Any liabilities in respect of the disclaimed property were, by virtue of the law as
> laid down, for example, in *Stacey v Hill* [1901] 1 KB 660, discharged by the   B
> disclaimer.'

Mr Fancourt and Mr Hodge pointed out that, although this was under s. 652, 656 and
657, Hoffmann J, at the foot of p. 118 and top of p. 119, said:

> '. . . the effect of the disclaimer is the same as if the property had been disclaimed
> by a liquidator under the Insolvency Act immediately before the dissolution of the
> company. The effect of a disclaimer by a liquidator is, by virtue of s. 178(4) of the   C
> Insolvency Act, to determine as from the date of the disclaimer the rights, interests
> and liabilities of the company in or in respect of the property disclaimed.'

Had he, they ask, lost sight of the difference between a liquidator's disclaimer, which
must of necessity precede dissolution, and a Crown disclaimer, which is deemed to take
effect immediately before dissolution although in fact dissolution precedes disclaimer?

Re Yarmarine (IW) Ltd [1992] BCC 28 (Millett J) – The essential facts were the   D
same as in *Re No. 1 London.* Dealing with the surety's future liabilities, Millett J said at
p. 30G:

> 'But s. 178(4)(b) is, to all intents and purposes, in the same terms as its predecessors
> going right back to s. 55(2) of the *Bankruptcy Act* 1883, and it was decided in
> *Stacey v Hill* that that section required the release of the surety in order to release
> the tenant, since otherwise the continuing liability of the surety and the surety's   E
> continuing right of indemnity would not bring about the release of the tenant.
> Accordingly a disclaimer by a liquidator under s. 178(4) of a lease brings to an end
> the surety's obligation in respect of future liabilities under the lease. Consequently
> the effect of Crown disclaimer under s. 656 of the *Companies Act* 1985 has the
> same effect by virtue of s. 657(2).'

At p. 31C, Millett J added: F

> 'The language of s. 657(2) is very narrow. It does no more than apply certain
> specified sections of the Insolvency Act as if there had been a liquidation. It does
> not deem there to have been a liquidation or provide that leases and other
> contractual arrangements should have effect as if the Crown disclaimer were a
> disclaimer by a liquidator.'

Mr Fancourt and Mr Hodge drew attention to this passage in support of the point they
take that a distinction can and should be drawn between the different forms of disclaimer.   G

*Murphy v Sawyer-Hoare & Anor [1993] 27 EG 127 (Mr Grabiner QC, sitting as a
deputy judge of the Chancery Division)* – The second defendant was the guarantor of the
assignee of a lease. The assignee went into liquidation and the liquidator disclaimed the
lease. The deputy judge, following *Warnford Investments Ltd v Duckworth*, held that the
lease continued to exist and that the position as between lessor and lessee was unaffected.
However, he took the view that *Stacey v Hill* applied as between assignee and surety (at   H
p. 129):

> 'If, on the true construction of the covenant given by the surety, he would be
> discharged if the principal debtor ceases to have any liability, then, in my view, it
> is necessary for the purpose of releasing the company from any liability that the
> liability of the surety is affected.'

A He also expressed the view that Parliament, by continuing to use the wording of s. 55(2) of the 1883 Act, was impliedly adopting the decision in *Stacey v Hill* in s. 178(4).

Were the matter res integra, I would have regarded the arguments advanced by Mr Fancourt and Mr Hodge as very persuasive. However, while acknowledging that there is a fundamental distinction between a liquidator's disclaimer taking effect from the date of the disclaimer and a Crown disclaimer deeming the property never to have vested in the Crown at all; and between a disclaimer taking effect some time before dissolution
B and one that takes place after dissolution though deemed to take place immediately before it, I feel constrained by the decisions of Hoffmann J and Millett J to accept that *Stacey v Hill*, a decision of the Court of Appeal, is binding on me both as to covenants to Allied and the covenants to Pneumatic. Counsel took the points that *Murphy v Sawyer-Hoare* and, more importantly, *Stacey v Hill*, were wrongly decided.

C Mr Fancourt picked up a point made by Mr Grabiner QC at p. 129 of *Murphy v Sawyer-Hoare* that a covenant could be so drafted as to ensure that a surety's liability continued notwithstanding the liquidation of the obligor, whether original tenant or assignee, and submitted, perhaps in a somewhat muted way, that the sureties' covenants to the plaintiffs did so continue. Their covenants are contained in the licence of 22 December 1987 which is in what can best be described as a law stationer's common form designed for use for an underlease as well as an assignment. The relevant words under
D the headings 'Appendix, General Conditions, 9' are:

> 'Where a surety joins this licence it covenants that in consideration of this licence being issued, then throughout the term of the lease (including any continuation of that term) the assignee ... will comply with the lessee's covenants and the conditions in the documents [the lease and any earlier licences, assignments, guarantees or indemnities] ... and that in default of compliance (notwithstanding
E any time or indulgence given to the defaulting person) the surety will comply with those obligations ...'

In my view this covenant falls a long way short of the sort of provision to be found in chattel leasing agreements, contracts for the sale and delivery of goods, or in construction contracts providing for retention of property in materials delivered to the site but not incorporated in the works, or if incorporated, not yet paid for.

F **(2) Is the sureties' liability revived?**

I therefore pass to the larger question: what happens when the company is revived under s. 653(3)? Is it an 'as you were' situation with the company liable from the moment of dissolution and the sureties likewise; or, as Mr Lightman submits, are the sureties at any rate excused all liability from 7 April 1992 to 30 September 1993?

G *The arguments*

The argument for Allied and Pneumatic can be summarised in the following way:

(1)   The effect of s. 653(3) is that on 30 September 1993 KGP was 'deemed to have continued in existence as if its name had not been struck off'. The lease therefore is deemed never to have vested in the Crown so that no question of bona vacantia ever arose.

H (2)   If the lease is deemed never to have vested in the Crown, the Crown cannot have disclaimed. However, if there had in fact been a disposition while the company's property was vested in the Crown, s. 655 provides for the necessary 'tidying up' but a disclaimer is not a disposition. The construction of the section requires a disposition to a third party. A mere divesting from the Crown does not fall within the section. If it did, two undesirable consequences would follow:

(a) The Crown's right to disclaim is to protect the Crown from having to assume   A
burdens: if, in the event, the lease is shown to have had some value on
assignment, the Crown would have to pay compensation under
s. 655(2)(b)(ii).

(b) A company (or interested surety, e.g. a director) could obtain relief from
liability by the company failing to file returns, being struck off, persuading
the Crown to disclaim, being revived (at very modest cost) and then   B
continuing to trade, but without liability for the period from dissolution to
revival.

Mr Lightman QC accepted that prior to the enactment of s. 108 of the Companies Act
1981 the effect of subsequent restoration to the register would have been to revest the
lease in KGP as was the case in *Re C W Dixon Ltd* [1947] Ch 251 and *Tyman's Ltd v
Craven* [1952] 2 QB 100. However, he submitted that the legislative scheme introduced
by s. 108 and now found in s. 654(2) and 655 is that restoration of the company cannot   C
effect any 'disposition' by the Crown of the lease during the period before KGP was
restored to the register. On restoration, the Crown would be liable to account for any
consideration received for it, or if none was received, an amount equal to the value of the
lease at the date of disposition (see s. 655(1) and (2)). If, therefore, a Crown disclaimer is
a 'disposition', it would have the effect of releasing the sureties from liability and any
subsequent restoration could not revive such liability. The central issue is accordingly   D
whether a Crown disclaimer constitutes a disposition. While acknowledging that the
word has to be construed in its context, Mr Lightman QC looked to other statutes and
situations in support of his submission that it was sufficient that there should be a
disposition *from* without there being a disposition *to*.

The meaning of disclaimer

It was submitted that an appropriate definition is 'a renunciation of all rights and   E
obligations in respect of the property disclaimed'. Reference was made to *Re Finley. Ex
parte Clothworkers' Co* (1888) 21 QBD 475. The decision concerned the construction and
effect of s. 55 of the *Bankruptcy Act* 1883 where a trustee in bankruptcy had disclaimed a
lease which the bankrupt had mortgaged by subdemise and the original lessor applied for
an order under subs. (6) vesting the property in the mortgagee. At p. 482, Lindley LJ
said: F

'The effect of the disclaimer, speaking roughly and generally, is plain enough; it is
to put an end to both the rights and the liabilities of the bankrupt and his trustee
in respect of the disclaimed property. That is the primary object. By the disclaimer
the trustee elects to have nothing to do with the property, which is onerous, and
from which nothing can be got for the benefit of the creditors. He is at liberty to
disclaim it, and the effect of the disclaimer is to extinguish all the rights and
liabilities, both of the bankrupt and of the trustee himself.'   G

The Court of Appeal again considered the meaning of the section in *Re Lister. Ex
parte Bradford Overseers and Bradford Corporation* [1926] Ch 149. The bankrupt
occupied a small house under an oral tenancy. The official receiver, as trustee, entered
the premises and took possession of the furniture, remaining in occupation from 8
February until 15 May when he sold the furniture. On 1 June he disclaimed the tenancy.
The local authority claimed rates during the period of the trustee's occupation. The Court   H
of Appeal held that although he had incurred liability by his voluntary occupation of the
premises, that liability was discharged by s. 54 as one flowing from the vesting in him of
the property disclaimed. At p. 165, Sargant LJ said:

'The use throughout s. 54 of the words "disclaim" and "disclaimer" is in itself a
strong indication of the scope of the section. The words, in my view, connote a

A   renunciation of, or refusal to claim, rights or property which would automatically devolve on or accrue to the person making the disclaimer. They are precisely applicable to a renunciation of a property which with all its rights, interests and liabilities has vested in the trustee under s. 53(2) of the Act. They are not appropriate to any interests, rights or liabilities that have been acquired or undertaken by the voluntary act of the trustee himself, and independently of devolution of the bankrupt. "Disclaime, disclamare ... signifieth utterly to

B   renounce" Co. Litt. 102a ... And the word is habitually used in this sense at the present day with reference to the non-acceptance or renunciation of the office and estate of a trustee under a deed or of an executor and trustee under a will.'

Mr Lightman pointed to the decisions in *Re No. 1 London Ltd* and *Re Yarmarine (IW) Ltd* treating a disclaimer by a liquidator on the same footing as a disclaimer by the Crown.

C

The meaning of disposition

It was submitted that a disclaimer by a liquidator is a disposal or disposition on the authority of *Re Nottingham General Cemetery Co* [1955] Ch 683. The liquidator of a company incorporated by special Act of Parliament and which prohibited it from selling or disposing of any of its land which had been consecrated, set apart or used for the burial of the dead, sought an order that he be at liberty to disclaim the land constituting

D   the company's cemetery together with all implied contracts with holders of grave certificates and all contracts for the upkeep of the graves. The actual decision, summarised in the headnote, was:

'... (1) the land was "burdened with onerous covenants" within the meaning of section 323 of the Companies Act, 1948; (2) the subject-matter of the disclaimer was not necessary for the carrying on of the company's business, which had come to an end; and (3) the right to disclaim property which had become a liability was

E   exercisable personally by the liquidator ... so that no question as to whether such a disclaimer was ultra vires the company could arise.'

Mr Lightman directed my attention to a passage in the judgment of Wynn-Parry J at p. 694 where he said:

'In the present case the act for which authority is sought is the disposal of land because the undertaking has by force of circumstances come to an end, or is about

F   to come to an end. There can be no reason for retaining land which was used for the purpose of carrying on the undertaking when the undertaking has come to an end. Further, unlike the case of a sale, the liquidator in making a disclaimer does not have to use the name of the company. The right to disclaim is a right conferred on the liquidator, as such, by section 323 of the Companies Act, 1948 – a right which did not exist prior to 1929.'

G

The disclaimed land would have vested in the Crown as bona vacantia because there was no other person entitled to the freehold. There would accordingly in a broad sense be both a disposition *from* the company, in whom the land remained vested until disclaimer, *to* the Crown in which it would vest as bona vacantia.

For my own part, I take the view that Wynn-Parry J was using the word 'disposal' in the widest and most informal sense and I do not regard it as an indication of the meaning

H   of the word in s. 655.

Mr Lightman passed to gifts inter vivos and by will conceding that a disclaimer operates by way of avoidance or extinguishment not disposition, although an oral direction to hold property on trust was a purported 'disposition' within the *Law of Property Act* 1925, s. 53(1)(c) and ineffective because it was not in writing. Reference was made to *Re Stratton's Disclaimer* [1958] Ch 42 where, at p. 55, Jenkins LJ said:

'As to the second question, I entirely agree with the judge that the disclaimer must   A
be held to have operated as an extinguishment of Mrs Stratton's right in respect of
the specific bequest and devise. It seems to me that a disclaimer such as this is a
typical example of the extinguishment of a right.'

Re Paradise Motor Co Ltd [1968] 1 WLR 1125 is to the same effect. A donee disclaimed
a gift of shares. The point was taken that because the disclaimer would by retransfer be a
disposition of an equitable interest in the property, it was required to be evidenced in
writing signed by the donee by virtue of s. 53(2) of the *Law of Property Act* 1925.   B
Danckwerts LJ delivering the judgment of the court, dealt with the point very shortly
(p. 1143B):

'We think that the short answer to this is that a disclaimer operates by way of
avoidance and not by way of disposition. For the general characteristics of
disclaimer we refer briefly to the discussion in *In re Stratton's Disclaimer* . . .'
   C

Mr Lightman submits that that part of the decision was per incuriam and referred to the
note in *Wolstenholme and Cherry* vol. 1, p. 131.

'The Court of Appeal has held that the disclaimer of a beneficial interest in shares
is not within para. (c) supra [s. 52(2)(c)] for the short reason that a disclaimer
operates by way of avoidance and not by way of disposition. But no reference was
made to the fact that the Act defines 'disposition' as including a conveyance and   D
defines 'conveyance' as including a 'disclaimer': s. 205(1)(ii) infra'.

Section 52(1) provides:

'All conveyances of land or of any interest therein are void for the purpose of
conveying or creating a legal estate unless made by deed.'

Subsection (2):

'This section does not apply to–   E

   (b)   disclaimers in accordance with [s. 178–180 or s. 315–319 of the Insolvency
         Act 1986], or not required to be evidenced in writing;

   (c)   surrenders by operation of law, including surrenders which may, by law, be
         effected without writing.'

Section 205(1)(ii) defines 'conveyance' as including: F

'a mortgage, charge, lease, assent, vesting declaration, vesting instrument,
disclaimer, release and every other assurance of property or of an interest therein
by any instrument, except a will.'

Mr Hodge pointed out that s. 205 is prefaced by the phrase 'In this Act unless the
context otherwise requires' and that notwithstanding the amendment to s. 52 to include
reference to the Insolvency Act, no reference has been made to Crown disclaimers under
s. 656 of the *Companies Act* 1985 which provides that a disclaimer is by notice signed by   G
the Crown representative, whereas s. 52 of the Law of Property Act requires a deed
subject to the exceptions set out in subs. (2). Mr Hodge therefore submits that Crown
disclaimers stand alone outside the provisions of the Law of Property Act. He also
submits that *Re Paradise Motor Co Ltd* was correctly decided, pointing out that Russell
LJ had been counsel for the plaintiffs in *Re Stratton* and that Danckwerts LJ had been
the judge of first instance whose decision was upheld by the Court of Appeal. The court   H
cannot, he submits, have simply ignored s. 201: subs. (2)(b) of s. 52 then read:

'disclaimers made in accordance with s. 54 of the Bankruptcy Act 1914 or not
required to be evidenced in writing.'

Allied and Pneumatic rely on *Re Paradise Motor Co Ltd*; a disclaimer, they submit,
operates by way of avoidance, s. 655 does not include a disclaimer under s. 656.

A   *Policy*

Mr Lightman answered Mr Fancourt's points to which reference has already been made, first by accepting that if a Crown disclaimer is a disposition, the Crown may have to pay for the consequences. Probably most property disclaimed will be of no or negative value, but, if it is not, and the Crown has to make up its mind within 12 months overall or three months on application, compensation becomes payable. Secondly, Mr Lightman asks how far should a landlord be left at risk of a company being restored to the register and the lease being revived after disclaimer?

B

Counsel for Allied and Pneumatic made the following points:

(1)   A lessor can under s. 656(3)(b) force the Crown to make up its mind rather than wait for the 12-month period to expire.

(2)   Until disclaimer, the lessor can forfeit as against the Crown: reference was made to *Re A E Realisations (1985) Ltd* (1987) 3 BCC 136 at pp. 140–141.

C

(3)   An alternative to (2) above would be peaceful re-entry.

(4)   The lessor is entitled to apply under s. 181 and 182 of the Insolvency Act for a vesting order or exclusion order but it was conceded that the wording of subs. (2) and (3) of s. 181 (and of the corresponding sections of the *Bankruptcy Act* 1883) were 'somewhat opaque'. This is because if the landlord is the 'person who claims an interest in the disclaimed property' the court may make a vesting order in favour of 'the person entitled to it'. To what is the lessor entitled? He may in fact recover his reversion by the exclusion of someone claiming under the company or seek an order vesting the lease in a surety who had covenanted to accept a lease should the tenant or assignee default, but he is not on the face of it entitled to the unexpired term.

D

E   (5)   The court would have power, on the restoration of the company to the register, to grant relief against forfeiture in any event.

Policy arguments based on lacunae in detailed legislation are a legitimate guide to construction but should be used with caution. There are bound to be anomalies and uncertainties where matters are deemed to have taken place quite contrary to what happened in actual fact: the deeming required by s. 653(3) and 657(1) is bound to create some anomalies.

F

Conclusion

The answer to the central issue 'Is a Crown disclaimer a disposition for the purposes of s. 655?' must, in my judgment, be 'No'. I accept the arguments advanced by Allied and Pneumatic which I have summarised earlier. In my view, both the natural meaning of the words used and the policy of Ch. VI of Pt. XX of the 1985 Act point to an 'as you were'

G   situation once the company is restored to the register, subject to the court's power to 'tidy up' under s. 653(3) and 655. Accordingly, I dismiss the appeals.

(Order accordingly)

H

Securum Finance Ltd v Camswell Ltd.

A

Chancery Division (Companies Court).
His Honour Judge Weeks (sitting as a High Court judge).
Judgment delivered 8 February 1994.

> *Winding-up petition – Prospective creditor – Striking-out application – Whether
> petition by prospective creditor should be struck out – Insolvency Act 1986, s.
> 122(1)(f), (g), 123(1)(e), 123(2).*

B

**This was an application to strike out a winding-up petition. The company which was the
subject of the petition used to occupy a hotel. The petitioner had a charge over the property
and brought proceedings against the company claiming possession and damages for trespass.
The petitioner obtained an order for possession and an order for damages to be assessed by
an inquiry and an order for costs. The petition was based on the prospective debts payable
by the company for the costs, when taxed or agreed, and the damages, when determined on
inquiry or agreed.**

C

Held, refusing to strike out the petition:

**1. If the petition had contained no more than the general allegation that the company
was insolvent and unable to pay its debts, it would have been an abuse. All the more so
because the verifying affidavit was taken as prima facie evidence of that statement. A
petitioner had to put in the petition more than a bare statement of the ground on which it
was seeking to wind up the company.**

D

**2. The petition did contain material from which the court could infer that the company
was presently insolvent and unable to pay its debts. Whether or not the petitioner had to go
further and show that the company would be unable to pay the petitioner's prospective debt
when that debt fell due as well, was not a matter which had to be decided at present.**

E

The following case was referred to in the judgment:

Company No. 003028 of 1987, Re a (1987) 3 BCC 575.

Christopher R Parker (instructed by Denton Hall Burgin & Warren) for the petitioner.

Fernanda Pirie (instructed by Holman Fenwick & Willan) for the company.

JUDGMENT

F

His Honour Judge Weeks: I have before me a winding-up petition, an application to
strike out the petition by the company which it is sought to wind up and an application
by the petitioner for leave to amend.

The petitioner is Securum Finance Ltd, which had a previous name of Nordbanken
(UK) Ltd. The company, which is the subject of the petition, is Camswell Ltd. Camswell
Ltd used to occupy a well-known hotel at Maidenhead called the Skindles Hotel. The
owner of that hotel was Abbeyom Properties Ltd, who charged the property to
Nordbanken (UK) Ltd or Securum Finance Ltd, as it is now known. Securum brought
proceedings under its charge against Camswell Ltd in the Chancery Division, an action
which was later transferred to the Mayor's and City Court, claiming possession and
damages for trespass. On 26 November 1993, they were successful to the extent that they
had an order for possession, suspended, on conditions which were complied with, until
7 January 1994, an order for damages to be assessed by an inquiry and an order for
costs in their favour on the High Court scale.

G

H

The petitioning creditor, therefore, has two prospective debts payable by the company:
one is for the costs when those costs have been taxed or agreed, which they have not yet
been, and the other is for the damages when those damages have been determined on the
inquiry or agreed. Neither of those debts is presently payable, but that does not prevent

A   Securum Finance Ltd from presenting a winding-up petition. The relevant provisions of the *Insolvency Act* 1986 are as follows:

> '122(1) A company may be wound up by the court if–
>
> (f) the company is unable to pay its debts . . .
>
> . . .

B

> 123(1) A company is deemed unable to pay its debts–
>
> (e) if it is proved to the satisfaction of the court that the company is unable to pay its debts as they fall due.
>
> (2) A company is also deemed unable to pay its debts if it is proved to the satisfaction of the court that the value of the company's assets is less than the amount of its liabilities, taking into account its contingent and prospective liabilities.'

C

Application for winding up

> 124(1) Subject to the provisions of this section, an application to the court for the winding up of a company shall be by petition presented either by the company, or the directors, or by any creditor or creditors (including any contingent or prospective creditor or creditors), contributory or contributories . . .'

D

Then there are restrictions on petitions by contributories in subs. (2) and (3) and provision for winding-up petitions presented by the Secretary of State or the official receiver.

But, clearly, a prospective creditor whose debt is not currently due does have a right to petition. What he has to prove is that the company is unable to pay its debts as defined in s. 123. He has a difficulty, which is not faced by those creditors whose debts are currently due, in that he cannot rely on a statutory demand, as those creditors who have current debts exceeding £750 can.

E

In *Re a Company No. 003028 of 1987* (1987) 3 BCC 575 at p. 585 there is an interesting passage in Scott J's judgment where he is dealing obiter with what a contingent creditor might have to prove. He said:

F

> 'Mr Elland (counsel for the company) relied also on the feature that there appears in the books no case in which a petition to wind up on the just and equitable ground by a contingent creditor or any creditor has succeeded. That may be right, but it is no ground for a submission that a contingent creditor has no locus standi. If a contingent creditor seeks to wind up on the just and equitable ground, the court would have to look very closely at what was alleged in support of the petition to see whether the contingent creditor did in fact have such an interest in the company as to make it proper to wind up on that ground. Ordinarily, the interest of a creditor is in obtaining repayment of his debt. If his debt is repayable and is not repaid, the creditor can apply to wind up on the ground that the company cannot pay its debts: s. 122(1)(f). If the petitioner were a contingent creditor, the debt would not be immediately repayable, and in order to obtain a winding-up order the contingent creditor would have to show something in the affairs of the company to justify the apprehension that when the time for repayment of the debt arrived, the company would be unable to repay, and that in those circumstances the company ought to be at once wound up. Current inability on the part of a company to pay its debts would not necessarily entitle a contingent creditor to succeed in a winding-up petition. The contingent creditor would, I think, be expected to show, not only and not necessarily a current inability by the company to pay its debts, but rather an inability to pay its debts at the time when the

G

H

contingent debt became payable. A case of that character would in my opinion fall   A
more clearly within para. (g) than para. (f) of s. 122(1).'

There was no submission in the present case that this petition was based on the just
and equitable ground, although I note that there is an allegation at the end of the petition
that it is just and equitable to wind up the company.

This petition is based on an allegation that the company is insolvent and unable to pay
its debts. Whether or not the petitioner must go further and show that the company is   B
not only unable to pay its debts at present, but will be unable to pay the petitioner's
prospective debt when that debt falls due as well, is not a matter that I need to decide for
present purposes.

What I do find from the words of the statute is that the minimum that a petitioner has
to show is current inability on the part of the company to pay its debts, if it is going to
succeed under para. (f) of s. 122(1). Here in the present case we have a general allegation   C
that the company is insolvent and unable to pay its debts and it is submitted by counsel
on behalf of the petitioner that that in itself is sufficient to comply with the requirements
of a petition. Moreover, an affidavit verifying that statement must, so counsel says, be
taken as prima facie evidence of the statements in the petition to which it relates, including
the statement that the company is insolvent and unable to pay its debts. That is because
r. 4.12(6) provides that the affidavit verifying the petition is prima facie evidence of the
statements in the petition to which it relates.   D

If the petition had contained no more than the general allegation that the company is
insolvent and unable to pay its debts, I would have regarded the petition as an abuse. All
the more so because the verifying affidavit is taken as prima facie evidence of that
statement. It seems to me that a petitioner who is seeking to wind up a company must do
more than put in the petition a bare statement which only states the ground on which it
is seeking to wind up the company.   E

The matter, however, does not stop there, because this petition does contain reasons
from which the court could infer that the company was unable to pay its debts. There is
an allegation in para. 5 that the company occupies as its sole premises the freehold
property known as the Skindles Hotel and later the allegation, which is not disputed, that
the petitioner has a possession order in respect of the hotel.

There is the further allegation that the company's last filed audited financial statements   F
are for the year ended 31 December 1991, so that the company is at least three months in
arrears in its statutory obligation to file annual accounts.

There is, finally, the allegation in the petition that the amount of costs is likely to
amount to not less than £80,000 and the amount of damages for trespass is likely to be at
least £30,000. There is £110,000 on the face of the petition, supported by the statutory
affidavit, which is likely to be payable by a company which has lost its sole trading   G
premises and has not filed any accounts later than 1991. That does seem to me to be
evidence from which a court might infer that the company was unable to pay its debts
and on which it might, if so persuaded at the hearing, make a winding-up order.

In those circumstances, it would seem to me wrong to strike out the petition altogether.

The amendments which are sought to be made to the petition are to allege that, in an
exchange of correspondence between the respective solicitors after the petition had been   H
issued, the company's solicitors failed to respond positively to allegations by the
petitioner's solicitors that this company was insolvent. There has been an objection to
leave to amend on the basis that I ought not to grant leave in respect of a new cause of
action. This does not seem to me to be a new cause of action, but an additional piece of
evidence, the worth of which will be assessed by the judge hearing the petition in due
course, as to the solvency or insolvency of this company at the present time.

A   Accordingly, in all the circumstances, I think it right to give leave to amend the petition to make this further allegation, which will probably have to be verified by affidavit in due course.

     It would seem to me to be unfair to proceed with the hearing of the petition without giving the company a chance to respond to the amendments and to deal with the general basis of the petition, because, of course, it has not done so while its application to strike out as demurrable was proceeding. In those circumstances, I will adjourn the hearing of the petition to a date to be fixed and will hear submissions as to the time for filing evidence.

(Order accordingly)

Re a Debtor No. 32 of 1993.

A

Chancery Division (in bankruptcy).
Timothy Lloyd QC (sitting as a deputy High Court judge).
Judgment delivered 11 February 1994.

Bankruptcy – Creditor's petition – Petition dismissed where debtor's offer unreasonably refused – Whether creditor's refusal of offer was unreasonable – Insolvency Act 1986, s. 271(3).

B

This was an appeal by the petitioning creditor against the refusal of the county court to make a bankruptcy order on its petition on the ground that the petitioning creditor had unreasonably refused an offer by the debtor within s. 271(3) of the Insolvency Act 1986 to compound for the petition debt.

The debt of over £33,000 (at presentation of the petition) arose under an agreement for services between the petitioning creditor, Commercial Union, and the debtor made in 1989 when the debtor was in partnership as an estate agent. The agreement was terminated in 1990 and sums then outstanding became due. Payment by instalments was made at the rate of £800 per month for some time up to June 1991 when the creditor demanded a greater payment. In June 1992 an offer was made to pay the sum of £9,000 representing back payments, and to continue at the same rate. The creditor asked for the same lump sum plus payment of £1,000 per month. In August 1992, £10,000 was offered and paid but then no more than £450 per month was offered by way of continuing payment. Against that the creditor offered to accept £600 per month but nothing was agreed. At that point payments ceased and in due course the statutory demand and the petition followed. There were further negotiations when the petition was due for hearing. The offer in issue was then made on behalf of the debtor by reference to s. 271(3) for the provision of £15,000 by third parties in full settlement of all claims against the debtor. The offer was refused by the creditor and a counter-offer made requiring payment in full with interest and costs. The county court refused the creditor's petition. The creditor appealed.

C

D

E

Held, allowing the appeal:

1. If a debtor had only one creditor seeking to use the bankruptcy procedure, there was no reason in principle why he should not be able to make an offer to that one creditor which would come within s. 271(3). An actual composition with that creditor resulted in the dismissal of the petition under s. 271(1) in the absence of another supporting creditor who wished to be substituted.

F

2. The test under s. 271(3) was whether a reasonable creditor, in the position of the petitioning creditor, and in the light of the actual history as disclosed to the court, would have accepted or refused the offer. However, there could be a range of reasonable positions on the part of hypothetical reasonable creditors. In order to conclude that the refusal was unreasonable, the court had to be satisfied that no reasonable hypothetical creditor would have refused the offer, and that the refusal of the offer was therefore beyond the range of possible reasonable actions in the context.

G

3. The district judge had adopted an approach which was wrong in principle in three respects; first, he approached the matter on the basis that there was only one course that could reasonably be taken; second, inconsistently with his own test, he looked at the matter subjectively; thirdly, he took the wrong view of the relevance of the past history of offers and payments, and of the prospect of limited or negligible recovery in bankruptcy.

H

4. The hypothetical reasonable creditor, on the facts of this case, might well be influenced, in deciding whether to accept the offer or to press for a bankruptcy order, by the unsatisfactory record of the debtor's past dealings. Also the hypothetical reasonable creditor might well regard it as relevant that, whatever the eventual outcome of the bankruptcy in

A   financial terms for the creditors, a bankruptcy order would at least result in a full investigation. The hypothetical creditor would not simply regard the issue as one of comparing the economic outcome of two different propositions, nor would the risk of a nil return for the creditors from the bankruptcy necessarily lead the creditor to favour the offer.

The following cases were referred to in the judgment:

B   *Debtor (No. 2389 of 1989), Re a* [1991] Ch 326.
Gilmartin (a bankrupt), Re [1989] 1 WLR 513.
Ladd v Marshall [1954] 1 WLR 1489.

Lexa Hilliard (instructed by Kingsford Stacey) for the appellant.

Jeremy Bamford (instructed by Anstey Sargent & Probert, Exeter) for the respondent.

JUDGMENT

C   **Timothy Lloyd QC:** The Commercial Union Life Assurance Co Ltd, the petitioning creditor, appeals to this court against the refusal of the Exeter County Court in bankruptcy to make a bankruptcy order on its petition. The ground for the refusal was that the petitioning creditor had unreasonably refused an offer made to it which fell within s. 271(3) of the *Insolvency Act* 1986 to compound for the debt on which the petition is based.

D   On this appeal I have to consider whether the offer was one which fell within the section, which is a matter of law, and if so whether the district judge's conclusion that the refusal was unreasonable is one that can successfully be challenged. Since the latter point is one of judgment and this appeal is a true appeal, not a rehearing, the creditor can only succeed on this point if the district judge's decision was based on a misdirection and is therefore wrong in principle.

E   I consider first the question whether the offer was within the section. The subsections which need to be considered are (1) and (3). They are as follows:

'(1) The court shall not make a bankruptcy order on a creditor's petition unless it is satisfied that the debt, or one of the debts, in respect of which the petition was presented is either–

F   (a) a debt which, having been payable at the date of the petition or having since become payable, has been neither paid nor secured or compounded for, or

         (b) a debt which the debtor has no reasonable prospect of being able to pay when it falls due.

(3) The court may dismiss the petition if it is satisfied that the debtor is able to pay all his debts or is satisfied–

G   (a) that the debtor has made an offer to secure or compound for a debt in respect of which the petition is presented,

         (b) that the acceptance of that offer would have required the dismissal of the petition, and

         (c) that the offer has been unreasonably refused;

H   and, in determining for the purposes of this subsection whether the debtor is able to pay all his debts, the court shall take into account his contingent and prospective liabilities.'

Thus, on hearing the petition, there must be at least one debt, on which the petition is based, as to which, if it is already due and payable, it has neither been paid nor secured nor compounded for or, if it is a future debt, there is no reasonable prospect that the debtor will be able to pay it when it falls due. Payment is a question of fact, securing or

compounding I take to be a matter of agreement between the debtor and the creditor,   A
and the prospects of payment of future debts must be a question of evidence.

If the threshold conditions of subs. (1) are satisfied the court may nevertheless dismiss
the petition if it is satisfied that the debtor is able to pay all his debts. Alternatively it may
dismiss the petition if an offer within subs. (3) has been made and has been unreasonably
refused.

The debt on which the present petition was issued on 8 January 1993 is now stated as   B
£33,638.86. It is a joint debt of the debtor and a Mr Buxton, arising from a loan made by
the petitioning creditor in February 1989. During 1992 and 1993 a number of proposals
were made by the debtors for the satisfaction of the debt. On 20 May 1993 a formal offer
was made on behalf of both debtors by reference to s. 271(3), for the provision of £15,000
by third parties in full settlement of all claims against both debtors, to be paid within two
months of acceptance or earlier if funds were made available sooner by realisation of
investments, the petition to be withdrawn and no further proceedings to be made in   C
respect of the claim. This offer was refused by the petitioner and was then reiterated by
the debtor in his evidence on the petition. He said:

> 'If the offer were to be accepted, then I would arrange for my solicitors to be put
> in funds thereby securing the payment. Irrevocable undertakings would be given
> and the sum would be paid over to the petitioning creditors or to their solicitors
> on the petition being either dismissed or withdrawn.'   D

The debtor says that an offer of £15,000 in respect of a debt of £33,000 is an offer to
compound for the debt. On behalf of the creditor Miss Hilliard says that that would be
so as a matter of the ordinary usage of language, but says that a special and more limited
meaning applies in this context. As a matter of the ordinary use of language I agree that
the offer is one to compound. Composition with creditors normally involves accepting a
partial payment, whether by a lump sum or instalments. It seems to me that composition   E
with a single creditor has exactly the same scope.

Miss Hilliard for the petitioning creditor relies on a passage in the judgment of Vinelott
J in *Re a Debtor (No. 2389 of 1989)* [1991] Ch 326. That case was concerned with a
situation where a proposal was put to all a debtor's creditors for a voluntary arrangement
but was voted down by the petitioning creditor whose debt was worth about half the
total. It was said that that vote was equivalent to a refusal to accept the offer and was
unreasonable. The judge rejected this argument and said that the regime concerning   F
voluntary arrangements was entirely distinct. Part of his reasoning involved examining
s. 271(3) in detail, particularly subpara. (b), and considering the implications of his
conclusion as to the scope of the section. At p. 333A he said:

> 'This is not the only difficulty. Under section 271(3) the court can dismiss a petition
> if an offer is unreasonably refused and if acceptance of the offer "would have
> required the dismissal of the petition." But if a voluntary arrangement is accepted   G
> at the meeting of creditors then, on the expiration of 28 days from the date when
> the report of the meeting was made to the court, the bankruptcy petition "is
> deemed, unless the court otherwise orders, to have been dismissed."
>
> Mr. Hamer submitted that the words in section 271(3)(b) "would have required
> the dismissal of the petition" can be read as "would have required or would have
> resulted in the dismissal of the petition." I accept, of course, that it would be wrong   H
> to attach too great importance to the literal meaning of the words used in
> paragraph (b). The court must look at the scheme of the legislation as a whole and
> the purpose to be inferred from it. However, in the instant case, the literal
> construction of paragraph (b) avoids the anomalies to which I have referred. The
> acceptance of a proposed voluntary arrangement at the creditors' meeting does not
> itself require or have the consequence that the petition falls to be dismissed. That

A   consequence only follows if no application to the court is made under section 262(1).

In my judgment, therefore, a proposed voluntary arrangement is not to be treated as an offer to each creditor capable of being accepted or refused by the petitioning creditor within the meaning of section 271(3). The offer is made to the creditors affected by it as a class, and the consequences of acceptance or refusal are to be

B   found in Part VIII of the Act alone.

It is suggested in *Muir Hunter on Personal Insolvency* (1987) (release of 3 April 1989), p. 3050, that so construed section 271(3) has very limited scope. The tender of payment in full with costs is covered by section 271(1)(a) (which must read with r. 6.25 of the Rules of 1986); further, if a composition for less than the full amount of the debt is accepted a petition cannot be withdrawn without the leave of the

C   court. It is difficult, therefore, to see how it can be said that in such a situation acceptance would have required the dismissal of the petition. That leaves only the possibility – in practice rare – where a [debtor] might offer to pay off one or more of the debts, leaving the balance of debt less than the statutory minimum; for in such a situation the petition would have to be dismissed on that ground.

However, as I see it, construed in the sense I have indicated, there is a plain and

D   important area for the operation of section 271(3). If, after a petition has been presented, a debtor were to offer a composition to all his creditors conditionally on acceptance by them all, which was accepted by all the creditors except the petitioning creditor, it could, it seems to me, be said that the offer was an offer to each of the creditors individually and that acceptance by the petitioning creditor (as well as the other creditors) "would have required the dismissal of the petition;"
since if all the creditors had agreed to accept the composition, there would be

E   simply no ground on which the court could properly refuse to dismiss the petition.

What the debtor cannot do, as I see it, is to invoke the coercive machinery in Part VIII of the Act in order to bind dissentient or inactive creditors (creditors, that is, who do not attend the meeting of creditors in person or by proxy) and then claim that a creditor who votes against the resolution to approve the voluntary arrangement has unreasonably withheld his consent to it. What the debtor can do

F   in these circumstances (that is, if all except the petitioning creditor accept a proposed voluntary arrangement which provides for payment by way of composition) is to offer the composition to each creditor conditionally on acceptance by all and then, if the petitioning creditor refuses, apply for the dismissal of the petition. The court would have jurisdiction to stand over the petition, if necessary, while these steps are being taken or completed.'

G   Mr Bamford for the debtor says that this was said in an entirely different context and that the judge was not considering the present sort of case. However the judge clearly had in mind the notes to the section in the then text of *Muir Hunter on Personal Insolvency*. In what respects that text has changed since the state it was in then, apart from dealing with the decision in the case itself, I cannot tell, but it seems likely from what the judge says that it already included text similar to or the same as the present para. 3-095 on p. 3051 in which the scope of the sort of offers to which the section is

H   relevant is considered. That text now includes the following:

'*(2) Debtor alleges offer to secure or compound with petitioning creditor*

This is where the debtor satisfies the court:

(a) that he has made an offer to secure or compound for "a debt" in respect of which the petition is presented, and

(b) that the acceptance of that offer would have required the dismissal of the   A
petition, and

(c) that the offer has been "unreasonably refused".

This limb of the subsection presents difficulties. The reason for the use of the
phrase "a debt" (rather than "the debt or debts") is obscure; it would only be
relevant to deal with "a" (i.e. one) debt in the petition if it was the only debt, or if
its payment off reduced the aggregate petition debt or debts below the bankruptcy   B
level (£750). The debt in question, however, is not visualised as being paid, but as
being only secured or compounded for, i.e. by the acceptance of an offer either of
less than 100p in the £ or by a request for forbearance. There is some bankruptcy
case-law on the analogous words in section 2 of the Act of 1914 . . . but only as to
securing or compounding to the satisfaction of the creditor, not to the satisfaction
of the court. The operation of the "compounding or securing" clause in . . . section   C
2 and in the statutory forms of bankruptcy notices . . . took effect also outside the
relationship between creditor and debtor; if in fact a valid compounding or
securing had taken place within the currency of the notice, it suspended the notice,
and no act of bankruptcy was committed which could be "available" to other
creditors. For a case of a debtor claiming to be able to pay, though failing to do
so, see *Re Gilmartin. . .*

To what kind of "offer" does subsection (3) apply?   D

It is not clear, under clause (b), what would be the kind of offer, the acceptance of
which would have required the dismissal of the petition; and no guidance is given
on this issue. The offer must be something other than the tender of payment in full
with costs, for that situation is covered by section 271(1)(a) . . . (and cf. r. 6.25), as
a ground for dismissal. But in consideration of something less than payment in
full, as already pointed out in the note to section 266(2) . . . no petition can be   E
withdrawn (or presumably dismissed by consent) without the leave of the court.
No bargain made between the debtor and the creditor could therefore compel the
court to dismiss the petition. Clause (b) may perhaps be referring to such a bargain,
but in the context of what the parties have agreed should happen, rather than what
they can compel the court to perform, in order to carry out their bargain.

Another possible construction is that the debtor might, in the case of a multi   F
creditor petition, offer to pay off one (or more) of the debts, so as to bring the
remaining balance down below the statutory minimum, so that the petition would
have to be dismissed on that ground. A yet further hypothesis is that this may refer
to a creditor who has refused to assent to a voluntary arrangement under Part
VIII, where his assent would have led to the dismissal of the petition: see notes to
section 258.

    G
The situation of an offer, which if accepted would have necessitated the dismissal
of the petition, can only arise where no other creditor is seeking to be substituted.'

Mr Bamford says this is a case which, at the hearing, there was no other creditor
seeking to be substituted so that the case falls within the last sentence of that note.

As mentioned in that note, by virtue of s. 266(2) a bankruptcy petition may not be
withdrawn without the leave of the court. By r. 6.30 of the *Insolvency Rules* 1986, where   H
a petitioner consents to withdraw his petition or to allow it to be dismissed, or in other
comparable circumstances, the court may, on such terms as it thinks just, order that there
be substituted as petitioner any creditor who has given notice of his intention to appear
at the hearing and who is desirous of prosecuting the petition and who at the date on
which the date the petition was presented would have been in a position at that date to
present a bankruptcy petition in respect of relevant debts owed to him by the debtor.

A   Rule 6.32 is also relevant. It provides that where the petitioner applies to the court for the petition to be dismissed or for leave to withdraw it he must, unless the court otherwise orders, file in court an affidavit specifying the grounds of the application and the circumstances in which it is made. He must put certain relevant matters in evidence and it is also provided that no order giving leave to withdraw a petition should be given before the petition is heard.

B   In the present case there had been one creditor who had given notice of intention to appear at the hearing but it did not in fact appear and therefore could not have been regarded as at that stage being desirous of prosecuting the petition. At that point therefore the matter could be fairly regarded as if there had been no supporting creditor.

     It is thus said that, if the petitioning creditor had applied for leave to withdraw or had consented to dismissal, the court could not do other than accede to that application, so that the offer was one which would have required the dismissal of the petition. That

C   would be similar to the multi-creditor situation envisaged by Vinelott J in respect of which he said at p. 333H that 'if all the creditors had agreed to accept the composition, there would be simply no ground on which the court could properly refuse to dismiss the petition'.

     Of course, the offer here was in terms of withdrawal, not dismissal, but that seems to me to be a distinction without a difference in the present case and I would not hold the

D   offer to be outside the section on that ground.

     Miss Hilliard said that the offer could not be within the section in respect of present debts unless either it reduced the total petition debt to less than £750 or it fell within the case of an offer to each of several creditors as envisaged by Vinelott J. She submitted that, as another case in which the section could apply, there might be a case where both present and future debts were at issue and there might be an offer only to pay the present

E   debts, accompanied by evidence of prospective ability to pay future debts. That, she submitted, would be within the section but subject to those cases she submitted that an offer to compound must involve paying the whole value of the debt. If it is paid by instalments she submits that it would have to carry interest.

     As a matter of policy, she submitted that if the debtor wishes to deal with only one out of several creditors through the bankruptcy procedure, he cannot do a deal on the basis of paying less than the full value of the present debt (unless it is a case of paying the full

F   value less an amount not exceeding £749). If creditors are to be persuaded to accept less, she submitted, it must be on a collective basis through the individual voluntary arrangement procedure. The underlying policy, she said, was that a debtor must face up to his insolvency for the benefit of all creditors as a class.

     I cannot accept these submissions. Of course if there are several creditors wishing to use the bankruptcy procedure, in practice the debtor has to come to terms with each of

G   them, or another will be substituted as petitioning creditor. But if a debtor has only the one creditor seeking to use the bankruptcy procedure, I see no reason in principle why he should not be able to make an offer to that one creditor which would come within s. 271(3). Clearly an actual composition with that creditor results in the dismissal of the petition under s. 271(1) in the absence of another supporting creditor who wishes to be substituted. Miss Hilliard submitted that it would be inappropriate for the courts to have

H   to investigate reasonableness as between one creditor and the debtor in isolation, and that this would lead to inconsistency of practice, allowing too wide a scope for the discretion of individual bankruptcy courts. For that reason she submitted that the section should be construed narrowly.

     I see some force in her comment about the consequences of a wide discretion and possible inconsistent practice. But on the ordinary language of the section it seems to me that there is nothing to take this offer outside it and I am unable to accept Miss Hilliard's

arguments as being sufficient to give the words used in the section a special limited   A
meaning narrower than that which they would bear on the ordinary meaning of the
words.

For these reasons I hold that the district judge was right to decide that the offer was
within the section and I go on to consider the question of whether the refusal was
unreasonable.

To do this I must set out more of the factual history, from the evidence before the   B
district judge.

The debt arises under an agreement for services dated 1 February 1989 between the
petitioning creditor and the debtor and Mr Buxton, then practising in partnership as an
estate agent. The agreement was terminated in October 1990 and the sums outstanding
then became due. In the meantime a third person had been brought into the partnership
in August 1990 and it is said that it was he who enabled payments to be made to   C
the petitioning creditor from time to time by permitting drawings by the debtor and
Mr Buxton.

Payments seem to have been made at the rate of £800 per month for some time up to
about June 1991 when the creditor demanded a greater payment. In June 1992 an offer
was made to pay the sum of £9,000, representing back payments at that rate, and to
continue at the same rate. The creditor asked for the same lump sum plus payment of   D
£1,000 per month. In August 1992 £10,000 was offered and paid but by then no more
than £450 per month was offered by way of continuing payment. Against that the creditor
offered to accept £600 per month and nothing was agreed. At that point payments ceased,
and in due course the statutory demand and the petition followed. In February 1993
Touche Ross were assisting the debtor, in place of a firm of local solicitors who had been
acting and discussion was had between the accountants and the creditor's solicitors as to
terms of payment. The petition was due for hearing on 23 March 1993. On 11 March the   E
debtor offered to pay £2,000 immediately, £1,600 by the end of April and £600 per
month. On 16 March that offer was improved by the tender of two cheques provided by
the debtor's wife amounting to £4,200 but on the express basis that if they were to be
accepted the petition must be withdrawn. The creditor responded by requiring that in
addition to that sum there should be payments of £1,200 per month thereafter and
accordingly the petition hearing went ahead. On that date however the debtor was   F
represented by new solicitors, Anstey Sargent and Probert, who now act for him, and the
petition was adjourned. On 25 March the creditor withdrew the offer in the light of this
development and called for payment of the whole sum. On 20 May the offer at issue in
the proceedings was made and on 27 May it was rejected with a counter-offer to accept
£5,400 immediately and instalments of £1,200 per month continuing until payment of the
outstanding debt with interest, and the costs were to be paid as well.

On 3 June 1993 the debtor put in an affidavit deposing as to his means and to the offer.   G
In para. 10 he said that, 'for the reasons that I will mention, it was quite impossible for
me to contemplate, either alone or alone or jointly with Mr Buxton, the payments at a
level of £1,200 per month. That is still the case'. He deposes to the fact that his capital
account in the partnership is in deficit to the tune of some £110,000, that whilst the
business is improving as the result of the gradual pickup of the property market, he has
received no income whatsoever from the business since October 1992 and is wholly   H
dependent on his wife's income, she being employed by Devon County Council. He says
that although the financial position of the business is precarious, the third person who
was brought in is a man of substance and it is unlikely that he will allow the business as
such to collapse, and he, the debtor, hopes to negotiate a dissolution of the partnership
in due course and to enter into an arrangement under which he is employed by the third
person. He deposes to his financial position more generally and, although he has assets,

A   it is clear that they are charged for far more than their value and so the evidence overall suggests a substantial net deficiency in his current financial position. He says in particular:

> 'it is quite clear that if I am made bankrupt, then the petitioning creditor will, most unfortunately, receive nothing at all unless during the period of my bankruptcy, I become entitled to any after acquired assets, or which is most unlikely my income is such that I might be liable for an income payments order.'

B   In the course of his affidavit he refers to the fact that the £15,000 offered would have been made available by relatives and by implication it is reasonably clear that that would have been by way of loan to the debtor.

Mr Buxton also put in an affidavit of means. His position is less severe in terms of a deficiency but it too suggests that he has no net assets and that he also has no income of his own. In response to the debtor's affidavit an affidavit was put in by the solicitor for C   the petitioning creditor in which it was said that the creditor's attitude had always been reasonable, that the debtor had prevaricated and delayed, and reference was made to the several changes of adviser who had the conduct of negotiations with the petitioner's solicitors, and the point was made that the correct procedure would be an individual voluntary arrangement which it was pointed out could have been made even after a bankruptcy order.

D   The hearing took place on 24 August. The district judge reserved judgment and delivered a written judgment on 2 September. He held that the refusal had been unreasonable but gave the creditor until 24 September to reconsider its position. On that day there was a further hearing at which the petitioning creditor sought to rely on a further affidavit to make good what the district judge had seen as gaps in its evidence. That was rejected, and I have already dismissed an appeal against that rejection. The E   creditor did not accept the offer and accordingly the petition was dismissed.

The consequence of that, if it stands, seems to be that the debt is still owing but that, in the absence of any material change of circumstances, the petitioning creditor could not expect to be able to obtain a bankruptcy order on fresh proceedings. However, if any other creditor were to obtain a bankruptcy order, the petitioner's debt would be proved in the bankruptcy and there seems no obvious basis for holding that the petitioner could not enforce in any other way available to it after obtaining judgment for the outstanding F   debt.

The district judge's judgment indicates a number of factors on which reliance was placed by him in coming to the conclusion that the refusal was unreasonable. One was that nothing would be immediately available to the creditors and the prospect of anything being available to the creditors at any time was not hopeful. He referred to the fact that the debtor's solicitors, 'a reputable firm experienced in this field', had expressed their own G   view of the matter in the letter in which the offer was made. Then he referred to the fact that affidavits of means had been offered but not taken up by the petitioning creditor. Then he referred to the fact that the petitioning creditor had submitted that a bankruptcy order would result in a full investigation of the situation but that there was no evidence that this was a consideration present to the mind of the petitioning creditor. Then he referred to the fact that the funds were to be provided by a third party and therefore H   there was no risk of that payment being set aside on a subsequent bankruptcy. He alluded to the history of offers and payments by instalments but he said that this was of little relevance to a decision whether one should accept a proposal of payment from a third party of a substantial part of the debt or risk obtaining nothing in a bankruptcy. He referred to the fact that no reasons were given for the petitioning creditor's refusal of the offer. He referred to the fact on which reliance was placed by the creditor that it would have been possible to proceed by way of an individual voluntary arrangement but he

rejected that submission and held that the court could have regard to the position
concerning the petitioning creditor alone.

He then posed, as his test, whether a reasonable man in the position of the creditor
would have refused or accepted the offer. He said that at first sight it was unreasonable
to refuse an offer of £15,000 from a third party in favour of a serious risk of getting
nothing. He said that the creditor could have required to investigate the debtor's means
and their disclosure and then come back on the basis of inadequate disclosure. He says
that the creditor could have relied on commercial reasons for example to maintain
standards in the industry but that because nothing was said about this it was to be
disregarded. On this basis he said that there was nothing to alter his prima facie view that
the refusal was unreasonable.

Miss Hilliard submits that this conclusion was based on a number of errors of principle
or self-misdirection. The reference to the opinion of the debtor's solicitors is one of these
errors. The fact that the refusal might mean that the creditor would get nothing in a
bankruptcy is also said to have been a wrong consideration to bear in mind. The failure
to state any subjective grounds for the refusal is also criticised as irrelevant as is the
district judge's consideration of the point purely on economic terms as between creditor
and debtor. She also criticised his failure to take into account established principles of
bankruptcy law. For example she said that a petitioner was ordinarily entitled to be paid
in full at the hearing unless the petition is adjourned on the ground that there is a
reasonable prospect of him being paid within a reasonable time. In support of that, she
referred to *Re Gilmartin* [1989] 1 WLR 513. That case was cited to the district judge. She
said that on established principles the absence of assets was no reason for refusing a
bankruptcy order unless proved cogently by evidence other than that of the debtor. She
referred to the class remedy status of the bankruptcy system and in that context to the
fact that if third party money is provided on loan, as appears to be the case, it merely
exchanges one liability for another. She referred to the availability of the individual
voluntary arrangement procedure.

It seems to me correct that the reference to the statement by the debtor's solicitors was
misplaced but probable that no substantial reliance was placed on that. A more material
point is the district judge's comment that the debtor's evidence of means should be
accepted in the absence of investigation and challenge by the creditor. As to that Miss
Hilliard referred to another passage in Vinelott J's decision *Re a Debtor (No. 2389 of
1989)*, at p. 337B. There he says:

> '. . . it is, in my judgment, essential that a debtor who puts forward a proposed
> voluntary arrangement should be not only honest but should take care to put all
> relevant facts before the creditors. It is said by Mr. Hamer that there was a genuine
> misunderstanding as to the amount of the debt due to the bank. It is said that
> £45,000 was held in a frozen account of M.I.T., which the debtor thought he was
> entitled to have set off against the total debt. However, even if the debtor did hold
> that view, his solicitor (in March) had told the petitioning creditor what the bank's
> claim was and, on any view, the creditors should have been told what the bank
> claimed to be due and what the debtor's answer to their claim was. If they had
> been told the amount of the claim, then the nominee, in framing her report, would,
> I think, plainly have had to draw attention to the fact that if the bank's claims were
> valid, the total debt due to the petitioning creditor was unsecured.

> It is not, in my judgment, enough to say, as the registrar thought, that the
> petitioning creditor was in a position to correct the facts revealed by the proposal
> and the nominee's report at or before the meeting. It should not be left to a
> petitioning creditor to circulate other creditors to correct errors in the proposals
> which ought not to have been made.'

A   I can see some analogy between that case and that of an offer under s. 271. It is up to the debtor to put his position and its implications fully. But, apart from some lack of detail, it is not shown that that has not been done. It is reasonably clear that the third party moneys will be lent even though the terms of the loan are not stated and may not have been settled. More particularly, where only one creditor is concerned, as would be usual under s. 271, rather than a body of creditors and a nominee as in the case of an individual voluntary arrangement, the second paragraph of that citation simply is not
B   relevant. Any process of investigation, questioning or challenge can be done on a purely bilateral basis between debtor and creditor.

    As to the relevance of the wider body of creditors, it seems to me that, on the facts of this case, the district judge was entitled to take the view that what mattered was the impact on this creditor, not on the entire body of creditors. It is true that, at the time when the offer was made, the creditor knew that there was another creditor who might
C   well attend and support, namely the Legal & General. If that had turned out to be the case the petitioning creditor would not necessarily have been able to do a deal on its own with the debtor. That may have a bearing on the reasonableness of their refusal to accept the offer on 27 May. However it leaves open the question as to whether the unreasonableness needs to be satisfied in respect of the date of the actual refusal, or at the date of the hearing. The statutory words 'has been unreasonably refused' suggest that one should look only at the date of actual refusal. No submissions were addressed to me
D   on this point and I am prepared to proceed on the basis that the position has to be reviewed by reference to the position at the date of the hearing, on the basis that at least in this case the offer was kept open until the hearing and it was therefore the creditor's continued opposition, and finally its opposition at the hearing, which amounted to the definitive refusal on which the debtor relied. That being so, although there could have been another creditor to take into account, in fact at the hearing there was not. I therefore
E   do not disagree with the district judge's approach of taking into account only the circumstances of this debtor and this creditor.

    Looking at the matter in that way, a number of criticisms of the judgment seem to me to fall away, in particular his refusal to consider that an individual voluntary arrangement was the more proper procedure, and any criticism on the basis that the third party money was on loan so as to make no substantial difference to the debtor's overall position.

F   In large part I can accept the district judge's formulation of the appropriate test, which I would express more fully, but not differently in substance, as being whether a reasonable creditor, in the position of this petitioning creditor, and in the light of the actual history as disclosed to the court, would have accepted or refused the offer.

    However, I think it has to be borne in mind that there could be a range of reasonable positions on the part of hypothetical reasonable creditors. In order to conclude that the refusal was unreasonable, it seems to me that the court has to be satisfied that no
G   reasonable hypothetical creditor would have refused the offer, and that the refusal of the offer was therefore beyond the range of possible reasonable actions in the context.

    On that basis it seems to me that the district judge has in fact adopted an approach which is wrong in principle in three respects. The first is that he has approached the matter on the basis that there is only one course that could reasonably be taken. A second is that, inconsistently with his own test, he has looked at the matter as if it had been
H   subjectively considered, and has drawn conclusions from the fact that certain points which might have been relied on were not said to have been relied on by the petitioning creditor. On the objective test it seems to me that what the court has to consider is whether the reasonable creditor would have considered any of these matters and if so whether it would have come to any particular conclusion.

    Thirdly, it seems to me that the district judge took the wrong view of the relevance of the past history of offers and payments, and of the prospect of limited or negligible

recovery in bankruptcy. It seems to me that the past history would be of substantial   A
relevance to the hypothetical reasonable creditor when deciding whether or not to accept
an offer or rather to press for a bankruptcy order.

In that regard, I consider that the petitioning creditor's criticisms of the attitude
adopted on behalf of the debtor as being a tale of prevarication and delay, while perhaps
over severe, have a good deal of justification. It may be that the debtor was doing his
best to reach an accommodation which would be acceptable to his creditors, and that the
several changes of professional advisers handling the dealings with the petitioner – one   B
of them at a moment which gave the debtor a tactical advantage by necessitating an
adjournment of the hearing of the petition – arose for reasons which cannot fairly be laid
at the door of the debtor. However, it seems to me that it is incumbent on a debtor, if he
wishes his proposals to be looked at with sympathy, to be full, frank and open with his
creditors in respect of his statements of his position, and the record of this debtor is not
all that satisfactory. Despite what I have said earlier about the ability of the creditor to   C
investigate and challenge the specific evidence of means and so on in relation to the actual
proposal, it seems to me that the hypothetical reasonable creditor, on the facts of this
case, might well be influenced, in deciding whether to accept the offer or to press for a
bankruptcy order, by the unsatisfactory record of the debtor's past dealings.

In that context, it also seems to me that the hypothetical reasonable creditor might
well regard it as relevant that, whatever the eventual outcome of the bankruptcy, in
financial terms for the creditors, a bankruptcy order would at least result in a full   D
investigation, fuller than could be achieved by enquiries on behalf of the creditor on an
ad hoc basis.

I agree with the district judge that the third party offer is a bird in the hand, and that
this is a factor which the reasonable creditor would take into account. I do not agree that
the hypothetical creditor would simply regard the issue as one of comparing the economic
outcome of two different propositions, nor that the risk of a nil return for the creditors
from the bankruptcy would necessarily lead the creditor to favour the bird in the hand.   E

For these reasons, I consider that the district judge's examination of the issue was
flawed, and in material respects. It therefore falls to me to make my own assessment as
to whether the creditor's refusal should be categorised as outside the range of what is
reasonable.

It seems to me to be appropriate to start from the premise that a creditor such as the
Commercial Union, with extensive dealings with professional men such as the debtor and
Mr Buxton, and no doubt with much experience of bad debts such as that on which the   F
petition is based, is relatively unlikely to adopt an attitude which no reasonable creditor
would adopt. There is no evidence here of motives of oppression or other ulterior
purpose, which could well arise in the case of a less commercial creditor.

I can well see that a different creditor might have accepted the offer. But, taking all the
evidence into account, and accepting that the position should be considered only as
between this actual creditor and the debtor (and Mr Buxton), without regard to the   G
position of whatever other creditors there may be, it seems to me that I cannot conclude
that no reasonable creditor could refuse this offer. It follows that I cannot uphold the
debtor's opposition to the application for a bankruptcy order on the basis that the
petitioning creditor's refusal was unreasonable, and that s. 271(3) is therefore satisfied.

Mr Bamford submitted that, if I came to that view, the debtor should be allowed to
put in more evidence to amplify his explanation of his position. I consider it too late for
that to be done, it not being suggested that the evidence would satisfy the *Ladd v Marshall*   H
[1954] 1 WLR 1489 test for evidence admissible on appeal. I will therefore allow the
petitioning creditor's appeal, but I will hear submissions from counsel as to what order
should be made.

(Order accordingly)

A
Re ELS Ltd.
Ramsbottom & Anor v Luton Borough Council & Anor.
Chancery Division (Companies Court).
Ferris J.
Judgment delivered 16 February 1994.

B
Receivership – Floating charge – Crystallisation – Distress for non-domestic rates
– Councils obtained liability orders against company for unpaid non-domestic
rates and sought to levy distress – Receivers appointed under floating charge
contained in debenture – Whether goods over which councils sought to levy distress
remained goods of the company after receivers appointed and charge crystallised.

C
This was a summons by administrative receivers seeking the court's decision on the question whether the crystallisation of a floating charge on the receivers' appointment completed the assignment of the company's goods covered by the floating charge to the debenture holder with the consequence that such goods were no longer 'goods of' the company against which the local authority could levy distress for non-domestic rates.

The company was the subject of liability orders for non-domestic rates made in favour of local authorities. Bailiffs attempted to levy distress but receivers were appointed by the bank as debenture holder and the question whether the goods over which the councils sought to levy distress were goods of the company once the receivers were appointed was referred to the court.

D

The receivers accepted that goods owned by a company subject to a floating charge which had not crystallised were 'goods of' the company against which distress could be levied. Once the floating charge had crystallised the goods ceased to be goods of the company because crystallisation completed the assignment of title to the chargee which was made when the debenture was created. The receivers relied on the decision of the Court of Appeal in Re Roundwood Colliery Co [1897] 1 Ch 373 that chattels over which distress had been levied remained chattels 'belonging to' lessees at the time of the distress where the charge in favour of the debenture holder was a floating charge which had not crystallised at the relevant time; the implication being that if the floating charge had crystallised when the distress was levied, the chattels would no longer have been chattels belonging to the lessees.

E

F
However, in Re Marriage Neave & Co [1896] 2 Ch 663 the Court of Appeal allowed a distress for unpaid rates to be levied notwithstanding the existence of a charge in favour of debenture holders and the appointment of receivers. It was said that an equitable charge did not prevent the goods subject to the charge from being goods of the company.

Held, declaring that the crystallisation of the bank's floating charge completed the assignment of the goods of the company effected by the floating charge contained in the debenture; consequently such goods were thereafter no longer the goods of the company for the purpose of the regulations relating to non-domestic rating:

G

1. The charge in the present case arose under a formal debenture executed under seal, there was an express power to appoint a receiver without any application to the court, and a receiver who was an administrative receiver was expressly given the powers specified in Sch. 1 to the Insolvency Act 1986, including the power to take possession of and sell the assets charged. Once the charge had crystallised the goods over which the councils sought to levy distress did not remain the property of the company. Re Marriage Neave & Co [1896] 2 Ch 663 applied only to a mere charge which did not operate by way of assignment and which conferred no power, without the assistance of the court, to appoint a receiver, take possession or sell.

H

2. If, however, Marriage Neave was not to be confined in that way, then it was in conflict with the reasoning in later decisions of the Court of Appeal in Re Roundwood Colliery Co

[1897] 1 Ch 373, N W Robbie & Co Ltd v Witney Warehouse Co Ltd [1963] 1 WLR 1324   A
and George Barker (Transport) Ltd v Eynon [1974] 1 WLR 462 which the court would
follow in preference to Marriage Neave.

3. It was not necessary to decide a subsidiary argument that if distress could be levied
notwithstanding the appointment of a receiver the practical result would be that, to the
extent of the value of goods distrained, a charging authority could obtain preference even
over preferential debts, and that, accordingly, s. 40 of the Insolvency Act 1986 should be   B
treated as having impliedly excluded the levying of distress after the appointment of a
receiver under a floating charge.

The following cases were referred to in the judgment:

Adolphe Crosbie Ltd, Re (1910) 74 JP 25.
Barker (George) (Transport) Ltd v Eynon [1974] 1 WLR 462.
Biggerstaff v Rowatt's Wharf Ltd [1896] 2 Ch 93.   C
Carreras Rothmans Ltd v Freeman Mathews Treasure Ltd & Anor (1984) 1 BCC 99,210;
[1985] Ch 207.
French's Wine Bar Ltd, Re (1987) 3 BCC 173.
Marriage Neave & Co, Re [1896] 2 Ch 663.
Metropolitan Life Assurance Co of NZ Ltd v Essere Print Ltd (1990) 5 NZCLC 66,775;
(1990) 5 NZCLC 67,115 (CA).
National Mutual Life Nominees Ltd & Ors v National Capital Development Commission   D
& Ors (1975) 37 FLR 404.
Robbie (N W) & Co Ltd v Witney Warehouse Co Ltd [1963] 1 WLR 1324.
Roundwood Colliery Co, Re [1897] 1 Ch 373.
Taggs Island Casino Hotel Ltd v Richmond upon Thames BC [1967] RA 70.

Gabriel Moss QC and Peter Havey (instructed by Addleshaw Sons & Latham,
Manchester) for the applicants.   E

Christopher Brougham QC and Lexa Hilliard (instructed by Luton Borough Council
and Wrekin District Council solicitors) for the respondents.

JUDGMENT

Ferris J: Can a local authority having a power of distress in order to recover business
rates exercise that power over the goods of a company which are subject to a floating   F
charge after that floating charge has crystallised? This case has been brought in order to
determine the answer to that question.

The facts are agreed and are set out in an agreed statement. It is not necessary for me
to set out the whole of that statement in this judgment. It will suffice to summarise the
salient facts as follows:

(1)   At all material times ELS Ltd, formerly English Lifestyle Ltd, carried on the
       business of retailing furniture from premises in the districts for which Luton   G
       Borough Council and Wrekin District Council are respectively the local
       authorities.

(2)   Each of these authorities is the charging authority in relation to non-domestic rates
       in its area.

(3)   By a debenture dated 15 October 1990 ELS created in favour of National
       Westminster Bank Ltd ('the bank') charges over all its assets including a charge by   H
       way of floating security over its undertaking and all its property not charged by
       way of specific charge. The debenture was to secure all money covenanted to be
       paid by ELS to the bank.

(4)   Clause 8 of the debenture conferred an express power to appoint a receiver who, if
       appointed as an administrative receiver within the meaning of the *Insolvency Act*

A   1986, was to have all the powers of an administrative receiver specified in Sch. 1 to the Act. These include power to take possession of and to sell the property of ELS.

(5)   On 14 February 1992 the bank appointed the applicants, Philip Ramsbottom and Alan Athol Elmslie Benzie ('the receivers'), to be joint administrative receivers under the debenture.

(6)   On 19 September 1991, on the application of Luton District Council, the South Bedfordshire magistrates' court made a liability order against ELS in the sum of £191,644.48 in respect of unpaid non-domestic rates. Before the appointment of the receivers ELS made payments which reduced the amount due to Luton District Council to £151,644.48. After the appointment of the receivers bailiffs appointed by Luton District Council endeavoured to levy a distress over property of ELS at its premises in that council's district in respect of this unpaid liability, but they were restrained by injunctions from continuing to levy such distress.

(7)   On 17 March 1992 Telford magistrates' court made a liability order against ELS in the sum of £65,654.61 in respect of unpaid non-domestic rates. In late March 1992 bailiffs acting for Wrekin District Council endeavoured to levy a distress over property of ELS at its premises in that council's district. The completion of such distress has been suspended by agreement pending the determination of the point of principle which is at issue in this case.

(8)   For the purpose of this application it is agreed that the court should proceed on the assumption that the goods over which the two councils have respectively sought to levy distress were, until the appointment of the receivers, goods owned by and belonging to ELS.

In contrast to the right of a landlord to levy distress for unpaid rent, which is a common law right, the right of an authority to levy distress in respect of unpaid rates is entirely statutory. By the *Poor Relief Act* 1606 (43 Eliz 1 c. 2) provision was made for the churchwardens and overseers of the poor of every parish to levy and assess a rate for certain prescribed statutory purposes. By s. IV of the Act, so far as it is material, it was provided that it should be lawful for the churchwardens and overseers to levy the sums due:

'from every one that shall refuse to contribute according as they shall be assessed, by Distress and Sale of the Offender's Goods.'

In default of such distress the non-payer was liable to be committed to prison by the justices. No power was given to sue for unpaid rates in debt.

The legislation has, of course, changed from time to time over the years and the reference to a non-payer as 'the offender' has been dropped. But throughout successive enactments the goods in respect of which distress may be levied have been defined, in one way or another, as the non-payer's goods. The current provisions are contained in Pt. III of the *Non-Domestic Rating (Collection and Enforcement) (Local Lists) Regulations* 1989 (SI 1989/1058). The procedure can be summarised as follows:

(1)   A billing authority must, before taking other enforcement steps, serve a reminder notice on the ratepayer.

(2)   If the relevant rates remain wholly or partly unpaid seven days after a reminder notice has been served the billing authority may apply to a magistrates' court for a liability order.

(3)   By reg. 14(1), which is the material provision for present purposes:

'Where a liability order has been made, the authority which applied for the order may levy the appropriate amount by distress and sale of the goods of the debtor against whom the order was made.'

It will be noted that the relevant words are 'the goods of the debtor'.

(4)   Provision is made for committal to prison (reg. 14); for a creditor's petition in   A
bankruptcy or for a winding-up order on the basis that the amount due under an
unsatisfied liability order is a debt (reg. 18); and for recovery by means of a money
judgment obtained from an appropriate court (reg. 20). Committal is available
only when distress has been attempted and has been unsuccessful. The insolvency
remedies and the ability to seek a money judgment are available whether or not
distress has been attempted.

B

There is one further part of statute law which it is convenient to deal with at this stage.
Under s. 32 of the *Bankruptcy Act* 1869, rates due within 12 months next before a
bankruptcy were (together with certain other debts) made preferential debts in the
bankruptcy. The bankruptcy rule was applied to company liquidations by the *Supreme
Court of Judicature Act* 1873. Preference for one year's rates was reaffirmed by s. 1 of the
Preferential Payments in Bankruptcy Act 1888. A similar principle was applied in the case
of receiverships arising pursuant to a floating charge by the *Preferential Payments in*   C
Bankruptcy Amendment Act 1897. It is not necessary to trace the development of the
legislation in full. The preference was retained in a winding up by s. 319 of the *Companies
Act* 1948 and in receivership under a floating charge by s. 94. This situation was changed
when the *Insolvency Act* 1986 came into force. Although, under s. 40 of that Act, a
receiver appointed under debentures secured by a charge which, as created, was a floating
charge remains liable to pay the company's preferential debts in priority to the principal   D
and interest in respect of debentures, preferential debts, which are defined in s. 386 and
Sch. 6, no longer include rates. The existence of a preference in respect of the rates until
1986 and its abolition in that year may provide a partial explanation why the extent of
the power of distress for rates has not been the subject of litigation during this century
although, as will be seen, there were a number of decisions in this field in the 1890s. While
unpaid rates were preferential there may have been little reason for the remedy of distress
to be resorted to in the case of insolvent companies.   E

The originating summons in this case seeks the decision of the court on the question:

'Whether the crystallisation of a floating charge upon the appointment of
administrative receivers completes the assignment of the goods of the company
covered by a floating charge to the debenture holder with the consequence that
such goods are no longer "goods of" the company for the purposes of reg. 14(1) of
the *Non-Domestic Rating (Collection and Enforcement) (Local Lists) Regulations*   F
1989 (SI 1989/1058).'

There is a second substantive question which I will come to later.

The receivers accept that where goods owned by a company are subject to a floating
charge which has not crystallised they are 'goods of the company'. Thus where the
company is a debtor against which a liability order has been made, those goods are
'goods of the debtor' for the purposes of reg. 14(1) and distress can be levied. The   G
receivers argue, however, that once the floating charge has crystallised, whether by the
appointment of administrative receivers or for any other cause, the goods cease to be
'goods of the debtor' because crystallisation completes the assignment of title to the
chargee which was made when the debenture was created.

The difference between the operation of a charge created as a floating charge before
crystallisation and its operation after crystallisation has been recognised for 100 years, if   H
not longer (see the reasoning in *Biggerstaff v Rowatt's Wharf Ltd* [1896] 2 Ch 93). In *N
W Robbie & Co Ltd v Witney Warehouse Co Ltd* [1963] 1 WLR 1324 it was considered in
relation to a claim that a debtor of a company in receivership could set off against the
debt owed by it to the company a debt owed by the company which had been assigned to
it after the commencement of the receivership. One issue in the case was whether a sum
which had become due to the company from the debtor during the receivership fell to be

A   treated in the same way as a debt due from the debtor prior to the receivership. A majority of the Court of Appeal (Sellers and Russell L JJ, Donovan LJ dissenting) held that it did. In respect of these combined debts Russell LJ said (at p. 1338):

> 'It was next argued that if the charge in favour of the debenture-holder existed on such future assets, it was really of the same quality as a floating charge, since the debenture-holder, by procuring the agreement of the company that the receiver
B   and manager should be agent for the company, permitted the company to continue to trade through its agent without immediate regard to the debenture charge; therefore, it was argued, such charge no more precluded set-off than did the original charge while floating, as to which see the *Biggerstaff* case. I confess that I do not find this argument easy to follow. Why does it not apply equally to the charge upon the assets existing at the time of the appointment? And what then is meant by crystallisation of a floating charge in such a case? I venture to think that
C   in rejecting this argument I would have the whole-hearted support of the members of this court who decided the *Biggerstaff* case and who were at such pains to point out the radical difference produced by crystallisation.

> Thus far, in my judgment, by force of the debenture charge an equitable charge attached in favour of the debenture-holders not only on the £95 debt existing at the date of the appointment of the receiver and manager, but also upon the other
D   debts constituting the total of £1,346 as they came into existence on delivery of goods to the defendants after such appointment. These choses in action belonging to the company became thus assigned in equity to the debenture-holders, at times when the defendants had no cross-claim of any kind against the company and consequently no right of set-off. Before the defendants acquired by assignment this cross-claim the defendants must be fixed with knowledge of this equitable assignment to the debenture-holders (by way of charge) of the debt owed by the
E   defendants to the company. A debtor cannot set off his claim against X against a claim by X against him which the debtor knows has been assigned by X to Y before the debtor's claims arose. Just as an assignee of a chose in action takes subject to an already existing right of set-off, so a debtor with no existing right of set-off cannot assert set-off of a cross-claim which he first acquires after he has notice of the assignment of the claim against him: here, for instance, no part of the
F   £852 could have been set off against the £95.'

This accords with the reasoning of Sellers LJ.

   In *George Barker (Transport) Ltd v Eynon* [1974] 1 WLR 462 the point arose in relation to a lien. In that case a road haulage company was owed money for haulage by a meat importing company which had charged all its goods to its bank by way of floating security. The road haulage company asserted a general lien over goods transported after
G   the appointment of a receiver under the debenture in respect of money which had become due to it before the appointment of the receiver. The precise reasoning by which this claim was resolved is not relevant for present purposes but in the Court of Appeal there were some observations as to the effect of a floating charge and its crystallisation. Edmund Davies LJ said (at p. 467E):

> 'A floating charge is ambulatory and hovers over the property until some event occurs which causes it to settle and crystallise into a specific charge . . . One of the
H   events which causes crystallisation is the appointment of a receiver, which, as we know, occurred in the present case on August 31, 1971. . .

> One consequence of the receiver's appointment by the debenture holders was that the incomplete assignment constituted by the 1970 deed became converted into a completed equitable assignment to them of the assets charged and of the company's rights . . .'

Stamp LJ said (at p. 471):   A

'. . . the appointment of a receiver operates as an equitable assignment (by way of charge) of the property of the company to the debenture holder . . . and so in this case operated as an equitable assignment (by way of charge) of (a) the company's property in the goods, and (b) the company's rights under the contract of carriage.'

Sir Gordon Willmer observed (at p. 475B) that:

'Upon the appointment of the defendant as receiver the rights of the debenture   B holders crystallised, and they became equitable assignees of the rights of the company.'

Similar reasoning, applying the English authorities, is to be found in Australia in *National Mutual v National Capital Development Commission* [1975] 37 FLR 404 at pp. 408–410 and in New Zealand in *Metropolitan Life Assurance v Essere Print Ltd* (1990) 5 NZCLC 66, 775. (There was an appeal in the last mentioned case and the decision at first   C instance was upheld, but without reference to the principle with which I am concerned.)

The importance of whether a floating charge has or has not crystallised has been recognised in relation to distress in *Re Roundwood Colliery Co* [1897] 1 Ch 373. In that case a mining company was lessee of two adjoining coal mines, A and B. There was no shaft on mine B, both mines being worked by the shaft on mine A. In both leases the landlord reserved a right of distress, not only upon chattels upon the demised premises   D but also upon chattels 'belonging to the lessees' in or about adjoining or neighbouring collieries. The landlord of mine B levied a distress upon chattels on mine A. The proceedings were brought to determine the validity of this distress. At first instance the case was decided against the landlord on a point under the Bills of Sale Acts on which the Court of Appeal reversed the judge. The Court of Appeal had then to determine whether the distress was good against the debenture holders of the mining company. It   E was held that the distress, having been levied before the commencement of the winding up and before a receiver was appointed by the debenture holders, was valid against the debenture holders.

Lindley LJ said (at p. 393):

'This ground [i.e. the Bills of Sale Acts point] being, in my opinion, erroneous, it becomes necessary to consider the respective rights of the landlord and of the   F debenture-holders to the goods seized. These rights depend upon the question whether the landlord distrained while the debentures were still a floating security, or whether the debentures are to be regarded as having definitively attached to the goods seized, so that, as between the landlord and the debenture-holders, those goods had become the property of the latter before the landlord seized them.

It is not contended that the landlord could distrain off the property on goods which were not the goods of the company, both at law and in equity. The debenture-   G holders contend that the goods seized were not the goods of the company, except subject to the equitable charge created by the debentures. As between the debenture-holders and the company this proposition is true; but it does not decide the respective rights of the lessor and the debenture-holders, which is what we have to consider. The goods seized by the lessor were seized under a power conferred either before the debentures were issued or whilst they were clearly a floating   H security, and in either case that power could be exercised before the debentures ceased to be floating securities. They did not cease to be so before the distress was put in. The winding-up did not commence until after that date, nor was any effectual order for a receiver made until after the same date. The order of October 7 was never really effective. It was never drawn up, the lessor had no notice of it, and before the receiver could take possession he had to give security. The distress,

A   having been made before the commencement of the winding-up of the company, and before a receiver was effectively appointed, was, in my opinion, valid as against the debenture-holders.'

The other two members of the Court of Appeal (A L Smith LJ and Rigby LJ) agreed.

The decision in *Roundwood* is relied upon by Mr Moss, on behalf of the receivers, as being, in substance, the converse of the present case. The decision of the Court of Appeal

B   in favour of the landlord was that the chattels over which distress had been levied remained chattels 'belonging to the lessees' at the time of the distress. The reason why this was so was that the charge in favour of the debenture holder was a floating charge which had not crystallised at the relevant time. The clear implication of the passage cited from Lindley LJ is that, if the floating charge had crystallised when the distress was levied, the chattels would no longer have been chattels 'belonging to the lessees' and the distress would have been held to be bad. The present case, it was argued, is precisely

C   covered by this implication.

However another case in the Court of Appeal, decided some six months earlier by a court of which Lindley and Rigby L JJ were both members, is said to stand in the way of this conclusion. The case is *Re Marriage Neave & Co* [1896] 2 Ch 663. There, on the face of it, the Court of Appeal allowed a distress for unpaid rates to be levied notwithstanding the existence of a charge in favour of debenture holders, the appointment of receivers on

D   behalf of those debenture holders and a resolution for the voluntary winding-up of the company. In order to see whether this is indeed the effect of the decision it is necessary to consider the facts, arguments and judgments in that case in some detail.

In *Marriage Neave* the company had, on 30 June 1890, executed two debenture trust deeds to secure issues of first and second mortgage debentures respectively. Each deed constituted a floating security. The report then goes on to state (at p. 664) that:

E   'The company, by each debenture, charged with the payment of the principal sum and interest thereby secured "all its property whatsoever and wheresoever, both present and future, not comprised in or subject to the trusts of or effectually charged by" the trust deed.'

It appears, therefore, that there were potentially three different assignments or charges to be considered, namely (1) that contained in the first mortgage debenture trust deed; (2) that contained in the second mortgage debenture trust deed; and (3) that contained in the

F   debentures. In 1896 the company became insolvent. On 6 February 1896 receivers and managers were appointed under the second mortgage debenture trust deed; on 17 February 1896, in a debenture holders action brought by the first mortgage debenture holders, the court appointed the same persons to be receivers and managers under the first mortgage debenture; and on 19 February 1896 the company passed an extraordinary resolution to wind up, one of the receivers and managers being appointed liquidator. On

G   12 November rates for the half year which was to end on 25 March 1896 had been demanded of the company and, when these remained unpaid, steps were taken to enforce payment. On 2 March 1896 a distress warrant for the unpaid rates was issued by the justices. It was accepted that, in view of the existence of court appointed receivers and managers, distress could not be levied without the leave of the court. Such leave was sought by a summons which came before Kekewich J.

H   The argument presented to Kekewich J appears to have been that a 'change of occupation' for the purposes of the relevant rating legislation had taken place when receivers and managers were appointed by the court on 17 February. Kekewich J upheld this argument, with the consequence that rates could not be levied after that date in respect of rates which became due partly before and partly after that date. The receivers and managers subsequently paid the part of the rates which was apportioned to the period after the commencement of the receivership. An appeal was brought to determine whether the power of distress could be exercised after that time in order to recover rates due for the period preceding that time.

The first argument on behalf of the first debenture holders was that, notwithstanding the subsequent reversal of an authority on which Kekewich J had relied, there was indeed a change of occupation when the receivers and managers were appointed by the court. This argument, which failed, need not be explored further. The second argument, which is relevant for present purposes, was that the goods over which it was sought to levy the distress were not the goods of the company but the goods of the debenture holders, by reason of the assignment contained in the first mortgage debenture trust deed or the charges contained in the debentures. As reported, it appears that the argument was that the assignment or the charges by themselves caused the goods to cease to be the goods of the company, no reliance being placed upon the crystallisation of the floating charge which had been created by the first mortgage debenture trust deed.

In his judgment Lindley LJ dealt first with the change of occupation point, holding that there had been no change of occupation. He went on, at p. 672:

'The next point is this. These rates can only be distrained for upon goods of the person assessed and who has made default; that is the "offender", I agree. The "offender" here is the company. The company is assessed; the company has made default; and the only goods which can be taken under the distress warrant are the goods of the company. Then, are there any goods of the company on these premises which are liable to distraint? It is said, No. It is said, first of all, that the goods belong in point of law to the trustees for the debenture-holders. That turns upon the true construction of the trust deed . . .'

He then considered the first mortgage debenture trust deed and concluded that it was not in terms which caused the goods to pass to the trustees for the debenture holders. Then he said (at p. 673):

'The next point is this. The debentures appear to be expressed in language so large as to include the goods of the company, although the trust deed does not, but their only effect is to give the debenture-holders an equitable charge upon these goods. That is all the debenture-holders want. They do not require to take possession, and they have no right even to take possession. Their only right is to institute an action and get a receiver appointed. The goods are not theirs: they are the goods of the company, subject to the equitable charge created by the debentures.'

Lindley LJ then considered the duties of the bailiff in respect of the proceeds of sale of the goods distrained and concluded (at p. 674) that the bailiff's duty,

'does, in effect, give these rates priority with regard to the proceeds of the goods when seized and sold under that distress.'

The second member of the court, Lopes LJ, dealt similarly with the change of occupation point. He dealt with the effect of the trust deed and the debentures as follows (at pp. 675–676):

'Then it is said that these goods which it is sought to seize were not the goods of the company – that they passed under a certain deed of trust. When that trust deed is examined, it appears that these goods were excepted, and did not pass under the deed at all: they cannot, therefore, be said to belong to the debenture-holders. The position with regard to the goods is really this, that they belong to the company subject to an equitable charge in favour of the debenture-holders.

A Then another question was raised as to the effect of the equitable charge. It was said that these goods have been subjected to this equitable charge of the debenture-holders, and that therefore no distress can be issued against them or is enforceable against them. . . . I am conversant with the practice as to enforcing the payment of rates such as these, and I never heard of this point being raised before. However, when the point is looked into, it really comes to this, that there is a preferential charge in favour of rates – that rates are to be paid in preference to any equitable

B charge such as this. What leads me to that conclusion is, amongst other things, this, that there is power given by statute to distrain for rates, and no action can be brought to recover them.'

Rigby LJ, the third member of the court, agreed with the others as to change of occupation. On the other main point he said this (at pp. 677–678):

C 'I have nothing to add respecting the construction of the debenture trust deed, which to my mind did not carry the goods and chattels; but there is a charge given by the debentures. Does that prevent the goods from being the goods of marriage Neave & Co? I apprehend not. Putting aside the Bills of Sale Act, and, considering the state of the law before any Bills of Sale Act was passed, can it be said that because a man writes on a piece of paper, "I charge my household furniture with the payment of £1 in favour of So-and-So", that the man is thereby securing

D himself practically from the payment of rates? The argument put forward virtually goes as far as that, for the contention is that furniture so charged becomes the property of the person in whose favour the charge is made, and that it cannot be seized by way of distress. I think that the construction of the statute is really this, that the overseers take the goods of the "offender" as they find them, that they must distrain and sell, and pay the rates first. When they have paid the rates, I

E apprehend that they may be called upon in a proper way to account for the surplus, it may be to the equitable mortgagee, if any, or if there is no equitable mortgagee, then to the owner of the goods. They have to pay the rates, and that practically gives them a preferential charge on the goods.'

These extensive quotations from the judgments in *Marriage Neave* demonstrate, to my mind, two points. First they seem to confirm what appears from the report of the

F argument that what was being contended on behalf of the debenture holders was that it was the charge itself, as executed in 1890, which had caused the goods to cease to be the goods of the company, not the events of 1896. Secondly, going hand in hand with the first point, there is nothing in any of the judgments to suggest that crystallisation of a floating charge had anything to do with the case.

Marriage Neave, apart from being referred to in argument in *Roundwood*, has been

G followed in one reported case, namely *Re Adolphe Crosbie Ltd* (1910) 74 JP 25. There the relevant power of distress arose under the *Gasworks Clauses Act* 1871. The relevant charge was undoubtedly created as a floating charge and had crystallised on the appointment of receivers before there was any distress. Neville J held that the case was covered by *Marriage Neave*, but added no reasoning of his own.

Mr Brougham, on behalf of Luton and Wrekin, accepted that the decision in *Marriage*

H *Neave* did not depend in any way on crystallisation. He argued that what *Marriage Neave* establishes is not the proposition that crystallisation of a floating charge over goods makes no difference to liability to distress but the wider proposition that an equitable charge over a company's goods does not cause them to cease to be 'goods of the company' for the purposes of the law of distress in respect of unpaid rates. As a charge over goods to be acquired after the date of the charge must, of necessity, be only an equitable not a legal charge this would mean that few, if any, debentures created in the usual form could

A

ever cause goods to cease to be the goods of the company until such goods are actually   A
sold to a third party.

Mr Brougham argued that expressions such as 'goods of the debtor', 'chattels of any
person' or 'the company's property' are not terms of art which have an invariable or even
a prima facie legal meaning. Thus in the New Zealand case of *Metropolitan Life v Essere
Print* the New Zealand Court of Appeal had regarded as finely balanced the question
whether a statutory limitation precluding the levying of distress by a landlord on any   B
chattels save those of the tenant required that, in order to be liable to distraint, the goods
must belong to the tenant in equity as well as law. (The actual decision of the court was
that where both the tenant and a debenture holder under a debenture created by the
tenant had substantial interests in the chattel, it was not the chattel of the tenant for the
purpose of the statute.) In *Re French's Wine Bar Ltd* (1987) 3 BCC 173 there was serious
argument whether property which, at the time when a company went into liquidation,
was subject to a contract of sale which could be enforced by specific performance was   C
'the company's property' for the purposes of s. 522 of the *Companies Act* 1985. Vinelott
J held that it was not, so that the completion of the contract after the commencement of
the winding up did not require validation under the section (now s. 127 of the *Insolvency
Act* 1986).

Mr Brougham sought to obtain some assistance from a passage in the judgment of
Peter Gibson J in *Carreras Rothmans Ltd v Freeman Mathews Treasure Ltd & Anor*   D
(1984) 1 BCC 99,210. One of the issues in that case was whether a particular agreement
created a charge on the book debts of a company which was registrable under s. 95 of the
Companies Act 1948. At p. 99,222 Peter Gibson J said:

> '"Charge" is not defined for the purpose of s. 95 (save to extend its meaning to
> include a mortgage) and so must, in the absence of any indication to the contrary
> (and none is suggested), bear its ordinary meaning. The type of charge which it is   E
> said was created is an equitable charge. Such a charge is created by an
> appropriation of specific property to the discharge of some debt or other obligation
> without there being any change in ownership either at law or in equity, and it
> confers on the chargee rights to apply to the court for an order for sale or for the
> appointment of a receiver, but no right to foreclosure (so as to make the property
> his own) or take possession . . .'

F

As I understood the argument, it was that an equitable charge over chattels, including
the charge under consideration in *Marriage Neave* and the charge created by the
debenture in this case, was of this character. However I cannot accept, if it was intended
so to suggest, that the description of Peter Gibson J is to be taken to apply to every case
in which a charge operates in equity, so making the term 'equitable charge' appropriate.
It will be recollected that in the present case the charge arises under a formal debenture
executed under seal, there is an express power to appoint a receiver without any   G
application to the court, and a receiver who is an administrative receiver is expressly
given the powers specified in Sch. 1 to the *Insolvency Act* 1986, including the power to
take possession of and sell the assets charged.

I do not find *Marriage Neave* a particularly easy case to understand. On the language
used by all the members of the court it does seem that what was being said was that a
mere equitable charge did not prevent the goods subject to the charge from being 'goods   H
of the company'. But if that were so as a general proposition it is difficult to see why,
some six months later, a division of the Court of Appeal which included two of those
who had decided *Marriage Neave* gave the reasons which were given for the decision in
Roundwood. The actual decision in *Roundwood*, like that in *Marriage Neave*, was in
favour of the distress. But if the fact that the debenture holders were only equitable
assignees was sufficient to prevent them from challenging the distress it is difficult to see

A   why Lindley LJ and Rigby LJ did not simply refer to their earlier judgments in *Marriage Neave* and say that this was sufficient to dispose of the appeal in *Roundwood*. If *Marriage Neave* had decided what Mr Brougham contended that it decided it is surprising, to say the least, that Lindley LJ should have said in *Roundwood* at p. 393 that the rights of the landlords and the debenture holders to the goods seized,

B   'depend upon the question whether the landlord distrained while the debentures were still a floating security, or whether the debentures are to be regarded as having definitively attached to the goods seized, so that, as between the landlord and the debenture-holders, those goods had become the property of the latter before the landlord seized them.'

Indeed the way in which the court dealt with the argument on the debenture trust deed in *Marriage Neave* is somewhat surprising if Mr Brougham is correct. It would have been different if the debenture trust deed had carried the chattels. But if Mr Brougham is right

C   the result would have been the same, because the debenture trust deed created only an equitable charge.

Mr Brougham's argument concerning the scope of the decision in *Marriage Neave* is also, to my mind, impossible to reconcile with what has been said about the effect of the crystallisation of a floating charge in *Biggerstaff v Rowatt's Wharf* (to which Lindley LJ was a party); or in the passages from the *Robbie* and *George Barker* cases which I have

D   quoted above. This argument would also lead to the conclusion that the abolition of preferential status for unpaid rates which was brought about by the passing of the *Insolvency Act* 1986 was to a large extent irrelevant because, by resorting to the remedy of distress, an authority entitled to receive rates can establish a de facto preference ranking above that accorded to debts which remain preferential.

I cannot accept that what was said in *Marriage Neave* applies to every type of equitable charge, whatever the formality of its creation, whether or not effected by means of an

E   assignment or created as a floating charge and, if created as a floating charge, whether or not it has crystallised. In my judgment the decision applies only to a mere charge which does not operate by way of assignment and which, like the type of charge described by Peter Gibson J in the *Carreras* case, confers no power, without the assistance of the court, to appoint a receiver, take possession or sell. This view of the decision would, I think, avoid conflict between *Marriage Neave* and *Roundwood* and with the description of the

F   effect of crystallisation in the other case I have cited. Viewed in this way the decision lends no support to the argument that in the present case the goods over which Luton and Wrekin seek to levy distress remain the property of ELS notwithstanding crystallisation of the floating charge.

If, however, *Marriage Neave* is not to be confined in this way then it is, in my view, in conflict with the reasoning in the later decisions in *Roundwood*, *Robbie* and *George*

G   *Barker*. These are all decisions of the Court of Appeal and I am, I think, entitled to follow them in preference to *Marriage Neave*.

I therefore answer the question posed by para. 1 of the originating summons by declaring that the crystallisation of the bank's floating charge in this case completed the assignment of the goods of ELS effected by the floating charge contained in the debenture dated 15 October 1990, with the consequence that such goods were thereafter no longer the goods of ELS for the purpose of reg. 14 of the regulations referred to. So expressed

H   the declaration relates to this particular case rather than following the generalised proposition put forward in the originating summons, but in my view that is as far as I ought to go.

Paragraph 2 of the originating summons raises a separate question, albeit one designed to arrive at the resolution of the same point of substance as the first. In its original form the paragraph sought the determination of the question:

'Whether administrative receivers appointed under a floating charge who have a   A
statutory duty to pay preferential creditors are entitled in principle to an injunction
to restrain the levy of distress for non-domestic rates by a charging authority which
would have the effect of giving the charging authority levying distress priority over
preferential creditors of the company.'

After I had expressed some concern about the court being asked to declare that a party
is 'entitled in principle to an injunction' Mr Moss formulated a different question, which   B
I gave the applicants leave to add to the originating summons by amendment. This
question is in the following terms:

'Whether administrative receivers appointed under a floating charge who have a
statutory duty pursuant to s. 40 of the *Insolvency Act* 1986 to pay preferential
creditors are entitled to a declaration that a charging authority is not entitled to
levy distress for non-domestic rates pursuant to reg. 14(1) of the *Non-Domestic
Rating (Collection and Enforcement) (Local Lists) Regulations* 1989 (SI 1989/1058)   C
unless and until all preferential debts (within the meaning given to that expression
by s. 386 of the *Insolvency Act* 1986) have been paid out of the assets coming to the
hands of the administrative receivers.'

Both the original and the amended question sought, so far as the applicants are
concerned, to take advantage of the decision of Ungoed-Thomas J in *Taggs Island Casino
Hotel Ltd v Richmond upon Thames BC* [1967] RA 70. In that case a debenture holder   D
had appointed a receiver and manager under the debenture. After the appointment the
rating authority sought to levy a distraint over property on the company's premises in
respect of rates which had become due before the receiver and manager was appointed.
An application was then made to the court for an interlocutory injunction to restrain
completion of the proved distress. Much of the argument was concerned with the
question of occupation, which the judge held to be largely irrelevant. There was, however,
an alternative argument which was that s. 94 and 319(1) of the *Companies Act* 1948,   E
whose effect was to require the receiver to pay certain rates and taxes as preferential
debts, was inconsistent with the existence of a power of distress. On this Ungoed-Thomas
J referred to the relevant sections and continued, at pp. 80–81:

'It therefore appears to me prima facie to follow that, when provision is made as it
is under s. 94 for the application of assets in the receiver's hands, none of the
persons in whose favour those assets are to be administered can levy distress and,   F
in effect, obtain priority over other creditors, who, according to the Act, are to
rank pari passu with the creditor levying the distress. It may be that it is so, but it
seems to me to be a matter which requires the consideration and investigation
which is proper for the trial of the action. This consideration appears to me to
govern quite a number of arguments and submissions which were made to me with
regard to the receiver's liability to pay these rates and the consequential, so it was
said, liability of the goods in his hands to be available for distress. These were   G
powerful considerations submitted on behalf of the rating authority, but, as I have
indicated, there appeared to me to be powerful considerations on the other side
too.'

Ungoed-Thomas J then turned to the balance of convenience and, finding this to be in
favour of restraining the distress, granted an injunction until trial.

Clearly Ungoed-Thomas J did not himself decide the point at the interlocutory stage   H
in that case and there is no record of the matter ever having gone to trial. The precise
argument which was presented then is no longer available since the abolition of
preference for rates. Nevertheless it was submitted by Mr Moss that the essential point is
still a good one, if not indeed now reinforced. Whereas at the time of the decision in
Taggs Island the law was that one year's rates were to be paid pari passu with certain

A   taxes and other specified debts and in preference to the debt due to the debenture holder, the law is now that rates no longer have any preference. If, however, distress can be levied notwithstanding the appointment of a receiver the practical result is that, to the extent of the value of goods distrained, a charging authority can obtain preference even over preferential debts. This, argued Mr Moss, cannot be the law. Section 40 of the *Insolvency Act* 1986, like s. 94 of the *Companies Act* 1948, should therefore be treated as having impliedly excluded the levying of distress after the appointment of a receiver under a floating charge.

B

This argument certainly has some attraction, but I am not wholly convinced by it. If I am right in my conclusion on the arguments under question 1 of the originating summons there is no need to uphold this alternative argument as a means of avoiding conflict with the statutory provisions as to priority. In any event it is an argument which, if correct, benefits only the preferential creditors, not the bank as debenture holder. In all the circumstances I do not propose to answer either of the questions raised by para. 2 of the originating summons.

C

(*Order accordingly*)

D

E

F

G

H

Re Bank of Credit and Commerce International SA (No. 3).   A

Chancery Division (Companies Court).
Rattee J.
Judgment delivered 9 March 1994.

> *Liquidation – Set-off – Loans by bank to principal debtors secured by third party*
> *deposits with bank – Bank went into liquidation – Whether liquidators only*   B
> *entitled to recover from principal debtors so much of loans as exceeded deposits –*
> *Whether security documents imposed personal liability on depositors – Whether*
> *liquidators had to realise security and give credit for it – Whether deposits*
> *impressed with specific purpose trust – Whether unconscionable for liquidators to*
> *insist on full legal rights.*

This was an application by the liquidators of Bank of Credit and Commerce International   C
SA ('the bank') for determination of the question whether the liquidators could recover the
whole of loans outstanding from principal debtors where repayment of the loans was secured
by purported charges over third party deposits with the bank.

The depositors contended that the liquidators were only entitled to recover from the
principal debtors so much of the outstanding loans as exceeded the amounts of the deposits
purportedly charged by depositors to secure those loans. The liquidators argued that they   D
were entitled to recover the whole of the outstanding loans from the principal debtors,
leaving the depositors to prove for their deposits in the liquidation of the bank.

A similar question arose in relation to other loans made by the bank in M S Fashions Ltd
and High Street Services Ltd v Bank of Credit and Commerce International SA [1993]
BCC 360, in which the Court of Appeal held that the effect of the security documents
executed by the depositors was to subject the depositors to personal liability to the bank for
the debts due from the principal debtors. There was therefore mutuality leading to set-off   E
under r. 4.90 of the Insolvency Rules 1986 such that the indebtedness of the principal debtors
was extinguished by the amount standing to the credit of the depositors' deposit accounts
with the bank.

The respondents submitted, first, that the effect of the security documents in this case was
to make the amount of the deposit a sum 'due from' the depositor as a result of mutual
dealings within r. 4.90 leading to the same result as in M S Fashions. The liquidators argued   F
that the security documents did not impose a personal liability on the depositors and that
therefore the reasoning in M S Fashions could not apply. An alternative submission by some
respondents (relying on dicta in Re Charge Card Services Ltd (1986) 2 BCC 99,373) was
that the attempt by the depositors to create security over their deposits in favour of the bank
was ineffective to create a charge in favour of the bank, but was effective to give a right of
set-off in the bank's liquidation in accordance with r. 4.90.   G

As a further alternative the respondents argued, on the basis that the security documents
did create charges in favour of the bank, that since the bank was not in a position to restore
to the depositors the right to repayment of their deposits in full, the bank had to give credit
for the full amount of those deposits on any claim against the principal debtors for
repayment of the loans secured by the security documents (on the principle in Ellis & Co's
Trustee v Dixon-Johnson [1925] Ch 489). The liquidators argued that the principle in Ellis   H
& Co's Trustee v Dixon-Johnson had no application because the bank was able to restore
the security taken by it from the depositors since that was not the cash paid to the bank by
the depositors, but the right to repayment. Furthermore, under the terms of the security
documents the bank was entitled to withhold repayment of the charged deposits until the
principal debtors had repaid their loans from the bank in full and since such repayment had
not been made the bank had never failed to comply with a valid demand for repayment of

A   the deposits. The liquidators remained entitled to elect whether to realise the security or to proceed against the principal debtors.

The respondents further argued that on the principle in Barclays Bank Ltd v Quistclose Investments Ltd [1970] AC 567 the deposits were provided to the bank specifically for the purpose of discharging the indebtedness. Finally the respondents argued that even if the liquidators were entitled to claim against the principal debtors in full with no set-off for the deposits, such claim would be so unmeritorious that the court should not authorise the

B   liquidators to pursue it.

Held, finding that nothing in the security documents or the Insolvency Act 1986 or the rules made thereunder affected the prima facie right of the liquidators to seek to recover from the principal debtors the full amount of their indebtedness:

1. The security documents did not have the effect of subjecting the depositors to any personal liability for the principal debts, and therefore did not make any part of the principal

C   debts 'due from' the depositors within the meaning of r. 4.90. (M S Fashions Ltd and High Street Services Ltd v Bank of Credit and Commerce International SA [1993] BCC 360 distinguished.)

2. The security documents did not impose any personal liability for the principal debts on the depositors, and the depositors were under no such liability aliunde. There was therefore nothing on which set-off could operate in accordance with r. 4.90.

D   3. Assuming (without deciding) that the security documents created charges on the deposits, the security provided by the depositors was their entitlement to the charged deposit, which remained intact notwithstanding that it was enforceable only by proof in the liquidation of the bank. There was nothing in the principle in Ellis & Co's Trustee v Dixon-Johnson [1925] AC 489 to compel the liquidators to realise the security rather than pursuing the principal debtors. Other arguments based on the proposition that the bank could not

E   restore the security unimpaired to the depositors were unsound for similar reasons.

4. The Quistclose argument was not supported by the security documents, which charged whatever credit balances might from time to time be standing to the credit of the depositors on accounts in the books of the bank. Neither in the security documents nor in any of the affidavit evidence sworn on behalf of the depositors was there any suggestion of payments made to the bank for the specific purpose of paying the indebtedness of the principal debtors.

F   5. The facts of the case did not come anywhere near the kind of facts to fall within the principle that the court would not direct liquidators to insist on their full legal rights where it would be unacceptable to do so.

The following cases were referred to in the judgment:

Barclays Bank Ltd v Quistclose Investments Ltd [1970] AC 567.
Charge Card Services Ltd, Re (1986) 2 BCC 99,373; [1987] Ch 150.

G   *Ellis & Co's Trustee v Dixon-Johnson* [1924] 2 Ch 451 (CA); [1925] AC 489 (HL).
Mackay, Ex parte. Re Jeavons (1873) LR 8 Ch App 643; LJ(NS) Bankruptcy 68.
Middleton v Pollock (1875) LR 20 Eq 515.
M S Fashions Ltd & High Street Services Ltd v Bank of Credit and Commerce International SA [1993] BCC 70; [1993] BCC 360, [1993] Ch 425 (CA).
Multi Guarantee Co Ltd, Re [1987] BCLC 257.
Stein v Blake [1993] BCC 587; [1994] Ch 16.

H   *Stephens, Ex parte* (1805) 11 Ves Jun 24; 32 ER 996.
Vulliamy & Anor v Noble & Ors (1817) 3 Mer 593; 36 ER 228.
Welsh Development Agency v Export Finance Co Ltd [1992] BCC 270.

Robin Dicker (instructed by Lovell White Durrant) for the liquidators.

John McDonnell QC and Jonathan Russen (instructed by Gagrat Gardi & Co) for the first respondents.

Christopher Carr QC and Michael Todd (instructed by Charles Russell) for the second   A
respondents.

JUDGMENT

Rattee J: The court is asked by the liquidators of bank of Credit and Commerce
International SA ('the bank') for directions in the following circumstances.

The bank lent money to a borrower company ('the principal debtor'). The repayment   B
of the loan was secured by inter alia a purported charge granted to the bank by a third
party ('the depositor') of a deposit or deposits made by the depositor with the bank.
Before the loan was repaid the bank went into liquidation.

The liquidators seek directions as to whether they should seek to recover the whole of
the outstanding loan from the principal debtor (leaving the depositor to prove in the
liquidation of the bank for the deposits purportedly charged to the bank) or only so
much of that loan as exceeds the amount of the deposits. The question arises in relation   C
to several loans made to several different principal debtors purportedly secured by
charges over deposits given by several different depositors.

There are two groups of respondents to this application before me. The first comprises
a principal debtor called Rayners Enterprises Inc and Mr Jessa, a depositor who
purported to charge deposits with the bank to secure loans to Rayners Enterprises Inc.
The second group comprises a group of principal debtors, to which I shall refer as 'the   D
agrichemicals group', and Société Générale de Gestion et Services SA, a depositor who
purported to charge deposits with the bank to secure loans to the agrichemicals group.

All the respondents contend that the liquidators are only entitled to recover from the
principal debtors so much of the outstanding loans as exceeds the amounts of the deposits
purportedly charged by depositors to secure those loans. Although the application is one
by the liquidators for directions, Mr Dicker, counsel for the liquidators, very properly   E
and helpfully put the contrary argument, to the effect that the liquidators are entitled to
recover the whole of the outstanding loans from the principal debtors, leaving the
depositors to prove for their deposits in the liquidation of the bank.

A similar question arising in relation to other loans made by the bank secured by
purported charges in its favour over deposits with it was considered by Hoffmann LJ
sitting as a judge of the Chancery Division and by the Court of Appeal in *M S Fashions*
Ltd v Bank of Credit and Commerce International SA [1993] BCC 360. Those proceedings   F
concerned loans made by the bank to three different companies, namely M S Fashions
Ltd, High Street Services Ltd and Impexbond Ltd. Hoffmann LJ ([1993] BCC 70) held,
in relation to the loans to all three companies, that the effect of the documents executed
by the depositors was that the indebtedness of the principal debtors was extinguished by
the amount standing to the credit of the depositors' deposit accounts with the bank.
There was no appeal in relation to the loans to M S Fashions Ltd. The liquidators   G
appealed in relation to the loans to the other two companies. The Court of Appeal
affirmed the decision of Hoffmann LJ. The documents executed by the depositors in the
present case are in terms different from those of the documents in the cases considered
by the court in the *M S Fashions Ltd* case, and the question I have to answer is whether
these differences make the decision of the court in the latter case inapplicable to the loans
to Rayners Enterprises Inc and the agrichemicals group.

H
I think it convenient at this stage to summarise the effect of the decision in the *M S*
Fashions Ltd case. The court held that the effect of the security documents executed by
the depositors in that case was to subject the depositors to a personal liability to the bank
for the debts due from the principal debtors. This personal liability of the depositors on
the one hand and the bank's liability to the depositors for the deposits on the other hand
constituted liabilities arising from mutual dealings between the depositors and the bank

A falling to be set off under r. 4.90 of the *Insolvency Rules* 1986. The result was to reduce the debts due from the principal debtors by the amount of the deposits standing to the credit of the depositors on their accounts with the bank.

Mr Dicker, counsel for the liquidators, submitted that because the security documents in the present case, unlike those in the *M S Fashions Ltd* case, were not apt in form to impose any personal liability on the depositors for the indebtedness to the bank of the
B principal debtors, but merely created charges on the deposits concerned to secure payment by the principal debtors, there is no room for set-off in accordance with the principles applied in the *M S Fashions Ltd* case. The result, submitted Mr Dicker, is that the liquidators can sue the principal debtors for the full amount of their indebtedness to the bank.

If Mr Dicker's submission is right, it appears to produce the surprising result that the liquidators are in a better position in the case of loans by the bank in respect of which it
C did not take personal guarantees in addition to charges on deposits from depositors than in the case of loans such as those considered in the *M S Fashions Ltd* case, in respect of which the bank did take personal guarantees as well. Of course this does not mean that the submission is necessarily unsound.

It is therefore necessary at this point to consider the terms of the documentation signed by the depositors in the present case to see whether it can also be said to have created a
D situation within the principles applied in the *M S Fashions Ltd* case.

There are two different forms of document signed by depositors in the present case, but it was not suggested by any of the parties that for present purposes there is any difference in their effect. One form is as follows:

'*LETTER OF LIEN*

The Manager

E Bank of Credit and Commerce International SA

Dear Sir,

In consideration of the advances already made and of those which the bank may at its discretion make to [the principal debtor] from time to time, I/we hereby give the bank a lien on the balances maintained by me/us in my/our Demand Deposit/ Call Deposit/Term Deposit/Current Accounts with your bank for the outstanding
F general balance of all and every loan, overdraft, or other accounts of [the principal debtor] with the bank and so that the bank shall have the power to WITHDRAW and utilise the proceeds thereof or of any other Demand Deposit/Call Deposit/ Term Deposit/Current Accounts for the adjustment of the various accounts of [the principal debtor] with the bank without reference to me/us. I/We undertake to execute such deeds and instruments as the bank may require hereafter further to
G secure the Demand Deposit/Call Deposit/Term Deposit/Current Accounts and I/ we shall bear the cost thereof.

I/We hereby declare that I/we have not encumbered, assigned or otherwise dealt with the Demand Deposit/Call Deposit/Term Deposit/Current Accounts in any way and that they are free from all encumbrances, and THAT I/WE WILL NOT ENCUMBER, ASSIGN OR DEAL WITH THEM OR ANY RENEWAL THEREOF.

H It is understood that the balances held in the Demand Deposit/Call Deposit/Term Deposit/Current Accounts under the bank's lien are not to be released to me/us, my/our heirs or assignees unless or until the amount of loan/overdraft/ accommodation and facilities have been fully repaid with interest etc. to the bank by [the principal debtor].

Please mark your lien up to . . . in my account . . . in favour of your . . . branch.'

At least some of the relevant deposits in respect of which letters of lien in this form   A
were signed were made with the Luxembourg branch of the bank. However the parties
accept that the issues to be determined by me should be determined on the footing that
the relevant law is, or is the same as, English law.

The other form of document signed by some of the depositors was as follows:

'*LETTER OF LIEN/CHARGE*

The Manager   B

BANK OF CREDIT & COMMERCE INTERNATIONAL SA

Dear Sir

In consideration of your branch, or any other branch of Bank of Credit and
Commerce International SA or any affiliate or correspondent bank at our request
providing/agreeing to provide from time to time loans, advances, letters of credit
facility, guarantee facility and/or other accommodation, banking services or   C
facilities ("banking facilities"), (the branch/bank actually providing banking
facilities is hereinafter referred to as the 'bank')

to [the principal debtor]

of [address of borrower] (the 'borrower')

I/we [the depositor]   D

of [address of account holder]

hereby give a lien/charge on the balances maintained by me/us in my/our Demand
Deposit/Call Deposit/Term Deposit/Current Accounts with you for all of the
outstanding liabilities of the borrower in respect of the banking facilities and so
that you shall have the power to WITHDRAW and utilise the proceeds thereof or
of any other Demand Deposit/Call Deposit/Term Deposit/Current Account(s) for   E
the reduction or adjustment of the outstanding liabilities of the borrower with the
bank, without reference to me/us. I/We undertake to execute such deeds and
instruments as you may require hereafter further to secure my/our Demand
Deposit/Call Deposit/Term Deposit/Current Account(s) and I/we shall bear the
cost thereof.

I/We hereby declare that I/we have not encumbered, assigned or otherwise dealt
with the Demand Deposit/Call Deposit/Term Deposit/Current Account(s) in any   F
way and that they are free from all encumbrances and THAT I/WE WILL NOT
ENCUMBER, ASSIGN OR DEAL WITH THEM OR ANY RENEWAL
THEREOF.

It is understood that the balances held in the Demand Deposit/Call Deposit/Term
Deposit/Current Account(s) under lien/charge are not to be released to me/us, my/
our heirs or assignees unless or until the entire outstanding liabilities of the   G
Borrower whether actual or contingent are fully repaid with interest, fees,
commission etc., and the bank is under no obligation to provide or make available
banking facilities to the borrower.

Please mark lien up to . . . or equivalent amount in any other currency in any of
my/our account(s) No(s) . . . in your favour/in favour of your following branch/
affiliate/correspondent   H

Name BANK OF CREDIT & COMMERCE

Address . . .'

It is immediately apparent that there is no reference in either form of document (unlike
the relevant documents in the *M S Fashions Ltd* case) to any personal liability on the
depositor for the debt due from the principal debtor. Nonetheless the first group of

A respondents ('the Rayners Enterprises respondents') submitted by Mr McDonnell that the effect of these letters of lien or charge ('the security documents') was to make the amount of the relevant deposit a sum 'due from' the depositor as a result of 'mutual dealings' between the depositor and the bank within the meaning of r. 4.90 of the *Insolvency Rules* 1986. The result, said Mr McDonnell, was (as in the *M S Fashions Ltd* case) that the debt due from the principal debtor was reduced by the amount of the depositor's deposit.

B Mr McDonnell sought to reach this conclusion by two alternative routes. First (with some support from Mr Carr, counsel for the agrichemicals group respondents, at least in his skeleton argument) he submitted that the effect of the security documents was to entitle the bank to satisfy the debts due from the principal debtors out of the depositors' deposits. This made the debts also 'due from' the depositors. I do not accept this argument. In my judgment the security documents (whatever else may be their true effect)

C do not have the effect of subjecting the depositors to any personal liability for the principal debts, and therefore do not make any part of the principal debts due from the depositors within the meaning of r. 4.90.

Mr McDonnell's alternative argument on this point was based on a dictum of Millett J in *Re Charge Card Services Ltd* (1986) 2 BCC 99,373 at p. 99,393. In that case Millett J held that it is impossible for a creditor to charge a debt by way of security to the debtor

D by whom the same debt is owing. I must return to this part of the decision later. Having reached that conclusion, Millett J said:

> 'It does not, of course, follow that an attempt to create an express mortgage or charge of a debt in favour of the debtor would be ineffective to create a security. Equity looks to the substance, not the form; and while in my judgment this would not create a mortgage or charge, it would no doubt give a right of set-off which would be effective against the creditor's liquidator or trustee in bankruptcy,
E provided that it did not purport to go beyond what is permitted by s. 31 of the *Bankruptcy Act* 1914.'

Section 31 of the *Bankruptcy Act* 1914 was the precursor of r. 4.90 of the *Insolvency Rules* 1986.

Mr McDonnell submitted that as in *Re Charge Card Services Ltd*, so in the present case, the attempt by the depositors to create security over their deposits (debts due to

F them from the bank) in favour of the bank was ineffective to create a charge in favour of the bank, but was effective to give a right of set-off in the bank's liquidation in accordance with r. 4.90.

In my judgment this reliance on the dictum of Millett J which I have quoted is misconceived. In the case before Millett J the purported creator of the security was itself under a personal obligation to the bank, and the purported charge was intended to secure

G performance of that obligation. If, as Millett J held, the charge was ineffective, the prior obligation of the 'chargor' remained as a liability eligible for set-off under s. 31 of the *Bankruptcy Act* 1914. In the present case, as I have already held, the security documents did not impose any personal liability for the principal debts on the depositors, and the depositors were under no such liability aliunde. There is therefore nothing on which set-off can operate in accordance with r. 4.90.

H Mr Carr did not adopt Mr McDonnell's argument based on *Re Charge Card Services Ltd*. Indeed he submitted (and this submission was relied upon also by Mr McDonnell on behalf of the Rayners Enterprises respondents as a further alternative to his submissions to which I have already referred) that I should decline to follow the decision of Millett J to the effect that a charge over a debt in favour of the debtor is a conceptual impossibility, and should hold that the security documents did indeed create charges in favour of the bank over the depositors' rights to their deposits with the bank. The respondents' purpose in this submission was to rely on what Dillon LJ referred to in the *M S Fashions Ltd* case at p. 367H as:

> 'the rule in equity, stated by Viscount Cave LC in *Ellis & Co's Trustee v Dixon-Johnson* [1925] AC 489 at p. 491, and stated also by Sargant LJ in the court below ([1924] 2 Ch 451 at p. 473), that if a creditor holding security sues for his debt he is under an obligation on payment of the debt to hand over the security, and if, having improperly made away with the security he is unable to return it to his debtor, he cannot have judgment for the debt.'

Mr Carr submitted that I should not follow the decision of Millett J to the effect that a creditor cannot create a charge over his debt in favour of the debtor, having regard to (1) the fact that the decision is inconsistent with the decision (not cited to Millett J) of the Court of Appeal in *Re Jeavons. Ex parte Mackay* (1873) LR 8 Ch App 643, and (2) the criticism of the decision by Dillon LJ in *Welsh Development Agency v Export Finance Co Ltd* [1992] BCC 270 at p. 284F.

In *Ex parte Mackay* (1873) LR 8 Ch App 643, A sold a patent to B in consideration of royalties payable by B to A. At the same time B lent A £12,500, and it was agreed between the parties that B should retain one half of the royalties, as they became payable, towards repayment of the loan, provided that if A became bankrupt B should be entitled to retain the whole of the royalties in satisfaction of the loan. The court held that the proviso expressed to enlarge B's rights on the bankruptcy of A was void, but that B was entitled to a charge on half A's right to royalties. At p. 647 of the report James LJ said:

> 'I entertain no doubt that there is a good charge upon one moiety of the royalties, because they are part of the property and effects of the bankrupt.'

Mellish LJ agreed. As appears from another report of the same case in (1873) LJ(NS) Bankruptcy 68, at p. 69, counsel in the course of argument had posed the question 'How can a man have a charge on a debt to become due from himself?', to which Mellish LJ responded 'Why cannot a man have a charge on a debt due from himself as well as on a debt due from another?' Counsel apparently failed to give an answer to this question satisfactory to the court.

In *Welsh Development Agency v Export Finance Co Ltd* [1992] BCC 270 at p. 284F Dillon LJ said:

> 'So far as the decision in *Re Charge Card Services Ltd* is concerned, I have very considerable difficulty with the view expressed by Millett J at p. 99,391 that a book debt due to the company (Charge Card Services Ltd) from Commercial Credit could not be charged in favour of Commercial Credit itself because a charge in favour of a debtor of his own indebtedness to the chargor is conceptually impossible. I see no basis for this conclusion in the judgment of Millett J himself. I see no reason why the transaction which took place in *Ex parte Mackay* (1873) LR 8 Ch App 643 (better reported in (1873) LJ (NS) Bankruptcy 68) and was upheld by this court – viz. that a creditor who was entitled to royalties from a debtor but was also indebted to the debtor in a sum by way of loan bearing interest could give the debtor a continuing right, which would subsist as security despite the bankruptcy of the creditor, to apply half the royalties in reduction of the loan and interest – should not be valid in law. The same applies to the auctioneer's lien on his client's moneys in his hands which was upheld in *Webb v Smith* (1885) 30 ChD 192. However I do not see that this arises in the present case.'

The other members of the court did not think it necessary to express a view on the point. The comment made by Dillon LJ on the question whether a creditor can charge his debt in favour of the debtor was obiter, but nevertheless of considerable weight, expressing as it did the same view as appears to have been applied by the Lords Justices in *Ex parte Mackay*.

A   I see considerable force in the argument that it would be impossible, consistently with the decision of the Court of Appeal in *Ex parte Mackay* (1873) LR 8 Ch App 643, to hold that the security documents could not create charges in favour of the bank over the credit balances on the accounts referred to in those documents. For the purpose of considering the further submissions made on behalf of the parties I will for the moment assume (without deciding) that the security documents did create such charges.

B   On the assumption that the security documents created charges on the depositors' credit balances with the bank the respondents rely on the principle of equity enunciated in *Ellis & Co's Trustee v Dixon-Johnson* [1925] AC 489, the application of which the Court of Appeal found it unnecessary to decide in the *M S Fashions Ltd* case. The respondents' submission is that the effect of the application of that principle in the present case is as follows. Since the bank is not in a position to restore to the depositors the right to repayment of their deposits in full, which right was the property charged to the bank

C   by the security documents, the bank must give credit for the full amount of those deposits on any claim against the principal debtors for repayment of the loans secured by the security documents.

In *Ellis & Co's Trustee v Dixon-Johnson* the defendant opened an account with a firm of stockbrokers, Ellis & Co, and deposited with them by way of security for any debit balance that might from time to time be owing by him on that account the indicia of title

D   to certain bonds and shares. The firm sold some of the shares without the authority or even knowledge of the defendant. The firm was then adjudicated bankrupt. The trustee in bankruptcy sought to sue the defendant to recover the balance of the amount owing on the defendant's account with the firm, after giving credit for the proceeds of sale of the shares which the firm had wrongly sold. At first instance Lawrence J remitted the matter to a master in chambers to certify the amount of the indebtedness of the defendant, to ascertain the market value of the shares wrongly sold by the firm as at the date of the

E   master's certificate and to set that value off against the defendant's debt. In fact the value of the shares had risen since their sale to the extent that a deduction of their current value pursuant to the order made by Lawrence J left nothing due to the firm.

The firm's trustee in bankruptcy appealed. The appeal was dismissed by the Court of Appeal (Warrington and Sargant L JJ, Pollock MR dissenting) ([1924] 2 Ch 451). In his judgment, at pp. 469–471, Warrington LJ said:

F   'Under these circumstances all that the defendant asks us to say is that the judgment of the judge, if it errs at all, does so in being too favourable to the plaintiff, but that, whether this be so or not, it is right in principle in giving effect to the rule in equity that a mortgagee who cannot or will not return the mortgaged property on payment is not entitled to sue for the debt. There can, I think, be no question that such was and is the rule in equity. In *Palmer* v. *Hendrie* (1859) 27

G   Beav. 349, 351 the rule was there stated by Romilly M.R.: "These then are the relative duties and reciprocal obligations between mortgagor and mortgagee:– The mortgagee has a right to make use of all his remedies against the mortgagor for obtaining payment of his money; but as soon as the mortgage money has been fully paid, he is bound to deliver over the mortgaged estate to the mortgagor. The question is, whether, when the mortgagee has made it impossible to restore the property mortgaged, he can proceed against a mortgagor to recover the amount of

H   the mortgage money. He can undoubtedly, at law, sue upon the covenant, and, consequently, the executors of Hendrie are, at law, entitled to recover from the plaintiff the unpaid mortgage money:– but the mortgagees must perform their reciprocal obligations: they are bound, on payment, to restore the property to the mortgagor, and" – this is a most important part – "if it appear, from the state of the transaction, that, by the act of the mortgagee, unauthorized by the mortgagor,

it has become impossible to restore the estate on payment of all that is due, I am   A
of opinion that this Court will interfere and prevent the mortgagee suing the
mortgagor at law.''

This statement of the law was cited and adopted by Stirling J. in *Kinnaird* v.
Trollope (1888) 39 Ch.D. 636, 644, and has never, so far as I am aware, been
questioned or doubted. Is there any reason why it should not be applied to such a
mortgage as that in question in this case? I agree with the judge that there is none.   B
The rule is based on the very nature of a mortgage security, and the reciprocal
obligations of mortgagor and mortgagee, and is, in my opinion, in accordance
with justice and common sense. But obviously, as the judge has pointed out, its
application to a case where the mortgaged property or property identical in all
material respects therewith is readily purchasable on the market may very well be
different to its application to an ordinary mortgage of land. It would be absurd to
insist on a retransfer of the identical shares mortgaged when other shares of the   C
same nature are available, and so also, I think, the judge is right in substituting for
the actual shares the value thereof, in as much as the money representing the value
could, if the mortgagor so pleases, be at once invested in the purchase of shares.'

Sargant LJ at pp. 472–473 said:

'First, then, as between the firm and the defendant, what is the right of a
mortgagor? The cases of *Walker* v. *Jones* LR 1 PC 50, *Palmer* v. *Hendrie*. . . and   D
Kinnaird v. *Trollope*. . . have definitely recognized that, in general, a mortgagee or
his assignee cannot recover his debt from the mortgagor except upon performing
his reciprocal obligation of reconveying the mortgaged property to the mortgagor.
And, accordingly, where the security for the debt was a specific estate, and through
the unauthorized acts of the mortgagee it has become impossible to restore the
estate at law, the mortgagee lost the right to sue for the mortgage debt. In a case   E
like the present, where the security that has been wrongly disposed of in part by
the mortgagees consisted of freely marketable shares which can readily be replaced
by others of precisely similar value, there is no necessity for insisting on the
restoration of the particular shares charged. The obligation of the mortgagee can
be sufficiently performed by the replacement of the shares by others of the same
denomination, or even by furnishing the mortgagor with funds sufficient to enable
him so to replace the shares. But I see no reason for further relaxing the clear   F
general principle, that, as a condition of recovering his debt or the balance of it,
the mortgagee must perform the reciprocal obligation of restoring the security, or
so much of it as has not been properly disposed of by him.'

The trustee in bankruptcy appealed to the House of Lords. The appeal was dismissed
([1925] AC 489). Viscount Cave LC said at p. 491:

'I have always understood the rule in equity to be that, if a creditor holding security   G
sues for his debt, he is under an obligation on payment of the debt to hand over
the security; and if, having improperly made away with the security, he is unable
to return it to his debtor, he cannot have judgment for the debt. If that rule had
been strictly applied on the hearing of this action, the action must have been then
and there dismissed. But Lawrence J took note of the fact that in this case the
missing security consisted of shares which could be replaced by purchasing them   H
on the market; and he applied the rule with this variation, that he directed the
master to whom it was remitted to ascertain the amount of the respondent's debt,
to ascertain the market value at the date of his certificate of the missing shares, and
to set that value off against the debt. Whether this direction so given took precisely
the right form, need not now be considered. Speaking generally, it was a reasonable
course to take, and if the shares had fallen in price it would have been

A   advantageous to the trustee in bankruptcy; but as it turned out, the modification adopted by the judge was of no advantage to the trustee, as the value of the shares when ascertained in accordance with his direction exceeded the amount of the debt and there was nothing for the trustee to recover; and the action has now been dismissed.'

Lord Buckmaster at p. 493 said, referring to the endorsement on the writ:

B   'Had all the admitted facts been stated on that endorsement the action would have been demurrable, because the plaintiffs were not in a position to hand over the securities, and consequently were not able to maintain the action. It is perfectly true that originally such an action was maintainable at law and was restrained in equity, but now whenever the principles of law and of equity are in conflict the principles of equity prevail.'

C   As I have said, the respondents submit that this principle of equity applies in the present case, because the bank is unable to restore to the depositors the property charged by them to secure the indebtedness of the principal debtors, namely the right to receive in full from the bank the credit balances on the depositors' deposit accounts. Therefore, runs the argument, the bank (and thus the liquidators) will not be allowed by equity to claim the principal debts without giving credit for those credit balances. It makes no difference to the application of this equitable principle that the security was provided by D   a third party (the depositor) and not by the principal debtor itself.

Mr Dicker, counsel for the liquidators, submitted that the equitable principle applied in *Ellis & Co's Trustee v Dixon-Johnson* [1925] AC 489 has no application to the present case, because the bank is able to and will restore the security taken by it from the depositors as a condition of suing the principal debtors. Once the principal debts are recovered in full, the depositors' deposits will be released from the charges presently E   affecting them, and the depositors will be free to prove in the liquidation of the bank for their deposits. The property charged by the security documents was not the cash paid to the bank by the depositors, which on general principles became the property of the bank, but the choses in action consisting of the depositors' rights to repayment of the deposits. Once the principal debts are recovered in full from the principal debtors (if they are), these choses in action charged by the security documents will be restored intact to the depositors. The fact that the choses in action will now be subject in the hands of the F   depositors to the restrictions on enforcement imposed by law as a result of the liquidation of the bank, and will therefore almost certainly be worth very much less than when charged to the bank, does not alter the fact that the depositors will recover the property they charged to the bank.

Mr Dicker on behalf of the liquidators further submitted that the bank has not 'improperly made away with the security' in the words of Viscount Cave LC in *Ellis &* G   *Co's Trustee v Dixon-Johnson* [1925] AC 489. Under the terms of the security documents the bank is entitled to withhold repayment of the charged deposits until the principal debtors have repaid their loans from the bank in full. Such repayment has still not been made. Accordingly the bank has never failed to comply with a valid demand for repayment of the deposits. It or now the liquidators in its place remain entitled to elect whether to realise the security provided by the security documents or to proceed against the principal debtors to recover the outstanding loans from them. There is no legal basis H   on which they can be compelled to rely on the security as opposed to suing the principal debtors for the full amount of the outstanding loans.

Mr Dicker submitted that although, on one view, the result might seem unduly favourable to the general body of the bank's creditors, in that they will have the benefit of the depositors' deposits as well as (subject to any question of the solvency of the principal debtors) full recovery of the loans for which the deposits were charged as

security, this is merely the consequence of the rights of the depositors being subject to the
rules governing the application of the bank's assets in liquidation, just as are the rights of
all other persons unfortunate enough to have placed deposits with the bank.

Although I was initially concerned by the apparent unfair advantage that the
liquidators' argument would give the general body of the creditors of the bank, I am
persuaded that the argument is sound in law and should be accepted. It is, in my
judgment, wrong in principle that the creditor (now represented by the liquidators)
should be compelled against its own choice to realise its security rather than pursuing the
principal debtor. There is, in my judgment, nothing in the principle of equity applied in
Ellis & Co's Trustee v Dixon-Johnson [1925] AC 489 to require or even justify such a
departure from legal principle. Accordingly I reject this submission of the respondents.

An alternative argument relied upon by both sets of respondents was based on the
principle applied in *Barclays Bank Ltd v Quistclose Investments Ltd* [1970] AC 567 to the
effect that money paid and received with the mutual intention that it should be used for
a specific purpose is held by the payee on trust to apply it for that purpose and as to any
balance left after effecting the purpose on trust for the payer. It was submitted that in the
present case the deposits were provided to the bank by the depositors specifically for the
purpose of discharging the indebtedness of the principal debtors and accordingly were
held by the liquidators on trust to use them for that purpose.

In my judgment this argument is not supported by the security documents, which
charge whatever credit balances may from time to time be standing to the credit of the
depositors on accounts in the books of the bank. Neither in the security documents nor
in any of the affidavit evidence sworn on behalf of the depositors is there any suggestion
of payments made to the bank for the specific purpose of paying the indebtedness of the
principal debtors.

A further alternative argument put by Mr McDonnell on behalf of the Rayners
Enterprises respondents was based on an implied obligation owed by the bank to the
principal debtors as well as to the depositors to preserve the security provided to it. The
bank is in breach of this obligation, in that it cannot restore the security unimpaired to
the depositors. The resultant liability of the bank can be set off against the principal
debts. In my judgment this argument is unsound for reasons similar to those for which I
have rejected the argument based on the principle in *Ellis & Co's Trustee v Dixon-Johnson*
[1925] AC 489. The security provided by the depositors – their entitlement to the charged
deposit – remains intact, notwithstanding that it is now enforceable only by proof in the
liquidation of the bank.

Next Mr McDonnell submitted that by reason of the doctrine of marshalling of
securities, the bank, which has the benefit of two securities, namely the depositors'
charges over the deposits and charges granted by the principal debtors over property
purchased with the money borrowed from the bank, must, if it cannot return one security
(the deposits), be treated as satisfying the principal debts out of that, leaving the property
charged by the principal debtors to satisfy the depositors' rights to indemnity from the
principal debtors. Again this argument seems to me fallacious (even if otherwise sound,
which I do not decide) because it is based on the false premise that the bank is unable to
restore to the depositors the property charged by them.

Finally Mr McDonnell submitted that the depositors are entitled as a matter of law to
insist on discharging the principal debts out of the credit balance on the depositors'
deposit accounts with the bank, reimbursing themselves by claims against the principal
debtors. For this submission Mr McDonnell relied on *Ex parte Stephens* (1805) 11 Ves
Jun 24 and *Vulliamy v Noble* (1817) 3 Mer 593. In my judgment, neither case supports
the respondents' argument in the present case. As explained in *Middleton v Pollock* (1875)
LR 20 Eq 515, *Ex parte Stephens* decided no more than that in equity a right of set-off

A was not destroyed by fraudulent concealment of the facts from the party entitled to exercise that right, and *Vulliamy v Noble* no more than that where a bank had sold security held by it for a debt due from the provider of the security and another jointly, without notice to the debtors, it must be treated as having appropriated the proceeds of sale in satisfaction of the joint debt. In other words, the latter case was no more than an example of the principle applied later in *Ellis & Co's Trustee v Dixon-Johnson* [1925] AC
B 489, which I have considered earlier in this judgment. It is to be noted that in both *Ex parte Stephens* and *Vulliamy v Noble* the party seeking to enforce a right of 'set-off' was (unlike the depositors in the present case) a surety who had undertaken a personal liability jointly with the principal debtor for the debt concerned.

Thus I reject all the arguments put by the respondents on the assumption that the security documents were effective to create charges over the relevant deposit accounts. In my judgment, therefore, it is unnecessary and inappropriate for me to decide whether I
C should follow the decision of Millett J in *Re Charge Card Services Ltd*, to the effect that such a charge is conceptually impossible, in the light of the other authorities on the point to which I have earlier referred. For, in my judgment, whether or not the security documents created charges, the liquidators are entitled to recover the full amount of the debts due from the principal debtors without any set-off or other allowance for the deposits affected by the security documents.

D I accept that this conclusion produces the prima facie surprising result that the liquidators are in a stronger position as against the principal debtors in the cases with which I am concerned, where the depositors undertook no personal liability for the principal debts, than they have been held to be in the cases considered by the court in the *M S Fashions Ltd* case, in which the depositors did undertake such a liability. But the fact is that the court's decision in that case in favour of set-off clearly depended on the construction of the security documents in that case as imposing on the depositors a
E personal joint liability for the principal debts, which, in my judgment, the depositors did not undertake in the present case. Moreover the difference in result is perhaps not so striking when one bears in mind that in a case where the liquidators' right against the principal debtor is potentially subject to set-off, because of the joint personal liability of the depositor, it must, in my judgment, be open to the liquidators to release the depositor from his personal liability and thereby avoid any set-off of the deposit, provided the
F release is effected before the operative date of set-off under r. 4.90 of the *Insolvency Rules* 1986.

According to the decision of the Court of Appeal in *Stein v Blake* [1993] BCC 587 the statutory set-off provided for by s. 323 of the *Insolvency Act* 1986 in the case of the bankruptcy of an individual does not operate automatically at the date of the bankruptcy, but only at the date when an account of the relevant liabilities falls to be taken – for
G example on a proof being admitted. In the meantime the mutual liabilities concerned remain in existence and can be assigned. Section 323 of the *Insolvency Act* 1986 is in terms indistinguishable for present purposes from r. 4.90 of the *Insolvency Rules* 1986. It seems to me, therefore, to follow that the set-off provided for by r. 4.90 does not operate to prevent dealings with the relevant mutual debts until an account in respect thereof falls to be taken for the purpose of the liquidation. Consequently, after the bank went into liquidation, it would still be open to the liquidators, in the case of principal debts (such
H as those considered in the *M S Fashions Ltd* case) in respect of which the depositors had entered into joint personal liability with the principal debtors, to release that liability of the depositors before the taking of any account of the position as between those depositors and the bank and thereby avoid the effect of r. 4.90.

This possibility does not appear from the report of the *M S Fashions Ltd* case to have been considered by the Court of Appeal in that case, the decision of the Court of Appeal

in *Stein v Blake* not yet having been made. On the other hand the court in the latter case   A
was, not surprisingly, not referred to the decision of the Court of Appeal on the
application of r. 4.90 in the *M S Fashions Ltd* case, because that decision was delivered
less than a fortnight before the hearing in *Stein v Blake*. In my respectful opinion the two
decisions do not stand entirely happily together. The decision of the Court of Appeal in
the *M S Fashions Ltd* case appears to be based on the assumption that the effect of
r. 4.90 was to crystallise the rights of the parties as at the date of the winding up of the   B
bank. This was certainly the view taken by Hoffmann LJ in his judgment at first instance
(see [1993] BCC 70 at p. 73F–G). It now seems, with great respect, inconsistent with the
decision in *Stein v Blake* on the application of s. 323 of the *Insolvency Act* 1986.

However, whatever the true view of the application of r. 4.90 in a case in which it is
applicable, in my judgment, for the reasons which I have attempted to explain, that rule
has no application in the present case.   C

It follows that I reject all the alternative arguments eloquently put by counsel on behalf
of the two classes of respondents to the effect that the liquidators cannot recover the
indebtedness of the principal debtors from them without giving credit for the deposits the
subject-matter of the security documents.

Finally I should deal with an argument of last resort put on behalf of the respondents
to the effect that, even if (which I have held they are) the liquidators are entitled as a
matter of law to claim against the principal debtors for the full amount of their debts   D
with no set-off for the deposits, such claim would be so unmeritorious that the court
should not authorise liquidators to pursue it. The principle relied on for this argument is
that restated by Nourse LJ in *Re Multi Guarantee Co Ltd* [1987] BCLC 257 at p. 269e:

'The principle . . . is that the court will direct a trustee in bankruptcy not to insist
on his full legal rights if it would be unacceptable for him to do so. The principle is
subject to qualifications, of which the most important is that the court will only   E
take that course in a case where it would be dishonest or shabby or the like for the
trustee to insist on his full legal rights.'

In my judgment, as the Court of Appeal decided in that case, so in this, the facts do
not come anywhere near the kind of facts which fall within the principle. I do not consider
that the court should restrain the liquidators enforcing what I have held are their rights
against the principal debtors for the benefit of the general body of the bank's creditors.   F
The unfortunate position of the depositors, who are left to prove in the bank's
liquidation, is, like that of all other depositors in and creditors of the bank, the inevitable
consequence of the financial collapse of a bank.

Thus, in my judgment, nothing in the security documents or the *Insolvency Act* 1986
or the rules made thereunder affects the prima facie right of the liquidators to seek to
recover from the principal debtors the full amount of their indebtedness. However, I was
told by counsel that, if that should be my decision, the respondents wished to have an   G
opportunity to adduce evidence of facts surrounding the relevant transactions on which
the respondents wish to mount an argument that the liquidators are somehow estopped
from enforcing their prima facie rights against the principal debtors, and I was told that
it was agreed between the parties that I should be asked to give directions as to the
manner in which these issues of fact should be dealt with. I will hear counsel further on
the question of what directions should be made.   H

(*Order accordingly*)

Re Saul D Harrison & Sons plc.

Chancery Division (Companies Court) and Court of Appeal (Civil Division).
Vinelott J; Neill, Hoffmann and Waite L JJ.
Judgment delivered 9 March 1992 and 25 March 1994.

Unfair prejudice petition – Striking out application – Petition alleged company run for benefit of director shareholders – Petition did not allege any special relationship between shareholders – Petition alleged bad faith by directors – Whether evidence supported inference of bad faith – Companies Act 1985, s. 459.

This was an appeal against the striking out as an abuse of process of a contributory's petition for an order under s. 459 of the Companies Act 1985 and to wind up on the just and equitable ground.

The petition alleged that the directors and the holders of the A shares, which had voting rights, were running the company solely for their own benefit and were ignoring the interests of, inter alia, the C shareholders of which the petitioner was one, and that whereas in a winding up the C shareholders would receive a substantial distribution, as a result of the way in which the company was being run the C shareholders received no benefit and were unlikely to receive any benefit in the future.

The petition alleged that the directors had acted in ways contrary to the petitioner's legitimate expectations in that the directors had not acted bona fide in the best interests of the company in deciding whether to pay dividends and how much to pay, in managing the business and in agreeing directors' remuneration, but had acted in their own interests and had not in all respects complied with the provisions of the Companies Act.

The judge found that the petition did not allege anything in the history of the company or the relationship between the shareholders which could be relied on as superimposing an equitable fetter on the exercise of the rights conferred by the articles of association of the company. It could not be said that the petition on its face did not disclose any cause of action. But it was not sufficient simply to allege that a company was making a loss or insufficient profits and that there was no real prospect that it would make a profit or a sufficient profit in the future. There had to be some evidence which, if substantiated at the trial, could found the inference that the directors' decision to continue to trade was influenced by self-interest, or at least that no reasonable board of directors mindful of their duty to the company and its members could have decided that it was in the interests of the company and its members that it should continue to trade. The judge held that the petitioner had not adduced any evidence which, if accepted at trial, would support the allegations in the petition and justify the relief sought. He therefore struck out the petition. The petitioner appealed.

Held, dismissing the appeal:

1. There were no special circumstances and the petitioner's rights were laid down by the articles. Her legitimate expectations amounted to no more than an expectation that the board would manage the company in accordance with their fiduciary obligations and the terms of the articles and the Companies Act.

2. As there were no grounds for saying that it would be unfair for the board to act in accordance with the bargain between the petitioner and the company contained in the articles, the minimum required to make out a case of unfairness was that the powers of management had been used for an unlawful purpose or the articles otherwise infringed. The claims for relief under s. 459 and winding up depended on whether the petitioner could make out the allegation that the board acted in bad faith, carrying on the business in order to provide themselves with salaries rather than because they genuinely thought that it was in the interests of the shareholders as a whole.

3. The consequences for the company of a petition meant that the court should be willing
to scrutinise with care the allegations in a s. 459 petition and, if necessary, the evidence
proposed to be adduced in support, in order to see whether the petitioner really had an
arguable case, particularly when the petition rested on allegations of bad faith.

4. The evidence could not support an inference that the board had acted unfairly in
relation to the petitioner.

The following cases were referred to in the judgments:

Cayne & Anor v Global Natural Resources plc [1984] 1 All ER 225.
Company No. 007623 of 1984, Re a (1986) 2 BCC 99,191.
Company No. 00370 of 1987, Re a (1988) 4 BCC 506.
Company No. 002470 of 1988, Re a, ex parte Nicholas [1992] BCC 895.
Company No. 00314 of 1989, Re a [1990] BCC 221.
Ebrahimi v Westbourne Galleries Ltd [1973] AC 360.
Elder & Ors v Elder & Watson Ltd 1952 SC 49.
Elgindata Ltd, Re [1991] BCLC 959.
Foss v Harbottle (1843) 2 Hare 461.
Harmer (H R) Ltd, Re [1959] 1 WLR 62.
Jermyn Street Turkish Baths Ltd, Re [1971] 1 WLR 1042.
Lundie Brothers Ltd, Re [1965] 1 WLR 1051.
Rica Gold Washing Co, Re (1879) 11 ChD 36.
Ringtower Holdings plc, Re (Company No. 005685 of 1988 (No. 2)) (1989) 5 BCC 82.
Scottish Co-operative Wholesale Society Ltd v Meyer & Anor [1959] AC 324.
Smith (Howard) Ltd v Ampol Petroleum Ltd [1974] AC 821.
Weller (Sam) & Sons Ltd, Re (1989) 5 BCC 810; [1990] Ch 682.
Wenlock v Moloney & Ors [1965] 1 WLR 1238.

Charles Purle QC (in the Court of Appeal) and Peter Griffiths (instructed by Nabarro
Nathanson) for the petitioner.

Daniel Serota QC (in the Court of Appeal) and John Brisby (instructed by Wallace &
Partners) for the respondent shareholder directors.

Michael Todd (in the High Court) (instructed by Boodle Hatfield) for a shareholder.

HIGH COURT JUDGMENT
(Delivered 9 March 1992)

Vinelott J: This is an application to strike out a petition presented by a minority
shareholder in the company named in the title to the petition. I will refer to it as 'the
company'. The petition seeks an order for the compulsory winding up of the company
pursuant to s. 459 of the *Companies Act* 1985 on the ground that it is just and equitable
that it be wound up or, alternatively, an order that the petitioner's shares be purchased
by two other shareholders, whom I shall call Alan and Marian respectively, at a price
equal to the amount the petitioner would have received in a winding up of the company.
The registrar directed that the petition be served on Marian, Alan and two other
shareholders, to whom I shall refer as David and Stephen. They, together with Alan, are
the directors of the company. It has not yet been served on the other shareholders. In this
application the directors seek an order striking out the petition on the grounds set out in
O. 18, r. 19 or, alternatively, under the court's inherent jurisdiction.

The company was incorporated in 1947 and took over an existing business, the
conversion of waste textiles into cleaning and wiping cloths; it was, in a literal sense of
the words, engaged in the rag trade. This business had been started in 1891 by the person
whose name the company now bears. In 1947 it was run by the founder's four sons who
were, in order of age, Alfred, Harold, Bernard and Lionel. It is unnecessary to say

A   anything about the original capital structure of the company. It was restructured in 1960 with a view to ensuring that the control of the company was retained by Alfred, Bernard and Lionel (Harold had died in the meantime without having married and his shares had passed to his brothers) while enabling them to pass on to the next and subsequent generations shares which entitled the holders to all the distributed profits and on a winding up to all the assets of the company. As reconstructed the nominal capital comprised £125,000 redeemable preference shares of £1 each, 30 A ordinary shares of ten

B   pence each, 174,300 B ordinary shares of ten pence each, 825,670 C ordinary shares also of ten pence each, and 250,000 unclassified shares of ten pence each. The redeemable preference shares were issued but have since been redeemed. Only the A, B and C ordinary shares are now in issue. They are all fully paid. The rights attaching to them are shortly as follows. The A shares alone carry voting rights but they carry no rights to any dividend nor to any of the company's assets in a winding up. Profits available for

C   distribution are applicable in the first instance in paying a fixed cumulative dividend of ten per cent on the B shares and then paying an equivalent dividend on the C shares; any surplus of the profits available for distribution are then divisible pari passu between the holders of the B and C shares. On a winding up the surplus assets are to be applied in repaying to the holders of the B shares the amount paid up on their shares with any arrears of the fixed dividend; the balance is then to be distributed amongst the holders of the C shares.

D   Ten A shares were issued to each of the three brothers. They also had some B shares. The other shares were issued to their respective children and issue. Alfred died in 1977. His ten A shares passed to his only son, Seymour. Bernard died in 1985 or 1986. He had no son though he had a daughter, Rebecca. His A shares passed, as to five to Seymour, and as to five to Alan who is Lionel's only son. Seymour died on 24 April 1987 and his 15 shares passed to his widow, Marian. Lionel died on 10 June 1987 and his ten shares

E   also passed to Alan. So, since the death of Lionel, the 30 A shares have been equally divided between Marian and Alan. Alan had been appointed a director jointly with Lionel and Seymour before 1985. Following the deaths in quick succession of Seymour and Lionel, two new directors were appointed, David (who is Seymour's only son and who is 37 years old) and Stephen (who is Alan's only son and who is 30 years old). They were both appointed on 1 September 1987.

F   As to the remainder of the shares, the B shares are held as to part by Marian, as to part by Alfred's daughter Bernice, as to part by Bernard's widow Simone, and as to part by Lionel's executors. The C shares are all held by grandchildren of the brothers (the four children of Seymour, the petitioner, who is Bernice's only child, the two children of Alan and the three children of Alan's sister Susan), by Beatrice and by nominees for the Royal Bank of Scotland, the trustee of a settlement made by or for the benefit of

G   Bernard's only child, Rebecca. The holding of nominees for the Royal Bank of Scotland is far the largest of the holdings of C shares – over 50 per cent. The others are comparatively small. The petitioner's C shares are only eight per cent of the total of the C shares.

   After Lionel's death and the appointment of David and Stephen as directors, there was another major change. The company, and before its incorporation, the partnership, had

H   for many years carried on the business on premises in Hackney, which I will call 'the old premises'. In 1960 the ownership of the old premises was split between two wholly-owned subsidiaries. A long lease was granted to a company which I will call 'the F company', the freehold was conveyed to another wholly-owned subsidiary. The F company then granted an underlease of the larger part of the old premises back to the company. The old premises comprised a number of units, 12 in all. One was a self-contained unit and was surplus to the company's needs. It was sub-let to a company with no connection with

the company. The rent from the sub-letting is passed up to the company by the F   A
company.

In December 1989, London Regional Transport (LRT) introduced a bill for the
purpose of enabling it to extend the Jubilee line. It conferred powers of compulsory
acquisition. The directors decided to petition against the bill on the footing that the
company's bargaining position would be stronger than if it negotiated after an Act had
been passed and after steps had been taken to acquire the old premises compulsorily. An   B
agreement was later entered into between the company and its two subsidiaries, which I
will call collectively 'the group', and LRT, under which the group agreed to refrain from
opposing the bill and LRT agreed to treat with the petitioner in advance of Royal Assent
so as to assist the petitioners in finding alternative accommodation without undue
pressure of time. In the event, the old premises were sold for £2.27m and LRT granted to
a company in the group a lease for nine months at a peppercorn. The F company then   C
purchased other premises, which I will call 'the new premises', conveniently near to the
old premises. The period of nine months was sufficient to enable the company to find and
have the new premises altered and equipped to meet its requirements and to move its
business there with little interruption. The cost of acquiring and altering the new premises
was £4.2m but the group has received compensation amounting in all to £4.14m,
substantially all of which will attract roll-over relief for the purposes of corporation tax
on capital gains. The company has also received an improvement grant of £185,000 from   D
a local authority. Thus, so far the move has cost the company nothing. In addition, the
company has received or has outstanding claims for compensation for loss of profit
resulting from the disruption caused by the move.

Turning to the petition, the first five paragraphs set out details of the incorporation of
the company, its registration and re-registration in 1983 as a public limited company, its
issued share capital, its objects, and the material provision of the articles (which, apart   E
from special rights for the various classes of shares, are substantially those set out in
Table A). Paragraphs 6 and 7 set out details of the present shareholdings and the names
of the directors. Paragraph 8 then sets out what are described as the petitioner's
'legitimate expectations'. The legitimate expectations are in substance that the directors
will act bona fide in the best interests of the company and that in deciding whether to pay
dividends and how much to pay in managing the business and in agreeing directors'
remuneration, they will so act without regard to their own interests and will in all respects   F
comply with the provisions of the Companies Act, in particular those relating to accounts
and the disclosures which ought to be made in the accounts and in the directors' reports.
Paragraph 9 sets out details of the ways in which it is said the directors have acted in
ways contrary to the petitioner's legitimate expectations. I will return to this paragraph
in more detail later. Paragraph 10 alleges that the directors and the holders of the A
shares are running the company 'solely for their own benefit and are completely ignoring
the interests of, inter alia, the C shareholders'. It is then said that in a winding up the C   G
shareholders will receive a substantial distribution and that as a result of the way in
which the company is now being conducted the C shareholders will receive no benefit
and are unlikely to receive any benefit in the future.

The significant feature of the petition is that it is nowhere alleged that there is anything
in the history of the company or the relationship between the shareholders which could
be relied on as superimposing an equitable fetter on the exercise of the rights conferred   H
by the articles of association of the company. Any legitimate expectation of the
shareholders must be found in the articles of association or in the general principles
applicable to the conduct of the directors of a limited liability company.

The acts which are said to be contrary to the petitioner's legitimate expectations can
be grouped under five heads.

A

Subparagraphs (1) and (2)

The charges in essence are that the directors have continued the business of the company notwithstanding that it is making losses and that its future prospects of making a profit are poor and that in deciding to continue that business the directors have been and are being influenced by their desire to receive remuneration and other benefits and are not acting in the best interests of the company. It is said that the directors are content

B

that the company should continue to make losses or a small profit and that it should 'appear' to need its profits for the purpose of its business in order to justify and excuse its failure to pay a dividend.

Subparagraph (3)

The charge is that the decision of the directors to negotiate the sale of the old premises and the purchase of the new premises was not made bona fide in the interests of the

C

company but that the directors were again influenced by their desire to receive remuneration notwithstanding the company's poor profit record and expectation.

Subparagraphs (4), (6) and (7)

The charges in essence are that the directors have caused the company to pay substantial salaries and to give other benefits to their respective wives for no return; that

D

the notes to the accounts do not give proper particulars of their own remuneration package and that they have not acted bona fide in the interests of the company in agreeing the remuneration package of each of the directors. Reliance is placed on an assertion that despite falling margins and profits and the non-payment of dividends, the directors' remuneration packages and their respective wives' salaries and benefits have substantially increased.

E

Subparagraph (5)

The charge is that the old works were entered into the accounts of the group at a figure of just over £450,000 (a sum far less than its market value; the old works were sold for £2.275m); that the difference between the value stated in the accounts and the market value of the old premises was not a matter apparent from the accounts and the directors' reports, and that 'no reasonable director could have been of the opinion that the

F

difference was not of such significance as to require that the attention of the members of the company should have been drawn to it'.

Subparagraph (8)

The charge is that the directors have failed to keep proper and complete accounting records with the result that the auditors qualified the financial statements for the years to

G

31 March 1989.

I can deal with these last two charges very briefly. As to subpara. (5) reliance is placed on the provisions in Sch. 7, para. 1(2) to the *Companies Act* 1985. That subparagraph provides that if in the case of fixed assets which consist of interests in land, their market value at the end of a financial year differs from the amount at which they are included in the balance sheet and the difference is, in the directors' opinion, of such significance as to

H

require that the attention of members of the company or holders of debentures should be drawn to it, then the directors' report must indicate the difference with as much precision as is possible. This subparagraph clearly does not impose an unqualified duty to draw the attention of members and debenture holders to a difference between market value and book value whenever the difference is substantial. The difference must be such as to 'require' that their attention be drawn to it. The subparagraph has obvious application to, for instance, a case where a decline in the market value of land is such that there is a

risk that sums advanced on the security of the land may become immediately repayable,   A
or to a case of a quoted investment company whose assets on revaluation are either
substantially less or substantially more than their book value. But, in my judgment, it
can have no possible relevance in the circumstances of this case. The old works were
entered into the company's books at cost. Over the years the market value increased
substantially above cost. Every shareholder and any other person concerned with what
was revealed by the accounts must have been well aware that the book value would have   B
afforded no reliable guide to the market value of the old premises. But there was no need
to call for a revaluation or to remark upon this obvious fact in the directors' report until
the directors became aware that the old premises might have to be compulsorily acquired.

As to subpara. (8) of para. 9 of the petition, the charge is founded on the fact that the
accounts for the year up to 31 March 1989 and for earlier years contained a statement by
the auditors that:

      'In common with many businesses of similar size and organisation the company's   C
      system of control is dependent upon the close involvement of the directors . . .
      Where independent confirmation of the completeness of the accounting records
      was therefore not available we have accepted assurances from the directors that all
      the company's transactions have been reflected in the records.

      Subject to the foregoing, in our opinion the financial statements, which have been   D
      prepared under the historical cost convention, give a true and fair view of the state
      of the company's affairs at 31 March 1989 and of its loss and source and
      application of funds for the year then ended and comply with the *Companies Act
      1985.*'

No sinister influence can be drawn from this qualification. The company is, for the
purposes of the auditing standards, a 'small enterprise'. It is a classic example of a private
family company; it was only re-registered as a public limited company because at the   E
relevant time some of its redeemable preference shares were held by institutional
investors. The auditing standards appropriate to small enterprises are explained in the
Institute's auditing standards and guidelines in a passage which I should, I think, read in
full:

      'However, the operating procedures and methods for recording and processing
      transactions used by small enterprises often differ significantly from those of large   F
      enterprises. Indeed, many of the controls which would be relevant to the large
      enterprise are not practical, appropriate or necessary in a small enterprise. The
      most effective form of internal control for small enterprises is generally the close
      involvement of the directors or proprietors. This involvement will, however, enable
      them to override controls and purposely to exclude transactions from the records.
      This possibility can give rise to difficulties for the auditor not because there is a
      lack of controls but because of the insufficient evidence as to their operation and   G
      the completeness of the records. In many situations it may be possible to reach a
      conclusion that will support an unqualified opinion on the financial statements by
      combining the evidence obtained from extensive substantive testing of transactions
      with a careful review of costs and margins.

      However, in some businesses such as those where most transactions are for cash
      and there is no regular pattern of costs and margins, the available evidence may be   H
      inadequate to support an opinion on the financial statements. There will be other
      situations where the evidence available to the auditor is insufficient to give him the
      confidence necessary for him to express an unqualified opinion but this uncertainty
      is not so great as to justify a total disclaimer of opinion. In such situations the most
      helpful form of report may be one which indicates the need to accept the assurances
      of management as to the completeness or accuracy of the accounting records. Such

a report should contain a "subject to" opinion. It would only be appropriate to use this form of report if the auditor has taken steps to obtain all the evidence which can reasonably be obtained and is satisfied that (a) the system of accounting and control is reasonable having regard to the size and type of the enterprise's operations and is sufficient to enable management to give the auditor the assurances which he requires; (b) there is no evidence to suggest that the assurances may be inadequate.'

In an earlier passage explaining the forms of qualification, it is said that in a 'subject to' opinion the auditor 'effectively disclaims an opinion on a particular matter which is not considered fundamental'. The particular 'subject to' qualification which is relevant to the acceptance of management assurances in the case of small businesses is that set out in the qualification in the report of the company's auditors which I have read.

That is not all. The senior partner in the firm of chartered accounts responsible for the company's audit for the year ended 31 March 1988 (and which took over from the firm which previously audited the company's accounts on the latter firm's acquisition by merger with the present auditors) has deposed to an affidavit in support of the company's application. He explains:

'(6) . . . the qualification to the company's accounts in respect of those for the years prior to 1990 did not arise as a result of any failure on the part of the directors to keep proper and complete accounting records. The qualification arose

out of the company's inherent management and shareholder structure in which the system of control was dependent upon the close involvement of the directors and A shareholders and their family with the system of control. The A shares being the only shares conferring the right to vote at shareholders' meetings of the company were held by two full-time working directors until April 1987 and a full-time working director and the widow of a full-time working director thereafter. Until

such time as the accountancy profession auditing guideline relating to the qualification in the auditor's report on small companies' accounts was reviewed in 1989, it was appropriate to qualify the company's accounts in the manner they were. Following the change in auditing guideline, the accounts have been unqualified.

(7) In the period in which my firm has audited the company's accounts and so far

as I have been able to ascertain in the preceding years when the same were audited by Messrs Tessier, Son & Randall, there has never been occasion to send a management letter to the directors. Instead of sending after the annual audit a management letter identifying areas of weakness in the financial controls of the company, my firm conducted periodic reviews including the preparation of interim accounts. From time to time, advice has been given and letters written to the

directors as to improvements that could be made in the manner in which the company's accounting records are kept. For example, advice was given on the company's computer system. Where such advice has been given, it has been accepted by the directors and the acceptance of such advice has greatly facilitated the conduct of the audit of the company's accounts.'

This evidence has not been challenged and indeed it is difficult to see how it could be challenged. In the light of this evidence the claim that the qualification in the accounts

points to or even hints at some possible irregularity or inadequacy in the company's accounts falls to the ground.

The remaining charges in para. 9 of the petition can, I think, be conveniently grouped under two heads. There is, first, the claim that in continuing a loss-making trade the directors have disregarded the interests of the company and its members and have had regard primarily to their own interests and the related claim that the company would not

have moved to the new premises if the directors had had regard solely to the interests of   A
the company and its members and had not been influenced by consideration of their own
interests. There are, secondly, the group of charges related to the level of remuneration
paid to the directors and to remuneration and benefits provided for directors' wives.

Trading at a loss

There can be no doubt that if the directors of a company continue to trade when the   B
company is making losses and when it should have been apparent that there was no real
prospect that the company would return to profitability, the court may draw the inference
that the directors' decision was improperly influenced by their desire to continue in office
and in control of the company and to draw remuneration and other benefits for
themselves and others connected with them. So also if the company is trading at a profit
which yields a return which does not reflect the value of the assets employed and which
would be available for distribution in a winding up, and if there is no real prospect that   C
the profits will ever represent a reasonable return on the capital employed. If that
inference is drawn, the court may conclude that the affairs of the company are being
conducted in a way which is unfairly prejudicial to the members or to members other
than the directors and those who obtain such benefit. It cannot therefore be said that the
petition on its face does not disclose any cause of action. But it is not sufficient simply to
allege that a company is making a loss or insufficient profits and that there is no real   D
prospect that it will make a profit or a sufficient profit in the future. There must be some
evidence which, if substantiated at the trial, could found the inference that the directors'
decision to continue to trade was influenced by self-interest or at least that no reasonable
board of directors mindful of their duty to the company and its members could have
decided that it was in the interests of the company and its members that it should continue
to trade.

The evidence relied on by the petitioner consists of two affidavits by a Ms Paradise, a   E
partner in the firm of solicitors acting for her, which in large measure repeats advice given
to the petitioner by an accountant, a partner in Binder Hamlyn. That advice is founded
on the company's accounts and directors' reports for the years to 31 March 1990, the
most recent accounts when the petition was presented. The view advanced by the expert,
in summary, is that the company has been making trading losses for many years which
would have been larger if the company had paid an economic rent for the premises it   F
occupies; that the field in which it operates is of declining importance leaving little, if any,
scope for expansion and that the company's gross profit margins have declined and
cannot reasonably be expected to recover. The conclusion drawn is that the company's
business is doomed, that the losses now being made can never be recovered and that in
these circumstances no reasonable board of directors acting in good faith and without
regard to their own interests (in particular their desire to hang on to executive positions
and to continue to draw remuneration) could have formed the opinion that it was in the   G
interests of the company and its members that the company should continue to trade.

The accounts relied on are the accounts of the company for the year to 31 March 1985
and for subsequent years up to and including the year 31 March 1990. These accounts
show that during those years the company's turnover increased steadily from £1.82m to
£3.33m. Although the accounts show an overall (though declining) profit during those
years, the trading activities of the company (disregarding income from investments and   H
what is described in the accounts as 'other operating income') show a loss. Moreover,
gross profit margin declined from 35 per cent in the year to 31 March 1985 to 32 per cent
in the year to 31 March 1986, 33 per cent in the year to 31 March 1987, 22 per cent in the
year to 31 March 1988, 20 per cent in the year to 31 March 1989, and 19 per cent in the
year to 31 March 1990. The sudden drop from 33 per cent to 22 per cent occurred in the
year when the two older directors died – in the summer of 1987.

A   In a subsequent affidavit in answer, Alan explains that the decline in gross profit margin after 31 March 1987 is only an apparent and not a real decline. In 1988 there was a change in the company's accounting practice. Some costs which before 31 March 1987 had been shown below the line were later shown above the line as a deduction from the gross profit. If the figures are recalculated to give the gross profit on the basis used in the earlier years, the gross profit margin for the years to 31 March 1988, 31 March 1989 and 31 March 1990 is 24.6, 24.4 and 27.7 per cent respectively. Looked at in the light of these figures, while there was a drop in the year to 31 March 1988 the gross profit margin has remained steady since.

B

     Turning to the net profit or loss figures, the accounts show, first, a deduction for distribution costs and administrative expenses and then the addition of 'other operating income' and a net figure then described as 'operating profit/loss'. There is in every year up to and including the year to 31 March 1990, a loss after distribution costs and administrative expenses are deducted and before the addition of other operating income – in round figures £6,673 for the year to 31 March 1985, £114,000 for the year to 31 March 1986, £40,000 for the year to 31 March 1987, £183,000 for the year to 31 March 1988, £119,000 for the year to 31 March 1989 and £27,000 for the year to 31 March 1990. There is still an 'operating loss' in all the years after 31 March 1985 (profit £30,000) up to the year to 31 March 1990 after 'other operating income' has been added – £89,000 for the year to 31 March 1986, £20,000 for the year to 31 March 1987, £74,000 for the year to 31 March 1988 and £53,000 for the year to 31 March 1989. In the year to 31 March 1990 there is for the first time after many years a profit, £46,000. The loss is turned into a profit for all these years by the addition of income from a subsidiary company, from investments and interest received. It is unnecessary to give these figures.

C

D

     The criticism that is made of the directors I have already outlined. It is that the company has made a trading loss on its core business in every year since 31 March 1986 which is disguised in the years to 31 March 1989 and turned into a profit in the year to 31 March 1990 only by the inclusion of 'other operating income'. The company has only been able to show a profit (and in the years up to the year to 31 March 1988 to distribute a dividend) because it has investment income. That the company did make a trading loss up to 31 March 1989 is clear. Whether the loss should be taken to be the trading loss before the addition of 'other operating income' is less clear. The other operating income consists substantially (at least in the year to 31 March 1988 when it is analysed in notes to the accounts) of the rent received from the let part of the old works. That rent was derived from part of the premises from which the company traded which could not easily have been severed and sold, and in part from a service charge from a company in which the company had a 50 per cent shareholding and which prima facie was a source of trading income. Moreover, the investment income includes income from the subsidiary.

E

F

     However, it is unnecessary to go into these refinements. Alan's evidence is that since the new team took over in the summer of 1987 strenuous efforts have been made to turn round a company which at that time and while it was under the control of the older generation had in short got stuck in a groove in a business of declining profitability. The company has diversified. The company has entered into two new fields: the sorting and sale of second hand clothing, mostly in Africa (which now represents 23 per cent of its turnover) and the sale of non-woven industrial cleaning wipes manufactured by a leading public company of which it is now the leading distributor. That business now represents 36 per cent of its turnover. It is said that both these fields provide an opportunity of further expansion which will more than off-set the decline in the company's traditional trade. The acquisition of the new custom-built premises will enable the company to trade more efficiently and, it is hoped, more profitably.

G

H

     The effect of the move to new premises cannot yet be gauged. The move was completed on 2 October 1991. However, the accounts to 31 March 1991 (dated 31 October 1991) show a further increase in turnover (to £3.71m). The accounts show a loss (after deducting administrative expenses of £495,492 and operating charges of £246,982) of £93,497 which is turned into an operating profit of £398 by the addition of other operating income of £93,895. However, the company was paid compensation by LRT (of some £66,262) for disturbance which is attributable to that year and, if that figure is added in, it made a significant profit after deducting other operating income and only a small loss if it is excluded. The audited accounts for the six months to 31 September 1991 show a further increase in turnover (to nearly £2m) for the six months and a profit before taking into account other operating income of £13,745 (the other operating income for the period is a minus figure, £4,678 which reflects the lower rents recovered for that period and a figure of £13,590 paid in respect of pensions). But further compensation is expected to be paid by LRT for disturbance to the company's trade and will properly be included in the company's profit and loss account for the year to 31 March 1992.

These accounts clearly support the evidence of Alan that under its new management the company is diversifying and expanding and has at least a prospect of earning a level of profit in future years which will reflect the value of the assets employed in the business. It must be borne in mind that at the date of the last six-monthly accounts the company had not moved into its new premises. That move took place a few days later. The directors expect considerable cost reductions and room for expansion as a result. Further, during the past few years the company's capital position has been strengthened by the acquisition at no net cost to the company of the new premises which have been valued by professional valuers instructed by the company's bankers who attribute a market value of £3.35m to the new premises as compared with the value of £2.5m which was put on the property by valuers instructed by the directors at the time of the negotiations with LRT.

In the light of this evidence it is, to my mind, simply perverse to allege that the board have carried on the business with no or no substantial expectation that they will succeed in making a profit reflecting the value of the assets employed and only with a view to furthering their own interests in preference to the interests of the company and its shareholders. At the very lowest, this complaint is premature. The major change has just taken place. In time no doubt the directors will have to revise the position and the future profitability of the company, but that time has not yet arrived. No injury has been suffered by the company by the arrangements entered into with the LRT and the acquisition of the new premises. As I have pointed out, the company's capital position has been enhanced.

There is one other matter to which I should draw attention. Under s. 309 of the *Companies Act* 1985 the directors of a company are required to have regard to the interests of its employees as well as the interests of its members. This company has over 100 employees and because it has been able to find new premises in the same neighbourhood, the company has been able to ensure that their employment has not been jeopardised. The company's duty to its employees was clearly a matter which the directors were entitled to take into account if they were of the opinion that there was a reasonable prospect that the company's business could be salvaged.

Remuneration

The accounts show the total emoluments paid to directors and the emoluments paid to the chairman for the year to 31 March 1986 as £147,400 and £23,400 respectively; for the year to 31 March 1987 as £145,529 and £33,050; for the year to 31 March 1988 as £105,770 and £51,000; for the year to 31 March 1989 as £110,570 and £41,000; for the year to 31 March 1990 as £125,570 and £38,250; lastly, for the year to 31 March 1990 the figures are £144,010 and £41,000. The drop in the year for 31 July 1988 and the increase

A   in the emoluments of the chairman and chief executive during that year reflect the deaths of the two senior directors and Alan's appointment as chairman and chief executive. Since then the annual increase has slightly exceeded the rate of inflation generally.

In his affidavit in support of this application, Alan explains that two of the directors' wives received small salaries. The amount paid to the wives is in effect treated as part of the directors total 'package' and is calculated as an amount sufficient to cover each wife's personal allowances and any other available tax reliefs. He gives the total paid to the wives in the year to 31 March 1990, the last year for which accounts were available when he deposed to his first affidavit, as £13,920. This evidence is criticised in Ms Paradise's affidavit. She draws attention to the amount of travel expenses (£16,659 in the year to 31 March 1987, £13,731 in the year to 31 March 1988 and £16,543 in the year to 31 March 1989) and to directors' expenses in those years (£20,590, £13,098 and £13,206 respectively). She also claims that 'in the light of the refusal of those acting for the directors to disclose details of remuneration paid to directors and the wives', Alan's evidence should be 'ignored'.

In a further affidavit in answer, Alan gives a more complete breakdown for the year to 31 March 1990. The figures are: Alan, £38,250, wife, £8,640; David £21,070, wife £5,280; Stephen £26,250. The total paid to David and his wife is thus almost exactly equal to the remuneration paid to Stephen. Alan then gives details of other benefits provided for directors (a company car, petrol, home telephone bills and private medical insurance) and for their respective wives (a company car of modest value and petrol expenses and the benefit of the private medical insurance). The company also has set up a retirement benefit scheme for the directors and their widows: £40,000 was paid into the scheme in each of the years to 31 March 1989 and 31 March 1990. Alan's evidence is that the company has been advised by its pension advisers that the scheme is underfunded and that the annual contributions are less than the pension advisers recommended. As to the travelling and directors' expenses, Alan's explanation is that as a result of the expansion of the company's business, in particular in the sorting and export of second-hand clothes, the directors have incurred considerable travelling and allied expenses at home and abroad. All these expenses have of course been accepted by the Inland Revenue as properly incurred. Ms Paradise then in a further affidavit in answer claims that despite these explanations full information as to the remuneration paid to each director and his wife, including pension and other benefits, has still not been given and that 'in any event the petitioner does not accept the truth of what Alan says as regards benefits given to the directors and their wives and the travel expenses. What he says as regards benefits and travel expenses can only be tested after discovery and cross-examination'. There is no evidence that the directors are paid in the aggregate (including benefits received by their wives) more than the company would have had to pay to secure suitable replacements or that the level of remuneration is out of line with that paid to executive directors of other companies of comparable size and turnover.

I have set out this evidence in some detail for two reasons. First, the information that has been given to the petitioner is far more detailed than a minority shareholder is entitled to require. Secondly, there is, in my judgment, no ground for the claim, if it is made, that the level of remuneration and benefit to directors and their wives is 'disguised' by the accounts. In his affidavit Mr Neville says:

> '(5) It appears to be implied in . . . Ms Paradise's affidavit that the directors have deliberately procured the accounts to be prepared in a manner which disguises the level of remuneration payable to the directors and the value of the company's property. I would categorically state that at no stage have the directors of the company ever suggested that the level of remuneration payable to the directors or the value of the company's property should be disguised. I would similarly

categorically state that no such consideration has been in my mind in preparing   A
the company's accounts.'

I should nonetheless say a little more about two specific criticisms. There is, first, the practice of, in effect, diverting part of Alan's and David's remuneration to their respective wives. Alan explains that this practice is common in small businesses and has been adopted in this company for upwards of 20 years. Whatever may be said as to the propriety of this practice (and I am anxious not to say anything that could be read as in   B any way approving it) it has not adversely affected the company or its shareholders. Moreover, I understand that it has now ceased. Secondly, the accounts up to the year 31 March 1988 did not strictly comply with the provisions of the Companies Acts which require the chairman's salary to be shown separately and to show remuneration paid to the other directors in bands. That defect in the context of this case is trivial. It is also out of date. The accounts have been rectified in this respect for the year to 31 March 1988   C and subsequent years.

The gravamen of the petitioner's complaint is not that the remuneration and benefits paid to the directors and their wives is either excessive or disguised. It is that the company should not have continued its business and that the decision to do so was motivated solely or primarily by the directors' desire to hang on to their employment. I have already expressed my conclusions on that point.   D

Conclusion

In my judgment, the petitioner has not adduced any evidence which, if accepted at the trial, would support the allegations in the petition and justify the relief sought. The petitioner's case in substance is that something might be revealed on discovery in the course of cross-examination of the directors that could be relied on as justifying the   E petition. That is not a proper ground for presenting a petition. The damaging effect which the presentation of the petition may have on the business of a company, even if it is not advertised, has often been the subject of judicial comment. A petition should not be presented unless it can be supported by evidence which, if accepted at the trial, would found a claim for relief.

The petitioner faces other difficulties which I have not found it necessary to explore.   F The relief sought is the compulsory winding up of the company or the compulsory purchase of the petitioner's C shares by Marian and Alan. Neither Marian nor Alan alone has voting control of the company. The other directors do not hold voting shares. It is not said that Marian has joined with Alan in maintaining the present board in office for any selfish or even ulterior purpose. As at present advised, I do not see how a claim that Alan and Marian should buy the petitioner's shares can be supported. However, the point has not been argued and I say no more about it.   G

(Petition struck out with costs. Costs of the hearing to be taxed on the indemnity basis. Costs incurred prior to the hearing to be taxed on the standard basis. Additional costs incurred by the company to be included in the directors's costs. Leave to appeal on striking-out and costs refused)

H

COURT OF APPEAL JUDGMENT
(Delivered 25 March 1994)

Hoffmann LJ: This is an appeal from an order of Vinelott J striking out as an abuse of process a contributory's petition for an order under s. 459 of the *Companies Act* 1985 and to wind up on the just and equitable ground.

A

(1) The company

The company was formed in 1947 to take over the business founded by the petitioner's great-grandfather in 1891 and subsequently carried on by four of his sons. Its original and until recently main business was the manufacture and sale of industrial cleaning and wiping cloths made from waste textiles. But it also sells Johnson & Johnson J-Cloths and wiping products made from paper and it sorts and sells second-hand clothing (mainly for

B   export to Africa).

For many years the company owned a factory called the Stronghold Works in West Ham. In December 1989, London Regional Transport promoted a bill in Parliament for the extension of the Jubilee Line which included a power compulsorily to purchase the Stronghold Works. The company negotiated with London Regional Transport in advance of the passage of the bill and in October 1990 it entered into an agreement to sell

C   the Stronghold Works for £2,750,000 and at the same time bought new premises in Hackney for the same price. The move to Hackney was completed in October 1991.

In 1960 the company's shares were reorganised into three classes. There are 30 A shares, 174,300 B shares and 825,670 C shares. The A shares carry votes but no right to dividend. The B and C shares carry no votes but are entitled to a dividend, with the B shareholders entitled to ten per cent before payment to the C shareholders. For the

D   purpose of avoiding estate duty, most of the C shares were allotted to or in trust for the grandchildren of Saul Harrison's sons, including the petitioner. But the A shares were allotted to the three surviving sons of the founder, including the petitioner's grandfather Alfred. They have since devolved upon the petitioner's aunt Marion and her second cousin Alan. The petitioner's 87,563 C shares represent 8.76 per cent of the issued share capital of the company, all of which is still held by or on trust for members of the family. At the time of the hearing before Vinelott J the directors were Alan, his son Stephen and

E   the petitioner's first cousin David.

(2) The allegations

The essence of the petitioner's complaint is that although the company has substantial net assets, the prospects for its business have for some years been so poor that by the time the petition was presented any reasonable board would have closed it down and

F   distributed the assets to the shareholders. Instead, the directors have allowed the assets to be dissipated in losses in order to preserve their own inflated salaries and perquisites. The petitioner relies in particular upon the purchase of new premises in 1990. She says that any reasonable board would have regarded the proposed compulsory purchase by London Regional Transport as a golden opportunity to realise the company's principal asset and cease trading. The decision to buy new premises to continue a loss-making

G   trade could not have been bona fide.

In addition to these central allegations the petition also complains that the directors have caused the company to pay substantial salaries and benefits to their wives for little or no consideration. The accounts are said to be deficient; first, because the Stronghold Works were shown until sale at historic cost (£456,000) when they were plainly worth a great deal more, and secondly, because proper particulars of the directors' remuneration

H   were not given. Finally, it is said that the accounts for periods up to 31 March 1989 were qualified because the directors did not keep proper accounting records.

On these grounds the petitioner says that the affairs of the company have been conducted in a manner unfairly prejudicial to the C shareholders, including herself, within the meaning of s. 459 of the *Companies Act* 1985 and that it is just and equitable that the company should be wound up.

(3) 'Unfairly prejudicial' and 'just and equitable'

A

What must a petitioner show in order to justify an order under s. 459 or an order to wind up? The grounds for winding up are that it is 'just and equitable' to do so. The grounds for an order under s. 459 are that:

> 'the company's affairs are being or have been conducted in a manner which is unfairly prejudicial to the interests of its members generally or of some part of its members (including at least [the petitioner]) . . .'

B

If these grounds are made out, the court has a discretion to make such order as it thinks fit for giving relief in respect of the matters complained of; including in particular the relief sought in this case, which is an order that other members or the company itself buy the petitioner's shares: see s. 461(2)(d).

'Unfairly prejudicial' is deliberately imprecise language which was chosen by Parliament because its earlier attempt in s. 210 of the *Companies Act* 1948 to provide a similar remedy had been too restrictively construed. The earlier section had used the word 'oppressive', which the House of Lords in *Scottish Co-operative Wholesale Society v Meyer* [1959] AC 324 said meant 'burdensome, harsh and wrongful'. This gave rise to some uncertainty as to whether 'wrongful' required actual illegality or invasion of legal rights. The Jenkins Committee on Company Law, which reported in 1962, thought that it should not. To make this clear, it recommended the use of the term 'unfairly prejudicial', which Parliament somewhat tardily adopted in s. 75 of the *Companies Act* 1980. This section is reproduced (with minor amendment) in the present s. 459 of the *Companies Act* 1985.

C

D

Mr Purle, who appeared for the petitioner, said that the only test of unfairness was whether a reasonable bystander would think that the conduct in question was unfair. This is correct, so far as it goes, and has some support in the cases. Its merit is to emphasise that the court is applying an objective standard of fairness. But I do not think that it is the most illuminating way of putting the matter. For one thing, the standard of fairness must necessarily be laid down by the court. In explaining how the court sets about deciding what is fair in the context of company management, I do not think that it helps a great deal to add the reasonable company watcher to the already substantial cast of imaginary characters which the law uses to personify its standards of justice in different situations. An appeal to the views of an imaginary third party makes the concept seem more vague than it really is. It is more useful to examine the factors which the law actually takes into account in setting the standard.

E

F

In deciding what is fair or unfair for the purposes of s. 459, it is important to have in mind that fairness is being used in the context of a commercial relationship. The articles of association are just what their name implies: the contractual terms which govern the relationships of the shareholders with the company and each other. They determine the powers of the board and the company in general meeting and everyone who becomes a member of a company is taken to have agreed to them. Since keeping promises and honouring agreements is probably the most important element of commercial fairness, the starting point in any case under s. 459 will be to ask whether the conduct of which the shareholder complains was in accordance with the articles of association.

G

The answer to this question often turns on the fact that the powers which the shareholders have entrusted to the board are fiduciary powers, which must be exercised for the benefit of the company as a whole. If the board act for some ulterior purpose, they step outside the terms of the bargain between the shareholders and the company. As a matter of ordinary company law, this may or may not entitle the individual shareholder to a remedy. It depends upon whether he can bring himself within one of the exceptions to the rule in *Foss v Harbottle* (1843) 2 Hare 461. But the fact that the board are protected by the principle of majority rule does not necessarily prevent their conduct from being

H

A
unfair within the meaning of s. 459. Enabling the court in an appropriate case to outflank the rule in *Foss v Harbottle* was one of the purposes of the section. So in *Re a Company No. 00370 of 1987* (1988) 4 BCC 506, where the complaint was of a consistent refusal by the board to recommend payment of a dividend, Harman J said that such conduct could make it just and equitable to wind up the company. He did so by reference to the seminal judgment of Lord Wilberforce in *Howard Smith Ltd v Ampol Petroleum Ltd* [1974] AC 821 on the principles by which the court decides whether the board has acted within its
B
fiduciary powers and said that on the facts alleged it was arguable that the board had exceeded them. This seems to me in principle the correct point at which to start the inquiry into both whether the conduct in question could justify a just and equitable winding up and also whether it is unfair for the purposes of s. 459. It seems clear that but for a technical objection which was removed when the section was amended in 1989, Harman J would have allowed the petition to proceed on both grounds, as Peter Gibson
C
J did before the amendment in *Re Sam Weller & Sons Ltd* (1989) 5 BCC 810. I should however add that while I respectfully think that Harman J was right in asking himself whether the board had abused its fiduciary powers, I would not necessarily subscribe to the theory of corporate hubris on which he decided that it arguably had.

Although one begins with the articles and the powers of the board, a finding that conduct was not in accordance with the articles does not necessarily mean that it was unfair, still less that the court will exercise its discretion to grant relief. There is often
D
sound sense in the rule in *Foss v Harbottle*. In choosing the term 'unfairly prejudicial', the Jenkins Committee (at para. 204) equated it with Lord Cooper's understanding of 'oppression' in *Elder v Elder & Watson* 1952 SC 49 at p. 55:

> 'a visible departure from the standards of fair dealing, and a violation of the conditions of fair play on which every shareholder who entrusts his money to a company is entitled to rely.'

E
So trivial or technical infringements of the articles were not intended to give rise to petitions under s. 459.

Not only may conduct be technically unlawful without being unfair: it can also be unfair without being unlawful. In a commercial context, this may at first seem surprising. How can it be unfair to act in accordance with what the parties have agreed? As a general rule, it is not. But there are cases in which the letter of the articles does not fully reflect
F
the understandings upon which the shareholders are associated. Lord Wilberforce drew attention to such cases in a celebrated passage of his judgment in *Re Westbourne Galleries* [1973] AC 360 at p. 379B which discusses what seems to me the identical concept of injustice or unfairness which can form the basis of a just and equitable winding up:

> 'The words [just and equitable] are a recognition of the fact that a limited company is more than a mere legal entity, with a personality in law of its own: that there is
G
> room in company law for recognition of the fact that behind it, or amongst it, there are individuals, with rights, expectations and obligations inter se which are not necessarily submerged in the company structure. That structure is defined by the Companies Act and by the articles of association by which the shareholders agree to be bound. In most companies and in most contexts, this definition is sufficient and exhaustive, equally so whether the company is large or small. The
H
> "just and equitable" provision does not, as the respondents suggest, entitle one party to disregard the obligation he assumes by entering a company, nor the court to dispense him from it. It does, as equity always does, enable the court to subject the exercise of legal rights to equitable considerations; considerations, that is, of a personal character arising between one individual and another, which may make it unjust, or inequitable, to insist on legal rights or to exercise them in a particular way.'

Thus the personal relationship between a shareholder and those who control the   A
company may entitle him to say that it would in certain circumstances be unfair for them
to exercise a power conferred by the articles upon the board or the company in general
meeting. I have in the past ventured to borrow from public law the term 'legitimate
expectation' to describe the correlative 'right' in the shareholder to which such a
relationship may give rise. It often arises out of a fundamental understanding between
the shareholders which formed the basis of their association but was not put into
contractual form, such as an assumption that each of the parties who has ventured his   B
capital will also participate in the management of the company and receive the return on
his investment in the form of salary rather than dividend. These relationships need not
always take the form of implied agreements with the shareholder concerned; they could
enure for the benefit of a third party such as a joint venturer's widow. But in *Re
Westbourne Galleries* Lord Wilberforce went on to say:

> 'It would be impossible, and wholly undesirable, to define the circumstances in   C
> which these considerations may arise. Certainly the fact that the company is a
> small one, or a private company, is not enough. There are very many of these
> where the association is a purely commercial one, of which it can safely be said
> that the basis of association is adequately and exhaustively laid down in the
> articles. The superimposition of equitable considerations requires something more
> . . .'
                                                                                          D

Thus in the absence of 'something more', there is no basis for a legitimate expectation
that the board and the company in general meeting will not exercise whatever powers
they are given by the articles of association.

In this case, as the judge emphasised, there is nothing more. The petitioner was given
her shares in 1960 pursuant to a reorganisation of the share capital which vested the
entire control of the company in the A shareholders and the board whom they appointed.   E
This scheme is binding upon her and there are no special circumstances to modify its
effects. Although the petition speaks of the petitioner having various 'legitimate
expectations', no grounds are alleged for saying that her rights are not 'adequately and
exhaustively' laid down by the articles. And in substance the alleged 'legitimate
expectations' amount to no more than an expectation that the board would manage the
company in accordance with their fiduciary obligations and the terms of the articles and   F
the Companies Act.

Thus it seems to me that in this case one can be a good deal more precise than to ask
in general terms, as Mr Purle suggested, whether a bystander would think that the board
had been unfair. As there are no grounds for saying that it would be unfair for the board
to act in accordance with the bargain between the petitioner and the company, the very
minimum required to make out a case of unfairness is that the powers of management   G
have been used for an unlawful purpose or the articles otherwise infringed. Hence the
allegation in the petition that the board acted in bad faith, carrying on the business in
order to provide themselves with salaries rather than because they genuinely thought that
it was in the interests of the shareholders as a whole.

Mr Purle said that it was not necessary for this purpose that the petitioner should have
to show that the board was motivated by self-interest. It would be sufficient that the
decision to continue the business was irrational: one which no reasonable board of   H
rational businessmen could have thought was in the interests of the company. There may
be cases in which this distinction makes some sense but in this one it does not. If no
rational board could honestly have thought that carrying on the business was in the
interests of the company, the conclusion must inevitably follow that the board acted from
some improper motive of their own. The petition recognises this and squarely alleges bad

A   faith. In my judgment the claims for relief under s. 459 and winding up stand or fall by whether this allegation can be made out.

(4) The application to strike out

The respondents applied to strike out the petition under RSC, O. 18, r. 19 and the court's inherent jurisdiction on the grounds that it disclosed no cause of action or was

B   frivolous, vexatious or otherwise an abuse of the process of the court. The first ground was not seriously pursued: the allegations of bad faith on the part of the directors and A shareholders plainly disclosed a cause of action. The real attack was that the petition was an abuse of process because the incontrovertible facts showed that the allegations of bad faith could not succeed and that without them the petition was bound to fail.

The petition largely confined itself to the general allegations which I have summarised

C   and did not go into detail. This is in accordance with the modern practice, by which after service of the petition there is a return day at which the registrar gives directions for the filing of evidence and, if appropriate, the delivery of particulars of claim and defence: see r. 5 of the *Companies (Unfair Prejudice Applications) Proceedings Rules* 1986 (SI 1986/ 2000) and r. 4.22(3) of the *Insolvency Rules* 1986 (SI 1986/1925). The result was that the first statement in any detail of the facts concerning the company's business came in the affidavit of Mr Alan Harrison, chairman of the company, in his affidavit in support of

D   the application to strike out. A full statement of the petitioner's case emerged from the evidence sworn in answer and depended almost entirely upon the expert opinion of Mr Simmons, a chartered accountant who had examined the company's financial statements. Further exchanges of evidence followed and the judge gave his decision on 9 March 1992. In this court leave was given to both sides to adduce further evidence exhibiting financial statements which have since come into existence.

E   Mr Purle reminded us that the court's power to strike out a petition under RSC, O. 18, r. 19 or the inherent jurisdiction should be exercised only in a plain and obvious case. He referred us to a well-known passage in the judgment of Danckwerts LJ in *Wenlock v Moloney* [1965] 1 WLR 1238 at p. 1244B:

'. . . this summary jurisdiction of the court was never intended to be exercised by a minute and protracted examination of the documents and facts of the case, in order to see whether the plaintiff really has a cause of action. To do this is to usurp

F   the position of the trial judge, and to produce a trial of the case in chambers on affidavits only, without discovery and without oral evidence tested by cross-examination in the ordinary way.'

I entirely accept that the court cannot ordinarily resolve disputes of fact on affidavit and I agree with Mr Purle that the filing of an affidavit in reply by the applicant (as happened in this case) is usually a symptom of the existence of issues which can be

G   resolved only at a trial. In this case, however, the primary facts concerning the company's history and financial performance are not in any serious dispute. The question is whether those facts could arguably support an inference that the directors had abused their powers.

Mr Purle said that similar questions of inference as to motives arose in *Cayne v Global Natural Resources plc* [1984] 1 All ER 225 where the court was concerned with whether

H   the company's board had agreed to issue shares for the improper purpose of maintaining itself in office. Eveleigh LJ said at p. 230c:

'The plaintiffs' evidence, as I have said, clearly pointed to the inference which they asked the court to draw. Global's evidence, if true and accepted, of course clearly destroyed that inference. But the great question that has to be determined is whether the defendants' case is accepted or not. The mere fact it is deposed to does not make it incontrovertible. Therefore, when the evidence is not accepted by the plaintiffs, I am left in doubt as to the outcome of the trial on that issue.'

Kerr LJ said at p. 236d:

'Admittedly, the plaintiffs have strong inferences about the defendants' real motives on their side. There are considerable grounds for suspicion. But Global has strong evidence on oath on its side, and, when this is read together with the exhibits, it is quite clear that Global has a fully arguable case, which it is entitled to have tested on its merits at a full trial.'

So Mr Purle said that in this case, the board's denial of improper motive could not be regarded as conclusive. It was not accepted by the petitioner and the issue could therefore be determined only after discovery and cross-examination at the trial.

I do not think it is very useful to reason from what was said about the facts of another case. Clearly in *Cayne* the court thought that the plaintiffs had a strong prima facie case, considerable grounds for suspicion. There was a case to answer. But the question in this case is whether on the evidence taken as a whole and assuming in favour of the petitioner any disputed questions of primary fact, there is any case to answer. Of course it is always possible that discovery and cross-examination may produce some written or oral confession that the board were indeed acting in bad faith. But I do not think that the petition can be allowed to proceed to trial simply in the hope that something may turn up.

In exercising his discretion to strike out the petition, the judge referred to the damaging effect of the presentation of a petition under s. 459 and the burdensome nature of the proceedings, which may involve a lengthy and detailed investigation of the company over a long period. Mr Purle said that this was not a proper consideration to take into account. If the petitioner had a statutory cause of action, she was entitled to have it tried, whatever the consequences for the company.

I accept that the notoriously burdensome nature of s. 459 proceedings does not lighten the burden on the respondent who applies to have the petition struck out. He must still satisfy the court that the petitioner's case is plainly and obviously unsustainable. But I think that the consequences for the company mean that a court should be willing to scrutinise with care the allegations in a s. 459 petition and, if necessary, the evidence proposed to be adduced in support, in order to see whether the petitioner really does have an arguable case. This is particularly so when the petition rests on allegations of bad faith akin to fraud: see Sir George Jessel MR in *Re Rica Gold Washing Co* (1879) 11 ChD 36.

(5) The primary facts

The judge had audited accounts for the years ending 31 March 1986–1991 and unaudited management accounts for the six months to 30 September 1991. The supplementary evidence consists of the audited accounts for the years ended 31 March 1992 and 1993. Mr Simmons makes certain criticisms of the accounting methods but there is no challenge to the underlying financial facts which the accounts reveal. For convenience I shall summarise in tabular form the essential primary information disclosed by the accounts for the years ending 31 March 1986–1993.

Saul D Harrison & Sons plc
£000

Year to 31 March	Turnover	Gross profit	% Gross margin	Trading profit (loss)	Net profit (loss)
1986	2,118	684	32	(114)	53
1987	2,380	795	33	(39)	109
1988	2,560	563	22	(183)	(36)
1989	2,706	535	20	(119)	(8)
1990	3,230	634	19	(27)	95
1991	3,715	649	17	(93)	(25)
1992	4,379	861	20	40	71
1993	5,068	539	11	(349)	(336)

The petitioner's case before the judge was that the company's trading activities had made losses in every year since 1986. It had in some years reduced those losses and in others converted them into a net profit only because it had 'other operating income' which consisted principally of rent from letting part of its premises and investment income. But this income would accrue to the company whether or not it continued to trade. The company's trade showed steadily declining gross margins and nothing to suggest that they were likely to recover. Furthermore, the accounts did not charge against profits a commercial rent for the premises which the company owned and occupied. In assessing the viability of the business, one should take into account the opportunity cost of not letting the premises to someone else or selling them and investing the proceeds. On this basis the company's business was wholly uneconomic. In the light of these facts, the petitioner said that the proposed compulsory purchase of the Stronghold Works had been an ideal opportunity to cease trading.

(a) *Changes in the company's business*

The company's financial record must however be seen in the light of other facts deposed to by the respondents and not challenged by the petitioner. Until their deaths in 1987, Lionel Harrison (the founder's last surviving son) and his nephew Seymour (son of the founder's eldest son Alfred) had been the senior directors. Upon their deaths, Lionel's son Alan (who had previously been a director) became chairman and his son Stephen and cousin David (both young men) were appointed to the board. In his affidavit in reply sworn in January 1992, Mr Alan Harrison said that there had been a change of emphasis in the company's business. The original business of manufacturing industrial cleaning and wiping cloths from waste textiles now constituted only 35 per cent of turnover. It was exceeded by the sale of Johnson & Johnson J-Cloths, which accounted for 36 per cent. Of the remaining business, 23 per cent arose from export sales of second-hand clothing and six per cent from the sale of paper and ancillary wiping products. The most expanding part of the business was the J-Cloths, sales of which had increased from £709,000 in 1988-9 to £1.3m in 1990-1 and were forecast to reach £1.6m in 1991-2. Alan gave reasons why the directors were optimistic about this side of the business although it was highly competitive and margins were relatively low. He said that in his view the company's business was viable and capable of expansion. He produced management accounts for the six months to 30 September 1991 which showed an increased turnover and a trading profit of £13,745 without taking into account compensation for disturbance which was due to be paid by London Regional Transport.

(b) *Gross profit margins*

Mr Alan Harrison also pointed out that the decline in gross profits over the period 1988–1991 had not been as steep as the figures in the table would suggest. In each of the

years 1988–1990 there had been changes in accounting practice by which costs previously   A
taken 'below the line' were treated as costs of sales and deducted from gross profits. This
had led in each year to a restatement of the previous year's gross profit, so that for
example in 1990 the previous year's figure of £535,000 had for purposes of comparison
been restated as £492,000, which would produce a gross profit margin of 18 per cent for
that year as against 19 per cent in 1991. Similar adjustments had to be made to earlier
figures. Mr Harrison also said that the overall gross profit margin had been affected by
the changes in the sales mix. The expanding sectors such as the J-Cloths and clothing had   B
lower margins than the manufactured rags.

(c) *The move to Hackney*

Mr Harrison also explained what had happened when the company moved to
Hackney. The Stronghold Works was an outdated building which had value only as a
site for redevelopment. But in 1990 the value of redevelopment sites in London was   C
notoriously on the slide. When the Jubilee Line extension proposals were announced, the
company faced a potentially lengthy period of uncertainty while it waited to see whether
the bill passed and then whether London Regional Transport would obtain the money to
carry out the scheme. No one could predict when the compulsory purchase powers would
be exercised or what the value of the site would then be. The board therefore decided to
petition against the bill as a negotiating tactic with a view to securing an early agreement   D
with London Regional Transport. The outcome was the agreed sale of the Stronghold
Works, but the contract shows that it was a condition of that sale that the company
should have acquired new premises into which it would move. Mr Harrison said that
London Regional Transport made it clear that they had power to buy the premises in
advance of the passage of the bill only in order to enable the company to relocate its
business. If the company had decided to cease trading, it would have had to wait for the
compulsory purchase powers to be exercised. The premises could not have been sold   E
because they were blighted by the Jubilee Line proposals.

The terms of relocation are accepted to have been very favourable. The company
acquired new premises for the same price as it sold the old ones and London Regional
Transport paid the cost of fitting them out and compensation for disturbance. It also
allowed the company nine months' free occupation of the old premises to enable the
move to take place without pressure. Mr Harrison says that throughout the transaction   F
the company was advised by various professionals such as surveyors, management
consultants, accountants and solicitors. As a result, said Mr Harrison in January 1992,
the company had newly equipped and modern premises in which it could expand its
business.

The petitioner's solicitor Ms Paradise says on affidavit that she does not accept that
London Regional Transport would not have bought the premises for just as much even   G
if the company had decided to cease trading. Nor does she accept that it would not have
been better to wait for the compulsory purchase to go through. But these are simply
expressions of opinion which do not challenge the underlying facts or offer any additional
evidence to support the allegation that the board was motivated by self-interest. Where
the respondents have offered such explanations, it cannot be sufficient for a petitioner
simply to say that she does not accept them and wants to cross-examine.

H

(d) *The employees*

The importance of having regard not only to the petitioner's allegations but also to the
primary and unchallenged facts put in evidence by the respondent is shown very clearly
by the evidence about the company's employees. Mr Alan Harrison said that one of the
matters which the board took into account was the interests of the company's employees.

A   This is a matter to which they are required to have regard by s. 309 of the *Companies Act 1985*. Ms Paradise dismissed this claim with the sentence:

> 'I am informed by the petitioner and verily believe that almost all the employees, except for the directors, are very badly paid and rarely stay with the company for any significant period of time.'

In answer, Mr Alan Harrison went into some detail about the employees. There were over 100. The average length of service of the sales staff was over 22 years and that of the 30 labourers, textile cutters and graders over nine years. Some of the labourers were educationally sub-normal and would find it difficult to get other jobs. They were paid in excess of the Wages Council recommendation. In reply, Ms Paradise said that she 'did not accept' this evidence. But in my view this is not good enough and highlights the way in which the petitioner's case has been presented.

C   (e) *The directors' remuneration*

The allegation is that the directors have preferred their interests as salary earners to the interests of the shareholders. One is however bound to observe that the two younger directors have between them 109,454 C shares to the 87,563 held by the petitioner and that the siblings of the younger directors have 197,018 more. While this does not remove the possibility that they may be deliberately prejudicing their own interests as shareholders, it makes such an inference rather less plausible. When one turns to the salaries they earn, the inference is even less plausible. In the year to 31 March 1990 Mr Alan Harrison as chairman was paid £46,890 and the two younger directors £26,250 each. In the case of Mr Alan Harrison and Mr David Harrison, a part of their earnings was paid in the form of a salary to their wives. It is said that the wives rendered no services for this salary or for the modest cars which they were also allowed at the company's expense. This is a common enough practice in small companies and may or may not pass muster with the Inland Revenue. But given the scale of the overall earnings in relation to a company employing 100 people with a turnover of over £3m a year, the payment to the wives does not begin to form the basis of a claim of unfairly prejudicial conduct. The same can be said of the other subsidiary complaints made in the petition which the judge rightly dismissed as of no account.

F   **(6) Conclusion**

Looking at the matter in March 1992, six months after the company had moved into its new premises in Hackney, the judge said that the petition was 'at the very lowest' (by which I think he meant 'at best') premature. He said (at p. 484) that in the light of the evidence it was:

> 'simply perverse to allege that the board have carried on the business with no or no substantial expectation that they will succeed in making a profit reflecting the value of the assets employed and only with a view to furthering their own interests in preference to the interests of the company and its shareholders . . . The major change has just taken place. In time no doubt the directors will have to revise the position and the future profitability of the company but that time has not arrived.'

I agree. It follows that the petition as presented was on the evidence before the judge an abuse of process and was rightly struck out.

H   **(7) Postscript**

Is this conclusion affected by the evidence of subsequent events? The latest financial statements put before the judge were, as I have mentioned, the management accounts for the six months ended 30 September 1991. Since then, the audited accounts for the year to 31 March 1992 have become available and these showed, as appears from the table, a

trading profit of £40,000 and a net profit of £71,000. Mr Simmons has criticised these   A
accounts and explained why in his view they should be restated to show a trading loss of
£199,914. For example, he says that £66,262 received from London Regional Transport
should be excluded, even though the money was compensation for loss of profit caused
by disturbance. I do not propose to debate the accounting niceties because I do not think
that they matter. The issue is whether the directors acted improperly in carrying on the
business and for this purpose they must in my opinion have been entitled to rely upon
their audited accounts.   B

Finally, the accounts for the year ended 31 March 1993 show that that year was a
financial disaster. Mr Simmons says that this only confirms the predictions he was
making earlier, as reported by Ms Paradise. It may indeed show that Mr Simmons was
better at predicting the future than the board. But it does not retrospectively cast doubt
upon the motives of the board in carrying on the business in earlier years. It has led to
the reappraisal which Vinelott J predicted. The company has ceased the manufacture of   C
industrial wiping rags and is concentrating on its other forms of trade. Mr Alan Harrison
has retired with effect from 31 January 1994 and Mr David Harrison has given up his
employment with the company and become a non-executive director. In other words, the
members of the board appear to have responded to the crisis and taken what they
considered to be appropriate measures. There is nothing to show that the board have
acted unfairly in relation to the petitioner.   D

I would dismiss the appeal.

Waite LJ: I have had the opportunity of reading in draft the judgments of Hoffmann
and Neill L JJ. I agree with both and have nothing to add.

Neill LJ: The appellant, Mrs Rosemary Burr, is a minority shareholder in Saul D
Harrison & Sons plc ('the company'). The company was incorporated in 1947 to take   E
over an existing family business which had been founded by the late Saul Harrison in
1891. At the time of incorporation the business was run by Saul Harrison's four sons –
Alfred, Harold, Bernard and Lionel. The share capital of the company now in issue
consists of 30 A ordinary shares, 174,300 B ordinary shares and 825,670 C ordinary
shares. The A shares alone carry voting rights but they carry no rights to any dividend
nor to any share in the company's assets on a winding up. The B and C shares carry
rights to a dividend, the B shareholders being entitled to ten per cent before any payment   F
to the C shareholders. On a winding up the surplus assets are to be applied in making a
repayment on the B shares of the amount paid up together with any arrears of the fixed
cumulative dividend of ten per cent; the balance is then to be distributed to the holders
of the C shares. Mrs Burr holds 87,563 C shares, which represent 8.76 per cent of the
issued share capital of the company.

The present holders of the 30 A shares are Marian, the widow of Alfred's son, Seymour   G
Harrison, and Alan, the only son of Lionel. Mrs Burr (the appellant) is a granddaughter
of Alfred.

By a petition presented on 19 July 1991 the appellant applied to the court for an order
that the company should be wound up by the court, or alternatively for an order that the
A shareholders should purchase the appellant's shares at such price as was equal to the
amount that would be distributed to her on a winding up. The petition was presented   H
pursuant to s. 459 of the *Companies Act* 1985 (as amended) and under the *Insolvency Act*
1986. It was alleged in the petition that the affairs of the company were being conducted
in a manner which was unfairly prejudicial to the interests of some part of the members
of the company including the petitioner, and further, that it was just and equitable that
the company should be wound up. The petition included a consent by the petitioner to
an order under s. 127 of the *Insolvency Act* 1986.

A   By a summons issued on 1 October 1991 the directors of the company applied to the
court for an order under RSC, O. 18, r. 19 or under the inherent jurisdiction of the court
to strike out the petition on the ground that it disclosed no reasonable cause of action or
was scandalous, frivolous or vexatious or otherwise an abuse of the process of the court.

The summons to strike out came on for hearing before Vinelott J in March 1992. By
an order dated 9 March 1992 Vinelott J struck out the petition with costs. In the course
of his judgment (at p. 482C) the judge accepted that the petition disclosed a cause of
B   action. It seems therefore that the order was made on the basis that the petition was
vexatious or otherwise an abuse of the process of the court. At the end of the judgment
the judge expressed his conclusion (at p. 486):

'In my judgment, the petitioner has not adduced any evidence which, if accepted
at the trial, would support the allegations in the petition and justify the relief
sought. The petitioner's case in substance is that something might be revealed on
C   discovery in the course of cross-examination of the directors that could be relied
on as justifying the petition. That is not a proper ground for presenting a petition.
The damaging effect which the presentation of the petition may have on the
business of a company, even if it is not advertised, has often been the subject of
judicial comment. A petition should not be presented unless it can be supported by
evidence which, if accepted at the trial, would found a claim for relief.'

D   The appellant has now appealed to this court by leave of the single Lord Justice. She
does not any longer seek a winding up of the company but intends, if the petition is
allowed to proceed, to seek an order under s. 461(2)(d) that her shares should be
purchased by the holders of the A shares.

The protection of shareholders

E   Section 210 of the *Companies Act* 1948 introduced a new provision designed to furnish
shareholders who claimed that they were being oppressed with an alternative remedy to
the winding up of the company. The section, so far as is material, provided:

'(1) Any member of a company who complains that the affairs of the company
are being conducted in a manner oppressive to some part of the members
(including himself) . . . may make an application to the court by petition for an
order under this section.

F   (2) If on any such petition the court is of opinion–

(a) that the company's affairs are being conducted as aforesaid; and

(b) that to wind up the company would unfairly prejudice that part of the
members, but otherwise the facts would justify the making of a winding-up
order on the ground that it was just and equitable that the company should
be wound up;

G   the court may, with a view to bringing to an end the matters complained of, make
such order as it thinks fit, whether for regulating the conduct of the company's
affairs in future, or for the purchase of the shares of any members of the company
by other members of the company . . .'

When, however, s. 210 came to be considered by the House of Lords in *Scottish Co-
operative Wholesale Society Ltd v Meyer* [1959] AC 324, Viscount Simonds at p. 342
H   adopted the dictionary meaning of the word 'oppressive' and equated an oppressive
manner with a manner which was 'burdensome, harsh and wrongful'. Furthermore, at
p. 364 Lord Keith said that 'oppressive' suggested a lack of probity and fair dealing in
the affairs of the company. It may also be noted (1) that in *Re H R Harmer Ltd* [1959] 1
WLR 62 Jenkins LJ attached importance to the words 'burdensome, harsh and wrongful'
used by Viscount Simonds; and (2) that in *Re Lundie Brothers Ltd* [1965] 1 WLR 1051

Plowman J accepted at p. 1057 that in a case under s. 210 the petitioner had to 'establish   A
some element of lack of probity or fair dealing to him in his capacity as shareholder in
the company'; in reaching this conclusion Plowman J followed the approach of Lord
Keith in *Elder v Elder* 1952 SC 49 at p. 60 and in *Scottish Co-operative Wholesale Society
Ltd v Meyer* [1959] AC 324 at p. 364.

Further guidance as to the meaning of the word 'oppressive' in s. 210 of the 1948 Act
was given in the judgment of the Court of Appeal delivered by Buckley LJ in *Re Jermyn*   B
Street Turkish Baths [1971] 1 WLR 1042 at p. 1059G:

'What does the word "oppressive" mean in this context? In our judgment,
oppression occurs when shareholders, having a dominant power in a company,
either (1) exercise that power to procure that something is done or not done in the
conduct of the company's affairs or (2) procure by an express or implicit threat of
an exercise of that power that something is not done in the conduct of the   C
company's affairs; and when such conduct is unfair or . . . "burdensome, harsh
and wrongful" to the other members of the company or some of them, and lacks
that degree of probity which they are entitled to expect in the conduct of the
company's affairs. . . We do not say that this is necessarily a comprehensive
definition of the meaning of the word "oppressive" in section 210, for the affairs
of life are so diverse that it is dangerous to attempt a universal definition. We
think, however, that it may serve as a useful definition for the present purpose.   D
Oppression must, we think, import that the oppressed are being constrained to
submit to something which is unfair to them as a result of some overbearing act or
attitude on the part of the oppressor.'

Section 210 was one of the matters which were considered by the Jenkins Committee
in 1962. The committee considered that in some respects the section was too restrictive.
As a result of these and other criticisms s. 210 of the 1948 Act was repealed and   E
superseded by the provisions of s. 75 of the *Companies Act* 1980. It is, however,
unnecessary to refer further at this stage to s. 75 of the 1980 Act because that section was
itself replaced by s. 459 of the 1985 Act. Section 459 (as amended from 4 February 1991
by the *Companies Act* 1989) is, so far as is material, in these terms:

'(1) A member of a company may apply to the court by petition for an order
under this Part on the ground that the company's affairs are being or have been   F
conducted in a manner which is unfairly prejudicial to the interests of its members
generally or of some part of its members (including at least himself) or that any
actual or proposed act or omission of the company (including an act or omission
on its behalf) is or would be so prejudicial.'

The powers of the court on a s. 459 petition are contained in s. 461. Section 461(1)
provides:
                                                                                     G
'If the court is satisfied that a petition under this Part is well founded, it may make
such order as it thinks fit for giving relief in respect of the matters complained of.'

Section 461(2) includes the following provision:

'Without prejudice to the generality of subsection (1), the court's order may–

    . . .
                                                                                     H
(d) provide for the purchase of the shares of any members of the company by
    other members or by the company itself and, in the case of a purchase by
    the company itself, the reduction of the company's capital accordingly.'

It may be noted that s. 459–461 are in Part XVII of the 1985 Act which has the heading
'Protection of company's members against unfair prejudice'.

A **Unfair prejudice**

It is against the background of the earlier legislation relating to oppression that one must consider the statutory ground for an order under s. 459, that is that:

'the company's affairs are being or have been conducted in a manner which is unfairly prejudicial to the interests of its members generally or of some part of its members (including at least [the petitioner]) . . .'

B The scope of the protection afforded by s. 459 and by the remedies available under s. 461 is clearly intended to be more extensive than that provided by s. 210 of the 1948 Act. At this stage, however, the precise boundaries of the protection are unclear and they will have to be worked out on a case by case basis. Nevertheless it seems to me that it is already possible to collect from the cases decided under the 1948 Act and under the 1985 Act the following guidelines as to the correct approach to the concept of 'unfairly prejudicial' in s. 459.

C (1) The words 'unfairly prejudicial' are general words and they should be applied flexibly to meet the circumstances of the particular case. I have in mind the warning which Lord Wilberforce gave in *Ebrahimi v Westbourne Galleries Ltd* [1973] AC 360 at p. 374H in relation to the words 'just and equitable':

'Illustrations may be used, but general words should remain general and not be reduced to the sum of particular instances.'

D It is also relevant to bear in mind that whereas a winding-up order on just and equitable grounds will terminate the existence of the company a wider range of remedies is available under s. 461. In *Re a Company No. 00314 of 1989* [1990] BCC 221 Mummery J put the matter as follows (at p. 227B):

'Under s. 459–461 the court is not, therefore, faced with a death sentence decision dependent on establishing just and equitable grounds for such a decision. A court is more in the position of a medical practitioner presented with a patient who is alleged to be suffering from one or more ailments which can be treated by an appropriate remedy applied during the course of the continuing life of the company.'

(2) On the other hand, as Hoffmann J pointed out in *Re a Company No. 007623 of 1984* (1986) 2 BCC 99,191 at p. 99,196 in relation to a s. 459 petition:

F '. . . the very width of the jurisdiction means that unless carefully controlled it can become a means of oppression.'

These words have been echoed in later cases.

(3) The relevant conduct (of commission or omission) must relate to the affairs of the company of which the petitioner is a member: see Peter Gibson J in *Re Ringtower Holdings plc (Company No. 005685 of 1988 (No. 2))* (1989) 5 BCC 82 at p. 90.

G (4) The conduct must be both prejudicial (in the sense of causing prejudice or harm to the relevant interest) and also unfairly so: conduct may be unfair without being prejudicial or prejudicial without being unfair, and it is not sufficient if the conduct satisfies only one of these tests: see Peter Gibson J (ibid).

(5) In construing the word 'unfairly' in this context it will be necessary to take account not only of the legal rights of the petitioner but also consider whether there are any H equitable considerations such as the petitioner's legitimate expectations to be weighed in the balance.

(6) For the purpose of determining the legal rights of the petitioner one turns to the memorandum and articles of the company because the articles constitute the contract between the company and the member in respect of his rights and liabilities as a shareholder. Furthermore, it is to be remembered that the management of a company is

entrusted to the directors, who have to exercise their powers in the interests of the company as a whole.

(7) In order to establish unfairness it is clearly not enough to show that some managerial decision may have prejudiced the petitioner's interest. A shareholder on joining a company will be deemed to have accepted the risk that in the wider interests of the company decisions may be taken which will prejudice his own interests. Thus it may be necessary for the directors to take steps which are prejudicial to some of the members in order to secure the future prosperity of the company or even its survival: cf. *Re a Company No. 002470 of 1988, ex parte Nicholas* [1992] BCC 895 at p. 913 per Ralph Gibson LJ.

(8) Though it is open to the court to find that serious mismanagement of a company's business constitutes conduct that is unfairly prejudicial to the interests of the shareholders the court will normally be very reluctant to accept that managerial decisions can amount to unfairly prejudicial conduct: see *Re Elgindata Ltd* [1991] BCLC 959 at p. 993.

(9) A shareholder can legitimately complain, however, if the directors exceed the powers vested in them or exercise their powers for some illegitimate or ulterior purpose.

(10) Though in general members of a company have no legitimate expectations going beyond the legal rights conferred on them by the constitution of the company, additional legitimate expectations may be superimposed in certain circumstances. These may arise from agreements or understandings between the members or between the members and the directors. Thus I am satisfied that the concept of fairness in the phrase 'unfairly prejudicial' is capable of introducing considerations similar to those explained by Lord Wilberforce in the *Westbourne Galleries* case [1973] AC 360 at p. 379 where he said that the 'just and equitable' provision in s. 222(f) of the *Companies Act* 1948 enabled the court to subject the exercise of legal rights to equitable considerations. Lord Wilberforce continued:

'. . . considerations, that is, of a personal character arising between one individual and another, which may make it unjust, or inequitable, to insist on legal rights, or to exercise them in a particular way.

It would be impossible, and wholly undesirable, to define the circumstances in which these considerations may arise. Certainly the fact that a company is a small one, or a private company, is not enough. There are very many of these where the association is a purely commercial one, of which it can safely be said that the basis of association is adequately and exhaustively laid down in the articles. The superimposition of equitable considerations requires something more, which typically may include one, or probably more, of the following elements: (i) an association formed or continued on the basis of a personal relationship, involving mutual confidence – this element will often be found where a pre-existing partnership has been converted into a limited company; (ii) an agreement, or understanding, that all, or some (for there may be "sleeping" members), of the shareholders shall participate in the conduct of the business; (iii) restriction upon the transfer of the members' interest in the company – so that if confidence is lost, or one member is removed from management, he cannot take out his stake and go elsewhere.'

The application to strike out the petition

Counsel for Mrs Burr very properly reminded us that the court's power to strike out a petition under RSC, O. 18, r. 19 or the inherent jurisdiction of the court should be exercised only in a plain and obvious case. He referred us to the judgment of Danckwerts LJ in *Wenlock v Moloney* [1965] 1 WLR 1238. In addition Mr Purle drew our attention to the approach of the Court of Appeal in *Cayne v Global Natural Resources* [1984] 1 All

A   ER 225. It is clear, however, that in that case, as Kerr LJ said at p. 236c, there were 'considerable grounds for suspicion'.

Each case depends on its own facts.

In his judgment the judge gave careful consideration to what were described in the petition as the petitioner's 'legitimate expectations'. At p. 478 the judge made this comment:

B   'The significant feature of the petition is that it is nowhere alleged that there is anything in the history of the company or the relationship between the shareholders which could be relied on as superimposing an equitable fetter on the exercise of the rights conferred by the articles of association of the company. Any legitimate expectation of the shareholders must be found in the articles of association or in the general principles applicable to the conduct of the directors of a limited liability company.'

C   The judge then proceeded to deal with the matters set out in the petition which he grouped under five heads.

It is plain that this is not a case in which the equitable considerations to which Lord Wilberforce referred can have any application. One must therefore examine the petition and the evidence filed in support of it to see whether there is an arguable case that the directors have either exceeded their powers or have exercised their powers for some illegitimate or ulterior purpose.

D   I have had the advantage of reading the judgment of Hoffmann LJ in draft. Both Hoffmann LJ and the judge have subjected the facts alleged in the petition and the affidavits to detailed analysis. It is therefore unnecessary for me to attempt a further exposition.

E   I am quite satisfied that the facts alleged by Mrs Burr do not begin to establish a case of unfairly prejudicial conduct within the meaning of s. 459. Like Hoffmann LJ I can see no adequate basis for the allegation that the directors have carried on the business with no or no substantial expectation that they will succeed in making a profit which will reflect the value of the assets employed. The company has clearly passed through a difficult time, but looking at the matter objectively I can find no justification for the suggestion that the company has been kept going simply to further the selfish interests of the directors. As Hoffmann LJ has pointed out, the petitioner's evidence pays scant

F   regard to the obligations imposed on the board by s. 309 of the 1985 Act to take account of the interests of the employees of the company, of whom there are over 100.

I recognise that the words of s. 459 of the 1985 Act are very wide. I also recognise the exceptional nature of the jurisdiction to strike out a petition before discovery is complete and before there has been any cross examination. I have therefore taken time to look

G   carefully at the law and at the facts set out not only in the original evidence but also in the further evidence which was before us. Like Hoffmann LJ, however, I have come to the clear conclusion that there is nothing to show that the directors of the company have acted unfairly towards the petitioner or, applying as one must an objective test, she has been unfairly prejudiced by the manner in which the company has been or is being conducted.

I too would dismiss the appeal.

H

(Appeal dismissed)

Re BML Group Ltd.

A

Chancery Division (Companies Court) and Court of Appeal (Civil Division).
His Honour Judge Paul Baker QC (sitting as a deputy High Court judge);
Dillon, Leggatt and Henry L JJ.
Judgment delivered 8 February and 28 March 1994.

B

Company meetings – Class rights – Shareholders' agreement – Quorum – Power of court to order meeting – Shareholders' agreement provided that company meeting would not be quorate without B shareholder – On majority shareholders' application court ordered meeting without B shareholder – Appeal – Whether court order overrode class rights – Materiality of pending unfair prejudice petition – Companies Act 1985, s. 371, 459.

This was an appeal from a judge's order for a company meeting to be held under s. 371 of the Companies Act 1985.

C

There were five shareholders in the company, one of whom, 'B', held B shares. All were directors. Under a shareholders' agreement B, whose shares were 38 per cent of the issued shares, was entitled to remain in office as a director of the company for so long as he owned the B shares and a shareholders' meeting would not be quorate unless a B shareholder or proxy was present.

B became concerned that two of the shareholders, holding 52 per cent between them, were taking money out of the company to which they were not entitled. At a meeting the majority shareholders were removed as directors by a three to two vote on a show of hands without a poll. The majority attempted to requisition a further meeting but B refused to attend. They then applied to the court for a meeting to be held to reinstate them as directors.

D

The court ordered a meeting to be held at which any two members, not necessarily including the B shareholder, would constitute a quorum. The order was on terms relating inter alia to a pending petition under s. 459 of the Companies Act 1985 presented by B. The company appealed.

E

Held, allowing the appeal:

1. It was not right to invoke the s. 371 machinery to override the right of B, as the holder of the B shares, to be present in the quorum. That was a class right imposed for the protection of the minority by the shareholder agreement which had the same effect as if the rights had been set out as class rights in the articles.

F

2. The mere fact that a s. 459 petition had been presented did not lead to an automatic conclusion that the court's jurisdiction under s. 371 was ousted. But it might be a relevant factor and the judge had not given sufficient weight to the situation of the s. 459 petition and the allegations therein.

3. The company was in a situation with large numbers of legal proceedings started in which the shareholders were likely to find that their and the company's moneys had all been dissipated on legal costs. The ultimate result was likely to be the majority buying out B or vice versa or a winding up. It was not the function of the court to intervene by requiring various cross-undertakings to achieve the conduct of the company's business on sensible terms. That was for the parties' advisers. It was not for the court to make a new shareholders' agreement and impose it on them.

G

The following cases were referred to in the judgments:

Bushell v Faith [1970] AC 1099.
Consolidated Nickel Mines Ltd, Re [1914] 1 Ch 883.
El Sombrero Ltd, Re [1958] Ch 900.
Morris Funeral Service Ltd, Re (1957) 7 DLR (2d) 642.

H

A   *Opera Photographic Ltd, Re* (1989) 5 BCC 601; [1989] 1 WLR 634.
Paul (H R) & Son Ltd, Re (1973) 118 SJ 166.
Sticky Fingers Restaurant Ltd, Re [1991] BCC 754.
Whitchurch Insurance Consultants Ltd, Re [1994] BCC 51.

Nicholas Merriman QC (in the Court of Appeal) and Catherine Roberts (instructed by Scates Rosenblatt) for the company.

B   Patrick Howell QC (in the Court of Appeal) and Leslie Michaelson (instructed by Blaser Mills, Rickmansworth) for the first respondent.

HIGH COURT JUDGMENT
(Delivered 8 February 1994)

His Honour Judge Paul Baker QC: This is an application under s. 371 of the
C   *Companies Act* 1985 for the holding of an extraordinary general meeting of BML Group Ltd for the purpose of confirming or appointing the applicants as directors and removing two others.

I will start by looking at the section. It is headed: 'Power of the court to order a meeting'. The first subsection reads thus:

'(1) If for any reason it is impracticable to call a meeting of a company in any
D   manner in which meetings of that company may be called, or to conduct the meeting in the manner prescribed by the articles or this Act, the court may, either of its own motion or on the application–

(a) of any director of the company, or

(b) of any member of the company who would be entitled to vote at the meeting,

order a meeting to be called, held and conducted in any manner the court thinks
E   fit.'

There is no question but that the applicants here are entitled to make an application under that section, being members of the company. The second subsection reads:

'(2) Where such an order is made, the court may give such ancillary or consequential directions as it thinks expedient; and these may include a direction that one member of the company present in person or by proxy be deemed to
F   constitute a meeting.'

The third subsection reads:

'(3) A meeting called, held and conducted in accordance with an order under subsection (1) is deemed for all purposes a meeting of the company duly called, held and conducted.'

G   I may say that that section in the 1985 Act has been in the successive Companies Acts for many years now and certainly was in the *Companies Act* 1948, that being the Act in force at the date of one of the authorities I shall mention.

The proceedings before me are part of a dispute between the five directors and shareholders of this company which broke out in July 1993. I am sorry to notice that it is one of five sets of proceedings going on in the Companies Court and the Chancery Division, all arising out of the same set of facts, to which I now turn.

H   The BML Group Ltd was formed in 1988 as a holding company of a much older company which still exists and trades in business machines. That company is called BML Office Technology plc ('BMLO'). Before 1988, BMLO, which was then not a subsidiary but an independent company, was owned as to 80 per cent by Mr Humphries. The balance of 20 per cent was owned as to 15 per cent by Mr Roger Harman, who is one of the applicants here and was at all material times the managing director of the companies.

The remaining five per cent was owned by the other applicant here, Mr Paul Mills, who   A
is the finance director, or was at all material times.

Two other directors are Mr Iain Boyle and Mr Michael Mills. They looked after the
sales. Also before 1988 there was a company known as Team Leasing (Southern) Ltd.
That was a finance company which carried on a complementary business. It provided
finance for customers of BMLO and no doubt for other companies who wished to lease
office machinery rather than buy it outright. The chief person in that company and the   B
owner as I understand it was Mr Stephen Blumenthal.

Towards the end of 1987 or the beginning of 1988, Mr Humphries wished to retire
from business. As one sees, he was virtually the owner of the company which had formed
his livelihood. He offered to sell out his shares to the working directors, that is to say,
principally Mr Harman and Mr Mills. They could not afford on their own to buy out Mr
Humphries on any terms that he was willing to accept and hence Team Leasing, the
complementary company, came in as an investor and lender to assist. In that way Mr   C
Blumenthal and his company became direct shareholders of BMLO.

It was thought it would be convenient to structure the deal through a holding company
with BMLO becoming a subsidiary and to that end, on 18 February 1988, BML Group
Ltd was incorporated. It was then known as Bardrow Ltd. It has certain special articles,
but in the main BMLO Ltd adopted large parts of Table A. In particular it adopted
Table A, reg. 40, under which the quorum of meetings for the company had to be at least   D
two members. It is a standard article. There were a few special articles, mainly relating to
purchases of shares of retiring members and that sort of thing.

That having been set in place, on 8 April 1988 there was a shareholders' agreement.
Because it has been superseded, I do not need to go into this shareholders' agreement in
any detail. I think the only point I would mention about it is that it showed there that the
new company, Bardrow, had an authorised capital of £1m, divided into 500,000 A   E
ordinary shares of £1 each and 500,000 B ordinary shares of £1 each. In cl. 13 and 14 of
that agreement, one can see the relationship between the two classes of shares. But as I
say, I do not propose to go into that in detail, because it was replaced in circumstances I
shall mention.

Later in that year, on 31 May, the name of Bardrow was changed to its present name,
BML Group Ltd. In the following year, on 4 December 1989, there was a director's   F
service agreement in favour of Mr Harman. I should look at some parts of that. One
feature is that there is some confusion in it as between the two companies, BML Group
Ltd and BMLO, the operating subsidiary. The agreement was obviously not drawn up
to take full account of the coming into existence of the holding company. Those
discrepancies are the subject of one of the proceedings which I have mentioned. For my
purposes today, I think it is sufficient if I look at para. 14 of the agreement:

'On termination of this agreement howsoever occasioned the director shall: G

   14.1 Forthwith deliver to the company any property of the company or any
          company within the group and all records and documents letters and papers
          of every description within his possession or relating to the affairs and
          business of the company or any company within the group whether or not
          they were originally supplied by the company and shall not retain any copies
          thereof.'   H

That has come into issue in other proceedings, particularly I think relating to motor
cars, but again it is not a matter which I have to go into. Then the second one deals with
termination:

   '14.2 At any time or from time to time thereafter upon request of the company
          resign without claim for compensation from office as a director of the company

A and such offices held by him in the group (if any) as may be so requested and should he fail to do so the company is hereby irrevocably authorised to appoint some person in his name and on his behalf to sign and do any documents or things necessary or requisite to give effect thereto.'

Then it says he has to offer to sell his shareholding to the other shareholders of the company pro rata according to their existing shareholding and otherwise in accordance B with the provision in the articles of association.

I think that is all I need refer to, at any rate at this stage, in that service agreement. It had a large number of other provisions of the sort which you see in such arrangements.

That was back in 1988–1989 and the company went on trading so far as I know successfully throughout that period. The four men I have mentioned, that is to say, Messrs Harman, Mills, Boyle and Lees, were conducting the business of the company on C a day-to-day basis. Mr Blumenthal and his company did not play an active part in the management of the company. Then what happened was nothing to do with this company, but with Mr Blumenthal's company which, as I have said, had become an investor and lender of this company. Team Leasing, which I have described as a finance company, lending on leases of office machinery and so forth, owing to changes in the law as to tax allowances regulating that business, was forced into liquidation. The tax laws changed adversely. That had this impact on BML Group and its subsidiary: that Team Leasing's D shares in BML group had to be sold, no doubt to satisfy the creditors of Team Leasing.

The solution reached was that Mr Blumenthal personally would take over those shares at I think a sum of £85,000, but again, I am not concerned with the details of it. But it did require, among other things, a new shareholders' agreement, because there had been an important change in the shareholding, quite apart from the fact that Team Leasing, its business associate, had gone under.

E The new shareholders' agreement came into being on 15 June 1992 and there are some parts of that to which I must refer. It was made between the five directors and shareholders, that is to say, Mr Harman, Mr Mills, Mr Lees and Mr Boyle as the existing shareholders and Mr Blumenthal, who was coming in as the new shareholder. It recites that immediately prior to the execution of the agreement, Midland Bank, on behalf of Team Leasing, transferred 190,000 B shares held by that company in BML to Mr F Blumenthal and the existing shareholders agreed to waive their pre-emption rights as to the shares. Then I should note in the operative provisions this about remuneration:

'The present annual remuneration (exclusive of bonus and/or dividends) of each of the existing shareholders shall be as is provided for in their respective service contracts and letter signed immediately thereafter.'

That letter is dated 4 December 1989, so that it is the same date as the original G shareholders' agreement, and is addressed by Mr Mills to his colleague, Mr Harman. It says:

'Clause 3 of the schedule of the service agreement you have entered into with the company today refers to a profit-sharing bonus in addition to your basic salary. It is intended, until otherwise agreed between us in writing, that you will be entitled to receive an additional sum each month equivalent to the monthly amount you pay in respect of the loans taken out to purchase your shares in BML Group Ltd. H This is to be treated as part of your basic remuneration before calculation of any profit-sharing bonus or dividend.'

That letter has led to part of the area of dispute in this company. Mr Blumenthal claims that he was unaware of it until shortly before this agreement was entered into, i.e. in 1992. On the face of it, it shows the company providing some assistance by way of loan to assist Mr Harman to purchase his shares back in the 1988 takeover. That has

come under challenge as being an improper use of the company's assets by providing
that assistance in the purchase of its own shares. There again, that is not a matter which
is before me today, but that also is part of the contention between these parties.

The parties' current shareholdings in BML are set out in the first schedule of the 1992
agreement. That shows Roger Charles Harman as having 210,000 A shares, Paul Ronald
Mills as having 50,000 A shares, Michael John Lees as having 25,000 A shares and Iain
Douglas Boyle, 25,000 A shares. Lastly, there is Stephen Jeffrey Blumenthal, who has
190,000 B shares. The total of that is 500,000 shares, the aggregate of the A and B.
Therefore the issued capital of BML Group has been unchanged; it has an authorised
capital of £1m, but it has been unchanged at 500,000. That shareholding remains the
same today.

Before parting with this, it is of great significance that if Mr Harman and Mr Mills (as
they do) act together, then their combined shareholding is 260,000 shares, which is more
than 50 per cent of the total issued shares. Mr Harman has broadly 42 per cent; Mr Mills
ten per cent; Mr Blumenthal has 38 per cent and the other two gentlemen have five per
cent each. That is how it works out in percentages roughly, but the actual shares are as I
have stated in the schedule.

Going back to the shareholders' agreement, I have just mentioned the remuneration.
Then cl. 2.2 deals with Mr Blumenthal's remuneration, but that is not a matter I need go
into here. Clause 2.3:

'The amounts payable to existing shareholders pursuant to cl. 2.1' – which I have
read out – 'may only be increased by agreement between the parties. In the event
of any increase being agreed for Mr Harman and Mr Mills the amount payable to
the company pursuant to cl. 2.2 shall increase pro rata or if increases for Mr
Harman and Mr Mills differ pro rata to the increase which is the greater.'

I must now look at the ranking and status of shares. This is cl. 3:

'The A shares and the B shares in BML shall rank pari passu with each other in all
respects save:

3.1.1. in respect of the pre-emption rights which are set out in the second schedule;

3.1.2. that Mr Blumenthal shall be entitled to transfer the B shares in their entirety
to a company controlled by him and members of his immediate family . . .'

That is subject to a number of conditions, which I need not read out. Then:

'3.1.3. that Mr Blumenthal shall be entitled to remain in office as a director of the
company for so long as he or any company referred to in cl. 3.2 owns the B shares.
Such right shall be personal to Mr Blumenthal except that he may appoint an
alternate director . . .'

Then this is very important:

'3.1.4. that a shareholders meeting shall not have a quorum unless a B shareholder
or proxy is present.'

Then under 'Management and control' there is this:

'4.2. Mr Blumenthal shall be entitled to:

4.2.1. quarterly management accounts for the group;

4.2.3. to receive at least 14 days' notice of any board meeting.'

Then under cl. 5: 'Obligations of BML and other group companies':

'5.2. BML on behalf of itself and all other group companies undertakes that they
will not without Mr Blumenthal's written consent (such consent not to be
unreasonably withheld):

5.2.1. amend the memorandum and articles of association . . . save to give effect to the terms of this agreement;

5.2.2. issue any further shares in the company save in accordance with the provisions of the articles . . .

5.2.3. declare and distribute dividends save as authorised by cl. 2.4 hereof;

5.2.4. sell the whole or a substantial part of the business . . .

5.2.5. increase its directors' remuneration . . .'

Then under cl. 8, 'General' – I am passing over cl. 7 which deals with procedure on termination:

'8.4. Each of the parties hereto shall do all acts and things and execute all such further deeds and documents as may be reasonably necessary to more fully implement the intention of the parties as expressed in this agreement and in particular and without prejudice to the generality of the foregoing shall ensure that the articles of BML are altered to give effect to the provisions of this agreement and pending such alterations the provisions of this agreement shall prevail.'

As far as I understand from the evidence, there has been no alteration of the articles pursuant to that. The articles I have here show nothing of that sort. Then there is an exclusion:

'8.5. Nothing in this agreement shall constitute or be deemed to constitute a partnership . . .'

Then:

'8.6. For the avoidance of doubt Mr Blumenthal as a director and controlling shareholder of Team Leasing (Southern) Ltd and the existing shareholders confirm that the terms of the existing agreement shall no longer apply.'

So that is why I did not dwell in any detail on the 1988 shareholders' agreement. That is the current shareholders' agreement, or as much of it as I need refer to.

Of course, this brought Mr Blumenthal himself much more closely connected with the running of this business. He did not become an executive director, but he became quite an active one and was entitled to receive management accounts and other information. He was a director as well as a shareholder of this company. The trouble which has unfortunately come about here started when he discovered what he believed to be serious irregularities. If I go to para. 29 of his affidavit in response to this application, he says this:

'. . . Since about August 1992' – so that was a couple of months after the shareholders' agreement – 'I had begun to become concerned about the conduct of Mr Harman and Mr Mills in managing the affairs of the company. Up until that point, I had taken virtually no active role in its affairs at all. Mr Harman was the managing director and Mr Mills the finance director and I was aware that they managed the affairs of the company on a day-to-day basis, with Mr Lees and Mr Boyle confining their duties mainly to sales. I was alerted to this initially because of my discovery during my negotiations with the shareholders' agreement of 15 June 1992 of the existence of the letter of 4 December 1989 addressed to Mr Harman . . .'

I have read that letter earlier. Then he deals in more detail with that and says he has been advised that it is a breach of s. 151 of the *Companies Act* 1985. Then I can go to para. 33:

'Having been alerted to this unlawful arrangement I then began to investigate the extent to which Mr Harman and Mr Mills had been benefiting themselves out of

BML and BMLO and it came to my attention that they had systematically been   A
withdrawing sums of money far in excess of their contracted salaries and Mr
Harman in particular was procuring that bonuses were declared payable to himself
and other directors without proper consultation or authority, particularly in view
of the provisions of cl. 2.1 of the shareholders' agreement . . .

34. It also came to my attention that Mr Harman had run up a substantial
unauthorised 'loan account' with BML or BMLO and was generally acting in   B
breach of his fiduciary duties. Amongst other things, it became clear that Mr
Harman, with the assistance of Mr Mills, had maintained what is known as a
'notional loan account' in which was recorded expenditure made by Mr Harman
of a personal nature, but charged to BML or BMLO.

35. It also became clear that Mr Harman had been procuring that the company
declare or pay bonuses to him, without approval of the board, without approval   C
of shareholders, in breach of his obligations under the 15 June 1992 shareholders'
agreement, to enable him to utilise the value of those bonuses to offset against the
outstanding balance on his notional loan account. Furthermore, this notional loan
account was kept separately from the books and records of the company and was
kept secretly by Mr Harman and Mr Mills. The balance outstanding on this
notional loan account represented by personal expenditure incurred by Mr
Harman, but paid for by the company, is some £84,000.'   D

I think that is the gist of the complaints that Mr Blumenthal has against Mr Harman
and Mr Mills. It is in effect an accusation against Mr Harman of taking out of the
company money of the company to which he is not entitled. That is the broad nature of
those allegations. At that stage at any rate it did not seem that he was critical of his
conduct of the company's business.

Having made those investigations, Mr Blumenthal brought matters to a head at a   E
board meeting on 7 July 1993, that is almost a year after the revised shareholders'
agreement. It was a meeting that went on for some time, I think an hour and 15 minutes
the minutes record. I must look at what occurred at that meeting.

All five of these gentlemen were present. It was in the morning. Mr Blumenthal had
criticisms to make of the accounts, but that is not a matter which concerns me today.
Coming to directors' remuneration and emoluments, Mr Blumenthal made a number of   F
enquiries on that subject, asking for further information and explanations. There was
obviously a substantial and possibly heated discussion about those matters, but the
conclusion of it as far as Mr Blumenthal is concerned in this very long minute, which I
understand was compiled from notes made by Mr Blumenthal, is as follows:

'Mr Blumenthal said that he was not happy with the way the company was being
run. Issues, as he had said, were not discussed with the rest of the board time after   G
time, in spite of protests to this behaviour. Mr Harman appeared to be running
this business as if it was his and being aided by Mr Mills like a cartel and to the
detriment of the other directors and shareholders.

Mr Blumenthal also said that he felt his investment had been diminished, as it must
be for the others as well, and that the best interests of the company were not being
served by Mr Harman's actions, including these. The morale of the company was   H
down and there was dissention in the ranks.

Mr Blumenthal then moved therefore a vote of 'no confidence' in Mr Harman as
managing director and to remove him from office. The vote was carried by three
votes to two. Mr Harman and Mr Mills voting against.

Mr Mills said this could not be, as the meeting was not a shareholders' meeting.

A Mr Blumenthal rejected this by saying the vote is valid, this is a board of directors meeting and one does not need a shareholders' meeting.

Mr Blumenthal then proposed three further motions:

1. that Mr Lees be appointed the managing director with immediate effect;

B
2. the bank mandate for signing cheques be altered to Mr Lees and any other director (with the exception of Mr Harman); and

3. that Farrell Cheeseman, a firm of chartered accountants, be appointed forthwith to carry out an investigation of the company's records.

All of these motions were carried by a show of hands . . .'

The minute records that Mr Harman made several comments to Mr Blumenthal:

C 'Mr Harman asked if he was still to be salaried, Mr Blumenthal replied no.

Mr Blumenthal then handed out to each director, including Mr Harman, a notice of intention to remove him as a director at a meeting on 3 August 1993.

Mr Blumenthal pointed out to Mr Harman that he was still a director with the rights carried therein and a shareholder, also that he should go and obtain legal advice and that he would be contacted in 10–14 days with a view to discussing his shares.'

D
So Mr Harman, as I understand the evidence, was confronted on that occasion without warning and removed as managing director. There was a notice given, of which I have not seen a copy in the papers, to remove him as a director at a meeting on 3 August 1993.

Farrell Cheeseman were engaged to conduct an investigation. Their terms of reference were on these lines:

E 'According to the decision at the board meeting, we have been appointed by the board of directors following Mr Harman's dismissal as an employee of the company to review the accounting systems, policies and records of BML Group and in particular its trading subsidiary, BML Office Technology, and to report on areas of weakness and on any transactions which came to light and which we were are unable to satisfy ourselves were either appropriately approved by the board of directors and/or shareholders or were not in the best interests of the shareholders as a whole.'

F
This was shortly after 7 July. They completed their investigations and it is no part of my function here to look into what they found – that will be the subject of these other proceedings – but they were critical of Mr Harman and what he had done. They completed their report and handed it in certainly by 20 July. It does not appear exactly when they had completed it, but certainly by 20 July. That is because on that date both Mr Harman and Mr Mills were sent a letter:

G
'Please find enclosed notice of a forthcoming board meeting for Friday, 23 July at 11 am.'

This was on 20 July. The notice says:

'Notice is hereby given of a board meeting of the above companies:

H (1) to consider the report of Farrell Cheeseman. Attached is this document.'

So that document was sent to Mr Harman and Mr Mills on 20 July for a meeting two or three days later. At the board meeting which took place on 23 July, Mr Harman and Mr Mills were not present. It opened at 11 o'clock in the morning and it took about half an hour to hold the meeting. Mr Lees, Mr Boyle and Mr Blumenthal were present. The minute of the meeting says:

'Neither Mr Harman nor Mr Mills or alternate directors acting on their behalf   A
attended in spite of having had good notice.'

It may be good under the articles, but it certainly was not very long. The purpose of
the meeting was to discuss the report by Farrell Cheeseman commissioned by the board
at their meeting. Then these conclusions were reached:

'The board members present discussed the report mentioned and agreed that it was
very unpalatable and the behaviour of both Mr Harman and Mr Mills was   B
unforgivable and very damaging to the group. It was stated that the board had no
alternative but to sue and it was resolved by a unanimous show of hands to instruct
Scates Rosenblatt . . . to do so and for the avoidance of doubt the board ratified
the position of their decision previously taken to retain Scates Rosenblatt on behalf
of the group . . .

It was then moved that in the light of the foregoing and the implicated behaviour   C
of Mr Paul Mills in the report, to remove him from office and his position of
financial director and company secretary thereby terminating his contract with the
group, as we did with Mr Harman . . .'

Again, I cannot avoid noticing that no notice that that was being proposed was given
to Mr Mills. Then:

'It was further moved that cl. 14.2 in the service contracts of both Mr Harman and   D
Mr Mills be revoked and that they should both resign as directors and Mr Mills as
company secretary from all and any of the companies within the group and of
which they are directors and company secretary. Again, a vote was taken and by a
show of hands, unanimously passed by the board.

As neither Mr Harman or Mills or alternative directors representing them bothered
to attend the meeting, the board authorised Mr Lees to sign their resignations on   E
their behalf and to register the relevant documents at Companies House.'

The validity of that is I understand under challenge in other proceedings. Certainly no
notice was given so far as these documents show that that was going to be done. That
was on 23 July. On 30 July, the second of the proceedings which I mentioned at the outset
was launched. That was a petition under s. 459 of the *Companies Act* 1985, under which
the relief sought by Mr Blumenthal, if not by the others, was that the shares of Mr   F
Harman and Mr Mills should be purchased. In computing the price which they should
be purchased for, they should be at full value after taking into account the unauthorised
payments. So that petition under s. 459 was launched by the end of July.

On 3 August, we have a further meeting, this being a meeting of the company. There
are two minutes of what occurred at that meeting. The shorter one says that there were
present the five gentleman:

'Mr Lees opened the meeting at 3 pm to ratify the following motion pursuant to a   G
decision of the board that Roger Charles Harman be removed from office of
director of the company forthwith. Mr Lees asked for a show of hands on the
resolution. Three were in favour and two against. Therefore the motion was
carried. Mr Lees declared the meeting closed at 3.01 pm.'

The longer minute has this to say. There were the five gentlemen, plus Mr Charles
Lumsden, appointed by the chairman of the meeting to take notes: H

'Just before 3 pm, Mr Harman and Mr Mills were shown into the room and had
Mr Bennett, a solicitor, from Blaser Mills & Co' – that is the firm which is acting
for the applicants here – 'with them. When challenged as to his purpose, he replied
he was attending as an observer. The shareholders immediately objected and asked
him to leave. After not much of an attempt to stay, he departed to wait downstairs.

A
However, just before going, he enquired as to Mr Lumsden's purpose and was told that he was here officially by the chairman of the meeting's request and that Mr Lumsden was adviser to the company. Everybody was seated and the meeting declared open by Mr Lees, who thanked all for attending.'

Perhaps I should recall that Mr Lees had been appointed managing director of the company when Mr Harman was removed earlier in the year. Going on with the minute:

B
'Mr Lees said that the shareholders were here to vote on the resolutions before them and to ratify what had been done on the matter at our last meeting. Mr Lees then called for a show of hands, saying, 'All those for', to which Mr Lees, Mr Boyle and Mr Blumenthal voted. He then called for those against and both Mr Harman and Mr Mills voted against. Mr Lees paused, then said, 'By a show of three votes to two', the motion was passed. Mr Lees then declared the meeting closed at 3.01 pm. After this, Mr Harman enquired if this was an EGM. He was
C
told that it was. He said, 'I think you're wrong', stood up to go and said, 'You'll be hearing from us'. Mr Mills then said, 'This is a shareholders' meeting'. Mr Blumenthal told him that they should have asked in certain ways at certain times for that, i.e. at no time did Mr Harman or Mr Mills ask for a poll.'

Some of the evidence before me is directed to supplement what occurred there. Mr Blumenthal said in para. 40 of his affidavit:

D
'Mr Harman and Mr Mills attended the above-mentioned extraordinary general meeting with their solicitor, so they clearly had the benefit of legal advice. The meeting lasted precisely one minute. Mr Lees took the chair without any objection from either Mr Harman or Mr Mills. Mr Lees conducted the meeting and informed the meeting that its purpose was to vote on the resolution to remove Mr Harman as a director. The articles of BML are governed by Table A of the *Companies Act*
E
1985 and, accordingly, Mr Lees called for a show of hands in favour of the resolution. Mr Lees, Mr Boyle and myself put up our hands and then Mr Lees called for a show of hands for those voting against and Mr Harman and Mr Mills put up their hands. After a pause, Mr Lees said that by a show of hands, the resolution was passed. Mr Lees paused and waited for a reaction from Mr Harman and Mr Mills, but there was no reaction at all and accordingly he declared the meeting closed. At no time did Mr Harman or Mr Mills demand a poll. Neither
F
Mr Harman or Mr Mills indicated any desire to say anything at all, nor did they indicate even after the meeting was closed that they had the right to demand a poll.'

Mr Harman in his evidence had this to say about it:

'It is not clear to me why there exist two versions of the minutes of the meeting of 3 August. In any event, the correct position is set out in (3) of the letter from my
G
solicitors to the solicitors acting on behalf of Mr Blumenthal, Mr Lees and Mr Boyle. In short, my legal adviser, Mr Bennett, was denied access to the meeting and neither I nor Mr Mills was given a chance to demand a poll until after the meeting had been declared closed. The allegations that Mr Lees paused before declaring the meeting closed and that neither of us indicated, either during the meeting or immediately after it had closed, that we had the right to demand a poll are completely untrue. Mr Mills made it perfectly clear that he thought that such a
H
resolution was a matter for the shareholders, as opposed to the directors, to vote on.'

So that is how the evidence stands about that and the validity of that is also the subject of later proceedings, but on any score, even on Mr Blumenthal's evidence, it was a very hasty meeting and there was no specific reference at the meeting that it was a shareholders' meeting and that therefore voting rules were different and included the

right to demand a poll. Nothing of that was said to Mr Harman and Mr Mills. That   A
seems to be clear from Mr Blumenthal's evidence. It is of course also Mr Harman's
evidence. That was 3 August.

A week later on 10 August, what is called the fiduciary action was started. This is in
the name of the company and seeks to recover from Mr Harman the amounts which it is
said he has wrongfully taken from the company. In addition to cash sums, there had
evidently been a serious dispute about motor cars. There have been interlocutory   B
proceedings about that, I think in the way of injunction proceedings and O. 14
proceedings. So there has been quite a lot of activity in relation to that action, but the
present position there is that the dispute concerning cars has been resolved and the main
issues for an account of allegedly unlawful drawings has to go to trial by consent. Leave
to defend was granted, subject to the payment of certain funds which is itself evidently a
matter of dispute between the parties.

On the same day – this must be coincidental – Mr Harman gave notice requisitioning   C
an extraordinary general meeting:

> 'Notice is hereby given that an extraordinary general meeting of the above named
> company will be held at BML House . . . at 10 o'clock in the morning on Thursday,
> 9 September for the purpose of considering and if thought fit passing the following
> ordinary resolutions:
>
> 1. That Michael John Lees be removed from office of director of the company   D
>   forthwith.
>
> 2. That Iain Douglas Boyle be removed from office of director of the company
>   forthwith.
>
> 3. That Stephen Jeffrey Blumenthal be removed from the office of director of
>   the company forthwith.'

That produced a letter from Scates Rosenblatt, the solicitors, two days later. It said: E

> 'Mr Harman's purported notice of extraordinary general meeting for 9 September
> is invalid as his original requisition does not comply with s. 368(3) of the *Companies
> Act* 1985 as it was not deposited at the company's registered office. Furthermore,
> may we yet again refer you to the shareholders' agreement of 15 June 1992, and in
> particular, cl. 3.1.3 and 3.1.4. Mr Blumenthal cannot be removed as a director and
> any proposed shareholders' meeting is inquorate in the absence of his attendance.   F
> Irrespective therefore of the validity or otherwise of Mr Harman's notice, Mr
> Blumenthal does not intend to be present at this proposed meeting nor indeed do
> any of our other clients.'

Then they say that he called the meeting at BML House, but they will be denied access.
It ends up:

> 'Finally on this point and for reasons given in this paragraph our clients will not   G
> consider themselves bound by any resolution purportedly passed on 9 September.'

Just to complete the history of that aspect of it, on 9 September, Mr Harman and Mr
Mills did turn up at the company's offices, but they were refused access and held the
meeting, or alleged meeting, in the car park. The two of them purported to pass the
resolutions and the validity of those is a further matter which is the subject of other
proceedings. Indeed, an action to that end was started by these two gentlemen on 14   H
October 1993. That was an action by Mr Harman and Mr Mills concerning the validity
of that meeting and a number of other meetings and resolutions, some of which I have
gone over in the course of this judgment.

Then on the same day, 14 October, these proceedings were started. So on that day, Mr
Harman and Mr Mills started two sets of proceedings, one to test the validity of the

A   various meetings and resolutions passed thereat, and these proceedings. Now I should look at the originating summons. It is issued by Mr Harman and Mr Mills against BML Group Ltd and says:

'(1) that one or more extraordinary meetings of the company may be convened by the court for the purpose of considering and if thought fit passing the resolutions set forth in the schedule hereto;

B   (2) that the court may give directions as to the manner in which the said meetings are to be called, held and conducted and all such ancillary and consequential directions as it may think expedient;

(3) that the costs of this application may be provided for.'

In the schedule it says:

C   '(1) That it may be affirmed that Mr Roger Charles Harman is a director of the company alternatively that Mr Roger Charles Harman be appointed to the office of director of the company immediately.'

Then (2) is similarly as to Mr Mills.

(3) That Mr Iain Douglas Boyle be removed from the office of director of the company forthwith;

D   (4) That Mr Michael John Lees be removed from the office of director of the company forthwith.

(5) That any director of the company appointed since 23 July be removed from the office of director of the company forthwith.

(6) That it be confirmed that the only present directors of the company are Mr Stephen Jeffrey Blumenthal, Mr Roger Charles Harman and Mr Paul Ronald Mills.'

E   No attempt is being made to remove Mr Blumenthal. So that is the application before me. Just to round this off, I said there were five proceedings. The final one is on 21 December 1993. Mr Blumenthal started an action for rectification – he may be joined by others, but it is certainly by him – against Mr Harman and Mr Mills for rectification of the service agreement which I mentioned earlier.

F   That is a somewhat long review, but that I think is as far as I need go in reviewing the various resolutions. I have already read out the section which we are governed by, but I must just look at some of the authorities under which this section or its predecessor has come under consideration from the courts.

The earliest case is *Re El Sombrero Ltd* [1958] Ch 900, a decision of Wynn-Parry J. The situation there was a somewhat simpler one than I have before me, in that this was a company with 1,000 shares. The applicant held 900 and the two respondents, who were the only directors of the company, each held 50. No general meeting of the company had ever been held. The applicant, who was dissatisfied with the directors, wished to hold a meeting, but as two members were required for the meeting and the two other shareholders each refused to go, no meeting could be held which was quorate. So he applied under what was then s. 135 of the Companies Act, directing the convening of a meeting, and that was opposed. What the judge held was:

H   '(1) that the question raised by the word "impracticable" was merely whether in the particular circumstances of the case the desired meeting of the company could as a practical matter be conducted.

(2) That on the true construction of section 135 there was nothing to prevent the court intervening in a proper case and where the application before it was opposed by other shareholders.

(3) That the present case was eminently one in which the court ought to exercise   A
its discretion, because otherwise it would be depriving the applicant of his statutory
right under section 184(1) to remove the respondents as directors, because the
respondents had failed to perform their statutory duty to call an annual general
meeting.'

I think that statutory right is now in s. 303 of the *Companies Act* 1985. That of course
was a fairly simple case, nothing like the more elaborate facts we have here. The judge   B
had this to say about the general approach to this, having noted that the respondents
could frustrate the meeting by neither of them attending it (at p. 906):

'They (the respondents) have, it is true, a power to prevent him from doing so, but
that power is not derived from the articles; it is derived from the accidental
distribution of the shareholding in this company, and that, to my mind, explains
the whole difficulty which has arisen.

  C

I therefore arrive at the stage where I hold that I have jurisdiction in this case, and
there is nothing to prevent me exercising the discretion which is given under the
section if I choose to exercise it. It is true that I am sitting as an appellate court . . .'

That is because, before him, the registrar had refused the order and the shareholder had
taken the appeal to the judge.

'. . . but I am entitled to consider the question of discretion, because, in my view,   D
as I have held, the registrar has misdirected himself on a question of law. In my
judgment, this is eminently a case in which the court ought to exercise its discretion;
first, because if the court were to refuse the application it would be depriving the
applicant of a statutory right, which, through the company, he is entitled to
exercise under section 184(1), to remove the respondents as directors; secondly
(and I think this is a proper matter to take into account as part of the reasons for
deciding to exercise my discretion), the evidence disclosed that the respondents are   E
failing to perform their statutory duty to call an annual general meeting.'

So he made an order. The only other point which perhaps I should mention before
leaving the judgment is this. At p. 907, he said:

'Reference was made to other proceedings between the parties and to a motion for
the committal of the applicant for the alleged offence of endeavouring to procure
that one of the respondents should not be present in court. It appears to me that I   F
cannot properly take those other matters into account; I have no knowledge of
them at all, and were I in any way to take them into account, I would be, at any
rate to some extent, prejudging the issues between the parties one way or the other.'

The other authority which I was referred to by Mr Michaelson was *Re Opera
Photographic Ltd* (1989) 5 BCC 601, a decision of Morritt J. Again, there were quorum
difficulties. There were just two shareholders, holding the 100 issued shares. The applicant   G
held 51 per cent. They were the only directors and they had fallen out. The applicant
requisitioned a meeting of the company to remove the second respondent as director, but
the second respondent refused to attend any board meeting to convene the meeting. The
applicant convened the meeting himself, but the second respondent did not attend and
there was no quorum. So an order was sought under s. 371 and the judge held that the
applicant as the 51 per cent shareholder had the statutory right to remove the second
respondent as a director. The quorum provisions could not be regarded as conferring   H
some form of veto on the second respondent. Deadlock existed which had to be resolved
one way or another. The wrongfulness or otherwise of the conduct of either individual
would have to be determined in other proceedings.

He cited with approval a decision of Brightman J in an earlier case very briefly reported
(*Re H R Paul & Son Ltd* (1973) 118 SJ 166), in which Brightman J had said:

A
'His Lordship did not accept that the quorum provisions should be regarded as a right vested in the minority to frustrate the wishes of the majority, and he would therefore grant the relief sought.'

The other point which perhaps I should refer to here is the presence of other proceedings (at p. 603D):

B
'If he is, as no doubt he will be, removed if I make the order sought it may then well be that further proceedings will have to be undertaken by one side or another to procure the purchase of the other shares, but that seems to me to be inevitable in any event. It would be in those proceedings that the wrongfulness or otherwise of the conduct of either of the individuals would have to be determined in order to decide what order to make and in what form the relief should be.'

Something which takes the matter of other proceedings a little further is the presence, when an application of this sort comes before the court, of other proceedings. It is a C decision of Mervyn Davies J in *Re Sticky Fingers Restaurant Ltd* [1991] BCC 754 in which again there was frustration by a failure to attend a meeting, just involving two directors and shareholders. Having gone into the facts, which I do not propose to do for the purposes of my judgment, the judge held that M's (the respondent's) refusal to attend meetings should not prevent the company from dealing with its accounts, VAT etc. The discretion under s. 371 of the 1985 Act should be exercised to enable an effective board D to be brought into being but not so as to give W (the majority shareholder) the opportunity of harming M pending the outcome of (M's) s. 459 petition by causing him to be dismissed as a director or excluded from participation in the company's affairs. Accordingly, the order sought would be made subject to the proviso that each of the directors appointed pursuant to it would be restrained from acting as a director until he delivered to M's solicitors an undertaking that pending the outcome of the petition, he E would not exercise his rights to exclude M from his directorship; or interfere in M's day-to-day conduct of the business; or effect any alteration in the constitution or capital of the company.

In the circumstances of that case, that proviso would seem to me to be eminently justified under the subsection that a court may give such ancillary and consequential directions as it thinks convenient (s. 371(2)). If that was all there was to it, one would not particularly notice this case, but what has led to some division of opinion is the fact that F the judge prefaced his consideration of the detailed facts and other submissions with this statement on p. 757G:

'The difficulty, as I see it, arises from the fact that (1) it may be proper to use s. 371 to overcome the difficulty of achieving a quorum, but (2) it is not a proper use of s. 371 to use it indirectly to secure the removal of a director while a s. 459 petition is pending. As to (1) see *Re H R Paul & Son Ltd. . .*' – that is Brightman J's case –
G
'and *Re Opera Photographic Ltd. . .* In those cases, apart from other differences with this case, there was not the complication of a subsisting s. 459 petition.'

If one accepted that as of general application, it would mean that wherever there was a s. 459 petition pending in an application of this sort, an order can be made under it, but it must not be used so as to secure the removal of directors. It seems to be laying down as a general proposition that that would be an improper use of s. 371.

H
That is how matters stood when the case came before Harman J. of *Re Whitchurch Insurance Consultants Ltd* [1994] BCC 51. Harman J disagreed with the statement as a matter of principle that Mervyn Davies J had laid down. Again, this was a case of two directors of a company. I need not deal with the facts. He said at the end, after referring to this decision:

'Counsel observed by reference to the facts in this case where the s. 371 application

was on the very verge of coming on for hearing today, Monday 2 November, when   A
on Friday 30 October the s. 459 petition was presented, that he was not prepared
to argue that in every case where a s. 459 petition is presented apparently with a
view, at least in part, of frustrating an already pending s. 371 application there
should be a bar to the exercise of the discretion given by s.371. That concession by
counsel seems to me to be right. With the greatest possible respect to Mervyn
Davies J, whose views on the Companies Act I would always follow if possible, I   B
cannot think that the mere existence of a s. 459 petition at the date of the hearing
of the s. 371 application is inevitably a bar. It may be a bar. It is obviously a matter
which bears on the discretion of the court, but it is not something which prevents
the court exercising its powers.'

I respectfully align myself with the observations of Harman J in that case. It seems to
me that the s. 459 petition is a matter which has to be taken into account. It may result,
having done so, in the sort of order that Mervyn Davies J gave in the particular   C
circumstances, but it is not a bar to an order under s. 371, either in whole or in part.

Those are the authorities from which I have derived assistance in this matter. There is
one other I shall mention later, a Canadian authority.

Mr Michaelson makes these points in support of his application. This is a very brief
summary of them. The conduct of the meetings, and particularly that on 3 August, was
unfair. Then he says that the quorum provision which requires the attendance of a B   D
shareholder for a meeting to be valid is being abused. It is not being used to protect Mr
Blumenthal as a minority shareholder, but it is being used to attack Mr Harman and Mr
Mills and to get hold of the company in advance of the s. 459 petition, the proper forum
for the resolution of those sort of disputes.

Then he says that Mr Harman and Mr Mills, as over 50 per cent shareholders, should
not be denied their right to control the company and, in particular, denied their right to   E
remove directors and appoint other directors which is given them by statute.

Those I would accept are some forceful points, but I should have to mention at this
stage certain of the events regarding a letter that came to light during the course of the
proceedings. The applicants had obtained a letter, admittedly which was privileged and
obtained improperly, by the respondents' solicitors to the respondents. I do not propose
to go into the details. Suffice it to say it was to be used in cross-examination, but Mr   F
Michaelson failed to create an opportunity to use it in cross-examination.

The gravamen of the allegation is that the letter suggests that the costs of the individual
respondents can be taken from the company, but it may in the end be insupportable. It is
said that that conflicts with the categorical statement by the solicitor in para. 6 of his
recent affidavit. From that, he invites me to draw the inference that it was in furtherance
of a fraud and it goes to the heart of the stewardship issue. I do regard that intervention   G
as unfortunate.

Up to that point, the applicants had run the application in a way I found persuasive
based, as it was, on the incontrovertible facts of the previous meetings. They had
specifically declined to enter into undisputed facts on the very reasonable grounds that
they were not relevant to these proceedings. The disputed allegations are that the
applicants have been taking improper funds from the company. It is possible that the
defendants may be taking improper amounts. That is not a matter I am prepared to   H
entertain or look into at this stage. If that was so, then it may conceivably be relevant in
exercising the discretion which I have to exercise under the section, but I am not prepared
to infer that such serious allegations are true merely by looking at the documents which
I am invited to. In consequence, I have not taken that point into account in any way in
coming to my conclusion.

A   Miss Roberts addressed me carefully and fully on the matter both as to the construction of the section and the purpose of quorate provisions and the discretionary matters. Some arguments were addressed on the lines:

'Well, the difficulties are a matter of contract between the parties. They are not to be found in the articles. All the articles say is that any two members will be a meeting . . .'

B   and then sought to persuade me that it was impracticality, but not impossibility, that the section is aimed at.

There was also the point that none of the cases have dealt with where there are two classes of shareholding. Going back to the section, it seems to me that all that one has to find is that it is impracticable to call a meeting. There are to be no glosses on it, such as whether it is to be found in the articles or anything like that. The difficulties which I have recounted and the disputes which have broken out between these parties and the
C   expedients they have resorted to on both sides in calling meetings and getting things through do show to me that it is impracticable to have a meeting pending the resolution of the various proceedings which are going on. The very existence of the proceedings makes it impracticable to call a meeting in this case.

In her observations about the two classes of shares, Miss Roberts asked:

D   'What is the purpose of having enhanced quorum provisions? It is a mechanism to protect a minority shareholder. It is a tried and tested mechanism, protecting the shareholders who are a significant minority.'

I have no difficulty in accepting that as a general proposition, but I do not find it applicable to the situation we have here. Mr Blumenthal was not under attack. Mr Blumenthal was carrying the attack to the applicants.

E   That fact clearly differentiates the case from the Canadian case of *Re Morris Funeral Service Ltd* (1957) 7 DLR (2d) 642, which was a decision of the Ontario Court of Appeal. There, the applicants for a meeting were the newcomers. They were trying to get in to oust the sitting director, who was in a position, by using the quorum provisions, to resist it. Aylesworth JA said at p. 647:

'Applying – as I do – these principles to the application of s. 309 of the Act to the facts as revealed in this case, the order appealed from must be set aside. The alleged
F   difficulty is an artificial one, caused in great part at least by the respondents, who seek to invoke the section. In my opinion, except in extraordinary circumstances – none of which are present here – the section may not be invoked successfully for the express and sole purpose of placing in control of the company's directorate and affairs one of two or more contending factions among the shareholders. The present disagreement, among the three executors jointly entitled under the will to registration in their names of 147 shares, renders those shares ineffective so far as
G   voting is concerned. It is the championing by the widow of the cause of her fellow respondent which has brought about that disagreement. She and he ought not to be allowed to capitalise upon that fact by securing, through the Court's intervention under s. 309 of the Act, the ouster of bona fide directors who may not see fit to agree with them and the substitution in their place of directors more malleable to their will.'

H   But that is clearly distinguishable because here, the majority have been ousted. There, newcomers were trying to take over the existing management. So I do not find persuasive points of that sort, but Miss Roberts went on to make a number of other points which I think stand very differently.

Firstly, although there are independent proceedings, in substance this is interlocutory. Section 371 proceedings are independent proceedings and in substance they are

interlocutory. Who is to control the company pending the resolution of the various   A
disputes? Secondly, if this application is granted, it would put alleged wrongdoers back
in control. One course open to them, which they are likely to take, is to discontinue the
proceedings against them in the name of the company. That is the fiduciary action. The
right course is to preserve the status quo.

    I found those arguments very powerful, but I have come to the conclusion that they
should not prevail. The reason I have come to that conclusion is this. First, Mr Harman   B
and Mr Mills joined this company in 1974 and they have been the executive directors for
a long time, as well as being the controlling shareholders. Secondly, Mr Blumenthal, the
other substantial shareholder, has not hitherto been an executive director. Thirdly, the
allegations against Mr Harman and Mr Mills relate to unauthorised payments from the
company and not to mismanagement of the day-to-day business of the company.
Fourthly, while some of the allegations against Mr Harman are admitted, many are
disputed on substantial grounds. Fifthly, I notice that there is little or no notice of board   C
meetings or of the hostile resolutions which were to be passed at them. Sixthly and lastly,
the rights of Mr Harman and Mr Mills, if exercised correctly as regards a poll, would
have resulted in defeat of the moves to remove them as directors.

    I would regard the meeting of 7 August as conducted unfairly. There was confusion as
to the time of the meeting from what notice was given, their own solicitor was excluded.
They may have been entitled to do that, but he was excluded. The whole thing was rushed   D
through and no proper opportunity was given to Mr Harman and Mr Mills to consider
their rights.

    It is for those reasons I propose to make an order: a meeting of only two members and
the terms of it, it will not be necessary for a B shareholder to be present. Not necessary;
but of course he would not be excluded. But having regard to the interlocutory nature of
this application, the ongoing disputes on other matters, I am certainly going to impose
conditions. The two I have in mind – but I will discuss the details with counsel – are first   E
that pending the hearing of the petition, the emoluments of Mr Harman and Mr Mills
will be restricted to some level. Secondly, if Mr Lees and Mr Boyle are removed as
directors, then they will be given information of the company's financial affairs which a
director would normally be entitled to. Thirdly, if they are removed as directors, they will
not be dismissed as employees.

    Other conditions I have considered and do not see my way to enforcing at the moment   F
at any rate, are that Mr Lees and Mr Boyle would not be removed as directors – that is
looking at a condition something of the order that Mervyn Davies J found favourable.
But it seems to me that if one did that, the board meetings would then become
unworkable. Another is whether I should in some way stop any discontinuance of the
action which is going on in the name of the company against the directors.

    I have come to the conclusion that Mr Harman and Mr Mills are the controllers of the
company and the others must proceed in the position of minority shareholders.   G

(Order accordingly)

COURT OF APPEAL JUDGMENT
(Delivered 28 March 1994)

    Dillon LJ: This is an appeal against a decision of His Honour Judge Paul Baker QC
sitting as a deputy judge of the High Court given on 8 February 1994, whereby he   H
ordered that a meeting of the company BML Group Ltd be held pursuant to s. 371 of
the *Companies Act* 1985 whereat any two members of the company do constitute a
quorum of the members of the company.

    The company is a company whose shareholding consists of A and B shares. The
applicants to the judge, Mr Harman and Mr Mills, on whose application he made the

A   order convening a meeting, hold between them 260,000 A ordinary shares. Mr Harman holds 210,000 and Mr Mills 50,000. There are three other members of the company: Mr Lees and Mr Boyle, who each hold 25,000 A ordinary shares, and Mr Blumenthal, who holds 190,000 B ordinary shares. So Mr Blumenthal is the sole holder of the B ordinary shares and the others are holders of A ordinary shares. But it so happens that in the disputes that have broken out Mr Lees and Mr Boyle at present side with Mr Blumenthal.

B   Nonetheless Mr Harman and Mr Mills, between them holding 260,000 out of 500,000, hold over 50 per cent of the ordinary shares.

The history of the matter is that there was a company which has for some time carried on an active business which is now a wholly owned subsidiary of this company, BML Group Ltd. It came into business in effect to acquire the share capital of the subsidiary. The back history was that Mr Harman and Mr Mills, Mr Lees and Mr Boyle, were engaged in the running of the business. A director who had the control of the business to

C   a very substantial extent, 80 per cent, Mr Humphries, desired to retire. At some stage around the beginning of 1988 he retired and a company called Team Leasing Ltd came in to hold the B ordinary shares. There was a shareholders' agreement at that time, but that came to an end after Team Leasing had dropped out and Mr Blumenthal had acquired the B ordinary shares.

We therefore have the current shareholders' agreement between all the present

D   shareholders which deals with all sorts of matters, including the rights attached to the different classes of shares.

The company's articles are basically Table A. It is provided that the A shares and the B shares rank pari passu in all respects, save certain pre-emption rights which are set out. Furthermore, it is provided that Mr Blumenthal shall be entitled to transfer the B shares in their entirety to a company controlled by him and members of his immediate family.

E   It is also provided that Mr Blumenthal shall be entitled to remain in office as a director of the company for so long as he or any company referred to, that is to say family company to which he has transferred his shares, owns the B shares. Such rights shall be personal to Mr Blumenthal, except that he may appoint an alternate director.

Then, in cl. 3.1.4, it is provided that a shareholders' meeting shall not have a quorum unless a B shareholder or proxy is present.

F   There are then provisions for Mr Blumenthal to have quarterly management accounts and to receive at least 14 days' notice of any board meeting. There are various things that are not to be done without Mr Blumenthal's written consent. That is the general nature of the agreement. Unfortunately, difficulties arose last year when Mr Blumenthal came to suspect that Mr Harman and Mr Mills were paying themselves more than they were entitled to under the shareholders' agreement. Therefore, various meetings were held in July, which purported to be board meetings, at which Mr Blumenthal, with the support

G   of Mr Lees and Mr Boyle, terminated the employment of Mr Harman and later Mr Mills with the company. There was furthermore provision taken, purportedly under the shareholders' agreement, for notices to be given purporting to terminate Mr Harman's and Mr Mills' directorships of the company by resignations signed on their behalf. We are not concerned with the validity of those steps. There was then a very strange extraordinary general meeting of the company on 3 August 1993, convened for the

H   purpose of removing the majority shareholders, Mr Harman and Mr Mills, from office as directors of the company; possibly not Mr Mills but merely Mr Harman. It does not matter. The meeting began at three o'clock. It ended at one minute past three. Before the meeting began Mr Harman's solicitor, who attended, had been refused permission to remain. A show of hands was held on the removal of Mr Harman and it was carried on a show of hands three to two – Mr Blumenthal, Mr Lees and Mr Boyle against Mr Harman and Mr Mills. The meeting was declared closed immediately afterwards before

A

any reaction in the way of calling for a poll had time to take place. That is said to have been effective.

It seems to me extraordinarily difficult to see how it could have been.

Behind all this lies the fear that Mr Harman and Mr Mills had been taking money improperly from the company. To find out about that a firm of chartered accountants were instructed by the company, under the control of Mr Blumenthal, Mr Lees and Mr Boyle, to prepare an investigation. The accountants made a report. That includes a number of matters which amount to serious allegations against Mr Harman in particular. That being the state of affairs it is fairly apparent – indeed Mr Harman and Mr Mills purported to hold a meeting in the car park which was invalid in the absence of Mr Blumenthal – that there would be difficulty in holding any meeting of the company which was for the purpose of transacting any business that was not acceptable to Mr Blumenthal.

B

C

Section 371 of the *Companies Act* 1985 provides as follows:

'(1) If for any reason it is impracticable to call a meeting of a company in any manner in which meetings of that company may be called, or to conduct the meeting in manner prescribed by the articles or this Act, the court may, either of its own motion or on the application–

(a) of any director of the company, or

(b) of any member of the company who would be entitled to vote at the meeting,

order a meeting to be called, held and conducted in any manner the court thinks fit.

D

(2) Where such an order is made, the court may give such ancillary or consequential directions as it thinks expedient; and these may include a direction that one member of the company present in person or by proxy be deemed to constitute a meeting.

E

(3) A meeting called, held and conducted in accordance with an order under subsection (1) is deemed for all purposes a meeting of the company duly called, held and conducted.'

There are statutory antecedents of that section going back to the *Companies Act* 1862. The wording of the section is wide. The sort of circumstances in which it was commonly invoked, so far as my experience goes, up until 1958, were where for instance a company with a large number of shareholders or members had failed to comply with the provisions of the articles as to the retirement of directors by rotation and thus by the operation of the rule in *Re Consolidated Nickel Mines* [1914] 1 Ch 883 suddenly found, contrary to its belief, that it had no directors and it was necessary to have directors appointed. Other circumstances would be where the company's share register and records of its membership had been destroyed by wartime bombing or in a fire, and a meeting was necessary to resurrect the membership of the company and carry out the necessary formalities until that could be done. Equally there could be a case where, under the articles, notices of meetings had to be given to overseas shareholders and there were hostilities in foreign parts which prevented that being done and that could have prevented meetings being validly convened. So other directions could be given by the court.

F

G

However, in 1958, Wynn-Parry J decided the case of *Re El Sombrero Ltd* [1958] Ch 900. That was a case where there was a dispute between the majority shareholder, who held 900 shares of 1,000 shares in a private company, and two minority shareholders, who were the only directors and each only held 50 shares. It appeared that the two directors were happy with the situation and were not willing to attend a general meeting which might have involved their removal from office. They could prevent it de facto

H

A   because the articles provided that two members had to be present in person or by proxy to constitute a quorum for a general meeting. Wynn-Parry J held that the general right to have a quorum of two members, whoever they might happen to be, could not be regarded as a class right attached to any particular shares and so could be overridden by the court directing a meeting to be held at which one shareholder would be a quorum.

B   That has been many times followed and applied. Judge Baker purported to apply it in the present case.

I can refer for interim decisions to the decision of Brightman J in *Re H R Paul & Son Ltd* (1973) 118 SJ 166 and a decision of Morritt J in *Re Opera Photographic Ltd* (1989) 5 BCC 601. There Morritt J cites with approval a passage in Brightman J's judgment in *H R Paul and Son Ltd*, where he says:

C   'The jurisdiction conferred by the section was discretionary and his Lordship was therefore not bound to make an order. But to refuse B Ltd's application would deprive a majority shareholder of the right to alter the articles of association, and confer on a minority a right of veto not commensurate with their shareholding. His Lordship did not accept that the quorum provisions should be regarded as a right vested in the minority to frustrate the wishes of the majority, and he would therefore grant the relief sought.'

D   Those were in both cases the ordinary Table A quorum provisions. But it is entirely novel to seek to use the machinery of convening a meeting under s. 371 to override class rights.

It is not uncommon in private companies for steps to be taken to prevent a minority holding being overridden by the majority shareholders by entrenching voting rights on particular questions. Mr Howell accepts that if there were entrenched voting rights (as in *Bushell v Faith* [1970] AC 1099) it would not be appropriate to try to override them under

E   s. 371. Here we have, in the shareholders' agreement signed by all the shareholders attaching rights to the shares – which must have the same effect as if the rights had been set out as class rights in the articles – the provision that Mr Blumenthal is to be entitled to remain in office as a director of the company for so long as he or any family company to whom he had transferred the B shares owns the B shares. Then there is the quorum provision that a shareholders' meeting shall not have a quorum unless a B shareholder or proxy is present. That is essential to entrench Mr Blumenthal's right to remain a

F   director. With nothing else to protect it that would be overridden by an ordinary resolution.

The provision as to quorum is not just the mere chance that that is how the number of shares are held. It is a special provision to secure the directorship of Mr Blumenthal. I do not see why it is not equally entrenched as a provision which enables Mr Blumenthal to preserve in office any people who are his allies for the time being on the board, like Mr

G   Lees and Mr Boyle. The resolution which the applicants to the judge want to put forward at the meeting which the judge ordered would, besides confirming Mr Harman and Mr Mills in office, have the effect of removing Mr Lees and Mr Boyle from the board.

There is also the question of the petition which has been presented under s. 459 of the *Companies Act* 1985 by Mr Blumenthal and others, complaining about misapplication of funds by Mr Harman and Mr Mills. I entirely agree with Harman J in the case of *Re*

H   *Whitchurch Insurance Consultants Ltd* [1994] BCC 51, that the mere fact that a petition has been presented under s. 459 making serious allegations against directors does not lead to an automatic conclusion that the court's jurisdiction under s. 371 is ousted. But it may be a relevant factor. While we are not concerned to express any conclusion on the allegations that have been made, they are founded on an accountant's report. Some seem to have been admitted, although many are disputed. The judge, in setting out the reasons which led him to his conclusion, says:

A

'First Mr Harman and Mr Mills joined this company' – it was the operative company rather than the holding company – 'in 1974 and they have been the executive directors for a long time, as well as being the controlling shareholders. Secondly, Mr Blumenthal, the other substantial shareholder, has not hitherto been an executive director. Thirdly, the allegations against Mr Harman and Mr Mills relate to unauthorised payments from the company and not to mismanagement of the day-to-day business of the company. Fourthly, while some of the allegations against Mr Harman are admitted, many are disputed on substantial grounds.'

B

As to those points, I am bound to say that I attach great importance to the fact that there are allegations of unauthorised payments from the company and I do not regard it as an automatic conclusion that these gentlemen should have control of the board and of the day-to-day running of the company because they have not mismanaged the day-to-day business, even though they may have taken very substantial unauthorised payments. You do not want in charge of the company's business people who are strongly suspected of having stolen the company's moneys. One does not need to press that point very far. Mr Howell did not seek to support that particular part of the judge's reasoning.

C

Then he says:

'Fifthly, ... there is little or no notice of board meetings or of the hostile resolutions which were to be passed at them.'

D

Then he refers to the fact that if Mr Harman and Mr Mills had on 3 June correctly exercised their rights to demand a poll, the attempt to remove them as directors would have failed. It seems to me obvious that this company is in a situation, with large numbers of legal proceedings started, in which the shareholders are likely to find that their, and the company's, moneys have all been dissipated on legal costs, and the goose that they hoped to lay the golden eggs has been well and truly slaughtered. There are few companies that can afford the feast of litigation which these parties seem to be looking forward to. It is therefore strongly to be hoped that their legal advisers will be able to instil a measure of common sense into all parties to achieve an interim regime until any necessary litigation is decided, and to ensure that litigation is concentrated in the appropriate channels if there has to be litigation without a multiplicity of forays on different points in different proceedings.

E

It would seem that the ultimate result must be either (1) that Mr Harman and Mr Mills buy out Mr Blumenthal, or (2) that Mr Blumenthal buys out Mr Harman and Mr Mills, or (3) that the company is wound up very possibly at the suit of a creditor, when all its assets have been dissipated on litigation.

F

For present purposes I do not regard it as the function of the court to intervene in these sort of proceedings by requiring various cross-undertakings to achieve the conduct of the business of the company on sensible terms. That is for the parties' advisers to achieve. It is not for the court to make a new shareholders' agreement between the parties and impose it on them.

G

Beyond that, however, I am of the view that the judge has not given sufficient weight to the situation of the s. 459 petition and the allegations there. He has misdirected himself.

Much more, it is not right, in my view, to invoke s. 371 to override class rights attached to a class of shares which have been deliberately – in this case by the shareholders' agreement – imposed for the protection of the holders of those shares, although they are a minority. It is not the case that the overriding position is that the majority shareholders must prevail on everything.

H

Class rights have to be respected and I regard the right of Mr Blumenthal, as the holder of the B shares to be present in the quorum, as a class right for his protection which is not to be overridden by this machinery.

A   I would therefore allow this appeal.

Leggatt LJ: I agree that, for the reasons given by Dillon LJ, this appeal should be allowed.

Henry LJ: I agree. After some initial doubts I am persuaded that Mr Blumenthal's rights were entrenched as a class right in the shareholders' agreement; that those rights gave him an effective veto and that, as the company was deliberately set up this way,

B   s. 371 should not be pressed into use to rewrite the shareholders' agreement.

(*Appeal allowed. Order of judge set aside. Summons seeking convening of a meeting dismissed. Mr Harman and Mr Mills to pay the company's costs in the court below. Order not to be enforced against Mr Harman without leave in relation to costs incurred after he became an assisted person. Legal aid taxation of Mr Harman's costs in the Court of Appeal and below*)

Re a Debtor No. 32 of 1991 (No. 2).

A

Chancery Division (Bankruptcy).
Vinelott J.
Judgment delivered 30 March 1994.

Bankruptcy – Statutory demand – Power of court exercising insolvency jurisdiction to review order – Creditor served statutory demand for professional fees – Debtor disputed amount of fees – Whether statutory demand should be set aside – Insolvency Act 1986, s. 375(1).

B

A firm of accountants should not have served a statutory demand for its fees before the fees properly chargeable had been agreed or determined by the court. Accordingly the statutory demand was set aside. Where a demand was made for payment of reasonable remuneration for services rendered or for a reasonable price for goods supplied, the creditor ought to quantify his claim by obtaining a judgment before serving a statutory demand (except in exceptional cases where the minimum sum due could be ascertained by reference to some objective standard: where the rate of charging was agreed and the minimum time that had to be spent on the task for which remuneration was sought could be similarly established, or advance or periodic payments had been agreed). In the instant case the charges were based solely on the assertion of the creditor as to the time that had been spent and as to the quality of the staff employed to do the work.

C

D

The following cases were referred to in the judgment:

Debtor No. 32 of 1991, Re a [1993] 1 WLR 314.
Debtor No. 517 of 1991, Re a [1991] TLR 534.
Debtor No. 90 of 1992, Re a [1993] TLR 387.

Thomas Graham (instructed by Wright-Morris & Co) for the appellant.

David Holland (instructed by Beveridge Ross & Prevesers) for the respondents.

E

JUDGMENT

Vinelott J: This is an appeal from the decision of District Judge Hewetson-Brown given in the Hertford County Court in June and September 1993 on the rehearing of an application under s. 375(1) of the *Insolvency Act* 1986 which had been remitted to the county court by Millett J on 16 October 1992. Under s. 375(1) a court exercising bankruptcy jurisdiction has power to review, rescind or vary an order made by it.

F

The application under s. 375(1) was first made to District Judge Willers, also in the Hertford County Court, and sought a review and rescission by her of an order she had made on 12 March 1992 dismissing an application by Mr J D Perrin to set aside a statutory demand served by a firm of accountants, J B Morphew & Co, on 9 September 1991, and giving that firm leave to present a bankruptcy petition not earlier than seven days after the order. The application under s. 375(1) was dismissed by District Judge Willers on 3 June 1992. Mr Perrin appealed. Millett J discharged the order of 3 June 1992 and remitted the application to the county court for consideration whether the order of 12 March 1992 should be rescinded or varied and expressed the opinion that the application should be heard by a different district judge. He also ordered that the costs of the appeal should be costs of the rehearing. I shall return to explain the complex order made by District Judge Hewetson-Brown on the rehearing later.

G

H

The background which led to the service of the statutory demand and the subsequent history are fully set out in the judgment of Millett J which is reported at [1993] 1 WLR 314. However, the course which these proceedings have taken has caused me considerable concern and I think that to make this judgment complete and comprehensible I should briefly summarise the events which preceded the hearing before Millett J.

A   Mr Perrin was a sole trader. He dealt in motor cars and to a lesser extent in buying and selling small residential properties. In 1989 his tax affairs were in disorder. He had not filed accounts or returns for many years and the Inland Revenue had commenced a back duty enquiry. It is the usual if not the invariable practice of the Revenue in these circumstances to require a taxpayer to instruct an accountant with whom they can deal. The taxpayer instructed J B Morphew & Co ('the firm') to prepare accounts, to report to the Inland Revenue enquiry branch and to negotiate a settlement. There was no agreement as to the rate to be charged, as to the maximum time that could be spent without prior reference to Mr Perrin, no estimate was given of the likely amount of the bill, and no arrangement was made for interim payments on account.

In the early stages three small bills for some £2,000 each were submitted and paid. Then for a period of six months no bills were submitted. In August 1990 the firm submitted a bill for a further £24,000 including VAT of some £3,000. The debtor responded by expressing his shock at the amount of the bill. However, he paid £8,000 on account. That was in October 1990. He did not ask the firm to stop work, but he did ask to see the accounts that had been so far prepared. In the result he was not able to see the accounts because Mr Morphew, the senior partner of the firm, insisted that Mr Perrin should come to his offices and examine the accounts with him, a course which Mr Perrin declined to take because he feared that it would not give him sufficient time fully to understand what had been done.

There was further correspondence in which Mr Perrin expressed his anxiety at the amount of the bill which he described as 'horrendous'. Another six months passed and on 27 March 1991 the firm wrote asking Mr Perrin to pay the balance outstanding on the August bill, some £16,000. They also enclosed a further fee note of just under £19,000 including VAT of some £2,500. Mr Morphew said that he would not carry out any further work until his fees were paid, or an arrangement had been entered into for their payment. Mr Perrin sent him a further cheque for £8,000. At this stage he had paid approximately £20,000. The balance claimed was £28,000.

There followed some inconclusive correspondence. Mr Perrin asked for further information as to, amongst other things, the likely tax liabilities. His bank manager had asked him to obtain this information so that he could consider an application by Mr Perrin for an extension of his overdraft facility. The estimate of the tax liability given by Mr Morphew was £102,000 less payments on account of £26,000 (increased in a later estimate to £36,000), possible penalties of a further £76,000 and interest of £44,000 – a total of over £200,000. He refused to give an estimate of his future fees. He recommended that Mr Perrin should make a payment on account of the outstanding tax liabilities of £50,000.

In subsequent correspondence Mr Morphew said that the inspector wanted to see the business records and working papers in his possession which he said he would only supply if, amongst other things, outstanding fees were paid or secured. He also said that he had decided that:

> 'In view of the long delay in settling my fees I now intend to exercise my right of lien where appropriate and I shall not therefore release those items over which I have any such right until my fees have been paid in full.'

Immediately after that letter, on 3 August 1991, Mr Perrin received a letter from the firm's solicitors to say that unless the outstanding fees were paid proceedings would be commenced which 'might involve commencement of bankruptcy proceedings'. As I have said, the statutory demand was served on 6 September 1991. The claim including interest was now over £30,000. An application to set aside the statutory demand was made on 26 September for hearing on 16 October. There were a series of adjournments until it was finally heard on 12 March 1992. Mr Perrin filed a number of affidavits including an

affidavit by Mr Donnen, an articled clerk in the firm of solicitors instructed by him, in
which Mr Donnen made it clear that Mr Perrin regarded the fees charged as 'excessive in
the extreme'.

Mr Morphew filed an affidavit on behalf of the firm exhibiting the correspondence
between the firm and Mr Perrin. He pointed out that Mr Perrin had not put forward his
own estimate of what would be a reasonable fee and said that the final bill reflected a
reduction he had made of just under £6,000 because some of the work done had been
done by an inexperienced clerk who might have spent more time than was strictly
necessary. He exhibited the firm's costs sheets and claimed that there can be no genuine
triable issue on the paltry and unsubstantiated allegations made in the affidavit of Mr
Donnen. That was answered by the principal of the firm of solicitors instructed by Mr
Perrin who claimed that:

> 'It is apparent from the information received that Perrin was in business in a small
> way and it is quite inconceivable that a competent accountant could properly incur
> professional fees in undertaking proper work in respect of such a matter which fees
> would amount to or exceed the actual tax which could have been payable. It would
> have been infinitely wiser and easier for Perrin simply to have paid those moneys
> to the tax man and entered into an agreement which cleaned the slate.'

There was then a remarkable development. While the application to strike out the
statutory demand was pending Mr Perrin himself negotiated with the Revenue. The
Revenue had obtained the documents they required from the firm either in exercise or
under threat of the exercise of the powers conferred by the Taxes Management Act. At
the hearing before District Judge Willers Mr Donnen tendered a further affidavit
exhibiting letters from the Inland Revenue. The first, dated 2 March 1992, said that the
Commissioners had decided to accept an offer made by Mr Perrin in a letter of 2 March;
the second, dated 3 March, acknowledged receipt of a cheque for £30,000 which was said
to have been sent to the collector to be placed on deposit.

There is a manuscript addition to that letter which reads as follows:

> 'To cover all liabilities inclusive of penalties and interest for the years under
> investigation.'

It later transpired that the manuscript had been added by Mr Perrin and his conduct
was severely criticised in a subsequent affidavit by Mr Morphew. Mr Perrin's
explanation, which is not now in dispute, is that he had in fact reached an agreement
covering all penalties and interest and added these words to make it clear to his solicitors
that that was the basis on which the £30,000 had been paid. The position therefore on 12
March was that Mr Perrin had reached an agreement with the Revenue settling all
liabilities for a fraction of Mr Morphew's estimate and for a sum less than they had
recommended him to pay on account. It was also less than the total fees charged by the
firm, £20,000 of which had been paid.

District Judge Willers nonetheless refused to set aside the statutory demand. She gave
the firm leave to present a bankruptcy petition after seven days. I should, I think, make
it clear at the outset that in my judgment she was plainly wrong. It is said in a Practice
Note issued on 5 January 1987 that 'the court will normally set aside a statutory demand
if in its opinion on the evidence there is a genuinely triable issue'. The expression 'a triable
issue' is a useful formula, but it is, I think, important to bear in mind the context in which
this question has to be determined. If a statutory demand is not set aside and if the sum
claimed, or that part which is held to be indisputable, is not paid, the debtor faces the
serious consequences of a bankruptcy petition from which he may be unable to extricate
himself without considerable additional expense. The court must therefore always be
alert to the danger that a statutory demand may be used to put pressure on a debtor to
pay a debt, liability for which has not been established by judgment and which is disputed.

A   It must also be borne in mind that when an application is made for summary judgment
     under O. 14 or the corresponding rule in a county court (the jurisdiction from which the
     phrase 'triable issue' originates) the court can give leave conditionally on the sum or part
     of it being paid into court. That is a course which the court frequently takes in cases
     where it is 'very nearly prepared to give judgment for the plaintiff' or where the court is
     satisfied that the defence is a shadowy one and 'almost one in which summary judgment
B   should be given'. The court may also give judgment for an amount to be determined on
     an enquiry and conditionally on a sum being paid into court to await the enquiry. By
     contrast the court cannot set aside a statutory demand conditionally on the sum claimed,
     or part of it, being paid into a separate and secure account pending the outcome of an
     action to determine a debtor's liability. I respectfully agree with the decision of Knox J in
     Re a Debtor No. 90 of 1992 [1993] TLR 387 when he held that a demand must be either
     set aside or upheld and disagreed with the decision of Ferris J in *Re a Debtor No. 517 of*
C   *1991* [1991] TLR 534 where he set aside a statutory demand on terms that the sum
     claimed was paid into an account in the joint names of the creditor and the debtor's
     solicitors. The court must be confident that the debt is one liability for which cannot be
     honestly and reasonably disputed if it is to refuse to set aside the statutory demand which
     is not founded on a judgment.

          These principles are particularly important where a demand is made for payment of
     reasonable remuneration for services rendered or for a reasonable price for goods
D   supplied. I do not say that a statutory demand can never properly be presented in such
     case – that the creditor must always quantify his claim by obtaining a judgment before
     serving a statutory demand. There may be cases where the minimum sum due can be
     ascertained by reference to some objective standard. There may be cases where the rate
     of charging is agreed and the minimum time that had to be spent on the task for which
     remuneration is sought can be similarly established; or advance or periodic payments
E   may have been agreed. But these cases must be regarded as exceptional. In the instant
     case the charges were based solely on the assertion of the creditor as to the time that had
     been spent and as to the quality of the staff employed to do the work. Mr Perrin was
     denied access to the working papers, save on terms that he inspected them at the firm's
     offices, an offer which was withdrawn when the bill was not paid. There was simply no
     material by reference to which the court could judge the reasonableness of the firm's
     charges. Moreover, the purpose of employing the firm was to enable Mr Perrin to
F   negotiate a settlement with the Revenue and the charge made was out of all proportion
     to the compromise which Mr Perrin himself negotiated with the Revenue.

          However, although Mr Perrin issued a notice of appeal the appeal was not pursued.
     Those advising him apparently took the view that it would be unsafe to proceed further
     without independent evidence from an expert demonstrating that the charge was
     excessive, and meeting the criticism made by Mr Morphew in his affidavit evidence that
G   Mr Perrin had not put forward what he regarded as a reasonable charge. This further
     evidence would not be admissible on appeal and accordingly recourse was had to the
     jurisdiction conferred by s. 375(1). The application under s. 375(1) was supported by an
     affidavit by Mr Morphakis (wrongly spelt in the report of the decision of Millett J as
     Mulphakis) a chartered accountant of seven years' standing and a partner in a medium-
     size London firm. He had not examined the working papers and he gave his opinion on
     the basis of the papers in Mr Perrin's possession. It is not clear whether Mr Morphew
H   was asked to allow him access to the papers. District Judge Hewetson-Brown, in a
     judgment to which I will refer later, expressed the opinion that if a request had been
     made it would have met with 'a dusty answer', a view which was not dissented from at
     the hearing before me.

          However, Mr Morphakis saw the papers in Mr Perrin's possession and Mr Morphew's
     affidavit and he gave it as his opinion that the overall total of the work done should not

have exceeded £16,406 plus VAT giving a total of £19,277.05 just short of the £20,000   A
already paid by Mr Perrin. He added that:

> 'It would be my professional view that Mr Perrin has paid enough and should not
> pay any more without first a full investigation into (Mr Morphew's) assertions and
> full disclosure of his working papers.'

That affidavit was sworn on 2 June 1992. The application to vary or review under
s. 375(1) came before District Judge Willers on 3 June. The application was dismissed   B
after a hearing lasting only a few minutes. There is a dispute as to precisely what
transpired. A note agreed by counsel and comments on the note made by the district
judge are fully set out in the judgment of Millett J. He concluded (at p. 317H) that:

> 'Although there is a discrepancy between those two accounts I do not think that
> there is much doubt as to what happened or what the views of the district judge
> were. She clearly considered that there was no ground for seeking a review of the   C
> order; that (Mr Morphakis's) evidence should have been obtained in time for the
> hearing on 12 March; and that accordingly it was not material upon which an
> application for review could be founded. She does not seem to have recognised the
> distinction between a review and an appeal, or that the affidavit evidence of (Mr
> Morphakis) could not be admitted on appeal because of the doctrine laid down in
> the well known case of *Ladd v Marshall*. . .'
>   D
Millett J dealt fully with the question whether a decision refusing to set aside a statutory
demand was capable of being reviewed in an application under s. 375(1). He referred to
cases on s. 108(1) of the *Bankruptcy Act* 1914, the predecessor of s. 375(1), and concluded
that the court had jurisdiction to review a refusal to set aside the statutory demand (at
p. 320D):

> '. . . any fresh evidence must be cogent evidence that the debt is bona fide disputed.
> Where credible – it obviously need not be incontrovertible – it must be such that if   E
> unanswered it would undoubtedly lead to the setting aside of the statutory demand
> if made at the appropriate time.
>
> I turn to deal with the floodgates argument. It seems to me that the problem can
> safely be left to the discretion of the district judges who have great experience of
> debtors who make excuses for non-payment and take every advantage of the rules
> to delay the day of judgment. I do not believe that by confirming the existence of   F
> this jurisdiction and the admissibility of fresh evidence upon an application under
> section 375, notwithstanding that it could have been made available at the initial
> hearing, will lead to chaos in the county court.'

I respectfully endorse those observations. The court's power of review under s. 375(1)
is an exceptional power, not to be found in any other jurisdiction. The reason for
conferring this exceptional power on the court in exercising bankruptcy jurisdiction must,   G
I think, lie in the fact that bankruptcy results in a serious restriction on the debtor's
freedom of action and on his reputation. It should not be resorted to in place of the
ordinary process of appeal, save in cases where the court is satisfied that there has been
something amounting to a miscarriage of justice which cannot be corrected by the
ordinary process of appeal.

Millett J also held that on the evidence District Judge Willers had either not exercised
her discretion or, if she had exercised it, had done so on the wrong basis. He said (at   H
p. 320G):

> 'She did not consider whether the fresh evidence was admissible. She gave no
> consideration to its cogency or whether it was sufficient, if unanswered, to show
> that any outstanding liability was disputed. She does not appear to have recognised
> the difference between the appeal and review procedures and she seems to have

A   considered that because the case had been previously investigated the only proper course now was to appeal it.'

He accordingly remitted the case to the district judge and expressed the view that the application should be heard by a different district judge.

Further evidence was then filed. Mr Morphew deposed to a further affidavit questioning Mr Morphakis' standing and experience. One criticism made is that Mr B   Morphakis had not seen his working papers or the accounts prepared by Mr Perrin's previous accountants or his working papers. Mr Morphew at an earlier stage had, of course, refused to allow Mr Perrin access to the papers over which he asserted a lien and Mr Perrin and his advisers clearly took the view that it would be a waste of time to raise this question again. I have already referred to District Judge Hewetson-Brown's inference that any request would have met with a dusty answer.

C   Mr Perrin filed an affidavit by Mr Austin, a partner in a well-known London firm of accountants, with wide experience in handling back duty enquiries. He was very critical of Mr Morphew's conduct of the case, of his failure to ask for fees in advance, and of his conduct in continuing work after Mr Perrin had expressed dissatisfaction with the amount of the August 1990 bill and had paid only £8,000 on account. He thought that:

D   'Work should not have been recommenced until a fee had been agreed for the work done and a proposed fee agreed for work needed to complete the case as well as agreeing payment terms. I would expect such an approach to fees from an experienced professional. Mr Morphew's failure to adopt such an approach would indicate to me a lack of professional management skills.'

Mr Austin, like Mr Morphakis, did not see Mr Morphew's working papers. However, he took the view that the hours spent were excessive and said that:

E   'I would not therefore expect the total fees for the work carried out by Mr Morphew to be in excess of £20,000 excluding VAT even allowing for the nature of the work and the quality of the information and records provided.'

£20,000 plus VAT is some £2,500 more than the total moneys paid by Mr Perrin.

The application for review then came before District Judge Hewetson-Brown. He gave a written decision which was served on the parties' solicitors on 26 June 1993. His decision F   contains a very careful review of the earlier history and of the further evidence. He observed that:

'The respondent [that is Mr Morphew] exercised his lien over the papers and has refused to allow them to be inspected. It is not clear if they were asked to make them available to the appellant applicant's expert but if they had been I am satisfied he would have been given a dusty answer.'

G   His conclusion was that Mr Perrin had established grounds justifying a review but that, 'on the evidence he has himself submitted, namely that of Mr Austin, he may well owe another £2,500'. The order he made was that if within 11 days of service Mr Perrin paid £2,488.17, the statutory demand would be set aside and if not the application to set aside the statutory demand would be dismissed and the firm would be at liberty to present a petition. He also ordered that period for appeal should commence on the first date H   upon which both solicitors had received their copies of his judgment and had agreed a costs order or, if later, on the date of the county court determination of the costs issue by the county court. He then invited the parties' solicitors to agree an order for costs and directed that if no agreement had been reached within 14 days of the posting of his judgment a date should be fixed for hearing argument as to costs. No agreement was reached and on 14 September he ordered that the costs of the appeal and of the subsequent review should be paid by Mr Perrin; the firm's costs after 30 July 1993, when

Mr Perrin was granted a legal aid certificate, not to be enforced without leave. He refused   A
leave to appeal on costs.

The reason given by District Judge Hewetson-Brown for giving Mr Perrin 11 days in
which to pay the £2,500 was that:

> 'Time for compliance with this demand ceased to run on 26 September 1991 when
> that application to set it aside was filed and was never restarted again. As a demand
> was served on 16 September 1991, and he was given 21 days in which to pay it, he   B
> had a further 11 days in which to pay the sum of £2,488.17. If he does I will set
> aside the demand as to the balance. If he does not then the application to set aside
> the demand will be dismissed. This time-limit is critical because once the 21 days
> has passed I probably have no power to enlarge it.'

The district judge must, I think, have taken as his guide r. 6.5(1) of the Insolvency
Rules under which the court has power to set aside a statutory demand summarily and   C
without notice to the creditor; then:

> 'As from (inclusive) the date on which the application is dismissed, the time limited
> for compliance runs again.'

A closer analogy is r. 6.5(6) under which if an application to set aside a statutory
demand is dismissed after a contested hearing the court has a discretion to make an order
authorising the creditor to present a bankruptcy petition either forthwith or after a date   D
specified in the order. Rule 6.5(6) is not, I think, strictly applicable where an application
is for the review of a refusal to set aside a statutory demand. However, if the court
considers that the statutory demand ought to be set aside it must have a discretion, as
under r. 6.5(6) to fix a date after which the creditor is to be at liberty to present a petition.

The order of District Judge Hewetson-Brown is also open to the criticism that it is in
terms a conditional order and one which the court has no jurisdiction to make. Neither   E
of these criticisms affects the substance of his order. He could have reached the same
result by setting aside the statutory demand save as regards the sum of £2,500, and by
giving the firm leave to present a petition after a stated period thereby giving Mr Perrin
the opportunity of meeting the reduced demand.

The more substantial criticism is that by giving the firm leave to present a bankruptcy
petition if the £2,500 was not paid within 11 days after the date when his order was sent   F
to the parties' solicitors and then directing that the period of appeal should commence
when the costs had been agreed, or if not agreed within 14 days from the posting of his
judgment, when an order for costs was made by the court, the district judge effectively
put Mr Perrin in a position in which he could only avoid the presentation of a bankruptcy
petition by paying the £2,500 to the firm before the period for appealing against the order
began to run, and before the incidence of costs had been decided. By this time the costs   G
must have been very considerable and in the ordinary course liability for costs when
determined would be a matter which Mr Perrin and his advisers would want to take into
account before deciding whether or not to appeal.

Mr Perrin might have escaped from this dilemma by applying to the court for leave to
appeal and for a stay. However, he did not, he paid the £2,500. In an accompanying
letter his solicitors said the cheque was enclosed to comply with the terms of the court   H
order setting aside the statutory demand:

> 'Therefore, as the judge confirmed that it was an order for the decision to be
> reviewed and as the statutory demand will now be set aside it is clear that our
> client's application has been successful and therefore is entitled to costs. Would
> you kindly confirm your agreement to this so that we can notify the court
> accordingly.'

A   That, as I have indicated, was not acceptable to the firm's advisers and the question of costs was then decided by the district judge.

I was at one time troubled as to whether Mr Perrin having paid the £2,500 'to comply with the terms of the court order setting aside the statutory demand', it was open to him to appeal against the whole of the order made by the district judge. He had refused leave to appeal on the costs alone.

B   I have come to the conclusion on further consideration that these doubts are ill-founded. The court, in deciding whether to set aside or to refuse to set aside a statutory demand, is not called on to decide and has no jurisdiction to decide whether the debt claimed to be due is in fact due. The issue is whether on the evidence before the court the claim appears to be so plainly established as to justify the bankruptcy petition. The court does not exercise a summary jurisdiction comparable to its jurisdiction under O. 14. It follows that if the court does decide on an application to set aside a statutory demand on
C   the ground that there is no genuine dispute as to the debtor's liability, and if the debtor pays the debt to avoid the presentation of a bankruptcy petition, it is still in principle open to him to commence proceedings to recover the sum paid as money had and received. So also if the court decides that there is no genuine dispute as to part of the sum claimed and gives leave to present a petition if that part is not paid within the specified period. That is in substance the result of the order made by District Judge Hewetson-
D   Brown.

The last chapter in this sorry story of litigation is that on 8 October 1993 the firm commenced an action in the Queen's Bench Division claiming a balance due (after deducting the £2,500) of some £26,250. By his defence Mr Perrin claims that reasonable remuneration was £19,277.05 (Mr Morphakis' figure) or alternatively £22,644.17 (Mr Austin's figure) and by counterclaim seeks repayment of £3,366.95 or, alternatively, £2,487.88.

E   I must now turn to the issue in this appeal. I can deal with it very briefly. In my judgment District Judge Hewetson-Brown erred in treating the passage I have cited from Mr Austin's affidavit as an admission that Mr Perrin was liable to pay £22,644.29 less the sums paid on account. The most that can be said is that Mr Morphakis took the view that the value of the work done should be no more than £19,277.05 including VAT and that Mr Austin 'would not expect' the total fees for work carried out to be in excess of
F   £22,642 including VAT. Neither had had access to the papers in the possession of the firm and neither, therefore, was in a position to give any final opinion as to what would have been a reasonable sum. I have already pointed out more than once that District Judge Hewetson-Brown thought it immaterial whether they asked to see these papers or not because any request would have been refused.

In the action that has now been commenced the firm will have to give discovery and the court can decide in the light of the opinion of experts who have seen the documents
G   what is a reasonable charge for the firm's services. It may be less than the figure put forward by Mr Morphakis and Mr Austin as maxima. In my judgment the short answer to this case is that the firm should not have served a statutory demand before the fees properly chargeable had been agreed or determined by the court. I will accordingly set aside the statutory demand. The firm must pay the costs of the application for review by District Judge Willers and the costs subsequently incurred.

H   In my judgment the service of the statutory demand was an abuse of the bankruptcy procedure. However, the costs of the original application to set aside the statutory demand were ordered to be borne by Mr Perrin. There was no appeal from that decision and I do not think it is open to me on a review to vary that order.

(Order accordingly)

Re Ellis, Son & Vidler Ltd & Anor.

Chancery Division (Companies Court).
His Honour Judge Paul Baker QC (sitting as a High Court judge).
Judgment delivered 22 April 1994.

Administrative receivership – Directions – Whether goods were property of companies in receivership or of customers – Whether goods were ascertained – Whether resulting trust of purchase moneys arose – Whether companies were trustees or fiduciaries for customers – Sale of Goods Act 1979, s. 16.

These were applications for directions under s. 35 of the Insolvency Act 1986 by the receivers of companies which carried on business as wine merchants, in relation to stocks of wine held on behalf of customers. The respondents were representative customers.

The claimants had all bought wine, paid for it in full, left it with the wine merchants for storage, paid storage, and drawn it out in part as they wished. The wine merchants for their part segregated it from their own trading stock and did not consider that it belonged to them. The receivers took the view that it was impossible to allocate specific cases of wine to specific customers. Therefore they had not been appropriated to individual customers and were the property of the companies. The claimants sought to show that the goods were ascertained within the meaning of s. 16 of the Sale of Goods Act 1979 so that property had passed; alternatively that the seller had become a trustee or fiduciary of the goods for the claimants (thus circumventing the section). The wine which one claimant, 'J', had ordered and paid for had not left France when the receivers were appointed: he argued that there was a resulting trust of the purchase money.

Held, giving directions:

1. From the evidence it could readily be inferred that the parties intended the property in the goods to pass when they were set aside for storage. The segregation of the stock from the company's trading assets, whether done physically, or by giving instructions to a bonded warehouse keeper, caused the goods to be ascertained for the purposes of s. 16. If a number of cases or bottles of identical wine were held, not mingled with the trading stock, in store for a group of customers, those cases or bottles would be ascertained for the purposes of s. 16 even though they were not immediately appropriated to each individual customer. Property passed by common intention. They took as tenants in common.

2. J had no proprietary interest. The wine that he had ordered had not left France when the receivers were appointed. It remained part of the generic stock of the vineyards, but subject to a contract for its sale to the company. It plainly had not been ascertained under the contract between the company and J. There was no question of any trust of the purchase money which was used, and intended to be used, to finance the purchase of the wine in France. There was no question of segregating it in a separate trust account to await the import of the wine into this country.

3. None of the wine in one bonded warehouse had been appropriated to specific customers either by marks on the cases or by an inventory. There had been no attempt by the company to allocate any of the wine to customers' orders. At the time of the receivers' appointment those wines had not been ascertained. (Re London Wine Co (Shippers) Ltd [1986] PCC 121 applied.)

4. On the question of a fiduciary or constructive trust existing between the companies and their customers, the court was bound by authority to hold that a contract for the sale of goods did not of itself create equitable rights: a contractual obligation to store the goods of another did not give rise to a trust. The respective rights and obligations of the parties were governed exclusively by the terms of the two contracts. Nor could any kind of equitable interest be based on estoppel or specific performance. (Re Wait [1927] 1 Ch 606 applied.)

A   The following cases were referred to in the judgment:

Federspiel (Carlos) & Co SA v Charles Twigg & Co Ltd & Anor [1957] 1 Ll L Rep 240.
Healy v Howlett & Sons [1917] 1 KB 337.
Indian Oil Corporation Ltd v Greenstone Shipping SA (Panama) ('The Ypatianna') [1988] QB 345.
Karlshamns Olje Fabriker v Eastport Navigation Corporation ('The Elafi') [1981] 2 Ll Rep 679.

B

Kayford Ltd, Re [1975] 1 WLR 279.
Liggett v Kensington [1993] 1 NZLR 257.
London Wine Co (Shippers) Ltd, Re [1986] PCC 121.
Napier and Ettrick (Lord) & Anor v Hunter & Ors [1993] AC 713.
Spence & Anor v Union Marine Insurance Co Ltd (1868) LR 3 CP 427.
Wait and James v Midland Bank Ltd (1926) 24 Ll L Rep 313.

C   *Wait, Re* [1927] 1 Ch 606.

Peter Arden (instructed by Wilde Sapte) for the receivers.

Roger Ter Haar QC and Norman Palmer (instructed by Rubinstein Callingham Polden & Gale) for the respondents.

JUDGMENT

D   **His Honour Judge Paul Baker QC:** The applicants, Nigel John Vooght and Christopher John Hughes, are the joint administrative receivers of Ellis, Son & Vidler Ltd ('ESV') and Stapylton Fletcher Ltd ('SFL') appointed on 29 May 1992 by National Westminster Bank plc ('the bank') under debentures dated 14 April 1987 and 17 May 1982 respectively. Both companies were in the business of wine merchants. Until a few weeks before the appointment of the receivers they were independent of each other but the shares of both were then acquired by Mr Nigel Baring or his company, Nigel Baring & Co Ltd. The receivers seek directions under s. 35 of the *Insolvency Act* 1986 in relation to stocks of wine held on behalf of the companies' customers. It is not the first time that this problem has come before the courts. In 1975 Oliver J determined *Re London Wine Co (Shippers) Ltd* [1986] PCC 121, but not all questions were then resolved, and the facts in the present case are markedly different. Most of the questions arise in connection with ESV so I shall deal with that first and then at the end come briefly to SFL.

F   About 70 customers of ESV have wine stored with the company, mostly small amounts of high quality wine. The respondents are representative customers. I will explain their positions after recounting the facts, which are not in dispute.

The present company was incorporated on 24 April 1986, but the business in some form or other had been in existence for some 200 years. In 1970 the then company, also known as Ellis, Son & Vidler Ltd, came under the control of Major Shand. At that time it operated in Hastings where it had offices and three warehouses. For a description of the mode of operation at that stage I go to the statement of Mr Brian Steedman. He was at all material times in charge of office management and customer relations. He explains that when a warehouse received instructions on an order to reserve a particular quantity of a specified wine, a warehouseman would physically remove the wine from the general trading stock area of the warehouse to customers' reserve area. He continues at para. 10:

H   'A very occasional practice at Hastings which came to light when I did the audit at Cliffe on the stock which came over from Hastings was where a customer had ordered a case or cases of a certain vintage of, for example, a Chablis 1977 in customers' reserve, one of the those cases had been taken out of that customer's reserve to keep another, subsequent customer happy. When the replacement shipment came in, the vintage had changed, and that created a problem with the original customer and the records of the customers' reserve. Because [ESV's]

original customer had ordered a particular vintage and the company had replaced A
it with a different vintage from a subsequent shipment, the customer would not be
particularly happy about that. That did happen on a couple of occasions, and this
came to light when we did the audit at Cliffe. We made sure it didn't happen again.'

In 1984 the Hastings operation was moved to Lewes, into premises at Units 12/13
Cliffe Industrial Estate. Some 6,000 cases of customers' reserve were moved. The trading
stock was put into unit 13 and the customers' reserve was put into unit 12. Though the B
two units were in one shell, the shelving for each unit was separate. The customers'
reserve was stored by type and vintage. Accompanying each stack of wine was a master
card or slate showing the names of the customers and the numbers of cases allocated to
each one of them. The wines were all checked following the move and reconciled with the
records of wine held for the individual customers. Any wine which had been moved into
unit 12 was only moved out thereafter in response to a customer's order for delivery, or
for resale. ESV would undertake the resale of a customer's wine for a commission on the C
resale price.

In the middle of 1986 Major Shand sold out his interests in ESV and its holding
company to a group headed by Sir Hugh Bidwell. The sale was effected by an agreement
for the sale and purchase of assets between the ESV companies as vendors and a new
company then called Hopepass Ltd as purchaser. Sir Hugh Bidwell joined in as
guarantor. The importance of the agreement for present purposes is the segregation in it D
of the customers' stocks from other stocks. Thus in cl. 1, the interpretation provision,
'Customers' stocks' are defined as:

> 'the stocks of wine not belonging to ESV but stored or held by or to the order of
> ESV on behalf of other persons whether or not a rent is paid to ESV in respect of
> such stocks.'

'Stock' generally is defined as: E

> 'all the stocks of wines beers and spirits belonging to ESV at the completion date
> (including the stocks known as 'the directors' stocks') including bottles and other
> containers . . .'

In cl. 3 the purchase price for the 'Stock' is to be the value thereof as at the close of
business on 27 June 1986. No value is to be placed on 'customers' stocks'. In cl. 9 we find
the following: F

> 'The vendors hereby agree to indemnify the purchaser against all claims losses
> damage or expenses made against suffered or incurred by the purchaser in
> connection with the customers' stocks for a period of three years from the
> completion date.'

The fifth schedule contains a number of representations, warranties and undertakings
by the vendors. It includes the following: G

'C. *STOCK*

1. The stock is in good condition and capable of being sold in the ordinary course
of the business in accordance with the current price list of ESV without rebate or
allowance to a purchaser other than any normal trade discounts.

2. None of the stock is held on consignment or is otherwise subject to the rights or H
claims of suppliers or other third parties.

D. *CUSTOMERS' STOCKS*

The customers' stocks are in good condition and all stocks comprising the
customers' stocks shall have been delivered to or made available to the purchaser
on completion.'

A   I would note three points about this agreement:

(1)   It proceeds on the basis that the customers' stocks belong beneficially to the customers.

(2)   The customers' stocks are not confined to stocks clearly appropriated to individual customers.

B   (3)   The custody of the customers' stocks is transferred to the new company which would appear to take as bailees or trustees for the customers.

At or shortly after completion, Hopepass Ltd, the purchaser, changed its name to Ellis, Son & Vidler Ltd. The former ESV abandoned that name and was in due course dissolved.

I must now describe in greater detail the company's method of selling wines to be held in customers' reserves. It falls into two parts, wines purchased from existing duty paid stock, and wines purchased *en primeur*, or other imported stock held in a bonded warehouse, and on which duty would have to be paid at some stage before delivery to the customer.

Existing stock

D   In the company's list for 1983–84 the following term is set out.

'*Reserves*

Customers may reserve wine purchased from our lists in our duty paid cellars at a rental of £2.20 per dozen per annum exclusive of VAT. Customers' reserves purchased elsewhere will be charged at £3.30 per annum exclusive of VAT. Reserves can only be accepted in multiples of 12 bottles of any wine or spirit. All reserves are covered by insurance against all major hazards (except theft, larceny, etc.) at invoice price only. We do not hold ourselves responsible for loss of condition, ullages, dry breaks, unless these arise from our negligence. Should customers wish for extra cover against these contingencies we would ask them to make their own arrangements. Arrangements can be made for storage of vintage ports in bond. A minimum of 14 days' notice is required for withdrawals of reserves held in our duty paid cellars or in bond.'

F   I have not seen any later list but I understand that this term remained the same save as to alterations in the rental charge. I call attention to the offer to store wines not purchased from ESV, albeit at a greater rental.

When an order was received for the purchase of wine to be retained in reserve, the company raised an invoice. When that was paid an appropriate entry was made in what was known as 'the Bible'. This consisted of a Roneo Vickers Cardex System. It contained a card for each customer showing what wines were held in store for that customer. After that entry was made the wine was taken physically out of the trading stock in unit 13 and placed in the customers' reserve storage in unit 12. If the wine was of a kind and vintage for which a stock already existed, the cases would be added to that particular stock. If there was no existing stock, a new stack was started. Different wines were never mixed in the same stack. When wine was thus added to the reserve, the relevant master card would be adjusted to reflect the addition, or a new card started, as the case might be. The cases themselves were not systematically marked with the individual customer's name, though some of them might be. When a customer wished to have his wine or some of it delivered, or wished to collect it, it would be booked out in the Bible and a case or cases would be taken off the appropriate stack and the master card adjusted. Occasionally mistakes or omissions would occur in amending the master card, but the Bible, according to Mr Steedman, 'was virtually 100 per cent accurate in its reflection of the stocks of wine (other than any which may have "disappeared").' Others have testified to the excellence of Mr Steedman's record keeping and his management of the stocks.

I have been told and can accept that labelling each box of reserve wine would have been totally impracticable. Mr Steedman in para. 31 and 32 of his statement explains:

> 'If a customer had wanted (his) individually labelled box at the bottom of a stack it would have been necessary to disassemble the whole stack to get it out; and this would prevent storage facilities being run efficiently and increase the risk of disturbance (thus damaging very valuable wine which should be moved as little as possible other than for turning) and breakages.
>
> . . .
>
> Another reason for not labelling each case was purely practical; the cellarman obviously takes the easy way out and so he always took the top case off the stack. If the boxes had all been named he would probably have had to change the names round on the boxes, and this could have resulted in a series of two or three name changes on the same box which was just not practical.'

In some instances, exceptionally, wines were stored separately for an individual customer and labelled with his name. This could occur where a very large quantity of a particular wine was ordered, or small quantities of a rare wine had been purchased by an individual customer.

The physical arrangements for the storage of ports differed, but the system of recording was similar. There were a number of purpose-built bins at unit 12. Each bin contained a separate brand and vintage. To economise on space many were stored by bottles rather than cases. All bottles and cases had been bought by customers. None of it was the trading stock of ESV. When a customer required a case of port a dozen bottles would be taken off the top of the relevant bin, put in a case and the master card duly marked.

En primeur

A number of customers bought wine *en primeur* rather than from the existing stock of ESV. One advantage of this is that the wine could be stored in a bonded warehouse and payment of duty and VAT deferred until the customer required delivery. ESV used a bonded warehouse at Corsham in Wiltshire owned and operated by an independent company known as Octavian Ltd. Purchases *en primeur* are purchases direct from the producers of wine. Each year ESV would provisionally order supplies from a number of selected chateaux. At that stage the grapes would have been harvested but the wine not bottled and ready for sale and delivery. ESV would then canvass its customers inviting them to place orders. The terms and conditions of the offer for 1990 clarets were as follows:

> '1. Offer closes 30-vi-91 subject to stocks remaining unsold.
>
> 2. Shipment late 1992/early 1993.
>
> 3. Quotations are ex cellars Bordeaux.
>
> 4. Duty, freight, insurance and VAT will be charged at the time of shipment at prevailing rates.
>
> 5. Delivery from UK bond to customer's address will be charged at prevailing rates.
>
> 6. PAYMENT MUST BE MADE WITH ORDER.'

The vintages of previous years were offered on similar terms. Indeed the 1989 and subsequent clarets have not left France because ESV could not pay for them.

These customers placed orders and paid for the wine net of duty and VAT. Having obtained those payments ESV concluded contracts with the chateaux for sufficient wine

A   to satisfy the customers' orders at whatever price it could negotiate, frequently arranging to pay by instalments. When the wine was ready for shipment, the customers would be required to pay freight, insurance and the warehouse charges. On arrival at the bonded warehouse, Octavian Ltd would send by post a stock certificate to ESV. There would be no immediate method by which Octavian could tell which part of the consignment belonged to an individual customer. What happened thereafter is best described by Mr Steedman in para. 99 and 100 of his statement.

B

> '99. As soon as the stock certificate arrived at ESV I would have the entries made in the Bible to allocate the bonded wine so ordered to each ESV customer. The ESV records would therefore reflect who was entitled to what wines in the bonded warehouse (but of course there would be no physical separation between various customers' holdings of the same wines unless only one customer ordered one specific wine).

C

> 100. ESV stored all its customers' bonded wines in ESV's name. This enabled ESV to get a better storage rate out of Octavian, and ESV made a turn on the storage and insurance. The customer was billed by ESV for the storage and insurance, in respect of which the wines were insured to replacement value. ESV paid Octavian's charges directly.'

D   Each parcel or type of wine arriving in the bond was given what is known as a rotation number which was used as a check by the customs. If one customer had ordered a large quantity of a particular wine, that wine was given its own unique customer rotation number. If there were various customers who had each ordered a smaller quantity of a particular wine, that wine was given a rotation number applicable to that group of customers. These rotation numbers could not be confused with any of the trading stock of ESV in bond which had separate rotation numbers.

E   In the period when Major Shand was in control the then company had purchased wines *en primeur* over and above those ordered by the customers. That practice was not followed by subsequent owners of ESV. At the time of the appointment of the receivers, ESV had no wine in bond to its own account which was the same type and vintage as any of the wines held by ESV for its customers.

F   Mr Steedman could not recall ever having to seize any stock from the customers' reserve to satisfy unpaid storage charges. It was his understanding that ESV owned none of the wine bought *en primeur* from the chateaux by customers through ESV and held in bond.

Other, more mature wines were sometimes bought by ESV for customers and imported into bond and retained there for them. A customer could get his wine out of bond at any time by paying ESV the duty and VAT (for transmission to the customs) and any other outstanding charges. Such wine could be delivered to him or it could be transferred to G   the customer reserve at Cliffe where it would be documented and stored in the same way as wines added to the store from the trading stock of ESV.

Other classes of documents produced or acquiesced in by the company are also consistent with the absence of any beneficial interest of ESV in any part of the customers' reserve. The first of these are the annual accounts of ESV. They show the amount of the trading stock but they contain no entry for the customers' reserve stocks as forming any H   part of the assets of the company. In the notes to the profit and loss account, however, are set out the reserve rents receivable, £29,020 in the year to 30 June 1991.

Secondly, there are documents relating to insurances held by ESV. An early document (March 1977) from the brokers refers to the insurance valuation of the stock in the following terms:

> '(a) Where such goods are your property, market value plus duty paid or payable;

(b) where such goods are the property of customers for which you are responsible, the values indicated on the appropriate invoices plus duty paid or payable.'

This accords with the terms in the 1983–84 list which I have already set out. A later document (6 March 1989) discusses throughput arrangements, that is insurance on moving stock. Though the stock is valued at £950,000, 'of this 500,000 is customers stock held for them and as such would be excluded from any throughput arrangements'.

Thirdly, and most significantly, are the documents from the debenture holders, the bank. On 14 April 1987 ESV granted a mortgage debenture to the bank. It was executed as part of the terms of an overdraft facility negotiated in the previous July when the new ESV took over. The accounts and other documents presented to the bank by the company made clear that (1) the company held stocks on behalf of customers, (2) these stocks were not included in the assets of the company, and (3) rent on wine reserves, described as such, was a significant element of the company's income. In July 1990 an officer of the bank visited the premises at Cliffe and noted:

'The double unit on an industrial estate in Lewes holds approximately £100,000 of customers' stock and £200,000 of bottled wine, being the property of clients and for which a rental of £5 per case per annum is charged. This rental covers the cost of maintaining the Lewes property.'

In the following month the bank became aware that sales were well below budget. In January 1991 it was noticed that while the basic administration, stock control and bookkeeping were particularly good, the company was insolvent and had been for several months. The bank's recommendation was not encouraging:

'Frankly the prospects look particularly gloomy and it would appear that without our continued support at the existing level, the company will need to call in the receiver.'

Nevertheless the bank temporarily increased the overdraft limit to allow trading to continue, while the company sought further finance.

Before passing to the final phase of the history I must refer to two further matters. First, the company at its Cliffe reserve provided storage facilities for wine which customers had bought elsewhere, mostly from other failed vintners. All such consignments were separately marked with the customer's name on each case when they came in, and the cases of each customer were stored separately from those of other customers and from the general customers' reserve.

The second matter is this. Although the unit was well managed, some losses and breakages occurred. Usually the broken bottle or missing bottle or case could not be replaced from the trading stock which normally would not include the relevant type and vintage, especially if it was of some age. The practice was to assign the missing bottle or case to a customer with a large holding and give him a credit for it. Mr Steedman could not recall being required to replace it in specie. If he had had such a request, he would have attempted to buy in the market. It appears that losses by theft and breakage were very small.

I now pick up the narrative in 1991 when as we have seen, the company was seen to be insolvent but trading temporarily with the assistance of the bank while looking for outside rescue. At this point, Mr Nigel Baring appeared on the scene. By December 1991 he had acquired the shares of ESV and in the following March or April those of Stapylton Fletcher Ltd also. In March 1992 he took three steps in relation to the stock of ESV.

First, he caused the administration and the trading stock of ESV to be moved from Cliffe to SFL's office and warehouse in Maidstone. No part of the customers' reserve went there. The trading stock was eventually sold by the receivers.

A   Secondly, he directed that all customer reserve wines held in bond at Octavian's warehouse should be transferred from ESV's named account to the named account there of Nigel Baring & Co Ltd. Mr Steedman accordingly sent to Octavian by fax a manuscript inventory containing the rotation numbers of each wine and identifying the customer or customers to whom each wine had been allocated. He further describes the inventory in para. 106 of his statement:

B   'Upon my suggestion in March 1992 wine in bond was also given a code using the customer's initials e.g. Charlie Brown would be CB1. Where a wine belonged to several customers it was given a product code of VA for various and was broken down into individual entries in the company reserve records. The bond sent a stock certificate every month which agreed with the company records, otherwise VAT and duty was payable on differences.'

C   Thirdly, Mr Baring directed that all customer reserve stocks at Cliffe be moved to Ardington House, a private residence of his with ample cellars at Wantage, Oxfordshire. The move was a substantial operation. It involved more than 2,000 cases, and took two to three weeks to organise and carry out. Before any wine was moved, Mr Steedman and his assistants checked all the wines in the reserve against the entries in the Bible. They satisfied themselves that all was correct. They tried to ensure that any label on a stack reflected the number of cases in that stack. The cases were loaded on the lorries as far as

D   possible in such a way as to keep each different type of wine segregated. On arrival at Ardington House, however, they were offloaded in no sort of order. Mr Steedman and one of his assistants went to Ardington House on 13 and 14 April to sort out the customers reserve wine. 'It was obvious', he says, 'when we got there that the stacks had been broken up and many cards had been lost en route'. This included some cards attached to the customers' own stocks which they had bought elsewhere. His statement

E   continues:

'79. We sorted out three rooms during two days. We sorted out *all the port* during that period. Indeed by the time we had finished we had reconciled every bottle of previously binned port and the 1977 ports against customers reserve records for the binned and 1977 ports.

F   80. All the wines in these three rooms were clearly labelled individually or with master slates using the same stacking procedures.

81. That was all we were able to do and we were unable to get back down to Oxford to complete the operation before the administrative receivers were appointed.'

As previously mentioned, the receivers were appointed on 29 May 1992.

G   On 10 June 1992 Mr Steedman assisted the receivers' representatives to check the stock at Ardington House. The three rooms which he had previously sorted out were as he had left them. That accounted for about 1,000 of the 2,000 cases sent to Ardington House. The rest of the wine needed remarking. They went through the lot on 10 June. They noted the cases which had been marked, but there were quite a few boxes with only the name of the wine on them. On returning to Maidstone, Mr Steedman checked the lists against the Bible as far as he could. He never went back to Ardington House again. He

H   concludes:

'By the time I left working for the receivers on 3 July, there were only 50 cases which could not be tied up to the reserve cabinet; which I put down to either miscounting or incorrect description of the wines in the cases. Another day's visit would have solved it. I am confident that the transporters who took the wine from Lewes were honest.'

After the appointment of the receivers a dispute arose between them and Mr Baring regarding the custody of the wine at Ardington House. Mr Baring maintained that it belonged to the customers and the receivers had no right to it. The receivers obtained an order of the court for its delivery up. Accordingly, the wine was moved again. It went on the orders of the receivers to the warehouse of Smith & Taylor Ltd. The operation was carefully carried out and recorded even to the extent of having a video recording made of it, together with a full inventory. The operation took about 12 days. It was found that some cases had had a bottle removed, and some cases of champagne were missing. It must be inferred that those losses occurred while the wine was at Ardington House.

We have now come to end of the history and can look at the claims. The claimants might be forgiven for thinking that the matter was straightforward. They are all people who have bought wine, in some instances many years ago, paid for it in full, left it with wine merchants for storage, paid storage, drawn it out in part as they wished. The wine merchants for their part have segregated it from their own trading stock, and did not consider that it belonged to ESV. The claimants would not be too particular that the precise cases which were set aside for them were those which were ultimately delivered so long as the latter were of identical type and vintage. Accordingly they would regard the stored wine as their own and expect to call for its delivery even though the vintner had become insolvent.

The reality is somewhat different. The receivers, in assessing whether or not ESV's action was sufficient to pass title, have applied the test on appropriation as set out in *Carlos Federspiel SA v Charles Twigg & Co Ltd* [1957] 1 Ll L Rep 240, which I shall refer to later. Applying that test the receivers admitted the following claims and allowed the removal of the wine concerned.

(1)   Where an individual case of wine had a specific customer's reference on it and the allocation tallied with the company's records of wine ordered and paid for.

(2)   Where a stack of cases had a label showing the cases as belonging to one individual.

(3)   Where the records show that other cases in a stack have already been removed leaving a number of cases which exactly tally with a remaining individual's order. This is appropriation by exhaustion.

(4)   In the Octavian bond, where the faxed inventory showed one or more cases earmarked for a specific customer and bearing a single rotation number.

These examples in the view of the receivers are to be contrasted with those where the customers had 'entitlements' to wines rather than an actual allocation of individual cases. They identify five classes of customers of ESV who had such entitlements and who are represented by the five respondents.

1. Mr Jeffrey Bonas represents those customers for whom wine in bond is allocated in the faxed inventory under VA or 'various'. Each such entry related to a specific vintage. While Mr Steedman, using the Bible, has been able to allocate these entries in the inventory to specific customers, Mr Vooght, the receiver, in his statement said that upon inspection, it proved impossible to allocate specific cases of wine to specific customers as there were no discernible features identifying a particular case or cases as belonging to an individual customer. Therefore, he believed that these wines had not been appropriated to individual customers and were the property of ESV. He went on to note that although for the most part the totals of stock matched the total customer entitlement, there were discrepancies, and he instanced one example where there was an excess of 14 cases.

2. Mr Mark Shand represents those customers who claim to share in composite stacks originally at Cliffe and which were still identifiable as stacks at Ardington House. The receivers do not believe that the formation of a composite stack is sufficient to pass the property to each customer whose cases are somewhere in that stack.

A   3. Lord Ashcombe represents those who claim to share in composite stacks at Cliffe which have become to a greater or less extent dispersed at Ardington House. Mr Arden, for the receivers, accepts that where property has passed, later mixing will not reverse that, though there may be problems of identification. Thus this category does not differ in principle from the last, though special directions may be required.

B   4. Mr Richard Beharrell represents those who purchased wine elsewhere. The difficulty here is that, while title is admitted, the claimant's cases or bottles cannot now be identified as they have been mixed with other cases or bottles of the same, or believed to be the same, vintage.

5. Finally, Mr Peter Jamieson represents those customers who had ordered and paid for *en primeur* wines which at the appointment of the receivers had not been dispatched from the vineyards concerned. None had been labelled with the name of ESV and in some cases the wine had not even been bottled.

C

I can now come to the law. The basic difficulty in the way of the claimants here stems from s. 16 of the *Sale of Goods Act* 1979 as interpreted in the courts. That section, unchanged from the *Sale of Goods Act* 1893, reads:

> 'Where there is a contract for the sale of unascertained goods no property in the goods is transferred to the buyer unless and until the goods are ascertained.'

D   I add parts of the following sections.

> '17(1) Where there is a contract for the sale of specific or ascertained goods the property in them is transferred to the buyer at such time as the parties to the contract intend it to be transferred.
>
> (2) For the purpose of ascertaining the intention of the parties regard shall be had to the terms of the contract, the conduct of the parties and the circumstances of the case.
>
> 18. Unless a different intention appears, the following are rules for ascertaining the intention of the parties as to the time at which the property in the goods is to pass to the buyer.
>
> . . .

F

> *Rule 5.*–(1) Where there is a contract for the sale of unascertained or future goods by description, and goods of that description and in a deliverable state are unconditionally appropriated to the contract, either by the seller with the assent of the buyer or by the buyer with the assent of the seller, the property in the goods then passes to the buyer; and the assent may be express or implied, and may be given either before or after the appropriation is made.'

G   The prohibition in s. 16 has proved too restrictive in the case of sales of goods forming part of a bulk and consequently has recently been considered and its modification proposed by the Law Commission (Paper No. 215). However, I have to deal with the law as it is. Many of the sales of wine to be considered here are sales of goods forming part of a bulk. The claimants approach this problem with two separate lines of argument. First, they seek to show that the provision has been satisfied by ascertainment of the goods claimed. Secondly, they seek to show that the seller has become a trustee or fiduciary of some description, thus circumventing the section.

H

Both lines were pursued unsuccessfully in *Re London Wine Co* [1986] PCC 121. The company had substantial stocks of wine in a number of warehouses. Large quantities were sold but in many instances remained warehoused with the company. There was no appropriation from the bulk of any wine to answer particular contracts, but the customer received from the company a 'certificate of title' describing the wine for which he had

paid. He was charged storage and insurance periodically. When receivers were appointed,   A
there were sufficient stocks to satisfy all claims.

The court considered three types of transaction: (a) a single purchaser of the total stock
of a particular wine; (b) a number of purchasers whose combined purchases exhausted
the total stock of a particular wine; (c) a number of purchasers whose combined
purchases did not exhaust the relevant stock. Oliver J. held that legal title had not passed
in any case. There was no ascertainment. Orders could have been fulfilled from any   B
source, not necessarily existing stocks. There was no undivided interest. There might be
an estoppel resulting from the representations in the 'certificate of title', but that did not
give a proprietary interest good against the debenture holder, but would merely preclude
a defence to an action for damages.

There was no trust for there was no certainty of subject matter. No proprietary right
arose from the payment of purchase money. The existence of a right to specific
performance does not necessarily imply a proprietary interest in the subject matter. The   C
carrying out of the order would bring about the ascertainment of the goods, but there
would not necessarily be any pre-existing equitable right. Hence the claims wholly failed.

Points in the judgment I would note are the following: at pp. 134–135:

> '[A fourth] category consists of purchasers in respect of whose orders wine was not
> only allocated but segregated and appropriated (so that the goods became   D
> ascertained goods) but whose goods cannot now be identified because they have
> been mixed with other batches of similar wine. Mr Bingham on behalf of the bank,
> however, has (clearly rightly, if I may say) denied that this would have the effect of
> reversing the property or giving the bank any charge on the wine of purchasers in
> this category . . .'

On p. 137 Oliver J said that a farmer: E

> '. . . could by appropriate words, declare himself to be a trustee of a specified
> proportion of his whole flock and thus create an equitable tenancy in common
> between himself and the named beneficiary, so that a proprietary interest would
> arise in the beneficiary in an undivided share of all the flock and its produce. But
> the *mere* declaration that a given number of animals would be held upon trust
> could not, I should have thought, without very clear words pointing to such an
> intention, result in the creation of an interest in common in the proportion which   F
> that number bears to the number of the whole at the time of the declaration. And
> where the mass from which the numerical interest is to take effect is not itself
> ascertainable at the date of the declaration such a conclusion becomes impossible.'

I do not regard that decision as inevitably governing the case before me. One obvious
difference in the present case is the segregation of the wine purchased by the customers
in a separate part of the warehouse and the careful maintenance of records within the   G
company. Further as the London Wine Co was free to sell its stock and satisfy the
customers from any other available source, there was no ascertainable bulk in that case.

Both counsel have submitted careful and illuminating skeleton arguments for which I
am grateful. The submissions of Mr Arden for the receivers appear from the description
above of the claims which the receivers have allowed and those which are in issue here.
The only additional point he made, and which I should mention, was in connection with   H
a removal on payment of duty of a parcel of wine for a specific customer from the bond
to Cliffe. That operation of itself, he said, would not necessarily lead to appropriation. It
would depend on what happened at Cliffe. If it was added to a stack containing wines of
the same vintage belonging to several customers there would be no appropriation. In
support of his submissions he referred to a number of authorities to which I must now
turn.

A   The first case is that particularly relied on by the receivers, *Carlos Federspiel & Co SA v Charles Twigg & Co Ltd* [1957] 1 Ll L Rep 240. The contract was one for the sale of cycles FOB. The purchasers had paid for them. Preparations for shipment were made, the goods got ready but had not been shipped before a receiver was appointed. It was held that the property in the goods did not pass before shipment and so the receiver could retain them. Pearson J, after a review of the authorities, said at p. 255:

B   'On those authorities, what are the principles emerging? I think one can distinguish these principles. First, Rule 5 of Sect. 18 of the Act is one of the Rules for ascertaining the intention of the parties as to the time at which the property in the goods is to pass to the buyer unless a different intention appears. Therefore the element of common intention has always to be borne in mind. A mere setting apart or selection of the seller of the goods which he expects to use in performance of the contract is not enough. If that is all, he can change his mind and use those goods

C   in performance of some other contract and use some other goods in performance of this contract. To constitute an appropriation of the goods to the contract, the parties must have had, or be reasonably supposed to have had, an intention to attach the contract irrevocably to those goods, so that those goods and no others are the subject of the sale and become the property of the buyer.

D   Secondly, it is by agreement of the parties that the appropriation, involving a change of ownership, is made, although in some cases the buyer's assent to an appropriation by the seller is conferred in advance by the contract itself or otherwise.

        Thirdly, an appropriation by the seller, with the assent of the buyer, may be said always to involve an actual or constructive delivery. If the seller retains possession, he does so as bailee for the buyer. There is a passage in Chalmers' Sale of Goods

E   Act, 12th ed., at p.75, where it is said:

            "In the second place, if the decisions be carefully examined, it will be found that in every case where the property has been held to pass, there has been an actual or constructive delivery of the goods to the buyer."

        I think that is right, subject only to this possible qualification, that there may be after such constructive delivery an actual delivery still to be made by the seller

F   under the contract. Of course, that is quite possible, because delivery is the transfer of possession, whereas appropriation transfers ownership. So there may be first an appropriation, constructive delivery, whereby the seller becomes bailee for the buyer, and then a subsequent actual delivery involving actual possession, and when I say that I have in mind in particular the two cases cited, namely, *Aldridge v. Johnson, sup.*, and *Langton v. Higgins, sup.*'

G   In each of those two cases the buyers had sent their own containers for the goods, with instructions to fill and deliver them. The sellers had filled them but had not delivered them. Instead they emptied them, and disposed of the contents elsewhere. It was held that the property had passed. I emphasise the possibility recognised there of appropriation by the seller assuming the character of bailee, albeit temporarily and without the buyers' assent.

H   The next case to look at is *Healy v Howlett & Sons* [1917] 1 KB 337. A fish exporter in Valentia in south-west Ireland sent 190 boxes of mackerel by rail and sea to London via Dublin and Holyhead. They were intended for three separate customers, but the boxes were not individually marked when put on rail at Valentia. They were dispatched to the shipper's order. He did not wish to reveal the customers' names at that stage. He wired instructions to his agent in Holyhead who consigned them on to the separate customers. The goods had been delayed en route and by the time they arrived in Holyhead some at

least had become unmerchantable. The essence of the case may be collected from the   A
opening sentences of the judgment of Avory J at p. 345:

> 'The whole question is whether the twenty boxes of mackerel became the property
> of the buyer, or, in other words, whether they were at the buyer's risk when they
> were put on rail at Valentia. That depends on whether there was an appropriation
> of the twenty boxes at that time to the defendants.'

It was thus a case on risk. The precise timing of the appropriation was critical. The   B
commodities in the present case could not be more different. Unlike fish, wine improves
with keeping. If one applies that case slavishly one arrives at the situation where wine
under a contract for sale may be set aside, but because it is with some other identical
wine, not be appropriated pursuant to the sale contract until possibly years, if not
decades, have elapsed.

We next come to the decision of the Court of Appeal in *Re Wait* [1927] 1 Ch 606. W   C
bought 1,000 tons of wheat to be shipped from Oregon. He subsold 500 tons to the
claimants who paid in full. It was shipped but before it arrived W went bankrupt. His
trustee claimed to receive the whole of the 1,000 tons, leaving the claimants to their rights
in damages. The majority held that the 500 tons due to the claimants had not been
appropriated and so was not specific or ascertained goods in respect of which specific
performance could be ordered under s. 52 of the Act. The interest of the case lies in the
acute division of opinion in the court. Sargant LJ would have held that the claimants had   D
an equitable assignment of part enforceable against the whole. The view of the majority
can best be taken from the following passage in the judgment of Atkin LJ (at pp. 629–
630):

> 'In any case, however, I am of opinion that the claimants fail, and that to grant the
> relief claimed would violate well established principles of common law and equity.
> It would also appear to embarrass to a most serious degree the ordinary operations   E
> of buying and selling goods, and the banking operations which attend them . . .'

–and p. 636:

> 'The rules for transfer of property as between seller and buyer, performance of the
> contract, rights of the unpaid seller against the goods, unpaid sellers' lien, remedies
> of the seller, remedies of the buyer, appear to be complete and exclusive statements
> of the legal relations both in law and equity. They have, of course, no relevance   F
> when one is considering rights, legal or equitable, which may come into existence
> dehors the contract for sale. A seller or a purchaser may, of course, create any
> equity he pleases by way of charge, equitable assignment or any other dealing with
> or disposition of goods, the subject-matter of sale; and he may, of course, create
> such an equity as one of the terms expressed in the contract of sale. But the mere
> sale or agreement to sell or the acts in pursuance of such a contract mentioned in   G
> the Code will only produce the legal effects which the Code states.'

This landmark decision demonstrates that normally a contract for the sale of goods
takes effect at law, and gives rise to no equitable interest in favour of the buyer.

The last case I have to mention in this line is *Karlshamns Olje Fabriker v Eastport
Navigation Corporation ('The Elafi')* [1981] 2 Ll Rep 679. It concerned four separate
contracts for the sale of copra totalling 6,000 tons shipped in bulk with other copra. The   H
rest was offloaded leaving that attributable to the four contracts which in the meantime
had become held by the same person. it was held that the goods had become ascertained
by exhaustion following the decision of Roche J in *Wait and James v Midland Bank Ltd*
(1926) 24 Ll L Rep 313, described as a common sense decision, 'common sense' because
in strict logic there would need to be appropriation to each contract for the property to
pass even though by assignment the contracts had come into one hand. In reply to

A   criticisms along those lines Mustill J (at p. 684) made the following observations relied on by the receivers here:

> 'First Mr. Eder contends that Mr. Justice Roche was mistaken in giving a broad interpretation to s. 16. If the section is looked at in isolation, there is force in this argument. The section refers to "a contract for the sale of unascertained goods", and says that the property shall not pass "unless and until the goods are ascertained". In their most natural sense the words "the goods" would be read as referring to the goods which are the subject of the contract in question, so that one can say of them that "*these* are the goods which refer to *that* contract". But when one comes to deal with an unusual situation, such as exists here, it is in my view legitimate to look at the reasoning which underlies the legislation. This is quite plain. The passing of property is concerned with the creation of rights in rem, which the purchaser can assert, not only against the vendor, but against the world at large, and which he can alienate in such a way as to create similar rights in a transferee. Where there are multiple contracts of sale in the hands of different buyers, in relation to an undivided bulk, there are only two possible solutions. First, to hold that the buyers take as joint owners in undivided shares. English law has rejected this solution. The only alternative is to hold that the property does not pass until the goods are not only physically separated, but separated in a way which enables an individual buyer to say that a particular portion has become his property under his contract of sale: for until then . . . no one can say which part of the whole quantity the seller has agreed to deliver. There is, however, no need to impose this solution on a case where there are parallel contracts between the parties, together comprising the whole of the bulk.'

The reference to English law as rejecting the solution of undivided shares is a reminder that in the USA that solution has been adopted. As will be seen, English law does not reject the possibility of a tenancy in common in relation to goods in all circumstances. Mustill J was considering the case where in order to perform a number of individual contracts for sale, a bulk has to be divided. He was not considering a case where there was an intention to segregate and retain goods in bulk. In all the cases so far considered, other than *Re London Wine Co*, there was simply a contract for the sale of goods to be delivered in the normal course of business. The transactions with which I am concerned present the following features.

From the point of view of ESV, the reserve stocks were completely segregated from the trading stock, and the documentation was in good order. The company did not regard the wine as still belonging to them, even to the extent of refraining from borrowing it. This can be contrasted with the situation revealed as existing at the London Wine Co.

The customers were looking to have their wine properly stored and not unduly disturbed. Further, the nature of the commodity is such that it would be pointless for them to inspect the cases or bottles, and impracticable to inspect their contents. One case of wine of a particular type and vintage is in practice to be regarded as identical with every other case of the same wine, breakages and missing bottles apart. From this two consequences follow. First, it is of secondary importance that the customer's name should be attached to any particular case. Secondly, the customer's assent to any appropriation of specific cases without consultation can be safely inferred. Accordingly, it must seem strange to those not acquainted with the Sale of Goods Act 1979 that a customer's entitlement should differ according to whether a stack of identical cases is allocated to a single customer or is to be shared between two or more.

Having regard to those considerations, the proper legal analysis must begin by recognising that we are not here dealing only with a contract for the sale of goods, but

A

with two separate, if related, contracts, the second with its own consideration being a contract to store wines indefinitely.

Let us assume that each buyer of duty paid wine went to Cliffe, took delivery of his wine from unit 13, then handed it back to Mr Steedman to be added to a stack in unit 12, knowing that the stack already contained wine belonging to others and that he would not necessarily get the identical cases or bottles back for very good reasons connected with the proper care of his and the other owners' wine. The proper inference there, in my judgment, is that he agreed to become a tenant in common of the entire stack in the proportion that his cases bear to the total number of the cases in the stack for the time being, that total being liable to increase by additions and decrease by removals, where the tenancy in common is determined pro tanto by partition. That such a tenancy in common in goods can exist is not open to doubt, despite the cautionary words of Oliver J, cited above. In fact, in *Re London Wine Co* at p. 152 Oliver J refers to *Spence v Union Marine Insurance Co Ltd* (1868) LR 3 CP 427 as a case where 'specific goods which undoubtedly were in separate individual ownerships to start with become so mixed as to be indistinguishable'. A ship carrying cotton bales was wrecked. Each of the bales had been marked with the name of its consignee. Some of the bales were lost. Others were salvaged, many were damaged, all had lost their distinguishing marks. The remedy for that situation can be taken from the judgment of Bovill CJ at p. 438:

B

C

D

> 'The goods being before they are mixed the separate property of the several owners, unless, which is absurd, they cease to be property by reason of the accidental mixture, when they would not so cease if the mixture was designed, must continue to be the property of the original owners; and, as there would be no means of distinguishing the goods of each, the several owners seem necessarily to become jointly interested, as tenants in common, in the bulk.'

The *Spence* case was one of those cited by Staughton J in his full survey of the authorities in *Indian Oil Corporation Ltd v Greenstone Shipping SA (Panama) ('The Ypatianna')* [1988] QB 345. In that case shipowners had wrongfully mixed crude oil they had been chartered to transport with their own oil. Thus it was not precisely what had happened here where the goods of a number of innocent claimants have been mixed. Staughton J's judgment contains this passage at pp. 368–369:

E

> 'Two points of significance in my view emerge from the authorities. First, in some cases a decision had to be made "not upon the notion, that strict justice was done, but upon this; that it was the only justice, that could be done," *per* Lord Eldon L.C. in *Lupton v. White*, 15 Ves. Jun. 432, 440. Or as Lord Moulton put it, such cases "have been little more than instances of cutting the Gordian knot – reasonable adjustments of the rights of the parties in cases where complete justice was impracticable of attainment," in *Sandeman & Sons v. Tyzack and Branfoot Steamship Co. Ltd.* [1913] A.C. 680, 695.'

F

G

So one may use the tenancy in common as a tool for remedying an unforeseen mixing, damage or loss. If the creation of a tenancy in common can be brought about by the construction of law, it can equally be brought about by agreement either express or to be inferred from the circumstances.

I now return to the contracts for sale. From the evidence, one can readily infer that the parties intended the property in the goods to pass when they were set aside for storage: in Cliffe that occurred when they were moved from unit 13 to unit 12; in the Octavian bond, when they were recorded as belonging to customers and thereafter ceased to be part of the assets of the company in its records. The question remaining is at what point did the goods become 'ascertained' for the purposes of s. 16. For this one must start from the statute itself. There is no definition of 'ascertained'. Where, as is normal, the contract is to be performed on the part of the seller by delivery, the goods must be ascertained by

H

A the time delivery occurs, but may be ascertained earlier. As we have seen, in the case of goods forming part of a bulk, ascertainment does not occur until they are separated from the bulk, usually immediately prior to delivery. But what if there is to be no delivery, but merely a segregation in the hands of the seller for retention by him? There is no compelling reason why ascertainment should mean the same in such circumstances. A customer orders 20 cases of a particular wine. They are put in a stack which never contains less than 40 cases. Over the next five years the customer takes delivery of a case

B at a time. It seems absurd that the 20 cases the subject of his contract for sale should thus become ascertained one by one. The sale contract was that 20 cases should be delivered into the customers' reserve. What happened to them thereafter is regulated by the storage contract, whether the terms of that were part of a single contract for sale and storage, or were in a separate contract. It is the segregation of the stock from the company's trading assets, whether done physically, or by giving instructions to a bonded warehouse keeper,

C which causes the goods to be ascertained for the purposes of s. 16. The goods are then identified as those to be handed over for storage in performance of the contract for sale. It could not be doubted that if, by agreement with a number of customers, the aggregate number of cases of a specific vintage bought by them were handed over en bloc to another company to hold on their behalf, the cases would be ascertained. The selling company would not be seeking to retain any interest in them. This is quite different from *Healy v Howlett & Sons* where for his own purposes the seller retained control of the

D appropriation of the goods, and from *Carlos Federspiel* where he had not completed the arrangements for shipment of the goods and could still withdraw them and replace them with others if it suited him. Where goods were to go to another company for storage there would be an actual delivery. Where the selling company was going to store them and *segregated them for that purpose*, there will be a constructive delivery. Further at that stage, where the price has been paid in full, there would appear to be nothing to embarrass

E the ordinary operations of buying and selling goods, and the banking operations which attend them, to which Atkin LJ referred in *Re Wait*.

In summary, on the facts here, I conclude that if a number of cases or bottles of identical wine are held, not mingled with the trading stock, in store for a group of customers, those cases or bottles will be ascertained for the purposes of s. 16 of the *Sale of Goods Act* 1979 even though they are not immediately appropriated to each individual customer. Property will pass by common intention and not pursuant to s. 18, rule 5. They

F will take as tenants in common.

At this point I can conveniently return to the transfer of assets in June 1986 from the former ESV to the present company. According to my analysis, the property in the goods then in the customers' reserve at Cliffe would have already passed to the customers. The present ESV simply took over the storage contracts and became bailees. The customers accepted this by continuing to pay the storage charges to the new company. Had anyone

G objected, he could have removed his wine.

Therefore I determine and give directions in the representative cases as follows.

(1) Mr Bonas claims two cases of Chateau Palmer 1988. They are part of 117 cases listed among the 'various' entitlements and sub-listed by Mr Steedman. I regard the sub-listed names as holding the 117 cases as tenants in common in the proportion the number of cases against each name bears to 117. In his statement dealing with this category Mr

H Vooght mentions a surplus of 14 cases of Chateau Palmer 1987 (para.33). Any such surplus in Octavian would belong to ESV either as unclaimed goods, or as a mistake in ordering from the vineyards.

(2) Mr Shand claims three cases of port held as part of 32 cases at the Cliffe reserve and transferred intact to Ardington House. Here, too, I regard Mr Shand as a tenant in common with the others named as entitled to the 32 cases.

(3) Lord Ashcombe represents those who shared in a composite stack at Cliffe which   A
has become dispersed at Ardington House. It is conceded that this dispersal does not of
itself deprive the owners of their property in the stack at Cliffe to which I have found
they would have been entitled. It seems that, taking the example given by Mr Vooght
(para. 44) of Chateau Coufran 1985, all the cases have been located at Ardington House.
If there are examples of shortfall, the common owners of the relevant stack at Cliffe
would be entitled to what remained as tenants in common in their original shares. That
might mean that some or all of the available cases would have to be sold and the proceeds   B
distributed pro rata.

(4) Mr Beharrell has an interest in eight cases of Graham Port 1963 purchased
elsewhere, but stored with ESV. These have never been the property of ESV but have
become mixed with other cases of the same vintage. If I have read para. 48 of Mr
Vooght's statement and para. 75 and 79 of that of Mr Steedman correctly, there is no
shortfall: there are 23 and 2/12 cases distributable to Mr Beharrell (eight), Mr Lawston   C
(eight) and others (seven and 2/12). As at present, Mr Beharrell has an interest as tenant
in common in the cases in the proportion 8 to 23 and 2/12.

(5) I have to reject the claim of Mr Jamieson to any proprietary interest. The wine that
he had ordered had not left France when the receivers were appointed. It remained part
of the generic stock of the vineyards, but subject to a contract for its sale to ESV. It
plainly had not been ascertained under the contract between ESV and Mr Jamieson. It is   D
true that Mr Jamieson had paid in full in advance. However there can be no question of
any trust of the purchase moneys as was found in *Re Kayford* [1975] 1 WLR 279. The
money was used, and intended to be used to finance the purchase of the wine in France.
There was no question of segregating it in a separate trust account to await the import of
the wine into this country.

Finally, I come to the application concerning SFL (Stapylton Fletcher Ltd). This   E
company, too, used a bonded warehouse and a duty paid warehouse in which customers'
wines were held. The bonded warehouse is known as Lenham Bond and is managed by
Freightflow International Ltd. In SFL's duty paid warehouse all wines held for customers
were placed on separate cling-film wrapped pallets and clearly labelled as the wine of a
particular customer. Unlike ESV, all stacks were individually allocated. Accordingly, the
receivers have been able to release that wine to the customers concerned. On the other
hand, the situation in the Lenham bonded warehouse was not as clear-cut as in the   F
Octavian warehouse. None of the wine there had been appropriated to specific customers
either by marks on the cases or by an inventory such as Mr Steedman had sent to
Octavian. There had, in short, been no attempt by SFL to allocate any of the wine to
customers' orders. Mr John Macarthur, who appeared in person and submitted an
informative affidavit, claims a case of each of six different 1989 clarets. He describes how,
after payment for *en primeur* wines, an appropriate entry was made in the stock book   G
against the name of the customer. There was no further documentation or any attempt
to allocate wines in the warehouse, even as between SFL and its customers generally, let
alone between individual customers. Accordingly, I am unable to differentiate this case
from *Re London Wine Co*, and have therefore to hold that at the time of the receivers'
appointment the wines claimed by Mr Macarthur had not been ascertained and hence
his remedy lies in damages.

   H

As I have found for the first four claimants in the case relating to ESV on the basis of
the passing of property at law, I do not have to consider the alternative lines of argument
based on trusts, fiduciary relationships or other equitable principles in relation to these
claims. Further, I have dealt with the only equitable principle (in *Re Kayford*) that might
apply to the fifth ESV claimant, Mr Jamieson. However, I have had to reject Mr
Macarthur's claim in relation to SFL so far as it rests on the passing of property at law.

A   As he appeared in person, I should consider whether the alternative lines of argument might apply to his case, though he did not specifically put them forward.

There was much discussion of the possibility of a fiduciary relationship or constructive trust existing between the companies and their customers. The submissions drew support from the decision of the Court of Appeal in New Zealand in *Liggett v Kensington* [1993] 1 NZLR 257, currently under appeal to the Privy Council. The case concerned the

B   insolvency of a company, Goldcorp Exchange Ltd (Exchange), that dealt in gold. The company offered to sell gold coins and bullion to customers to be retained by the company for delivery or resale at the customer's order. Although no specific gold was allocated to each customer, it was represented that the company maintained sufficient stocks to cover its contractual commitments. In fact it did not do so, but held only such stocks it considered necessary to meet likely demands for delivery, so that when it became insolvent there was a substantial shortage. The issue addressed was whether there existed

C   between the company and the customers a fiduciary relationship so that the moneys paid to the company were held upon trust to finance the purchase of bullion to be set aside, and consequently could be traced into the company's assets in priority to the debenture holders. By a majority, the court held that there was a fiduciary relationship. Sir Robin Cooke P. expressed the principle at p. 271 as follows:

D   'This is that the fiduciary, Exchange, received all the moneys of the non-allocated claimants, from the moment of their payment, upon trust. The purpose of the trust was to finance the setting aside and holding of sufficient bullion for all the claimants. Exchange was free to allocate from its own existing stocks or to buy in at such price as it saw fit, but its fiduciary obligation was to do one or the other. The moneys were received on that basis only; it was a breach of trust to utilise them for the general purposes of Exchange without allocating the bullion. That seems to me a fair and realistic interpretation of the transactions with the non-

E   allocated clients. That being so, Exchange was in breach of trust. As Exchange well knew, there was never any intention that it should have the funds unless it made the allocations. Exchange having failed to do so, the clients retained their beneficial interests in the moneys. Those interests never passed to Exchange; on the contrary Exchange appropriated the moneys in breach of trust.'

F   The other member of the majority, Gault J, agreed with this: see p. 281.

I am unable to accept the reasoning of the majority as applicable to this case. Obviously, there is a considerable difference in the subject-matter. The company in New Zealand was in effect dealing in a type of investment. Save by a few specialist users like manufacturing jewellers and dentists, gold is bought as an investment or speculation. Hence the company would appear to be as much an investment broker as a seller of goods. This feature clearly influenced the judges in that case. Thus Cooke P at p. 267:

G   'The contracts between Exchange and its "non-allocated" clients, however, were much more than contracts of sale and purchase or ordinary commercial contracts. Essentially Exchange was holding itself out as vesting title to bullion in the purchasing member of the public, certifying that title, holding the bullion in safe custody as the client's agent, and providing easy dealing facilities for the client. It was a system in which the client was totally dependent on Exchange. The company

H   solicited the client to repose trust in it.'

Gault J said at p. 282:

'The company held itself out as a trusted and expert dealer in bullion and as being in a position to assist members of the public to engage in investment in precious metals. It was an unsophisticated clientele being attracted to an unregulated market by representations of assurance and trust. The nature of bullion is such that the

company stood in a position akin to an investment broker or adviser rather than   A
merely as a seller of goods.'

In the present case we are concerned with the buying and selling of consumables. I am
bound by the decision of *Re Wait* to hold that a contract for the sale of goods does not
of itself create equitable rights. Furthermore, as Gault J himself commented (at p. 279):
'A contractual obligation to store the goods of another does not give rise to a trust.' The
respective rights and obligations of the parties are governed exclusively by the terms of   B
the two contracts.

I also cannot accept the submissions based on estoppel and specific performance as
creating some kind of equitable interest binding on the bank. On estoppel I respectfully
adopt the reasoning of Oliver J in *Re London Wine Co*. Any estoppel here does no more
than provide a defence to some action against the companies under the contracts for sale
or storage. Any suggestion of a proprietary estoppel seems quite hopeless. It is notable   C
that Gault J in *Liggett v Kensington* at p. 279, rejected this.

The availability of the remedy of specific performance does not of itself import the
existence of some equitable interest. All it imports is the inadequacy of the common law
remedy of damages in the particular circumstances. Here, too, I respectfully associate
myself with the reasoning of Oliver J.

Equally untenable as leading to an equitable interest are the arguments based on total
failure of consideration or what was described as a remedial equitable lien. The former   D
cannot be supported from the facts. Even if it could, it would lead to a personal claim
only. Authority for the latter is said to be found in *Lord Napier and Ettrick v Hunter*
[1993] AC 713. That case deals with the right of an insurer to claim by subrogation sums
recovered by the assured after payment of the claim. I see no way in which that can be
extended to give customers a lien as and when their sellers or bailees go into receivership.
The court must be very cautious in devising equitable interests and remedies which erode   E
the statutory scheme for distribution on insolvency. It cannot do it because of some
perceived injustice arising as a consequence only of the insolvency. Perhaps that is an
appropriate note on which to end this judgment.

(Order accordingly)

F

G

H

A Re Rex Williams Leisure plc.
Secretary of State for Trade and Industry v Warren & Anor.

Court of Appeal (Civil Division).
Russell, Staughton and Hoffmann L JJ.
Judgment delivered 27 April 1994.

B *Disqualifying unfit directors of insolvent companies – Procedure – Whether evidence of DTI examiner should be struck out as hearsay – Whether respondents had to file affidavit evidence before hearing – Whether disqualification proceedings should be stayed pending outcome of litigation by company – Companies Act 1985, s. 447; Company Directors Disqualification Act 1986, s. 8, 16; Insolvent Companies (Disqualification of Unfit Directors) Proceedings Rules 1987 (SI 1987/2023), r. 2–4, 6, 7.*

C This was an appeal by the respondents to a director disqualification application against preliminary rulings by the Vice-Chancellor (see [1993] BCC 79).

The respondents were directors of Rex Williams Leisure plc which went into administration in April 1990. In 1991 the Secretary of State appointed an inspector under s. 447 of the Companies Act 1985 to investigate a payment of £200,000 by the company to one of the respondents and authorised by the other. The Secretary of State in 1992 issued D disqualification proceedings under s. 8 of the Company Directors Disqualification Act 1986. The proceedings were defended. Affidavit evidence was filed in support of the application by the Secretary of State. The directors then made an application seeking to have the proceedings stayed pending the outcome of proceedings against them by the administrators; seeking to have parts of the evidence struck out as hearsay; and arguing that they did not need to file affidavit evidence but could wait until trial and submit that there was no case to answer or then call evidence.

E The Vice-Chancellor dismissed the respondents' application on all three issues. The respondents appealed.

Held, dismissing the appeal:

1. The rules required a respondent to adduce his evidence in the form of affidavits which he had to file within the stipulated time.

F 2. Hearsay evidence obtained under s. 447 was admissible because s. 8 of the Disqualification Act created an implied exception to the hearsay rule.

3. The Secretary of State had a public duty to apply for the disqualification of unfit directors. He could not be held up by other proceedings over which he had no control.

The following cases were referred to in the judgment of Hoffmann LJ:

Armvent Ltd, Re [1975] 1 WLR 1679.
G *City Investment Centres Ltd, Re* [1992] BCLC 956.
Grosvenor and West-end Terminus Railway Hotel Co Ltd, Re (1897) 76 LT 337.
Keypak Homecare Ltd, Re (No. 2) [1990] BCC 117.
Koscot Interplanetary (UK) Ltd, Re [1972] 3 All ER 829.
Laurie v Raglan Building Co Ltd [1942] 1 KB 152.
Moonbeam Cards Ltd, Re [1993] BCLC 1099.
H *Practice Note* [1921] WN 356.
R v Erdheim [1896] 2 QB 260.
R v Harris [1970] 1 WLR 1252.
R v Scott (1856) Dears & Bell 47; 169 ER 909.
St Piran Ltd, Re [1981] 1 WLR 1300.
SBA Properties Ltd, Re [1967] 1 WLR 799.
Travel & Holiday Clubs Ltd, Re [1967] 1 WLR 711.

Clive Hugh Jones (instructed by Garstangs, Bolton) for the appellants.   A

Elizabeth Gloster QC and Guy Newey (instructed by the Treasury Solicitor) for the Secretary of State.

JUDGMENT

Hoffmann LJ: This is an appeal by leave of the judge from three interlocutory rulings of the Vice-Chancellor ([1993] BCC 79). They concern the procedure to be followed in an   B application by the Secretary of State to have company directors disqualified. Two of them raise questions of general importance. One is whether a respondent to such an application must file his evidence in opposition before the hearing or whether he can wait until then and give or call oral evidence. The other is whether the Secretary of State as applicant can rely upon statements taken from third parties in the course of an official investigation into the affairs of a company.   C

1. The facts

The appellants (respondents to the application to disqualify) are Mr Frank Warren and Mr Peter Sealey. Mr Warren is, among other things, a boxing promoter. Mr Sealey is a solicitor. Both were directors of a company called Rex Williams Leisure plc. Its principal business was the supply of amusement machines. It obtained a quotation on   D the Unlisted Securities Market. Members of the public subscribed for shares. Early in 1988 it appears to have entered into some kind of transaction to buy from Mr Warren the shares in another company which he controlled for over £2m. In the end the purchase did not proceed. But as part of the transaction the company on 21 March 1988 paid Mr Warren £200,000. Mr Sealey authorised the payment. After the share sale fell through, Mr Warren did not return the money. It remained unpaid on 30 April 1990, when the company was placed in administration. The estimated deficiency for creditors is £4.4m.   E

2. Procedural steps so far

The joint administrators sued Mr Warren for the return of the £200,000. He gave notice of intention to defend the action. For the last three years the action has been asleep. The last thing that happened was on 9 January 1991, when a summons for summary judgment issued by the administrators was adjourned to the judge.   F

On 2 April 1991 the Secretary of State took an interest. There is no evidence as to why, but the chances are that he had received a report from the administrators under the *Insolvent Companies (Reports on Conduct of Directors) No. 2 Rules* 1986 (SI 1986/2134). This requires administrators within six months of the date of the administration order to furnish the Secretary of State with a report on the persons who have been directors within the preceding three years. At any rate, the Secretary of State authorised Mr Desmond   G High, a chartered accountant, to investigate the £200,000 payment pursuant to s. 447 of the *Companies Act* 1985.

Section 447 is one of a battery of powers contained in Pt. XIV of the *Companies Act* 1985, which is headed 'Investigation of companies and their affairs; requisition of documents'. The best known is s. 432(2), which empowers the Secretary of State to appoint inspectors to investigate the affairs of a company and report if it appears to him   H that there are circumstances suggesting various kinds of misconduct, including misfeasance by the persons concerned in its management. Section 431, more rarely used, provides for inspection on the application of some of the members or the company itself. Sections 442 and 446 deal with more limited investigations into share ownership and share dealings. Section 447 has the side-note 'Secretary of State's power to require production of documents'. For present purposes, these are the relevant provisions:

A
'(3) The Secretary of State may at any time, if he thinks there is good reason to do so, authorise an officer of his or any other competent person, on producing (if so required) evidence of his authority, to require a company to produce to him (the officer or other person) forthwith any documents which he (the officer or other person) may specify.

(4) Where by virtue of subsection . . . (3) the Secretary of State or an officer of his
B
or other person has power to require the production of documents from a company, he or the officer or other person has the like power to require production of those documents from any person who appears to him or the officer or other person to be in possession of them . . .

(5) The power under this section to require a company or other person to produce documents includes power–

    (a) if the documents are produced–
C
      . . .

        (ii) to require that person, or any other person who is a past or present officer of, or is or was at any time employed by, the company in question, to provide an explanation of any of them . . .

    . . .

(8) A statement made by a person in compliance with such a requirement may be
D
used in evidence against him.'

The product of a s. 447 investigation will therefore consist primarily of documents which were already in existence but also explanations and commentary by former officers of employees. It is an offence knowingly or recklessly to provide an explanation which is false in a material particular: s. 451. But, unlike an inspector under s. 431 or 432, a person authorised to conduct an investigation under s. 447 is not required to write a report expressing his opinion in the matters under investigation. His formal duty is simply to
E
gather information.

Informally, however, Mr High told the investigations division at the Department of Trade and Industry that as a result of his investigations, he had come to the conclusion that Mr Warren and Mr Sealey had acted unlawfully and in breach of their fiduciary duties to the company. They had simply extracted its cash. The result was that the Secretary of State decided to apply to the court under s. 8 of the *Company Directors*
F
Disqualification Act 1986 for the disqualification of Mr Warren and Mr Sealey as directors on the ground that their conduct made them 'unfit to be concerned in the management of a company'.

Sections 6–10 of the *Company Directors Disqualification Act* 1986 provide for various circumstances in which such an application may be made. The most common is under s. 6, which deals with persons who have been directors of insolvent companies and whose
G
conduct shows them to be unfit. If it appears to the Secretary of State 'expedient in the public interest' that a disqualification order should be made under s. 6, he may either make the application himself or, in the case of a person who has been a director of a company in compulsory liquidation, he may direct that the application be made by the official receiver. In either case, the information upon which the Secretary of State will act in deciding whether an application for a disqualification order is expedient in the public interest will be primarily derived from the 'office-holder' (i.e. the liquidator, administrator
H
or administrative receiver). He has a statutory duty under s. 7 of the Act and also under the *Insolvent Companies (Reports on Conduct of Directors) No. 2 Rules* 1986 to report to the Secretary of State on matters which may indicate that a director is unfit.

An alternative route is s. 8, which can be used even if the company has not become insolvent. Leaving out reference to a number of statutory powers which do not for present purposes matter, these are the relevant provisions:

'8(1) If it appears to the Secretary of State from a report made by inspectors under   A
section 437 of the Companies Act . . . or from information or documents obtained
under section 447 . . . of the Companies Act . . . that it is expedient in the public
interest that a disqualification order should be made against any person who is or
has been a director or shadow director of any company, he may apply to the court
for such an order to he made against that person.

(2) The court may make a disqualification order against a person where, on an   B
application under this section, it is satisfied that his conduct in relation to the
company makes him unfit to be concerned in the management of a company.'

In this case the Secretary of State applied under s. 8.

The procedure governing applications for disqualification orders is for the most part
contained in the *Insolvent Companies (Disqualification of Unfit Directors) Proceedings
Rules* 1987 (SI 1987/2023) ('the disqualification rules'). Rule 2(a) says that an application   C
in the High Court shall be made by originating summons and that the appropriate
provisions of the Rules of the Supreme Court shall apply accordingly, except when the
disqualification rules make provision to inconsistent effect. The Secretary of State issued
the originating summons in these proceedings on 27 April 1992.

Rule 3 of the disqualification rules is headed 'The case against the respondent'. It reads
as follows: D

'(1) There shall, at the time when the summons is issued, be filed in court evidence
in support of the application for a disqualification order; and copies of the evidence
shall be served with the summons on the respondent.

(2) The evidence shall be by one or more affidavits, except where the applicant is
the official receiver, in which case it may be in the form of a written report (with or
without affidavits by other persons) which shall be treated as if it had been verified   E
by affidavit by him and shall be prima facie evidence of any matter contained in it.

(3) There shall in the affidavit or affidavits or (as the case may be) the official
receiver's report be included a statement of the matters by reference to which the
respondent is alleged to be unfit to be concerned in the management of a company.'

The evidence filed by the Secretary of State under r. 3(1) and (2) consisted of three
affidavits. One was by Mr Burns, a deputy inspector of companies. It was fairly formal   F
and said pursuant to r. 3(3) that the matters upon which the Secretary of State would
rely were those concerning the £200,000 payment. The second affidavit was by Mr Copp,
one of the administrators. He exhibited his affidavit in the O. 14 application, setting out
the results of his investigations. The third was by Mr High. He explained the progress of
his investigations, describing and exhibiting some of the documents which he had
obtained and his notes of the explanations which he had been given. He recorded his   G
conclusion that the payment had been unauthorised, unlawful and in breach of fiduciary
duty.

Ordinarily, the next step would have been for the respondents to file their evidence in
answer. This is what is contemplated by r. 6 of the disqualification rules, to which I shall
return in a moment. But instead, on 10 July 1992, the respondents took out a summons
seeking the following relief. First, an order striking out the summons on the ground that   H
it was an abuse of the process for the application to be heard while the action to recover
the £200,000 was still proceeding. The Vice-Chancellor had little difficulty in refusing this
application and I shall deal with it last. Secondly, a declaration that the respondents were
'entitled' to appear at the hearing and give evidence or call witnesses without having filed
affidavit evidence. Thirdly, an order striking out those parts of the affidavits of Mr Copp
and Mr High which recorded or exhibited statements by persons other than the

A respondents themselves. The summons was adjourned to the Vice-Chancellor who refused all three applications (see [1993] BCC 79). The respondents appeal.

3. Oral evidence or affidavits?

The appellants claim that they need not file affidavit evidence in answer. Instead, they say that they are entitled as of right to wait until the hearing and then give oral evidence
B or call witnesses. Or if the court has a discretion in the matter, they say that it should be exercised in favouring of ordering pleadings followed by a trial with oral evidence.

The disqualification rules are not the most hospitable terrain on which to mount such a submission. Rule 6 says:

'(1) The respondent shall, within 28 days from the date of service of the summons, file in court any affidavit evidence in opposition to the application he wishes the
C court to take into consideration and shall forthwith serve upon the applicant a copy of such evidence.

(2) The applicant shall, within 14 days from receiving the copy of the respondents evidence, file in court any further evidence in reply he wishes the court to take into consideration and shall forthwith serve a copy of that evidence upon the respondent.'

D The imperative 'shall' in r. 6(1) suggests that if the respondent wants his evidence taken into consideration, he must file it within the stipulated time. Perhaps it could have been clearer still: 'shall file in court any affidavit evidence' might at first sight leave open the possibility that he could adduce other forms of evidence (e.g. oral evidence) which does not have to be filed in court. But then why does it say 'he wishes the court to take into consideration'? Presumably he wishes the court to take all his evidence into consideration.
E These words only make sense if they mean that the evidence he wishes the court to take into consideration must be filed on affidavit. Furthermore, r. 6(3), which deals with the Secretary of State's evidence in reply, makes it clear that it must be on affidavit. How is this to be done unless the respondent has filed affidavits?

The question is put beyond doubt if one takes into account the way the 1987 disqualification rules amended the previous version in the *Insolvent Companies*
F *(Disqualification of Unfit Directors) Proceedings Rules* 1986 (SI 1986/612). In the 1986 rules, r. 6 said that the respondent 'may' within 28 days file affidavit evidence. It left out the words 'he wishes the court to take into consideration'. Now 'may' has been replaced by 'shall'. And to the various notices which by r. 4 have to be endorsed on the originating summons, the 1987 rules have added the following:

'(e) that any evidence which the respondent wishes to be taken into consideration by the court must be filed in court in accordance with the time limits imposed
G under Rule 6 (the provisions of which shall be set out on the summons).'

This could hardly be clearer.

In the face of this language Mr Jones (who appeared for the appellants) has deployed some of the familiar weaponry of statutory construction: the argument from a priori incredulity ('it is impossible to believe that the legislator intended by such language to take away such a fundamental human right') and the various forms of argument from
H inconsistency with other parts of current and earlier legislation. Some of these linguistic arguments would carry greater weight if the *Companies Act* 1985 and associated legislation were, as the Old Testament was once thought to be, the work of a single faultless author. In fact the legislation is a vast legislative mosaic, the work of many hands, parts of which date back to the *Companies Act* 1862 and the Bankruptcy Act 1849. Interpretation must take this into account.

I could simply say that the language of the disqualification rules is now so clear as to   A
be impervious to arguments of this kind. But out of respect to Mr Jones's skilful
argument, I shall deal with them in more detail.

(a) *History*

Mr Jones pointed out that when a power to disqualify directors was first introduced in
s. 217 of the *Companies Act* 1929, the procedure was assimilated to that of the misfeasance   B
summons, a summary procedure which went back to the *Companies Act* 1862: see r. 66
of the *Companies (Winding-up) Rules* 1929. Misfeasance summonses had originally
followed the traditional Chancery procedure of having all the evidence on affidavit, but
in 1921 the Companies Court adopted a more common law approach. Astbury J issued
a Practice Note [1921] WN 356:

> 'In a recent case tried in this Court various defects in the present practice relating
> to the trial of misfeasance summonses . . . were made apparent. The practice of   C
> allowing witnesses to give their evidence in chief by affidavits, prepared or settled
> for them by others, in cases where real disputes of fact exist and/or where various
> charges of misfeasance or breach of trust are involved, is open to grave objection,
> and when numerous or complicated issues of law or fact exist, the points relied
> upon are under the practice at present prevailing, as and when occasion demands,
> amended or raised for the first time and from time to time during the progress of
> the trial, which causes confusion, recalling of witnesses, possible injustice, waste of   D
> time and increased costs . . . in future the practice in these cases shall be as follows:
> On the return of the summons the Registrar shall give directions as to whether
> points of claim and defence are to be delivered or not, as to the taking of evidence
> wholly or in part by affidavit or orally, as to cross-examination, and generally as
> to the procedure on the summons. No report or affidavit shall be made or filed
> until the Registrar shall so direct.'   E

Rule 66 of the *Companies (Winding-up) Rules* 1929 reflected this Practice Note,
providing that no affidavit or report was to be filed in advance of the first appointment
before the registrar and giving him a wide discretion 'as to the taking of evidence wholly
or in part by affidavit or orally'. Mr Jones says that against this background of practice,
the legislation on disqualification reflected an expectation that the procedure would be
primarily oral. Section 217(2) of the *Companies Act* 1929 said that the official receiver   F
should give the respondent not less than ten days' notice of his intention to make an
application 'and on the hearing of the application that person may appear and himself
give evidence or call witnesses'. This was the language of trial at common law rather than
Chancery affidavits. Section 217(2) has been carried forward into successive statutes
dealing with disqualification and still exists as s. 16(1) of the *Company Directors
Disqualification Act* 1986. Therefore, said Mr Jones, the disqualification rules should not
be construed to exclude the oral procedure envisaged by Astbury J in an appropriate   G
case: where 'real disputes of fact exist and/or various charges of misfeasance or breach of
trust are involved'. The present was such a case. Mr Jones went so far as diffidently to
suggest that if the 1987 disqualification rules did exclude oral evidence by or on behalf of
the respondent, they would be ultra vires as purporting to exclude a right conferred by
Parliament in s. 16(1).

No doubt there are many cases in which the most effective method of trial is to have a   H
brief statement of the issues and then have the protagonists into the witness box as soon
as possible to tell their stories in their own words. It happens daily in County courts all
over the land. But in the High Court it has been largely abandoned. The 1987
disqualification rules are only part of a general trend towards greater emphasis on written
procedure in advance of the hearing, which is also reflected in the rules of the exchange
of witness statements (RSC, O. 38, r. 2A) and the use of skeleton arguments. Misfeasance

A proceedings under s. 212 of the *Insolvency Act* 1986 are once more tried on affidavits: see the *Insolvency Rules* 1986, r. 7.7. So the short answer to Mr Jones's submission based on the history of disqualification procedure is that times have changed. The advantage of allowing both sides to discover each other's cases in detail before trial and cross-examination is perceived to outweigh the loss of spontaneity and the increase in costs at the pre-trial stage.

B As for the submission of ultra vires, I do not think that s. 16(1) and its predecessors were ever intended to confer an absolute right to give or call oral evidence. Even the 1921 Practice Note (and the subsequent winding-up rules) gave the court power to direct that evidence should be wholly by affidavit. All that has happened is that this has become the norm. So in my judgment, 'give evidence or call witnesses' confers a right to give evidence or adduce the evidence of other witnesses, but the manner in which that may be done is a matter for the rules.

C Of course the court retains a residuary discretionary control over its own procedure (see, for example, RSC, O. 2, r. 1). A judge will commonly allow a witness in proceedings under the *Company Directors Disqualification Act* 1986 to supplement his affidavit with a few answers in chief before being cross-examined. And no doubt if a respondent wishes to call a witness over whom he genuinely has no influence and who has refused to swear an affidavit, the court will allow him to do so on subpoena. But the circumstances in

D which oral evidence in chief will be allowed at the hearing are exceptional and neither applicant nor respondent is entitled to insist on it.

(b) *No case to answer*

Mr Jones said that a requirement that the respondents put their evidence on affidavit would deprive them of an effective opportunity to submit that they had no case to answer. A submission of no case to answer, i.e. that there is no evidence upon which a notional

E jury could find for the plaintiff or applicant, is, in civil proceedings without a jury, an arcane and almost obsolete procedure of which the collective experience of the court could recall only one instance. The reason for its disappearance is that in *Laurie v Raglan Building Co Ltd* [1942] 1 KB 152 at p. 155, Lord Greene MR (with whom the other two members of the Court of Appeal agreed) said that the proper practice is for the judge to refuse to rule on a submission of no case to answer unless counsel for the defendant has

F said that he proposes to call no evidence. If this is the invariable practice, a submission of no case to answer would appear to offer no advantage over closing one's case without calling evidence and submitting that the plaintiff has not discharged the burden of proof.

Mr Jones accepted that, one way or the other, he would have to elect whether or not to call evidence. But he said that in an ordinary civil trial, he could postpone this decision until after the applicant's evidence had been tested by cross-examination. Even if there

G had been an order for exchange of witness statements under RSC, O. 38, r. 2A, so that his right to call evidence was conditional on having served a witness statement, he could still decide not to call the witness. If so, the witness statement could not be used as evidence against him: see r. 2A(4). But once he and his witnesses had committed themselves to affidavit, their evidence was available for both sides.

This may represent a difference between trial on affidavits and trial with oral evidence

H preceded by exchange of witness statements. But I do not regard the difference as sufficient to cast any doubt upon the construction or vires of the disqualification rules. Until O. 38, r. 2A, a litigant had a privilege to withhold until trial the contents of the proofs taken from his witnesses. Now it can be made a condition of his calling their evidence that he should have waived that privilege in advance of the trial. Likewise, the disqualification rules advance the moment at which a respondent must elect whether or not he is going to call evidence. Both changes are in my view purely procedural and

within the rule-making power to regulate the 'practice and procedure' of the court   A
exercising jurisdiction under s. 6–10 of the *Company Directors Disqualification Act* 1986:
see s. 21(2) of the Act, applying s. 411 of and para. 2 of Sch. 8 to the *Insolvency Act* 1986.

(c) *Expense*

Mr Jones next submitted that to require affidavits to be filed often placed an unfair
burden upon respondents to disqualification applications. Affidavits were expensive.   B
They were usually drafted by lawyers. Respondents whose companies had become
insolvent tended to be short of money. It would be much cheaper if they could simply go
into the witness-box and tell their stories. Mr Jones, who has great experience of the
Companies Court, said that disqualification applications not infrequently went
undefended because the director could not afford to oppose them.

I think, speaking for myself, that this was Mr Jones's best point. The 'cards on the
table' philosophy, as exemplified by RSC, O. 38, r. 2A and the disqualification rules, may   C
save costs overall by promoting settlements and shortening oral hearings. But it does
undoubtedly produce a 'front-loading' of the costs at the pre-trial stage when affidavits
or witness statements have to be prepared. This is capable of being used oppressively,
enabling the state or the richer party to drown his opponent in documents and testimony.
I do not suggest that anything of the kind has happened in this case, but it is something
which requires careful handling on the part of the department and vigilance on the part   D
of the registrar and judges.

But although I think that the point has substance, it does not advance Mr Jones's
argument in this case. It is a general complaint about the spirit of the times rather than a
reason for not giving the disqualification rules the effect they were obviously intended to
have.

   E

4. The use of hearsay

The second point of principle is the use by the Secretary of State, in the affidavits in of
Mr High and Mr Copp and their exhibits, of statements made to them by third parties.
The statements by the respondents themselves are of course admissible at common law
as admissions. But the remaining statements are at common law inadmissible under the
hearsay rule. They can be admissible in disqualification proceedings only by virtue of   F
some statutory exception to that rule.

Miss Gloster, who appeared for the Secretary of State, relied upon an implied
exception in the case of information obtained under statutory powers which the Secretary
of State is required to take into account in deciding whether it is expedient in the public
interest that certain proceedings should be brought under the Companies Act or
associated legislation. In such cases she says that there is an implied hearsay exception   G
which allows the court to receive the same information in evidence.

The exception originates in two decisions of Pennycuick J sitting in the Companies
Court in 1967: *Re Travel & Holiday Clubs Ltd* [1967] 1 WLR 711 and *Re SBA Properties
Ltd* [1967] 1 WLR 799. Each concerned a winding-up petition presented by the Board of
Trade under s. 169(3) of the *Companies Act* 1948, which said that the board could present
such a petition on the just and equitable ground if it appeared from a report of inspectors
appointed under s. 169(1) or (2) (now s. 431 and 432 of the *Companies Act* 1985) that it   H
was expedient to do so. In *Travel & Holiday Clubs* Pennycuick J said at p. 715E:

> 'It seems to me that it would not be in accordance with the apparent intention of
> the section that, where inspectors appointed under the Act have made a report, the
> court should not be entitled to look at that report and accept it not as hearsay
> evidence but as material of a different character altogether, and should have to be

A
satisfied anew by evidence of the ordinary nature as to the facts found in the report.'

In *SBA Properties* he distinguished a case concerning a report of inspectors under the *Companies Act* 1862, in which the Court of Appeal had said that the report was not 'evidence in a court of justice of the existence of any fact mentioned in it': per Lord Esher MR in *Re Grosvenor and West-End Railway Terminus Hotel Co Ltd* (1897) 76 LT 337 at
B
p. 338. Under s. 169(3), he said (at p. 806E), the question was:

'whether the court can treat the inspector's report not as evidence in the ordinary sense but as material upon which, if it is not challenged, the court can proceed to make a winding-up order on the ground that it is just and equitable to do so.'

These decisions left two matters for later clarification: first, the somewhat mysterious distinction between 'evidence' and 'material', and secondly, the suggestion that if the
C
report was 'challenged', it might cease to be evidence or 'material', leaving all the relevant facts to be proved de novo.

Both points were resolved by later decisions. *Re Koscot Interplanetary (UK) Ltd* [1972] 3 All ER 829 shows recognition that the report is hearsay evidence and that s. 169(3) of the *Companies Act* 1948 (by then replaced by s. 35 of the *Companies Act* 1967) created an implied statutory exception to the hearsay rule. In *Re Armvent Ltd* [1975] 1 WLR 1679
D
the petition was opposed. Templeman J said at p. 1685H:

'It seems to me even if the report of the inspectors is challenged nevertheless it ought to be treated as prima facie evidence and that it ought to be left to a judge in any case having read the report and having seen the witnesses to make up his own mind whether it is just and equitable to wind up the company. The whole machinery of the inspectors' report was evolved in order to enable the Secretary of
E
State to present a winding-up petition where the Secretary of State considers the public interest so demands. It would be unfortunate if once the Secretary of State has reached that conclusion on proper grounds based on the inspectors' detailed report, that the court should be right back to square one and start again as though the inspectors had never come on the scene at all.'

Finally in *Re St Piran Ltd* [1981] 1 WLR 1300 at p. 1306B, Dillon J referred to the principle which had evolved as an exception to the hearsay rule and stated its basis as
F
follows:

'it would be nonsensical if the court could not take the report into consideration in deciding whether it was just and equitable that the company should be wound up when on the very terms of section 169(3) of the 1948 Act as of section 35 of the Act of 1967, it is on the basis of his consideration of the report that the Secretary of State has concluded that it is expedient that the winding-up petition should be
G
presented or that the company should be wound up.'

The provisions which derive from s. 169(3) of the 1948 Act have been amended and extended on a number of occasions. The latest version is s. 124A of the *Insolvency Act* 1986, which was inserted by the *Companies Act* 1989. These are the relevant provisions:

'(1) Where it appears to the Secretary of State from–

H
(a) any report made or information obtained under Part XIV of the Companies Act 1985 (company investigations, etc.),

. . .

that it is expedient in the public interest that a company should be wound up, he may present a petition for it to be wound up if the court thinks it just and equitable for it to be so.'

Thus the material which the Secretary of State may take into consideration includes   A
whatever is gathered under the inspection and investigation powers of Pt. XIV of the
Companies Act 1985, including s. 447.

Miss Gloster says that if the exception applies to public interest petitions under s. 124A
of the *Insolvency Act* 1986, it should equally apply to disqualification applications under
s. 8 of the *Company Directors Disqualification Act* 1986. The relevant phraseology of the
two sections is almost identical. The Vice-Chancellor found the analogy a powerful one   B
and so do I.

But Mr Jones submitted that disqualification applications were quite different from
public interest petitions for winding up. In the latter, no particular facts had to be proved.
In *Re Armvent Ltd* [1975] 1 WLR 1679 at p. 1683B, Templeman J said:

> 'I am not here to establish whether every charge made by the inspectors and every
> conclusion is right. In my judgment there is no way in which the truth about this   C
> company can be established save by winding up.'

All that the evidence had to establish was that it was in the public interest that the
company should be wound up to enable the official receiver to investigate its affairs. But
in a disqualification application the Secretary of State must prove facts which show that
the director is unfit.

In my judgment these distinctions go to weight rather than admissibility. In a   D
disqualification application, hearsay evidence untested by cross-examination of the
informant may be insufficient to satisfy the burden of proof against opposing evidence.
It will depend upon the facts and probabilities of each case. Once the Secretary of State
knows from the opposing affidavits which material facts are seriously in dispute, he may
be well advised to reinforce his case by affidavits from the appropriate informants. But
that is no reason why their hearsay evidence obtained under s. 447 should be inadmissible.
Much of what they say may be uncontested, in which case it would have been a waste of   E
time and money to insist that they swear affidavits.

Mr Jones relies upon two further arguments on construction. First, he draws attention
to s. 447(8) of the *Companies Act* 1985, which I have quoted above. He says that if the
statute expressly makes the respondent's own statements admissible against him, surely
it follows that statements by other people are not. In my judgment, however, s. 447(8)
has nothing to do with the hearsay rule. At common law a statement by a party to   F
litigation is always admissible against him. No statutory exception to the hearsay rule is
needed. Section 447(8) is one of a number of sections scattered over various statutes
which are intended to deal with a different problem, namely an early nineteenth century
opinion that statements made under statutory compulsion were not 'voluntary' for the
purposes of the confession rule in criminal proceedings. In fact this view was decisively
rejected in *R v Scott* (1856) Dears & B 47, but starting with s. 17(8) of the *Bankruptcy Act*
1883, Parliament has been constantly vigilant in case it should again raise its head. The   G
result is that powers to obtain information in the Companies Act, Insolvency Act and
associated legislation are almost invariably accompanied by a provision that the answers
are to be admissible against the informant. They may have served little purpose except to
stir up arguments of the *expressio unius* variety (see for example *R v Erdheim* [1896] 2 QB
260 and *R v Harris* [1970] 1 WLR 1252) and in *Re Keypak Homecare Ltd (No. 2)* [1990]
BCC 117 Harman J (probably unfairly) declared one of them to be absolutely
meaningless. But they were not intended as exceptions to the rule against hearsay.   H

Mr Jones based a similar argument on r. 3(2) of the disqualification rules, which I have
already quoted. The 1986 version of the rules had merely equated the official receiver's
report to an affidavit. It said that the report 'shall be treated as if it had been verified by
affidavit by him'. The 1987 version added the words 'and shall be prima facie evidence of
any matter contained in it'. The effect of these words is to make any assertion in the

A report, whether or not within the personal knowledge of the official receiver, prima facie evidence of its truth: see *Re City Investment Centres Ltd* [1992] BCLC 956 and *Re Moonbeam Cards Ltd* [1993] BCLC 1099. There is no similar provision for assertions in affidavits sworn on behalf of the Secretary of State and so Mr Jones says that if the amendment was necessary to make hearsay admissible in reports by the official receiver, it must follow that it is not admissible in affidavits.

B The formal answer to this submission is that subordinate legislation such as the disqualification rules cannot repeal an exception to the hearsay rule which Parliament has impliedly created by primary legislation in s. 8. The more realistic answer is that it is indeed odd that in reports by the official receiver any hearsay should be admissible, whereas affidavits should be limited to hearsay which is admissible under specific exceptions such as s. 8 or the *Civil Evidence Act* 1968. The new r. 3(2) seems another example of legislation which has not been sufficiently thought through and, in a C praiseworthy attempt to improve or clarify one detail of the law, produces inconsistency or uncertainty in other parts. But this is not in my judgment sufficient to prevent statements obtained under s. 447 of the *Companies Act* 1985 from being impliedly admissible in proceedings under s. 8 of the *Company Directors Disqualification Act* 1986. It is therefore unnecessary for me to deal with the Secretary of State's alternative submissions that the hearsay passages in the affidavits should not be struck out because D they might be admissible under the *Civil Evidence Act* 1968 or RSC, O. 38, r. 3. The Vice-Chancellor dealt separately with hearsay statements, exhibited documents and conclusory assertions, but I agree that there are no grounds for striking out any parts of the affidavits and the appeal against his ruling therefore fails.

5. Stay pendente lite

E Finally, I return to the first order sought on the respondents' summons, which was an order striking out the disqualification proceedings as an abuse of process because they were launched while the action by the administrators to recover the £200,000 was still proceeding. This action, as I mentioned earlier, has been dormant for more than three years. In this court, Mr Jones put forward the more modest proposal that there should be a stay of these proceedings until the action had been concluded. Even this was not pursued with great enthusiasm. For my part, I think it would be quite absurd. The F Secretary of State has a public duty to apply for the disqualification of unfit directors. He cannot be held up indefinitely by other proceedings over which he has no control.

6. Conclusion

I think that the judgment of the Vice-Chancellor was entirely right and I would dismiss this appeal.

G

Staughton LJ: I agree that this appeal should be dismissed. Of the two points which seem to me most significant, the first is whether the *Insolvent Companies (Disqualification of Unfit Directors) Proceedings Rules* 1987 are ultra vires. It is said that they are, if and to the extent that they do not allow a respondent to call evidence unless he has filed an affidavit of the proposed witness. That is said to conflict with s. 16(1) of the *Company Directors Disqualification Act* 1986, which provides that the person against whom an H order is sought may appear and himself give evidence or call witnesses.

The Disqualification Act contemplates in s. 21, although somewhat indirectly, that rules may be made. In my judgment it enables rules to deal with how evidence shall be given and witnesses called; and in particular it permits a requirement that affidavits shall first be filed. This is essentially a rule as to how the right conferred by s. 16(1) shall be exercised, and not a derogation from that right.

A

The second point that has troubled me concerns hearsay evidence. Order 41, r. 5 of the Rules of the Supreme Court provides that, subject to a number of exceptions which do not apply in the present case, an affidavit may contain only such facts as the deponent is able of his own knowledge to prove.

How then can the Secretary of State be entitled to use affidavits of information and belief in disqualification proceedings? As Hoffmann LJ has shown, this stems from an implied statutory provision as to the use of hearsay as evidence, or at any rate as provisional evidence until it is challenged. That doctrine is now of respectable antiquity, having been established between 1967 and 1975. I would for my part have hesitated to accept it when first propounded. But as it has existed for a substantial period of time, during which relevant statutory provisions have been repealed and re-enacted or amended, I would not now alter it.

Russell LJ: I also agree.

(Appeal dismissed)

A # Re G E Tunbridge Ltd.

Chancery Division (Companies Court).
Sir Mervyn Davies.
Judgment delivered 27 April 1994.

Administration – Debenture – Debenture expressed to create fixed charge over
B *certain assets – Assets not to be disposed of without debenture holder's consent –*
Whether charge was fixed or floating – Materiality of parties' intention to create
fixed charge.

This was an application in the administration of a company by a debenture holder who
claimed that the proceeds of sale of certain assets covered by a fixed charge in the debenture
were payable to him.

C   The company was engaged in the sale and repair of motor cars. The debenture contained
a fixed charge over 'the fixed assets and the proceeds and products thereof' and a floating
charge over 'the floating assets and the proceeds and products thereof'. The floating assets
comprised new and used motor vehicles, spare parts and other assets acquired by the chargor
for the purpose of resale. The fixed assets included freehold properties and 'all other assets
(not being floating assets) now owned or hereafter acquired by the chargor or in which it
D now has or in the future acquires an interest'. The question was whether the debenture was
effective to create a fixed charge over not only such assets as various chattels which were
sold at auction but also intangible assets such as book debts. The debenture prevented the
chargor disposing of the fixed assets without the debenture holder's consent.

Held, dismissing the application:

1. The debenture created a charge on a class of assets present and future and clearly
E contemplated that the company was to carry on business in the ordinary way as far as those
assets were concerned. The debenture was not apt to create a specific charge over the book
debts or the chattels. It was unrealistic to suppose that a considerable number of the chattels
would not or might not be changed or removed from time to time. The debenture as a whole
disclosed a situation in which a floating charge arose over the assets despite the parties
having supposed that they were creating a specific charge.

F   2. The position might have been otherwise had the debenture contained a schedule in
which there were itemised the particular chattels that the parties regarded as being
susceptible of a fixed charge. (National Provincial Bank of England Ltd v United Electric
Theatres Ltd [1916] 1 Ch 132 considered.)

3. The restriction on the company selling the assets without the debenture holder's
consent did not convert what was otherwise a floating charge over the assets into a specific
charge. (Re Brightlife Ltd (1986) 2 BCC 99,359 considered.)
G
The following cases were referred to in the judgment:

Brightlife Ltd, Re (1986) 2 BCC 99,359; [1987] Ch 200.
Illingworth v Houldsworth & Anor [1904] AC 355.
National Provincial Bank of England Ltd v United Electric Theatres Ltd [1916] 1 Ch
132.
H *Siebe Gorman & Co Ltd v Barclays Bank Ltd* [1979] 2 Ll Rep 142.
Tailby v Official Receiver (1888) 13 App Cas 523.
Welsh Development Agency v Export Finance Co Ltd [1992] BCC 270.
Yorkshire Woolcombers Association Ltd, Re [1903] 2 Ch 284 (CA); [1904] AC 355 (HL).

Henry Harrod (instructed by Keene Marsland) for the applicant.

David Marks (instructed by Taylor Joynson Garrett) for the respondent.

JUDGMENT

Sir Mervyn Davies: This is an application concerning a company called G E Tunbridge Ltd. The application, dated 23 September 1993, is by Mr Alan Howard Tunbridge.

Before mentioning the purpose of the application I must set out some facts concerning the company. The company was engaged for some years in the sale and repair of motor cars. There was a distributorship agreement for Fiat and Lancia cars. The company fell into difficulties in 1991. On 6 August 1991 an administration order was made under s. 8 of the *Insolvency Act* 1986. Mr J C Heath and Mr A D Killington were appointed the joint administrators. The petition had been presented by Mr Tunbridge with the consent of the other directors of the company. The company accounts showed money owing to the National Westminster Bank and £85,000 to Mr Tunbridge. The bank had no charge over the specified assets that I will be mentioning later.

It was supposed that the business of the company could be sold as a going concern but in the event that course was not taken, the joint administrators discontinued the business and arranged an auction sale of the company's chattels on site. The sale took place on 23 June 1993. The sale catalogue is exhibit AHT4 to an affidavit of Mr Tunbridge, sworn on 22 September 1993. It shows nearly 676 items. The sale realised £50,380.

On 14 June Mr Tunbridge's solicitor had written to the solicitors for the joint respondents, contending that Mr Tunbridge had a charge over assets of the company, assets that included many of the chattels that were being put up for auction. In consequence it was said that a sum of about £40,000 is payable to Mr Tunbridge out of the £50,380 auction proceeds. That contention was not accepted. In consequence, the application dated 23 September 1993 was issued with the joint administrators being the respondents thereto. The application seeks a declaration that some of the assets of the company sold by auction ('the specified assets') are subject to a fixed charge in favour of Mr Tunbridge by virtue of a debenture dated 29 November 1982. The specified assets are identified by their lot numbers in the auction catalogue. I am told that those lot numbers total 337.

The lot numbers cover an assortment of the articles one expects to see in a business engaged in selling and repairing motor cars. There is office furniture, typewriters, electronic equipment, a multitude of receptacles or articles designed to house spare parts and tools, as well as the spare parts, tools and fixed or semi-fixed equipment for dealing with motor car repairs.

The debenture dated 29 November 1982 is exhibit AHT1 to Mr Tunbridge's first affidavit. It has been duly registered. It is made between the company, therein called 'the chargor', of the one part and Mr Tunbridge, therein called 'the lender', of the other part. Clause 5.1 of the debenture reads:

'The chargor, as beneficial owner, hereby charges to the lender as security for the payment of the chargor's monetary liability and the performance of its other obligations to the lender from time to time:

    (a) By way of fixed charge the fixed assets and the proceeds and products thereof (and in the case of the assets described in pt. 1 of the first schedule, such charge shall be by way of legal mortgage);

    (b) By way of floating charge, the floating assets and the proceeds and products thereof.'

Clause 5.2 explains when the floating charge crystallises. It is common ground that there has been no crystallisation of the floating charge. The fixed assets referred to in cl. 5.1 are said to be the assets described in the first schedule. The floating assets are said to be the assets described in the second schedule. 'The property' means the fixed and floating assets. The first schedule I have mentioned is in two parts. Part 1 itemises the

A   freehold properties; I am not concerned with pt. 1. Part 2 includes two paragraphs. I am not concerned with the first paragraph in pt. 2 but the second paragraph reads in this way:

> '2. All other assets (not being floating assets) now owned or hereafter acquired by the chargor or in which it now has or in the future acquires an interest.'

The second schedule – that is the schedule which specifies the floating assets – reads as

B   follows:

> 'The floating assets:
>
>   (1) New motor vehicles;
>
>   (2) Used motor vehicles;
>
>   (3) Spare parts for (1) and/or (2) or other assets acquired by the chargor for the

C   purpose of resale.'

Although the application before me seeks the declaration I have already described, it was agreed by counsel that the true question that falls for decision is whether or not the debenture was effective to create a fixed charge over the property described in the second paragraph of pt. 2 of the first schedule; that is to say over what I refer to as 'the para. 2(2) assets'; that is to say, disregarding the freehold land, is there a fixed charge in favour

D   of Mr Tunbridge over all the assets of the company other than the assets specified in the second schedule (i.e. the motor cars and spare parts, etc., as they are referred to, being stock regularly bought and sold). Put shortly, is there a fixed charge over the para. 2(2) assets?

Mr Harrod, for Mr Tunbridge, submitted that, construing the debenture, it is plain that the parties intended to create a fixed charge over the para. 2(2) assets. That, he said,

E   is what the debenture says. He also drew attention to para. 6 of the debenture, which is in these terms:

> '6. Until the crystallisation of the floating charge under cl. 5 the chargor shall be at liberty to dispose of any of the floating assets by way of sale or hire purchase in the ordinary course of business and on such terms usual in a business of that kind but save as aforesaid the chargor shall not without the prior written consent of the

F   lender dispose of the property, nor shall it permit the property to become the subject of any lien, distress, execution or other legal process.'

Mr Harrod referred to *Siebe Gorman v Barclays Bank* [1979] 2 Ll Rep 142. That case was concerned with a charge over book debts. The circumstances in which that charge was regarded as a fixed charge do not appear in the case before me, see *Siebe Gorman* at p. 159.

G   I begin by referring to the well known observations of Romer LJ in the *Yorkshire Woolcombers* case [1903] 2 Ch 284 at p. 295. There Romer LJ says:

> 'I certainly do not intend to attempt to give an exact definition of the term 'floating charge', nor am I prepared to say that there will not be a floating charge within the meaning of the Act, which does not contain all the three characteristics that I am about to mention, but I certainly think that if a charge has the three characteristics

H   that I am about to mention it is a floating charge. (1.) If it is a charge on a class of assets of a company present and future; (2.) if that class is one which, in the ordinary course of the business of the company, would be changing from time to time; and (3.) if you find that by the charge it is contemplated that, until some future step is taken by or on behalf of those interested in the charge, the company may carry on its business in the ordinary way as far as concerns the particular class of assets I am dealing with.'

In my view the Tunbridge debenture created a charge on a class of assets present and future – i.e. the assets described in para. 2(2). The debenture clearly contemplates that the company was to carry on business in the ordinary way as far as concerns the para. 2(2) assets. Thus characteristics (1) and (3) appear. There is then characteristic (2) above.

The debenture contemplates new and used motor vehicles and spare parts and other assets acquired for resale (see the second schedule) would be changing from time to time. But there is a question whether the para. 2(2) assets are also assets that would be changing from time to time.

I bear in mind that the para. 2(2) assets include not only such assets as the chattels that were sold by auction but also intangible assets such as book debts. In *Illingworth v Houldsworth* [1904] AC 355 (that is the *Yorkshire Woolcombers* case in the House of Lords) Lord Macnaghten said at p. 358:

'I should have thought there was not much difficulty in defining what a floating charge is in contrast to what is called a specific charge. A specific charge, I think, is one that without more fastens on ascertained and definite property or property capable of being ascertained and defined; a floating charge, on the other hand, is ambulatory and shifting in its nature, hovering over and so to speak floating with the property which it is intended to affect until some event occurs or some act is done which causes it to settle and fasten on the subject of the charge within its reach and grasp.'

With that guidance I cannot see that the debenture was apt to create a specific charge over the company's book debts – see *Tailby v Official Receiver* (1888) 13 App Cas 523 at p. 541.

As to whether the debenture created a specific charge over the company's chattels other than the second schedule chattels I refer to the judgment of Astbury J in *National Provincial Bank v United Electric Theatres Ltd* [1916] 1 Ch 132. In that case there was a charge on property which included chattels then or thereafter lying in various specific business premises. The charge was not expressed to be fixed or floating. The judge construed the charge as creating a floating charge. The argument, as reported, is instructive. After referring to some words of Lord Macnaghten at p. 541 in the *Tailby* case Astbury J said at p. 139:

'In *In re Yorkshire Woolcombers Association*. . . a similar question arose. Two years after issuing debentures secured by a trust deed the company by an apparently specific charge assigned to Illingworth all the book and other debts then owing, or which might at any time during the continuance of the security become due and owing to the company, and the full benefit of all securities for the present and future and other debts in trust for certain guarantors in proportion to their respective liabilities. The question was whether that was a specific or a floating charge. It is quite true it was stronger than in the present case, because it was a charge only on the book debts, and the provisions of the mortgage showed that they could be collected from time to time by the company. Farwell J. held that the mortgage was merely a floating charge.'

After reading the words of Romer LJ that I have set out above Astbury J continued:

'That category applies to this case. Of course all cases differ in degree. This not being a mortgage by a manufacturing company, the chattels charged would not change with the same frequency as in a manufacturing business; but where a company like the defendants carry on a considerable number of theatres, and charge the whole of their present and future stock in trade, furniture, loose effects, plant, machinery and so on that may be upon the various premises, and agreed to carry on their business in the ordinary course, I think that is a charge upon a class

A   of chattels all of which in the ordinary course of business would or might be changed or removed from time to time.'

As in that case the Tunbridge company was not a manufacturing company but when one looks at the range of chattels itemised in the auction particulars it is, in my view, unrealistic to suppose that a considerable number of the auction chattels would not or might not be changed or removed from time to time. So it is that I regard as present characteristic (2) referred to by Romer LJ. The position might have been otherwise had

B   the debenture contained a schedule in which there were itemised the particular chattels that the parties regarded as being susceptible of a fixed charge (see Astbury J at p. 141).

I do not regard cl. 6 of the debenture as operating to convert what I regard as a floating charge over the para. 2(2) assets into a specific charge. For present purposes, the effect of cl. 6 is not to allow the company to sell para. 2(2) assets without Mr Tunbridge's consent. That restriction does not seem to me to be conclusive in making what is otherwise a

C   floating charge into a fixed charge. In *Re Brightlife Ltd* (1986) 2 BCC 99,359, Hoffmann J says at p. 99,363:

> 'It is true that cl. 5(ii) does not allow Brightlife to sell, factor or discount debts without the written consent of Norandex. But a floating charge is consistent with some restriction on the company's freedom to deal with its assets.'

D   There remains for consideration Mr Harrod's persuasive submission that whether or not the charge appears to have the characteristics of a floating charge, nevertheless, the charge must be construed as a fixed charge because the parties' intention in the deed manifestly shows an intent to create a fixed charge. I do not accept that submission. No doubt the parties intended to create and supposed that they were creating a fixed charge over the para. 2(2) assets but that intention was not fulfilled. The effect of the debenture was to create a situation in which a floating charge arose.

E   Hoffmann J in the *Brightlife* case appears to have found no difficulty in this regard. He says at p. 99,362:

> 'Secondly, although cl. 3(A)(ii)(a) speaks of a "first specific charge" over the book debts and other debts, the rights over the debts created by the debenture were in my judgment such as to be categorised in law as a floating charge (compare *Street v Mountford* [1985] AC 809 at p. 819).'

F   In *Welsh Development Agency v Export Finance Co Ltd* [1992] BCC 270 the Court of Appeal considered (see p. 279B) the question:

> '. . . where, without any question of sham, there is some objective criterion in law by which the court can test whether the agreement the parties have made does or does not fall into the legal category in which the parties have sought to place their agreement.'

G   At p. 280B Dillon LJ says:

> 'In my judgment there is no one clear touchstone by which it can necessarily and inevitably be said that a document which is not a sham and which is expressed as an agreement for sale must necessarily, as a matter of law, amount to no more than the creation of a mortgage or charge on the property expressed to be sold. It is necessary therefore to look at the provisions in the master agreement as a whole

H   to decide whether in substance it amounts to an agreement for the sale of goods or only to a mortgage or charge on goods and their proceeds.'

Following that approach, I have considered the provisions of the Tunbridge debenture as a whole. My conclusion is that the document as a whole discloses a situation in which a floating charge arises over the para. 2(2) assets, despite the parties having supposed that they were creating a specific charge. Taken against the background of the evidence

A

as to the chattels and other property on which the charge was to operate, it seems to me that all three indicia referred to by Romer LJ are present, and a reading of the debenture as a whole does not lead to the conclusion that, despite those indicia, the debenture is to be read as creating a specific or fixed charge over the para.2(2) assets, albeit that the debenture refers to the charge created as being a fixed charge.

It follows that I hold that the debenture was not apt to create a fixed charge over the para. 2(2) assets.

B

(Application dismissed with costs)

C

D

E

F

G

H

A # Pinewood Joinery v Starelm Properties Ltd.

Chancery Division (Companies Court).
His Honour Judge Moseley QC (sitting as a High Court judge).
Judgment delivered 27 April 1994.

B *Transactions defrauding creditors – Whether transfer of property was at an undervalue – Whether applicants were capable of being prejudiced by transaction – Whether purpose of transfer was to put assets beyond reach of claimants – Insolvency Act 1986, s. 423.*

This was an application under s. 423 of the Insolvency Act 1986 (transactions defrauding creditors).

The applicants were a firm engaged in general building work who claimed to be owed
C money by a property developer, 'A & T'. The dispute had given rise to an action in the official referee's court. A & T owned a property which was in use as a hotel but which did not have planning permission for that use. A loan of some £2.65m was secured on the property. The property was sold by A & T in 1993 to a related company, which was the respondent. A & T had made profits until 1990 but made losses in 1991 and 1992. A & T had advice that it was necessary to sell the property to obtain tax relief which might otherwise not be available. The equity of redemption in the hotel property was sold by
D A & T to the respondent for £1. The property remained mortgaged to the bank; A & T remained liable on its personal obligation to the bank.

The applicants agreed that in the circumstances and for the purposes of s. 423(1)(c) £1 was more than the value of the property transferred unless the value of the property was more than £2.65m.

E *Held*, dismissing the application:

1. There were valuations in being showing the value of the hotel on various assumptions as being more than £2.65m, but those assumptions had not been realised. A property with a hope of obtaining planning permission which would increase the value of that property, had 'hope' value. However, there was no evidence of what that 'hope' value was. That was a question requiring expert evidence.

F 2. Section 423(5) was widely enough drafted to enable a person who was a litigant in proceedings and who had a chance of success in those proceedings to qualify as a victim of the transaction under s. 423(5) as being a person capable of being prejudiced by the transaction.

3. However, the applicants were not prejudiced by the transaction or capable of being prejudiced by it because they were no worse off after it than before. Before the transaction they had no hope of recovering anything because the respondents had no funds other than
G funds which were subject to the security in favour of the bank. After the transaction the position remained unchanged. The property had been transferred, subject to the mortgage, but what had been transferred was a property which had a greater sum secured on it than its value.

4. The evidence established that the dominant purpose of A & T in transferring the property was not to put the property beyond the reach of the applicants but to gain a tax
H advantage. That being the dominant purpose, the applicants had failed to establish the purpose requisite under s. 423(3).

The following cases were referred to in the judgment:

Chohan v Saggar & Anor [1992] BCC 306.
Lloyds Bank Ltd v Marcan & Ors [1973] 1 WLR 1387.
Moon v Franklin The Independent 22 June 1990.

James Todd (instructed by Quintons) for the applicant.   A

Timothy Harry (instructed by Abbott King) for the respondent.

JUDGMENT

His Honour Judge Moseley QC: This is an extempore judgment given after three days
of evidence and argument and immediately at the conclusion of the argument. In normal
circumstances, in a case of this complexity I would reserve the matter at least overnight   B
before giving judgment. However, I give my judgment now for two reasons: the first is
the practical reason that I am sitting in London only for these three days and leaving this
evening; the second more important reason is that the parties are locked in litigation in
the Official Referees' Court and the hearing is due to begin at the beginning of May. It is
important, therefore, for both parties that they should know the outcome of this litigation
in the Companies Court so that they can arrange their affairs in relation to that other
litigation.   C

I would be grateful to counsel, if they think that I have omitted anything from this
extempore judgment which they think is important, if they would, at the termination of
my judgment, remind me of it so that I can add it to the judgment.

The application is an application under s. 423 of the *Insolvency Act* 1986. That is the
successor of the old *Law of Property Act* 1925, s. 172, which had its roots in legislation
dating from the seventeenth century, a statute of Elizabeth I. The purpose and effect of   D
s. 423 is to enable a person who is a victim of a transaction defrauding creditors to have
it set aside. Under the section the court has a discretion as to whether or not it will set
aside the transaction and there has been brought to my attention a decision of Mervyn
Davies J, *Moon v Franklin* (reported, so far as I know, only in the Independent of 22 June
1990), in which he exercised that discretion by making a declaration rather than setting
aside the transaction.   E

Looking at the section, the matters that are important for the purposes of this litigation
are numerous. First of all, s. 423(1)(c) is important and I will read it. It reads:

'(1) This section relates to transactions entered into at an undervalue; and a person
enters into such a transaction with another person if–

(c) he enters into a transaction with the other for a consideration the value of
which, in money or money's worth, is significantly less than the value, in   F
money or money's worth, of the consideration provided by himself.'

Then subs. (2), which I need not read, contains provisions relevant to the exercise of the
discretion of the court.

Section 423(3) is also important in the present application:

'In the case of a person entering into such a transaction, an order shall only be
made if the court is satisfied that it was entered into by him for the purpose–   G

(a) of putting assets beyond the reach of a person who is making, or may at
some time make, a claim against him . . .'

The next section which is important is s. 424(1)(c). That reads:

'(1) An application for an order under section 423 shall not be made in relation to
a transaction except–   H

(c) in any other case, by a victim of the transaction.'

To find out what is meant by a 'victim of the transaction' one then has to go back to
the previous section, s. 423(5), and that reads:

'In relation to a transaction at an undervalue, references here and below' – 'below'
means s. 424 – 'to a victim of the transaction are to a person who is, or is capable

A   of being, prejudiced by it; and in the following two sections the person entering into the transaction is referred to as "the debtor".'

Each of those sections that I have quoted has given rise to argument to which I will return after referring to the facts.

The relevant facts are these: the applicant, Pinewood Joinery, is a firm, as I understand it a partnership of two people, concerned inter alia with joinery but also, as I understand
B   it, engaged in general building works. In 1990 they performed building works for the company which is the first defendant to the present proceedings, A & T Investments Ltd. In round terms they performed some £300,000 worth of work to a building which is now being used as an hotel, then owned by A & T Investments. They were paid, again in very round terms, £200,000 and allege that they have not been paid, again in round terms, £100,000. They have brought proceedings in the Official Referees' Court to recover the
C   debt. The exact sum was of the order of £132,000.

Staying for the present with those proceedings, they were commenced by writ followed by a statement of claim, and a summons under O. 14 was then issued for summary judgment. That came before Master Prebble who gave the defendant, A & T Investments, unconditional leave to defend. A defence and counterclaim was then served, and a reply and defence to counterclaim was in turn served. Thus it was that there arises in the Official Referees' Court a disputed building claim.

D   Leaving for the present that dispute in the Official Referees' Court I turn to the business activities of A & T Investments, which are central to the present application. A & T Investments were engaged during the period until about 1990 in the trade of buying properties, converting them and re-selling them at a profit and it appears that they engaged in that trade with some success. During the year 1990 in particular they made a very substantial profit which would make them liable to pay corporation tax in the sum
E   of the order of £111,000. Unfortunately, they were far less successful in subsequent years. They made a loss in the year ending March 1991 – which is their accounting year – and an even greater loss in the accounting year ending March 1992.

In 1988 they purchased a building which was at that time in use as a hostel. Their purpose in buying it, I am satisfied, was to convert it into residential accommodation, but with the decline in the value of residential accommodation in London in or about 1990 their intentions relating to the property altered. They formed the intention of
F   converting the property for use as a luxury hotel and for that purpose engaged the services of the plaintiffs in the Official Referees' Court and applicants in the present case, Pinewood Joinery.

It was at first thought that the building could lawfully be used as an hotel, given that it was in use as a hostel and, as it was thought, had been in use as a hostel since 1964. Under the Town and Country Planning Act – to which I have not been referred in detail,
G   so I refer to it in general terms – it is possible to use a property lawfully for a use which is established, provided that it has been established since 1964. The law was altered, as I understand it, in 1990 and from thenceforward it is possible to enjoy an established use without obtaining fresh planning permission, provided one can show that that use has been established for the past ten years.

Believing, as they did at the time, that the hostel could lawfully be used in the future as
H   an hotel, the directors of A & T decided, as I have said, to abandon their scheme to convert the property into residential use and decided instead to use it as an hotel.

The money for that purpose was borrowed from National Westminster Bank and as at the date which is important for this application, 29 March 1993, the amount of money outstanding on the security of the property owed by A & T Investments Limited to National Westminster Bank was of the order of £2.65m. Valuations of the property were

obtained by the bank in 1990, but it is clear that those valuations, and indeed all A
valuations obtained by the bank, have been on various assumptions. The assumption on
which the 1990 valuation, obtained from W G Edwards, was based was the assumption
that an established use certificate could be obtained enabling the building lawfully to be
used as an hotel. In those circumstances Knight Frank & Rutley, and on that assumption,
valued the building in its completed state, which is on another assumption that it would
be completed, at the figure of £3.1m, £3.5m if the property were in use as an hotel.

The hope of the directors that an established use could be proved was unfortunately
not realised and as time proceeded the company became more and more embroiled in
difficulties relating to planning permission. As at 29 March 1993, the date of the transfer
– to which I will come back in a moment – the situation was that the only planning
permission which the building had was planning permission for the conversion of the
property into residential accommodation. The company attempted to tackle the problem
of the absence of planning permission in other ways (i.e. other than by arguing that there C
was an established use) but hitherto the company and its successor company, Starelm
Properties Ltd, have been unsuccessful. So as at March 1993 and, in fact, as at the present
also, the property, though in use as an hotel and though converted as a luxury hotel, has
no planning permission for use as an hotel, with a result that the assumptions made in
the various valuations I have referred to have not, as yet, been realised.

I return to the profit which A & T Investments made in 1990. As a result of that profit D
it owed to the Inland Revenue corporation tax of the order of £111,000. However, it had
the advice of a very competent accountant, Mr Cooper, whom I found a straightforward
and impressive witness and whose evidence I accept. Mr Cooper pointed out to the
directors of the company that the legislation which was then in force – in 1993 – enabled
the company to set off subsequent losses against earlier gains, provided those subsequent
losses were incurred on or after 1 April 1991. The legislation which enabled the company
to set off those later losses against earlier gains was the *Income and Corporation Taxes* E
Act 1988, s. 393A(1), which found its way into the Taxes Act 1988 by virtue of an
amendment arising under the *Finance Act* 1991. The effect of that would be that the
losses made in the accounting year ending March 1992 could be set off against the gains
made in 1990, resulting in a very substantial saving of corporation tax for the company.

The setting-off of subsequent losses against earlier gains is, however, dependent upon
the taxpayer, which is the company, establishing to the satisfaction of the Inspector of F
Taxes that it carries on 'the trade'. The words 'the trade' appear both in the new section,
s. 393A, and the old section, s. 393, which enabled losses to be carried back only for one
year.

Mr Cooper pointed out to the directors of the company that during the accounting
year ending in March 1993 it was possible to obtain that tax relief but that there was a
danger that the Inspector of Taxes would not allow the setting-off of the loss against G
earlier gains on the basis that the company was not carrying on the same trade. The
reason for his fears that that might be the outcome of negotiations with the Revenue I
accept were these: the company had acquired the building – which I will refer to as the
hotel building – in 1988 when it was engaged in buying, improving and re-selling land. It
had bought the hotel building, it had improved it, but it had not sold it. Neither was it
buying and selling other property in 1993. So there was a risk, Mr Cooper felt, that unless
the property were sold, the tax advantages of s. 393A would not be available to the H
company, A & T Investments.

I am quite satisfied from the correspondence between Mr Cooper and the Inland
Revenue, which was exhibited to Mr Cooper's affidavit, that the matter was gone into in
depth with the Inspector of Taxes and that it was Mr Cooper's firm view that the
retention of the hotel was an impediment to the successful advancing of his argument

A   under s. 393A and that in those circumstances it was desirable that the property be sold. So the property was sold in March 1993 to a related company, Starelm Properties Ltd, the first respondent to this application.

The situation immediately before the sale was this: £2.65m was owed by A & T Properties to the bank and secured by a mortgage on the hotel property. The bank knew – it was clear that it did know from the various valuations before it – that the property B   did not enjoy planning permission for use as an hotel. With the benefit of the planning permission which it did enjoy for conversion into flats the property had been valued by a valuer engaged by the bank in January 1992 in the sum of £750,000.

For practical purposes a mortgagor, such as A & T Investments Ltd, owning property worth £750,000 encumbered by a mortgage of £2.65m can only sell that property to another company with the consent of the mortgagee, the bank. Thus it was that shortly C   before the transfer there was a round table discussion in Luton between A & T Investments' directors, in particular Mr Fode, a firm of accountants, Stoy Hayward, engaged by the bank, and a representative of the bank. As a result of the discussions in that meeting documents which are now exhibited to the affidavits and which are dated 29 March 1993 were drafted by the bank and supplied to A & T Investments for signature.

The effect of those documents was that the equity of redemption in the hotel property was sold by A & T Investments to its related company, Starelm Properties Limited, for D   £1. By the transfer the transferee, Starelm Properties, gave A & T Investments an indemnity whereby Starelm covenanted with A & T Investments to observe and perform the covenants, conditions and obligations contained in the charges. It is clear from the documents that A & T Investments was not released from its personal obligation under the charge to National Westminster Bank. So National Westminster Bank acquired an additional advantage in the form of a fresh covenant by Starelm Properties. The property E   remained mortgaged to the bank and was now owned by Starelm Properties. A & T Investments remained liable to the bank under its personal cover.

That suffices as a summary of the documents. There were other documents brought into being but they are peripheral documents. The important one is the transfer of 29 March 1993.

As I analyse the circumstances surrounding that transfer, £1 was more than the value F   of the property transferred unless the property transferred was valued at more than £2.65m. I understand that that analysis is agreed by Mr Todd on behalf of the applicants. The reason for that is obvious: whatever the value of the property is – unless it be more than £2.65m – if a debt of £2.65m is secured on it its value is nil and consequently £1 is more than its value.

It seems to me to follow that unless the applicants can prove that the value of the hotel G   property exceeded £2.65m on 29 March 1993 the applicants will fail. They will fail because they fail to satisfy the requirements of s. 423(1)(c). In order to succeed they must show that A & T Investments enter into a transaction with Starelm Properties for a consideration the value of which in money or money's worth is significantly less than the value in money or money's worth of the consideration provided by themselves. Unless the value of the hotel was more than £2.65m then, far from being significantly less in value, £1 was significantly more in value.

H   So one of the issues which arises between the parties is whether the property was on 29 March 1993 worth more than £2.65m. Mr Todd has struggled valiantly against evidence to the contrary to attempt to persuade me that the hotel was worth more than £2.65m. What he has succeeded in persuading me is that there are valuations in being showing the value of the hotel on various assumptions as being more than £2.65m, but unfortunately those assumptions have not as yet been realised.

As a matter of common sense it seems to me to follow that if property has a hope of   A
obtaining planning permission which would increase the value of that property
considerably, persons in the market for that sort of property are likely to be willing to
pay more for the property if there is a hope of a significant increase in value once planning
permission has been obtained. I accept as a general proposition, therefore, that a property
may have 'hope' value if there is a hope for an increase in value.

However, what the applicants have failed to adduce before me is any evidence of what   B
that 'hope' value is and in particular that the 'hope' value of the hotel exceeds £2.65m.
Mr Todd at one point in his argument attempted to persuade me that that was a matter
which I could decide for myself. I disagree fundamentally with that proposition. If the
hotel property has a 'hope' value it is a question of fact and as to what those facts are it
is a question of opinion to be placed before the court by an expert in the field. As a judge,
I cannot possibly reach a decision as to what, if any, 'hope' value the property enjoyed
without any evidence to enable me to reach a conclusion.   C

So, in my view, the applicants have failed to show that the property was valued in
excess of £2.65m as at 29 March 1993 and, having done so, they fail to establish their
case under s. 423.

That, however, is not the end of the argument. The respondents to the application
have put before me a number of other powerful arguments turning on the other sections
to which I have referred. One of the arguments can be put very shortly. It is the argument   D
which turns on s. 423(5). They have put before me under that section two arguments, one
of which I reject and one of which I accept. The argument which I reject was to the effect
that because the applicants have not yet succeeded in their action in the Official Referees'
Court they were not persons who were capable of being prejudiced by the transaction.
That involved referring me to a passage in a text book going back to the law as it was
under the *Law of Property Act* 1925, s. 172, and on putting into subs. (5) the proposition   E
that the applicant must be a creditor and that an applicant is not a creditor when all he
has is the possibility that in the future he may be a judgment creditor. I do not accept
that argument. In my view, subs. (5) is widely enough drafted to enable a person who is
a litigant in proceedings and who has a chance of success in those proceedings to qualify
as a victim of the transaction under subs. (5) as being a person capable of being prejudiced
by the transaction.

The other argument, however, which Mr Harry advanced on behalf of the respondent,   F
I accept as a valid argument. The argument is this: immediately before the transaction
the applicants had no hope of recovering anything against the respondents because the
respondents had no funds other than funds which were subject to the security in favour
of National Westminster Bank. Unless the respondents owned a property worth more
than £2.65m, of which in my view there is no evidence, the respondents had no property
from which it could satisfy a claim by the applicants before the transaction. After the   G
transaction the position remained unchanged. The position now is that after the
transaction the property has been transferred, subject to the mortgage, but what has been
transferred is a property which has a greater sum secured on it than its value. So the
plaintiffs are no worse off now after the transaction than they were before. They are not
a person, in those circumstances, prejudiced by the transaction or capable of being
prejudiced by it. So, for that additional reason, the application also fails.

I now come to s. 423(3) which is the vital subsection in the whole of this litigation. In   H
order to succeed under s. 423 the applicants must not only prove that the transaction was
entered into at an undervalue and that they are a victim of the transaction – I have dealt
with those two points – but must also establish to the satisfaction of the court that the
transaction was entered into – in this case by A & T Investments – for the purpose of
putting assets beyond the reach of, in this case, the applicants who are making a claim.

A   That has been the subject of interpretation in the case of *Chohan v Saggar* [1992] BCC 306, a decision of Mr Evans-Lombe QC. The relevant passage which was brought to my attention in that case is at p. 323B, in which Mr Evans-Lombe says as follows:

'I see no reason to give s. 423 a different meaning and to approach it differently from the way in which the Court of Appeal approached its predecessor, s. 172, in the *Marcan* case.'

B   He was referring there to *Lloyds Bank Ltd v Marcan* [1973] 1 WLR 1387, a decision of the Court of Appeal. Mr Evans-Lombe goes on to say:

'I propose to construe s. 423(3) as requiring a plaintiff to demonstrate a dominant purpose to remove assets from the reach of actual or potential claimants or creditors, but as not excluding the possibility that there might also be other purposes behind the relevant transfer.'

C   I have not read *Lloyds Bank v Marcan* before delivering this judgment, neither have I read *Chohan v Saggar* in full. There has been no time to do so. I have expressed the view during the course of the argument doubting the proposition that a dominant purpose must be established, but I reach no view on that issue given the fact that I have not read either of the two cases in detail. I merely state, subject to those observations, that it seems to me odd that if a transferor has two purposes which are equally paramount in his mind that he fails altogether because one of those purposes is not dominant and because the dominant purpose, therefore, is not the purpose required under s. 423(3). It does not matter, however, in the present case.

D   It seems to me that the evidence establishes on a balance of probabilities, if not to a higher standard even than that, that the dominant purpose of A & T Investments in transferring the property was not to put the hotel property beyond the reach of the applicants but to gain the tax advantage which Mr Cooper successfully negotiated with the Inspector. That being the dominant purpose the applicants have also failed to establish the purpose requisite under s. 423(3).

E   In those circumstances, I must find for the respondent and do so.

(Application dismissed with costs)

F

G

H

Re Cranley Mansions Ltd.
Saigol v Goldstein.

Chancery Division (Companies Court).

Ferris J.

Judgment delivered 13 May 1994.

> *Company voluntary arrangement – Creditors' voting rights – Challenge of*
> *decisions for unfair prejudice or material irregularity – Claim of £900,000 valued*
> *at £1 for purpose of entitlement to vote – Claimant complained of unfair prejudice,*
> *material irregularity and appealed chairman's decision – Whether claimant should*
> *have been allowed to vote in respect of a substantially greater sum or not at all –*
> *Insolvency Act 1986, s. 5, 6; Insolvency Rules 1986 (SI 1986/1925), r. 1.17.*

This was an application by a creditor, 'S', of Cranley Mansions Ltd ('the company'),
seeking an order under s. 6 of the Insolvency Act 1986 revoking or suspending the approval
of a company voluntary arrangement in respect of the company; alternatively, equivalent
relief was sought by way of appeal under r. 1.17(5) of the Insolvency Rules 1986.

The company held the freehold of a property containing long-leasehold flats. The
shareholders were the leaseholders including S. In 1988 the company decided to undertake
a programme of major works. S wished to carry out some alterations to her flat. Both sets
of work were carried out by the same contractors under a single building contract. S
complained of poor workmanship and refused to pay her share of the cost. The company in
turn failed to pay the contractor. The company started legal proceedings against S who
claimed damages against the company in respect of defects. The contractor started
proceedings against the company. The actions were consolidated with S as plaintiff.

In 1993 the directors of the company realised that, as a result of the building contract and
legal proceedings, the company had become insolvent. An insolvency practitioner, 'G',
devised a proposal to be put to the company's creditors for a company voluntary
arrangement under Pt. I of the Insolvency Act 1986. The statement of affairs set out the
company's unsecured creditors which included the sum of £1 in respect of S's 'unliquidated
and unascertained contingent claim' against the company in the building proceedings.

S's claim had been lodged in the sum of £900,000 but at the meeting G, as chairman,
considered that as the value of the debt was not ascertained it was proper for him to place
an estimated minimum value of £1 on the debt for voting purposes under r. 1.17(3) of the
Insolvency Rules. The voluntary arrangement was approved. If S's vote against the
arrangement had been valued at anything over about £1,700 the proposal would have been
defeated.

S sought an order under s. 6 of the 1986 Act revoking or suspending the approval of the
voluntary arrangement; she alleged unfair prejudice under s. 6(1)(a) and material
irregularities at the creditors' meeting under s. 6(1)(b). Alternatively, she appealed the
chairman's decision on her entitlement to vote under r. 1.17(5) of the Insolvency Rules and
sought equivalent relief under r. 1.17(7). The essence of S's complaint was that she ought
either to have been allowed to vote in respect of a substantially greater debt than £1 or she
ought not to have been allowed to vote at all. G was made a party to the proceedings so that
an order for costs could be sought against him personally.

Held, setting aside G's decision as chairman to put upon S's claim a value of £1 for the
purpose of entitlement to vote and declaring that S was not entitled to vote at the creditors'
meeting:

1. S's complaints of unfair prejudice were misconceived.

2. S's claim could not be subject to r. 1.17(3) and r. 1.17(4). The scheme of the rules only
made sense if r. 1.17(3) was treated as the only rule which was relevant to unliquidated or

A   unquantified claims and r. 1.17(4) and (6) were confined to disputed claims for liquidated amounts. (Re a Debtor (No. 222 of 1990), ex parte Bank of Ireland [1992] BCLC 137 considered.)

3. G's valuation of S's claim at £1 was suspect but it could not be said that G should have valued the claim at some other, higher figure and that his failure to do so was a material irregularity in relation to the creditors' meeting.

B   4. G should not have put any value at all on S's claim. The word 'agrees' in r. 1.17(3) required some element of bilateral concurrence between the chairman and the creditor in question. S claimed to vote in respect of £900,000 but G treated her as voting only in respect of £1, the latter figure being attributable not to any bilateral consensus between S and G but to a unilateral determination made by G alone. Accordingly there was an irregularity at the creditors' meeting in that S's vote was admitted in respect of £1, whereas she was precluded from voting by r. 1.17(3). That was a material irregularity.

C   5. It followed that S's application failed so far as it was made under s. 6 because, by virtue of s. 6(2), S was entitled to apply under that section only if she was a person entitled, in accordance with the rules, to vote at the creditors' meeting.

6. There was no point in ordering another meeting to be summoned. It would not be right to revoke or suspend the approval of the proposals given by the creditors' meeting, since that arose by virtue of votes whose validity had not been impeached.

D   7. As regards the application for costs against G personally, S could only appeal under r. 1.17(5) because she had no standing to apply under s. 6. Rule 1.17(9) thus provided an absolute bar to the making of the order for costs which S sought against G. However the application for costs against him was rejected on substantive as well as technical grounds. Although there was a material irregularity in G's treatment of S's vote, there was no doubt that he acted in good faith.

E   The following cases were referred to in the judgment:

Debtor (No. 222 of 1990), Re a, ex parte Bank of Ireland & Ors [1992] BCLC 137.
Debtor (No. 222 of 1990), Re a, ex parte Bank of Ireland & Ors (No. 2) [1993] BCLC 233.
English, Scottish and Australian Chartered Bank, Re [1893] 3 Ch 385.
Naeem (a bankrupt), Re [1990] 1 WLR 48.

F   *Nuneaton Borough Association Football Club Ltd, Re* (1989) 5 BCC 377.
Ruffle, Ex parte. Re Dummelow (1873) LR 8 Ch App 997.
Sherratt (W A) Ltd v John Bromley Ltd [1985] QB 1038.

Raquel Agnello (instructed by Alan Taylor & Co) for the applicant.

Mary Stokes (instructed by Binks Stern) for the company.

Michael Green (instructed by Sprecher Grier) for the insolvency practitioner.

G

JUDGMENT

Ferris J: In this case Mrs Kathleen Megan Saigol, who is or claims to be a creditor of Cranley Mansions Ltd ('the company'), seeks an order under s. 6 of the *Insolvency Act* 1986 revoking or suspending the approval of a company voluntary arrangement in respect of the company given at a meeting held under s. 3 of the Act on 15 June 1993. In

H   the alternative, equivalent relief is sought by way of appeal under r. 1.17(5) of the *Insolvency Rules* 1986.

The facts giving rise to the propounding of the arrangement and to this application are somewhat complex and need to be stated in a little detail.

The company is the freehold owner of a property known as Cranley Mansions, 160 Gloucester Road, London SW7. That property consists of seven apartments, each of

which was, at 12 December 1986 when the company acquired the freehold, let on a long   A
lease at a low rent. The company was formed as a vehicle by means of which the owners
of the leasehold apartments could own and control the freehold. Each owner of an
apartment subscribed for shares in the company and there were no outside shareholders.
The purchase price for the freehold was £10 plus the outstanding service charges due
under the leases and this price was funded by the shareholders. Mrs Saigol was the
leaseholder of flat 6 and she subscribed for 18 of the 94 issued shares in the company,
being approximately 19 per cent of the total number of shares.   B

In September 1988 one of the flats, No. 1(a), came onto the market and the company
purchased it as accommodation for a resident caretaker. The cost was £45,000 which was
borrowed from the company's shareholders, the loans being secured by the issue of
interest free unsecured loan notes with no fixed date for repayment. Each shareholder
provided a proportion of the total loan commensurate with his shareholding.

In 1988 the company decided to undertake a programme of major works of repair and   C
maintenance of the property. Mrs Saigol also desired to carry out some alterations to her
own apartment. It was decided that both sets of work would be carried out by the same
contractors under a single building contract placed by the company. Mrs Saigol agreed
to pay to the company the cost of those works carried out under the contract which
related to her apartment and were done at her request, in addition to paying 19 per cent
of the cost of the work done to the structure and common parts of the property for which   D
she was liable under her lease.

The company arranged for the work to be carried out by a contractor named Cosmur
Construction Ltd ('Cosmur') under a formal contract in one of the well-known standard
forms. It engaged the services of Congreve Horner to act as architects or supervising
surveyors under the contract. Mrs Saigol also had her own architect or surveyor, Mr
Goldsbrough.   E

For a time all appeared to go well under the building contract. Various certificates
were issued in relation to the works in the summer of 1988 and were duly met by Mrs
Saigol and the company. But difficulties began to arise later in the summer of 1988.
According to the company the main cause of these difficulties was that Mrs Saigol and
her architect requested Cosmur to carry out a large number of variations to the contract,
including one particular major variation affecting the west elevation of the building.
According to Mrs Saigol the workmanship of Cosmur was poor. Whatever the reason,   F
in August and September 1988 Mrs Saigol refused to pay her share of the amount due to
Cosmur under the certificates. The company in turn failed to pay Cosmur. This led to the
commencement of legal proceedings by the company against Mrs Saigol and by Cosmur
against the company.

The action by the company against Mrs Saigol was the first action to be commenced,
the writ being issued on 21 November 1988. The company complained initially of Mrs   G
Saigol's non-payment of service charges payable under her lease and said to amount to
£46,694.93 as at 9 August 1988. This claim seems to have been based on the assumption
that money payable by Mrs Saigol in respect of the work done by Cosmur to her own
apartment was recoverable as part of the service charge. The company claimed to have
forfeited Mrs Saigol's lease by the service of the writ. It claimed possession and a money
judgment. On 17 April 1989, on the company's application for judgment under O. 14,   H
Master Turner gave the company liberty to sign judgment for £8,649.89, but gave Mrs
Saigol unconditional leave to defend as to the balance of the company's claim. Mrs
Saigol appealed to the judge and on 20 October 1989 her appeal was allowed and the
company was ordered to pay her costs of the appeal. On 28 November 1989 Master
Turner made an order under which the company had to pay into court the sum of £8,000
as security for Mrs Saigol's costs. The company was also ordered to pay Mrs Saigol's

A   costs of the application for security in any event. The company duly paid £8,000 into court as security.

For reasons which are not apparent to me, Mrs Saigol's defence in the company's action was not served until 1 October 1990. The defence consists mainly of denials of the company's main allegations. In a counterclaim Mrs Saigol alleged contractual and other duties on the part of the company of which she claimed that the company was in breach. The breaches related to the choice of Cosmur as contractor and to allowing Cosmur to

B   carry out defective work. Mrs Saigol counterclaimed for a large sum of special and general damages. The main items of special damage were £100,000 for the cost of remedial works, £400,000 for loss of value of her apartment and over £156,000 for interest on loans. Other items added a further £153,000, making a grand total for special damages of over £800,000. On 4 July 1991 the company served on Congreve Horner a third party notice in which it alleged various defaults in the performance by Congreve Horner of

C   their duties as supervising surveyor and architect. Mr Goldsbrough was also brought in to the proceedings as a third party.

On 19 August 1991 a bankruptcy order was made against Mrs Saigol and she remains an undischarged bankrupt. So far as I am aware the bankruptcy petition was not presented by any of the parties with whom I am concerned in these proceedings. Although it involves jumping ahead in the chronology it is convenient to mention now that, by a

D   deed of assignment dated 15 April 1992, Mrs Saigol's trustee in bankruptcy assigned to her the benefit of all claims advanced on her behalf in relation to her apartment against the company and others, including her counterclaim in the company's action.

At some stage the company's action was made official referee's business and on 8 October 1981 the company served an amended statement of claim. The main effect of the amendment was to add a claim based upon an agreement between Mrs Saigol and the company under which Mrs Saigol was alleged to have agreed to the employment of

E   Cosmur as contractor and to pay the company 19 per cent of the cost of the works to the common parts and the whole of the cost of the works to her apartment. The claim for unpaid service charges (including Mrs Saigol's proportion of the cost of the works done to the common parts) was put at £37,813.19; and the claim for the cost of the works done to Mrs Saigol's apartment was put at £46,842.95.

At an early stage of the proceedings Mrs Saigol's mortgagee, Dunbar Bank plc, was

F   joined as second defendant in the company's action. It seems that Mrs Saigol had defaulted under her mortgage and that Dunbar Bank obtained an order for possession against her. On 4 November 1991 an order was made in the company's action under which, subject to the payment by Dunbar Bank of agreed sums (amounting to more than £53,000) in respect of rent and service charge arrears and interest thereon, Dunbar Bank was granted relief from forfeiture and the lease of Mrs Saigol's apartment was vested in it. Dunbar Bank duly paid the required sum and has since sold the apartment with

G   vacant possession to a purchaser with whom I am not concerned. The payment made by Dunbar Bank in order to obtain relief against forfeiture must have satisfied the company's claim against Mrs Saigol for unpaid service charges. It did not satisfy the company's claim for the cost of the works done to Mrs Saigol's apartment.

In the third party proceedings between the company and Congreve Horner various pleadings have been served including, on 26 August 1992, a detailed response by the

H   company to a request by Congreve Horner for particulars of the third party claim, especially in respect of the defaults alleged.

I turn now to the proceedings brought by Cosmur against the company. The writ was issued on 13 February 1989. At that stage Cosmur's claim was for the liquidated sum of £49,584.01 due under certificates issued by Congreve Horner on 8 August and 28 September 1988. It was later amended to become a claim for £57,216.01, the additional amount having become due under a certificate issued on 15 December 1989. On 16 March 1989 Cosmur signed judgment against the company in default of defence for the sum of £49,584.01 which it then claimed and £570.36 interest and costs. The company applied successfully for this judgment to be set aside but it had to pay into court the sum of £50,000 or thereabouts. The defence and counterclaim of the company was served on 29 January 1990. The counterclaim sought damages for breach of contract on the ground of late completion and defective work, although the defects were not at that stage specified.

On 29 January 1990 the company joined Mrs Saigol as third party in the Cosmur action, seeking determination, as between Mrs Saigol and the defendant as well as between Cosmur and the company, of the question whether the company was liable to pay to Cosmur the amount claimed by it and whether Cosmur had carried out the works in breach of contract.

On 7 August 1990 the company served further and better particulars of its counterclaim against Cosmur which included, in the form of a schedule, particulars of the defective work alleged.

In 1991 there were further developments in the third party proceedings. A third party statement of claim was served on 25 January 1991. Mrs Saigol served her defence on 14 February 1991 in which she relied on her defence and counterclaim in the action brought against her by the company. She also made a counterclaim against Cosmur. The basis of this counterclaim was a contention that, if the company was not liable to her in respect of the building defects which she complained of, then Cosmur must be liable to her in breach of contract or negligence. Mrs Saigol relied on the particulars already served by her in the company's action.

Eventually on 13 January 1993 an order was made consolidating the actions commenced by the company and Cosmur and all the counterclaims and third party proceedings to which these actions had given rise. It was ordered that Mrs Saigol should be the plaintiff in the consolidated action and that the company, Cosmur, Congreve Horner and Mr Goldsbrough should be defendants. On 24 February 1993 a new statement of claim in the consolidated action was served on behalf of Mrs Saigol. Mrs Saigol's primary claim was for damages against all the defendants. The statement of claim made no attempt to apportion to particular defendants the loss and damage alleged. The main heads of loss and damage claimed were as follows:

(1) loss of value of Mrs Saigol's apartment by reason of Mrs Saigol's inability to sell it or to pay the money due to Dunbar Bank, resulting in its repossession and sale by Dunbar Bank;

(2) diminution in the value of the apartment by reason of defective building works; and

(3) the cost of remedying the defective work to the apartment.

These heads of claim were supplemented by a Scott schedule particularising numerous building defects which was served on 6 April 1993 and a separate schedule of loss, dealing with other heads of loss, which was served on 28 October 1993.

Each of the defendants in the consolidated action has served a defence and in some cases a counterclaim. Various contribution notices have been served as well. I do not think it necessary to go into these except to mention that the company's counterclaim against Mrs Saigol is for £46,842.95 with interest; and the company served a contribution notice on Congreve Horner on 4 May 1993.

In order to finance its involvement in this welter of litigation the company has raised further loans from certain of its shareholders, not including Mrs Saigol. These loans are secured by a debenture dated 28 June 1989 under which the loans, together with interest

A   thereon at two per cent per annum over National Westminster Bank base rate, are charged upon the entirety of the assets of the company. Neither principal or interest is payable before final settlement of the company's action against Mrs Saigol. Interest is compounded annually. As at 27 May 1993 the principal sum secured by the debenture was £106,950 and a further £68,438.07 was outstanding in respect of interest.

B   By early in 1993 the directors of the company realised that, as a result of the building contract and the subsequent proceedings, the company had become insolvent. On 1 March 1993 they approached Mr Mark Stephen Goldstein, a licensed insolvency practitioner and a partner in the firm of Morley & Scott, chartered accountants, with a view to devising a company voluntary arrangement to be put to the company's creditors pursuant to Pt. I of the *Insolvency Act* 1986. Mr Goldstein became the nominee in relation to the proposal for such an arrangement. The proposed company voluntary arrangement was promoted by means of the following documents, each of which is dated 27 May

C   1993:

    (1)   A statement of the proposals which were put forward on behalf of the directors of the company by Mr Llewellyn, one of those directors. Annexed to the statement was an estimated financial statement of the company's position as at 27 May 1993. Presumably this was intended to satisfy the requirement for a statement of affairs imposed by r. 1.5 of the *Insolvency Rules* 1986.

D   (2)   Mr Goldstein's comments, as nominee, on the company's proposal, pursuant to r. 1.7(2) of the Insolvency Rules.

    (3)   A report to the court by Mr Goldstein as nominee pursuant to s. 2 of the Act and r. 1.7(1). In this report Mr Goldstein stated, amongst other things, that he considered that a meeting of the company and its creditors should be summoned pursuant to s. 3 and that the meeting of creditors would be held at the offices of

E   Morley & Scott on 15 June 1993.

    (4)   A notice to the creditors of the meeting to be held on 15 June 1993.

It is necessary for me to comment in some detail on the estimated financial statement of the company's position as at 27 May 1993 ('the statement of affairs'). This began with a statement of assets specifically pledged, of which there were two. The first consisted of a sum of £67,350 in court. This represented the sum of £50,000 or thereabouts which had

F   been paid into court by the company as a term of setting aside the default judgment obtained by Cosmur. The excess over the sum paid in represented interest earned while the money had been in court. In the statement of affairs there was set off against the total sum of £67,350 an identical sum which was stated to be due to Cosmur. The rationale behind this appears to have been that Cosmur was probably a creditor for a sum in excess of £67,350 and that, in accordance with *W A Sherratt Ltd v John Bromley Ltd* [1985] QB

G   1038, it was a secured creditor to the extent of the money in court.

The second asset specifically pledged was the freehold interest in Cranley Mansions which was valued at £120,000, most of which represented the value of the caretaker's flat. There was set off against this the sum of £106,950 said to be due to the debenture holders, giving a surplus of £13,050. In fact this was erroneous. The £106,950 was the amount due to the debenture holders in respect of principal only. A further £68,438.07 was due to the debenture holders in respect of interest. In the result the statement of affairs should have

H   shown a deficit as against the debenture holders of more than £55,000, not a surplus of about £13,000.

The next part of the statement of affairs dealt with assets not specifically pledged. The first of these is stated as 'Debtor £38,293'. The explanation of this item, which appears in a footnote, is that it represents the £46,842.95 which is counterclaimed against Mrs Saigol in the building proceedings less a claim for £8,550 which Mrs Saigol's trustee in bankruptcy had against the company in respect of Mrs Saigol's unsecured loan to the company made when the caretaker's flat was purchased. In view of Mrs Saigol's bankruptcy the net debt of £38,293 is understandably estimated to realise nothing either on a liquidation or under the proposed voluntary arrangement.

The only other asset mentioned as being not specifically pledged was the company's cash at bank amounting to £14,957. Adding this to the supposed surplus of £13,050 as against the debenture holders yielded an apparent surplus of £28,007 for unsecured creditors on a liquidation. In fact, of course, if the interest due to the debenture holders had been taken into account there would on these figures have been nothing for the unsecured creditors.

The statement of affairs then proceeded to set out the company's unsecured creditors of whom six were mentioned. The first was Congreve Horner for £4,650, being the amount the unpaid fees claimed by that firm. Next was Lawrence Graham, who had acted as solicitors for the company at one stage, to whom £3,280 was due. The Inland Revenue was owed £200. After that came 'unsecured shareholder loans £36,450'. This represents the amount borrowed from shareholders at the time of the purchase of the caretaker's flat, after deducting the £8,550 which had been lent by Mrs Saigol and which was notionally satisfied by being set off against the company's claim against her as mentioned above. The final item was described as 'Mrs Saigol – unliquidated and unascertained contingent claim £1'. This was intended to represent a valuation of Mrs Saigol's claim against the company in the building proceedings. It is an item to which I shall have to return.

The total of these liabilities amounted to £44,581 which, when set against the erroneously assumed surplus against debenture holders of £28,007, yielded a deficiency 'subject to contingent liabilities' of £16,574. The statement of affairs ended with certain other calculations which do not matter for present purposes.

Now that the statement of affairs has been examined against the known facts in some detail in these proceedings it can be seen that, leaving aside argument as to the valuation of Mrs Saigol's claim against the company in the building proceedings, it contained a number of errors and omissions. These can be summarised as follows:

(1)   As already mentioned, the sum of approximately £68,000 due to the debenture holders in respect of accrued interest was left out of account.

(2)   Cosmur's claim against the company was not quantified except to the extent that it was treated as being exactly equal to the amount in court. In fact, as later transpired, Cosmur put its claim against the company at about £93,000 at the time of the proposal.

(3)   No mention was made of Mrs Saigol's position as a creditor in respect of the orders for costs made in her favour on her successful appeal against the O. 14 judgment obtained against her and on her successful application for security for costs. As no order for immediate taxation of these costs had been made and the proceedings were still pending, Mrs Saigol was a future rather than an immediate creditor in respect of such costs, but she was nevertheless a creditor.

(4)   No mention was made of the £8,000 paid into court as security for Mrs Saigol's costs. This sum represented an asset of the company, subject to Mrs Saigol's security interest. As Mrs Saigol's own estimate of her costs of the appeal against the O. 14 judgment is £5,000 and the application for security involved only a single application to the master, it is unlikely that the amount prospectively due to Mrs Saigol under the orders for costs previously made in her favour is as much as £8,000, so that some part of this amount is likely to become available for unsecured creditors if the company incurs no further liability to pay costs to Mrs Saigol in the building proceedings.

A   It might seem that the statement of affairs was also erroneous in its failure to attribute any value to the company's counterclaims and contribution claims in the building proceedings, apart from the counterclaim against Mrs Saigol. In my view, however, the statement of affairs adopted a tenable position in respect of these matters. The company was, in effect, accepting that it could not pursue its claim for damages against Cosmur and Congreve Horner, with the result that the liquidated claims of these creditors (under the architect's certificates in the case of Cosmur and in respect of unpaid fees in the case

B   of Congreve Horner) would have to be met in full. There is no inconsistency between the adoption of this position against these creditors and the treatment of the company's claim against Mrs Saigol as valid. This claim was for a liquidated sum representing the certified cost of the work done to Mrs Saigol's own apartment. I will consider later the difference, such as it was, between the valuation of Mrs Saigol's unliquidated claims against the company at £1 and the implied valuation of the company's unliquidated

C   claims against Cosmur and Congreve Horner at nil.

      The proposals advanced as the basis of the voluntary arrangement are not, to my mind, very clearly or systematically expressed in the statement submitted by the directors to the nominee. The essence of these is, however, relatively straightforward. The caretaker's flat was excluded from the proposals and was not to be treated as an asset available to unsecured creditors. But the company's cash amounting to £14,959, plus a

D   sum of £15,000 to be provided by the debenture holders, was to be made available for distribution among the company's unsecured creditors, excluding the shareholders. There would thus be nearly £30,000 available for distribution to creditors whose debts, on the figures given in the statement of affairs, came to £8,131. If, therefore, the figures worked out in accordance with the statement of affairs, these unsecured creditors would be paid in full. This contrasted with the prospective figures on liquidation (erroneously optimistic from the unsecured creditors' point of view) under which there would be only £28,007

E   for distribution between creditors for a total of £44,581. If, however, Mrs Saigol's claim against the company proved to have a value substantially in excess of the nominal value of £1 attributed to it or if Cosmur had (as it now claims) an entitlement to significantly more than the sum in court, the dividend to unsecured creditors under the proposals might be less than that expected to be payable in a liquidation.

      A number of features of the proposals call for particular mention. These are as follows:

F   (1)   The property to be made available for those unsecured creditors who were to benefit (i.e. all unsecured creditors except the company's own shareholders) consists of all the company's assets except the caretaker's flat. Thus if any part of the sums of £67,350 and £8,000 now in court remains after satisfying the claim of Cosmur and Mrs Saigol's right to costs respectively, these balances will be available for the unsecured creditors.

G   (2)   Secured creditors such as Cosmur, Mrs Saigol (in respect of her orders for costs) and Lawrence Graham (which asserted a lien) remain entitled to resort to all the assets charged as security in their favour.

  (3)   The figures given for the debts due to unsecured creditors in the statement of affairs are in no way binding on either the company or the relevant creditor. A single regime for the quantification of debts is made applicable to all unsecured creditors.

H   Wherever a debt is not agreed by the supervisor of the arrangement there is to be negotiation in good faith and, where necessary, the use of mediation or arbitration. If necessary, of course, the decision of the court might be obtained under s. 7 of the *Insolvency Act* 1986.

  (4)   If the £30,000 or so available for unsecured creditors proves insufficient to satisfy their claims in full, those claims are to abate rateably as between themselves.

(5)   The debenture holders agree not to seek to enforce their debentures during a period   A
which is not very satisfactorily defined but which appears to be intended to last for
two years unless the final payment to unsecured creditors is made earlier. The
shareholders also agree to defer any requirement for repayment of their unsecured
loans (amounting to £36,450) during the same period.

(6)   Unsecured creditors whose claims are agreed are to receive an interim dividend of
not less than ten pence in the pound as soon as sufficient funds are available for   B
that purpose.

(7)   In return for the benefits made available under the proposals it is provided as
follows:

> 'Save as referred to in para. 12 and 16 above' – which do not matter for present
> purposes – 'and save as regards the rights of secured creditors, the arrangement
> shall operate as an accord and satisfaction of all monetary claims (whether   C
> actual or contingent and whether or not liquidated or ascertained) existing as
> at the date creditors approve the proposal and any adverse costs for which the
> company may at any time become liable in respect of proceedings commenced
> prior to the date of this proposal. Such accord and satisfaction shall take effect
> upon the supervisor certifying that the company has complied with all its
> obligations under this arrangement. Creditors shall not, in the meantime, be
> entitled to commence or continue any action or other legal process against the   D
> company or its property in the meantime except with the consent of the
> supervisor or with the leave of the Companies Court.'

In the notice convening the creditors' meeting on 15 June Mr Goldstein stated:

> 'To be entitled to vote at the meeting, a creditor must give written details of his
> debt (including the amount) and lodge any necessary proxy form duly completed
> at the offices of Morley & Scott, Lynton House, 7–12 Tavistock Square, London   E
> WC1H 9LT, on or before 15 June 1993 or deliver the same to the chairman at the
> meeting.'

In response to this requirement Mrs Saigol, through her solicitors, submitted a prescribed
proof of debt form which is dated 10 June 1993. In s. 3 of the form Mrs Saigol's claim
was stated to be '£900,000 estimated, plus legal costs'. In pt. 4 of the form, where the
creditor is to give details of any document by reference to which the debt can be   F
substantiated, the answer given was:

> 'By reference to a consolidated statement of claim where Mrs Saigol is plaintiff
> and Cranley Mansions is the first of four defendants in Action No. 1990 ORB 516
> & 1990 ORB 804, Queen's Bench division, official referee business.'

I come now to the meeting of creditors itself. There were present Mr Goldstein, who
acted as chairman; another representative of Morley & Scott; two directors of the   G
company and the company's solicitor; a solicitor representing Cosmur; Mr Horner of
Congreve Horner; Mrs Saigol and her legal representative; and a representative of Mrs
Saigol's trustee in bankruptcy. There is in evidence a note of the meeting made by the
representative of Mrs Saigol's trustee and Mr Goldstein's formal report of the meeting.
From these records the material statements made and acts done at the meeting appear to
have been as follows:

(1)   Mr Goldstein, as chairman, commended the proposals to the creditors and there   H
was general discussion about the litigation.

(2)   It was indicated that Cosmur had submitted by fax a proof of debt claiming
£93,575.11 and a proxy voting against the proposals. Mr Goldstein pointed out
that in the statement of affairs Cosmur was fully secured. Cosmur's representative
expressed the view that Cosmur was not secured but could not explain the reason

A   for the difference between Cosmur's debt as shown in the statement of affairs and its proof for more than £93,000. Ultimately Mr Goldstein refused to accept Cosmur's vote against the proposals on the ground that a faxed proxy was not valid. Cosmur's representative was unable to produce the original proxy.

(3)   Lawrence Graham claimed to be secured to the extent of £3,000 but voted by proxy for the proposals in respect of the unsecured balance of their debt amounting to about £665.

B

(4)   Mr Horner voted for the proposals on behalf of Congreve Horner.

(5)   Mr Llewellyn and Matlodge Ltd, two of the shareholders in the company who had provided loans to the company, had lodged proxies in favour of the proposals but as they were connected parties their votes were left out of account.

(6)   According to Mr Goldstein's report, Mrs Saigol's position was dealt with as follows:

C

> 'Mrs Saigol's claim had been lodged in the sum of £900,000 as an estimated amount. The chairman, in accordance with r. 1.17(3) of the *Insolvency Rules* 1986 considered that as the value of the debt was not ascertained it was proper for him to place an estimated minimum value of £1 for voting purposes.'

The note of Mrs Saigol's trustee in bankruptcy reads:

D

> 'The chairman then stated that as Mrs Saigol's claim of £900,000 is unsubstantiated, in accordance with r. 1.17(3) of the *Insolvency Rules* 1986 it is the chairman's right to put a minimum value on it, that being £1.'

Mr Goldstein annexed to his report a summary of creditors present and voting in person or by proxy. This summary shows that the votes of Mr Horner and of Lawrence Graham in favour of the proposal were accepted by Mr Goldstein in the sums of £4,650

E   and £665.05 respectively. The vote of Cosmur in the sum of £93,575.11 against the proposals was rejected by Mr Goldstein as invalid. The vote of Mrs Saigol in the sum of £900,000 against the proposals was given a value of £1 for voting purposes, the chairman's remarks in the summary stating that, in respect of £1, the vote was 'valid in accordance with r. 1.17(3) of the *Insolvency Rules* 1986'.

The notice of application in this matter was issued on 8 July 1993, within the periods

F   of 28 days prescribed by s. 6(3) of the *Insolvency Act* 1986 and r. 1.17(8). It joins as respondents not only the company but Mr Goldstein personally. The purpose of joining Mr Goldstein was to seek an order for costs against him, which is something I shall consider later. The application does not state whether it is made under s. 6 or by way of appeal against the decision of the chairman of a meeting under r. 1.17(5), but the substantive relief sought is formulated in accordance with the terms of s. 6(1). Miss Agnello, on behalf of Mrs Saigol, opened the case on the basis that it was a s. 6

G   application. At a later stage, however, it became apparent that one line of argument urged on behalf of Mrs Saigol might lead to the conclusion the Mrs Saigol was not entitled to make an application under s. 6 because, if the argument is correct, Mrs Saigol was not entitled to vote at the creditors' meeting. Miss Agnello then asked for leave to amend the notice of application in such a way as to make it clear that it is made alternatively under r. 1.17(5). Such an amendment could cause no prejudice to the respondents and I allowed it. The relief claimed under r. 1.17(5) is for practical purposes

H   the same as that sought under s. 6.

The grounds of Mrs Saigol's application fall under two heads which correspond with para. (a) and (b) of s. 6(1). Under the first head Mrs Saigol claims that the voluntary arrangement unfairly prejudices her interests as a creditor of the company. Under the second head she complains of what are said to be material irregularities at the creditors' meeting.

(1) Unfair prejudice

The first matter complained of by way of unfair prejudice is that there is disparity of treatment of the claims of the parties to the building litigation. It was said that the company's claim of £46,829.95 against Mrs Saigol is treated as valid in full, while Mrs Saigol's claim of £900,000 against the company is given a token value of only £1. The claim of Congreve Horner for £4,650 is said to be admitted in full without any deduction for the company's claim against Congreve Horner under its contribution notice. Further, nothing is brought into the statement of affairs in respect of the company's contribution claim against Mr Goldsbrough.

In my judgment these complaints are misconceived. They are based primarily upon the figures set out in the statement of affairs. It is clear, however, that the statement of affairs is not itself part of the proposals. It merely contains information (now accepted to be incomplete or inaccurate in the respects I have mentioned) intended to assist creditors and others in their appraisal of the proposals. When this is appreciated it becomes clear that Congreve Horner's claim for £4,650 is not 'admitted'. Congreve Horner will, like any other unsecured creditor, have to agree their claim with the supervisor of the arrangement before they can receive any payment. It may be, of course, that they will have little difficulty in reaching agreement. The only answer that the company has ever suggested that it has to Congreve Horner's claim is a set off in respect of the unliquidated damages claimed in the building proceedings. Neither the supervisor nor the company will be in any position to pursue this claim. But even if Congreve Horner's task of satisfying the supervisor proves to be an easy one, this does not affect the principle that the arrangement itself does not fix Congreve Horner's debt at £4,650 or any other figure. Likewise it does not fix Mrs Saigol's claim at £1. That was the amount for which her vote was counted. But within the limits of the procedures available under the arrangement Mrs Saigol will be entitled, if she can, to seek to satisfy the supervisor that the debt due to her is indeed the £900,000 or more which she claims.

Similar comments apply to the suggestion that the arrangement treats the company's claim against Mrs Saigol as recoverable in full. It does no such thing. The claim remains unsatisfied and, if the company sought to recover anything in respect of it, it would first have to make it good. So far as liability is concerned there might be no great difficulty, as the claim seems to depend on architects' certificates. In practice, however, there is no real prospect of the company making any actual recovery in respect of the claim because of Mrs Saigol's bankruptcy. The statement of affairs merely recognises this.

As to the contribution claims against Congreve Horner and Mr Goldsbrough, nothing in the arrangement extinguishes or qualifies these. Here again the prospect of the company making any recovery is practically non-existent, because the company is not in a position to pursue the building litigation to a successful conclusion. The statement of affairs was, in my view, right to reflect this.

The second matter complained of is closely akin to the first. It is said that Mrs Saigol is the only unsecured creditor who is required to agree her claim with the company. This is not the case. It is true that Mrs Saigol will, before a distribution is made to her, have to agree the amount of her claim with the supervisor or have it determined by appropriate machinery. But exactly the same applies to the other unsecured creditors including Congreve Horner, Cosmur (so far as its claim is unsecured) and Lawrence Graham.

The third complaint is that Cosmur is treated as a secured creditor to the extent of the money in court to the credit of its action against the company, whereas Mrs Saigol is not treated as a secured creditor in respect of her orders for costs to the extent of the £8,000 paid into court as security for her costs. Here again the argument erroneously treats the statement of affairs as part of the arrangement. The arrangement itself does not affect the rights of secured creditors. To the extent, therefore, that Mrs Saigol can establish that

A   she is a creditor in respect of costs (which may not be the case, because the orders for costs in her favour were made before her bankruptcy and the benefit of these orders belongs prima facie to her trustee in bankruptcy) she will be at liberty to assert the same right of security in respect of the £8,000 in court as Cosmur can assert in respect of the £67,350 in court.

      The fourth complaint is of the failure of the company to treat Mrs Saigol as a creditor, save to the extent of £1, in respect of her claim against the company in the building

B   proceedings. This complaint ignores the fact that the valuation of £1 does not bind Mrs Saigol in respect of the quantification of her claim against the company for the purpose of obtaining a distribution under the arrangement.

(2) Material irregularities

C   Turning to the second head of claim, the material irregularities complained of fall into two categories, namely (a) irregularities relating to the presentation of the proposals and (b) irregularities relating to the conduct of the meeting.

(a) *Presentation*

      There is, in my judgment, nothing in the complaints as to presentation of the proposals. In substance many of these came to a repetition of matters relied upon as giving rise to

D   unfair prejudice. Particular complaint was made of the appraisals of the various claims and counterclaims of the company, Mrs Saigol, Cosmur and Congreve Horner which are raised in the building proceedings. Precision in these appraisals was unattainable in advance of a trial of the building proceedings. In my view the approach which was adopted by the directors in setting out the statement of affairs was a tenable and consistent one. It was assumed that the liquidated claims of Cosmur and Congreve

E   Horner against the company and of the company against Mrs Saigol were likely to succeed. It was further assumed that the unliquidated claims of Mrs Saigol against the company and of the company against Cosmur and Congreve Horner could not be given a positive value, save to the extent of £1 in the case of Mrs Saigol's claim. Both these assumptions appear to me to have been permissible. (I am not at this stage commenting on the value of £1 attributable to Mrs Saigol's vote.) Even if they were not, the arrangement itself contained nothing which precluded anyone from arguing for a

F   different result.

      A separate complaint as regards presentation relates to the failure to refer, either in the proposals or in the statement of affairs, to the costs orders in favour of Mrs Saigol and the £8,000 in court as security for Mrs Saigol's costs. The directors of the company say that they had forgotten about these matters, which occurred while the company was represented by different solicitors from those now representing it. Mr Goldstein says that

G   he never knew about them because he was not told. I see no reason to reject either of theses explanations. Mrs Saigol herself seems to have forgotten about these matters. The statement of affairs certainly ought to have dealt with these items as liabilities and assets. However its failure to do so was not, in my judgment, a material matter. That failure cannot, in my view, have affected the appraisal of the proposals by Mrs Saigol or any other creditors. Moreover, as I have already said, the arrangement did not adversely affect any secured rights arising from the costs order in favour of Mrs Saigol or her

H   estate.

(b) *Conduct of the meeting*

      Mrs Saigol's complaints concerning the conduct of the meeting are, however, of a different order. They relate to (i) the acceptance of Mrs Saigol's vote in respect of £1; and (ii) the rejection of Cosmur's proxy vote against the proposals in respect of £93,575.11. If

I find that there was an irregularity under either of these heads I must consider also whether that irregularity was material.

(i) Acceptance of Mrs Saigol's vote in respect of £1

In order to deal with the complaint about Mrs Saigol's own vote I must begin with r. 1.17 of the Insolvency Rules, relating to the voting rights of creditors. So far as material r. 1.17 provides as follows:

'(1) Subject as follows, every creditor who was given notice of the creditors' meeting is entitled to vote at the meeting or any adjournment of it.

(2) Votes are calculated according to the amount of the creditor's debt as at the date of the meeting or, where the company is being wound up or is subject to an administration order, the date of its going into liquidation or (as the case may be) of the administration order.

(3) A creditor shall not vote in respect of a debt for an unliquidated amount, or any debt whose value is not ascertained, except where the chairman agrees to put upon the debt an estimated minimum value for the purpose of entitlement to vote.

(4) At any creditors' meeting the chairman has power to admit or reject a creditor's claim for the purpose of his entitlement to vote, and the power is exercisable with respect to the whole or any part of the claim.

(5) The chairman's decision on a creditor's entitlement to vote is subject to appeal to the court by any creditor or member of the company.

(6) If the chairman is in doubt whether a claim should be admitted or rejected, he shall mark it as objected to and allow the creditor to vote, subject to his vote being subsequently declared invalid if the objection to the claim is sustained.'

Subrules (7), (8) and (9) are not relevant for present purposes, although I shall have to come back to r. 17(9) for a different purpose later on. It is to be noted that provisions in terms which are in all material respects the same as those in r. 1.17(1)–(6) are to be found also in r. 5.17, which applies to creditors' voting in relation to individual voluntary arrangements. There is also a close identity of language between some of the provisions of r. 1.17 and the equivalent provisions in r. 2.22 (votes at meetings of creditors in an administration); r. 3.11 (votes at meetings of creditors in an administrative receivership); r. 4.67 (votes at meetings of creditors in a company liquidation); and r. 6.93 (votes at meetings of creditors in a bankruptcy).

The essence of Mrs Saigol's complaint is that she ought either to have been allowed to vote in respect of a substantially greater debt than £1 or she ought not to have been allowed to vote at all. On the basis of the votes actually cast in favour of the arrangement, namely for a total of £5,316.05, she could have prevented the arrangement being approved by the necessary three quarters majority (see r. 1.19(1)) if the value of her debt had been fixed at any sum in excess of about £1,722. Having regard to the fact that her full claim was £900,000, she contends that a valuation of at least £1,772 is not an unreasonable minimum value and is no less likely to be right than a valuation of £1. By valuing her debt at £1 Mr Goldstein, as chairman of the meeting, has ensured that Mrs Saigol is in the worst possible position. The valuation gave Mrs Saigol an entitlement to vote, with the result that the arrangement, if approved, would become binding upon her – see s. 5(2)(b); but it gave her no real voting power and she was thus outvoted by creditors whose claims were much less in value than her own.

At the heart of Mrs Saigol's argument is r. 1.17(3), which I read again:

'A creditor shall not vote in respect of a debt for an unliquidated amount, or any debt whose value is not ascertained, except where the chairman agrees to put upon the debt an estimated minimum value for the purpose of entitlement to vote.'

A   There can be no doubt that Mrs Saigol claimed to have a debt for an unliquidated amount or a debt whose value was not ascertained at the date of the meeting. The argument on her behalf is that, instead of putting a value of £1 upon the debt, Mr Goldstein should have either (1) allowed Mrs Saigol to vote for her full claim of £900,000, marking the claim as objected to, pursuant to r. 1.17(6); or (2) put upon the debt a value much higher than £1; or (3) declined to put a value on the debt, so leaving Mrs Saigol without a vote but, as she contends, not bound by the arrangement. I shall consider each

B   of these possibilities in turn.

     As to (1), in *Re a Debtor (No. 222 of 1990), ex parte Bank of Ireland [1992] BCLC 137* (which I shall refer to as the *Bank of Ireland* case) Harman J was concerned with five creditors for large sums whose claims arose out of guarantees given by a debtor whose enforceability was disputed by the debtor. At a creditors' meeting convened to consider an individual voluntary arrangement these creditors were not allowed by the chairman

C   to vote on the ground that their debts were for unliquidated amounts, or amounts whose value was not ascertained, with the result that r. 5.17(3) (whose terms are indistinguishable from those of r. 1.17(3)) precluded them from voting. In fact the creditors' claims were for ascertained and liquidated sums, but there were disputes about whether the claims were valid. Harman J held that their debts were not within r. 5.17(3) but were disputed debts within r. 5.17(4). As it was not plain and obvious that they were

D   not recoverable debts, the correct course for the chairman of the meeting to have taken was to admit the creditors' claims for the purpose of entitlement to vote but to mark them as objected to under r. 5.17(6). Miss Agnello, on behalf of Mrs Saigol, contended that Mr Goldstein should have taken an equivalent course in this case, namely to allow Mrs Saigol to vote for the full £900,000 claimed by her, but to mark her vote as objected to. On this basis the arrangement would not have been approved unless, in subsequent proceedings, it is established that Mrs Saigol's vote was either wholly invalid or invalid

E   except in respect of an amount which falls short of the 25 per cent level required to defeat the proposals.

     I cannot accept this argument. So far as the *Bank of Ireland* case is concerned, Harman J (at p. 144h) limited his decision to debts:

     'which are not within sub-rule (3) but are said to be disputed within sub-rule (4)'.

F   In one sense all claims which are for unliquidated sums, or sums which have not yet been ascertained, are disputed debts, because there is a dispute about their quantum. But it cannot, in my judgment, be the case that such debts are within subr. (4) as well as subr. (3). The machinery of the two subrules is quite different and a single debt cannot, in my view, be covered by both of them. Under subr. (3) the person claiming to be a creditor cannot vote at all unless the chairman puts upon his debt an estimated minimum value. Under subr. (4), taken in conjunction with subr. (6), he can vote in respect of his full

G   claim (subject to it being marked as disputed) unless the chairman rejects his claim, or some part of it, which he should only do in a plain case. The scheme of the rules makes sense, in my view, only if subr. (3) is treated as the only rule which is relevant to unliquidated or unquantified claims and subr. (4) and (6) are confined to disputed claims for liquidated amounts. On this footing the *Bank of Ireland* case is distinguishable because it concerned debts of the latter kind, while Mrs Saigol's claim is of the former kind.

H   I turn to the second possibility contended for, namely that Mr Goldstein should have put upon Mrs Saigol's claim a value substantially in excess of £1. Clearly the valuation of Mrs Saigol's claim is a matter of extreme difficulty. Anyone who examines the pleadings in the building litigation and Mrs Saigol's claimed heads of loss is bound to have the greatest degree of scepticism whether, even if she could establish that Cosmur's work was defective and that the company was liable to her in respect of such defective work, her damages against the company would amount to anything like £900,000 or even a modest proportion of this sum. It is not possible, however, to exclude all possibility that Cosmur's work was defective. Mr Llewellyn himself seems to have thought that it was, at least in some respects (see the copy of his letter sent by fax to the managing agents employed by the company and exhibited as 'DM1' to the affidavit of Mr Maloney). Likewise it is not impossible that the company, having undertaken to engage Cosmur to carry out work to Mrs Saigol's apartment, is liable to her for defects in such work. If these issues were resolved in favour of Mrs Saigol it seems to me to be much more probable that she would recover a substantial sum from the company than that she would recover only £1. Indeed the real alternatives, so far as her claim against the company is concerned, seem to be that it will either fail altogether or that it will succeed in respect of a sum that would be in excess of the amount required to enable Mrs Saigol to prevent the proposal for a voluntary arrangement gaining the necessary three quarters majority in the value of the votes cast.

Mr Goldstein's explanation of his valuation of Mrs Saigol's claim at £1 is contained in para. 17 of his affidavit sworn on 18 October 1993. After referring to Mrs Saigol's estimate of £900,000 plus costs and exhibiting the proof of debt lodged on her behalf he continues:

> 'As I have said, in the consolidated statement of claim, no figures had been put on the damages claimed. Furthermore, in view of the contribution notices, it was impossible to predict which party, if any, might be liable for what amount. Generally, it seemed to me that the nature of the applicant's claim in the litigation was such that the only practical course was to assign a minimum value of £1 to her claim. I could not realistically put it any higher. It is my interpretation that this was in accordance with r. 1.17(3) of the Insolvency Rules. It was clear from the proposal that this was the procedure that was to be adopted and in the comments annexed to my report to the court dated 27 May 1993 [I] specifically dealt with [this] aspect.'

While Mr Goldstein's statement that no figures were put upon Mrs Saigol's claim in the consolidated statement of claim is correct so far as it goes, it does not, in my view, paint a true picture. As I have already mentioned, Mrs Saigol's original counterclaim against the company, served on 1 October 1990, had quantified her claim at a sum in excess of £800,000 and nothing had happened since then to suggest that her claim had in any way diminished. Moreover on 6 April 1993 there had been served on Mrs Saigol's behalf a Scott schedule particularising numerous building defects which included items (being almost all of the items 201–342) which related only to Mrs Saigol's apartment and which amounted together to a substantial sum. The original quantification of Mrs Saigol's counterclaim and the existence and contents of the Scott schedule are matters which must either have been known to Mr Goldstein or would have been discovered by him if he had made reasonable enquiries about the buildings proceedings.

I find it impossible to resist the conclusion that Mr Goldstein made no real attempt to value Mrs Saigol's claim or even to arrive at a minimum value for that claim. Not unreasonably, he must have considered it impossible to carry out any realistic valuation. Equally he must have realised, from the time when he was first instructed to assist in the preparation of proposals for a voluntary arrangement, that it was essential for him to put *some* value on Mrs Saigol's claim. If he did not do so then Mrs Saigol might claim, as she has indeed now claimed as one way of putting her case in these proceedings, that she was not entitled to vote on the proposals and so not bound by the approved voluntary arrangement pursuant to s. 5(2)(b) of the Act. It was an essential part of the proposals which Mr Goldstein devised to be put forward by the directors that a value should be put upon Mrs Saigol's claim so that she was clearly entitled to vote at the creditors' meeting pursuant to r. 1.17(3). Equally, as it must have been apparent to everyone that Mrs

A   Saigol would oppose anything which was put forward on behalf of the company or its directors, it was important that the value of Mrs Saigol's vote should be low. The last sentence in the passage from Mr Goldstein's affidavit which I have quoted shows, in my view, that the valuation of Mrs Saigol's claim at £1 for the purposes of r. 1.17(3) was an essential part of the plan from the outset.

B   In these circumstances the valuation of £1 is, to say the least, deeply suspect. But I find it impossible to say that Mr Goldstein ought to have valued Mrs Saigol's claim at some other, much higher, figure and that his failure to do so was a material irregularity in relation to the creditors' meeting. The difficulty is that Mrs Saigol's claim was and is incapable of having a realistic value attributed to it. The real question, as it appears to me, is whether Mr Goldstein could or should, in all the circumstances, have put any value at all on Mrs Saigol's claim. In other words the crucial matter is whether the third possibility advanced on behalf of Mrs Saigol is correct.

C   Essentially the issue is whether Mr Goldstein, as chairman at the meeting of creditors, was entitled to put a value on Mrs Saigol's claim whether or not she had invited him to do so and whether or not she concurred in the value proposed by him. On behalf of the company and Mr Goldstein it was said that Mrs Saigol did not herself put forward any value which should be attributed to her claim under r. 1.17(3), nor did she abstain from voting on the basis that the prohibition arising from the opening words of r. 1.17(3) was

D   applicable. I do not consider that either of these criticisms is well-founded as a matter of fact. It is true that Mrs Saigol did not, by herself or her legal representative, invite Mr Goldstein to put upon her claim a value in excess of £1 but less than £900,000 as being the estimated minimum value of that claim for the purpose of entitlement to vote. Her position, as it seems to me, was that her claim should be valued at £900,000 and, in voting, she claimed to vote in respect of that sum. Certainly the evidence showed nothing in the nature of a consensus between Mrs Saigol and Mr Goldstein as to the valuation at

E   £1. Moreover it has not been suggested that any estoppel arises from the fact that Mrs Saigol voted in the knowledge that her vote would be given a value of only £1.

On behalf of Mrs Saigol Miss Agnello pointed out that r. 1.17(3) imposes a prohibition upon voting by a creditor in Mrs Saigol's position unless a particular exception applies. Moreover the wording of that exception begins:

'except where the chairman agrees to put upon the debt an estimated minimum
F   value . . .'

If it had been intended that the chairman should be entitled to act unilaterally the rule would surely have said:

'except where the chairman puts upon the debt an estimated minimum value . . .'

While the word 'agrees' does not necessarily import a requirement for an offer followed
G   by acceptance and supported by consideration, so as to give rise to a contract (cf *Re Nuneaton Borough Association Football Club Ltd* (1989) 5 BCC 377), Miss Agnello argued that it does require an element of bilateral consensus.

Miss Stokes on behalf of the company and Mr Green on behalf of Mr Goldstein argued against this. They relied upon one of the dictionary definitions of 'agree', namely 'To accede, consent to, grant'. I do not think that this helps them. Both 'accede' and 'consent to' imply a bilateral element, in that something proposed by one party is being
H   assented to by another. As to 'grant', I find it somewhat difficult to see how agreeing to put a value on a debt involves anything which can be regarded as equivalent to a grant; and even a grant in the form of a voluntary gift requires acceptance by the grantee before it is complete.

Both Miss Stokes and Mr Green said that Mrs Saigol could not complain of Mr Goldstein having put a value of £1 on her claim when she herself had attended the

creditors' meeting with a view to voting, and had in fact voted, without herself putting   A
forward a figure for the purpose of r. 1.17(3). As I have already indicated, I do not think
this is a correct factual analysis of Mrs Saigol's position. She was asserting that her claim
had a value of at least £900,000.

Miss Stokes cited to me *Ex parte Ruffle. Re Dummelow* (1873) LR 8 Ch App 997.
There a creditor claimed to vote at a meeting of creditors not only in respect of a
judgment for £357 for which he had obtained judgment but also in respect of the untaxed   B
costs which had been awarded to him, which he estimated at £200. It was held that he
was not entitled to vote in respect of the £200. The reasoning of the court turned upon
the fact that the creditor had neither converted his claim into a liquidated one by having
the costs taxed nor proved the £200 as a debt in accordance with the relevant rules then
in force. This case supports the argument that Mrs Saigol cannot complain that the
valuation of her claim took no account of her claim for costs which had not yet been
taxed under the order made in her favour. Such complaint is, in my view, in any event   C
precluded by the fact that, having regard to the payment of £8,000 into court, Mrs Saigol
was a secured creditor in respect of her costs, with the result that her vote, if cast in
respect of her claim for costs, would have had to be left out of account under r. 1.19(3)(b)
(and, on the facts, almost certainly under r. 1.19(3)(a) as well). Beyond providing this
support *Re Dummelow* does not, in my view, assist the company's argument because it
depends upon quite different rules from those applicable to this case.   D

Both Miss Stokes and Mr Green pointed out that unless the chairman is entitled to put
a value upon the claim of a creditor which is unliquidated or unascertained without
regard to the wishes of that creditor, the utility of the statutory provisions in respect of
corporate voluntary arrangements (and, indeed, individual voluntary arrangements and
other matters to be decided at meetings governed by rules as to voting equivalent to
r. 1.17) would be greatly reduced. If a creditor is not entitled to vote in respect of such a   E
claim without a value being put upon the claim under r. 1.17(3) or its equivalent (which
is a matter to be considered in a moment) a disaffected creditor could stultify proposals
for a voluntary arrangement by the simple expedient of failing to concur in a value being
put on his claim. The arrangement might then be approved by the requisite majorities of
those entitled to vote on it, but it would not be binding on the disaffected creditor. In
most, if not all, cases there will be no point in having an arrangement which is not binding
upon all creditors.   F

I see the force of this submission, which causes me some anxiety because my decision
is likely to affect many other cases. Nevertheless I cannot escape the fact that the relevant
words of r. 1.17(3) are 'where the chairman agrees to put upon the debt an estimated
minimum value', not 'where the chairman puts upon the debt an estimated minimum
value'. Moreover I think it would be perverse to say that the requirement imported by
the word 'agrees' can be satisfied by an agreement between the chairman and someone   G
other that the creditor, such as the company, as was suggested in argument. In my
judgment 'agrees' requires some element of bilateral concurrence between the chairman
and the creditor in question. If the creditor puts forward an estimated minimum value
without prejudice to a contention that his real claim is much larger and if the chairman
accepts this, the words of the rule would, in my view, clearly be satisfied notwithstanding
that there is nothing in the nature of a contract between the chairman and the creditor.
The same would be the case if the chairman took the initiative in suggesting a value and   H
the creditor concurred in this suggestion for the purpose of r. 1.17(3), although not for
the purpose of limiting the claim. The matter would be more difficult if the chairman put
forward a value for the purpose of r. 1.17(3) and the creditor rejected this for all purposes
but nevertheless insisted upon voting. The outcome would, in my view, then depend upon
an evaluation of precisely what was said and done.

A   The present case has some similarities with the third type of case suggested above. On the evidence I take the view that what was said and done was not sufficient to satisfy what the word 'agrees' requires. It seems to me that Mrs Saigol claimed to vote in respect of £900,000 but Mr Goldstein treated her as voting only in respect of £1, the latter figure being attributable not to any bilateral consensus between Mrs Saigol and Mr Goldstein but to a unilateral determination made by Mr Goldstein alone. Moreover the evidence does not, in my judgment, justify any inference that it was made clear to Mrs Saigol or

B   her representative that if she voted at all she would be concurring in Mr Goldstein's determination.

     I conclude, therefore, that there was an irregularity at or in relation to the meeting of creditors, in that Mrs Saigol's vote was admitted in respect of £1, whereas she was precluded from voting by the opening words of r. 1.17(3), the exception to the general prohibition not being applicable because no 'estimated minimum value' had been put

C   upon her debt in accordance with the requirements of the latter part of the subrule.

(ii) Material irregularity

     I must therefore consider whether this irregularity was a material one. It is in this context that I propose to consider whether Mrs Saigol is a person who:

> 'in accordance with the rules had notice of, and was entitled to vote at, [the creditors'] meeting . . .'

D

If she is, the arrangement is, as matters now stand, binding upon her under s. 5(2)(b).

     There is no doubt that Mrs Saigol had proper notice of the creditors' meeting. Equally there can be no doubt that, if her claim had effectively been valued at £1 under r. 1.17(3), she was entitled to vote at the meeting. Mrs Saigol contends that, on my finding that her claim had not effectively been valued under r. 1.17(3), she was not entitled to vote at the

E   meeting, her purported vote ought to have been disregarded and the arrangement is not binding upon her. On behalf of the company it was contended that, whether or not a value was properly put upon Mrs Saigol's claim under r. 1.17(3), she comes within the description of 'a person who in accordance with the rules . . . was entitled to vote at' the creditors' meeting.

     The company's argument was founded upon the contention that entitlement to vote is

F   governed by r. 1.17(1), which provides:

> 'Subject as follows, every creditor who was given notice of the creditors' meeting is entitled to vote at the meeting or any adjournment of it.'

Entitlement is thus governed by the possession of the status of being a creditor and the receipt of notice of the creditors' meeting. Mrs Saigol herself asserts that she has the requisite status and it is not in doubt that she was given notice of the meeting. Although

G   this simple scheme is qualified by the words 'subject as follows', it was argued that nothing in the subsequent parts of r. 1.17 imposes any relevant limitation upon the entitlement to vote conferred by subr. (1). In particular it was said that the general prohibition upon voting by creditors in respect of unliquidated or unascertained claims which is imposed by r. 1.17(3) is expressed in terms which do not take away entitlement to vote. The relevant words are:

H

> 'A creditor shall not vote in respect of a debt for an unliquidated amount, or any debt whose value is not ascertained . . .'

These words, it was said, leave entitlement to vote unaffected but merely preclude the exercise of that entitlement.

     I reject this argument for three reasons. First it appears to me that the concept of a person being entitled to vote but precluded from voting is such a contradictory one that

it would be wrong to find that it is embodied in the rules without the clearest language to A
show that this was intended. I do not find such clear language here.

Secondly r. 1.17(3) does not, in my judgment, relate to the exercise of an entitlement as
distinct from the existence of the entitlement. The exception to the general prohibition
imposed by that subrule exists:

'where the chairman agrees to put upon the debt an estimated minimum value *for
the purpose of entitlement to vote.*' (emphasis added)   B

In other words the chairman can, by applying the requisite procedure, confer an
entitlement to vote. I find it impossible to resist the conclusion that where the exception
does not apply there is no entitlement to vote.

Thirdly this view of the matter is consistent with r. 1.17(4) and (5) which provide:

'(4) At any creditors' meeting the chairman has power to admit or reject a
creditor's claim for the purpose of his entitlement to vote, and the power is   C
exercisable with respect to the whole or any part of the claim.

(5) The chairman's decision on a creditor's entitlement to vote is subject to appeal
to the court by any creditor or member of the company.'

I cannot read r. 1.17(4) in any sense which does not have the consequence that (subject
to appeal) a creditor whose claim is admitted by the chairman is entitled to vote in respect
of that claim and a creditor whose claim is rejected by the chairman is not entitled to vote   D
(as distinct from not being allowed to exercise his entitlement) in respect of that claim.
This is reinforced by r. 1.17(5), which clearly shows that, in admitting or rejecting claims
under subr. (4), the chairman is deciding upon entitlement to vote, not the exercise of
entitlement. Moreover r. 1.17(5) is not confined to decisions taken under subr. (4). It
must apply equally to decisions taken under subr. (3). Thus in the *Bank of Ireland* case
the chairman erroneously determined that the creditors were precluded from voting by a   E
rule equivalent to the opening part of subr. (3). Harman J decided the case both under r.
5.17 (the equivalent of r. 1.17) and under s. 262 (the equivalent of s. 6) – see [1992] BCLC
at p. 146a and 147h and the report of the second stage of that case at [1993] BCLC 233
at p. 234d. He thus treated r. 5.17(3) as governing entitlement to vote; and r. 1.17(3) must
do likewise.

In the result I conclude that Mr Goldstein's error in putting a value of £1 on Mrs   F
Saigol's claim was a material irregularity. If correct it gave Mrs Saigol an entitlement to
vote which she would not otherwise have had, with the consequence that, on the face of
it, she is bound by an arrangement which would not otherwise be binding upon her.

(iii) Cosmur's faxed proxy

As I indicated earlier, it was argued on behalf of Mrs Saigol that there was also a
material irregularity at the meeting in that Mr Goldstein rejected Cosmur's vote against   G
the proposals on the ground that the copy of Cosmur's proxy received by fax, which was
the only proxy document produced on behalf of Cosmur, was not a valid proxy. It was
argued that there is no general rule of law that the original proxy, as distinct from a copy
of it or other evidence proving its contents, must be produced to the chairman of the
meeting. Reliance was placed upon *Re English, Scottish and Australian Chartered Bank*
[1893] 3 Ch 385. It was argued that Pt. 8 of the Insolvency Rules imposes no requirement
for such production and that the supervisor, when convening a creditors' meeting, had   H
no power to impose such a requirement.

Against this it was contended that r. 8(4) and 8(5) of the Insolvency Rules (which
provide for the retention and inspection of proxies used at any meeting) necessarily
envisage that proxies, which must mean the originals, not copies, will be lodged with the
chairman of the meeting. It was also drawn to my attention that the Insolvency Service

A   takes the view that the rules do not allow faxed proxies to be accepted and that this view is acted upon by official receivers and has been widely communicated to insolvency practitioners. It was pointed out to me that not only has Cosmur not itself appealed against the rejection of its proxy but it has indicated that it would now wish to support the arrangement. In these circumstances it was argued that even if the rejection of Cosmur's proxy was an irregularity it was not a material irregularity.

B   As my decision on the r. 1.17(3) point is enough to dispose of this case I have reached the conclusion that it is neither necessary nor wise for me to express a view on the proxy point. If the case proceeds further and the point becomes a decisive one the Court of Appeal will, I think, be in at least as good a position as I am to decide it. I therefore propose to say nothing further about it.

C   (iv) Consequences of material irregularity

I now turn to the consequence of my decision on the r. 1.17(3) point. I find that, by reason of the prohibition imposed by the opening part of that rule, Mrs Saigol had no entitlement to vote and Mr Goldstein fell into error in purporting to confer upon her such entitlement. Paradoxically it follows that Mrs Saigol's application must fail so far as it is made under s. 6 because, by virtue of s. 6(2), Mrs Saigol is entitled to apply under D   that section only if she is a person entitled, in accordance with the rules, to vote at the creditors' meeting.

However there is also the appeal under r. 1.17(5). It will be recalled that I gave leave for the application to be amended so as to make it clear, if it was otherwise in doubt, that it was brought by way of such appeal as well as under s. 6. It was not suggested that Mrs Saigol had no right of appeal under the rule, although it must be somewhat unusual for E   a creditor to complain of a decision to admit his vote and to argue that it ought not to have been admitted. The court's powers on an appeal are governed by r. 1.17(7) which provides:

> 'If on an appeal the chairman's decision is reversed or varied, or a creditor's vote is declared invalid, the court may order another meeting to be summoned, or make such other order as it thinks just.

F
> The court's power to make an order under this paragraph is exercisable only if it considers that the matter is such as gives rise to unfair prejudice or material irregularity.'

For the reasons which I have stated I find that 'the matter' (which in this case is Mr Goldstein's decision under r. 1.17(3)) is such as gives rise to material irregularity. I can therefore make an order under subr. (7). In my judgment it would be right to do so. If I G   do not Mrs Saigol will be bound by an arrangement which ought not to have become binding upon her. The fact that she, along with other creditors, is likely to be worse off if there is no arrangement is, in my view, immaterial.

It appears to me that the order which I should make is to set aside the chairman's decision to put upon Mrs Saigol's claim a value of £1 for the purpose of entitlement to H   vote and to declare that Mrs Saigol was not entitled to vote at the creditors' meeting held on 15 June 1993. As at present advised I see no point in ordering another meeting to be summoned. I do not think it would be right to revoke or suspend the approval of the proposals given by the creditors' meeting, since that arose by virtue of votes whose validity has not been impeached. The consequence of an arrangement having been approved but not being binding upon Mrs Saigol will, I think, have to be worked out later.

(3) Claim against Mr Goldstein

It remains to deal with Mrs Saigol's application for costs against Mr Goldstein. As I have said, the making of that application was the only reason for Mr Goldstein being joined as a respondent.

Re Naeem [1990] 1 WLR 48 concerned an appeal from a decision made on an application to revoke the approval of an individual voluntary arrangement given at a creditors' meeting. After deciding to allow the appeal Hoffmann J said (at pp. 50–51):

'Accordingly I have come to the conclusion that the registrar was wrong to revoke the consent to the arrangement and that the appeal must be allowed. I should add that it was also, in my judgment, wrong to make the bankrupt's nominee and the creditors respondents to the application and even more wrong to order them to pay the costs.'

In the *Bank of Ireland* case, Harman J took a poor view of the conduct of the nominee who had acted in relation to a proposal for an individual voluntary arrangement. He referred to the case before him as being an exceptional case and to the possibility which Hoffmann J had envisaged in *Naeem* that an order for costs might be made against the nominee if there has been some personal conduct on his part which would justify this. Harman J continued ([1993] BCLC at p. 235):

'It seems to me that Hoffmann J in *Naeem* when he referred to the nominee acting simply as an agent of the bankrupt, was entirely accurate in his use of that word in the context of that case, but was not directing his mind at all to the position of the nominee when he has a duty to report to the court his own opinion upon the debtor's proposals. That cannot be an opinion given as agent for anybody. Further, the nominee's duties as chairman of the meeting are plainly not to act merely as agent of the debtor, but to perform his duties under the 1986 rules in an independent fashion acting with regard to the rules and his duties and nothing else. The instructions of his principal, if he were a mere agent, could not possibly override those duties.'

In the *Bank of Ireland* case, Harman J held that the nominee had fallen so far below the proper standard of duty required of a professional insolvency practitioner that it would be right to visit some part of the costs upon him. He then mentioned what he described as an 'odd factor', namely that r. 5.17(9) provides that:

'The chairman is not personally liable for any costs incurred by any person in respect of an appeal under this Rule.'

Rule 1.17(9) is in precisely the same terms. Harman J considered that this provision did not preclude him from making an order for costs against the nominee on the application under s. 262 (the equivalent in that case of s. 6) which was before him. Nevertheless, as I read his judgment, he made some allowance in favour of the nominee for the fact that in so far as the application was made by way of appeal under the rule no order for costs could be made against the chairman.

In the present case, for the reasons which I have indicated, Mrs Saigol can only appeal under r. 1.17(5) because she has no standing to apply under s. 6. Rule 1.17(9) thus provides an absolute bar to the making of the order for costs which she seeks against Mr Goldstein.

However it would not, in my judgment, be satisfactory to leave the matter there. Mrs Saigol and her representatives have at all times made it clear that the purpose of joining Mr Goldstein as a respondent was to seek an order for costs against him personally. He has been subjected to criticism in his professional capacity and he has been put to substantial expense in being represented in these proceedings. In these circumstances it would be unfair if I did not make clear my view that the application for costs against him

A was misconceived on substantive as well as on technical grounds. The main ground of complaint against him, which was to the effect that he had failed to appreciate that the proposals treated some creditors, notably Mrs Saigol, in a discriminatory way, was without foundation. While it would have been better if the errors in the statement of affairs which I have noted above had been avoided or had been dealt with in Mr Goldstein's comments or in his report to the court as nominee, there was nothing before me which would support the view that these errors and Mr Goldstein's failure to

B appreciate their existence were the result of culpable conduct on his part. The want of clarity in the formulation of the proposals, even if attributable to Mr Goldstein rather than to someone else, would not justify the making of an order for costs against him. The one specific error on his part which has been proved is his treatment of Mrs Saigol's vote. While I have held that this was a material irregularity I have no doubt that Mr Goldstein acted in complete good faith. Even if r. 1.17(9) did not preclude an order for costs against

C Mr Goldstein, the making of this error would not justify the making of such an order.

(*Order accordingly*)

R A Securities Ltd v Mercantile Credit Co Ltd.

A

Chancery Division.
Jacob J.
Judgment delivered 27 May 1994.

Company voluntary arrangement – Assignee of lease subject to company voluntary arrangement – Landlord claimed rent from original tenant – Whether voluntary arrangement extinguished liability of original tenant – Insolvency Act 1986, s. 5.

B

This was a claim by the plaintiff landlords for rent and service charges due under a lease granted to the defendants ('T1'). The lease had been assigned first to Barclays Bank ('T2') and by them to a company called HLM Design ('T3'). Later T3 entered into a voluntary arrangement pursuant to Pt. I of the Insolvency Act 1986. At the time of that arrangement rent and service charges were due and unpaid. The claims of preferential creditors were such that the landlords would not receive any pre-arrangement rent from T3. Nor would they receive from T3 any of the post-arrangement rent and service charges. So the landlords claimed both the pre-arrangement and post-arrangement rent from the original lessees, T1.

C

T1 argued that its liability had been extinguished by the voluntary arrangement. As to the pre-arrangement rent, T1 was liable for it (so far as unpaid by T3) until the voluntary arrangement. But the arrangement amounted to a settlement with T3 by way of accord and satisfaction for the sums due, because the landlord accepted a surrender of the lease. Since there was no reservation of any claim against T1 that accord and satisfaction enured for his benefit. It was said that the landlord accepted a surrender of the lease because it was bound by the arrangement which proposed that the landlord should accept a surrender. T1's liability to pay post-arrangement rent fell with the lease.

D

Held, giving judgment for the landlord:

E

1. T1 could not take advantage of the arrangement to which it was not a party. The binding effect of the arrangement was solely as between those entitled to vote, whether they did so or not. An outsider, such as T1, could get no assistance from the terms of the voluntary arrangement as such. If something was actually done as a result of the arrangement, e.g. surrender of a lease, then an outsider could rely upon that. But it was plain that the landlord had not accepted any surrender in this case.

2. There was no equivalent to accord and satisfaction by virtue of the arrangement. The landlord was bound by the voluntary arrangement, but did not in fact voluntarily accept some other performance under the lease. There was no 'accord' in truth – just a statutory binding. Failure to exercise the option to turn up at the creditors' meeting and argue for some other arrangement did not amount to a true 'acceptance'.

F

The following cases were referred to in the judgment:

G

Cranley Mansions Ltd, Re. Saigol v Goldstein [1994] BCC 576.
Deanplan Ltd v Mahmoud & Anor [1993] Ch 151.
Hill v East and West India Dock Co (1884) 9 App Cas 448.
Jacobs, Ex parte (1875) LR 10 Ch App 211.
Walton, Ex parte. Re Levy (1881) 17 ChD 746.

Stephen Jourdan (instructed by PJW Sidwell) for the plaintiff.

H

Paul Emerson (instructed by Fladgate Fielder & Co) for the defendant.

JUDGMENT

Jacob J: The plaintiff landlords claim rent and service charges due under a lease granted to the defendants ('T1'). The lease had been assigned first to Barclays Bank ('T2') and by them to a company called HLM Design ('T3'). Later T3 entered into a voluntary

A   arrangement pursuant to Pt. I of the Insolvency Act 1986. At the time of that arrangement rent and service charges were due and unpaid ('the pre-arrangement rent'). The claims of preferential creditors are so great that the landlords will not receive any pre-arrangement rent from T3. Nor will they receive from that source any of the post-arrangement rent and service charges ('the post-arrangement rent'). So the landlords claim both the pre-arrangement and post-arrangement rent from the original lessees, T1. I have here summarised the essence of the case, omitting unnecessary detail.

B   The landlords say their claim is so plain that they are entitled to summary judgment under RSC, O. 14. Determination of this may involve the decision of a point of law arising from the effect of the voluntary arrangement. In any event the landlords invite me to decide this point one way or the other under RSC, O. 14A. They would like to know if they are wrong as soon as possible.

C   Despite a suggestion otherwise there is no real dispute as to the sums involved. No conflict of fact arises. I am told there is no authority on the points which arise for the first time under the *Insolvency Act* 1986. That is no reason not to determine them under O. 14A. I am clearly of the view that this is the sort of case to which this comparatively new rule applies – the parties can get a speedy determination of a point of law which lies at the heart of their dispute.

D   Matters might have been different if I had thought the points involved a prior determination of seriously disputed factual questions. But, as I have said, that is not the case here. The nearest approach to such a conflict was a suggestion that the landlords had actually accepted a surrender of the lease from T3 following the voluntary arrangement. Although T3 wrote a letter unilaterally purporting to terminate the lease with effect from the date of the voluntary arrangement it is plain that the landlords never accepted such termination. There is no triable issue as to a factual termination. That leaves the effect of the voluntary arrangement as such to be determined.

E   The original lease provided that the 'lessees' (as defined) were to pay rent and service charges for the demised term. There were review provisions which have operated in the usual way. 'Lessees' by definition include T1's successors in title and assigns. T1 covenanted to pay the rent and service charges. So, in the usual way, notwithstanding assignment of the lease, T1 retain their own primary liability to pay. T1 are primary debtors, not mere sureties. Whether it is rational for the law to permit such a liability to remain in force when the original tenant has long parted with the lease is debatable. Certainly the rule can often produce harsh results. But so far as this case is concerned the primary liability of T1 exists and remains unless in some way or other it has been extinguished.

F   T1 suggest such extinguishment by virtue of the voluntary arrangement. The landlords were duly summoned to the creditors' meeting called under s. 3 of the Act but did not attend. T2, but not T1, were also summoned and were parties to the arrangement. The

G   meeting approved the voluntary arrangement. Section 5(2) of the Act provides:

> 'The approved voluntary arrangement–
>
> (a) . . .
>
> (b) binds every person who in accordance with the rules had notice of, and was entitled to vote at, that meeting (whether or not he was present or

H   represented at the meeting) as if he were a party to the voluntary arrangement.'

So the landlords are deemed to be a party to the arrangement and bound by it. The terms of the arrangement (so far as material) are:

> 'At present the company leases business premises . . . [and equipment]. These leases are onerous to the company's business and in a receivership the receiver would

A

probably repudiate the leases and in a liquidation they would probably be surrendered or disclaimed. This would leave the lessors with unsecured claims in respect of their damages but with very little prospect of a dividend from the company. . . . It is therefore proposed that each lessor . . . accepts a surrender of the respective lease and takes immediate steps to mitigate its claim for damages.'

B

It is said that thereby the landlords accepted a surrender of the lease and that accordingly T1's liability to pay post-arrangement rent fell with the lease. This is said to be so even though in fact no surrender was accepted and there was no compliance with the statutory requirements for an effective surrender set out in s. 2 of the *Law of Property (Miscellaneous Provisions) Act* 1989.

As to the pre-arrangement rent, T1 accepts he was liable for it (so far as unpaid by T3) until the voluntary arrangement. But, he says, the arrangement amounted to a settlement with T3 by way of accord and satisfaction for the sums due: because the landlord accepted a surrender of the lease. Since there was no reservation of any claim against T1 that accord and satisfaction enures for his benefit.

C

I prefer to consider the matter as a question of principle first. The purpose of voluntary arrangements is to enable a company (or individual, for which case provision is made in Pt. VIII) to come to a composition with creditors so that the more drastic step of liquidation or bankruptcy can be avoided, if possible. It is better to keep the show on the road than close it down even if creditors have to accept less than their nominal (but not achievable) entitlement. The whole scheme is not for the benefit of solvent parties who happen to owe debts also owed by the debtor. It would in my judgment be unfair if a solvent debtor escaped liability as a side-wind of the voluntary arrangement system.

D

In so saying I am doing no more than echoing what other, more distinguished, judges said, in trenchant Victorian terms, in relation to earlier insolvency legislation. Thus in *Hill v East and West India Dock Co* (1884) 9 App Cas 448 at p. 454 Earl Cairns recoiled from a construction of s. 23 the *Bankruptcy Act* 1869 to the effect:

E

'that a solvent man who has entered, with his eyes open, into a covenant with the owners of property to pay rent to them and to be liable to them for that rent and for other covenants, and who upon an assignment has recognised that liability and has stipulated that it shall continue, shall nevertheless be delivered from that liability, not by reason of anything which has passed between him and the lessors, but from a misfortune which has happened to the lessors, namely that the person to whom the lease has been assigned has become a bankrupt.'

F

James LJ in *Ex parte Walton. Re Levy* (1881) 17 ChD 746 at p. 757 described the proposition that a solvent original tenant was released by reason of the assignee's insolvency as leading to a 'most grievous injustice and the most revolting absurdity'. These considerations led to a narrow construction of s. 23 of the *Bankruptcy Act* 1869 which provided that a disclaimed lease was 'deemed to have been surrendered'. It was not so deemed as between the landlord and solvent original lessee.

G

Turning back to s. 5, does 'binds every person' have any effect outside the voluntary arrangement? I think not. The effect of the binding is solely as between the parties bound – those entitled to vote, whether they did or not. An outsider, such as T1 can get no assistance from the terms of the voluntary arrangement as such. Of course if something is actually done as a result of the arrangement (e.g. property transferred, or as might have but did not happen here, surrender of a lease) then an outsider can rely upon that. But his right to rely upon it must result from an actual act done, not the arrangement.

H

That to my mind ends the case, both for pre-arrangement and post-arrangement rent. T1 cannot take advantage of the arrangement to which they were not a party. However I must go on to deal more fully with the points made by Mr Emerson.

A   First he said that the 1986 Act was a new code and that earlier authorities were irrelevant. He is right. But that does not mean that it was intended to create a 'most revolting absurdity'. Nor is it likely that a voluntary arrangement can extinguish a landlord's rights against a solvent non-party, when the more drastic effect of a liquidation or bankruptcy does not do so.

B   Second he said that things were different under this Act as compared with the position, for instance, in *Hill*, because under this Act the landlords could have protected themselves. This would be by turning up to the creditors' meeting and seeking an express preservation of their right to claim rent from an original tenant. Thus instead of agreeing to a surrender they could instead come to some accommodation about the rent due (past and future) from T3. Mr Emerson says that is what the landlord should have done, even though his prospects of actually getting any money pursuant to the arrangement were

C   minimal. His argument applied even if no rent were due at all, and only the future liability for rent was under consideration. I find that bizarre, and all the more so when Mr Emerson contended that if there had been such an attendance, the landlord would very probably get protection for his claim against T1, either from the meeting, or, were it not granted there, on appeal to the court pursuant to s. 6 of the Act. If Mr Emerson were right, whether or not an outsider could escape his own primary liability would depend on how well advised the landlord was. It is by no means self-evident that a creditor should

D   have to attend a meeting dealing with the debts of X when he has a claim against Y. Moreover, even well-advised creditors would have to incur the expense and trouble of attendance even where they had, in their own mind, written off any chance of significant recovery from the debtor concerned.

      Further, even if the landlord did attend to oppose an agreement to surrender, things might not go as smoothly as Mr Emerson suggests. Consider the simple case where the

E   company seeking an arrangement is the first assignee of the original tenant. His assignor is a contingent creditor, for if his assignor pays the rent he has a right of indemnity from his assignee pursuant to the usual implied covenant (see s. 77 of the *Law of Property Act* 1925). Suppose the landlord simply agrees to forego his claim for rent against the assignee, retaining his right to claim against the assignor. Then the assignor will be able to turn on the assignee. So, if the assignor is not a party to the voluntary arrangement,

F   nothing will have been achieved by the landlord giving up his financial claim against the assignee. The assignor will make the claim instead. The other parties to the arrangement would not want this and would therefore not readily allow the landlord to retain his claim against the assignor. Things would be different if both the landlord and original lessee (as a contingent creditor) were parties to the voluntary arrangement. Thus it may well be that for a voluntary arrangement effectively to deal with a lease held by assignment, the assignor should be summoned too.

G   Here the position is more complicated. T3's assignor is T2, who is a party to and bound by the arrangement. T2 has, as it seems to me accepted (as between him and T3) that there will be no post-arrangement rent due. So he could not bring a claim against T3 in respect of any unrecovered rent (supposing, that is, that T1 claims indemnity from him).

H   Mr Emerson's third point relied upon *Deanplan Ltd v Mahmoud & Anor* [1993] Ch 151. The plaintiff landlord had accepted goods and a surrender of the lease 'in full and final settlement' in respect of rent due from an ultimate assignee of the lease. He then turned on an earlier assignor for the rent unpaid less the value of the goods (which turned out to be minimal). It was held that by the settlement the landlord had accepted accord and satisfaction for the rent. So none was due. Judge Paul Baker QC's exhaustive analysis of the law was summarised by him as follows (at p. 170E):

'... where the obligations are non-cumulative, i.e. the obligation of each is to   A
perform in so far as it has not been performed by any other party, the acceptance
of some other performance in lieu of the promised performance relieves the others.
The covenantee cannot have both the promised performance and some other
performance which he agrees to accept.'

Here it is said there was an equivalent to accord and satisfaction. I do not think so. True
it is that the landlords are bound by the voluntary arrangement. But they did not in fact   B
voluntarily accept some other performance. There was no 'accord' in truth – just a
statutory binding. I do not regard failure to exercise the option to turn up at the creditors'
meeting and argue for some other arrangement as amounting to an 'accord' – a true
'acceptance'.

In my judgment the release of the debtor is, as Bailey, Groves and Smith say in
Corporate Insolvency Law & Practice at para. 25.15, an act of law. The same result was
achieved under earlier legislation, namely the *Bankruptcy Act* 1869, see e.g. *Ex parte*   C
Jacobs (1875) LR 10 Ch App 211. I only mention this case because Mr Emerson relied
upon a passage in vol. 2 of the current edition of *Chitty on Contract*, para. 5048:

'The position therefore appears to be that voluntary arrangements made under the
1986 Act are in the same position as were compositions under the 1869 Act: they
are "voluntary acts" which discharge the surety, in the same way as do
compositions and arrangements made at common law.'   D

Mr Emerson said that accordingly the landlords had by a 'voluntary act' agreed to accept
a different performance than payment of the rent due, namely gained at least a right to
accept surrender of the lease. Whether that was valuable or not was irrelevant – it was a
different performance. *Chitty* relies upon *Jacobs* but assumes that it held that a
'composition' under s. 126 of the 1869 Act was equated with a voluntary act. This is
simply not so. The judgment of Mellish LJ (read by James LJ) could not be clearer: E

'We think that a discharge of a debtor under a liquidation or a composition is
really a discharge in bankruptcy by operation of law.'

Another work relied upon by Mr Emerson was Andrews and Millett's *Law of Guarantees*.
This does not adopt the *Chitty* view, suggesting as a better analysis, the notion that a
voluntary arrangement is in effect a statutory variation of pre-existing contractual rights.
It follows, the authors argue, that the common law effect of discharge of a surety by a   F
consensual discharge of the debtor (without reservation of a right against the surety) will
apply in a voluntary arrangement. This analysis to my mind turns a statutory binding
into a consent and is in error.

So the third point fails.

My remaining concern was, what is to happen for the future? Can the landlords simply
stand by and collect the rent as and when due from T1, even though the lease continues   G
to exist and is assigned to T3? There is no provision for a vesting order such as, for
instance, can be made to vest a lease back in an original tenant after a liquidator of his
assignee disclaims a lease under s. 178 (see s. 181). It was made plain that this is a
theoretical concern in this case because the landlords are willing to let T1 back into
possession or to allow them to find new tenants. No doubt that would be the practical
answer in most cases.

However the theoretical problem must be addressed. I do not have complete confidence   H
in the answer which I have reached and which did not arise directly on the points in
dispute. The problem arises from the fact that the statutory scheme of voluntary
arrangements has not dealt with what happens to things like leases. Indeed it is possible
that the whole scheme only relates to creditors as such, and can only bind parties qua
their position as creditors. But assuming a landlord can be bound qua landlord, the

A   solution is, I think, as follows. The original tenant will remain liable for the rent and have an indemnity claim against his assignee. If that assignee enters into a voluntary arrangement he will either summon the assignor or not. If he does summon both then they will be bound and the assignor will get the benefit of any surrender called for by the arrangement. If the assignor is not summoned, then his right of indemnity will be enforceable. If the assignee cannot pay, then it can be wound up and liquidated. Then the liquidator would disclaim and the assignor could invoke the vesting order machinery.

B   In practice a vesting would be achieved by agreement by reason of the threat of this machinery.

Since I wrote the foregoing paragraph my attention has been drawn to a very recent decision of Ferris J, *Saigol v Goldstein* [1994] BCC 576. This was not available when the matter was argued before me. Ferris J held that a creditor for an unliquidated claim whose amount is not agreed at the meeting of creditors ought not to be bound by any

C   figure put on the claim at the meeting. That may well have an impact on what I wrote. This is because the claim of an assignor may well be uncertain in amount: although there is a fixed amount due, how much he will be owed depends upon how much is paid by the debtor, or, when there have been several assignments, by intermediate assignees and the debtor. If that is right then even if the assignor is summoned to the meeting, unless all is agreed, he may not be bound and my solution will not work. This might result in a failure of the voluntary arrangement altogether, for in some cases there would be no point in it

D   so far as other creditors were concerned. This again points to a flaw in the system as it stands.

Here the theoretical point does not arise so far as T1 is concerned. His indemnity is against T2. The fact that T2 cannot enforce his indemnity against T3 is a consequence of T2 being party to the arrangement.

In the result the claim succeeds.

E

(*Order accordingly*)

F

G

H

Burford Midland Properties Ltd v Marley Extrusions Ltd & Ors.

Chancery Division.

His Honour Judge Roger Cooke (sitting as a High Court judge).

Judgment delivered 6 June 1994.

Company voluntary arrangement – Whether arrangement covered rent becoming due after scheme date – Whether arrangement bound assignee of reversion – Whether assignee could recover from original tenant – Whether arrangement involved variation of lease or accord and satisfaction – Effect of term of arrangement prohibiting action likely to increase company's indebtedness – Insolvency Act 1986, Pt. I.

This was a preliminary issue whether a company voluntary arrangement under Pt. I of the Insolvency Act 1986 relating to a tenant by assignment ('Chancery') prevented the plaintiff, an assignee of the reversion, from pursuing claims under the lease against the original tenant ('Marley') and/or Chancery, and, if so, to what extent.

The plaintiff acquired the reversion at the time when the arrangement was becoming effective. The original landlord was bound by the arrangement. Rent becoming due before the arrangement date was dealt with under the arrangement. The plaintiff sought to recover rent due subsequent to implementation of the arrangement.

Chancery and Marley resisted the plaintiff's claim on the grounds that (1) the plaintiff's only rights were rights under the arrangement and those had the effect of inhibiting immediate recovery; (2) those rights were binding upon the plaintiff against both Chancery and Marley; but (3) if for any reason the arrangement did not give Marley the right to resist recovery on the ground that the arrangement was effective as between Marley and the plaintiff, Chancery could and would apply for an injunction restraining the plaintiff from pursuing Marley, under a clause in the arrangement (cl. 4.2) which prohibited claims which would have the effect of increasing Chancery's indebtedness.

Held, deciding the preliminary issue in favour of the plaintiff landlord:

1. The liability for future rent under a lease was not a prospective debt within the arrangement. The arrangement involved a compromise of debts, not of obligations, and future rent did not fit into either the definition of 'liabilities' in the arrangement, or the compromise. The arrangement only covered rent and service charges already due and owing at the scheme date.

2. The arrangement bound the plaintiff as the assignee of the reversion, as a matter of property law.

3. If future rent was within the arrangement, Chancery's liability to pay was within the arrangement and Chancery could enforce cl. 4.2 by injunction and limit its liability to claims directly within the scheme.

4. If future rent was within the arrangement, that would constitute a variation of the lease which could be taken advantage of by the original tenant. (Baynton v Morgan (1888) 22 QBD 74 and Centrovincial Estates plc v Bulk Storage Ltd (1983) 46 PCR 393 applied.)

5. The arrangement did not amount to accord and satisfaction which discharged the tenants. That was because cl. 4.2 prohibited suing a co-debtor without consent. That was a reservation of rights and it followed that, as regards the position of co-debtors, the arrangement was an agreement not to sue the assignee with a limited right reserved against the original tenants.

The following cases were referred to in the judgment:

Antaios, The [1981] 2 Ll Rep 284.

Baynton v Morgan (1888) 22 QBD 74.

A   *British Equitable Bond and Mortgage Corp Ltd, Re* [1910] 1 Ch 574.
Centrovincial Estates plc v Bulk Storage Ltd (1983) 46 PCR 393.
City of London Corporation v Fell [1994] AC 458.
Deanplan Ltd v Mahmoud & Anor [1993] Ch 151.
European Life Assurance Society, Re (1869) LR 9 Eq 122.
EWA, a Debtor, Re [1901] 2 KB 642.
Hockley (William) Ltd, Re [1962] 1 WLR 555.
B   *Matthey v Curling* [1922] 2 AC 180.
Naeem (a Bankrupt), Re [1990] 1 WLR 48.
Prenn v Simmonds [1971] 1 WLR 1381.
R A Securities Ltd v Mercantile Credit Co Ltd [1994] BCC 598.
Stonegate Securities Ltd v Gregory [1980] Ch 576.
Weg Motors Ltd v Hales & Ors [1962] Ch 49.

C   Mark Warwick (instructed by Green David Conway) for the plaintiff.

Joseph Karas (instructed by Thomson Shell & Passmore) for the first defendant.

Peter Sheridan QC (instructed by Rosling King) for the second defendant.

Rosalind Nicholson (instructed by D J Freeman) for the third defendant.

D   JUDGMENT

His Honour Judge Roger Cooke: I have before me a preliminary issue directed by the Chief Master by an order of 27 January 1994, which is, put shortly, whether a voluntary arrangement under the Insolvency Act by Chancery (as I will call them), the tenant by assignment of certain premises, prevents the plaintiff, an assignee of the reversion, from pursuing claims under the lease against (1) Marley, the original tenant, and/or (2) Chancery as tenant by assignment and, if so, to what extent. The issue in fact raises a series of questions which have been posed by counsel and I propose to answer all of them, irrespective of whether, in view of some of the answers which I have reached, all are necessary to the result.

The facts can be comparatively shortly stated.

On 9 April 1979, Wessex (the second defendant) entered into a lease with Marley (the first defendant) whereby Wessex lent to Marley the eighth floor of a block called Tricorn House, Hagley Road, Edgbaston ('the premises') for 25 years from the Christmas quarter day of 1978. The rent under the lease was, following the final relevant review, £13,900 per annum. On 19 May 1986 Marley assigned the lease to Chancery, the third defendant.

Chancery were, and are, a well-known banking enterprise who in 1990–91 had got into difficulties. An administration order was made on 18 February 1991 under the *Insolvency Act* 1986. The order was made with a view to seeing if a scheme could be devised and in due course a voluntary arrangement was entered into by the creditors pursuant to Pt. I of the Insolvency Act. I shall need later to come to the scheme in some detail.

While the scheme was in gestation, Wessex was in the process of selling the reversion to the present plaintiffs and the dates on the pleadings would indicate that the negotiations and the contract were prior to the arrangement becoming effective and that the actual transfer was after. For the purpose of the arrangement, Wessex was accepted as being a creditor for an estimated sum, but it is clear from a short piece of evidence I heard that this estimate was specifically for the purpose of giving their debt some value rather than relating to a part of the debt; it is not of much significance beyond that.

Following completion of the purchase and the implementation of the arrangement, the plaintiffs attempted to recover as it fell due the rent and service charges for the subsequent quarters both from Chancery and from Marley as original tenants. It was met by a

refusal from both. The lease has now, in circumstances which do not matter, been   A
forfeited.

Both Chancery and Marley resist the claim on the grounds that (1) the plaintiffs' only
rights are rights under the arrangement and those have the effect of inhibiting immediate
recovery; (2) those rights are binding upon the plaintiff against both Chancery and
Marley; but (3) if for any reason the arrangement does not give Marley the right to resist
recovery on the grounds the arrangement is effective as between Marley and the plaintiffs,   B
Chancery can and will apply for an injunction restraining the plaintiffs from pursuing
Marley.

I should say for the sake of completeness and emphasise that I am only concerned with
rent arising due after the critical date in the arrangement. Rent becoming due before then
has been dealt with under the arrangement in ways with which I am not concerned.

I am concerned to answer two fundamental questions, namely, (1) does the   C
arrangement affect rent which becomes payable after what I will call 'the arrangement
date'; (2) if it does, then does it do it in any way which affects the rights and liabilities
between the plaintiff, the assignee of the reversion, and Marley, the original tenant?

It is perhaps easiest to start with what the position would have been had Chancery
simply defaulted at the relevant date and the plaintiff decided, for whatever reason, not
to pursue Chancery or not to pursue it alone. In that case, the law would have been   D
totally clear. Generally speaking, assignment does not discharge the covenanted liabilities
of the original tenant. The landlord can always sue the original tenant on the covenant
to pay rent and the tenant can seek to recover that rent from the assignee. If the assignee
is not good for the money, the ultimate loss rests on the original tenant: see a line of
authority having as its most recent expression, so far as I know, *City of London
Corporation v Fell* [1994] AC 458 at p. 465E.

Under s. 141 of the Law of Property Act, the assignee of the reversion can sue the   E
original lessee not only prospectively but in respect of arrears accrued due at the date of
the assignment. So here, says Mr Warwick, the plaintiffs can recover from Marley both
the post-arrangement date arrears as they stood at completion on 23 December 1991 and
all the rent payable to it from and after completion. Nobody doubts that proposition is
accurate and it is for the parties to show that the arrangement effectively inhibits the
plaintiff from enforcing those rights.   F

With that preliminary, I turn to the arrangement itself. The voluntary arrangement as
an institution is a creature of Pt. I of the Insolvency Act. Under the old law, under the
1948 Companies Act, the effective choice on insolvency was either a s. 206 scheme, which
was slow and cumbersome and required the intervention of the court (not least because
the court usually had to be persuaded to adjourn the winding-up petition while that was
done with all the damages that a pending petition could do to a company's prospects of
survival) or the winding-up petition itself, the effect of which was a very blunt and   G
economically wasteful instrument, where a company might be insolvent but stood a
chance of survival in the long term.

The object of the legislation is to provide a swift and comparatively informal
arrangement whereby the majority of the company's creditors can bind the minority to
some arrangement (and there are many) inhibiting the immediate enforcement and/or
total enforcement of the debts, thereby avoiding a creditors' free-for-all and giving the   H
company often a period in which it can trade untrammelled by the need for payment of
the debts comprised in the arrangement. Not unusually, as here, such an arrangement
comes about when a company has already been regulated by an administration order.

The Act provides that the scheme shall become binding on all creditors (in essential) if
more than 75 per cent in value of the creditors present and voting approve it, but subject

A   to a right of application to the court. It is of course binding on the creditor whether or not he attends the meeting.

There is no doubt whatever on the facts (and nobody seeks to assert the contrary) that Wessex had notice of the meeting, that the requisite majority approved the arrangement and that nobody applied to the court to cancel it. That being so, the arrangement is beyond argument binding upon Wessex for whatever it does.

B   With that I turn to the detailed arrangement. In short summary, what it did was to convert a percentage of each debt into B shares in Chancery and reschedule the balance over a six-year period with percentage instalments being paid on fixed dates over that period. The date as at which the liabilities were fixed (I use this deliberately neutral expression to cover a controversial concept) was 18 February 1991, the date of the administration order ('the arrangement date'). The pure regime of the arrangement affected liabilities that as of the arrangement date were treated as ascertained. Those

C   debts defined as unascertained caught up, as it were, by means of a formula as and when they became ascertained, if indeed they did, at a date prior to the conversion date. The conversion date was, at the earliest, 1 October 1996.

The definitions of the arrangement are critical and I turn to these next.

'*Unascertained liabilities* – From time to time those of the liabilities which are not ascertained liabilities but which subsequently become so at a date prior to the

D   conversion.

Ascertained liabilities – Subject to cl. 7(i) [which does not matter] and to the extent not yet paid, those are liabilities which are from time to time both (a) liquidated in amount and ascertained in value; and (b) such as would but for the provisions of this voluntary arrangement be presently due and payable.

Liabilities – From time to time to the extent that they are still subsisting, any and

E   all liabilities of Chancery at 18 February 1991 are creditors howsoever such liabilities arise and whether at that date they were liquidated or unliquidated, their value ascertained or otherwise, present or future, contingent or otherwise, but excluding preferential debts.'

Those last few lines require underlining, because they are critical to this case.

F   '*Creditors* – Any creditor of Chancery as at 18 February 1991 bound by the voluntary arrangement by virtue of the provisions of the Act whose claims were at that date liquidated or unliquidated, ascertained in value or otherwise present or future, contingent or otherwise, including, wherever the context permits, but subject always to cl. 5.6, the successors and assigns of any such person as aforesaid.'

I should also look at cl. 4 of the arrangement, which is critical in a number of ways

G   and I think there is no alternative but to read it in full so far as at least 4.1 and 4.2 are concerned:

'4.1 The provisions of cl. 5, 6 and 7 shall have effect in full and final settlement of all claims against and obligations of Chancery present and potential in relation to the liabilities including, without limitation, in respect of damages, interest, costs or any other matters relating to the liabilities whether such claims or obligations are

H   liquidated or unliquidated, their value ascertained or unascertained, future or present, contingent or otherwise,'

–a form of language that is already familiar to readers of the arrangement.

'4.2 Accordingly, except with the prior written consent of the supervision committee or with the written consent given prior to entry into force of the creditors committee, any claim by any creditor against any person other than

Chancery or the Deposit Protection Board is hereby, for the benefit of Chancery,   A
prohibited to the maximum extent permitted by law if such claim would or might
lead to the recovery by such creditor or such person of moneys equal or
corresponding to all or part of the liabilities of such creditor when the direct or
indirect effect of such claim would be or was likely to be to increase the aggregate
amount from time to time becoming payable by Chancery (a) whether pursuant to
this voluntary arrangement or howsoever; and (b) whether in consequence of a   B
claim by such person against Chancery or for any other reason.'

I need not go into cl. 4.3.

I pause to say that cl. 4.1 is oddly drafted in that it purports to repeat part of the
definition of 'liabilities' but by reference to claims and obligations relating to the
liabilities: it does not aid clarity; but I doubt that it makes much material difference to
the point I have to decide. I shall have to come back to cl. 4.2 in more detail later.   C

I can now come to the issues themselves and I propose to define those in the same way
as Miss Nicholson and Mr Karas did in their submissions to me on behalf of Chancery
and Marley.

**(1) What is the effect of the arrangement on the obligations of Chancery to those bound by
the arrangement, and, in particular, does it extend to the rent accruing due after the**   D
arrangement date?

This to my mind must be the fundamental question. It is Chancery and Marley's case
that all rent falling due under the lease until at least the conversion date (in the event the
liability was terminated by forfeiture) is caught by the arrangement, so that the landlord
does not get paid his rent according to his covenant but receives it partly in B shares and
partly in rescheduled instalments so arranged in accordance with the catch-up provisions
as being an unascertained liability. And it follows that the landlord and all those similarly   E
bound are obliged to accept that regime.

In the original argument as opened by Miss Nicholson, it seemed to me this point was
taken to be a point of no great difficulty and that the difficulties in the case perhaps lay
elsewhere; however, Mr Sheridan QC launched a powerful attack on the whole concept,
to which he directed almost the whole of his argument. To my mind, it is this aspect of
the case that gives the greatest trouble.   F

I go back in trying to find what liabilities are caught by the arrangement to the
definition clause which I have already quoted. Running through the definitions, there is
one common thread which needs to be isolated at once. It is this: the central importance
of the arrangement date. The creditor thus is any creditor *as at* the arrangement date,
and his assigns, and liabilities are liabilities *at* the arrangement date. So if somebody is
not a creditor at the arrangement date or a liability is not a liability at the arrangement   G
date, the arrangement does not affect them.

If those words stood alone (which unhappily they do not), I would have very little
difficulty with this case. In the ordinary sense of liability, i.e. something which the
company is liable to pay, the company was not at the arrangement date liable to pay
future rent: it might be liable to pay it at some time in the future, but a statement of the
assets and liabilities of the company as they stood then would not have included it.   H
Adopting a simple test, a writ issued for the rent on the date of the arrangement date
would be struck out as disclosing no cause of action. But, say Miss Nicholson and Mr
Karas, it does not in fact end there. The definition of liabilities, repeated mutatis mutandis
in cl. 4.1, includes liabilities that were not liabilities at the arrangement date because of
the critical words 'present or future, contingent or otherwise'. I pause to say that these
are two pairs of alternatives: 'future' and 'contingent' are not alternatives. A contingent

A debt is pretty well inevitably a future debt, but not necessarily the only type of future debt.

On the basis of this, what they say is that a future debt is any debt which may, in the future, be payable to a creditor who is within the scheme. I think Mr Karas in argument accepts this could not extend so far as a debt incurred on a wholly new contract and that must plainly be right; but he does say that it is any debt arising in respect of an existing

B obligation, even though the date for performance of the obligation (on either side it must be) has not arrived.

Contingent and prospective debts are a concept that is not unfamiliar in the law of company insolvencies; thus under a succession of Companies Acts a contingent or prospective creditor has been a competent petitioner and in testing in appropriate cases whether a company is able to pay its debts, account is taken of contingent or prospective debts. I think 'prospective' and 'future' must really be taken to have the same meaning.

C I was referred to two authorities under the 1948 Act: *Re William Hockley Ltd* [1962] 1 WLR 555 (Pennycuick J) and *Stonegate Securities v Gregory* [1980] Ch 576, a decision of the Court of Appeal. In *Hockley* at p. 558, Pennycuick J said:

'The expression "contingent creditor" is not defined in the Companies Act, but must, I think, denote a person towards whom under an existing obligation, the company may or will become subject to a present liability upon the happening of

D some future event or at some future date. (See Buckley on the Companies Act, 13th ed., notes at pp. 460 to 462).'

In *Stonegate* at p. 579E, Buckley LJ says:

'. . . "contingent creditor" means a creditor in respect of a debt which will only become due in an event which may or may not occur; and a "prospective creditor" is a creditor in respect of a debt which will certainly become due in the future,

E either on some date which has been already determined or on some date determinable by reference to future events.'

It is I think useful to look at the passage in *Buckley* which Pennycuick J must be taken to have cited with approval. What the textbook says in the notes to s. 223 of the 1948 Act is that contingent and prospective liabilities are those:

'. . . under contracts and engagements already existing, and not . . . liabilities which

F the company may incur in the future in carrying on its business.'

It must be remembered the context of the note is a section directed to solvency as opposed to insolvency and it is therefore no surprise when the note goes on to say that:

'The court will not . . . take into account the possible liabilities or profits which may accrue in respect of future business.'

G That is amply supported by the authority which it cites, *Re British Equitable Bond and Mortgage Corp* [1910] 1 Ch 574 and the old case of *Re European Life Assurance Society* (1869) LR 9 Eq 122. In the latter case the court put the test rather vividly, saying one should look at the company as if it had completed business on the relevant day and did not intend to do any more.

Oddly, no authority has been discovered by counsel, despite considerable industry,

H that relates directly to the position of rent under an existing lease in the context of these definitions, although one authority to which I was referred may point that way and I will come to it in due course.

As the authorities stand, I think the following is clear: (1) a future prospective debt cannot include a debt that arises out of a future transaction; (2) that it can and will include a debt that arises out of an existing transaction as a result of which the basic liability is incurred which depends on the reaching of a future date or the happening of a

future event to make it payable if it is ever to be payable. Where there is less clarity is   A
whether a prospective future debt includes a liability under a subsisting series of
obligations when the future event goes to the whole root of the obligation. Thus one
might contrast a case where goods are delivered but the price is paid 50 days from
delivery (a clear future debt within the definition) and a case where under a contract there
is an obligation to supply goods at a future date and the obligation to pay is only to arise
when the goods have been supplied. Or, to put it in another way, the debt only becomes
a debt when the consideration for it has been supplied and the obligation has been   B
completed, even though there is a future obligation to supply the consideration.

For my part, I would have thought even for 1948 Act purposes one would readily see
the latter case as being outside the category of prospective debts, and that because what
one is really concerned with is what (time and contingency apart) the company is known
to owe at the relevant date as opposed to what the company will owe at a future date
when it receives some benefit which at present it does not have – for example, continued   C
possession under a subsisting lease and the continued benefit of the landlord's covenant.

In a way this is, I suppose, a digression, though I think a helpful illustration given that
the basic object of an arrangement is to create a moratorium or composition with the
creditors at the relevant date, those creditors being usually and inevitably the creditors
who will be proving in the liquidation if there was no arrangement and the company was
wound up. I would incline anyway to construe the expression in conformity with what,   D
as I have indicated, I think is the right way of construing the Companies Act approach
rather than as something that is radically different.

To my mind, a more general approach to construction of such terminology (but which
would produce a result in line with the way in which I think the Companies Act cases are
formulated) is this: ask the question, 'What is a debtor and what is a creditor?' and
indeed, 'What is a debt or liability?' Inevitably I would have thought the answer to that   E
question must be:

> 'An obligation to pay that is no longer dependent on executory matters on either
> side but where subject only either to date or to some uncertain inhibiting factor it
> is fully crystallised.'

I cannot to my mind see how something that depends on future executory matters can be
properly called a debt or liability or somebody who will be entitled to payment only when   F
executory matters have been performed can properly be called a creditor: he has not got
there yet.

If that is right, where would liability for future rent under a lease fit in? This is a right,
essentially one of property, tied into a bundle of rights and obligations, the enjoyment of
the estate for a period by the tenant and also consideration of the landlord's covenants.
The obligation to pay a service charge, which is in general terms the indemnity for the   G
performance of the landlord's covenants, is a fortiori this. I cannot see it is any different
from the executory contract scenario that I have just postulated.

Some help is given in general terms by Hoffmann J's decision in *Re Naeem* [1990] 1
WLR 48, a case of a voluntary arrangement in a personal insolvency where the court
concluded that an arrangement relating to arrears of rent related only to the landlord's
rights qua creditor and did not affect his property rights qua landlord. The reasoning
must, I would have thought, point to the conclusion that in terms of defining a creditor   H
there is a difference between a right to be paid something that has accrued due and has
become a debt and a right in respect of something that is an obligation (a fortiori I would
have thought an executory obligation) relating to and arising out of property.

I am conscious that these general principles, which seem to me to be of central
importance, were really not much touched on in argument and have occurred to me in

A the course of preparing this judgment, but although they may suffer from the lack of that refinement that reasoned argument might have given them, I do not myself feel much doubt that they afford a means of general guide to one's approach. Necessarily, of course, much may turn on the words used and their context.

I turn now to this case. Mr Sheridan made powerful submissions to me on basic principles of construction and those submissions to my mind support the approach which I have suggested above may be the way of construing such expressions in a Companies Act context and suggest strongly that it ought to apply to this arrangement. I hope it is no discourtesy to his substantial and helpful submissions if I can really take the point quite shortly.

He says this arrangement, like any other commercial arrangement, ought to be construed as follows: (1) in its surrounding factual matrix and having regard to what is objectively its aim (*Prenn v Simmonds* [1971] 1 WLR 1381); (2) in accordance with business common sense; *and* (3) producing a reasonable result rather than an unreasonable one (see, inter alia, *The Antaios* [1981] 2 Ll Rep 284). As to (3), I think it could only arise where there is some element of ambiguity so that the court has the opportunity of choosing between the reasonable and unreasonable result. If it is clear on the plain language the parties have agreed to do something silly, there is I think not a lot the court can do about it.

D Before considering Mr Sheridan's approach, I start by trying to see, using the language and applying by analogy the Companies Act approach to which I have referred, what the expressions used may mean. For this purpose, one has to look at more than just the bare definition section, defining liabilities, alone. A number of things are clear from cl. 6.3 as a whole. Thus, (1) liabilities are 'at 18 February 1991', i.e. the arrangement date; (2) creditors are creditors at that date; (3) as and when liabilities are ascertained prior to the conversion date they enter the scheme; (4) the conversion date is five years hence at least; (5) what turns an unascertained liability into an ascertained liability is that it becomes presently due and payable but not that the company becomes liable to pay it.

One then looks at cl. 4.1 where what the scheme is expressed as doing is to create a full settlement of all claims against Chancery, 'present and potential', in relation to the liabilities, necessarily liabilities at the arrangement date. It then goes on, of course, with a further definition of what those claims might be, sweeping in future and contingent. Why it has to distinguish claims relating to liabilities and the liabilities themselves is a mysterious oddity of drafting that, as I have said, may not matter.

Just trying to see what the ordinary language might mean – I find considerable difficulty in saying that as at the arrangement date the company has a liability (defined as a liability at the arrangement date) to its landlord for rent when that rent has not become due in any sense at the arrangement date but is payable in the future in respect of a quarter's, a future quarter's, enjoyment of the estate created by the lease. I have in mind the distinction drawn in *Naeem*. Nor can one see why it obviously fits into a compromise of liabilities (whether or not immediate or definitely payable) of the company at the arrangement date when there is no suggestion of compromising the rights, including the covenant under the lease, which continue to be performable in consideration of, inter alia, the rent.

H Essentially compromise of debts as I see it is a concept whereby the only obligation is the debt itself. Therefore the ambit of the compromise relates to the way in which the debt may be paid or postponed, while compromise of a future payment which is in consideration of other executory obligations would, one would think, involve compromise of those obligations, which this arrangement does not. Clearly and on its face, it assumes the non-existence of any other obligation, which is consistent entirely with a debt where all obligations have been performed and all that is left is payment of

money on some date and in some eventuality. So therefore the scheme makes at best   A
dubious sense defining the liabilities as including future rent/service charge, and makes
better sense defining debts/liabilities as I suggest in general terms (as a matter of language
dehors any special meanings or context in the arrangement) those expressions ought to
be defined.

Thus far and applying these considerations, I could not see how with any ease or
consistency future rents, as opposed to past rents, would fit into either the definitions or   B
the compromise.

Mr Sheridan's submissions are entirely in line with and supportive of this approach
and I can really take them very briefly.

(1)   It is part of the factual matrix that the explanatory document sent with the
arrangement makes it clear that the object of the exercise is to enable the company
to trade for five years according to a business plan and secure that its existing debts   C
will be dealt with in a tightly structured way which will not unduly interfere with
its ability to trade. If it is not legitimate to look at the explanatory documents, this
can I think be gathered in any event from the arrangement itself.

(2)   The other side of the coin must inevitably mean that for the five year period it is
business as usual: trade will take place, current trade debts will be paid as and
when they fall due.   D

(3)   Part of the trading business pattern of the post-arrangement world will be the
continued occupation of business premises with the landlord performing his
covenants and the tenant paying the rent and the service charges.

In that factual matrix and given that objective of the scheme, how can it be, says Mr
Sheridan rhetorically, that the current rent relating to current occupation and, a fortiori,
the service charge relating to current services, which is future payment for what is   E
presently the executory performance of the landlord's obligations, should be frozen in
time and the landlord be made to give the tenant continuing credit, some of it in the form
of B shares, continue to perform all its obligations under the lease and take the risk that
the company will be able to pay at the postponed date: it is totally inconsistent with the
concept and purpose of the scheme. I agree with Mr Sheridan. In that context, the
company's construction makes little sense.   F

For the same reason if in the end there is an ambiguity, which I do not think there is,
the tenants' construction makes commercial nonsense because it forces giving continuing
future credit for obligatory future services within what is meant to be a moratorium
scheme with business as usual, and the landlord's construction makes commercial sense,
i.e. it is consistent with drawing a line at the arrangement date and thereafter trading
normally.

For all these reasons, I adopt the landlord's construction and reject the tenants'   G
construction. I accordingly hold that the arrangement only covers rent and service
charges already actually due and owing at the scheme date.

I pause to say that just before I delivered this judgment I was very helpfully referred
by Mr Sheridan to a decision *R A Securities Ltd v Mercantile Credit Co Ltd* [1994] BCC
598, a decision of Jacob J as recently as 26 May 1994. That appears to be entirely in line
(though the reasons are somewhat different) with what I have said and gives me some   H
comfort at least that I have reached the right conclusion.

That is, in fact, enough to dispose of the application, but I am conscious that this
matter may well go further and in any event the parties may wish to know where they
might be, so I was asked by counsel and I propose to express a conclusion on each of the
questions which were raised.

A **(2) Was Wessex bound by the voluntary arrangement?**

In my judgment, there can be only one answer and nobody sought to argue the contrary. Section 5(2) of the Insolvency Act provides that once a creditor has notice of the meeting, being a creditor entitled to vote at it then, subject to the right to apply to the court, it is bound by the arrangement if the arrangement is approved. Wessex received notice of the meeting. This was the unchallenged evidence of Mr Masney who gave

B evidence before me. A spot value – again Mr Masney's evidence – was put on its debt in order to entitle Wessex to vote.

Wessex did not actually attend the meeting or give a proxy. This does not matter. What matters is the notice and their entitlement to attend. Accordingly, the meeting having approved the arrangement, Wessex was bound, subject only to its right to apply to the court under s. 6. No such application was made; Wessex is accordingly finally and

C irretrievably bound to whatever the arrangement bound it to.

(3) Is Burford bound by the arrangement?

The arrangement purports to bind successors and assigns. It cannot, of course, directly bind them as parties because they are not parties, but the provision in the arrangement clearly shows that the arrangement is not merely something personal between the contracting parties but affects the rights intended to be assigned.

D I find no difficulty at all in the concept that any assignee of the benefit of a contract which has been modified by an arrangement would take the contract as effectively so modified.

It was, however, submitted to me that where, as here, there has been no specific assignment of the benefit of the contract but there has been assignment of the reversion, the arrangement will, as a matter of property law, bind the purchaser.

E Mr Karas referred me to s. 142 of the Law of Property Act which subjects the reversion to the burden of what might loosely be called 'landlord's covenants'. And he submits (which I accept) that an obligation to bind the reversion need not be contained in the lease (see *Weg Motors v Hales* [1962] Ch 49). For my part, however, I think this makes rather heavy weather of it. I would have thought the more obvious approach is not to take this as a landlord's covenant to accept payment of rent by a peculiar route, but

F rather to treat it as a modification of the tenant's covenant to pay rent, the benefit of which would pass under s. 141, so that an assignee could only enforce the tenant's covenant as modified.

Referring again to *Re Naeem*, it is to be remembered that the proposition found by the court was that an arrangement relating to arrears related only to the landlord's right qua creditor and did not affect his property rights. As is obvious from what I have already said, I would not dissent from this, but of course once assuming against my construction

G that the arrangement comprehends future rents then I think it follows that these, as opposed to accrued arrears, must be in the nature of rights under the covenant in the lease and will transmit to an assignee of the reversion under one or other of the sections, my own preference being for s. 141.

Burford, I am told (and there is no evidence to the contrary), denied it had notice of the arrangement. In my judgment, notice is irrelevant: it is no prerequisite to the passing

H of liability under the sections.

(4) Assuming Burford to be bound, is Chancery released and, if so, to what extent?

I must of course again make the assumption that my construction is wrong and that post-arrangement instalments of rents are capable of being within the arrangement. I think it is beyond argument that once the rents are within the arrangement Chancery's

liability to pay them is necessarily within the arrangement and not otherwise. It is clear   A
the whole object of the arrangement is to release Chancery from liability for whatever
debts are within the arrangement to prevent a creditor from recovering payment from a
third party when the effect of so doing is to give the third party a right of recovery against
Chancery.

It is for this reason that cl. 4.2 appears in the arrangement. This clause attracted a
good deal of criticism in argument, and I am not surprised. I do not think I need read it   B
in full again, but it should be borne in mind in the remaining part of this section of the
judgment. In particular (a) and (b) at the end seem to be a typical draftsman's 'sweep-up'
device when he does not quite know what he might be talking about. To remind oneself
of that, it is amounts falling due and payable by Chancery:

'(a) whether pursuant to this voluntary arrangement or howsoever; and (b) whether
in consequence of a claim by such person against Chancery or for any other
reason.'   C

I can see that there could well be substantial construction problems on the outside edges
of this clause, though I do not doubt the proposition that a creditor thereby agrees with
Chancery that it will not pursue a third party if the effect of making such a successful
claim would give the third party rights of recovery against Chancery in respect of that
debt, i.e. to put it in practical terms, the creditors within the scheme cannot use their
rights against third parties to cause Chancery to pay the full amount, albeit indirectly.   D
This is a right which enures specifically to the benefit of Chancery. I do not think it is a
right which the third party can directly take advantage of: he is not a party to the scheme,
nor is he anybody's assignee. So only Chancery, as a party to the scheme, can enforce it
and of course it is for Chancery's benefit that it can be enforced. So, as it were, by the
back door Chancery can effectively limit its liability to the claims directly within the
arrangement. Such enforcement will be necessarily by way of injunction and I cannot see   E
why, all other things being equal, such an injunction should not be granted.

(5) To what extent is Marley released from liability for rent?

Making again the general assumption that future rents are within the arrangement, the
question would divide into two: (a) is there, in effect, a modification of the lease; (b) is
there accord and satisfaction?

F

(a) *Modification of the lease*

It was submitted that an assignee can by arrangement with his landlord alter the terms
on which he holds the estate and that this having been done the estate, so altered, binds
the original tenant. On first sight, this is a startling proposition. Examination of authority
shows it to be firmly settled in the last decade by four first instance decisions, the lead
decision, perhaps one might say, being *Centrovincial Estates plc v Bulk Storage Ltd* (1983)   G
46 PCR 393 and having as its ancestor an old decision of the Court of Appeal in *Baynton
v Morgan* (1888) 22 QBD 74.

I would for my part be concerned as to the full extent of the doctrine, notably as to
how far it can be said that an assignee can actually increase the burden on the original
tenant as opposed to decrease it. It is clear that I ought to follow these authorities: they
are four first instance decisions in the High Court, all consistent with each other, all in
line with the seminal authority of *Baynton v Morgan* and nobody can point to anywhere   H
where they might be said to be per incuriam. If these authorities are to be doubted, I
think that is for the Court of Appeal and not for me.

Once given the construction for which the tenants contend, then I think it has to follow
that the mode of recovery of rent under the lease has been varied for the future and the
only sensible way of construing it is as a variation of the lease. If once one gets that far,

A then necessarily the lease as altered binds, and can be taken advantage of, by the original tenant as well as the assignee. I therefore hold on this ground that were there such an alteration as is contended for, Marley could qua tenant directly take advantage of it by way of defence.

(b) *Accord and satisfaction*

B Does the arrangement amount to an accord and satisfaction which discharges both debtors? The basic principle long established is that where there are joint debtors the release of one releases both. It is curious the point appears not to have been argued in relation to the situation of original tenant and assignee prior to the decision of His Honour Judge Baker QC sitting in this division in *Deanplan v Mahmoud* [1993] Ch 151. From that authority I get the following propositions.

C (i) The principle is the same whether the debt is joint, joint and several or several with each liable to perform the same obligation.

(ii) Original tenant and assignee necessarily fall into the third of these categories.

(iii) Accordingly, a release of the assignee is a release of the original tenant.

As one would expect with a novel decision, it has not been without its critics. I was referred in argument to an interesting article in the *Solicitors' Journal* of 17 December

D 1993 at p. 1272, which Mr Warwick adopted as his argument. The nub of the criticism rests upon whether the law does in truth recognise a class of non-cumulative several covenants. If one assumes that it does not, then (so the article recites Professor Glanville Williams' argument in his work on *Joint Obligations*) the covenant must be regarded as joint and several. There can be no doubt the covenants exist and if they are joint and several then the principle that release of one releases both must obviously apply. But the article, and therefore Mr Warwick, then argues that on the authority of *Baynton v*

E *Morgan*, the seminal authority for the variation of lease cases I referred to earlier, unless the liability was regarded as joint a variation by the assignee could not discharge both.

So far as it is material to my decision, I think there are two answers to this:

(i) The dictum of Younger LJ in the Court of Appeal in *Matthey v Curling* [1922] 2 AC 180 at p. 208 which recognises that an original lessee may have a defence that the assignee has been absolved from performance is at least supportive of the view

F reached by Judge Baker that accord and satisfaction does extend to this group of obligations.

(ii) *Baynton v Morgan* does not actually decide that which Mr Warwick must argue it does in order to get his argument home. All it decides is that the assignee has the power to assign again, which includes surrender of part, something very different from a discharge of liability and which (I agree with Judge Baker at p. 161 of

G *Deanplan*) has little to do with this part of the discussion.

Thus far I see no reason why I should feel any concern about following the decision in *Deanplan*, which, in the absence of some clear indication that it was wrong, I would normally do with a first instance decision in the High Court and I propose to follow it.

This is not at all the end of the matter because there remains a point of real substance. Not everything that at first sight discharges a debt necessarily meets the criteria of an

H accord and satisfaction. In *Re EWA, a Debtor* [1901] 2 KB 642, cited at length in *Deanplan* at p. 168, Collins LJ at pp. 648–649 says:

'It is clear that, although a document in terms purports to release one of two joint debtors, yet it may contain in terms a reservation of rights against the other joint debtor. Where you find those two provisions you construe the document, not as a release, but merely as an undertaking not to sue a particular individual, and the

result is that the right to proceed against the co-debtor is reserved and can be put   A
in force against him.'

As far as I am aware this remains good law; it is also clear commercial common sense. To regard a transaction that reserved rights as one that in fact discharged would be to invite Mr Bumble's well-known strictures on the law.

With that, I turn to the relevant clause. I have already referred to cl. 4.1, the drafting of which was subjected in argument to some well-reasoned abuse. If, as I think, the   B accord and satisfaction point is in general a good one, then one would hardly need cl. 4.2 at all. In fact, the draftsman has sought by a rather cumbersome 'belt and braces' scheme to protect co-debtors and by doing so has, I think, exposed them to more danger than is necessary. The critical provision is the inhibition on suing a co-debtor except with the prior written consent of the supervision committee.

No criteria for consent are stated, although it is hard to think of a situation where such   C consent would (in accordance with the purposes of the arrangement) be given, it remains it could be given in any case. If the consent is given, then the co-debtor could be sued. What to my mind can this be but a reservation of rights, i.e. the creditors say:

'We reserve the right, subject to permission, which we may be able to obtain, to sue the co-debtor. If we do not get permission, we will not sue.'

This is not a total discharge. A total discharge can only mean no suit in any   D circumstances. Here, in some circumstances, there can be a suit. In my judgment, this is a reservation of rights and it follows that, as regards the position of co-debtors, the arrangement is to be construed as an agreement not to sue the assignee, with rights, albeit limited, being reserved against the original tenants. If, therefore, I had to answer this question I would conclude it in favour of the landlords.

I think and hope I have now dealt with all the points. It remains for me to express my   E indebtedness to all four counsel who have argued this matter with considerable interest and difference of approach and I will now hear them on the form of the order which I am asked to make and as to costs.

Order

I will deal first of all with how to dispose of the proceedings substantively.   F

The preliminary issue as formulated by the master is whether and if so to what extent the voluntary arrangement which is identified there prevents the plaintiff pursuing claims under the lease identified in paragraph one of the amended statement of claim. I propose to answer that by saying that the voluntary arrangement as defined in the order will not prevent the plaintiff pursuing claims arising under the lease identified in paragraph one of the amended statement of claim. That is all I need say about that.

It is always attractive when a preliminary issue is raised and having been determined   G in a particular way gives a fairly strong indication that there may be no further dispute left in the action for the court to go ahead and try to dispose of the entire action. Commonly, of course, that happens in claims under Pt. II of the *Landlord and Tenant Act* 1954. But I am mindful of this. The master's order in fact says that until the issue has been determined all further proceedings in the action, except for the purpose of determining the issue, be stayed, and that there is not any degree of consensus for that   H stay to be removed. If there was agreement to remove it, I would of course remove it and deal with the matter by consent in some short and summary way.

In practical terms I am told in any event by the two tenant defendants that there may be some issue on quantum, although, quite frankly, Mr Karas is not able to tell me what it is; but there it is. One can see such an issue might arise.

A   The larger temptation, perhaps, is to do what Mr Sheridan wants me to do, which is to dismiss his clients from the action at this stage, the preliminary issue having totally disposed of the question of liability against him and that he should go away with his costs. But, tempted though I am to take that course, and practical though it might be to do so, I think I am not going to give in to temptation and I ought to follow, strictly speaking, the master's order for all or for none. That being so, I do not propose to do more substantively than simply dispose of the preliminary issue.

B

Costs

     We then come to the question of costs, which in the nature of things can only at this stage be the costs of the preliminary issue and I am not concerned with the costs of the action, which will fall to be dealt with by somebody else at some other time. So far as the preliminary issue is concerned, the plaintiffs have undoubtedly succeeded. The two tenant

C   defendants have undoubtedly failed. That being so, it seems to me that Mr Warwick is entitled as against Chancery and Marley in any event to a joint and several order for the costs of the preliminary issue, and I make that order. Mr Sheridan, who is for the assignor defendants, who is there because the plaintiffs have sued him in the alternative, also seeks his costs either against Chancery and Marley direct or against the plaintiffs in the confident expectation the plaintiffs will pass the bill on down the line. Short of technicalities, the riposte made to that by the tenant defendants is the nice riposte that,

D   although Mr Sheridan's clients were represented, they were really making common cause with the plaintiff and there was no need for them to be here separately.

     I think that does, with respect, ignore the fact that although there is a common argument, nevertheless the plaintiff and Mr Sheridan's clients are in very different positions on the pleadings; they cannot effectively, I think, have their interests properly represented even for the purposes of the preliminary issue by the same counsel. They are

E   actually on opposite sides of the record and between them there is hostile litigation. That being so, I think Mr Sheridan's clients will both be entitled to be represented on this hearing and to put their own case, which they did. Having done so and having succeeded, I think they must have their costs and Chancery and Marley will have to pay those on a joint and several basis as well.

F   *[Plaintiffs' application for costs to be taxed and paid forthwith]*

     I think there is a difference between Burford and Wessex. In Wessex's case, it seems to me realistically that there is absolutely nothing left in these proceedings. Although I think para. 2 of the master's order inhibits me from actually dealing with the action, it seems most improbable that any further costs will be incurred which Wessex would have to pay which might be set off against these costs. I think that realistically Wessex should have their costs to be taxed and paid forthwith and I so order.

G   Where Burford are concerned, I simply do not know what is left in this action. It may well be there is very little left, but one can see the possibility that where the action remains alive, if only on the question of quantum, there might be orders for costs that might not all go Burford's way, I simply do not know, and they could be set off against an order for costs made now. In that case, to make an order for costs to be taxed and paid forthwith would be oppressive and, on balance, I do not think I should make it, and I do

H   not.

                  (*Order accordingly. Leave to appeal granted*)

Re Northern Engineering Industries plc.

Court of Appeal (Civil Division).
Neill, Leggatt and Millett L JJ.
Judgment delivered 10 May 1994.

Reduction of capital – Preference shares – Variation of class rights – Company proposed reduction of capital involving cancellation of preference shares – Articles required preference shareholders' consent to variation of rights – Articles deemed rights to be varied by 'reduction of capital' – Whether cancellation of preference shares was a 'reduction' – Companies Act 1985, s. 135.

This was an appeal by the company from Ferris J's refusal to confirm a reduction of capital: [1993] BCC 267.

The reduction involved paying off preference shares and cancelling them. The company had resolved upon the reduction in general meeting. The preference shareholders argued that their approval at a separate class meeting was required. The company's articles required the preference shareholders' consent or the sanction of an extraordinary resolution passed at a separate class meeting for a variation of their rights (art. 6); a 'reduction of the capital paid up on' such shares was deemed to be a variation (art. 7(B)). The question, therefore, was whether the cancellation of the preference shares and the return to the shareholders of the whole of the capital paid up on them was a reduction of the capital paid up on those shares within the meaning of art. 7(B). The judge upheld the objecting shareholder's contention that it was.

Held, dismissing the company's appeal:

Article 7(B) applied to the proposed reduction. The company's argument that 'reduction' did not include reduction to zero was rejected. The separate class consent of the preference shareholders was a prerequisite of the proposals, and accordingly the court had no jurisdiction to confirm the reduction in the absence of such approval.

The following cases were referred to in the judgment of Millett LJ:

Anglo-American Insurance Co Ltd, Re [1991] BCC 208.
Chatterley-Whitfield Collieries Ltd, Re [1948] 2 All ER 593.
Eastern Extension Australasia and China Telegraph Co Ltd v The Commonwealth (1908) 6 CLR 647.
House of Fraser plc v ACGE Investments Ltd & Ors (1987) 3 BCC 201; [1987] AC 387.
Saltdean Estate Co Ltd, Re [1968] 1 WLR 1844.

David Oliver QC and John Cone (instructed by Freshfields) for the company.

Richard Sykes QC (instructed by Herbert Smith) for the Commercial Union.

JUDGMENT

Millett LJ: This is an appeal by Northern Engineering Industries plc (now Rolls-Royce Power Engineering plc) ('the company') from the dismissal by Ferris J on 12 February 1993 of the company's petition seeking the confirmation by the court of a proposed reduction of the company's share capital: see [1993] BCC 267.

The company has four classes of shares in issue. These consist of a very large number of ordinary shares of 25 pence each, and three different and much smaller classes of preference shares of £1 each, of which one class is redeemable. The respective rights of the different classes of shares in respect of dividends, return of capital on a winding up or otherwise and redemption are set out in art. 3 of the company's articles of association which was adopted by special resolution passed in November 1988.

A   Since August 1989 the company has been a member of the Rolls-Royce group of companies. All the ordinary shares in the company are owned beneficially by Rolls-Royce plc or by one of its associated companies. The preference shares are owned by institutions and members of the general public. The directors of the company have for some time considered that the additional costs of administration which result from the maintenance of separate classes of ordinary and preference shares are not justified, and have sought to eliminate such costs by extinguishing the preference shares. In October
B   1989 the company proposed a scheme of arrangement under which all the preference shares would be cancelled in consideration of the payment by Rolls-Royce plc of a fixed amount for each share. The amount payable was calculated so as to provide a premium above the middle-market price of the shares of each class on a specified day. Despite this inducement, however, the scheme of arrangement was rejected when it was put to separate meetings of the holders of each class of preference shares.

C   The company then sought to achieve its object by a different route, that is to say by means of a reduction of capital subject to the confirmation of the court under s. 135 of the *Companies Act* 1985. It proposed to reduce the company's share capital by the cancellation of all the authorised preference shares of each class and the repayment of capital and accrued dividends to the holders of the issued preference shares in each class in accordance with their respective rights on a winding up. Resolutions to carry these proposals into effect were put to an extraordinary general meeting of the company held
D   on 6 January 1993. Under the company's articles of association the holders of the preference shares were entitled to attend the meeting and vote on the resolution to reduce the company's share capital, but they were heavily outvoted by the Rolls-Royce companies which held the ordinary shares and which voted in favour of the resolution. No separate class meetings of preference shareholders were held to approve the resolution.

E   When the company's petition for the confirmation of the reduction of its share capital came before the court, it was opposed by an institutional preference shareholder which successfully argued that a provision in the company's articles of association had the effect that the cancellation of any class of preference shares and the return to the shareholders of the whole of the capital paid up on those shares required the approval of a resolution passed by the appropriate majority at a separate class meeting of the holders of such
F   shares. The judge upheld the objection and dismissed the company's petition. The company now appeals to this court.

It is well established that, in the absence of an article which has the contrary effect:

(1)   the cancellation of a particular class of shares and the return of the capital paid up thereon does not require the separate consent of the holders of the shares of that class unless it involves a variation of the rights attaching to the shares; and

G   (2)   such cancellation and return of capital while the company is a going concern do not constitute a variation of the rights attaching to the shares if the return of capital is made strictly in accordance with those rights on a winding up. The reason is that stated by Lord Greene MR in *Re Chatterley-Whitfield Collieries Ltd* [1948] 2 All ER 593 (CA) at p. 596E that 'the risk of a reduction of capital taking place is as much an element in the bargain as the right to a preferential dividend' and by Buckley J in *Re Saltdean Estate Co Ltd* [1968] 1 WLR 1844 at p. 1849–1850:

H   'The liability to prior repayment on a reduction of capital, corresponding to their right to prior return of capital in a winding-up . . . is part of the bargain between the shareholders and forms an integral part of the definition or delimitation of the bundle of rights which make up a preferred share. Giving effect to it does not involve the variation or abrogation of any right attached to such a share.'

In the absence of special provision in the company's articles of association, therefore, preference shareholders are in an unenviable position. Locked into their investment when the general level of interest rates is higher than the fixed yield on their shares, they could find themselves bought out by the company against their will when interest rates fall below it. As a result it has become common for special provisions to be included in companies' articles of association to protect such shareholders from the risk which Lord Greene MR identified as 'the risk of a reduction of capital taking place' at their expense but without their consent. Where such provisions are included in the articles, of course, they too form part of the bargain between the shareholders; and to the extent that the preference shareholders are protected against a reduction of capital without their consent, to that extent the right of the ordinary shareholders to effect a reduction of the company's share capital by obtaining the passage of a special resolution and the confirmation of the court is diminished. The question is whether such an article exists in the present case.

Article 6 of the company's articles of association permits the variation or abrogation of the rights attached to any class of shares, either while the company is a going concern or during or in contemplation of a winding up, but only with the consent in writing of the holders of three-fourths in nominal value of the issued shares of that class. That article alone would not protect the preference shareholders from what is proposed in the present case, since it is common ground, as I have said, that the proposed repayment of capital is in accordance with the rights attached to the various classes of shares on a winding up and accordingly does not constitute a variation of those rights as a strict matter of law.

Article 7(B) of the articles of association of the company, however, provides, so far as material:

> '(B) The rights attached to any shares shall be deemed to be varied by the reduction of the capital paid up on those shares . . .'

The question, therefore, is whether the cancellation of the preference shares and the return to the shareholders of the whole of the capital paid up on them is a reduction of the capital paid up on those shares within the meaning of art. 7(B). The objecting shareholder says that it is. The company argues that it is not. 'Reduction', submits the company, means diminution or lessening from one number, quantity or amount to another and smaller number, quantity or amount. It does not include diminution or lessening to zero. That, it is said, is extinction, not reduction. After a reduction, it seems, there must always be something left, even if only an absurdity.

The company supports its contention by submitting that, while the ordinary shareholders may have been content to agree not without the consent of the preference shareholders to repay their investment piecemeal and in dribs and drabs, they should not lightly be assumed to have been content to forgo their right, without such consent, to repay it altogether and at a single stroke.

For my part I agree that in its ordinary meaning the word 'reduction' connotes diminution and not extinction; just as 'increase' strictly means increasing from something and not from nothing, and does not mean the same as 'growth' (as in 'Topsy just growed').

The *Oxford English Dictionary* gives the relevant meaning of 'reduce' as to lower, diminish or lessen to a smaller amount, extent etc., or to a single thing.

In *Eastern Extension Australasia and China Telegraph Co Ltd v The Commonwealth* (1908) 6 CLR 647 where the question was whether an agreement which conferred power on the government to reduce the rate charged for telegrams empowered the government to abolish the rates altogether, Griffith CJ said at p. 664:

A   '. . . the words 'shall have power to reduce,' do not, etymologically, include a power to reduce to nothing or abolish.'

Barton J said (at p. 668):

> 'Primarily the reduction of a charge means its diminution. when we are offered goods at reduced prices we do not expect to get them for nothing, however cheap they may have been before the reduction. But then it is said that the power may be exercised by successive steps until next to nothing remains, so that when an infinitesimal sum is reached by way of residuum, the charges have been practically abolished. To this there is a plain answer. Assuming the successive exercises of the power, there must be something left, and when that ultimate something is reached, *ex vi termini* there is neither a reduction to nothing nor an abolition. In truth, the power to reduce involves a direction to leave something, and therefore entire abolition is not an exercise of the power granted.'

O'Connor J also said that the word in its ordinary meaning does not mean abolish.

I have no doubt that what was the primary and ordinary meaning of the word in Australia at the beginning of the present century is still its primary meaning in the UK as the century draws towards its end. We still speak correctly of an 'irreducible minimum', meaning an amount which cannot be reduced further but can only be eliminated altogether.

But words take their meaning and effect from their surroundings. They are not always used in their ordinary or primary or, still less, their etymologically correct meaning. To speak of 'reducing' an amount to nothing rather than merely to 'vanishing point' may not be an etymologically correct use of the word, but it is a permissible one. What matters, however, is not what the word 'reduction' means as a matter of etymology, or even ordinary language, but what it means in art. 7(B) of the company's articles of association.

In my judgment, there are two contexts, one general and one particular, which point to the correct conclusion in the present case. In the first place, art. 7(B) is dealing with the general subject of variation of class rights, and in particular the reduction of the company's share capital. The mischief which it sets out to remedy is that early repayment of capital (whether partial or total) to one class of shareholders by means of a reduction of capital is not a variation of their rights and does not need their consent. The article is limited to the reduction of the capital paid up on their shares, which could be to their disadvantage, and does not extend to the reduction of any uncalled capital on their shares which could only be to their advantage. But the context in which the article must be construed is the right of the company, with the sanction of a special resolution of the members, to reduce its share capital. In this context the word 'reduction' must mean a reduction within, and governed by, s. 135(1) of the *Companies Act* 1985. Articles 6 and 7 are both concerned with the variation of class rights and constitute provisions in the articles of association of the kind foreshadowed by s. 125 of the *Companies Act* 1985 which provides for the consent of separate class meetings of the holders of separate classes of shares to be convened to approve any variation of class rights; and provides in particular that provision to such effect may be included in the company's articles of association. Section 125(3)(c) refers to the requirement for this purpose that:

> '. . . the variation of those rights is connected with the giving, variation, revocation or renewal of an authority for allotment under section 80 or with a reduction of the company's share capital under section 135.'

In the context of the reduction of a company's share capital, the word 'reduction' is constantly used in the sense of reduction to nothing. Indeed s. 135(1) itself provides:

'Subject to confirmation by the court, a company limited by shares or a company   A
limited by guarantee and having a share capital may, if so authorised by its articles,
by special resolution reduce its share capital in any way.'

It is not disputed before us that this allows a company to which the section applies to
reduce its share capital to nil, even though by reason of other requirements of the
Companies Acts it must immediately increase its share capital to a positive amount. Such
confirmations are frequently confirmed by the court. They cannot be justified by arguing   B
that in s. 135(1) the word 'reduction' refers to the end result of the reduction *and* the
increase, since this would preclude the court from confirming a reduction of the capital
to nothing and a subsequent increase to the original or greater amount. Such reductions
too are frequently confirmed by the court.

In *Re Anglo-American Insurance Co Ltd* [1991] BCC 208 the court confirmed the
reduction of the company's share capital from £50m divided into 50m shares of £1 each   C
to nil, followed by an increase in the capital to such number of shares of US$10 each as
would amount in value to £50m at a specified rate of exchange. The court approved only
the resolution for reduction and not for the subsequent increase. The form of the minute
which the company proposed to register recorded the fact that the company's share
capital had been reduced from £50m divided into 50m shares of £1 each to nil. Harman J
approved the minute, though he directed that an additional minute recording the
subsequent increase in the company's share capital should also be registered. He did so   D
because he considered that the registration of the one without the other would be
misleading. But he did not doubt that the reduction of the company's share capital to nil
was authorised by s. 135(1) nor that his confirmation thereof was proper, nor that it
constituted a reduction of capital and was correctly described as such in the minute.
Indeed, throughout the judgment, he adopted the same usage himself.

More compelling, in my judgment, is the particular context provided by art. 7(B) itself.   E
The 'reduction' of the capital paid up on shares of a particular class is made to require
the consent of the holders of the class affected. That is obviously Intended to be a
protection for those shareholders. It is idle to speculate whether it was included in the
articles at the insistence of those who applied to be issued with preference shares or at the
instigation of the ordinary shareholders as an inducement to investors to apply for
preference shares. That it was intended to protect them from some risk is undeniable.
The question is: what was the risk against which the preference shareholders were to be   F
protected? In my judgment, the conclusion is inescapable: it was to protect them from
the risk which was identified by Lord Greene MR, that of being subjected, without their
consent, to a premature repayment of their investment, in whole or in part, a risk which,
absent such an article, is inherent in the shares themselves. The company's argument
that, without their consent, it cannot reduce the capital paid up on their shares from £1
to 99 pence, or from £1 to one penny, but that it does not need their consent to reduce it   G
to nothing, in my view makes a nonsense of the protection which has been afforded them.
It would protect the preference shareholders from a partial repayment which would leave
them with something, however large and however small, but not from a complete
repayment which would leave them with nothing. Yet this is a fortiori. The suggestion
that the preference shareholders were to be protected merely from the piecemeal
repayment of their investment and not from its complete repayment outright appears to
me to be fanciful.   H

The company accepts that art. 7(B) confers a measure of protection on the preference
shareholders. The question, it submits, is whether the article confers full protection or
only a limited protection. That is true; but in my judgment the question answers itself
once it is realised that what is contended for by the company is not limited protection
against the greater invasion of their rights rather than the smaller; but limited protection

A   against the smaller invasion of the rights not the greater. No doubt the preference shareholders needed and they certainly obtained protection from the partial repayment of their investment; but it remains a mystery to me why that should be thought sufficient protection of their interests. It is not as though the company needed to withhold from them the protection against full repayment. If it wished to retain the right to repay the whole of the capital paid up on any class of preference shares, without seeking the consent of the preference shareholders, it had only to issue such shares as redeemable shares in B   the first place.

    I am not myself convinced that the solution lies in ascribing a secondary and etymologically inexact meaning to the word 'reduction' in art. 7(B). I believe that it is to be found in the principle that the greater includes the less. As the Latin derivation of the word indicates, 'reduction' literally means a 'bringing back', and describes a continuous process leading from a higher point to some lower point. It follows that it is possible to C   reduce something without eliminating it altogether; it is not possible to eliminate something without going through the process of reducing it. The effect of the word 'reduction', therefore, may depend on whether it is used in what in substance is a permissive context or a restrictive one. Confer a power on the committee of a club to reduce subscriptions of members who are suffering financial hardship, and I would not expect the committee to have power to waive such subscriptions altogether; the greater is D   not included in the less. The Australian case was just such an example. But restrain a defendant from disposing of his assets or diminishing their value below a stated amount, and I would expect him to be prohibited from rendering them valueless. Such a prohibition is directed to the maintenance of the value of the defendant's assets. In that context the greater cannot be achieved without going through the process of the (prohibited) less, and is therefore prohibited also.

E   So too in the present case. Article 7(B) is only a definition of those transactions which are to be taken as constituting a variation of class rights; but it is directed to the maintenance of those rights unless the shareholders consent to a variation. The reduction of the amount of the capital paid up on their shares is deemed to be a variation of their rights and cannot be effected without their consent. The context is therefore restrictive. The elimination of the paid up share capital on those shares is an a fortiori case. It cannot be achieved without a reduction. The greater includes the (prohibited) less. The greater is F   therefore prohibited.

    In my judgment, the company's arguments to the contrary are without substance and, in some cases, plainly misconceived. First, it is submitted that if 'reduction' in art. 7(B) has the wider meaning contended for by the objecting shareholder, it defeats the clear intention of the parties expressed in art. 3(B). Article 3(B) sets out the rights attached to the preference shares, including their rights to the return of capital 'on a liquidation or G   otherwise'. Thus the preference shareholders have agreed in advance that, on a return of capital while the company is a going concern, they shall be entitled to a fixed and ascertained amount in respect of each share and no more. If, the company points out, their consent is required to any such reduction, they can hold the company to ransom by demanding a far higher sum as the price of their consent. This, the company submits, cannot have been the intention of the parties.

H   The short answer, in my judgment, is that by art. 3(B) the preference shareholders agreed to what their entitlement should be on a reduction of capital in a liquidation or otherwise, *if one takes place*; they did not agree in advance that any reduction should take place. On the contrary, if and so far as art. 7(B) so provides, it was agreed that no reduction should take place while the company was a going concern without their consent. In short, art. 7(B) is as much as part of the bargain between the shareholders as art. 3(B) and the two must be read together.

Secondly it was submitted that, in the context of a variation of rights, the word   A
'reduction' cannot encompass a cancellation as this extinguishes the rights in toto whilst
a variation of rights presupposes a continued existence of the right in an altered form
after the variation. This submission is founded upon an observation by the Lord Justice-
Clerk, approved by Lord Keith of Kinkel in *House of Fraser plc v ACGE Investments Ltd*
(1987) 3 BCC 201 at p. 207 where it is said:

> 'In our opinion, the proposed cancellation of the preference shares would involve   B
> fulfilment or satisfaction of the contractual rights of the shareholders, and would
> not involve any variation of their rights. Variation of a right presupposes the
> existence of the right, the variation of the right, and the subsequent continued
> existence of the right as varied. A different situation obtains where a right is
> fulfilled and satisfied and thereafter ceases to exist.'

It is common ground that a reduction of capital, whether partial or total, does not in
fact constitute a variation of class rights, and that what art. 7(B) sets out to do is to deem   C
it to be a variation. It follows, therefore, that no inference can be drawn from the use of
the word 'variation' in what is necessarily an artificial sense.

But the company points out that all the other dealings mentioned in art. 7 affect the
rights attached to the shares or their value while they continue in existence and are,
therefore, true variations in the sense mentioned by the Lord Justice-Clerk. Only
art. 7(B) – and then only if the word 'reduction' is given an extended meaning – involves   D
the cancellation of the shares. For my own part, I do not find that at all surprising. There
are many different ways of affecting the value of existing shares, and they all need to
be guarded against. There is, however, only one way to eliminate them altogether. In
my judgment, therefore, no inference can be drawn from the fact that there is only
one dealing among several which, on one construction, extinguishes the shares.

At this stage it is necessary to note the bizarre argument advanced by the company   E
that, even if art. 7(B) does extend to the reduction of the amount paid up on the shares
to nil, it does not apply to the subsequent cancellation of the shares. If that is right then
by adding a further step (to which the preference shareholders could not possibly object
but, on the contrary, would welcome) the company can escape the need to obtain their
consent to the step to which they do object. In my judgment, the argument is quite
untenable.

The company's main thesis has been that art. 7(B) is intended to protect continuing   F
shareholders, that is to say, shareholders who continue to be members of the company;
and not shareholders who cease to be members of the company. But the short answer to
this contention is that art. 7(B) does not protect the shareholders after the notional
variation and is not intended to do so. It is intended to protect them from the notional
variation which cannot take place without their consent.

It was then submitted that various absurd consequences would follow if the objecting   G
shareholders' construction of the word 'reduction' were correct. In my judgment, none
of them is well-founded. In particular, it was submitted that the solvent liquidation of the
company would involve a return of capital to holders of preference shares, and
accordingly the company could net be put into liquidation without the prior approval of
the holders of the preference shares at separate class meetings.

The nominal capital of the issued shares of a company represents the protection for   H
creditors in the event of a winding up. It is a fundamental part of our company law that
that capital must be maintained and must not be returned to shareholders except in
strictly controlled circumstances. The reduction of any part of the nominal capital in
respect of issued shares, whether paid up or not, and whether or not accompanied by a
return to the shareholders while the company is a going concern, generally speaking
requires the confirmation of the court because it reduces the protection to the creditors

A   in a winding up, either by reducing the amount the shareholders may be called upon to contribute to the assets of the company in the event of a winding up, or by reducing the assets available to the creditors in the winding up.

But the repayment of capital to the shareholders on a winding up as part of the distribution of its assets after the creditors have been paid in full is simply not a process of reduction of capital at all. It is, in my judgment, an application of the company's share capital and not a reduction. It satisfies the rights of the shareholders to the repayment of their capital in the winding up after the company's debts have been paid. It cannot be said to reduce the entitlement which is thereby satisfied.

It was then submitted that the wider construction of the ward 'reduction' would conflict with the right of the company under art. 3(C) to redeem the redeemable preference shares because, it is said, redemption involves the reduction of the capital paid up on those shares by the repayment thereof to the holders. There are a number of answers to this, but it is sufficient to mention only two. The first is that reduction of capital and redemption of redeemable shares are, and are treated by the Companies Act as, essentially different processes. And if, as I consider, art. 7(B) is concerned with reduction of capital under s. 135 and not otherwise, it does not extend to a redemption of redeemable preference shares under s. 160.

The second is that, in any event, the specific provisions of art. 3 (C), which confer on the company the right to redeem shares issued as redeemable preference shares, must override art. 7(B) since they give a specific right to the company to redeem the shares without the prior consent of the shareholders in question. This is in sharp contrast to the provisions of art. 3(B) which confer no such right upon the company.

In my judgment, for the reasons which I have endeavoured to give, I consider that art. 7(B) applied to the proposed reduction of capital in this case; that the separate class consent of the preference shareholders was a prerequisite of the proposals; and the court has, accordingly, no jurisdiction to confirm the reduction in the absence of such approval. I would dismiss the appeal.

Leggatt LJ: I agree that for the reasons given Millett LJ, the judge came to the right conclusion. The appeal should be dismissed.

Neill LJ: I also agree.

(Appeal dismissed with costs)

Re Cimex Tissues Ltd. A

Chancery Division (Companies Court).
Mr S J Burnton QC (sitting as a deputy High Court judge).
Judgment delivered 15 July 1994.

Debenture – Whether debenture created fixed or floating charge over manufacturing machinery – Whether debenture conferred power to deal with charged property without lender's consent – Whether power to deal with charged property without lender's consent incompatible with fixed charge – Insolvency Act 1986, s. 175(2)(b). B

This was an application by a liquidator for determination of the question whether the charge created by a debenture was fixed or floating.

The debenture (cl. 2.1) charged 'by way of fixed charge' plant and machinery specified in C a valuation annexed to the debenture. The business of the company was that of toilet roll manufacturer and the machinery was located at its premises and used in the manufacturing business. It was undisputed that the machinery was not of a type which would be sold or replaced very often.

The drafting of the debenture was defective in that it contained provisions of little relevance to its subject-matter. It appeared to be an adaptation of a precedent for bank lending (although the lender was not a bank) which probably created both a fixed and a D floating charge, and related to book debts and to real property (although the subject-matter of the charge was the machinery). Clause 3.2 of the debenture provided that the company would not 'without the previous consent in writing of the lender ... sell, mortgage or otherwise deal with the charged property otherwise [than] for the purpose of getting in and realising them in the ordinary course of, and for the purposes of, carrying on its trading business' (cl. 3.2:1.1) nor 'sell the whole or, except in the ordinary course of, and for the E purpose of carrying on its trading business any other part of the charged property' (cl. 3.2: 1.2).

Preferential creditors argued that the debenture created a floating charge: cl. 3.2 conferred on the company liberty to deal with the charged assets in the ordinary course of business without the consent of the chargee, and such a power was inconsistent with a fixed charge; alternatively, the extent of that liberty was inconsistent with a fixed charge. The F debenture holder submitted that cl. 3.2 conferred no such liberty; but that if it did, the debenture took effect as a fixed charge on the equipment specified together with a power, contained in cl. 3.2, for the company to release the whole or part of the charged property from the charge thereby created.

Held, determining that the charge over plant and machinery created by the debenture was a fixed charge:

1. The inappropriateness of the words 'getting in and realising' to the subject-matter of G the debenture, compelled the conclusion that the words 'for the purpose of getting in and realising them' in cl. 3.2:1.1 were inapplicable to the charged property, by reason of its nature. Therefore cl. 3.2:1.1 did not confer on the company power to deal with the charged property.

2. The 'trading business' referred to in cl. 3.2 was the sale of stock, and was to be contrasted with the manufacturing business of the company. So interpreted, cl. 3.2:1.2 H conferred no relevant power on the company: the sale of capital manufacturing equipment could not be 'in the ordinary course of ... its trading business'.

3. The words 'or ... any other part of the charged property' in cl. 3.2:1.2 had no application; because of the lack of any previous reference to any part of the charged property, there was no 'other part of the charged property'. That reading avoided any

A   inconsistency with the fixed charge purportedly created by cl. 2.1 and avoided any conflict between cl. 3.2:1.1 and 3.2:1.2. It followed that cl. 3.2 did not confer any right on the company to sell the charged property or any part of it without the consent of the lender and there was no reason why the charge created by the debenture should not have taken effect as a fixed charge.

4. A licence for the chargor to deal to some extent with the charged assets was not necessarily inconsistent with a fixed charge, although if the licence to deal was extensive the

B   charge would be floating. The extent to which the licence to deal was compatible with a fixed charge would depend on the circumstances and the nature of the charged property. On the assumption that cl. 3.2 conferred on the company the right to sell any part of the charged property without the consent of the lender, the charge over the manufacturing machinery was nonetheless fixed.

The following cases were referred to in the judgment:

C   *Armagh Shoes Ltd, Re* [1982] NI 59; [1984] BCLC 405.
Atlantic Computer Systems plc, Re [1990] BCC 859; [1992] Ch 505.
Atlantic Medical Ltd, Re [1992] BCC 653.
Bond Worth Ltd, Re [1980] Ch 228.
Brightlife Ltd, Re (1986) 2 BCC 99,359; [1987] Ch 200.
Coates v Moore [1903] 2 KB 140.

D   *Evans v Rival Granite Quarries Ltd* [1910] 2 KB 979.
Evans, Coleman & Evans Ltd v R A Nelson Construction Ltd (1958) 16 DLR (2nd) 123.
Hi-Fi Equipment (Cabinets) Ltd, Re (1987) 3 BCC 478.
Holroyd & Ors v Marshall & Ors (1862) 10 HL Cas 191; 11 ER 999.
Mitsui Construction Co Ltd v A-G of Hong Kong (1986) 33 BLR 1.
New Bullas Trading Ltd, Re [1993] BCC 251; [1994] BCC 36 (CA).
Priestman (Alfred) & Co (1929) Ltd, Re [1936] 2 All ER 1340.

E   *Seed v Bradley* [1894] 1 QB 319.
Siebe Gorman & Co Ltd v Barclays Bank Ltd [1979] 2 Ll Rep 142.
Welsh Development Agency v Export Finance Co Ltd [1992] BCC 270.
Yorkshire Woolcombers Association Ltd, Re [1903] 2 Ch 284 (CA); [1904] AC 355 (HL).

Philip Gillyon (instructed by Streathers & Co) for the debenture holder.

Launcelot Henderson (instructed by the Treasury Solicitor) for the Department of

F   Employment and Commissioners of Customs & Excise.

Ceri Bryant (instructed by Foot & Bowden) for the liquidator.

JUDGMENT

Mr S J Burnton QC: This is an application by Mr Malcolm Cork, the liquidator of Cimex Tissues Ltd ('Cimex'), under s. 112 of the *Insolvency Act* 1986, for determination of the question:

G   'whether on the true construction of the debenture dated 6 December 1991 and made between (Cimex) and the first respondent, George Harvey-Bathurst, the charge over the plant and machinery created by cl. 2 thereof was, as created, a fixed or a floating charge.'

The first respondent to the application is Mr Harvey-Bathurst, the lender and referred to in the debenture as the chargee; the second and the third respondents are the

H   Department of Employment and the Commissioners of Customs and Excise, who are of course interested in the debts owed by Cimex to its preferred creditors being paid out of the proceeds of sale of the assets charged by the debenture in priority to the debt to Mr Harvey-Bathurst. The dispute in this matter is between Mr Harvey-Bathurst on the one hand, who contends that the charge created by the debenture was a fixed charge, and the Department of Employment and the Commissioners of Customs and Excise on the other, who contend that it created a floating charge.

The form of the question I have to determine reflects the recognition of all parties that   A
the answer turns on the construction of the debenture, a written instrument. It follows
that the subjective intentions of the parties to that instrument are irrelevant and
inadmissible for present purposes. The background, or factual matrix, against which the
debenture was executed may however be relevant. None of those facts is in dispute, and
there has been no cross-examination of any of the deponents.

The business of Cimex was that of toilet roll manufacturer. For the purpose of its   B
business, it owned and used certain machinery, and in particular machinery specified in a
valuation of Colebrook Evans and McKenzie dated 12 March 1990. The machinery
specified in that valuation was the subject of the debenture in issue in these proceedings.
It appears from the valuation that the machinery was acquired by Cimex on some date
after 12 March 1990 from the liquidator of Veltex Tissues Ltd. The valuation described
each item of machinery in question and, with certain exceptions, gave its individual
identifying number. The first, and most valuable item, was a series 150 automatic toilet   C
roll rewind line, manufactured by Paper Converting Machinery Co Ltd, and numbered
59122. It fed into a model R204 W log saw cutting unit. The valuation gave a figure of
£50,000 for that equipment valued on a break-up basis, and £95,000 on a going-concern
basis. According to Mr Harvey-Bathurst's first affidavit, that equipment was in excess of
27 feet in length, and the third item, a series 100 automatic toilet roll rewind line, valued
at £15,000 on a break-up basis and £30,000 on a going-concern basis, was in excess of 36
feet in length. Mr Harvey-Bathurst deposed that of the seven items of equipment   D
individually valued in the valuation (two of which were rewind lines incorporating more
than one item of machinery), only one was moveable, namely the fork-lift truck No.
243939 and reel clamp, together valued at £2,500 on a break-up basis and £7,000 on a
going-concern basis. There is evidence that with one exception none of the machinery
was fixed to the floor, but whether it was fixed in any physical sense is irrelevant to the
question before me. It is undisputed that the machinery was not of the type which would   E
be sold or replaced very often. Some had originally been manufactured in 1964, and had
been in use for some 30 years. The liquidator deposed that there was no reason to
suppose that that machinery could not continue in use for the same length of time
provided that replacement parts could be purchased. According to the affidavit of Mr
Robert Levy, the former managing director of Cimex, the fork-lift truck was special to
the extent that it had a clamp for moving large reels of paper, and most of the value of
the truck lay in that clamp. He stated that the truck was not one which 'one would readily   F
dispose of within, say, two or three years'.

In December 1990, Mr Harvey-Bathurst made a temporary loan to Cimex of the sum
of £50,000 to fund its costs in commencing to trade. The principal amount of that loan
had been reduced to £35,000 by the beginning of November 1991. At the end of 1991,
Mr Harvey-Bathurst agreed to extend the time for repayment of the existing loan, and to
make further advances, to be secured on machinery of Cimex. Pursuant to this agreement,   G
the debenture was duly executed on 6 December 1991. It was registered in the companies
register, the registration describing it as a 'fixed charge'. Mr Harvey-Bathurst lent
additional moneys to Cimex in consideration of the debenture, and when it went into
liquidation on 4 August 1992, the sum of £65,385 was outstanding by way of capital
amount. In addition, Mr Harvey-Bathurst is a creditor in the sum of £8,441.49 in respect
of interest on the principal amount lent.

I turn to the debenture itself. Regrettably, its drafting was defective. It contains   H
provisions of little or no relevance to its subject matter. By way of example, cl. 1.2 refers
to 'banking facilities offered to the company'; but the lender was not a banker. Clause
3.2:1.1 refers to the 'getting in and realising' of the charged property. 'Getting in and
realising' may be relevant to book debts of a company, but can have no relevance to
machinery in the possession of a company, physically located in its premises, and used

A   by it for the purpose of its business. Clause 4.1 refers to a power to enter upon the charged property, as if it were real property. Clause 5 refers to s. 103 'of the Act' without identifying the statute in question. Restrictions or prohibitions on the mortgage of the charged property are to be found both in cl. 3.2:1.1 and in cl. 5, in different terms. The defects in the drafting of the debenture create a number of problems in construing it. At this stage, I mention only that in my judgment an approach appropriate to a well-drafted instrument may be inappropriate in relation to this debenture: cf. *Mitsui Construction Co*

B   *Ltd v A-G of Hong Kong* (1986) 33 BLR 1, per Lord Bridge of Harwich.

Clause 1 of the debenture defined the indebtedness of Cimex to the lender to which it related. Clause 2 was as follows:

> 'The company as the beneficial owner and to the intent that the security created by this debenture shall rank as a continuing security for all of the liabilities described in cl. 1 above
>
C
> 2.1 Charges by way of fixed charge the machinery referred to in Messrs Colebrook Evans and McKenzie's letter of 12 March 1990 attached hereto
>
> 2.2 All property assets and rights of the company charged by or pursuant to any provision of this debenture are referred to below as "the charged property" . . .'

As mentioned above, Colebrook Evans and McKenzie's letter of 12 March 1990

D   identified the machinery subject to the debenture with considerable particularity. The charge created by the debenture is clearly a charge of specific assets.

Clause 3 of the debenture contained a number of covenants by Cimex with the lender. Clause 3.1 is a covenant to provide to the lender information relating to the company's affairs. Clause 3.2 is central to the issue raised by the second and the third respondents:

'3.2:1   RESTRICTIONS ON THE COMPANY

E   Not without the previous consent in writing of the lender (and then only to the extent that such consent permits and in accordance with any conditions attached to such consent[)]:

3.2:1.1   To sell, mortgage or otherwise deal with the charged property otherwise and [than] for the purpose of getting in and realising them in the ordinary course of, and for the purposes of, carrying on its trading business and:

F   3.2:1.2   To sell the whole or, except in the ordinary course of, and for the purpose of carrying on its trading business any other part of the charged property.'

Clauses 3.3 and 3.4 concerned insurance of the charged property. Clause 3.3 is as follows:

> 'To insure and keep insured such parts of the charged property as are of an insurable nature against loss or damage by fire and other usual risks and such other risks as the lender may require in the full amount of their reinstatement value

G
> . . . in such name and in such offices or at Lloyd's as the lender shall in writing approve on terms requiring the insurers not to cancel the policy without giving at least 14 days' prior notice to the company and to pay all premiums and money necessary for effecting and keeping up such insurances . . . and to have the interest of the lender noted on any such policy or policies and if required to deliver to the lender such policy or policies and the receipt (or other evidence of payment

H   satisfactory to the lender) for every premium payable in respect of such policy or policies.'

Clause 3.4 provided:

> 'To add all money received on any insurance whatsoever in respect of loss or damage to the charged property on trust for the company to be applied in making good the loss or damage in respect of which the money is received or in or towards

discharge of the sums for the time being owing under this debenture as the lender   A
may in its absolute discretion require.'

Clause 3.5 was a prohibition on the creation of other charges:

'Not without the previous consent in writing of the lender (and then only to the
extent that such consent permits and in accordance with any conditions attached
to such consent) to create or attempt to create any mortgage, pledge, charge
(whether fixed or floating) or other encumbrances on or over the whole or any part   B
of the charged property or permit any lien to arise on or to affect any part and not
(save as mentioned above) to increase or extend any liability of the company
secured on any of the above forms of security.'

Clause 3.6 required the company to perfect the security constituted by the debenture
and to do all such things as the lender might reasonably require for exercising the powers
conferred by the debenture on the lender or any receiver appointed by him.   C

The debenture contained no covenant by the company to repair the charged property.
Nonetheless, cl. 4.1 was as follows:

'If default shall at any time be made in keeping the charged property or any part
of it in such state of repair as specified above or in effecting or keeping up such
insurances as specified above or producing any such policy or policies or receipt .
. . to the lender on demand the lender may put or keep the charged property or   D
any part of it in repair (with power to enter upon the charged property for that
purpose) and/or, as the case may be, may insure . . . the charged property and all
costs incurred by the lender under this provision shall be deemed to be properly
incurred by the lender.'

Clause 5 provided:

'Section 103 of the Act shall not apply and all money secured shall be immediately   E
payable on demand at any time or times and failing payment immediately of any
money so demanded this security shall become immediately enforceable and the
power of sale conferred upon mortgagees by the Act immediately exercisable
without the restrictions contained in the Act as to the giving of notice or otherwise.'

Clause 5 continued by specifying a number of common acts of default, none of which
is relevant to the question before me. Similarly, it was not submitted that either cl. 6 or
cl. 7, headed respectively 'Effect of delay or omission by lender' and 'Waiver of terms   F
and conditions' was relevant.

It is apparent from the above recital of the provisions of the debenture that it was
neither a standard form nor, as I have already mentioned, well drafted. It would appear
to be an adaptation of a precedent for bank lending which probably created both a fixed
and a floating charge, and related to book debts (see cl. 3.2:1.1) and to real property (see
cl. 4.1). Indeed, it seems clear that the debenture is derived from the precedent for a   G
debenture to secure bank lending at p. 145 of vol. 4 of the *Encyclopaedia of Forms and
Precedents* (5th edn). It should be noted that that precedent has been altered in important
and relevant respects in the service to that volume. The original precedent was imperfectly
adapted in the drafting of the debenture in this case. I should add that the wording of the
original precedent is irrelevant to the interpretation of the debenture before me.

But for the provisions of cl. 3.2, it would not have been questioned that the debenture   H
did indeed create a fixed charge as was expressly provided by cl. 2.1. However, cl. 3.2
contains provisions relating to the sale by the company of the charged property without
the consent of the lender. It contains no provision for bringing the proceeds of sale of the
charged property into the charge. On the basis of cl. 3.2, it is submitted by Mr Henderson,
counsel for the second and third respondents, that the debenture, on its true construction,
created a floating charge. He submitted that cl. 3.2 conferred on the company liberty to

A   deal with charged assets in the ordinary course of business without the consent of the chargee, and that such a power is inconsistent with a fixed charge; or that, alternatively, the extent of that liberty, in the present case, was inconsistent with a fixed charge. Mr Gillyon, counsel for the first respondent, Mr Harvey-Bathurst, submitted that on its true construction cl. 3.2 conferred no such liberty; but that if it did, the debenture took effect as a fixed charge on the equipment specified together with a power, contained in cl. 3.2, for the company to release the whole or part of the charged property from the charge thereby created.

B

     The approach of the court to a case such as the present was not in dispute. Clause 2.1 of the debenture purported to create a fixed charge. That description of the nature of the charge created by the debenture is relevant but not decisive of the nature of the charge in fact created. If, on an examination of all of the terms of the debenture, it appears that the debenture, on its true construction, created a floating charge, the court will so determine,

C   notwithstanding the wording of cl. 2.1. Similar questions may arise where it is argued that an agreement created a licence rather than a lease, and vice versa. In the present case, it is not alleged that the debenture was in any way a sham, that is, a document the terms of which were not intended by the parties to represent their transaction. There is no claim for rectification of the debenture, although there is, at the very least, considerable doubt, for reasons indicated above, whether certain of its provisions reflect the intentions of the parties. I was referred to the helpful judgment of Staughton LJ in

D   *Welsh Development Agency v Export Finance Co Ltd* [1992] BCC 270 at p. 302A:

> 'There was here no sham, no collateral agreement or common intention to be bound by different terms, and no subsequent variation to that effect. So I can leave the external route, and turn to an internal consideration of the master agreement itself. This must be carried out on the basis that the parties intended to bound by its terms, and by nothing else.

E

> If one part of the agreement purports to create a particular legal transaction, it may happen that other provisions are inconsistent with such a transaction. The task of the court is then to ascertain which is the substance, the truth, the reality. That was plainly the approach of Lord Herschell LC in *McEntire v Crossley Brothers Ltd* [1895] AC 457 at pp. 463–466, where there are repeated references to inconsistency. See also the speech of Lord Watson at p. 467:

F

>> "The duty of a court is to examine every part of the agreement, every stipulation which it contains, and to consider their mutual bearing upon each other; but it is entirely beyond the function of a court to discard the plain meaning of any term in the agreement unless there can be found within its four corners other language and other stipulations which necessarily deprive such term of its primary significance."

G   Mr Moss argued that the court is free to disregard the label which the parties have attached to a transaction. If by label one means the description which is found on the backsheet, or even in a preamble or a recital, I can see that it should be given little if any weight. A label can also be found elsewhere. Thus in *Street v Mountford* [1985] AC 809, Mrs Mountford agreed to "take" a furnished room; the references to "licence" in the agreement were in truth labels and nothing more. "Licence" was the name by which the agreement described itself. And in *A G Securities v*

H   *Vaughan* [1990] AC 417 in the Court of Appeal at p. 444, Bingham LJ said that:

> ". . . the true legal nature of a transaction is not to be altered by the description the parties choose to give it."

     In my judgment the correct process, when one is following the internal route, is to look at the operative parts of the document, in order to discover what legal transaction they provide for. If some parts appear to be inconsistent with others in

A

this respect, a decision must be made between the two. This is what I understand by ascertaining the substance of the transaction.'

These principles of construction are applicable to the present case, although here the words 'fixed charge' in cl. 2.1 were not intended merely as a label to the transaction constituted by the debenture: they are part of an operative provision of the debenture. Having regard to cl. 2.1, and the nature of the assets charged by the debenture, I should readily hold that it created a fixed charge. However, cl. 2.1 does not stand alone, and what would appear, from cl. 2.1, to have been the intention of the parties, may have been defeated by the subsequent provisions of the debenture. In the course of argument, Mr Henderson submitted that if the debenture had stated, in cl. 2.1, that the charge created by it was a floating charge, it could have taken effect as such with no alteration to its other provisions. I agree. Conversely, however, but for cl. 3.2, there would have been no argument that the debenture created anything other than the fixed charge referred to in cl. 2.1.

B

C

I first have to determine the effect of the provisions of cl. 3.2 of the debenture. Whether that clause is inconsistent with the creation of a fixed charge must depend on the effect of cl. 3.2 itself. First, two minor points: it is, I think, common ground that cl. 3.2 must be read as if there were a bracket immediately after the word 'consent' at the end of 3.2:1 and immediately before 3.2:1.1. Secondly, the phrase 'otherwise and for the purpose of getting in and realising them' in cl. 3.2:1.1 must be read as 'otherwise than for the purpose of getting in and realising them', since otherwise cl. 3.2:1.1 makes no sense. However, even so read, as mentioned above, I do not see how the words 'otherwise than for the purpose of getting in and realising them in the ordinary course of, and for the purposes of, carrying on its trading business' can be applied to manufacturing machinery forming part of the working capital of the company. The words are 'getting in and realising' and not 'getting in or realising'. These words, as I have stated above, are appropriate to book debts; they are wholly inappropriate to the manufacturing equipment of a manufacturing company. I must seek to give all of cl. 3.2:1.1 some meaning and effect if I can: I must assume that the parties intended all of the provisions of this debenture to have some effect. However, given the inappropriateness of the words 'getting in and realising' to the subject-matter of this debenture, I find myself compelled to conclude that the words 'for the purpose of getting in and realising them' in cl. 3.2:1.1 are inapplicable to the charged property, by reason of its nature. I reach this conclusion reluctantly, but I am comforted in rejecting these words by the fact that the general standard of drafting of the debenture indicates that little care was taken in adapting it to the circumstances of the case; and indeed Mr Henderson accepted that cl. 3.2:1.1 was redundant. I therefore conclude that cl. 3.2:1.1 did not confer on the company power to deal with the charged property.

D

E

F

Regrettably, this does not conclude the questions relating to cl. 3.2:1.1. I have to determine whether the prohibition in its first two lines ('Not . . . to sell, mortgage or otherwise deal with the charged property') is effective, notwithstanding the inapplicability of the remainder of that subclause and notwithstanding the general prohibition on charging the charged property in cl. 3.5 (which partly duplicates cl. 3.2:1.1), and the reference to sale of the charged property in cl. 3.2:1.2. I cannot finally answer this question without resolving the questions of construction relating to cl. 3.2:1.2. But for cl. 3.2:1.2, I should hold that the general restriction in the first two lines of cl. 3.2:1.1 should be given effect, notwithstanding the matters referred to above, on the basis that by so doing I should be rejecting as little as possible of that subclause; and that the general restriction is consistent with the fixed charge provided for in cl. 2.1.

G

H

I turn to cl. 3.2:1.2. Read together with the introductory words of cl. 3.2:1, it is as follows:

A   'Not without the previous consent in writing of the lender (and then only to the
           extent that such consent permits and in accordance with any conditions attached
           to such consent[)]:

           3.2:1.2 To sell the whole or, except in the ordinary course of, and for the purpose
           of carrying on its trading business any other part of the charged property.'

           A number of questions arise in connection with this provision. First (and this question
B   would arise equally in relation to cl. 3.2:1.1 if the whole of it were applicable to the
           charged property), what is meant by 'its *trading* business'? Secondly, what is the meaning
           of 'any other part of the charged property', given that no 'part' (as opposed to 'the
           whole') of the charged property has previously been mentioned in the debenture? Lastly,
           what is the relationship between cl. 3.2:1.2 and cl. 3.2:1.1 and the unequivocal wording
           of cl. 2.1? All these question are, of course, interrelated.

C   I find it convenient to deal first with the second of these questions. Does the word
           'trading' add anything to 'business'? The phrase 'in the ordinary course of its business' is
           frequently to be found in debentures and other instruments. The word 'trading' was
           presumably added to qualify 'business'. The company did not trade in machinery or
           equipment. Mr Gillyon, however, submitted that 'trading' must add something to
           'business'. The 'trading business' referred to was the sale of stock, and is to be contrasted
           with the manufacturing business of the company. So interpreted, cl. 3.2:1.2 conferred no
D   relevant power on the company: the sale of capital manufacturing equipment could not
           be 'in the ordinary course of . . . its trading business'. 'Business', unqualified by 'trading',
           appears in cl. 5.4. Mr Henderson submitted that, in effect, 'trading business' included the
           whole of the manufacturing and selling activities of the company. Some meaning should,
           if possible, be given to 'trading', and if so I see no alternative to Mr Gillyon's
           construction.

E   I turn to the words 'any other part of the charged property'. Here, there are only two
           possibilities. The first, and that adopted in argument by Mr Henderson, is to read cl. 3.2:
           1.2 as if 'other' were not there. So to read cl. 3.2:1.2 does minor violence to its wording.
           However, if Mr Henderson's submission as to the meaning of 'trading business' is correct,
           it results in cl. 3.2:1.2 being read as conferring on the company a licence to sell any part
           of the charged property, no matter how substantial, and presumably ultimately the whole
F   in parts, free of the charge. Both counsel accepted that the consequence of sale within
           cl. 3.2:1.2 would be that the charge created by cl. 2.1 would cease to attach to the
           equipment sold and would not apply to its proceeds of sale or to any equipment acquired
           in substitution for it. I agree that this is what cl. 3.2:1.2, so read, would provide. Whether
           or not this consequence is consistent, as a matter of law, with the fixed charge purportedly
           created by cl. 2.1 is a question I consider below. It is, however, difficult to see the
           commercial sense of cl. 3.2:1.2 so construed, at least from the point of view of the lender.
G   So construed, the company could, without reference to him, remove the entirety of the
           charged property, or major parts of it, from the scope of the charge, leaving the lender
           wholly or partly unsecured. Nor is it easy to see why, given the nature of the charged
           property, the company should have sought such a right of sale. In addition, it is difficult
           to reconcile cl. 3.2:1.2 so construed with cl. 3.4, which purports to keep insurance moneys
           received by the company in the event of, for example, loss of part of the charged property,
           within the scope of the charge. Lastly, this reading involves a contradiction between
H   cl. 3.2:1.2 and the first two lines (i.e. from 'To sell' to 'property') of cl. 3.2:1.1.

           The alternative interpretation of cl. 3.2:1.2 gives the word 'other' full effect. On this
           reading, because of the lack of any previous reference to any part of the charged property,
           there is no 'other part of the charged property', and the words 'or . . . any other part of
           the charged property' have no application. Although such a reading may involve
           practically discarding a large part of the clause (depending on the meaning ascribed to

'trading business'), it results in a far more commercially sensible reading of the debenture   A
as a whole. It avoids any inconsistency with the fixed charge purportedly created by
cl. 2.1. It avoids any conflict between cl. 3.2:1.1 and 3.2:1.2 and is consistent with the
commercial object of cl. 3.4. In my judgment, the second interpretation of cl. 3.2:1.2 is to
be preferred. It follows that cl. 3.2 did not confer any right on the company to sell the
charged property or any part of it without the consent of the lender and there is no
reason why the charge created by the debenture should not have taken effect as a fixed
charge.   B

I appreciate that on the construction of cl. 3.2:1.2 which I have accepted, cl. 3.2 is
redundant in so far as it appears to envisage a sale, mortgage or other dealing with the
charged property. However, Mr Henderson and Mr Gillyon were in agreement that the
power to deal in cl. 3.2:1.1 is redundant and is inapplicable to the charged property. If
so, it is a smaller step than it would otherwise be to reach a similar conclusion in relation
to cl. 3.2:1.2. Mortgage of the charged property is in any event separately dealt with in   C
cl. 3.5.

In these circumstances, it is unnecessary for me to come to a concluded view on the
argument before me, based on the assumption that cl. 3.2 conferred on the company the
right to sell any part of the charged property without the consent of the lender, that the
purportedly fixed charge created by the debenture was in fact a floating charge. In
deference to that argument, however, I set out below my provisional view.   D

The primary submission of counsel for the lender is that the debenture created a fixed
charge coupled with a licence for the company to release part of the charged property
from the charge without the lender's consent. Mr Gillyon submitted that there was no
restriction in the present case on the parties' freedom to contract. They were therefore
free to create a fixed charge coupled with a licence to the company to sell the charged
property in certain circumstances. I agree that the parties had complete freedom to   E
contract. The crucial question is, however: what kind of charge did they create by their
contract? If a licence for the company to sell the charged property in the ordinary course
of its business is, as a matter of law, inconsistent with a fixed charge, they may have
chosen, perhaps unwittingly, to create a floating charge; on the other hand, if there is no
such inconsistency, they did not necessarily do so. And so the central question raised by
this submission is: is a liberty to sell in the ordinary course of business necessarily
inconsistent with a fixed charge?   F

In the present case, no question arises of the debenture applying to any future property
of the company, except possibly 'money received on any insurance' under cl. 3.4. With
this exception, the charge created by the debenture attached to present specific assets
only. It would not attach to the proceeds of sale of charged property by the company
without the consent of the lender pursuant to cl. 3.2:1.2. Counsel for the lender submitted
that it was an essential quality of a floating charge that it should be capable of attaching   G
to future assets. Counsel for the second and third respondents conceded that a floating
charge usually did relate to future, as well as to present, assets; but he submitted that a
charge over future assets was not essential to the nature of a floating charge.

Before discussing the central issues on these arguments, I can dispose of some minor
points. First, in the present case, the debenture did not apply to the whole, or possibly
even substantially the whole, of the assets of the company. This, however, would not of
itself affect the nature of the charge created: a floating charge of part of the assets of a   H
company is perfectly possible and was found to have been created in *Re Yorkshire
Woolcombers Association Ltd* [1903] 2 Ch 284 (CA) and [1904] AC 355 (HL) itself and
other cases. Secondly, unlike the precedent in the *Encyclopaedia of Forms and Precedents,*
the debenture contains no provisions for the appointment of a receiver (although a
receiver appointed by the lender is referred to in cl. 3.6). Any well-drawn floating charge

A   includes such provisions; but they are not essential to the creation of a floating charge: see *Re Bond Worth* [1980] Ch 228 and *Re Armagh Shoes Ltd* [1984] BCLC 405, where floating charges were held to have been created and there were no such provisions. Thirdly, the existence of some restrictions on the company's dealings with the charged property is not inconsistent with a floating charge: debentures creating floating charges commonly contain such restrictions, as indeed does the bank debenture in evidence in the present case; and see *Re Brightlife Ltd* (1986) 2 BCC 99,359 at p. 99, 363. Lastly, I do not

B   receive any assistance from cl. 3.3, which is in my judgment equally consistent with a fixed and a floating charge. I reject Mr Gillyon's submission that it points to a fixed charge. In particular, I do not see why a floating chargee does not have an insurable interest in the charged assets, and no authority was cited for the proposition that he does not.

     Both a fixed and a floating charge are present securities. In my judgment, the difference

C   between them relates to the nature of the interest of the lender in the charged property immediately created by the debenture before any crystallising event occurred. A fixed charge attaches to the charged property in specie either immediately or as soon as it is acquired by the chargor. The interest of a floating chargee is not specific prior to crystallisation. The floating chargee is, in effect, given a security interest in the fund of assets over which the charge is created.

D   If the crucial difference between a fixed charge and a floating charge is in the nature of the interest of the chargee prior to any event of crystallisation, it would follow that a licence for the chargor to deal to some extent with the charged assets is not necessarily inconsistent with a fixed charge. If, however, the licence to deal given to the chargor is extensive, the charge will be floating, since in these circumstances there is in effect no attachment of the charge to any specific asset: see Goode, *Legal Problems of Credit and Security*, at p. 56. The extent to which the licence to deal is compatible with a fixed charge

E   must depend on all the circumstances of the case, and in particular on the nature of the charged property. Where the charged property is stock, or book debts – i.e. where the assets are naturally fluctuating – the court will readily conclude that a liberty for the chargor to deal with the charged assets is inconsistent with a fixed charge. Where, as in the present case, the assets are specific and do not necessarily fluctuate, some liberty to release the charged assets may not be inconsistent with a fixed charge. Conversely,

F   however, on this basis a floating charge over present goods, not extending to future goods, is not a conceptual impossibility.

     If this analysis is correct, one would expect to find cases where there was a fixed charge notwithstanding that, under the instrument creating the charge, the chargor had the right to deal, to some extent, with the charged assets. *Holroyd v Marshall* (1862) 10 HL Cas 191 is such a case. It concerned a charge on machinery in a mill. The deed of charge contained a covenant by the owner that all machinery placed in the mill in addition to,

G   or in substitution for, the original machinery should be subject to the charge. It must be implicit in such a covenant that the owner may deal with the original machinery, for example by selling it, with a view to substituting new machinery. The chargor did indeed sell and exchange some of the original machinery, and introduced new machinery. The new machinery was not conveyed to the chargees or to the trustee for the chargees, and nothing was done by or on behalf of the chargee to constitute a taking of possession of the new machinery. On 2 April 1860 the chargees served the chargor with a demand for

H   payment of the amount secured by the charge. On 14 April 1860 at the instance of an unsecured creditor the sheriff executed a writ of scire facias against the chargor. The only machinery claimed by the execution creditor consisted of items purchased by the chargor after the date of the deed. On 30 April 1860, the chargees took possession of the remaining machinery. The issue in the appeal was whether the chargees had an equitable estate in the added machinery. If they did, it could not be taken in execution by the judgment

creditors. If, however, the chargees had no equitable estate in the added machinery (as A
would have been the position if the charge had been a floating charge prior to
crystallisation) the execution creditors would have been entitled to succeed. The claim of
the execution creditors failed. Lord Westbury LC said, at p. 211–212:

> '. . . immediately on the new machinery and effects being fixed or placed in the
> mill, they became subject to the operation of the contract, and passed in equity to
> the mortgagees, to whom Taylor was bound to make a legal conveyance, and for B
> whom he, in the meantime, was the trustee of the property in question.

> There is another criterion to prove that the mortgagee acquired an estate or interest
> in the added machinery as soon as it was brought into the mill. If afterwards the
> mortgagor had attempted to remove any part of such machinery, except for the
> purpose of substitution, the mortgagee would have been entitled to an injunction
> to restrain such removal, and that because of his estate in the specific property. C
> The result is, that the title of the Appellants is to be preferred to that of the
> judgment creditor.'

I therefore agree with Professor Goode, *Commercial Law*, at p. 786, footnote 3, and Dr
Gough, *Company Charges*, at p. 82, that the charge in that case was fixed not floating.
Such a power of substitution of new machinery for old was permitted by the Bills of Sale
Acts: see s. 5 and 6 of the *Bills of Sale Act (1878) Amendment Act* 1882, *Seed v Bradley*
[1894] 1 QB 319 and *Coates v Moore* [1903] 2 KB 140. In *Seed v Bradley*, Kay LJ said at D
p. 326:

> '[Section 6(2) of the 1882 Act] allows certain trade chattels which may be
> afterwards acquired to be included, not merely for the purpose of maintaining the
> security, but for the obvious reason that, unless this could be done, a manufacturer
> who had given a bill of sale could not make any alteration or improvement in his
> plant, fixtures, or machinery without lessening the security – that is, practically, E
> without the consent of the mortgagee. In the interest of trade he is to be allowed to
> do this on the terms that the security is to cover the substituted articles.'

In *Coates v Moore* the dispute was between the holder of the bill of sale and an
execution creditor. It was assumed that the holder of the bill of sale, provided it was
valid, had a good title as against the execution creditor. If the charge had been only a
floating charge, this would not have been the case. F

I accept Mr Henderson's submission that *Holroyd v Marshall* itself is authority only
for the proposition that a contract for the mortgage of future acquired property will take
effect in equity as soon as the property is acquired, provided the contract is capable of
specific performance. But it was assumed in that case that the liberty of the chargor to
substitute new machinery for old was valid and consistent with a fixed charge over the
original machinery. G

I turn to the authorities on floating charges. I was of course referred to the classic
statement of the law in *Re Yorkshire Woolcombers Association Ltd* in the Court of
Appeal, at [1903] 2 Ch 284, and in the House of Lords at [1904] AC 355. That case
concerned an assignment of the present and future book and other debts of the
mortgagor. The judgment of Romer LJ, which I note with admiration was unreserved, is
regarded as a locus classicus (at p. 295):

H

> 'I certainly do not intend to attempt to give an exact definition of the term "floating
> charge", nor am I prepared to say that there will not be a floating charge within
> the meaning of the Act, which does not contain all the three characteristics that
> I am about to mention, but I certainly think that if a charge has the three
> characteristics that I am about to mention it is a floating charge. (1.) If it is a
> charge on a class of assets of a company present and future; (2.) if that class is one

A which, in the ordinary course of the business of the company, would be changing from time to time; and (3.) if you find that by the charge it is contemplated that, until some future step is taken by or on behalf of those interested in the charge, the company may carry on its business in the ordinary way as far as concerns the particular class of assets I am dealing with.

In the present case those three characteristics do in my opinion distinguish the
B charge we have to consider. In the first place, the charge is one upon all the debts of the company present and future, not even limiting them (though I do not think it makes any difference) to the trade debts, present and future. In the second place, it obviously contemplates a class of asset which, in the ordinary course of the life of the company, must continually, and of necessity, change; and, thirdly, in the present case, if I look at the deed which created the charge here, to my mind it is clearly contemplated that until some step is taken by or on behalf of those who are
C to have the benefit of the charge, the company would be able to receive the debts due to the company in its ordinary course of business, and to deal with them for the ordinary purposes of the business.'

In the instant case, characteristics (1) and (2) are not present; (3) is, on the basis on which I now consider the matter, present at least in part. The judgments of Vaughan Williams LJ and Cozens-Hardy LJ were in somewhat different terms. Vaughan Williams
D LJ focused on the unilateral right of the mortgagor to dispose of the charged property: he regarded this as being inconsistent with a 'specific security': see p. 294. However, I consider that his judgment must be read in context. He was concerned with a charge on book debts, a constantly changing class of assets. I do not think that Vaughan Williams LJ had in mind cases like *Holroyd v Marshall*. The reasons given by Cozens-Hardy LJ were closer than those given by Romer LJ: see at p. 298.

E In the House of Lords, Lord Macnaghten said ([1904] AC 355 at p. 358):

'A specific charge, I think, is one that without more fastens on ascertained and definite property or property capable of being ascertained and defined; a floating charge, on the other hand, is ambulatory and shifting in its nature, hovering and so to speak floating with the property which it is intended to affect until some event occurs or some act is done which causes it to settle and fasten on the subject of the
F charge within its reach and grasp.'

A power on the part of the chargor in limited circumstances to release part of the charged property from the scope of a charge would not be necessarily inconsistent with a specific charge, on this definition.

In *Evans v Rival Granite Quarries Ltd* [1910] 2 KB 979, the Court of Appeal considered the nature of the interest of a mortgagee in property subject to a floating charge. The
G charge in question was not described as either fixed or floating; it was a charge of the entire undertaking of the company. It was not disputed that the security was a floating charge: the question before the court was as to the priority between the mortgagee and an execution creditor prior to crystallisation. Fletcher Moulton LJ, at p. 994, cited the passage from the speech of Lord Macnaghten referred to above, and continued:

'I think that Lord Macnaghten was here keeping in view the two characteristic
H features of floating charges – (1.) the non-permanence of the property which is the subject of the charge, and its constant change from time to time, and (2.) that a floating charge does not of itself fasten and settle even on the property existing at the moment. This explanation removes all difficulties arising from decisions which speak of a floating charge as an existing charge. It is an existing charge, and is rightly termed so, but care must be taken to remember that it has not settled down and fastened on the property which is the subject of the charge.'

Buckley LJ said, in a frequently cited passage at p. 999:   A

'The outcome of the decisions may be thus summarized. A floating security is not a future security; it is a present security, which presently affects all the assets of the company expressed to be included in it. On the other hand, it is not a specific security; the holder cannot affirm that the assets are specifically mortgaged to him. The assets are mortgaged in such a way that the mortgagor can deal with them without the concurrence of the mortgagee. A floating security is not a specific mortgage of the assets, plus a licence to the mortgagor to dispose of them in the course of his business, but is a floating mortgage applying to every item comprised in the security, but not specifically affecting any item until some event occurs or some act on the part of the mortgagee is done which causes it to crystallize into a fixed security.'

In that passage, Buckley LJ would seem to have envisaged at least the possibility of a fixed charge coupled with a licence to the mortgagor to dispose of the charged assets in the ordinary course of business. He was so understood by Davey JA in *Evans, Coleman & Evans Ltd v R A Nelson Construction Ltd* (1958) 16 DLR (2nd) 123 (a decision of the British Columbia Court of Appeal referred to by Slade J in *Siebe Gorman v Barclays Bank* [1979] 2 Ll Rep 142 at p. 159), and by Knox J in *Re New Bullas Trading Ltd* at first instance [1993] BCC 251 at p. 265. However, the contrary view was taken by Hutton J in *Re Armagh Shoes Ltd* [1984] BCC 405 at p. 415, in which it was held that a purportedly fixed charge over 'all receivables debts plant machinery fixtures fittings and ancillary equipment now or at any time hereafter belonging to the mortgagor' created a floating charge. In that case, the generality of the assets charged, the fact that they would necessarily change from time to time, and the implicit right of the company to deal with the charged assets, were inconsistent with a fixed charge.

Mr Gillyon placed reliance on *Re Alfred Priestman & Co (1929) Ltd* [1936] 2 All ER 1340. That case is authority for the proposition that a floating charge will generally be construed as applying to future property of the chargor within the description of the charged property. However, it is not authority for the proposition that a charge which does not purport to apply to future property of the chargor is necessarily a fixed charge.

In *Re Bond Worth Ltd* [1980] Ch 228, Slade J considered the effect of a title retention clause in contracts for the sale of fibre to a carpet manufacturer which processed it and wove it into carpet. He held that the title retention clause created a floating, not a fixed, charge over the fibre itself and the products manufactured from it. He said at p. 266B:

'Does the authority and freedom of Bond Worth, to which I have last referred, by itself negative the existence of a valid trust by way of equitable charge? In my judgment, in so far as it might be suggested that the clause operated to create in this manner an immediate *specific* charge, the answer to this question must be "yes". It is in my judgment quite incompatible with the existence of an effective trust by way of specific charge in equity over specific assets that the alleged trustee should be free to use them as he pleases for his own benefit in the course of his own business.

There is, however, one type of charge (and I think one type only) which, by its very nature, leaves a company at liberty to deal with the assets charged in the ordinary course of its business, without regard to the charge, until stopped by a winding up or by the appointment of a receiver or the happening of some other agreed event. I refer to what is commonly known as a "floating charge": see for example *Wheatley* v. *Silkstone and Haigh Moor Coal Co.* (1885) 29 Ch.D. 715, 724 *per* North J. and *George Barker (Transport) Ltd.* v. *Eynon* [1974] 1 W.L.R. 462, 467 *per* Edmund Davies L.J. Such a charge remains unattached to any particular property and leaves the company with a licence to deal with, and even sell, the

A   assets falling within its ambit in the ordinary course of business, as if the charge had not been given, until it is stopped by one or other of the events to which I have referred, when it is said to "crystallise"; it then becomes effectively fixed to the assets within its scope.'

That statement must be read in its context. For example, I do not think that Slade J would have regarded a specific charge over manufacturing machinery used by a manufacturing company as a legal impossibility, notwithstanding that the company

B   retained possession of the machinery and was free to use it in its business, and even notwithstanding that the company might be free to sell the machinery and substitute other machinery for it. I do not think that he had in mind cases such as *Holroyd v Marshall* which was not cited to him. he was concerned with a charge on raw material which, on the raw material being processed, transferred over to the products manufactured from it and to their proceeds of sale. He said at p. 268B:

C   'In the present case, in my judgment, the respective charges on each of the four categories of charged assets were ambulatory and shifting in their nature, and were intended to hover over them until the happening of an event which caused them to crystallise. The assets comprised in each of the four categories were of a fluctuating class, albeit in the case of the first category liable to fluctuate only by diminution. Until a crystallising event occurred, it was clearly not intended that any restriction

D   should be placed on Bond Worth to deal with them in the ordinary course of its business.'

In contrast, the charge created by the debenture in the present case was not ambulatory at all.

In *Re Hi-Fi Equipment (Cabinets) Ltd* (1987) 3 BCC 478, Harman J considered the interpretation of the words 'fixed plant and machinery' in a debenture. Cases such as *Holroyd v Marshall* were not before him. At p. 483 he said:

E   'It would be, to my mind, extremely surprising if a large fork-lift truck, which I think is undoubtedly a piece of machinery, were to be within the fixed charge upon the property of the company because, amongst other things, it would mean that the company would have no right to sell that fork-lift truck when it came to the end of its normal useful life in three or five years and replace it with another without the express consent of the mortgagee bank. Such a conclusion seems to me

F   highly improbable and I would expect normal mobile machinery of that sort to be within the floating charge but not within the fixed charge in any ordinary contemplation of a debenture of this sort.'

However, it does not follow that a charge on a fork-lift truck cannot be fixed rather than floating; and *Holroyd v Marshall* is authority for the proposition that it is as a matter of law possible for the chargor of machinery subject to a fixed charge to have the right to

G   sell it and replace it with other machinery without, so far as appears from the report, the requirement of any consent of the chargee.

Re Atlantic Computer Systems plc [1990] BCC 859 concerned charges on subleases of computer equipment. The Court of Appeal held that these were fixed, not floating charges, because they were not ambulatory and the company was not at liberty to deal with its rights under the subleases without the consent of the chargee. The decision was followed by *Vinelott* J in *Re Atlantic Medical Ltd* [1992] BCC 653. These cases were

H   concerned with charges over subleases of equipment, and I do not find them of particular assistance in the present context.

Lastly, in *Re New Bullas Trading Ltd* [1994] BCC 36, the Court of Appeal was concerned with a debenture expressed to create a fixed charge over book and other debts, requiring the company to pay the proceeds of its book debts into a designated account and, in the absence of directions by the debenture holder, for such moneys to be released

from the fixed charge and to become subject to a floating charge. At first instance, *Knox*   A
J, following *Re Brightlife Ltd* (1986) 2 BCC 99,359, held that the charge over book debts
was in law a floating charge. The Court of Appeal held that the debenture did create a
fixed charge over the book debts. This case was particularly relied upon by Mr Gillyon
in support of his proposition that the parties to a debenture are free to make such
arrangements as they wish, and that their agreement must prevail. However, as I have
already indicated, this does not enable the parties to agree to create a charge unknown to
the law, any more than the parties to an instrument concerning land are free to create a   B
lease under which the occupier is not entitled to exclusive possession. In my judgment it
was crucial to the decision in *New Bullas Trading* that the company had no liberty to deal
with the charged book debts: their proceeds had to be paid into the designated account
subject to the floating charge, in the absence of a contrary direction by the debenture
holder: see the judgment of the Court of Appeal at p. 41F.

The authorities on floating charges to which I have been referred do not lead me to   C
conclude that, in the case of a charge over specific manufacturing machinery, a liberty
for the chargor to deal to some extent with that machinery without the consent of the
chargee is necessarily inconsistent with the creation of a fixed charge. I see no reason
why, if the facts of *Holroyd v Marshall* were to recur today, in the case of a company, it
could not be held that the charge created was a fixed charge.

In the present case, on any basis the company was prohibited from creating any charge
over the secured property by virtue of cl. 3.5 of the debenture. At most, the licence   D
conferred implicitly by cl. 3.2:1.2 entitled it to sell parts of the charged machinery 'in the
ordinary course of, and for the purpose of carrying on its trading business'. If I assume
that 'trading' adds nothing to 'business', this licence is scarcely different from that of the
chargor in *Holroyd v Marshall*, except that in that case, substitute machinery had to be
brought within the scope of the charge. I do not consider that that difference is sufficient
to require me to find that the charge created by the debenture in the present case was,   E
contrary to its description, and notwithstanding that only specific assets were charged, a
floating charge. The difference relates to the commercial sense of the transaction from
the point of view of the chargee, rather than the legal classification of the charge created.
In this connection, I must say that I should be reluctant to be compelled to conclude, in
the case of a charge on specific manufacturing equipment of a manufacturing company,
that the unequivocal words of cl. 2.1, explicitly referring to a fixed charge, could be
overridden by what is in the present debenture a highly ambiguous and uncertain   F
provision for sale in cl. 3.2.

It follows that if I had concluded that cl. 3.2:1.2 of the debenture had conferred a
licence on the company without the subsequent consent of the chargee to sell parts of the
specific manufacturing machinery constituting the charged property 'in the ordinary
course of, and for the purpose of carrying on its business', I should nonetheless have
found that the charge created was a fixed charge.

It does not, however, follow that a charge created by a debenture in the form of the   G
precedent at p. 145 of vol. 4 of the *Encyclopaedia of Forms and Precedents* (5th edn)
(unaltered by the service to that volume), would necessarily create a fixed charge over the
classes of assets referred to in cl. 2.1, 2.2, 2.3, 2.4 and 2.5 of the precedent. The charge
created by such a debenture would be ambulatory in the full sense of the expression. The
scope of the charge in the present case is very different. It certainly should not be assumed
that if I had had before me a charge in the form of that precedent, covering existing and   H
future assets of the company, and fluctuating classes of assets, the decision would have
been the same.

In the result, I determine that on the true construction of the debenture the charge over
plant and machinery created by cl. 2 thereof was, as created, a fixed charge.

(Order accordingly)

Hamilton & Anor v Naviede & Anor.
Re Arrows Ltd (No. 4).
House of Lords.
Lord Keith of Kinkel, Lord Jauncey of Tullichettle, Lord Browne-Wilkinson,
Lord Lloyd of Berwick and Lord Nolan.
B Judgment delivered 25 July 1994.

*Insolvency – Private examination – Whether liquidators should supply transcripts
of private examination to Serious Fraud Office – Judge ordered disclosure subject
to restrictions on use of transcripts as evidence – Appeal – Insolvency Act 1986,
s. 236, 433; Criminal Justice Act 1987, s. 2(3), (8); Insolvency Rules 1986
(SI 1986/1925), r. 9.5.*

C This was an appeal against the Court of Appeal's reversal of Vinelott J's decision that
the Serious Fraud Office's access to transcripts of the examination of 'N' under s. 236 of
the Insolvency Act 1986 should be restricted by undertakings not to use the transcripts in
evidence against N save in the circumstances specified in s. 2(8) of the Criminal Justice Act
1987.

N was concerned with the running of a company. When it collapsed, he was examined by
the liquidators under s. 236 of the Insolvency Act 1986. Acting under powers conferred by
D s. 2(3) of the Criminal Justice Act 1987, the Serious Fraud Office ('SFO') required the
liquidators to produce those transcripts with a view to the SFO using them as evidence in
criminal proceedings against N. The liquidators applied to the Companies Court for
directions and the judge ordered that transcripts should not be handed over to the SFO
except upon an undertaking not to use the transcripts in evidence in the criminal proceedings:
see [1992] BCC 987. The judge's decision was reversed by the Court of Appeal [1993] BCC
E 473. N appealed.

Two issues arose on the appeal: (1) did Vinelott J have any discretion to refuse to permit
the liquidators to hand over the transcripts save upon the SFO giving the undertaking
required by the judge; (2) if so, did the judge exercise his discretion in accordance with the
right principles.

Held, dismissing N's appeal:

F 1. Subject to limited exceptions s. 3(3) of the 1987 Act expressly overrode any duty of
confidence imposed by or under any statute other than the Taxes Management Act 1970.
Similarly, the fact that the 1987 Act expressly preserved two specific duties of confidence
(legal professional privilege and banking confidence) showed that all other common law
duties of confidence were overridden. Therefore even if N could demonstrate a private law
duty of confidence owed by the liquidators to him, such duty would provide no excuse to the
liquidators for a failure to comply with a notice under s. 2(3).

G 2. Section 3(3) overrode statutory obligations of secrecy expressly imposed by statute: it
did not override obligations arising under the general law on the grounds of policy, e.g.
national security.

3. The rights (if any) of the SFO to obtain the liquidator's records of informal answers
given under s. 235 were not to be equated with its right to obtain records of formal
examination under s. 236. N's case was concerned only with the record of an examination
H under s. 236; no view was expressed on records of information obtained under s. 235 beyond
saying that the public interest in ensuring the free flow of such informally obtained
information was much greater than it was in relation to transcripts of s. 236 examinations.

4. The statutory framework imposed a wide range of duties on liquidators to report,
directly or indirectly, to the DTI and prosecuting authorities cases of suspected criminal and
dishonest conduct and to furnish them with all documents and information they required.

Such documents included transcripts of evidence given on a s. 236 examination, which A
evidence was admissible in evidence. The liquidator could not be under any duty of
confidence which would prevent the performance of those statutory duties. Therefore
liquidators could not in any event give any assurance to a person examined under s. 236 that
his answers would not be disclosed to prosecuting authorities. In the absence of such
assurance there could not be any maintainable claim that such answers enjoyed public
interest immunity on the grounds either of the public interest in preserving confidentiality or
the public interest in giving an assurance to witnesses that their information would be B
confidential.

5. Rule 9.5(4) conferred on the court a discretion to decide who could inspect the records
of the s. 236 examination. This was not mere machinery. The extraction of private and
confidential information under compulsion from a witness otherwise than in the course of
inter partes litigation was an exorbitant power. Such information should not be generally
available but should be used only for the purposes for which the power was conferred. C
Although there were severe limitations on the way in which such discretion could be exercised
where prosecuting authorities were involved, no doubt should be cast on the discretion of the
court to decide who should have access to such information.

6. Insolvency was a process conducted by, or under the control of, the court acting
through its officers, the liquidators. Documents held by liquidators were held by them to the
order of the court. The 1987 Act did not override the powers of the court to control the use D
of property under the administration of the court, including documents. If the court, acting
properly under a discretion, directed its officers not to produce documents, that would
provide a reasonable excuse to those officers for failure to do so.

7. It was not for the Companies Court judge to exercise any discretion so as to prevent
the prosecuting authorities (including the SFO) from obtaining and leading in evidence the
transcripts of the s. 236 examination. He should not himself have sought to limit the use of
the transcripts but should have left the matter to be decided by the judge at the criminal E
trial. (Rank Film Distributors Ltd & Ors v Video Information Centre & Ors [1982] AC 380
applied.)

8. The judge at the criminal trial would know all the facts both as to the means whereby
the documents were obtained and their significance or impact in the criminal proceedings.
He would have a discretion to refuse to allow the prosecution to rely on the transcripts under
s. 78(1) of the Police and Criminal Evidence Act 1984. There was no satisfactory answer to F
the question why Parliament, having taken care to include the s. 2(8) protection to witnesses
required to answer in response to a s. 2(2) notice did not provide similar protection against
the use of self-incriminatory answers given in other investigations to which the privilege did
not attach. It was an unexplained anomaly which the judge of the criminal trial could take
into account in exercising his powers under s. 78.

The following cases were referred to in the speeches: G

A & Ors v B Bank (Bank of England intervening) [1993] QB 311.
Arrows Ltd, Re (No. 2) [1992] BCC 125, [1992] Ch 545; [1992] BCC 446.
AT & T Istel Ltd & Anor v Tully & Anor [1992] QB 315 (CA); [1993] AC 45 (HL).
Bank of England v Riley & Anor [1992] Ch 475.
Barlow Clowes (Gilt Managers) Ltd, Re [1991] BCC 608; [1992] Ch 208.
Bishopsgate Investment Management Ltd, Re [1992] BCC 222; [1993] Ch 1.   H
Conway v Rimmer & Anor [1968] AC 910.
Crompton (Alfred) Amusement Machines Ltd v C & E Commrs (No. 2) [1974] AC 405.
Esal (Commodities) Ltd, Re (No. 2) [1990] BCC 708.
Funke, Cremieux and Miailhe v France (82/1991/334/407, ECHR).
London United Investments plc, Re [1992] BCC 202; [1992] Ch 578.
Marcel & Ors v Commissioner of Police of the Metropolis & Ors [1992] Ch 225.

A   *Norton Warburg Holdings Ltd, Re; Re Norton Warburg Investment Management Ltd* (1983) 1 BCC 98,907.

Orkem v Commission of the European Communities (Case 374/87) [1991] 2 CEC 19; [1989] ECR 3283.

Otto BV v Postbank NV (Case C-60/92) (10 November 1993, not yet reported).

R v Director of the Serious Fraud Office, ex parte Smith [1993] AC 1.

B   *R v Gray & Ors* (unreported, 18 May 1992, Judge Laughland QC).

R v Saunders (unreported, 29 January 1990, Henry J).

Rank Film Distributors Ltd & Ors v Video Information Centre & Ors [1982] AC 380.

Sociedade Nacional de Combustiveis de Angola UEE & Ors v Lundqvist & Ors [1991] 2 QB 310.

Tate Access Floors Inc & Anor v Boswell & Ors [1991] Ch 512.

C   Gavin Lightman QC and Matthew Collings (instructed by Burton Copeland, Manchester) for Mr Naviede.

John Jarvis QC and Ewan McQuater (instructed by Lovell White Durrant) for the liquidators.

Roger Kaye QC and Richard Ritchie (instructed by the Treasury Solicitor) for the Director of the Serious Fraud Office.

D   AWH Charles (instructed by the Treasury Solicitor) for the Secretary of State for Trade and Industry.

SPEECHES

Lord Keith of Kinkel: For the reasons given in the speech to be delivered by Lord Browne-Wilkinson, which I have read in draft and with which I agree, I would dismiss this appeal.

E   **Lord Jauncey of Tullichettle:** For the reasons given in the speech to be delivered by Lord Browne-Wilkinson, which I have read in draft and with which I agree, I too would dismiss this appeal.

Lord Browne-Wilkinson: This is yet another case in which the courts have had to grapple with the impact of statutory provisions on the privilege of an individual not to be required to incriminate himself.

F   Shortly stated the position is as follows. The appellant was concerned with the running of a company. When it collapsed, he was examined by the liquidators under s. 236 of the *Insolvency Act* 1986 ('IA 1986'). There are transcripts of that examination. Acting under powers conferred by s. 2(3) of the *Criminal Justice Act* 1987 ('CJA'), the Serious Fraud Office ('SFO') required the liquidators to produce those transcripts with a view to the SFO using them as evidence in criminal proceedings against the appellant. The liquidators applied to the Companies Court for directions and the judge ordered that

G   transcripts should not be handed over to the SFO except upon an undertaking not to use the transcripts in evidence in the criminal proceedings: see [1992] BCC 987. The question is whether the judge (whose decision was reversed by the Court of Appeal [1993] BCC 473) was entitled to impose such undertaking precluding the use of the appellant's answers as evidence in the pending criminal trial.

H   **The statutory provisions**

(1) *Insolvency*

When a company becomes insolvent, the liquidators or administrators need to obtain information as to the company's affairs for the purposes of the winding up or administration of the company. IA 1986 provides two procedures for this purpose, one informal, the other formal.

Section 235 of IA 1986 imposes on a wide class (consisting of all those who have been   A
concerned with the running of the company) a duty to give to the liquidators:

> '(2)(a) ... such information concerning the company and its promotion, formation, business, dealings, affairs or property as the office-holder may at any time after the effective date reasonably require . . .'

Failure to comply with that obligation is punishable by a fine under s. 235(5) of IA 1986
and r. 7.20(1)(c) of the *Insolvency Rules* 1986 (SI 1986/1925).   B

The second procedure is under s. 236 which is the material section in the present case.
It is more formal. The court, on the application of the liquidator, can summon to appear
before it:

> '(2)(c) any person whom the court thinks capable of giving information concerning the promotion, formation, business, dealings, affairs or property of the company.'   C

An examination under s. 236 takes place before a registrar or judge, both the
liquidators and the respondents being entitled to be represented by solicitors and counsel.
Under r. 9.4(6) of the Insolvency Rules a record of the examination, usually a transcript,
must be made. A statement made by the respondent in the course of a s. 236 examination
may be used as evidence against him in any proceedings whether or not under the
Insolvency Act: IA 1986, s. 433; IR 1986, r. 9.4(7).   D

Rule 9.5 of the Insolvency Rules lays down a special procedure regulating the custody
of transcripts and affidavits obtained under the s. 236 procedure. They are not to go on
the court file and, unless the court so orders, are not available for inspection by anyone
other than the liquidators or other persons who could have applied for an order under
s. 236. Rule 9.5(4) provides:

> 'The court may from time to time give directions as to the custody and inspection   E
> of any documents to which this Rule applies, and as to the furnishing of copies of,
> or extracts from, such documents.'

Until recently, it was thought that a person examined under s. 236 could refuse to
answer self-incriminatory questions. However in *Re Bishopsgate Investment Management
Ltd* [1992] BCC 222 the Court of Appeal held that the statutory provisions of IA 1986
impliedly overrode the privilege against self-incrimination. Leave to appeal to your   F
Lordships' House in *Bishopsgate* was refused. On this appeal, no attempt has been made
to persuade your Lordships to overrule it.

In sum, therefore, a person examined under s. 236 can be compelled to give self-
incriminating answers which are admissible against him in criminal proceedings.
However, the record of his answers is not available to outsiders without an order of the
court under r. 9.5(4) of the Insolvency Rules.   G

(2) *The Serious Fraud Office*

The CJA conferred on the director of the SFO special powers to assist him in the
investigation and prosecution of serious fraud. When the director has launched an
investigation under s. 1, s. 2 confers on him two exceptional powers, one to put questions,
the other to obtain documents.

The inquisitorial power is contained in s. 2(2) which provides: H

> 'The Director may by notice in writing require the person whose affairs are to be
> investigated ("the person under investigation") or any other person whom he has
> reason to believe has relevant information to answer questions or otherwise furnish
> information with respect to any matter relevant to the investigation at a specified
> place and either at a specified time or forthwith.'

A   This House has recently decided in *R v Director of Serious Fraud Office, ex parte Smith* [1993] AC 1 that the privilege against self-incrimination has been impliedly overridden by the CJA. Therefore a person required to answer questions by a subs. (2) notice is bound to answer the questions put to him by the SFO even if by so doing he may incriminate himself. Failure to do so gives rise to criminal sanctions including imprisonment: s. 2(13). However, s. 2(8) provides the person interrogated with a valuable safeguard which, to a substantial extent, protects him against the consequences of giving

B self-incriminating answers. It provides:

> 'A statement by a person in response to a requirement imposed by virtue of this section may only be used in evidence against him–
>
> (a) on a prosecution for an offence under subsection (14) below; or
>
> (b) on a prosecution for some other offence where in giving evidence he makes

C   a statement inconsistent with it.'

Proceedings under subs. (14) are irrelevant in the present case. Therefore the section effectively prevents the answers being used by the prosecution unless, at the criminal trial, the accused elects to give evidence. The protection afforded by this subsection in relation to answers given in response to a subs. (2) notice lies at the heart of this case.

The special power to obtain documents is conferred on the SFO by s. 2(3) which

D provides:

> 'The Director may by notice in writing require the person under investigation or any other person to produce ... any specified documents which appear to the Director to relate to any matter relevant to the investigation or any documents of a specified description which appear to him so to relate; and–
>
> (a) if any such documents are produced, the Director may–

E
>
> (i) take copies or extracts from them;
>
> (ii) require the person producing them to provide an explanation of any of them;
>
> (b) ...'

Failure to comply with a notice served under subs. (3) 'without reasonable excuse' is a

F criminal offence punishable with imprisonment (s. 2(13)). In the present case, the SFO acting under subs. (3) has demanded from liquidators production of the transcripts of an examination of the appellant under s. 236 of IA 1986.

The protection afforded by s. 2(8) does not apply to documents obtained under s. 2(3): the liquidators are not required to make a 'statement' and the appellant's statements contained in the transcripts were not made 'in response to a requirement imposed by

G virtue of this section' but in response to a requirement under s. 236 of IA 1986. There is no other provision in the CJA restricting the use that may be made by the SFO of documents obtained by use of a subs. (3) notice.

(3) The combined effect of the statutory provisions

Unless the court has some discretion to restrict the use to which s. 236 transcripts can

H be put, the result of these statutory provisions, read together, is this. Self-incriminating answers given by the appellant in the course of the s. 236 examination (which he could not refuse to give) will be obtained by the SFO and will be admissible in evidence against him in criminal proceedings. Whereas, if the SFO had itself asked the same questions acting under the inquisitorial procedure laid down by s. 2(2) of the CJA, the appellant's answers to such questions would not have been admissible against him in criminal proceedings.

The privilege against self-incrimination

A

One of the basic freedoms secured by English law is that (subject to any statutory provisions to the contrary) no one can be forced to answer questions or produce documents which may incriminate him in subsequent criminal proceedings. The principle evolved from the abhorrence felt for the procedures of the Star Chamber under which the prisoner was forced, by the use of torture, to answer self-incriminating questions on the basis of which he was subsequently convicted. Although physical torture is a thing of the past, the principle remains firmly embedded in our law: a witness can refuse to answer self-incriminating questions without punishment and a judge in civil proceedings customarily warns a witness that he need not answer such questions. Similarly, the privilege entitles a party to civil litigation to refuse to give discovery of documents which may incriminate him: *Rank Film Distributors Ltd v Video Information Centre* [1982] AC 380; *AT & T Istel Ltd v Tully* [1993] AC 45. As Lord Wilberforce said in the *Rank* case (at p. 442C) the principle 'has been too long established in our law as a basic liberty of the subject – in other countries it has constitutional status – to be denied'.

B

C

The principle has been carried over into the jurisprudence of all common law countries, including the US. It is one of the basic rights protected by the European Convention on Human Rights. In *Funke, Cremieux and Miailhe v France* (82/1991/334/407), art. 6 of the convention was held to render unlawful a demand to produce self-incriminating documents. Similarly in *Orkem v Commission of the European Communities* (Case 374/ 87) [1991] 2 CEC 19; [1989] ECR 3283 at p. 3350 the European Court of Justice held that under the law of the European Union an individual could not be compelled to give incriminating answers to the Commission since to do so would infringe 'the general principles of Community law, of which fundamental rights form an integral part . . .': compare *Otto BV v Postbank NV* (Case C-60/92, 10 November 1993, not yet reported).

D

The inevitable effect of a witness in civil proceedings claiming the privilege against self-incrimination is to deprive the opposite party and the court of evidence relevant to the dispute under consideration. Until recently, this has not given rise to much litigation. But the recent upsurge of financial fraud, particularly in relation to companies, has raised in an acute form the conflict between the witness's basic right to rely on the privilege on the one hand and the public interest in successfully pursuing and recovering the fruits of such fraud.

E

Thus in relation to claims for Mareva injunctions and Anton Piller orders, the defendant relies on the privilege to refuse disclosure or discovery of documents which would enable the assets to be traced. He is entitled to claim the privilege: see the *Rank* case [1982] AC 380, *Sociedade Nacional de Combustiveis de Angola UEE v Lundqvist* [1991] 2 QB 310, *Tate Access Floors Inc v Boswell* [1991] Ch 512; *AT & T Istel Ltd v Tully* [1993] AC 45. The serious consequences flowing from a successful claim to the privilege has led Parliament in certain cases to override the privilege but to substitute an alternative protection. Thus under s. 31 of the *Theft Act* 1968 the privilege cannot be claimed in civil proceedings on the grounds that it might incriminate the witness of an offence under that Act; the witness is bound to answer but the answers given cannot be used in evidence against him in subsequent criminal proceedings. This is also the method adopted by Parliament in relation to answers given in response to a notice under s. 2(2) of the CJA.

F

G

However, in other cases Parliament has not expressly provided whether or not the privilege is overridden by the statutory powers. The primary purpose of an inspection under s. 432 of the *Companies Act* 1985, or an examination by liquidators under s. 236 of IA 1986 is to enable the true facts to be elicited from those who know them. Frequently it is suspected fraud which has given rise to the investigation or examination. If witnesses in such proceedings were able to rely on the privilege against self-incrimination, the whole investigation could be frustrated by a refusal to answer sensitive questions. Although the

H

A   statutes establishing such inquisitorial rights for the purpose of discovering the true facts about the conduct of a company are silent on the question whether the privilege is to apply, the courts have been ready in recent years to hold that Parliament has impliedly overridden the ancient privilege against self-incrimination. Thus recently it has been held that a witness cannot rely on the privilege so as to refuse to answer questions put by inspectors under the Companies Act: *Re London United Investments plc* [1992] BCC 202 or by liquidators on an examination under s. 236 of IA 1986: see *Bishopsgate Investment*
B   *Management Ltd* [1992] BCC 222.

This recent erosion of the privilege against self-incrimination in the interests of aiding the tracing and recovery of property extracted from companies by fraud is taken one stage further in this case. The SFO is seeking to obtain answers given in the course of investigations initiated for the purpose of safeguarding the company's property (and for that purpose deprived of the privilege against self-incrimination) for use in evidence in a
C   criminal prosecution. The question is whether the statutory machinery permits this further erosion to take place.

The facts

The appellant, Mr Naviede, was a director and principal shareholder of Arrows Ltd ('the company'). In September 1990 the SFO began an investigation into the affairs of
D   the company. Between then and 15 August 1991 the director of the SFO served on Mr Naviede seven notices pursuant to s. 2(2) of the CJA requiring Mr Naviede to answer certain questions. On 8 August 1991 Mr Naviede was arrested and charged with offences of obtaining money by deception. His criminal trial is pending.

In the meantime, on 30 July 1991 the respondents, Mr Hamilton and Mr Martin, were appointed provisional liquidators of the company: they became the liquidators when the
E   company was compulsorily wound up on 13 December 1991. On 29 October 1991, Hoffmann J made an order for the examination of Mr Naviede pursuant to s. 236: *Re Arrows Ltd (No. 2)* [1992] BCC 125. At that date it was still thought that a person examined under s. 236 was entitled to refuse to answer questions which might incriminate him. With a view to discouraging Mr Naviede from relying on the privilege the order of Hoffmann J by a proviso directed that the transcript of evidence obtained by the
F   liquidators should not be disclosed to the SFO. Subsequently, the Court of Appeal decided the *Bishopsgate* case [1992] BCC 222 and for the first time held that a person examined under s. 236 could not rely on the privilege against self-incrimination. An appeal by the director of the SFO against the decision of Hoffmann J was accordingly allowed by consent: the proviso to the order was deleted but without prejudice to the right of Mr Naviede to apply to set aside the original order for his examination under s. 236. Mr Naviede made such an application but it was rejected by Vinelott J (*Re Arrows*
G   *Ltd (No. 2)* [1992] BCC 446) whose decision was upheld by the Court of Appeal (unreported).

Mr Naviede's examination under s. 236 started on 1 July 1992 before Millett J. The examination related to the same matters as formed the subject-matter of the criminal charges. At the start of the first day, Millett J directed that in the event of the director of the SFO giving the liquidators notice of an intention to serve a notice under s. 2 of the
H   CJA relating to the transcripts of the examination, the liquidators:

'do within 48 hours apply to the High Court for directions or determination as to whether and if so how they should deal with such transcripts and respond to the Serious Fraud Office or to such notice.'

–and that they should not comply with any such notice until after the determination by the court of such application.

On 15 September 1992, the SFO requested from the liquidators copies of the s. 236   A
transcripts, it being clear that in the event of a refusal a formal notice would be served
under s. 2(3) of the CJA. Pursuant to the order of Millett J the liquidators applied to the
Companies Court for directions how they should deal with the request. Mr Naviede and
the SFO were respondents to that application. It came before Vinelott J (*Re Arrows Ltd
(No. 4)* [1992] BCC 987) who held that he had a discretion under r. 9.5(4) of the
Insolvency Rules whether or not to allow the SFO to receive copies of the transcripts. In
the exercise of that discretion the judge refused to make such an order unless the director   B
of the SFO undertook not to use the transcripts in evidence against Mr Naviede save in
the circumstances specified in s. 2(8) of the CJA and to procure a similar undertaking
from any party to whom the director supplied the transcripts. The director gave such
undertaking under protest, on the footing that he would appeal against its extraction.
Copies of the transcripts were then handed over to the SFO.

On appeal the Court of Appeal (Dillon, Steyn and Rose L JJ) unanimously reversed   C
the judge's decision and released the director of the SFO from his undertaking ([1993]
BCC 473). In general terms the Court of Appeal held that the Companies Court judge
had no discretion whether or not to permit the SFO to have copies of the transcripts and
that, in any event, Vinelott J had exercised his discretion on the wrong principles. Mr
Naviede appeals to your Lordships' House.

The issues   D

Mr Lightman QC, for Mr Naviede, accepted that the transcripts of the s. 236
examination were 'documents' within the meaning of s. 2(3) and (18) of the CJA.
Accordingly, he accepted that the director could validly serve a notice on the liquidators
requiring production of the transcripts. It follows that the liquidators were bound to
produce the transcripts to the SFO unconditionally unless first there is a court order
restricting such production and, second, such order provides a 'reasonable excuse' for   E
the failure to comply with such a notice within the meaning of s. 2(13) of the CJA.

The following issues therefore arise on the appeal:

(1)   did Vinelott J have any discretion to refuse to permit the liquidators to hand over
       the transcripts save upon the director giving the undertaking required by the judge;

(2)   if so, did the judge exercise his discretion in accordance with the right principles.   F

(1) *Did the judge have a discretion?*

Mr Lightman submitted that the judge had a discretion whether or not to order the
handing over of the transcripts on three different grounds which I will consider in turn.

(a) A private law right to confidentiality

Mr Lightman submitted that where information is extracted from an individual under   G
statutory powers such information can only be used for the purposes for which those
powers were conferred. The person who so obtains the information owes a private law
duty of confidentiality not to disclose such information to others: *Marcel v Commissioner
of Police of the Metropolis* [1992] Ch 225. He accepts that, like any other duty of
confidentiality, this duty is not absolute but the court has a discretion to override it in the
public interest: *Marcel*.

In my view there are many reasons why this argument must fail. It is not necessary to   H
consider them all since, on any footing, there is one short and decisive answer. Subject to
limited exceptions the CJA expressly overrides any duty of confidence 'imposed by or
under' any statute other than the Taxes Management Act 1970: CJA, s. 3(3). Similarly,
the fact that s. 2(9) and (10) of the CJA expressly preserves two specific duties of
confidence (legal professional privilege and banking confidence) shows that all other

A   common law duties of confidence are overridden. Therefore even if Mr Lightman could demonstrate a private law duty of confidence owed by the liquidators to Mr Naviede, such duty would provide no excuse to the liquidators for their failure to comply with a notice under s. 2(3).

(b) Public interest immunity

B   Mr Lightman submitted that public interest immunity attached to the transcripts and that accordingly the judge had a discretion to decide whether, in the present case, such immunity was overridden by the public interest in insuring that all admissible evidence should be available in the criminal proceedings. Mr Charles (who with leave intervened on behalf of the Department of Trade and Industry) supported Mr Lightman in his contention that there was a discretion: however, Mr Charles contended that the proper exercise of such discretion in this case required the handing over of the documents. Mr
C   Lightman was also supported by Mr Jarvis for the liquidators.

The claim to public interest immunity was advanced on two separate, but related grounds. First it was submitted that even though Mr Naviede's own private law right to the confidentiality of information extracted from him under statutory powers is overridden by the CJA, there is a wider public interest in ensuring that information so extracted is only used for the purposes for which the statutory power was conferred:
D   *Conway v Rimmer* [1968] AC 910 at p. 946; *Alfred Crompton Amusement Machines Ltd v C & E Commrs (No. 2)* [1974] AC 405. So it was submitted, Mr Naviede's answers in the transcripts, having been extracted under the compulsion of an order under s. 236 of IA 1986, could only be used for the purposes of the liquidation. Secondly, it was submitted that there is a public interest in ensuring that those from whom liquidators and other officeholders seek essential information as to the company's affairs can be assured that what they say will not be communicated to others; in the absence of such confidentiality
E   the free and speedy flow of essential information will be impeded and the proper winding up of the company's affairs (including the recovery from wrongdoers of its property) rendered more difficult or impossible.

In the Court of Appeal, Dillon LJ [1992] BCC 473 at pp. 478–480 held that some confidentiality did attach to answers obtained under a s. 236 examination but that such public interest in confidentiality did not outweigh the right of prosecutors to use such
F   answers in criminal proceedings. As to the immunity based on providing reassurance to those giving information to liquidators, he held (p. 483A) that the court had 'no relevant discretion'. The other statutory provisions envisaged so many lawful leakages of information obtained by liquidators that those giving the information to the liquidators could not properly have or be given any assurance of confidentiality. Steyn LJ held that the court had no discretion.

G   Mr Kaye, for the SFO, submitted that the court had no discretion in the matter. First, he submitted that s. 3(3) of the CJA overrides any public interest immunity based on confidentiality of information obtained under statutory powers. Second, adopting and developing the reasoning of the Court of Appeal, he submitted that the statutory provisions authorising or requiring the disclosure of information obtained under s. 235 or 236 were such that there could be no relevant confidentiality and that accordingly no witness could feel any reassurance that any information he gives will not be disclosed to
H   others.

As to Mr Kaye's first argument based on s. 3(3) of the CJA, I reject it. The subsection provides as follows:

> 'Where any information is subject to an obligation of secrecy *imposed by or under any enactment* other than an enactment contained in the Taxes Management Act 1970, the obligation shall not have effect to prohibit the disclosure of that

information to any person in his capacity as a member of the Serious Fraud Office   A
. . .' (emphasis added)

If Mr Kaye's argument is correct it would mean that even the clearest public interest immunity was automatically overridden if the information had been obtained under statutory powers. Say, for example, that the security services had obtained highly sensitive information as a result of the tapping of a telephone. If Mr Kaye's argument is correct, the security services could not refuse to hand over to the SFO any record of that   B information even though to do so might jeopardise national security. Wide as are the powers of the SFO, I cannot accept that Parliament intended any such result. Section 3(3) overrides statutory obligations of secrecy *expressly* imposed by the statute: it does not override obligations arising under the general law on the grounds of policy. I agree with Hoffmann J in *Re Arrows Ltd (No. 2)* [1992] BCC 125 at p. 129B:

> 'Section 3(3) deals with statutory obligations of secrecy but not, in my judgment,   C the heads of public policy which may justify non-disclosure. When one considers the various heads of policy, such as national security, diplomatic relations and the administration of central government, which have been held to justify non-disclosure even for the purposes of justice, I find it impossible to suppose that the only public interest which Parliament thought capable of taking precedence over the investigation of fraud was the efficient collection of the revenue. The reason, in   D my judgment, why s. 3(3) overrides most statutory obligations of secrecy is that these are expressed in absolute terms, or at any rate in terms which permit no exception for the needs of the SFO. But the doctrine of public policy, which may well underlie some of the statutory provisions, permits a balance to be struck between the public interest in preserving secrecy and the public interest in the investigation of fraud. There was no reason why these heads of public policy should have to be excluded from the concept of 'reasonable excuse' and in my judgment   E s. 3(3) does not have this effect.'

For these reasons I reject Mr Kaye's first argument under this head.

Before dealing with Mr Kaye's second argument (as to the reassurance of persons giving information to liquidators) I must draw a distinction between information obtained by liquidators under s. 235 and that obtained under a s. 236 examination. The   F evidence in this and earlier cases shows that all the leading insolvency practitioners attach much greater importance to the confidentiality of information obtained under s. 235 than they do to information obtained under a formal examination under s. 236. The reason is obvious. When a liquidator or other 'office-holder' (see IA 1986, s. 234(1)) is appointed he normally has little information about the affairs of the company and, in cases of suspected fraud, the documentation is frequently deficient or unreliable. He is therefore largely dependent on information obtained from those who have been concerned with   G the running of the company. For the purpose of protecting the company's assets (including the recovery of its assets which have been plundered by the fraud) he needs to obtain speedy and reliable information from those who have been concerned with the company. They will include not only those centrally involved with the alleged fraud but also those in an equivocal position (who may feel themselves at risk) and those apparently not implicated in any wrongdoing. Ultimately the liquidator's right to require such   H informal provision of information depends on the duty imposed on such person by s. 235 to give him the necessary information. Therefore if, as he will, the liquidator keeps records of what he is told and if the SFO is entitled to obtain such records of informal unprepared statements by means of a notice under s. 2(3) of the CJA, the insolvency practitioners say, and I agree, there will be a severe impairment of their ability to obtain the necessary information. It can be argued (although I express no view on the point)

A   that such information informally asked for and recorded is provided 'in pursuance of a requirement imposed by' IA 1986 and is therefore admissible in evidence under s. 433.

Quite different considerations apply to information obtained under s. 236. The evidence shows that liquidators do not normally have recourse to the formal procedures under s. 236 unless a witness has proved unco-operative. The examination takes place before a judge or registrar. The witness is entitled to legal representation. He is entitled

B   to advance notice in general terms of the topics on which he is to be examined: *Re Norton Warburg Holdings Ltd* (1983) 1 BCC 98,907; *Re Arrows Ltd (No. 2)* [1992] BCC 446. The record of such examinations is not part of the liquidator's private records but is subjected to special statutory provisions relating to its custody and release.

I am therefore not prepared as were the Court of Appeal to equate the rights (if any) of the SFO to obtain the liquidator's records of informal answers given under s. 235 with its right to obtain records of formal examination under s. 236. This case is concerned

C   only with the record of an examination under s. 236; I express no views on records of information obtained under s. 235 beyond saying that the public interest in ensuring the free flow of such informally obtained information is much greater than it is in relation to transcripts of s. 236 examinations.

I turn therefore to consider Mr Kaye's second argument in relation to records of s. 236 examinations. He submits that there can be no relevant duty of confidence in relation to

D   information obtained under the statutory powers if there are statutory provisions permitting the wide disclosure of such information. He submits that the machinery laid down by IA 1986 requires such wide disclosure. Therefore, since the liquidator is bound to disclose information obtained to others, he cannot either expressly or implicitly give any assurance of confidentiality to the person examined under s. 236. Therefore the public interest relied on (the free flow of information based on an assurance of confidentiality) does not exist.

E   The fundamental question is the extent of the duty of confidentiality owed by liquidators to persons who are examined under s. 236. In *Re Esal (Commodities) Ltd (No. 2)* [1990] BCC 708 at p. 723H Millett J said:

'. . . where leave is sought to make use of material obtained by the use or under the threat of s. [236] proceedings, then, save in exceptional circumstances, leave should be granted only if the use proposed to be made is within the purpose of the

F   statutory procedure, that is to say, that the use proposed to be made of the material is to assist the beneficial winding up of the company.'

He reaffirmed this view in *Re Barlow Clowes (Gilt Managers) Ltd* [1991] BCC 608 at p. 614. In the present case, Dillon LJ at p. 481 and Steyn LJ at p. 487 considered these remarks were too wide. I agree. Although the primary purpose of a s. 236 examination is to assist the beneficial winding up of the company, it is not its only purpose. In my view,

G   where information has been obtained under statutory powers the duty of confidence owed on the *Marcel* principle cannot operate so as to prevent the person obtaining the information from disclosing it to those persons to whom the statutory provisions either require or authorise him to make disclosure.

IA 1986 contains a series of provisions which envisage that information and documents in the hands of the liquidators is to be disclosed to others, including disclosure for the

H   purposes of criminal proceedings. First, under s. 433 statements made to the liquidator in pursuance of a requirement imposed by or under IA 1986 are made admissible in criminal or civil proceedings. Second, in a compulsory winding up, if it appears to the liquidator that a criminal offence is being committed he must report the matter to the court (s. 218(3)) which can direct the liquidator to refer the matter to 'the prosecuting authority' (s. 218(1)). The definition of 'the prosecuting authority' does not include the SFO but means, in England, the Director of Public Prosecutions and, in Scotland, the

Lord Advocate (s. 218(2)). There can be no doubt however that the DPP could hand on   A
to the SFO the information so received. In Scotland, the functions and powers exercised
by the SFO in England are vested in the Lord Advocate himself. Third, in the case of a
voluntary winding up, if it appears to the liquidator that there has been a criminal offence
he is required to report the matter to 'the prosecuting authority' and provide to that
authority such information and documents as the authority requires (s. 218(4)). The
court can also direct the liquidator to take that course (s. 218(6)). Fourth, it is the duty   B
of the liquidator of a company in compulsory liquidation to provide to the official
receiver such information and documents and give such other assistance as the official
receiver may reasonably require for the purposes of carrying out his functions (section
143(2)). The official receiver is appointed by and must act in accordance with the
directions of the President of the Board of Trade. Information and documents supplied
by the liquidator to the official receiver will become widely available within the Insolvency
Service and, in practice, the DTI would refer cases of suspected crime to the prosecuting   C
authorities including the SFO.

In addition to these requirements of disclosure contained in IA 1986, under s. 7 of the
Company Directors Disqualification Act 1986 the liquidator is bound to report to the DTI
any case in which it appears to the liquidator that it may be appropriate for a
disqualification order to be made. The liquidator is bound to supply to the DTI or the
official receiver such information and documents as they may require.   D

The statutory framework thus imposes a wide range of duties on liquidators to report,
directly or indirectly, to the DTI and prosecuting authorities cases of suspected criminal
and dishonest conduct and to furnish them with all documents and information they may
require. Such documents include transcripts of evidence given on a s. 236 examination,
which evidence is admissible in evidence. The liquidator cannot be under any duty of
confidence which will prevent the performance of these statutory duties. Therefore
liquidators cannot in any event give any assurance to a person examined under s. 236   E
that his answers will not be disclosed to prosecuting authorities. In the absence of such
assurance there cannot be any maintainable claim that such answers enjoy public interest
immunity on the grounds either of the public interest in preserving confidentiality or the
public interest in giving an assurance to witnesses that their information will be
confidential.

F

(c) Rule 9.5(4) of the Insolvency Rules

The court is required to keep records of all insolvency proceedings, which records are
open to inspection by the public: r. 7.27 and 7.28 of the Insolvency Rules. In addition the
court is required to open and maintain a file for each case: r. 7.30. This latter file is open
to inspection by a wide range of persons concerned with insolvency, but not without
special leave of the court by the general public: r. 7.31. Thus in general there is widespread   G
access to the records of insolvency proceedings.

In contrast r. 9.5 contains a special code regulating the records of examinations
conducted under s. 236. Rule 9.5(1) directs that the record of the respondent's
examination shall not be placed on the court file. Moreover the record of the examination
is not open to inspection without an order of the court by anyone other than a person
who made, or was entitled to make, an application for a s. 236 examination.

H

In the present case, Vinelott J made his order in reliance on the special discretion
apparently conferred on the court in relation to records of s. 236 examinations by
r. 9.5(4) (which I have set out above). In the Court of Appeal at p. 483B Dillon LJ held
that the rule was 'mere machinery as to how the transcripts in the possession of the court
are to be kept'. Steyn LJ held that any discretion under the rule was overridden by
the CJA.

A   I prefer the view of Vinelott J. Rule 9.5(4) confers on the court a discretion to decide who can inspect the records of the s. 236 examination. In my judgment this is not mere machinery. The extraction of private and confidential information under compulsion from a witness otherwise than in the course of inter partes litigation is an exorbitant power. It is right that such information should not be generally available but should be used only for the purposes for which the power was conferred. Although, as will appear, in my view there are severe limitations on the way in which such discretion can be

B   exercised where prosecuting authorities are involved, it is important that no doubt should be cast on the discretion of the court to decide who shall have access to such information. That is particularly so in the present case where, at the outset of the examination, Millett J made it clear by his order that the examination was being conducted on the basis that the court would decide what, if any, access to the record should be afforded to the SFO.

     In this context I should notice an argument advanced by Mr Kaye that, even if the

C   court could properly make an order prohibiting disclosure to the SFO, that would not provide the liquidators with a 'reasonable excuse' (within the meaning of s. 2(13) of the CJA) for failing to produce to the SFO copies of the transcripts in their possession. I do not accept this argument. Section 2(3) of the CJA does not expressly limit the documents in relation to which production can be demanded to documents which are in the possession or under the control of the recipient of the notice. But it must be clear that, if

D   the recipient of the notice cannot, directly or indirectly, procure the production of a document he must have a 'reasonable excuse' for not producing it. Insolvency is a process conducted by, or under the control of, the court acting through its officers, the liquidators. Documents held by liquidators are held by them to the order of the court. In my judgment a statute would need to use very clear words if it is intended to override the powers of the court to control the use of property under the administration of the court, including documents. If the court, acting properly under a discretion, directs that its

E   officers shall not produce documents, this must provide a reasonable excuse to those officers for failure to do so.

     In this connection Mr Kaye relied on the decision in *A v B Bank (Bank of England intervening)* [1993] QB 311. In that case A had obtained an injunction restraining the B bank from disclosing documents and information. The Bank of England had served on the B bank a notice under s. 39 of the *Banking Act* 1987 which confers on the Bank of England powers similar to those of the SFO under s. 2(3) of the CJA. It was held that the

F   injunction did not provide a reasonable excuse to the B bank for failure to comply with the notice. In my judgment that decision casts no light on the present case. The documents belonged either to A or to B bank: they were not in the custody of the court. The injunction was granted to secure compliance with a banking duty of confidence which is itself overridden by the Banking Act.

G   (2) *The exercise of the discretion*

     Vinelott J exercised his discretion under r. 9.5(4) of the Insolvency Rules by ordering the release of the transcripts to the SFO but only on the SFO giving an undertaking which would provide to Mr Naviede the same protection which the transcripts would have enjoyed had the SFO proceeded directly to question Mr Naviede under s. 2(2) of the CJA, i.e. an undertaking not to use them in evidence against Mr Naviede in the

H   criminal proceedings save for the purposes permitted by s. 2(8) of the CJA. The basis on which the judge acted was, in essence, that it was unfair for the SFO to use against Mr Naviede answers given to a third party (the liquidator) under s. 236 when Parliament had demonstrated by s. 2(8) that answers given directly to the SFO could not be so used. In his view, the SFO is seeking by the back door to achieve what it cannot do by the front door. The Court of Appeal held that it was not for the judge of the Companies Court to exercise his discretion, if any, on such grounds. The judge of the Companies Court had

no right to impose conditions on prosecuting authorities as to their use of documents   A
relevant in criminal proceedings. Steyn LJ (with whom Rose LJ agreed) also expressed
the view that the discretion, if exercisable by the Companies Court judge at all, had been
exercised wrongly.

I agree with the conclusion of the Court of Appeal that it was not for the Companies
Court judge to exercise any discretion so as to prevent the prosecuting authorities
(including the SFO) from obtaining and leading in evidence the transcripts of the s. 236
examination. In the *Rank* case [1982] AC 380 (which unfortunately was not specifically   B
drawn to the attention of Vinelott J) an Anton Piller order had been obtained against the
defendants who were video pirates. The order required the defendants, inter alia, to give
discovery of documents and answer interrogatories. The defendants claimed that to
comply with the order would incriminate them on criminal charges and consequently the
order was improperly made. This House, with regret, upheld that claim. In the course of
argument counsel for the plaintiffs contended that the court could impose a condition in   C
its order to the effect that the documents and information disclosed should not be
admissible in evidence. This House held that such a condition would be ineffective and
improper. Lord Wilberforce said at p. 442G:

> '. . . I cannot accept that a civil court has any power to decide in a manner which
> would bind a criminal court that evidence of any kind is admissible or inadmissible
> in that court.'   D

Lord Fraser of Tullybelton said at p. 446D:

> 'At one stage, the argument seemed to depend on the possibility that the court
> which ordered the discovery might place an express restriction on the use of any
> information disclosed. In my opinion, any argument on that basis must be rejected.
> A restriction by the court making the order would, no doubt, be effective to bind
> the party who obtained the order, but it can hardly be suggested that it would be   E
> effective to prevent a prosecutor in the public interest from using, or an English
> criminal court (a fortiori a Scottish criminal court if a conspiracy were prosecuted
> in Scotland) from admitting the information in evidence at a trial. All evidence
> which is relevant is prima facie admissible in a criminal trial, although the trial
> judge has a discretion to exclude evidence which, though admissible, has been
> obtained by unfair means from the accused after commission of the offence . . .'
>   F

That decision was applied by this House in 1992 in the *Istel* case [1993] AC 45, although
it was distinguished in a case where the prosecuting authority had itself, voluntarily,
agreed not to use the information disclosed. In the present appeal, no attempt was made
to challenge the correctness of the *Rank* decision. Mr Lightman sought to distinguish it
on the basis that in the present case the condition required by the judge did not seek to
make the transcripts inadmissible but to make the imposition of a condition against use
a precondition to the prosecuting authority obtaining possession of the documents at all.   G
In my judgment the *Rank* case [1982] AC 380 cannot be read as permitting any such
distinction to be drawn. The passage which I have quoted from the speech of Lord Fraser
applies to any express restriction on the use by prosecuting authorities of the information
disclosed: this applies as much to the ability of the prosecuting authority to obtain the
documents as it does to the admissibility of the documents once obtained. In my
judgment, the judge did not have power to force upon the SFO an agreement not to use
the documents. If the judge could not himself properly impose such a condition restricting   H
the use of the transcripts he could not properly exercise his discretion by forcing the SFO
to agree to the condition.

For these reasons, in my judgment, Vinelott J should not himself have sought to limit
the use of the transcripts but should have left the matter to be decided by the judge at the
criminal trial, as did Millett J in the *Barlow Clowes* case [1991] BCC 608. The judge at

A   the criminal trial will know all the facts both as to the means whereby the documents
were obtained and their significance or impact in the criminal proceedings. Under s. 78(1)
of the *Police and Criminal Evidence Act* 1984 the judge will have a discretion to refuse to
allow the prosecution to rely on the transcripts:

'. . . if it appears to the court that, having regard to all the circumstances, including
the circumstances in which the evidence was obtained, the admission of the
B   evidence would have such an adverse effect on the fairness of the proceedings that
the court ought not to admit it.'

Mr Lightman and Mr Jarvis, in their attempts to uphold the validity of the exercise of
his discretion by the Companies Court judge, submitted that the judge at the criminal
trial could not under s. 78 of PACE exclude the transcripts. If that were so, I would have
been very reluctant to hold that no judge had the necessary power to ensure that only
fair use could be made of the transcripts obtained under a s. 236 examination. Mr Kaye,
C   for the SFO, accepted that the judge at the criminal trial would have a discretion under
s. 78 which he would have to exercise in the light of all the circumstances, including the
circumstances under which the transcripts were obtained. I am satisfied the judge would
have the necessary discretion. In R v Saunders (unreported, 29 January 1990), Henry J
excluded under s. 78 records of interviews by DTI inspectors with the accused after the
accused had been charged, notwithstanding the fact that such records were technically
D   admissible against the accused. He based his decision, in part, on the fact that neither the
right to silence nor the privilege against self-incrimination applied to the interviews and
that, as in the present case, they took place after the accused had been charged. The
Court of Appeal upheld his decision (unreported). See also *R v Gray & Ors* (unreported,
18 May 1992, Judge Laughland QC).

I would therefore dismiss the appeal on the grounds that, although the judge had a
E   discretion under r. 9.5 of the Insolvency Rules whether or not to authorise the
unconditional release of the transcripts, it was an improper exercise of that discretion by
a judge of the Companies Court to seek to prevent the use by the SFO of those transcripts
in the criminal proceedings. Parliament having made the transcripts admissible, it is for
the judge at the criminal trial alone to decide, in the light of all the circumstances known
to him but not to the judge of the Companies Court, whether the admission of the
transcripts will prejudice a fair criminal trial.

F

Additional points

1. There are passages in the judgments of the Court of Appeal [1993] BCC 473 with
which I do not agree and which would, in my view, lead the judge of the criminal trial to
exercise his discretion on a wrong legal basis if he applied them.

First, Steyn LJ (p. 486B) expresses the view that Parliament, in enacting s. 2(3) of the
G   CJA, must have had in mind that the transcripts of inquisitorial proceedings under s. 236
of IA 1986, the *Companies Act* 1985, the *Banking Act* 1987, and the *Financial Services
Act* 1986 would be available and that the privilege against self-incrimination would not
have been available in such inquisitorial proceedings. I cannot agree. At the time the CJA
was enacted it was thought that the privilege against self-incrimination was applicable to
such investigations. Only since the passing of the CJA has it been established by recent
decisions of the Court of Appeal that the privilege against self-incrimination is not
H   applicable in such inquisitorial proceedings: the *Bishopsgate* case [1992] BCC 222; *Bank
of England v Riley* [1992] Ch 475; *Re London United Investments plc* [1992] BCC 202. I
have considerable doubts whether, in using the word 'documents' in s. 2(3) of the CJA
Parliament directed its mind to documents other than those which formed part of the
transactions under investigation. But if I am wrong on this and Parliament did intend the
word to comprehend post-transaction records of investigations made by other people

under different statutory powers, in 1987 Parliament would have been under the   A
impression that the privilege against self-incrimination applied to such other
investigations or at least that the matter was doubtful.

Secondly, Steyn LJ sought to account for the disparity between the protection afforded
by s. 2(8) to answers given directly to the SFO under s. 2(2) and the lack of any such
protection afforded to transcripts of investigations conducted by others. He found the
reason for this distinction in the fact that s. 236 examinations take place before the court   B
which would protect the witness from unfair treatment whereas questions put by the SFO
under s. 2(2) would not enjoy such protection. In my judgment this distinction provides
no logical answer to why Parliament did not extend s. 2(8) protection to self-
incriminatory answers given to liquidators and others. It overstates the role of the court
in s. 236 examinations which, while protecting the witness against oppressive questioning,
is concerned to discover what has happened to the company's property, not to protect
the witness from conduct which might infringe the requirements of PACE. Moreover,   C
although I have deliberately expressed no view as to records of informal meetings with
liquidators under s. 235 of IA 1986, Steyn LJ was treating such records as being
indistinguishable from records of examinations under s. 236. Yet s. 235 examinations are
informal and do not take place before the court, any more than investigations under the
Companies Act, the Banking Act or the Financial Services Act.

In the circumstances, I can find no satisfactory answer to the question why Parliament,   D
having taken care to include the s. 2(8) protection to witnesses required to answer in
response to a s. 2(2) notice did not provide similar protection against the use of self-
incriminatory answers given in other investigations to which the privilege does not attach.
In my judgment it is an unexplained anomaly which the judge of the criminal trial can
take into account in exercising his powers under s. 78 of PACE.

2. The Court of Appeal in the present case and this House in the *Istel* case expressed   E
the hope that Parliament would address the interaction between the ancient privilege
against self-incrimination and the need in civil proceedings (including statutory
inquisitorial proceedings) to discover what has happened to the property obtained by
fraud. In expressing such hope they were merely echoing the sentiments which have been
expressed in very many cases over the last ten years. Although the question was the
subject-matter of a consultation paper issued by the Lord Chancellor's Department in   F
July 1992 legislation has not been introduced.

Only Parliament can weigh the conflicting public interests between the demands of
justice to the accused, the need to obtain the information for the purposes of civil
proceedings (including investigatory proceedings) and the public interest in the successful
prosecution of those guilty of fraud. In some areas of the law Parliament has shown that
the solution lies in removing the privilege in civil proceedings (including investigatory   G
proceedings) but then providing partial protection to the witness against the use in
subsequent criminal proceedings of the self-incriminating answers: see *Theft Act* 1968,
s. 31 and s. 2(8) of the CJA. The extent to which such partial protection is appropriate to
cases where those in a fiduciary position (such as directors of companies) are suspected
of fraud is a matter which only Parliament can resolve bearing in mind the uniform view
of insolvency practitioners that the protection of the company's property may be
prejudiced if they cannot give assurances of confidentiality to those from whom they seek   H
essential information.

For these reasons I would dismiss the appeal. Mr Naviede must pay the costs of the
SFO. Since Mr Naviede is legally aided such order cannot be enforced without further
order of the court. There will be no order as to the costs of the liquidators or the Secretary
of State.

A   **Lord Lloyd of Berwick:** For the reasons given in the speech delivered by Lord Browne-Wilkinson, which I have read in draft and with which I agree, I too would dismiss this appeal.

    Lord Nolan: I have had the advantage of reading in draft the speech prepared by Lord Browne-Wilkinson. I agree with it in every respect and wish to add only a few words of my own.

B   It is hard to believe that Parliament, when authorising the director under s. 2(3) of the *Criminal Justice Act* 1987 to require the production of 'documents' meant that he should have a free hand to obtain the records of admissions made by the defendant to other authorities and to use them as part of the prosecution case. It seems anomalous in the extreme that the director should thus be allowed to obtain and use evidence in the form of admissions made by the defendant to others when by s. 2(8) Parliament has expressly prohibited, save within narrow limits, the use in evidence of admissions made in response

C to a requirement under s. 2(2) from the director himself. Yet that is the result which is produced by the language of s. 2(3).

    For the reasons given by Lord Browne-Wilkinson, I can see no ground in principle to support the distinction thus drawn between admissions obtained by way of s. 2(2) and evidence of admissions obtained by way of s. 2(3). There may, in fact, be a stronger case for affording some protection to the defendant in respect of the latter. A defendant

D responding to inquiries under s. 236 of the *Insolvency Act* 1986 may well have been less cautious in his answers than if he were being subjected to a s. 2(2) inquiry by the director.

    The director fully accepts, and to some extent relies upon, the overriding power of the criminal court, under s. 78 of the *Police and Criminal Evidence Act* 1984, to exclude the documentary evidence obtained under s. 2(3) if it would be unfair to admit it. The full terms of s. 78(1) are that the court may refuse to allow the evidence:

E   '. . . if it appears to the court that, having regard to all the circumstances, including the circumstances in which the evidence was obtained, the admission of the evidence would have such an adverse effect on the fairness of the proceedings that the court ought not to admit it.'

    It seems strange that evidence of admissions by the defendant may be excluded on these grounds, even though it was obtained in strict compliance with an express statutory

F power. Yet that, as I understand the speech of Lord Mustill in *R v Director of the Serious Fraud Office, ex parte Smith* [1993] AC 1 at p. 43F–G, is undoubtedly the law in relation to answers obtained from the defendant under s. 2(2), and is, as I have said, accepted by the director, rightly in my view, as applicable to evidence obtained by way of s. 2(3). It follows that s. 78 is the one remaining solid bulwark against the possibility of excessive or unfair use by the director of his powers under s. 2.

G   The type of fraud which led to the passing of the *Criminal Justice Act* 1987 is an exceptionally pernicious form of crime, and those who commit it tend to be as devious as they are wicked. It is not in the least surprising or regrettable that Parliament should have entrusted the SFO with the power to call upon a suspected person to come into the open, and to disclose information which may incriminate him. It would be highly regrettable if the power has, in fact, been created in terms which go significantly wider than was intended. But that is a matter which only Parliament can debate and, if

H necessary, resolve.

    I concur in the order proposed by Lord Browne-Wilkinson.

(Order accordingly)

Re Leyland Daf Ltd; Re Ferranti International plc. Talbot & Anor v Cadge & Ors.

A

Chancery Division (Companies Court).
Lightman J.
Judgment delivered 26 July 1994.

Administrative receivership – Whether administrative receivers had 'adopted' contracts of employment – Whether receivers were personally liable on contracts – Whether receivers could contract out of 'adoption' – Insolvency Act 1986, s. 44(1)(b).

B

These were applications by the administrative receivers of two companies ('Leyland Daf' and 'Ferranti') for directions whether under s. 44(1)(b) of the Insolvency Act 1986 they had adopted certain contracts of employment between the companies and their employees and if so as to the extent, if any, of the receivers' personal liability.

C

Under s. 44(1)(b) the administrative receiver of a company was 'personally liable . . . on any contract of employment adopted by him in the carrying out of [his] functions'. The receiver was entitled in respect of that liability to an indemnity out of the assets of the company. Under subs. (2) the receiver was not to be taken to have adopted a contract of employment by reason of anything done or omitted to be done within 14 days after his appointment.

D

In the case of both companies the receivers wrote to the employees stating that they 'ha[d] not adopted, do not adopt, and will not at any future date adopt' contracts of employment with the companies. Sending such letters followed the accepted practice in receivership cases. The Leyland Daf receivers intended to pay, and in fact paid, employees' wages post-receivership as and when the liability to pay arose. Some 957 Leyland Daf employees made redundant after the 14-day period in s. 44(2) had claims relating to pay in lieu of notice, pension contributions, redundancy payments, benefits under company car and medical and accident insurance policies, and holiday pay. The Ferranti receivers caused Ferranti to pay the employees' wages for the periods in which they continued to work. Some 106 employees were made redundant after the 14 day period. Their claims related to payments in lieu of notice, severance payments, holiday pay, pension contributions, and company car benefits.

E

The issues raised on the application were: (1) the meaning of 'adoption' and whether the Leyland Daf and Ferranti receivers had adopted the contracts of employment of the companies' employees; (2) if the answer to (1) was in the affirmative, whether the personal liability of the receivers in respect of such adopted contracts (a) could legally be excluded and if so (b) whether it had been in this case; and (3) if the answer to (2) was to the effect that there was no exclusion, the extent of the obligations under the adopted contracts to which personal liability extended. It was common ground that the receivers had no obligation to pay interest.

F

G

Held, determining that the receivers had adopted the contracts of employment; had not contracted out of their personal liability; were personally liable (coextensively with the companies) in respect of all contractual (but no other) liabilities under the contracts of employment of the employees irrespective of the dates on which they accrued or the periods in respect of which the liability arose (there was no dispute as to which of the items detailed in the applications were contractual); and were bound to pay forthwith:

H

1. In s. 44 the word 'adopted' meant 'treated as continuing in force'. The receivers' letters stating that they were not by so treating the contracts as continuing adopting them did not negate or qualify the legal effect of their actions.

2. No distinction could be drawn between the meaning of adopted in s. 44 and s. 19 applying to administrators. The decision of the Court of Appeal in *Powdrill & Anor v*

A   Watson & Anor; Re Paramount Airways Ltd (No. 3) [1994] BCC 172 on the cc
of the word in the context of s. 19 was to the same effect.

3. There was no statutory prohibition on employees contracting out of the protection
afforded by s. 44. Exclusion by the receivers of the statutory incident of personal liability
required a contract to that effect between the receiver and the affected employees.

4. The receivers' letters could not reasonably have been understood by the recipient
B   employees as an offer requiring acceptance or rejection. They constituted merely unilateral
declarations of 'non-liability'. But even if they did constitute offers, since the exclusion of
personal liability of the receiver had no immediate practical effect on the employees, it would
be unrealistic and unfair to treat the continued performance by the employees of their
contracts of employment as an acceptance of a new contract by way of variation of their
contract of employment excluding the statutory incident of personal liability.

C   5. The liability of the 'adopting' receiver extended to all liabilities whenever incurred of
whatever kind under the adopted contract.

6. The liability attached at and from the date of adoption and was not retrospective to
the date of appointment.

The following cases were referred to in the judgment:

Anchor Line (Henderson Brothers) Ltd, Re [1937] Ch 1.
D   *Atlantic Computer Systems plc, Re* [1990] BCC 859; [1992] Ch 505.
Botibol, Re [1947] 1 All ER 26.
Davis (S) & Co Ltd, Re [1945] Ch 402.
Diesels & Components Pty Ltd, Re (1985) 3 ACLC 555.
Greenwood v Martins Bank Ltd [1933] AC 51.
Jones v Associated Tunnelling Co Ltd [1981] IRLR 477.
E   *Lawson v Hosemaster Co Ltd* [1966] 1 WLR 1300.
Leyland Daf Ltd v Automotive Products plc [1993] BCC 389.
Mack Trucks (Britain) Ltd, Re [1967] 1 All ER 977.
Nicoll v Cutts (1985) 1 BCC 99,427.
Phoenix Bessemer Steel Co, Re (1876) 4 ChD 108.
Powdrill & Anor v Watson & Anor; Re Paramount Airways Ltd (No. 3) [1994] BCC
172.
F   *R v Grantham* (1984) 1 BCC 99,075.
R v Lockwood [1986] Crim LR 244.
Specialised Mouldings Ltd, Re (unreported, 13 February 1987, Harman J).

Patrick Elias QC and Mark Phillips (instructed by Wilde Sapte and Allen & Overy) for
the receivers.

Charles Purle QC and David Bean (instructed by Rowley Ashworth) for the employees.
G

JUDGMENT

Lightman J: 1. Introduction

I have before me originating applications by the administrative receivers of Leyland
Daf Ltd and Ferranti International plc seeking directions whether they have adopted
certain contracts of employment between their respective companies and these
H   companies' employees and if so as to the extent (if any) of the personal liability assumed.

The applications raise important and far-reaching questions as to the meaning and
effect of s. 44(1)(b) of the *Insolvency Act* 1986. This section imposes on administrative
receivers personal liability in respect of contracts of employment adopted by them.
Section 19(5) of the Act provides that sums payable in respect of debts and liabilities
incurred during an administration under contracts of employment adopted by an

administrator shall be charged on the property of the company in administration in his   A
custody or under his control. The legislature was impelled to make these specific
provisions (initially in s. 50(1)(b) and 37(3)(b) of the *Insolvency Act* 1985, replaced by and
consolidated in the sections in the Act) providing special protection for employees in case
of both administrative receivership and administration by the lack of protection under
the pre-existing law made apparent by the decision of the Court of Appeal in *Nicoll v
Cutts* (1985) 1 BCC 99,427. Section 37(1) of the Act provides like protection in case of
non-administrative receiverships. The meaning and effect of s. 19(5) was considered by   B
Evans-Lombe J and the Court of Appeal in the case of *Paramount Airways Ltd (No. 3).
Powdrill v Watson* [1994] BCC 172. The decision of the Court of Appeal occasioned the
legislature to give second thoughts to this special protection and whether it went too far,
and to pass the *Insolvency Act* 1994 which strictly limits that protection in case of
contracts adopted on or after 15 March 1994 by administrators and administrative
receivers, but not non-administrative receivers. The applications before me concern   C
contracts adopted (if adopted at all) by administrative receivers prior to that date, and
accordingly must be decided without regard to the provisions of the 1994 Act. The
problems raised on these applications and in *Powdrill* are not isolated incidents. I am
told that between 1987 and 1994 there have been 27,210 administrative receiverships and
1,172 administrations. Accordingly whilst the 1994 Act lays down the code for the future
in respect of adoptions by administrative receivers and administrators, since it is not
retrospective and does not extend to adoptions by non-administrative receivers, for many   D
contracts *Powdrill* and the applications before me will be test cases. An appeal from the
decision of the Court of Appeal in *Powdrill* is due to be heard by the House of Lords on
5 December 1994. It is proposed that, whatever I decide, the losing party will seek to
'leap-frog' the Court of Appeal and obtain a hearing of an appeal by the House of Lords
at the same time as the pending appeal in *Powdrill* so as to obtain definitive guidance on
both sections.   E

Sections 19(5) and 44(1)(b) plainly have an affinity, but their language and operation
are not identical. Accordingly the decision of the Court of Appeal is not necessarily
determinative of the issues before me. In these circumstances, it seems to me appropriate
that I should in my judgment give a full and detailed judgment reviewing the statutory
legal context in which the sections fall to be considered, and first reach a view of my own
as to the construction and ambit of s. 44; and then, and then only, consider whether this   F
view is confirmed or precluded by the decision in *Powdrill*.

2. Facts and questions raised

The parties have helpfully agreed the facts and questions to be answered in respect of
both companies and I can set these out briefly.
   G
Leyland Daf

(1) History of receivership

(a) The Leyland Daf receivers were appointed on 3 February 1993, following the
collapse of Leyland Daf's Dutch parent company. At the date of the appointment
Leyland Daf owed approximately £570m to secured and unsecured creditors.
   H
(b) Leyland Daf owned six plants over the country and employed 5,371 individuals.
The monthly wage bill was £7m and the Leyland Daf receivers had no access to cash to
fund it. On the day of their appointment the Leyland Daf receivers wrote to all employees
a letter ('the Leyland Daf letter') intended to state their attitude to future trading and the
status of employment contracts during the period of receivership trading. The key terms
of the letter are as follows:

A
'. . . the receivers currently contemplate causing the company, for such period as the receivers think fit, to continue to pay remuneration to you in accordance with your contract of employment . . .

. . . Section 44(1)(b) of the *Insolvency Act* 1986 provides that an administrative receiver of the company is "personally liable on any contract of employment adopted by him in the carrying out of his functions".

B
The receivers have not adopted, do not adopt, and will not at any future date adopt your contract of employment with the company . . .

. . . Section 44(1)(b) also provides that "an administrative receiver of the company is personally liable on any contract entered into by him in the carrying out of his functions (except in so far as the contract otherwise provides)". The receivers themselves have not intended to enter nor do they intend to enter into any contract of employment with you. Nevertheless, to avoid any doubt, it is stressed that in
C
any event, the receivers have not assumed and will not at any future date assume any personal liability in relation to your present or future employment.'

The Leyland Daf receivers intended to pay, and in fact paid, employees' wages post-receivership as and when the liability to pay arose. Sending this letter followed the accepted practice in receivership cases.

D
(c) On 12 February 1993, 1,552 employees were made redundant. On 16 February 1993 a further 74 employees were made redundant. These redundancies were made within the 14-day period provided in s. 44 of the Act. Between 26 March 1993 and 10 September 1993, 957 employees were made redundant. As a consequence of the circumstances at the time, contractual notice was not given to these employees.

(d) As a result of Leyland Daf's continued trading and a series of sales between 24 April 1993 and March 1994, 2,700 jobs were saved. This was achieved on the assumption
E
that the claims of any employees not transferred to the purchasers would fall to be dealt with in a subsequent liquidation.

2. The contractual position of the employees

(a) There are two classes of employee:

(i)   'Workshop employees', represented by the second respondent, Mr Sumner. There are 582 former employees who fall into this category. Mr Sumner was a fitter and
F
latterly a workshop inspector for various Leyland Daf companies from 1958 until he was dismissed on 31 March 1993. His contract is in essence set down in the collective agreement covering pay, working practices and conditions of employment.

(ii)   'Staff employees', represented by the first respondent, Mr Cadge. There are 375 former employees who fall into this category. Mr Cadge was a principal engineer
G
who had been employed since September 1946 and was made redundant on 26 March 1993. His contract is primarily set out in the letter dated 2 February 1981.

(b) The contracts of employment of these employees are contained in a series of collective agreements, letters sent to individual employees and Leyland Daf employee manuals. Under these contracts the employees are or may be entitled to benefits under six heads:

H
(i)   *Notice*

(a) Workshop employees are generally entitled to one week's notice for each year of service up to a maximum of 12 weeks. Mr Sumner was entitled to 12 weeks' notice, making a claim (subject to mitigation) of £2,915.28.

(b) Staff employees have different periods of notice. Mr Cadge is entitled to three months' notice, making a claim (subject to mitigation) of £6,671.08.

(ii) *Pensions*–The letters sent to employees encouraged them to join the pension scheme   A
and advised them that unless they contracted out it would be assumed that they
wished to be a member.

    (a) Mr Sumner's claim for pension payments falling due during his notice period
is £116.61.

    (b) Mr Cadge's claim for pension payments falling due during his notice period
is £266.84.   B

The total value of the potential claims under this head together with claims in
respect of medical insurance is £148,463.45.

(iii) *Redundancy policy*– Leyland Daf had a negotiated redundancy policy. The
minimum sum payable was six weeks' pay. The provision for payment of
compensation for loss of office, which constitutes an element of severance pay, is
not contractually binding. The relevant policy document on employee redundancy   C
compensation is stated in terms that the payment for compensation for loss of
office 'is neither a right nor a contractual entitlement'.

    (a) Mr Sumner would have a claim under this policy of £4,372.92.

    (b) Mr Cadge would have a claim under this policy of £12,315.84.

(iv) *Company car policy*– Certain employees claim to be entitled to purchase their cars
on termination at a discounted price. There are 142 employees who qualified for   D
this benefit. Mr Cadge's loss for being unable to participate in the car purchase
scheme is £692.51. The opportunity to purchase cars on termination was not part
of the contracts of employment. The relevant policy document setting out the
principles applicable states in terms that 'this policy does not establish any
contractual entitlement or "right" to the privilege of discounted cars'.

(v) *Medical and accident insurance*–Some employees (and in particular Mr Cadge, but   E
not Mr Sumner) were entitled to participate in Leyland Daf's BUPA scheme.

(vi) *Holiday Pay*

    (a) Mr Sumner was entitled to 25 days' holiday in accordance with cl. 3-12 of
the collective agreement. His claim to holiday pay is £291.53.

    (b) Mr Cadge's claim to holiday pay arises under cl. 1-5 and 1-6 of the staff
employment terms and conditions. He claims £307.90 under this head.   F

The total potential claims to holiday pay are £143,573.41.

    (c) Part VII of the *Employment Protection (Consolidation) Act* 1978 (as
amended) provides for the National Insurance Fund to guarantee employees
the payment of certain debts owing from insolvent employers. The
employees of Leyland Daf either have been paid, or are entitled to be paid,
the guaranteed sums out of this fund. Their claims against the Leyland Daf   G
receivers fall to be reduced accordingly, although the Secretary of State is
subrogated to those claims. Payment out of the fund accordingly does not
affect any liability of the receivers.

(3) Questions raised

The questions raised by the Leyland Daf receivers are as follows:

(1) Whether the contracts of employment of Mr Cadge and Mr Sumner were adopted   H
by the receivers as such in carrying out their functions as administrative receivers
within the meaning of s. 44 of the Act.

(2) Assuming that the contracts were adopted, whether the receivers in principle are
personally liable on such contracts to make payment (together with interest or not)
in respect of the following:

A
(a) sums payable by way of damages for wrongful dismissal effected by them during the receivership:

(i) in lieu of contractual notice under the respondents' contracts of employment;

(ii) in respect of pension benefits to the extent that such benefits would have accrued to the respondents during their contractual notice periods;

B

(iii) sums payable under Leyland Daf's policies in relation to private medical insurance and accident insurance that the first respondent was entitled to;

(b) holiday pay falling due by reason of the respondents' contracts of employment;

C

(c) sums payable under Leyland Daf's redundancy policy;

(d) sums payable to the first respondent under Leyland Daf's car policy.

(3) Whether such of the sums referred to above as the court directs should be paid to the respondents, should be paid:

(a) forthwith; or

D

(b) on the vacation of office by the receivers; or

(c) on the winding up of Leyland Daf.

Ferranti

(1) History of the receivership

E
On 1 December 1993 the Ferranti receivers were appointed. They were appointed receivers of Ferranti International plc, Ferranti Control Group plc, Ferranti International Holdings Ltd, Dundridge College Ltd, ISC Technologies Ltd and Ferranti Dynamics Ltd: I shall call the companies collectively 'Ferranti'. At the date of the appointments Ferranti owed approximately £111m to secured creditors, £5m to preferential creditors and £44.7m to unsecured creditors.

F
Ferranti's business was organised into four business units within which there were a number of different operations located throughout the UK. There were approximately 3,200 employees and the monthly wage bill was about £4.7m. The businesses of the Ferranti group were sophisticated and highly complex. Whether the businesses survived depended upon the continued performance of hundreds of contracts and on Ferranti's ability to secure future contracts. This gave rise to a number of difficulties and approximately 70 members of the Ferranti receivers' staff were used to conduct urgent investigations.

G
To ensure that Ferranti had the funds to continue trading whilst the Ferranti receivers carried out their investigations, the Ferranti receivers borrowed £5m on the basis of personal liability.

On 2 December 1993 (the day after their appointment) the Ferranti receivers wrote to all employees a letter ('the Ferranti letter') intended to inform them in unambiguous terms that there was no question of the Ferranti receivers adopting their contracts of employment if they were kept on after the 14-day period stipulated in s. 44(2) of the Act and that there was no intention on the part of the Ferranti receivers to incur any personal liability on those contracts of employment. The key terms of the letter are:

H

'1. The receivers themselves are not and will not become your employer.

2. On the contrary, the companies have remained and, for so long as your employment continues, will remain your employer.

3. The receivers have not assumed, and will not at any future date assume, any personal liability in relation to your employment.

4. Section 44(1)(b) of the *Insolvency Act* 1986 provides that an administrative receiver of a company is "personally liable on any contract of employment adopted by him in the carrying out of his functions". The receivers have not adopted, do not adopt and will not at any future date adopt, your contract of employment with the companies.

5. Section 44(1)(b) provides that "an administrative receiver of a company is personally liable on any contract entered into by him in the carrying out of his functions (except in so far as the contract otherwise provides)". The receivers themselves have not intended to enter into nor do they intend to enter into any contract of employment with you. Nevertheless, to avoid any doubt, it is stressed that in any event the receivers have not assumed and will not at any future date assume any personal liability in relation to your present or any future employment.'

The Ferranti receivers caused Ferranti to pay the employees' wages for the periods in which they continued to work.

On 10 December 1993, 611 employees were made redundant. The redundancies were discussed with the management and unions of Ferranti but it was impracticable to give the employees contractual notice. These redundancies were made within the 14-day period provided by s. 44 of the Act.

Since 16 December 1993 106 employees have been made redundant, seven of whom were employed on the 'executive contract' and the remaining 99 on the 'non-executive contract'. As at 26 April 1994, 2,243 employees were still employed by the Ferranti group.

As a result of Ferranti's continued trading, two of the business units have been sold to GEC and 1,017 jobs saved. There is, at present, interest in the remaining business units.

(2) The contractual position of the employees

There are two classes of employee employed under one of two standard forms of contract:

(a) 'Executive staff' represented by Mr Parry. This contract applies only to senior managers and 85 members of staff who were employed under this contract at the commencement of the receivership. Mr Parry was a materials manager at Ferranti's Oldham site. His employment with Ferranti began on 11 August 1986 and he was made redundant on 14 January 1994. Subject to mitigation Mr Parry's claim is for £27,062.17.

(b) 'Non-executive staff' represented by Mrs Grundy. This contract applies to all other grades of staff and 3,108 members of staff who were employed under this contract at the commencement of the receiverships. Mrs Grundy was a process worker at Ferranti's Oldham site. Her employment began on 28 March 1977 and she was made redundant on 4 February 1994. Subject to mitigation Mrs Grundy's claim is for £4,564.33.

Under their contracts the respondent employees are or may be entitled to benefits under five heads:

(1) *Notice–*

    (a) Under clause 12 of the Executive contract Mr Parry was entitled to six months' notice of termination and claims £17,336.52. The total potential claims under this head are £1,397,012.

A (b) Non-executive staff are entitled to four weeks' notice plus an additional week for every year after five years' service up to a maximum of 12 weeks. Mrs Grundy was entitled to 12 weeks' notice and claims £1,845.72. The total potential claims under this head are £356,054.

There is a potential claim of £570,000 by Mr Davies, the former finance director who is one of a number of 'super-employees'.

B (2) *Severance payment–*

(a) Under a severance payment and redeployment agreement dated 14 April 1991 Mr Parry was entitled to a severance payment of one month's pay plus 5 weeks' pay, totalling £6,376.63. The total potential claims under this head are £108,037.

C (b) Under the severance payment and reemployment agreement Mrs Grundy was entitled to a severance payment of one month's salary plus the maximum additional severance payment of 12 weeks' pay under cl. 5. Her claim is for £2,514.80. The total potential claims under this head are £385,029.

(3) *Holiday pay–*

D (a) Under the executive contract Mr Parry was entitled to 33 days of paid holiday. Under cl. 6(d) of his contract holiday pay on termination was calculated based on the number of completed weeks of service from 1 January until the date of termination less holiday taken. Mr Parry claims £132.85.

(b) Under the non-executive contract Mrs Grundy was entitled to 37 days of paid holiday. Holiday pay on termination was calculated based on the number of completed weeks of service from 1 January until the date of

E termination less holiday taken. Mrs Grundy claims to be entitled to 2 weeks of holiday pay totalling £132.85. The Ferranti receivers believe that her claim is for £76.91.

The total potential claims for holiday pay are £50,218, of which £12,375 is the potential liability to Mr Davies.

F (4) *Pensions–*

(a) Mr Parry was a member of Ferranti's pension scheme. Clause 9 of the executive contract refers to the Ferranti pension schemes. Mr Parry entered the Ferranti pension scheme.

(b) Mrs Grundy was a member of Ferranti's pension scheme. The booklet given to employees is referred to in cl. 5 of the non-executive contract. The booklet

G provides that 'the company meets the balance of the cost of providing the scheme benefits' and '[t]he company . . . has undertaken to meet the balance of the cost, as advised by the scheme's actuary, of providing all the scheme benefits'.

The claims for payment to the pension scheme are considerable. Personal liability of receivers in respect of these claims is not in issue before me. Under the non-

H executive contract there are claims for damages for non-payment of pension contributions of £39,086. Under the executive contract the claims total £361,296. Mr Davies has a claim for £60,000. If the Ferranti receivers are personally liable to meet the contributions required to top up the pension scheme for the year commencing 1 April 1993, the liability is approximately £4,485,000 notwithstanding the fact that part of that liability is due in respect of the period prior to the appointment of the receivers.

(5)   *Mr Parry's company car–*   A

Under cl. 2.4 of his contract Mr Parry was provided with a car. The total claim for motor cars is £8,157 under the non-executive contract and £22,986 under the executive contract. Mr Davies has a claim for £15,387.

The employees of Ferranti either have been paid, or are entitled to be paid, the guaranteed sums out of the National Insurance Fund. Their claims against the Ferranti receivers fall to be reduced accordingly, although the Secretary of State is subrogated to   B
those claims. Any personal liability of the receivers is accordingly unaffected by payments out of the fund.

The total liability of the Ferranti receivers to employees who have been made redundant since 15 December 1993 is about £1,735,000. In addition there is a claim by the pension fund trustees (which again is not in issue) of £4,485,000 and potential liabilities to those staff still employed of £10,114,000. The Ferranti receivers' potential   C
personal liability is accordingly over £17m.

(3) Questions raised

The questions raised by the Ferranti receivers are as follows:

(1)   Whether the contracts of employment of Mrs Grundy and Mr Parry were adopted by the receivers as such in carrying out their functions as administrative receivers within the meaning of s. 44 of the Act.   D

(2)   Assuming that the contracts were adopted, whether the receivers in principle are personally liable on such contracts to make payment (together with interest or not) in respect of the following:

   (a)   sums payable by way of damages for wrongful dismissal effected by them during their receivership:

      (i)   in lieu of contractual notice under the respondents' contracts of   E
      employment;

      (ii)   in respect of pension benefits to the extent that such benefits would have accrued to the respondents during their contractual notice periods;

      (iii)   in respect of health care scheme benefits to which the second respondent was entitled by reason of cl. 5 of his contract of   F
      employment to the extent that such benefits would have accrued to the second respondent during his contractual period;

      (iv)   in respect of the benefits of the provision of a motor car to the second respondent in accordance with cl. 2.4 of his contract of employment to the extent that such benefits would have accrued to him during his contractual period;   G

   (b)   sums due to the first respondent in respect of holiday pay falling due by reason of cl. 3 of the first respondent's contract of employment;

   (c)   sums due to the second respondent in respect of holiday pay falling due by reason of cl. 6(d) of the second respondent's contract of employment;

   (d)   sums due to the respondents under the terms of a severance payment and redeployment agreement dated 14 February 1991.   H

(3)   Whether such of the sums referred to in (2) above as the court directs should be paid, should be paid to the respondents:

   (a)   forthwith; or

   (b)   on vacation of office by the receivers; or

   (c)   on the winding up of Ferranti.

A   ### 3. Relevant legal context

Before examining the relevant legislation, it is, I think, appropriate to consider the rights and duties of employees and receivers under the pre-existing law, which subject to the changes thereby effected remain in force.

(a) *Liquidation and receivership expenses*

B   In the case of a liquidation, a liquidator is ordinarily required to pay out of the assets of the company as liquidation expenses in priority to other creditors, not merely new debts incurred by the liquidator on behalf of the company, but also sums due under continuing obligations, e.g. under contracts of employment and supply agreements, which the liquidator chooses to continue (or 'adopt' as it is expressed in the cases: see *Re Anchor Line (Henderson Brothers) Ltd* [1937] Ch 1 and *Re S Davis & Co Ltd* [1945] Ch 402) for the benefit of the winding up, in respect of and limited to the period of

C   liquidation. But there is no requirement of a receiver in a receivership to make any such payment. The reason for the distinction is that in the case of a liquidation the creditor is precluded during the liquidation from taking proceedings against the company to enforce his right to payment, but there is no such constraint on the creditor in case of a receivership: see *Re Atlantic Computer Systems plc* [1990] BCC 859 at pp. 862–866 (CA).

(b) *Receivers' liability under contracts*

D   (i) New contracts

It has always been a regular feature of a floating charge that it authorises the receiver to enter into contracts in the name and on behalf of the company, an authority which terminates on liquidation. Under the law of contract, a receiver should incur no personal liability under the contract any more than any other agent. But since the enactment of s. 87(2) of the *Companies Act* 1947, which was immediately superseded by s. 369(2) of

E   the *Companies Act* 1948, statute has imposed personal liability on the receiver, 'except in so far as the contract otherwise provides'. Such liability is not a term of the contract, but a statutory incident: see *Lawson v Hosemaster Co Ltd* [1966] 1 WLR 1300 at p. 1313. The current legislation in respect of the imposition of this incident is contained in the first part of s. 44(1)(b).

F   (ii) Continuing contracts

The appointment of a receiver out of court does not automatically determine continuing contracts (e.g. of employment or for the supply of goods) in effect at the date of his appointment unless the contract expressly or implicitly provides to the contrary or could no longer be performed consistently with the appointment and role of the receiver: see *Re Mack Trucks (Britain) Ltd* [1967] 1 All ER 977 at p. 982 approved by Dillon LJ in *Nicoll v Cutts* (1985) 1 BCC 99,427 at p. 99,430. In the case of continuing contracts

G   (subject to one qualification) the receiver is entitled on behalf of the company to require the employee or supplier to continue to honour the contracts. The qualification is that the insolvency of the company may amount to a declaration of inability to meet engagements when they become due and on this ground may entitle the employee or supplier to treat the contract as discharged: see *Re Phoenix Bessemer Steel Co* (1876) 4 ChD 108 (CA).

H   (c) *Pre-receivership liability*

Pre-receivership unsecured debts and liabilities of the company continue after receivership as debts of the company, but they are debts which (save and to the extent that they are statutorily preferred under the provisions of the Act) the receiver is under no obligation to pay, whether personally or out of the charged assets. Save with the statutory exception of certain public utilities (see s. 233 of the Act) the creditor may (if

his contract terms so permit) refuse to continue to supply or refuse to enter into a new   A
contract with the company unless arrears are paid or the receiver accepts personal liability
or both: see *Leyland Daf v Automotive Products* [1993] BCC 389 (CA) and the earlier
cases which led to the statutory limitation on the exercise of monopoly power by utilities
to achieve this advantage cited in Lightman & Moss, *Law of Receivers of Companies*
(1986) p. 60, footnote 2a. If the receiver accedes to such a demand, the creditor will
obtain priority over other creditors including those on whom the status of preferential
creditor is specifically conferred by the Act.   B

(d) *Fraudulent trading*

Under s. 213 of the Act, if in the course of the winding up of a company it appears that
the business of the company has been carried on with intent to defraud the creditors of
the company, the court may on the application of the liquidator declare that any persons
who were knowingly parties to the carrying on of the business in such manner are liable   C
to make such contribution (if any) to the company's assets as the court thinks proper.
The required intent to defraud is subjective, and not objective, and accordingly it is
necessary to show that there was either an intent to defraud or a reckless indifference
whether or not the creditors were defrauded: see *R v Lockwood* [1986] Crim LR 244. But
there is a sufficient intent to defraud if credit is obtained at a time when the person knows
that there is no good reason for thinking that funds will become available to pay the debt
when it becomes due or shortly afterwards. It is unnecessary to establish knowledge that   D
funds will never become available: see *R v Grantham* (1984) 1 BCC 99,075.

A receiver carrying on the business of a company is exposed to a claim for fraudulent
trading if he allows debts or liabilities to be incurred by the company (of particular
relevance in this case) under continuing contracts during the receivership for which he
has no personal liability and in respect of which he knows there is no good reason for
thinking that they can or will be paid. Honesty requires no less. The responsibility of   E
receivers in respect of such creditors has perhaps been insufficiently regarded in the past.
Section 213 has scope for application in situations such as that which arose in *Nicoll v
Cutts* (below).

4. The decision in Nicoll v Cutts

Nicoll v Cutts (1985) 1 BCC 99,427 was decided whilst the 1985 Insolvency Bill was   F
progressing through Parliament. In that case Mr Nicoll, the company's managing
director, was the company's only working director. He was in charge of the day-to-day
running of the company. He had a five-year contract and an annual salary of £7,500. Mr
Nicoll was injured and spent five or six months in hospital. After the appointment of
receivers no step was taken to determine Mr Nicoll's contract. Instead, Mr Nicoll
discussed the company's business with the receiver from his hospital bed. At no stage did
the receiver make it clear (or even suggest) to Mr Nicoll that it was not his intention to   G
pay him for the services which he was providing. Subsequently Mr Nicoll was given
notice terminating his employment which was effective about two months after the
appointment of the receiver. Mr Nicoll claimed his salary for the period during which his
employment had not been terminated. The receiver replied that he had no personal
liability to pay and that Mr Nicoll could only prove for this remuneration in the
company's liquidation which had supervened. In view of the company's insolvency, such   H
a proof would not have resulted in any dividend. Mr Nicoll contended that it made no
sense that an employee, whose service contract is continued by the bank's receiver in
order to assist in realising the company's assets to the best advantage, should, as
remuneration for the period of that continuation of his service contract, be relegated to a
claim against the company and get nothing. The Court of Appeal held that, whilst they
had considerable sympathy for Mr Nicoll, they could do nothing because the court had

A   no power to order the receiver to pay him. This holding, that the receiver was not liable to pay for services provided by an employee, was the trigger for legislative reform.

5. Sections 44 and 19(5)

The Act included two provisions for the protection of employees in the case of an administrative receivership in s. 44 and in the case of an administration in s. 19. These

B   sections read as follows:

'44(1) The administrative receiver of a company–

(a) is deemed to be the company's agent, unless and until the company goes into liquidation;

(b) is personally liable on any contract entered into by him in the carrying out

C   of his functions (except in so far as the contract otherwise provides) and . . . on any contract of employment adopted by him in the carrying out of those functions; and

(c) is entitled in respect of that liability to an indemnity out of the assets of the company.

(2) For the purposes of subsection 1(b) the administrative receiver is not to be

D   taken to have adopted a contract of employment by reason of anything done or omitted to be done within 14 days after his appointment.

19(4) His [the administrator's] remuneration and any expenses properly incurred by him shall be charged on and paid out of any property of the company which is in his custody or under his control at that time in priority to any security to which section 15(1) then applies.

E   (5) Any sums payable in respect of debts or liabilities incurred, while he was an administrator, under contracts entered into or contracts of employment adopted by him or a predecessor of his in the carrying out of his or the predecessor's functions shall be charged on and paid out of any such property as is mentioned in subsection (4) in priority to any charge arising under that subsection.

For this purpose, the administrator is not to be taken to have adopted a contract

F   of employment by reason of anything done or omitted to be done within 14 days after his appointment.'

Both sections have one thing in common, namely the concern to make specific provision in the case of contracts of employment 'adopted' by the receiver and administrator. The subject of both sections is the same, namely adopted contracts. But there are in particular two immediately apparent and significant distinctions between the

G   two sections:

(1) s. 44(1)(b) imposes personal liability on the receiver, who is entitled to an indemnity out of and a charge on the assets in the hands of the receiver, whilst s. 19(5) merely creates a charge on the assets the subject of the administration; and

(2) under s. 44(1)(b) the receiver's liability is 'on' the adopted contracts, whilst under s. 19(5) the charge is limited to sums payable in respect of debts and liabilities

H   incurred whilst he is an administrator under the adopted contract.

In short the intended legal consequences are different.

The statutory purpose of these sections was to overrule the effect of *Nicoll v Cutts*: see Nicholls V-C in *Atlantic Computer Systems plc* at p. 865H. But whilst Parliament clearly wished to be seen to act, it was less anxious to make plain what it had done, and this has given rise to the issues in this action.

6. The issues
A

The issues raised on the application are threefold:

(1)   the meaning of 'adoption' and whether in this case Leyland Daf and Ferranti adopted the contracts of employment of their employees;

(2)   if the answer to (1) is in the affirmative, whether the personal liability of the receivers in respect of such adopted contracts (a) can legally be excluded and if so (b) whether it was in this case; and
B

(3)   if the answer to (2) is to the effect that there was no exclusion, the extent of the obligations under the adopted contracts to which personal liability extends.

(1) *Meaning of 'adoption'*

The word 'adoption' in respect of a contract has a variety of different meanings in different contexts. It may mean 'novation': see e.g. Lord Tomlin in *Greenwood v Martins* C *Bank* [1933] AC 51 at p. 57 and Evershed J in *Re Botibol* [1947] 1 All ER 26 at p. 28. It may (in case of a contract entered into by an agent without authority) mean 'ratify'. Adoption however in cases of receivership has a special meaning. 'What is meant by saying that a receiver has power to "adopt" a pre-receivership contract is that he may refrain from repudiating it' per McPherson J in *Re Diesels & Components Pty Ltd* (1985) 3 ACLC 555 at 557. Adoption has the same meaning in the context of a liquidation when D the question arises whether the liquidator has so acted as to render the liability to the other party part of the costs of the liquidation, as opposed to a mere provable debt: see *Re Anchor Line (Henderson Brothers) Ltd* [1937] Ch 1 and *Re S Davis & Co Ltd* [1945] Ch 402. Accordingly as it seems to me, in the context of s. 44, the word 'adopted' must be given the meaning 'treated as continuing in force'. It is fair to say that this is the view expressed in Lightman & Moss (above), pp. 203–206 and I can see no reason to resile from it (or indeed the views expressed on the other issues raised on these applications).
E

No distinction can be drawn, as it seems to me, from the meaning of the word 'adopted' in s. 44 and 19. The construction of the word in the context of s. 19 adopted by the Court of Appeal in *Powdrill* [1994] BCC 172 by Dillon LJ at p. 178H and Leggatt LJ at p. 183 is to this very effect, namely the express or implied acceptance of the contract's continuance, a restatement of the language of Professor R M Goode in *Principles of Corporate Insolvency Law* (1990), cited with approval by Evans-Lombe J and Dillon LJ F at p. 403, namely acts or acquiescence after expiry of the 14-day period indicative of the intention to treat the contract as on foot.

In these circumstances there can be no dispute that the contracts of employment of the employees of Leyland Daf and Ferranti were adopted by the respective receivers. The protestations by the receivers in their letters that they were not by so treating the contracts as continuing adopting them cannot negate or qualify the legal effect of their actions.
G

(2) *Exclusion of liability*

Before considering questions of exclusion it is appropriate to consider the character of the liability imposed on the receiver by s. 44. It seems to me quite clear that the character is the same as that imposed on receivers who contract without excluding personal liability. The liability is not a term of the contract, but a statutory incident of it.

(a) Power to exclude
H

Mr Purle for the employees submits that the language and policy of the Act precludes any arrangement or agreement between the receiver and employee excluding this personal liability. He draws attention to the way that the section specifically permits a receiver to contract out of personal liability in case of contracts entered into by him as receiver, and the absence of any like provision in respect of adopted contracts, and he stresses the

A   statutory policy underlying the section to protect employees, which (he says) would be undermined if the receiver could as a matter of course contract out of his liability.

There are, as it seems to me, a number of answers to this submission. First, as a matter of language the proviso requiring a provision in the contract excluding personal liability if personal liability is to be avoided in case of contracts entered into by the receiver is quite inapposite in case of the adoption of a contract by the receiver. The act of adoption

B   does not require and in any ordinary case will not take the form of a contract between the receiver and employee, and accordingly a statutory proviso that liability may be excluded by a term in the contract would not be appropriate. Accordingly I do not think that the absence of an express provision for an agreement excluding personal liability in case of adopted contracts is of particular significance.

Of far greater significance are the facts that: (1) in many cases it may only be sensible for a receiver to adopt a contract of employment if he can agree some limitation on his

C   personal liabilities, his only alternative being to dismiss. I can see no reason why Parliament should forbid him to enter into such an agreement, which may be for the benefit of the employees as well as himself; (2) the receiver can in any event dismiss and re-engage employees on terms excluding personal liability. Again I can see no reason why this should be necessary instead of an agreement to allow the existing employment to continue, but excluding personal liability. There is plainly nothing to prevent receivers in

D   new contracts of employment contracting out of personal liability.

As it seems to me, the statutory policy is not to confer upon employees a basic right which they cannot contract out of, but to prevent receivers encouraging expectations of payment and then disappointing them; and in particular the unfair exploitation of employees by receivers, in the absence of the unequivocal and informed agreement of the employees, taking the benefit of their services without at the same time accepting legal

E   responsibility for payment.

I can see no hint of, or reason for, any statutory prohibition on employees contracting out of the protection afforded by s. 44. I am comforted by the fact that in *Powdrill* Evans-Lombe J at first instance took the same view in respect of administrators contracting out of s. 19(5). The Court of Appeal expressed no view on the question as it did not arise.

(b) Actual exclusion

F   For exclusion of the statutory incident of personal liability, it is plain that what is required is a contract to this effect between the receiver and the affected employees and nothing less will do. The statutory incident of personal liability should be capable of removal whatever the capacity in which the receiver contracts for its removal, whether personally or as agent for the company. But as it seems to me the court should be slow to infer that the employees have entered into such contract surrendering their statutory

G   rights unless it is plain that they have given a full and informed consent.

Mr Elias has very properly in this context brought to my attention the case of *Jones v Associated Tunnelling Co Ltd* [1981] IRLR 477. The Employment Appeal Tribunal (albeit obiter) gave consideration in that case to the question how far the assent to a variation in the contractual terms of employment should be implied from the mere failure of an employee to object to the unilateral alteration by the employer of the terms of his employment contained in a statutory statement. Browne-Wilkinson J giving the decision

H   of the tribunal, in a passage which I gratefully adopt, said (at p. 481):

> 'In our view, to imply an agreement to vary or to raise an estoppel against the employee on the grounds that he has not objected to a false record by the employers of the terms actually agreed is a course which should be adopted with great caution. If the variation relates to a matter which has immediate practical application (e.g., the rate of pay) and the employee continues to work without objection after effect

has been given to the variation (e.g., his pay packet has been reduced) then   A
obviously he may well be taken to have impliedly agreed. But where, as in the
present case, the variation has no immediate practical effect, the position is not the
same. It is the view of both members of this Tribunal with experience in industrial
relations (with which the chairman, without such experience, agrees) that it is
asking too much of the ordinary employee to require him either to object to an
erroneous statement of his terms of employment having no immediate practical
impact on him or be taken to have assented to the variation. So to hold would   B
involve an unrealistic view of the inclination and ability of the ordinary employee
to read and fully understand such statements.

Even if he does read the statement and can understand it, it would be unrealistic of
the law to require him to risk a confrontation with his employer on a matter which
has no immediate practical impact on the employee. For those reasons, as at
present advised, we would not be inclined to imply any assent to a variation from   C
mere failure by the employee to object to the unilateral alteration by the employer
of the terms of employment contained in a statutory statement.'

It seems to me clear beyond question that neither the Leyland Daf nor the Ferranti
letter was or should reasonably have been understood by the recipient employees as an
offer requiring acceptance or rejection. They constituted merely unilateral declarations
of 'non-liability'. But even if they did constitute offers, since the exclusion of personal   D
liability of the receiver had no immediate practical effect on the employees, it would be
totally unrealistic and unfair to treat the continued performance by the employees of
their contracts of employment as an acceptance of a new contract by way of variation
of their contracts of employment excluding the statutory incident of personal liability.
The statutory personal liability accordingly continues to attach to the receivers.

Mr Elias did at one point submit that a more relaxed attitude should be adopted in   E
inferring an arrangement or agreement to displace personal liability. He explained with
conviction the heavy burden on receivers on taking office, the impracticality of obtaining
written acceptances by employees of offers within the statutory 14-day period, and the
damaging consequences for all concerned if the receiver is obliged in order to protect
himself from personal liability to dismiss all employees and then re-engage them. He also
made a plea that the finding of the requirement for an agreement excluding liability   F
operated harshly on receivers who had acted and developed an established practice based
upon the decision in *Re Specialised Mouldings Ltd* (unreported but referred to by Dillon
LJ in *Powdrill* at p. 179E) to the effect that sending letters in terms of the Leyland Daf
and Ferranti letters was effective to exclude personal liability.

I can only respond that Parliament in the Act plainly did not intend that liability in
respect of adopted contracts should be avoided by anything less than liability under new   G
contracts entered into by the receiver. The receiver was given the free choice between
adoption and repudiation: he was not given the third free choice of adoption in the
absence of agreement of the employees without assuming personal liability. This may be
unfortunate for the receiver and the receivership, but would negate the protection
intended for employees and restore the position to that prevailing in *Nicoll v Cutts*.

As regards reliance on the decision in *Re Specialised Mouldings* and the established   H
practice of insolvency practitioners based upon it, it is difficult to believe that there was
not involved on the part of such practitioners some degree of wishful thinking. This
decision in *Re Specialised Mouldings* cannot (as Dillon LJ pointed out in *Powdrill* at
p. 180B) have been intended by the judge as a precedent in other cases. Certainly even
before *Powdrill*, the decision, given without reasons, was regarded by lawyers at best as
one 'to be treated with caution' (see e.g. *Employment Insolvency Handbook* by Tim

A   Marshall, pp. 22–25), and was indeed authoritatively stated to be wrong (see e.g. Professor R M Goode (above), p. 101).

By the end of his argument I think that Mr Elias fairly and correctly accepted that nothing less than a contract with the employees was required, in effect conceding that the decision in *Re Specialised Mouldings Ltd* was not even arguably sustainable.

B
(c) *Extent of liabilities*

Mr Elias has submitted that as a matter of construction of s. 44 there are three possible alternatives regarding the extent of the liabilities assumed by the 'adopting' receiver:

(1)   all liabilities whenever incurred of whatever kind under the adopted contract;

(2)   liabilities incurred under the contract whilst receiver;

(3)   liabilities for services rendered to the company during the receivership.

C
The second alternative equates the liability of the receiver to that of the administrator in respect of adopted contracts under s. 19(5) as held in *Powdrill*. The third alternative equates the liability to that imposed in respect of contracts adopted on or after 15 March 1994 under the 1994 Act.

Whilst there may be doubt whether Parliament really intended such a windfall for employees and indeed anything more than the third alternative as the antidote to *Nicoll*

D   *v Cutts*, as a matter of language it seems to me the only tenable construction is the first alternative. As Leggatt LJ said in respect of a related question in *Powdrill* at p. 183D: 'Whatever the consequences for insolvency law . . . the point is in my judgment too plain for argument.' Section 44(1)(b) equates the statutory incident of personal liability of the receiver in case of liability on employment contracts adopted by the receiver in carrying out his functions, to the statutory incident of personal liability on new contracts which do not exclude personal liability entered into by him in the carrying out of his functions.

E   In both cases the liability is co-extensive with that of the company. I can find no handle within the language used on which to fasten any limitation, nor could Mr Elias suggest any.

Mr Elias has helpfully and forcibly addressed me as to the damaging consequences that will ensue from such a construction on receiverships and the achievement of corporate rescues which the Act is designed to achieve. He submits that the first

F   construction should be rejected because it (1) goes beyond the mischief in *Nicoll v Cutts* which s. 44(1)(b) was designed to remedy; (2) involves receivers being required to assume blind open-ended commitments; (3) creates difficulties for receivers and in particular in respect of distributions and the discharge of the receivership; and (4) subverts the rescue culture in respect of companies in difficulties which the Act was designed to promote.

1. As regards remedying the mischief revealed by the decision in *Nicoll v Cutts*, the

G   mischief could be remedied in a multitude of ways and it seems to me that all three alternative constructions remedy the mischief: the mischief rule affords no light as to which construction should be adopted.

2. I am concerned that the decision by receivers whether or not to adopt employment contracts (a course which may be critical to saving a business and the jobs of employees) if the decision is to be made within the statutory 14 days must frequently be made without any adequate opportunity to investigate, let alone evaluate, the possible claims in respect

H   of which an open-ended personal liability is to be assumed. The potential liability makes adoption a risky course which receivers must think twice about (and on occasions consult their appointors) before undertaking. The answer to this dilemma for receivers, as I read the Act, is that if they are not prepared to take this risk, they must decline to adopt. Any other answer, limiting their exposure, must be found in legislation (as in the 1994 Act) and not a forced construction of the Act.

3. As regards distribution and discharge, I recognise that the personal liability on   A
adopted contracts will continue to subsist until the liability is discharged and that this
may create problems in the way of distribution of realisations and the discharge of the
receivership. But the problem is no different in kind from that posed in respect of new
contracts entered into by the receiver which do not exclude personal liability. The
receivers may be compelled to proceed on a 'worst case' estimate, but this course is not
an unfamiliar one, e.g. when there is outstanding litigation, and to insist on protection
by way of indemnity, security or otherwise before they pay their appointor or agree to be   B
discharged. Whilst I appreciate the practical advantages for the receiver and receivership
in this respect of adopting the other constructions and the disincentive which my
preferred construction may create on the adoption of employment contracts, I do not
think that this construction is so obviously unreasonable that another should be adopted
which finds no like basis in the statutory language.

4. As regards the rescue culture which prevails today, no doubt one of the most   C
important resources of a business over which a receiver is appointed is likely to be the
employees, and it will facilitate a rescue if the receiver can keep the workforce together
without incurring any or any substantial personal liability. But the legislation recognises
that the employees in respect of their labour are not to be treated in the same way as
other suppliers of goods and services under continuing contracts. They merit special
protection. They are specially vulnerable and unlikely to have the muscle to be able to
insist (as may some other suppliers under continuing contracts) on payment or special   D
treatment in respect of sums already accrued due or to accrue in the future. I do not think
it is inconceivable or absurd to infer from the section that Parliament intended the
receiver, if he intended to exploit this resource, to honour the employees' contracts in
full; nor do I think it inconceivable or absurd to infer that Parliament may have
considered that the real issue in many cases such as the present is not really one of
personal liability of the receivers, but of priorities in payment between the debenture   E
holder (generally a bank) and the employees. This is the case here where the assets of
both companies subject to the crystallised floating charge are more than ample to pay the
employees in full. The receiver has a charge on these assets to secure his liability. When
the assets are not sufficient or there is any risk of the personal liability exceeding the
value of the assets to which the receiver can look for payment, no doubt the receiver can
and will before incurring personal liability require an indemnity from his appointor. It
may be that this 'priority' of the employees may deter some rescues; some appointors will   F
not wish to take the risk that the costs of discharging all liabilities to employees under
adopted contracts will fall upon them if the rescue fails to achieve a sufficient return. But
I cannot think that this consequence must be seen to be so inconsistent with the legislation
or its purpose as to deny the employees under adopted contracts the protection which
prima facie the language affords them.

I should add that nothing decided in *Powdrill* on the different wording of s. 19(5)   G
impinges on my decision as to the extent of the liability imposed on receivers by
s. 44(1)(b).

7. Date of commencement of personal liability

I have been asked to decide the date on which the personal liability of the receiver
attaches, namely retrospectively to the date of appointment or the date of adoption. This   H
question does not have the significance it would have if I had reached a different view on
the extent of liabilities arising on adoption. Mr Elias argues that retrospectivity to the
date of appointment has the advantages (1) of consistency with the practice in liquidation
where payment as a liquidation expense for continuing services and supplies runs from
the date of liquidation; (2) of certainty, avoiding possible difficult inquiries as to the date
of adoption; and (3) of harmonising with the existing preference given to employees

A   which relates to the period immediately prior to the appointment. But it seems to me plain on the language of the section that liability attaches at and from the date of adoption and is not retrospective to the date of appointment. By virtue of s. 44(2), this will be on day 15 after the appointment or the earliest date thereafter on which adoption takes place. It would appear that it is not legally possible for a receiver deliberately to adopt a contract earlier than day 15 though this may be thought the only or best method of holding on to essential employees. Earlier than this date he can however contract to

B   adopt after the statutory period for taking stock has expired or contract immediately to assume an equivalent obligation.

8. Answers to questions

In view of my decision on the construction of the Act, the answer to all questions raised is simple, namely the receivers (1) have adopted the contracts of employment; (2)

C   have not contracted out of their personal liability; and (3) are personally liable co-extensively with the companies in respect of all contractual (but no other) liabilities under the contracts of employment of the employees irrespective of the dates on which they accrued or the periods in respect of which the liability arose.

The receivers are bound to pay forthwith, as they are bound to discharge forthwith all immediate obligations under new contracts they enter into without an exclusion of

D   personal liability. It is common ground that the receivers have no obligation to pay interest: any such obligation can only arise when and if the employees sue for payment. This is clearly correct.

It is, I think, agreed that there is no dispute as to which of the items detailed in the originating application are contractual. The detailed answers are as follows.

E   *Leyland Daf*

1. The contracts of employment of the first respondent, Mr Cadge, and the second respondent, Mr Sumner, have been adopted by the administrative receivers of Leyland Daf Ltd in the carrying out of their functions as such receivers within the meaning of s. 44 of the Act.

2. (1) The administrative receivers in principle are personally liable on such contracts

F   to make payments in respect of the following:

(a)   sums payable by way of damages for wrongful dismissal effected by them during the receivership:

    (i)   in lieu of contractual notice under the respondents' contracts of employment;

    (ii)   in respect of pension benefits to the extent that such benefits would have

G   accrued to the respondents during their contractual notice periods;

    (iii)   in respect of Mr Cadge's entitlement under Leyland Daf's policies in relation to private medical insurance and accident insurance;

(b)   all holiday pay falling due under the respondents' contract of employment.

But the administrative receivers are not liable to pay:

H   (c)   under Leyland Daf's redundancy policy, compensation for loss of office; or

(d)   under the Leyland Daf company car policy, for loss of opportunity to purchase cars at a discounted price on termination of employment.

(2) The administrative receivers are not presently liable to pay interest on any sum so due.

(3) The sums referred to in 2. above should be paid to the respondents forthwith.

Ferranti International plc   A

1. The contracts of employment of the first respondent, Mrs Grundy, and the second respondent, John Parry, have been adopted by the administrative receivers of Ferranti International plc in the carrying out of their functions as such receivers within the meaning of s. 44 of the Act.

2. (1) The administrative receivers in principle are personally liable on such contracts to make payments in respect of the following: B

(a)   sums payable by way of damages for wrongful dismissal effected by them during the receivership:

    (i)   in lieu of contractual notice under the respondents' contracts of employment;

    (ii)   in respect of pension benefits, to the extent that such benefits would have accrued to the respondents during their contractual notice periods;   C

    (iii)   in respect of health care schemes, benefits to which the second respondent was entitled by reason of cl. 5 of his contract of employment to the extent that such benefits would have accrued to him during his contractual notice period;

    (iv)   in respect of the benefit of the provision of a motor car to Mr Parry in accordance with cl. 2.4 of his contract of employment to the extent that such   D benefits would have accrued to him during his contractual notice period;

(b)   all sums due to Mrs Grundy in respect of holiday pay falling due by reason of cl. 3 of her contract of employment;

(c)   all sums due to John Parry in respect of holiday pay falling due by reason of cl. 6(d) of his contract of employment;   E

(d)   all sums due to the respondents under the terms of the severance payment 1and redeployment agreement dated 14 February 1991.

(2) The administrative receivers are not presently liable to pay interest on any sum so due.

3. The sums referred to in 2. above should be paid to the respondents forthwith.

(*Order accordingly. Certificate under s. 12 of the Administration of Justice Act 1969 for*   F
appeal to House of Lords. Costs against administrative receivers on indemnity basis
agreed)

G

H

A # McKillop & Anor (Joint receivers of Rowan Leisure Ltd), Petitioners.

Court of Session (Outer House).
Lord MacLean.
Judgment delivered 29 March 1994.

B *Receivership – Rates – Whether receivers were liable for rates on company premises.*

This was a petition for directions brought by the receivers of Rowan Leisure Ltd seeking determination of the question whether they were liable as joint receivers of the company to make payment to the respondent council of rates in respect of the occupation of premises by the company in the period from 6 March 1991 (appointment of the receivers) to 18 June
C **1992 (sale of premises).**

Held, giving directions accordingly:

The receivers were not personally liable to pay rates in respect of the occupation of the premises from 6 March 1991 until 18 June 1992, and the rates were not a receivership expense in terms of s. 60(1)(c) of the Insolvency Act 1986.

The following cases were referred to in the opinion:

D *Assessor for Renfrewshire v Old Consort Co Ltd & Anor* 1960 SC 226.
Lord Advocate v Aero Technologies Ltd (in receivership) 1991 SLT 134.
Ratford & Anor v Northavon District Council (1986) 2 BCC 99,242; [1987] QB 357.
Taggs Island Casino Hotel Ltd v Richmond-upon-Thames London Borough Council [1967] RA 70; (1966) 14 RRC 119.
Westminster Council v Southern Railway Co & Ors [1936] AC 511.

E P S Hodge (instructed by Dorman Jeffrey & Co) for the receivers.

OPINION

Lord MacLean: This is a petition for directions in terms of s. 63(1) of the *Insolvency Act* 1986 brought by the joint receivers of Rowan Leisure Ltd who were appointed by Scottish and Newcastle Breweries plc by instrument of appointment dated 6 March 1991 to be joint receivers of the property charged by a floating charge granted by the company
F in favour of Scottish and Newcastle Breweries dated 3 August 1990. The floating charge, according to its terms, was granted over the whole of the company's property (including uncalled capital) which was or might be from time to time while the instrument was in force comprised in the company's property and undertaking. Amongst the company's property were licensed premises in Dundee known as Morgan's Bar, and after the appointment, the petitioners as joint receivers continued the company's business carried
G on in the premises with a view to selling the heritable property as a going concern. The licensed premises were later closed on 25 February 1992 and sold on 18 June 1992.

Tayside Regional Council, who are called as respondents in this action, thereafter sought as rating authority payment of rates directly from the petitioners as joint receivers for the period from 6 March 1991 to 18 June 1992. On 12 October 1993 the respondents sent two letters to the firm of chartered accountants in which the petitioners are partners. In one they demanded payment of rates amounting to £27,788.56. In support of that
H demand they said:

'As the receiver and agent of the company I consider that you are responsible for acting on behalf of the company in receivership. In my opinion this responsibility also extends to post-receivership rates liability and although I am aware of the decision in the case of *Ratford & Anor v Northavon District Council*, I would point out that the ruling was made under English law and until a ruling is made by a

court in Scotland, the fact of whether or not the decision would be persuasive to a　A
Scottish court can be only speculation. In these circumstances, payments of the
amount listed above should be made by return. A copy of this letter has been
passed to Sheriff Officers, Scott & Co.'

In the other letter, they wrote:

'I refer to your letter of 5 July 1993 the contents of which have been noted. The
example case that you quote namely *Ratford & Anor v Northavon District Council*　B
was ruled upon under English law and to the best of my knowledge no test case
has yet been brought before a court in Scotland.

Although I appreciate the case in question may well be persuasive in the Scottish
court, I must advise you that until such ruling is made under Scottish law, it is my
intention on behalf of Tayside Regional Council to pursue by means of summary
warrant if necessary, all cases where post-receivership rates are due and remain　C
unpaid.'

In the face of these letters and the demand made by the respondents the petitioners
seek the directions of the court as to whether they are responsible as joint receivers of the
company to make payment to the respondents of rates in respect of the occupation of the
licensed premises by the company in the period from 6 March 1991 to 18 June 1992.
Prior to the petition being heard, solicitors acting for the respondents intimated to
solicitors acting for the petitioners by letter dated 23 February 1994, that the respondents　D
did not intend to lodge answers; that the petition would not be opposed; and that the
respondents were prepared to mark their consent on any motion made in terms of the
petition. There is, therefore, no contradictor to the petition; and so the first question
which I must consider is whether I should exercise the discretion I have in terms of
s. 63(1) of the 1986 Act and give directions to the petitioners. I have reached the
conclusion that I should do so because, although the respondents have not opposed this　E
petition, and, indeed, would if asked have, it appears, consented to the directions sought
being given, they have not, as a rating authority, expressly retracted the demand they
made in their letters of 12 October 1993.

Mr Hodge, who appeared for the petitioners, said that the question upon which I was
called upon to make directions was whether the petitioners as joint receivers of the
company were in rateable occupation of the licensed premises during the period when the
parties continued the operation of the company's business at Morgan's Bar. In support　F
of his submission that it was the company who were in rateable occupation he referred,
first, to *Armour on valuation for rating* (5th edn) para. 14-01–14-03; to the cases of
Westminster Council v Southern Railway Co & Ors [1936] AC 511 and the speech of Lord
Russell of Killowen at pp. 529–530; and *Assessor for Renfrewshire v Old Consort Co Ltd*
1960 SC 226 per Lord Guest at p. 233. At para. 13-11 the editors of *Armour* say with
reference to receivers of a Scottish company:　　　　　　　　　　　　　　　　　　　G

'In *Ratford v Northavon District Council* [(1986) 2 BCC 99,242], it was held that a
company was still in the rateable occupation of its premises even although they
were in possession of receivers. The basis of this decision was that the receiver was
according to the terms of the debenture and his appointment, to be treated as the
agent of the company. A receiver of a Scottish company is deemed to be the agent
of the company in relation to such property of the company as is attached to the
floating charge by virtue of which he was appointed. In the ordinary case where a　H
receiver is appointed, therefore, it would appear to be proper to retain the company
in the Valuation Roll as rateable occupier.'

In *Ratford* the Court of Appeal held that, subject to the terms of the debenture and the
appointment, a receiver appointed by a debenture holder would, normally, not be under
personal liability if he properly carried out his functions since he would be acting simply

A   as an agent either for the debenture holder or the company. Where an agent had to occupy heritage in order properly to carry out his duties, his occupation should be treated as that of his principal. Thus, if both the debenture and the instrument of appointment provided for the receiver to be treated as the company's agent, the company remained the rateable occupier and was not dispossessed merely by the receivers taking possession. The case of *Taggs Island Casino Hotel Ltd v Richmond-upon-Thames London Borough Council* (1968) 14 RRC 119 was regarded as a special one, principally because the receiver

B   had deponed in an affidavit that he himself had taken possession of the company's premises, but also because the view of the judge at first instance was a preliminary one given at an interlocutory stage. In England, at least, it may be possible to show, either from the terms of the receiver's appointment, or from what he has actually done, or from both, that he has taken possession of the premises adversely to the company. But, as the editors of *Kerr on Receivers* (17th edn) write at p. 367:

C   'Since the decision in *Ratford v Northavon District Council*, however, it is clear that some totally unusual circumstances are required to produce such a result; in any usual case, the receiver is not in possession otherwise than as agent for the company, or, if perchance he is an agent for the debenture holders, for such debenture holders.'

In Scotland, of course, the receiver is wholly a creature of statute, and s. 57(1) of the

D   *Insolvency Act 1986* provides that:

'A receiver is deemed to be the agent of the company in relation to such property of the company as is attached by the floating charge by virtue of which he was appointed.'

In terms of s. 57(2) of the Act he is personally liable on any contract entered into by him in the performance of his functions, unless he specifically excludes his personal liability

E   in the contract, although he is entitled to be indemnified out of the property in respect of which he was appointed (s. 57(3)). Mr Hodge drew my attention to a single sentence in St Clair and Drummond Young *The Law of Corporate Insolvency in Scotland* (2nd edn) at p. 147 which reads as follows:

'A receiver becomes liable to pay rates in respect of the period of his occupancy.'

Mr Hodge submitted that this statement, which was based solely on the *Taggs Island*

F   *Casino* case, was incorrect in the light of the *Ratford* case. It was not, he said, sound law in Scotland either. I agree with Mr Hodge's criticism of the statement, and I shall therefore disregard the statement. I shall adopt as correct the statement in *Palmer's Company Law*, vol. 2, para. 14.224 that:

'A receiver may be regarded as the occupier of company premises (jointly with the company) for the purposes of enforcing a statutory duty imposed on the occupier of premises but not for the purpose of liability for rates.'

G   In considering the duty of receivers under s. 23 of the *Explosives Act* 1875 as occupiers of a factory, Lord Sutherland in *Lord Advocate v Aero Technologies Ltd (in receivership)* 1991 SLT 134 said this at p. 136D:

'I see no reason in principle why both the company and the receivers, who are after all acting on behalf of the company and as managers for the company, should not be regarded as joint occupiers. Counsel for the receivers accepted that there was

H   nothing in principle to prevent there being more than one occupier. The position may be different for the purposes of payment of rates, and accordingly I find the case of *Ratford* of little assistance, particularly as what was sought there was decree against the receivers as individuals. Having regard to the fact that the receivers are acting as managers for the company they are for practical purposes in occupation of the premises in order that they can carry out their task. The requirement to

A

comply with statutory duty is a management function and accordingly I see no reason in principle why the receivers should not be occupiers for the purposes of the Explosives Act.'

Mr Hodge submitted on first principles that since no one ever suggested that directors of a company who were its controlling minds, were in fact occupiers, by a parity of reasoning neither could it be suggested that receivers were occupiers. Mr Hodge distinguished the situation in which the receiver entered into contracts in the performance of his functions in which he incurred personal liability, from the occupancy of rateable property by a receiver on behalf of the company. The statutory scheme, said Mr Hodge, made it clear that the receiver acts as agent for the company in relation to the property which is subject to the floating charge under which he was appointed. Accordingly, when he was carrying on the business of the company from the heritable property owned by the company, it was the company which remained in rateable occupation during the receivership.

B

C

I agree with Mr Hodge's submissions. As I am asked to do in terms of the prayer of the petition, I shall give directions in terms of s. 63(1) of the *Insolvency Act* 1986, and these directions are to the effect that the receivers are not personally liable to pay rates in respect of the occupation of the licensed premises known as Morgan's Bar, Dundee, from 6 March 1991 until 18 June 1992, and that the rates are not a receivership expense in terms of s. 60(1)(c) of the Act.

D

(*Order accordingly*)

E

F

G

H

A Tottenham Hotspur plc & Ors v Edennote plc.

Chancery Division.
Rattee J.
Judgment delivered 12 May 1994.

B *Winding-up petition – Petitioners claimed to be creditors by virtue of order for costs – Whether petitioners had standing to petition – Whether court should make winding-up order – Insolvency Act 1986, s. 122(1)(f); Insolvency Rules 1986 (SI 1986/1925), r. 13.12.*

This was a petition under s. 122(1)(f) of the Insolvency Act 1986 to wind up a company on the ground that it was unable to pay its debts.

The petitioners claimed to be creditors within the meaning of s. 124 of the Insolvency Act C by virtue of an order for costs which was made in their favour against the company respondent to the petition by Chadwick J on 13 September 1993, those costs being the costs of an abortive petition under s. 459 of the Companies Act brought by the company against the petitioners. On 27 October 1993 the petitioners delivered a bill of costs to the company in the sum of £460,130. On 12 January 1994 the petition was presented. On 25 and 26 January 1994 taxation was conducted and a total of some £335,000-odd remained as the sum due on the bill after taxation. However, notices of objection to that taxation had been D lodged by both sides and had yet to be determined. On 21 February 1994 the taxing master gave an interim taxing certificate in the sum of £183,750. No payment had been made in respect of that sum by the company.

The company did not dispute that it was unable to pay its debts, but submitted, first, that the petitioners had no standing to petition and, secondly, that the court should exercise its discretion against the making of a winding-up order because the order was sought for the E improper purpose of stifling an action brought by the company against the wholly owned subsidiary of one of the petitioners.

Held, making the usual compulsory winding-up order:

1. At the date of the petition the company was under an obligation to the petitioners to pay the costs ordered by Chadwick J to be paid by the company when taxed. Such obligation was a debt within the definition in r. 13.12(1)(b) and r. 13.12(3) of the Insolvency Rules. It F followed that the petitioners were accordingly creditors of the company and had the locus standi necessary to present the petition by virtue of s. 124 of the 1986 Act. In the absence of any other express definition of the word 'creditor' for the purposes of s. 124, it meant a person to whom a debt (within the meaning of the Insolvency Act) was owed by the relevant company.

2. In all the circumstances it was right to make a winding-up order. It would not be right to refuse such an order and to adjourn the petition merely because the company had a claim G not against the petitioners or any of them, but against a subsidiary company of one of the petitioners, which claim, if the liquidator considered it to be prima facie a good claim, could be pursued by him with an indemnity for the costs incurred in doing so from the company's owner and major creditor, which claim he would be likely to have to finance in any exent even if there were no winding-up order.

The following cases were referred to in the judgment:

H *Burnet v Francis Industries plc* [1987] 1 WLR 802.
Company No. 001573 of 1983, Re a (1983) 1 BCC 98,937.
FSA Business Software Ltd, Re [1990] BCC 465.
Laceward Ltd, Re [1981] 1 WLR 133.
LHF Wools Ltd, Re [1970] Ch 27.

David Oliver QC and Jonathan Crow (instructed by Herbert Smith) for the petitioners.

A

Sonia Proudman QC and Michael Jefferis (instructed by John Bowden Trainer) for the company.

JUDGMENT

Rattee J: This is a petition under s. 122(1)(f) of the *Insolvency Act* 1986 to wind up a company on the ground that it is unable to pay its debts within the meaning of s. 123(2) of the same Act because the value of its asset is less than the amount of its liabilities.

B

The petitioners claim to be creditors within the meaning of s. 124 of the Insolvency Act by virtue of an order for costs which was made in their favour against the company respondent to the petition by Chadwick J on 13 September 1993, those costs being the costs of an abortive petition under s. 459 of the Companies Act brought by the company against the petitioners. The s. 459 petition was presented on 17 May 1993 against the present petitioners on the petition which I have to determine, namely Tottenham Hotspur plc ('Tottenham plc'), a public quoted company, Mr Sugar (its chairman and a significant shareholder in it) and Amshold Ltd, a company wholly owned by Mr Sugar.

C

The s. 459 petition arose from a dispute which was well publicised at the time, between Mr Sugar and Mr Terry Venables over the management of Tottenham plc and its subsidiary Tottenham Hotspur Football and Athletic Co Ltd ('Tottenham Ltd').

On 17 August 1993 a writ was issued by the company respondent to the present petition ('the company') and Mr Venables, including a claim by the company against Tottenham Ltd for damages for alleged wrongful termination of a management agreement between the company and Tottenham Ltd and a claim by Mr Venables, the indirect beneficial owner of all the shares in the company, against Tottenham plc, claiming damages for alleged wrongful termination of a service contract between Tottenham plc and Mr Venables.

D

An application has been made in the proceedings begun by that writ by the defendants to the action for security for costs to be provided by the company. I am told that the application for an order for such security has been adjourned by the master dealing with the application to await the outcome of this petition.

E

On 25 August 1993 the company granted charges over certain shares in Tottenham plc owned by it, being charges for approximately £1.2m in favour of Mr Venables and £450,000-odd in favour of the company's solicitors in the s. 459 proceedings. Those charges were registered on 10 September 1993. On 13 September 1993 Chadwick J dismissed the s. 459 petition because of the company's failure to comply with an order for security for the costs that had been made, and ordered the company to pay the costs of each of the three petitioners on the present petition, that is to say the three respondents to the s. 459 petition.

F

On 27 October 1993 the petitioners delivered a bill of costs to the company in the sum of £460,130. On 12 January 1994 the present petition was presented. On 25 and 26 January 1994 taxation was conducted of the costs ordered by Chadwick J to be paid by the company; and a total of some £335,000-odd remains as the sum due on the bill after taxation. However, notices of objection to that taxation have been lodged by both sides and have yet to be determined. On 21 February 1994 the taxing master gave an interim taxing certificate in the sum of £183,750. That then is the minimum amount due from the company in respect of the order for costs made by Chadwick J, and no payment has been made in respect of that sum by the company.

G

H

At some stage since the execution of the charges by the company which I have mentioned, the shares charged were sold; and I understand that the proceeds were paid out by the company as to part to a prior chargee bank and as to part to the company's former solicitors, in favour of whom one of the charges which I have mentioned had been

A created. The company now owes, apart from the costs due to the petitioners by virtue of Chadwick J's order, approximately £1.2m, being a debt due to Mr Venables, and a sum £2,000-odd to one supporting creditor supporting this petition.

The company's only assets are a claim for repayment of tax against the Commissioners of Inland Revenue in the sum of some £100,000, which has yet to be determined, and the claim made by the company against Tottenham Ltd in the action which I have already

B mentioned. It is not disputed on behalf of the company that at the date of the presentation of the present petition and now it was and is unable to pay its debts having regard in particular to the debt owed to Mr Venables. The petitioners accordingly seek a winding-up order on the present petition on the ground that the company is unable to pay its debts within the meaning of s. 123(2) of the *Insolvency Act* 1986.

The petition for a winding-up order was resisted by Miss Proudman at the hearing before me on behalf of the company in a very able and attractively presented argument

C on two separate grounds. First, she submitted that the petitioners had at the date of the presentation of the petition no locus standi to present the petition. For that submission Miss Proudman relied on two first instance decisions made under the 1948 Companies Act legislation, the first of them being *Re a Company No. 001573 of 1983* (1983) 1 BCC 98,937 and the second *Re Laceward Ltd* [1980] 1 WLR 133. In *Re a Company* the petition presented to wind up the relevant company was based on an order for the costs of

D separate litigation made earlier on the same day as that on which the petition was presented; and the petition was presented before in fact any bill of costs had been delivered to the company. Harman J dismissed the petition, because he held that it would achieve an improper purpose, that is to say improper as a purpose for a winding-up petition, in that it would confer on the petitioner an advantage not shared by other creditors of the company because the effect of a winding-up order would be to entitle the petitioner to a lease of certain property that was currently occupied by the company

E itself.

However, in a passage which seems to me clearly obiter, Harman J suggested that it was also arguable that the petitioner's debt for costs was still disputed and unascertained and would remain so until either taxation or agreement of the costs concerned; and that it was therefore not a proper ground for a winding-up petition. Harman J found support for that argument in the other decision relied on by Miss Proudman, namely *Re Laceward*

F *Ltd*. In that case the petition was also based on a debt for costs, being costs incurred for non-contentious work done by solicitors on behalf of the company. A bill was presented by the solicitors to the company but the solicitors had omitted to tell the company of its right to have the bill taxed. Slade J held that the petition was bad as being in breach of art. 3(2) of the *Solicitors' Remuneration Order* 1972.

As an alternative ground for dismissing the petition, Slade J held that the petitioner had no locus standi to present the petition as a creditor because, said Slade J at p. 137A–

G B:

> 'Before such taxation takes place [that is to say, taxation of the bill of costs concerned] there is no certainty whatever as to whether all or any specific part of the debt alleged by the petition will be found truly due to the petitioners. In these circumstances, it seems to me that, in the events which have happened, the alleged debt on which the petition is founded is manifestly disputed on bona fide and

H substantial grounds.'

In the last paragraph of his judgment, also on p. 137, Slade J said:

> 'In the present case, as I have indicated, there is no clearly ascertained sum in respect of which the petitioners have a claim to be creditors in advance of a taxation. Correspondingly, in my judgment, they have no locus standi to present a petition on this second, alternative ground.'

In my judgment I should beware of placing too much reliance on either of those cases, given that both were decided on the effect of earlier legislation replaced by a completely new code in the form of the 1986 Insolvency Act and the rules made thereunder.

What I must consider is whether the petitioners are creditors within the meaning of s. 124 of the 1986 Act. Section 124 provides that a petitioner can be a contingent or prospective creditor. The word 'creditor' is not otherwise defined for the purposes of s. 124, but I was rightly referred by counsel to the provisions of r. 13.12 of the *Insolvency Rules* 1986. Rule 13.12(1) is in these terms:

' "Debt", in relation to the winding up of a company, means (subject to the next paragraph) any of the following–

    (a) any debt or liability to which the company is subject at the date on which it goes into liquidation;

    (b) any debt or liability to which the company may become subject after that date by reason of any obligation incurred before that date; and

    (c) any interest provable, as mentioned in Rule 4.93(1).'

Subrule (2) contains a provision not relevant for present purposes. Subrule (3) is in these terms:

'For the purposes of references in any provision of the Act or the Rules about winding up to a debt or liability, it is immaterial whether the debt or liability is present or future, whether it is certain or contingent, or whether its amount is fixed or liquidated, or is capable of being ascertained by fixed rules or as a matter of opinion; and references in any such provision to owing a debt are to be read accordingly.'

Subrule (4), again, is not material for present purposes.

The petitioners before me submitted that a creditor for the purposes of s. 124 of the 1986 Act is a person to whom a debt within the meaning of the Act is owed. Rule 13.12(3) shows, submit the petitioners, that the relevant debt can be future and unascertained. To the extent that the judge in either *Re a Company* or *Re Laceward Ltd* – the cases to which I have referred – decided that a liability for untaxed, unagreed costs could not be a debt capable of founding a winding-up petition, because the amount of the indebtedness was unascertained and unascertainable at the date of the petition, the petitioners submitted that that decision is no longer valid in the context of the 1986 legislation. I accept this argument.

At the date of the petition the company was under a present obligation to the petitioners to pay the costs ordered by Chadwick J to be paid by the company when taxed. Such obligation was, in my judgment, a debt within the definition in r. 13.12(1)(b) and r. 13.12(3) of the Insolvency Rules. In my judgment, it follows that the petitioners were accordingly creditors of the company and had the locus standi necessary to present the petition by virtue of s. 124 of the 1986 Act. I accept the submission on behalf of the petitioners that, in the absence of any other express definition of the word 'creditor' for the purposes of s. 124, it must be taken to mean a person to whom a debt (within the meaning of the Insolvency Act) is owed by the relevant company.

Miss Proudman's second argument against the making of a winding-up order on the petition was that the court should exercise its discretion against the making of such an order because the effect of such an order would be (as Miss Proudman submitted the petitioners intend that it should be) to stifle the existing action brought by the company against the wholly owned subsidiary of one of the petitioners. This, submitted Miss Proudman, is an improper purpose which the court should not allow to be achieved by a winding-up petition.

A   In support of that proposition Miss Proudman relied on the decision of the Court of Appeal in *Re LHF Wools Ltd* [1970] Ch 27. In that case the relevant petition was presented by a bank to wind up a company which had a pending claim against the bank justiciable under Belgian law although not under English law. The company had ceased trading and had no assets other than the alleged claim against the petitioner bank. An individual in Belgium, who claimed a right against the bank similar to that claimed by the company, had agreed to finance the company's action against the bank in Belgium. The judge of first instance, Plowman J, had made a winding-up order. The Court of Appeal held that the judge had erred in principle in the exercise of his discretion. The petitioner in that case had argued that if the winding-up order was made the claim by the company against the petitioner bank could perfectly well be pursued by the liquidator, just as it could by the company were it not wound up. At p. 39B, Harman LJ said this:

C   'What in the end, then, are the considerations which I think ought to weigh with the court. First, that there is no object in this winding up and no purpose to be served by going on with it. There are no assets: there is nothing to collect: there is nothing to claim except this one alleged debt, which is, in my opinion, better served by being pursued by a person who understands the wool trade, who has allies in Belgium and who is more likely than the most able official who comes into it from outside to be able to make some progress with a matter which is undoubtedly of great complication. I, therefore, think that the balance goes in favour of allowing the company to continue.'

Miss Proudman, on behalf of the company in the present case, submitted that were the claim brought in the action by the company a claim against the petitioners themselves, the approach adopted by Harman LJ in *Re LHF Wools Ltd* would apply equally in this case and mean that at the very least the petition, if not dismissed, should be stood over to await the outcome of that action. The fact, submitted Miss Proudman, that the claim brought by the company is not against the petitioners or any of them but against a wholly-owned subsidiary of one of the petitioners should make no difference. For that proposition Miss Proudman relied on *Burnet v Francis Industries plc* [1987] 1 WLR 802, and in particular to a passage in the judgment of Bingham LJ, as he then was, at p. 811 in which his Lordship explained that in special circumstances, which he found did not exist in the case before the court, the court could under O. 47 of the Rules of the Supreme Court stay the execution of a summary judgment awarded in favour of A against a company, B, to await the outcome of an unresolved claim by C, a company associated with B, against A.

      In connection with that proposition, Miss Proudman also relied on a dictum of Warner J in *Re FSA Business Software Ltd* [1990] BCC 465, in which at p. 469G Warner J expressed the view that there is a close analogy between the jurisdiction of the court to stay an O. 14 judgment pending the prosecution of a counterclaim and the jurisdiction of this court to stay a winding-up petition pending the prosecution of a cross-claim.

      The petitioners responded to these arguments of Miss Proudman's on the exercise of the court's discretion with the following argument. The petitioners submitted that the making of a winding-up order would not stifle the prosecution of the action brought by the company against Tottenham Ltd. In any event, even if there is no winding-up order, the prosecution of that action will have to be financed by Mr Venables himself because the company has no available assets for the time being, and Mr Venables appears to be the only source of finance for costs. Mr Oliver on behalf of the petitioners submitted that, if a winding-up order is made, a liquidator will be able to continue the action just as effectively as Mr Venables, if the liquidator thinks fit so to do, with an indemnity from Mr Venables as to the costs of so doing. In deciding what action to take with regard to prosecuting that action, submitted Mr Oliver, the liquidator will have to take into

account Mr Venables' wishes as being one of the principal creditors, indeed the largest   A
creditor, of the company.

Unlike the situation in *Re LHF Wools Ltd*, Mr Oliver submitted that in the present
case there is no particular advantage in the company rather than a liquidator of the
company pursuing the alleged claim, and there is some point in a liquidation, that point
being that the petitioners claim that the charges executed by the company in favour of
Mr Venables and their former solicitors, and any payments made out of the proceeds of   B
the shares charged to either, would be voidable as improper preferences within the
meaning of s. 239 of the *Insolvency Act* 1986. Indeed, Mr Oliver told me that the reason
for the issue of the petition in this case at as early a stage as that at which it was issued,
was to preserve the petitioners' position in relation to the argument that the grant of the
charges were improper preferences within s. 239 of the Act, having regard to the six-
month period provided by s. 240 of the Act which may be relevant to the question of   C
whether any charge or payment made in favour of the company's former solicitors was
an improper preference.

The petitioners further rely on the fact (which is admitted by the company) that the
company will still be substantially insolvent even if its present claim against Tottenham
Ltd succeeds to its fullest possible extent. The petitioners also point out that, according
to a company search made in the course of the hearing as a result of something said on
behalf of the company by Miss Proudman, the petitioners have discovered that Mr   D
Venables as recently as 5 March of this year transferred all his shares in the company to
another company apparently owned by him at a time when only 25p was paid up on each
of the £1 shares. Finally, the petitioners rely on the fact that Tottenham plc, whose
subsidiary is the defendant to the claim relied upon by the company, is not the only
person interested in having the company wound up. The persons so interested include
Mr Sugar and his company, the third petitioner on this petition, who are not parties to
any claim by the company, and, indeed, the supporting creditor for the sum of £2,000,   E
although I am told by Miss Proudman that Mr Venables has come to some terms with
that creditor to pay off that creditor in the event of the company not being wound up.

That I have a discretion to make a winding-up order is clear from the decision of the
Court of Appeal which I have already cited in *Re LHF Wools Ltd*. It seems to me that in
exercising that discretion I should have regard in particular to the following
considerations. First, the company is insolvent and was insolvent at the date of the   F
petition. Secondly, the petitioners are entitled now to at least the sum of £183,750 in
respect of the interim taxation certificate, which the company has made no attempt to
pay and made no proposals to pay. Thirdly, the petitioners claim that the company's
assets have already been applied by way of improper preference – a proposition which
should be investigated, irrespective of the outcome of the company's claim against
Tottenham Ltd, and which can only be properly investigated in the context of a winding-
up order.   G

Fourthly, on the other hand, the company has an alleged substantial claim which may
or may not be made out at the end of the day against a wholly-owned subsidiary of one
of the petitioners, which claim has been made in proceedings started before the
presentation of the present petition. Fifthly, at the time of the events leading to that claim
five out of seven of the directors of the defendant to the claim, Tottenham Ltd, were also
directors of the petitioner Tottenham plc and Mr Sugar was the chairman of both   H
companies.

Sixthly, Mr Venables, the indirect beneficial owner of the company, also has a claim
made in the same action started before the presentation of the petition against Tottenham
plc, one of the petitioners – a claim arising out of the same facts as those on which the
company's claim against Tottenham Ltd is based. Seventhly, a winding-up order will

A   take the prosecution of the action by the company against the subsidiary of Tottenham plc out of the hands of the company but will enable a liquidator appointed in a winding up to pursue it if he thinks fit, taking account of the strength of the claim and of the wishes of Mr Venables as the largest creditor of the company with the benefit of an indemnity if proffered by Mr Venables as to costs, in circumstances where, if there were no winding-up order, Mr Venables anyway would appear to be the only person in a position to finance the further prosecution of the claim for the time being.

B   Eighthly, the company does not purport to have any cross-claim against any of the petitioners themselves. In particular, it alleges no claim against Mr Sugar or the third petitioner, a company owned by Mr Sugar, both of whom (that is to say Mr Sugar and his company) are likely to be the major beneficiaries of the order made by Chadwick J for costs against the company, since the largest burden of the costs of the respondents to the s. 459 petition fell upon them rather than on Tottenham plc.

C   Ninthly, a significant delay in the final resolution of the question whether the company should be wound up will ensue if the petition is stood over to await the trial of the company's action, at any rate if that action survives the present pending application for security for the costs against the company.

Tenthly, meanwhile, pending any adjournment of the petition to await the determination of the company's action, the company will be dormant and not trading but will remain insolvent throughout that period of delay and, indeed, will remain substantially insolvent even if the claim brought in the action succeeds to the fullest extent hoped for by the company.

D

In all these circumstances, I consider it right to exercise my discretion in favour of making a winding-up order. In particular I am not satisfied that it would be right to refuse such an order and to adjourn the petition merely because the company has a claim – good or bad I know not – not against the petitioners or any of them, but against a subsidiary company of one of the petitioners, the petitioner itself being a public quoted company, which claim, if the liquidator considers it to be prima facie a good claim, can be pursued by him with an indemnity from Mr Venables for the costs incurred in doing so, which in any event he would be likely to have to finance even if there were no winding-up order. Accordingly, I shall make the usual compulsory winding-up order on the petition.

E

(Order accordingly)

F

G

H

Agricultural Mortgage Corp plc v Woodward & Anor.

A

Court of Appeal (Civil Division).
Neill and Saville L JJ and Sir Christopher Slade.
Judgment delivered 19 May 1994.

Transactions defrauding creditors – Whether transaction was at an undervalue –
Whether detriment suffered by transferor was part of consideration – Whether
consideration given by transferee was significantly less than that given by
transferor – Insolvency Act 1986, s. 423(1)(c).

B

This was an appeal which raised the issue whether a tenancy purportedly created by the
first defendant in favour of his wife, the second defendant, was a transaction caught by
s. 423 of the Insolvency Act 1986.

The first defendant owned a farm in Warwickshire. He borrowed £700,000 from the
plaintiff secured on the farm. He fell into arrears. Shortly before a deadline agreed with the
plaintiff for the arrears to be cleared, the first defendant granted the second defendant a
tenancy of the mortgaged property. The value of the mortgaged farm with vacant possession
was over £1m, whereas its value, subject to the tenancy, was less than £500,000, leaving the
plaintiff unsecured for a substantial part of the debt owed to it. It was accepted that the rent
reserved under the tenancy represented a full market rent. The judge held that the
transaction was entered into by the first defendant for the purpose of prejudicing the interests
of the plaintiff, within s. 423(3)(c) of the 1986 Act. That finding was not challenged on
appeal.

C

D

The issue on the appeal was whether the tenancy agreement was a transaction 'entered
into at an undervalue' within s. 423(1)(c), the judge having rejected the argument that the
detriment suffered by the first defendant, consisting of a substantial diminution in the value
of his freehold interest in the property, fell to be treated as part of the consideration provided
by him for the purpose of s. 423(1)(c) (and that, when it was so treated, the monetary value
of the obligations assumed by the second defendant under the tenancy agreement was shown
to be significantly less than the value of the consideration provided by the first defendant).

E

The plaintiff's first principal submission on the appeal was that the judge had erred in law
in holding that, in the application of s. 423(1)(c), the detriment to the first defendant was
irrelevant. The second defendant argued that there was no warrant for treating the detriment
suffered by the first defendant as part of the consideration provided by him unless that
detriment was in truth part of the bargain entered into by him with his wife, which it was
not. It was merely an incidental result of the transaction.

F

The plaintiff's second submission was that the transaction plainly conferred, and was
intended to confer, on the second defendant significant benefits beyond the rights granted by
the tenancy agreement itself, for which enhanced benefits she did not pay. The second
defendant argued that the plaintiff had to show that the annual rent under the tenancy was
significantly less than the market rent, and had not done so; and that the alleged benefits
conferred on the second defendant were irrelevant and would have been available to any
person who took a tenancy of the farm.

G

Held, allowing the plaintiff's appeal:

1. It was unnecessary to decide whether mere detriment to the person entering into the
relevant transaction, unaccompanied by a corresponding benefit to the other party, could
not properly be treated as part of the consideration provided by such person for the purpose
of applying s. 423(1)(c) unless the incurring of the detriment was actually part of the bargain,
as opposed to being merely an incidental result of the transaction.

H

2. The 'transaction' for the purposes of s. 423(1)(c) was wider than the tenancy
agreement. Due weight had to be given to the facts that the land in question was mortgaged

A   and that the wife, through the grant of the tenancy, would be placed in 'a ransom position' vis-à-vis the mortgagee. It was clear that, when the transaction was viewed as a whole, the benefits which the first defendant thereby conferred on the second defendant were significantly greater in value, in money or money's worth, than the value of the consideration provided by her. To hold otherwise would fly in the face of reality and common sense. On the facts, the substantial detriment incurred by the first defendant under the transaction was largely matched by a substantial benefit conferred on the second defendant beyond the rights

B   specifically conferred on her by the tenancy agreement.

The following cases were referred to in the judgment of Sir Christopher Slade:

Bolton v Madden (1873) LR 9 QB 55.
Lloyds Bank Ltd v Marcan & Ors [1973] 1 WLR 1387.
M C Bacon Ltd, Re [1990] BCC 78.
Menzies v National Bank of Kuwait [1994] BCC 119.

C   Gabriel Moss QC (instructed by Bond Pearce, Plymouth) for the appellant.

Nicholas Dowding (instructed by Burgess Salmon, Bristol) for the respondent.

JUDGMENT

Sir Christopher Slade: With the leave of the judge, the plaintiff in these proceedings,

D   Agricultural Mortgage Corporation plc, appeals from an order of His Honour Judge Weeks made in the Bristol District Registry on 3 March 1993. He had before him an application by the plaintiff under RSC, O. 14 for final judgment in the proceedings (1) against both defendants setting aside a tenancy agreement dated 16 April 1992 made between the first defendant, Mr Woodward, and the second defendant, his wife, Mrs Woodward, and (2) against the first defendant for payment of all sums due under a mortgage by way of legal charge made on 18 April 1989 between the first defendant and

E   the plaintiff. The judge dismissed the summons as regards the second defendant and ordered her to serve a defence within 14 days. He gave the plaintiff liberty to restore the summons as regards the first defendant for hearing by the district judge. The issue raised on this appeal is whether the tenancy purportedly created by the first defendant in favour of his wife was a transaction caught by s. 423 of the *Insolvency Act* 1986 ('the 1986 Act').

The relevant facts are not in dispute and I can take them largely from the judgment in

F   the court below. The first defendant is a farmer who owns a farm in Warwickshire. He borrowed £700,000 from the plaintiff. By the legal charge dated 18 April 1989 he charged his farm to the plaintiff to secure repayment of the loan and interest. Before this charge was executed, the plaintiff obtained the second defendant's signature to a document dated 7 March 1989 in which she stated:

'I agree to the mortgage being granted on the clear understanding that [the

G   plaintiff] can exercise its rights in priority to any rights I may have in the property.'

The first defendant soon fell into arrears. Eventually, at a meeting on 14 January 1992, the plaintiff gave him a deadline of 18 April 1992 for the arrears to be cleared. It confirmed the deadline in a letter of 16 January 1992 and in subsequent discussions. The first defendant did not clear the arrears. By 18 April 1992 the total arrears of capital and interest were about £850,000. The first defendant had other creditors who were also pressing him to repay substantial debts to them. The first defendant represented to the

H   plaintiff that he would clear the arrears by selling property, but all he did for this purpose was to sell one small part of the land and make a small payment.

Shortly before the deadline expired (if the document is correctly dated), the two defendants signed a tenancy agreement dated 16 April 1992 by which the first defendant granted the second defendant a tenancy of the mortgaged property stated to begin on 16 April 1992 and to continue until 29 September 1992 and thereafter to continue from year

to year until determined by 12 months' notice to quit. No consent to this tenancy was   A
sought or obtained from the plaintiff, as provided for by the legal charge. However, it is
common ground that this absence of consent is remedied by s. 99 of the *Law of Property
Act* 1925 which confers limited powers of leasing on a mortgagor and that para. 12 of
Sch. 14 to the *Agricultural Holdings Act* 1986 makes it impossible to contract out of those
powers in regard to agricultural land.

If the tenancy were valid and binding on the plaintiff, the consequences for the plaintiff   B
would be serious because, on the undisputed evidence, the value of the mortgaged farm
with vacant possession is over £1m, whereas its value, subject to the tenancy, is less than
£500,000, that is to say far below the debt owing to the plaintiff. The plaintiff would thus
be left without security for a substantial part of the debt owed to it.

In May 1992 the plaintiff issued a writ against both defendants, which was followed
by a statement of claim served on 17 July 1992 and subsequently amended on 18
September 1992. The plaintiff then issued a summons under RSC, O. 14 seeking the relief   C
which has been summarised at the start of this judgment.

At the hearing before Judge Weeks, the first defendant, who has not appeared before
this court, was not represented, but the second defendant appeared by counsel. The
plaintiff's counsel, having accepted that there were triable issues in relation to a number
of the other grounds upon which the relief was sought in the statement of claim, based
the plaintiff's claim to summary judgment on two grounds only. The first was based on   D
the acknowledgment dated 7 March 1989 signed by the first defendant. The judge, in my
view, clearly rightly rejected this point, holding that the words in the document 'any
rights I may have in the property' referred only to then existing rights of the first
defendant in the property and not to future rights which she might acquire thereafter.
This part of his decision is not challenged on this appeal.

The second and main ground upon which the plaintiff based its case for summary   E
judgment in the court below was s. 423 of the 1986 Act. This section is contained in
Pt. XVI of that Act, which is headed 'Provisions against debt avoidance (England and
Wales only)' and, so far as material, provides:

'*Transactions defrauding creditors*

(1) This section relates to transactions entered into at an undervalue; and a person
enters into such a transaction with another person if–   F

    (a) he makes a gift to the other person or he otherwise enters into a transaction
    with the other on terms that provide for him to receive no consideration;

    (b) he enters into a transaction with the other in consideration of marriage; or

    (c) he enters into a transaction with the other for a consideration the value of
    which, in money or money's worth, is significantly less than the value, in
    money or money's worth, of the consideration provided by himself.   G

(2) Where a person has entered into such a transaction, the court may, if satisfied
under the next subsection, make such order as it thinks fit for–

    (a) restoring the position to what it would have been if the transaction had not
    been entered into, and

    (b) protecting the interests of persons who are victims of the transaction.

(3) In the case of a person entering into such a transaction, an order shall only be   H
made if the court is satisfied that it was entered into by him for the purpose–

    (a) of putting assets beyond the reach of a person who is making, or may at
    some time make, a claim against him, or

    (b) of otherwise prejudicing the interests of such a person in relation to the claim
    which he is making or may make.

A

. . .

(5) In relation to a transaction at an undervalue, references here and below to a victim of the transaction are to a person who is, or is capable of being, prejudiced by it . . .'

Section 424 specifies those persons who may apply for an order under s. 423. The plaintiff is such a person.

B

By s. 423(3) the court in the present case is required to investigate the purpose of the first defendant in entering into the tenancy agreement. As to the purpose for which the tenancy agreement was entered into, the second defendant gave the following evidence in an affidavit:

'6. In order to continue to produce an income for the family I needed to take over the farming business and I clearly needed land and machinery and livestock to be
C
able to do so. The first defendant and I had heard from other farmers that it was possible for a farmer to grant a tenancy even where there was a mortgage on the property and after I had taken advice from my solicitors, the first defendant and I agreed that I should take a tenancy over Sole End Farm and should acquire the live and dead stock. I took the tenancy and, by an agreement of the same date ('the sale and purchase agreement') I purchased machinery equipment and livestock
D
from the first defendant at a price of £23,969 . . .

7. I was aware of the fact that the action which I was taking would have the effect that the plaintiff would be unable to sell the farm with vacant possession and, indeed, my aim could not be achieved if that were not the case. Mr Drew is correct when he says in para. 9 of his affidavit that there would be no point in taking over the business unless I gained some security of tenure since without security of tenure
E
it would be inevitable that the plaintiff would realise its security. It was therefore imperative that I took a tenancy over the freehold land as well as acquiring the machinery and live and dead stock. I will refer to this aspect in more detail below but it is clear that in order to achieve my aims, a fully protected tenancy with security of tenure which was binding on the AMC as mortgagee was necessary. I was also aware of the fact that the value of the farm to the plaintiff with a tenancy was significantly less than without a tenancy. However, my understanding was that
F
the first defendant as mortgagor was entitled to grant such a tenancy and, as I have said, I took it primarily in order to enable me to provide for my young family.

8. . . . It is correct to say that I consider that the tenancy was granted for commercial reasons to enable me to take over the farming business in my own right and for my own benefit. Mr Drew says that he cannot see what commercial purpose was served by the tenancy, but he concentrates on the position of the first
G
defendant. I accept that it was unlikely that the payments due under the sale and purchase agreement and the tenancy would be sufficient to enable the first defendant to pay off his indebtedness, but the commercial purpose served was to enable me to take over the farming business and to produce an income in the likely event that the first defendant would cease to be able to do so.'

H
On the evidence before him, the judge inferred that the first defendant's purposes in entering into the tenancy agreement were (inter alia) to ensure that the plaintiff did not get vacant possession of the property. Indeed, as the second defendant had admitted, the tenancy was purposeless unless she obtained security of tenure. In these circumstances, the judge found on the evidence that the transaction was entered into by the first defendant for the purpose of prejudicing the interests of the plaintiff, within s. 423(3)(c) of the 1986 Act. This finding has not been challenged on this appeal.

The principal issue before the judge, as before this court, was whether the tenancy   A
agreement was a transaction 'entered into at an undervalue', falling within the definition
of such a transaction contained in s. 423(1)(c) of the 1986 Act.

In this context, some helpful guidance was to be found in the judgment of Millett J in
Re M C Bacon Ltd [1990] BCC 78. There he had to consider whether the granting of a
debenture by a company was a transaction entered into by the company at an undervalue
within s. 238(4)(b) of the 1986 Act, which reads: B

> '(b) the company enters into a transaction with that person for a consideration the
> value of which, in money or money's worth, is significantly less than the value, in
> money, or money's worth, of the consideration provided by the company.'

Millett J said (at p. 92):

> 'To come within that paragraph the transaction must be: C
>
> (1) entered into by the company;
>
> (2) for a consideration;
>
> (3) the value of which measured in money or money's worth;
>
> (4) is significantly less than the value;
>
> (5) also measured in money or money's worth; D
>
> (6) of the consideration provided by the company.
>
> It requires a comparison to be made between the value obtained by the company
> for the transaction and the value of consideration provided by the company. Both
> values must be measurable in money or money's worth and both must be
> considered from the company's point of view.
>
> In my judgment, the applicant's claim to characterise the granting of the bank's E
> debenture as a transaction at an undervalue is misconceived. The mere creation of
> a security over a company's assets does not deplete them and does not come within
> the paragraph. By charging its assets the company appropriates them to meet the
> liabilities due to the secured creditor and adversely affects the rights of other
> creditors in the event of insolvency. But it does not deplete its assets or diminish
> their value. It retains the right to redeem and the right to sell or remortgage the F
> charged assets. All it loses is the ability to apply the proceeds otherwise than in
> satisfaction of the secured debt. That is not something capable of valuation in
> monetary terms and is not customarily disposed of for value.
>
> In the present case the company did not suffer that loss by reason of the grant of
> the debenture. Once the bank had demanded a debenture the company could not
> have sold or charged its assets without applying the proceeds in reduction of the
> overdraft; had it attempted to do so, the bank would at once have called in the G
> overdraft. By granting the debenture the company parted with nothing of value,
> and the value of the consideration which it received in return was incapable of
> being measured in money or money's worth.
>
> Mr Vos submitted that the consideration which the company received was, with
> hindsight, of no value. It merely gained time and with it the opportunity to lose
> more money. But he could not and did not claim that the company ought to have H
> received a fee or other capital sum in return for the debenture. That gives the game
> away. The applicant's real complaint is not that the company entered into the
> transaction at an undervalue but that it entered into it at all.'

An assessment of the value in money or money's worth of the consideration provided
by each of the respective parties to the transaction is thus of crucial importance. As to

A   this, s. 99(6) of the *Law of Property Act* 1925, pursuant to which section the tenancy in
the present case was purportedly granted, provides:

'Every such lease shall reserve the best rent that can reasonably be obtained, regard
being had to the circumstances of the case, but without any fine being taken.'

For the purposes of the O. 14 application before the judge, the plaintiff's counsel
accepted that there was a triable issue as to whether the grant of the tenancy was validly
B   made in exercise of the powers of leasing contained in s. 99. The argument before the
judge thus proceeded on the basis that the annual rent of £37,250 reserved under the
tenancy represented a full market rent, being the best rent that could reasonably be
obtained. Nevertheless, it was argued by the plaintiff that the value of the consideration
in money or money's worth received by the first defendant for the transaction was
significantly less than the value in money or money's worth of the consideration provided
by him. It appears that the principal grounds for this argument were (in substance) that
C   by virtue of the transaction the first defendant suffered a detriment, consisting of a
substantial diminution in the value of his freehold interest in the property, that this
detriment fell to be treated as part of the consideration provided by him for the purpose
of s. 423(1)(c) and that, when it was so treated, the monetary value of the obligations
assumed by the second defendant under the tenancy agreement was shown to be
significantly less than the value of the consideration provided by the first defendant.

D   The judge rejected this argument, saying:

'I turn to the question whether the jurisdiction opens under s. 423(1)(c). This
requires that a transferor enters into a transaction with another the value of the
consideration for which is significantly less than the value provided by himself.
This requires a comparison between the consideration the first defendant received
in money or money's worth compared with the consideration provided by the first
E   defendant. What one does not have to do is value the detriment suffered by the
first defendant as a result of the transaction. A simple example of this which will
be familiar in a fiscal context is a set of chairs the aggregate value of which is
greater than the value of each chair added together. If a person sells one he may
do so at market value and the consideration which he receives is full value and will
equal the consideration provided by the vendor. The vendor would still have
suffered a detriment because he would have devalued his estate, because he would
F   have only five chairs left which would be worth less as individuals than as
components of a set. The fiscal legislation meets this by looking at the way the
estate is diminished.

I do not think that the same approach has been adopted in the Insolvency Act.
That Act compares simply the consideration provided by the donor with the
consideration received, translated into money or money's worth and compared
G   with each other.'

A little later, the judge, having quoted the passage from Millett J's judgment in *Re
M C Bacon Ltd* [1990] BCC 78 cited above, said:

'As I understand that part of the judgment Millett J decided that there was no
consideration in money or money's worth. The sentence which troubles me is:

"both values must be measurable in money or money's worth and both must
H   be considered from the company's point of view."

I have to consider a different section. I reach the firm conclusion (as I consider I
am bound to do on a question of law on O. 14) that I should compare the
consideration provided by the donee with the consideration provided by the donor,
both in money or money's worth, and that I am not directed to look at incidental
detriment to the donor.

There is evidence that the annual rent of £37,250 for the first year is equal to   A
market value and is the best rent reasonably obtainable. Taking the two
considerations in money or money's worth they appear equal provided one
disregards the incidental detriment as a result of the loss of vacant possession.
Therefore the tenancy is not within s. 423. I reach this conclusion with some regret
because it appears to me that this tenancy was designed to prejudice the interests
of the mortgagor and if I am right there is a lacuna in the insolvency provisions
under which it is open to a debtor deliberately to prejudice a creditor in   B
circumstances which depreciate the value of his assets but do not confer a
corresponding advantage on the donee. This may not be an unintentional lacuna;
it may be unfair to subject a donee to a burden where no gratuitous benefit has
been conferred upon him. Be that as it may I have reached a firm decision and
dismiss the application.'

The judge, as he said, reached his decision with regret. If it was correct, the results are   C
surprising as well as disturbing. For, as he found, the very purpose of the relevant
transaction was to prejudice the interests of the plaintiff as creditor-mortgagee, by
conferring on the second defendant a tenancy which gave her security of tenure and
thereby procuring that the plaintiff could not get vacant possession of the property for
the purpose of enforcing its security. Furthermore, its effect, if it was valid, was to deplete
the value of the first defendant's assets available for his creditors, including the plaintiff,   D
by over £500,000. On similar facts the Court of Appeal in *Lloyds Bank Ltd v Marcan*
[1973] 1 WLR 1387 held that a lease of a dwelling house and market garden granted by a
mortgagor-debtor pursuant to his statutory powers under s. 99 of the *Law of Property
Act* 1925 but with the intent of depriving the mortgagee bank of its ability to obtain
vacant possession 'because he wanted to remain with his wife and family in their home
and with the market garden business' (see at p. 1390A), was a transaction made with
intent to defraud the bank within s. 172 of the *Law of Property Act* 1925; and that since   E
the wife knew of the intent, the lease was voidable at the instance of the bank. Russell LJ
(at p. 1391B) made the following comment:

> 'The intention of Mr Marcan is perfectly plain: the lease to his wife was designed
> expressly to deprive the bank of the ability to obtain the vacant possession to
> which the bank plainly attributed value, and to diminish to that extent the strength
> of the bank's position as creditor. To take that action at that juncture, in my   F
> judgment, was, in the context of relationship of debtor and creditor, less than
> honest: it was sharp practice, and not the less so because he was advised that he
> had power to grant the lease. It was, in my judgment, a transaction made with
> intent to defraud the bank within section 172 and would have been within the
> Statute 13 Eliz. I, c. 5.'

The relevant transaction in the present case would plainly have fallen within s. 172 of   G
the *Law of Property Act* 1925. Section 423 of the 1986 Act, which was first introduced as
s. 212 of the *Insolvency Act* 1985 and replaced s. 172, following the recommendations of
the *Report of the Review Committee on Insolvency Law and Practice* (Cmnd 8558) ('the
Cork Report'), is one of a series of provisions against debt avoidance and, as the heading
to the section shows, is intended to deal with 'transactions defrauding creditors'. Prima
facie it seems most unlikely that the legislature would have intended a transaction of the
Lloyds Bank v Marcan type to escape the net of the section. Nevertheless, the wording of   H
s. 423 is very different from that of the old s. 172 and, while having due regard to the
purpose of the section, we must apply that wording as we find it.

As his first principal submission for the plaintiff on this appeal, Mr Gabriel Moss QC
submitted that the judge plainly erred in law in holding that, in the application of
s. 423(1)(c), the detriment to the first defendant was irrelevant. As he pointed out, it is

A   elementary law that detriment to the promisor is capable of constituting consideration
for a contract: see for example *Bolton v Madden* (1873) LR 9 QB 55. Millett J, he
submitted, in the passage from his judgment in *Re M C Bacon* quoted above, had held
that (1) an undervalue was created where the transaction depleted the debtor's assets or
diminished their value; and (2) both items of consideration had to be considered from the
point of view of the debtor trying to prejudice his creditors. This judgment, it was
B   contended, made it clear that detriment to the debtor's estate is a crucial factor which can
be taken into account, and Judge Weeks erred in declining to follow that judgment in
applying s. 423(1)(c) merely because it dealt with a different section (s. 238). His decision,
it was suggested, ignored the mischief with which s. 423 was intended to deal. Mr Moss
referred us to (inter alia) para. 1215 of the Cork Report which recommended that s. 172
of the *Law of Property Act* 1925 be reenacted in an amended form so as to make it clear
(inter alia):

C
'(b) that the necessary intent is an intent on the part of the debtor to defeat, hinder,
delay or defraud creditors or to put assets belonging to the debtor beyond their
reach . . .'

–and:

'(c) that the section applies to any disposition made with the necessary intent, even
D   if supported by valuable consideration, where that does not consist of full
consideration in money or money's worth received by the debtor . . .'

In the present case, the first defendant incurred a very substantial detriment under the
transaction, since the value of his freehold interest in the farm was diminished by more
than £500,000. This detriment, it was submitted, was part of the 'consideration provided
by himself' for the purpose of applying s. 423(1) and its value far exceeded the value of
E   the consideration given by the second defendant in entering into the obligations imposed
by the tenancy agreement.

The relevant passage from Millett J's judgment in *Re M C Bacon* was approved by the
Court of Appeal in *Menzies v National Bank of Kuwait* [1994] BCC 119 which held that
on the facts of that case his analysis of s. 238(4)(b) applied mutatis mutandis to
s. 423(1)(c) of the 1986 Act (see at pp. 128–129 per Balcombe LJ, with whose judgment
F   Butler-Sloss LJ agreed). I would therefore agree that the grounds on which Judge Weeks
regarded Millett J's analysis of the law in the *Re M C Bacon* case as inapplicable in the
present case were not valid grounds. Furthermore, it is true that one of the grounds upon
which Millett J reached his decision in *Re M C Bacon* was that the creation of the
debenture in that case did not deplete the company's assets or diminish their value.
However, I do not read his judgment as specifically supporting the converse proposition,
namely that if the debenture *had* depleted the company's assets or diminished their value,
G   the detriment to the company would have by itself have sufficed to bring the transaction
within s. 238(4)(b). As is pointed out in *Chitty on Contracts* (26th edn) para. 154, in the
context of contractual relations usually detriment and benefit are merely the same thing
looked at from different points of view. The present case, however, is not the usual case.
As Mr Dowding pointed out on behalf of the second defendant, under the transaction
she did not receive the £500,000 diminution in value suffered by the first defendant. Even
H   accepting that, following the guidance given by Millett J, one must look at the transaction
from the debtor's point of view, there is, in Mr Dowding's submission, no warrant for
treating the detriment suffered by the first defendant as part of the consideration provided
by him *unless that detriment was in truth part of the bargain entered into by him with his
wife.* Consideration, in his submission, is what you get or give for a bargain; it would be
wholly artificial and incorrect to regard the diminution in value of the freehold as
something for which the second defendant had bargained and thus as forming part of the

consideration provided by the first defendant. This diminution in value was merely an   A
incidental *result* of the transaction.

I see some force in the argument that mere detriment to the person entering into the
relevant transaction, unaccompanied by a corresponding benefit to the other party,
cannot properly be treated as part of the consideration provided by such person for the
purpose of applying s. 423(1)(c) unless the incurring of the detriment is actually part of
the bargain, as opposed to being merely an incidental result of the transaction. However,   B
I have some doubts as to whether this is what Parliament would have intended and would
prefer to leave this question open for decision in another case. For I am of the clear
opinion that Mr Moss is correct in his second main submission on this appeal.

This submission focused attention not so much on the detriment to the first defendant
as on the benefit to the second defendant conferred by the transaction. 'Transaction', it
was pointed out, is a wide word, defined by s. 436 as including 'a gift, agreement or   C
arrangement'. The tenancy, if effective, gave her the threefold benefits of safeguarding
the family home, enabling her to acquire and carry on the family farming business, and a
surrender value. Furthermore, and most significantly, the transaction, if effective, placed
her vis-à-vis the plaintiff in what Mr Moss described as a 'ransom' position. If the tenancy
was effective, the plaintiff would have had to negotiate with and no doubt pay a high
price to her before it could obtain vacant possession of the farm and sell it for the purpose
of enforcing its security and repaying the debt owed to it by the first defendant. Thus, it   D
was submitted, the transaction plainly conferred, and was intended to confer, on her
significant enhanced benefits beyond the rights granted by the tenancy agreement itself,
for which enhanced benefits she did not pay.

Mr Dowding, in answering these submissions, naturally relied strongly on the
concession that the annual rent of £37,250 reserved under the tenancy represented a full
market rent, being the best rent that could reasonably be obtained. A proper assessment   E
of the market rent of property will, in his submission, always take account of the existence
of a potential purchaser, such as the second defendant in the present case; the only
relevance of the presence of a potential special purchaser is that it may inflate the market
value. It is not enough for the plaintiff to assert that because of the second defendant's
special position, she might or would have been willing to pay a higher rent than any other
tenant. In Mr Dowding's submission, to bring the case within s. 423(1)(c), the plaintiff
would have to show that the annual rent of £37,250 was *significantly* less than the market   F
rent and this has not been shown. The alleged threefold benefits relied on by the plaintiff
are, he contended, irrelevant. They would all have been available to any person who took
a tenancy of the farm. Any such tenant could have acquired the farming business and
lived in the farmhouse. Any such tenant would have acquired the benefit of the surrender
value. All these potential advantages were part and parcel of the factors which would be
reflected in the assessment of the market rent, which, together with the other obligations   G
entered into by the second defendant under the tenancy agreement, constituted full
consideration for the benefits conferred on her.

Persuasively though these submissions were advanced, I am not persuaded by them. In
applying s. 423(1)(c) to the facts of the present case, one must look at the transaction as
a whole; the tenancy agreement cannot be considered in blinkers. Due weight must be
given (inter alia) to the facts not only that the agreement was entered into by the first   H
defendant with his wife for the purposes outlined above, but that the land in question
was mortgaged and that the wife, through the grant of the tenancy, would be placed in
the 'ransom' position described above. Accepting that she agreed to pay for her yearly
tenancy a rent which was the best rent reasonably obtainable for that tenancy viewed in
isolation, and that she undertook the other tenant's obligations imposed by the tenancy
agreement, it seems to me nevertheless clear that, when the transactions are viewed as a

A   whole, the benefits which the first defendant thereby conferred on her were significantly greater in value, *far* greater in value, in money or money's worth than the value of the consideration provided by her. To hold otherwise would seem to me to fly in the face of reality and common sense. No further evidence was, in my judgment, required to establish that the transaction was one falling within s. 423(1)(c); the agreed facts speak for themselves. On the facts of this case, the substantial detriment incurred by the first defendant under the transaction was largely matched by a substantial benefit conferred
B   on the second defendant beyond the rights specifically conferred on her by the tenancy agreement.

As a long-stop argument Mr Dowding pointed out that the effect of para. 12 of Sch. 14 to the *Agricultural Holdings Act* 1986 is that the statutory power of leasing conferred by s. 99 of the *Law of Property Act* 1925 cannot be excluded in relation to a mortgage of agricultural land; the policy of that Act is therefore to allow farmers who
C   have mortgaged their farms to grant tenancies binding the mortgagee even where they have expressly agreed not to do so. He submitted that accordingly s. 423 of the 1986 Act can have no application to a tenancy to which the last-mentioned provisions apply. A similar argument was advanced in *Lloyds Bank v Marcan* (above) and rejected (see at p. 1390D–E per Russell LJ). I for my part would unhesitatingly reject it in the present case. The whole object of s. 423 is to enable the setting aside, in the particular circumstances
D   mentioned in the section, of transactions which would otherwise be valid. The fact that in the present case the tenancy agreement might or would have been perfectly valid but for s. 423 is neither here nor there.

We have had the benefit of excellent arguments from counsel on both sides. For the reasons stated, I would allow the appeal and order that there be final judgment against both the defendants setting aside the tenancy referred to in the statement of claim. I reach this conclusion without regret because a contrary conclusion would, in my view, subject
E   the plaintiff to a substantial injustice.

Saville LJ: I have had the opportunity of reading in draft the judgments of Sir Christopher Slade and Neill LJ and I agree with them both.

Neill LJ: I agree that this appeal should be allowed for the reasons set out in the judgment of Sir Christopher Slade. I add a few words of my own only because we are differing from the decision of the judge.
F

The central question which arises in this case is whether the tenancy agreement dated 16 April 1992 was a transaction which fell within s. 423 of the *Insolvency Act* 1986. Sir Christopher Slade has already set out the material provisions of that section and it is sufficient for me to confine my citation to that part of s. 423(1) which provides:

> 'This section relates to transactions entered into at an undervalue; and a person enters into such a transaction with another person if—
G
>   . . .
>
> > (c) he enters into a transaction with the other for a consideration the value of which, in money or money's worth, is significantly less than the value, in money or money's worth, of the consideration provided by himself.'

The principal submission put forward on behalf of the plaintiffs was that in calculating the consideration provided by Mr Woodward one was entitled to take account of the
H   detriment which he suffered by reason of the reduction in the value of his property consequent upon the grant of the tenancy. This reduction in value was of the order of £500,000.

It is of course true that a detriment suffered by one party to a contract is *capable* of constituting good consideration. Like Sir Christopher Slade, however, I would wish to leave over for another occasion any conclusion as to whether the 'detriment' suffered by

Mr Woodward in the present case constituted 'consideration provided by' Mr Woodward   A
for the purpose of s. 423(1)(c).

Counsel for the plaintiff, however, had a subsidiary argument which I found to be
unanswerable. I am not clear how far, if at all, this argument was advanced before the
judge, but the matter is raised in the notice of appeal and explained more fully in the
skeleton argument lodged on behalf of the plaintiff. This alternative argument was to the
effect that the agricultural tenancy granted to Mrs Woodward had three intended   B
consequences which were additional to any benefit which she received from the tenancy
itself:

(1)   the safeguarding of the family home;

(2)   the acquisition by Mrs Woodward of the farming business free from its previous
       creditors; and

(3)   the benefit of the surrender value of the tenancy, which was of particular   C
       importance in view of the fact that the property was mortgaged.

It was argued on behalf of Mrs Woodward, inter alia, that these suggested benefits had
already been taken into account in fixing the annual rent which, as was accepted by the
plaintiff, represented the full market rent. It was further argued that the value of any of
these additional benefits could not be calculated 'in money or money's worth' and,
accordingly, could not be taken into account for the purpose of s. 423(1)(c).   D

I am quite unconvinced by these arguments. The purpose of the grant of the tenancy
agreement was to ensure that the plaintiff did not get vacant possession of the property
and was for the purpose of prejudicing the interests of the plaintiff. By the grant of the
tenancy Mrs Woodward acquired the benefit of the surrender value which placed her, as
counsel for the plaintiff put it, in 'a ransom position' in any future dealings with the
mortgagee. On the facts of this case it is unnecessary to attempt to calculate the value of
the surrender value. In view of the existence of the mortgage it must be a large sum and   E
may approach the value of the 'detriment' suffered by Mr Woodward. In the
circumstances I see no answer to the argument that, quite apart from any value which
may be attributed to the securing of the family home and the acquisition of a debt-free
business, the surrender value constituted 'consideration provided by' Mr Woodward
which was significantly greater than the payment made by Mrs Woodward for the grant
of the lease.   F

I too would allow the appeal and order that there be final judgment against both the
defendants setting aside the tenancy agreement referred to in the statement of claim.

*(Appeal allowed with costs in Court of Appeal and below, not to be enforced without leave
of the court or further order. Leave to appeal to House of Lords refused)*

G

H

W H Smith Ltd v Wyndham Investments Ltd.

Chancery Division.

His Honour Judge Paul Baker QC (sitting as a judge of the Chancery Division). Judgment delivered 18 May 1994.

Liquidation – Disclaimer of leaseholds – Whether original lessee continued to be liable for rent after assignee went into liquidation and liquidator disclaimed lease – Insolvency Act 1986, s. 178.

This was a case raising the question whether the original lessee of a lease which had been assigned continued to be liable for the rent after the assignee had gone into liquidation and the liquidator had disclaimed the lease.

The original lessee argued that if its liability continued, the assignee company would not be released from liability as it would continue to be liable to indemnify the lessee for the rent the lessee had to pay. Therefore it was necessary to release the lessee from that liability so as to release the assignee company from its liability as required by s. 178 of the Insolvency Act 1986. The original lessee argued that Warnford Investments Ltd v Duckworth [1979] Ch 127 was wrongly decided and reserved for a higher court the submission that Hill v East and West India Dock Co (1884) 9 App Cas 448 (HL) was wrongly decided. The original lessee relied on Stacey v Hill [1901] 1 KB 660 and argued that if it was necessary to release a surety because of his right to seek indemnity from the bankrupt, the original lessee must be similarly relieved because of his right of indemnity against the bankrupt assignee.

An alternative submission on behalf of the plaintiffs was that the lease remained in being only during the three-month period allowed for an application for a vesting order under s. 181 of the Act of 1986. After that the lease became defunct and with the disappearance of the lease, the liability of the original lessor would be at an end.

Held, declaring that the liability of the plaintiffs under the lease continued until the lease expired by effluxion of time or was determined earlier:

1. The obligation of the original lessee towards the lessor was quite separate from that of the assignee to indemnify. Ex hypothesi, the former came into existence before the latter. There was no difficulty in abrogating the right of the original lessee to claim an indemnity from the assignee without any necessity to abrogate the obligation of the original lessee to pay the lessor. (Warnford Investments Ltd v Duckworth [1979] Ch 127 followed; Stacey v Hill [1901] 1 KB 660 distinguished.)

2. The period for applying for a vesting order was set at three months under the Insolvency Rules, but that limit could be extended at the discretion of the court under the rules. In any event the lease did not become defunct following the removal of all possibility of an application for a vesting order. The lease was ownerless until a vesting order was made. If none was made the lease did not disappear on that account. It would not disappear until the occurrence of one of the normal means of termination, effluxion of time, surrender or retaking of possession by the landlord.

The following cases were referred to in the judgment:

Hill v East and West India Dock Co (1884) 9 App Cas 448.
Stacey v Hill [1901] 1 KB 660.
Warnford Investments Ltd v Duckworth & Ors [1979] Ch 127.

Nicholas Patten QC and John McGhee (instructed by Bircham & Co) for the plaintiff lessees.

Lawrence Cohen QC and Elizabeth Weaver (instructed by Edge & Ellison) for the defendant lessors.

JUDGMENT   A

His Honour Judge Paul Baker QC: The question in this case is whether the original lessee of a lease which has been assigned continues to be liable for the rent after the assignee has gone into liquidation and the liquidator has disclaimed the lease.

This question has been answered in the affirmative by the House of Lords in *Hill v East and West India Dock Co* (1884) 9 App Cas 448, and by Sir Robert Megarry V-C in a characteristically comprehensive and careful judgment in *Warnford Investments Ltd v*   B *Duckworth* [1979] Ch 127.

The plaintiffs here are the original lessees under a lease which has been assigned to a company which went into liquidation followed by disclaimer of the lease. They ask the court to determine whether their liability in respect of rent and other obligations under the lease is limited to any liability which accrued due before the date of disclaimer, or alternatively is limited to liabilities which accrued before the expiry of the time allowed   C for an application for a vesting order in respect of the disclaimed property, normally three months after receipt of notice of the disclaimer.

In seeking an affirmative answer to one or other of these questions, the plaintiffs' counsel, Mr Patten, boldly submitted that the Warnford case was wrongly decided, or that it ought not to be followed in relation to s. 178 of the *Insolvency Act* 1986, the provision now governing disclaimer by liquidators. When we came to examine the   D statutory provisions it did not appear that there was any significant difference between the current provision and that obtaining when Warnford was decided, viz. the *Companies Act* 1948, s. 323. Hence we are left with the submission that I should not follow the decision of Megarry V-C. Mr Patten did not argue in this court that *Hill v East and West India Dock Co* was wrongly decided. He reserved that submission for a higher court. To me he submitted that that case was based on a statutory provision which is markedly different from the later provision. In that Mr Patten is right; it is markedly different as   E may by seen from the following.

The *Bankruptcy Act* 1869, s. 23, the provision considered in *Hill v East and West India Dock Co*:

'When any property of the bankrupt acquired by the trustee under this Act consists of land of any tenure burdened with onerous covenants . . . the trustee . . . may, by writing under his hand, disclaim such property, and upon the execution of such   F disclaimer the property disclaimed shall, if the same is a contract, be deemed to be determined from the date of the order of adjudication, and if the same is a lease be deemed to have been surrendered on the same date . . .'

Under this provision the House of Lords held, by a majority, that the deemed surrender consequent on a disclaimer did not mean:

'that to all intents and purposes, as between all persons, persons actually concerned   G in the bankruptcy and those not so concerned, it shall be a surrendered lease and shall be altogether out of the case.'

The surrender was to be qualified as operating only 'as between the lessor on the one hand and the bankrupt, his trustee and estate, on the other hand' (pp. 455, 456). In his speech Earl Cairns noted that s. 23 of the 1869 Act had been repealed and replaced for the future by 'an enactment of a very different and much more explicit kind' (p. 453).   H

The new provision was the *Bankruptcy Act* 1883, s. 55, which survived unchanged in the *Bankruptcy Act* 1914, s. 54. That provides:

'(2) The disclaimer shall operate to determine, as from the date of the disclaimer, the rights, interests, and liabilities of the bankrupt and his property in or in respect of the property disclaimed, and shall also discharge the trustee from all personal

A   liability in respect of the property disclaimed, as from the date when the property vested in him, but shall not, except so far as necessary for the purpose of releasing the bankrupt and his property and the trustee from liability, affect the rights and liabilities of any other person.'

The *Companies Act* 1929, s. 267, conferred on liquidators of companies for the first time a power of disclaiming onerous property. So far as material it was in the same terms

B   as the power conferred on trustees in bankruptcy, save that the liquidator had to get the leave of the court to disclaim. The power reappeared as s. 323 of the *Companies Act* 1948. It is now in the *Insolvency Act* 1986, s. 178. The most important change in that Act is that leave of the court is no longer required, thus putting company insolvency on the same footing as personal insolvency as regards disclaimer. The material subsection of s. 178 for present purposes is the fourth:

C   '(4) A disclaimer under this section–

         (a) operates so as to determine, as from the date of the disclaimer, the rights, interests and liabilities of the company in or in respect of the property disclaimed; but

         (b) does not, except so far as is necessary for the purpose of releasing the company from any liability, affect the rights or liabilities of any other

D   person.'

The corresponding provision for personal bankruptcy is to be found in s. 315(3) of the same Act, replacing s. 54(2) of the *Bankruptcy Act* 1914.

What is said is that if the original lessee's liability continues, the assignee company would not be released from liability as it would continue to be liable to indemnify the lessee for the rent the lessee had had to pay. Therefore it is necessary to release the lessee from that liability so as to release the assignee company from its liability. Before turning

E   to the authorities, I set out the brief and undisputed facts.

By a lease dated 28 February 1979 and made between Tannergate Ltd and the plaintiffs, premises at 205/206 Sloane Street, London SW1, were demised to the plaintiffs for a term of 25 years from 29 September 1978. The initial rent was £52,500 subject to review every five years. Rent and service charge are payable quarterly in advance on the usual quarter days. The current rent payable is £400,000 per annum. In that lease the

F   plaintiffs covenanted with the lessor to pay the rent and service charge. By a licence to assign dated 12 February 1990 the defendants (in whom the reversionary interest was by then vested) gave the plaintiffs licence to assign the residue of the term of the lease to Hecuba Ltd. Mandisa Investments Ltd and the Honourable Mrs Jaqumine Bromage entered into the licence as sureties for the lessee's obligation for the remainder of the term. The lease was assigned to Hecuba Ltd pursuant to that licence. On 21 February

G   1992 both Hecuba Ltd and Mandisa Investments Ltd went into creditors' voluntary liquidation. On 1 April 1993 the liquidator disclaimed the lease.

The defendants have demanded from the plaintiffs, and the plaintiffs have paid rent falling due on the March and June 1993 quarter days, that is, in respect of a period falling after the disclaimer, but the plaintiffs now seek to resist any further demands. The plaintiffs do not now seek recovery of the sums already paid, though that formed part of their claim in the originating summons. What remains is a question whether the liability

H   of the plaintiffs is limited to liability for rent which accrued before the date of disclaimer, or alternatively before 1 July 1993, being the time limited for an application for a vesting order, or whether that liability continues throughout the remainder of the term.

We now come to the authorities. The sheet anchor of the plaintiffs' claim is the decision of the Court of Appeal in *Stacey v Hill* [1901] 1 KB 660. In that case, the defendant had guaranteed the payment of rent which might from time to time be in arrear for 21 days

under a lease. There had not been any underlease or assignment of the lease. The lessee   A
having become bankrupt, the trustee in bankruptcy disclaimed the lease. The lessor sued
the defendant for an amount which he claimed as rent in arrear in respect of a period
subsequent to the disclaimer. It was held that as the lease was determined from the date
of disclaimer as between the lessor and the lessee, the liability of the defendant for future
rent was also determined. Collins LJ based his judgment on the proposition that as the
surety was liable only if the rent payable by the lessee was in arrears, no rent accruing
after the disclaimer was payable by the lessee. Hence the surety could not be liable   B
because his liability was dependent upon the existence of a liability of the lessee as
principal debtor. That reasoning does not assist the plaintiffs in the present case as an
original lessee is a principal covenantor, not a surety. Mr Patten, however, seeks to rely
on the broader ground put forward by the other two judges, with reference to the
expression 'except so far as may be necessary for the purpose of releasing the bankrupt
and his property, and the trustee from liability'. A L Smith MR said (at p. 664):   C

> 'If the surety is liable to pay rent in futuro on his guarantee, he would be entitled
> to indemnity against the bankrupt or his property. It is therefore necessary, in
> order to release the bankrupt and his property from liability under the lease
> subsequently to the disclaimer, that the words at the end of the subsection should
> be brought into play in such a case.'

After referring to the statutory words already cited ('except so far' etc.) Romer LJ   D
continued (at pp. 666–667):

> 'Bearing in mind the facts that in this case no person had any estate in the demised
> premises except the lessor and the bankrupt lessee, and that the liability alleged
> against the defendant is that of a surety for the payment of rent due upon the lease,
> it appears to me that the case comes within those words of the subsection; and that
> it is necessary, for the purpose of releasing the bankrupt, and his property, and the
> trustee in bankruptcy from future liability in respect of the lease, that the liability   E
> of the defendant should be determined by the disclaimer. The section does not
> operate so as to cast upon third persons liabilities different in kind from what they
> Were under before the disclaimer. Here, if the appellant was right in his contention,
> the section would so operate. For the defendant has only agreed to be liable as
> surety for the payment of rent by a lessee under a lease: and yet the appellant seeks
> to make him liable to pay money, though there is no rent payable, no lease, and no   F
> person in the position of lessee.'

It is said here that the position of an original lessee following an assignment of the
lease is no different. If he is compelled to pay the rent he would have a right of indemnity
against the assignee. Accordingly, if the latter becomes bankrupt, and the lease is
disclaimed, it is necessary for the purpose of releasing the bankrupt, to release the original
lessee also. I will return to that submission after looking at *Warnford Investments Ltd v*   G
Duckworth [1979] Ch 127.

In *Warnford* the plaintiffs had granted a lease to the defendants for a term of 20 years.
Three years into the term the defendants had assigned the lease with the consent of the
plaintiffs to a company. Less than two years later the company went into liquidation and
the liquidator disclaimed the lease. In an action for arrears of rent against the defendant
as the original lessee and covenantor Megarry V-C held that the defendant remained
liable throughout the whole term of the lease. In a general review of the position the Vice-   H
Chancellor said at pp. 138, 139:

> '(3) Generally speaking, the guarantor of rent due under a lease is in a very
> different position towards the lessor from that of an original lessee. Like any other
> guarantor, from the start the liability of a guarantor is merely collateral, or
> accessory, or secondary: the terms used in the authorities vary. There never is a

A period when the guarantor alone is liable to the lessor for the rent, in the way that initially the lessee is alone liable for it to the lessor. Instead, the guarantor is merely liable to pay if the principal debtor does not. It follows that once the liability of the principal debtor for future payments is at an end, so also is the liability of the surety.'

The Vice-Chancellor then discusses *Stacey v Hill* and continues:

B '(5) On the other hand, where the lease had been assigned, and the bankruptcy is that of the assignee in whom the lease is vested&, and not that of the original lessee, the position of the original lessee is very different. The disclaimer does not destroy the lease, but leaves it in existence, though without an owner until a vesting order is made. The original lessee is a person who, as principal, undertook towards the lessor the obligations of the lease for the whole term; and there is nothing in the process of assignment which replaced this liability by the mere collateral

C liability of a surety who must pay the rent only if the assignee does not. The bankruptcy of the assignee had for the time being destroyed the original lessee's right against the assignee to require him to discharge the obligations of the lease, and it has impaired the lessee's right of indemnity against him when he has to discharge the obligations himself; but it has not affected his primary liability towards the lessor, which continues unaffected. At no time does an original lessee

D become a mere guarantor to the lessor of the liability of any assignee of the lease.'

Later the Vice-Chancellor addresses specifically the provision that the disclaimer will not release anybody save the bankrupt except so far as it necessary to do so 'for the purpose of releasing the bankrupt and his property and the trustee from liability'. He said at pp. 139–140:

E 'Where the lease has been assigned, I can see nothing which requires the original lessee to be released from liability in order to release the bankrupt, his property or his trustee. Whether he is released or not, the lease continues in existence, and the rent under it continues to fall due. If it were to be held that the lessee remains liable for the rent, he could prove for it in the bankruptcy as "injury" under s. 54(8) of the Bankruptcy Act 1914. If instead it were to be held that the lessee is released from liability for the rent, then it is the lessor who could prove for it in the bankruptcy, also as an "injury" under subsection (8). The release of the lessee

F could thus in no way be said to be "necessary for the purpose of releasing" the bankrupt, his property or his trustee from liability, for it would not achieve any release.'

Section 54(8) of the *Bankruptcy Act* 1914 is now s. 315(5) of the *Insolvency Act* 1986. The corresponding provision for companies is s. 178(6) of the Act of 1986.

G I now return to the submission for the plaintiffs, based on *Stacey v Hill*, that if it is necessary to release a surety because of his right to seek indemnity from the bankrupt, the original lessee must be similarly relieved because of his right of indemnity against the bankrupt assignee. Attractively as it was put, I have to reject that submission. I am not persuaded by it that the decision of the Vice-Chancellor in *Warnford* was wrong. Indeed, it is the decision in *Stacey v Hill* which has failed to win universal acceptance, but accepting it as I have to, there is a clear distinction between the obligation of a surety and that of an original lessee. The obligation of a surety to the creditor is conditioned upon

H the existence of a principal debtor coupled with a right to look to the principal debtor for indemnity. Accordingly, if the principal debtor becomes bankrupt, and his future liability to indemnify is determined by disclaimer, the obligation towards the landlord also has to go as being necessary for the purpose of releasing the debtor. Otherwise, as Romer LJ observed in *Stacey v Hill*, the disclaimer would cast upon the surety an obligation different in kind and more onerous than that which he was under before the disclaimer.

By contrast, the obligation of the original lessee towards the lessor is quite separate from   A
that of the assignee to indemnify. Ex hypothesi, the former came into existence before
the latter. Accordingly, I see no difficulty in abrogating the right of the original lessee to
claim an indemnity from the assignee without any necessity to abrogate the obligation of
the original lessee to pay the lessor. To compensate for the loss of the right to be
indemnified against future rent, the original lessee can prove for any loss or injury under
s. 178(6). I may add, with all respect, that I do not see the necessity for any equation
between the lessee's claim for injury and that of the lessor as expounded by the Vice-   B
Chancellor in the passage set out above. The position as I see it is that the liability of the
assignee to indemnify the original lessee against *future* payments of rent is removed and
a right to assess the loss and prove for it once and for all is substituted without regard to
claims for loss or injury from any other party.

An alternative submission on behalf of the plaintiffs challenged the assumption that in
cases of disclaimer of a lease by the liquidator of an insolvent assignee, the lease remains   C
in being only pending the making of a vesting order under s. 181 of the Act of 1986. It
was submitted that as any vesting order has to be applied for within three months of
receipt of notice of disclaimer, any such lease would become defunct at an early stage.
With the disappearance of the lease, the liability of the original lessor would be at an end.

I am unable to accept this line of reasoning. First, while the period for the application
for a vesting order is set at three months under r. 4.194 of the *Insolvency Rules* 1986, that   D
limit can be extended at the discretion of the court: see r. 4.3. No doubt the discretion
would not be exercised if the property had been retaken by the landlord and relet, but in
that case the liability of the original tenant would have ended anyway as on an implied
surrender of the original lease.

Secondly, I do not consider that the lease becomes defunct following the removal of all
possibility of an application for a vesting order. It is true that in *Warnford* the Vice-   E
Chancellor said at p. 138:

> 'the disclaimer does not destroy the lease, but leaves it in existence, though without
> an owner until a vesting order is made.'

This merely states that the lease is ownerless until a vesting order is made. If none is made
the lease does not disappear on that account. It will not disappear until the occurrence of
one of the normal means of termination, effluxion of time, surrender or retaking of   F
possession by the landlord. I shall accordingly declare in answer to the questions on the
originating summons that the liability of the plaintiffs under the lease continues until the
lease expires by effluxion of time or is determined earlier.

(Order accordingly)

—————————————

   G

   H

A
Hindcastle Ltd v Barbara Attenborough Associates Ltd & Ors.
Court of Appeal (Civil Division).
Sir Stephen Brown P, Rose and Millett L JJ.
Judgment delivered 15 June 1994.

B
Liquidation – Disclaimer of leaseholds – Whether original lessee continued to be liable for rent after assignee went into liquidation and liquidator disclaimed lease – Insolvency Act 1986, s. 178.

This was an appeal with the leave of the judge by the second and third defendants from orders of a deputy High Court judge giving summary judgment under RSC, O. 14 for arrears of rent due under a lease after the lessee had gone into insolvent liquidation and the liquidator had disclaimed the lease. The second defendant was an intermediate assignee of the lease which entered into a direct contractual relationship with the lessor. The third C defendant was a surety which guaranteed the contractual obligations of the second defendant. The first defendant was the original lessee under the lease. The first defendant, which was also in liquidation, did not appeal.

The appellants relied on Stacey v Hill [1901] 1 KB 660 and argued that there was no relevant distinction between the position of a surety for the bankrupt original lessee (who was released from liability on a disclaimer) and the original lessee with an unbroken chain D of indemnity from the bankrupt assignee.

Alternatively the second and third defendants submitted that their liability extended only to the initial rent reserved by the lease and not to the increased rent agreed between the company and the lessor in accordance with the provisions of the rent review clause. That agreement was reached without reference to the second or third defendants.

E
Held, dismissing the appeals:

1. It was necessary to distinguish between two different liabilities of the bankrupt estate: first, the liability which was put an end to by the disclaimer, for example, the liability to pay the rent due under the lease; and, secondly, the statutory liability under s. 178(6) which replaced it. When s. 178(4)(b) spoke of something being 'necessary for the purpose of releasing the company from any liability', the words 'any liability' referred to a liability of the first kind and not the second, i.e. a liability in or in respect of the property disclaimed
F and capable of being determined by s. 178(4)(a).

2. It was not necessary to extinguish the liability of the original lessee in order to release the estate of the bankrupt: it was sufficient to extinguish the liability of the bankrupt assignee to indemnify the original lessee. (Warnford Investments Ltd v Duckworth [1979] Ch 127 not followed.)

3. In order to release the estate of the bankrupt assignee from its liability to indemnify
G the original lessee, it was necessary to extinguish the right of the original lessee to be indemnified. Abrogating the right of the original lessee to an indemnity from the assignee did not necessitate abrogating the obligation of the original lessee to the lessor. (Stacey v Hill [1901] 1 KB 660 distinguished.)

4. On the plain construction of the language of the lease, the rent reserved by the lease after the first review date was the rent agreed between the lessor and the then lessee in accordance
H with the lease. The argument that the only rent which the second defendant had covenanted to pay which the third defendant guaranteed was the original rent was completely untenable since that rent was reserved by the lease until the first review date and not afterwards.

The following cases were referred to in the judgment of Millett LJ:

Hill v East and West India Dock Co (1884) 9 App Cas 448.
Smith (W H) Ltd v Wyndham Investments Ltd [1994] BCC 699.

Stacey v Hill [1901] 1 KB 660.
Warnford Investments Ltd v Duckworth & Ors [1979] Ch 127.

David Oliver QC and Carolyn Walton (instructed by Stallards) for the appellants.

Jonathan Arkush (instructed by Chethams) for the respondent.

JUDGMENT

Millett LJ: This is an appeal with the leave of the judge by the second and third defendants from two orders both dated 14 October 1993 of Mr Simon Goldblatt QC sitting as a deputy High Court judge of the Queen's Bench Division whereby he gave summary judgment under RSC, O. 14 for arrears of rent due under a lease after the lessee had gone into insolvent liquidation and the liquidator had disclaimed the lease.

The second defendant is an intermediate assignee of the lease which entered into a direct contractual relationship with the lessor. The third defendant is a surety which guaranteed the contractual obligations of the second defendant. The first defendant is the original lessee under the lease. The deputy judge gave judgment against all three defendants, but the first defendant, which I understand is now also in liquidation, has not appealed.

The question for decision is whether the disclaimer of a lease under s. 178 of the *Insolvency Act* 1986 by the liquidator of a company which has taken an assignment of the lease operates to determine the liability of the original lessee and any surety for the original lessee, for the position of an intermediate assignee of the lease which has entered into direct contractual relationship with the lessor is indistinguishable from that of the original lessee. Although in form the appeal is an appeal from the decision of Mr Simon Goldblatt QC, it is, in reality, an appeal 15 years out of time from a decision of Sir Robert Megarry V-C in 1979, and it has been argued by the same counsel who appeared for the unsuccessful party in that case.

The lease was granted on 20 October 1983 for a term of 20 years from 12 September 1983 at an initial rent of £13,626 per annum with periodic upwards only rent reviews. It was made between the respondent as lessor and the first defendant as original lessee. It was not assignable except with the consent of the lessor. In 1987 it was assigned to the second defendant pursuant to a licence to assign which contained a covenant on the part of the second defendant with the lessor to pay the rent and observe and perform the covenants in the lease during the remainder of the term thereby granted. The third defendant joined in the licence to assign in order to guarantee the performance of the obligations thereby undertaken by the second defendant. The obligations of the third defendant as surety were limited to expire after the end of ten years from the date of the lease.

In 1989 the second defendant assigned the lease to Prest Ltd ('the company'). The assignment was made with the lessor's consent. In 1990 the company and the lessor agreed that the rent payable under the lease in accordance with the rent review provisions should thenceforth be £37,500 per annum. None of the defendants took any part in the negotiations which led to the revised rent. On 31 October 1992 the company went into creditors' voluntary liquidation. On 8 December 1992 the liquidator gave notice of disclaimer of the lease pursuant to s. 178 of the *Insolvency Act* 1986. No one has applied for a vesting order under s. 181 of the Act and the time-limit for doing so prescribed by the Insolvency Rules has now expired, though it may of course be extended by the court. Writs were issued by the lessor claiming arrears of rent in respect of different rental periods. The writs were issued on 28 January 1993 and 22 July 1993 respectively, and summary judgment in both actions was entered against all the defendants following Mr Goldblatt's judgment in November 1993.

A   The effect of a disclaimer by the liquidator of an insolvent company is laid down by
s. 178 of the *Insolvency Act* 1986, and in particular by subs. (4) and (6) thereof. Subsection
(4) provides:

'A disclaimer under this section–

(a) operates so as to determine, as from the date of the disclaimer, the rights,
interests, and liabilities of the company in or in respect of the property
B   disclaimed; but

(b) does not, except so far as is necessary for the purpose of releasing the
company from any liability, affect the rights or liabilities of any other
person.'

Subsection (6) provides:

C   'Any person sustaining loss or damage in consequence of the operation of a
disclaimer under this section is deemed a creditor of the company to the extent of
the loss or damage and accordingly may prove for the loss or damage in the
winding up.'

Provisions in identical terms are contained in s. 315 of the *Insolvency Act* 1986 in relation
to disclaimer by the trustee in bankruptcy of an individual bankrupt.

D   Provisions to the like effect have been contained in every Companies Act since the
right to disclaim onerous property was first extended from personal to corporate
insolvency by the *Companies Act* 1929, and in every Bankruptcy Act since the *Bankruptcy
Act* 1883. The *Insolvency Act* 1986 introduced two changes primarily of a procedural
character, though having some substantive effect. Before the Act the liquidator of an
insolvent company needed the leave of the court to disclaim in all cases, whereas a trustee
E   in bankruptcy did not need such leave in most cases, and in particular did not need leave
to disclaim a lease unless the bankrupt had sublet the premises or mortgaged the lease
and the lessor, sublessee or mortgagee had objected to the disclaimer after being given
notice thereof. The changes introduced by the 1986 Act brought the law and practice of
disclaimer in corporate insolvency into line with that prevailing in personal bankruptcy.
They were not without substantive effect, however, for the court had normally refused
leave to disclaim where this would prejudice the lessor by discharging a surety from
F   liability. Under the 1986 Act, however, the lessor has no opportunity to object to the
disclaimer taking effect.

Mr Oliver QC, who appeared for the second and third defendants, acknowledged that
the changes introduced by the *Insolvency Act* 1986 did not affect the consequences of a
disclaimer, which are laid down by s. 178(4) and (6) in substantially the same terms as
the corresponding provisions of the Bankruptcy Acts of 1883 and 1914. For ease of
G   exposition I shall, throughout the rest of this judgment, refer to the relevant provisions
of the earlier legislation by the numbers of the corresponding provisions in the *Insolvency
Act* 1986, that is to say, subs. (4) or (6).

The consequences of disclaimer of leasehold property have been considered by the
courts on a number of occasions. The leading authorities, which consist of one decision
of the House of Lords on the effect of the *Bankruptcy Act* 1869 and one decision of this
court on the effect of the *Bankruptcy Act* 1883, established that there is a clear distinction
H   between the case where the lease was still vested in the original lessee immediately before
the disclaimer (which is not the present case), and the case where it is vested in an assignee
of the original lessee (which is). The burden of Mr Oliver's submissions was that there is
no relevant distinction to be drawn between the position of a surety for the bankrupt
original lessee and the original lessee with an unbroken chain of indemnity from the
bankrupt assignee. Each of them is liable to the lessor and is entitled to be indemnified

by the bankrupt's estate. I shall deal in turn with the two situations as they appear from   A
the relevant authorities.

1. Lease vested in the original lessee

Disclaimer by the trustee in bankruptcy of the lessee determines the lease and the
lessee's obligations thereunder, with the result that the liability of any surety for the lessee
is necessarily discharged. This was decided in *Stacey v Hill* [1901] 1 KB 660, a decision of   B
this court. Two grounds for the decision can be detected:

(1)   No other person being interested in the lease, the determination of the lessee's
rights and liabilities thereunder – including his right to possession – has the effect
of determining the lease altogether and accelerating the reversion. The effect of
determining the liability of the lessee is to discharge the surety, for the secondary
liability of a surety cannot survive the extinction of the primary guaranteed debt.   C

(2)   Subsection (4)(b) does not have the effect of preserving the liability of the surety,
because the existence of the surety's right of indemnity by the principal debtor
makes it necessary to release the surety if the bankrupt's estate is to be released
from liability.

Two points may be noticed. The first and main ground for the decision, in which all
three Lords Justices concurred, was that the determination of the lessee's rights and
obligations had the effect of determining the lease. The lessee's right to possession being   D
determined, and there being no one else with a similar right, there was no obstacle to the
lessor's resumption of possession with a view to re-letting the property. Strictly speaking,
it was unnecessary to decide that the lease was determined or the reversion accelerated; it
was sufficient for the decision that the liabilities of the lessee under the lease had been
determined.

The second ground for the decision, to which only two of the Lords Justices subscribed,   E
is not fully explained in the judgments and is not as straightforward as it appears at first
sight. I shall have to return to this aspect of the case later.

2. Where the lease is vested in an assignee

Prior to the *Bankruptcy Act* 1883 a disclaimer by the trustee in bankruptcy of an
assignee of the lease had no effect on the continuing liability of the original lessee or his   F
surety. This was decided by the House of Lords in *Hill v East & West India Dock Co*
(1884) 9 App Cas 448. That case was decided under the *Bankruptcy Act* 1869, the relevant
provisions of which were in very different terms from those introduced by the *Bankruptcy
Act* 1883, and which in particular did not include any provision corresponding to subs.
(4)(b). The House of Lords held that the determination of the rights and liabilities of the
assignee, which took effect by way of a deemed surrender of the lease, operated only as
between the lessor and the bankrupt assignee; so far as the original lessee was concerned,   G
the lease continued to subsist (as did his liability) unless and until the lessor resumed
actual possession and brought the lease to an end for all purposes.

Two points may be made about that decision. (1) Mr Oliver submitted that the concept
of a lease continuing to exist but having no owner is not a particularly easy one to grasp;
nor is it easy to understand what obstacle there is to the lessor's resumption of possession
and re-letting the property, seeing that the right to possession of the bankrupt assignee   H
has been determined and that he is the only person entitled to possession as against the
lessor. These difficulties are inherent in the decision itself; they do not derive from the
potential reactivation of the lease by the making of a vesting order, since there was no
power to make such an order prior to the *Bankruptcy Act* 1883. Both suggested difficulties
disappear, however, once it is recognised that the question is not whether the lease
actually exists or not, but whether it is to be deemed or treated as continuing to exist.

A   The result of the decision in *Hill v East & West India Dock Co* is that, as between the lessor and the bankrupt assignee the lease is *deemed* to have been surrendered; as between the lessor and the original lessee and his surety, it is not deemed to have been surrendered. In the real world a lease must either exist or not. In the world of statutory hypothesis, however, there is no such requirement.

B   (2) The basis of the decision in *Hill v East & West India Dock Co* is that the liability of the original lessee is a primary and direct liability and is not dependent on the continued liability of the assignee. There are two separate and distinct obligations, and the statutory determination of the one does not discharge the other. In *Stacey v Hill*, by contrast, there was only one obligation, namely that of the lessee, though two different parties were liable in respect of it; and the statutory determination of that obligation necessarily discharged the liability of both of them.

C   The question, therefore, is what difference, if any, to the liability of the original lessee and any surety for him resulted from the introduction in 1883 of subs. (4)(b); for we are bound in this court by the decision in *Hill v East & West India Dock Co* to hold that an original lessee is not discharged from his liability to the lessor by reason of the disclaimer of the lease by the liquidator of an assignee 'except so far as is necessary for the purpose of releasing the company [that is to say, the insolvent assignee] from any liability'.

D   This question was considered by Sir Robert Megarry V-C in a characteristically clear and comprehensive judgment in *Warnford Investments Ltd v Duckworth & Ors* [1979] Ch 127. He held that the introduction of subs. (4)(b) by the *Bankruptcy Act* 1883 made no difference. Accordingly, he applied *Hill v East & West India Dock Co* and distinguished *Stacey v Hill*. He pointed out that the situations dealt with by the two cases were entirely different. In the one case the lease itself was determined and with it the liability of the bankrupt; and the guaranteed liability having been brought to an end, the surety was

E   necessarily discharged. In the other the liability of the original lessee was primary and direct, and was not dependent on any continued liability on the part of the bankrupt. The Vice-Chancellor dealt with the argument that the liability of the original lessee was determined (or more accurately not preserved) by subs. (4)(b) by saying that the bankrupt's estate was not released from liability in any event: any loss sustained by reason of the disclaimer was susceptible of proof under subs. (6) (a provision which has been in every Bankruptcy Act since 1869). The only question was whether the proof

F   should be lodged by the lessor or by the original lessee. If the original lessee was discharged from liability, the proof would be lodged by the lessor; if not, it would be lodged by the original lessee, relying on the chain of indemnity. In either case, the bankrupt's estate would not be released from liability. Since the discharge of the original lessee did not in fact lead to the release of the bankrupt estate, it could not be necessary in order to secure its release.

G   If that reasoning is correct, then in my judgment the second ground of the decision in *Stacey v Hill* cannot be supported; for there is no relevant distinction to be drawn between the position of the original lessee and that of a surety for the bankrupt assignee, each being liable to the lessor and having a claim for indemnity against the bankrupt estate. Either the determination of the liability to the lessor results in the release of the bankrupt estate or it does not, and if it does not (whether because of subs. (6) or otherwise) then the discharge of the person entitled to be indemnified is not necessary for the purpose of

H   securing the release of the bankrupt estate from liability.

But in my judgment this part of the reasoning of the Vice-Chancellor is untenable. It is necessary to distinguish between two quite different liabilities of the bankrupt estate. There is, first, the liability which is put an end to by the disclaimer, in the present case, for example, the liability to pay the rent due under the lease. There is, secondly, the statutory liability under subs. (6) which replaces it, that is to say, the liability to

compensate any person who has sustained loss or damage in consequence of the   A
disclaimer. These liabilities may or may not be identical in amount, but they are different
and distinct liabilities, the effect of a disclaimer being to extinguish the one and to replace
it by the other. In my judgment, when subs. (4)(b) speaks of something being 'necessary
for the purpose of releasing the company from any liability', the words 'any liability'
refer to a liability of the first kind and not the second. There are two reasons for this. In
the first place, the effect of the disclaimer under subs. (4) must be determined as an
anterior question before the identification of the party sustaining loss as a result and the   B
quantification of his loss can be undertaken for the purposes of proof under subs. (6). In
the second place, the bankrupt's estate can never be released from its potential liability
under subs. (6). In my judgment, therefore, subs. (4)(b) means: 'necessary for the purpose
of releasing the company from any such liability as aforesaid', that is to say, a liability in
or in respect of the property disclaimed and capable of being determined by subs. (4)(a).

The rejection of this part of the reasoning of the Vice-Chancellor, however, also   C
disposes of Mr Oliver's main argument, which is that subs. (4) should be given a
purposive construction; that its purpose is to release the bankrupt estate from liability to
the greatest extent possible; that this means giving subs. (4) that effect which would lead
to the smallest possible claim under subs. (6); and that this in turn means extinguishing
the liability of the original lessee and substituting a claim by the lessor, who would
inevitably have a smaller claim than the original lessee, since the lessor, being able to re-   D
let the premises, would have to give credit for the current rental value of the premises,
whereas the original lessee would have nothing for which he could be required to give
credit. The whole elaborate argument breaks down, however, once it is recognised that
the amount of the loss sustained by reason of the disclaimer and provable under subs. (6)
cannot be considered until the effect of the disclaimer under subs. (4) has first been
determined.

It follows in my judgment (and to this extent I disagree with the judgment of Sir Robert   E
Megarry V-C) that the case of the original lessee with an unbroken chain of indemnity
cannot be distinguished from that of the surety of the bankrupt lessee by praying in aid
the existence of subs. (6). The question, however, remains: is it necessary to extinguish
the liability of the original lessee to the lessor in order to release the liability of the
bankrupt assignee to indemnify him? The question only has to be asked to be answered
in the negative. It cannot be necessary to extinguish the liability of the original lessee in   F
order to release the estate of the bankrupt: it is sufficient to extinguish the liability of the
bankrupt assignee to indemnify the original lessee. Moreover, the extinction of the
liability of the bankrupt estate to indemnify the original lessee, is in my judgment the
plain effect of the subsection. Subsection (4)(a) determines all the liabilities of the
bankrupt assignee in respect of the disclaimed property. These are not restricted to
liabilities owed to the lessor. They include not only the liability to pay the rent to the
lessor, but also the liability to indemnify the original lessee in respect of rent payable to   G
the lessor: both in my judgment are equally 'liabilities in respect of the disclaimed
property'. In order to release the estate of the bankrupt assignee from its liability to
indemnify the original lessee, however, it is necessary to extinguish the right of the
original lessee to be indemnified; what subs. (4)(b) does, however, is to make it clear that
the liability of a bankrupt assignee is determined notwithstanding its effect on the right
of the original lessee to an indemnity against his liability.   H

This was the solution adopted by His Honour Judge Paul Baker QC in *W H Smith Ltd
v Wyndham Investments Ltd* [1994] BCC 699. He said (at p. 704A):

'. . . I see no difficulty in abrogating the right of the original lessee to claim an
indemnity from the assignee without any necessity to abrogate the obligation of
the original lessee to pay the lessor. To compensate for the loss of the right to be

A   indemnified against future rent, the original lessee can prove for any loss or injury under s. 178(6). I may add, with all respect, that I do not see the necessity for any equation between the lessee's claim for injury and that of the lessor as expounded by the Vice-Chancellor in the passage set out above. The position as I see it is that the liability of the assignee to indemnify the original lessee against future payments of rent is removed and a right to assess the loss and prove for it once and for all it substituted without regard to claims for loss or injury from any other party.'

B   Mr Oliver's response to this solution was to submit that we are precluded from adopting it by the decision of this court in *Stacey v Hill*. We are, of course, bound by that decision and by both grounds for it, and we cannot take refuge in the fact that the second ground for the decision has not won universal acceptance, or that the first ground was sufficient for the decision, or that the second ground is not fully explained. Mr Oliver submitted that the solution which I have suggested (and which was adopted by His Honour Judge Paul Baker) was equally open to the court in *Stacey v Hill*; and that since that court undoubtedly decided that it was necessary to discharge the surety in order to release the bankrupt lessee, it must be taken to have decided that it was not sufficient (or appropriate or possible) to leave the surety's obligation unaffected and extinguish his right to indemnity; and that the same must necessarily apply to the case of an original lessee.

D   As a strict matter of stare decisis, that submission is not acceptable. We are bound by what the court in *Stacey v Hill* actually decided, but not by any conclusion which can be logically deduced from what was decided but which was neither argued nor considered. But in any case I do not accept the submission. The right of the surety to be indemnified by the principal debtor, although arising from contract express or implied, is inherent in the relationship between them. It is coextensive with and arises eo instanti as his liability. The two may be regarded as inseparable; or, as is sometimes said, as two sides of the same coin. It would, in my judgment, require very clear statutory language to deprive a statutory surety of his right to indemnity while leaving his liability unimpaired. No such language is to be found in subs. (4)(b), and it is not surprising that the possibility of extinguishing the surety's right to indemnity while leaving him exposed to liability did not occur to any member of the court, except possibly Romer LJ who rejected it. No such inhibitions need constrain the court when considering the position of the original lessee. His obligation arises when he takes the lease; it continues after assignment. If he is prudent, therefore, he takes a covenant of indemnity from his assignee when he assigns the lease. But his right to indemnity is quite separate from his obligation. The two arise at different times and by virtue of different instruments; and the existence of the obligation in no sense imports the right. Like Judge Paul Baker QC, I see no objection to abrogating the right of the original lessee to an indemnity from the assignee without any necessity to abrogate the obligation of the original lessee to the lessor; and in my judgment we are not precluded by the decision in *Stacey v Hill* from deciding that that is the effect of subs. (4).

In an alternative and subordinate submission, Mr Oliver submitted that the liability of the second and third defendants extended only to the initial rent reserved by the lease and not to the increased rent agreed between the company and the lessor in accordance with the provisions of the rent review clause. That agreement was reached without reference to the second or third defendants. The question depends on the true construction of the covenants entered into by the second and third defendants in the licence to assign.

The second defendant covenanted with the lessor:

    'that as from the date when the lessee's estate and interest in the lease shall be assigned to the assignee pursuant to the licence hereinbefore contained and thenceforth during the residue of the term created by the lease the assignee will pay the rents thereby reserved . . .'

That takes one back to the lease in order to ascertain what was the amount of the rent reserved thereby during the relevant rental period. That takes one to cl. 5 of the lease, which (so far as material) provided:

'5. IT IS HEREBY FURTHER AGREED AND DECLARED as follows:

The yearly rents reserved by this lease are those stated in or ascertained in accordance with this clause . . .

(2) The yearly rent shall be:

(a) until the first review date the yearly rent of thirteen thousand six hundred and twenty six pounds (13,626), and

(b) during each successive review period a yearly rent equal to the yearly rent previously payable hereunder or such revised yearly rent as may be ascertained as herein provided whichever be the greater, and

(3) Such revised yearly rent for any review period may be agreed at any time between the lessor and the lessee or (in the absence of agreement) determined . . .'

(I should add that the word 'lessee' was defined as including the original lessee and its successors to title.)

Accordingly, on the plain construction of the language of the lease, the rent reserved by the lease after the first review date was the rent agreed between the lessor and the then lessee in accordance with cl. 5(2)(b) and (3) of the lease. Indeed, the argument that the only rent which the second defendant has covenanted to pay which the third defendant was covenanted to guarantee is £13,626 is completely untenable since that rent was reserved by the lease until the first review date and not afterwards.

In a powerful argument, Mr Oliver submitted that the time has come to re-examine the position of the original lessee. The continuing liability of the original lessee after assignment of the lease and the possible operation of a rent review clause has been the subject of a report by the Law Commission, and may well merit consideration by Parliament. We are not concerned with that, but only with a narrower question: the continuing liability of the original lessee after the disclaimer of the lease by the liquidator of his assignee. In my judgment his liability was established by *Hill v East & West India Dock Co*, a decision of the House of Lords which is binding on us, and the introduction of subs. (4)(b) by the *Bankruptcy Act* 1883 has not affected it. Accordingly, for my part, I would dismiss this appeal.

Rose LJ: I agree.

Brown P: I agree that the appeal shall be dismissed for the reasons given by Millett LJ.

(*Appeal dismissed with costs. Leave to appeal to the House of Lords refused. Stay granted pending the lodging of a petition on terms that £10,000 be paid into court*)

C T Bowring & Co (Insurance) Ltd v Corsi & Partners Ltd.

Court of Appeal (Civil Division).
Dillon, Millett L JJ and Sir Michael Kerr.
Judgment delivered 16 June 1994.

Costs – Security for costs – Plaintiff obtained Mareva injunction against defendant on cross-undertaking in damages – Mareva injunction discharged by consent – Defendant sought security for costs from plaintiff for inquiry into damages – Whether application in existing proceedings 'an action or other legal proceedings' or 'an action or other proceeding in the High Court' – Whether defendant making application in position of plaintiff – Whether jurisdiction to order defendant to pay plaintiff's costs – Companies Act 1985, s. 726; Rules of the Supreme Court, O. 23, r.1.

This was an appeal against the dismissal of the plaintiff's application for security for costs of the defendant's application to enforce the plaintiff's cross-undertaking in damages given to obtain a Mareva injunction later discharged by consent.

The plaintiff issued a writ against the defendant on 3 December 1985 claiming balances due in respect of insurance and reinsurance business. In anticipation the plaintiff obtained a Mareva injunction against the defendant on 2 December 1985 on the usual cross-undertaking in damages. On 30 January 1986 the Mareva injunction was discharged by consent. The action did not proceed to trial, the defendants having repaid to the plaintiff £60,000, which represented the sum claimed apart from an amount extinguished by set-off. The defendants sought an inquiry into damages under the cross-undertaking claiming £3.75m although the Mareva injunction was in force for just under two months. The plaintiff's application for security for costs in relation to the defendant's application for an inquiry into damages was refused. The plaintiff appealed.

Held, dismissing the plaintiff's appeal:

1. It was a rule of practice, not a matter of discretion, that a defendant was to be at liberty to defend himself. A court therefore could not award security for costs against a defendant.

2. The 'proceedings' in s. 726 of the Companies Act 1985 and RSC, O. 23, r. 1 referred to proceedings in the nature of an action and therefore encompassed the entire proceedings between the parties, not an application in existing proceedings.

3. It was necessary to consider the whole litigation between the parties to determine which was the plaintiff and which the defendant. A party making an application in proceedings in which he was not a plaintiff did not thereby become a 'plaintiff' for the purposes of that application. It followed that there was no jurisdiction to order the defendant to provide security for the plaintiff's costs of the application under s. 726 of the 1985 Act or under RSC, O. 23, r. 1.

4. It was an abuse of the process of the court for a defendant to make an exorbitant claim for damages with no genuine belief in its merits and reject all reasonable offers of settlement. The court could exercise its discretion to refuse to order an inquiry into damages under its inherent jurisdiction to release or vary an undertaking given to it. That was the remedy available to the plaintiff if the defendant was making an exorbitant claim, rather than an application for security for costs. Since there was no evidence that the defendant's claim amounted to an abuse of the process of the court, the appeal was dismissed.

The following cases were referred to in the judgments:

Accidental and Marine Insurance Co v Mercati (1866) LR 3 Eq 200.
B (Infants), Re [1965] 1 WLR 946.
Cheltenham and Gloucester Building Society v Ricketts & Ors [1993] 1 WLR 1545.

City of Moscow Gas Co v International Financial Society (1872) LR 7 Ch App 225.

Eden v Weardale Iron and Coal Co (1887) 35 ChD 287.

Lonrho plc v Fayed & Ors (No. 2) [1992] 1 WLR 1.

Naamlooze Vennootschap Beleggings Compagnie 'Uranus' v Bank of England & Ors [1948] 1 All ER 465.

Neck v Taylor [1893] 1 QB 560.

New Fenix Compagnie Anonyme D'Assurances de Madrid v General Accident, Fire, and Life Assurance Corp Ltd [1911] 2 KB 619.

Newcomen v Coulson (1878) 7 ChD 764.

Taly NDC International NV v Terra Nova Insurance Co Ltd & Ors [1985] 1 WLR 1359.

Unisoft Group Ltd, Re [1994] BCC 11.

Washoe Mining Co v Ferguson (1866) LR 2 Eq 371.

Watteeu v Billam (1849) 3 De G & Sm 516; 64 ER 586.

Yorke (MV) Motors v Edwards [1982] 1 WLR 444.

Steven Gee QC (instructed by Clyde & Co) for the plaintiff.

Andrew Fletcher (instructed by Norton Rose) for the defendant.

JUDGMENT

Dillon LJ: This is an appeal, pursuant to leave granted by Beldam and Saville L JJ, by the plaintiff in this action C T Bowring & Co (Insurance) Ltd against an order of Waller J made on 7 October 1993. By that order the judge dismissed an application by the plaintiff that the defendant in the action, Corsi & Partners Ltd – which is the respondent to the appeal – should provide security for costs in circumstances to which I shall come. That application by the plaintiff had been made by a summons in the action dated 23 July 1993, which, in the original form and as it stood when it was before the judge, sought:

> 'that the defendant give security for the plaintiff's costs in relation to the defendant's application for an inquiry into damages to the satisfaction of the judge on the ground that there is reason to believe that the defendant will be unable to pay the plaintiff's costs if the plaintiff is successful in its defence of the defendant's application for an inquiry (s. 726 of the *Companies Act* 1985) and that in default by the defendant in providing any security so ordered, the defendant's said application be struck out.'

At the end of the argument in this court Mr Gee QC for the plaintiff sought leave to amend the summons to raise alternatives which had been canvassed in the course of the argument in this court. His formulation of the amendments he seeks makes the relief sought in the existing summons para. 1 and adds after the reference to the *Companies Act* 1985 the words 'and under RSC, O. 23, r. 1(1)(b) on the grounds that the defendant is a nominal plaintiff for the purposes of that rule'. There is then added to the summons a new para. 2 as follows:

> '2. The defendant's application by summons dated 28 August 1992 for an inquiry as to damages be stayed unless the defendant do provide security for costs in such amount as the court may determine and/or upon such other terms as may be prescribed by the court on the grounds that there is jurisdiction to make such order under the inherent jurisdiction of the court and/or by reason of the fact that the undertaking in damages has been furnished to the court, and in the circumstances of the case the said application for an inquiry is an abuse of the process of the court and/or in the circumstances of the case it is just that such an order be made.'

Despite the objections to para. 2 of Mr Fletcher on behalf of the defendant – which were to the general effect that, if the plaintiff wanted to put forward arguments not covered by the summons of 23 July 1993 as actually issued, the plaintiff should issue a

A fresh summons returnable before a judge at first instance and to be dealt with at his discretion – I would allow the summons to be amended as now asked, so that this court can deal so far as necessary with all the issues of law which have been argued before us. So far as the facts are concerned, we can only consider the issues on the evidence which is now before us; there is no application to admit further evidence.

An application for security for costs as against a defendant in an action (otherwise than in respect of costs of a counterclaim) is, at the least, unusual. But it is not necessary
B to go into the facts of the case or the history of the litigation in any great detail.

The writ was issued as long ago as 3 December 1985. In anticipation, the plaintiff obtained a Mareva injunction against the defendant from Leggatt J on 2 December 1985, and the plaintiff had, of course, as the price of obtaining the injunction, to give to the court the usual cross-undertaking in damages, viz. an undertaking to abide by any order
C the court might make as to damages in case the court should thereafter be of the opinion that the defendant shall have sustained any loss by reason of the injunction which the plaintiff ought to pay.

The Mareva injunction was discharged by consent on 30 January 1986. The inquiry as to damages, in respect of the costs of which, and of obtaining which, the plaintiff seeks security, is the inquiry which the defendant seeks as to damages under the cross-undertaking routinely given by the plaintiff to the court when the Mareva injunction was
D granted.

The substance of the plaintiff's claim in the action was for balances alleged to be due from the defendant to the plaintiff in respect of insurance and reinsurance business placed either in the Italian market by the plaintiff as producing broker through the defendant as placing broker or in the London market by the defendant as producing broker through the plaintiff as placing broker.

E It is said for the plaintiff (though this we have not been concerned to check) that of the total principal sum claimed, some £600,000 in aggregate had been repaid by the defendant to the plaintiff by December 1986, while the balance was extinguished by set-off of cross-claims by the defendant against an associated company of the plaintiff. The action has never come on for formal trial, but all that remains in it is a claim by the plaintiff, which has not been vigorously pursued, for interest on the principal sums repaid, plus costs.

F Although the Mareva was only in force for just under two months, the damages claimed by the defendant as a result of its imposition amount to no less than £3.75m. It is not uncommon for defendants claiming damages under a cross-undertaking, whether in relation to a Mareva injunction or a more traditional interlocutory injunction prohibiting some act, to put forward apparently exorbitant claims, as if, had the injunction not been granted, they would have enjoyed the Midas touch and achieved economic success not remotely within their reach before or since.
G
Apart however from disputing the amount of damages claimed by the defendant under the cross-undertaking, the plaintiff asserts that this is not an appropriate case for any inquiry as to damages to be ordered. It is not a case in which the Mareva has been set aside by the court as improperly or inappropriately granted, nor is it a case in which the court has rejected the plaintiff's claims in support of which the Mareva was obtained. The first stage, therefore, for the costs of which the plaintiff seeks security, is the
H determination whether there should be any inquiry as to damages at all. To determine this first stage a hearing has been fixed for 11 July 1994, with an estimated duration of five days. If an inquiry were to be ordered, the plaintiff would also claim security for the costs of the inquiry.

It is clear from the decision of this court in *Cheltenham and Gloucester Building Society v Ricketts* [1993] 1 WLR 1545 that whether or not a cross-undertaking in damages should

be enforced by an order for an inquiry is a matter for the discretion of the court to be   A
exercised on equitable principles. The factors to be considered may be various but in
some cases the conduct of the defendant may be a reason why an inquiry should not be
ordered.

Section 726 of the *Companies Act* 1985, which is the only authority for awarding
security for costs relied on in the summons of 23 July 1993 as issued, provides as follows:

'(1) Where in England and Wales a limited company is plaintiff in an action or   B
other legal proceeding, the court having jurisdiction in the matter may, if it appears
by credible testimony that there is reason to believe that the company will be
unable to pay the defendant's costs if successful in his defence, require sufficient
security to be given for those costs, and may stay all proceedings until the security
is given.'

Subsection (2) applies to Scotland.   C

In the present case we are not concerned with whether or not the defendant will if
unsuccessful be able to pay the plaintiff's costs of its application for the inquiry as to
damages, or the plaintiff's costs of the inquiry, if ordered. Before the judge, the case did
not reach that stage; he held that the defendant was a defendant and not a plaintiff and
so it cannot be ordered to provide security for the plaintiff's costs.

The earliest legislative antecedent of s. 726 is s. 24 of the *Joint Stock Companies Act*   D
1857 which provided:

'Where a limited company is plaintiff or pursuer in any action suit or other legal
proceeding any judge having jurisdiction in the matter may, if it be proved to his
satisfaction that there is reason to believe that if the defendant be successful in his
defence the assets of the company will be insufficient to pay his costs, require
sufficient security to be given for such costs, and may stay all proceedings until
such security be given.'   E

Similarly worded sections appeared in the successive Companies Acts of 1862, 1908,
1929 and 1948. With the passage of time, the word 'suit' was dropped as obsolete.

Section 24 of the 1857 Act represented an innovation, and it and its successors
represent even now the only established exception to the general rule of practice that a
party who desires to litigate a claim shall not be prevented by the court from doing so, at
any rate at first instance, on the grounds of his poverty and consequent inability to pay   F
the costs of his adversary if his adversary were to be successful.

There was, even before 1857, a power which the courts exercised, under their inherent
jurisdiction, in certain cases to order a plaintiff to give security for costs. But again there
was a strongly established rule of practice that a person who is in the position of a
defendant is to be at liberty to defend himself and is not to be called on to give security.
See the judgment of Sir William Page Wood V-C in *Accidental and Marine Insurance Co*   G
v Mercati (1866) LR 3 Eq 200 at p. 203. I regard this as a rule of practice, and not a mere
matter of discretion to be determined on the facts in each individual case – although of
course any decision even to order a plaintiff to give security is a matter for the court's
discretion, as is pointed out in *New Fenix Compagnie Anonyme D'Assurances v General
Accident Fire and Life Assurance Corporation Ltd* [1911] 2 KB 619 at pp. 624 and 630. I
regard this rule of practice as of the same class as the rule of practice under which any   H
litigant, other than the Crown or a public authority as law enforcer, who obtains an
interlocutory injunction is required to give a cross-undertaking in damages. That is not a
matter for discretion in the individual case.

Although the word counterclaim is not used in s. 726 or any of its predecessors – no
doubt because the counterclaim, as we have long known it, did not exist as a form of
procedure in 1857 or 1862 – it is clear that an impecunious company which makes a

A   counterclaim which is more than a mere formulation of its defence can be ordered to give security for the plaintiff's costs of the counterclaim. The distinction taken in the old cases of *Accidental and Marine Insurance Co v Mercati* and *Watteeu v Billam* (1849) 3 De G & Sm 516 on the one hand and *Washoe Mining Co v Ferguson* (1866) LR 2 Eq 371 and *City of Moscow Gas Co v International Financial Society* (1872) LR 7 Ch App 225 on the other, in relation to cross suits or cross bills by defendants which were not, and those which were, more than mere defences to a plaintiff's suit or bill remains valid nowadays,

B   but is not relevant to the present case. The continuing validity of the distinction was accepted by this court in *Neck v Taylor* [1893] 1 QB 560.

The cases, outside the Companies Acts, in which the courts used to order security for costs in the exercise of their inherent jurisdiction, are now formulated in the Rules of the Supreme Court. Order 23 deals with security for costs and r. 1, 2 and 3 provide as follows:

C   '*Security for costs of action, etc.* (O. 23, r. 1)

1(1) Where, on the application of a defendant to an action or other proceeding in the High Court, it appears to the Court–

    (a) that the plaintiff is ordinarily resident out of the jurisdiction, or

    (b) that the plaintiff (not being a plaintiff who is suing in a representative capacity) is a nominal plaintiff who is suing for the benefit of some other person and that there is reason to believe that he will be unable to pay the

D   costs of the defendant if ordered to do so, or

    (c) subject to paragraph (2) that the plaintiff's address is not stated in the writ or other originating process or is incorrectly stated therein, or

    (d) that the plaintiff has changed his address during the course of the proceedings with a view to evading the consequences of the litigation,

E   then if, having regard to all the circumstances of the case, the Court thinks it just to do so, it may order the plaintiff to give such security for the defendant's costs of the action or other proceeding as it thinks just.

(2) The Court shall not require a plaintiff to give security by reason only of paragraph (1)(c) if he satisfies the Court that the failure to state his address or the mis-statement thereof was made innocently and without intention to deceive.

F   (3) The references in the foregoing paragraphs to a plaintiff and a defendant shall be construed as references to the person (howsoever described on the record) who is in the position of plaintiff or defendant, as the case may be, in the proceeding in question, including a proceeding on a counterclaim.

Manner of giving security (O. 23, r. 2)

2. Where an order is made requiring any party to give security for costs, the

G   security shall be given in such manner, at such time, and on such terms (if any) as the Court may direct.

Saving for enactments (O. 23, r. 3)

3. This Order is without prejudice to the provisions of any enactment which empowers the Court to require security to be given for the costs of any proceedings.'

H   To add a new category, not covered by any enactment, to those listed in r. 1(1) in which a plaintiff can be ordered to give security would now be a matter for the Rules Committee, and not for the discretion, as a matter of inherent jurisdiction, of the individual judge in the individual case.

In so far as O. 23, r. 1 is relied on in the amended summons, it is not said that the defendant is ordinarily resident out of the jurisdiction; the defendant is a company

incorporated in England, albeit controlled by Italian shareholders. It is said, if the   A
defendant can be regarded as a plaintiff for the purposes of the application for an inquiry
as to damages under the cross-undertaking, that the defendant is a nominal plaintiff,
within sub-head (b) of the rule, who is suing for the benefit of some other person. With
the details of that we are not concerned.

The relevance to this appeal of O. 23 is rather different. Mr Gee advances an intricate
argument on the following lines, viz: B

(1)   Under O. 1, r. 3 the Interpretation Act applies for the interpretation of O. 23.

(2)   Therefore expressions used in O. 23 have (unless the contrary intention appears)
the meanings which they bear in the interpretation sections in the statutes under
which the Rules of the Supreme Court were made, viz. since 1925 s. 225 of the
Supreme Court of Judicature (Consolidation) Act 1925, and before that, from 1873,
s. 100 of the *Supreme Court of Judicature Act* 1873.   C

(3)   The interpretation of expressions used in s. 225 of the 1925 Judicature Act colours
all references to the same expressions in the successive Companies Acts.

As to the last point, Mr Gee relies in particular on the statement of Scott LJ in giving
the leading judgment, with which the other members of this court concurred, in *Re
Unisoft Group Ltd* [1994] BCC 11 at p. 13F that:

'In my opinion that broad definition of plaintiff' – sc. in s. 225 – 'colours all   D
references to "plaintiff" in the rules and colours the references to "plaintiff" in the
successive Companies Acts.'

Therefore Mr Gee submits that the word 'plaintiff' in s. 726 of the *Companies Act* 1985
is to be interpreted in accordance with the definition of 'plaintiff' in s. 225 of the 1925
Judicature Act which Mr Gee submits is so wide as to give the court jurisdiction to order
an impoverished company which is a defendant in an action to provide security for the   E
costs of any interlocutory summons or motion which may be issued by that defendant in
the course of the action brought against it.

Since the wording of s. 726 is plainly derived, via the intermediate general Companies
Acts, from the first general Companies Act, the 1862 Act, and thenceforth from s. 24 of
the 1857 Act, I have personal difficulty in seeing how the wording of s. 726 can be said to
be 'coloured' by interpretation sections in a different line of statutes which started some
years after 1862. But that is of minor importance.   F

By s. 225 of the 1925 Judicature Act the term 'plaintiff' is defined as follows:

' "plaintiff" includes every person asking for any relief (otherwise than by way of
counterclaim as a defendant) against any other person by any form of proceedings,
whether the proceeding is by action, suit, petition, motion, summons or otherwise.'

The definition of 'plaintiff' in s. 100 of the 1873 Judicature Act was for all practical   G
purposes identical.

Mr Gee submitted that in both definition sections the definition of the term 'cause' was
expressly limited to 'original' proceedings and that showed that the definition of 'plaintiff'
was not limited to 'original' or originating process but extended to any one who asked
for relief by any interlocutory summons or motion in any proceedings. I do not see that
that follows at all. In statutes as complex as the Judicature Acts one term may be carefully   H
defined for its own purposes in the Act without the definition casting any light by
implication on the scope of the definition of a different phrase. Thus as there are common
phrases like 'costs in cause', it is desirable that it should be emphasised in the definition
of 'cause' that it refers to the original proceeding. But I do not derive any assistance from
that towards a conclusion that in the definition of 'plaintiff' summonses and motions are
to include interlocutory summonses and motions with the consequence that a defendant

A   who issues an interlocutory summons or motion in the plaintiff's action is to be regarded as himself being the plaintiff for the purposes of that summons or motion.

Indeed the express exclusion from the definition of 'plaintiff' of the person who seeks relief by way of counterclaim as a defendant indicates to me that the 'relief' referred to in the definition of 'plaintiff' is the relief claimed by the originating process, and not mere interlocutory relief. To say that a defendant who counterclaims is not a plaintiff but a B   defendant who issues an interlocutory summons or motion in the plaintiff's action is a plaintiff makes no sense at all to my mind.

For my part, I agree respectfully and emphatically with the passage in the judgment of Parker LJ in relation to O. 23, r. 1 in *Taly v Terra Nova Ltd* [1985] 1 WLR 1359 at p. 1361 where he said:

C   'I will deal first with the suggestion that the application for specific discovery and leave to deliver interrogatories should be regarded as proceedings within the rule. I have no hesitation, myself, in coming to an opposite conclusion. In my judgment the proceedings referred to in the rule, if they are not an action, are at least proceedings of the nature of an action and refer to the whole matter and not to an interlocutory application in some other proceedings. Were it otherwise, it appears to me that chaos would reign, for every time an interlocutory application was taken out by a defendant the plaintiff would be able to say, "The plaintiff is in the D   position of the defendant in this application and the defendant is in the position of the plaintiff. They are proceedings. Therefore I ought to have security for the costs of this application." One has only to examine that to see that it cannot have any foundation whatever.'

In the same case, Croom-Johnson LJ said at p. 1363C–D:

E   'As to the point on jurisdiction, it really proceeds upon the proper construction of R.S.C., Ord. 23, r. 1, and I have no doubt myself that the purpose of that Order is that the proceeding, which is referred to there, is the proceeding as a whole, whether it is an action or something equivalent to an action . . . . . The right to ask for security for costs under Order 23, where the plaintiff is not resident within the jurisdiction, is purely devoted to people who are plaintiff and defendant in the proceeding as a whole.'

F   Again, I agree.

The natural meaning of the term 'plaintiff' in a context of litigation is the plaintiff in the proceedings as a whole or original proceedings. The definition in s. 225 should be construed in accordance with that natural meaning.

Accordingly, I reject Mr Gee's submission that by route of the definition of 'plaintiff' in s. 225 an impoverished corporate defendant who makes an application by interlocutory summons or motion in some other plaintiff's action thereby constitutes itself a 'plaintiff' G   which can be ordered to give security for the costs of its application under s. 726, 'plaintiff' in s. 726 bears its ordinary meaning and that does not include a defendant which makes an interlocutory application.

Mr Gee also relied, in relation to s. 225, on general observations of Cotton LJ in *Eden v Weardale Iron and Coal Co* (1887) 35 ChD 287 at p. 295 that:

H   'the words of definition of "plaintiff" and "defendant" in the 100th section of the *Judicature Act* [1873] are so wide as to include all persons who litigate one against the other in any proceeding any question which the Court may properly decide.'

There however what was in issue was whether parties who had been given leave to defend proceedings could interrogate the plaintiff. It was held that, as defendants, they could; but there was no question of using the definition to turn a defendant into a plaintiff. The observations do not, therefore, assist Mr Gee.

To be fair to Mr Gee, he accepted that for most practical purposes it would make no
difference whether or not on its strict construction the term 'plaintiff' in O. 23, r. 1 or
s. 726 included, quoad that application, a defendant who made application for relief by
interlocutory summons or motion in another plaintiff's action; any plaintiff who sought
security for costs of such an interlocutory application against a defendant would still be
met by what I have called the rule of practice that a person who is in the position of a
defendant is to be at liberty to defend himself and is not to be called on to give security.
Therefore Mr Gee accepted that a plaintiff would not obtain security for costs against a
foreign defendant who applied to set aside service under O. 11 or who applied to set aside
or curtail a Mareva or other interlocutory injunction obtained ex parte by the plaintiff or
who applied for specific discovery or further and better particulars against the plaintiff.
This would be so even though the issues raised by such an application might be complex
and might involve a protracted and expensive hearing and possibly appeals to a higher
court. But Mr Gee submitted that what I have referred to as a rule of practice was no
more than a matter of discretion, which, although prima facie the rule, was capable of
being departed from by any individual judge in any particular case in the light of the
facts and circumstances of that case.

The strength of the rule of practice, as I have called it that a defendant cannot be
compelled to give security for costs, is emphasised by the judgment of Lord Greene MR
in *Naamlooze Vennootschap Beleggings Compagnie 'Uranus' v Bank of England* [1948] 1
All ER 465. In that case a Dutch plaintiff had brought an action against English
defendants. Two Dutch resident parties were added as defendants in the action, and these
Dutch defendants then applied for security for costs against the Dutch plaintiff and the
Dutch plaintiff consequently made a cross-application for security for costs against the
Dutch defendants. The Dutch defendants' application was allowed, but the cross-
application by the Dutch plaintiff was dismissed by the judge and its dismissal was upheld
by this court on appeal.

In his judgment, with which Evershed LJ concurred, Lord Greene said at p. 466F–H:

'The idea that a foreign defendant properly joined in an action in these courts is to
be impeded in defending himself by being forbidden to do so unless he gives
security for costs is one which, at first sight, is not an attractive one . . .

It is said that where there is a foreign plaintiff and a foreign defendant and the
foreign defendant exercises what is *prima facie* his right to require security from
the foreign plaintiff, the court ought to make it a condition of granting such an
order that the defendant himself should give security. I do not find that at all an
attractive proposition.'

Lord Greene continued at pp. 467H–468B:

'It is a proposition which, to my mind, runs counter to the whole of one's ideas of
the difference in the positions of plaintiff and defendant. I should be sorry to think
that the time should ever come when a defendant should be deprived of the right
to defend himself in the courts merely because he has done what every defendant,
English or foreign, is *prima facie* entitled to do, namely, to apply against a foreign
plaintiff for security for costs. It seems to me that, if such a principle as that for
which counsel for the plaintiffs has argued were to be admitted, it ought to be
applied in every case where security can be ordered and the circumstances are
comparable. There are many cases in which, according to the ordinary practice,
the court will order security against a plaintiff who is resident in this country.
Supposing that such a plaintiff sues a defendant who happens to be impecunious
so that the plaintiff, if successful, will not recover a pennyworth of costs, is it to be
said that such a defendant is to be deprived of his right to get security from such a
plaintiff unless he submits to an order to do something which *ex hypothesi* would

A

be impossible because he is impecunious? I cannot see any justification for a principle that might lead to such a result. The position of a plaintiff and the position of a defendant are quite different in these respects, and, after all, the foreign plaintiff who chooses to sue here knows quite well before he issues his writ that he is going to be made subject to the ordinary practice of the court if an application is made to provide security.'

B

So equally the plaintiff in the present action knew the risks it ran in the way of recovery of its costs in bringing proceedings against a company which it believed to be without assets.

If a defendant, including a foreign defendant or a defendant which is an impecunious company, puts in a defence which is extravagant and without foundation, the plaintiff may be able to have the defence struck out as an abuse of process, or in an appropriate case to obtain summary judgment under O. 14. But I know of no case in which it has been held, or could be held, that if a defence could not be struck out but appeared, on a preliminary trial on affidavits and statements without cross-examination to be weak, the defendant ought to be ordered to give security for the plaintiff's costs of the action. Even where under O. 14 conditional leave to defend is granted, conditionally on a sum being brought into court in respect of the claim, it has not been the practice to order the defendant to give security for the plaintiff's costs of the action, and the sum to be brought into court must not be such as would necessarily prevent the defence being pursued to trial – *Yorke Motors v Edwards* [1982] 1 WLR 444.

C

D

Although para. 2 of the amended summons suggests that the defendant's summons for an inquiry as to damages is an abuse of process, Mr Gee accepted – as I understood him – that he could not ask the court, or at any rate could not ask this court, to strike the defendant's summons out as an abuse of process; it would have to go forward to a hearing. The plaintiff certainly could not ask the court to order the defendant to provide security for the costs of the plaintiff's application to strike out the defendant's summons.

E

Mr Gee accepts, as I have mentioned, that the rule that a defendant cannot be ordered to give security when he has been brought before the court and is seeking to defend himself (as opposed to counterclaiming in respect of matters which go beyond his defence) would preclude a plaintiff from claiming security against a defendant, whether a foreign resident or an impoverished company, in respect of an application by that defendant to set aside or curtail a Mareva or other injunction obtained ex parte by the plaintiff. In my judgment, an application by the defendant for an inquiry as to damages under the cross-undertaking when the Mareva or other injunction has been discharged is likewise a mere matter of defence.

F

For this conclusion there are several reasons which are cumulative (or different aspects of the same point), viz: (1) the cross-undertaking is the price which the plaintiff has to pay for obtaining an injunction before the action can be finally tried and decided, (2) the damages under the cross-undertaking are not strictly damages but compensation to the defendant for loss suffered if it is subsequently established that the interlocutory injunction should not have been granted, and (3) there is no separate cause of action for the damages and it can only be enforced by application in the action in which the injunction was granted. See generally the observations of Neill LJ in *Cheltenham & Gloucester Building Society v Ricketts* [1993] 1 WLR 1545 at pp. 1550H–1552G. Therefore the general rule as to not awarding security for costs against a defendant is applicable.

G

H

Mr Gee submits alternatively that the rationale of the immunity of a defendant from giving security for costs is that the defendant is not to be hampered in his defence of the action by having to give security. Mr Gee therefore submits that the rationale ceases to apply, and the immunity should cease to apply when because the action has been tried or for some other reason there is no longer any claim outstanding against which the defendant needs to defend himself. He submits that in the present case there is no subsisting lis, except the application by the defendant for an inquiry under the cross-undertaking. I do not, however, find that line of argument persuasive. It is often the case that an interlocutory injunction is discharged before trial, but the court cannot know enough to decide whether to order an inquiry as to damages until after judgment at the trial. Moreover if a plaintiff, having obtained an interlocutory injunction, terminates the proceedings by serving notice of discontinuance, it will inevitably happen that the question of ordering an inquiry as to damages will only be brought before the court at a time when there is no longer any outstanding claim by the plaintiff – see *Newcomen v Coulson* (1878) 7 ChD 764. I prefer the view that as the interlocutory injunction will have been obtained against the defendant as a defendant (or potential defendant) and as the damage in respect of which he claims to be compensated will have been suffered by him while the injunction was in force and thus while he was still a defendant, it is only fair and just that his immunity against having to give security should continue until all matters under the cross-undertaking have been worked out. Such matters are part of the defendant's defence to the claim for the interlocutory injunction, even if not – particularly in the case of a cross-undertaking in a Mareva or Anton Piller order – part of his defence to the substantive issues in the action.

In theory, as the courts originally ordered security for costs under their inherent jurisdiction, there must be still inherent jurisdiction in the court to order security in cases not covered by s. 726 or any other statutory provision or by O. 23 or any other rule of court. But the issues of policy involved are such that I find it difficult to envisage the court creating a new category of case in which a plaintiff or defendant can be required to give security, without leaving that to the Rules Committee or Parliament.

In the present case, whether under para. 2 of the amended summons the security for costs is sought under the inherent jurisdiction of the court to order security or under the inherent jurisdiction of the court to release a party from an undertaking given to the court even if the undertaking is given under a well-established rule of practice, what is really in issue is not the nature of a cross-undertaking in damages, but that the defendant is making a case, which appears to be of doubtful validity, to get an inquiry in which an apparently excessive sum is claimed as compensation. It may be that it would be a good idea that a defendant company, as to which there is reason to believe that it will be unable to pay the plaintiff's costs if unsuccessful in its defence, or a defendant who is resident abroad, could be ordered to give security for the plaintiff's costs of any proceedings, or part of any proceedings, if it appears that the defendant is making a case of doubtful validity or putting forward what appear to be excessive or extravagant claims. But in my judgment it is not for this court to make new law to that effect.

I would therefore dismiss this appeal. I can see no basis on the material before us, on which the court could make an order for security for costs against the defendant either under para. 1 or para. 2 of the amended summons.

Millett LJ: The question to be determined on this appeal is whether a defendant which has obtained the discharge of an interlocutory injunction against it and which seeks to enforce the plaintiff's cross-undertaking in damages can be ordered to give security for the plaintiff's costs, whether of resisting the application for an inquiry as to damages or, if such an inquiry is ordered, of the inquiry itself.

In the court below the plaintiff confined its application for security to the costs of the defendant's application for an inquiry, and invoked the statutory jurisdiction conferred on the court by s. 726 of the *Companies Act* 1985 to order security for costs against a limited company which there is reason to believe will be unable to satisfy an order for costs made against it. The judge dismissed the application. He held that there was no

A   jurisdiction to make the order sought because an application in existing proceedings for an inquiry as to damages was not 'an action or other legal proceeding' within the meaning of the section. The plaintiff has invited us to consider also the position under RSC, O. 23 and the inherent jurisdiction of the court, and has obtained leave to amend the summons in order to invoke O. 23, r. 1(1)(b) (nominal plaintiff) and the inherent jurisdiction (where the grounds relied on include an unparticularised allegation that the defendant's application for an inquiry is an abuse of the process of the court). Whether the plaintiff

B   can establish the facts necessary to substantiate any such case has not been considered by the court below or explored before us, and I express no opinion whatever on that subject.

It is convenient to defer consideration of the court's inherent jurisdiction until after the scope of s. 726 and O. 23 has been determined. Whether either of them has any application depends upon the answers to two questions:

C   (1)   Is an application by a defendant in existing proceedings to enforce the plaintiff's cross-undertaking in damages 'an action or other legal proceeding' within the meaning of s. 726 or 'an action or other proceeding in the High court' within O. 23, r. 1(1)?

(2)   Is a defendant who makes such an application substantially in the position of a plaintiff?

D   Only if both questions are answered in the affirmative is the relevant jurisdiction established.

Section 726: 'an action or other legal proceeding'

Section 726(1) of the *Companies Act* 1985 provides:

E   '(1) Where in England and Wales a limited company is plaintiff in an action or other legal proceeding, the court having jurisdiction in the matter may, if it appears by credible testimony that there is reason to believe that the company will be unable to pay the defendant's costs if successful in his defence, require sufficient security to be given for those costs, and may stay all proceedings until the security is given.'

A similar provision has been enacted in every Companies Act almost from the first. It is part of the price which Parliament has required to be paid for the advantages of limited

F   liability. The earliest such provision was s. 24 of the *Joint Stock Companies Act* 1857. It applied to a limited company which was 'a plaintiff in any action, suit or other legal proceedings'. It was re-enacted in the same terms by s. 69 of the *Companies Act* 1862, which remained in force throughout the remainder of the nineteenth century.

Before 1873 the word 'action' was ordinarily used to describe civil proceedings in the Common Law Courts which were commenced by writ, and the word 'suit' to describe

G   proceedings in Chancery which were commenced by bill or information. The *Supreme Court of Judicature Act* 1873 ('the Judicature Act'), however, provided (by para. 1 of the Schedule) that all suits which had previously thereto been commenced by bill or information in the High Court of Chancery should thenceforth be instituted in the High Court of Justice by a proceeding to be called an action, and (by para. 2) that every action in the High Court should thenceforth be commenced by writ. The expression 'suit' thus became obsolete. Accordingly it was omitted from the corresponding s. 278 of the

H   *Companies (Consolidation) Act* 1908, the first Companies Act to be enacted after the passing of the Judicature Act, which referred to 'a plaintiff in any action or other legal proceeding'. The expression has remained the same in successive Companies Acts down to the present day.

'Proceedings' (whether in the singular or the plural) has always had two possible meanings: (1) the entirety of any action or other legal proceedings commenced by some

originating process; or (2) a step or application in an existing action or proceedings. The   A
word has not been given a statutory definition in any of the Companies Acts or Judicature
Acts.

In *Re Unisoft Group Ltd* [1994] BCC 11 this court held that a contributory's petition
under s. 459 of the *Companies Act* 1985 was an 'other legal proceeding' within the
meaning of s. 726. It upheld the decision of the judge below that the expression 'action'
refers to proceedings commenced by writ and 'other legal proceedings' to proceedings in   B
which the jurisdiction of the court is invoked by an originating process other than a writ.
The present question, however, was not considered, and while the case is an authority
binding on this court that the expression 'other legal proceeding' in s. 726 includes
proceedings by whatever form of originating process they may be commenced, it is not
strictly binding authority for the proposition that it is confined to such proceedings.
Nevertheless I have no doubt that the proposition is correct.

The legislative history of the section demonstrates that there has been no material   C
change of language since its statutory predecessor was first introduced in 1857. Apart
from the omission of the word 'suit' after it had become obsolete and an immaterial
substitution of the singular 'proceeding' for the plural 'proceedings', the relevant
expression has not changed at all. If s. 726 confers jurisdiction on the court to order
security for costs against a defendant who applies to enforce the plaintiff's cross-
undertaking in damages, then this must be because s. 24 of the 1857 Act did so. Yet in   D
my judgment the proposition that the expression 'action, suit or other legal proceedings'
in the 1857 or 1862 Acts included a step or application in existing proceedings is really
unarguable. Every consideration points to the opposite conclusion. The words 'action'
and 'suit' both described the entirety of proceedings begun by an originating process, in
the one case a writ and in the other a bill or information. But these were not the only
forms of originating process before 1873, and not all forms of proceedings could be
subsumed in the expression 'action or suit'; hence the need for the words 'or other legal   E
proceedings'. Ordinary principles of construction, including the eiusdem generis rule,
confine those words to other legal proceedings comparable to an action or suit in that
they are commenced by a form of originating process.

Other considerations of language, history and policy point in the same direction. Had
Parliament intended to confer power on the court to order security for costs against the
applicant (whether a plaintiff or a defendant in existing proceedings) who makes an   F
application to the court in the course of those proceedings, it would hardly have restricted
the operation of the section to 'a plaintiff in an action, suit or other legal proceedings'.

Moreover, by enacting s. 24 of the 1857 Act Parliament was extending the existing
power of the court under its inherent jurisdiction to order security for costs by adding an
additional circumstance in which it could be exercised. It was well settled long before
1857 that the court would not order security for costs against a plaintiff who was resident   G
within the jurisdiction merely because he was impecunious and unlikely to be able to
meet an order for costs made against him. Henceforth that would be a ground for
ordering security for costs against a plaintiff which was a company incorporated in the
UK with limited liability. Yet no case has been cited to us to suggest that the court had
ever ordered security for costs before 1857 against a party who happened to make an
application in existing proceedings in which he was a defendant. Such a possibility
appears to have been first canvassed in 1965: see *Re B (Infants)* [1965] 1 WLR 946.   H

Policy considerations support the same conclusion. The purpose of the jurisdiction to
order security for costs is to prevent the injustice which would result if a plaintiff who
was in effect immune from orders for costs were free to litigate at the defendant's expense
even if unsuccessful. Such an order can be made only against a plaintiff; it cannot be
made against a defendant. That is because a plaintiff institutes proceedings voluntarily.

A   If he chooses to bring proceedings against an insolvent company with limited liability, he does so with his eyes open; he takes the risk that he may not recover his costs even if successful, but it is his own decision to take that risk. The defendant, however, has no choice in the matter. He is compelled to litigate or submit to the plaintiff's demands. He must be allowed to defend himself without being subjected to the embarrassment of having to provide security for the plaintiff's costs. This involves being free to take whatever steps and make whatever applications are necessary in order to enable him to

B   defend the proceedings. In *Taly NDC International NV v Terra Nova Insurance Co Ltd* [1985] 1 WLR 1359 (a case under O. 23, r. 1(1)) Parker LJ held that the proceedings referred to were proceedings in the nature of an action and referred to the whole matter and not to an interlocutory application in existing proceedings, observing that were it otherwise 'chaos would reign'. I respectfully agree. I have entertained myself by supposing an action by a foreign resident against an insolvent English company. If the

C   plaintiff's argument in the present case is right, only the defendant could obtain an order for security for costs of the entire proceedings; but if he applied for such an order the plaintiff could immediately apply for security for costs of the defendant's application – and so ad infinitum, each application for security provoking a cross-application for security for that application.

The plaintiff has sought to support its argument by invoking the definition of the word 'plaintiff' in s. 100 of the Judicature Act and its statutory successor s. 225 of the *Supreme*

D   *Court of Judicature Act* 1925; (the *Supreme Court Act* 1981 contained no definition of the word). Section 100 of the Judicature Act defined 'plaintiff' as including,

> 'any person asking any relief (otherwise than by way of counterclaim as a defendant) against any person by an form of proceeding, whether the same be taken by action, suit, petition, motion, summons or otherwise . . .'

It is not necessary to consider whether the reference to motion and summons was a

E   reference to originating motion and originating summons, as I suspect it was. In my judgment the definition cannot help the plaintiff, for two reasons. In the first place, the definition applied only for the purpose of construing the language of the Judicature Act (and of delegated legislation made under it). It cannot possibly have governed the meaning of the words used in the Acts of 1857 and 1862 which had been passed years before. With all respect to Scott LJ who expressed the contrary view in *Re Unisoft Group*

F   *Ltd*, given the legislative derivation of s. 726 from the 1857 Act I cannot accept that its meaning is affected by the definitions contained in the Judicature Acts. In the second place, even if I were persuaded that the word 'plaintiff' in s. 726 taken in isolation was wide enough to include a defendant who made an interlocutory application in existing proceedings (which I am not), I would conclude that that meaning was cut down by the following words 'in an action or other legal proceeding'.

G   **Order 23, r. 1(1): 'an action or other proceeding in the High Court'**

Order 23, r. 1(1) so far as material provides:

> '(1) Where, on the application of a defendant to an action or other proceeding in the High Court, it appears to the Court . . .
>
> then if, having regard to all the circumstances of the case, the Court thinks it just to do so, it may order the plaintiff to give such security for the defendant's costs of

H   the action or other proceeding as it thinks just.'

The order is taken from the 1962 revision of the Rules of the Supreme Court and replaces (with changes not material to be here considered) the former O. 65, r. 6 which was introduced in 1883 and embodied the previous case law on the subject.

The language of O. 23 and that of s. 726 and its predecessors are closely similar and if possible ought to be similarly construed. That is not because either was taken from or is

coloured by the other, but because they have a common source. The order represents a   A
codification of the case law dealing with the power of the court to order security for costs
which had formed the model for the statutory power conferred by the various Companies
Acts. The only difference is that O. 1, r. 3 provides that the *Interpretation Act* 1978 applies
for the interpretation of the Rules of the Supreme Court with the result that expressions
used in the rules have the same meaning (unless the contrary intention appears) as the
same expressions in the statutes under which they were made. The 1883 rules were made
under the Judicature Act and the 1962 revision under its 1925 successor. Accordingly   B
expressions used in O. 65 of the 1883 rules fell to be construed in accordance with s. 100
of the former Act, while since 1962 O. 23 must be construed in accordance with s. 225 of
the latter.

In *Taly NDC International NV v Terra Nova Insurance Co Ltd* plaintiffs resident
abroad brought an action against defendants who brought third party proceedings
against a third party. The plaintiffs obtained orders for specific discovery and   C
interrogatories against the third party. The third party then applied under O. 23, r. 1(1)
for an order that the plaintiffs provide security for the third party's costs. The judge
dismissed the application on the ground that he had no jurisdiction to make the order.
This court dismissed the appeal, holding that the word 'proceeding' in O. 23, r. 1(1)
meant proceedings in the nature of an action and referred to the whole matter and not to
an interlocutory application in other proceedings. That is a clear authority binding on   D
this court that a party who makes an application in the course of proceedings in which
he is not a plaintiff does not thereby become a plaintiff in any 'proceeding' for the
purpose of O. 23, r. 1(1) and cannot be ordered to give security for costs. The plaintiff
has sought to distinguish that case on the ground that there was no lis between the
plaintiff and the third party, the only 'proceeding' between them being the plaintiff's
application for discovery and interrogatories; yet the third party was seeking security for
the whole of its costs of defending the action. In the present case, by contrast, the   E
defendant is making an application in the course of an action instituted against it by the
plaintiff, and the plaintiff is not seeking security for its costs of the action – it plainly
could not do so, since it is a plaintiff in the action and not a defendant – but only of the
application, in which it claims that the roles of the parties are reversed. These features,
however, formed no part of the ratio of the *Taly* case. The court did not base its decision
on the absence of any lis between the parties, nor on any mismatch between the
proceedings between the parties and those in respect of which an order for security for   F
costs was being sought. It based its decision squarely on the fact that an interlocutory
application in existing proceedings is not a 'proceeding' for the purpose of O. 23, r. 1(1).
Parker LJ said ([1985] 1 WLR 1359 at p. 1361):

> 'Were it otherwise, it appears to me that chaos would reign, for every time an
> interlocutory application was taken out by a defendant the plaintiff would be able
> to say, "The plaintiff is in the position of the defendant in this application and the   G
> defendant is in the position of the plaintiff. They are proceedings. Therefore I
> ought to have security for the costs of this application." One has only to examine
> that to see that it cannot have any foundation whatever.'

The reason why it had no foundation was that the application would not be a
'proceeding' within the meaning of O. 23, r. 1(1). In the same case Croom-Johnson LJ
said at p. 1363:   H

> '. . . I have no doubt myself that the purpose of [O. 23] is that the proceeding,
> which is referred to there, is the proceeding as a whole, whether it is an action or
> something equivalent to an action . . . The right to ask for security for costs under
> Ord. 23, where the plaintiff is not resident within the jurisdiction, is purely devoted
> to people who are plaintiff and defendant in the proceeding as a whole.'

A   The plaintiff submitted in effect (though not in terms) that the decision in *Taly* was per incuriam because it disregarded the statutory definitions in the Judicature Acts. I do not accept this because I do not accept that reference to those definitions would make any difference. In O. 23, r. 1(1) it is the word 'defendant' rather than 'plaintiff' which is the key word, and that is very widely defined in the Judicature Acts; but its meaning is necessarily cut down by the words 'to an action or other proceeding in the High Court' which follows. It is, therefore, the meaning of that expression which falls to be considered.

B

The word 'action' is defined by s. 100 of the Judicature Act as meaning 'a civil proceeding commenced by writ or in such other manner as may be prescribed by rules of court'. An identical definition of the word is to be found in s. 225 of the 1925 Act. Accordingly, the word 'action' in O. 23, r. 1(1) has a wider meaning than the same word in s. 726, and the scope of the expression 'other proceeding in the High Court' is correspondingly reduced. But not all proceedings in the High Court are commenced by a form of originating proceedings prescribed by the rules. Many proceedings are brought under statutory provisions and are commenced by the form of originating process prescribed in the statute under which they are brought. Examples are winding-up petitions and contributories' petitions brought under s. 459 of the *Companies Act* 1985, but there are many others. All such proceedings are outside the statutory definition of the word 'action' in the Judicature Acts, but are 'other proceedings in the High Court'.

C

D   In my judgment, therefore, the statutory definitions in the Judicature Acts do not affect the conclusion that the word 'proceeding' in O. 23, r. 1(1) means an original proceeding commenced by a form of originating process and not an interlocutory application in other proceedings. While the demarcation between 'action' and 'other proceeding' in O. 23, r. 1(1) is not precisely the same as that in s. 726, I have no doubt that the scope of the combined expression 'action or other proceeding' is the same.

E

Is the defendant in the position of a plaintiff?

It has long been firmly established by authority that the court cannot award security for costs against a defendant, and that in considering whether a party is a plaintiff or a defendant the court must have regard to the substantial and not the nominal position of the parties. The question in every case is whether the party against whom an order for security is sought is in the position of plaintiff in the proceeding in question. This rule is made explicit in O. 23 by r. 1(3). The same rule applied to the statutory jurisdiction under the Companies Acts. In *Accidental and Marine Insurance Co v Mercati* (1866) LR 3 Eq 200 a policy-holder brought an action at common law against a limited company to recover the amount due under a policy of marine insurance. The company filed a bill in Chancery for a declaration that the policy had been obtained by fraud and was void. On a petition for the insolvent winding-up of the company being presented the policy-holder applied in the Chancery proceedings for security for costs. In those proceedings the company was clearly the plaintiff and the policy-holder was the defendant; yet the application was refused. Sir William Page Wood V-C said at p. 202:

F

G

'But in this case, as in *Watteeu v Billam* (1849) 3 De G & Sm 516, the company, though called a plaintiff, is really a defendant. The principle is not based on the narrow ground that the plaintiff in the original suit, having admitted the jurisdiction, is not at liberty to deny it: the true ground is, that a person who is in the position of a defendant (though nominally a plaintiff) is to be at liberty to defend himself. So likewise a person in contempt is considered to be at liberty, in the same way, to ask justice at the hands of the court. He may defend himself freely, although he is not at liberty to initiate proceedings as plaintiff, as an ordinary person may.'

H

A

Where a company is defending itself, it must be regarded as, in substance, a defendant, and, therefore, is not to be called upon to give security. In this instance the company must be considered as a defendant, and not as a 'plaintiff or pursuer', within the meaning of the Act, this being virtually a cross-suit.'

In *Watteeu v Billam* the plaintiff had filed a bill in Chancery to restrain an action at law against him. He was held to be a person in the position of a defendant, so that security for costs of the suit in Chancery could not be ordered against him.

B

The distinction between a bill and a true cross-bill, reflected in modern times by the distinction between a counterclaim which is purely defensive and one which is not, can be a distinction of some nicety, but it is a necessary adjunct to the fundamental principle that the court will not order security for costs against a defendant. That principle reflects the difference between the position of a plaintiff and that of a defendant to which I have already referred. A plaintiff chooses to sue and voluntarily assumes the risk that he may not recover his costs if he is successful; a defendant has no choice in the matter. The rule, which represents a settled practice of the court for over 200 years, is made explicit by the terms of s. 726 and O. 23. In my view it must now be regarded as going to the jurisdiction of the court.

C

If attention is concentrated on the defendant's application to enforce the plaintiff's cross-undertaking in damages, the defendant certainly has the appearance of a plaintiff. It claims that it has suffered loss for which the plaintiff is responsible and it seeks compensation for that loss. If the plaintiff recognises that it is likely to be ordered to pay something, though not as much as the defendant claims, it can protect its position by making a payment into court. It certainly looks like a defendant. But as the cases which I have cited in this part of my judgment demonstrate, it is necessary to consider the whole litigation between the parties in order to determine which of them is really in the position of a plaintiff and which a defendant. If the proceedings are considered as a whole, then it is apparent that the parties have never exchanged roles, and that the defendant has done nothing to justify being treated as a plaintiff.

D

E

It was the plaintiff which chose to bring the proceedings and take the risk of failing to recover its costs even if successful. It was the plaintiff which chose to apply for interlocutory relief and to offer the court a cross-undertaking in damages as the price of obtaining such relief. It must have known that the injunction which it obtained might cause the defendant loss, that it might subsequently be established that the injunction should not have been granted, and that the defendant might seek to recover its loss by applying to enforce the cross-undertaking. It must have known that, if it chose to resist such an application, it might incur further irrecoverable costs. It did not qualify its cross-undertaking by making its enforcement conditional on the defendant providing security for costs. Had it attempted to do so, its cross-undertaking would have been rejected and its application for an injunction refused. Having offered the court an unqualified cross-undertaking, it now seeks to protect itself against a situation which it must have been able to foresee. That it should succeed is not an attractive proposition.

F

G

As for the defendant, it has had no choice in the matter. It has done nothing beyond reacting to the steps which the plaintiff has taken against it. The plaintiff brought the proceedings; the defendant has been compelled to defend them. The plaintiff obtained an injunction against it which the defendant claims ought not to have been granted; the defendant has obtained its discharge. The defendant claims that the existence of the injunction caused it loss; it seeks to recover the loss. It seeks only to be restored, so far as compensation can achieve it, to the position it was in before the proceedings began. The defendant must counter-attack to recover ground lost by an earlier defeat, but it makes no territorial claim of its own; it cannot fairly be described as an aggressor.

H

A   Although the defendant is claiming monetary compensation for loss which it alleges it has sustained as a result of the injunction, it has no independent cause of action to recover such loss. It cannot bring separate proceedings, whether by writ or counterclaim in the existing proceedings. Its claim arises out of and is wholly dependent upon the plaintiff's cross-undertaking. Its only remedy is to enforce the cross-undertaking by applying under the liberty to apply in the proceedings in which the cross-undertaking was given. Analogies tend to be imperfect, but the closest analogy which occurs to me is the enforcement by a successful defendant of an order for costs made in his favour. Security for the plaintiff's costs of resisting enforcement would not be ordered for other reasons, but I cannot think that such a defendant could properly be regarded as being in the position of a plaintiff.

The inherent jurisdiction of the court

C   The plaintiff has also sought to invoke a residual inherent jurisdiction of the court. In my judgment there is none. There is clearly no inherent jurisdiction to order security for costs against an impoverished plaintiff merely on the ground that he would be unable to satisfy an order for costs against him if unsuccessful. Any such jurisdiction was disclaimed by the courts long before 1857; it cannot be revived now. Section 726 of the *Companies Act* 1985 and its predecessors represent a special statutory exception to the principle thus established. Apart from this, all the surviving grounds upon which security for costs may be ordered have for over 100 years been set out in the Rules of the Supreme Court which embody and codify the case law on the subject. In my judgment O. 23 must be regarded as a complete and exhaustive code. I agree with Dillon LJ that if there should emerge a need for a new category of case in which it is desirable that the court should have power to order security for costs, that will have to be dealt with by Parliament or the Rules Committee.

E   In a powerful argument we were strongly pressed by the plaintiff to avoid this conclusion because, it was said, it would curtail the powers of the court to redress the mischief which Parliament had sought to redress by s. 726. We were told that in an increasing number of cases defendants who have obtained the discharge of an interlocutory injunction have claimed exorbitant damages under the plaintiff's cross-undertaking, exploiting their inability to satisfy any order for costs which may be made against them to extract an offer of payment out of all proportion to the loss truly suffered.

I express no view whether this is happening, nor whether the present case is an example. In my judgment, the remedy lies in the power of the court to prevent abuse of its own process, not in its jurisdiction to order security for costs.

Abuse of the process of the court

G   It is an abuse of the process of the court to bring a claim with no genuine belief in its merits but in bad faith and for an ulterior purpose. Such a claim may be struck out in limine: see *Lonrho plc v Fayed (No. 2)* [1992] 1 WLR 1. A party who makes an exorbitant claim with no genuine belief in its merits, rejecting all reasonable offers of settlement, and exploiting his own inability to satisfy an order for costs in order to bring pressure on the other party to settle for an excessive sum, is abusing the process of the court.

H   Where such a claim is made by way of an application to enforce the plaintiff's cross-undertaking in damages, the solution lies in the fact that the court's power to order an inquiry as to damages is discretionary. This is not because of the words 'may' and 'ought' in the usual form of cross-undertaking, which is 'to abide by any order which the court may make as to damages . . . which the defendant ought to pay'. The word 'may' merely reflects the fact that at the time when the cross-undertaking is given it is not certain that the defendant will ever be in a position to enforce it; while the word 'ought' reflects the

fact that only damages for loss properly referable to the existence of the injunction are A
recoverable. The source of the court's discretion to refuse to order an inquiry is its
inherent jurisdiction to release or vary an undertaking which has been given it. It will not
do so except in special circumstances; but the need to prevent an abuse of the process of
the court would certainly justify such a course.

If the court is satisfied that the plaintiff has made a reasonable offer, that there is no
realistic prospect of the defendant obtaining more, and that in rejecting the offer and B
pressing for an inquiry the defendant is not acting in good faith and with a genuine belief
in his claim the court can release the plaintiff from his cross-undertaking and substitute
an undertaking to pay a fixed amount or (which comes to the same thing) refuse the
inquiry on the plaintiff's undertaking to pay such an amount. If the court has power to
refuse the inquiry altogether, it has power if appropriate to order the inquiry but to put
the defendant on terms; and these may include the provision of security for costs.

I must stress, however, that this should not be regarded as letting in by the back door C
a jurisdiction to order security for costs which does not exist. The kind of order I have
described should be unusual, not commonplace. The plaintiff must ask the court to refuse
the inquiry, and must make out a case for it. It will not be enough for him to show that
he has made a reasonable offer and that the defendant will be unable to meet the costs of
the inquiry if he fails to obtain more and is ordered to pay them. Nor will it be enough
for him to show that, if the jurisdiction to order security were available, the circumstances D
of the case would justify its exercise, leaving it to the defendant to show that he has a
reasonable claim which an order for security would stifle. The plaintiff will have to go
much further. He will have to satisfy the court that the defendant's application is an
abuse of the process of the court. If the court is satisfied that the defendant's claim has
no realistic prospect of success, and that the defendant is not pursuing it in good faith
and with a genuine belief that it may succeed, but in order to extract an excessive offer of
settlement by exploiting its inability to pay the plaintiff's costs of the inquiry if ordered E
to pay them, then the court can and should refuse the inquiry. If the court is left in real
doubt that the claim is genuine, it should order the inquiry but it may require the
defendant to provide security for costs as an earnest of its good faith.

Conclusion

In my view the only ground put forward in para. 2 of the amended summons which is F
sufficient to justify the relief sought is that the defendant's application for an inquiry is
an abuse of the process of the court. That ground is not supported by evidence.
Accordingly, I would dismiss the appeal with the result that the amended summons
would stand dismissed. This would not, of course, preclude the plaintiff from filing
evidence in opposition to the defendant's application for an inquiry or from attempting
to establish that the application is an abuse of the process of the court. But I repeat that G
if the judge who hears the application comes to the conclusion that an inquiry should be
ordered, he should not put the defendant on terms as to security for costs unless he is left
in real doubt that the defendant is acting in good faith.

Sir Michael Kerr: While agreeing that the appeal should be dismissed, I had somewhat
greater doubts than Dillon and Millett L JJ on the question whether the court had
jurisdiction to consider an order for security for costs in this case under s. 726 and/or H
RSC, O. 23, r. 1(1)(b), and had drafted a judgment to this effect. However, having seen
the judgments of my Lords and reflected on the matter, I entirely agree with their
conclusion that the appellants' case breaks down at the first and greatest hurdle in their
way on the ground that, despite Mr Gee's ingenious arguments, it is impossible to
conclude that an interlocutory or other step in an action or other form of legal
proceedings can fall within the expression 'other legal proceeding' at 'other proceeding'

A   in s. 726 and O. 23 respectively. I therefore agree that on this ground there is no jurisdiction to make an order for security for costs against Corsi under either of these provisions, and it is unnecessary to consider the other obstacles in Bowring's way.

However, I would also like to add my full agreement with the passage in the judgment of Millett LJ under the heading 'Abuse of the process of the court'. Indeed, I think that the powers which the court may exercise in deciding what action to take in relation to an

B   undertaking or cross-undertaking as to damages are somewhat wider than this heading suggests, bearing in mind that it is applicable to all proceedings in any event. The reason may lie in the special features of such an undertaking. It is given to the court, not to any opposite party. No action, set-off or counterclaim can be founded upon it. In relation to such undertakings the court acts or declines to act in its own right, not merely as an umpire in an adversarial process between the parties, though obviously having full regard to the position of the parties and to the interests of justice. In deciding how to deal with

C   such an undertaking the court exercises a broad equitable jurisdiction: see *Cheltenham and Gloucester Building Society v Ricketts* [1993] 1 WLR 1545 (CA). In these circumstances, and bearing in mind that the court may release such undertakings altogether, it must be entitled to impose terms on parties seeking to enforce them, in whatever way appears to be just in the circumstances; and some form of security for costs may be an appropriate requirement in some cases. We have not been referred to the evidence in this case except by way of a summary of the allegations made on behalf of

D   Bowring. These were strong, but they were not investigated on either side. I therefore agree with Dillon LJ that on the material seen by this court there is no basis for any order for security for costs against Corsi under either paragraph of the amended summons. But, beyond this, I prefer not to seek to define the limits of the court's discretion in this or other cases, save that – as already mentioned – its scope is in my view wider than the inherent jurisdiction to deal with abuses of the court's process.

E

(*Appeal dismissed with costs. Leave to appeal to House of Lords refused*)

————————

F

G

H

Re Bishopsgate Investment Management Ltd (No. 2).

A

Chancery Division (Companies Court).
Hoffmann J.
Judgment delivered 15 July 1992.

Insolvency – Liquidation – Private examination – Whether liquidator's confidential statement of grounds should be disclosed – Whether order for examination should be discharged – Insolvency Act 1986, s. 236.

B

These were an application to discharge an order for oral examination made by the registrar under s. 236 of the Insolvency Act 1986, and a preliminary application for disclosure of the liquidators' confidential statement of grounds supporting their application for an order under s. 236.

Held, dismissing both applications:

C

1. Having read the confidential annexure the court was satisfied that it could dispose of the matter fairly without the need for the disclosure of that information to the applicant. Furthermore if the annexure were disclosed to the applicant in advance of any oral examination, it would have the effect of defeating the purpose for which the liquidators wished to interrogate rather than submit questions in writing. (Re British & Commonwealth Holdings plc [1992] BCC 165 (CA) applied.)

D

2. The liquidators had shown a genuine need to examine on grounds which accorded with the legislative purpose of s. 236. The submission of a questionnaire would be followed ultimately by an examination and would simply lead to delay and extra cost. While it was certainly burdensome upon the applicant to have to submit to oral interrogation, that burden was not sufficient to outweigh the need for the office-holder to obtain the information in the manner best calculated to elicit it.

E

The following cases were referred to in the judgment:

British & Commonwealth Holdings plc, Re [1992] BCC 165 (CA).
British & Commonwealth Holdings plc, Re (No. 2) [1992] BCC 172 (CA); [1992] BCC 977 (HL).
Cloverbay Ltd, Re (No. 2) [1990] BCC 414; [1991] Ch 90.
Gold Co, Re (1879) 12 ChD 77.
Rolls Razor Ltd, Re (No. 2) [1970] Ch 576.

F

John Brisby (instructed by Stephenson Harwood) for the liquidators.

Charles Aldous QC and Robert Hildyard (instructed by Freshfields) for the respondent.

PRELIMINARY RULING

G

Hoffmann J: This is an application by Mr Mark Haas, who is an employee of Lehman Brothers International Ltd, to set aside an order of Mr Registrar Buckley made on 11 June 1992 requiring him to appear for oral examination under s. 236 of the *Insolvency Act* 1986. In accordance with the practice laid down in *Re British & Commonwealth Holdings plc* [1992] BCC 165 (CA) and *Re British & Commonwealth Holdings plc (No. 2)* [1992] BCC 977 (HL) the office-holder, who in this case is one of the joint liquidators of Bishopsgate Investment Management Ltd, has put before the court a confidential report which has been disclosed to Mr Haas, but there is also exhibited to that report a strictly confidential annexure containing further information which has not been disclosed to him. I am asked to give a preliminary ruling on whether it appears to me in accordance with the guidance given in the *British & Commonwealth* case that that annexure ought to be disclosed as well.

H

A   The application to interrogate Mr Haas arose out of arrangements for stock lending which were entered into between Bishopsgate Investment Management Ltd ('BIM') and a company in the Lehman Brothers group in November 1989 and pursuant to which stock was transferred from BIM to Lehman Brothers over a period until the end of 1991. BIM was the company which controlled the common investment fund of the Maxwell pension schemes.

B   Stock lending, as I understand it from the evidence, is an arrangement under which the holder of stock, which is being held as an investment, can earn extra fees by lending that stock to brokers who needed to satisfy a commitment in the market. That loan is made against collateral to secure the position of the lender and from the point of view of the borrower it enables him to satisfy a commitment for delivery of stock and yet in effect to maintain an open position for as long as the loan of the stock lasts. From the point of view of an investment fund, such as a pension fund, it provides the opportunity to

C generate income from the fees for the lending, additional to the normal income which the fund would receive by way of dividends on that stock; it preserves their right to any capital appreciation and provided it is sufficiently secured by the collateral it does not involve any additional risk to the fund.

     In the case of the arrangements with Lehman Brothers there appears from the evidence to have been two so-called stock-lending agreements. One was intended to be along the

D lines I have described but does not appear ever to have been operated. The second involved the lending by Lehman Brothers to BIM of US treasury bills against collateral provided by BIM in the form of fund investments which it held. The treasury bills are as close as one can get to cash and indeed immediately upon being lent by Lehman Brothers were converted into cash for the benefit of BIM by another Lehman Brothers entity. On the face of it, therefore, this arrangement, although designated as stock lending, was

E nothing more than a secured loan of money by Lehman Brothers to BIM and it is the liquidators' case that BIM never received the benefit of that money, or a great part of it. Instead it was diverted to the support of other companies in the Maxwell empire. These have since become insolvent and Lehman Brothers lay claim to the pension fund securities which were deposited as collateral for the advances.

     It is the liquidators' contention that this transaction was an unusual one to be

F undertaken in the guise of stock lending. It was, they say, unusual for a pension fund to be borrowing very large sums of money against the security of its investment and they are investigating among other things the question of what the extent of Lehman Brothers' knowledge was as to the true nature of these transactions, where the collateral stock was really coming from and where the money was really going to.

     Mr Haas was the employee at Lehman Brothers who from August 1990 was

G responsible for these stock-lending arrangements and the liquidators in the disclosed part of the confidential report say this about why they want to interrogate:

> 'Information is now coming to my possession on a strictly confidential basis which suggests that officers and employees of Lehman Bros were aware of the unorthodox nature of the stock-lending arrangement, and in particular of the fact that the real purpose of the arrangement was to generate very substantial amounts of cash ostensibly for BIM but in reality to support the requirements of other
>
H > Maxwell companies such as MCC. It appears from this information that the Respondent Mark Haas is in a position to give me relevant information concerning these matters. The source of my information and belief and an account of the information I have received is set out in a strictly confidential annexure. That information has been obtained in circumstances has been obtained where I am under a strict duty of confidentiality to the person concerned.'

The strictly confidential annexure discloses the identity of the informant and the   A
particular information which he gave which leads the liquidators to the conclusion that
Mr Haas may be able to assist.

This application to discharge is made on the ground that Lehman Brothers have, since
the liquidators were appointed in December 1991, been extremely co-operative and made
available a great deal of documentation at the liquidators' request. Mr Haas, they say,
would be willing to provide within reason any further documentation which the   B
liquidators might want on the matters which have come to their attention, and would be
willing to answer any questions submitted to him in writing. They say, however, that it
would be oppressive and unfair for Mr Haas to have to answer questions by way of
interrogation when he would not have had the same opportunities to consider and take
advice upon his answers.

It seems to me that whether that objection is reasonable or, on the other hand, the   C
liquidators are right in saying that this is a matter in which oral interrogation is the only
practical method of obtaining the information they need, is a fairly short point in which
the arguments one way or the other appear sufficiently from the report which has been
disclosed and the affidavit evidence which has been filed. In the *British & Commonwealth*
case Nourse LJ said ([1992] BCC 165 at p. 170G):

> 'In my judgment inspection of the statement should prima facie be allowed where
> the court is of the opinion that it will or may be unable fairly and properly to   D
> dispose of the application if part of the evidence is withheld from the person against
> whom the order is sought. It will then be for the office-holder to satisfy the court
> that confidentiality in whole or in part is nevertheless appropriate.'

Having read the confidential annexure I am satisfied that it will be possible for the
court to dispose of the matter fairly without the need for the disclosure of that
information to the respondent. I am further of the opinion that if that annexure,   E
containing as it does the identity of the informant and some of the details as to which the
liquidators wish to interrogate, were disclosed to Mr Haas in advance of any oral
examination, it would have the effect of defeating the purpose for which the liquidators
wish to interrogate rather than submit questions in writing. I say that without prejudice
as to whether they are right to take that view or not, but my ruling is that the strictly
confidential annexure should not under the *British & Commonwealth* guidelines be
disclosed to Mr Haas.   F

(Ruling accordingly)

JUDGMENT

Hoffmann J: This is an application to discharge an order for the oral examination of
Mr Mark Haas made by Mr Registrar Buckley on 11 June 1992 under s. 236 of the   G
Insolvency Act 1986. Mr Haas is an employee of Lehman Brothers International Ltd
which for convenience I shall refer to with other companies in the Lehman group simply
as Lehman Brothers.

The application to examine him arises out of the business dealings between Bishopsgate
Investment Management Ltd ('BIM'), a company now in liquidation, and Lehman
Brothers, during the period from November 1989 until the provisional liquidation of the   H
company. That relationship involved, as I explained in a ruling which I gave this morning
on the disclosure of the liquidators' report, a stock-lending agreement which was said to
have been operated by BIM in a somewhat unorthodox manner. Since their appointment
the liquidators have requested information from Lehman Brothers about the operation
of the stock-lending agreement and Lehman Brothers has disclosed a good deal of
documentation.

A   Mr Cooper, one of the liquidators, says however that he has now reached the stage at which he needs orally to examine Mr Haas. In an affidavit sworn on 15 April in connection with a similar application for the production of documents he said that there were a number of matters which he needed to know about. In particular, he wants to know what the representatives of BIM told Lehman Brothers; what Lehman Brothers understood about the purpose of the transactions; what Lehman Brothers told BIM about the nature of the stock-lending agreement; what the representatives of Lehman B   Brothers knew about or what enquiries they made from time to time about the BIM status and functions and place in the Maxwell group of companies; whether and when Lehman Brothers became aware that BIM was a pension fund trustee; what the representatives in Lehman Brothers knew and what enquiries they made about BIM's directors and employees; and what Lehman Brothers thought about the status of the persons who were giving instructions for the operation of the agreement.

C   Mr Cooper says that the documents which have been disclosed, while no doubt very informative as to the mechanics of the operation of the stock-lending agreement and what stock actually passed, are not particularly informative on the critical question of what Lehman Brothers were told by the persons purporting to act on behalf of BIM and what they knew and understood about the way the agreement was being operated. For that purpose he seeks therefore to invoke the provisions of s. 236 of the Insolvency Act. D   That section provides that the court may, on the application of the office-holder, summon to appear before it any person whom the court thinks capable of giving information concerning the business, dealings, affairs or property of the company. Under s. 237(4) any person who appears before the court under s. 236 may be examined on oath either orally or by interrogatories concerning the company or the matters I have mentioned.

This power to interrogate has been conferred on liquidators and other office-holders because of the public interest in the speedy, cheap and efficient prosecution of their duties E   as liquidators. The need for the public interest in liquidators being able to carry out their duties in this way could hardly be better illustrated by the present case. The operation of the stock-lending agreement which is here under enquiry has been instrumental in enabling many millions of dollars of assets of the pension funds to be converted into cash which according to the evidence was used to prop up other parts of the late Mr Robert Maxwell's empire. This has caused a considerable deficiency in the pension funds and loss and distress to many innocent employees and ex-employees of the Maxwell F   companies. It is properly a matter of national concern and illustrates the need for the sort of powers which s. 236 confers.

The most recent guidance on the way in which the court should exercise the discretion which that section gives it is in the decision of the Court of Appeal in *Re British & Commonwealth Holdings plc* [1992] BCC 165 and an earlier decision of the Court of Appeal in *Re Cloverbay Ltd (No. 2)* [1990] BCC 414. In the *British & Commonwealth* G   case Woolf LJ at p. 201B says that the matter which in his judgment:

'. . . must be given most weight by the court in exercising its discretion is the policy disclosed by Parliament in giving the powers under s. 236 to the court . . . It surely must be the intention of Parliament that the court should normally be prepared to use those powers in a way which will facilitate the purposes of the administration.'

That remark was echoed at p. 194H where he said:
H
'The nature and range of these summary powers make clear the importance that Parliament attached to administrators and other office-holders being able to perform their functions in an effective and expeditious manner. They illustrate that, in relation to a company in liquidation or administration, a liquidator or administrator is intended to be in quite a different position from that of the directors of a company which is not in administration. The court must therefore,

in accord with the intention of Parliament, use these powers so as to assist
administrators to perform their functions and must not use them in a way which
would frustrate this intent which can be discerned from the Act. At the same time
the fact that exercise of these powers is capable of having an onerous and
oppressive effect upon those against whom the orders are made must not be
ignored. The problem is striking the correct balance between the interests of the
office-holder on the one hand and those against whom orders can be made on the
other.'

The exercise therefore involved in a case such as this, is to balance, as Sir Nicolas
Browne-Wilkinson V-C said in the *Cloverbay* case, the requirements of the office-holder
to obtain information against the possible oppression to the person from whom the
information is sought.

Let me start by considering what appears on the evidence the need of the office-holder
to obtain the information. He says on affidavit that he needs the information primarily
to decide whether the company in liquidation has any claim against Lehman Brothers to
recover the stock belonging to the pension funds which was pledged to it under the stock-
lending agreement. That is a matter which depends primarily upon whether Lehman
Brothers through its officers or agents knew or ought to have known the truth about the
way in which the stock lending was being operated.

Mr Cooper says in an affidavit which he has sworn on 9 July that at the moment no
decision on whether to sue Lehman Brothers has been taken and:

'we simply do not have anything like enough material on which to make a rational
decision either to sue or not to sue Lehman Brothers.'

It has frequently been said in earlier cases that the view of the office-holder upon such a
matter is something to which the court should attach very considerable weight.

The purpose of the enquiry is, as I have said, primarily to discover whether there is a
case against Lehman Brothers. Mr Cooper says that information from the officers of
Lehman Brothers as to what they were told by officers of BIM and other persons acting
for other companies within the Maxwell group who appear to have been involved in
these transactions will also assist in deciding what remedies, if any, the company has
against them, but even if that was not the case, the obtaining of information as to a
specific claim against a specific person who is sought to be interrogated would,
nevertheless, be within the power of s. 236 (see Ralph Gibson LJ in *British &
Commonwealth* at p. 184C).

Furthermore one is here concerned not only with discovering facts which may show
that he has a claim against Lehman Brothers, but also if necessary with discovering that
there is nothing in the particular line of enquiry which he is intending to pursue. The
liquidator may thereby avoid the considerable cost and delay which would follow from
commencing expensive and ultimately fruitless litigation. This is a point made by Sir
George Jessel as long ago as 1879 in *Re Gold Co* (1879) 12 ChD 77 where he said (at
p. 85) that one of the purposes of the statutory power was to enable the office-holder:

'. . . to find out facts before they brought an action, so as to avoid incurring the
expense of some hundreds of pounds in bringing an unsuccessful action, when they
might, by examining a witness or two, have discovered at a trifling expense that an
action could not succeed.'

In this case, as I have said this morning, the liquidators have information from an
informant which suggests to them the line of enquiry that they wish to pursue with Mr
Haas, but it is possible that the result of their questioning may be to satisfy them that
their information is entirely unreliable and that line of enquiry is not worth pursuing any

A further. The achievement of cost savings in that way is also a significant part of the purpose of s. 236.

In the *Cloverbay* case considerable emphasis was placed upon the distinction between interrogation which is intended to reconstitute the knowledge of the company, that is to say, about matters of which the company ought properly to have had knowledge through its officers or fiduciary agents, and interrogation to secure information to which the

B company would not have been entitled if it were solvent and a going concern.

The effect of *British & Commonwealth* is somewhat to reduce the significance of that distinction, but the majority of the judges in that case still nevertheless give it some significance. The fact that the interrogation is intended to provide the company with information to which it was entitled from its officers or agents is an additional factor to be taken into account in deciding whether the examination is justified.

C In this case the matters which are set out in Mr Cooper's affidavit of 15 April, to which I have made reference, do in part involve a reconstitution of the company's knowledge in the sense that they are matters related to the acts and states of mind of persons who were acting for the company. But for present purposes it seems to me that the more significant aspect of the information which is being sought relates to the acts and states of mind of the persons in Lehman Brothers and therefore does not fall within that category. I do not

D therefore attach particular importance to the aspect of the case which does involve reconstitution of the company's knowledge.

Looking at the case from the point of view of the needs of the office-holders it therefore seems to me that the office-holders have shown a genuine need on grounds which accord with the legislative purpose of s. 236. It has been submitted that though they may have shown a need to obtain the information, it is not necessary that it should be done by an immediate interrogation. Instead it has been suggested that the office-holders should

E submit to Mr Haas a written questionnaire which he can deal with upon proper consideration and that the question of whether he should also answer to an oral interrogation should be deferred until his written answers have been given.

In *Re Rolls Razor Ltd (No. 2)* [1970] Ch 576 Megarry J said (at p. 595H):

'There may well be some cases in which it would plainly be oppressive or

F unreasonable not to submit written questions first. There will also be other cases in which there plainly ought to be an oral examination without the prior submission of any written questions. Between these two categories there may be many cases in which the court must determine which course is best suited to discover the relevant facts without being oppressive, vexatious or unfair. In order to do this, the court must, I think, look at the facts of the case as a whole, without yielding to preconceptions; and in doing this, the court should give all proper

G weight to the views of the liquidator without, of course, abandoning the proper exercise of its discretion, or treating the liquidator's views as being in any way decisive of the matter.'

The liquidator in this case says in his confidential statement that he is concerned that a questionnaire would lead to carefully drafted answers prepared by lawyers acting for the respondent, and that such answers will not assist him in arriving at what actually

H happened. 'In any event', he says,

'I do not consider that a questionnaire would be a practical or effective way to proceed as the subject matter of the enquiry is such that there will always be the need to follow up initial questions with a live exchange and the progressive procedure of questionnaires followed ultimately by an examination is simply likely to lead to delays and extra costs being incurred.'

I do not think it would be deferring excessively to the liquidators' view if I say I accept   A
that proposition. Now I turn to the other side of the scale, which is the question of
whether the making of an order for interrogation would be oppressive. In the authorities
to which I referred there is considerable guidance on what can in an appropriate case
constitute oppression. Thus in *British & Commonwealth* at p. 184H Ralph Gibson LJ
says that the case for making an order against an office-holder or former officer of the
company would usually be stronger than it would be against a third party because officers
owe a fiduciary duty to the company. Thus an interrogation which might be perfectly   B
legitimate against somebody owing fiduciary duties may be oppressive if imposed on a
stranger. There are however third parties and third parties. It is true that Lehman
Brothers were not officers or agents of the company, but by virtue of the stock-lending
agreement they had a continuing and no doubt profitable relationship with the company
over a period of nearly two years. As a result of that relationship they were, and whether
wittingly or unwittingly and whether they knew or ought to have known is a matter to be   C
investigated, instrumental in causing the pension funds very great losses. In those
circumstances it does not appear to me that a request that they should assist the
liquidators by providing information could be described as oppressive. Indeed until this
application Lehman Brothers had recognised this to be the case. They had been willing
to provide documents and respond to written enquiries. I think therefore that I am only
concerned with the much narrower question of whether that obligation should stop short   D
at providing documents and answering questionnaires or whether it should extend to
having one of their employees orally examined.

That takes me on to the next point. It is said by Ralph Gibson LJ that an order for
oral examination is more likely to be oppressive than an order for the production of
documents. That point is forcibly made on behalf of Mr Haas. Mr Lawrence in his
affidavit of 30 June says that a witness who is examined orally without previous notice of
the questions that he is to be asked will have no realistic opportunity to review in advance   E
the documents which might be put to him or to refresh his memory and,

> '. . . any differences however small between his answers to questions put to him
> and in respect of which he has had no opportunity to consider, and his considered
> evidence at trial would then doubtless be used against him in my submission most
> unfairly.'
                                                                                          F
In a later affidavit he says again,

> 'There is an important distinction between on the one hand seeking information
> that is necessary to understand the transactions and on the other hand seeking the
> opportunity not so much of testing the facts as of testing the witness and seeking
> the chance of provoking admissions or inconsistencies, which although they may
> be the product of confusion, over-hasty reaction or poor recollection may be used   G
> against the witness in any subsequent proceedings.'

I recognise at once that there is a burden in being subject to oral examination rather
than having to answer a questionnaire at leisure with the assistance of one's solicitors.
To that extent what is proposed here would be more oppressive than the course which
Mr Haas's lawyers suggest. I think however that they exaggerate the degree of unfairness
which this involves. The judge at the trial is well aware that witnesses occasionally give   H
answers which on further consideration they would wish to correct. Cross-examining
counsel does frequently make a great deal of minor discrepancies between what is being
said at the trial and what was said on an earlier occasion, but I am confident that the
tribunal has sufficient common sense to be able to detect what is a really significant
change in evidence and what is simply human error. While, therefore, I bear this factor
in mind it does not seem to me sufficient to outweigh what in this case would be the

A   advantage to the liquidator in being able to proceed by oral examination rather than by submission of the questionnaire.

The next element of oppression which is relied upon is that in answering the questions Mr Haas may be exposing himself or his employers to liability. It is said that it is particularly oppressive to interrogate someone who is suspected of wrongdoing and to require him to prove the case against him out of his own mouth. That appears to have

B   been one of the main reasons why in the *Cloverbay* case the Court of Appeal thought it would be oppressive to allow the examination to proceed. The *Cloverbay* case however was one in which there was a direct accusation of fraud against the persons sought to be interrogated and the court is always particularly careful in the protection of persons against whom allegations of fraud are made. There is no suggestion in this case of fraud on the part of Mr Haas. What the liquidators are concerned with is the extent of Lehman Brothers' knowledge and perhaps even more important what, having regard to those

C   matters of which they were on notice, they ought to have ascertained.

In the *British & Commonwealth* case Ralph Gibson LJ, after referring to what had been said in *Cloverbay*, said (at p. 189H) that he did not regard that case as,

> 'setting up some sort of barrier to the making of such an order where fraud is suspected or alleged. If the office-holder reasonably requires the information to be obtained by oral examination of a third party, the mere fact that the witness is or

D   > is expected to be accused of fraud would provide, in my judgment, no proof of opposition which must be treated as outweighing the requirement of the office-holder. As has been stated so many times, each case must depend on its own facts.'

Equally in the *British & Commonwealth* case it was accepted that the fact that answering the questions might expose the accountants in that case to civil liability was on its own facts not a factor to which very great weight needed to be attached.

E   It was until the *Cloverbay* decision the practice of this court not to allow interrogation under s. 236 or its predecessors in a case where the office-holder had made up his mind to bring legal proceedings against the person whom he was seeking to interrogate. The *Cloverbay* case has released the court from any restriction on its discretion to order interrogation. Nevertheless the old doctrine retains a certain germ of truth. It has been said in a number of cases that the purpose of s. 236 is to assist the office-holder in carrying

F   out his duties as liquidator or administrator, but not, once he is or is about to become a litigant, to give him an advantage as litigant over what ordinary parties would have under the normal rules of civil procedure.

In this case Mr Haas says that in practice the liquidators are committed to litigation. He refers to press cuttings which are said to be based on interviews with the liquidator and in which the view is expressed that sooner or later Lehman Brothers are going to be sued.

G   The submission was, as I understand it, that there was sufficient public pressure upon the liquidators to bring proceedings to ensure that that happened, whether or not, to use Mr Cooper's words, there was any rational basis for the decision. Accordingly the battle lines were drawn and the application was oppressive because the liquidators were simply in their capacity as litigants seeking to have an advance cross-examination of Mr Haas before he gave his evidence in court.

H   I do not think there are facts on which such a submission can be based. I accept that the liquidator wants to discover facts which he needs to know before deciding whether he can bring any proceedings and not merely to test Mr Haas as a witness. I also accept that the liquidator has genuinely not yet decided and does not have the material upon which he could decide whether to sue Lehman Brothers or not. Looking at it therefore from the point of view of Mr Haas it seems to me that while it is certainly burdensome upon him

A

to have to submit to oral interrogation and no doubt worrying for his employers that he should have to do so, that burden is no where near sufficient to outweigh what appears to me to be the need for the office-holder in this case to obtain the information in a manner best calculated to elicit it.

I would therefore exercise the discretion in favour of upholding the order of the registrar and dismiss the application.

B

(*Application dismissed with costs*)

C

D

E

F

G

H

A **Re Maxwell Communications Corporation plc.**
Homan & Ors. v Vogel & Ors.
Chancery Division (Companies Court).
Vinelott J.
Judgment delivered 21 April 1994.

B *Insolvency – Administration – Private examination and production of documents*
– Whether administrators were wrong to apply ex parte for private examination –
Whether order for production of documents was too widely drawn – Whether
order for examination should be discharged – Whether court had jurisdiction to
order that the examination could be conducted by a US attorney – Insolvency Act
1986, s. 236.

C   This was an application to set aside an order for production of documents and oral
examination made by the registrar under s. 236 of the Insolvency Act 1986 on the ex parte
application of the administrators of Maxwell Communications Corporation ('MCC'). The
respondents were five individuals, all partners or employees (or former employees) of a firm
of solicitors, ('TSW') and TSW itself.

   Very large sums of money were improperly abstracted from MCC by the late Mr Robert
Maxwell and members of his family and companies, commonly referred to as 'the private
D side companies', owned or controlled directly or indirectly by them. There were two
categories of transactions in relation to which the administrators wished to obtain access to
TSW's documents and to interview the partners and employees: the first was a group of
transactions which involved the disposal of properties to a Liechtenstein trust company ('the
Corry transactions'); the second involved the sale of assets of a US subsidiary of MCC ('the
Intertec transaction'). It was said that as a result of the transactions MCC was owed £58m
E and US$127m, which sums were irrecoverable.

   The questions on the application were whether it was necessary to obtain an order for the
production of documents, whether the documents were sufficiently clearly described for
TSW to be able to comply with the order and whether if TSW had been given notice of the
application an order would have been unnecessary. There was also a question whether the
transactions were sufficiently clearly described to enable the respondents to prepare for
examination. There was a further question whether the registrar had jurisdiction to order
F that the examination could be conducted by a US attorney.

   Held, ruling accordingly:

   1. TSW's claim that the administrators had not sufficiently explained the grounds for the
claim that the documents fell within s. 236 was unfounded. The documents were clearly
material in ascertaining how assets of MCC were extracted and sold or charged through the
medium of vehicle companies and how they came to be charged to secure loans to the private
G side. Thus they clearly fell within s. 236(2)(c).

   2. Although the administrators were justified in seeking an order under s. 236, they were
not justified in making the application ex parte and, when it became apparent that there
would be considerable delay before an application could be heard, in failing to give TSW
notice so that they could attend the hearing. In many cases, the circumstances did justify the
making of the application ex parte and without notice to the person against whom the order
H was sought. However, some good reason had to be shown justifying an application ex parte.
In the instant case there was no good ground for proceeding ex parte and without notice.

   3. There was no justification in the light of the information available to the administrators
for making an application for disclosure of documents relating to the Intertec transaction.

   4. Weighing the factors, the balance came down in favour of making an order for
examination of the respondents. In relation to the Corry transactions the administrators

should supply the respondents with a note of the topics they wished to pursue and copies of   A
documents to which they might wish to refer.

5. The court had no jurisdiction to make an order for an examination except upon the
application of an office-holder and under r. 9.4(1) of the Insolvency Rules it was only the
applicant office-holder (or solicitor or counsel instructed by him) who was entitled to put
questions to the witness. The only exception was that contained in subpara. (2) which dealt
with the rare case where there were two office-holders and an order was made for the   B
examination by one of them; then the other (being 'a person who could have applied for an
order under the applicable section') might ('with the leave of the court and if the applicant
did not object') attend and question the examinee, but only through the applicant.

The following cases were referred to in the judgment:

Bishopsgate Investment Management Ltd, Re (No. 2) [1994] BCC 732.
British & Commonwealth Holdings plc, Re (No. 2) [1992] BCC 172 (CA); [1992] BCC
977 (HL).   C
North Australian Territory Co, Re (1890) 45 ChD 87.
Norton Warburg Holdings Ltd, Re (1983) 1 BCC 98,907.
Silkstone and Dodworth Coal & Iron Co, Re. Whitworth's Case (1881) 19 ChD 118.

John Higham QC (who did not appear before the registrar) (instructed by Norton
Rose) for the administrators.

Colin Rimer QC (instructed by Reynolds Porter Chamberlain) for the respondents.   D

JUDGMENT

Vinelott J: This is an application to set aside an order made pursuant to s. 236 of the
Insolvency Act 1986 by Mr Registrar Simmonds on 14 March 1994. It was made on the
application of the administrators of Maxwell Communications Corporation ('MCC').
The respondents to that application were five individuals, all partners or employees (or
former employees) of a firm of solicitors, Titmuss Sainer & Webb ('TSW') and TSW   E
itself. A statement by Mr JGA Phillips, one of the administrators, in support of the
application is dated 11 February. I understand that an attempt was made as soon as the
statement had been signed to obtain a date for the hearing of the application: 14 March
was the first date available even for an application ex parte. The application was made ex
parte. I shall have to say more about the practice of making orders under s. 236 on an
application ex parte later.   F

As is well known, the administration of the affairs of MCC has been complex and
protracted. Very large sums were improperly abstracted from MCC by the late Mr
Robert Maxwell and members of his family and companies, commonly referred to as 'the
private side companies', owned or controlled directly or indirectly by them. Amongst the
many transactions investigated by the administrators two are relevant. First, there is a
group of transactions which involved the disposal of properties to a Liechtenstein trust
company known as the Corry Stiftung ('Corry').   G

The usual sequence of events consisted of four successive stages. MCC would transfer
a property to companies created or acquired as the vehicle through which the property
would be indirectly disposed of. The vehicle companies were incorporated or acquired by
the Robert Fraser group who acted as financial intermediaries and the properties were at
least ostensibly acquired as a partnership venture between the vehicle companies (possibly
for tax reasons). So, for example, properties in Worship Street and Vandy Street were   H
acquired by two companies, Worship Street (No. 2) Ltd and Leesmere Properties Ltd,
and formed the subject-matter of the Worship Street (No. 2) Partnership. The properties
were purchased on terms that the whole, or substantially the whole, of the purchase price
would be deferred, often for a period of several years. That is stage 1.

The shares in the vehicle companies would then be sold to Corry prior to the date
when the deferred consideration was payable and at a time, therefore, when the shares of

A the vehicle companies had little value. That is stage 2. In some cases at least, Corry guaranteed the payment of the consideration payable at stage 1.

The shares would then be transferred by Corry to one or more of the private side companies. That is stage 3.

The property would then be charged as security for loans to the private side companies. That is stage 4.

B The detail varied from case to case. Moreover, it is not clear on the evidence I have seen whether the payment of the deferred consideration was secured on the assets of the vehicle companies and if it was, how charges were created by the vehicle companies ranking ahead of the charge in favour of MCC. However, it is said that the sums outstanding to MCC are very large. The transactions within this group fall within three sub-groups. The first involves properties in Worship Street where the amount outstanding

C is £22m. The second comprises properties known as 'the UK property portfolio' (which includes a property in Worship Street and in Vandy Street which was the subject-matter of the Worship Street (No. 2) Partnership) where the amount at stake is £27m. The third group comprises properties sold to Perham Securities Ltd and Pierrepont Investments Ltd. It is said in Mr Phillips' affidavit that the shares in Perham Securities Ltd have remained in the control of Corry through its subsidiary, Pierrepont Investments Ltd, and that Corry are liable for the consideration outstanding which amounts to £7.7m. The

D total owed to MCC, which is now thought to be largely irrecoverable, is some £58m.

The second transaction is referred to as the Intertec transaction. Macmillan Incorporated ('Macmillan'), a wholly owned US subsidiary of MCC, owned directly or indirectly all the stock of another US company, Intertec Inc ('Intertec') and another US subsidiary of Macmillan (Macmillan (Delaware)) owned all the assets of Webb Publishing Corporation. By an agreement dated 30 December 1988 an acquisition

E vehicle, Intertec Publishing Corporation, formed by three investment banks acquired all of the Intertec and Webb assets for a total consideration of US$17m in cash and US$154m in long-term notes ('the Intertec notes') which were secured on the assets acquired.

Then in July 1989 the new Intertec Publishing Corporation sold the assets for US$167m (thereby making a small loss). It was a term of the sale that if the assets were

F subsequently disposed of by the purchaser the Intertec notes (which prior to the sale would be secured on the assets) would be secured by irrevocable letters of credit and similar securities provided in effect out of the proceeds of sale. At this stage the new Intertec Publishing Corporation had been renamed IW Corporation. However, Mr Robert Maxwell and members of his family and others associated with them procured Macmillan and its subsidiaries to waive their right to letters of credit, and proceeds of sale of the assets totalling US$127m were lent to a private side company, Pergamon

G Holdings Ltd, and are irrecoverable.

Those are the two categories of transaction in relation to which the administrators wish to obtain access to TSW's documents and to interview the partners and employees of TSW. The first three individuals, Mr Vogel, Mr Hutchinson and Mr Harding, are and have at all material times been partners in TSW. The other two, Ms Coldwell and Ms Hyde, were assistant solicitors employed by TSW at the material time but are no longer

H so employed.

The first part of the order of 14 March is directed to documentary evidence. Paragraph 1 reads as follows, that TSW produce to the administrators all files, records and other documents in their possession which relate to:

'(i) MCC's UK property portfolio (and all transactions relating to the Robert Fraser group and Corry Stiftung) and (ii) to the Intertec transaction. Category (i)

includes transactions concerning properties on Worship Street in London and a   A
portfolio of UK properties owned by MCC (as well as shares in Perham Securities
Ltd), which were disposed of by MCC in a series of transactions involving Corry
Stiftung.'

Then there is a list of files which TSW are required to produce 'without prejudice to
the generality of the foregoing' and para. 1 continues:

'Category (ii) concerns the sale of assets of Intertec Inc, an indirect US subsidiary   B
of MCC, in December 1988 to Intertec Publishing Corporation (later renamed IW
Corporation) and the subsequent dealings in those assets. In particular, a large
proportion of the proceeds of the sale of the assets was lent by IW Corporation to
Pergamon Holdings Ltd, for whom [TSW] acted as the legal advisers in the
transaction. Production of files, records and the other documents referred to in
categories (i) and (ii) above is to be made even to the extent that such files, records
and documents may otherwise be privileged, since privilege has been waived by the   C
administrators of the private side and Corry Stiftung in respect of such production
of these documents.'

Then there follows an exception of a specific file which had already been produced.
Paragraph 2 reads as follows:

'Production of the files and documents referred to above be made by [TSW] by
way of their supplying copies of all such files, records and documents to the   D
applicants within seven days of the date of service of this order.'

It was conceded by Mr Higham, who appeared for the administrators, that the registrar
had no jurisdiction to order TSW to supply copies of documents in its possession. Under
s. 236(3) the court can order a respondent to produce documents in his possession or
under his control relating to the company; the court cannot order him to provide copies
of such documents. However, there is no longer any issue on this part of the order.   E
Arrangements have been made between TSW and the administrators for the
administrators to have access to the files, the production of which is sought, and
themselves to copy any documents they require. The only questions are whether it was
necessary to obtain an order for the production of these documents, whether the
documents to be produced were initially described sufficiently clearly for TSW to be able
to comply with the order and whether if TSW had been given notice of the application
an order would have been unnecessary.   F

The second part of the order relates to the examination of the individual respondents.
Paragraph 3 requires them to appear before the court:

'. . . to give information and answer questions relating to the transactions referred
to in para. (1) above.'

–and so raises the same question, whether the transactions are described in sufficient
detail to enable the respondents to prepare for the examination.   G

Paragraph 7 requires Mr Vogel, Mr Harding and Ms Coldwell to attend to be
examined on 21 April (when it is intended that the examination will be confined to the
Intertec transaction); para. 8 requires Mr Vogel, Mr Hutchinson and Ms Hyde to attend
on 19 May (when it is intended that the examination will be confined to the Corry
transactions). Paragraph 4 provides that subject to the consent of the registrar hearing
the examination: H

'Mr Adlai S Hardin Jr, a US attorney in the New York law firm of Milbank
Tweed, be entitled to conduct part or all of the interviews referred to in para. (3)
above.'

Mr Harding had been concerned on behalf of the administrators and the supervisors
of concurrent insolvency proceeding in the US who were investigating the Intertec

A   transaction. There is an important question whether the registrar had jurisdiction to make this part of the order.

The documentary evidence

Corry

In the course of correspondence after 11 February (the date of Mr Phillips' statement
B   and the date when arrangements were made for the hearing of the ex parte application) and in the evidence filed on the application to discharge the registrar's order, the extent of the property files which the administrators wished to see (in particular the reference to MCC's 'UK property portfolio') has been clarified. It has also been made clear and is accepted by the administrators that TSW acted for Corry in relation to the Corry transactions (and not for MCC or, in relation to stages 3 and 4, the private side
C   companies) and that TSW did not act for the Robert Fraser group in relation to the Corry transactions.

Following the service of the order, arrangements were made for the relevant files to be inspected by the administrators and I understand that that inspection was completed and copies were made where necessary before the end of March. The question is whether in the light of the correspondence before the application was made the administrators were justified in making an application under s. 236.

D   It is unnecessary to review the whole of the correspondence. The administrators obtained the consent of Dr Holzhacker representing Corry and of Allen & Overy ('A & O'), the solicitors acting for the administrators of all the private side companies, to inspect the relevant files in the possession of TSW and waiving any privilege or duty of confidence, in or before March 1993. They first asked TSW to provide a list of all files opened between 1 January 1988 and 20 April 1990 for the Maxwell private companies.
E   In their reply TSW said that the operation would cost between £5,000–£8,000. Norton Rose ('NR'), the solicitors acting for the administrators, suggested ways in which a list of files could be produced at less cost. TSW's reply was that the method suggested by NR would be impractical. They also asked NR to say why the investigation was required and under which provision of the Insolvency Act the request was made. TSW nonetheless provided Dr Holzhacker with a list of files and asked for confirmation that Corry had waived privilege and any duty of confidentiality. Dr Holzhacker gave NR a copy of a list
F   and gave TSW the necessary assurances as to privilege and confidentiality. Some months have now passed since the request to see these files was first made.

On 26 November NR sought to inspect the files itemised on Dr Holzhacker's list. That was at first agreed in a letter of 30 November, but on 1 December TSW sought confirmation that NR would be 'responsible for any costs involved'. They also said it would help them if NR could identify the aspects of the transactions in which NR was
G   interested and repeated their request that NR should explain why the administrators required access and under which provisions of the Insolvency Act they claimed to be entitled to inspect.

The reply on 8 December 1993 was that NR wished to see the files relating to the Worship Street partnerships, Pergamon Securities, Pierrepont Investments and 'the properties known as the UK property portfolio'. TSW on 13 December repeated their
H   claim that time and expense would be saved if the information sought was first set out in a memorandum followed by a discussion before any inspection took place. That was rejected by NR on 11 January. NR also pointed out that they did not need to rely on any provision of the Insolvency Act, since they had Corry's consent to the inspection. At that point TSW, replying on 17 January, claimed that Corry could not consent to NR having access to the documents because TSW had a lien on the documents for unpaid fees. But they offered to permit inspection 'subject to hearing satisfactorily from Corry' and NR

agreeing to meet their expenses 'incurred in dealing with your clients' request in providing   A
facilities for inspection and photocopying'. They raised a further objection, that NR were
engaged in 'a fishing expedition', aimed in part at fishing for information which might
assist in a claim against TSW. They concluded by saying that they were 'not prepared to
assist in enquiries which appear not to fall within the ambit of the relevant authorising
legislation and which also appear to be made for an inappropriate purpose'.

The earlier objection that the inspection would not be permitted without a further and   B
specific authority from Dr Holzhacker was not pursued in the letter of 17 January, no
doubt because Dr Holzhacker had written to TSW on 13 January in very strong terms
objecting that:

> 'Your policy adopted [by TSW] puts Corry itself in an embarrassing situation. In
> order to avoid any misunderstanding I may stress that Corry is ready to back steps
> undertaken by the administrators in order to gain access by means of court orders
> if said question cannot be resolved in due course as envisaged by Norton Rose's   C
> letter to Titmuss Sainer & Webb dated 11 January 1994.'

Norton Rose replied on 25 January to TSW's letter of 17 January pointing out the
claim to assert a lien had not previously been made and claiming that TSW were not
entitled to rely on their lien as against the administrators. They made it clear that the
administrators had not decided to institute proceedings against TSW and concluded with
a paragraph which I should I think read in full.   D

> 'We have provided you with an opportunity to assist the joint administrators
> voluntarily, which you have declined. We are entitled to rely upon s. 236 of the
> *Insolvency Act* 1986 and are of the view that it is neither necessary nor appropriate
> to enter into further lengthy debates in correspondence about the ambit of the
> section. You have referred more than once to "fishing": it is our view that the
> expression is neither apt to describe the exercise upon which we are engaged nor a   E
> good objection to our request.
>
> Since you are clearly not prepared to assist voluntarily, there seems little purpose
> continuing correspondence on this issue.'

The last letter relating to the Corry documents before Mr Phillips' statement was
signed and arrangements were made for the hearing of an ex parte application, is a
lengthy letter from TSW dated 28 January. In that letter TSW asserted that in so far as
NR relied on Corry's authority to inspect, they were entitled to rely on their lien. They   F
claimed that any thorough inspection would be a lengthy exercise and that the enquiry
could be more efficiently and cheaply carried out if preceded by a memorandum and
discussions. They rejected the claim that NR had not explained how the claim to inspect
the documents fell within the ambit of s. 236.

In my judgment it is intelligible in the light of this correspondence and the time that
had elapsed since NR first made its request to inspect the Corry documents, that NR and   G
the administrators should feel, as Mr Higham expressed it, 'frustrated' by the apparent
unwillingness of TSW to make the files in their possession available for inspection and, it
may be, should have come to feel even more anxious to inspect documents which TSW
appeared reluctant to produce. The claim that NR had not sufficiently explained the
grounds for the claim that the documents fell within s. 236 is I think unfounded. The
documents were clearly material in ascertaining how assets of MCC were extracted and
sold or charged through the medium of the vehicle companies and how they came to be   H
charged to secure loans to Pergamon. Thus they clearly fell within s. 236(2)(c). Waivers
of privilege and confidentiality had been obtained from Corry and the solicitors to the
administrators of the private side companies.

The claim that TSW were entitled to exact an undertaking that it would be paid all
expenses incurred in dealing with the administrators' request in providing facilities for

A   inspection and of copying was, I think, too widely framed. However, although NR were I think justified in seeking an order under s. 236, I am not satisfied that they were justified in making the application ex parte and, when it became apparent that there would be considerable delay before an application could be heard, in failing to give TSW notice so that they could attend the hearing. In many if not in most cases where application is made under s. 236, the circumstances do justify the making of the application ex parte and without notice to the person against whom the order is sought. It is not infrequently

B   the case that it is apparent when the application is made that documents which fall clearly within s. 236 will not be produced voluntarily and there may be good reasons for insisting on the confidentiality of the statement by the office-holder in support of the application. It is not infrequently the case that the production of documents is urgently required and that the delay in obtaining an inter partes hearing or in giving notice to the person affected would unduly hamper the office-holder's task. There are cases, though less

C   frequent, where notice in advance of the service of the order might lead to the disappearance of the documents which the office-holder wishes to inspect.

However, an application under s. 236 must not be seen as an all embracing exception from the general rule that a person is entitled to be heard before an order of the court is made against him, more particularly if it is a mandatory order requiring the production of documents. Some good reason must be shown justifying an application ex parte. In

D   the instant case there was no good ground for proceeding ex parte and without notice, at least when it became apparent that the application could not be heard before 14 March. The administrators' statement has in fact been made available and confidentiality has not been claimed. In these circumstances I think the inference is that if TSW had been given notice they could have satisfied themselves that the order sought fell within the scope of s. 236(2)(c) and have raised objection to the unduly wide and vague terms in which para. 1 was framed. I have no doubt that if this course had been taken the extent

E   of the documents to be produced would have been clarified and the arrangements later made for inspection and taking of copies would then have been made. The order would either not have been necessary or if necessary would not have provided for copies of all the documents to be made and supplied by TSW. The costs of the application to set aside the order would therefore have been saved.

The Intertec documents

F   TSW acted for Pergamon in relation to the loans by IW Corporation. Their file relating to the transaction was made available for inspection on 25 May 1993 and copies of the documents requested were provided on 4 June. This file is excepted from the order (though it is inaccurately described).

The next reference to the Intertec transaction is contained in a letter from NR to TSW of 26 November 1993 which contains a brief description of the transaction. NR asked

G   TSW whether Mr Vogel, Mr Harding and Ms Coldwell would be made available for an interview with Mr Harding in December. Nothing was said in that letter or in a further letter dated 8 December (making it clear that no order had been sought under s. 236 for their attendance at an interview and that their voluntary assistance was sought) as to the disclosure of further documents. TSW replied on 13 December to the letter of 8 December saying categorically that they would not be prepared to participate in the interviews, though they offered to reconsider their position if given details of the purpose of the

H   request, a list of the questions to be raised and an indemnity as to any costs incurred by them.

In para. 30 of his statement, Mr Phillips asserts that in this letter TSW said that they 'were not prepared to provide further documents in relation to this transaction'. That does not, I think, accurately reflect the position as at 13 December. The production of documents relating to the Intertec transaction was not taken up in the subsequent

correspondence before Mr Phillips' statement was signed. It was not until 23 March that   A
TSW learned in the course of a telephone conversation that the administrators took the
view that TSW might have further documents relating to the Intertec transaction. It is
now clear and is accepted by the administrators that TSW were not concerned in the sale
of the assets of Intertec to IW and that the only documents in the possession of TSW are
documents relating to the loan to Pergamon and advice given to MCC in relation to a
circular to shareholders explaining the acquisition of Macmillan Inc and the disposal of
assets of subsidiaries of Macmillan Inc to IW.   B

The administrators have accepted an assurance given by Mr Russell on behalf of TSW
that he has enquired from his partners and has inspected his firm's file and is satisfied
that there are no documents relating to the Intertec transaction except those contained in
the file disclosed in May last year (which include the documents relating to the circular).

In my judgment there was no justification in the light of the information available to
the administrators for making an application for disclosure of documents relating to the   C
Intertec transaction. The reason for making the application set out in para. 30 of Mr
Phillips' affidavit rests on a misreading of TSW's letter of 13 December. The
administrators' subsequent request for clarification as to the role played by TSW should
have been raised in correspondence before any application was made. Similarly, if notice
of the application had been given to TSW the matter could have been resolved before the
application came before the registrar.   D

Interviews

I have already summarised NR's first request in the letter of 26 November for the
attendance of Mr Vogel, Mr Harding and Ms Coldwell at a voluntary interview and the
correspondence leading to TSW's reply of 13 December. The question of interviews was
taken up again by NR on 25 January when they said that they wished to interview also
Mr Hutchinson and Ms Hyde, but that in the light of the earlier replies they assumed   E
that TSW would not cooperate in voluntary interviews. TSW responded on 27 January
asking the purpose of the proposed interviews and whether the request was made
pursuant to s. 235–236. NR replied to say that the interviews with Mr Hutchinson and
Ms Hyde were sought in relation to the Corry transactions and that the request was that
they attend voluntarily.

At the time when the application was made, it was I think clear that TSW would not   F
assist in making any of the persons whom the administrators wished to interview
available for interview unless an order was obtained under s. 236 or unless the
requirements stated in their letter of 13 December were met. In subsequent
correspondence TSW repeated their contention that it was unreasonable for NR to seek
to interview members of their firm without providing the information and undertakings
they sought. The undertakings included an undertaking to meet TSW's costs 'in
providing the answers'. Under r. 9.6(4) of the Insolvency Rules: G

'A person summoned to attend for examination . . . shall be tendered a reasonable
sum in respect of travelling expenses incurred in connection with his attendance.
Other costs falling on him are at the court's discretion.'

It is well settled that the power conferred on the court by s. 236 is an extraordinary
power and that the discretion must be exercised after a careful balancing of the factors
involved; on the one hand the reasonable requirements of the administrator to carry out   H
his task and on the other a need to avoid making an order which is wholly unreasonable,
unnecessary or oppressive to the persons concerned (see per Lord Slynn in *British &
Commonwealth Holdings plc v Spicer & Oppenheim* [1992] BCC 977 at p. 984E).

In *British & Commonwealth Holdings* the application was for the production of
documents. An application for oral examination is more intrusive and burdensome and

A so more likely to be oppressive than an order for the production of documents. Amongst the other factors mentioned by Ralph Gibson LJ in the *British & Commonwealth Holdings* case in the Court of Appeal are the following (see [1992] BCC 172 at p. 184H):

'(a) The case for making an order against an officer or former officer of the company will usually be stronger than it would against a third party because officers owe a fiduciary duty to the company and they are under a statutory duty
B (s. 235 of the 1986 Act) to assist the officer holder.

(b) If, by giving the information sought, a third party risks exposing himself to liability, that involves an element of oppression: per Sir Nicolas Browne-Wilkinson V-C in *Cloverbay (No. 2)* [1990] BCC 414 at p. 420E.

(c) An order for oral examination is more likely to be oppressive than an order for the production of documents: per Sir Nicolas Browne-Wilkinson V-C in *Cloverbay*
C at p. 420F.

(d) If someone is suspected of wrongdoing, and in particular fraud, it is oppressive to require him to prove the case against himself on oath before any proceedings are brought: per Sir Nicolas Browne-Wilkinson V-C in *Cloverbay* at p. 421A.'

In the instant case TSW are in a position of third parties; they did not act for MCC or its subsidiaries save in relation to the MCC circular disclosing the sale of the Intertec
D assets.

As regards (b) I do not think that any significant weight should be attached to the risk that answers given in the interviews may lead to and be relied on in civil litigation brought by the administrators against TSW. The transactions in question are complex and unusual and resulted in very serious losses to MCC. The administrators must clearly make a full investigation into all the surrounding circumstances and if their enquiries reveal any shortcoming on the part of any of the professional advisers concerned with
E the transactions giving rise to recoverable compensation, they must take appropriate action. But the investigation is not designed to furnish evidence which can be relied upon to support a claim against TSW, though a claim may be the consequence of investigations designed to uncover the full circumstances surrounding them.

The factor mentioned by Ralph Gibson LJ in (d) has no relevance in this case.

In addition to these specific factors I must, of course, bear in mind that an oral
F examination is not only intrusive and to that extent oppressive, but will also entrench upon the no doubt valuable time of professional men and women. As against that I must bear in mind also that the collapse of the Maxwell group is a matter of wide public concern and that it has resulted in grave hardship to a large number of innocent employees and pensioners; the interests of pensioners are indirectly affected in that pension funds administrated by Bishopsgate Investment Management Ltd (another
G company controlled by Mr Maxwell) has very large claims against MCC. In these circumstances the administrators must make and be seen to have made the fullest possible investigations.

I have no doubt whatever that, weighing these factors, the balance comes down in favour of making an order for the examination of the respondents. Mr Rimer submitted that the examination should be preceded by a questionnaire and by interrogatories and should only be proceeded with if the information forthcoming is found insufficient. Mr
H Phillips' answer is that this course:

'. . . would result in the long run in a more drawn out and less effective process. At an oral examination supplementary questions designed at getting to the truth of the events that are the subject-matter of the investigations can be asked immediately and directly. In addition, written answers to the administrators' questions are likely to prompt yet further questions which would result in further

delay. Furthermore, given the history of the correspondence between TSW and   A
Norton Rose, I have no confidence that a submission of written questions will not
be met by further and repeated requests for the administrators to justify their
entitlement to receive answers to such questions. At an oral examination the
registrar will be able to rule on any objections to the questions to be put, whether
founded on confidentiality, privilege, or the width of the information sought.'

In *Re Bishopsgate Investment Management Ltd (No. 2)* [1994] BCC 732, Hoffmann J   B
rejected a similar claim by a respondent that an oral examination was oppressive because
he would be exposed to the danger that answers would be elicited in the examination
which might be 'the product of confusion, over hasty reaction or poor recollection' and
might be relied upon in subsequent litigation. As to that Hoffmann J said (at p. 738G):

'I recognise at once that there is a burden in being subject to oral examination
rather than having to answer a questionnaire at leisure for the assistance of one's
solicitors. To that extent what is proposed here would be more oppressive than the   C
course which is suggested [by the respondent] in that case. I think, however, that
they exaggerate the degree of unfairness which this involves. The judge at the trial
is well aware that witnesses occasionally give answers which on further
consideration they would wish to correct. Cross-examining counsel does frequently
make a great deal of minor discrepancies between what is being said at the trial
and what was said on an earlier occasion, but I am confident that the trial had   D
sufficient common sense to be able to detect what is a really significant change in
evidence and what is simply human error. While, therefore, I bear this factor in
mind it does not seem to me sufficient to outweigh what in this case would be the
advantage to the liquidator in being able to proceed by oral examination rather
than the submission of the questionnaire.'

I have no hesitation in the context of this case in taking the same course. The only   E
question, it seems to me, is whether the administrators should supply the respondent not
with a questionnaire, but with a note of the topics which they wish to pursue as well as
copies of documents to which they may wish to refer, a course which I suggested in *Re
Norton Warburg Holdings* (1983) 1 BCC 98,907 at p. 98,913. The administrators are
willing to adopt this course at the examinations in relation to the Corry transactions
which is due to take place on 19 May. The Intertec transaction, to the extent that TSW
were involved, was far simpler and the documents are much less extensive. I do not think   F
that I should insist upon the respondents being supplied with a list of topics in advance
of the examination in relation to that transaction which has now been deferred.

Examination to be carried out by a US attorney

Under s. 236(2) the court has jurisdiction to order any such person as is therein
mentioned to appear 'on the application of the office-holder'; s. 237(4) provides that any   G
person brought before the court on an application under s. 236(2) 'may be examined on
oath'. These provisions must be read together with the Insolvency Rules which were
made under the powers conferred by s. 411 of the Insolvency Act. Rules governing
examinations under s. 236 are set out in Pt. 9. The first two subparagraphs of r. 9.4 read
as follows:

'(1) At any examination of the respondent, the applicant may attend in person, or
be represented by a solicitor with or without counsel, and may put such questions   H
to the respondent as the court may allow.

(2) Any other person who could have applied for an order under the applicable
section in respect of the insolvent's affairs may, with the leave of the court and if
the applicant does not object, attend the examination and put questions to the
respondent (but only through the applicant).'

A   The question is whether the court has any jurisdiction to make an order authorising a person who is not an office-holder entitled to apply for an order under s. 236 or a solicitor or counsel instructed by him to conduct an examination.

     I was taken by Mr Higham through the history of the provisions which were replaced by s. 236 starting with s. 115 and 117 of the *Companies Act* 1862 and ending with s. 561 of the *Companies Act* 1985. It will, I think, be sufficient to refer to the familiar s. 268 of

B   the *Companies Act* 1948 which is a direct descendant of s. 115 and s. 117 and which is repeated in s. 561. Section 268(1) and (2) read as follows:

> '(1) The court may, at any time after the appointment of a provisional liquidator or the making of a winding-up order, summon before it any officer of the company or person known or suspected to have in his possession any property of the company or supposed to be indebted to the company, or any person whom the
>
C   court deems capable of giving information concerning the promotion, formation, trade, dealings, affairs or property of the company.
>
> (2) The court may examine him on oath concerning the matters aforesaid, either by word of mouth or on written interrogatories, and may reduce his answers to writing and require him to sign them.'

     It was well settled under these provisions that if a liquidator was not willing to make an application a contributory might do so (see *Whitworth's Case* (1881) 19 ChD 118) and

D   there is support in the notes of the 14th edition of *Buckley on the Companies Acts* for the proposition that the court might make an order of its own motion. The examination was an examination by the court and it was for the court to decide who should be entitled to question the witness and the extent of the questions that ought to be allowed.

     In *Re North Australian Territory Co* (1890) 45 ChD 87, Fry LJ at p. 96 explained that:

E   > 'The whole of the proceeding, therefore, is a proceeding by the Court, and the liquidator or the contributory or the other person whom the Court allows to intervene and to be active in the proceedings only does so by the leave of the Court, because he is a person supposed to have the means of addressing inquiries to the witness; but it is an entirely different proceeding from that in which a litigant summons a witness and examines that witness before the Court. The liquidator,
>
F   > therefore, in insisting, as he seems to me to have done in the argument before us, upon the right to any question, has, I think, entirely mistaken his position. Each question is put by the liquidator only by the leave of the Court, and on behalf of the Court.'

     The position under s. 236 is radically different. The court has no jurisdiction to make an order for an examination except upon the application of an office-holder and under r. 9.4(1) it is only the applicant office-holder (or solicitor or counsel instructed by him)

G   who is entitled to put questions to the witness. The only exception is that contained in subpara. (2) which deals with the rare case where there are two office-holders and an order is made for the examination by one of them; then the other (being 'a person who could have applied for an order under the applicable section') may ('with the leave of the court and if the applicant does not object') attend and question the examinee, but only through the applicant.

H   Mr Higham submitted that this construction of the rules is likely to give rise to serious practical difficulties in cases where (as here) an administrator or liquidator is a partner in a large firm of accountants and parts of the administration of the affairs of the company have been entrusted to partners or assistants. The office-holder himself may know little about the matters upon which the respondent is to be examined. The difficulty is particularly acute where, as in the instant case, the administration is carried out in conjunction with concurrent proceedings in the US (under Chapter 11) and the matters

on which the respondent is to be examined relate to transactions there. In practice I
imagine no objection would be raised by a respondent to the presence of the person
charged with an investigation into matters on which the respondent is to be examined to
assist the office-holder or solicitors or counsel instructed by him. In the instant case it
may well be that the respondents will not object to the presence of Mr Gerdts III (who
has taken over the investigation of the Intertec transaction from Mr Harding) for that
purpose.

If objection is raised the only solution I think will be for the administrators (or solicitor
or counsel instructed by them to conduct the examination) to apply to adjourn (if
necessary) from time to time and to seek leave to disclose the transcript to Mr Gerdts so
that he can be satisfied that all the questions he wishes to ask are answered. That course,
if insisted upon, will of course greatly protract and increase the expense of the
examination to no one's advantage. The additional costs incurred will of course be in the
discretion of the court. I can see no alternative if that objection is persisted with.

Costs

Costs I think are probably the most difficult of the questions that I have to decide in
this application. I had given some thought to it before this morning. I have reached the
conclusion that the right course is to make no order as to costs.

I will express my reasons very briefly. The administrators made an application ex parte
because it was thought (and it is, I think, perhaps too widely thought) that such
applications are always made ex parte. In that I think they were wrong. If the application
had been made inter partes or if notice had been given to Titmuss Sainer & Webb before
it was heard, I have myself little doubt that by the time the matter came before the
registrar matters relating to documentary evidence would have been sorted out and
agreement reached. So if that had been done either no order would have been needed or,
if one was needed, it would have been in a form which TSW would not challenge.

To that extent I am bound to say that I think the administrators were at fault, though
I think that it is an excusable fault bearing in mind the way in which these applications
have come to be made. When I say 'excusable', I do not mean that it is one in which the
costs of applying to discharge the order ought not to fall prima facie upon them.

But as regards the application for an examination, it is I think not enough for TSW to
say, 'We have got a list of topics as regards one limb of it and we have got rid of Mr
Gerdts except so far as he attends with our consent for the assistance of the person
conducting the examination.' To my mind it is quite clear from the correspondence that
objection was made, and would have been made even if notice had been given, to oral
examinations on grounds which I have held to be insufficient. In substance I think there
were two quite distinct subject-matters. The administrators have lost upon one and TSW
have lost upon the other. In all the circumstances I think the right course is to make no
order.

(Order accordingly)

A   # Re Wimbledon Village Restaurant Ltd.
Secretary of State for Trade and Industry v Thomson & Ors.

Chancery Division.
Michael Hart QC (sitting as a deputy High Court judge).
Judgment delivered 18 March 1994.

B   *Disqualifying unfit directors of insolvent companies – Whether executive directors were unfit – Whether non-executive director was unfit – Whether past impropriety necessarily led to finding of present unfitness – Company Directors Disqualification Act 1986, s. 6.*

This was an application by the Secretary of State for Trade and Industry under s. 6 of the Company Directors Disqualification Act 1986 for disqualification orders against three
C   **respondents who were directors of 'WVR Ltd', which carried on business as a restaurant proprietor from March 1985 until late September 1989 and went into creditors' voluntary liquidation in November 1989 with an estimated deficiency of £327,356 as disclosed by the statement of affairs.**

The first and second respondents were brothers who were involved in the management of the restaurant. The third respondent, 'W', retained a directorship in order to protect her
D   **own position as the unlimited guarantor of the company overdraft.**

Held, declining to make disqualification orders:

1. The way in which the business of the company was run from the end of March 1989 onwards was not the way it ought to have been run, given the possible consequences for trade creditors. The first and second respondents paid insufficient regard to the interests of creditors during that period. It was the responsibility of both of them to make an early and informed decision on what would be in the best interests of the company and its creditors.
E   **That did not happen. The financial information about the business on which they were relying had never been subjected to the scrutiny of audit; and, while they might have genuinely believed that they would be able to sell the business and lease should the worst come to the worst, they did not have reasonable grounds for such a belief.**

2. The respondents failed to ensure that accounts for the period ended 31 March 1988, which ought to have been filed by the end of January 1989, were prepared and delivered for
F   **filing to the registrar of companies. All the directors ought to have concerned themselves with the progress of the audit at a much earlier date. However 'non-executive' a non-executive director might be there was nothing to stop him or her from showing an interest in the progress and timing of the statutorily required audit. In this case there were particularly strong reasons why all the directors should be interested in the results of an audit of the accounts of the year to 31 March 1988. The external audit provided the only objective check on the accuracy of the figures on the basis of which the company was pursuing its precarious**
G   **strategy.**

3. The law rightly exacted high standards of those who claimed the privilege of trading with limited liability. Those standards were particularly appropriate where, as here, the adventure was fraught with risk from the outset. The lapses from those standards in the case of the first and second respondents demonstrated a failure to appreciate their responsibilities, and that failure did in the event damage trade creditors of the business. It was not, however,
H   **every past impropriety which should lead to a conclusion that the director responsible was unfit. Having regard to all the circumstances there was a significant measure of doubt as to whether the lapses properly attributable to either of them were sufficiently serious as to compel a finding that either was unfit. That doubt was to be resolved in their favour.**

4. W retained a directorship simply as a means of being able to protect her position as the unlimited guarantor of the company overdraft and neither asserted nor accepted any

wider responsibility. **In taking that attitude, she wholly misconceived her duties as the**   A
director of a limited liability company. She seemed completely unaware of the wider
responsibilities owed by her to the company and its creditors. However, the mere fact that
she had that attitude did not lead inexorably to the conclusion that she was unfit. The court
had to consider her actual responsibility in relation to the allegations which had been proved.
In all the circumstances her misconduct in relation to WVR was not so serious as to justify
finding her to be unfit.

B

The following cases were referred to in the judgment:

Bath Glass Ltd, Re (1988) 4 BCC 130.

Swift 736 Ltd, Re [1993] BCC 312.

Paul Girolami (instructed by the Treasury Solicitor) for the Secretary of State for
Trade and Industry.

Philip Gillyon (instructed by Leach & Co) for the first respondent.   C

Ashley Underwood (instructed by Hill Taylor Dickinson) for the second respondent.

Cyril Kinsky (instructed by Edmonds Bowen & Co) for the third respondent.

JUDGMENT

Michael Hart QC: This is an application by the Secretary of State for Trade and
Industry under s. 6 of the *Company Directors Disqualification Act* 1986 for   D
disqualification orders against the three respondents. Each of them was a director of
Wimbledon Village Restaurant Ltd ('WVR'), which carried on business as a restaurant
proprietor from premises in Wimbledon from March 1985 until late September 1989. It
went into creditors' voluntary liquidation on 10 November 1989, with an estimated
deficiency of £327,356 as disclosed by the statement of affairs.

Much of the debate before me has been as to the roles and responsibilities of each of   E
the respondents within WVR. To set that in context it is necessary to say something of
the history of the business, although (for reasons which will become apparent) the events
of the last 12 months trading have a particular significance.

For all practical purposes the founder of WVR was the third respondent ('Mrs
Woods'). She is aged 57, and has been involved in the restaurant business since the early
1970s. Between 1979 and 1988 she was managing director of Langben and Devonshire
Street Restaurant Ltd, the proprietor of, inter alia, the well-known Odins and Langans   F
Bistro restaurants. In 1984 she conceived the idea of opening a quality English restaurant
in Wimbledon, with a particular view to giving a start in life to a young chef whose
talents she admired, Mr Nicholas Rochford. She acquired WVR, holding 99 of the 100
issued shares therein, and negotiated on its behalf the acquisition of licensed premises in
a favourable location at 8, The High Street, Wimbledon Village. The premises were held
under a 14-year lease due to expire in December 1990. There was evidence that WVR   G
paid some £140,000 for the benefit of this lease and the fixtures and fittings of the existing
business. She obtained on WVR's behalf a business development loan in the amount of
some £60,000 from National Westminster Bank, Westminster Branch, where she had a
good relationship with the manager, Mr Halsey, who gave evidence before me, and in
whose favour she gave an unlimited, all-accounts guarantee. A further £50,000 was raised
by loans from Mr Rochford, the chef, and from Ms Pamela Leighton, who was to be the
new restaurant's head waitress. Daniel Auerbach & Co (with whom Mrs Woods was   H
familiar from her full-time employment) were retained as accountants to WVR.

By late 1986, it had become clear that, despite the restaurant having established a good
reputation, it had not achieved financial success. This can be seen from the accounts to
the years ending 31 March 1986 and 31 March 1987, which were not finalised until
September 1987. In addition, things seem not to have worked out with Mr Rochford and

A   Ms Leighton, each of whom wished to leave and withdraw their money. Against that background Mrs Woods approached the second respondent, Robert Graham Thomson ('Graham'), with a view to getting him interested in opening a wine bar in the basement. Graham was already known to her as a successful manager of wine bars, an activity for which he had already acquired a good reputation in the trade.

B   Through Graham, Mrs Woods met other members of the Thomson family, in particular the first respondent, Ian Cadzow Thomson ('Ian'), and his brother William David Thomson ('David'). The Thomson brothers were shareholders in a company called Diga Wines Ltd ('Diga'). An agreement was eventually arrived at between Diga and Mrs Woods, some elements of which are the subject of continued dispute between the parties, but the broad outlines of which were that Diga would acquire 75 per cent of the equity of WVR, Diga would lend WVR £50,000 to replace the moneys taken out by Mr Rochford and Ms Leighton, the management of WVR and its business was to be put C   entirely into the hands of the Thomson brothers, and Mrs Woods was to be indemnified by individual covenants against any liability to National Westminster Bank in excess of £112,000. The figure of £112,000 was at that time considered to be the amount of the liability incurred as a result of WVR's trading up to the date of the takeover. The takeover duly took place in February 1987. Ian and Graham became directors, and David, a professional accountant, became the company secretary. Mrs Woods remained a D   director, but without any intention of playing any future role in WVR save that of being in a position to monitor its progress in reducing her liability under the guarantee.

At this stage (as subsequently appearing from the audited accounts to 31 March 1987) there was a balance sheet deficiency of some £129,444, and the company was trading at a loss on a turnover of some £200,000 per annum. The thinking behind Diga's acquisition was explained in evidence before me by the Thomsons' father, William Cran Thomson. The father is a chartered accountant by profession, the chairman of Nickerson Group E   Rothwell Ltd, a non-executive director of Shell Transport and Trading plc and of Coats Viyella plc. Until his retirement in 1986 he had been group managing director of Royal Dutch Shell group with particular responsibility for finance. He was therefore a useful person for his sons to have available to consult. Mr Stanley Rose, the insolvency practitioner who in due course became WVR's liquidator doubted whether that background equipped him as well as Mr Rose was equipped to evaluate the dangers of F   trading through the medium of a company in WVR's position, but the Crown did not, in the event, challenge his account of the nature of the decision taken by Diga. His evidence was as follows:

> '(2) In about February 1987 my sons, Ian and Graham, informed me that they had learnt of a potential investment opportunity in an ailing restaurant business, namely [WVR] . . . Owing to my accountancy and business experience I was asked to review the acquisition, and in particular to consider the viability of WVR and G   whether it could be turned to profitability.
>
> (3) It was realised and accepted that WVR had made losses in each of its first two accounting periods and that as a consequence WVR showed a deficit on its balance sheet. The business could be said to be technically insolvent, but the bank overdraft was covered by Mrs Wood, one of the shareholders. This fact alone caused all concerned to realise that the acquisition required careful planning and detailed H   calculations if it was to proceed, and in my view the acquisition was given the consideration it merited.
>
> (4) In the most general terms the strategy envisaged was that during the unexpired portion of WVR's lease (approximately 2 years 10 months) WVR should generate sufficient trade profits before depreciation to eliminate the bank borrowings. Thereafter, if the lease was renewed (as it was confidently anticipated), Ian and

Graham would be able to continue and develop the profitable business devoid of liabilities.

(5) It was my general opinion that subject to detailed consideration of the figures there was no reason why the above strategy should not succeed. In my experience businesses which have been consistently loss-making can be and have been returned to profitability by (a) a change in management; (b) a consequent change in direction; and (c) tighter cost controls. I considered this was the case with WVR's restaurant business, particularly if a decreasing clientele could be restored by an appropriate new manager with a record in the trade of attracting new custom.

(6) My sons David (also an accountant), Ian, Graham and I all considered and discussed whether the general strategy put forward in para. (4) above could be achieved in light of the figures involved. We considered that it could be achieved. From figures obtained from Daniel Auerbach & Co (WVR's accountants) it appeared that a deficit on the profit and loss account of the order of £100,000 would require to be eliminated by the time the lease of the property was due to expire at the end of 1989 – a period of 2 years and 10 months. (Subsequent production of the actual accounts to 31 March 1987 revealed a deficit of £129,000.) It was realised that it would be over-optimistic to assume that this could be achieved within such a time-scale but if WVR could not renew the lease and the bank debts had been eliminated, then there would be sufficient funds available from debtors and the realisation of stocks to satisfy the remaining creditors.

The business plan was to change WVR from a very high-priced restaurant to one at lower prices, but still of high quality and to open a wine bar in the basement.

To achieve the stated financial objective it would be necessary to raise annual sales from approximately £200,000 to £340,000, i.e. a level of £6,600 per week.

The sales would be split £3,000 in the wine bar, generating a 60 per cent gross margin and £3,600 in the restaurant generating a 55 per cent gross margin. (The gross margin had been 60 per cent.)

Costs would require to be contained to their 1986/87 level (these included a depreciation charge of £34,000). This would produce a profit of some £10,000 per annum or, allowing for slippage, some £25,000 over the period being considered. After adding back depreciation totalling say £100,000 this would produce a cash profit of £125,000 – comfortably in excess of the £100,000 thought to be required to settle the obligations to the bank.

It was recognised that the shareholder's loan of £50,000 from DIGA would probably still be outstanding.

As background and to appreciate the sensitivities in the calculations, £3,600 per week in the restaurant implied 24 diners at each of 10 sessions, spending of the order of £17.50. The restaurant had 46 seats.

These calculations in the round were thought to be balanced and reasonably conservative.

(7) It was a further important factor in the decision to acquire a controlling interest in WVR, that WVR's bankers the National Westminster Bank plc ("the bank") was prepared to continue WVR's loan facilities. This was an important point for two reasons: first it indicated that the bank was also satisfied that the business strategy formulated was viable; and secondly it enabled WVR to establish profitability methodically, by building up the clientele and turnover. In other words, the continued loan facilities meant that WVR did not have to achieve instant profitability to discharge creditors (which would not be possible) but could take a long-term view of the "rescue" of WVR.

A
(8) The working papers relating to the foregoing calculations have not been retained by me.

(9) I believe that the general business plan as conceived was sound . . .'

I note that this business plan assumed that the lease would in due course be renewed under the provisions of the *Landlord and Tenant Act* 1954. Unless it was renewed, not only would Diga not recover its £50,000 but the Thomsons would get nothing from the
B
business apart from the modest salary which it was contemplated that Graham would draw as the full-time manager.

The company duly began to trade under its new management as a restaurant with a wine bar in the basement. I find that the division of responsibilities as between the two Thomson brothers was that Graham was to be the full-time manager, with the responsibility of running the business at the premises and recording the raw financial
C
data. That data was passed to David whose job it was to keep the basic books, draw up management and statutory accounts, and advise which creditors were due to be paid. For this purpose a room above the premises was made available, which David visited at least once a week. During the first year's trading, Graham had the assistance of a full-time manager, Mr Paul Wallen. Ian's active role was limited to establishing the basic accounting systems for WVR – i.e. management accounts, weekly return sheets, 'goods in' sheets for both drink and food, and payroll sheets. Thereafter (until the events of
D
1989) his role was limited to monitoring the financial progress at meetings convened for the purpose at regular (approximately monthly) meetings of the three brothers, sometimes attended by Mr Thomson senior. It was the custom of the brothers on these occasions to receive a verbal report from David on performance and prospects.

During the first year's trading the strategy proved partially successful in that turnover increased to some £302,217. It was clear, however, that the business was trading at a loss.
E
Unaudited accounts available to the brothers showed a loss for the period ended 31 March 1988 of £12,248 before charging interest and depreciation. The balance sheet deficiency at 31 March 1988 had increased to £187,386. The overdraft at the bank (of £94,300) was at (indeed apparently above) the limit of the facility then available. The problem appeared to lie in an inability to achieve the gross margins anticipated by the business plan, but precise identification of the problem eluded the brothers. Some indication of the kind of calculations being done during this period can be seen from the
F
management trading and profit and loss account for the nine months to 31 December 1987 together with the forecast of the year to 31 March 1988, which were produced at the hearing before me by Mr Halsey, the bank manager. These show that gross margins (at 55.8 per cent) were down on the previous year's trading, although turnover had improved. The compiler of these accounts has also calculated that to achieve break-even, i.e. a level of trading which would achieve a profit after charging depreciation and
G
interest, it would be necessary to increase sales from £5,572 per week to £6,685 per week (i.e. from £289,768 in a full year's trading to £358,376). Inclusive of VAT, the break-even sales were shown as £7,687 per week, which would appear to equate to some £412,000 over a full year.

It seems that trading in the next nine months or so after 31 March 1988 encouraged the brothers to believe that, while profitability remained elusive, matters were not significantly deteriorating. Hard evidence for or against the reasonableness of this view
H
does not exist. Mr Halsey produced in evidence a wholly illegible balance sheet as at 31 July 1988 including forecast profit and loss to 31 March 1989. A draft manuscript trading and profit and loss account to 31 July 1988 which is before me shows a loss (after depreciation and interest) of some £14,000 for the four-month period and a forecast turnover (exclusive of VAT) to the end of March 1989 of £383,000. There is also a cash flow forecast (prepared by David) for the 12 months from September 1988. That forecast

showed budgeted sales over the period of £440,000, inclusive of VAT, and a bank   A
overdraft reducing from £106,900 to £56,400. In October 1988, however, the overdraft
facility of £90,000 was increased by £20,000. In November 1988 five cheques issued by
the company were bounced. At about this time, according to Ian's subsequent statement
to Mr Rose, Ian and Graham reviewed the position. It was concluded that the business
would not be able to achieve the necessary increase in profitability without a fundamental
change to a less formal 'brasserie' style operation, which would require the injection of
further capital. A provisional decision was made to take steps to sell the lease and the   B
business in the new year, the position to be reviewed in January or February 1989.
Whether Ian was correct in his statement to Mr Rose in placing this review in the autumn
of 1988 seems to me doubtful. The minutes which exist in relation to meetings in 1989
suggest that a review along these lines did not take place until 26 March 1989.

There is some contemporary documentary evidence for the early months of 1989. It is
sparse, but it nevertheless tells a story.   C

First, Mr Halsey rang Ian and voiced his concern at the viability of the company. A
meeting was held on 27 January 1989, attended by the three Thomson brothers and Mr
Halsey. From the internal evidence of the minute of that meeting drawn up by Ian, it was
plainly not the first such meeting. It appears that Mr Halsey was seeking on Mrs Woods'
behalf to procure that additional security be given by David and Graham for the
overdraft, and that they had at an earlier meeting agreed to give it. This was resisted by   D
Ian on the basis that this was inconsistent with the original agreement between themselves
and Mrs Woods, and that the bank lending was being serviced by WVR. Ian rebutted
suggestions made by Mr Halsey that the business was not being effectively managed,
asserting that gross profit margin was now rising again after the fall in 1988 caused by
the price reductions effected in pursuit of higher turnover. It was agreed to have a further
meeting in the second week of March.   E

On 29 January 1989 the Diga board met to consider WVR affairs. Present were the
three brothers and their father. The following points may be noted: first, it was decided
that Ian should deal with meetings with Mr Halsey in the future. From this I infer that
this had not previously been his prime responsibility, and that it was as a result of David
and Graham having attended one or more earlier meetings that the 'misunderstandings'
over the question of additional security had arisen. Secondly, it was reported that one M
Commins 'was prepared to take on both wages and accounts . . . on the basis that the   F
information is provided on time and is complete'. Thirdly, David complained that
Graham was not using the filing cabinet which had been installed, that he was failing to
carry out the basic weekly returns, that wages information was not being processed
correctly, and that the cash handling system which had been set up was being ignored.
The meeting put it to Graham that 'his presence was required at the restaurant and that
all the basic management functions in dealing with wages, weekly returns etc. have to be   G
done properly'. There was clearly considerable dissatisfaction with Graham's
performance. There must also have been considerable room for doubt, in the light of that
dissatisfaction, whether the financial information being received by Ian as a director was
reliable. Thirdly, there is in the minute of that meeting a reference to the 'audit date'
being agreed. With only two days to go before the date for filing of audited accounts this
entry is puzzling. Fourthly, there is no reference in the minute to any proposal to sell the
business. Finally, the date of the next meeting was agreed as 5 March. From this I infer   H
that no immediate sense of urgency was being felt. This may have been because the
Christmas and post-Christmas trading had been, or had at least been felt to be, unusually
good.

In late February, Ian had a telephone call from Daniel Auerbach & Co ('Auerbachs')
expressing dissatisfaction over the accounts to 31 March 1988, and in particular to the

A   fact that they had not been paid. They had not started doing the audit at all, and gave Ian the impression that they did not wish to continue as auditors. They suggested that their account be settled and that WVR find new auditors. They were also unwilling to continue to do the payroll. It was decided that the audit should be moved to Leslie Marshall, and that Auerbachs should be approached with a proposal to settle their account by scheduled payments. The note of this meeting records also that David would cease to be available on a daily basis from 27 February 1989, and notes the particular

B   need to keep paperwork up to date. It further records a complaint that the cash sheets were still not being balanced, and a rejoinder by Graham that he was unhappy about the weekly cash sheet. This confirms what Graham told me in evidence about his attitude to the irksome chore of completing what he regarded as 'big company' financial information for his brothers.

C   On 14 March 1989 Ian and Mrs Woods met, as the board of WVR, in preparation for a meeting to be held the following day with Mr Halsey. The minute notes that provisional figures supplied by David for the year ended 31 March 1989 showed a 'potential trading profit for the first time ever', but noted that the overdraft was not decreasing despite the trading figures, and that Ian should try to establish the reason for this. It is possible that the figures before the meeting were the management accounts to 28 February 1989 with a forecast to the year end which are before me, and which must have been produced in

D   March. If so, however, it is difficult to understand why the minute shows uncertainty as to the causes of the overdraft not being reduced, since these accounts show that insufficient profit was being made wholly to absorb the interest on the bank overdraft. These accounts show the following forecasts for the period ended 31 March 1989:

Turnover	£358,681
Gross profit (per cent):	54.25
Trading profit before charging depreciation and bank and Diga interest:	£5,191
Bank interest	£5,400
Interest on Diga loan	£5,000
Depreciation	£35,264
Net loss	£40,473
Balance sheet deficiency	£226,036

F   A note of a meeting on 26 March 1989 records that the March sales had been below target, and that there had been a poor record in March in getting in some £9,700 of debts. The note also records a discussion of a proposal from Graham of a possible move to a brasserie-style operation, and a decision that Graham should obtain two valuations of the business.

     Soon after this, two events of some significance occurred. First, by a letter dated 13

G   April 1989, Mr Harris announced that he would oppose a renewal of the lease on the grounds that he wanted to occupy for his own purposes. The brothers, and Mrs Wood, interpreted this as no more than a negotiating ploy on his part. He was a well-known local landlord, in his late sixties, who was unlikely to have a genuine intention to trade from the premises himself. Nevertheless, his reluctance to negotiate the terms of a new lease presented an obvious obstacle to any attempt to market the premises. Secondly, in May 1989, it was decided that Graham should cease to be the manager at the end of May

H   and be replaced by a new manageress, Susan James. In the event, however, Susan James did not take over until 10 July, so that Graham with some reluctance continued in the post until 14 July.

     From 10 July onwards Ian immersed himself more thoroughly in the business. By late August, it is clear that he appreciated the desperate state of affairs in which the company found itself. Business was at what a contemporary minute (of 21 August) described as a 'drastic' level. The Inland Revenue had taken walking possession of the company's A chattels on 31 July. In despair at producing proper books of account, Ian had persuaded his parents to spend a fortnight in August writing up the books. Mrs Woods was by late August requiring weekly updates on business levels. Mr Harris continued to stone wall over negotiations for a new lease: the only strategy the company had, namely negotiating a new lease and then selling, could not be implemented while Mr Harris maintained his attitude. In the event the business traded on until late September when, following advice B from Mr Rose, the decision was taken to close it down.

Against this background, the Secretary of State seeks disqualification orders on a variety of grounds.

First, it is alleged that the Thomson brothers ought to have known from the outset of Diga's takeover that there was no reasonable prospect of WVR avoiding an insolvent liquidation, but nevertheless they allowed it to continue trading. This ground was not C pressed before me by counsel on behalf of the Secretary of State, and, in the light of Mr Thomson senior's evidence I reject it. It is, however, relevant to note that from 1987 it was or should have been apparent to the directors that the company's ability to pay its debts from its trade receipts was going to be a finely balanced affair unless the original strategy worked perfectly, and that there was no room for any complacency that the value of the business and the lease either then did, or would subsequently continue to, suffice to meet any deficiency should the company have to cease trading. In my judgment D the circumstances required that particular care and attention be paid by the directors to the possible consequences for trade creditors of the company continuing to pursue a strategy of trading its way out of loss.

Secondly, it is alleged that by February 1989 at the latest the respondents knew that the company should not continue to trade, but that they nevertheless allowed WVR to continue to incur liabilities. As to this, a distinction has to be drawn first between what E the directors knew and what they ought to have known, and, secondly, between each of the respondents. As Mr Rose recognised in his evidence, it is difficult to pinpoint precise dates at which the respondents knew or ought to have known of certain facts. It must also be borne in mind that management accounts were being produced in the absence of any audit having been done of the figures produced for the year ended 31 March 1988. I find that by the end of February 1989, the respondents believed that it was possible that the business might for the first time be achieving a situation of profitability, and that they F genuinely hoped that this possibility would be realised. They believed that, if profitability could be achieved in the coming year, the business would gradually be able to trade itself into a better position. In other words there were grounds for hoping that the original strategy might continue to be appropriate, and there were no grounds for supposing that a new lease would not be obtained when the current one expired at the end of 1990. Nevertheless, such grounds for hope as existed at the end of February 1989 provided G only a faint glow of light in an otherwise threatening sky. From the end of February onwards it is clear that the business was having increasing difficulties in paying its current liabilities. In March, possibly as a result of a misunderstanding either by WVR or the bank over the overdraft facility, the bank bounced two substantial cheques. In April further cheques were bounced. Creditors were constantly pressing Graham for payment, and decisions had to be made as to who was to be paid, when and in what order. Graham accepted in evidence that to some extent suppliers had to be strung along with excuses H about computer breakdowns. Stringing suppliers along was, he thought, partly the nature of the business.

By late March 1989, it was apparent that trading in March had been loss-making. A typewritten document dated 13 May, with manuscript annotations, gives some indications of the calculations then being made to pay accrued VAT and PAYE liabilities.

A   Two further pieces of evidence show the extent to which the business was trading on the credit of its suppliers in its final stages. First, Mr Rose produced an analysis of aged creditors. While criticisms can undoubtedly be made of this document, and it remained unexplained in a number of aspects by Mr Rose, I am satisfied that it shows that a substantial number of creditors had not had significant amounts of debt paid for six months prior to the liquidation. Mr Rose's own statement in re-examination that the document ages the debts from the date shown on it (23 April 1990) I reject as quite simply

B   mistaken. Secondly, trade creditors at the date of liquidation were some £98,559 as compared with the £49,661 given in the management accounts as at 28 February 1989. It is, of course, possible that those management accounts were wrong, and this was a hypothesis relied on in evidence by Ian. Given, however, the deficiencies in the company's audit procedures, those responsible had only themselves to blame if the management accounts gave a false picture. As I have indicated, they could, even if accurately reflecting

C   the position, have provided comfort only when read with the eye of faith. However, even allowing for the possibility that those accounts were inaccurate I am satisfied that during the period from the end of March onwards, both Graham and Ian should have become increasingly aware that the business was only being sustained by the patience of its creditors, and at their potential expense.

In my judgment a dispassionate analysis at any point thereafter would have led to the

D   conclusion that continued trading could only be justified if there was a real prospect of selling the business in the very near future. In the event no such sober analysis took place. Apart from making oral inquiry as to the value of the lease and business from a customer in the wine bar, Graham took no steps to obtain the valuations which the meeting on 26 March had called for. It appears from the manuscript notes on the document dated 13 May that the oral valuation had come up with a figure of between £250,000 and £350,000. In evidence Graham recalled a figure of £300,000. The document dated 13 May also

E   made the point, however, that Mr Harris was maintaining his intransigent attitude. No doubt for that reason, and because of the impending change of management, no active steps were taken to see whether the lease could in reality be marketed for the expected figure, or to look carefully at the extent to which the strategy of continued trading was simply increasing the amount of trade debt being incurred and which (absent a successful and early sale) would not be capable of being paid.

F   It was urged on behalf of the Secretary of State that Ian and Graham were deliberately gambling during the last few months of trading, and that their motive for doing so was to drive down the bank overdraft so as to reduce or eliminate their exposure under the indemnity they had given to Mrs Woods against her liability to the bank in excess of £112,000, and disregarding the possible consequences for trade creditors. In my judgment, however, they had no such conscious motive. I believe that what happened was the result of a combination of factors. Graham almost certainly ceased to manage

G   the business effectively during the period of ten weeks or so prior to his departure in mid-July. The business was to have been his livelihood and principal occupation. He had been used to being, and being seen as, a successful wine bar operator, and he found himself in a position where the business appeared to be failing and he had lost the confidence of his brothers as a manager. His ability to keep abreast of the paperwork (which had been the subject of much criticism earlier in the year) can hardly have improved in a situation in

H   which he was overworked and demoralised, and from which he was looking forward to an early release. The day of freedom in fact had to be postponed from the end of May to the middle of July. A consequence of this was, no doubt, that the full disastrousness of the current trading situation was not made apparent to Ian until, in his own words, he plunged into the business in mid-July. Ian then found, over a period of some weeks, just how dire the situation was. Given the precariousness of the company's business, and the long-standing dissatisfaction with Graham's conduct of it (and particularly his ability to

supply relevant financial information) Ian ought to have taken more vigorous steps at an   A
earlier date to make sure that he was in a position to assess the company's state of health.
Both brothers allowed themselves to think throughout this period that Mr Harris might
at any moment relent, and render a sale possible. The picture I have is not one of a
deliberate strategy to reduce the overdraft at expense of trade creditors and then to scuttle
the ship, but rather one of allowing the ship to drift. Had the brothers been trading with
personal liability, I doubt whether events would have taken quite the same course. There
would have been an earlier decision to cut their losses, and do the best deal possible with   B
Mr Harris.

In my judgment the way in which the business of the company was run from the end.
of March onwards was not the way in which such a business ought to have been run,
given the possible consequences for trade creditors. I find that both Ian and Graham
paid insufficient regard to the interests of creditors during this period. It was the
responsibility of both of them to make an early and informed decision on what would be   C
in the best interests of the company and its creditors. This did not happen. The financial
information about the business on which they were relying had never been subjected to
the scrutiny of audit; and, while they may have genuinely believed that they would be
able to sell the business and lease for £300,000 should the worst come to the worst, they
did not have reasonable grounds on which to base such a belief. It was the product of
wishful thinking. In coming to that conclusion I bear in mind that Mr Rose was later (in   D
October 1989) advised that the business and lease should be marketed by inviting offers
above £200,000 but that, absent a new lease, it could not be expected to fetch more than
£75,000. That advice clearly assumed that the £200,000 offer would only be achieved on
the basis of a new lease being negotiated, and that Mr Harris would probably expect a
share of any such premium.

Before considering the conduct of Mrs Woods, I will examine the other grounds put
forward by the Secretary of State.   E

The third allegation is that the respondents made improper use of the company's bank
account by issuing cheques which they knew or ought to have known would not be
honoured on presentation. I do not find this allegation proved. While cheques
undoubtedly were issued which bounced (sometimes more than once), I do not find it
proved that either Graham (in relation to the cheques issued in November 1988 and in
March and April 1989) or Ian (in relation to cheques issued following the cessation of   F
trading) knew or must be taken to have been in a position where he ought to have known
that those cheques would not be met on presentation. So far as the earlier ones were
concerned, it was primarily David's responsibility to monitor the bank overdraft.

So far as all were concerned, there were difficulties in knowing the exact state of
account because of the unpredictable timing of certain credits (in particular Amex and
Diners Club credits). So far as the final flurry of cheques were concerned, I think it   G
probable that the issuing of these cheques was in part the result of a misinterpretation by
Ian of what he was told by Mr Rose of the position of staff wages in a liquidation. At
any rate his action in issuing these cheques drives a further nail into the coffin of the
theory that there was a deliberate policy of driving down the overdraft.

The fourth allegation is that the respondents failed to co-operate in the liquidation.
This was an allegation made without the slightest foundation against Mrs Woods but
maintained by the Secretary of State until the close of Mr Rose's evidence when it was   H
abandoned. As against Ian and Graham, it was maintained throughout, but on grounds
which I find tenuous. In each case, information was given by the brother able to supply
it within a reasonable time of being asked. I reject this allegation.

The fifth allegation is that the respondents failed to ensure that accounts were prepared
and delivered for filing to the registrar of companies in accordance with s. 227, 241 and

A   242 of the *Companies Act* 1985. This is an allegation which relates solely to the accounts for the period ended 31 March 1988 which ought to have been filed by the end of January 1989. There is no denying the fact that these accounts never were delivered for filing. The question is how seriously I should view the lapse, and who was responsible for it. The reason for the failure lay in Auerbachs' unwillingness to act, which Ian first heard of in February 1989. Graham and David must have known of their complaints about not being paid at a much earlier date. Moreover it seems to me that all the directors ought at

B   a much earlier date have concerned themselves with the progress of the audit. However 'non-executive' a non-executive director may be there is nothing to stop him or her from showing an interest in the progress and timing of the statutorily required audit. In this case there were particularly strong reasons why all the directors should be interested in the results of an audit of the accounts of the year to 31 March 1988. Those accounts covered the first year of the Diga management, and were therefore based on the book-

C   keeping and recording systems instituted by the Thomsons in February 1987. The external audit provided the only objective check on the accuracy of the figures being produced by those systems, and on the basis of which the company was pursuing its precarious strategy. Without the verification of an audit, the merits of a continued pursuit of the original strategy could not be safely assessed. In the event, at least one of the directors, Ian, has concluded with hindsight that the management accounts produced in March 1989 cannot have been correct. The seriousness of a failure of the strategy has in

D   the event been felt by the £90,000-worth of trade creditors who have not been paid a penny in the liquidation. My conclusion is that this lapse, albeit a single one in the sense of relating to only one year's accounts, does form part of the pattern of carelessness to which I have referred in dealing with the second allegation and, if Ian's belief as to the inaccuracy of the 1989 management accounts is correct, directly contributed to it. I will consider Mrs Woods' position in relation to this later in this judgment.

E   The final allegation relates to the filing of annual returns. Again this allegation relates to only one lapse, and both Ian and Graham allege, and David accepts, that the fault was David's. Without in any way wishing to understate the importance which those who trade with the privilege of limited liability ought to attach to the obligations inherent in that privilege (an importance which has been emphasised on many occasions by this court and which has recently been the subject of forceful reiteration in the Court of Appeal (see *Re Swift 736 Ltd* [1993] BCC 312 at p. 315D–G per Nicholls V-C), I do not

F   think that on the facts of this particular case this lapse compels me to a finding of unfitness.

     I turn then to consider whether my findings in relation to the second and fifth allegations lead to the conclusion that either of them, Ian and Graham, is unfit to be concerned in the management of a company. I have found that each of them was careless in the final months of trading of the proper interests of WVR's creditors. In evidence

G   each brother sought to blame the other while seeking to exculpate himself, although Graham did admit to overwork having led him to be deficient in fulfilling accounting requirements. In relation to the material period and the material matters, however, the extent of each brother's responsibility qua director of the company seems to me to have been equal. Graham cannot excuse himself on the basis that his role was really that of a glorified employee, and Ian cannot excuse himself on the basis that Graham was being left in sole control of the business. As directors each had the same duties to see that the

H   accounts were prepared, audited and delivered for filing, and to ensure that the company did not trade to the prejudice of its creditors.

     In reaching my conclusions I have had regard to what seem to me to be some special factors which contributed to the ultimate debacle:

     (1) The economic climate in which the business plan was conceived and executed was one which, in retrospect, encouraged a degree of false optimism across a wide section of

the business community. It was also one which suffered from instabilities which were not easily predictable by the ordinary businessman. As an example of the latter, bank minimum lending rates rose from 7.5 per cent in May 1988 to 14 per cent in May 1989.

(2) The brothers' belief that the lease could be sold for some £300,000 was genuinely held. Their failure to obtain a formal valuation, which would have dispelled their illusions, was a commercial misjudgment. But in the heady days of the explosion of commercial property prices in Wimbledon Village High Street in 1988 and early 1989, it was an understandable misjudgment. Their belief that Mr Harris was merely bluffing when he refused to discuss a renewal and claimed to be intending to trade from the premises himself was probably justified. Again, however, they misjudged the effect of his continuing to maintain that attitude on their ability to market the existing lease.

(3) The failure to get to early grips with the deteriorating situation was not the result of innate or invincible incompetence on the part of either of them. The lack of management cohesion experienced in 1989 owed as much to a breakdown in the relationship between the two brothers as to anything else.

(4) Given some grounds for optimism as to trading prospects in early 1989, the nature of the business was such as to make it difficult to forecast whether a subsequent bad period of trading was a merely temporary phenomenon, or indicative of a deeper malaise. With hindsight it can be seen that the poor trading in March and April was the beginning of the death throes of the business. At the time it appeared to be no more than a seasonal down-turn which could be expected to reverse itself in the period up to and including the peak time of the Wimbledon fortnight. Furthermore, the picture which might otherwise have emerged more clearly was obscured by the management changes, themselves scheduled for the end of May but which had to be postponed to mid-July. The decision to put in a new manager at that stage demonstrates the genuineness of the belief that the business was still viable.

(5) Throughout the relevant trading history, WVR had available to it accountancy and business expertise to a degree unusual for such a small business. This was the result of the direct involvement in the business of David, a professional accountant, and the indirect involvement of the father. Neither dog barked as loudly or as early as might have been expected in the circumstances. Their mute presence was, however, perhaps a reason why professional advice was not sought earlier. As counsel for the Secretary of State observed, this might well have been a suitable case in which to have applied for an administration order.

(6) Neither brother prolonged the trading life of WVR with any view to personal advantage.

These factors mitigate, though they do not excuse, the deficiencies in the conduct of WVR to which I have referred. I have to decide in each case whether Ian's and Graham's acts and omissions were in 1988 and 1989 such as to demonstrate their unfitness now to be concerned in the management of a company. The Act requires me to consider whether the unfitness then displayed makes them unfit now to be so concerned: see *Re Bath Glass Ltd* (1988) 4 BCC 130 at p. 132 per Peter Gibson J. The law rightly exacts high standards of those who claim the privilege of trading with limited liability. Those standards are particularly appropriate where, as here, the adventure was fraught with risk from the outset. In my judgment the lapses from those standards in the case of both Ian and Graham demonstrated a failure to appreciate their responsibilities, and I have found that this failure did in the event damage trade creditors of the business. To that extent they may be said to have been shown to have been unfit to be concerned in the management of a company. It is not, however, every past impropriety which should lead to a conclusion that the director responsible is unfit. Having regard to what seem to me to have been the peculiar combination of family and commercial circumstances in which

A   they found themselves in relation to WVR, I find myself left with a significant measure of doubt as to whether the lapses properly attributable to either of them were sufficiently serious as to compel a finding that either is now unfit to be concerned in the management of a company. That doubt is sufficiently strong to make me conclude that the correct course is to resolve it in their favour.

I turn now to the position of Mrs Woods. This has given me some difficulty. Mrs

B   Woods played no role whatsoever as a director of WVR following the Diga takeover. The Thomsons appeared to her, as indeed they were, to be experienced in the relevant catering skills and to have available to them within their family all relevant accountancy and business skills. They were men of some personal worth. Her agreement with them was that they would be wholly responsible for the running of the business, she retaining a directorship simply as a means of being able to protect her own position as the unlimited guarantor of the company overdraft. In those circumstances, she neither asserted nor

C   accepted any wider responsibility. In taking that attitude, she seems to me wholly to have misconceived her duties as the director of a limited liability company. She seems to have been completely unaware of the wider responsibilities owed by her to the company and its creditors. This attitude (or lack of one) in relation to WVR certainly points in the direction of her being unfit to be concerned in the management of a company. I do not, however, think that the mere fact that she had this attitude drives me inexorably to the conclusion that she is so unfit. I must measure her actual responsibility in relation to the

D   allegations which I have found proved. Given the division of responsibilities on the board, while she must bear some responsibility for not having ascertained the state of the audit of the 1988 accounts, I have no doubt that Ian would have advised her after February 1989 that this matter was well in hand. Equally I have no doubt that until August 1989, the noises she had heard from Ian about the business were on the whole reassuring. I should add that her ability to take a more active interest was in any case

E   compromised at the material time by her own domestic pressures: she had an adolescent daughter and a husband with Parkinson's disease to care for. She alone of the directors has in the event suffered financially, having found herself at the end of the day liable to the bank in the sum of some £140,000. I would also add that the allegations made against her appear to have been made and maintained by Mr Rose in the wholly mistaken belief that she was occupied full-time at the restaurant as 'a meeter and greeter'. In all the circumstances, while her failure to appreciate that she had duties as a director beyond

F   those that she owed to herself was regrettable, and while I accept the argument that, had she appreciated the fact, events might have taken a different course, I do not find her misconduct in relation to WVR to have been so serious as to justify my finding her to be unfit to be concerned in the management of a company.

(*Order accordingly. Respondents' costs on standard basis*)

G   ───────────────

H

Re Unisoft Group Ltd (No. 2). A

Chancery Division (Companies Court).
Harman J.
Judgment delivered 8 June 1993.

> *Unfair prejudice petition – Points of claim ordered to be delivered – Petition*
> *amended – Amended points of claim to be delivered – Whether amended points of* B
> *claim should be struck out – Particularity of points of claim – Companies Act*
> *1985, s. 459.*

This was a motion by respondents to a petition under s. 459 of the Companies Act 1985
seeking to have amended points of claim supporting the petition struck out on grounds that
they did not show conduct of the affairs of or acts of the company and so did not show a
cause of action within O. 18, r. 19 or were otherwise in breach of that rule; the amendments
were also attacked for want of particularity. C

Held, striking out amendments:

1. Order 18, r. 12 which required particularity of pleadings did apply to points of claim
under a s. 459 petition. Various amendments would be struck out for want of particularity.

2. There was no way in which the acts of any one of several directors of a company in
complying with the directions of an outsider could constitute that outsider a shadow director D
of that company. Unless the whole of the board or at the very least a governing majority of
it were accustomed to act on the directions of an outsider such an outsider could not be a
shadow director. Further, there had to be more than one act and a course of conduct. The
allegation that 'H' was a shadow director was accordingly unsustainable.

3. The distinction between acts or conduct of the company and the act or conduct of a
shareholder in his private capacity had to be kept clear. The first type of act would found a
petition under s. 459; the second type of act would not. A number of paragraphs in the points E
of claim were about shareholders' activities and not about activities of the company. Upon
that basis they raised no cause of action within O. 18, r. 19 and were not proper to be
pleaded.

4. The complaints made in certain paragraphs were about the relationship of landlord
and tenant between 'SH Ltd' and the company. They were not about SH Ltd's position as a
member of the company. There could be exactly the same complaints between them if they F
were wholly unrelated companies. The allegations showed a course of conduct which was
not the conduct of the company's affairs which had caused prejudice to the member as a
member.

The following cases were referred to in the judgment:
Bradford Corp v Pickles [1895] AC 587.
Company No. 004475 of 1982, Re a [1983] Ch 178. G
Company No. 008699 of 1985, Re a (1986) 2 BCC 99,024.
Lundie Brothers Ltd, Re [1965] 1 WLR 1051.
North-West Transportation Co Ltd & Anor v Beatty (1887) 12 App Cas 589.

John Davies and Nicholas Cherryman (instructed by Pothecary & Barratt) for the
petitioner.

Michael Lyndon-Stanford QC and Catherine Roberts (instructed by Herbert Smith) H
for the respondents.

JUDGMENT

Harman J: This is a motion in a pending petition. That simple statement grossly
understates the unusual nature of the application.

A   The petition was presented by a contributory on 8 January 1991. It is based upon s. 459 of the *Companies Act* 1985; that is it alleges that 'the company's affairs are being or have been conducted in a manner which is unfairly prejudicial to the interests of its members generally or of some part of its members (including at least himself)'. Those words are, on the face of them, extraordinarily wide and general. They allow, on the face of them, every sort and kind of conduct which has taken place over an almost unlimited

B   – certainly upwards of 20 years – period of time in the management of a company's business to be dug up and gone over. The words are, however, limited by the reference to 'the company's affairs' in respect of which the conduct must be alleged.

     The section also enables a member to apply to the court on the ground that 'any actual or proposed act or omission of the company (including an act or omission on its behalf) is or would be so prejudicial'. Again the words are wide and anything that the company

C   does or fails to do can be relied upon. But wide as the category of acts may be it is necessary that the act or omission is done or left undone by the company itself or on its behalf. Thus voting at a general meeting, whether annual or extraordinary, may result in a resolution being passed or defeated. The resolution is, obviously, an act of the company notwithstanding that the votes which pass or defeat it are the votes of members which are their private rights which, on the longstanding authority of *North-West*

D   *Transportation Co Ltd & Anor v Beatty* (1887) 12 App Cas 589, can be exercised by members as they choose. The acts of the members themselves are not acts of the company nor are they part of the conduct of the affairs of the company and cannot found a petition under s. 459.

     Petitions under s. 459 have become notorious to the judges of this court – and I think also to the Bar – for their length, their unpredictability of management, and the enormous and appalling costs which are incurred upon them particularly by reason of the volume

E   of documents liable to be produced. By way of example on this petition there are before me upwards of thirty lever-arch files of documents. In those circumstances it befits the court, in my view, to be extremely careful to ensure that oppression is not caused to parties, respondents to such petitions or, indeed, petitioners upon such petitions, by allowing the parties to trawl through facts which have given rise to grievances but which are not relevant conduct within even the very wide words of the section.

F   The section requires there to have been conduct of the company's affairs, or an act or omission of the company, so one has to look and see that the activity complained of is an activity in the course of conduct of the company's affairs or is by the company, so that the petitioner can show that the affairs have been conducted in a manner prejudicial to the interests of the members. The requirement of prejudice means that the conduct must be shown to have done the members harm and I believe harm in a commercial

G   sense, not in a merely emotional sense. The further requirement that the prejudice is 'unfair' is a more uncertain but necessary thing to show, but before the fairness or unfairness of the conduct or act is considered 'prejudice' – that is harm or damage – must be shown. Those requirements set out the basic rules that the court must in my view be careful to insist upon to restrain this procedure from breaking all reasonable bounds.

H   This petition followed a routine and normal course in that it came before the registrar of the Companies Court and an order was made on 28 January 1991. That order directed that points of claim be served and filed by 11 February 1991. The registrar went on to direct points of defence by 25 February, reply, discovery and so forth. Such are conventional directions regularly given by the registrar on applications to him under the *Companies (Unfair Prejudice Applications) Proceedings Rules* 1986 (SI 1986/2000). The rules start off by providing, under r. 2.2, that:

'Except so far as inconsistent with the Act and these Rules, the Rules of the   A
Supreme Court and the practice of the High Court apply to proceedings under
Part XVII of the Act in the High Court . . .'

– which includes s. 459 petitions amongst others.

Mr Lyndon-Stanford specifically drew my attention – in my view rightly – to the
reference to the practice of the High Court and that is a point to be borne in mind; it is
also to be noticed that r. 5(b) provides that the court may give directions: B

'whether particulars of claim and defence are to be delivered, and generally as to
the procedure on the petition . . .'

It is, of course, a habitual practice, to my knowledge in this court for many years, under
s. 459 and its predecessors, that points of claim are ordered to be delivered rather than
the phrase in the rule 'particulars of claim'. But the words 'points of claim' were adopted
– and I suspect that I may have had something to do with that adoption as a regular   C
formulation – from actions in the Commercial Court. That is because there are so many
cases nowadays which are interchangeable between that court of the Queen's Bench
Division and this court and are regularly swapped between the divisions according to the
state of business.

Commercial Court actions are governed, of course, by O. 72. That provides specifically
by O. 72, r. 7 that the pleadings in an action in the Commercial List must be in the form   D
of points of claim or of defence, counterclaim etc., and must be as brief as possible. That
injunction has been one well in mind and the reference in directions upon s. 459 petitions
to points of claim has certainly been intended to be a reference to a document intended
to be a 'pleading' in the full sense of that word, to which all the Rules of the Supreme
Court as to pleadings, particularly O. 18, r. 12 and O. 18, r. 19, shall apply, and of which
requests for further and better particulars and so forth may be made and which must
state fact and not plead law and should be as brief as possible.   E

Mr Davies for the petitioner herein, whose petition is sought to be struck out, drew my
attention specifically to O. 18, r. 19(1), the striking-out rule, which provides that:

'The Court may at any stage of proceedings order to be struck out or amended any
pleading on the ground that–

     (a)   it discloses no reasonable cause of action . . .   F

     (b)   it is scandalous, frivolous or vexatious . . .

     (c)   it may prejudice, embarrass or delay the fair trial of the action; or

     (d)   it is otherwise an abuse of the process of the Court . . .'

–and, notably, O. 18, r. 19(3):

'This rule shall, so far as applicable, apply to an originating summons and a   G
petition as if the summons or petition, as the case may be, were a pleading.'

From that Mr Davies derived the proposition which is unanswerable, which I entirely
accept, that a petition is not a pleading. One cannot get further and better particulars of
a petition and a petition by itself cannot be dealt with under the ordinary rules of pleading
and is not intended to be in the form of an ordinary pleading. It is intended to be and
regularly is a more discursive and free-running document – in more ordinary daily   H
language rather than the precise dry averments of bare facts which a pleading proper
ought to contain.

From that, Mr Davies went on to say that O. 18, r. 12 had no application to a petition,
which is right, and that therefore O. 18, r. 12 which requires particularity could not apply
to points of claim under a petition under s. 459. I understand the argument. I admire its
ingenuity. I hope I may reject it with complete and total conviction, on the ground that

A
     if it be right it will reduce the practice of this court – which is very widely used – to a farce. It may be that the rules require that to be the conclusion. I refuse to reach that conclusion. In my judgment the attempt to use the phrase 'points of claim' was by reference to the Commercial Court rules where points of claim are defined as a pleading and the points of claim directed on this petition by the registrar were intended to be and will be treated by me as a pleading within the full rules of court, to which the whole practice of the High Court in relation to pleadings will apply.

B
     I understand that this is a new point and it may well be reviewed in some other place. It is, in my view, a complete contradiction of all good sense and practice if the court cannot direct pleadings on a petition under s. 459 without using the phrase 'statement of claim' which I suppose it could do under the r. 5(b) directions, which are allowed. To require such a formalistic view of the words 'points of claim', which are, to my mind, more apt for points under a petition than the words 'statement of claim' would be, would

C
be to take an attitude I will not adopt unless forced to do so. For that reason I reject Mr Davies' fundamental objection to a great many of Mr Lyndon-Stanford's points.

     Having said that, I turn back to the history of this petition in brief terms. An order for substantial security for costs was made on 14 October 1992, the question having been litigated in higher places as to whether there was any jurisdiction to make such an order (see [1994] BCC 11). The petition eventually came on for hearing, set down for I think

D
15–20 days on 21 April this year before me. On the second or third day of the hearing I was informed by counsel on both sides that the estimate of 15–20 days was in their view a serious underestimate and that three months was a more likely period. Such a change of estimate can do nothing but depress a judge to whom it is made, and probably also the parties.

     The hearing then continued with the opening of the petition by Mr Davies, labouring

E
under great difficulties but with considerable ability, for some eight or ten days at the least – I am not precisely sure of the number, nor does it matter. But on Tuesday, 11 May 1993, Mr Davies having come to the end of the reading of these formidable bundles of documents, or at least the end as he then saw it, applied to amend the petition. He introduced substantial new averments in the draft amendment. The respondents had not seen them in advance and asked me for time to consider the amendments so that they could see how to deal with them. I granted that time and the hearing resumed on

F
Wednesday, 12 May.

     Upon that day, Mr Davies for the petitioner had before me a full draft of the intended amended petition. He had no draft of amended points of claim, although the petition was, pursuant to the order of Mr Registrar Scott in January 1991, to be conducted by pleadings in the form of points of claim, etc. I took – I hope I may legitimately say with the encouragement of counsel, but I took and I am responsible for the decision – the view

G
that it was practical and sensible to try and get on with this case and see whether one could not get it towards some form of conclusion by limiting issues and defining points. I decided that I should deal there and then with the intended amendments to the petition and leave until later a further order about amendments to the points of claim, which plainly would be necessary. I now wonder whether that was, in fact, a sensible order to have made and whether I should not have said that in the circumstances, without a draft of amendments to the points of claim, I would not entertain any application to make any

H
amendments to the petition at all and thereby prevent the situation which has to some degree arisen now.

     However, I did not take that course. I made on 12 May an order which is in the file before me. I took the petition out of the list and put it back for the Michaelmas term, I gave leave to amend the petition in the form of a draft before me but without prejudice to an application to strike out to be made later, I ordered that unless amended points of

claim supporting the amended petition were delivered by 5 o'clock on Monday, 17 May,   A
the petition was to be struck out. I ordered a time for amended points of defence, I gave
various other directions and, in particular, under para. (6) of the order I said that the
respondents were to be at liberty to apply (a) in respect of costs of and occasioned by the
amendments to the petition and to the points of claim (that being a future amendment)
and how such costs would be paid, (b) for striking out the amended petition and the
amended points of claim, (c) for further security and (d) for issues of valuation to be
determined separately. I then reserved to myself further interlocutory applications. I gave   B
direction that if any application by motion was to be made this term, it should be made
by notice by Friday, 21 May.

On Monday, 17 May a document headed 'Amended points of claim' was delivered by
the petitioner to the respondent's solicitor. The amendments were substantial and were
in large parts lifted – and I use that word deliberately – from the amended petition into
the amended points of claim. I confess that that was not what I had envisaged or hoped   C
for – I had hoped for a much more pithy and short sentence definition of facts to be
alleged in the points of claim, but by itself that is a stylistic and not a fundamental
criticism.

The respondents' motion was launched on 21 May as permitted and it seeks, first, a
declaration that the petitioner had failed to comply with para. 3 of my order of 12 May
and that the petition had therefore been struck out – para. 3 required the amended points   D
of claim supporting the petition to be delivered in a short time.

Secondly, and alternatively, the motion seeks an order striking out the amended points
of claim and the amended petition for failure to comply with the order. That was upon
the footing that the automatic order nisi provision had not operated but that the amended
points of claim did not, as they were required to do, support the petition in themselves,
leading to an order to strike out upon that ground alone; and, thirdly in the further   E
alternative, that the amended points of claim and the amended petition be struck out on
the grounds in (a)–(d) of O. 18, r. 19 and under O. 18 r. 12 and under the inherent
jurisdiction.

I took the view fairly early during the hearing of this motion, which has occupied
several days, that the document produced by the petitioner within the relevant time was
a document proper to be called 'Amended points of claim' and did satisfy para. 3 of the
order and that, therefore, the petition had not been struck out under the automatic order   F
nisi which I made on 12 May. I took that view because, although the amended points of
claim were capable of and have been very extensively and severely criticised, yet nobody
could say that they were a pretence at a compliance with my order. The draft was a
serious attempt, even if the attempt may not have been wholly successful, to comply with
the order and the amended points of claim were bona fide and properly to be described
as points of claim which attempted to at the very least – intended to certainly – support   G
the petition, and on that ground, in my view, there is no automatic strike-out.

Further I took the view that the attack to be made upon the points of claim was better
made under para. 3 of the notice of motion, rather than under para. 2 of the notice of
motion, where Mr Lyndon-Stanford referred to my order having included the words
'supporting the petition' in reference to the points of claim which he said they failed to
do. To my mind it was cleaner and better to go back to the ordinary and familiar and
established rules of court under O. 18, r. 19 and O. 18, r. 12, than to rely upon the form   H
of my order. For that reason I will not strike out under para. 2 of the notice of motion.
However, the substantive, serious and, in parts, in my view, well-founded argument by
Mr Lyndon-Stanford arises under para. 3 of the notice of motion.

I shall start by making an observation which I believe to be founded upon a general,
long-standing and far-reaching practice of the court. I found it upon my own experience

A   as counsel before the courts from the years 1955–1982 when I had an extensive litigation practice (I hope I may properly say) and upon applications before me in court since November 1982. During those years I have conducted it must be hundreds and heard many other applications made for leave to amend a pleading. In my judgment it is the invariable practice of the court to require late amendments, a fortiori amendments sought during trial, to be completely and fully particularised in every respect when made, leaving no lacuna and no uncertainty of allegation.

B

    The reason is, in my belief, obvious. The point of pleadings is not, of course, to win a game of skill, although litigation such as this is conducted by skilled players, and thereby avoid informing the other side. The point of pleadings is to give warning to the other side of what is to be said against them, so that they may prepare themselves with documents and evidence to deal with those allegations. If parties to proceedings do not know the precise and detailed charges they are going to meet, they cannot fully and properly defend

C   themselves. That can lead to grave and serious injustice. In my belief pleadings are an essential instrument in the achievement of much greater ends than the objectives of players of games of skill, that is the achievement of substantial justice between parties. Notice I say 'substantial' justice – perfect justice is not, in my view, a thing attainable in human courts but only in a higher court.

    Thus I believe that it is vital, when parties are faced at a late stage during trial or

D   shortly before trial with new averments, that all proper particulars be given in the proposed amendment. That principle must be reinforced by the practical consideration – perhaps not quite so prevalent in this particular case, but prevalent in most – that there is no time to go round formulating a request for further and better particulars, receiving a refusal or an unsatisfactory answer, going back to the judge or master for an order and then considering the particulars and getting your material and evidence together. All that

E   elaborate procedure Mr Davies observed to me might be possible in this particular petition, since I have taken it out of the list until after 1 October.

    In my view that is not a proper answer to the general proposition. First, there is the time taken in getting counsel to formulate the request in detail in the course of a busy practice where there are other people in the queue who are entitled to have their business dealt with in proper turn. Secondly, there are difficulties in getting back before the court to get detailed answers. There are the difficulties inevitably raised by vacations – not only

F   that the court does not sit in the long vacation although many things are nowadays done in the long vacation which would never have been done in the old days – but the difficulty that solicitors, clients, witnesses all have holidays and that July, August and September are notoriously times when people are away and difficult to reach. In my view, Mr Davies' bland assertion that a request for further and better particulars where particulars are lacking in his amended points of claim could, in this case, make up for the deficiency

G   in particularity is not a proper or adequate answer. The general rule, I repeat, must be that any late amendment, a fortiori an amendment during trial, must be fully and completely particularised and if the pleader is to say 'so-and-so acted' he must say how, when and where so-and-so acted. Or if the pleader is to say that 'so-and-so intended something' then he must state every fact upon which it is intended to rely for the argument that so-and-so must have formed such an intent. In my view, unless particulars are so given injustice is almost certainly to be caused, probably to the defendant, possibly to the

H   plaintiff (or in this case respondent and petitioner). I therefore conclude that the ordinary rules and practice of the High Court apply to these amended points of claim as much as to any other pleading where leave is sought to amend late and that at this stage of the proceedings the amendments proposed must give all necessary particulars.

    Further, in my judgment, the initial observations I made as to the scope of s. 459 petitions and the obvious opportunities for alleging a whole series of ugly, unattractive

acts and saying that, as a result, the judge should infer that there has been conduct of the   A
affairs of the company unfairly prejudicial to someone, must be borne well in mind. I,
during the opening, expressed views from time to time about the conduct of various of
the individuals who have been engaged in or acting in relation to the history of this
company, judging by the letters and the documents they wrote. Many of the documents
and letters are, in my view, thoroughly unattractive and portray attitudes of mind which
I find utterly deplorable. Nonetheless, I have to go back and say, 'Do those events   B
constitute, as alleged in the points of claim, acts unfairly prejudicial to the petitioner in
the conduct of the affairs of this company or do they show acts of this company?'

The attack upon the amended points of claim thus falls into two parts. It falls into one
part where the original allegations can be attacked on the ground that they do not show
conduct in the affairs of or acts of this company and so do not show a cause of action
within O. 18, r. 19, or are otherwise in breach of that rule, and in the other part the
amendments can be attacked for want of particularity, simply upon that ground alone.   C
The attack really starts at para. 8 of the points of claim in the original pleading. The first
seven paragraphs are, I think, purely history and may or may not be central but do not
in themselves plead conduct of the company's affairs unfairly prejudicial to the petitioner.

Paragraph 8 alleges that the third to tenth respondents 'have allowed the authority of
the monitor to be exercised by Mr Hatch'. It alleges that Mr Hatch, together with Mr
Twigger, thereby came to gain control over the company and that that arose as a result   D
of the appointment of the monitor represented by Mr Hatch who came to have voting
control. The control was given de facto recognition – I think the pleader must have meant
de jure recognition rather than de facto but perhaps he did not know Latin very well –
when Mr Hatch was appointed a director and chairman of the company at a board
meeting on 12 July 1990. So far the allegation appears to be about control of the company
in the ordinary sense, that is shareholder control exercised at and through general,
whether annual or extraordinary, meetings. The points of claim then refer in para. 9 to a   E
supplemental subscription agreement and to an agreement whereby the petitioner was
bound to vote its A shares in the same way as the other A shares. That resulted in all the
A shareholders' votes being cast by Mr Hatch and with the addition of the votes of Mr
Twigger the A shareholders had voting control. Thus the paragraphs are all about
agreements between shareholders, such as are commonplace in this court, called
shareholders' agreements, and not about the ordinary conduct of the affairs of the   F
company or about acts or omissions of the company.

Paragraph 10 is purely factual and of no particular significance.

The original allegations were thus, at this stage, about control of the company and
further and better particulars were asked of that allegation and were given. It was asked
'What is meant by the phrase "gain control over the company"?'.

Regrettably the request did not ask at what date that allegation of gaining control was   G
said to have occurred. The answer was 'The phrase is used in its commonly understood
sense'. In my view, the commonly understood sense is voting control in general meeting,
giving control of the company by determining membership of the board, by authorising
the creation of shares and so forth. But the particulars go on to say, 'Mr Hatch
transformed the role of the monitor into that of controller of the board of the company'.
That is a pleading by way of particulars which, as I see it, departs wholly from para. 8   H
and 9 of the points of claim as drawn. It alleges control of the board but such is not
alleged in the pleading itself. That, in my view, is an improper form of pleading.

The further and better particulars go on to refer in para. 2 of the particulars (1) to
voting control of the company, which must mean voting control in general meeting and
not board control, (2) to the third to tenth respondents' votes, which can only be votes in

A   general meeting, and (3) references to the monitor and its contacts which have nothing to do with the matter at all.

By para. 6 of the particulars there is made a sudden allegation that Mr Hatch directed – how Mr Hatch directed or by what power or capacity is wholly unspecified – that fees should no longer be paid by the company to the petitioner, that he procured – again how is wholly unparticularised – the removal of Mr Bradley as company secretary, and that B   he (Mr Hatch) systematically undermined the relationship between Mr Saunderson, then the chairman of the company, and Mr Thomas, the chief executive of the company. The whole of these particulars appear to me to be a serious departure from the request and in no sense proper particulars of any of the allegations in the paragraphs of the points of claim themselves. The particulars seek to add new matter to the pleadings and simply, in my view, confuse matters.

C   The petition and points of claim go on to allege unfair exclusion of the petitioner, which is called Saunderson Holdings Ltd, a company controlled by Mr Saunderson, because of Mr Saunderson's personal involvement in the incorporation of the company. No attack was made upon those paragraphs by themselves. We come on to para. 15 which alleges the unfair removal of Mr Saunderson as a director, which was unfairly prejudicial to the petitioner.

D   There then appears a new para. 15A. Paragraph 15A, with all respect to the pleader, I find extremely unhappy and confusing. It refers to a 'scheme', more particularly described in new para. 22A and 22B of the amended points of claim. Those allege that the objective of that 'scheme' was the removal of Mr Saunderson as chairman and subsequently as a director of the company. The pleading alleges that Mr Hatch sought to influence Mr Thomas to act in a manner unfairly prejudicial to the petitioner's interest. Now, Mr Hatch's action in seeking to influence Mr Thomas cannot of itself be the conduct of the E   affairs of the company. Further, on the documents that Mr Davies for the petitioners has read to me in opening, it is clear that Mr Saunderson was never 'removed' as chairman of the company in any proper sense of the word removed. Mr Saunderson himself voted at a board meeting in favour of a new chairman being appointed, and agreed to cease to be chairman at midnight on 11 July 1990. No scheme or plan to remove him as chairman was needed since he agreed to cease to hold that office. In my judgment it cannot be proper to plead a fact contrary to the known and uncontested documentary evidence. F   The paragraph is in a wholly unsatisfactory form because it refers to the 'scheme' but then does so by reference to later paragraphs, to which I will now turn, para. 22A and 22B.

Paragraph 22A asserts that the scheme was a plan followed by Mr Hatch in relation to Mr Saunderson and Saunderson Holdings Ltd, the objective of which was to compel the petitioner to sell its shares. That can only be read as an assertion of a plan to make the G   petitioner sell its shares. When that plan was formed is not stated, with whom, if anybody, it was formed, or whether by Hatch alone is not stated and the motive for it is entirely unclear. The purpose, it seems, was to compel the petitioner to sell its shares – apparently quite generally, the petitioner must just sell its shares somehow to somebody. It then says:

> 'if to CMC' – that is a potential purchaser who appears in the picture later – 'at a H   substantial differential price, if to management, then at a much discounted price to the true market value thereof.'

Unhappily, the paragraph goes on by saying:

> 'The petitioner does not allege that the scheme followed any predetermined plan.'

So one has a plan which does not follow any predetermined plan which is an unhappy piece of English at the very lowest. The pleading asserts that Mr Hatch's actions were all

consistent with seeking the objective, and the objective is to compel the petitioner to sell   A
its shares.

The amended points of claim then refers in para. 15A to para. 22B, which asserts that
the scheme also produced an additional commercial benefit to Venture Link, that was
the company designated as the monitor, the issued capital of which was substantially in
the ownership of Mr Hatch and therefore a benefit to Venture Link will be beneficial to
Mr Hatch. The points of claim then aver that the commercial benefit to Mr Hatch was   B
damaging to the petitioner. There is no allegation of specific damage to the petitioner nor
of facts which would lead to an inference of damage. How that can hang together is
entirely unclear because, assuming there was a commission payable to Venture Link and
therefore beneficial to Mr Hatch, it does not follow for a moment that there is any
damage to the petitioner thereby. The price to be paid for shares is not affected by the
commission paid to the broker who effects the deal, unless it is suggested that the
purchaser paid the broker an inducement to accept a lower price for his vendor, which is   C
not this averment.

Thus the petitioner repeats para. 21A and avers that the conduct of Mr Hatch in
pursuing the scheme and towards Mr Thomas and so on, was in breach of his duty as a
director or shadow director of the company. The whole of that paragraph seems to me
utterly unsatisfactory.

Paragraphs 22A and 22B do not, in my view, justify inclusion by way of amendment   D
into points of claim at this stage of a trial. They do not do so because they are grossly
unparticularised in very material respects. They raise allegations which are wholly
inconsequential one upon another, such as, for example, that there was a plan but it was
not a predetermined plan and there was a commercial benefit to Mr Hatch which was,
for no stated reason, damaging to the petitioner, and they are almost impossible to plead
to. The new paragraphs contain embarrassing averments, which is also a ground under
O. 18, r. 19 for striking out and would be a ground for refusing an amendment, which is   E
what I must consider in dealing with para. 22B, because they assert payment of a
commission to Venture Link with no possible connection with the petitioner that I can
see, save the general assertion that it was damaging to the petitioner, wholly
unparticularised and wholly unsubstantiated. The paragraph contains allegations about
shadow directorships by repetition of para. 21A and from that raises a fiduciary duty
which must depend on there being a shadow directorship. If there be no shadow   F
directorship the whole of the second part of 22B must go for that reason alone.

Paragraph 21A asserts that the petitioner will aver that the conduct of Mr Hatch was
such that at all material times until the board meeting of 12 July 1990 he was a shadow
director within the meaning of s. 741(2) of the *Companies Act* 1985. The new pleading
goes on to allege, alternatively, without prejudice to the generality of the foregoing (that
must refer to the allegation 'at all material times'), that Mr Hatch became a shadow   G
director, by reason of the facts and matters pleaded, from 8 January 1990 or, in the
further alternative, from early May 1990. All those must turn on the averment that Mr
Hatch became a shadow director of the company from one or other of three different
dates.

In order to consider the propriety of that allegation, one must go back to s. 741 and
see what a shadow director is because the term as used in the pleading is expressly in the
defined sense of the Act and not in any other and more general sense, if there be such,   H
which I know not. Section 741 of the Act contains a definition in subs. (1) of 'Director'
and contains in subs. (2) the following provisions:

> 'In relation to a company, "shadow director" means a person in accordance with
> whose directions or instructions the directors of the company are accustomed to
> act.

A   However, a person is not deemed a shadow director by reason only that the directors act on advice given by him in a professional capacity.'

In my view, those words can only mean what Mr Lyndon-Stanford suggested, that the shadow director must be, in effect, the puppet master controlling the actions of the board. The directors must be (to use a different phrase) the 'cat's-paw' of the shadow director. They must be people who act on the directions or instructions of the shadow director as

B   a matter of regular practice. That last requirement follows from the reference in the subsection to the directors being 'accustomed to act'. That must refer to acts not on one individual occasion but over a period of time and as a regular course of conduct.

In my view, there can be no way in which the acts of any one of several directors of a company in complying with the directions of an outsider could constitute that outsider a shadow director of that company. Of course, if the board of the company be one person

C   only and that person is a 'cat's-paw' for an outsider, the outsider may be the shadow director of that company. But in a case such as this, with a multi-member board, unless the whole of the board or at the very least a governing majority of it – in my belief the whole, but I need not exclude a governing majority – are accustomed to act on the directions of an outsider such an outsider cannot be a shadow director. Further, there must be, as I say, more than one act and a course of conduct.

D   Here the averments alleging that Mr Hatch became a shadow director are primarily by reason of the facts and matters pleaded in para. 15A(i) from 8 January. Paragraph 15A(i) alleges an ugly, probably unnecessary and at the very least, grossly abusive letter, from Mr Hatch to Mr Thomas about Mr Saunderson. Why he thought it necessary to write in such terms passes my understanding. He described Mr Saunderson in terms which are extremely unpleasant and alleged that he was a lunatic, that is mentally unbalanced. It seems a remarkable assertion to make about a man in substantial commercial business.

E   How such a fact, for the letter is a fact, amounts to an allegation from which the court could infer that Mr Hatch was in command of the board and able to make four persons, including Mr Saunderson, or three if Mr Saunderson is excluded and a majority of the board is sufficient, dance to his call is entirely impossible to understand. The same letter offered Mr Thomas, the chief executive, the temporary chairmanship of the company but that does not make Mr Thomas Mr Hatch's cat's-paw since it does not allege for a

F   moment that Mr Thomas accepted the offer, and the other directors are wholly ignored. There were in fact at that time on the board of the company four persons – Mr Saunderson, the chairman, Mr Schlee, an associate (perhaps is the proper word) of Mr Saunderson, being a fellow shareholder in Saunderson Holdings Ltd, but a person of apparent integrity who acted regularly as a director, Mr Thomas, the chief executive, and Mr Twigger who is not mentioned in this paragraph. This averment concerning Mr Hatch's letter to Mr Thomas cannot in my view amount to any particulars on which an

G   allegation of shadow directorship could possibly be based.

The rest of the conduct supposed to have taken place at all material times is wholly unparticularised and therefore not permissible. In my judgment it is not legitimate in an amended pleading such as para. 21A(i) to allege conduct 'at all material times' but give no details whatever of the conduct. Thus there are no details from which shadow directorship could be inferred. The facts and matters pleaded in para. 29 from early May

H   are to do with an allegation that Mr Twigger's votes at general meeting were bought with company money. That, again, would be an improper act by the company if it were proved but would not, in my view, in any sense go to show that Mr Hatch was the shadow director of the company. In my view, the whole of para. 21A(i) is wholly unsustainable because it is grossly unparticularised, embarrassing and incapable of satisfying the statutory definition which it alleges. It follows that para. 21A(ii) falls because that starts by relying on Mr Hatch's capacity as shadow director, and if the capacity goes, the whole of the rest of the paragraph goes.

The difficulty, as I have found repeatedly with this pleading, is that one starts with one paragraph and is led to another, is then led to a third and then has to go back to the beginning. In my view, the true conclusion is that para. 15A is unmaintainable because unparticularised, embarrassing and not a proper form of pleading by way of amendment, and should be disallowed. The particulars given under it, (i)–(vi), fall with the substantial pleading and the whole of that part of the amended points of claim must be refused.

There then comes a cross-heading in the points of claim with which I am uncertain how to deal. It says 'Consequential lack of proper management'. I do not know whether this is intended to be an averment that there was in consequence of something a lack. If so it is grossly unparticularised and there is no way that anyone can properly deal with it now. There is then an allegation as to the suspension of Mr Schlee which is set out in para. 16 of the points of claim. Mr Schlee was removed by the board as a cheque signatory, suspended as managing director, but has refused to resign as a director. His dismissal was proposed but not achieved. He has been a minority shareholder – there is nothing in the rest of para. 16.

Paragraph 17 goes on to assert that Mr Lovell resigned from the post of president of the American subsidiary, four other senior employees also resigned, since (not 'in consequence of') Mr Saunderson's removal, and finally that the loss of key personnel is a result of severe lack of confidence – it does not say by whom – in the present management and coupled with the dismissal of Mr Schlee, it having been noted in the previous paragraph that Mr Schlee had not been dismissed. In my view, para. 16 and 17 are not properly contained in this pleading as an allegation of conduct within s. 459 of the Act because there is no substantive allegation that damage was done to the petitioner due to Mr Saunderson's removal from the board, or that these resignations by staff were directly consequential upon it. The pleading is self-inconsistent between para. 16 (no dismissal of Mr Schlee) and para. 17 (dismissal of Mr Schlee) and it is therefore not a proper pleading which should remain on the file, and I shall direct that it be struck out.

I then come on to the allegations about an attempted share sale. It is headed 'Prejudicial interference with CMC transaction'. The paragraph starts out 'Mr Hatch on behalf of the monitor' which is an unhappy start to an allegation about conduct of the affairs of the company. That the monitor was a party to the shareholders' agreement and had duties, rights, and powers under it is plain, and that those contractual rights could be exercised between shareholders without there being any form of unfair conduct of the company's business is plain to anyone. It is a familiar matter when new capital is brought into a private company for there to be shareholders' agreements giving powers to the new outside shareholders by contract with the present shareholders. If every such agreement is a ground for a petition under s. 459, the court will sink under the weight of them.

The averments go on and it becomes quite clear that the averments are all about a share sale agreement. A share sale was negotiated by Mr Saunderson and it appears on the face of it to have been a good and sensible share sale. Why Mr Hatch chose, as he apparently did, to frustrate it, passes my understanding and it seems in retrospect to have been singularly ill-advised and ill-considered by Mr Hatch. Nonetheless Mr Hatch, acting on behalf of Venture Link, was a representative of the A shareholders who appointed him under the monitoring agreement. Any dealing with the A shares plainly concerned Mr Hatch. Mr Saunderson was a shareholder controlling large blocks of ordinary shares. He negotiated with CMC for the sale of the shares and reached heads of agreement which are referred to in the pleading and incorporated by reference. When read those heads of agreement do not make the company a party and they are plainly to do with shareholders'

A   activities as such. The heads of agreement are, in my judgment, clearly concerned with shareholders' private rights over their shares and nothing whatever to do with s. 459 and the conduct of the affairs of the company.

It is important to remember that shareholders' rights to deal with or vote their shares are separate from the rights of the company as a corporate entity and shareholders' relationships with it. Shareholders are entitled to sell their shares, to vote their shares, to

B   take any course they like in general meeting without regard to any other person's rights or position. In my judgment the law is that a shareholder may act with malice in voting his shares against a particular resolution and there can be no objection to that, just as in *Bradford Corp v Pickles* [1895] AC 587 a landowner acted on his own land with malicious intent to harm his neighbour, but was not in breach of any legal obligation. Of course, if a trustee holds shares on trust, he may have obligations to his beneficiaries which cause him to exercise the rights attached to those shares in the interest of the beneficiaries, but

C   that is nothing whatever to do with an individual's position as a shareholder and his relationship with his co-shareholders.

In my judgment, it is vitally important to hold that shareholders' disputes concerning dealings with their shares are not the same as unfair conduct of the company's business. Shareholders must be kept distinct from the company so far as their private position as shareholders is concerned.

D   It is of course obvious that a company may act or conduct itself in a manner affecting a shareholder's rights in respect of his shares, for example the board may refuse to sanction a transfer of shares for improper reasons. The action of the board is conduct of the affairs of the company and so, if damage is alleged, may raise the ground of 'unfair' prejudice, and a petition under s. 459 may be presented to the court. Further, a shareholder by exercising his own private right to vote his shares may cause the company to act, by the passing of some resolution in general meeting, in a matter alleged to be

E   unfairly prejudicial to some members. Again it is not the act of the shareholder in voting that will found a petition but the result of that act if it produces action, or inaction, by the company. In my judgment the vital distinction between acts or conduct of the company and the act or conduct of the shareholder in his private capacity must be kept clear. The first type of act will found a petition under s. 459; the second type of act will not.

F   It is only when a shareholder is affected qua member of the company by the company's action which causes damage that s. 459 comes into operation. There is a clear and important distinction, in my judgment, to be drawn between actions by shareholders affecting other shareholders directly and actions by the company affecting shareholders. The whole of these paragraphs in the points of claim, right on to para. 23, are all, in my view, about shareholders' activities and are none, in my view, about activities of the

G   company. Upon that basis they raise no cause of action within O. 18, r. 19(a) and they are not proper to be pleaded.

There are then para. 24 in the original and 24A in the pleading by amendment. Paragraph 24 alleges that Mr Hatch on behalf of the monitor has refused permission to seek out possible purchasers. Such an averment can have no place in a s. 459 petition in my judgment. It is a pure shareholder activity, pursuant to a contractual right negotiated outside the articles of the company. Nothing was done by the board or by any officer of

H   the company. In my view this is not a matter which can be maintained in this petition.

Paragraph 24A incorporates by reference a board report dated 31 January 1991. That, in fact, is post-petition and, of course, on classic rules of practice, averments about activities post the inception of originating proceedings cannot properly be brought in. But more seriously than that, the paragraph depends upon an assertion that a document refers to discussions for the acquisition of shares. When the document is referred to, as is

proper, since it is incorporated by reference, there was no mention of any such   A
discussions. There was reference to a consideration of a merger of part of the operations
of the company. Paragraph 24A does not allege that these negotiations were improperly
conducted or improperly refused for motives that were other than commercial motives.
There is an averment that the directors, or two of them, should have informed the
petitioner of the interests of the parties. That seems to me an impossible averment to
make. This was a matter plainly within the charge of the board in the conduct of the day-
to-day business of the company and in no sense to do with the relationship of the   B
company to its members. The averment that it was a breach of fiduciary duty is one
which, in my view, is impossible to maintain upon the facts alleged. I hold that there is
no proper cause of action here alleged that could arise within s. 459 and that in the
circumstances it is wrong to allow an amendment to include that averment.

There are then paragraphs about excessive payments to Mr Thomas and Mr Twigger.
Paragraphs 25, 26 and 27 are in themselves not objected to as they stand. The amendment   C
at the end of para. 26 is of no substantial importance and can be left alone.

Paragraph 27A is not, in my judgment, objectionable. However, para. 27B is
objectionable because it refers to para. 15A which I have already held should be struck
out. Paragraph 27C is attacked by Mr Lyndon-Stanford. It is attacked as being
embarrassing because it adds in, in para. 27C(ii) an allegation about the scheme, which it
will be remembered was defined as being a plan but not a plan, which included the   D
removal of Mr Saunderson as chairman when Mr Saunderson had agreed that he would
give up that office. No such averment appears in the petition and therefore it cannot
properly be pleaded in the points of claim under the decision of Plowman J in *Re Lundie
Brothers Ltd* [1965] 1 WLR 1051 at p. 1058E–F.

The paragraph also refers to the removal of Mr Saunderson as a director of the
company and the appointment to the board of Mr Hatch. The appointment to the board   E
of Mr Hatch was by virtue of the powers of the A shareholders under the monitoring
agreement, which they were contractually entitled to exercise, and which they did, in fact,
exercise as is agreed upon the documents properly referable to upon this matter. It must
be embarrassing for an averment flatly contradictory of the documentary evidence to
remain upon the file.

In my view there are also very gross wants of particularity in this part of the amended
pleading. In para. 27C(i) there is an averment that a payment was made without any   F
consideration being given by Mr Thomas. It is quite clear from the documents which are
incorporated by reference, that the payment purported to be in consideration of Mr
Thomas agreeing to continue in service beyond the expiry of his service contract. It is
also clear that the service contract did expire but that Mr Thomas continued to serve the
company. It may be – and Mr Lyndon-Stanford accepted – that if there were no proper
consideration by the board of the scale of award to Mr Thomas as against a proper   G
inducement causing him to remain, that that could be an act of the company causing
improper prejudice to the petitioner. But to allege that there was no consideration is an
allegation which raises an argument of law and is plainly not maintainable on these facts.
It should not remain on the file.

It seems to me in the end that the only way to deal with these averments is to strike
them out. I am led to that decision by a compound of reasons within the O. 18, r. 19
provisions, ending with the inherent jurisdiction of the court to control abuse of process   H
and, in my view, this set of paragraphs do come to that.

The next paragraph is para. 28 which is, in itself, not attacked, and the amendment at
the end of para. 28 depends upon the following paragraphs. Paragraph 29 asserts that a
payment was made to Mr Twigger as a reward to vote in the manner in which he did.
The averment includes an allegation that Mr Twigger had agreed to act in concert with

A   Mr Hatch and Mr Thomas, to assist Mr Hatch in implementing the scheme. There had heretofore been, so far as I know, no assertion that Mr Thomas was assisting Mr Hatch in implementing the scheme in general terms and the allegation that Mr Twigger had agreed to act in concert is wholly and unwarrantably unparticularised. If Mr Twigger is said to have been agreeing to act in concert with Mr Hatch, some particulars must surely be given, failing which, at this stage of an action, it must not be permitted to stand. In particular in para. 29A there is an averment that Mr Twigger had been given an assurance that he would not be made a defendant to a claim by the respondents on warranties. At the same time as the amendments were being considered the solicitor instructing Mr Davies and acting for the petitioner swore an affidavit in para. 2(iv) of which he asserts that he is not in a position to aver any such agreement. It must be embarrassing and, as Mr Lyndon-Stanford put it, overreaching to make an averment which, upon oath, the solicitor conducting the litigation says he cannot properly make. I accept that Mr Warren is entirely right and proper in what he says, but that must mean that the pleading is wrong and improper and should not be allowed to stand.

In the result, para. 29 in my view, in its amendments, is objectionable. Its original part is not objectionable but is totally unimportant and immaterial by itself and para. 29A is objectionable upon the ground that it is overreaching, embarrassing and unparticularised. In my view, the correct thing to do in those circumstances is to strike out the whole of para. 29 and 29A as an abuse of the process.

There follow para. 30 and 31 – the chapter headed 'Unfairly using the company to influence your petitioner's bankers'. This is attacked as disclosing no cause of action within s. 459. The allegation is that Mr Hatch, exercising the authority of the monitor, wrote to the bankers with whom the petitioner had its accounts. The letter was odd – in my view quite unnecessary and irresponsible for Mr Hatch to have written – and one which I deplore totally. Nonetheless, it does not seem to me that the writing of this letter can in any way possibly be an act in the conduct of the company's business, or by the company, nor is there any allegation that the disgraceful (as I would call it) letter from Mr Hatch to the bankers in any way damaged either the petitioner or Mr Saunderson. Mr Davies observed to me that a letter like that lying on the file might in the future damage the petitioner. I quite agree, it might. The allegation that it did so damage the petitioner is not there and I believe at the present time cannot be made in the light of correspondence. But whether an allegation of a risk of future damage could be made or could not be made it is, in fact, not made and there is thus neither prejudice alleged nor an act by the company nor in the conduct of the company's business. Those para. 30 and 31 in my judgment disclose no cause of action within s. 459.

Paragraphs 32–36 are all about the failure to pay rental charges from the company to the petitioner and to pay management charges. In my view, these are not matters which affect the petitioner qua member of the company. The decision of Lord Grantchester QC in *Re a Company No. 004475 of 1982* [1983] Ch 178, particularly at p. 189D–F, is entirely relevant and in my view a correct view of the law. The complaints made in these paragraphs are about the relationship of landlord and tenant and the relationship of service provider and service user between Saunderson Holdings Ltd and the company. They are not, in any sense, about Saunderson Holdings Ltd's position as a member of the company. There could be exactly the same complaints between them if they were wholly unrelated, in Companies Act terms, companies. The allegations show a course of conduct which is curious, it may be objectionable, but it is not activities in the conduct of the company's business which have caused prejudice to the member qua member. They are decisions by the company in respect of its tenancies.

The criticism of Lord Grantchester's decision in a case called *Re a Company No. 008699 of 1985* (1986) 2 BCC 99,024 by Hoffmann J, does not, in my judgment, address the point which Lord Grantchester makes at the passage I cite and, in my judgment, Hoffmann J had no intention of dissenting on that point, which seems to me unquestionably good law and which stands.

I therefore hold that the whole of para. 32–36 should be struck out as disclosing no cause of action because not affecting the petitioner as a member and, in addition, in para. 35 of the points of claim there are a string of additional amounts, so called, totalling £123,000, none of which appear in the petition at all. Those matters must go on the *Re Lundie Brothers* principle, which I have already cited, apart from any other matter.

Paragraphs 37, 38 and 39 are all about the removal of the company from the premises of the petitioner. They include averments, which I have criticised and I am sorry I remain of the view I should criticise, such as 'the petitioner believes that', which plainly should not appear in points of claim which should allege facts and not matters of belief. But, apart from that, they assert that the relocation of the offices of the company was motivated by a wish to inflict financial harm upon the petitioner and that the relocation has cost the company an unnecessary sum and depleted (the pleading says 'diluted' but that cannot be the right word) the company's assets. If the company's assets can be shown to have been depleted by activities motivated by a wish to inflict financial harm upon the petitioner, that could plainly be (a) conduct of the company's affairs, (b) prejudicial to the petitioner and (c) probably unfairly prejudicial to the petitioner. Those paragraphs, therefore, in my view, do raise a claim which can and should remain upon the file.

Paragraphs 40 and 41 are somewhat inconsequential. In my view, given the draconian remedy of striking out, although I regard them as thoroughly unhelpful to anybody, I do not think that I ought to take the draconian step of striking them out of the petition, although I cannot see that if they are proved – if they can be proved – they will advance the petitioner very far. In my view, there is nothing that I should touch in those.

Paragraph 41A is, on the other hand, in my view, seriously objectionable. Firstly, it is post-petition, and so not proper to be litigated on this petition; secondly, it alleges that actions, some of which are in the Queen's Bench and one in this division, were founded upon unjustifiable grounds. That must amount to an assertion that the actions ought to have been struck out as improperly brought for some reason within the rules, but they have not been so struck out and no application to strike out has been made. To attempt to litigate in these proceedings the justifiability or not of the pleaded proceedings can only be an abuse of process as being double litigation upon the same point.

Thirdly, the allegations are seriously and, indeed, grossly unparticularised in very late amendments and, fourthly, they are not averments, as to para. 41A(iii), in the petition at all. Upon all those grounds they amount, in my view, to an abuse of process or an embarrassing set of pleadings and the whole of para. 41A should be struck out.

Paragraphs 42 and 43 are plainly proper paragraphs and can properly remain.

I think I have now dealt with all the paragraphs in the points of claim, save para. 8 and 9, which I referred to long ago. Those paragraphs do seem to me to be entirely concerned with voting control of the company by members at general meeting acting as shareholders. It seems to me, as I have said, of great importance to maintain the distinction between acts of shareholders in general meeting in conduct of their individual rights as shareholders, and the conduct of the company's business. That being so, it seems to me, it is wrong to allow para. 8 and 9 to remain, since they contain no averments which could properly come within s. 459 and they should also be struck out on the ground that they disclose no cause of action.

(*Order accordingly*)

Re Macro (Ipswich) Ltd & Anor.

Chancery Division (Companies Court).
Arden J.
Judgment delivered 16 November 1993 and 25 April 1994.

Unfair prejudice petition – Minority shareholders complained of mismanagement – Respondents applied to strike out certain allegations – Valuation of shares for buy-out order – Companies Act 1985, s. 459–461.

These were petitions under s. 459 of the Companies Act 1985 in respect of two companies (and an associated action and counterclaim). There was also a motion to strike out passages in the petitions as disclosing no cause of action.

The companies were substantial landlords of residential property and garages. The principal relief sought in the action was a declaration that the majority shareholder, 'T', held shares (which gave him control) on trust for the plaintiffs/petitioners. (The counterclaim by the majority shareholder sought a declaration that agreements entered into in May 1993 between the plaintiffs had triggered pre-emption provisions in the companies' articles of association.) The petitions under s. 459 of the Companies Act 1985 were based on T's conduct (as sole director) of the affairs of the companies and they sought an order requiring T to buy the plaintiffs' shares or vice versa.

T sought to strike out allegations in the petitions that there was an agreement for him to restore control to the petitioners.

Held, dismissing the motion to strike out, dismissing the action, giving judgment for the defendant on the counterclaim and ordering the majority shareholder to acquire the minority's shares:

1. T's failure to transfer his shares in accordance with the alleged arrangement was not an act or omission of the company. That was an arrangement he made personally and not as agent for the company. (Re Unisoft Group Ltd (No. 2) [1994] BCC 766 followed.)

2. However on the wording of s. 459 it was open to the court to consider the position of the person who was actually conducting the affairs of the company, i.e. T. On that basis it was open to the petitioners to argue that the conduct of the company's affairs by T as sole director was, following the date on which he should have implemented the alleged assurances, unfairly prejudicial to them. The interests of the petitioners for the purposes of s. 459 were capable of including an expectation on their part that they would acquire voting control upon implementation of the alleged assurances and that such an expectation was of a kind justiciable under s. 459.

3. The plaintiffs' claims in the action failed on the facts.

4. The pre-emption article imposed an obligation to serve a sale notice (as defined) on a 'member desiring to sell a share'. In the context, the relevant desire was to transfer a share. The article applied to the petitioners who had executed transfers for their shares. There was nothing further for them to do. They had done more than merely sell the beneficial interest in the shares. They had agreed also to sell the legal title to their shares and provided forms of transfer executed by them. They had to serve sale notices under the pre-emption article, but had no right to be offered each other's shares. They had waived their rights under the pre-emption article.

5. Based on the findings of fact, the companies had suffered prejudice in consequence of various failures of management. All the matters were within the responsibility of the companies' managing agents but they were attributable to lack of effective supervision by T on behalf of the companies. This conduct of the companies' affairs by T was prejudicial in a financial sense to the companies, and therefore also prejudicial to the interests of the holders of its shares. The specific acts of mismanagement by the managing agents which T failed to

prevent or rectify were sufficiently significant and serious to justify intervention by the court   A
under s. 461.

6. The court rejected a valuation method which aimed to find the fair value of the minority
shareholding by reference to net asset value and a market valuation was inappropriate
because the transaction resulting from the order of the court was not in the open market.
The approach adopted involved ascertaining the value per share of the minority
shareholdings in the companies using a gross dividend yield basis, (A); ascertaining the net   B
asset values per share of each company and deducting ten per cent for lack of total control,
(B); then deducting (A) from (B) to ascertain the value of control, (C). To find the fair value
of the minority shareholdings, (C) should be divided between the controlling and minority
shareholders; this was done on a 35:65 basis (i.e. the minority getting 65 per cent).

7. So far as concerned the loss suffered by the companies as a result of prejudice which
the petitioners had alleged and proved, the court could order an inquiry, but preferred to fix
a sum.   C

The following cases were referred to in the judgment on the striking-out application:

Dyson v A-G [1911] 1 KB 410.
Elgindata Ltd, Re [1991] BCLC 959.
Hubbuck & Sons Ltd v Wilkinson, Heywood & Clark Ltd [1899] 1 QB 86.
Unisoft Group Ltd, Re (No. 2) [1994] BCC 766.   D

The following cases were referred to in the judgment on the petitions:

Bird Precision Bellows Ltd, Re (1985) 1 BCC 99,467; [1986] 1 Ch 658.
Ebrahimi v Westbourne Galleries Ltd [1973] AC 360.
Elgindata Ltd, Re [1991] BCLC 959.
Harmer (H R) Ltd, Re [1959] 1 WLR 62.
Lyle & Scott Ltd v Scott's Trustees [1959] AC 763.
Safeguard Industrial Investments Ltd v National Westminster Bank Ltd & Anor [1982] 1   E
WLR 589.
Sprange v Lee [1908] 1 Ch 424.
Tett v Phoenix Property and Investment Co Ltd & Ors (1986) 2 BCC 99,140.
Thomas v H W Thomas Ltd (1984) 2 ACLC 610.

Michael Driscoll QC and Timothy Harry (instructed by Penningtons) for the
petitioners.   F

J Owen Rhys and Gregory J S Hill (instructed by Graham & Oldham) for the
respondents.

JUDGMENT ON STRIKING-OUT APPLICATION

Arden J: This is a motion to strike out passages in the petition under s. 459 of the
Companies Act 1985 against Earliba Finance Co Ltd ('the company') as disclosing no   G
cause of action. There is also before the court an application for leave to make further
amendments to the petition. Since it is submitted that the amendments to the petition
disclose no cause of action under s. 459, the matter has effectively been argued as if the
new allegations appeared in the petition. For the purposes of this application, the
allegations in the petition and the proposed amendments must be assumed to be true.
My ruling on this matter will apply (with necessary modifications) to the petition against   H
Macro (Ipswich) Ltd which has been consolidated with the petition against the company.

The principles which apply on an application to strike out under O. 18, r. 19(1) are
well established. It is only in 'plain and obvious cases' that an order striking out a claim
can be made (see per Lindley MR in *Hubbuck & Sons Ltd v Wilkinson, Heywood & Clark
Ltd* [1899] 1 QB 86 at p. 91). A party is not to be 'driven from the judgment seat' except
where the claim is obviously bad or almost incontestably bad (per Fletcher Moulton LJ

A   in *Dyson v A-G* [1911] 1 KB 410 at p. 419). Order 18, r. 19(1) applies to a petition as if it were a pleading (O. 18, r. 19(3)). The material parts of the petition, including para. 27A as proposed to be inserted by amendment, are as follows:

> '14. Mr Macro senior and Mr Thompson senior acquired Earliba in about 1962 with the mutual intention and understanding that they and their respective families would each own one half of the company. Mr Macro senior and Mr Thompson
>
> B   senior each became directors of Earliba, and they each had one share in Earliba.
>
> 15. Mr Macro senior and Mr Thompson senior on a number of occasions from 1964 onwards orally declared to members of their respective families that the shares in Earliba were held for the benefit of their families and that after the deaths of Mr Macro senior and Mr Thompson senior and their then wives the shares would pass to their respective children so that the children of each family owned one half of the company.
>
> C   . . .
>
> 17. In 1964, Mr Macro senior and Mr Thompson senior acting as aforesaid similarly caused the issued share capital in Earliba to be increased to 100 shares of £1 each, and, as in the case of Macro, the shares in Earliba to be issued amongst members of Mr Macro senior's family and members of Mr Thompson senior's
>
> D   family in such a way as to ensure (i) that Mr Macro senior and Mr Thompson senior did not have controlling interests and (ii) that each family (that is to say Mr Macro senior's family on the one hand and Mr Thompson senior's family on the other) had an equal number of shares in Earliba. Accordingly of the 100 issued shares, 20 were held by Mr Macro senior, 12 by Mrs Macro senior, nine by Ian Macro, and nine by Neil Macro. The balance of 50 shares were held as to 20 shares by Mr Thompson senior, 12 by Mrs Thompson senior and as to nine shares each
>
> E   by his sons John and Julian Thompson.
>
> 18. The object of the changes described above was both to achieve an estate duty saving and to ensure that both companies remained in the ownership of the two families with each family owning one half of each company, and with the shares passing on the death of a member of one generation to the members of the next generation. Accordingly with the same object and as part of the same arrangement, then orally agreed between Mr Macro senior and Mr Thompson senior, as that
>
> F   under which the changes in share ownership were made:
>
> 18.1 Mr Macro senior and Mrs Macro senior made wills leaving their shares in Macro and in Earliba to their sons Ian and Neil Macro, and provided for the devolution of the office of permanent director to their sons;
>
> 18.2 Mr Thompson senior and Mrs Thompson senior made wills leaving their shares in Macro and in Earliba to their sons John and Julian Thompson, and
>
> G   provided for the devolution of the office of permanent director to their sons;
>
> 18.3 the articles of association of both companies were altered so as to ensure that shares were transferred only to the issue (or brother) of the deceased member; and
>
> 18.4 Ian Macro and John Thompson were invited orally by Mr Macro senior and Mr Thompson senior to become directors of Macro but in the event it was agreed that neither should be appointed directors if both could not be and neither was
>
> H   then appointed because Ian Macro was then advised that the directorship was not compatible with the terms of his employment with Barclays Bank Ltd.
>
> 19. On 11 March 1965, Mrs Thompson senior died. Shortly before her death, pursuant to the arrangement pleaded in para. 18 above and on the oral instructions of Mr Thompson senior, Mrs Thompson senior transferred her shares in Macro and Earliba to John and Julian Thompson.

20. In 1969 Mr Thompson senior requested the other shareholders in Macro and   A
Earliba to agree to a new arrangement in relation to the shares in Macro and
Earliba which would give him temporary control of both companies. In order to
persuade the petitioners and John Thompson to agree to this new arrangement,
Mr Thompson senior orally assured them that the only reason for the new
arrangement was because (as he claimed) the companies were not financially sound
and that once they were financially sound he, Mr Thompson senior, would ensure
that the shareholdings in the companies were divided equally between the two   B
families, and that, after the deaths of Mr Thompson senior and Mr and Mrs
Macro senior, the shares would be vested in John and Julian Thompson as to 50
per cent and in Ian and Neil Macro as to the remaining 50 per cent and that in the
meantime he, Mr Thompson senior, would hold the shares held by him in the
companies in trust to give effect to the arrangement pleaded to in para. 16 and 18
above.   C

. . .

21. Persuaded by those assurances and acting upon them the petitioners and John
Thompson agreed to the new arrangement of shares namely in the case of Macro
a new issue of 601 shares made to Mr Thompson senior giving him 701 shares out
of 1401 issued shares, and in the case of Earliba an increase in its authorised share
capital and a new issue of 61 shares made to Mr Thompson senior giving him 81   D
shares out of 161 issued shares.

22. Each of the shareholders in Macro and Earliba believed at the time when they
agreed to the new arrangement because of the assurances given as pleaded by Mr
Thompson senior that the transfer of control of both companies to Mr Thompson
senior would be temporary only and that when the companies were on a sound
financial footing the shareholdings in the companies would be restored to the same   E
ownership as envisaged by the arrangement pleaded to in para. 16–18 above.

23. On a number of occasions since 1969 Mr Thompson senior has further assured
the petitioners and John Thompson that he would abide by the assurances which
he had given in 1969 as hereinbefore pleaded and indeed that he would transfer to
them his shares in Macro and Earliba once the companies were in a sound financial
position, and more recently that he would do so when he had reached the age of   F
80 (which he reached in 1990).

24. Notwithstanding all the assurances given (as hereinbefore pleaded) and that
Macro and Earliba have been in a sound financial position for at least 4 years, Mr
Thompson senior has not taken or indicated that he is willing to take any step to
ensure that the shares in the companies are held equally by the two families or that
on his death his shares in the companies will pass in such a way as will give effect
to the arrangement pleaded in para. 16–18 above.   G

. . .

26. By letter dated 14 March 1991 solicitors acting for the petitioners and John
Thompson called upon Mr Thompson senior to give effect to the assurances which
he had given and to the arrangement pleaded in para. 16–18 above, but Mr
Thompson senior has not done so nor indicated that he would do so.   H

27. In the premises Mr Thompson senior has conducted and continues to conduct
and will conduct the affairs of Macro and Earliba in a manner which is unfairly
prejudicial to the interest of the petitioners in that he has not taken any step nor
does he intend to take any step to give effect to the assurances hereinbefore pleaded
and to transfer to the petitioners the shares necessary to give effect to the
arrangement pleaded in para. 16–18 above.

A   27A. Further or alternatively:

27A(1) Mr Thompson senior required voting control in 1969 in order to enable him to continue to manage the businesses of Macro and Earliba without the need to obtain the approval of or consult with the other shareholders;

27A(2) by assuring as hereinbefore pleaded the other shareholders that he would give up voting control when the companies were financially sound Mr Thompson

B   senior meant and was understood by the other shareholders to mean that he would give up his right to manage the businesses of Macro and Earliba without the need to obtain such approval or to consult with them;

27A(3) because Mr Thompson senior has not taken any such step and has not reduced (whether by the transfer of shares or the issue of new shares) the proportions of his own shareholdings in Macro and Earliba to the total issued

C   share capital of those companies, to the proportions borne by them to the total issued share capital of those companies prior to the 1969 issue of shares hereinbefore pleaded, namely to 12.5 per cent and 20 per cent respectively (i) Mr Thompson senior has not only deprived the other shareholders of the shareholding interests in those companies which they expected to have (as hereinbefore pleaded) but also deprived them of the right (which they also expected to have) to participate in if not determine the management of the business of the companies and (ii) at the

D   same time Mr Thompson senior has been able to continue to manage those businesses without the need to seek the approval of or consult with the other shareholders; and

27A(4) accordingly the conduct of the affairs of each of Macro and Earliba has been and is being and will continue to be conducted in a manner unfairly prejudicial to the interests of the other shareholders in those companies in that

E   those businesses are being managed in a manner contrary to the expectation of those other shareholders.

. . .

7. Mr Thompson senior's disregard for the interests and wishes of the minority shareholders

36. As already pleaded, Mr Thompson senior refuses to countenance the

F   appointment of any of the petitioners as additional directors of Macro and Earliba, notwithstanding that they are, by experience, qualification and age, well suited to act as directors.

. . .

The petitioners therefore pray as follows:

(1) that Mr Thompson senior be ordered to transfer 17 shares in Earliba to each

G   of John Thompson and Julian Thompson, seven shares in Earliba to each of Ian and Neil Macro, and one share to all four of the three petitioners and John Thompson and to execute a deed of trust in respect of his remaining 32 shares in Earliba under which he has a life interest in those shares and after his death those shares vest in the petitioners equally;

(2) alternatively to (1), that such order be made so as to ensure that Mr

H   Thompson senior gives effect to the assurances pleaded in so far as they relate to Earliba; . . .'

Section 459(1) of the *Companies Act* 1985 provides:

'A member of a company may apply to the court by petition for an order under this Part on the ground that the company's affairs are being or have been conducted in a manner which is unfairly prejudicial to the interests of its members

generally or of some part of its members (including at least himself) or that any
actual or proposed act or omission of the company (including an act or omission
on its behalf) is or would be so prejudicial.'

Section 461(1) and (2) of the *Companies Act* 1985 provide:

'(1) If the court is satisfied that a petition under this Part is well founded, it may
make such order as it thinks fit for giving relief in respect of the matters complained
of.

(2) Without prejudice to the generality of subsection (1), the court's order may–

    (a) regulate the conduct of the company's affairs in the future,

    (b) require the company to refrain from doing or continuing an act complained
        of by the petitioner or to do an act which the petitioner has complained it
        has omitted to do,

    (c) authorise civil proceedings to be brought in the name and on behalf of the
        company by such person or persons and on such terms as the court may
        direct,

    (d) provide for the purchase of the shares of any members of the company by
        other members or by the company itself and, in the case of a purchase by
        the company itself, the reduction of the company's capital accordingly.'

Mr Driscoll made the following submissions:

(1)   In this case, ownership and management went hand in hand. Voting control carries
        with it control of management. Therefore voting control meant the right to
        participate in management in this case.

(2)   By reason of the pleaded assurances, the petitioners had a legitimate expectation
        that voting control/management control would be restored to them. The interests
        of a member for the purposes of s. 459 include legitimate expectations which he
        has: see per Warner J in *Re Elgindata Ltd* [1991] BCLC 959 at p. 985a–d.

(3)   There can be unfairly prejudicial conduct of a company's affairs as a result of an
        agreement between shareholders where the agreement is translated into the actual
        running of the company.

Mr Rhys made the following submissions:

(1)   The petitioners have remedies in contract, trust or estoppel if their allegations are
        well-founded. Section 459 is available only where no other remedy is available.

(2)   Until the proposed para. 27A was formulated, it was no part of the petitioners'
        case that they had any right to participate in the management of the company.

(3)   The petitioners' legitimate expectation was at most that at some future date they
        would obtain control of the company. Participation in management is simply a
        consequence of having that control.

(4)   The decision of Harman J in *Re Unisoft Ltd (No. 2)* [1994] BCC 766 should be
        applied. In that case, the judge struck out certain parts of amended points of claim
        in s. 459 proceedings. Although the relevant parts of the points of claim are not set
        out in the judgment, it appears that the allegations included an allegation that a
        person appointed to act as a 'monitor' under a shareholders' agreement had acted
        in a manner which the petitioners who were parties to that agreement alleged to be
        unfairly prejudicial to them. The company was not a party to the agreement.

On the question whether the activities of the respondents in relation to the
shareholders' agreements were within s. 459, Harman J held (at p. 777C):

'In my judgment, it is vitally important to hold that shareholders' disputes

A   concerning dealings with their shares are not the same as unfair conduct of the company's business. Shareholders must be kept distinct from the company so far as their private position as shareholders is concerned.

It is of course obvious that a company may act or conduct itself in a manner affecting a shareholder's rights in respect of his shares, for example the board may refuse to sanction a transfer of shares for improper reasons. The action of

B   the board is conduct of the affairs of the company and so, if damage is alleged, may raise the ground of 'unfair' prejudice, and a petition under s. 459 may be presented to the court. Further, a shareholder by exercising his own private right to vote his shares may cause the company to act, by the passing of some resolution in general meeting, in a matter alleged to be unfairly prejudicial to some members. Again it is not the act of the shareholder in voting that will found a petition but the result of that act if it produces action, or inaction, by

C   the company. In my judgment the vital distinction between acts or conduct of the company and the acts or conduct of the shareholder in his private capacity must be kept clear. The first type of act will found a petition under s. 459; the second type of act will not.'

(5)   A company is not bound by any trust on which its shares may be held: see s. 360 of the *Companies Act* 1985.

D   With regard to *Unisoft*, Mr Driscoll's submission was that the decision in that case was distinguishable. The present case was one of a family-owned company with a clear and obvious link between voting control and management. Mr Driscoll submitted that the affairs of the company were being conducted in a manner prejudicial to the interests of the petitioners in this case because they were being managed by a person who is only able to manage the company's business because he has gone back on a promise to give up control.

E   I agree with Mr Driscoll that Mr Rhys' first submission should not be accepted. It would involve reading words into s. 459. His second submission is rather more a point for argument than one available on a strike-out application. Submission (5) is right but is only valid in so far as the company is being asked to recognise a trust.

That leaves Mr Rhys' submissions (3) and (4). There is much force in (3). All the petitioners' complaints (on this part of their case) stem from the failure of Mr Thompson

F   to implement the alleged arrangement. This is an arrangement which he made personally and not as agent for the company.

On *Unisoft*, I agree with Mr Driscoll that the decision in that case concerns the activities of shareholders under a share agreement. It does not (as far as I can tell) deal with the conduct of the company's affairs as a consequence of those activities. It was the activities under the share agreement which the judge found were outside s. 459.

G   With the assistance of the reasoning in *Unisoft* and applying the words of s. 459, I have come to the conclusion that Mr Thompson's failure to transfer his shares in accordance with the alleged arrangement was not an act or omission of the company. Had the matter stopped there I would have had grave doubt whether this part of the petition stood any chance of success in law. However the jurisdiction under s. 459 also arises when the company's affairs 'are being or have been conducted in a manner which is unfairly

H   prejudicial' to the interests of the petitioner. The fact that these words appear in the intransitive make it arguable that it is open to the court to consider the position of the person who is actually conducting the affairs of the company and to ask whether the conduct of the company's affairs by that person is unfairly prejudicial to the interests of the petitioners. On the basis of this distinction, I consider that Mr Driscoll's submission (3) is arguable. I therefore hold that it is open to the petitioners to argue that the conduct of the company's affairs by Mr Thompson (its sole director) was, following the date on

which he should have implemented the alleged assurances, unfairly prejudicial to the   A
petitioners as contended by them. What the petitioners contend is that since that date
they have, in consequence of Mr Thompson's alleged wrongful act, been deprived of the
opportunity of securing representation on the board of the company.

I further consider that the interests of the petitioners for the purposes of s. 459 are
capable of including an expectation on their part that they would acquire voting control
upon implementation of the alleged assurances (see Mr Driscoll's submission (2)) and   B
that such an expectation is capable of being of a kind justiciable under s. 459. On this
basis it is unnecessary for me to deal with Mr Driscoll's submission (1). Whether there
was such an expectation and whether it was of the relevant kind, and whether Mr
Thompson conducted the affairs of the company in a manner prejudicial to that
expectation (or other relevant interests of the petitioners) cannot be determined at this
stage.

I therefore dismiss the motion to strike out.   C

As to the proposed amendment (para. 27A), it follows from this ruling that what the
court will be concerned with in this part of the case, if the petitioners show a relevant
legitimate expectation, will be the conduct of the affairs of the company by Mr Thompson
following his failure to implement the alleged arrangements. Accordingly, of the actions
by Mr Thompson pleaded in the proposed para. 27A(3), it is only that pleaded in para.
27A(3)(ii) which as at present advised I consider to be within s. 459 but that is enough to   D
persuade me that I should allow the amendment.

I should add that at this stage I have not heard full argument on the circumstances
which have to be shown in this case to exist for there to be a legitimate expectation of a
kind justiciable under s. 459. Accordingly I express no view on that matter.

(Motion to strike out dismissed)
                                                                                         E
JUDGMENT ON PETITIONS
INDEX

1. Introduction

These proceedings concern two companies, Macro (Ipswich) Ltd and Earliba Finance
Co Ltd, to which I will refer as 'Macro' and 'Earliba' respectively. The proceedings
consist of an action, in which there is a counterclaim, and a petition against each company
under s. 459 of the *Companies Act* 1985. The principal relief in the action is a declaration
that Albert Henry Victor Thompson, to whom I shall refer as Mr Thompson, holds 526
of the 1,401 ordinary shares of £1 each in Macro and 49 of the 161 ordinary shares of £1

A each in Earliba presently registered in his name on trust for the plaintiffs/petitioners ('the plaintiffs') and in addition for Mr John Thompson, in specified proportions. The plaintiffs are Mr Julian Thompson, Mr Ian Macro and Mr Neil Macro. For ease I will refer to the plaintiffs as respectively Julian, Ian and Neil and to Mr John Thompson as John. The counterclaim, which is brought by Mr Thompson, seeks a declaration that the provisions of the articles of association of Macro and Earliba, which confer rights of pre-emption on transfer, have been triggered by agreements entered into in May 1993

B between the plaintiffs. The petitions under s. 459 of the *Companies Act* 1985 are based on the conduct by Mr Thompson (as sole director) of the affairs of the companies and they seek inter alia an order requiring Mr Thompson to buy the plaintiffs' shares or vice-versa. My findings of fact are below.

 John was originally one of the plaintiffs/petitioners in these proceedings but on 11 October 1993 he was given leave to discontinue the proceedings. The defendants/

C respondents ('the defendants') are Mr Thompson, Macro and Earliba. Mr Rhys and Mr Hill have appeared for all the defendants but I have been informed that no additional costs are thereby being incurred by the companies.

2. The companies and the shareholders

 2.1 Macro and Earliba were incorporated on 31 December 1945 and 26 April 1960

D respectively. The following table, adapted from a table provided by the plaintiffs' expert accountant, Mr Ingram, sets out the movements in shareholdings.

Movements in shareholdings (all numbers of £1 ordinary shares)

MACRO

	1. 1948*	2. 1962	3. 1965	4. 1969	5. 1987		6. Proposed Redistribution
Mr Thompson	100	100	100	701	701	(50.04%)	175
Mrs Thompson		100					
John Thompson		100	150	150	150		308**
Julian Thompson (P)		100	150	150	150		306
Mr Macro	100	100	100	100		(49.06%)	
Mrs Macro		100	100	100			
Ian Macro (P)		100	100	100	200		306
Neil Macro (P)		100	100	100	200		306
TOTALS	200	800	800	1401	1401		1401

EARLIBA

	1. 1960#	2. 1964	3. 1965	4. 1969	5. 1987		6. Proposed Redistribution
Mr Thompson	1	20	20	81	81	(50.31%)	32
Mrs Thompson		12					
John Thompson		9	15	15	15		33**
Julian Thompson (P)		9	15	15	15		32
Mr Macro	1	20	20	20		(49.69%)	
Mrs Macro		12	12	12			
Ian Macro (P)		9	9	9	25		32
Neil Macro (P)		9	9	9	25		32
TOTALS	2	100	100	161	161		161

P= Plaintiff/Petitioner.

* = First allotment.

** = Two Macro shares and one Earliba share to be held jointly with Julian Thompson and Ian and Neil Macro.

\# = After transfers by original holders.

1965: Mrs Thompson transferred shares to her two sons shortly before her death. Mrs Thompson was the first wife of Mr Thompson.

1969: Additional shares allotted to Mr Thompson giving him control.

1987: Mr Macro died in 1983 and Mrs Macro in 1987 and in each case their shares were transferred to their sons.

Column 6 shows the effect of the transfers sought in the action.

2.2 John and Julian are the sons of Mr and Mrs Thompson. Mrs Macro was the late wife of the late Mr Macro and their sons are Ian and Neil.

2.3 *Business*

The current business of both companies is that of letting residential properties and garages principally in Ipswich. Neither company has, or has had since 1987, any borrowings. Originally Macro was a building company. Macro acquired land for investment some of which it in due course sold to Earliba for development and retention or sale. Macro now has 88 residential properties and 22 garages. Earliba now has 150 residential properties and about 70 garages. With the exception of the sale by Earliba of some building land in its financial year ended 31 March 1986, there has been little change in the composition of the companies' property portfolios since 1969. The portfolios are now very valuable, but the increase in their value from 1969 to the present day is due to the effects of inflation and the retention of investments, not to any programme of development carried out by the companies nor yet from the purchase or sale of properties.

2.4 *Financial information.*

The following is relevant financial information extracted from the published accounts of Macro and Earliba for the last ten years.

EARLIBA

EARLIBA	1983	1984	1985	1986	1987	1988	1989	1990	1991	1992	1993
Net assets	49,273	64,912	78,506	144,880	193,916	244,763	265,933	301,101	380,722	442,449	556,189
Borrowings	214,812	190,043	157,712	19,181	8,077	—	—	—	—	—	—
Cash	—	—	—	—	—	10,499	7,829	10,179	197,637	251,082	292,516
Rents receivable	101,376	112,255	121,283	129,445	139,227	147,572	165,415	201,705	241,705	263,022	295,389
Managing agents' fees & (in some years) expenses	11,604	11,196	12,159	14,968	21,653	22,108	25,413	29,446	86,355*	138,070*	90,366*
Repairs/property maintenance	48,043	47,263	60,206	93,417	36,515	34,816	55,599	34,660			
Net profit [loss] for the year before tax	6,856	22,396	19,420	94,819**	69,135	79,081	59,205	97,637	158,912	113,463	191,005

(Note: * = No breakdown of this figure appears in the published accounts
         ** = Includes a profit received on the sale of land of £99,848)

MACRO

MACRO	1993	1992	1991	1990	1989	1988	1987	1986	1985	1984	1983
Net assets	278,205	213,842	155,459	91,804	50,271	23,958	(10,912)	681	30,548	36,745	31,656
Borrowing	—	—	—	—	—	—	—	4,372	4,219	8,477	15,434
Cash	167,758	116,312	59,986	10,316	7,732	9,094	4,634	—	—	—	—
Rents receivable	153,392	147,376	132,980	111,531	81,684	67,763	58,286	54,011	46,169	41,776	35,801
Managing agent's fees & (in some years) expenses	68,224*	68,762*	35,221*	12,230	8,337	6,678	5,818	5,322	5,264	4,803	4,134
Repairs/property maintenance				28,946	45,525	24,108	64,619	80,261	44,576	30,283	28,704
Net profit [loss] for the year before tax	97,109	90,883	102,269	64,766	28,156	36,804	(11,593)	(29,867)	(6,198)	36,745	31,656

(Note: * = No breakdown of this figure appears in the published accounts)

A   2.5   *Principal provisions of the companies' articles*

      2.5.1   Under Macro's articles adopted in 1964 and amended in the same year:

(i)   Unless otherwise determined by the company in general meetings, shares must be offered to the members before being allotted to non-members.

(ii)   With certain exceptions, shares must be offered to existing members before being sold to non-members, thus giving members a right of pre-emption (see further art. 7 in para. 2.5.3 below).

B

(iii)   All directors must hold one qualification share.

(iv)   Mr Thompson and Mr Macro were appointed permanent directors entitled to hold office for life.

(v)   A permanent director may by deed or will appoint a new permanent director in his place. The appointment is not subject to the approval of the other permanent directors or anyone else. The relevant article is the same in both companies. In the case of Macro it is art. 13 which is in these terms:

C

> '13(A) A permanent director shall have power, from time to time, by deed or by will or codicil, to appoint any one person as a permanent director in his place, such appointment taking effect upon the death or resignation of the permanent director making the appointment.

D

> (B) If a permanent director shall die whilst a member of the company, his executors or administrators shall have power to appoint a permanent director where there is no person appointed by the deceased permanent director under para. (A) hereof.'

(vi)   The chairman has no casting vote.

E   (vii)   Directors may vote at board meetings on contracts or arrangements in which they are interested.

(viii)   Unless otherwise determined by the company in general meeting, the minimum number of directors is two.

      2.5.2   As from 1964 Earliba's articles contained the same provisions.

      2.5.3   With respect to pre-emption, the relevant articles are (in the case of Macro)
F   art. 7 (as amended) and (in the case of Earliba) art. 13 (as amended). They are in the same form and accordingly I will set out only the material provisions of art. 7 of Macro (as amended):

> '7(A) Upon the death of any member any share held by such deceased member may in due course of administration be transferred to his or her legal personal representatives or by such legal personal representatives to the issue or brothers of
G   such deceased member and shares standing in the name of legal personal representatives may be transferred to the trustees from time to time of the will or estate of any deceased member, but in so far as such legal personal representatives or such trustees of the will or estate as aforesaid are required under the applicable trusts to transfer any share to or hold any share in trust for any person other than a person by this paragraph hereinbefore authorised to be a transferee, such trustees or legal personal representatives shall be deemed to have served a sale notice under
H   the provisions of para. (B) hereof.

> (B) A share shall not be transferred otherwise than as provided in para. (A) of this article unless it first be offered to the members at a fair value to be fixed by the company's auditors. Any member desiring to sell a share (hereinafter referred to as a 'retiring member') shall give notice thereof in writing to the company (hereinafter referred to as a 'sale notice') constituting the company his agent for

the purpose of such sale. No sale notice shall be withdrawn without the directors' sanction. The directors shall offer any share comprised in a sale notice to the existing members, and if within 28 days after the sale notice has been given a purchasing member is found, such purchasing member shall be bound to complete the purchase within seven days. Notice of the finding of the purchasing member shall be given to the retiring member, who shall be bound on payment of the fair value to transfer the share to the purchasing member. If the retiring member fails to complete the transfer, the directors may authorise some person to transfer the share to the purchasing member and may receive the purchase money and register the purchasing member as holder of the share, issuing him a certificate therefor. The retiring member shall deliver up his certificate and shall thereupon be paid the purchase money. If within 28 days after the sale notice has been given the directors shall not find a purchasing member for the share and give notice accordingly, or if through no default of the retiring member the purchase is not duly completed, the retiring member may at any time within six months after the sale notice was given, but subject to reg. 3 of Table A, Pt. II, sell such share to any person and at any price.

(C) No share shall be issued or transferred to any infant, bankrupt or person of unsound mind.

(D) Any direction (by way of renunciation, nomination or otherwise) by a member entitled to an allotment of shares, to the effect that such shares or any of them be allotted or issued to some person other than himself, shall for the purposes of reg. 3 of Table A, Pt. II, be deemed to be a transfer, and the directors shall accordingly be entitled to decline to register such person as the holder thereof except where he is a person to whom a transfer of shares might be made by the member pursuant to para. (A) of this article.'

2.6 *Auditors*

Brearey & Co, accountants and auditors, were auditors of the companies from about 1965 to 1985. Mr D K Brearey handled the companies' affairs. Thereafter Ford du Cane & Co, chartered accountants, were appointed as auditors of the companies and the affairs of the companies were handled by Mr J E Bullin FCA. In about July 1991, Ford du Cane & Co resigned and Fisk & Co, certified accountants, became, and remain, the auditors of the companies. According to Mr Thompson, Ford du Cane resigned because Mr Bullin did not fulfil the companies' requirements. 'We were at loggerheads', he added.

3. Witnesses

3.1 The following witnesses gave evidence:

Witnesses of fact

Called by the plaintiffs	*Called by the defendants*
Julian	Mr Thompson
Ian	Gary Richard Farley
Neil	Arthur Jackson
Colin Robert Holmes	David Kenneth Brearey
William Charles Studd	Graham Martell
Cyril Wyard	Marjorie June Woolterton
Bessie Hessey	Mary Rose Holden
Peter George Bumphrey	John Thompson Winlow
John Samuel Howard	Frances Doreen Claxton
Terence Parfitt	John Ling
	Ada Collins

Expert witnesses

Called by the plaintiffs	*Called by the defendants*
Peter Wells	Thomas Morton Balch
(chartered quantity surveyor)	(chartered surveyor)
Peter Woods	Graham Clive Pooley
(architectural technician)	(chartered quantity surveyor)
Richard Brunt	Robert Driver
(chartered surveyor)	(certified accountant)
Hugh James Law ARICS	John Mullett CA
Timothy W Ingram CA	D J Wass FRICS

3.2 John did not give evidence.

3.3 Julian was a conscientious and sensitive witness and exhibited no enmity towards his father. However I was not satisfied that his recollection of past events was totally sound, although he convinced me that he was a man of integrity and not given to invention of past events. Mr Thompson was confident in his answers; he has a powerful personality and considerable stamina. On many issues I accept his evidence, but on some matters his answers were unconvincing. Ian and Neil were careful and straightforward witnesses, but obviously they could give evidence on fewer matters than Julian or Mr Thompson. Neil was also a conscientious witness. He has had a career in horticulture and latterly as a commercial fisherman. His knowledge of the mechanics of share ownership and company administration was less than that of Julian or Ian whose careers have been in property and banking respectively.

3.4 Neither Ian nor Neil demonstrated any personal animosity to Mr Thompson. This was in striking contrast to some of the background in the case and led me to the conclusion that it was unlikely to be the case that any of the plaintiffs had conducted themselves towards Mr Thompson personally in a manner of which he could complain.

3.5 Mr Thompson's achievements are considerable. His father died when he was a young boy and he has made his own way in life. He is now 83 years old. I have already mentioned the value of the companies. However Mr Thompson's own evidence shows that in his personal relationships he has not had similar success. He experienced disagreements with his first wife and her parents, Mr and Mrs Macro, Ian and Neil and to a much greater extent John and Julian. He is uninhibited in his criticisms of his sons. Mr Thompson is a patriarchal figure. He refers to himself as the provider for all, and he has clearly done much for the purely financial well-being of both families. The implicit suggestion however in his emphasis on this is that those who benefited from his success have failed to demonstrate to him sufficient respect or gratitude. He feels that, because of his generosity and success, he can direct and criticise.

3.6. I have already referred to the fact that I found some parts of Mr Thompson's evidence unconvincing. For example, in his witness statement signed before there emerged in these proceedings allegations as to Mr Wyard's improper activities, of which Mr Thompson then knew, Mr Thompson described Mr Wyard as a 'faithful servant'. There was no indication in that statement of the matters which Mr Thompson discovered about him after he left and to which I refer later in this judgment. The explanation that Mr Thompson was referring to his opinion of him before he left is unsatisfactory. In a later statement Mr Thompson said how badly he felt he had been let down by Mr Wyard.

3.7 Mr Wyard, formerly general manager of Thompsons, gave evidence and indeed was recalled as a witness when leave to call other evidence was given in the course of the trial. In view of his admitted dishonesty he has an obvious motive in implicating Mr Thompson in his improper activities. In the circumstances I concluded that where there was a conflict of evidence I could give little weight to that of Mr Wyard. His evidence was on occasions not frank.

3.8 Mr Farley, currently general manager of Thompsons, had by his own admission
been involved as an employee of Thompsons in Mr Wyard's dishonesty. I accept the
explanation that he, like others, became involved because he was misled by Mr Wyard.
At the time, he was under Mr Wyard's direction and he was at a relatively early stage in
his career. Mr Farley is now about 29 years old and he has been with Thompsons since
finishing his formal education. He joined Thompsons in September 1982. Mr Farley is
now overall manager of Thompsons with a staff of about ten. On financial matters, Mr
Farley's evidence tended to be imprecise.

4. Events up to 1990

4.1 *Early history*

Mr Thompson, now sole director of Macro and Earliba, has throughout his life had
property or property related businesses. Before the Second World War he had a building
business and he set up an estate agency called Thompsons. He came into contact with
Mr Macro in the early part of his career and in 1936 his sister married Mr Macro. Mr
Thompson when a child made a promise to his dying father that he would look after his
sister and mother. Subsequently Mr Thompson married Mrs Thompson. On 30 April
1941, Mr Thompson made a will in which, after making specific bequests of personal
property, he left the remainder of his estate including the estate agency and building
business to be held on trust for life in four shares, one each for his wife, his mother, his
sister and Mr Macro. The reversion was to go to his children and to those of Mr Macro.
The relationship between Mr Macro and Mr Thompson was sufficiently close and
trusting for Mr Thompson to appoint Mr Macro to act as his attorney in conduct of and
management of his affairs during 1941–1945 when Mr Thompson served in the army
although this is partially explained by the fact that Mr Macro's health was such that it
was unlikely he would be called up. Mr Thompson complained of mismanagement (and
worse) in his absence but these complaints have to be seen in context. They did not
prevent Mr Thompson from setting up Macro, or acquiring Earliba, with Mr Macro.

In 1942 John and Ian were born. In 1947 Julian and Neil were born.

On 31 December 1945 Macro was incorporated. The two subscribers were Mr Macro,
who was described as a builder, and Mr Thompson, who was described as an estate agent
and auctioneer. The articles registered on incorporation name both Mr Macro and Mr
Thompson as the first directors. There was a share qualification of 100 shares. Mr
Thompson suggests in his evidence that Mr Macro was a subscriber only because there
needed to be two of them. But Mr Macro's involvement was clearly intended to be
substantial. At the first meeting of directors he became secretary at a salary of £5 per
week which exceeded that earned by a carpenter in those days. He also drew a salary for
his services and he gave his name to the company (Mr Thompson suggests that this was
because he had found an association with a building business embarrassing in the past).
On the other hand, Mr Thompson did not draw a salary. He acted as permanent
chairman and paid for the 200 shares issued on incorporation. Mr Thompson's evidence
was:

> 'We both knew it was my company. He was my front man. I took all the trading
> and investment decisions with reference to Macro. He had a directorship as my
> way of looking after my sister and because I needed someone else to form the
> company with and he needed shares to be a director . . . On the other hand I would
> not describe him as a nominee.'

The business of Macro was building houses. Mr Thompson provided some materials
from his earlier operations to enable it to start up.

On 8 February 1956 Mrs Thompson made a will leaving all her property to John and
Julian on their attaining 21. In my judgment Mr Thompson would have known about

this will when it was executed. Many of Mrs Thompson's assets derived from Mr Thompson, but, as Mr Thompson now accepts, his assertions to John and Julian at the time of her death that he had shortly before her death persuaded her to give those assets to John and Julian (rather than presumably back to him), were unwarranted. By a codicil dated 13 December 1963, Mrs Thompson made John an executor of her will with Mr Thompson and her solicitor, Mr Symes. Mr Macro made a will in 1958 in which he left 60 per cent of his shares in Macro to his wife, and the remainder to his sons on their reaching specified ages. The will directed that while his sons were under age all the shares were to be held by Mrs Macro so that she could be a director.

In April 1962 Mr Thompson acquired Gippeswyk Investment Co Ltd ('Gippeswyk'). This was a property investment vehicle for the Thompson family only. In October 1962, Earliba, which had been formed by company formation agents, was acquired by Mr Thompson and Mr Macro. They each became directors and Mr Macro became also company secretary. In its early years Earliba was primarily a vehicle to hold and develop land which Macro transferred to it.

4.2 *1962–64 share distribution*

In 1962–63, Mr Macro and Mr Thompson became concerned about estate duty. Because of this concern, a further 600 shares in Macro were allotted in December 1962, 300 to the Thompson family and 300 to the Macro family. The new shareholders received their shares by way of gift. Mr Thompson paid for them. The allotment anticipated advice by Turner Martin and Symes, solicitors of Ipswich, that the control vested in Mr Thompson and Mr Macro should be removed by spreading the shares over the widest practical field, that the directors' share qualification, previously 100 shares, be reduced to one share, that new articles should be adopted and the maximum number of directors increased from four to eight. Mr Thompson and Mr Macro were made permanent directors. Mr Thompson wanted to become permanent chairman of the company and to have control through the chairman's casting vote. He also wanted the board to control the appointment of new directors. However, Mr Thompson was advised that for estate duty reasons he could not have a casting vote. One of the reasons for increasing the number of directors was that the directors envisaged that their wives would at some time be appointed directors of the company. There was no suggestion of non-family members becoming directors.

In December 1963, Turner Martin and Symes submitted instructions to counsel. The point on which counsel was asked to advise is not material, but the terms of the instructions are. Macro was described as 'a family concern'. It was said that 'by virtue of his greater ability and stronger personality' Mr Thompson ran Macro. Its business was stated to be that of builders and contractors and that it was 'immensely strong and wealthy so that its shares are extremely valuable'. The instructions then continued:

'On 10 December 1962, 600 further shares were issued for cash, half to Mr Thompson's family and half to Mr Macro's family, and the necessary return of allotments made. The issue was decided upon as a first step to reduce the burden of estate duty on Mr Thompson's estate in the event of his death, he being in his fifties, and being worth upwards of £250,000.

Both Mr Thompson and Mr Macro have wives and two sons, and it is intended, in general, that these should be made directors of the company, but it is not intended that Mr Thompson and Mr Macro shall surrender their absolute control; and Mr Thompson feels that as long as equality is maintained between the two seniors during their lives, he will continue to control and run the company as he has done in the past.

It was intended to achieve the desired result by the method of making Messrs

A

Thompson and Macro permanent directors, and to go forward by conferring on each of them the right to appoint a permanent director in his stead on his resignation or death, and by deed, will or codicil, and art. 13 of the new articles was drafted with this end in view.'

Mr Thompson's plan therefore was to make himself (as far as he could) irremovable as a director by making himself a permanent director and to retain control by the power of his personality even if additional directors were appointed. He intended that, so long as he wished to do so, he should direct and dictate the affairs of Macro.

B

However, the building operations of Macro were carried on by Mr Macro. The works office was his home and surveyors and suppliers would come there to discuss matters arising out of its building operations. Thus in a letter dated 6 January 1964, the branch manager of the Co-operative Permanent Building Society, from whom Earliba was proposing to raise money, referred to Macro as 'Mr Macro's building company' and to Mr Thompson and Mr Macro as 'both principals' who 'have been in business for a number of years'. Macro obviously built a large number of houses between 1945 and 1969, many of which have been retained by Earliba.

C

By special resolution passed on 19 February 1964 Macro adopted new articles of association. These introduced a right of pre-emption on transfer, and reduced the directors' share qualification to the holding of one share. The maximum number of directors was increased from four to eight and Mr Macro and Mr Thompson were made permanent directors. In November 1964 similar changes were made to Earliba's articles.

D

At about this time, in my judgment, Mr Thompson appointed Mrs Thompson a permanent director upon his death although he does not now recall doing so. The document does not survive but the appointment is recited in codicils dated 28 February and 18 November 1964 whereby Mrs Thompson appointed John (or in default Julian) permanent directors of the companies upon her death subject to her being a permanent director at her death.

E

In March 1964, it was proposed by Mr Thompson and Mr Macro that their elder sons, John and Ian, should be appointed directors of Macro. Mr Thompson assisted Ian to write to his new employers, Barclays Bank Ltd ('Barclays'), for permission to be a director of Macro. Moreover, although Mr Thompson cannot now recollect the occasion, the contemporaneous documentation (see the letter dated 18 March 1964 from Barclays to Mr Thompson) shows that Mr Thompson actually went to see Barclays to discuss the matter. However Barclays refused its permission and accordingly the proposal for the appointment of the new directors proceeded no further. On this issue, I prefer the evidence of Julian and Ian to that of Mr Thompson who contended that the proposal was only that Ian should be a director, and not John, and that he had only gone along with it to please his sister. I find that at this stage both Mr Thompson and Mr Macro contemplated that their sons would join them on the board. Mr Thompson was in my judgment not then, as he is now, critical of the potential ability of Ian and John to act as directors of the companies.

F

G

In May 1964, Earliba charged certain of its properties to Ipswich Benefit Building Society Ltd to secure the advance of £100,000. Repayment of this advance was guaranteed by both Mr Thompson and Mr Macro. Mr Thompson said that the lenders would in practice look to him and not Mr Macro if a demand was made under any guarantee they had both given of the companies' liabilities, but this was because he had negotiated the loans guaranteed and was therefore known to the lenders.

H

On 12 November 1964, 98 shares in Earliba were allotted so as to result in the shareholdings shown in column 2 of the table on p. 790. The new shareholders received their shares by way of gift: Mr Thompson paid for them. At the annual general meeting held on 17 December 1964, Brearey & Co (Mr D K Brearey, FAIA) were appointed

A   auditors for the company in place of the retiring auditor and Mr Cyril Wyard was appointed company secretary upon the resignation of Mr Macro. In November and December 1964 the articles of Macro and Earliba were altered with respect to the pre-emption article which I have set out above.

The plaintiffs say that the object of the allotment of shares in Macro and Earliba in 1963 and 1964 was both to save estate duty 'and to ensure that both companies remained in the ownership of both families, with each family owning one-half of each company,

B   and with the shares passing on the death of a member of one generation to the members of the next generation'. The pre-emption articles certainly contemplate that the ownership of shares will pass in this way because transfers from one generation of the same family to another are excepted from pre-emption. However, I find that there was no agreement or arrangement that shares could only be transferred in this way.

C   There is an issue as to the nature of Mr Macro's role in the companies. For Mr Thompson it was contended that Mr Macro began his working relationship with Mr Thompson as one of his employees and that that relationship continued. Mr Thompson emphasised his own qualities as a manager but endeavoured to diminish Mr Macro's contribution. He said that Mr Macro was a man of 'extraordinary failings'. He further claimed that all the management decisions were taken by him and that he in practice had control. The secretarial and book-keeping functions, and the administration of Macro's

D   large labour force, were carried on from Thompsons' offices free of charge. The acquisition of investment properties was done by Mr Thompson without consultation with Mr Macro. Nevertheless the building operations were supervised by Mr Macro from the works office at his home. I accept that Mr Thompson had control so that, if there was some disagreement on a matter of policy, Mr Macro would have accepted Mr Thompson's wishes. However, save in that event, Mr Macro in my judgment exercised managerial responsibility in the sphere of the companies' building operations. In my

E   judgment he was empowered to act in this sphere without obtaining Mr Thompson's approval. This conclusion is supported by the evidence of Mr Holmes, a quantity surveyor who worked closely with him from about 1957 to 1966. I do not accept Mr Thompson's explanation that it was really the experienced foreman, Mr Dickens, who was in control. Mr Thompson was rarely on site or at the works office and the evidence points to Mr Macro rather than Mr Dickens having overall responsibility for building

F   operations.

4.3 *Further testamentary dispositions*

On 9 December 1964 Mrs Macro made a will whereby she appointed Ian (or in default Neil) to be a permanent director if she herself was a permanent director when she died and she left her shares in Macro and Earliba to her two sons in equal shares.

G   In 1965 Mrs Thompson became ill. She transferred her shares in Macro and Earliba to her two sons in equal shares. There is no evidence that she did this (as the plaintiffs suggest) in pursuance of some agreement between all the shareholders that the shares of each family should pass to their sons on the death of the parents. On 11 March 1965 Mrs Thompson died. Her will dated 8 February 1966 was duly proved and Mr Thompson, John and Mr Symes became executors.

H   On 9 June 1966, Mr Thompson executed a further will appointing John and Julian and Mr Symes, his family solicitor, as executors and leaving his residuary estate including his shares in Macro and Earliba to John and Julian in equal shares and appointing one of them to be a permanent director of Macro and the other to be a permanent director of Earliba, with a direction that his shares in Macro and Earliba were to be retained for the benefit of his sons and not sold. On 22 February 1968, however, Mr Thompson executed a second codicil to his will whereby he excluded John from all benefit under his will and

appointed Julian a permanent director of both Macro and Earliba on his death. There   A
was friction between Mr Thompson and John from about 1967. The friction extended to
the distribution of Mrs Thompson's estate. This led to Mr Thompson seeking advice in
February 1968 as to whether he could resign as one of her executors.

In June 1971, Mr Thompson made a further will in anticipation of his second marriage
but the provision for Julian (and the exclusion of John) remained as before.

Whatever the causes of the friction with John may have been, the result was that Mr   B
Thompson was not speaking to John from about 1967 to 1977. For quite separate reasons
Mr Thompson likewise was not speaking to Ian. He saw little of Neil so the only member
of the second generation with whom he was in regular communication was Julian. There
is no evidence that John knew he had been cut out of his father's will.

From time to time Mr Thompson was not on good terms with his sister, Mrs Macro. I
therefore accept Julian's evidence that when Mr Macro was about to retire what   C
concerned Mr Thompson was that the other shareholders, particularly Ian, Neil and
John, would combine to out-manoeuvre him in the companies.

4.4 *Declarations of trust*

Julian's evidence was that in the 1950s, 1960s and 1970s Mr Thompson regularly made
oral statements to the effect that the companies were family companies and that
ownership would ultimately devolve on the 'four boys'. I do not think things were quite   D
as Julian suggests. Up to the mid or late 1960s, Julian would not in my view have been of
a sufficient age to determine the significance of such statements and therefore I can place
no reliance on his recollection as to whether any such statements prior to (say) 1965
constituted declarations of trust or were merely statements of intention. Even Mr
Thompson accepted that the original plan was that the shares would go to the sons when
their parents died. In my judgment, the statements were at all times merely statements of
what was expected to happen. I do not consider that either Mr or Mrs Thompson or Mr   E
or Mrs Macro were bound to transfer their shares to their children. After all, the articles
contemplated the sale of shares to non-members once rights of pre-emption were
exhausted. There could be no such sales if the shares were impressed with a trust. Ian
described the statements as to future ownership as 'plans' or 'intentions'. In my judgment
the statements he recalled being made by his father and his uncle as to shares devolving
in time on the four boys have to be seen in that context. What the four sons fairly   F
assumed and expected would happen in time, namely that they would inherit all the
shares in the companies, has wrongly become confused in their minds with the idea of a
trust.

There were a number of testamentary dispositions (including that by Mrs Thompson)
which show that Mr and Mrs Thompson and Mr and Mrs Macro each proposed to give
their shares in the companies to their sons in the period 1945–1985. It is said that the
making of these dispositions provides evidentiary support for the alleged declarations of   G
trust. The making of wills was done by each couple independently of the other. The
disposition of the shares would not have been necessary if the shares were already held
on trust. Accordingly in my view the proper analysis is that these various testamentary
dispositions do not support the plaintiffs' case regarding the declarations of trust.

4.5 *Mr Macro's retirement and the 1969 reconstruction*   H

Mr Macro was some eight years older than Mr Thompson. Prior to 1969 Mr Macro
decided to retire from the companies because of ill-health. In 1969 Mr Macro sought a
valuation of his shareholdings in Macro and Earliba from Brearey & Co. The advice was
that his shares in Macro were each worth par and that his shares in Earliba were each
worth £40. Mr Thompson did not however regard the shares as of such little value: he
had confidence in his own ability to make the companies valuable.

A   On 14 October 1969, Mr Thompson and Mr Macro as directors of Macro resolved that Macro should cease to carry on building operations save to the extent that it would carry out work for Earliba and do maintenance work for itself and Earliba. The minutes record that Mr Macro's resignation with effect from 7 November 1969 was accepted but that 'on the question of shareholdings' his retirement was delayed until the matter had been fully discussed. Mr Macro evidently wanted a pension. Consistently with his approach in 1963, Mr Thompson was not prepared to approve this unless at the same time he obtained sufficient shares to have voting control. Mr Macro was offered a pension satisfactory to him provided the shareholders agreed to an allotment of new shares, which gave Mr Thompson control. Mr Macro was prepared to accept this. Turner Martin & Symes were instructed to write, and on 30 October 1969 did write, to each of the shareholders in the company setting out the arrangement and asking them to sign a consent to the allotment of new shares in favour of Mr Thompson alone. The letter to Ian was in the following terms (so far as material) and the others were in similar terms:

> 'Mr AHV Thompson has seen me in regard to the shareholdings in the above companies and I gather that these proposals are part of the overall arrangements for the retirement and pension of your father. The proposals include, as a matter of caution, that Mr Thompson shall obtain voting control which at the present time he has not, as shown by the following details:

Company	Authorised		Issued
Macro	£5,000	AHVT	100
		AJVT	150
		JGNT	150
		ERM	100
		ABM	100
		IAM	100
		NLRM	100
			800
Earliba	£100	AHVT	20
		JPVT	15
		JGNT	15
		ER	20
		ABM	12
		IAM	9
		NLRM	9
			100

> In the case of Macro there is abundant unissued capital to provide the further capital to provide the further 601 shares required, but in the case of Earliba it will be necessary to increase the company's capital to provide the additional 61 shares required.

> I am informed that you have been advised of the proposals and have agreed. Accordingly I send you three forms for signature and I hope that they are self-explanatory.

> Although in your trustee banking career you must have much experience with companies, I feel that, in sending you the enclosed three forms for signature, I must warn you that the effect of the proposals must inevitably be to reduce the value of your shares, both as regards voting rights, and as regards break up on liquidation,

A

and I think, in fairness to yourself, you should take independent advice either within your own organisation, or from a solicitor or accountant.'

It is clear from the other copies of this letter that the word 'caution' in the second sentence should read 'condition'. I do not accept Ian's evidence that he placed reliance on the word 'caution' or that it indicated that the passing of control was to be temporary.

B

The consents requested were given and new shares were then allotted in Macro and Earliba as appears from column 4 of the table set out in para. 2.1 above. Accordingly Mr Thompson obtained voting control, in each case, by a single vote. The articles were not altered and in particular the provisions as to permanent directors remained unchanged. I will call the new allotments 'the 1969 reconstruction'. On 9 December 1964 the board of Macro resolved to pay Mr Macro £5,000 by way of 'golden handshake', to give him his company car (worth £680) and an annual pension of £2,300 subject to annual review. (There was no argument on the propriety or otherwise of this arrangement from Macro's point of view and I express no view thereon.)

C

In 1972, the Inland Revenue queried whether the golden handshake was a deductible expense but Mr Thompson maintained throughout that the handshake was wholly and exclusively expenditure for Mr Macro's past services and not part of the arrangement whereby he obtained voting control of Macro and Earliba. He maintained (through Brearey & Co – see their letter dated 1 November 1973) that he required control because he was going to be responsible for management. The fact that Mr Macro remained a director of Macro was one of the grounds for the Inland Revenue's query. Eventually at the 1977 annual general meeting Mr Macro agreed to resign as a director apparently with effect from 9 December 1969. The Inland Revenue accepted that the golden handshake was a deductible expense and ceased their enquiries in November 1977.

D

Julian's evidence was that Mr Thompson made promises to him in the summer of 1969 (and subsequently) that when the companies were on a sound financial footing Mr Thompson would be prepared to revert to the status quo, meaning the distribution of voting power between the two families which existed in the two companies prior to the 1969 reconstruction. This was also to happen if Mr Thompson died or retired. The specific occasion in 1969 is said to have taken place after a walk in the garden at Mr Thompson's farm outside Ipswich. Moreover he discussed the letter from Turner Martin & Symes dated 30 October 1969 with John. As respects the 1969 reconstruction, Julian's evidence was that he gave the consents requested because of 'the statements, promises and the future intentions as expressed by' Mr Thompson.

E

F

Ian's evidence was that he only agreed to the 1969 reconstruction because ownership was in the end to devolve on the four boys and strictly on the basis that the shareholdings would revert so as to be held 50:50 by the two families. He points out that (as he calculated at the time) on a net asset basis the 1969 reconstruction resulted in a passing to Mr Thompson of substantial value. However he does not point to any statement made to him in 1969 by Mr Thompson or on his instructions. He says that later at annual general meetings Mr Thompson indicated that they would become involved at age 40 and then aged 50. He says Mr Thompson made these statements at annual general meetings attended by Neil who reported back to Ian or attended by Ian. He also says that Mr Thompson regularly promised to retire at age 80. Neil did not remember any specific representations in 1969 that control would be handed back when the companies were put on a sound financial footing. He simply assumed that ownership would descend to the second generation as it had been expected to before the 1969 reconstruction. Neil gave evidence that at the 1989 annual general meeting Mr Thompson said that he would pass over ownership of the companies to the four boys when he became 80 years old.

G

H

In my judgment Mr Thompson did not agree or represent in 1969 that he would cause control to revert to the pre-1969 reconstruction position or otherwise. I accept Mr

Thompson's denial. The real reason why Ian and Neil agreed to the arrangement was so that Mr Macro could have his pension. In my judgment it is improbable that Mr Thompson would have agreed to hand shares back to Mr and Mrs Macro. Moreover the companies have been on a firm financial footing since at least 1985.

The position of John and Julian was quite different and I have to consider their motivation for entry into the 1969 reconstruction. In my judgment, they did not, as Mr Thompson contends, act out of the commercial motivation that it would secure the continuation of Mr Thompson in management, there being no other management realistically on offer. There is no evidence that consideration was given to any alternative management. If there had been a commercial arrangement, I would have expected to see some reference in writing to Mr Thompson promising to continue in management. In my judgment Mr Thompson had given his sons to believe that in the fullness of time they would have an involvement in the companies and they as respectful sons concurred in the 1969 reconstruction in the expectation that the business would one day be handed over from father to son. No one would have foreseen the depth of the breach with John, or the breach that was to come with Julian. As far as I can see there is no other credible reason why John and Julian should concur in the 1969 reconstruction. But what was held out to Julian and John was no more than an expectation; they did not enter into any legally binding arrangement with their father and they did not conclude that he was not free to deal with the shares in some other way, if he chose to do so.

Julian says that he raised the question with his father orally on several occasions in 1978–79. I do not accept that he did. Nor did his solicitors raise it when they wrote in October 1990 to the companies' auditors in connection with short notice of AGM given with respect to the companies and a suggestion that Julian would be removed as a director of Gippeswyk. Julian said it was not mentioned in that letter because he was only dealing with his complaints over matters which concerned him as a director. But the claims arising out of the 1969 assurances would have made his then complaints in relation to the companies insignificant. If therefore he felt he had a good legal claim then he would in my view have raised it in that letter. So far as the latter alleged assurances by Mr Thompson that he would resign or that the boys would become involved in management, I think it likely that Mr Thompson gave all sorts of hints that he would resign and involve the plaintiffs in management but on the evidence I am not satisfied that he gave any binding assurance to this effect.

4.6 *1972 onwards*

In 1972 Mr Thompson made a yet further will, which was varied by codicil. In contrast to the 1971 will, Julian was no longer an executor. In his place Mr Wyard was appointed an executor. Mr Thompson left the goodwill of Thompsons to Mr Wyard together with a legacy of £500. The residue was left on trust as to half for Mr Thompson's second wife for life and then as to the balance on discretionary trusts for beneficiaries including John, Julian and their respective children. From about 1972 relations with Julian became strained. Much later (in 1985) Julian and Mr Thompson became totally estranged and they so remain. Speaking relations with John however were restored from 1977.

In 1973, Turner Martin & Symes submitted instructions to tax counsel. The point on which advice was sought is not material. In the instructions Macro was described as 'a company which [Mr Thompson] controlled in conjunction with his brother-in-law'. As to Mr Thompson the instructions stated that he was in rather poor health and wished to retire. The instructions further stated that Mr Thompson had kept his estate agency going because he hoped that one of his sons, who was an estate agent, would take it over. The son however was working in London and had indicated that he had no intention of returning to Ipswich.

In April 1975, further instructions were submitted to counsel. These stated that Mr   A
Thompson was at all times 'the controlling element' in Macro and Earliba and that 'for
family reasons' he had put a number of shares in the names of his sons.

4.7 *Annual general meetings*

Annual general meetings were held each year. From 1977, Julian usually attended. Ian
and Neil attended regularly from 1987 only. John attended regularly from 1980. I accept
that it was frequently difficult for Ian and Neil to attend these meetings. In some years   B
Ian sent queries with which Mr Brearey was instructed to deal. In November 1977 Ian
wrote to Mr Brearey querying the sum of £12,555 which had been left by the companies
with Thompsons. In 1978 Ian made the same complaint. At the 1978 annual general
meeting of Macro, the explanation given was that Thompsons needed to have 'a reserve
to meet the high costs of modernising several properties'.

Macro's annual general meeting in 1977 was attended by Mr Thompson, Mr Macro,   C
John and Julian. The question of the number of directors was discussed. The minutes
(which were signed by the chairman) record that

> 'Members present agreed that, for practical reasons, it would not be possible to
> appoint additional director(s) at the moment.'

In my view, the proper inference is that Mr Macro resigned at Mr Thompson's request.
In an answer provided to one of Ian's requests for information it was said that the   D
members had unanimously agreed to leave the appointment of additional directors in
Macro in abeyance 'pending clarification of the tax situation'. In Earliba, there continued
to be two directors as Mr Macro had not resigned as a director of that company.

By a will dated 23 January 1980, Mr Macro left his shares in Macro and Earliba to his
two sons and he appointed Mrs Macro to be a permanent director of both companies in
his place on his death. He clearly thought that he continued to be entitled to appoint a   E
permanent director of Macro in his place despite his own resignation in 1977: however,
it has not been suggested in these proceedings that a permanent director could be so
appointed or that the articles were by common agreement varied so that Mr Macro could
appoint a permanent director in his place even after his own resignation. Brearey & Co
again advised him that his Macro shares were only worth their nominal value. On 23
June 1980, a guarantee given by Mr Thompson and Mr Macro for £35,000 in favour of
Barclays to secure Macro's overdraft was released and property was substituted.   F

In September 1982, Mr Wyard wrote to Julian stating that 'the chairman wishes to
point out that it is not the intention to pay dividends in the foreseeable future as the
expenditure on maintenance is a continuous increase [sic] which it is thought will rise
considerably'. The accounts of Macro and Earliba for the year ended 31 March 1983 did
indeed show substantial sums being spent on repairs to properties.

On 5 August 1983, Mr Macro died. Macro agreed to pay the full amount of the   G
pension previously payable to Mr Macro to Mrs Macro. At the annual general meetings
of Macro and Earliba attended by all shareholders and held on 28 September 1983 it was
stated that Mrs Macro had been appointed a permanent director of Earliba by the terms
of Mr Macro's will but Mr Thompson opposed Mrs Macro taking up office as a
permanent director. In about October 1983 Mrs Macro gave written notice of her
resignation. Julian's evidence was that Mrs Macro was forced to resign because of Mr   H
Thompson's attitude to her. Ian's recollection of Mr Thompson's attitude was the same.
His evidence was that at the 1983 annual general meeting Mr Thompson told Mrs Macro
that she was not welcome as a director and that if she wanted to ensure the proper
management of the companies until it was right for the second generation to take over,
she should resign her directorship. If she did not do so, he would resign. It was agreed
that she should have four weeks to consider the position. At the end of the four-week

A   period she reluctantly decided to resign. Ian describes the pressure put on his mother to resign as extreme. Neil's recollection of the 1983 annual general meeting is the same as Ian's. Mr Thompson's explanation is entirely different. He denies having put pressure on Mrs Macro to resign. He says that in effect he said to her 'Really this is all beyond you and it would be better if the whole running of the companies remained as always with me your brother'.

B   I prefer the plaintiffs' evidence on this point to that of Mr Thompson. Given the nature of his personality I think it more than likely that he did put pressure on her. By his own admission he wanted to retain managerial control of Earliba. In my judgment this was contrary to the understandings on which Earliba had been established, as manifested in the article empowering a permanent director to appoint his successor. It was not for Mr Thompson to object to the choice of successor. It had been agreed between him and Mr Macro that Mr Macro could appoint a successor. Otherwise the article would not have

C   been adopted. It was never suggested that Mrs Macro's presence as a director would actually inconvenience him or adversely affect the management. I do not see on the evidence led how it would have done so. Everything indicates that Mrs Macro would have wanted to keep her role to a minimum. Unfortunately she likewise did not appoint a successor before she retired (no-one suggested that she should). In this way the Macros lost their right to representation on the board of both companies.

D   The 1984 and 1985 accounts of Macro and Earliba continued to show substantial sums being spent on repairs to properties. Starting in the 1980s Mr Thompson spent several months each winter in Lanzarote. In September 1985 Ford du Cane & Co replaced Brearey & Co as company auditors.

On 22 September 1986 Mrs Macro senior's pension was increased by an additional £15 per week. On 19 January 1987 Mrs Macro died.

E   On 11 March 1987 Mr Cyril Wyard suddenly left Thompsons. Mr Thompson was at this time in Lanzarote but he returned as soon as he received news of Mr Wyard's departure. Mr Wyard's duties were taken over by Mr Farley who was appointed general office manager of Thompsons and also company secretary of Macro and Earliba in 1988. The annual general meetings of both companies for 1990 were held on 5 November 1990. They were originally convened to be held on short notice at an earlier date but the date was altered by Mr Thompson so Julian could attend. Mr Thompson regarded Julian's

F   objection to the date originally chosen as a breach of a family understanding that meetings could be held on short notice. At the 1990 annual general meeting of one of the companies or Gippeswyk, Mr Thompson proposed that Mr Farley should be a director of the companies and be allowed one share on terms that it was transferred back to Mr Thompson or as the directors should direct on his ceasing to be a director. This was opposed by the other shareholders of Macro and Earliba. It was the proposal that Mr

G   Farley should be appointed a director of the companies that determined Julian to take some action against his father.

5. Allegations of mismanagement

I will now set out my findings of facts relative to the various allegations of mismanagement made by the plaintiffs.

H

5.1 *Commissions and key money*

5.1.1 Commissions

The plaintiffs allege that from about 1970–1988 builders employed by the companies, with Mr Thompson's knowledge, paid sums in cash to Mr Wyard which represented between five per cent and ten per cent of the total contract price and those cash sums

were divided equally between Mr Thompson and Mr Wyard. The plaintiffs further allege   A
that neither Mr Thompson nor Mr Wyard accounted to the companies for these sums.

Mr Wyard was employed by Thompsons from 1936 to 1987. He was responsible for
the collection of rents, supervision of repairs and to some extent the keeping of books for
properties managed by Thompsons. Latterly Mrs Hessey was employed as a bookkeeper
but she left in about October 1987 when she was about 77 years old.

Thompsons employed a small number of small builders to do repair work on the   B
properties they managed. They included Mr Studd, Mr Martell and Mr Parfitt. Mr
Wyard took commission ranging from five per cent to ten per cent from these builders,
often by cashing a cheque for a small amount drawn in their favour by Thompsons in
settlement of their invoices. In the case of Mr Studd, this happened from about 1963 to
1987; in the case of Mr Martell from the early 1950s to 1987 at the rate of five per cent;
and in the case of Mr Parfitt from about 1981 to 1987. Mr Wyard said that he kept part
of the commission without Mr Thompson knowing that he kept that part and handed   C
the balance to Mr Thompson. In my judgment Mr Wyard did take commission from
builders and Mrs Hessey knew that this was happening since she had to raise two cheques
on each occasion that it happened and cash one of them. She also received some benefit
in that Mr Wyard reimbursed her for the tax deducted from her wages out of the
commissions that he received.

Mr Wyard told Mrs Hessey that the balance of the commissions after his deduction   D
was going to Mr Thompson. He says that he left it in a drawer for Mr Thompson. On a
separate occasion he told Mr Parfitt that he was placing the money in a safe for Mr
Thompson at Mr Thompson's home. Mr Thompson denies that he ever received any
share of the commissions though he accepts that Mr Wyard from time to time paid him
cash as a reimbursement for out of pocket expenses. Neither Mrs Hessey nor Mr Parfitt
actually saw Mr Wyard give the money to Mr Thompson. Mr Wyard's estimate was that
Mr Thompson received some £300,000 out of commissions over a 17-year period.   E

In my judgment Mr Wyard was in fact keeping all the commission for himself other
than that which he paid Mrs Hessey. The suggestion that Mr Thompson himself kept
commissions came from Mr Wyard, whose evidence I have cause to doubt, and from
Mrs Hessey and Mr Parfitt who never saw Mr Wyard hand it to Mr Thompson.
Accordingly I prefer Mr Thompson's explanation of such cash as he did receive.

The companies' auditor, Mr Brearey, was not aware of the payment of commissions,   F
or key money, which I discuss later.

In March 1987 Mr Wyard left without giving notice for personal reasons. Shortly
before he left he told Mrs Hessey to retain five per cent out of the commission she would
be receiving from Mr Studd and to keep it for herself and to hand the balance to Mr
Thompson. In my judgment she gave the money so deducted initially to Mr Farley. Mr
Farley must then have kept that money for himself. Later in the year however she gave it   G
to Mr Thompson direct. Mr Thompson was surprised to receive it and thereupon
instituted enquiries to find out why he had been given this cash. He then discovered the
practice of retaining commissions and caused it to cease. The practice had originated in
the round sum payments that had been made to builders and Mr Thompson instituted
accounting procedures to prevent round sum payments being made in future without his
permission. I reject Mrs Hessey's explanation that the surprise shown by Mr Thompson   H
was only at the amount of the commission that she passed to him rather than the fact
that it was commission. I prefer the explanation that he was surprised in the latter way,
which was the explanation she originally gave to Mr Graham, Mr Thompson's solicitor,
in November 1993.

Mr Bumphrey, sales negotiator with Thompsons from 1984 to 1985 and sales manager
at Thompsons from 1985 to 1989, gave evidence that he was aware of commissions from

A   information given to him in the office. However I can attach little weight to this evidence which was clearly hearsay.

Mr Parfitt was one of the builders employed by Thompsons from February 1981 to July 1987. During that period his main employer was Thompsons and some of the work which he did for Thompsons was on the properties of the companies. He says that he saw Mr Wyard putting money into Mr Thompson's safe at Mr Thompson's house. However,

B   he subsequently clarified this as meaning that that was what Mr Wyard told him that he had done. In fact Mr Thompson denied having a safe at his home and I accept that evidence.

There was obviously considerable animosity from Mr Parfitt to Mr Thompson. In June 1987 Thompsons paid only £24,000 of a bill from Mr Parfitt for £33,447.70. Mr Parfitt signed a receipt saying that this was in fact the total sum due. Mr Parfitt was very angry and took the view that he had been forced to accept this lesser sum under duress.

C   He was under pressure from his bank at this time and ill. He had told Mr Thompson that he added ten per cent to his estimate at Mr Wyard's request and allowed Mr Wyard to retain ten per cent of his bill believing that Mr Wyard was paying the amounts retained over to Mr Thompson. In November 1987 he wrote to Mr Thompson in an effort to recover the balance but was unsuccessful in doing so. Mr Thompson's evidence was that the work that Mr Parfitt had done was unsatisfactory. His reply to Mr Parfitt contained

D   no statement disclaiming involvement in the taking of commission. However, in my judgment his failure to do so in the circumstances throws little light on the question whether Mr Thompson was implicated in the commissions which Mr Parfitt had been paying. Mr Thompson obviously did not wish to claim back the commissions from Mr Parfitt (who would not have been able to pay them) but did want to reduce Mr Parfitt's bill because of unsatisfactory work. I am satisfied that he was genuinely of the opinion that Mr Parfitt's work had been unsatisfactory and justified the deduction he had made.

E   There is some evidence on the question whether the companies were charged more for building work because of the commissions Mr Wyard was taking. Mr Parfitt admitted that he simply added the commission to his estimate. Mr Martell however contended that he simply absorbed the five per cent commission that he paid by shrewd buying of material at discounts. I do not accept that evidence. It is, in my judgment, more likely than not that the cost of the commissions was, in part at least, passed on to the companies

F   in one way or another.

5.1.2 Key money

The plaintiffs allege that, as a result of inadequate supervision by Mr Thompson (see further para. 5.5.1 below), persons left to grant new lettings have been, and are still, able to obtain secret payments in return for the grant of lettings of the companies' properties

G   ('key money'). They do not allege, however, that any such payments have been received since 1988. There is a further allegation that, when Mr Thompson learnt of these payments, he took no steps to discover the payments from those involved, and concealed the existence of the payments from the shareholders.

As regards key money, Mr Wyard, on his own admission, accepted small sums from tenants without the knowledge of Mr Thompson in connection with the grant of new tenancies. He says that he received these sums after contracts were signed. The plaintiffs

H   called two witnesses, Mrs Mary Rose Holden and Mrs Marjorie June Woolterton, who claimed that they had paid sums of £100 and £65 respectively to Mr Wyard when they signed their tenancy agreements. However it was not clear from their evidence whether these sums were key money or payments of rent in advance. A further witness called by the plaintiffs, John Thompson Winlow, gave evidence that he had paid Mr Wyard the sum of £300. Mr Wyard accepted that he had received this sum after the tenancy

agreement was signed and that he had kept it for himself. Mr Bumphrey confirms that   A
key money was offered to him (but refused) very shortly after Mr Wyard's departure. I
find that Mr Wyard did receive money from tenants, that the sums involved were not
small and that the payments were not voluntary as was suggested but required by Mr
Wyard.

Mr Wyard admitted that before he left in March 1987 he had set up an arrangement
with Mr Keith Miller, a director of Sallows Developments East Anglia Ltd, whereby   B
Thompsons would rehouse a sitting tenant of the latter (using one of the companies'
properties) as part of a deal involving the payment of a 'fee' to Mr Wyard personally. Mr
Wyard left Thompsons before the tenancy was signed and he did not receive the fee. In
my judgment the likelihood is that Mr Wyard had been involved in a number of other
similar deals over several years.

Mr John Samuel Howard, a director of a property company called Brentoak Properties   C
Ltd, gave evidence that he paid between £500 and £1,500 on some seven occasions over a
period of 18 months to Mr Farley to persuade Mr Farley to grant tenancies to sitting
tenants of his company whom it was desired to rehouse. Mr Thompson discovered that
key money payments were being made in the summer of 1987 shortly after Mr Wyard's
departure. Mr Farley's reaction was to say that he had never received money and on 5
August 1987 he wrote a letter to Mr Thompson stating that this was the position. Mr
Thompson then discovered that, contrary to what he said, Mr Farley had indeed accepted   D
key money. He decided however, but not without hesitation, to give Mr Farley a second
chance. Mr Farley admits that he received sums of about £500 from landlords which he
says in a statement served in the course of the proceedings that he paid to Mr Wyard and
out of which he would then receive back from Mr Wyard some ten per cent. Mr Wyard
denied that he received any key money except on a few occasions from tenants. Mr Farley
also admits that he was involved in four key money transactions after Mr Wyard left. I
accept Mr Howard's evidence and find that the seven payments to which he referred were   E
paid to Mr Farley. Mr Farley said that he now felt ashamed of his participation in key
money transactions. He admits retaining £2,600 out of key money received by him. The
reality in my judgment is that he knew at the time that what he was doing was wrong.

After Mr Thompson decided to keep Mr Farley, he caused Mr Farley to obtain letters
from Mr Miller and from Mr Howard saying that they had not paid him key money. Mr
Thompson's explanation was that he wanted those letters so that there could be no come-   F
back on Mr Farley. No one has explained to me how, in all the circumstances, those
letters could properly be used. Mr Thompson was instrumental in obtaining the letters.
In my judgment he knew they were untrue. In my judgment it was an error of judgment
for him to obtain the letters but it did not necessarily mean that he had been involved in
the key money transactions. In my judgment he retained Mr Farley again not because he
(Mr Thompson) had been involved in the key money transactions but because he had   G
been left in the lurch by Mr Wyard and had to keep Mr Farley. Mr Thompson felt that
Mr Farley had been influenced by Mr Wyard. This is correct to a limited extent: at first
Mr Farley was involved because of Mr Wyard, but there is evidence that subsequently he
acted independently of Mr Wyard. Trust and confidence have now been re-established as
between Mr Thompson and Mr Farley. I will have to consider whether the other
shareholders should be bound to accept Mr Thompson's assessment in this matter, by
which they would be bound as long as Mr Farley had the support of the majority   H
shareholder and (if he was appointed a permanent director) possibly even after Mr
Thompson's demise.

In all the circumstances I am satisfied that Mr Thompson was not involved in the
receipt of commissions or of key money. I am also satisfied that he did not know that
these moneys were being received at the time of their receipt.

A   The 1987 AGMs were held on 7 October 1987. I find that Mr Thompson told Ian, Neil and John (all of whom were present at those meetings) that Mr Wyard had left without giving notice if Mr Wyard's departure was not known to them already. However I find that he did not inform the plaintiffs then or on any other occasion prior to the commencement of these proceedings of the commission payments or key money payments which I have found were made to Mr Wyard and Mr Farley. Mr Farley was introduced as company secretary at the 1988 AGM.

B   There is no evidence that any steps have been taken to recover commissions or key money from Mr Wyard or Mr Farley for the benefit of the companies or that such steps would have yielded any benefit in the companies. There is an allegation that Mr Thompson has not put into effect any system which would ensure that Mr Farley or any other employee could not take key money without detection. In my judgment this allegation is not proved as the plaintiffs have not identified the system which they contend

C   would achieve this result.

5.2 *Management of properties*

The plaintiffs' case is that, in a number of respects, Thompsons (acting by Mr Wyard and latterly Mr Farley) mismanaged the companies' properties, that this is attributable to a failure on the part of Mr Thompson to supervise their activities, that this has affected

D   rental income and capital values adversely and continues so to do and that accordingly the plaintiffs have been unfairly prejudiced. At this stage I must set out the facts as I find them to be in respect of these alleged acts of mismanagement.

The plaintiffs make a number of allegations in this field with which I propose to deal under the subheadings set out below:

5.2.1 Competitive tendering

E   (i)   Thompsons have failed to obtain competitive estimates for repair work.

5.2.2 Repairs and maintenance

(ii)   Thompsons have paid too much for repair and improvement work;

(iii)   Thompsons have failed to exercise control over maintenance and improvement works; and in particular

F   (a)   Thompsons have permitted tenants to alter properties without the landlord's consent;

(b)   Thompsons have failed to supervise repairs and inspect properties regularly;

(c)   Thompsons have disregarded the long-term health and fabric of the properties;

(d)   Thompsons have failed to plan ahead for repairs;

G   (e)   Thompsons have wasted money by not repairing the properties since the cost would have been tax deductible.

5.2.3 Properties needing refurbishment

(iv) Several properties still need to be refurbished.

5.2.4 36 Reading Road

H   (v)   36 Reading Road was refurbished to a poor standard.

I find that Mr Wyard and Mr Farley have enjoyed a high degree of autonomy as managers at Thompsons. Mr Thompson has not imposed on either of them any detailed guidelines as to repairs or improvements or lettings. So far as repairs and improvements were concerned, Mr Thompson's general policy was to expend as little as possible because of the low rents being received.

Expert evidence of (inter alios) quantity surveyors and an architectural technician   A
was adduced on various of the allegations of mismanagement, but by an order dated
1 October 1993 Mr Registrar Buckley ordered that this expert evidence be confined to
specified properties specified in the schedule to the order, being the properties referred to
in the relevant part of the pleadings.

The schedule reads as follows:

' (1) 18 Finchley Road, Ipswich	B
 (2) 44 Finchley Road, Ipswich
 (3) 62 Finchley Road, Ipswich
 (4) 96 Hatfield Road, Ipswich
 (5) 448 Spring Road, Ipswich
 (6) 3-10 Middleton Close, Ipswich
 (7) 132 Finchley Road, Ipswich
 (8) 15 Blenheim Road, Ipswich	C
 (9) 78 Finchley Road, Ipswich
 (10) 130 Finchley Road, Ipswich
 (11) 36 Kingston Road, Ipswich
 (12) 12 Thompson Road, Ipswich
 (13) 154 Cauldwell Hall Road, Ipswich
 (14) Lakeside Close and Lakeside Road properties,	D
being those properties where works were carried out under the "window contract",
as referred to in the further and better particulars dated 19 July 1993.'

5.2.1 Competitive tendering

I find that Thompsons did not in general obtain competitive estimates for the repair
and improvement work carried out to the companies' properties (indeed small or urgent
work was done without even an estimate). Mr Farley accepted that this was the case. He   E
gave as his reason the fact that Thompsons used Mr Martell when he was available, and
explained that both Thompsons and the local authority were satisfied with his work. Mr
Farley accepted that Mr Martell was not the cheapest builder on the market but
contended that his work was priced reasonably. Mr Thompson thought that the
management of the business had not changed substantially and accordingly I infer that it
was not in general the practice of Mr Wyard either to obtain competitive tenders for   F
repair or improvement work to the companies' properties. Mr Farley said that the
majority of the work was small.

Both Mr Pooley and Mr Balch, two of the experts called by the defendants, saw merit
in using a small, reliable local builder who would do the routine maintenance work more
cheaply provided he was also offered the larger work. In my judgment this would not be
an unreasonable view to take, but there was no evidence that that was the reason for
failing to obtain competitive tenders. Mr Farley said that he tended to use Mr Martell   G
because his work was good and reasonably priced.

According to Mr Wells, the plaintiffs' expert, the estimates in respect of nine contracts
relating to similar properties and totalling £59,010 approximately were excessive by
£18,763 approximately.

Mr Wells reached this conclusion using accepted pricing books and ensuring the   H
inclusion of a ten per cent margin for a profit and overheads. However the plaintiffs did
not produce any builder to say that he would have been prepared to do the particular
work in question at these rates. In the opinion of Mr Pooley, however, such estimates
exceeded his estimate by ten per cent in only three cases (154 Cauldwell Hall Road –
excess £2,360; 18 Finchley Road – excess £1,364; 62 Finchley Road – excess £1,800). The
rest were in his opinion not unreasonable.

A   5.2.2 Property maintenance

The acid test of whether the failure to obtain competitive tenders had in fact resulted
in loss to the companies would be to examine the work done and the amount paid for it.
The same investigation would reveal whether the companies had paid too much for repair
or improvement work.

The plaintiffs have not approached the matter in this way. They adduced the expert
B   evidence of Mr Wells, chartered surveyor. He has priced the work required to be done,
as appearing from schedules of work prepared by the local authority, in respect of twelve
contracts for the repairs or improvements to twelve separate properties belonging to the
companies. Save in three cases, Mr Wells subsequently visited the sites in question. The
estimates of cost were then adjusted to take into account the results of physical inspection.
However Mr Wells did not have access to details of the work actually done on these
properties at the relevant time, nor did he see parts of the repairs which were inaccessible
C   even on those properties which he did visit. The defendants therefore call Mr Wells' work
a hybrid exercise blending the tender with what he considered should have been produced
on the final account.

In Mr Wells' opinion, the estimates were excessive and could have been beaten if
competitive tenders had been sought. He also expressed the view that the work done had
not been properly checked, and that payment had been made against unsubstantiated
D   invoices. He also stated that there was no planned programme of maintenance. There
was furthermore no documentation reconciling the final accounts which were paid
against the original estimates or recording agreement to additional costs or work. The
aggregate of the differences between the amounts estimated by the contractor, and the
amounts paid by the companies, in respect of nine of the contracts considered by him
was £60,000 approximately (before VAT). The work in question took place at various
dates between 1983 and 1991. The total amounts paid to builders in respect of these
E   contracts was approximately £140,000 (before VAT). All of these contracts (save two)
were carried out by Mr Martell. In the case of one contract (96 Hatfield Road) Mr
Martell's estimate was £7,797 (before VAT). On 19 March 1985 he produced a statement
showing final costings of £7,969 plus VAT but on the following day he produced an
invoice claiming £9,400 plus VAT. The explanation given by Mr Martell was that the
invoice dated 20 March 1985 included additional works done in compliance with a
F   structural engineer's report. I accept that explanation.

In the case of some contracts Mr Wells expressed the view that the contract work, or
in some cases earlier work, must have been done inadequately as further works were
needed. In respect of the largest contract in terms of value (known as the Lakeside Close/
Road windows contract) Mr Wells was unable to express a view as to a fair value for the
works because of the lack of documentation.

G   Mr Wells' starting point is the local authority schedules. However, Mr Martell
explained that these were not comprehensive, and he recalled that in the case of many of
the contracts in question there had been extra work. Five of the contracts in question
related to properties in Finchley Road which were notorious for the building problems
to which they gave rise. He strenuously denied overcharging (though it follows from my
earlier finding regarding the passing on to the companies of the cost of the commission
he was paying to Mr Wyard that there was some element of overcharging). Indeed in one
H   case (154 Cauldwell Hall Road) Mr Martell's final invoice was less than his estimate. To
a certain extent, as Mr Pooley, the quantity surveyor called by the defendants, says in his
report:

> 'The true condition of the works prior to commencement and the condition under
> which the work was carried out cannot now be properly established for work
> executed up to 11 years ago. Thus any estimate or comparison produced

retrospectively for work of this nature including those estimates proffered by [Mr   A
Wells] must in [my] opinion be regarded as theoretical.'

The opinion of each of the experts has to be read subject to this qualification.

In Mr Pooley's opinion, based on consideration of the estimates and invoices and physical inspection in most cases, the amounts paid in respect of only two of the eleven contracts could be described as unreasonable. (In respect of another contract he was unable to give an opinion.) One of the two contracts was for work done on 44 Finchley   B
Road where Mr Martell could recall additional work. The other was for work done at 448 Spring Road, the circumstances of which Mr Martell could not recall. In the opinion of Mr Pooley, the amount paid in respect of these two contracts (£20,470) was excessive by £9,251 of which £3,751 related to 44 Finchley Road.

Like Mr Wells, Mr Pooley was critical of the lack of detail in Mr Martell's final invoices. This means that Thompsons could only have given them limited scrutiny at the   C
time they were received. In cross-examination, Mr Pooley accepted that there was a third contract (15 Blenheim Road) where the amount alleged by the plaintiffs to have been paid (£6,376) exceeded his own calculation of what the final invoice should have been for the work done (£5,751). The difference of £625 was more than ten per cent of £5,751 (by a relatively small amount). Mr Pooley regarded variances of ten per cent or less from his own figures as reasonable.

Mr Wells and Mr Pooley did not analyse in full the estimates and invoices for all the   D
same properties. However the differences between their respective approaches can be seen from the following table giving the relevant figure in respect of work done on nine similar properties in respect of which they both analysed the estimates and invoices in full:

E

Name of property	Total amount paid to the builder (A)	Amount of overpayment in (A)		
		Per Mr Pooley		Per Mr Wells
		1. Starting from the builder's estimate	2. Starting from Mr Pooley's opinion of what the estimate should have been	
18 Finchley Road	14,700	713	2,077	5,030
44 Finchley Road	9,828*	3,751	3,751	4,648

F

G

H

Name of property	Total amount paid to the builder (A)	Amount of overpayment in (A)		
		Per Mr Pooley		Per Mr Wells
		1. Starting from the builder's estimate	2. Starting from Mr Pooley's opinion of what the estimate should have been	
62 Finchley Road	18,545	7,721	9,517	13,321
96 Hatfield Road	9,400	242	242	3,292
448 Spring Road	10,750	5,500	6,085	6,003
15 Blenheim Road	6,376*	400	400	1,500
132 Finchley Road	7,856	1,000	1,000	853
78 Finchley Road	7,945	—	—	1,480
154 Cauldwell Hall Road	11,880	−490	1,870	2,143
TOTAL(S)	97,280	18,837	24,942	38,270

(* = Defendants allege that the amounts paid were slightly smaller than the amounts shown)

I should add that, unlike Mr Wells, Mr Pooley made no deduction for the work which he considered had not been done.

The plaintiffs also called Mr Woods, who is an architectural technician. He has many years' experience of supervising the improvement and maintenance of properties including tenanted properties. I now set out my findings with respect to Mr Woods' evidence. Mr Woods' evidence was based on his inspection of 31 properties constituting 14 per cent in number of the companies' housing stock. He impressed me as being a person who was both familiar with and knowledgeable about work to properties. He was also in my judgment realistic and I accept his opinion as to the condition of property he inspected as frank and not overstated.

Mr Woods expressed the following conclusions based upon his inspections:

(1)   That there were numerous defects in the properties he visited.

Mr Woods inspected all but one (78 Finchley Road) of the scheduled properties.   A
His report identifies about 140 defects in these properties. I find that some of these
defects were, as Mr Woods accepted, not serious. However in my judgment a
significant number were substantial. For example, in relation to 62 Finchley Road,
there was only one 13 amp electrical socket for the first floor comprising two
bedrooms and a bathroom. In addition, as appeared from a photograph produced
by Mr Woods, the bricks to the steps at the rear of the property were worn and in
a dangerous condition. Mr Woods compared his list of defects with the schedule   B
of works required to be done, drawn up by the local authority. Several of the
matters mentioned in the local authority's schedule had either not been done at all
or had been done defectively. Mr Woods' opinion was that the condition of the
property was poor. He was cross-examined on this but in my judgment his
conclusion was not invalidated by any point on this property made to him in cross-
examination. I would accept that the number of defects in relation to this property   C
was by far the longest, but there was evidence of other serious defects on other
properties. Many of the defects were repeated from property to property.

(2)   That Thompsons had not inspected the properties before the work was carried out
nor sufficiently supervised the working during construction.

In my judgment, the nature of the defects, many of which ought to have been
obvious on inspection, amply justified this conclusion. Mr Martell's evidence was   D
that Mr Wyard would inspect the work he did. I accept that from time to time
both Mr Wyard and Mr Farley would go to see how work on a property was
progressing but I also find that there was no methodical or critical assessment by
them of work done. I do not think it is an answer that the local authority should
have inspected grant-aided work. In any event it is not clear to what extent or in
what manner the local authority did make an inspection of work done.

(3)   That Thompsons could not have operated a properly planned maintenance   E
programme.

I accept this conclusion, which was not challenged in cross-examination. In
particular I accept that it would be desirable and usual for property owners in this
situation to have had such a programme and that the companies ought to have
had such a programme. They certainly had a sufficient number of properties (238
in all) to justify it. The programme could be tailored to their requirements. Mr   F
Woods frankly accepted that it would be unrealistic to maintain properties of the
type which Macro had in Finchley Road up to the highest standards. However he
thought that a four-year programme giving the highest priority to structural
matters would be appropriate. Mr Pooley agreed with Mr Woods that the
companies should have had a planned programme of property maintenance.

(4)   That some decisions taken were not in the companies' interests.   G

He instanced the conversion of a third bedroom of a house in Finchley Road into
a bathroom when an extension to the house had been built in similar properties,
thus reducing rental potential. He also instanced the installation of wooden
window frames, rather than UPVC (unplasticised poly vinyl chloride), window
placements which would be generally more expensive but which would not require
maintenance. It was suggested to Mr Woods in cross-examination that the landlord   H
would have to consider such questions as the rate of return he would get from the
property once the investment had been made. Mr Woods accepted that this was a
relevant consideration but he pointed out that in some cases grants were also
available. The defendants did not adduce evidence to show that the matters to
which Mr Woods referred in his report could not have been avoided by more
prudent property management. The defects had in my judgment been allowed to

A   remain or happen because of Thompsons' failure to supervise repairs and improvements with even a basic degree of efficiency. If this was beyond Thompsons' capabilities, Thompsons should have declined to agree to supervise repairs and the work should have been given to someone else.

Another incident concerning the Chantry Estate in Lakeside Road supports the conclusion that Thompsons did not adequately inspect the companies' properties which they managed. On that estate there is, or should be, a fence at the edge of

B   the car park which protects people using the car park from a drop of several feet. The fence was broken down by vandals and lay unrepaired for about 12 months. Mr Farley had to admit in cross-examination that this damage was not seen and rectified as quickly as it ought to have been. This incident occurred in late 1992. In a separate incident the external lights in a block of flats had not been repaired for some 18 months and the insurers wrote to Thompsons drawing their attention to

C   the condition in the policy requiring the property to be kept in good repair. In about March 1992, the Environmental Health Officer was informed and there was some publicity about the matter. Mr Farley's explanation was that various options had been considered and the work 'was in the pipeline' by the time this happened. I do not accept this as the full explanation. In my judgment, Thompsons had not conducted a proper or regular inspection of the blocks of flats in question and the problem had lain undetected for some considerable time before Thompsons took

D   any action. These incidents also demonstrate the wisdom of regular inspection.

Moreover, the defendants did not seek to show that a system of regular inspection – or a policy of having a planned maintenance programme – was now in operation. So far as the inspection of building work, however, is concerned, Mr Farley's evidence was that there are now two members of staff who try to see the repairs being done but there was no indication as to their qualifications for this purpose

E   or the usefulness of their inspections. In any event, in the case of Macro only some 30 per cent of repairs are inspected in this way. In Earliba the percentage is higher. I do not consider that this system is sufficient to prevent the situation arising in which defective work is done, paid for and remains unrectified. It was accepted that there was no planned maintenance programme, but the defendants argued that in the case of these properties a policy of minimum repairs was acceptable.

F   Mr Rhys has submitted that there were good commercial reasons for not seeking competitive quotes. He relied on Mr Pooley's evidence which showed that the companies were only overcharged in three or four cases. On this, I do not accept that the overcharging was as limited as this because Mr Pooley has taken the estimate that was accepted as his starting point even when Mr Pooley thought it was excessive. However the more serious criticism of Thompsons' approach was that they failed to spot defective work or to have it remedied, and for that reason

G   were overcharged. It is apparent from the financial information in para. 2.4 above that in all years the figures for repairs were material and in some years, in the case of Macro, the outgoings of the companies, including repairs, resulted in a trading loss.

5.2.3 Properties needing refurbishment

H   The plaintiffs allege that some 21 properties need to be refurbished. The pleaded allegation is that a number of these properties lack even a bathroom or lavatory.

The property valuers instructed by both parties, namely Mr Brunt FRICS on behalf of the plaintiffs, and Mr Wass FRICS, on behalf of the defendants, have met and produced a joint report which has obviated the need for either of them to be called. On this they are to be commended: by so doing they saved the court time and the parties time and expense. According to the valuers' report some 31 properties require repairs at an aggregate cost of £104,500. The figure for the pleaded properties is £67,000 approximately. Only 13 of the properties alleged to have been in need of refurbishment were on the valuers' list, but the valuers' report in this respect is expressly stated to be based on information provided in the rent registration forms lodged with the local rent officer under the *Rent Act* 1977 as amended by the *Housing Act* 1980.

Of these 13 properties:

(i)   the work required on 70 and 140 Finchley Road and 4 Bloomfield Street principally relates to the installation of new bathroom facilities. There are written statements in evidence (by agreement) from the tenants of those properties showing that (for various personal reasons) they do not wish that work to take place. I do not think that the failure to effect that work (to which the valuers attribute £19,000) is an act of mismanagement.

(ii)   It is pleaded that there is no bathroom at 43 Oxford Road or 78 Finchley Road. Mr Farley has given evidence which I accept that there is, and therefore in my judgment the allegation that refurbishment is needed is not made out in respect of these properties. The costs of repairs attributed to these properties was £10,000.

(iii)   It is pleaded that there is no bathroom or hot water at 41 Tomiline Road. Mr Farley's evidence on this point, which I accept, is that this work has now been done. This property is therefore no longer in need of refurbishment. The cost of repairs attributed by the valuer to this property was £6,000.

(iv)   It is pleaded that 80 Finchley Road had no hot water. Mr Farley's evidence on this point, which I accept, was that it had hot water and that an inside lavatory (which the property had lacked) had been installed in April 1992. The cost of repairs attributed by the valuers to this property was £6,000.

(v)   It is pleaded that 122 Finchley Road has no hot water or bathroom and that 130 Finchley Road has no bathroom. Mr Farley's evidence on this point, which I accept, was that the tenants had made these improvements. The cost of repairs attributed by the valuers to these properties was £13,000.

(vi)   The valuers estimate the cost of repair of one of the properties (28 Handford Street) as nil.

The remaining properties are 50 and 52 Finchley Road and 88 Richmond Road, to which the valuers attribute £14,000 as the cost of repairs. In the case of each of these properties the improvement which the plaintiffs allege should be made has already been made by the tenant. The plaintiffs say that Thompsons should have had the work done so that a higher rent could be charged, the value of the properties would be higher, tax relief on the cost of the repairs obtained and any grants available utilised. They add that the information extracted from the annual accounts of the companies shows that they have, and have since 1987–88 had, sufficient cash resources for this purpose. What the defendants say is that many of these 13 properties are subject to regulated tenancies (i.e. the tenants cannot be evicted except for non-payment of rent). Mr Farley said that there was little that could be done to prevent the tenants from making alterations, but of course there would have been no need for them to alter a property to (say) install a bathroom if the companies had already done so and the companies might have obtained vacant possession if they had not 'turned a blind eye' to what the tenants were doing.

The defendants rely upon the evidence of Mr Balch in relation to repairs and regulated tenancies:

'There [is] little to be gained from adopting other than a minimum repairs policy. Apart from the considerable grant aided repair/improvement programme put in place in Macro in the early and middle 1980s, this would seem to be the way the

A

company has been run, and in that I consider the company to have been prudent and in line with that sector of the market in general.'

I accept that policy as being one which the companies could properly determine to adopt, but the installation of bathrooms and lavatories would be grant-aided work. In relation to the failure to obtain grants, Mr Balch's evidence was as follows:

B

'I would agree that the respondents may not have exhausted the grant route on every occasion open to them. It should be understood however that the procedures are and were administratively complex and involved delays. I think it to be expected in the context of a diminishing portfolio of regulated properties, that the respondents adopted a pragmatic attitude. They may have lost some long term asset value but they have minimised expenditure in revenue terms and they have not reduced opportunities to convert to shortholds by way of vacant possession.'

C

Again, I accept that this is a view which the companies could reasonably take even though the companies would necessarily also have suffered a loss in rental income as a result. It has not in my judgment been shown that this loss of income was in fact substantial in the case of either company. As a cross-check on his conclusions, Mr Balch examined the amounts spent by the companies on repairs (including improvements) as a percentage of gross rents for the period 1983–93. He found that the percentages in question (Macro, with older properties – 51.8 per cent; Earliba – 32 per cent) were consistent with what he would expect. Mr Balch stressed that this was a very broad brush approach but it provides some confirmation that the attitude taken with regard to the amount spent on repairs and improvements was not out of the norm.

D

5.2.4 36 Reading Road

The plaintiffs allege that the refurbishment of Reading Road in 1990 was carried out to a poor standard, which was reflected in the rent achieved on its subsequent letting which at £300 per month was some £80 per month less than the then open market rent for such a property. No evidence was led in support of this allegation which I therefore find not proved.

E

5.3 *Matters relating to lettings*

5.3.1 Poor lettings

F

The plaintiffs' case is as follows:

'Wyard lost money for the companies by committing them to lettings on poor terms, that properties were let on protected tenancies within the meaning of the *Rent Act* 1977 rather than protected shorthold tenancies. If they had been let on protected shorthold tenancies then subsequently to the commencement of the *Housing Act* 1988 (15 January 1989) such tenancies could have been terminated, and at a later date assured shorthold tenancies could have been granted which would have commanded higher rents than those payable under the protected tenancies.'

G

The plaintiffs gave particulars of 74 properties where there were lettings on protected tenancies, and where they alleged that the letting should have been on protected shorthold tenancies. Two forms of loss are alleged: loss in capital value and loss of income. Appendix D to the report of Mr Brunt FRICS contained details of the value of the properties as at 1993 if subject to assured shorthold tenancies and also as subject to protected tenancies and I set out my findings as regards this in section 6 below. As respects loss in rental income, Mr Law (who is experienced in property management), for the plaintiffs, gave evidence as to the loss in income which in his opinion resulted from letting some 16 properties on protected tenancies as compared with what would have been received if the properties had been let on an assured shorthold basis:

H

		£	A
12 Dunlin Road	(ground floor flat)	105 per month	
18a Dunlin Road	(first floor flat)	95 per month	
52 Finchley Road	(two bedroomed house)	100 per month	
1 Lakeside Close	(ground floor flat)	100 per month	
17 Lakeside Close	(three bedroomed house)	110 per month	
3 Lakeside Road	(three bedroomed house)	100 per month	
7 Lakeside Road	(three bedroomed house)	100 per month	B
9 Lakeside Road	(three bedroomed house)	100 per month	
29 Lakeside Road	(three bedroomed house)	100 per month	
41 Manchester Road	(first floor flat)	120 per month	
47 Manchester Road	(three bedroomed house)	100 per month	
70 Manchester Road	(three bedroomed house)	100 per month	
4 Middleton Close	(two bedroomed house)	90 per month	C
7 Middleton Close	(two bedroomed house)	90 per month	
9 Middleton Close	(two bedroomed house)	90 per month	
29 Royston Drive	(two bedroomed house)	90 per month	

(These figures take no account of additional income lost through the properties being let on protected tenancies at below market rent for such tenancies.)

The statutory history is as follows. Prior to the *Housing Act* 1980, the companies'   D
residential properties were let on protected tenancies, to which the rent registration regime applied. Under this system, the rent had to be registered with the local rent officer. He had to fix the rent and was required to do so without regard to the scarcity of the property in question. After the *Housing Act* 1980, the companies could (if certain conditions were complied with) have let their properties on protected shortholds. Under this type of tenancy, possession could be recovered after the end of the period on giving three months' notice prior to the date of expiry or any anniversary of that date. Initially   E
these tenancies too were subject to the rent registration system, and the rent could not exceed the registered rent, but this ceased to be required for tenancies of properties outside Greater London after 1 December 1981, although the tenant could apply for the fair rent to be determined. By the *Housing Act* 1988, assured shorthold tenancies were introduced. A market rent could be agreed, and possession could be recovered at the end of the fixed term. This new form of tenancy could not be granted to a person who was   F
previously a protected tenant of the property but could be granted to a tenant who had previously had a protected shorthold tenancy of the property. These proposals were made clear in the Housing Bill presented to Parliament in November 1987.

Subject to there being sufficient tenants in the market willing and able to take assured shorthold tenancies, the rental income of the companies and the capital values of their assets would increase most if properties were let on that form of tenancy. Moreover,   G
protected shorthold tenancies could be converted into assured shorthold tenancies, but protected tenancies could not.

Mr Thompson did not know about protected shorthold tenancies or assured shorthold tenancies. He left such matters to Mr Wyard and after 1987 to Mr Farley. His standing instructions to Thompsons were simply to get the best rental return available. Mr Farley said that there was no advantage to the companies in letting on protected shortholds   H
because (a) the companies wanted a long-term tenant anyway; (b) the properties would have to have money spent on them for a higher rent to be obtained; (c) the tenant could always have the rent registered in any event; and (d) if the tenancy was long term, the tenant would feel more inclined to improve the property at his own expense and to look after it. He said that 24 of the 74 properties listed by the plaintiffs were now let on assured shorthold tenancies, and that since Mr Wyard's departure, 20 tenancies had been

A   converted to assured shorthold tenancies. I do not accept that Thompsons were consciously looking for long-term tenants. Most of the tenancy agreements in evidence, covering the period from 1980, are for one year only. Mr Farley saw the force of this point. He said that soon after he took over he changed the policy and started to grant protected shorthold because he could see assured shortholds coming in and because he preferred to have the security of knowing the tenant could be evicted. I accept that Mr Farley realised the benefits of protected shorthold tenancies in late 1987 and started
B   granting protected shorthold tenancies after that date. However there is correspondence between Turner Martin Symes and Mr Farley in 1990 regarding a tenancy of 30 Manchester Road, from which it is clear that even by early 1990 Mr Farley was not familiar with the requirements for a valid protected shorthold or assured shorthold tenancy and that Thompsons' procedures permitted situations to arise in which the new forms of tenancy were not properly and effectively created.

C   The next question is whether Thompsons ought to have granted assured shorthold tenancies from an earlier date. Mr Balch, for the defendants, said that prior to the publication of the Housing Bill in 1987, there was no obvious advantage in letting on protected shorthold tenancies since the tenant could refuse to pay rent above the registered rent, and because there were a large number of properties available for rent there was a greater risk of 'voids' if protected shorthold tenancies were granted. He thought that Thompsons' policy of encouraging tenants to improve their properties was
D   prudent. He doubted whether there was much of a market for letting at higher rents. It might have been more difficult for the companies to obtain improvement grants for their properties if let on protected shorthold tenancies, but Mr Balch had no evidence that that was in fact the case. By granting protected shorthold tenancies, the companies stood to gain in terms of capital values but might lose the security of their rental income.

E   Mr Law, for the plaintiffs, thought that the protected shorthold had the following advantages:

> '(a) After the period of compulsory registration rents could be agreed at their market level notwithstanding that the tenant had a right to refer back to the rent officer for a reduction to the "fair rent";
>
> (b) The right of repossession on shortholds was mandatory irrespective of the merits of the application giving a good bargaining lever with a tenant.'

F   He added that it had been the practice of his firm to let on protected shorthold rather than protected regulated tenancies during the 1980s subject to the instructions of landlords.

Mr Law did not accept that there was a greater risk of voids if properties were let on protected shortholds since the rent could be reduced on a reletting. He thought that housing benefit tenants could take such tenancies because the benefit office of the local
G   authority would refer the matter to the rent officer who would fix a fair market rent. He also thought that better presented properties were easier to let, even to tenants on housing benefit, than poorly maintained properties. He considered that by letting as protected tenancies, the landlord gained security because the rent was low. A better rent could be obtained in his opinion by letting on protected shortholds. He had not himself encountered problems when applying for improvement grants for properties subject to protected shorthold tenancies.
H   Having considered the views of both experts, I prefer that of Mr Law. In my judgment the companies lost money through not taking advantage of the protected shorthold systems before 1987. In my judgment, no consideration was given to this question. In my judgment, professional managers such as Thompsons ought to have considered whether the change to protected shortholds would be advantageous to the companies, but failed to do so.

I now set out my findings as to the loss in rental income as a result of lettings on protected tenancies rather than assured shorthold tenancies. I am only concerned with the 16 properties listed above. The figures in the following table represent the likely rent per month in the opinion of Mr Law (for the plaintiffs) and Mr Balch (for the defendants) respectively if the properties were now let on assured shorthold:

			Mr Law	Mr Balch	
			£	£	
A1	12 Dunlin Road	(Ground floor flat)	225	170	
A2	18a Dunlin Road	(First floor flat)	235	220	
A3	52 Finchley Road	(2 bedroomed house)	225	225	(agreed)
A4	1 Lakeside Close	(Ground floor flat)	210	170	
A5	17 Lakeside Close	(3 bedroomed house)	280	280	(agreed)
A6	3 Lakeside Road	(3 bedroomed house)	275	265	
A7	7 Lakeside Road	(3 bedroomed house)	265	265	(agreed)
A8	9 Lakeside Road	(3 bedroomed house)	265	265	(agreed)
A9	29 Lakeside Road	(3 bedroomed house)	280	280	(agreed)
A10	41 Manchester Road	(First floor flat)	250	220	
A11	47 Manchester Road	(3 bedroomed house)	275	270	
A12	70 Manchester Road	(3 bedroomed house)	265	265	(agreed)
A13	4 Middleton Close	(2 bedroomed house)	240	240	(agreed)
A14	7 Middleton Close	(2 bedroomed house)	240	240	(agreed)
A15	9 Middleton Close	(2 bedroomed house)	250	250	(agreed)
A16	29 Royston Drive	(2 bedroomed house)	250*	240	

(* This subject to possible structural problems with this property)

I accept Mr Law's figures, which were supported by comparables. According to figures produced by Mr Balch similar one-bedroomed flats to A1 and A4 had been let recently at £170 per month, but Mr Law satisfied me that his valuation was nonetheless fair having regard to other recent lettings and the sizes of the respective properties. I therefore accept Mr Law's opinion as to rental values. The loss in income resulting from letting on protected tenancies rather than protected shorthold tenancies is therefore as already set out above.

5.3.2 Late registrations of rent

Mr Farley accepted that in the case of some 39 regulated tenancies, an application to register the rent was made late, in some cases by a matter of months and in other cases, by a matter of years. Late registration would generally delay the date when an application for an increase in the registered rent could be made. However only 26 of these applications were made after Mr Farley was appointed manager (i.e. in the last seven years). On the basis that the companies had 243 residential properties approximately and assuming a fresh registration for each property every two years (which Mr Farley thought would be a realistic assumption for 1993), Thompsons would be handling some 800 rent registrations over a period of seven years. I accept that if rent is registered late, the companies will have difficulty in recovering or raising it but the percentage of error here (3.25 per cent) was (on the assumptions I have made) not in my view material. In my judgment, a nil error rate would be unrealistic and a 3.25 per cent error rate is immaterial in this context.

5.4 *Retentions and management charges*

5.4.1 Retentions

The plaintiffs' allegations are as follows:

'42. For many years Mr Thompson senior permitted Thompsons to place money

A belonging to Macro and Earliba in non-interest bearing accounts, albeit that the moneys were retained in those accounts, and were likely to be retained in them, for several months. In Earliba's audited accounts for the year ended 31 March 1990 there was an item described as 'Sundry debtors' of £116,050; approximately £110,000 of this sum was money collected by Thompsons for Earliba but not paid to Earliba, albeit that it represented approximately 50 per cent of its gross annual rental income.

B 43. By letter dated 5 March 1990 Earliba's auditors reminded Farley that it was a contravention of the Estate Agency Accounting Regulations and/or gave rise to a potential charge under s. 419 ICTA 1988 and/or was prejudicial to the interests of the minority shareholders in Earliba for Thompsons to retain, as it was doing and as it had done for some time, substantial credit balances on Thompsons' rent accounts for Earliba.'

C (The allegation in relation to the Estate Agency Accounting Regulations has not been pursued).

The second sentence of para. 42 is factually correct. At the end of their financial years in 1981–1988 Macro and/or Earliba owed moneys to Thompsons. At the end of their financial years in 1989–1992, the position was reversed. It was an agreed fact that the amounts owed by Thompsons (and held in its clients' account) did not bear interest. The details of the relevant balances in 1988–1992 is as follows:

D

31 March		Due to Thompsons	Due by Thompsons	Total net due by Thompsons
1992	Macro		(5,800)	
	Earliba		(5,201)	(11.001)
1991	Macro		(23,112)	
	Earliba	13,771		(9.341)
1990	Macro		(18,416)	
	Earliba		(110,705)	(129.121)
1989	Macro	26,774		
	Earliba		(49,813)	(23.039)

F Accordingly the debtors item in the Earliba accounts for the period ended 31 March 1989 showed that Thompsons held a credit balance of some £49,813 on behalf of Earliba. The Inland Revenue queried the amounts held by Thompsons on behalf of Earliba but Thompsons claimed that the amount represented rents collected and not paid over because of repair work in hand. The Inland Revenue also asked for an explanation as to why the management charges had increased from 11.5 per cent to 15 per cent. By a letter dated 8 November 1989 to Ford du Cane & Co dealing with this query and the amounts held on accounts, Mr Farley replied that the increase in repairs was due to storm damage in 1987: 'We have had and still have a vast amount of repairs coming in and it was agreed at a meeting that Earliba as well as the other companies should hold a reserve to cater for such works' and further that he had in fact underestimated the amount required. He also claimed that Thompsons' management charges for Earliba would increase further because of the time he was having to spend on the companies' affairs, and that they were in proportion to charges for other customers.

H Subsequent events show that information contained in this letter, which was written so that it could be shown to the Inland Revenue, was incorrect. Mr Farley must have known it was not correct when he wrote it. Such an incident cannot simply be brushed aside as one which only concerns the Inland Revenue. It is relevant also to the question whether the plaintiffs should be locked into companies for whose affairs Mr Farley is being given increasing responsibility.

By letter dated 24 November 1989, the Inland Revenue expressed themselves as   A
satisfied regarding the management charges but not so as far as the credit balances were
concerned. The Inland Revenue referred to these as 'money lent'. By letter dated 27
November 1989, Ford du Cane advised Mr Farley to change the methods of accounting
for rent received for Earliba and Macro. They advised that the ideal arrangement would
be for Earliba and Macro to be paid the balance of rent accounts each month in the same
way as other landlords and then for the companies each to pay their own repairs and
improvements out of their own separate bank accounts. The letter added 'Mr Thompson   B
may not like this idea'. In a further letter dated 29 November 1989 they advised that as
Mr Thompson had the use of the companies' moneys the arrangements amounted to an
interest free loan. By letter dated 8 January 1990, Mr Farley claimed that 'for the first
few months of the tax year 1989–90 some £42,000 was spent on the companies'
properties'. He continued: 'Unfortunately these moneys will always have to be held back
as Thompsons' client account issues the orders and instructions and we ourselves will be   C
responsible for the payment of all such bills if Earliba refuse to pay'. By letter dated 31
January 1990, Ford du Cane advised that the Inland Revenue were still not satisfied as
to the balance held by Thompsons at 31 March 1989, and that at 'the next year-end the
balances should be small'. This advice was repeated by letter dated 5 March 1990. Ford
du Cane's view was that the companies should pay their expenditure out of their own
separate bank accounts. Mr Farley's attention was drawn to the matters pleaded in para.
42 (quoted above) and in particular to the loss of interest and to the prejudice to minority   D
shareholders. On the same date Ford du Cane confirmed to the Inland Revenue that
Thompsons would not normally hold any amounts due to the landlords on their rent
accounts.

In fact the accounts of Macro and Earliba for the year ended 31 March 1990 showed
that Thompsons held £129,121 which belonged to the companies in spite of Ford du
Cane's warnings. It was not until 23 May 1990 that Mr Farley transferred the sum of   E
£150,000 from Earliba's current account to a money market deposit account and it was
not until at least November 1990 that steps were taken to ensure that the companies paid
for their own repairs. In a letter dated 6 November 1990 to Julian, Ford du Cane observed
that:

> 'in fairness to Farley you have to bear in mind that the general policy covering this
> matter is obviously still very much dictated by your father and he is all for carrying   F
> on in the same way as things have been done in the past.'

In due course Mr Farley produced the invoices paid in the next quarter out of the
balances at 31 March 1989. It then became apparent that their value was £4,500. In the
circumstances, the Inland Revenue levied a charge under s. 419 of the *Income and
Corporation Taxes Act* 1970 (loans to participators).

In January 1991, the Inland Revenue again queried the retentions shown at the last   G
year-end by Macro's accounts. The amount shown as then owed to Thompsons was
£18,416. However the amount this time could be justified by reference to insurance
premiums and repairs payable in April 1990.

Accordingly I find the allegations in para. 42 and 43 (quoted above) proved. The years
in which Thompsons retained moneys due to the companies were the financial years
ended 31 March 1989–1992. However (taking the affairs of the companies together) the   H
retentions were in my judgment significant only in relation to Earliba and only in the
financial years ended 31 March 1989 and 1990. Moreover, in my judgment, there has to
be weighed against the retentions in 1989–1992, the balances the other way in the four
previous years. In the years 1989–1992, the average balance due *from* Thompsons to the
companies was £43,125.50. In the years 1985–1988, the average balance due *to*
Thompsons from the companies was £67,759. In those circumstances, I hold that the

A   retentions did not result in prejudice to the plaintiffs for the purposes of s. 459 of the *Companies Act* 1985.

The situation at 31 March 1993 is not wholly clear. At the next financial year-end (31 March 1993), there was again a substantial amount (approximately £65,000) owed to Earliba by Thompsons. Mr Farley said that this was because he had in error failed to pay dividends and tax out of this money before the year-end. So far as dividends are

B   concerned, this suggests that Mr Farley was retaining money in Thompsons' client account to pay the dividend to be paid after the next annual general meeting. In relation to both dividends and tax, it is not in my view necessary for Thompsons to retain moneys: the companies should draw cheques at the appropriate time on their accounts. It is accepted that the companies have sufficient cash to pay their bills as they become due. Mr Farley informed the court that Thompsons now transfers the balance of rents received to the companies on a monthly basis. In my judgment the present system is probably not

C   operating satisfactorily (see the position at 31 March 1993). The present system is therefore potentially prejudicial to the interests of minority shareholders in the present and future financial years of the companies. I find that the defective nature of the present system is due to incompetence on the part of Thompsons and that moneys are not being deliberately withheld from the companies.

D   5.4.2 Management charges

The plaintiffs' allegation is as follows:

> '44. Thompsons charges and has at all times charged Macro and Earliba management fees for its management services and receives the benefit of commissions paid by insurance companies from premiums in relation to Macro and Earliba's properties. The charges are fixed by Farley as an employee of Thompsons and agreed by him as company secretary of both companies. The fees
>
> E   charged and agreed by Farley have been excessively high.'

I find that Thompsons charge Macro and Earliba a management charge of ten per cent of rents received (plus VAT), and are reimbursed for their expenses. I also find that Thompsons retained commission for insurance placed by them. I further find that payment of the fee is authorised by Mr Farley on behalf of the companies. Prior to the inception of these proceedings, Mr Farley received £1,000 per annum from Macro for his

F   services as secretary. Mr Thompson draws no directors' fees. Earliba also pays a management charge to Macro to assist the latter to retain its trading status. Since 1988, Mr Farley has been an employee of Macro and in the financial year ended 31 March 1993 this cost Macro £7,132. In my judgment the companies should be liable to pay only a small sum for the secretarial services which Mr Farley provides. Since about 1987, there appears to have been a further charge of £5,000 per annum paid by Earliba to Thompsons for management services. This fee was included in the relevant item in the annual

G   accounts of Earliba which were adopted each year but it is not suggested that shareholders' attention was drawn to this additional charge.

The effect of the management fees paid by the companies to Thompsons can be seen from the following information extracted from a table prepared by Mr Driver:

'Year ended 31 March	Managing agents' fees as percentage of gross rents	
	MACRO	EARLIBA
1987	10.0 per cent	15.6 per cent
1988	9.9 per cent	15.0 per cent
1989	10.2 per cent	15.4 per cent
1990	11.0 per cent	14.6 per cent

1991	14.1 per cent	13.6 per cent	A
1992	11.9 per cent	14.4 per cent	
1993	11.7 per cent	13.5 per cent	

Notes

(a) Earliba is not VAT registered and cannot reclaim VAT charged to it. Therefore at the current VAT rate of 17.5 per cent a ten per cent commission charge by Thompsons will equate to 11.75 per cent of gross rents in the company's accounts. Macro is partially exempt and can reclaim only a tiny fraction of VAT charged.

(b) Fluctuations in the percentages are attributable to the fact that rents in the companies' accounts are stated on an accruals basis (i.e. collections are adjusted for arrears brought forward and carried forward) but commissions are charged on a payments basis (i.e. when deducted from collections). The abnormal percentage in Macro in 1991 reflects an addition in respect of a VAT adjustment not accounted for in previous years.'

There is expert evidence on the reasonableness of Thompsons' charges to the companies. I will summarise the experts' views as follows:

Mr Balch – in his opinion it would be reasonable for the following to be charged by Thompsons:

(1) Rent collection – ten per cent of rents plus VAT.

(2) Legal work/attendance at court – by arrangement.

(3) Registration of fair rents – £30 + VAT for each registration.

(4) Supervising building work (including making grant applications), for both companies – £5,000 + VAT.

(5) Letting fees on shortholds – £75 for each new letting, £37.50 for each renewal.

(6) Insurance commissions (in view of their size) – 50:50 companies and Thompsons.

Mr Balch expressed the view that in addition Mr Thompson would be justified in drawing a director's fee. In cross-examination, Mr Balch conceded that if there were separate charges for items (2)–(5) above, the ten per cent was 'generous', i.e. should be reduced by negotiation. He also accepted that he did not know what agents in Ipswich charged. The percentage on rents gives Thompsons an increased benefit when (as has happened) rents rise.

Mr Driver – ten per cent of rents. He considers items (4) and (5) in Mr Balch's list justify the additional management charge of £5,000 per annum and Mr Farley's salary so far as not referable to his secretarial services.

Mr Law – 7.5–10 per cent of rents, plus VAT for standard property management work, including new lettings.

In all the circumstances, I prefer Mr Law's evidence. It is based on his experience as one actively engaged in property management in Ipswich. Accordingly I find that unless Thompsons can show that exceptional work was done by them their reasonable remuneration would be ten per cent of rents received plus VAT. This is consistent with charges made by Thompsons to other customers. In my opinion, Mr Balch and Mr Driver (whose calculations were based on Mr Balch's opinions) were really considering the separate question whether the charges rendered by Thompsons could be justified. In consequence, in my judgment, the companies were overcharged by Thompsons as follows:

(i) the additional management charge of £5,000 per annum paid by Earliba to Thompsons since 1987; and

A   (ii)   all but say £1,500/£2,000 per annum of Mr Farley's salary of £7,000 charged to Macro.

In my judgment Thompsons are accountable to the companies for these sums with interest. I do not however find that Thompsons are accountable for the insurance commissions which they obtained as a result of insurances arranged for the companies' properties.

B

5.5 *Miscellaneous*:

5.5.1 Lack of supervision by Mr Thompson

When Mr Thompson is in England, he works at Thompsons' offices each day from about 10 am to 4 pm. From the evidence which I have heard, I find that it is Mr Thompson's practice to examine certain financial records (such as bank statements) regularly during this time and that otherwise his role is of a consultative nature. Mr

C   Thompson goes to his house in Lanzarote regularly during the winter of each year. Mr Thompson told the court that he usually only spent three months of the year in Lanzarote. However, it is clear from the dates appearing on correspondence between Mr Wyard and Mr Thompson that in 1984–85 Mr Thompson spent 4/5 months in Lanzarote. With regard to other years, Mr Farley's recollection was that Mr Thompson went to Lanzarote from shortly after the AGM in each year and returned to England before the

D   end of March. I accept this evidence; it is consistent with what occurred in 1984–85. It is true that Mr Brearey said in cross-examination that Mr Thompson was away from about October until even May of the following year, but he was speaking from memory. It means that I accept that from 1987 onwards the period which Mr Thompson spent abroad was in general 4/5 months in each year. Having rejected Mr Thompson's recollection for 1987 onwards, I conclude that this was also the period that he was abroad in the years before Mr Farley joined Thompsons. While he is abroad, he is sent only a

E   very limited amount of information by Mr Farley. Likewise the reports he received from Mr Wyard were of a very limited nature.

The fact that Mr Thompson could be the sole director and yet be abroad for prolonged periods each year underscores the non-interventionist nature of his management. His policy is to manage the existing portfolios and to delegate ministerial matters, such as decisions on lettings, types of tenancies, repairs, grants, instructions to solicitors and

F   negotiations with contractors to Thompsons, i.e. since 1987 to Mr Farley. Mr Thompson considers that he does provide effective supervision and control. He says he manages Thompsons while other staff are away and that he lays down policy and gives advice where necessary. The difficulty with that is that there are long periods when he is not there. Even when he was a younger man his management style undoubtedly fostered an environment in which staff at Thompsons were able to take key money and commissions, and commit administrative errors on the matters covered by my findings of fact. In truth

G   Mr Thompson and Mr Farley are dependent on each other. So far as Mr Thompson is concerned, Mr Farley is the means by which Mr Thompson can control the affairs of the companies even in his absence. Mr Farley is clearly dependent on Mr Thompson for his job.

5.5.2 Mismanagement of litigation

H   The plaintiffs allege that Thompsons caused the companies to engage in costly litigation which was not for the companies' benefit relating to the following properties:

> '*106 Finchley Road, Ipswich*
>
> Macro brought proceedings against the tenant for arrears of rent of £286.47. Counterclaim proceedings were brought against Macro by the tenant for Macro's breach of its repairing obligations under statute; Mr Farley swore an affidavit

A

saying he did not have certain documents relevant to the case which in fact have now been disclosed in discovery in these proceedings; he was 15 months late in not making the grant application or processing the improvement notice procedure, he only obtained one estimate from a builder for the works to be done; he did not properly inspect the works after the work was done and he made payment to the builder for work of poor quality. The total cost of the litigation to Macro was £7,959.25.

B

Garage No. 67, Lakeside Close, Ipswich

Mr Farley served notice to vacate the garage on the tenant which was undated and advised that the contents of the garage would be disposed of. The EHO served notice under s. 16 of the *Local Government and Miscellaneous Provisions* Act 1976 requiring Earliba to provide information about the occupiers of the garages only. Mr Farley instructed a contractor to clear the contents of Garage No. 67 which contained an 1967 Chevrolet Impala Convertible classic car. The contractor, on instructions from Mr Farley sold the car for £160. The tenant issued proceedings for damages of approximately £6,000 in respect of the unauthorised removal and sale of the car. Mr Farley and Mr Corbett took no action following the issuing of proceedings and judgment was entered against Earliba, which was later set aside with costs awarded against Earliba. Mr Farley alleged that the tenant was occupying the wrong garage and should have been using No. 65 not No. 67. It was eventually agreed that Earliba was to pay the tenant £2,500 and costs. The total cost of the action was approximately £11,243.81 which Earliba paid.

C

D

The plaintiffs/petitioners allege that this litigation conducted by the companies Earliba and Macro ought never to have been progressed. Having lost that litigation it cost those companies £11,243.91 and £7,959.25 respectively and the plaintiffs/petitioners maintain that Thompsons were responsible for the failure of those cases and they ought themselves to have paid for the costs and damages.'

E

I have been taken to a number of documents and, on the basis of those documents, I find these allegations proved. The relevant events occurred between 1991 and 1993. As regards 106 Finchley Road, Mr Farley said that he was pursing Thompsons' policy of not carrying out repairs when the tenant was in arrears. To settle the matter, Earliba paid the tenant £2,750 plus costs in respect of the counterclaim. The sum of £2,750 was wrongly described in Thompsons' client accounting records as a payment to Mr Martell.

F

Mr Martell explained how his wife who was his bookkeeper had raised an invoice for this amount in error and that he had countermanded it before it was paid. Mr Farley was accordingly asked by Mr Driscoll in cross-examination to produce the paid cheque for the entry in the accounting records. It then turned out that the cheque had been made payable to the companies' solicitors and represented the sum agreed to be paid to the tenant of £2,750. Mr Farley offered no explanation for the error in Macro's accounting records, save that he blamed the staff. In my judgment there was no explanation that he could properly give. Having observed him in the witness box, I find that Mr Farley caused the erroneous entry to be made.

G

5.5.3 Overpayment of insurance premiums

In 1989 and 1990 Mr Farley caused Earliba to overpay its insurance premiums on its properties in June Avenue, Ipswich by accepting the insurers' overvaluation by some ten times. The overpayments amounted to £33,032.15 and they were not corrected until March 1991 after the payments were questioned by John. In due course the excess amounts of premium were repaid but without interest. The companies' loss is limited to the loss of interest. What is remarkable however is that Mr Farley did not spot the error before the premium was paid. The error increased the insurance charge of £15,042 shown

H

A   in Earliba's 1989 accounts to £37,419. Accordingly the loss could not exceed interest on £22,377 for two years, say £5,000. I do not consider this figure material.

6. Expert evidence as to property values

As I have already indicated Mr Brunt and Mr Wass submitted a joint report. In this report, they together express the view that:

B   (1)   the value of the properties of the companies, subject to existing tenancies as stated by the valuers, was

Earliba:	£2,048,275		
Macro:	£3,142.825		
	£5,191,100	£5,191,100	

   (ii)   the value of the companies' garages was:

C

Earliba:	£76,250		
Macro:	£20,500		
	£96,750	£96,750	
		£5,287,850	

As I understand it these valuations are as at October 1993. The valuers also considered
D   the amount of the reduction in capital values due to the lettings on unfavourable terms of the properties listed in appendix D of Mr Brunt's report to be £595,875 (excluding 23 properties which have since been relet on assured shorthold tenancies and two properties which were vacant at the date of the joint report). This is a temporary reduction in values which would be reduced as more properties became vacant and available for reletting on new terms. However the diminution in value would, on past record, be likely to take some ten years to be eradicated.

E

7. Events from March 1991 to 1993

7.1 On 14 March 1991 a letter before action was written by Penningtons, solicitors, on behalf of the plaintiffs and John to Mr Thompson. This set out the claims based on the prior declarations of trust and the 1969 reconstruction and asserted that there had been unfair prejudice to the minority shareholders in the conduct of the companies' affairs.

F   On 23 March 1991 John and Julian took over management of Gippeswyk. Mr Thompson ceased to be a director, and he and Mr Farley ceased to be signatories on the bank account of that company. On 2 June 1991, these proceedings were commenced. In about July 1991, Ford du Cane & Co resigned as auditors of the companies, and Mr Thompson appointed Fisk & Co in their place.

By a letter dated 9 July 1991, Penningtons wrote requesting the companies' solicitors'
G   agreement to John and Ian being appointed as directors. However no such consent was given.

The proceedings have culminated in this trial. However there is one further event in the course of the proceedings to which I need to refer and that is the sale by Ian and Neil of their shares in the companies to Julian in May 1993.

7.2 *Share sale agreements May 1993*
H

By agreements in writing dated May 1993 ('the May 1993 agreements') Ian and Neil sold (a) with effect from the date of the agreement, the beneficial interest in all their shares in the companies, and (b) with effect from a final order in these proceedings in the plaintiffs' favour, the beneficial interest in all shares which Mr Thompson might be ordered to hold upon trust for them respectively in these proceedings. As consideration, for 'the transfer of' their existing shares, Julian agreed (i) to pay £2,500 each to Ian and

Neil, which sum was paid on the execution of the May 1993 agreement; (ii) to indemnify   A
Ian and Neil against the costs of these proceedings and (iii) to pay Ian and Neil a further
£15,000 each if the proceedings are successful or are compromised. Ian and Neil executed
declarations of trust of their shares in the companies and delivered the share certificates
and forms of transfer duly executed in blank in favour of Julian. Ian and Neil covenanted
in the declaration of trust (i) to transfer their shares, deal with distributions in respect of
them and exercise the voting rights attached to them in such manner as Julian directed;
and (ii) to agree to be appointed as director of the companies if so required by Julian and   B
to act as such directors in accordance with Julian's instructions. None of the agreements
were disclosed until the start of the trial of these proceedings.

When he gave evidence, Ian said that his understanding was that he had only sold the
beneficial interest in his shares. He explained that he had decided to sell his shares to
Julian because for personal reasons he had decided to take early retirement from Barclays
in the near future and wished to limit his liability for the costs of these proceedings.   C

In the course of giving his evidence, Mr Thompson stated that he was not interested in
buying the plaintiffs' shares.

8. The issues

8.1 *Issues in the action*

The principal issues in the action arise out of allegations of trust and estoppel. The   D
plaintiffs say that from about 1955 (in the case of Macro) and from about 1964 (in the
case of Earliba) Mr Thompson and Mr Macro declared that their shares in those
companies were held on trust for their respective families and that they would pass their
shares to their respective children after their deaths and the deaths of their wives. I will
call these declarations 'the prior declarations of trust'. With respect to the 1963–64
arrangements, the plaintiffs say that Mr Thompsons's interest in the shares then   E
registered in his name thereby became a life interest with the remainder vesting in John
and Julian. With respect to the 1969 reconstruction the plaintiffs say that Mr Thompson
induced the other shareholders to give their consents on the basis that when the
companies were financially sound he would ensure that the shares were vested 50:50 in
the Thompson and Macro families. It is further said that Mr Thompson is estopped from
failing to give effect to these assurances. The allegations are denied and laches, delay and
acquiescence are relied on.   F

8.2 *Issues on the counterclaim*

The principal question here is simply whether the execution by Ian and Neil of the sale
agreements has resulted in their becoming obliged to serve a sale notice pursuant to
art. 7 and 13 of the articles of Macro and Earliba respectively.

8.3 *Issues in the s. 459 proceedings*   G

The principal complaints in issue are as follows (the references are to the petitions):

8.3.1 The prior declaration of trust and 1969 reconstruction

8.3.1.1 The petitions claim relief arising out of the prior declarations of trust and the
1969 reconstruction. In relation to the latter there is, in addition to the claim that Mr
Thompson has failed to transfer shares in accordance with assurances given by him, a   H
claim that the plaintiffs have in consequence been deprived of any involvement in
management. (Macro, para. 24A; Earliba, para. 27A.)

8.3.2 Quasi-partnerships

8.3.2.1 It is also claimed in the petitions that both companies were 'quasi-partnerships'
both before and after Mr Macro's retirement in 1969. It is alleged that there has been a

A   breakdown of trust and confidence between the quasi-partners. (Macro, para. 25A; Earliba, para. 37A.)

8.3.3 Conflict of interest.

8.3.3.1 The plaintiffs contend that the management of the property portfolios by Thompsons on the one hand and the roles played by Mr Thompson and Mr Farley on the other hand give rise to a conflict of interest and duty which has caused the companies B   loss. (Macro, para. 28; Earliba, para. 31.)

8.3.4 Number of directors

8.3.4.1 Mr Thompson refuses to consider the appointment of one of the plaintiffs as a director. (Macro, para. 30, 33; Earliba, para. 33, 36.)

8.3.4.2 Mr Thompson would like to appoint Mr Farley as an additional director of C   the companies. (Macro, para. 22; Earliba, para. 25.)

8.3.4.3 The number of directors in each company is below the minimum required by the articles. (Macro, para. 32; Earliba, para. 35.)

8.3.5 Annual general meetings

8.3.5.1 Annual general meetings have been held on short notice and on dates inconvenient to the minority shareholders. (Macro, para. 34; Earliba, para. 37.)

D

8.3.6 Alleged mismanagement by Mr Thompson

8.3.6.1 Complaint is made of Mr Thompson's alleged failure to attend to the companies' affairs particularly while absent abroad during the winter. (Macro, para. 29–31; Earliba, para. 32–35.)

8.3.6.2 From the mid-1930's to 1987 property management was left to Mr Wyard E   who wasted money on repairs and committed the companies to poor letting. (Macro, para. 36; Earliba, para. 39.)

8.3.6.3 From (at least) 1970 to 1988 builders paid commissions to Mr Thompson and Mr Wyard for which they failed to account to the companies. (Macro, para. 36B; Earliba, para. 39B.)

8.3.6.4 In the same period employees of Thompsons took 'key money' for granting F   lettings of properties of the companies which they kept. Mr Thompson ought to have recovered them for the benefit of the companies when he found out about them. (Macro, para. 36C; Earliba, para. 39C.)

8.3.6.5 Currently property management is left to Mr Farley who is inexperienced and who has not (it is said) managed the properties properly. (Macro, para. 37; Earliba, para. 40.)

8.3.6.6 The companies are said to have suffered loss as a result of mismanagement. G   (Macro, para. 28, 38; Earliba, para. 38, 41.)

8.3.7 Retentions

8.3.7.1 Thompsons has retained excessive moneys belonging to the companies and has not obtained or paid interest. For instance, as at 31 March 1990, Thompsons held £110,000 of Earliba's cash, representing 50 per cent of its gross accrued rental income. H   This situation gave rise to a potential tax charge under s. 419 of the *Income and Corporation Taxes Act* 1988 (loans to participators). (Macro, para. 39, 40; Earliba, para. 42, 43.)

8.3.8 Management fees

8.3.8.1 The management fees paid to Thompsons are fixed by Mr Farley and are excessive. (Macro, para. 41; Earliba, para. 44.)

9. The plaintiffs' claims in the action and the defendants' counterclaim   A

9.1 The plaintiffs' claims in the action

In my judgment, these claims fail on the facts which I have found – see section 4. The related issues in the s. 459 proceedings (see para. 8.3.1) fail for the same reason.

9.2 The defendants' counterclaim

B

The defendants seek to resist the operation of the pre-emption articles by contending that, under the May 1993 agreements, all that Ian and Neil have disposed of is their beneficial interests in their shares. They rely particularly on cl. 4 of the declaration of trust which provides as follows:

> '4. I shall forthwith when called upon to do so by [Julian] transfer my interest in the shares to [Julian] or as [Julian] may direct and for such purpose a transfer of the shares has been duly executed by me and delivered to Julian together with the   C relative share certificates . . .'

The plaintiffs contend that para. (B) of the pre-emption articles apply only to transfers of the legal title in a share, and that until Julian calls for a transfer, the pre-emption articles do not take effect. This argument is based on *Safeguard Industrial Investments Ltd v National Westminster Bank Ltd* [1982] 1 WLR 589. In that case the member in question was the defendant bank which held shares as the executor of a former member.   D The beneficiaries under the will (and a deed of family arrangement) were not persons to whom the bank could transfer the shares without going through the pre-emption procedure. But the beneficiaries did not want the bank to transfer the shares to them and the bank had not executed any form of transfer. The Court of Appeal held that in the circumstances the bank was not a 'proposing transferor' for the purposes of the pre-emption article in that case. The mere fact that the beneficiaries could require the bank   E to make an immediate transfer to themselves was not enough. The Court of Appeal distinguished *Lyle & Scott Ltd v Scott's Trustees* [1959] AC 763. In that case, shareholders had entered into unconditional agreements to sell their shares which obliged them to transfer their shares when requested. As in this case, the shareholders had been paid the price and they had effectively agreed to vote as the purchaser directed. In those circumstances the House of Lords drew the inference that the shareholders had sufficiently evinced an intention to transfer their shares. As Lord Reid said in *Lyle &*   F *Scott Ltd v Scott's Trustees* at p. 779:

> '. . . a person who has agreed to sell with a view to a transfer at some future date cannot be heard to say that he is not desirous of transferring the shares merely because it suits him and the purchaser to delay execution and presentation of the transfers.'

The second sentence of para. (B) of the pre-emption article imposes an obligation to   G serve a sale notice (as defined) on a 'member desiring to sell a share'. I accept that, in this context, the relevant desire must be to transfer a share. Even that point, however, does not prevent the article from applying in the circumstances of this case. Ian and Neil have executed transfers for their shares. Despite the wording of cl. 4 of the declarations of trust, there is nothing further for them to do when Julian decides to register the shares in his own name. They have done more than merely sell the beneficial interest in the shares. They have agreed also to sell the legal title to their shares and provided forms of transfer   H executed by them.

Accordingly, in my judgment, if at the date of my order the May 1993 agreements stand, Ian and Neil must serve sale notices under the pre-emption articles. It was suggested that Ian and Neil might wish to undo the May 1993 agreements and that I should give Ian and Neil time for this purpose. In my judgment, they have had sufficient

A   time for this purpose already, and it would be wrong for me to give them further time for this purpose.

The plaintiffs seek an order altering the articles of the companies so that the relief which they seek in the s. 459 proceedings is not affected by the May 1993 agreements. In my judgment it would not be right to grant such relief because it would interfere with the accrued rights of Mr Thompson and John. Those rights crystallised in May 1993. The

B   plaintiffs say that their claims under s. 459 should have priority but in my judgment they only become entitled to relief under that section when the order is actually made in their favour. Nor am I satisfied that it would be right to interfere with Mr Thompson's rights because Ian and Neil became involved in this litigation as a result of Mr Thompson's actions. Those actions did not authorise them to disregard the pre-emption articles. Nor does this argument meet the situation of John in any event.

C   As regards Mr Thompson the plaintiffs further say that since (as I accept) he said in evidence that he did not wish to buy the plaintiffs' shares, no offer needs to be made to him under the pre-emption articles since 'it is a principle of equity that the court does not require unnecessary formalities to be gone through' (*Sprange v Lee* [1908] 1 Ch 424 at p. 430). In my judgment, however, Mr Thompson has not simply by giving the evidence to which I have referred waived his right to receive an offer under the pre-emption articles.

D   On the other hand, it seems to me that Ian cannot claim any right to be offered Neil's shares under the pre-emption articles or vice-versa. By allowing each other to enter into the May 1993 agreements, they elected to waive their right to receive an offer of the other's shares under the pre-emption articles. Accordingly in my judgment their shares should be offered to the remaining members at the same time with neither of them having a right to receive an offer of the other's shares. Furthermore, the shares must be offered to all the remaining members. The offer should be made on the basis that in the event of

E   competition acceptances will be scaled down on some equitable basis specified by the companies at the time of making the offer.

I do not accept the argument that Ian or Neil can choose the members to whom they wish to transfer their shares. This was held to be possible in *Tett v Phoenix Property and Investment Co Ltd* (1986) 2 BCC 99,140, but the article there was in a very different form. In the pre-emption articles in this case, the director must offer the shares comprised in a

F   sale notice 'to the existing members'.

In section 10 of this judgment I have proceeded on the basis that all the shares belonging to Ian and Neil will be sold by operation of the pre-emption articles. Any shares of Ian or Neil to which Julian becomes entitled by virtue of the pre-emption articles are shares of Julian for the purposes of section 10. It may, therefore, be necessary to delay the implementation of the order to be made under s. 459 until after the pre-

G   emption procedures have been completed. If at the end of those procedures, Ian or Neil remain the holders of any shares in the companies, the relief ordered in s. 10 will apply for their benefit too. I am not concerned with the position as between Julian, Ian and Neil.

10. Section 459 of the Companies Act 1985

H   Section 459 and 461 of the *Companies Act* 1985 provide in material part as follows:

'459(1) A member of a company may apply to the court by petition for an order under this Part on the ground that the company's affairs are being or have been conducted in a manner which is unfairly prejudicial to the interests of its members generally or of some part of its members (including at least himself) or that any actual or proposed act or omission of the company (including an act or omission on its behalf) is or would be so prejudicial.

461(1) If the court is satisfied that a petition under this Part is well founded, it may   A
make such order as it thinks fit for giving relief in respect of the matters complained
of.

(2) Without prejudice to the generality of subsection (1), the court's order may–

(a) regulate the conduct of the company's affairs in the future,

(b) require the company to refrain from doing or continuing an act complained
of by the petitioner or to do an act which the petitioner has complained it   B
has omitted to do,

(c) authorise civil proceedings to be brought in the name and on behalf of the
company by such person or persons and on such terms as the court may
direct,

(d) provide for the purchase of the shares of any members of the company by
other members or by the company itself and, in the case of a purchase by   C
the company itself, the reduction of the company's capital accordingly.

(3) If an order under this Part requires the company not to make any, or any
specified, alteration in the memorandum or articles, the company does not then
have power without leave of the court to make any such alteration in breach of
that requirement.'

I should add that s. 459 has only been in substantially the form set out above since   D
1980. However no-one has suggested that I should apply some different test to activities
prior to that date.

The question whether any action was or would be 'unfairly prejudicial' to the interests
of the members has to be judged on an objective basis. Accordingly it has to be
determined, on an objective basis, first whether the action of which complaint is made is
prejudicial to members' interests and secondly whether it is unfairly so. Based on the   E
findings of fact that I have made, I am satisfied that the companies suffered prejudice in
consequence of failure to have a planned maintenance programme, the failure to
supervise repairs, the failure to inspect properties regularly, the failure to let on protected
shorthold tenancies, the taking of commissions from builders doing work for the
companies by employees of Thompsons, the charging of excessive management charges
and secretarial salary and the mismanagement of litigation. The absence of an effective
system to prevent excessive amounts being retained on Thompsons' client account instead   F
of paying it over to the companies is also in my judgment likely to cause loss to the
companies in the future. All of these matters are within the responsibility of Thompsons
as the companies' managing agents but they are attributable to the lack of effective
supervision by Mr Thompson on behalf of the companies. It is this conduct of the
companies' affairs by Mr Thompson which, in my judgment, is prejudicial in the respects
I have mentioned. As the conduct is prejudicial in a financial sense to the companies, it   G
must also be prejudicial to the interests of the plaintiffs as holders of its shares.

The next question is whether the conduct of the companies' affairs in these respects is
unfairly prejudicial to the interest of the plaintiffs. As pointed out by Richardson J in
Thomas v H W Thomas Ltd (1984) 2 ACLC 610 in the Court of Appeal of New Zealand,
the concept of unfairness (under the similar provision in s. 209 of the 1955 New Zealand
Companies Act, as amended) involves the balancing of many considerations (at p. 618):

    H

'Fairness cannot be assessed in a vacuum or simply from one member's point of
view. It will often depend on weighing conflicting interests of different groups
within the company. It is a matter of balancing all the interests involved in terms
of the policies underlying the companies legislation in general and s. 209 in
particular: thus to have regard to the principles governing the duties of a director
in the conduct of the affairs of a company and the rights and duties of a majority

A   shareholder in relation to the minority; but to recognise that s. 209 is a remedial provision designed to allow the court to intervene where there is a visible departure from the standards of fair dealing; and in the light of the history and structure of the particular company and the reasonable expectations of the members to determine whether the detriment occasioned to the complaining member's interests arising from the acts or conduct of the company in that way is justifiable.'

B   To this I would add that the jurisdiction under s. 459 has an elastic quality which enables the courts to mould the concepts of unfair prejudice according to the circumstances of the case.

With respect to alleged mismanagement, the court does not interfere in questions of commercial judgment, such as would arise here if (for example) it were alleged that the companies should invest in commercial properties rather than residential properties. However, in cases where what is shown is mismanagement, rather than a difference of
C   opinion on the desirability of particular commercial decisions, and the mismanagement is sufficiently serious to justify the intervention by the court, a remedy is available under s. 459. The position was explained by Warner J in *Re Elgindata Ltd* [1991] BCLC 959 in the following passage (pp. 993–994):

> 'There is little authority on the extent to which negligent or incompetent management of a company's business may constitute conduct which is unfairly
D   prejudicial to the interests of members for the purposes of s 459. Mr Chivers referred me to *Re Five Minute Car Wash Service Ltd* [1966] 1 All ER 242, [1966] 1 WLR 745, where Buckley J held that allegations that the chairman and managing director of a company had been unwise, inefficient and careless in the performance of his duties could not without more amount to allegations of oppressive conduct for the purposes of s 210 of the Companies Act 1948. Mr Chivers rightly conceded,
E   however, that that authority afforded little guidance in a case under s 459, because the concept of oppressive conduct in s 210 was narrower than the concept of unfairly prejudicial conduct in s 459. Mr Nurse referred me to a paragraph in *Gore-Browne on Companies* (44th edn, 1986) vol 2, p. 28.021 which reads as follows:

>> "Another aspect of the enforcement of directors' duties by means of a petition under section 459 which remains unclear is the directors' duty of care. It would seem that the Jenkins Committee intended that the reformed statutory remedy
F   might be used in this regard, although the courts decided otherwise in the case of the old section 210."

> Then there is a reference to *Re Five Minute Car Wash Service Ltd*:

>> "Where serious mismanagement causes real economic harm to the company's business (and therefore to the value of the members interests) the general conceptual developments examined earlier should enable the courts to hold that
G   unfair prejudice has been established. The terminology in section 459(1) (referring to 'any actual or proposed act or omission of the company including an act or omission on its behalf' where this 'is or would be so prejudicial' should be of assistance here. Once again, however, a petition in the case of a public listed company may present greater difficulty."

> Lastly I was referred, on this point also, to the judgment of Peter Gibson J in *Re*
H   *Sam Weller & Sons Ltd* at the end of which (see [1990] Ch 682 at 694) he said that he had no doubt that the court would ordinarily be very reluctant to accept that managerial decisions could amount to unfairly prejudicial conduct. The point for which that judgment is mainly authority is, of course, that conduct may be unfairly prejudicial to the interests of minority shareholders even if those responsible for that conduct may. as members of the company. have suffered the same or even greater prejudice. That point is relevant here.

I do not doubt that in an appropriate case it is open to the court to find that serious   A
mismanagement of a company's business constitutes conduct that is unfairly
prejudicial to the interests of minority shareholders. But I share Peter Gibson J's
view that the court will normally be very reluctant to accept that managerial
decisions can amount to unfairly prejudicial conduct.

Two considerations seem to me to be relevant. First, there will be cases where there
is disagreement between petitioners and respondents as to whether a particular   B
managerial decision was, as a matter of commercial judgment, the right one to
make, or as to whether a particular proposal relating to the conduct of the
company's business is commercially sound. . . . In my view, it is not for the court
to resolve such disagreements on a petition under s 459. Not only is a judge ill-
qualified to do so, but there can be no unfairness to the petitioners in those in
control of the company's affairs taking a different view from theirs on such
matters.   C

Secondly, as was persuasively argued by Mr Chivers, a shareholder acquires shares
in a company knowing that their value will depend in some measure on the
competence of the management. He takes the risk that that management may
prove not to be of the highest quality. Short of a breach by a director of his duty
of skill and care (and no such breach on the part of either Mr Purslow or Mrs
Purslow was alleged) there is prima facie no unfairness to a shareholder in the   D
quality of the management turning out to be poor. It occurred to me during the
argument that one example of a case where the court might none the less find that
there was unfair prejudice to minority shareholders would be one where the
majority shareholders, for reasons of their own, persisted in retaining in charge of
the management of the company's business a member of their family who was
demonstrably incompetent.'

    E

The example given in the last sentence was only an example but it is not without
parallel here where the acts of mismanagement were carried out by Thompsons, Mr
Thompson's firm. In view of Mr Thompson's control and personality, there has since the
1969 reconstruction been no realistic possibility of the appointment of alternative
property managers. However, this is not a case where what happened was merely that
quality of management turned out to be poor (cf. *Re Elgindata Ltd* at pp. 994–1000).
This is a case where there were specific acts of mismanagement by Thompsons, which Mr   F
Thompson failed to prevent or rectify. Moreover, several of the acts of mismanagement
which the plaintiffs have identified were repeated over many years, as for example in
relation to the failure to inspect repairs. In my judgment, viewed overall, those acts (and
Mr Thompson's failures to prevent or rectify them) are sufficiently significant and serious
to justify intervention by the court under s. 461.

In addition to the acts of mismanagement which the plaintiffs have identified, there is   G
also the question of who should be the directors of the company. For some years Mr
Thompson has been the sole director of the companies. (Although the minimum number
of directors under the articles is stated to be two, the members have in my judgment
informally agreed to a reduction in this number to one.) Mr Thompson cannot continue
as sole director of the companies indefinitely. The plaintiffs believed that they would in
due course be appointed directors. Mr Thompson was originally in favour of the   H
appointment of the wives of himself and Mr Macro and their respective sons becoming
directors. Moreover, at one stage, steps were taken to obtain Barclays' approval to the
appointment of Ian as a director of the companies. It was proposed that John should be
appointed a director at the same time. However Mr Thompson's views have now
changed. Mr Thompson is now firmly of the view that the next director should come
from outside the family, and that none of the plaintiffs is fit to be a director of the

A   companies. Mr Thompson proposes that a single share should be allotted or transferred to Mr Farley so that he has the necessary share qualification. (He would however hold such share on terms that he transferred it to (say) Mr Thompson on his retirement.)

Whether or not Mr Thompson could properly issue or transfer a share to Mr Farley for this purpose (a question which has not been fully argued before me), there is the threat that he will do so. He has voting power to cause an additional director to be B   appointed by an ordinary resolution because he holds a majority of the shares. Mr Farley has, however, played a central role in some of the matters of mismanagement identified by the plaintiffs which I have found proved. He was also in my judgment involved to a small extent in the receipt of key money and commissions and in the misdescription of the payment of £2,750 in settlement of litigation in the companies' accounting records. Mr Farley is an employee of Mr Thompson. In my judgment he would continue to regard himself as such in the performance of his duties as a director of the companies if he was C   appointed to such office. Given the presence of minority interests, the absence of an independent director would in my judgment be prejudicial to the position of the plaintiffs as shareholders in the companies. If support were needed for such proposition, it can be found in the recent Report of the Committee on the Financial Aspects of Corporate Governance (the Cadbury Committee) published in December 1992. This report, which has been accepted by inter alia the Stock Exchange, emphasises that no one individual within a company should have unfettered powers of decision and that, where the D   chairman is also chief executive, there should be a strong and independent element on the board. While that report is directed to listed companies, the desirability of having a truly independent board is applicable to all cases where there are minority shareholders. In my judgment neither Mr Thompson nor Mr Farley would be able to act independently of Mr Thompson's position as majority shareholder and sole proprietor of Thompsons. That situation would in my judgment not only be prejudicial to the interests of the E   minority shareholders, but unfairly so.

In reaching this conclusion I have been concerned to carry out the balancing exercise which the concept of fairness requires (see *Thomas v H W Thomas Ltd* above). I have considered the weight to be attached to the personal contribution made by Mr Thompson to the current financial strength of the companies. He has made a major contribution in this regard. On the other hand, although he has not drawn directors' fees, he has in my F   view received substantial compensation through the fees paid by the companies to Thompsons (so far as properly paid), and through the acquisition at par of a further 37.54 per cent interest in Macro, and a further 30.31 per cent interest in Earliba, under the terms of the 1969 reconstruction. Moreover, on the authorities, the fact that shares are acquired by gift does not mean that the recipients cannot enforce the rights attached to those shares as against the donor (see *Re H R Harmer Ltd* [1959] 1 WLR 62 at pp. 83, 86). Indeed the contrary has not been suggested by Mr Rhys. Another consideration G   which has to be borne in mind is that the plaintiffs in effect agreed to Mr Thompson being in charge of the management of the companies. However in my judgment they did not consent to this on an indefinite basis, and they gave their consent (as it seems to me) on the basis that Mr Thompson would supervise what was done on his behalf by Thompsons. For the reasons explained earlier in this judgment, I find that such supervision was defective and that various acts of mismanagement identified by the plaintiffs did indeed occur.

H   The next question is the form of the order which the court should make under s. 461(1) of the *Companies Act* 1985. In my judgment it would be appropriate to order that Mr Thompson do purchase Julian's shares, and in section 11 I will deal with the question of the price. I decline to order that Mr Thompson do sell his shares in either or both of the companies to Julian: Mr Thompson is the majority shareholder and currently has management control (as against the plaintiffs) of the companies' affairs. I also decline to

order the appointment of additional directors. That course might well simply exacerbate,   A
rather than resolve, the disputes between the parties.

The plaintiffs contend that the companies constituted 'quasi-partnerships' for the
purposes of the well-known passage in Lord Wilberforce's speech in *Ebrahimi v
Westbourne Galleries* [1973] AC 360. This would probably result in an asset valuation of
the shares which would be more advantageous to the plaintiffs (see *Re Bird Precision
Bellows Ltd* [1986] 1 Ch 658). However, in *Ebrahimi* Lord Wilberforce observed that it   B
was not enough that the company was a small company. He pointed out that it would
also have one or probably more of the following characteristics: first, the company would
be an association formed or constituted on the basis of a personal relationship involving
mutual confidence; second, there would be an agreement that some or all of the members
will participate in the conduct of the business, and, third, there would be restrictions on
the transfer of shares. Whatever may have been the position in this case in (say) 1960,
mutual trust and confidence does not in my judgment exist between the members of the   C
companies at today's date. In all the circumstances, I hold that the companies are not
now, and have not at any stage in these proceedings been, quasi-partnerships.

Finally I note that complaint is made in the petitions about the length of notice given
for annual general meetings. I do not propose to go further into this matter as it would
not affect the conclusions I have reached on this part of the case.

   D

11. Valuation of shares

I now have to determine the price to be paid by Mr Thompson for the shares the
subject of my order. It has been agreed that I should deal with the issues of principle
only, with the details of any element of the valuation being left to an enquiry, if necessary.

Mr Ingram, the plaintiffs' expert accountant, expressed the view that in all the   E
circumstances of the case, but particularly given the size of the plaintiffs' shareholdings
when aggregated and the possibility of either the plaintiffs being bought out by the
defendants or vice-versa, the appropriate method of valuation was to find the net asset
value of a single share and to discount this by 10 per cent. The resultant figure would be
the *fair* value of a single share. Because this was a private company, the *market* value of
a share forming part of a minority shareholding would be very small. If the court accepted
this approach in principle, it would be necessary to find the appropriate asset value of the   F
companies net of corporation tax and so on. In addition, if account was to be taken of
the sums lost due to mismanagement, for example because properties were not let on
protected shortholds when they ought to have been, further adjustments to net assets
would be necessary. However, based on the companies' net assets as at 31 March 1993,
Mr Ingram's valuation produces a price of £1,188 for each Macro share and £17,329 for
each Earliba share.   G

Mr Mullett, the defendants' expert accountant, had a different approach. He started
by ascertaining the value per share of the minority shareholdings in the companies using
a gross dividend yield basis, (A), he then ascertained the net asset values per share of each
company and deducted ten per cent for lack of total control, (B), and then deducted (A)
from (B) to ascertain the value of control, (C), which he called 'the value gap'. Mr Mullett
accepted that, to find the fair value of the minority shareholdings, (C) should be divided   H
between the controlling and minority shareholders, and was of the opinion that this
should be done on a 50:50 basis. He arrived at this split on the basis of the plaintiffs'
individual shareholdings. This method produces a value of £826 for each Macro share
and £11,101 for each Earliba share at 31 July 1993. The plaintiffs do not challenge Mr
Mullett's gross dividend yield valuation as such of Macro, but contend that the figure he
arrives at for Earliba is too low given the strength of its earnings.

A   In principle I reject a valuation method which aims to find the fair value of the minority shareholding by reference to net asset value. The ability of the plaintiffs to unlock that value by liquidation is in my judgment uncertain. At the other end of the scale, I accept that as both experts agree a market valuation is inappropriate because the transaction resulting from the order of the court is not in the open market. In the circumstances, leaving aside the size of the split, in my opinion Mr Mullett's approach should be adopted.

B   So far as the net asset value per share of the companies is concerned ((B) in Mr Mullett's calculation), in my judgment it is appropriate to take the values of the companies' properties as agreed by the valuers, and the value of other net assets as at 31 March 1994, being the financial year-end nearest the date of my order. An appropriate deduction will have to be made for corporation tax on chargeable gains.

C   I then ask whether it is possible to build up a financial model of the companies as they would have been as at 31 March 1994 if the matters of prejudice which the plaintiffs have alleged and proved had not occurred. This can be done in the case of the wasted litigation costs and excessive management charges by writing back the amounts involved with interest which I will fix at one per cent over base rate for the time being (without compounding). Likewise the capital loss due to inappropriate lettings can be ascertained from the valuers' joint report and included in the financial model. A figure for loss in rental income can also be ascertained, and I am not aware of any serious dispute as to Mr Ingram's figures as to this amount.

D   However it will in my judgment be at the very least difficult to place a value on the loss suffered by the companies as a result of the failure to supervise repairs and improvements and other matters referred to in this judgment. I could order an enquiry but I have real doubts as to whether that would be the best course. I would prefer to fix a sum now in respect of those matters. My provisional view is that I should do so by directing the inclusion in net assets of a notional credit equal to the sum of ten per cent of the cost of repairs incurred in each of the years 1984–1994. I appreciate that this sum is to some extent arbitrary, but I formed the provisional view that that would be an appropriate figure in the light of the evidence I have heard in this action. However, I will hear argument on this point and on the question whether an enquiry should be instead directed.

E

F   I should add:

(1)   that no amount in my judgment falls to be included in the valuation in respect of retentions;

(2)   that no loss to the companies has in my judgment been proved in respect of the receipt of key money or the non-recovery of commissions;

(3)   that I have not included any amount in respect of the loss of interest on the insurance premiums.

G   Lastly there is the question of proportions in which the control premium should be split between Mr Thompson and Julian. In Mr Mullett's opinion, this should be 50:50. If Julian was selling his shares in the open market, he would probably obtain none of this premium since Mr Thompson does not wish to buy his shares voluntarily. However, as I see it, by selling his shares to Mr Thompson, Julian would be surrendering potentially valuable rights under the pre-emption articles and would enable Mr Thompson (subject to resolving John's position) to obtain the benefits of 100 per cent ownership of the companies. He would be able to run the companies as part of Thompsons or, if he chose, to sell them. Accordingly I consider that a fair split would be 35:65 in favour of Julian (so that Julian gets 65 per cent of the value gap). This adjustment makes it unnecessary for me to make any separate allowance for the difference of view between the two experts as to the appropriate gross dividend yield for Earliba.

H

On the assumption that I have (as I have hoped) determined all the questions of   A
principle on the matter of valuation, I will leave it to the experts to produce the final
figures. This is subject to the possibility of an enquiry (as I have indicated). If the figures
have not been done before the question of costs is argued, I will give parties liberty to
apply with respect to any matter arising on the valuation of the shares pursuant to this
judgment, but any enquiry I direct will be remitted back to chambers. The costs of such
enquiry will be reserved to the court hearing the enquiry.
                                                                                 B

12. Postscript

I would particularly like to record that this case was conducted with great skill by all
counsel. On several occasions they provided me with written summaries of the
propositions on which they relied which I believe saved time and additional costs. I
appreciate also of course the hard work done by both firms of solicitors, both in
conjunction with each other and separately.   C

It would have been very easy for this case, involving as it has examination of events
over some 40 years, to have become prolonged. However counsel did not allow this to
happen. I would record that this was greatly to their credit. It is easy for cases under
s. 459 to become very prolonged. I hope that the parties in similar cases will also bear in
mind the need to keep them with manageable bounds. The procedural difficulties of these
cases should not be allowed to make proceedings under s. 459 cumbersome. Section 459   D
is of particular importance in smaller companies where the burden of expensive litigation
is likely to be a crucial consideration.

There are two points however that I should specifically like to make arising out of this
case. The first relates to the presentation of the expert evidence. The experts' reports in
this case were only served shortly before the trial began. They are all very detailed, but
on many of the property management issues no attempt appears to have been made   E
before the trial began to collate the material in manageable form. There needed to be a
list of issues on which the experts were divided and which required a decision by the
court. The obvious way to deal with the voluminous expert evidence on the property
management issues in this case would have been to prepare Scott schedules, but because
trial preparation was left in this regard too late, and neither party applied for a pre-trial
review, that essential pre-trial work was not done. Only a very limited amount of material
was collated during the course of the trial itself.   F

The second point I wish to make is as to the contents of the bundles. Many documents
were duplicated or irrelevant to either side's case. Several bundles had simply not been
agreed: I assume that the parties had not started the work of agreeing the files sufficiently
far in advance of trial. It is very important, in this sort of case, to pay careful attention to
what is put into the bundles. I appreciate that the production of bundles requires a high
level of co-operation on all sides, and detailed work, starting well before trial, but, unless   G
it is done, a considerable amount of time and money is likely to be wasted, and
inconvenience to witnesses and the court is likely to result.

I hope that parties in other s. 459 proceedings will take note of these comments. These
matters may be relevant to questions of costs.

(Order accordingly)
                                                                                 H

A # Hasbro UK Ltd v Harris & Anor.

Chancery Division.
Chadwick J.
Judgment delivered 14 June 1994.

Takeovers – Rival offers for shares – Shareholders undertook to accept offer
B *unless higher offer 'publicly announced' within specified period – Whether and*
when higher offer had been publicly announced.

This was a motion (treated as the trial of the action) which raised the question whether a general offer for shares was 'publicly announced' within the meaning of the terms of letters of undertaking.

The defendants held shares in 'S plc' as trustees and signed letters of undertaking to accept the plaintiff's offer for the shares, with an escape provision if a third party publicly
C announced an improved offer. The deadline for such announcement was midnight on 2 June. A higher offer was approved by the board of a rival bidder, 'M Inc', at 11.30 pm on 2 June. A press release about that offer was faxed to the Stock Exchange at 11.41 pm. A copy was delivered to the Stock Exchange by hand at 11.50 pm. The press release was faxed to the Takeover Panel at 11.50 pm. One of the trustees was told of the contents of the press release at 11.50 pm. Copies of the press release were delivered to the plaintiff's merchant bank
D adviser by 11.55 pm. S plc's advisers were also told of the contents of the press release at 11.55 pm.

Held, dismissing the action with costs:

The effect of what was done – and in particular the effect of the telephone call to S plc's advisers and the delivery of the announcement to the Takeover Panel – was that the position which had been reached before midnight on 2 June meant that it would have been impossible in practice for M Inc to have declined to proceed with the offer without the consent of the
E Panel. It was the intention of the parties that the time at which the escape provision in the letters of undertaking should expire should be linked to the announcement by the third party of a firm intention to make an offer. M Inc became committed, by an announcement made to the public before midnight on 2 June, to make an offer and accordingly the condition in the letters was satisfied. It was immaterial that the investing public might not become aware of the announcement until the following morning.

F Ian Glick QC and Terence Mowschenson (instructed by Baker McKenzie) for the plaintiff.

Michael Crystal QC and Robin Dicker (instructed by Jeffrey Green Russell) for the defendants.

JUDGMENT

G **Chadwick J:** Spear plc is a public company incorporated in England whose principal activity is the manufacture and sale of toys and board games. Its shares are listed on the London Stock Exchange. Immediately before the events which I am about to describe 1,390,616 Spear shares (representing 26.7 per cent of its issued share capital) were held by the plaintiff, Hasbro UK Ltd. A further 1,297,550 Spear shares (representing 24.9 per cent of its capital) were held by the defendants, Philip Harris and Kenneth Crowhurst, as trustees of four settlements created by Jakob Richard Spear. It has not been suggested
H that there is any distinction between the position of the defendants as trustees of the individual settlements; and I shall refer to them simply as 'the trustees'.

On 27 May 1994 the trustees signed letters of undertaking addressed to Hasbro and its merchant bankers, J H Schroder Wagg & Co. The effect of those letters, in broad terms, was that the trustees bound themselves (subject to an escape provision to which I shall refer) to accept a cash offer in the amount of £9 per share which was to be made by

Hasbro for all the issued ordinary shares of Spear. Acceptance by the trustees would give   A
Hasbro control of Spear shares in excess of 51 per cent.

The material provisions in the letters of undertaking are these.

> '1.1 In consideration of the bank [that is Schroders] on behalf of the offeror [that
> is Hasbro] agreeing to make (subject to para. 4) within 28 days of the date of the
> issue of the press announcement referred to below (or within such extended period
> as the Panel on Takeovers and Mergers . . . may agree) the offer substantially on   B
> the terms and conditions in the attached press announcement . . . together with
> such additional terms and conditions as may be required to comply with the
> requirements of the . . . Stock Exchange . . . and the Panel, we Philip N Harris and
> Kenneth B S Crowhurst . . . irrevocably undertake, represent and agree [inter alia]
> that:
>
> . . .   C
>
> 1.1.3. subject to 1.2 below, we will no later than 9 am on the fourth business day
> (excluding Saturdays, Sundays and bank holidays) after the dispatch of the formal
> document containing the offer . . . duly complete and deliver to the bank or as it
> shall direct . . . a form or forms of acceptance of the offer . . . in respect of the
> shares . . .
>
> 1.2: Notwithstanding anything else contained in this undertaking we shall cease to   D
> be bound by the undertakings, representations and obligations contained herein if,
> within three clear business days (excluding Saturdays, Sundays and bank holidays)
> after the date of the press announcement, any third party shall publicly announce
> a general offer for all shares in the offeree (not already owned by such third party)
> which offer represents an improvement to the offer in the reasonable opinion of
> Neville Russell, chartered accountants of 246 Bishopsgate, London . . .'
>   E

The press announcement referred to in those provisions was made by or on behalf of
Hasbro on the same day, Friday 27 May. The effect of the weekend and the spring bank
holiday was that the three clear business days referred to in cl. 1.2 were Tuesday 31 May,
Wednesday 1 June and Thursday 2 June. It is common ground that the time at which the
escape provision in cl. 1.2 could operate would expire at midnight on 2 June. It is not
contended on behalf of Hasbro that a business day in that context means any period of
less than 24 hours.   F

The offer which was to be made by Hasbro in consideration of the undertakings was
in fact made on Saturday 28 May. Again, the effect of the holidays was that the obligation
on the trustees to deliver acceptances, subject always to the escape provision in cl. 1.2,
was to be performed by 9 am on Friday 3 June. The Hasbro offer for Spear shares did
not impress the board of Spear. The board, with the exception of one member, Mr
Francis Spear, considered the Hasbro offer to be wholly inadequate. The board   G
instructed its advisers, Baring Brothers, to solicit higher offers for the Spear shares. A
press release to that effect was issued by Barings on Sunday 29 May 1994.

Baring's efforts identified a potential third party bidder in the person of Mattel Inc, a
company incorporated and registered in the USA. It appears that Mattel's interest was
first notified to Barings at or about 4.45 pm in the afternoon of Thursday 2 June. There
was of course very little time before the expiry of the period of three business days limited
under cl. 1.2 of the letters of undertaking. Events moved quickly. Mattel instructed   H
Robert Fleming & Co to act on its behalf. Mr Swift of Flemings telephoned Mr Dowie
of Barings at 6 pm in order to make contact. By 10.45 pm Barings had been told by their
New York office that Mattel intended to bid £10 per share for the Spear shares and
would attempt to do so before the deadline expired at midnight. At 11 pm that
information was confirmed by Mr Swift of Flemings to Mr Burch of Barings.

A   In the meantime Flemings had prepared a press release setting out full particulars of the offer which Mattel was expected to make. That press release and the offer which it announced were approved by the board of Mattel at 11.30 pm on the evening of 2 June. It is dated 2 June 1994 and marked for immediate release. It announces that Mattel Inc is to make a cash offer through Robert Fleming & Co for the whole of the issued share capital of Spear. The offer was to be made on the basis of £10 in cash for each Spear share of 25p. That offer values the issued share capital of Spear at approximately £52m.

B   The press release goes on to indicate that Flemings on behalf of Mattel will dispatch the formal offer document as soon as practicable.

     Steps were then taken to make public the announcement contained in that press release. To put those steps into context, it is necessary to go back to an earlier stage in the events of the evening of 2 June. Shortly after 5 pm Mr Dowie of Barings had telephoned Mr Mummery at the City Panel on Takeovers and Mergers to seek his views on the form of

C   announcement which the Panel would require for the purposes of the City Code. Mr Dowie's note of that conversation, which has not been challenged, is in these terms:

> 'I also sought his advice on the form of an acceptable announcement of a third-party offer given that it was likely, if any third-party offer materialised, that an announcement would have to be made after the Stock Exchange RNS was off-screen for the evening. PM [that is Mr Mummery] confirmed that an acceptable

D   form for an announcement would be one where it was released down the wire to RNS, delivered by hand to the Stock Exchange, provided to Schroders and notified to PM at home on the telephone. All of this would, of course, have to be completed before midnight on Thursday, 2 June 1994.'

     Later on the same evening Mr Swift of Flemings also spoke to Mr Mummery on the telephone. He told Mr Mummery that he intended to deliver the press release to the Companies Announcements Office of the London Stock Exchange, to the Panel and to

E   Schroders before midnight. Mr Mummery agreed that that would constitute an announcement for the purposes of the City Code. I should perhaps add that Mr Mummery was not asked to express any view on the requirements in cl. 1.2 of the letters of undertaking. I have no doubt that he would not have thought it sensible or appropriate to do so.

     The steps taken in the late evening of Thursday 2 June to make public the Mattel press

F   release were these. First, a copy of the press release was faxed to the Stock Exchange at 11.41 pm. A further copy was delivered to the Stock Exchange by hand at 11.50 pm. Second, the press release was faxed to the Panel at 11.50 pm. Third, Mr Swift telephoned Mr Harris, one of the trustees, at 11.50 pm and told him of the contents of the press release. Fourth, six copies of the press release were delivered to Schroders' offices by 11.55 pm. Fifth, Mr Swift telephoned Mr Dowie at Barings at 11.55 pm and told him of

G   the contents of the press release.

     I am satisfied that the effect of what was done – and in particular the effect of the telephone call to Barings and the delivery of the announcement to the Panel – was that the position which had been reached before midnight on 2 June meant that it would have been impossible in practice for Mattel to have declined to proceed with the offer without the consent of the Panel. That this is also the view of the Panel is confirmed in an affidavit of its deputy director general, Mr Lee.

H   The question which I have to decide is whether the general offer for the shares in Spear which was announced in the Mattel press release was 'publicly announced' within the three clear business days limited by cl. 1.2 of the letters of undertaking. That is to say, whether the steps taken before midnight on 2 June for the purposes of making public that press release were sufficient to satisfy the requirement in that clause that the third party 'shall publicly announce' its general offer.

I am asked to construe the provisions of cl. 1.2 of the letters of undertaking in the light   A
of the circumstances which must be taken to have been in the minds of the trustees and
Hasbro and their respective advisers at the time when the letters of undertaking were
signed. This must be the correct approach. It is clear that those circumstances must have
included both the provisions of the Code itself and the requirements of the Stock
Exchange. There is express reference to both these bodies in the letters of undertaking.
The parties must have been well aware that the circumstances in which cl. 1.2 would be
invoked, if at all, were circumstances in which there was a rival offer to the offer made   B
by Hasbro. This is very much the territory in which the City Code is intended to operate.
Further, if a rival offer were to be made by a company listed on the Stock Exchange, the
requirements in the Stock Exchange's *Listing Rules* (the Yellow Book) might well have
to be satisfied by the new offeror.

The relevant provisions of the City Code are these. Rule 1(a) requires that an offer
must be put forward in the first instance to the board of the offeree company or to its   C
advisers. Rule 2.2 sets out the circumstances in which an announcement is required. In
particular an announcement is required:

> '(a) when a firm intention to make an offer (the making of which is not, or has
> ceased to be, subject to any precondition) is notified to the board of the offeree
> company from a serious source, irrespective of the attitude of the board to the
> offer'.   D

Rule 2.5 requires that:

> '(a) The announcement of a firm intention to make an offer should be made only
> when an offeror has every reason to believe that it can and will continue to be able
> to implement the offer. Responsibility in this connection also rests on the financial
> adviser to the offeror.'

It is clear that the point had been reached by 11.30 pm on the evening of 2 June at   E
which an announcement of a firm intention to make an offer was required from Mattel.
The effect was that the period within which the offer itself had to be made had
commenced to run: see r. 30.1. That this was the view of the Takeover Panel appears
from para. 5 of Mr Lee's affidavit.

Rule 2.7 of the Code sets out the consequences of an announcement of firm intention.
It is in these terms: F

> 'When there has been an announcement of a firm intention to make an offer, the
> offeror must, except with the consent of the Panel, proceed with the offer unless
> the posting of the offer is subject to the prior fulfilment of a specific condition and
> that condition has not been met.'

Rule 2 of the Code says nothing in terms about public announcement but it is clear
that the announcement of a firm intention to make an offer is intended to become public   G
knowledge. Rule 2.6 expressly imposes on the offeree company an obligation to send a
copy of the relevant announcement or a circular summarising the terms and conditions
of the offer to all its shareholders and to the Panel.

In my view, cl. 1.2 of the letter of undertaking must be construed against the
background that Hasbro and the trustees would have appreciated that any third party
who had a firm intention to make an offer for the shares of Spear would be bound to   H
make an announcement in compliance with the provisions of the Code to which I have
referred; that that announcement would become public knowledge; and that on the
making of the announcement the third party would be committed to making its offer.

Rule 19.7 of the Code provides for copies of announcements to be lodged with the
Panel and with the advisers to all other parties to the offer. In sending a copy of the press

A   release to the Panel and to Barings shortly before midnight on 2 June Mattel and its advisers were clearly seeking to comply with the requirements in that rule.

Mr Glick QC, who appears on behalf of Hasbro, has referred me to the provisions in r. 8 of the Code. That is a rule which deals with the disclosure of dealings in shares during the offer period. It is not a rule which would have had any direct relevance to the matters under consideration at the time the letters of undertaking were signed. But it is of some

B   relevance because it draws a distinction between the public disclosure of dealings in shares and private disclosure. In particular, note 4 to r. 8 of the Code explains how public disclosure is to be made. The note is in these terms:

'4. Method of disclosure . . .

(a) Public disclosure

Public disclosure is to the Stock Exchange, the Panel and the press.

C   Dealings should be disclosed in writing, by fax or by telex to the Stock Exchange (Company Announcements Office); they are published on the Regulatory News Service of the Stock Exchange. Copies of such disclosures are sent by the Stock Exchange to the Panel. Separate disclosure to the Panel and the press is, therefore, unnecessary . . .'

It is clear that the normal method of public disclosure under r. 8 is through the

D   Regulatory News Service of the Stock Exchange. I was taken to the relevant Stock Exchange publication regarding the Regulatory News Service. That service cannot be used after 6.00 pm for the publication of information that day. In the case of hand-delivered material, the service cannot be used after 5.30 pm. For out-of-hours publication, what is required under r. 8 of the Code is disclosure through two national newspapers and two newswire services operating in the UK.

E   Reference was also made to r. 9.15 of the Stock Exchange *Listing Rules*; the rules which will apply to offers, or to most offers, made by offeror companies who are themselves listed on the Stock Exchange. Mattel was not such an offeror. Publication under the Stock Exchange *Listing Rules* is either through the Regulatory News Service or in two national newspapers and two wire services.

It is clear that the steps that were taken on the evening of 2 June would not have been sufficient to satisfy the disclosure requirements under r. 8 of the Code or the requirements

F   under the Stock Exchange *Listing Rules*.

The question which I have to consider is whether, when the parties to the letter of undertaking used the phrase 'any third party shall publicly announce a general offer for all shares in the offeree', they intended to impose a requirement that such announcement should be made in a form which would satisfy the requirements for public disclosure under r. 8 of the Code (which would not apply to the announcement directly) or under

G   the Stock Exchange *Listing Rules* (which would apply only if the offeror company was subject to those rules): alternatively, whether what they intended was that the third party should have made an announcement of firm intention for the purposes of the Code; and so should have reached a position in which it was so committed to the offer which it announced that it could not withdraw: or whether they had some other form of public announcement in mind.

H   Having regard to the structure of the letter of 27 May it seems to me much more likely that it was the intention of the parties that the time at which the escape provision in cl. 1.2 should expire should be linked to the announcement by the third party of a firm intention to make an offer (which was an announcement which would, necessarily, have to be made by a serious third party offeror in due course) rather than to public disclosure under r. 8 of the Code or under the Stock Exchange Rules (which would or might have no application to the offer actually made). Looking at the letter as a whole, it is clear that

the purpose of cl. 1.2 was to provide an opportunity for a better offer than that which   A
Hasbro was proposing to make to be obtained within a limited time; and to give the
trustees the opportunity to accept that offer before being irrevocably committed to accept
what, on that hypothesis, would necessarily be a lesser price. If that is a correct view as
to the purpose of the letter, it is sensible that cl. 1.2 should be directed to the point at
which the third party becomes publicly committed to make an offer, rather than to the
point at which the investing public becomes aware of his intention to do so.

  B

A further indication that that was the parties' intention lies, I think, in Hasbro's
acceptance that the time for making a public announcement for the purpose of cl. 1.2 of
the letter of undertaking would not expire until after the time when the Regulatory News
Service would have closed for the day; and until after a time at which publication in
newspapers (and, probably, wire services) could be achieved for that day. If it was
contemplated that the relevant announcement could, and so might, be made shortly
before midnight, it must have been appreciated that the announcement would not appear   C
on the wire services, or in the press, until the following day. In those circumstances,
insistence on disclosure in accordance with the Stock Exchange *Listing Rules* would
clearly frustrate the intention that the period should continue until midnight; and the
parties must have appreciated this.

I am satisfied that Mattel became committed, by an announcement made to the public
before midnight on 2 June, to make an offer of £10 a share and that, accordingly, the   D
condition in cl. 1.2 was satisfied. It is immaterial that the investing public might not
become aware of the announcement until the following morning. Accordingly, I am
satisfied that the trustees ceased to be bound by the undertakings and obligations
contained in the letter of 27 May before 9 am on the following day and so did not become
obliged to deliver the forms of acceptance in accordance with cl. 1.1.3.

I have been asked by both parties to treat the hearing of this motion as the trial of the   E
action on the basis that there is no material dispute of fact between them and that there
are no further factual matters which either party would wish to put in evidence at a trial.
On that basis the question is a question of construction to be applied to agreed facts and
the order which I make dismissing this motion is to be regarded as a final order; subject,
of course, to any appeal.

(*Action dismissed with costs*)

  F

  G

  H

A **Scottish Exhibition Centre Ltd v Mirestop Ltd & Ors.**
Court of Session (Outer House).
Lord Morton of Shuna.
Judgment delivered 25 March 1994.

Administration – Whether service of notice under lease required leave – Whether
B *condition for serving notice satisfied by appointment of administrators ad interim*
– Insolvency Act 1986, s. 8–11.

This was an action in which landlords who had served a notice under a lease containing
an irritancy clause providing that if a receiver or other administrator or manager for
creditors were appointed to the tenant, the landlord was entitled by notice in writing to bring
the lease to an end forthwith, sought declarator that an irritancy had been incurred. It was
argued, inter alia, that the leave of the court was required for service of the notice, and that
C the requisite condition for service of the notice did not exist when it was served because the
administrators were then only appointed ad interim.

Held, determining preliminary pleas and directing proof before answer:

1. Leave was not required for the service of the notice required under the lease between
the pursuers and the first defenders to bring the irritancy into effect. The service of the
notice was not 'other legal process' nor was it 'proceedings' in terms of s. 10 and 11 of the
D Insolvency Act 1986. It was a non-judicial step required by the contract of lease. (Re
Olympia & York Canary Wharf Ltd [1993] BCC 154 followed.)

2. The appointment of administrators was made ad interim for the purposes of s. 8(3)(a)
and (d) of the Insolvency Act 1986. The situation was to that extent different from the
situation where the interim order was made under s. 9. The appointment ad interim was
sufficient to entitle the pursuers to give notice under cl. 5 of the lease. (Secretary of State
E for Trade and Industry v Palmer [1993] BCC 650 considered.)

The following cases were referred to in the opinion:

Air Ecosse Ltd v Civil Aviation Authority (1987) 3 BCC 492; 1987 SLT 751.
Armia Ltd v Daeiam Developments Ltd 1979 SC(HL) 56.
Atlantic Computer Systems plc, Re [1990] BCC 859; [1992] Ch 505.
Bristol Airport plc v Powdrill & Ors [1990] BCC 130; [1990] Ch 744.
F *Company No. 00175 of 1987, Re a* (1987) 3 BCC 124.
CIN Properties Ltd v Dollar Land (Cumbernauld) Ltd 1992 SLT 669.
Exchange Travel Agency Ltd v Triton Property Trust plc & Anor [1991] BCC 341.
HMV Fields Properties Ltd v Bracken Self-selection Fabrics Ltd 1991 SLT 31.
Olympia & York Canary Wharf Ltd, Re [1993] BCC 154.
Radford & Bright Ltd v D M Stevenson & Co (1904) 6 F 429.
Scottish Exhibition Centre Ltd, Noters [1993] BCC 529; 1993 SLT 1034.
G *Secretary of State for Trade and Industry v Palmer* [1993] BCC 650.

J R Doherty (instructed by Dundas & Wilson, CS) for the pursuers.

N J Mackinnon (instructed by Bishop & Robertson Chalmers) for the defenders.

OPINION

H **Lord Morton of Shuna:** The pursuers in this action leased to the first defenders in 1987
an area of ground and a building known as 'The Pump House'. The lease was for 99
years. On 4 June 1991 in a petition at the instance of the first defenders the court
appointed the second and third defenders as joint administrators *ad interim* of the first
defenders for the purposes specified in s. 8(3)(a) and (d) of the *Insolvency Act* 1986 and
made the usual order for advertisement and service. On 16 July 1991 no answers having
been lodged the court appointed the second and third defenders to be joint administrators

for the purposes specified in s. 8(3)(a) and (d) of the Act. The fourth defenders held a   A
standard security and floating charge over the first defenders' interest in the lease. On 22
January 1993 I granted to the pursuers leave to bring proceedings against the first
defenders. The present action is the action for the bringing of which I granted leave.

The lease contained an irritancy clause providing that if a receiver or other
administrator or manager for creditors were appointed to the tenant, the landlord was
entitled by notice in writing to bring the lease to an end forthwith. The pursuers served   B
such a notice on 18 and 19 June 1991 on the first, second and third defenders and in this
action seek declarator that an irritancy has been incurred and seek an order ordaining
the first defenders to flit and remove. On procedure roll I heard submissions in respect of
the preliminary pleas on either side. The defenders who are not separately represented
and who have lodged joint defences submitted that the pursuers' averments narrated that
the notices on which they founded did not fulfil the statutory requirements and argued
that the circumstances required to bring the irritancy into effect had not occurred and   C
that the pursuers were not entitled to terminate the lease.

In support of their relevancy plea, counsel for the defenders submitted, first, that there
was no relevant averment that the required notice under the irritancy clause of the lease
was served after leave to bring proceedings was granted; secondly, that the notice was
served prior to the appointment of the administrators on 16 July 1991 and therefore that
the requisite condition for the service of the notice did not exist at the date of the notice;   D
and, thirdly, that the pursuers' averments that a fair and reasonable landlord would not
have felt bound to refrain from seeking to rely on the provisions in cl. 5 of the lease were
wholly lacking in specification and as the onus was on the pursuers to establish this the
action was irrelevant. For the pursuers counsel submitted arguments that the defenders'
averment of waiver and the averments by the defenders in relation to the heritable
creditor serving a calling-up notice and in relation to the averment that the terms of the
lease caused a serious commercial imbalance were wholly lacking in specification and   E
irrelevant.

The defenders' first argument, that leave of the court was required to allow the pursuers
to give notice under cl. 5 of the lease to bring the irritancy into effect, was founded on
s. 10(1)(b) and (c) and s. 11(3)(c) and (d) of the *Insolvency Act* 1986. These provisions
stated that the various steps mentioned in the subsection required the leave of the court.
Section 10(1) deals with the periods between the presentation of the petition for an   F
administration order and ending with the making of such an order or the dismissal of the
petition. Section 11 applies to the period on and after the making of an administration
order. Subsections (b) and (c) of s. 10(1) are in similar terms to subs. (c) and (d) of
s. 11(3) which provide:

'(c) no other steps may be taken to enforce any security over the company's
property, or to repossess goods in the company's possession under any hire-   G
purchase agreement, except with the consent of the administrator or the leave of
the court and subject (where the court gives leave) to such terms as the court may
impose; and

(d) no other proceedings and no execution or other legal process may be
commenced or continued, and no distress may be levied, against the company or
its property except with the consent of the administrator or the leave of the court
and subject (where the court gives leave) to such terms as aforesaid.'   H

It was submitted that the service of the notice was within the meaning of the phrase 'other
legal process'. I was referred to *Air Ecosse Ltd v Civil Aviation Authority* (1987) 3 BCC
492 in which case the Second Division held that the word 'proceedings' in s. 11 was to be
given a restricted meaning applying the *eiusdem generis* rule. I was also referred to
Exchange Travel Agency Ltd v Triton Property Trust plc [1991] BCC 341 in which

A   Harman J, in a case where a landlord had exercised a right of re-entry under a lease where the tenant was in administration, held that the right of re-entry was the commencement of 'other legal process' under s. 11. I was also referred to *Radford & Bright Ltd v D M Stevenson & Co* (1904) 6 F 429 as authority for the proposition that leave of the court could not be retrospective. In answer to this argument counsel for the pursuers submitted that the *Air Ecosse* case gave no definition of proceedings and that the present situation was plainly different from the *Exchange Travel* case. In that case the

B   ground of decision was that the right of re-entry was a security right and the opinion of Harman J on 'other legal process' was secondary and in any event turned on questions of English law which did not apply in Scots law. The pursuers' relationship with the first defenders was purely contractual and did not depend on any notion of 'privity of estate'. In the later case of *Re Olympia & York Canary Wharf Ltd* [1993] BCC 154, Millett J declined to follow the decision of Harman J in *Exchange Travel* and held that the service

C   of a contractual notice purporting to make time of the essence or to terminate a contract by reason of the company's repudiatory breach did not require the consent of the administrator or the leave of the court. I was also referred to *Bristol Airport plc v Powdrill* [1990] BCC 130 and to the judgment of Browne-Wilkinson V-C at pp. 152–153 and to Ross & McKichan's *Drafting and Negotiating Commercial Leases in Scotland* (2nd edn) at para. 12.8.

D   In my opinion the pursuers' contention is clearly correct. I agree with Millett J in *Re Olympia & York Canary Wharf Ltd* at p. 157F where he said:

> 'It is not necessary in this case to consider where the line is to be drawn between the commencement or continuation of "proceedings" on the one hand or of "legal process" on the other. But in my judgment both concepts are well known. Together they embrace all steps in legal proceedings from the issue of initiating process, to their final termination in the process of execution or other means of enforcement
>
> E   of a judgment such as the appointment of a receiver by way of equitable execution or the making of a charging order or other steps for the enforcement of the court's judgment without execution. But the phrase is not apt to describe the taking of non-judicial steps such as the service of a contractual notice in order to crystallise the liability of the party on whom the notice is served.
>
> F   In my judgment support for that conclusion can be derived from the use of the words "commenced or continued" in s. 11(3)(d) of the 1986 Act. If the service of a contractual notice is part of a legal process, I am unable to understand what legal process it is supposed to commence or continue. The words "commence or continue" indicate a process which has an independent existence of its own apart from the step by which it is commenced or continued; a process which either continues after or was in existence before the taking of the relevant step.'

G   I consider that leave was not required for the service of the notice required under cl. 5 of the lease between the pursuers and the first defenders to bring the irritancy into effect. The service of the notice was not an 'other legal process' nor was it 'proceedings'. It was a non-judicial step required by the contract of lease.

The defenders' second argument turns on whether the first defenders were in administration when the pursuers served the notice on 18 and 19 June 1991. If the

H   company was not in administration the pursuers would have no basis under cl. 5 of the lease for the service of the notice. This clause as quoted in condescendence 3 is:

> 'If the tenant shall suffer a receiver or other administrator or manager for creditors to be appointed then, and in any such case, it shall be lawful for the landlord at any time thereafter by notice in writing to bring this lease to an end forthwith and to enter the subjects and repossess and enjoy the same.'

It appears that in England it has been held that the court has no power to appoint an
interim administrator, see *Re a Company (No. 00175 of 1987)* (1987) 3 BCC 124. Counsel
for the defenders submitted that the joint administrators were not appointed until 16 July
1991 and that it was inappropriate to treat an administrator *ad interim* in the same way
as an administrator, as the interim appointment was not an irrevocable step. I was
referred to the case of *Secretary of State for Trade and Industry v Palmer* [1993] BCC 650.
In that case on 3 October 1989 the directors of two companies presented petitions seeking
administration orders under s. 8 of the *Insolvency Act* 1986. Interim orders in terms of
s. 9(4) were pronounced on 3 October 1989 and on 1 November 1989 administration
orders were pronounced under s. 8 for the purposes of s. 8(3)(a), (b) and (d). The
petitioner brought a petition for a disqualification order against the respondent who was
a director of the company. The first order on the petition was on 31 October 1991. The
respondent argued that the petition was incompetent as it had been brought without
leave of the court more than two years after the company of which the respondent was a
director had become insolvent. Section 6(2) of the *Company Directors Disqualification
Act* 1986 provides inter alia that for the purposes of that section a company becomes
insolvent if an administration order is made in relation to the company. Lord MacLean
repelled the competency plea holding that the reference to an administration order in s.
6(2) of the Company Directors Disqualification Act referred to an administration order
made under s. 8 of the Insolvency Act and not to an interim order made under s. 9(4). In
his opinion Lord MacLean said (at p. 652E):

'I do also think that the language of s. 18(1) and (3) indicates a distinction between
an administration order per se and an interim order.'

He was referring to the *Insolvency Act* 1986.

For the pursuers counsel submitted that there was a distinction between an interim
order under s. 9(4) and an appointment *ad interim*. The interlocutor of 4 June 1991
appointing the second and third defenders to be the 'joint administrators *ad interim* of
Mirestop Ltd', 'for the purposes specified in s. 8(3)(a) and (d) of the said Act' made it
clear that it was an appointment under s. 8 and not an interim appointment under s. 9.
He also referred me to vol. 4 of the *Stair Memorial Encyclopaedia* at para. 615 where the
author states:

'In an English case *Vinelott* J held that there was no power under the *Insolvency
Act* 1986 to appoint an interim administrator, as opposed to an interim manager.
The practice of the Court of Session, however, has been to make an order
appointing an administrator *ad interim*. Such an order is clearly an 'administration
order' within the meaning given by the Act, but, even assuming that, at the time of
the first order, the court has been able to satisfy itself that the company is or is
likely to become unable to pay its debts and that the making of an administration
order would be likely to achieve one or more of the statutory purposes the court
has no power to dispense with notice of the petition to persons entitled thereto.'

Counsel also submitted that Lord MacLean would have been wrong if the initial
appointment in his case had been of an administrator *ad interim* under s. 8 and that he
was wrong in stating that the terms of s. 18(1) and (3) indicated a distinction between an
administration order per se and an interim order. I was also informed that Lord
MacLean's decision had been reclaimed against, although the reclaiming motion had not
yet been heard.

In *Scottish Exhibition Centre Ltd v Mirestop Ltd* [1993] BCC 529, which is the action
in which I granted leave to bring the present action, I narrated that the petition seeking
the appointment of administrators was at the instance of the first defenders on the basis
that the company was unable to pay its debts and that a valuation as a 'going concern'
was higher than a valuation on a 'forced sale' basis. The appointment of joint

A administrators was made *ad interim* for the purposes of s. 8(3)(a) and (d). The appointment of 16 July 1991 was made for exactly the same purposes and was unopposed, no answers having been lodged. The situation is to that extent different from the situation in *Secretary of State for Trade and Industry v Palmer* where the interim order was made under s. 9. In my opinion the whole purpose of the administration procedure is to provide an interim and temporary regime to give the company a breathing space and administration is for this reason different from receivership or liquidation: see

B *Re Atlantic Computer Systems plc* [1990] BCC 859). I consider that the appointment of the administrators on 4 June 1991 was sufficient to entitle the pursuers to give notice under cl. 5 of the lease.

For these reasons I shall sustain the pursuers' relevancy plea to the extent of holding that the defenders' averments that authority was granted after the date of the notice and the averments relating to the pursuers not being entitled to terminate the lease are

C irrelevant and should not be admitted to probation. I shall also repel the defenders' second and fourth pleas-in-law.

Both counsel made submissions regarding the averments relating to what a fair and reasonable landlord would have done in the circumstances. The concept of a fair and reasonable landlord appears in s. 5 of the *Law Reform (Miscellaneous Provisions) (Scotland) Act* 1985 which was enacted following a report of the Scottish Law

D Commission and clearly involves questions of fact on which evidence will be required. The pursuers aver in condescendence 4 the circumstances in which they claim that what they are attempting to do is what a fair and reasonable landlord would do, and in my opinion these averments give adequate notice of the case they seek to make. The defenders' averments were attacked for lack of specification but as the onus of proof is on the pursuers it would not appear appropriate to refuse probation to what is, in effect, a denial of the pursuers' averments. There is, however, a sentence in answer 4:

E
'In any event the terms of said lease caused a serious commercial imbalance between the pursuers and the company as tenants.'

It is not clear to me whether this sentence is meant to relate to the fair and reasonable landlord averments which it follows. The sentence clearly has its origin in the Scottish Law Commission report quoted by Lord Jauncey of Tullichettle in his speech in *CIN Properties Ltd v Dollar Land (Cumbernauld) Ltd* 1992 SLT 669 at p. 674. The defenders'

F averments are totally unspecific as to the nature or cause of the alleged imbalance in a tenancy entered into by the first defenders with the pursuers less than four years earlier. There is no suggestion of why the imbalance existed or its cause and one would have expected if the imbalance were serious that it would have been possible to aver why it existed and what it was.

The pursuers' counsel also attacked as irrelevant the defenders' averments relating to

G the service by the heritable creditor, who is the fourth defender, of a calling-up notice. No date is averred as to when this is said to have been served and this date must be within the knowledge of at least the fourth defender. The date of service of such a calling-up notice required, to be relevant, to be prior to the landlord's service of notice of irritancy. I shall sustain the pursuers' relevancy plea to the extent of excluding from probation the averments relating to the calling-up notice by the heritable creditor and the sentence relating to 'serious commercial imbalance'.

H
Finally the pursuers' counsel submitted that the defenders' averments of waiver and personal bar in relation to the cashing of a cheque from the first defenders for £1,250 in February 1992 were irrelevant. I was referred to *Armia Ltd v Daeiam Developments Ltd* 1979 SC(HL) 56 and to the passages in the speeches of Lord Fraser of Tullybelton at p. 68 and of Lord Keith of Kinkel at p. 72. It was submitted that the defenders' averments were not sufficient to demonstrate any giving up or abandoning of a right. In answer the

A

defenders' counsel referred me to *HMV Fields Properties Ltd v Bracken Self Selection Fabrics Ltd* 1991 SLT 31 where the First Division held that the question of whether or not a subsequent acceptance of rent amounted to an unequivocal act amounting to waiver of the notice of irritancy was a question of fact which had to be answered in the light of the surrounding circumstances. In the situation I consider it to be appropriate that the question of waiver and personal bar should be decided after proof of the facts, which proof should be a proof before answer.

B

(Order accordingly)

C

D

E

F

G

H

A   Bass Breweries Ltd v Delaney & Ors.

Chancery Division (Manchester).
His Honour Judge Maddocks (sitting as a High Court judge).
Judgment delivered 1 February 1994.

B   *Receivership – Chargees agreed that their charges should rank equally – Both appointed receivers – One chargee's receivers took possession – The other sought an order restraining the exclusion of its receivers – Whether receiver(s) should be appointed by the court.*

This was a dispute between two mortgagees for control of a receivership.

The mortgagees were breweries, 'B' and 'W', and each had a legal charge over certain public house premises and over the goodwill; they had entered into a deed of priorities by which they agreed that their charges ranked equally. Both mortgagees had invoked their powers to appoint a receiver, and W's receivers had taken possession and were proposing to grant a licence to the publican to continue to carry on the business at a weekly fee, thereby excluding B's receivers from control. B sought an order restraining the exclusion of its receivers, alternatively the appointment of an independent receiver by the court.

Held, ruling accordingly:

D   In order to protect the interests of B while causing the least disruption of the business in the conduct of the receivership, the court would appoint one of the W receivers together with one of the B receivers as receivers appointed by the court (one each to be nominated by the parties and subject to both consenting to act). They would be expected objectively to assess the merits of the licence and other courses open with any adjustments they saw fit to the arrangement, and if either party then wished to challenge the course proposed the matter could be referred back to the court if proper reason was shown. If any decision was made, at least it would be a joint decision.

The following cases were referred to in the judgment:

American Cyanamid Co v Ethicon Ltd [1975] AC 396.
Britannia Building Society v Crammer (unreported, 23 October 1990, Scott J).
Downsview Nominees Ltd & Anor v First City Corporation Ltd & Anor [1993] BCC 46; [1993] AC 295.
F   *Maskelyne British Typewriter Ltd, Re* [1898] 1 Ch 133.
Patel & Ors v W H Smith (Eziot) Ltd & Anor [1987] 1 WLR 853.

Anthony Elleray QC (instructed by Lopian Wagner, Manchester) for the plaintiff.

Peter Smith QC (instructed by Davies Wallis Foyster, Manchester) for the defendants.

JUDGMENT

G   **His Honour Judge Maddocks:** The subject-matter of this action is a public house, known as 'Jenny D's', formerly 'Three Lock Falls', situate at Salter Hebble near Halifax. The first defendant, Mr Christopher Delaney, is the licensee and registered proprietor. According to the latest accounts, Jenny D's has an annual turnover in excess of £0.5m but nevertheless has been running at a trading loss after meeting all overheads.

H   This dispute is, however, between two breweries, each of which is a supplier and each of which has a legal charge over the premises and over the goodwill. The first is the plaintiff, Bass Breweries Ltd, which has in fact three legal charges (which I will refer to as the Bass charges), the second is the second defendant, Samuel Webster & Wilson's Ltd (which I will refer to as Webster), which is associated with Courage Ltd (which I will refer to as Courage). As between the two sets of charges, there is no priority as they have entered into a deed of priorities by which they have agreed that the charges rank equally

and the sums due are to be repaid rateably. There are substantial sums due under both   A
mortgages and both mortgagees have invoked their powers to appoint a receiver.

This motion concerns the control of the receivership. More specifically, the Webster
receivers, being the third and fourth defendants who are partners in Coopers and
Lybrand or Cork Gully, have taken possession and are proposing to grant a licence to
Mr Delaney to continue to carry on the business at a weekly fee, thereby excluding the
Bass receivers from control. The plaintiff, Bass, seeks an order restraining the exclusion   B
of their receivers, Mr Lopian and Mr Wagner, who are partners in the solicitor's firm of
that name or, alternatively, the appointment of an independent receiver by the court.

The facts are fairly straightforward and are not in dispute. Mr Delaney became the
registered proprietor on 8 July 1985. The Bass charges were dated 14 May 1986, 29 May
1987 and 21 August 1990, the first two being in the name of Bass (North) Ltd but later
assigned to the plaintiff, Bass Breweries Ltd, by a transfer of 30 October 1989. The   C
Webster's charge was dated after the first two but before the third, being made on 20
June 1990. The deed of priorities was dated 3 September 1990.

I note in passing there has also been a legal charge to Yorkshire Bank plc, dated 27
May 1992, which does not affect the present issues but their solicitors have written to
draw the court's attention to it.

The state of the mortgage accounts, according to the most recent statement from the   D
parties, is as follows: Bass, on loan account £82,733.65, trading account £46,941.69,
interest £5,908.99 – a total of £135,584.33. Bass also has other accounts not covered by
these charges and the total sum due from Mr Delaney is in the region of £750,000. The
Webster account is as follows: loan account £105,096.25, interest £22,798.28, trade
account £34,864.96, interest on that £281.27 – a total of £163,040.76. The defendants'
initial valuation of the security – that is the freehold – of Jenny D's is £650,000 as a going
concern and £500,000 on a forced sale. It may be that Yorkshire Bank has some priority   E
over some part of the trade accounts but I am not concerned with that today.

For completeness, I should note that Bass has charges over two other licensed premises
of Mr Delaney, the Power Bar and Delaney's. As I have indicated, the total sum due to
them is in the region of £750,000.

The total debts of Mr Delaney have been assessed by the plaintiff at £2m. The evidence   F
is that in December 1993 he was contemplating a voluntary arrangement.

I come then to the recent events leading to this motion. In 1993 Bass issued proceedings
against Mr Delaney for payment only of the total sums due to them, being £742,072.72
as at 23 September 1993, for which Bass signed judgment on 10 January 1994. In the
meantime on Tuesday 4 January 1994 Mr Rhodes, regional investment manager of Bass,
saw Mr Delaney and told him of the intention of Bass to appoint a receiver under the   G
Jenny D's charges. The plaintiffs infer – and this has not been denied – that Mr Delaney
informed Webster of their intentions with the consequence that on the same day, 4
January, not only did Bass appoint their receivers but Webster did so as well. I should
just note in passing that the Bass appointment was expressed to refer only to their third
charge. Whether or not it had the effect of being appointment under all three charges,
Bass later entered, on 21 January 1994, into a deed of confirmation to confirm the
appointment as having that effect.   H

It was in fact the Webster receivers who were first off the mark. On 5 January 1994
(the next day), they took possession of the premises and came to a provisional
arrangement with Mr Delaney for him to continue to carry on the business under licence
from them, paying them £1,000 per week. Their intentions were and are to conclude a
more formal but temporary licence to the same effect pending a sale of the property.

A   The Bass receivers proposed a different arrangement: the appointment as managers of a firm that they had used on other public house receiverships, including the Power Bar and Delaney's, that firm being called DFD Management Consultants, at a remuneration linked to turnover. However, when the Bass receivers attempted to take possession they were turned away by the Webster receivers, who refused, and still refuse, to allow them access for the purpose of exercising their powers under the Bass charges, the Webster receivers relying upon their own prior taking of possession, albeit under a

B   contemporaneous appointment.

There was a final incident in relation to the chattels, being mainly the tables and chairs at the premises. These were not covered either by the Bass charge or the Webster charge. On 14 January, Bass instructed the sheriff to levy execution over these chattels under the judgment of 10 January. The sheriff was turned away by the Webster receivers and on the same day Mr Delaney sold all these chattels to Courage for £12,095 plus VAT under

C   a bill of sale of that date.

Following some correspondence, the writ and notice of motion in this action were both issued on 25 January 1994 and the latter came on for hearing before me last Friday, 28 January, being concluded yesterday on Monday, 31 January. By the motion Bass seeks, until trial of the action shortly, (a) an order restraining the defendants from selling the property or receiving the income or managing the premises except with the agreement of

D   Bass or as directed by the court, (b) an order restraining the defendant from denying possession to the Bass receivers or preventing them from managing the business. Finally, and as an alternative, they invite the court to appoint a receiver or receivers and propose as independent receivers partners in the firm of Grant Thornton.

At the hearing, Mr Elleray, for Bass, put this last form of relief at the forefront of his claim. He did so on the basis that for the purpose of this motion the parties should be

E   treated on a footing of equality.

I should finally note, although this is not in evidence, that each party, Bass and Webster, has offered to the other to redeem the other's charge and each of them has refused that offer.

As I have said, those facts are not really in dispute and I come back to the deeds to consider the rights of the parties as established by those deeds. Each charge confers a

F   legal charge over the freehold and over the goodwill but not over the chattels, book debts or other assets of the business. An attempted charge over chattels in the Bass charge is accepted to have been unenforceable for want of registration as a bill of sale and the chattels have now been purchased by Courage. The statutory power of sale has arisen and is exercisable in each case, as had the power to appoint a receiver at the time of the appointments. That power was supplemented by express powers in each charge: in the case of the second Bass charge by cl. 9(b) there is a power for the receiver to manage any

G   business carried on at the property, as there is in cl. 9.2.2 of the third charge, which confers power to appoint a manager for that purpose; likewise, under the Webster charge, under cl. 6.2 which in this case is by cl. 6.3 supplemented by a power to use the trade fixtures, fittings, furniture and equipment.

The critical document really is the deed of priorities dated 3 September 1990. Had it not been for that Bass would have had two prior charges and one subsequent charge to

H   the Webster charge. The deed recites all four charges, and the final recital is (7):

> 'It has been agreed between Webster and Bass that their respective charges shall rank equally.'

The deed continues (in the operative parts):

> '1. The Webster charge and the Bass charge shall rank equally and neither of them shall have any priority over the other.

2. Webster and Bass hereby mutually covenant and agree with each other that any sums of money or other property recovered from or arising out of any action or proceedings against the borrower or the exercise of the rights and obligations of Webster and Bass in relation to the mortgage property or any sums of money received by any party hereto under any insurance policy concerning the mortgage property or the licence relating thereto, or by way of compensation under the Licensing Consolidation Act 1910 or the Licensing Act 1964 or any amendment thereof shall, after payments of all property, costs, fees and commissions incurred under such recovery, be apportioned between Webster and Bass in the following manner.'

The deed then sets out the basis of the apportionment. I think I need read no more of that deed.

A preliminary question is whether that deed had the effect of creating equality for all purposes. Mr Elleray, for Bass, reserved the right to argue at trial that it covered receipts only so as to retain for Bass its priority for charges 1 and 2. I am bound to say I do not see how that could be sustained. The wording of cl. 1 could hardly be plainer. However, I was not asked to take any different view for the purposes of this motion. The consequence, it seems to me, must be that each has an equal right to appoint a receiver and neither can exclude the right of the other. Furthermore, any receiver or receivers so appointed must necessarily be appointed for the benefit of both chargees just as they would be if appointed under a debenture trust deed constituted for more than one debenture holder.

A further preliminary point to which I should also refer concerns the powers of a receiver in this case, whether appointed out of court or by the court. In this connection I was referred to the transcript of an unreported decision of Scott J in *Britannia Building Society v Crammer* (23 October 1990). That concerned a legal charge over property used as a nursing home. The charge did not extend to the chattels or trading debts, or indeed to anything beyond the building. Scott J concluded that it would be in vain for him to appoint a receiver as the receiver could only be appointed over the charged assets, which would not suffice to enable him either to carry on the existing business or a new nursing home business.

He distinguished an earlier decision concerning a colliery:

'Whether a receiver can carry on the business or a like business on the same premises must in each case depend on the subject-matter of the charge and the nature of the business and the powers concerned.'

In the present case both parties are faced with the same problem, that the charge is limited save for the slight advantage to Webster in relation to the use of the chattels themselves which it has purchased. It is, however, really the building itself which enables the trade to be carried on. With that and the goodwill, neither brewery feels unable to put the receiver in a position to be able to trade. If necessary, Bass could find the chattels. I do not think that aspect limits the relief which may be granted here.

I turn then to the rival contentions. Mr Smith takes the stand that the Webster receivers are in possession and lawfully so. The court should not, therefore, disturb them unless there is a clear case that the damages would not be an adequate remedy to the plaintiff and that the balance of convenience requires it. As the order would be mandatory, tantamount to an order for possession, strong reason would be required for that purpose.

On the evidence, he points to the fact that the Webster receivers are both reputable and experienced in this field. The correspondence shows that they have considered their duties with care; their decision to enter into the licence arrangement is, on the figures before the court, one which can be justified. It will produce a good income for the two

A   sets of chargees – and there is no question of the income not being applied equally for the benefit of Bass as for Webster – a total of £52,000 in a full year, and it will do so at minimal expense and with least disturbance to the business. If Bass are not satisfied, it is open to them to accept the offer to redeem. The assets are not in jeopardy and are fully protected by the receivers, who are already in place.

B   The case for the plaintiff is that Bass has established and has an incontestable right to appoint a receiver, which on any view ranks equally with that of Webster. This is not a case in which their right is in issue or could be challenged at the trial. That being so, the principles in *American Cyanamid Co v Ethicon Ltd* [1975] AC 396, do not apply, and Mr Elleray referred me to the case of *Patel & Ors v W H Smith (Eziot) Ltd & Anor* [1987] 1 WLR 853, and in particular the judgment of Balcombe LJ. He says there is nothing on this aspect to go to trial. The court is not therefore concerned to weigh the balance of convenience but is free to act as it would act at the trial. I simply have to decide whether

C   or not the case is one for an injunction as an equitable remedy. The case for an injunction as an equitable remedy is made out in support of the plaintiff's established right. Only if that itself were arguable would the balance of convenience enter into it.

From that point he says whatever the merits of the Webster receivers and their proposed licence they are not entitled to impose their decision unilaterally on Bass. Neither is entitled to oust the other from its remedies. If they both wish to act and cannot

D   agree to the action then the court should resolve the deadlock, which it can do either by appointing an independent receiver or by giving directions as to the specific area of difference after a proper hearing on that aspect. In this case that might involve the court in deciding whether or not the receivers should enter into the proposed licence with Mr Delaney.

The plaintiff reinforces his claim by saying that the circumstances of the Webster

E   appointment are questionable. It was plainly done in response to information supplied as to Bass's intention and as a pre-emptive step taken to keep Bass out of its rights. That should not be allowed.

Mr Elleray referred me to two decisions of the court as to the principles on which a power to appoint a receiver should be exercised. The first is *Re Maskelyne British Typewriter Ltd* [1898] 1 Ch 133, where it was held that, in relation to an appointment

F   under a debenture:

> 'The Corporation were trustees of this power on behalf of all the debenture-holders, and were bound to exercise it in their interest alone, and that as it was shewn that the appointment had been made in the interest of the shareholders, and not in that of the debenture-holders, the Court had jurisdiction to interfere to carry out the trust, and accordingly to appoint its own receiver.'

G   So here, he said, the appointment by Webster was tainted by the intention to pre-empt Bass. He referred me also to *Downsview Nominees Ltd & Anor v First City Corporation Ltd* [1993] BCC 46, a decision of the Privy Council on appeal from the Court of Appeal of New Zealand, which deals with the duties owed by receivers.

On the merits of this case the plaintiff takes the view that Mr Delaney ought not to be left in charge. It is a cash business and his records are, they say, unreliable. Proper records

H   should be kept, both for the purposes of obtaining the best return and for establishing the true worth of the company on a sale. I cannot, on the limited evidence available to me at this stage, say which approach is right. Indeed, in large measure, it may be a matter for commercial judgment. For what it is worth on the limited evidence before me, my inclination would be to follow the pragmatic approach adopted by the Webster receivers in proposing the licence, but Bass are entitled to be fully consulted and involved in any such decision.

A

I am prepared to accept that in making their decision to appoint a receiver on 4 January, Webster were acting in what they saw as their legitimate commercial interests. That action, however, having been taken at a time when to their knowledge Bass were also intent on appointing a receiver, it is not in my judgment open to them to rely on their possession as a ground for excluding Bass from its equal right to appoint a receiver. That right has been and is being infringed. As a consequence, Bass are being excluded from participation in the conduct of the receivership and management of the business. Bass, in turn, is entitled to rely on its own offer to redeem Webster if Webster wishes to exclude it.

B

In this situation, the parties being, in my judgment, on an equal footing and unable to resolve their differences, it is right that I should intervene. I have considered whether it would suffice to require undertakings from the defendants as to the supply of information and conduct of the receivership. That, however, would fall short of supporting the plaintiff's rights. At the other extreme, I might appoint an independent receiver, such as partners in Grant Thornton. A middle course suggested was to appoint the Webster receivers as receivers under both charges if willing to act, which today I am informed they are.

C

At one stage I was attracted to that proposal, but it would inevitably leave Bass with some grievance as the receivers have largely committed themselves to a course of action which Bass would wish to question, or certainly to consider in greater depth. It would also leave Bass in the position that the receivers nominated by Webster had remained with conduct of the receivership.

D

After some hesitation, the course I propose is one which I hope, with goodwill, may protect the interests of Bass while causing the least disruption in the conduct of the receivership of the business, and that is to appoint one of the Webster receivers together with one of the Bass receivers as receivers appointed by the court. I will leave it to the parties to nominate which one it should be and this, of course, will be subject to both those persons consenting to act. I would expect them then objectively to assess the merits of the licence and other courses open with any adjustments they see fit to the arrangement, and if either party then wishes to challenge the course proposed the matter can be referred back to the court if proper reason is shown. If a decision is made, at least it will be a joint decision.

E

For the reasons given, I consider that the plaintiff is entitled to relief and propose to make the order in those terms. I will now hear counsel as to any consequential orders which are required.

F

(Order accordingly)

G

H

A
Re Thundercrest Ltd.
Chancery Division (Companies Court).
His Honour Judge Paul Baker QC.
Judgment delivered 27 May 1994.

B
Allotment – Notice – Rectification – Letter of provisional allotment returned to company by Post Office – Shares were allotted to other members – Whether plaintiff entitled to rectification – Whether plaintiff had been given proper notice – Whether notice deemed delivered – Companies Act 1985, s. 89–96, 359.

This was a motion for rectification of a company's register of members pursuant to s. 359 of the Companies Act 1985.

The company had three shareholders including the plaintiff. Each held 50 shares. It was proposed to issue 30,000 new shares, 10,000 to each shareholder. A letter of provisional allotment and form of acceptance sent by recorded delivery post to the plaintiff was returned by the Post Office. The other two shareholders took up the plaintiff's shares. At that time they knew that the letter of provisional allotment had not been delivered to the plaintiff but had been returned to the company. They also knew that the plaintiff was desirous of taking up the shares.

C

The plaintiff argued that the allotment was invalid because it did not state a period of not less than 21 days for acceptance contrary to the Companies Act 1985, s. 90(6). The second point was that notice of the provisional allotment was not in fact given to the plaintiff. The defendants disputed both points. They also argued that in any event the matter could not be brought by an originating motion: the plaintiff's remedy, if any, lay in damages only under s. 92 of the 1985 Act, and an action for damages could not be brought by originating motion. In relation to notice the company's articles provided for the offer to be made by notice specifying the number of shares to which the member was entitled and 'limiting a time within which the offer if not accepted shall be deemed to have been declined . . .' and that the provisions of the statute were to have effect only in so far as they were not inconsistent with the article.

D

E

Held, avoiding the allotment of the shares and rectifying the register by cancelling the allotment of the additional 5,000 shares to the second and third defendants:

1. There was a case for having the register rectified by removing the names of the second and third defendants, justifying the commencement of proceedings by originating motion.

F

2. It was clear that the provisions of the statute were not excluded by the articles. Each provision of the statute had to be tested to see whether it was inconsistent with the article. The statute and the article could perfectly well stand together. The time-limit had to be specified but that time must not be less than 21 days. The notice which was given was defective in specifying less than 21 days.

G

3. The defendants could not rely on the provisions in the articles deeming the letter to have been delivered when it was manifest that the letter had not been delivered because it was returned by the Post Office to the defendants before the allotment of shares was made.

The following cases were referred to in the judgment:
Bishop (Thomas) Ltd v Helmville Ltd [1972] 1 QB 464.
TO Supplies (London) Ltd v Jerry Creighton Ltd [1952] 1 KB 42.

H
Adrian Jack (instructed by Slater Adams) for the applicant.

Edmund Cullen (instructed by Gregory Rowcliffe & Milnes) for the respondents.

JUDGMENT

His Honour Judge Paul Baker QC: This originating motion raises a number of points concerning an alleged allotment of shares in a company called Thundercrest Ltd. It has

A

only three shareholders, the plaintiff and the second and third defendants. I shall have to deal with the facts before coming to the particular issues, otherwise they cannot be understood.

The company was incorporated in 1983. It was in the building construction business but ceased trading in 1989. It was not then wound up, the reason being that it had very substantial claims which it was pursuing against other parties in that industry and is still continuing to pursue them. One was against Wates for some £20,000 to £30,000. Another was a claim against a firm called T Scudder Ltd for some £430,000 as to which a interim payment of something under £100,000 had been paid. That action is due to be tried in October 1994.

B

I need not go through the history of the company in detail. It did not always have the same three shareholders but by 1992 they were the parties now before me. Each had 50 shares which was the total issued capital of the company at that time. There is a relationship between the plaintiff and the second defendant in that they are brothers-in-law, the plaintiff being married to the second defendant's sister. The third defendant is a business colleague of theirs. In the period I am concerned with the second and third defendants were and still are the directors of the company. The plaintiff in the past has been a director but he is not currently a director.

C

Earlier this year the company needed to raise funds in order to carry on the litigation that I have mentioned. The sum of £30,000 was required for that purpose. The method proposed was to raise this sum from the three shareholders by increasing the share capital by that amount and offering it to the three shareholders equally. By that means each shareholder would have to put £10,000 into the kitty for the litigation fund. They evidently were advised that they had good prospects of success in the litigation but with that I am not concerned. By doing that and allotting shares pro rata it would maintain equality of shareholding between the three directors. The consequence of that would be that when the claims were fought to a conclusion or settled there would be some cash in the company, or so they hoped. The company could then be put into litigation or otherwise disposed of and the fruits shared equally between the shareholders. But, of course, if one shareholder put up all the money and took all the shares, that would manifestly dilute the shareholding of the others. That is by way of general background.

D

E

I now come to the immediate proceedings which led to this dispute. As I have said, the plaintiff and the second defendant were brothers-in-law but relationships were somewhat strained between them but that is not a matter into which I need go. At all events, on 7 March 1994 Mr Coyne, the second defendant wrote to his brother-in-law, Mr Murray, setting out the need to raise money. He mentioned the litigation and said:

F

'Existing funds are almost depleted and your board proposes to raise £30,000 by way of a rights issue of 30,000 new shares. The rights issue is being made on the basis of 200 new shares for every one share held at the price of £1 per share. . . .

G

Should you wish to subscribe to all or any of the new shares you must lodge the provisional allotment letter duly completed and signed, by post or by hand with Stoy Hayward at Fitzallan House [the company's auditors], . . . so as to arrive no later than 3.00 p.m. on Monday, 11 April 1994.'

Accompanying that letter was the notice of the meeting to enlarge the share capital. It gave notice of an extraordinary general meeting for Wednesday, 23 March, at 2.30 p.m. The resolutions to be considered were:

H

'(a) The authorised share capital of the company be and it is increased from £150 to £30,150 by the creation of an additional 30,000 shares of £1 each.

(b) The directors of the company be and are hereby authorised during the period of five years from the date of this resolution to allot, grant options over or

A   otherwise dispose of the unissued shares in the capital of the company to such persons at such times and on such conditions as they think fit, subject to the provisions of art. 3 and 4 of the company's articles of association and provided no shares shall be issued at a discount.'

There is then a note:

'A member entitled to attend and vote is entitled to appoint a proxy to attend . . .'

B   It was not convenient for Mr Murray to attend the meeting at the time and date specified and accordingly he sent a proxy, addressed to Mr Coyne, on 9 February saying:

'Please accept this letter as an instrument appointing you as a proxy to vote on my behalf at the meeting on 23 March for the adoption of resolutions A and B on the notice of meeting attached to the above letter.'

So at that point Mr Murray was in full agreement with what was proposed and gave
C   his proxy to his brother-in-law to help carry it into effect.

In response to a request by Mr Murray, on 14 March Mr Coyne gave further details of the litigation. It seems that that letter was not responded to by Mr Murray. That was the last contact, I think, by correspondence until a month later.

The meeting was held on 23 March and the resolutions were passed. On the following day a letter of provisional allotment and form of acceptance was sent out by recorded
D   delivery post to Mr Murray. The letter is addressed to Mr Murray and it is signed by Mr Coyne:

'Dear Jim,

With regard to the extraordinary general meeting held on 23 March I would confirm that the resolution proposed was adopted and as a result I can confirm your provisional allotment with regard to the rights issue advised in my letter of 7
E   March . . .

The rights issue, being made on the basis of 200 new shares for every old one share held, entitles you to subscribe to a maximum of 10,000 new shares at a cost of £10,000. You have been provisionally allotted your full entitlement. You may, of course, subscribe to a smaller number of shares and provision is made for this in the acceptance letter attached.'

F   Attached to that is a formal letter from the company which Mr Murray, if he was willing to accept the shares and pay the £10,000 or some lesser amount, should sign and return. It says:

'I have read an accept the terms of allotment in connection with the rights issue notified to me in a letter from the company dated 7 March.'

One alternative was to agree to subscribe to the full entitlement of 10,000 shares at the
G   cost of £1. Then the terms of the allotment had this:

'The final date for acceptance of your provisional allotment or a smaller number of shares as may be indicated by you in your acceptance letter is Monday, 11 April. Your acceptance of shares to which you are entitled must be lodged with Stoy Hayward by 3.00 p.m.

Full payment becomes due seven days after the final date for acceptance and therefore payment is due on 18 April. Payment must be made by post or by hand
H   so as to arrive at the offices of Stoy Hayward . . .'

That was sent by recorded delivery. It would seem from the evidence before me that the Post Office made one call but got no answer from the house of Mr Murray. There was no one at home. In accordance with the normal practice it would seem (though this is not fully established) that the postman would have left a card saying that the call had been made and the letter was available at some sorting office. The evidence is not clear

whether in fact a card was left or not. At all events the letter itself was marked to the A
effect that no answer was obtained from it and the procedure of leaving the card had
been followed. The defendants, on the other hand, say they did not get any card and
accordingly did not respond to the allotment letter.

On 15 April, which was a few days after the time-limit specified in the allotment letter,
there was a meeting of the directors of the company. The object of the meeting was to
discuss the recent rights issue and to decide what to do with the shares provisionally B
allocated to Mr Murray. They noted that they had received no response to the letter of
allotment from Mr Murray. They resolved that the company required to raise the full
£30,000 anticipated by the rights issue and, therefore, the shares provisionally allotted to
Mr Murray would be placed. They further resolved that the remaining 10,000 shares
would be allotted to Mr Kinsella and Mr Coyne in equal proportions as they had both
indicated that they would be willing to take up such shares. It was finally resolved that
the date for payment under the rights issue be extended from 18 April to 25 April to C
allow time to raise the additional moneys.

Three days later, on 18 April, the letter which had been sent to Mr Murray and had
not been delivered to him was returned by the Post Office to the company. It is clear that
there had been one attempt only to deliver the letter soon after 24 March, and it had been
retained thereafter at the Post Office in the expectation that Mr Murray or someone from
his household would call and collect it. This had not happened and, therefore, it was D
returned.

When he received that, Mr Coyne wrote to his brother-in-law on 18 April in the
following terms:

'Dear Jim,

Today the Post Office returned correspondence sent to you by recorded delivery
mail on 24 March as they were unable to obtain a signature when delivering to E
your address, and they have received no response to their card inviting you to
collect said mail from your local sorting office. In addition, I have received no
response to my letter dated 14 March which was sent by ordinary first class post. I
have enclosed copies of the above two items of correspondence for your records
and look forward to hearing from you should you have any comments.'

On receipt of that letter Mr Murray went to see his solicitors. Two days later the F
solicitor, Slater Adams & Co, wrote to Mr Kinsella:

'We refer to the above matter and our telephone conversation of today.

We have been instructed by Mr J Murray with regard to the allotment of shares in
respect of Thundercrest Ltd. Our client instructs us that he has been allotted 10,000
shares. We are instructed by our client that he did not receive the acceptance form
in respect of this allotment until yesterday, 19 April, when a copy of the form was
sent to him by Mr Coyne. Our client wishes to take up his full entitlement to the G
shares and please confirm that these are available to him. We are instructed to
inform you that if our client is denied his entitlement, then we will be issuing a
petition for unfair prejudice in the High Court and will pursue all legal remedies
available.'

On receiving that Mr Kinsella went to consult the company's solicitors, Gregory
Rowcliffe & Milnes. Two days later, on 22 April, the solicitors replied, setting out the H
facts as I have done, and concluding:

'The offers to the other shareholders were accepted but no acceptance was received
by Thundercrest and Mr Murray even though he was also aware of the relevant
dates from the letters sent by Thundercrest to him dated 7 March. In the
circumstances, we have advised Thundercrest that Mr Murray, having declined to

A   accept the offer, is not eligible to be allotted the shares in question and in accordance with the articles of association they are being allotted elsewhere.

In passing, we would mention that, for reasons best known to Mr Murray, he did not visit the Post Office to collect the recorded delivery letter dated 24 March despite being in possession of the Post Office's card which had been put through his letter box on 26 March.'

B   As I say, the allegation in that last paragraph is disputed.

Finally, following that exchange of correspondence, a further meeting was held in the morning of 25 April and the 10,000 shares were allotted equally between Mr Coyne and Mr Kinsella. The appropriate entries were made in the register of members showing that on that date 15,000 shares were allotted to each of those shareholders and the appropriate certificates of shareholdings were issued by the company. In the afternoon an ex parte application was made in this court to Arden J and an injunction was obtained to restrain the allotment although, as we have seen, it had already occurred.

C

That is the chronology and I must now refer to one or two passages in the evidence.

In Mr Murray's affidavit in para. 1 he explains he is the applicant and that although he is a successful entrepreneur he left school at the age of 13 and so his reading and writing is not very good. In para. 7 he talks of the resolution to allot the shares and says:

D   'I was fully in agreement with the resolution but I could not attend the meeting because I was due to be at a meeting in New Addington so I gave the second respondent my proxy to vote in favour of the resolution. Although the letter of 7 March 1994 referred to payment of the allotment by 11 April, after the meeting on 23 March I received nothing until 19 April when my wife, who was at home at the time, received a letter dated 18 April from the second respondent. My wife had been looking out for a letter from him because we knew that the letter of allotment could be expected.'

E

Mr Coyne in his evidence at para. 9 says:

'Offer letters were sent out pursuant to the articles of association on 24 March. Mr Murray's letter was sent by recorded delivery on 25 March, this being the date franked on the envelope, and arrived on 26 March.'

F   He produces that and says that there is written on the envelope 'NA' and the date 26 March 1994.

'I believe this was written by the postman who delivered it and indicates that the letter was delivered on 26 March and there was no answer. I also believe that 739 is the Post Office code for the usual practice with recorded delivery mail of putting a card through the door asking the addressee to collect the letter. Thus the stamped words 'No response to P.739B treatment' indicates that the letter was not collected. It was returned to Thundercrest on 18 April. I immediately wrote to Mr Murray.'

G

Mr Murray in his evidence in relation to using recorded delivery says:

'The second respondent states he was keen to ensure there was no room for any argument about receipt of the offer letter. There is no room for argument about receipt of the offer letter. I never received it. It was returned to the second respondent. Had he genuinely wished for me to have notice of the offer, he could also have sent the offer by first class post. I accept the relations between the second respondent and myself are strained. However, he could have telephoned his sister and told her about the offer letter.'

H

Mrs Murray says:

'At no time did I see any card which said the recorded delivery letter was waiting to be collected. I feel certain that had such a card been delivered through the door I would have seen it as I was looking out for the offer letter.'

A

That is the way the evidence stands with the documents in this case and it is manifest from that evidence that the directors knew two things on 25 April when the final allocation was made of these shares. First, that the letter of provisional allotment had not been delivered to Mr Murray but had been returned to the company. Secondly, they knew that the plaintiff was saying through his solicitors that he was desirous of taking up the shares. Nevertheless, on 25 April the directors went ahead and made the allotment to themselves and caused it to be registered in the register of members. Those I think are the indisputable facts that emerge in this case.

B

I now come to the issues that arise in respect of this matter. The plaintiff has issued an originating motion under RSC, O. 5, r. 2. The relief sought is an order pursuant to s. 359 of the *Companies Act* 1985 that:

> '... on the applicant paying £10,000 to the above-named company the register of members be rectified by inserting the name of the applicant as the holder of 10,050 £1 shares with such consequential orders as may be just and for a declaration that the purported offer is invalid and for an injunction restraining the respondents and each of them from allotting the 10,000 shares authorised to be issued by virtue of a resolution passed at the extraordinary general meeting of 23 April and from registering the ownership of the shares ...'

C

It then seeks damages and interest.

D

The plaintiff takes two points in support of an argument that the provisional allotment was invalid. The first point is that it does not state a period of not less than 21 days for acceptance. The actual period stated from the resolution to 11 April, which was the date specified, is several days less than 21. It is said that that is contrary to the *Companies Act* 1985, s. 90(6). The second point is that, having regard to the facts that I have outlined, notice of the provisional allotment was not in fact given to Mr Murray.

E

The defendants dispute both those points. They also say that in any event this matter cannot be brought by an originating motion. They say that the plaintiff's remedy, if any, lies in damages only under the *Companies Act* 1985, s. 92, and an action for damages cannot be brought by an originating motion. There is no case here for having the register rectified which alone would justify the commencement of proceedings by originating motion. Hence I must now examine the rules relating to such motions.

F

Order 5, r. 5, says:

> 'Proceedings may be begun by originating motion or petition if, but only if, by these rules or by or under any Act the proceedings in question are required or authorised to be so begun.'

In relation to companies one goes to O. 102, r. 3, which says:

> '(1) The following applications under the Act must be made by originating motion, namely, applications–
>
> . . .
>
> (g) Under section 359(1) for the rectification of the register of members of a company . . .'

G

There is nothing in there that could justify the action for damages or anything of that nature. So, so far as that point goes, the defendant is on strong ground, but the question is whether this is a viable application for rectification of the register.

H

The relevant section is s. 359 of the *Companies Act* 1985, which says:

> 'If–
>
> (a) the name of any person is without sufficient cause entered in or omitted from a company's register of members; or

A
    (b) default is made or unnecessary delay takes place on entering on the register the fact of any person having ceased to be a member, the person aggrieved or any member of the company may apply to the court for rectification of the register.'

The defendants' argument proceeds that here there is no contract at the moment between Mr Murray and the company to take the allotment of the shares, and there is

B
nothing that the court can enforce, hence there is no power to order rectification as required in the originating motion. That may be so, but that overlooks the fact that the court can order the names of persons who have been improperly entered on the register to be removed. Looking at it that way, then clearly the complaint of Mr Murray is in part that the directors have put themselves on the register and allocated to themselves shares that ought to go to him.

C
    In reply to that it is pointed out me that in *Gore Brown on Companies* (44th edn), para. 9.2 there is this:

    '. . . Section 92(1) does not appear to invalidate any allotment not complying with shareholders' pre-emptive rights. They are simply left to the civil remedy provided by the subsection. It has been left to the courts to determine the measure and scope of loss or damage that may be recovered. It is not clear whether the loss of 'control' of a company would be compensable over and above the market price for the

D
shares of that class. However, no such proceedings may be commenced after the expiration of two years from the delivery to the registrar of companies of the return of allotments . . .'

    One can see in the case of a large allotment the grave difficulties of undoing an allotment of shares where third party rights have become involved. If some mistake has occurred in allotting the shares among a group of shareholders when some have paid

E
their money, it may well be that the allotment cannot be undone and the register cannot be rectified where those rights have accrued. Hence the person who has suffered an injury or wrong because of the mishandling of the allotment is left with a remedy of compensation or damages. One can see the sense of all that. But, in my judgment, there is nothing to prevent the setting aside of allotments to directors in their own favour, the directors themselves being responsible for managing the allotments. In appropriate circumstances it would be possible to rectify by removing a name from the register.

F
Otherwise directors might be taking advantage of their own wrong. Therefore, I reject the submission that the proceedings are misconceived, having been brought by way of originating motion, but that does not mean to say that they are bound to succeed. We have to see whether there should be some degree of rectification of the register in the particular circumstances of this case, and that in turn depends on whether the supplementary allotment was valid.

G
    To test whether the allotment is invalid or not, I must look at some of the articles of association of the company, and the provisions of the statute. It is a private company. In the main its articles adopt the regulations contained in Pt. I of Table A of the First Schedule to the *Companies Act* 1948, with some omissions with which I need not deal and some special articles. I think I can go straight to art. 5 of the special articles.

    'Subject to any direction to the contrary that may be given by the company in

H
general meeting, any original shares for the time being unissued and any new shares from time to time to be created shall, before they are issued, be offered to the members in proportion as nearly as possible to the nominal value of the existing shares held by them and such offer shall be made by notice specifying the number of shares to which the member is entitled and limiting a time within which the offer, if not accepted, shall be deemed to be declined; and after the expiration of such time or on receipt of an intimation from the member to whom the notice is

given that he declines to accept the shares, the directors may dispose of the same   A
in such manner as they think most beneficial to the company. The provisions of
s. 17 of the *Companies Act* 1980 shall have effect only in so far as they are not
inconsistent with this article.'

That is relevant to one of the objections taken to the allotment, the fact that too short
a time was given.

As to service, I must go to Table A and read that before reading the relevant special   B
article. The material article in Table A of the 1948 Act is art. 131:

'*Notices*

A notice may be given by the company to any member either personally or by
sending it by post to him or to his registered address, or (if he has no registered
address within the United Kingdom) to the address, if any, within the United
Kingdom supplied by him to the company for the giving of notice to him . . .'   C

We now come to the important parts:

'Where a notice is sent by post, service of the notice shall be deemed to be effected
by properly addressing, prepaying, and posting a letter containing the notice . . .'

I omit to read the remaining words and I now pick up the special article, art. 22.

'In reg. 131 of Table A, all the words after the words 'letter containing the notice'
shall be omitted, and in substitution therefor there shall be inserted the words: D
Where a notice is sent by post, service of the notice shall be deemed to be effected
by properly addressing, prepaying and posting a letter containing the notice, and
if posted by pre-paid first class mail, to have been effected at the expiration of 24
hours after the letter containing the same is posted, and, if posted by any other
class of pre-paid mail, at the time at which the letter would be delivered in the
ordinary course of post.'   E

That is the article which regulates the giving of notices.

I return to the point on the length of notice. Article 5 refers to s. 17 of the *Companies
Act* 1980. This was a new provision introduced by that Act (which was an amending Act)
relating to pre-emption rights which is what we have under art. 5. The present statutory
provisions in relation to pre-emption rights are now to be found in s. 89–92 of the
Companies Act 1985. It is common ground between counsel that there is no material   F
difference between what was provided in s. 17 of the 1980 Act and what is now to be
found in the sections which I have mentioned of the 1985 Act in relation to offers to
shareholders on a pre-emptive basis. Section 89(1) says that:

'Subject to the provisions of this section and the seven sections next following, a
company proposing to allot equity securities–'

–and there is no doubt that that is what was proposed here–   G

'(a) shall not allot any of them on any terms to a person unless it has made an
offer to each person who holds relevant shares or relevant employee shares
to allot to him on the same or more favourable terms a proportion of those
securities which is as nearly as practicable equal to the proportion in nominal
value held by him of the aggregate of the relevant shares and the relevant
employee shares, and

(b) shall not allot any of those securities to a person unless the period during   H
which any such offer may be accepted has expired or the company has
received notice of the acceptance or refusal of any offer so made.'

There is then a provision that subs. (3) applies to a provision of a company's
memorandum or articles which requires the company, when proposing to allot equity
securities consisting of relevant shares of any particular class not to allow those securities

on any terms unless it has complied with the condition that it makes such offer as is described in subs. (1) to each such person; and, if the subsection applies, then there follows an exclusion which I do not propose to read at the moment.

Section 90 reads as follows:

'(1) This section has effect as to the manner in which offers required by section 89(1), or by a provision to which section 89(3) applies, are to be made to the holders of a company's shares.'

There are then a number of provisions including:

'(2) Subject to the following subsections, an offer shall be in writing and shall be made to a holder of shares either personally or by sending it by post (that is to say, prepaying and posting a letter containing the offer) to him or to his registered address or, if he has no registered address in the United Kingdom, to the address in the United Kingdom supplied by him to the company for the giving of notice to him.

If sent by post, the offer is deemed to be made at the time at which the letter would be delivered in the ordinary course of post.
. . .

(6) The offer must state a period of not less than 21 days during which it may be accepted; and the offer shall not be withdrawn before the end of that period.
. . .

91(1) Section 89(1), section 90(1) to 95 or section 90(6) may, as applying to allotments by a private company of equity securities or to such allotments of a particular description, be excluded by a provision contained in the memorandum or articles of that company.

(2) A requirement or authority contained in the memorandum or articles of a private company, if it is inconsistent with any of those subsections, has effect as a provision excluding that sub-section; but a provision to which section 89(3) applies is not to be treated as inconsistent with section 89(1).'

Section 92 deals with the consequences of contravening and the company and officers liable to compensate persons who have sustained any loss or damage by contraventions.

Mr Cullen for the defendants, first of all, took the point that none of those provisions apply. Section 90, which contains the provisions relied on by the plaintiffs, does not apply in this case. The argument starting with s. 91(1) ran that if the offer was required, s. 90 only bites, as it were, if the offer is required to be made in accordance with s. 89(1); s. 90(1) reads:

'This section has effect as to the manner in which offers required by section 89(1) . . . are to be made to the holders of a company's shares.'

It is said in this case that the offer is not required to be made by s. 89(1) and one sees that from s. 91(1), and as an example in a case of this company, one would not have to wait until the end of a period to place shares of a provisional allottee who immediately renounced them or indicated that he did not wish to take them up. To my mind that submission breaks down at the beginning because it overlooks the provision in art. 5 that:

'. . . The provisions of s. 17 . . . shall have effect only in so far as they are not inconsistent with this article.'

That is the forerunner to the present section and, in my judgment, it could not be that the predecessor of s. 90 never applies when, in the article itself, s. 17 is expressly incorporated and is to have effect, though qualified, only in so far as they are not inconsistent with the article. It seems that one has to test each provision to see whether any provision is inconsistent with the article. One first looks at subs. (6):

'The offer must state a period of not less than 21 days during which it may be   A
accepted; and the offer shall not be withdrawn before the end of that period.'

What the special article provides is that:

'. . . such offer shall be made by notice specifying the number of shares to which
the member is entitled and limiting a time within which the offer if not accepted
shall be deemed to have been declined . . .'

That is said to be inconsistent because it prevents the company limiting a shorter time,   B
whereas the article is wide-ranging and any such time can be limited. I find no difficulty
about the two provisions standing together, which I think is the true test. One looks at
the two provisions: is one inconsistent with the other in the sense that, can one stand with
the other? I was shown some cases on analogous situations in relation to objections to
inclusion in a voters' list or in arbitration proceedings. I have had some assistance from
those authorities but it seems to come down to the simple principle that I have mentioned: C
can the two provisions stand together? It seems that they can perfectly well stand
together. The time-limit has to be specified but that time must not be less than 21 days. It
is sensible that, in a case of an allotment where large sums may be involved and have to
be found to pay the call, some reasonable time should be allowed. It seems to me that the
notice which was given in this case was defective in specifying less than 21 days.

The other point is as to service. Applying the articles, one can say that the notice was
duly served because of the deeming provisions in art. 131 of Table A (as modified by   D
art. 22 of the special articles). I was shown authority in relation to what type of post can
be used. It includes the Recorded Delivery Post. I accept that authority and I would
have reached that conclusion anyway. When the article says 'by pre-paid first class mail',
that would include, in my judgment, recorded delivery post.

There is also authority to that effect in relation to another provision, which was referred
to me by Mr Cullen. This was the case of *TO Supplies (London) Ltd v Jerry Creighton Ltd*   E
[1952] 1 KB 42 in relation to s. 437 of the then *Companies Act* 1948. That provided that a
document may be served on a company by leaving it at or sending it by post to the
registered office of the company. It was held that the word 'post' in that section is wide
enough to include both ordinary and registered post and, therefore, a company was
properly served with a writ if it was sent by registered post to its registered address.

The argument against is that with registered post, and now recorded delivery, the letter   F
is not left at the address unless some signature is obtained for it, whereas in the ordinary
way a letter is left at the house whether it is empty or not. But that argument did not
prevail for reasons which, if I may say so, I find compelling.

Devlin J in *TO Supplies* was reversing a practice which was not to accept registered
post as adequate for the service of writs. At p. 44 he said:

'I am told that the reason for the practice of not using the registered post is to
overcome the difficulty that for some reason or other a registered letter will not be   G
taken in; and that that may happen is illustrated by the present case.'

The registered office was some accountants' office and they forwarded it on to the
business address of the company. When it got there it was handed to one of the sales
women who at that time was the only person in the office. She refused to accept it, as she
thought the contents of a registered letter would probably be too important for her to
attend to. So it was actually proffered to somebody at the company's business office and   H
refused.

Going back to the judgment:

'On the other hand, it may be said that by registering a letter one makes it more
likely that it will be delivered and its arrival is easier to prove. But while there is
the difficulty that a registered letter may not be taken in, the sender will, sooner or

A

later, be made aware of the loss, and the courts will know how to treat a plaintiff who, knowing that a writ has in fact not been delivered to a limited company's place of business, still tries to obtain a judgment on it.'

I was also referred to *Thomas Bishop Ltd v Helmville Ltd* [1972] 1 QB 464. In that case the plaintiffs posted a writ, claiming a sum of money, by first class mail to the defendants' company's registered office. The plaintiffs entered judgment in default of appearance.

B

The defendant company applied to have the judgment set aside. Their managing director swore by affidavit that no copy of the writ had been received. He was not cross-examined and the plaintiffs did not challenge the facts deposed to but contended that, the writ having been duly posted on 3 June and not having been returned undelivered, service was deemed to have been effected by reason of s. 26 of the *Interpretation Act* 1889. The master refused to set aside the judgment but varied it. The commissioner dismissed the appeal.

C

On appeal to the Court of Appeal it was held, allowing the appeal, that service of the writ on the defendant company could not be deemed to have been effected on the date specified or at all in the ordinary course of post since, by reason of the unchallenged facts deposed to by the defendant company's managing director the contrary had been proved and accordingly the whole judgment in default of appearance was defective and should be set aside. Reliance was placed there on s. 26 of the *Interpretation Act* 1889 dealing with the same subject-matter:

D

'Where an Act passed after the commencement of this Act authorises or requires any document to be served by post . . . then, unless the contrary intention appears, the service shall be deemed to be effected by properly addressing, prepaying, and posting a letter containing the document, and unless the contrary is proved to have been effected at the time at which the letter would be delivered in the ordinary course of post.'

E

In that case, of course, they had that qualification 'unless the contrary is proved'. There is, it must be said, no such qualification in the article before me.

The facts in the present case are even more compelling than the facts in those cases. Here not only have we the sworn evidence of the plaintiff and his wife that the letter was not received, but it was manifest that the letter had not been delivered because it was returned by the Post Office to the defendants before the allotment of these shares was made. The purpose of deeming provisions in the case of management of companies is

F

clear. In the case of uncertainty as to whether a document has been delivered, with large numbers of shareholders and so forth, there has to be some rule under which those in charge of the management can carry on the business without having to investigate every case where some shareholder comes along and says he has not got the document. The directors have to proceed and transact the company's business on the basis of the deeming provisions. But, in my judgment, all that falls away when you find it is established without

G

any possibility of challenge that the document has not been delivered. It would seem, if Devlin J had been confronted with those facts he would have dealt with the matter according to the true facts and not the deemed facts. So I find that that ground of objection also has been established. Accordingly, the order I propose to make under the originating motion is to avoid the allotment of the shares and rectify the register by cancelling the allotment of the additional 5,000 shares to the two defendants.

H

(*Order accordingly. Second and third defendants to pay the plaintiff's costs*)

Bishopsgate Investment Management Ltd v Homan & Ors.

Court of Appeal (Civil Division).
Dillon, Leggatt and Henry L JJ.
Judgment delivered 12 July 1994.

> *Administration – Priority – Tracing – Moneys of trustee company improperly
> paid to Maxwell companies – Trustee company sought equitable charge on all
> assets of payee company in administration – Whether trustee could trace through
> overdrawn account – Whether trustee could trace into asset acquired before
> misappropriation of trust moneys.*

This was an appeal by Bishopsgate Investment Management Ltd ('BIM'), which was the
trustee of various pension schemes for employees of companies with which the late Robert
Maxwell was associated, against an order of Vinelott J. BIM was in liquidation.

On the unexpected death of Robert Maxwell on 5 November 1991 it was discovered that
BIM had improperly paid pension fund moneys, during his lifetime, directly or indirectly,
into an account of Maxwell Communications Corporation plc ('MCC') with National
Westminster Bank. MCC was the most prominent of the Maxwell companies. At the time
of each wrongful payment of BIM's pension fund moneys into that account the account was
overdrawn.

MCC itself proved to be insolvent and administrators had been appointed. The company
was also in Ch. 11 bankruptcy in the US. A scheme of arrangement had been approved in
both jurisdictions. The administrators wanted to make an interim distribution among the
creditors of MCC, but BIM's liquidators claimed that BIM was entitled to an equitable
charge, in priority to all other unsecured creditors of MCC, on all the assets of MCC for
the full amount of the pension moneys of BIM wrongly paid to MCC. The administrators
applied to the Companies Court for directions.

Vinelott J declared that BIM was not entitled to any equitable charge over assets of
MCC acquired before any moneys or assets misappropriated from BIM were paid or
transferred to or so as to be under the control of MCC and were not acquired in anticipation
of or otherwise in connection with the misappropriation of such assets or moneys. He held
that BIM could only claim an equitable charge on any assets of MCC in accordance with
the recognised principles of equitable tracing which did not permit tracing through an
overdrawn bank account (whether the account was already overdrawn at the time the
relevant moneys were paid into it or was in credit but became overdrawn by subsequent
drawings). However, the judge reserved the position if it were shown that there was a
connection between a particular misappropriation of BIM's moneys and the acquisition by
MCC of a particular asset ('backward tracing'), e.g. where an asset was acquired by MCC
with moneys borrowed from the overdrawn account and there was an inference that when
the borrowing was incurred it was the intention that it should be repaid by misappropriations
of BIM's moneys. Another possibility was that moneys misappropriated from BIM were
paid into an overdrawn account of MCC in order to reduce the overdraft and so make
finance available within the overdraft limits for MCC to purchase some particular asset.

BIM appealed against the judge's order and the administrators cross-appealed against
his reservations.

Held, dismissing the appeal and the cross-appeal:

1. So far as BIM claimed to be entitled to an equitable charge over moneys standing to
the credit of MCC when the administrators were appointed in any bank account into which
any moneys of BIM, or the proceeds of any assets misappropriated from BIM, were paid,
the point was that the bank account into which the misappropriated BIM trust moneys were
paid happened to be in credit when the administrators were appointed. In the absence of

A   clear evidence of intention to make good the depredations on BIM it was not possible to assume that that credit balance had been clothed with a trust in favour of BIM and its beneficiaries. (James Roscoe (Bolton) Ltd v Winder [1915] 1 Ch 62 applied.)

2. As to equitable tracing, though devised for the protection of trust moneys misapplied, it could not be pursued through an overdrawn and therefore non-existent fund. It was not open to the court to say that because the moneys were trust moneys the fact that they were

B   paid into an overdrawn account or had otherwise been dissipated presented no difficulty to raising an equitable charge on assets of MCC for their amount in favour of BIM. Nor was it possible to trace misappropriated money into an asset bought before the money was received by the purchaser. (Re Diplock [1948] Ch 465 applied; Space Investments v Canadian Imperial Bank of Commerce Trust Co (Bahamas) Ltd & Ors (1986) 2 BCC 99,302 and Kensington & Anor (Receivers of Goldcorp Finance Ltd) v Liggett & Ors [1994] CLC 591 considered.)

C   3. However, if the connection between a particular misappropriation of BIM's money and the acquisition by MCC of a particular asset was sufficiently clearly proved, it was at least arguable, depending on the facts, that there ought to be an equitable charge in favour of BIM on that asset of MCC.

The following cases were referred to in the judgments:

D
A-G for Hong Kong v Reid & Ors [1994] AC 324.
Borden (UK) Ltd v Scottish Timber Products Ltd & Anor [1981] Ch 25.
Diplock, Re [1948] Ch 465.
Frith v Cartland (1865) 2 Hem & M 417.
Hallett's Estate, Re (1880) 13 ChD 696.
Kensington & Anor (Receivers of Goldcorp Finance Ltd) v Liggett & Ors [1993] 1 NZLR 257; [1994] CLC 591, [1994] 3 WLR 199 (PC).

E   *Napier and Ettrick (Lord) & Anor v Hunter & Ors* [1993] AC 713.
Roscoe (James) (Bolton) Ltd v Winder [1915] 1 Ch 62.
Space Investments v Canadian Imperial Bank of Commerce Trust Co (Bahamas) Ltd & Ors (1986) 2 BCC 99,302; [1986] 1 WLR 1072.

Philip Heslop QC and John Brisby (instructed by Stephenson Harwood) for the appellants.

F   Leslie Kosmin QC (instructed by Norton Rose) for the respondents.

JUDGMENT

Dillon LJ: This is an appeal, by leave of the judge, by Bishopsgate Investment Management Ltd ('BIM') against an order of Vinelott J made on 21 December 1993. BIM, which is now in liquidation, is the trustee of certain of the assets of various pensions schemes for employees of companies with which the late Robert Maxwell was associated.

G   The respondents to the appeal, Mr Homan and three colleagues who are partners in Price Waterhouse, are the court-appointed administrators of Maxwell Communication Corporation plc ('MCC'). The judge's order was made on an application by the administrators under the *Insolvency Act* 1986 for directions. MCC, which was known at an earlier stage as the British Printing Corporation Ltd, was a publicly quoted company and the most prominent of a large number of companies, for which it was the holding

H   company. There is a second group of companies, which have been referred to as the Maxwell 'private side' companies; essentially they were companies the share capitals of which were beneficially owned, directly or indirectly, by Robert Maxwell and members of his family or trusts established by him.

On the unexpected death of Robert Maxwell on 5 November 1991, it was discovered that very large amounts of pension fund moneys of BIM had been improperly paid,

during his lifetime, directly or indirectly into various bank accounts of the private side   A
companies and of MCC with National Westminster Bank. At the time of each wrongful
payment of BIM's pension fund moneys into MCC's accounts those accounts were
overdrawn, or later became overdrawn. It was also found that MCC was hopelessly
insolvent. Consequently on 20 December 1991 the administrators were appointed by the
Companies Court in England. Also, because MCC had substantial assets in the USA, on
16 December 1991 MCC was placed in Chapter XI protection under the US Bankruptcy
Code in the United States Bankruptcy Court, Southern District of New York.   B

To simplify administration and avoid difficulties because of differences between the
statutory provisions in the two jurisdictions, in July 1993 a scheme of arrangement was
approved by the Companies Court under the *Companies Act* 1985 and a plan for
reorganisation was approved by the US court under Chapter XI so that, in effect, the
funds in both jurisdictions could be dealt with as a single fund.

Naturally, therefore, the administrators, who have realised a substantial amount of   C
MCC's assets although the administration is far from complete, wanted to make an
interim distribution among the creditors of MCC. But the liquidators claimed that BIM
was entitled to an equitable charge, in priority to all other unsecured creditors of MCC,
on all the assets of MCC for the full amount of the pension moneys of BIM wrongly paid
to MCC. Accordingly the administrators applied to the Companies Court for directions.

Vinelott J approached the application on the basis that if the claims of BIM were   D
plainly not maintainable in law the court ought to make a declaration to that effect, in
order that an interim distribution could be made without regard to unfounded claims.
But, if it was possible that on a further investigation of the facts there might be a claim,
valid in law, by BIM to an equitable charge on a particular asset, the proceeds of that
asset ought not to be distributed until the particular facts had been investigated.

The judge declared by his order that the administrators were entitled to deal with   E
specified notices of claim as if they do not give rise to any proprietary claims, and he
declared also that BIM was not entitled to any equitable charge over the assets of MCC
in respect of proprietary claims notified to the administrators to the extent that such
assets were acquired before any moneys or assets misappropriated from BIM were paid
or transferred to or so as to be under the control of MCC and were not acquired in
anticipation of or otherwise in connection with the misappropriation of such assets or
moneys. In essence the judge held that BIM could only claim an equitable charge on any   F
assets of MCC in accordance with the recognised principles of equitable tracing and these
principles do not permit tracing through an overdrawn bank account – whether an
account which was already overdrawn at the time the relevant moneys were paid into it
or an account which was then in credit, but subsequently became overdrawn by
subsequent drawings.

The judge reserved, however, the position if it were shown that there was a connection   G
between a particular misappropriation of BIM's moneys and the acquisition by MCC of
a particular asset. The judge gave as an instance of such a case what he called 'backward
tracing' – where an asset was acquired by MCC with moneys borrowed from an
overdrawn or loan account and there was an inference that when the borrowing was
incurred it was the intention that it should be repaid by misappropriations of BIM's
moneys. Another possibility was that moneys misappropriated from BIM were paid into
an overdrawn account of MCC in order to reduce the overdraft and so make finance   H
available within the overdraft limits for MCC to purchase some particular asset.

By a respondent's notice by way of cross-appeal, the administrators ask us to overrule
these reservations of the judge, and hold that even if the possible facts which the judge
envisages were clearly proved, that could not in law give BIM any equitable charge on
the particular asset acquired. For my part I would not interfere at all with this aspect of

A the judge's exercise of his discretion. In my judgment, if the connection he postulates between a particular misappropriation of BIM's money and the acquisition by MCC of a particular asset is sufficiently clearly proved, it is at least arguable, depending on the facts, that there ought to be an equitable charge in favour of BIM on the asset in question of MCC.

B But the main claims of BIM are put much more widely as claims to an equitable charge on all the assets of MCC. These claims are not founded on proving any particular intention of Robert Maxwell or others in charge of MCC but on general principles which it is said that the court ought to apply. They are founded primarily on certain observations of Lord Templeman in giving the judgment of the Privy Council in *Space Investments Ltd v Canadian Imperial Bank of Commerce Trust Co (Bahamas) Ltd* (1986) 2 BCC 99,302. In particular, in that case Lord Templeman said at p. 99,304:

C 'In these circumstances it is impossible for the beneficiaries interested in trust money misappropriated from their trust to trace their money to any particular asset belonging to the trustee bank. But equity allows the beneficiaries, or a new trustee appointed in place of an insolvent bank trustee . . . to trace the trust money to all the assets of the bank and to recover the trust money by the exercise of an equitable charge over all the assets of the bank. . . . that equitable charge secures for the beneficiaries and the trust priority over the claims of the customers . . . and

D . . . all other unsecured creditors.'

What Lord Templeman there said was strictly obiter, in that on the facts the Privy Council held that the bank trustee was authorised by the trust instruments to deposit trust money with itself as banker and so there had been no misappropriation. The beneficiaries or their new trustee therefore could merely prove with the other general creditors of the insolvent bank trustee for a dividend in respect of the moneys so deposited.

E Vinelott J rejected the submissions of BIM founded on *Space Investments*. He considered that Lord Templeman could not have intended to effect such a fundamental change to the well-understood limitations to equitable tracing; Lord Templeman was only considering the position of an insolvent bank which had been taking deposits and lending money.

F In the notice of appeal to this court, BIM's first ground of appeal relies on *Space Investments* and it is said that the judge erred in his interpretation of what Lord Templeman had said. There is a second, and alternative, ground of appeal to which I will refer later.

The appeal was, for obvious reasons, expedited, and we heard full argument on 7 and 8 March 1994. By the end of the argument, however, it was clear that there were complicating factors that precluded us from giving judgment on the appeal then.

G One of the other members of the Board in the Privy Council which decided *Space Investments* was Sir Robin Cooke, the President of the Court of Appeal in New Zealand. In a later case in New Zealand, *Liggett v Kensington* [1993] 1 NZLR 257, which was concerned with deposits of gold coins and bullion, Sir Robin Cooke, as one of the majority in the Court of Appeal in New Zealand, treated the statements by Lord Templeman in *Space Investments* which I have quoted as authoritative general statements

H of the relevant law to be given wide application. He treated the governing distinction as being between trust beneficiaries, who do not expect to take any risk of the insolvency of their trustee, and lenders and others in commerce who do take the risk of insolvency of those with whom they deal. See at p. 274.

We learned in the course of the argument before us in March, that an appeal against the decision of the Court of Appeal in *Liggett v Kensington* had been argued before the

Privy Council, including Lord Templeman, before Christmas 1993, but the decision of   A
the Privy Council on that appeal was still awaited. Since that decision was likely to be
given within a relatively short time, and since the details of any interim distribution by
the administrators have yet to be approved by the US court, it became the obvious course
that we should not give our judgments on this appeal until after the decision of the Privy
Council was available.

In the event that decision was only given on 25 May 1994, immediately before the Whit   B
vacation, and it was not practicable to reassemble this division of this court and hear
further argument until 23 June. We have, however, had very helpful skeleton arguments
and oral argument of counsel on 23 June, in relation to the decision of the Privy Council
in *Liggett v Kensington* [1994] CLC 591. That decision reversed the majority decision of
the New Zealand Court of Appeal.

As I read the judgment of the Privy Council in *Liggett v Kensington* delivered by Lord   C
Mustill, it makes it clear that Lord Templeman's observations in *Space Investments* were
not concerned at all with the situation we have in the present case where trust moneys
have been paid into an overdrawn bank account, or an account which has become
overdrawn. Lord Mustill says in the clearest terms at p. 610C:

> 'Their Lordships should, however, say that they find it difficult to understand how
> the judgment of the Board in *Space Investments Ltd v Imperial Bank of Commerce
> Trust Co (Bahamas) Ltd* (1986) 2 BCC 99,302, on which the claimants leaned   D
> heavily in argument, would enable them to overcome the difficulty that the moneys
> said to be impressed with the trust were paid into an overdrawn account and
> thereupon ceased to exist; see, for example, *Re Diplock* [1948] Ch 465. The
> observations of the Board in *Space Investments* were concerned with a mixed, not
> a non-existent, fund.'

Thus the wide interpretation of those observations put forward by Sir Robin Cooke,   E
which is the basis of the first ground of appeal in the present case, is rejected. Instead the
decision of the Court of Appeal in *Re Diplock* is endorsed; there it was said at p. 521:

> 'The equitable remedies pre-suppose the continued existence of the money either
> as a separate fund or as part of a mixed fund or as latent in property acquired by
> means of such a fund. If, on the facts of any individual case, such continued
> existence is not established, equity is as helpless as the common law itself.'   F

Also endorsed, in my judgment, in the decision of the Board delivered by Lord Mustill
is the long-standing first instance decision in *James Roscoe (Bolton) Ltd v Winder* [1915]
1 Ch 62, which Mr Heslop QC for BIM, in his submissions in March, invited us to
overrule. That was a decision that, in tracing trust moneys into the bank account of a
trustee in accordance with *Re Hallett's Estate* (1880) 13 ChD 696, tracing was only
possible to such an amount of the balance ultimately standing to the credit of the trustee
as did not exceed the lowest balance of the account during the intervening period. Thus   G
as is said in the headnote to the report 'payments into a general account cannot, without
proof of express intention, be appropriated to the replacement of trust money which has
been improperly mixed with that account and drawn out'. That reflects the statement by
Sargant J at p. 69 that:

> '. . . it is impossible to attribute to him' – i.e. the account holder – 'that by the mere
> payment into the account of further moneys, which to a large extent he   H
> subsequently used for purposes of his own, he intended to clothe those moneys
> with a trust in favour of the plaintiffs.'

Mr Heslop QC for BIM refers however to later passages in the opinion of Lord Mustill.
First, at p. 614C Lord Mustill states that the law relating to the creation and tracing of
equitable proprietary interests is still in a state of development. He refers to two recent

A   decisions – *A-G for Hong Kong v Reid* [1994] AC 324 and *Lord Napier and Ettrick v Hunter* [1993] AC 713 – on facts not particularly relevant to the present case as instances where equitable proprietary interests have been recognised in circumstances which might previously have been regarded merely as circumstances for common law relief.

     Mr Heslop also refers to the fact that the claims of certain claimants in *Liggett v Kensington* referred to as 'the Walker & Hall claimants' were rejected without further

B   investigation of the law, on the ground that the Walker & Hall claimants were in no different position from any other claimants, and so it would have been inequitable to impose a lien in favour of the Walker & Hall claimants. Mr Heslop submits that the beneficiaries under the pension schemes of which BIM is trustee are in a different position from the other creditors of BIM, who are mainly banks. He does not, of course, adopt the simple populist approach that pensioners, like widows and orphans, are 'goodies' while banks, like usurers, are 'baddies' and so the court should use its powers to ensure

C   that the goodies are paid in full ahead of the baddies. But he does say that the beneficiaries under the pension schemes never undertook the risk that their pension funds would be misappropriated and paid into the overdrawn bank account of an insolvent company, whereas all the banks which lent money to MCC took their chance, as a commercial risk, on MCC's solvency.

     Mr Heslop therefore relies on the second ground in the notice of appeal, whereby BIM

D   claims (as it has been explained to us) to be entitled to an equitable charge as security for its claims against MCC (1) over any moneys standing to the credit at the time of the appointment of the administrators of MCC of any banking account maintained by MCC into which any moneys of BIM, or the proceeds of any assets of BIM misappropriated from it were paid and (2) over any assets acquired out of any such bank account, whether or not in credit as at the date such assets were acquired.

E   So far as (1) is concerned, the point is that the National Westminster Bank account into which the misappropriated BIM trust moneys were paid happened to be in credit when the administrators were appointed. BIM therefore claims a lien on that credit balance in the National Westminster Bank account for the amount of the misappropriated trust moneys. It is difficult to suppose, however, in the circumstances of Robert Maxwell's last days – and I know of no evidence – that Robert Maxwell intended to make good the misappropriation of the BIM pension moneys by the cryptic expedient

F   of arranging to put MCC's account with National Westminster Bank into credit – but without repaying the credit balance this created to BIM. But in the absence of clear evidence of intention to make good the depredations on BIM it is not possible to assume that the credit balance has been clothed with a trust in favour of BIM and its beneficiaries. See *James (Roscoe) Bolton Ltd v Winder*, above.

     As to (2), this seems to be going back to the original wide interpretation of what Lord

G   Templeman said in *Space Investments* and applying it to an overdrawn account because the misappropriated moneys that went into the account were trust moneys and thus different from other moneys that may have gone into that account. But the moneys in *Space Investments* were also trust moneys, and so, if argument (2) is valid in the present case, it would also have been valid, as a matter of law, in *Space Investments*. But that was rejected in *Liggett v Kensington* because equitable tracing, though devised for the protection of trust moneys misapplied, cannot be pursued through an overdrawn and

H   therefore non-existent fund. Acceptance of argument (2) would, in my judgment, require the rejection of *Re Diplock*, which is binding on us, and of Lord Mustill's explanation of Lord Templeman's statement in *Space Investments* given at p. 610 of the decision in *Liggett v Kensington*.

     It is not open to us to say that because the moneys were trust moneys the fact that they were paid into an overdrawn account or have otherwise been dissipated presents no

difficulty to raising an equitable charge on assets of MCC for their amount in favour of   A
BIM. The difficulty Lord Mustill referred to is not displaced.

Accordingly I would reject both grounds of appeal, and dismiss both the appeal and
the cross-appeal.

On consideration, I do not regard it as appropriate to give any further directions to
the judge.

Leggatt LJ: In *Space Investments v Canadian Imperial Bank* (1986) 2 BCC 99,302 the   B
bank trustee made authorised deposits with itself as banker. As it was entitled to do, it
used deposited money for its own purposes. On distribution of the assets in the winding
up of the bank trustee, the creditors ranked equally with the other secured creditors.
Since no money was misappropriated the comments in the judgment of the Board about
the right of beneficiaries following misappropriation to be paid in priority to the
customers and other unsecured creditors were obiter dicta. But all that was said related   C
specifically to deposits by a bank trustee with itself. The passage cited from Sir George
Jessel's judgment in *Re Hallett's Estate* (1880) 13 ChD 696 at p. 719 took the form of a
quotation from Wood V-C in *Frith v Cartland* (1865) 2 Hem & M 417 in which the
second principle (as explained by the Master of the Rolls) was 'that the trust property
comes first', while the first had been: 'If [a trustee] destroys a trust fund by dissipating it
altogether, there remains nothing to be the subject of the trust.' The corollary of that is,
as this court asserted in *Re Diplock* [1948] Ch 465, that it is only possible to trace in   D
equity money which has continued existence, actual or notional. That was why in *James
Roscoe v Winder* [1915] Ch 162 where trust funds had been mixed with private moneys in
a bank account and the credit balance reduced at one point to £25.18.0d before being
replenished, Sargant J held that the beneficiary's charge extended only to that sum. As
Buckley LJ said in *Borden v Scottish Timber* [1981] Ch 25 at p. 46F:

> '. . . it is a fundamental feature of the doctrine of tracing that the property to be   E
> traced can be identified at every stage of its journey through life . . .'

For the same reason there can be no equitable remedy against an asset acquired *before*
misappropriation of money takes place, since ex hypothesi it cannot be followed into
something which existed and so had been acquired before the money was received and
therefore without its aid. The concept of a 'composite transaction' is in my judgment
fallacious. What is envisaged is (a) the purchase of an asset by means of an overdraft,
that is, a loan from a bank, and (b) the discharge of the loan by means of misappropriated   F
trust money. The judge thought that the money could be regarded as having been used
to acquire the asset. His conclusion was that:

> 'It is sufficient to say that proof that trust moneys were paid into an overdrawn
> account of the defaulting trustee may not always be sufficient to bar a claim to an
> equitable charge.'

I see the force of Mr Kosmin's submission that if an asset were used as security for an   G
overdraft which was then discharged by means of misappropriated money, the
beneficiary might obtain priority by subrogation. But there can ordinarily be no tracing
into an asset which is already in the hands of the defaulting trustee when the
misappropriation occurs. In *Liggett v Kensington* [1993] 1 NZLR 257 Cooke P applied
the principle which he derived from *Space Investments* that those who do not take a risk
of insolvency are entitled to an equitable charge over all the assets of the trustee, giving   H
them priority over those who are to be regarded as having taken such a risk. That
decision is authority for no wider proposition than that where a bank trustee wrongly
deposits money with itself, the trustee can trace into all the bank's credit balances.
Consistently with Mr Kosmin's submissions on this appeal, Lord Mustill, delivering the
judgment of the Board in *Liggett v Kensington* [1994] CLC 591, stated (at p. 610) that
their Lordships found it difficult to understand how it would enable the claimants in that

A   case to 'overcome the difficulty that the monies said to be impressed with the trust were paid into an overdrawn account and thereupon ceased to exist.' Lord Mustill emphasised that the observations of the Board were concerned with a mixed, not a non-existent, fund. He also cited with approval the case of *James Roscoe v Winder* (above) as conventionally exemplifying the principles of tracing. I therefore consider that the judge came to the right conclusion, though I do not accept that it is possible to trace through an overdrawn bank account or to trace misappropriated money into an asset bought

B   before the money was received by the purchaser. I agree that the appeal should be dismissed.

     Henry LJ: I agree with both judgments.

(Appeal dismissed with costs. Leave to appeal refused)

C

D

E

F

G

H

Rutherford, Petitioner (for an order under s. 459 of the Companies Act 1985 re Lawrie & Symington Ltd).

Court of Session (Outer House).
Lord Caplan.
Judgment delivered 22 July 1994.

Unfair prejudice petition – Petitioner obtained interim interdict restraining company purchasing own shares – Whether price to be paid was excessive – Whether company could afford purchase – Whether purchase would prevent higher offer for shares – Balance of convenience; whether interim interdict should be recalled – Companies Act 1985, s. 459.

This was an unfair prejudice petition by which the petitioner sought an order in terms of s. 459 of the Companies Act 1985 on the basis that the company's proposal to buy back a block of shares (around 33 per cent of the shares) was unfairly prejudicial to the interests of the petitioner as a minority shareholder in the company.

First the petitioner averred that shares of the class which the company proposed to purchase are traded on the open market at 19p per share; accordingly the purchase price agreed for the shares of 64p per share was greatly in excess of their true market value. Secondly it was claimed that the company was not in a position to fund the purchase; it would have to borrow and the interest on such borrowings would exceed the annual profits of the company. The petitioner obtained interim interdict preventing the company from proceeding with the said purchase proposal. There was a possible rival offer for shares in the company of 72.5p per share.

Held, recalling the interim interdict:

1. The petitioner might be able to show that in recent times shares had passed at the price of 19p, but that did not lead to the conclusion that the shareholding in issue was only worth that price. The proposed share purchase was designed to stabilise the management of the company which might well elevate the price of the shares. More significantly the transactions referred to were in all probability of relatively small blocks of shares. The value of the dominant block of shares in the company around which a controlling interest could perhaps readily be formed was likely to be materially more valuable than a small minority interest. If a party had prospects of controlling the company then underlying commercial and asset values became much more significant. This was shown by the potential takeover offer at 72.5p a share or upwards to acquire a controlling interest.

2. It might not be easy for the petitioner to show that the company could not comfortably complete the proposed acquisition, but it was possible that he could do so. The court could not discount the fact that the petitioner might show that at the end of the day that the purchase of the shares would diminish the company in a manner which was both damaging and unfair. The petitioner has shown that there might well be an issue to try once the pleadings were completed, but even on the petitioner's presentation of the case the outcome for the petitioner had to be considered as problematical.

3. It was possible that the proposed contract to purchase the shares could affect the prospect of the takeover taking place, depriving the petitioner of a chance of accepting the higher offer. On the other hand, if the majority of the shareholders wanted to beat off the takeover bid because it was thought that they and the company would prosper better under widespread control then it would be a fine question as to whether the petitioner's decreased chance of securing the offer for his shares could be described as unfair.

4. The petitioner's case could not be described as prima facie a strong case. That factor would be taken into account in determining the balance of convenience. If the majority view were to be that it was better for the company to remain as it was then it would seem

A   unfortunate that the aspiration of such a majority could be defeated in the interests of a single shareholder. On the other hand, if the majority view of the shareholders was that the takeover bid should be accepted then they could achieve that objective even if the interdict was lifted. Furthermore, if the petitioner established unfair prejudice at the end of the day, although it might be too late for an effective interdict, there could be other remedies available to the petitioner including the right to ask that the company purchase his shares. The balance of convenience favoured the respondents.

B

The following cases were referred to in the opinion:

Elgindata Ltd, Re [1991] BCLC 959.
McGuinness v Bremner plc 1988 SLT 891; (1988) 4 BCC 161.
Ringtower Holdings plc, Re (1989) 5 BCC 82.

A Smith (instructed by Simpson & Marwick) for the petitioner.

C   N F Davidson QC (instructed by McGrigor Donald) for the respondents.

OPINION

Lord Caplan: The matter under consideration arises out of a petition by shareholders of Lawrie & Symington Ltd (hereinafter referred to as the company) for an order under s. 459 of the *Companies Act* 1985. The company are well known and long established, carrying on business as livestock auctioneers. Their principal place of business is at

D   Lanark.

The background to this dispute may be stated as follows. The called up share capital of the company is £860,000 comprising 3,440,000 ordinary shares of 25p each nominal value. The petitioner is a registered holder of 6,888 of these shares. The late Baroness Elliot of Harwood owned 1,146,664 of the company's shares and these are now registered in the name of her trustees. The Elliot Trust shares represent by far the largest block of

E   shares held in the company. The company has about 728 shareholders, most of these having relatively small holdings. Many of the shareholders are Borders farmers who because of their occupation are attracted to the company. Details of the shareholdings in the company are set up in excerpts from the register of members which were produced by the company who are respondents in this petition. The company is a private company. Until about April 1993 the control of the company rested in a group of shareholders coalescing around the Elliot shareholding. The petitioner was a director of the company.

F   On or about the date in question there was what was described by senior counsel for the respondents as 'a boardroom revolution'. Four directors were voted out of office and three others, including the petitioner, retired or resigned. The events in question apparently created tension between certain groups of shareholders and the chairman's statement attached to the accounts and annual report for 1993 suggests that the management of the company may have gone through a turbulent period. Certainly over

G   recent years the profits earned by the company seemed to have been disappointing.

It would appear that at some time in early 1994 the company reached agreement with the trustees of the Elliot Trust for the purchase by the company of the trust's shareholding of 1,146,664 shares. The price to be paid by the company was 64p per share which led to a total purchase price of £769,141.76. Accordingly on 17 June 1994 an extraordinary general meeting of the company was held at which it was proposed that the company should buy the said Elliot Trust shares at the said price and also buy at that price a block

H   of 55,120 shares from the executors of the late Baroness Elliot. The said purchases were to be in terms of a proposed contract which was tabled. These proposals were incorporated in a special resolution. On a show of hands 77 persons voted for the resolution. I understand that this vote represented 97 per cent of those present. The only member who voted against the resolution was the petitioner. No poll having been demanded, the resolution was accordingly taken as duly passed.

On 5 July 1994 the petitioner presented the present petition. The petition sought an   A
order in terms of s. 459 of the *Companies Act* 1985 on the basis that the said proposal
that the company should buy the said blocks of shares was unfairly prejudicial to the
interests of the petitioner as a minority shareholder in the company. In terms of the
petitioner's averments this complaint is based on two points. First it is said that shares of
the class which the company proposes to purchase are traded on the open market at 19p
per share. It was accordingly claimed that the purchase price agreed for the said shares
was greatly in excess of their true market value. Secondly it was claimed that the accounts   B
of the company for the year ended 31 December 1993 show a profit in ordinary activities
after taxation of £53,000 and a bank overdraft of £254,000. In the course of the said
extraordinary general meeting the chairman of the company is said to have explained
that it was proposed to fund the new shareholdings by further bank borrowings. It was
therefore claimed that the interest on such borrowings would exceed the annual profits
of the company. On the basis of the said allegations of unfair prejudice the petitioner   C
seeks to have the company interdicted from proceeding with the said purchase proposal
or from concluding any agreement with the proposed vendors to do so. By decree of the
same date, namely 8 July 1994, the petitioner was awarded interim interdict. There had
been no caveat lodged and the vacation judge accordingly granted the interdict on ex
parte representations on behalf of the petitioner.

The company have now lodged answers to the petition as respondents and the motion   D
I am presently considering is the respondents' motion for recall of the interim interdict.

Certain other significant facts require noting. On 24 June 1994 an Edinburgh based
investment trust called Caledonian Trust plc sent a letter to all shareholders of the
company indicating that the trust intended to make an offer for all the shares of the
company. The respondents have produced a copy of this letter. The consideration to be
offered by Caledonian Trust is somewhat complicated but subject to a maximum of   E
1,750,000 shares one of the options offered in respect of price is cash at the rate of 72.5p
per share. It would also be a condition of the offer that 50.1 per cent of the company's
shares would be the subject of acceptance. Another price option involves shares in
Caledonian Trust plc plus cash. It is claimed by the offerors that the consideration offered
would be worth £1 per share. It is stated in the letter that a formal offer will be sent to
shareholders within 28 days of 24 June 1994. For reasons which were never satisfactorily
explained to me, the existence of the Caledonian Trust offer was not put to the vacation   F
judge at the time he granted the interim interdict.

In advising me in support of the motion for recall of the interdict, senior counsel for
the respondents drew my attention to the foregoing history which in material terms is
undisputed. He drew attention to the fact that the minutes of the extraordinary general
meeting do not record the chairman stating (as is claimed by the petitioner) that the share
purchases would be financed out of borrowings, but rather these minutes record that the   G
chairman asserted that the purchase would be made out of distributable profits. However,
it was accepted that the chairman had added that in the event of distributable profits
being insufficient the bank would back the purchase. The difference between parties in
the matter of the prospective financing of the purchase may not be very material. Senior
counsel for the respondents contended that it was clear from the offer from Caledonian
Trust that the company had not overvalued the Elliot share blocks. Moreover the   H
contents of the 1993 accounts were discussed and it was claimed that the company had
ample financial resources to cover the proposed purchase. The purchase was necessary to
reform the structure of the company and to reflect the desire of the majority of the
members that there should be no dominant shareholding. The law relating to the
application of s. 459 was discussed and I was referred to *Palmer's Company Law* (25th
edn) vol. 1, para. 8.904–8.907 and *Re Elgindata Ltd* [1991] BCLC 959. It was further

A   argued that even if the petitioner has set out a prima facie case (which was disputed) the balance of convenience favoured the respondents.

Counsel for the petitioner in resisting the recall of the interim interdict contended that the completion of the proposed purchases would cause the petitioner a serious degree of unfair prejudice. He claimed that the action of the shareholders in passing the resolution was discriminatory in that the benefit was not available to all the shareholders. I was

B   referred to *Re Ringtower Holdings plc* (1989) 5 BCC 82 at pp. 102–103. The Caledonian Trust were likely to withdraw their offer if the purchase of the Elliot shares proceeded so that the petitioner would be deprived of the opportunity to sell his shares at 72.5p each. I was referred to *McGuinness v Bremner plc* 1988 SLT 891; (1988) 4 BCC 161. In any event the company will not be able to fund the purchases comfortably. This will put the future of the company in jeopardy and would diminish the value of the petitioner's shares. The petitioner has shown clearly that there is a case to try and that the balance of

C   convenience is in favour of the petitioner.

In deciding this matter I first have to consider whether the petitioner has set out a prima facie case. In doing so it would not be appropriate to criticise the petitioner's pleadings in detail (these at this stage necessarily being incomplete) nor to deal conclusively with any points of relevancy which may have to be decided at a later stage. However, on the material before me I have decided that the petitioner's case at least in

D   some respects is very doubtful even if all the averments are eventually established. There are really two cases made in the petition but the petitioner suggests that a further ground of complaint will be added, namely that the proposed purchase would prejudice prospects under the Caledonian Trust offer.

I do not think that the interpretation of s. 459 of the Companies Act presents much of a problem in this case. The test of conduct which is 'unfairly prejudicial' is of course a

E   narrower concept than the former test which was 'oppressive'. Of course, if the majority of shareholders act in a way which can be described as mala fide or oppressive that could strongly point to the conduct being 'unfairly prejudicial'. However, as Mr Davidson pointed out the petitioner does not attempt to brand the respondents' conduct as being improper other than in respect of fairness. It is clear that the conduct complained of must not merely be damaging to the petitioner but that it must also be such as could in all the circumstances be described as unfair. In certain circumstances persistent incompetent

F   management though backed by a majority could be such as to be unfair to a minority shareholder. On the other hand it is difficult to envisage that mere differences in commercial judgment would readily give rise to a foundation for complaints of unfairness even although a commercial decision (say, to sell assets to provide more working capital for the future) could cause a short-term diminution in share value. As would be expected it is a matter of circumstances and degree as to whether a damaging effect on a

G   shareholder can properly be described as unfair.

The first complaint of the petitioner is based on the assertion that since there have been recent share transactions when shares passed at 19p per share, the price offered to the Elliot interest is excessive. It may well be the case that the petitioner would be able to show that in recent times shares have passed at the price of 19p.

However, this in no way leads to the conclusion that the Elliot shareholding is only

H   worth that price. We do not know precisely when the shares referred to by the petitioner were sold but it seems quite likely that recent transactions could have been affected by the managerial problems which both parties admit have been experienced by the company. A situation which stabilised the management of the company may well elevate the price of the shares. The proposed share purchase is designed to do just that. However, more significantly the recent transactions referred to were in all probability those affecting relatively small blocks of shares. Such small parcels of shares in a private

company will generally have a restricted value. The value of the dominant block of shares   A
in the company around which a controlling interest could perhaps readily be formed is
likely to be materially more valuable than a small minority interest. If a party has
prospects of controlling the company then underlying commercial and asset values
become much more significant. This I think is shown by the fact that Caledonian Trust
seem anxious to take over the company and are prepared to pay 72.5p a share or upwards
to acquire a controlling interest. The 1993 accounts show that total assets less current
liabilities are £2,591,000. Moreover, the directors declare in their report that the value of   B
buildings and land of the group is in excess of the balance sheet figure which is based on
professional valuations and additions less sales since these valuations. Assuming that it
were thought valuable to the company to achieve the managerial and directorial flexibility
which may ensue from removing a dominant block of shares, then prima facie it seems
unlikely that the petitioner could ever demonstrate that such shares could be secured for
materially less than the price offered. It may be significant that there has been no attempt   C
made to refer to a professional valuation of such a large block of shares.

    The second feature of the petitioner's case is the assertion that the company could not
comfortably complete the proposed acquisition. It may not be easy for the petitioner to
show this but it is possible that he could do so. The company would have to devote a
substantial proportion of its free assets to acquire the Elliot shares and on any view it
may not get much immediate financial return. The shares would merely be absorbed by   D
the company although of course this could go towards elevating the value of the
remaining shares. However, it seems unlikely that the purchase could be catastrophic.
The balance sheet shows that the company has £220,000 cash in bank (although that has
to balanced against a bank overdraft of £254,000). However, as I have indicated, the
company has substantial net assets and there is no reason to doubt that the bank will
provide any necessary borrowing. I was informed that the purpose of the acquisition of
the Elliot interest is to satisfy the view of most of the shareholders of the company that   E
the shareholdings should be widely spread and that there should be no dominant block
of shares available to encourage individual shareholders to acquire a controlling interest.
It is notable that the present directors' share interests are shown in the accounts and that
no director has anything like a controlling share interest. It would appear that the
majority of members accept that removal of a possible source of trouble and friction
would be beneficial to the company. It may be the case that the assurance of the basis of   F
a more flexible management structure will greatly enhance the future progress of the
company's commercial activities. It is certainly obvious from the directors' report that
question marks existed over the management of the company at least until recently. The
letter from Caledonian Trust also advances the view that there is scope for improvement
in the management of the company. Nor can it be taken as obvious that the expenditure
of substantial funds in acquiring the Elliot shares would diminish the value of the
petitioner's holding. With a reduced number of shares in the company the value of the   G
remaining shares may be enhanced. Moreover, as I have indicated the value of a small
minority interest may not be anything like as asset-sensitive as a major block of shares.
The share value of the minority share interests seems to be relatively low (compared, say,
with the value of a controlling interest placed on the company by Caledonian Trust) and
an improvement in the prospect of sound and independent management controlled by a
wide spread of small shareholders could possibly more than compensate for any short-
term diminution in the company's assets. However, I cannot discount the fact that the   H
petitioner could show at the end of the day that the purchase of the Elliot shares would
diminish the company in a manner which is both damaging and unfair. The petitioner
has shown that there may well be an issue to try once the pleadings are completed, but
even on the petitioner's presentation of the case the outcome for the petitioner must be
considered as problematical.

A   It may be that the third element in the petitioner's case offers at least a degree more
potential. The petitioner at the moment has not said if he will accept the Caledonian
Trust offer assuming that it is made. However, assuming that he eventually declares it to
be his intention to accept the offer it is quite possible that the proposed contract with the
Elliot trustees could affect the prospect of the Caledonian Trust takeover taking place.
This transaction will not proceed unless a majority of shareholders accept the offer. It
may well be difficult to secure the necessary degree of acceptance if the Elliot trustees and
B   executors are deflected from accepting the Caledonian Trust offer by receipt of a better
offer from the company. I am told that the company's proposed offer to the Elliot interest
may be more valuable than it would appear at first sight because of tax implications. On
the other hand, if the majority of the shareholders want to beat off the takeover bid
because it is thought that they and the company would prosper better under the present
widespread control then it may be a fine question as to whether the petitioner's decreased
C   chance of securing the Caledonian Trust offer for these shares could be described as
unfair.

        My view is that at best for the petitioner his case on the merits presents him with
serious difficulties and that it cannot be described as prima facie being a strong case. This
would be a factor therefore that I would take into account in determining the balance of
convenience.

D   In my view the maintenance of the present interdict could be extremely damaging to
the respondents. It is perhaps unfortunate that the interdict arrived at a time when the
whole future of the company is in balance because of the pending takeover bid. The
acquisition of the Elliot interests may be an important element in a defeat of this bid if
that proves to be what the majority of members and the company want. The members
may of course decide to accept the takeover bid and it may be that the Elliot trustees will
be included among the number who accept. On the other hand, if an alternative disposal
E   of the Elliot trustees' shares is cut off by the interdict then they may feel that they have
no viable alternative but to accept the Caledonian offer and thus ensure the success of
the takeover bid. What is best for the interest of the company and its present shareholders
may be a matter of fine judgment but I think it would be unfortunate and damaging if
both the company and its shareholders were deprived of the chance to give full and open
consideration to the various options that may be available to them. The fact that the
F   extent of the prospective prejudice may prove difficult to quantify and define is itself a
reason for not maintaining the interdict provided it is clear, as I think to be the case, that
there is a prospect of such prejudice. If the majority view were to be that it is far better
for the company to remain as it is then it would seem unfortunate that the aspiration of
such a majority could be defeated in the interests of a single shareholder. On the other
hand, if the majority view of the shareholders is that the takeover bid should be accepted
then they can achieve that objective even if the interdict is lifted. As I understand the
G   position there is not as yet a formally concluded agreement between the company and
the trustees. The prospect of loss to the petitioner is less certain and significant. When the
petition was raised the petitioner's shares were on his own valuation worth only 19p each
and as I have already suggested it is not manifest to what degree the company's proposals
if implemented would affect the value of his shares if at all. On the other hand, if the
Caledonian Trust takeover does not proceed then there would certainly be a stronger
H   possibility that the petitioner would suffer more serious loss. Of course, as I have said, it
is not even certain that the petitioner personally would accept the Caledonian Trust offer.
He may choose to remain on as a minority shareholder in the hope that Caledonian Trust
would improve the value of the company. Even if the interdict is lifted the takeover may
proceed. If the view of the company and its members was that the takeover bid should be
accepted then it may be easier to mobilise a controlling interest if the number of
shareholdings is reduced particularly by the elimination of a substantial block of shares.

The petitioner's counsel suggested that the Caledonian Trust would not proceed if the Elliot shares were eliminated but he advanced that opinion somewhat tentatively and did not specify the basis of his assertion. Furthermore, if the petitioner were able to establish the foundation of his case to the effect that the company had acted unfairly towards him then although it might at that stage be too late for an effective interdict there could be other remedies available to the petitioner including the right to ask that the company purchase his shares.

A balance of convenience is rarely a comfortable exercise for the court since often, as here, it is necessary to take into account conjectural factors but my view is that the balance in this case favours the respondents.

In all the circumstances I shall grant the motion for the recall of the interdict.

(Order accordingly)

Re a Company No. 003061 of 1993.
Safinia & Anor v Comet Enterprises Ltd & Ors.

Chancery Division (Companies Court).
Elizabeth Gloster QC (sitting as a deputy judge of the Chancery Division).
Judgment delivered 22 June 1993.

Unfair prejudice petition – Petition alleged diversion of corporate opportunities – Whether petitioner entitled to interlocutory relief – Companies Act 1985, s. 459–461.

This was a motion for an interlocutory injunction in petition proceedings under s. 459 of the Companies Act 1985. The petitioners and the applicants on the motion were Mr and Mrs S, who together were 45 per cent shareholders in the company which was the subject of the petition. The respondents to the petition, apart from the company which was not represented, were Mr and Mrs M, who together were 55 per cent shareholders in the company.

For the purposes of the motion Mr M conceded that Mr and Mrs S had an arguable case that various agency contracts entered into by the company with suppliers had been entered into by the company in its own right and not as agent for an Iranian company of the same name and that, accordingly, Mr and Mrs S had an arguable case that the agency business, or at least that part of it which did not involve the Iran company's activities in Iran, belonged to the UK company. Mr M alone was respondent to the motion which sought an injunction restraining him (1) from procuring or endeavouring to procure the company's suppliers to cease dealing or reduce any of their dealings with the UK company or commence dealing or increase any of their dealings with the Iranian company, and (2) from procuring or endeavouring to procure the suppliers not to pay certain moneys to the UK company or to pay them to him or to the Iranian company or into a specified bank account.

Held, granting the relief sought subject to certain modifications:

1. The balance of convenience required some sort of relief to protect the UK company's and Mr S's position pending the hearing of the petition. The only apparent assets of Mr M within the jurisdiction were his flat and his shares in the company. Moreover, it might well be that an order could be made against the UK company requiring it to purchase Mr and Mrs S's shares under s. 461, and that would only be a possible course if there were sufficient assets in the company. The fact that Mr and Mrs S could be compensated at trial for any misappropriations of the UK company's assets was not per se an answer to the injunction sought.

2. In the absence of an injunction relating to the preservation of the commission payments, it would be difficult to value the UK company's goodwill and other assets for the purposes of the petition and any valuation of Mr and Mrs S's shares. Mr S, moreover, remained a director with obligations as well as rights in relation to the company's assets and liabilities. He was entitled to interlocutory relief which prevented active diversion of what, prima facie at least, were the UK company's receivables. However, the injunction would be limited to moneys payable under contracts with the suppliers, irrespective of whether the UK company was acting as principal or agent for the Iran company in entering into such contract.

3. In relation to seeking to restrain Mr M from diverting business or corporate opportunities or contracts to the Iranian company, it would be quite wrong given the wholly unclear nature of the relationship between the UK and Iranian companies and the roles respectively played by each company, to grant an interlocutory injunction which might have the effect of preventing the UK company from carrying on its legitimate separate business, or which would make it unclear what business Mr M was entitled to procure the Iranian

company to carry out. Mr and Mrs S were entitled to an injunction to restrain Mr M from   A
procuring or attempting to procure the suppliers to breach or terminate any existing contract
alleged by the petitioners to be with the UK company.

The following cases were referred to in the judgment:

Company No. 008126 of 1989 (Hailey Group Ltd), Re a [1992] BCC 542.
Posgate & Denby (Agencies) Ltd, Re (1986) 2 BCC 99,352.
Standard Chartered Bank v Walker & Anor [1992] 1 WLR 561.   B

Peter Griffiths (instructed by Clifford Harris) for the applicants.

Richard Snowden (instructed by Jepson Goff) for the respondents.

JUDGMENT

Elizabeth Gloster QC: This is a motion for an interlocutory injunction in petition   C
proceedings brought under s. 459 of the *Companies Act* 1985. The petitioners and the
applicants on the motion are Mr and Mrs Safinia, who together are 45 per cent
shareholders in Comet Enterprises Ltd, the company which is the subject of the petition
and which I shall refer to as 'Comet UK' or 'the company'. The respondents to this
petition, apart from the company which is not represented before me, are Mr and Mrs
Molavi, who together are 55 per cent shareholders in the company. Mr Molavi alone is
respondent to the motion. Mr and Mrs Molavi and Mr and Mrs Safinia are Iranians who   D
live in this country but whose business affairs are conducted not only in the UK but also
in Iran, where they have good business contacts. The injunction now sought against Mr
Molavi is to restrain him from:

'(1) procuring or endeavouring to procure the companies, firms or trading
organisations set out in the schedule hereto or any of them to cease dealing or
reduce any of their dealings with Comet Enterprise Ltd ('Comet UK') or   E
commence dealing or increase any of their dealings with Comet Enterprise Ltd
('Comet Iran') save on behalf of and for the benefit of Comet UK, and

(2) procuring or endeavouring to procure the companies, firms or trading
organisations set out in the schedule hereto or any of them not to pay any money
to Comet UK or pay money to himself, Comet Iran or into an account at the
Union Bank of Switzerland . . . save as agreed with the petitioners.'   F

On the first day of the hearing of the motion Mr Griffiths for the petitioners applied to
amend the notice of motion to its present form on terms that, so far as the relief sought
related to the companies and other institutions listed on the second page of the schedule
to the draft order in relation to which Mr Molavi had not had any opportunity of filing
evidence, the motion would be adjourned. On that basis leave to amend was not opposed
and I granted Mr Griffiths leave to amend accordingly.   G

Comet UK was incorporated on 26 May 1982 with an original issued share capital of
1,000 shares. Originally, Mr Molavi and his wife were 50 per cent shareholders with
another couple, Mr and Mrs Dimont, and Mr Molavi and Mr Dimont were directors,
Mr Molavi being appointed executive chairman, a post which he holds to this day. Mr
and Mrs Dimont left Comet UK in about 1984/1985 and Mr Molavi acquired their
shares. Mr Dimont was replaced by Mr Fred Mazhari, who likewise became a 50 per
cent shareholder and a director and was issued with 1,000 shares so that he and Mr and   H
Mrs Molavi were each 50 per cent shareholders. Mr Safinia originally became a director
of Comet UK on 7 December 1987 and subsequently he and his wife became 50 per cent
shareholders in Comet UK in mid-1988 when, after certain disagreements, Mr Mazhari
resigned as a director and transferred his 1,000 shares to Mr and Mrs Safinia, who
thereby became 50 per cent shareholders in the company. The circumstances in which

A   Mr Safinia became a director and the nature of his participation in the company are matters in dispute in the petition.

In about June 1992, as a result of an agreement covering various matters between the parties, Mr and Mrs Safinia transferred five per cent of their shareholding in Comet UK to Mr and Mrs Molavi so that at the present time, as I have said, Mr and Mrs Molavi own 55 per cent of the share capital and Mr and Mrs Safinia own 45 per cent.

B   The precise nature of Comet UK's business is in dispute and is an issue which will have to be decided in the petition. However, a little of the background is necessary in order to put the issues which arise on the motion into context, although I emphasise that many of these matters may well require further investigation at trial.

From about 1974 to 1982 Mr Molavi and his family conducted a commission agency business involving the sales of engineering equipment manufactured by suppliers in the west to buyers in Iran, principally Iranian government organisations. This business was C   effected through a company incorporated in Iran and based in Tehran called Comet Enterprise Ltd. I shall refer to that company as 'Comet Iran'. Mr Molavi has at all material times been, and is, the executive chairman of Comet Iran.

According to Mr Molavi, as a result of the political changes in Iran at the beginning of the 1980s and the American hostage crisis as well as other matters, doing business with American companies and suppliers from Iran became extremely difficult. American D   companies did not want to be seen dealing directly with Iranian companies. To overcome these problems Comet UK was incorporated in the UK. The main issue on the petition is the precise role played by Comet UK and its relationship with Comet Iran, at least after Mr Safinia became a director and shareholder.

According to Mr Safinia, he and Mr Molavi, through a number of vehicle companies, carry on a quasi-partnership or joint venture business together as agents for a number of E   suppliers and manufacturers in the aviation, broadcasting, telecommunications, marine and power generation fields who wish to do business in Iran. Comet UK, says Mr Safinia, is one of those companies which acts as agent principally in the aviation, broadcasting and telecommunications field and has entered into agency agreements with a number of western suppliers and manufacturers, including those on the first page of the schedule to the draft order. Under the terms of those agreements, says Mr Safinia, Comet UK is F   entitled to commission on all goods and services supplied to customers and end users in Iran. A similar situation exists in relation to another company incorporated in the UK called Genusis Ltd, which carries on business as commission agent in the marine and power generation field where Mr and Mrs Safinia are 55 per cent shareholders and Mr and Mrs Molavi 45 per cent shareholders. According to Mr Safinia, whilst the contracts with suppliers and the benefit of agency payments are with Comet UK, the role of Comet Iran, in which Mr and Mrs Safinia had no interest, is to find purchasers and end users in G   Iran who are interested in purchasing goods, and therefore Comet Iran and another Iranian company, Kaman Ltd, in which Mr and Mrs Safinia do have an interest, conduct the Iran side of the operation, for which Comet Iran and Kaman, as the case may be, are paid a commission by Comet UK or Genusis out of the commission payments received from western suppliers. Mr Safinia says that, if there is any profit on the business conducted by Comet UK, then the arrangement is that it is split 55 per cent/45 per cent between Mr Molavi and Mr Safinia respectively in accordance with their shareholdings H   in Comet UK. Mr Molavi's salary is paid from Comet UK and Mr Safinia's from Genusis.

On the other hand, according to Mr Molavi, the picture is quite different. He says that Comet UK acts really as a post box and message liaison centre for communications to and from Comet Iran and suppliers. It also handles the invoicing and processes certain moneys paid by suppliers and arranges for certain payments to be made on behalf of and to Comet Iran. Mr Molavi says that Comet UK has never treated the agency contracts, or the commissions received from suppliers, as belonging to it beneficially, that such contracts are in reality with Comet Iran and beneficially owned by Comet Iran, and that Comet UK enters into them merely as agent and on behalf of Comet Iran as undisclosed principal. Mr Molavi says that Comet UK neither makes nor retains any significant profits of its own; the profits of the business, he says, are made by Comet Iran, which is wholly owned by his family, and retained by Comet Iran in its sterling and dollar accounts in the Union Bank of Switzerland, Geneva (which I shall refer to as 'the UBS account') which was opened in or about 1984. However, some commissions which, according to Mr Molavi, have been earned by Comet Iran are paid into a Midland Bank account of Comet UK because, apparently, some suppliers prefer to pay commissions into an account in the UK. Mr Molavi seeks to explain this by saying that, since Comet UK's operating expenses are paid for by Comet Iran, commission moneys paid to Comet UK's bank account have been retained for paying these expenses. However, Mr Molavi describes the UBS account as 'the main operating account of the Comet companies' – not, it is to be noted, merely Comet Iran – and the Midland account as a subsidiary account. Mr Safinia, on the other hand, says that Comet UK's commission was only paid into the UBS account as a matter of convenience and to avoid any suggestion that its business was being conducted in the UK.

What the true position is and the relationship between the two Comet companies is, I have said, a matter that can only be resolved at trial. Certainly the audited accounts of Comet UK do not appear to reflect the position as described by either Mr Molavi or Mr Safinia. Thus, the latest audited accounts for the year ended 31 May 1992 describe the company's principal activity as commission agency and make no reference to the fact that its commission earnings have, as Mr Molavi says, been earned entirely by it as agent of and for the benefit of Comet Iran, to whom it is liable to account. Moreover, the profit and loss account shows sums in the region of £43,000 being paid for overseas representation, which I was told was a payment to Comet Iran for activities carried on by it, as well as almost £15,000 for overseas travel and accommodation, which appears at first sight to be inconsistent with Mr Molavi's description of how Comet UK's business is alleged to have been run.

However, the accounts do not sit happily with Mr Safinia's account either. The figures referred to in his evidence and in argument on his behalf for Comet UK's profit commission appear to be considerably in excess of the £281,000 figure for commission shown in the accounts, and there is no indication in the accounts of there having been any split of the profits 55 per cent/45 per cent of the type described by Mr Safinia, particularly in the light of the fact that no dividend appears to have been declared at any material time.

The suspicious mind might be forgiven for thinking that the parties have so arranged their affairs for tax purposes so as to ensure that the expenses of the business have been paid for by the British operation, Comet UK, whereas the profit has been taken abroad. But, again, no doubt, all these matters are matters that will have to be explained and investigated at trial.

For present purposes, however, I must proceed on the basis, as Mr Snowden for Mr Molavi conceded, that, for the purposes of this application at any rate, Mr and Mrs Safinia have an arguable case for saying that the agency contracts entered into with the suppliers referred to on the first page of the schedule to the draft minute of order had indeed been entered into by Comet UK in its own right and not as agent for Comet Iran and that, accordingly, Mr and Mrs Safinia have an arguable case for saying that the agency business, or at least that part of it that does not involve Comet Iran's activities in Iran, belongs to Comet UK.

A   This is not a surprising concession since many of the agreements with suppliers are clearly concluded with Comet UK, whatever may be the beneficial position and, moreover, the first time that the question appears to have been put forward in writing was in a letter dated 20 April 1993 from Mr Molavi's solicitors to the petitioner's solicitors after the petition had been presented and served on or about 5 April 1993 and after the issue and service of the notice of motion for an injunction.

B   The facts leading up to the present proceedings can be summarised as follows. In July 1990 Mr and Mrs Safinia transferred five per cent of their shareholding to Mr and Mrs Molavi. The reason for this transfer is in dispute. Mr Safinia says that it was the price of getting rid of a bonus incentive scheme for remuneration which Mr Safinia considered unfair as he was more concerned in the administrative side of the business rather than in getting in new business upon which the bonus incentive depended. Mr Molavi says that it was in consideration of Mr Molavi agreeing to continue subsidising Mr Safinia's salary

C   and expenses. Again, these are matters that can only be resolved at trial.

In March or April 1991 Mr Safinia and Mr Molavi agreed that, if Mr Safinia paid Mr Molavi £200,000, Mr Molavi would transfer 45 per cent of Comet Iran to Mr Safinia. Mr Molavi deposes that Mr Safinia said that he did not have the money to pay the £200,000 but proposed that, if Comet Iran had any surplus commissions after payment of all expenses and overheads and leaving a cushion for safety, those surplus commissions

D   could be split 75 per cent to Mr Molavi and 25 per cent to Mr Safinia, treating the extra 20 per cent paid to Mr Molavi over and above the 55 per cent/45 per cent split as a payment on account of the £200,000 purchase moneys, and Mr Molavi said he agreed to that.

Mr Safinia says that this agreement was consistent with his analysis, namely that he and Mr Molavi were partners in the joint venture whereby the profits of the business being carried out by Comet UK were going to be split 55 per cent/45 per cent. Mr Molavi

E   says that this did no more than recognise what was going to happen after Mr Safinia became entitled to his 45 per cent of Comet Iran upon completion of the agreement and that the proposal simply dealt with the outstanding payment of the purchase price for the shares.

At all material times up until May 1992 Mr Safinia was a signatory on the UBS bank account. In 1991 and early 1992 there were various disagreements between the parties

F   about transfers, which Mr Safinia had made from the UBS account. Whether these were unauthorised misappropriations as Mr Molavi suggests, or legitimate business payments as Mr Safinia asserts, is again a matter that will have to be resolved at trial. However, these disagreements led to Mr Molavi instructing UBS on 14 May 1992 to remove Mr Safinia as a signatory from the account without, Mr Safinia alleges, notifying him. According to Mr Safinia, this meant that bills which had to be paid in connection with

G   Comet UK's business could not be paid from that source, and it was therefore no longer appropriate for Comet UK's moneys to be paid into the UBS account from that date. However, it is fair to say that Mr Safinia does not appear to have complained, at least in writing, about his removal from the UBS account at that time.

Various discussions between the parties took place culminating in a meeting on 25 June 1992 with the company's current auditors. What was agreed precisely at that meeting is far from clear, if indeed anything was precisely agreed. But it appears to have

H   involved reiteration of matters that had already been agreed, such as the transfer of the 45 per cent of the shares in Comet Iran and the division of the shareholdings in the UK companies, including readjustment of the shareholdings in Genusis and Kaman, so that Mr Safinia would have 55 per cent of those companies and Mr Molavi 45 per cent. It also appears to have been agreed at this stage that Mr Molavi's salary would be paid by Comet UK and Mr Safinia would receive an equal salary from Genusis. There also appears to have been some recognition, at least on an operational basis, of a separation of the ways with Mr Safinia being responsible for running the business of Genusis and Kaman in the marine and power generation fields, and Mr Molavi being responsible for running the separate business of Comet UK in the broadcasting, aviation and telecommunications fields. However, Mr Safinia asserts that all companies were still to be part of one joint venture or partnership. He also says that at some stage between June and November 1992 he had told Mr Molavi that he was not interested any more in purchasing shares in Comet Iran because he did not trust Mr Molavi any longer and that, accordingly, the profit sharing ratio went back to 55 per cent/45 per cent as there was no longer any need for Mr Safinia to pay the £200,000 purchase price for the shares.

Mr Safinia then says that there was an agreement concluded in Tehran on 16 October 1992 whereby it was agreed that two commission payments due to be received from Telefunken in November and December 1992 would be split 55 per cent to Mr Molavi and 45 per cent to Mr Safinia. The November payment was expected to be about £130,000 or its equivalent and the December payment about £300,000. The parties appear to have signed a page of calculations confirming their agreement to this split and, although he disagrees about the detail of this agreement and the reasons for it, Mr Molavi appears to agree that such a profit share arrangement was indeed entered into about these particular commissions. The agency agreement with Telefunken was in fact with Genusis, not Comet UK. Again, Mr Molavi says that this Genusis contract was beneficially owned by Comet Iran and not by Genusis and that Genusis was simply entering into the contract as nominee or agent for Comet Iran. Be that as it may, the parties agreed that the first tranche of the Telefunken payment would be paid into the UBS account because, according to Mr Safinia, Mr Molavi was under pressure to make a number of payments. Mr Safinia saw no harm in that since the profit split had been agreed, and he wrote to Telefunken, asking them to pay the amount agreed into the UBS account. The surplus profit does appear to have been split between the parties in relation to the first payment, although the evidence is not very clear on this.

So far as the December Telefunken payment was concerned, that was a payment of about £300,000 which was received into the UBS account on or about 28 December 1992. There is a dispute as to whether Telefunken should or should not have paid the money into the UBS account, but there is no dispute that the money has been received by Mr Molavi or Comet Iran in the UBS account, that it has not been distributed in accordance with the profit share agreement concluded on 16 October 1992 and that it was, or has been, available, whether legitimately or otherwise, to meet the expenses of Comet Iran and/or Comet UK.

Matters then appear to have come to a head in December 1992 and early January 1993 with Mr Molavi complaining that Mr Safinia had failed to pay the £200,000 which he had promised to pay for the transfer of the shares in Comet Iran, and Mr Safinia complaining that Mr Molavi had taken the commission properly payable to Genusis so as to prevent Mr Safinia getting money under his control so as to continue the business of Comet UK, Genusis and Kaman. On 4 January 1993 Mr Molavi wrote to Mr Safinia, purporting to accept Mr Safinia's alleged repudiation of the agreement to purchase shares in Comet Iran.

Going back for a moment in time, Mr Safinia complains in his first affidavit that, after he was removed as a signatory from the UBS account in May 1992, Mr Molavi took steps to persuade suppliers with whom Comet UK had contracted to pay commission payments into the UBS account and he exhibits various letters to that effect sent by Mr Molavi in August and November 1992. Mr Molavi counters this by saying that these were merely routine letters and that there was nothing sinister in such direction since

A payment to the UBS account had been the norm. Again, these matters can only be resolved at trial.

On 20 January 1993 Mr Safinia sent a number of letters to suppliers and manufacturers with whom Comet UK dealt, stating (1) that it had come to his notice that payments due to Comet UK had been remitted to bank accounts other than the company's Midland Bank account; (2) that such payments had been without his authority or sanction; (3) B requesting details of all sums that had been paid; (4) requiring all payments in future to be made to Comet UK's account at Midland; and (5) stating that he would hold such suppliers responsible if payments were made in breach of his instructions. Of course, both Mr Molavi and Mr Safinia are signatories to the Midland Bank account, which is a Comet UK bank account.

Mr Safinia says that he wrote these letters because he could no longer trust Mr Molavi and that all he was doing was to ensure that the right companies were paid commissions C by suppliers. Mr Molavi took the view that Mr Safinia's letters of 20 January were an attempt to damage and sabotage the business and reputation of Comet Iran and obstruct Mr Molavi and, accordingly, countered by sending a series of letters dated about 17 February 1992 to suppliers and manufacturers, including those who had contracts with Comet UK and who are listed on the first page of the schedule to the draft order, in which he said that Comet's activities would be consolidated and centralised in Iran; that D Comet UK's role would diminish to that of a facilitating or satellite office; that Comet UK's office would be relocated in the near future; that in the meantime and until further notice all future correspondence should be addressed to Comet Iran's address in Tehran; that recipients of the letter should amend all contracts and agreements with Comet UK 'to show our operational changes' by deleting 'Comet UK' and replacing it with 'Comet Iran'; and, finally, that future payments to Comet should be deposited in accordance with the instructions given solely by Mr Molavi.

E In riposte Mr Safinia appears to have sent a further series of letters in February 1993, repeating the request that commission should be paid into the Comet UK Midland Bank account, which again Mr Molavi regards as an attempt to sabotage Comet Iran's business.

Not surprisingly, perhaps, the dissention between the two directors and the conflicting instructions has led a number of suppliers to terminate their contracts with Comet UK. F Mr Molavi blames Mr Safinia's letters for this. Mr Safinia blames Mr Molavi because, he says, all the suppliers thought that they were dealing with Comet UK, not Comet Iran. Again, where the blame lies is only something that can be adequately resolved at trial.

What is clear is that the uncertainty is extremely unsatisfactory and disrupting to the business and the proper collection of moneys which are due, at least prima facie, under G the terms of the contracts to Comet UK.

To deal with receipt of commissions from three designated suppliers the parties have sensibly come to terms that commissions from these suppliers should be received in a joint bank account in Jersey. However, no terms have been agreed as to the receipt of moneys from other suppliers.

Apart from allegations against Mr Safinia of wrongly diverting Comet Iran and Comet H UK's funds which, it was agreed between counsel, were matters for trial, Mr Molavi in his third affidavit alleges that Mr Safinia has attempted to divert the business of Comet UK and Comet Iran to a new company operated by Mr Safinia called Lamagrove Ltd. Mr Molavi refers to a letter dated 2 June 1993 from Mr Safinia on Lamagrove writing paper to Conrac Elektron which, according to Mr Molavi, is a customer of Comet Iran with whom it has a letter of understanding. The second and third paragraph of that letter read as follows:

'At the same time I think it is prudent that Conrac should send a message to Comet A
Enterprises Ltd of Iran and Comet Enterprises Ltd in the UK, advising them that
Conrac has determined to follow up their projects in Iran without the help of
Comet Enterprises Ltd and inform Comet that they can no longer be active on
behalf of Conrac. You need not mention who you are collaborating with, or how
you wish to proceed. It is however important that you cancel any agreement or
possible cooperation with Comet.

I would be grateful if you could send me copies of both letters and faxes to Mashad B
Airport Manager and Comet Enterprises Ltd. Please ensure that both letters are
sent without any reference to Lamagrove Ltd.'

Mr Molavi says that he believes that this letter shows without doubt that Mr Safinia's
protestations throughout his evidence that he is acting at all times in the best interests of
Comet UK and that he is seeking to preserve the business of Comet UK are false. He is,
says Mr Molavi, clearly attempting to divert the business of both Comet Iran and Comet C
UK, 'which is exactly what he accuses me of doing'.

Mr Safinia's answer to this is that it is common ground between the parties that Conrac
is not a client of Comet UK. Mr Safinia says also that he does not regard, and has never
regarded, Conrac as a client of Comet UK, and that what he said in the fax to Conrac
was a clumsy attempt to ensure that he was not pinching any business belonging to
Comet UK or Comet Iran because he did not want accusations such as are now being D
made against him being made against him.

In this morass of allegation and counter-allegation what, if any, injunction should be
made? Mr Griffiths submits that there is clearly a serious issue to be tried on the merits
as to whether the agency contracts are with Comet UK or Comet Iran. There is no
dispute on this point in the light of the concession made by Mr Snowden for Mr Molavi.
Mr Griffiths submits that damages is not an adequate remedy because, unless the business E
is preserved by the grant of the injunction sought, it will be very difficult, if not
impossible, to quantify the petitioners' claim on the petition, where the primary relief
which they seek is that their shares should be purchased by Mr and Mrs Molavi at a
value which takes into account the effect of the alleged misappropriations by Mr Molavi
and the value of the commission income business arising from agencies belonging to
Comet UK. Unless the business is preserved, submits Mr Griffiths, it will be very difficult
to quantify the company's business. Moreover, he says, no undertaking is in fact put F
forward to purchase Mr and Mrs Safinia's shares. All that is said in one of Mr Molavi's
recent affidavits is that he is prepared to purchase the Safinia shares. The fact that Mr
Molavi may be prepared to purchase the Safinia shares at a valuation is not a good
reason why in the meantime, Mr Griffiths submits, Mr Molavi should be allowed to
continue to divert Comet UK property to Comet Iran. As a shareholder, Mr Griffiths
submits that Mr Safinia is entitled to have the company's assets preserved and that the G
jurisdiction exercised by the court is similar to the Mareva jurisdiction and that the
business and assets should be available to meet the company's obligations to its creditors,
and also to be available for distribution amongst its shareholders. He also submits that
indirectly, since Mr and Mrs Safinia will be entitled to have recourse at the end of the
day to Mr Molavi's shares as assets within the jurisdiction to satisfy any claim against
him in these proceedings, the value in such shares should not be dissipated by means of
the misappropriation of the moneys to Comet Iran, thereby effectively transferring value H
out of the jurisdiction.

Mr Griffiths supported his submissions by reference to *Re a Company No. 008126 of
1989 (Re Hailey Group Ltd)* [1992] BCC 542 and *Standard Chartered Bank v Walker*
[1992] 1 WLR 561. I do not find either authority of much assistance to me in the present
case as the facts of both were very different. *Re Hailey Group Ltd* shows that a court may

A   make an order under s. 459 even though an administrative receiver has been appointed; for example, where the unfairly prejudicial conduct has prevented the sale of the petitioner's shares before the onset of insolvency, or the substantive relief sought is for the purchase of the petitioner's shares and that relief was sought at a time when the company was solvent. In other words, the court may take an earlier value of the petitioner's shares than the hearing date of the petition if it is appropriate in all the circumstances to do so. I do not think that this case helps Mr Griffiths for, as Mr

B   Snowden submits, it shows that the court need not have regard to present day values when valuing the petitioner's shares in circumstances where the petitioner is to be bought out. But the court may order a valuation at some earlier date based on a different or hypothetical basis. The facts of *Standard Chartered Bank* are so different that I regard the case as of no assistance.

C   Mr Griffiths submits that damages are an adequate remedy to Mr Molavi because there is no evidence that Comet UK or Mr Molavi are going to suffer any damage if the commissions are not received by Comet UK (a) because Mr Safinia is quite willing to seek commissions properly payable to Comet Iran by Comet UK funded out of receipts; (b) that there is no evidence to suggest that the £300,000 Telefunken commissions and other commissions received in the UBS account are not sufficient to fund any operating expenses of Comet Iran; (c) no detail has been given by Comet Iran or Mr Molavi of the

D   quantum or extent of these expenses; and (d) liberty to apply can be given in case any problems arise about payment of expenses. There is some force in these submissions, in my view.

So far as balance of convenience is concerned, Mr Griffiths says that the status quo should be preserved, the status quo being Comet UK's undoubted legal entitlement as party to the agency contracts to receive the commissions from the suppliers. Mr Griffiths

E   submits that the order which he seeks will preserve the balance of convenience.

Mr Snowden's submissions are helpfully set out in his written skeleton. His initial submission is that no relief at all should be granted, or at least the court should be very reluctant, or far less willing, to exercise its discretion in Mr Safinia's favour because Mr Safinia does not come to the court with clean hands. Mr Snowden points to the Conrac letter which he says shows that Mr Safinia is trying to lure business away from Comet

F   Iran and Comet UK to a company which he has formed. Mr Snowden submits that this gives the lie to Mr Safinia's protestations of seeking to protect the business of Comet UK.

I reject the submission that I should not grant any relief to Mr and Mrs Safinia on these grounds. First, there is no suggestion in the evidence that Conrac was ever a party with whom Comet UK had entered into a contract or had done business and, secondly,

G   it is impossible to determine on this motion what are the rights and wrongs of Mr Safinia's conduct on this matter. It is perfectly clear that both sides have attempted to secure business for their own companies and whether such activity was or was not a breach of fiduciary duty on their respective parts can only be determined at trial. In my judgment, it would be wrong to deny Mr Safinia relief on this ground alone.

However, Mr Snowden's principal submission is that the balance of convenience

H   clearly lies against the grant of any interim relief. He submits that Mr and Mrs Safinia simply seek an order that their shares in Comet be purchased on terms that permit for allowances to be made for the effect of any proven misfeasance by Mr Molavi in that valuation. He further submits that, provided that a record is kept of commissions paid and disbursements made under contracts which Mr Safinia claims belong to Comet UK, this can be taken into account on the valuation if Mr Safinia is proved correct at trial. He submits that Mr Molavi has offered to give undertakings to this effect.

Mr Snowden has handed up to the court a draft proposed undertaking as follows:

'Upon Mr Molavi by his counsel undertaking until trial or further order (as to which there be liberty to apply):

(1) whether by himself, his servants, agents or otherwise howsoever, not to cause or procure or attempt to cause or procure any of the companies, firms or trading organisations set out in the schedule hereto ('the suppliers') to breach or terminate any existing contract alleged to be with Comet UK;

(2) to provide to the petitioners' solicitors within a week of the end of each [six] week period, a statement setting out:

(a) details of any moneys received by or on behalf of Comet Iran from any of the suppliers within such [six] week period;

. . .

(c) details of payments made from such moneys within such [six] week period, provided that Mr Molavi be at liberty not to disclose the names of recipients of such moneys who are not officers of or employed by Comet Iran.'

Paragraphs 12–19 of Mr Snowden's skeleton amplify his principal submissions as follows:

'12. The argument that an interim injunction interfering with Mr Molavi's conduct of Comet business or dictating to whom commission payments must be made is necessary "to preserve something worth fighting about" (as stated in Mr Safinia's evidence) is entirely misconceived. Mr Safinia is not "fighting about" Comet UK or the business or the commissions themselves. He does not lay claim to the business or the company itself or the commissions. Instead he wishes to *sell* his shares in Comet UK at an assessed value.

13. Mr Safinia's claims in the petition can be protected in ways which do not require the court actively to attempt to intervene in and regulate the conduct of complex commercial transactions by Mr Molavi and Comet Iran. The terms of such intervention cannot be formulated with any precision to meet the current situation and the innumerable eventualities which might arise (see below) and the consequences of such intervention are difficult if not impossible to foresee.

14. The relief sought is clearly intended to restrict the activities of Mr Molavi and the payment of moneys in relation to future agency business which is conducted by Comet Iran. In effect it seeks to prevent Mr Molavi from fulfilling his duties to Comet Iran by obtaining any new business for Comet Iran from the companies mentioned and in some way to force Comet Iran to give its agency business to Comet UK.

15. There is no guarantee that the named companies will wish any longer to deal with Comet UK and indeed there is evidence to suggest that they might well not. It is also the case that there is nothing which obliges Comet Iran to operate through Comet UK or sets out how or on what terms that should be done.

16. The draft order also fails to deal with the question of how moneys are to be disbursed if required to be paid to Comet UK – thus risking serious damage to the business of Comet Iran.

17. The very impracticality of any such order as well as its restrictions mean that there would be a substantial risk that the business of Comet Iran (and thus Comet UK) and Mr Molavi's interests in that business will be harmed by an injunction as now sought. It would be impossible to quantify the extent of such harm caused as

A   a result. If Mr Safinia is found to be correct at trial, adjustments can be made to the price of Mr and Mrs Safinia's shares to reflect the business actually done and commissions received which ought to have benefited Comet UK: the damage suffered by Mr Molavi and the Comet companies as a consequence of any such injunction would be irremediable.

B   18. It is not clear how or on what basis Comet Iran could "take over" the business from Comet UK or recoup itself in respect of lost opportunities after the trial as suggested in Mr Safinia's evidence.

19. The balance of convenience is therefore clearly against the grant of the relief sought.'

Mr Snowden relies on the case of *Re Posgate & Denby (Agencies) Ltd* (1986) 2 BCC 99,352, a decision of Hoffmann J, to support his argument that the balance of

C   convenience lies against the grant of an injunction. Mr Snowden submits that, as in *Re Posgate & Denby*, if at trial it turns out that payments of commission have been wrongly misappropriated by Mr Molavi or Comet Iran or that business opportunities or contracts have been wrongly diverted to Comet Iran, Mr and Mrs Safinia can be fully compensated financially by an order which provides for them to be bought out on the basis of a valuation that takes account of such misappropriations or defalcations as may be proved.

D   Each case has, of course, to be decided upon its own facts but, in my judgment, the essential difference between the facts in the present case and *Re Posgate & Denby* is that in the latter case there was no allegation of impropriety against the board selling the syndicates nor any evidence that the sales were at an actual undervalue. Here, on the other hand, so far at least as receipt of commissions is concerned, prima facie on the face of the relevant contracts Comet UK is entitled to receive the relevant commissions and that remains the position until Mr Molavi has proved his case that, in reality, Comet UK

E   was merely a nominee and that Comet Iran is beneficially entitled to all commissions. Prima facie it is Mr Molavi who is seeking to disturb the status quo by asserting that all such receipts are Comet Iran's money and should be exclusively under his control, and not subject to any distribution of profits under the type of arrangement such as that which was apparently concluded between him and Mr Safinia in relation to moneys paid into the UBS account. The evidence, it seems to me, does show that in the past the parties did use the UBS account, as Mr Molavi himself accepts, as the joint bank account for the

F   companies, and that profits arising in that bank account would be distributed between the parties in the agreed ratio.

In my judgment, therefore, the balance of convenience does require some sort of relief to protect Comet UK and Mr Safinia's position pending the hearing of the petition. In particular, I am mindful at the end of the day that the only apparent assets of Mr Molavi within the jurisdiction are his flat and his shares in the company. Moreover, it may well

G   be that an order could be made against Comet UK requiring it to purchase Mr and Mrs Safinia's shares under s. 461, and that would only be a possible course if there are sufficient assets in the company. I accept Mr Griffiths' submissions that the fact that Mr and Mrs Safinia can be compensated at trial for any misappropriations of Comet UK's assets is not per se an answer to the injunction sought. Comet Iran is not a party to the petition. I have no indication as to whether it would be prepared, or indeed would be in a position, to compensate the Safinias in respect of diverted commissions or return such

H   payments to Comet UK. In the intervening period Comet Iran itself may have incurred obligations to its own creditors. So far as Mr Molavi is concerned, there is no evidence as to his ability to do so, once the commissions have left the jurisdiction or have been received by Comet Iran.

In my judgment and despite the undertakings offered by Mr Molavi, I do think that, in the absence of an injunction relating to the preservation of the commission payments,

it will be difficult to value Comet UK's goodwill and other assets for the purposes of the   A
petition and any valuation of Mr and Mrs Safinia's shares. Mr Safinia, moreover, remains
a director with obligations as well as rights in relation to the company's assets and
liabilities. He is entitled, in my judgment, to interlocutory relief which prevents active
diversion of what, prima facie at least, are Comet UK's receivables. Although, because
of the disputes between the shareholders, the company does not appear to be trading in
a very active way, debts must be paid and proper receipts and records maintained.

     B

Accordingly, I propose to grant the relief sought in para. 1(2) of the draft order subject
to certain modifications which will have to be the subject of further drafting by counsel,
or possibly further submissions on the terms of the order. The first modifications are that
the words 'any money' in the third and fourth line are, in my judgment, too wide. They
must be limited to any moneys payable under or in respect of contracts or arrangements
concluded between any one or more of the companies, firms or trading organisations set
out on the first page of the schedule, and irrespective of whether Comet UK was acting   C
as principal or agent for Comet Iran in entering into such contract. I am happy to hear
submissions from counsel as to the precise form of any such wording, but that is the gist
that it seems to me is necessary in order to make the words sufficiently certain.

Second, in my judgment, the wording of the order must make it clear that Mr Molavi
is at liberty to procure payment to a designated account or accounts of Comet UK over
which both parties have signing rights so that he can proceed to collect in moneys owed   D
to Comet UK without having to obtain further agreement from Mr and Mrs Safinia
before requiring suppliers to pay moneys to Comet UK. In other words, I require some
sort of amendment to the words 'save as agreed with the petitioners', but, again, that is a
matter for argument.

However, an injunction in this form will not deal with two problems which have been
identified by Mr Snowden. First, it will not deal with the situation where, despite no   E
procuration by, or attempt to procure on the part of, Mr Molavi, a supplier in fact pays
money into the UBS account, in accordance perhaps with previous instructions. This
would not constitute a breach by Mr Molavi of the injunction since the payment would
not be made as a result of conduct on his part. In my judgment, the best and most
practical course would be for an agreed circular letter to be signed by both directors,
directing all the company's suppliers to pay commissions due under p. 1 of the schedule
contracts to specified bank accounts, whether in the UK or out of the jurisdiction. Were   F
Mr Griffiths to seek a mandatory order in such terms (and he does not do so at the
present time), I would be minded, subject to any further submissions by Mr Snowden, to
make such a mandatory order, as it seems to me to be highly desirable that there should
be certainty as to where the commission payments referred to on p. 1 of the schedule are
to be paid. Accordingly, I propose to hear further submissions on the wording of this
part of the order.

     G

The second problem relates to the payment of Comet UK's expenses out of any
commissions collected. Clearly, any such sums can and should be applied in payment of
the proper expenses and liabilities of Comet UK. Again, I propose to hear submissions
on the form of order in this respect. Either the parties can agree a regime amongst
themselves for the payment of proper expenses and liabilities and the order can contain
merely general words authorising the payment of the same, or alternatively the regime
will have to be incorporated in the order of the court with liberty to apply in both cases.   H

I turn now to consider para. 1(1) of the draft order, which in effect seeks to restrain
Mr Molavi from diverting business or corporate opportunities or contracts to Comet
Iran. In my judgment, the relief sought in this subparagraph is of a very different nature
from that sought in para. 1(2). I agree with most of the criticisms of the substance and
drafting of this subparagraph which are set out in para. 23–26 of Mr Snowden's skeleton.

A   Given the wholly unclear nature of the relationship between Comet UK and Comet Iran
    and the roles respectively played by each company, in my judgment it would be quite
    wrong to grant an interlocutory injunction in the wide and vague terms sought in this
    subparagraph, which might have the effect of preventing Comet UK from carrying on its
    legitimate separate business, or which would certainly make it unclear as to what business
    Mr Molavi is entitled to procure Comet Iran to carry out. In this context there is, in my
B   judgment, a real difference between attempts by Mr Molavi to breach or terminate
    existing contracts with suppliers and the diversion of corporate opportunities, which is a
    much more nebulous concept. So far as the latter is concerned, that is to say the diversion
    of corporate opportunities, even if, as Mr Griffiths submits, Mr Molavi's letter of 17
    February 1993 suggests there have been and may continue to be attempts to divert
    corporate opportunities away from Comet UK to Comet Iran, that is something in
    respect of which Mr and Mrs Safinia can be adequately compensated at trial provided
C   that adequate records exist showing precisely what corporate opportunities have or may
    have been diverted.

        So far as the former is concerned, in my judgment, Mr and Mrs Safinia are, in the
    circumstances, entitled to an injunction to restrain Mr Molavi from procuring or
    attempting to procure any of the companies, firms or trading organisations set out on the
    first page to the schedule to breach or terminate any existing contract alleged by the
D   petitioners to be with Comet UK. In other words, I take the view that an injunction
    should be granted or an undertaking given by Mr Molavi in the terms of para. (1) of the
    draft undertakings offered by Mr Molavi, with the addition of the words 'by the
    petitioners' after the word 'alleged' in the last line. As I understand it, Mr Snowden has
    offered an undertaking in this form.

        However, to protect the petitioners' position in relation to the quantification of loss
E   arising from possible diverted corporate opportunities or contracts, they are, in my
    judgment, also entitled to an injunction or an undertaking in the form of para. 2(a) and
    (b) of Mr Snowden's proposed draft undertaking so that at trial adequate records will
    exist upon the basis of which Mr and Mrs Safinia's shares can be valued if it is held that
    business of Comet Iran constitutes the wrongful diversion of business properly belonging
    to Comet UK. However, I do not consider it necessary or relevant to this head that an
F   undertaking or injunction in the form of para. 2(c) should be given or ordered. Paragraph
    2(c) relates to the provision of details of payments made by Comet Iran and, as I
    understand it, such undertaking was offered merely in an attempt to persuade the court
    not to make the order sought in para. 1(2) of the amended notice of motion. As I have
    already indicated, I do propose to make such an order with modifications. However, the
    undertaking or order referring to the provision of details of payments does not seem to
G   me to be necessary in order to provide an adequate record of business that has or may
    have been allegedly improperly diverted and I would not propose to make such an order.

        If Mr Molavi is not prepared to give an undertaking in the form of para. 2(a) and (b)
    of the draft in connection with or in order to avoid the relief sought in para. 1(1) of the
    amended notice of motion, then I would be minded to make a mandatory order in the
    terms of para. 2(a) and (b) to support the undertaking which I understand is being offered
H   in para. 1 of the draft undertaking. However, I propose to hear further argument on this
    aspect also.

        Finally, it should be made clear, in my judgment, what precisely is being referred to by
    the word 'details' in para. 2(a) and (b) of the draft undertaking. All the petitioners need
    to know at this stage is a broad outline of the contracts or arrangements entered into by
    Comet Iran, so that they can be adequately recorded and identified at trial provided, of

A

course, that the detail of the arrangements would be forthcoming at trial by means of discovery or otherwise. That may require an undertaking by Mr Molavi to procure discovery of such agreements at trial; otherwise, the detail given may need to be more full than I would have thought was otherwise necessary. Again, I propose to hear argument as to the precise terms of the minutes of order.

(*Order accordingly*)

B

C

D

E

F

G

H

A # Orion Finance Ltd v Crown Financial Management Ltd.

Chancery Division.
Vinelott J.
Judgment delivered 30 March 1994.

> *Assignment of rents payable under leases of computer equipment – Whether*
> *assignment was binding on lessee – Whether assignment was by way of charge and*
> *registrable – Whether avoidance of assignment for non-registration meant that*
> *assignee had no claim against lessee – Companies Act 1985, s. 395, 396.*

These were two actions both raising the question whether the plaintiff ('Orion') was entitled to compensation for the refusal of the defendant ('Crown') to pay rent payable under leases of computer equipment made between Crown and Atlantic Computer Systems plc. In both cases the rents payable under the relevant leases were assigned by Atlantic to Orion. The main issues were whether the assignment was binding on Crown and whether an option agreed between Atlantic and Crown, under which Crown had the right to terminate the relevant lease without any penalty before the full period of the lease had expired, was a term of the lease binding on Orion, or was part of an arrangement (the 'management agreement') between Atlantic and Crown under which on exercise of the option Atlantic undertook to pay any remaining rentals due under the then unexpired term of the lease to Orion as assignee. Crown argued that the lease had been amended by a side letter which rendered invalid any purported assignment made without the prior written consent of Crown. It was further argued, in the alternative, that as the management agreement was executed before Crown received notice of the assignment to Orion, it created rights binding on Orion in equity.

In the first case there was a further question whether the assignment by Atlantic to Orion was an assignment by way of charge on book debts of Atlantic within s. 396 of the Companies Act 1985. The assignment was not registered pursuant to s. 395 and if registrable the assignment was void as against administrators of Atlantic who were appointed in April 1990 and liquidators of Atlantic subsequently appointed. Orion argued that the assignment was in substance an outright assignment. The assignment was made pursuant to the hire-purchase agreement under which Orion consented to Atlantic subletting the equipment to Crown on the terms of the annexed lease and which provided that Atlantic 'as security for its obligations hereunder' would assign to Orion all moneys then or to become payable under the lease 'to the intent that they may be charged with payment of all moneys now or hereafter owing to' Orion under the hire-purchase agreement. Orion submitted that Atlantic was left with no equity of redemption and that the assignment was accordingly incapable of operating as a security. If the assignment was void against the administrators and liquidators of Atlantic, the further question was whether the avoidance of the charge against the administrators and liquidators had the result that Orion as assignee had no enforceable right as against Crown. Those questions did not arise in relation to the second lease which was registered.

Held, giving judgment for Crown on the first lease and for Orion on the second:

1. When the first lease was executed Atlantic was not the owner of the equipment and would not become the owner unless and until an order was placed with IBM (if it had not already been placed) and IBM had agreed to enter into a novation agreement. It had been agreed between Crown and Atlantic that until Atlantic became the owner of the equipment and the equipment was installed rent would not be paid by Crown though when the equipment had been installed the rent would be paid retrospectively. By the time that the equipment had been installed Crown knew that the assignment to Orion had been executed and must be taken to have assumed that the assignment was also conditional upon Atlantic becoming the owner of the equipment and entitled to rent under the lease. By that time it must also

have been clear to Crown from the terms of the management agreement and an exchange of   A
letters that the assignment to Orion was an assignment of the rent payable over the full
seven year term and that the management agreement was a wholly separate agreement
binding between Crown and Atlantic alone. Orion's right to payment during the whole term
would not be affected but Crown would not have to pay the instalments of rent due after
termination 'to Atlantic'. In the circumstances if Crown wished to contend that the
assignment was invalid or that Orion was bound by the term of the management agreement,
it had to make those claims before the lease became unconditional and so before Orion   B
would act upon it by paying the purchase price which it had agreed to pay for the assignment
of the rental stream. The failure of Crown to do so amounted to a representation that Crown
accepted that the assignment was valid and would become binding when the lease became
unconditional and that Orion would take the benefit of it free from the management
agreement.

2. The hire-purchase agreement contained a provision for adjustment of the instalments   C
of hire (reflecting differences between the market rate of interest for the time being and a
fixed rate) so that the instalments of hire might be more or less than the rent payable under
the lease. If less then Atlantic was entitled to be repaid annually the amount of the difference.
Its entitlement reflected its right as chargor to a surplus over the amount required to
discharge its liability in the hands of Orion.

3. Section 395 clearly avoided the assignment as between Orion and the administrators   D
or liquidators of Atlantic. It followed that notice of the assignment would not afford any
defence to Crown if sued by the administrators or liquidators. Section 395 was a complete
defence to Orion's action on the first lease which had to be dismissed.

4. In relation to the second lease it was the duty of Crown when it received the notice of
assignment to draw the attention of Orion to the supplemental agreement and the
requirement for prior written consent to an assignment. Crown must have known when it   E
received the notice of assignment (if not before) that Orion had taken an assignment for
value of the rental stream in ignorance of the terms of the supplemental agreement and that
the assignment was the means by which a tripartite composite arrangement had been
financed. In these circumstances Crown should not have signed the acknowledgement at the
end of the notice of assignment but should have sent it to Orion and made it clear that it
would treat the assignment as invalid.

5. It was plain that it was intended and was known by Crown to be intended that the   F
lease and the management agreement would be treated as wholly separate agreements. The
bundle of rights created by the lease would bind Crown for the full term after the assignment
of the benefit of the lease – in effect Crown would be bound to pay rent during the entire
term. The other would be binding only as between Atlantic and Crown; following exercise
of the option Atlantic would take over Crown's obligations as lessee.

6. Crown returned the equipment comprised in the second lease to Atlantic's warehouse   G
in breach of the terms of the lease and asserted that it was not liable to pay rentals due in
respect of the quarter days following December 1992 (the expiry of five years from the date
of the lease). Orion accepted the conduct of Crown as amounting to a repudiation. Orion
was entitled to damages.

The following cases were referred to in the judgment:

Independent Automatic Sales Ltd & Anor v Knowles & Foster [1962] 1 WLR 974.   H
Linden Gardens Trust Ltd v Lenesta Sludge Disposals Ltd & Ors [1994] 1 AC 85.
Mangles & Ors v Dixon & Ors (1852) 3 HLC 702; 10 ER 278.
Paul & Frank Ltd & Anor v Discount Bank (Overseas) Ltd & Anor [1967] Ch 348.
Roxburghe v Cox (1881) 17 ChD 520.
Saunderson and Co (in liq) v Clark (1913) 29 TLR 579.

A   J V Martin QC and James Ayliffe (instructed by Berwin Leighton) for Orion Finance Ltd.

Colin Rimer QC and Christopher Pymont (instructed by Simmons & Simmons) for Crown Financial Management Ltd.

JUDGMENT

B   **Vinelott J:** Both these actions raise the same question – whether the plaintiff, Orion Finance Ltd ('Orion'), is entitled to compensation for the refusal of the defendant, Crown Financial Management Ltd ('Crown'), to pay rent payable under leases of computer equipment made between Atlantic Computer Systems plc ('Atlantic') and Crown. In both cases the rents payable under the relevant leases were assigned to Orion by Atlantic and in both cases the main issues are whether the assignment is binding on Crown and whether an option agreed between Atlantic and Crown under which Crown had the right to terminate the relevant lease without any penalty before the full period of the lease had expired was a term of the lease binding on Orion or was part of an arrangement between Atlantic and Crown under which on exercise of the option Atlantic undertook to pay any remaining rentals due under the then unexpired term of the lease to Orion as assignee.

In the first of the two cases there is a further question whether the assignment by Atlantic to Orion was an assignment by way of charge on book debts of Atlantic within s. 396 of the *Companies Act* 1985. The assignment was not registered pursuant to s. 395 and if registrable the assignment was void as against administrators of Atlantic who were appointed on 18 April 1990 and liquidators of Atlantic subsequently appointed. If the assignment was void against the administrators and liquidators of Atlantic the further question is whether the avoidance of the charge against the administrators and liquidators has the result that Orion as assignee has no enforceable right as against Crown. These questions do not arise in relation to the second lease which was duly registered. In this judgment I propose to deal, first, with all the questions which arise in relation to the first lease, and then with the questions which arise in relation to the second lease, although as regards the questions as to the initial validity of the assignment and whether the right of termination bound Orion there is a measure of overlap.

The first lease

It will be convenient first to clarify the meaning of certain terms in common use in this specialist field. A 'finance lease' is a lease of equipment by a lessor (normally a bank or finance company) under which equipment is leased for the full term of its expected useful life at a rent which will recoup to the lessor the full cost of the equipment with interest and with a return on the lessor's investment. An 'operating lease' is a lease for a shorter term under which the equipment will be returned to the lessor while it still has some useful life and a market value realisable either on sale or by subsequent letting. The distinction is not, of course, clear cut but the majority of leases can be recognised by anyone with experience in the field of computer leasing as belonging to one category or the other. Under SSAP 21 (which was issued by the Institute of Chartered Accountants in August 1984) a finance lease (like a hire-purchase contract) has to be recorded in the balance sheet of the lessee as an asset on the one side and as an obligation to pay future rentals on the other side. In the case of an operating lease the rent is charged in the profit and loss account on a straight line basis over the term of the lease.

Atlantic was prominent in the business of leasing computers. The transactions entered into by Atlantic fall broadly into three categories. Atlantic would sometimes itself purchase a computer needed by a customer and lease it direct to the customer either on a finance or on an operating lease. It would sometimes arrange the purchase of a computer and also arrange for it to be purchased either from it or more frequently direct from the manufacturer by a bank or finance company ('the funder') and leased by the funder to a customer on a finance lease. Atlantic would be remunerated either by the profit it made on the resale to the funder or by a commission. Leases of this kind are commonly called 'arranged leases'.

By far the most usual form of transaction was a complex tripartite transaction. Atlantic would buy or contract to buy the equipment wanted by the customer. It would negotiate the terms of a finance lease. At the same time it would approach a number of funders who would be asked how much they would be prepared to pay for, in effect, an assignment of the rents payable under the agreed period of the lease. Atlantic would then repurchase the equipment under a hire-purchase agreement which conferred on it a power to enter into the intended lease or sublease to the customer. The instalments payable under the hire-purchase agreement would normally match the rents payable under the lease both in date and amount. If Atlantic succeeded in matching the rents and instalments under the hire-purchase agreement, Atlantic's profit would be the difference between the price it paid for the equipment and the price paid by the funder. That latter price would, of course, be arrived at by the funder by discounting the rental payments at what it considered to be an appropriate rate of interest having regard to the current cost of borrowing. I will refer to these tripartite transactions as 'composite transactions'.

There were two subcategories within this category at least so far as transactions between Atlantic and Orion were concerned. If Orion was satisfied with the financial standing of the customer Orion would accept the assigned rents in satisfaction of the instalments payable under the hire-purchase agreement. An agreement of this sort was known as a 'non-recourse agreement' – Orion would bear the risk that the customer would not be able to meet the rental payments and would have no recourse against Atlantic if the customer failed to pay. As a refinement the hire-purchase agreement might provide for variation of the instalments payable according to whether the rate of interest measured by an agreed standard varied from the rate assumed by Orion in valuing the stream of rental payments. In effect Orion and Atlantic gambled on changes in the rate of interest from time to time. Orion would then have recourse to Atlantic if the change in the rate of interest was adverse to Atlantic. That was called a 'limited recourse agreement'. If Orion was not satisfied with the financial standing of the customer it would not accept an assignment of the rents under the lease as discharging Atlantic's liabilities under the hire-purchase agreement. It would then retain a right of recourse against Atlantic if the rents were not duly paid. That was known as a 'full recourse agreement'. Atlantic had a credit facility or ceiling up to which potential liabilities under full recourse agreements would be allowed ('the Atlantic recourse facility'). If a full recourse agreement would exceed that ceiling Orion might require Atlantic to deposit a sum to meet future instalments of hire. However, full recourse agreements were uncommon. Ninety per cent of the business transacted between Orion and Atlantic over the years was on a non-recourse or limited recourse basis.

Atlantic was not the only company which entered into arranged leases or composite transactions of the kind I have described. The field was a very competitive one. The margin between the rate of interest assumed in discounting the rental payments and the market rate of interest on borrowed money (which represented the funder's profit) was very fine, often less than one per cent. Moreover, during the late seventies and eighties radical advances were being made in the design and manufacture of computers and customers were increasingly reluctant to commit themselves to a lease of equipment which might become obsolete before the term had expired. Atlantic and other leasing companies developed a form of lease known as 'a flex lease' under which the customer was entitled to upgrade the equipment during the term of the lease. The leasing company would protect itself by requiring the new equipment to be provided by it and on terms which ensured that after making allowance for the cost of the new equipment it obtained

A   the same overall return. Later Atlantic, at least, added a further refinement, a right for the customer to terminate the lease after a given period. Within Atlantic leases which contained a right to upgrade the equipment ('the flex option') and the right to terminate the lease at the end of a longer period ('the walk option') were described by reference to the period of the lease and the period after which the walk and flex options were exercisable; thus a 7/5/3 lease was a lease for a term of seven years with a walk option after five years and a flex option after three years. It does not require much commercial

B   or financial experience to see that an arranged lease or a lease which formed part of a composite transaction and which in either case contained a flex or walk option (more particularly a walk option) would be unattractive to a funder unless the funder was given a right of recourse against Atlantic if the flex or walk option was exercised or unless the flex or walk option was made part of a separate transaction not binding on the funder – that is, a separate transaction under which Atlantic agreed with the customer that if the

C   flex or walk option were exercised it would accept liability for future rentals and would enter into any necessary arrangement with the funder relieving the customer from further liability. The disadvantage of including a walk option in an arranged lease or a lease which formed part of a composite transaction is obvious; if it were exercised the funder would not get the stream of discounted payments which formed the basis of its valuation of the lease and would almost inevitably make a loss unless the equipment could be sold at a price that would make up the deficiency. The disadvantage of a flex option even if so

D   framed as to ensure that the return over the whole period of the lease was not affected was that the funder had no control over the substituted equipment supplied by Atlantic and would not have the experience and expertise to operate the flex option itself.

     During the first half of the eighties Atlantic emerged as the leading leasing company in the field of computers in the UK and possibly in the world. Its expansion was largely due to the attraction of the flex lease and this attraction was increased when Atlantic began

E   to offer leases under which the rents were 'loaded' towards the end of the term, in some cases, after a walk option had become exercisable.

     In 1980 a company, United Leasing Ltd, which carried on business in this field, sent its clients or potential clients (data processing managers with large concerns) a circular drawing attention to the dangers of entering into leases containing flex and walk options. As regards the flex option the criticism made was that these options were often framed in

F   a way which enabled the leasing company to obtain the same overall return as that on which the lease was based with the result that the terms on which the new equipment was leased were more onerous than the terms that would have been offered if the same equipment had been acquired under a separate lease. As regards the walk option the author pointed out that, given the rapid rate of depreciation of computer equipment, the inclusion of a walk option in an arranged lease or in a lease forming part of a composite transaction would not make commercial sense to a funder unless either the funder was

G   given a right of recourse against the leasing company or the walk option was so framed that it did not effect the right of the funder as against the customer to rent payable during the entire term, the obligation after the operation of the walk option being thrown upon the leasing company. Moreover, if the walk option were exercisable at a time when the equipment had little if any resale value, the transaction would almost inevitably result in a loss to the leasing company which it could only make good from the 'front end' profit

H   derived from entering into subsequent transactions. The loss would more acute if the rentals were 'stepped up' towards the end of the lease after the period when the walk option was exercisable. In effect the liabilities would mount up and 'when increasing amounts of business cannot be written the dam may begin to crack and the total edifice will collapse overnight'. In the light of the subsequent history of Atlantic these words were prophetic. Similar warnings were given in an article in November 1980 issue of the Law Society's Gazette which may well have been inspired by the United Leasing circular.

However, they seem to have little effect. Atlantic continued to expand and reported growing profits. The profits, of course, represented the profit made by Atlantic at the inception of a composite transaction; the probable loss on the operation of the walk option would be a contingent liability which would not appear in the accounts but only in a note to the accounts.

Orion is a subsidiary of Orion Leasing Holdings Ltd, itself a direct or indirect subsidiary of the Royal Bank of Canada. In 1985 it was one of a number of funders who provided finance for Atlantic. The normal procedure when Atlantic sought finance for an arranged lease or a composite transaction was to negotiate the terms of the proposed lease with the customer and to circularise a number of funders with details of the proposed term and rentals and to invite them to quote the price they would pay to take over the benefit of the rental stream. In the case of Atlantic the customer would be asked to sign the front page of a lease containing these details which operated as an irrevocable offer by the customer to enter into the lease when signed by Atlantic. If Orion was the selected funder it would make an offer conditionally on being satisfied as to the financial standing of the customer. In the case of a substantial customer these checks might be completed within 12 hours or less. The credit check rarely took more than two days. On completion of the credit check, Orion would say whether they were willing to make finance available and, if so, how much they were willing to pay and whether the transaction would be accepted on a non-recourse or a recourse basis. If on a full recourse basis Orion would have to ensure that the potential liability of Atlantic fell within the Atlantic recourse facility or was otherwise adequately provided for. These negotiations were to large extent carried out on the telephone or by the exchange of faxes and under considerable pressure of time. Atlantic tended to bunch transactions towards the end of each quarterly accounting period.

Under its usual procedures, if Orion accepted the transaction the payment to Atlantic would be made when Atlantic had supplied the following documents:

(1) Two originals of the lease, one signed by the customer and one by Atlantic. The detailed terms of the lease were set out in a printed schedule of which Orion already had a copy. As I have already mentioned, the front page would contain details of the equipment, the term, the date of commencement of the term, of the rent and the signature of persons authorised to sign on behalf of the customer and of Atlantic. I shall have to say more about the conditions printed at the foot of the document later.

(2) An acceptance note in standard form signed on behalf of the customer and confirming that the equipment had been delivered, that the lease was in full force, that the lessee would enter into a maintenance agreement with the manufacturer, that the equipment would be fully insured in accordance with details provided on an insurance advice and that the premiums would be duly paid.

(3) An insurance advice signed on behalf of the customer confirming that the equipment had been insured against stated risks and that the broker and the insurance company had been authorised to provide any information needed as to the insurance of the equipment.

(d) An assignment by Atlantic to Orion of the benefit of the lease.

(e) A copy of the notice of assignment given to the customer and countersigned by the customer.

(f) Atlantic's invoice.

On production of these documents Orion would pay the agreed sum to Atlantic and Atlantic and Orion would enter into a hire-purchase agreement.

A   One curious feature of this procedure is that Atlantic would grant the lease of the equipment before the hire-purchase agreement had been executed and so at a time when it either had no title to the equipment (which might be sold direct to the funder) or more frequently when it had contracted to buy the equipment and had agreed to sell it to the funder free from encumbrances. However no practical difficulty arose from arranging things in this way; the documents were often all signed on the same day.

B   There were however important deviations from this procedure in the case of the two leases to Crown which I will explain a little later.

Crown is a member of an insurance group of which the parent is also a Canadian company. Atlantic was first approached by Crown with a view to the acquisition and leasing of a large IBM computer and ancillary equipment in November 1985. Atlantic had by this time emerged as the leader in the computer leasing field and had a turnover in excess of £100,000 per annum and apparent profits in excess of £10,000 per annum.

C   On 3 November Mr Cooke, the sales manager of Atlantic, wrote to Mr Wright, then the finance director of Crown, outlining Atlantic's proposals. He pointed out that, under the *Finance Act* 1984, the old system of capital allowances would be changed with effect from the end of March 1986 and that only a writing down allowance of 25 per cent (in place of a capital allowance of 50 per cent) would be available on equipment purchased and let by Atlantic after the end of March. The equipment wanted by Crown would not be

D   available for delivery until August. Mr Cooke suggested that capital allowances would be available if the lease was 'incepted' in March even though the equipment would be installed later. He set out comparative lease rentals on the footing that the lease was 'incepted' in March and in June. It is significant that the terms quoted were for a five year lease; the rentals were steeply graduated rising from £12,875 per quarter in the first year to £179,250 per quarter in the third year then reducing to £140,460 per quarter for the fourth and fifth years. Mr Cooke outlined a flex lease facility which would be available

E   to Crown giving Crown the right to upgrade the equipment after three years and stressed its advantages at a time of rapid technological change. He wrote again on 4 February to say that he had confirmed with the finance director of Atlantic that under SSAP 21 the lease would not need to be capitalised in Crown's balance sheet and elaborated the flex option pointing out that:

F   'the equipment can be changed to non-IBM equipment at no penalty. Rates for such replacement equipment would, again, be based on initial lease rentals quoted for the proposed equipment, though clearly flexibility cannot be offered on the replacement equipment in the same manner'.

Mr Tomkins, Atlantic's finance director, wrote on 10 February explaining that the lease would not have to be capitalised under SSAP 21. The reason he gave was that:

G   'Since under the terms of the proposal Crown have the right to terminate the lease at no penalty after five years, then by applying Crown's cost of funds to the lease rentals applicable a significant residual value in the equipment is retained by Atlantic. The risks and rewards of ownership of the asset are, therefore, clearly Atlantic's.'

He added that, as Crown would have the right to terminate the lease after three years and to enter into a lease for replacement equipment, there would be an even more

H   significant 'residual accounted for' by Atlantic.

The proposal elaborated in the letter of 10 February differs in one significant respect from the proposal put in Mr Cooke's letter of 3 February. In the earlier letter the proposal was that the lease be 'written over a committed period of five years'; in the letter of 10 February the proposal was that Crown would have 'the right to terminate the lease' after five years.

Crown had not then decided on the IBM computer to be purchased. But on 4 March   A
Mr Cooke wrote to Mr Wright to say that he understood that Crown had settled on a
particular IBM model and quoted revised quarterly rentals again over a five year period
– £11,960 for the first year rising to £165,010 for the third year and £128,440 for the
remaining two years. In an internal memorandum of Crown addressed to Mr Wright a
member of the staff of Crown set out modifications to the equipment which Crown
needed and stressed that:
                                                                                  B
'We need to be the "contracting party" with IBM so that we can obtain support
and services directly from IBM rather than through or from the leasing company.'

It seems probable from this memorandum that no order had then been placed with
IBM.

Atlantic went ahead with the preparation of the documentation. On 21 March there
was an important meeting attended by (amongst others) Mr Cooke, Mr Wright and Mr
Geiringer, Crown's in-house legal adviser. Draft documents were produced by Mr Cooke   C
and discussed. Mr Geiringer said that he would want to propose amendments to the
conditions in the standard schedule to the lease and, writing on 24 March, he enclosed a
schedule of amendments. They are for the most part of little importance but one is of
central importance. Condition 22 in the standard form provides that:

'This agreement shall be binding on the lessee its successors and assigns and shall
inure to the benefit of the lessor its successors and assigns. The lessor may assign   D
this agreement without the prior consent of the lessee.'

Mr Geiringer proposed the substitution for the last sentence of the words:

'The lessor may only assign this agreement with the prior written consent of the
lessee such consent not to be unreasonably withheld or delayed save in the event
of a proposed assignment to any overseas company or to an insurance company
whose activities may be in competition with the lessee's business in any way.'   E

There was a meeting of the finance committee of Crown to consider the proposed
arrangement on the same day, 24 March. A memorandum by Mr Wright prepared for
the committee said that the charge in the profit and loss account for 1986 would be
£33,000. That clearly assumes that the lease would not be a finance lease. He said that at
the end of the five year period the equipment would be returned to Atlantic:

'unless we take out a fresh lease based on the market values at that time. We do   F
not have the option to carry on using the kit after March 1991 for a peppercorn
rental'.

That indicates that Mr Wright had misunderstood the proposal which was that the
lease would be a seven year lease – although, of course, if the lease were terminated it
would be open to Crown to negotiate a new lease of equipment which at that time would
have little resale value. The last sentence of the memorandum reads as follows: G

'The lease will by financed by Barings, Orion, or taken onto Atlantic's own balance
sheet.'

Time was now pressing and things moved very fast. Also on 24 March, Mr Cooke
wrote to Mr Wright setting out 'the documentation which requires to be signed at latest
this Wednesday, 26 March in order for the lease to commence during March'. The
documents identified were the 'lease agreements' addenda to be drafted by Mr Geiringer,
the 'flex lease agreements' and an acceptance note. He enclosed copies of the lease   H
agreement. Mr Geiringer's suggested addenda were, of course, on the way. On 25 March
Mr Thomas of Atlantic wrote to Mr Geiringer approving substantially all his proposed
amendments including the vital amendment to cl. 22. He wrote a second letter to Mr
Geiringer on the same day confirming acceptance of other amendments suggested by
Mr Geiringer. The first sentence of that letter reads as follows.

A
'(a) We understand that Crown intend to operate the proposed lease as a finance lease for accounting purposes. Atlantic hereby undertake to complete and sign any further agreement which gives effect to this provision and does not materially impact Atlantic's rights under the existing lease agreement.'

It is clear that Mr Thomas was under a misapprehension as to what was meant by a 'finance lease'; the whole of the negotiations had been on the footing that the totality of
B
the arrangements between Crown and Atlantic would be such that Crown would not be obliged to pay rent for the whole period of the useful life of the equipment. This paragraph makes sense if 'finance lease' is read as meaning 'operating lease', the subsequent undertaking being an undertaking to enter into a management agreement conferring the agreed flex and walk options.

In the remaining paragraphs Mr Thomas confirmed that Atlantic would enter into a
C
novation agreement with Crown and IBM prior to delivery of the equipment and 'subsequent to such equipment being ordered direct from IBM by Crown' so that Crown would retain the benefit of warranties and representations by IBM. He confirmed that the lease would commence on 27 March 1986 and that Atlantic would pay Crown interest on delayed payments arising from delivery of the equipment after 1 September 1986. Precisely what is meant by this provision is obscure. As later appears the arrangement was that Crown would not pay rent until after delivery of the equipment. This letter
D
crossed with a letter from Mr Wilcox of Crown to Mr Thomas asking for confirmation of his understanding that Crown would 'place the equipment order directly with IBM following which novation agreements would be signed'. It seems therefore that at that stage the equipment had not actually been ordered by Crown. There is one other term agreed by Mr Thomas in his letter to Mr Geiringer of 25 March. Clause 23 of the scheduled lease contains provision for the variation of the rent if the lessor did not receive a full first year allowance of 50 per cent. Paragraph (f) of Mr Thomas's letter of 25 March
E
contains an undertaking by Atlantic to indemnify Crown against any 'charges' incurred due to the non-availability of 50 per cent capital allowances provided that this was not caused by Crown's wilful negligence. The reason for giving an undertaking rather than modifying cl. 23 must have been to cover the situation following an assignment of the benefit of the lease if the rent was subsequently varied.

F
On the following day Mr Cooke wrote an internal memorandum seeking approval of the proposed transaction by senior management. The memorandum is in a standard form. The equipment is specified with the cost, £1,392,511. The memorandum gives the 'lease structure' as finance term, seven years; committed term, five years; flex point, three years. There follows a calculation of the value of the rental stream, which is also set out, discounted to give a yield of eight per cent as £1,898,459. The difference between these two figures (the profit to Atlantic) is £505,848. The 'planned margin' given in the
G
memorandum is £588,329. The explanation is given in an attached memorandum in which the benefit to Atlantic of not having to pay for the equipment until January 1987 (because of the credit allowed by IBM under its usual terms) is calculated as £82,381.

Atlantic approached, amongst other funders, Orion. There is no record of the first approach which may have been made on the telephone but Orion's records include a memorandum by Mr Holmes, then the funding and operations manager for Orion
H
Leasing Holdings Ltd and its subsidiary Orion, addressed to Mr Vere Hodge, the managing director setting out again the term and the rental stream to be derived from the lease; the probable source of this information is the front page of a lease signed by Crown on 26 March which I will explain later. It is also apparent from this memorandum that Orion had been supplied with a balance sheet of Crown dated 30 November 1984 which it would need for its credit check. The price asked by Atlantic for the benefit of the assignment of the rental stream is given as £1,898,459, the figure given in Mr Cooke's

memorandum. The value put on the rental stream by Mr Holmes is £1,592,176.37 arrived   A
at by discounting at a rate of interest of 11.5 per cent plus 1.25 per cent margin. The
difference was made good in accordance with Orion's usual practice by paying the price
asked by Atlantic in full and adding the difference between the two values, £306,282.63,
to the first instalment under the hire-purchase agreement. On 26 and 27 March a number
of documents were executed; they are as follows.

The lease – The front page of the lease shows first the name and address of the lessee   B
and the date of the 'scheduled delivery' which is given as 'March 1986'. There follow a
description of the equipment, of the term, the date of commencement, the date of the first
rental payments and details of the quarterly rents payable thereafter. There follows an
important printed passage: 'This agreement shall remain in force for the term shown
above', and a statement that after completion of the term the lessee might terminate the
agreement on three months written notice and that 'until the notice becomes effective this
agreement shall be automatically renewed and extended on the same terms'. Next is the   C
signature of the person signing the lease on behalf of the lessee and the date of the
signature (in this case 26 March) and last the signature of the person authorised to sign
on behalf of the lessor and an entry for the date of that signature (which is not given).
Then at the foot there are three printed conditions which I must read in full.

   '*Conditions – Declaration of lessee*

   1. The lessee acknowledges that Atlantic Computer Systems plc being the vendors   D
   of the machines to the lessor have neither ever purported to be and are not the
   agents of the lessor nor made any representations, either in respect of the machines
   or which have induced the lessee to enter into this agreement, which are binding
   on the lessor.

   2. The within written agreement constitutes an irrevocable offer by the lessee by
   its execution hereof to hire the machines on the terms herein and therein contained   E
   and on the lessor's acceptance of such offer by its execution hereof the lessee will
   accept delivery of the machines specified herein in accordance with the scheduled
   delivery and will insure the machines as required under the provisions of the
   agreement.

   3. The lessee acknowledges that there are not and will not be any other agreements
   in respect of the machines above mentioned which are or may be binding on the   F
   lessor.'

It is clear from the second condition that the procedure adopted was to obtain the
signature of the customer to the front page of the lease before it was signed on behalf of
Atlantic; the front page signed by the customer would then be sent to the funder and
would form the basis of the arrangement between the funder and Atlantic. The purpose
and effect of the first condition (read in conjunction with the second part of the second   G
condition) is obscure. They may have been copied from an arranged lease.

The lease schedule – I need only refer to a few of the full terms of the lease set out in
the schedule. Clause 2 provides that the lease is to take effect when executed by the lessor.
Clause 12 gives the lessor power to terminate the lease – under para. (i) in the event of
the winding up of the lessee or on other usual events and under (ii) in the event of the
failure of the lessee to pay rent or to perform its obligations; para. (iv) provides for the
payment to the lessor on termination of outstanding rent of an amount equal to the   H
discounted value of future instalments but so that the discounted sum will leave the lessor
with its net after tax expenditure on the equipment. Clause 20 reads as follows:

   'This agreement is governed by the law of England and constitutes the whole of
   the agreement between the lessee and the lessor and shall not be altered or amended
   except by a written instrument executed by the parties hereto.'

A   I have already referred to cl. 22 which provides that the lease is not to be assignable by the lessor without the lessee's consent and to cl. 23 which provides for variation of the rents if the expected capital allowances were not obtained.

The side letters – I have already referred to the letter of 24 March and to certain of the modifications to the scheduled lease made therein. The letter also contains an important addition in para. (18) which reads as follows:

B   'In the event that the lessor is not Atlantic Computer Systems plc, but some other company, Atlantic shall procure that such other company accepts the amendments herein contained and performs all its obligation in the lease agreement as therein set as amended by the contents of this letter.'

The only relevant alteration to the front page of the lease is to condition 2 at the foot which was amended by the omission of the words 'and therein contained'.

C   I shall refer to this letter as 'the first side letter' to distinguish it from the second letter from Mr Thomas to Mr Geiringer dated 25 March which I shall refer to as 'the second side letter'. Neither was sent to Orion.

Atlantic's invoice – On 27 March Atlantic invoiced Orion for £1,898,459 plus VAT of £24,768.85.

D   *The acceptance note* – Crown also signed an acceptance note dated 27 March in the standard form I have already summarised. However, the last line of the printed form of note was amended by the addition to it of the words italicised in the following extract:

'We confirm that the machines leased *will be* fully insured in accordance with the details provided on the insurance advice *following installation on our premises* and that the premium for the said insurance will be paid.'

E   No insurance advice was in fact signed by Crown until much later.

The hire-purchase agreement – The hire-purchase agreement is a very elaborate document. It covered equipment leased by Atlantic to Allied Breweries Management Services Ltd as well as the equipment lease to Crown. It is unnecessary at this stage to refer to all its terms. The hire term is the same as the lease term and the equipment is described by reference to the lease. The total purchase price is given as £1,898,459 plus

F   VAT, the first instalment of hire is £317,137.63 and the subsequent instalments match precisely in amount and date the rentals payable under the lease. There is a provision for the adjustment of the quarterly rents (to be made annually) by reference to the difference between 11.5 per cent and a market rate ascertained by a given formula. Orion consents to Atlantic subletting the equipment to Crown on the terms of an annexed lease; the annexed lease is a copy of the lease and schedule signed on behalf of Crown but without the amendments made by the side letters. Clause 7 provides that Atlantic will assign to

G   Orion 'as security for its obligations hereunder' all moneys payable under the lease except VAT and 'any amounts payable under the lease on voluntary termination in excess of the amounts payable by the hirer on voluntary termination of this agreement'. There follows an important qualification. Under cl. 8(A) Atlantic agrees to pay the instalments of hire; subcl. (B) I must read in full.

H   '(B) The owner hereby acknowledges that the moneys assigned under the security granted to the owner under cl. 7 hereof shall be in satisfaction of the hirer's obligations in respect of the instalments set out in pt. 11 of the schedule save that nothing in this cl. 8(B) shall be taken as satisfying the hirer's obligations to pay the difference between the rentals under the lease and the hire-purchase instalments set out herein but so that the obligation of the hirer to pay such differences shall continue only for so long as the rental payments are duly paid under the lease.'

The effect of this subclause is, of course, that apart from any interest rate adjustment, Orion had no recourse to Atlantic for payments of hire except the payment of the first instalment (so far as it exceeded the first instalment of rent under the lease).

Under cl. 14(A) Atlantic had the right to terminate the agreement at any time after the first anniversary on giving three months' notice and was then required to purchase the equipment at a price ascertained in accordance with a specified formula. Other subclauses deal with other events of termination, and the payments to be made by Atlantic in those events. I shall have to refer in more detail to these provisions when I turn to the last question – whether the assignment and the hire-purchase agreement together operated as an assignment by way of charge. Clause 15 gave Atlantic the right on the expiry of the agreement to purchase the equipment for £1.

Orion's invoice – By an invoice which is undated but which gives a tax point of 27 March Orion invoiced Atlantic for the first instalment of £317,137.63 and VAT of £284,768.85. These payments were, no doubt, set off against Atlantic's invoice of the same date.

The assignment – By an assignment also dated 27 March 1986 Atlantic assigned to Orion all moneys to which Atlantic was or might become entitled under the lease and warranted:

> 'that there does not exist nor shall exist any other assignment of any of its rights or interests under the agreement and that there exist no debt or claim enforceable against the assignor by Crown which could effect the rights or interests hereby assigned to the assignee'.

The assignment also records an agreement that s. 93(1) and 103 of the *Law of Property Act* 1925 should not apply.

The notice of assignment – Atlantic also wrote a letter to Crown again dated 27 March (but not sent until later) giving notice of the assignment. The material part of the letter starts with confirmation:

> 'for the avoidance of doubt that Orion has taken an assignment of the lease agreement only and is not a party to any of the other agreements which are now or may hereafter be in force in respect of the equipment covered by this lease agreement'.

The letter goes on to ask Crown to countersign a copy of the letter to confirm the following to Orion:

> '1. The lease agreement No. 4927/1 dated 26 [March] 1986 is in full force and effect and neither party is in default thereunder.
>
> 2. The initial term of the lease agreement is seven years commencing on signature of the acceptance note by yourselves, the rentals payable thereunder are £10,855 + VAT × 4 quarterly in advance followed by £32,555 + VAT × 4 quarterly in advance followed by £143,410 + VAT × 4 quarterly in advance followed by £115,760 + VAT × 16 quarterly in advance, and that termination of the lease agreement prior to the expiry of the initial term may only take place subject to payment of the sum of the lease rentals outstanding upon termination, less a discount to reflect early settlement.
>
> 3. Any notice which you are required to give us under the lease agreement shall be sent to us with a copy to Orion.
>
> 4. You will not permit the lease agreement or any of the provisions contained therein to be amended or waived without the written consent of Orion.
>
> 5. You have not received notice of any prior charge or assignment of the rentals payable under the lease agreement.'

A   Pausing at this point the procedure followed differed in some important respects from Orion's usual procedure. The acceptance note was modified in a way which, to a careful reader, might have raised a doubt whether the equipment had in fact been received by Crown although, of course, it is consistent with the equipment having been received but not installed. Moreover, Orion had not received the usual insurance advice. Most important of all it had not received confirmation from Crown that it had been given notice of the assignment. However Orion, relying on the documents it had received, had

B   paid a net sum of £1,592,176.37 to Atlantic for the purchase of equipment which Atlantic did not own. Indeed, having regard to the terms of the letters from Mr Thomas of Atlantic and Mr Wilcox of Crown it must be doubtful whether any order for this equipment had been placed by Crown with IBM.

Nothing then happened until 7 April. In an internal memorandum of that date Mr Cooke instructed the accounts department of Atlantic that although an invoice had been

C   sent to Crown, Crown would not be paying it for some time and should not be chased for it. He said that as Crown was 'a large and particularly sensitive customer' the situation would have to be 'treated very carefully' and that if any questions arose they should be referred to him or to Nick Thomas, a director of Atlantic. On the same day he wrote to Mr Wright to say that there had been delay in returning all the documentation but confirmed that 'the lease has been financed by (Atlantic) and not directly with the bank,

D   since you did indicate that this was your preference'. This, must I think, relate to the agreement that the lease would not be an arranged finance lease. He added that the lease rentals would nonetheless be assigned to Orion and that he would 'enclose along with the lease documentation the various notices of assignment, etc. which will be required for your perusal'.

Next a management agreement containing a flex and walk option was entered into. The signature of the person who signed on behalf of Atlantic is dated 17 April; the date

E   of signature of the person who signed on behalf of Crown is not given. This agreement is again in printed form with space for details to be inserted. It is expressed to be made between 'Crown (the lessee) of the one part and Atlantic Computer Systems plc (Atlantic) of the other part' and to be made 'in respect of lease agreement Number 4927/1 (lease agreement)'. I must read the first paragraph in full:

    '1. Atlantic will arrange for the lease agreement to be terminated by the lessee after

F   a period of 5 years has elapsed at no penalty subject to the following terms and conditions:

    (i)   Six months' prior written notice having been given by the lessee to Atlantic at its London office.

    (ii) The return of all machines leased thereunder in good condition (fair wear and tear excepted) complete with all cables, accessories, manuals and other

G   items originally supplied with the aforesaid machines.

    (iii) All the other terms and conditions of the lease agreement having been strictly observed by the lessee at all times.

    (iv) All the lease rentals including VAT thereon up to and including the effective date of the said termination having been duly received by the lessor.

H   (v)   The machines leased under the lease agreement having not been moved to an alternative location or subleased without Atlantic's prior written consent, such consent which will not be unreasonably withheld.

    These terms and conditions having been duly observed, Atlantic hereby undertakes to settle in full all further charges due from the lessee to the lessor in respect of the lease agreement.'

Clause 2 contains a similar undertaking by Atlantic 'to arrange' for the equipment to   A
be replaced by other equipment of equal or greater value after three years:

> 'at no penalty subject to all the terms and conditions detailed in cl. 1(i-v) hereof,
> and subject to the remaining committed lease period being at least three years or it
> being extended to three years at least. These terms and conditions having been
> duly observed Atlantic hereby undertakes to settle in full all charges due from the
> lessee to the lessor arising out of the said replacement'.   B

It is unnecessary to read cl. 3. Clause 4 provides:

> 'This agreement constitutes the whole of the agreement between the lessee and
> Atlantic, and shall supersede all previous correspondence in respect of both this
> agreement and the lease agreement.'

The contrast drawn between 'Atlantic' and 'the lessor', the provision requiring Atlantic   C
to 'arrange' termination of the lease after five years and to meet all further charges from
the lessee to the lessor, and the provision that the agreement was to supersede all previous
correspondence in respect of both 'this agreement' and the lease are striking.

Mr Geiringer wrote on 11 April asking for copies of the lease agreement and subsidiary
documents 'as duly completed by the lessor or yourselves' and repeated the request on
2 May. On 6 May Mr Cooke wrote to Mr Wright enclosing a 'package of lease
documentation' which included 'two copies of an acknowledgement in respect of the   D
assignment of the lease which had been made in accordance with our rights under cl. 22
of the lease, to Orion . . .' That is the letter dated 27 March the terms of which I have
already set out in full. He asked Mr Wright to countersign the acknowledgement and
return it and added:

> 'you will remember that this was the way in which you requested the lease to be
> financed and you will see that (Atlantic) is the lessor as indicated on the front of   E
> the lease agreement. The alternative would have been to make Orion or another
> finance house the direct lessor and you did indicate that this was less attractive
> from your point of view'.

That again is a reference to the agreement that the lease would not be an arranged
lease. On 15 June Mr Cooke wrote to the treasurer of Crown to say that invoices for the
quarters commencing 27 March and 27 June would fall due for payment as soon as
installation had taken place and that the third quarter invoice would not become payable   F
until 27 September 1986. He asked for the acknowledgement of the notice of assignment
to be signed and returned. The treasurer of Crown, Mrs Hamer, replied on 19 June. She
asked for confirmation of a number of points of which only three are relevant:

> '1. The five year lease is between Atlantic and Crown.
>
> 2. The seven year lease is between Atlantic and Orion Finance only.   G
>
> . . .
>
> 7. The five year lease contains a three year flexibility option to allow Crown to
> change equipment, although the supplier must be Atlantic, after three years.'

Mr Wright replied on 7 July to say that as regards the first two points a seven year
lease was in place between Crown and Atlantic and:

> 'all of the financial benefits under this lease have been assigned to Orion Finance.   H
> However Crown have the absolute right to terminate this lease at no penalty after
> five years.
>
> What actually occurs is that as soon as Crown gives notice to Atlantic that they
> wish to terminate the agreement Atlantic, on the due date, pay all of the lease
> rentals which would be due from Crown to Orion under the assignment straight

A   over to Orion and agree that no further lease rentals will fall due by Crown unless some follow-on lease has been entered into.'

That seems not to have satisfied Mrs Hamer who wrote to Mr Cooke again on 11 July and asked for confirmation that 'if Crown give notice to terminate the seven year lease agreement on year five Crown will not have to pay the year six and seven instalments to Atlantic'. Mr Cooke replied on 21 July to confirm that 'if Crown give notice to terminate

B   the seven year lease agreement at year five, Crown will not have to pay the year six and seven instalment to Atlantic'. There matters rested until the end of July when Mr Cooke sent a telex to say that IBM had confirmed that the bulk of the hardware would be delivered on 12 August for installation by 15 August. On 14 August a novation agreement was entered into between IBM, Crown (described as 'the user') and Atlantic (described as 'the purchaser'). The novation agreement recited that the user wished to be released from his obligation to purchase the machines and that IBM was willing to agree the

C   novation upon the terms there set out. There were supplemental agreements relating to the survival of warranties in favour of Crown and the use of patent and copyright and matters of that kind. The equipment was duly installed. IBM invoiced Atlantic. On 27 August Mrs Hamer sent Mr Cooke a copy of the notice of assignment duly countersigned and said that she would arrange for bankers' orders to be signed and invoices approved within the next few days. Finally on 11 September Mrs Hamer sent Mr Cooke a signed

D   insurance advice in the printed form.

Two defences are relied on by Crown apart from the defence founded upon non-registration. First, it is said that cl. 22 of the scheduled lease as amended by the first side letter renders invalid any purported assignment made without the prior written consent of Crown; as the assignment is rendered wholly invalid the absence of consent cannot later be the subject of a waiver. Secondly, it is said that the lease was entered into as part of an arrangement under which Crown would have the benefit of a flex option after three

E   years and a walk option after five years (such terms being subsequently embodied in the management agreement) and that these options bound Atlantic as from the execution of the lease and accordingly bound Orion as its successor. It is said in the alternative that as the management agreement was executed before Crown received notice of the assignment to Orion it created rights binding on Orion in equity.

F   These contentions are advanced also in relation to the second lease and I shall deal more fully with them when I turn to that lease. In my judgment in the context of the first lease there is a simple answer to them.

The unusual, and in my judgment, critical feature of the first lease is that when it and the first and second side letters and the acceptance note were executed or signed Atlantic was not the owner of the equipment and would not become the owner unless and until an order was placed with IBM (if it had not already been placed) and IBM had agreed to

G   enter into a novation agreement. It had been agreed between Crown and Atlantic that until Atlantic became the owner of the equipment and the equipment was installed rent would not be paid by Crown though when the equipment had been installed the rent would be paid retrospectively with effect from 27 March. The lease and the first and second side letters and the acceptance note were in fact no more than window dressing 'incepted' (Mr Cooke's phrase) to obtain the higher rate of capital allowances. Crown

H   knew from before 24 March that there was a possibility that finance for the purchase of the equipment would be found from a funder but Crown must have assumed that a funder would not be asked to finance the purchase (by paying for an assignment of the rental stream) until Atlantic became the owners of the equipment and Crown had become bound to pay rent under the lease. Otherwise Crown in signing the lease documentation and the ambiguously worded acceptance note would have been party to a fraud. By the time that the equipment had been installed Crown knew that the assignment to Orion

had been executed and must be taken to have assumed that the assignment was also   A
conditional upon Atlantic becoming the owner of the equipment and entitled to rent
under the lease. By that time it must also have been clear to Crown from the terms of the
management agreement and the exchange of letters of 19 June, 7 July, 11 July and 31
July that the assignment to Orion was an assignment of the rent payable over the full
seven year term and that the management agreement was a wholly separate agreement
binding between Crown and Atlantic alone under which if the walk option was exercised   B
Atlantic would be bound to account to Orion for the rent due during the remaining
period of the seven year lease. Orion's right to payment during the whole term would not
be affected but Crown would not have to pay the instalments of rent due after termination
'to Atlantic'. These letters, in particular the letter of 21 July, must be understood in the
context of an arrangement under which rent was to be paid to Atlantic and paid over to
Orion by Atlantic; after the termination of the walk option Atlantic would continue to
pay or would compound for the rent payable under the lease so as to discharge Crown's   C
obligation to pay Orion.

In my judgment it was the duty of Crown if it wished to contend that the assignment
was invalid or that Orion was bound by the term of the management agreement to make
these claims before the lease became unconditional and so before Orion would act upon
it by paying the purchase price which it had agreed to pay for the assignment of the rental
stream. The failure of Crown to do so in my judgment amounted to a representation that   D
Crown accepted that the assignment was valid and would become binding when the lease
became unconditional and that Orion would take the benefit of it free from the
management agreement. If this claim had been raised the true position would have come
to light and it would have been open to Orion to set aside the whole transaction as
between it and Atlantic and to reclaim the consideration paid less instalments of rent
which it had received.

The further questions are whether the assignment was an assignment by way of charge   E
and if it was whether the avoidance of the charge by s. 395 has the consequence of
relieving Crown from any obligation to pay rent to Orion.

Was the assignment by way of charge?

The assignment was clearly an assignment of future book debts (rent due and to
become due) within s. 396(1)(e) (see *Independent Automatic Sales v Knowles & Foster*   F
[1962] 1 WLR 974 and *Paul & Frank Ltd v Discount Bank* [1967] Ch 348). The case for
Orion is that the assignment was in substance an outright assignment. The assignment
must clearly be read together with the hire-purchase agreement. It was made pursuant to
cl. 7 of the hire-purchase agreement which provided that Atlantic 'as security for its
obligations hereunder' would assign to Orion all moneys then or to become payable
under the lease 'to the intent that they be charged with payment of all moneys now or
hereafter owing to' Orion under the hire-purchase agreement; the assignment itself   G
contains provisions negating the operation of s. 93(1) and 103 of the *Law of Property Act*
1925 which, of course, relate to rights of consolidation and powers of sale under
mortgages. Mr Martin, who appeared for Orion, submitted that despite the terms of the
assignment and hire-purchase agreement Atlantic was left with no equity of redemption
and that the assignment was accordingly incapable of operating as a security. I have
already referred to cl. 8(B) under which Orion acknowledged that the assignment of the   H
rents was to be in satisfaction of Atlantic's obligations to pay instalments of hire. Mr
Martin subjected the other provisions of the hire-purchase agreement relating to
involuntary termination, to termination in event of default by Atlantic and to voluntary
termination, to a detailed analysis designed to show that although on voluntary
termination Atlantic had the right to repurchase the lease, in none of these events could
moneys payable under the lease operate as security for any obligation of Atlantic. The

A   difficulty which confronts this argument is that even if well founded (and I do not find it necessary to set out in detail all the provisions of the hire-purchase agreement and the payments to be made in the event of termination) nonetheless so long as the provision for adjustment of the instalments of hire (reflecting differences between the market rate of interest for the time being, ascertained in accordance with the formula in pt. 2 of the first schedule to the hire-purchase agreement and 11.5 per cent) remained in operation, the instalments of hire might be more or less than the rent payable under the lease. If less

B   then Atlantic was entitled to be repaid annually the amount of the difference. Its entitlement reflects its right as chargor to a surplus over the amount required to discharge its liability in the hands of Orion. Mr Martin pointed out that Atlantic is entitled to be paid the amount of a difference in its favour under the express terms of the schedule but that cannot, I think, be treated as a contractual right independent of its right as chargor. This can be illustrated by an invoice by Orion showing the amount due from Atlantic on

C   27 March 1987. The rental for the quarter then due was £32,555. The adjustments falling to be made in respect of that and the preceding four quarterly instalments left a net liability of £24,152.14. Of course, in fact nothing was paid by Orion to Atlantic; as I have said the arrangement was that Crown would pay Atlantic and that Atlantic would pay the rent due from Crown after any adjustment to its obligation to pay instalments made in accordance with the hire-purchase agreement. However, that was an arrangement made for reasons of convenience and the practical result was the same as if the rents had

D   been paid by Crown to Orion and if Orion had then accounted the difference between the rents and the adjusted instalments of hire to Atlantic as chargor.

Was the assignment void as against Crown?

Mr Martin submitted that the effect of s. 395 is to avoid the assignment as between the administrators and liquidators of Atlantic and Orion but not as between Crown and

E   Orion. He relied upon a short passage in the judgment of Lush J in *Saunderson and Co (in liq) v Clark* (1913) 29 TLR 579 where Lush J is reported as having said:

> 'He thought that S. 93 (the predecessor of S. 395) did nothing more than avoid the security as between the parties to the transaction.'

That statement must be read in the context of the argument addressed to Lush J. A company had executed an assignment to its bankers of a debt due from the defendant or

F   so much as might be necessary to indemnify the bank for a sum advanced to the company. Shortly thereafter the company wrote to the defendant requesting him to pay the debt due to the bankers. The company later went into voluntary liquidation. The assignment had not been registered. The defendant paid the bank and later the liquidator sued the defendant. One of the arguments advanced on behalf of the defendant was that the letter operated as an equitable assignment and that the defendant was entitled to pay the bank in reliance upon it. Lush J observed that:

G   > 'The company had already mortgaged the debt, and the letter was written to ensure the carrying out of the arrangement. It gave the bankers no right to demand a legal assignment, or payment, except on the terms of the indenture. If, however, the defendant had received the letter and nothing more and had complied with the directions and had paid accordingly, it was probably true that he would have been protected and would not have been compelled to pay the liquidator.'

H   I do not think that observation assists Mr Martin. I think Lush J was contemplating a situation where there had been no assignment by way of charge but a debtor had been directed by the company prior to the liquidation to pay a debt due to the company to another and had complied with his creditor's direction.

In my judgment the short answer to Mr Martin's submission is that s. 395 clearly avoids the assignment as between the administrators or liquidators of Atlantic and Orion.

It follows that notice of the assignment would not afford any defence to Crown if sued
by the administrators or liquidators in respect of a period prior to the exercise of the
walk option. So, if Mr Martin's submission were well founded, Crown might be faced by
two claims for the same rent. It cannot, I think, make any difference that the result of the
avoidance of the assignment as between Atlantic and Orion was to put Crown in a
position, when the walk option became exercisable, to terminate the lease and so prevent
Orion from recovering rent which could never have been an asset of Atlantic (in effect,
substituting an unsecured claim by Orion for instalments under the hire-purchase
agreement for the unsecured claim by Crown for the equivalent amount of rent which it
would have had to pay to Orion under the lease if it had not been terminated).

In my judgment, therefore, s. 395 is a complete defence to Orion's action on the first
lease which must accordingly be dismissed.

The second lease

The second lease was negotiated towards the end of 1987. Before the negotiations
started Crown had been alarmed and put on guard by an article in *Computing* headed
'Atlantic – your not so flexible leasing friend?'. The main points made in this lengthy
article are the same as the points made in the circular by United Leasing Ltd in 1980.
The difference is that the article is directed to Atlantic and details specific criticism made
by dissatisfied customers of Atlantic. The article takes as typical a 6/5/3 flex lease. One
point made early in the article is that the structure used by Atlantic, a six year lease which
is assigned to a funder coupled with an arrangement under which the lease can be
terminated after five years or 'flexed' after three years (Atlantic in either event agreeing
with the customer to pay any balance due to the funder), has the result that 'if for any
reason walking away turns out to be difficult: or if Atlantic were to go out of business the
customer would again be left to cover the full term'. The author cites a representative of
Atlantic whom he had interviewed as describing the six year lease as 'a hell or high water
contract'. By that is clearly meant one under which a funder taking an assignment of a
lease is entitled to be paid for the whole of the lease term come what may. The
representative of Atlantic interviewed was then reported as having said that 'worries
about Atlantic's future are ridiculous; any customer with doubts should simply not get
involved in a flex lease'. The author quotes the observation in the 1980 article that there
was a danger that with a lease financed in this way Atlantic would take its profit at the
front end but inevitably build up a contingent liability for the period after the exercise of
the walk option and until the end of the finance term which at a time when second hand
computers had little resale value would balloon and ultimately burst.

So far the article follows much the same territory as the 1980 circular. However the
larger part of the article is directed to specific criticisms of the flex option. The main point
that is made is that the advantage of the flex option may transpire to be only apparent.
It is said that, for example, on one construction of the standard flex option it can only be
exercised if the customer meets all payments up to the walk point; it is said that the
customer on exercising the flex option must return all original cables and manuals in
mint condition; it is said that under the standard flex option the customer is bound to
accept whatever price Atlantic puts on the substituted equipment and that the provision
that the rent charge will be 'based on current market leasing rates' gives Atlantic excessive
flexibility given the rate of return built into the calculation of rates payable under the
finance lease for the whole term. The article concludes with a list of difficulties
experienced by a number of well known customers in operating the flex option.

The publication of this article led to a number of meetings between Crown and Atlantic
in the course of which Crown sought modifications to the first lease and its related
documents. Orion were not a party to these negotiations and they are irrelevant to the

A   claim by Orion in relation to the first lease. They are only material as part of the background to negotiations for the second lease.

In July 1987 Crown had on order from IBM some further computer equipment (line interface couplers) ancillary to the equipment comprised in the first lease. Atlantic agreed to finance the acquisition of this equipment. The original proposal was that it would be bought on a five year finance lease with no walk or flex option. A novation agreement

B   was entered into between IBM and Crown and Atlantic in August. The front page of a lease and an acceptance note were signed by Crown – the lease on 7 August and the acceptance note on 15 September 1987. The benefit of the lease was offered to and accepted by Orion; a memorandum in standard form dated 30 September records Mr Vere Hodge's approval of a proposal by Mr Holmes to take an assignment of a level stream of rentals of £6,597 per quarter over a five year term. A hire-purchase agreement was signed on behalf of Atlantic on 30 October. However the transaction did not go

C   through in this form. A letter from Mr Foster, sales manager of Atlantic, to Mr Hudson, data manager of Crown, dated 16 November pointed out that the disc controllers and disc drives to which this new equipment would be attached were held on a lease terminating in March 1991 (that is the date on which the walk option in the first lease could be operated) and that the lease could be flexed after March 1989. He suggested ways in which the new equipment could be financed so as to match the existing

D   equipment. Both the ways suggested involved a five year committed lease term with an option to flex either in March 1991 or March 1989. That last proposal later emerged as the basis of a new front sheet of the proposed lease. However, the term is now six years at a flat rental of £6,969 per quarter. This front sheet was signed on behalf of Crown on 15 December. It is in the same form as the earlier front sheet except for cl. 3 of the 'declaration of lessee' at the foot which reads as follows:

E   '3. The lessee acknowledges that this is the entire agreement in respect of the leasing of the machines and that there are not or will not be any other agreements which may be binding on the lessor unless they are in writing signed by the lessor.'

The full terms of the lease set out in the schedule are unaltered. However as in the first lease there was an addendum or supplemental agreement also signed by Crown on 15 December. It is in substantially the same terms as the earlier supplemental agreement.

F   An internal memorandum of Atlantic dated 15 December 1987 gives the lease structure as finance term, six years; committed term, five years; flex point, one-and-a-quarter years; and values the rentals discounted at 9.5 per cent at £129,381 and gives Atlantic's profit as £23,961. The hire-purchase agreement was then modified by a substitution of a new schedule dated 31 December 1987 in which the hire term is increased to six years from 31 September 1987. The rentals as before match the payments under the lease except for the first rental payment due on 31 December 1987 which is £11,937.82. This again reflects

G   the difference between the invoice price charged by Atlantic and Orion's valuation of the stream of income, the difference being added to the first rental payment. The front page of the lease and the addendum were both then signed on behalf of Atlantic, also on 31 December, and the transaction so far as Orion was concerned was complete. An acceptance note and an insurance advice (dated 4 December 1987) had already been completed.

H   On 15 December a management agreement was signed on behalf of Crown. It was signed on behalf of Atlantic on 12 April. Clause 1 of the management agreement is in substantially the same terms as cl. 1 of the earlier agreement. There are significant differences to the flex option (exercisable after 1.25 years so as to match the flex option in the first lease) which was amended to take account of proposals put forward by Crown after the article in *Computing*.

The assignment by Atlantic to Orion is dated 20 January 1988. It is in the same terms
as the earlier assignment. On 2 February the assignment was registered at the companies
registration office as a mortgage or charge securing moneys due under the hire-purchase
contract, the date of which is there given as 30 October 1987.

A notice of assignment dated 20 January 1988 which is in the same terms as the earlier
assignment was sent to Crown together with the lease and related documents on 12 April
1988. Crown returned a copy of the letter duly signed on 6 July 1988. It seems not to
have been forwarded by Atlantic to Orion.

Between those two dates there was correspondence between Atlantic and Crown which
is of some importance in evaluating Crown's understanding of the position. On 7 March
1988 Mr Hughes, a branch manager of Atlantic, wrote to Mr Dziedzic of Crown setting
out two available options for the purchase of yet further equipment. He set out what he
described as a 'straight forward three year committed lease term' without a flex option
and commented 'we can achieve this reduction in rentals by using an extended financial
term of four years but keeping your committed term in both cases to only three years as
you have previously contracted with us'. It must have been plain to Mr Dziedzic that the
commercial effect of what was being offered was a term of four years which would be
purchased by a funder but under which Atlantic would have to arrange to buy out the
last year if a walk option was exercised. On 11 March Mr Wells of Crown writing to Mr
Hughes of Atlantic but in relation to the same proposal sought further information as to
the first of the two options set out in the letter of 7 March 1988 (a three year committed
lease term with a flex option after one year). The reply from Mr Burrows of Atlantic was
that should Crown elect to take the flex option in March 1989:

> 'then as stated within the agreement, Atlantic will settle in full all changes (sic) due
> from Crown to the lessor, subject to the stated terms and conditions. Therefore
> when the new equipment has been leased through Atlantic, (Crown) will not have
> any outstanding commitments under existing agreements'.

There again it is plain that the proposal was that the exercise of the flex option would
not affect the lessor (that is the funder to whom the lease was assigned) and that Atlantic
would make any necessary arrangements with the funder to whom the lease was assigned
which might be necessary to ensure that the exercise of the flex option was given effect.

Mr Wells then decided to approach Orion direct to clarify the position as between
Crown and Orion. On or about 17 March he telephoned Mr Fricker, a senior manager
with Orion (he became the managing director in April 1988). There is no direct evidence
as to what passed between them. There is no mention of this telephone conversation in
the pleadings nor was there in Mr Fricker's witness statement. Mr Martin sought leave
in the course of his opening to amend the pleadings to include an allegation founded on
evidence of Mr Fricker which had been set out in the witness statement. However, the
witness statement did not reach Crown's advisors until a very late stage (I was told by
Mr Rimer that he received it on the morning when the action commenced). Crown had
not traced Mr Wells' whereabouts (he is no longer employed by Crown) so as to obtain
a witness statement from him setting out his recollection of what transpired in the course
of this conversation. In these circumstances I declined to allow the amendment.

However, the documentary evidence does give some indication of what Mr Wells'
understanding of the position was at the time of this conversation. Immediately after this
conversation had taken place Mr Wells sent Mr Fricker a bundle of documents
comprising the front page of the first lease and the first side letter, the management
agreement relating to the first lease and a letter dated 24 June 1987 modifying the flex
option in that management agreement (this last letter followed the discussions with
Crown after publication of the article in *Computing*). On the same day Mr Wells wrote a
memorandum addressed to Mr Dziedzic which contains the following passage:

'*Flex lease with Atlantic*

We have a justifiable fear based on press report and market comment that should we take the flex option next year, Atlantic would structure any new agreement in order to recover the difference between the outstanding instalments, which they would have to pay to Orion Bank and residual values. Atlantic could do this by an inflated capital value for the new machinery or by a high interest rate on the new lease. However, when this fear was previously expressed, Atlantic and Crown signed an addition to the agreement which appears to have been prepared by Bruno Geiringer (as attached) and which seems to protect this situation. Discussions with Imperial Trident who have a similar agreement suggest that Atlantic will only tamper with price and interest rates if the customer refuses to take a new flex agreement and wants a straightforward lease. Atlantic would appear to pay for any losses on the old agreement out of profits on the new flex lease – a highly undesirable and risky practice.'

This paragraph is directed to the operation of the flex option which had been the main target of the article in *Computing*. I have already referred to improvements in the management agreement relating to the second lease which were designed to strengthen the position of Crown if it exercised the flex option; they are similar to the amendments which had been made to the management agreement relating to the first lease by the agreement dated 24 June 1987.

Mr Wells then sets out his summary of the position. Paragraph 3 of the summary reads as follows:

'3. Atlantic are indulging in high risk deals. Should they default we would have to pay Orion all the remaining instalments up to the seven year point.'

He concludes this note with the words:

'I am aware that you have a pressing need to implement the new upgrade but I feel as yet uncertain that we have any desirable solution.

I have spoken to Orion Bank (the lessor) and on the basis of our close connections in Canada they are looking at the lease documentation to see whether they can suggest a method of extracting us from the flex lease at low cost.'

Although Mr Wells' main concern was the operation of the flex option in the management agreement relating to the first lease, it seems clear from this memorandum that he was aware following his conversion with Mr Fricker that Orion's attitude was that following an assignment of rents under a lease between Atlantic and Crown, it was entitled to rent for the whole of the term of the lease and was not affected by any arrangements between Atlantic and Crown.

Not long after this conversation on 12 April Ms Davies, the customer services manager of Atlantic, wrote to Mr Hudson of Crown. That was on 12 April. She said that Atlantic had assigned the benefit of all moneys becoming due under the lease to Orion and asked him to 'sign the enclosed acknowledgement of this assignment and return it to us in the enclosed stamped addressed envelope'. That is the notice dated 20 January 1988.

On 6 July Mr Preston of Crown replied enclosing 'the signed letter assigning the lease to Orion' and a standing order mandate for the lease payments. He added that in addition the outstanding quarterly payments for the periods 31 March 1988 and 30 June 1988 would be paid and a cheque sent in the next seven days. It is not clear from the documentary evidence why these quarterly payments had not been made when they were due.

The question is whether Crown can escape liability to Orion either on the ground that as the assignment was not made with its prior written consent it is void as between Orion and Crown or alternatively on the footing that the management agreement is binding on Orion.

In answering these questions it is important to bear in mind the background to the second lease. At the time when the front page of the second lease was first signed Crown had already entered into one composite transaction and knew that it was the practice of Atlantic to finance the acquisition of equipment for leasing by selling the rentals under the lease to a funder and entering into a separate management agreement containing a flex and walk option which was not binding on the funder. They had seen the article in *Computing* which stressed both the disadvantageous terms in which the flex option was framed and the danger to a customer of entering into a composite transaction under which the customer had a walk option exercisable against Atlantic but not against the funder. It is clear from the subsequent discussions within Crown that what concerned Crown was not the possible inability of Atlantic to meet its obligations to the funder following the exercise of the walk option but the disadvantageous terms of the flex option which Crown then sought to modify (in the case of both leases). When the second lease was modified and became a six year term with a walk option after five years and a flex option after 1.25 years Crown must have been aware that the intention was to assign the benefit of the rentals during the six year term to a funder who would not be bound by the flex and walk option. No evidence by any of the persons concerned with these transactions at the time was adduced on Crown's behalf to contradict what, in my view, is the clear inference from the circumstances in which the second lease was entered into.

Consent to the assignment

The case for Crown is that as the prior written consent of Crown to the assignment was not obtained before the assignment was executed the assignment was wholly void as against it; as it was void the defect could not be cured by a subsequent consent. Crown relied upon the recent decision of the House of Lords in *Linden Gardens Trust Ltd v Lenesta Sludge Disposals Ltd* and *St Martins Property Corporation Ltd v Sir Robert McAlpine Ltd* [1994] 1 AC 85. Mr Martin sought to distinguish this decision upon the ground that in this case unlike the *Linden Gardens* case the provision prohibiting an assignment without the prior written consent of the lessee was qualified – consent could not be unreasonably withheld or delayed save in immaterial circumstances. He submitted that in the case of a qualified covenant an assignment is valid if it can be shown that the assignee is one to whom no reasonable objection could possibly have been made. Crown knew that the benefit of the lease would be assigned to a funder and had not previously raised any objection to Orion as assignee. I am not persuaded that this meets the difficulty. However, it is unnecessary to express any final opinion of this point. Mr Martin's further submission was that Crown is estopped from relying upon the breach of this requirement. Three grounds are relied on as founding the estoppel. First, the statement at the foot of the front page of the lease under which Crown acknowledged that 'this is the entire agreement in respect of the leasing of the machines and there are not and will not be other agreements which are or may be binding on the lessor unless they are in writing signed by the lessor' was a representation to a funder invited to take an assignment of the rental stream that there were no agreements between Atlantic and Crown which would prevent Atlantic from assigning the rental stream. Secondly, in the notice of assignment dated 20 January 1988 which Crown was asked to countersign, Crown was told that Orion had 'taken an assignment of the lease agreement only and is not a party to any of the other agreements which are now or may hereafter be in force in respect of the equipment covered by this lease agreement' and Crown must have been aware from the terms of the letter that Orion had taken an assignment in ignorance of the provision in the supplemental agreement under which the consent of Crown to an assignment was required. Lastly, in the last sentence in that letter Crown were asked to

A   sign a copy of the letter and to return it to Atlantic 'for onward transmission to the assignee'. This letter, of course, did not reach Crown until 12 April when it was enclosed with the letter from Ms Davies. What is said is that on receipt of this letter Crown must have known that Orion had taken an assignment in ignorance of any requirement for prior consent by Crown and should not have signed the letter. Instead, Crown should have immediately notified Orion that the assignment was not binding on it.

B   Mr Rimer's answer was that Orion cannot rely on Crown's signature of the letter as a representation to Orion; there is no evidence that the letter reached Orion or that Atlantic received it as Orion's agent. Orion cannot rely upon Crown's silence as amounting to a representation. It is clear that it is only in very exceptional circumstances that silence will be taken as founding a positive representation; the circumstances must be such as to impose a duty on the person whose silence is relied upon to correct an evident misapprehension on the part of another. I have, however, come to the conclusion after

C   some hesitation that it was the duty of Crown at least when it received the notice of assignment to draw the attention of Orion to the supplemental agreement and the requirement for prior written consent to an assignment. Crown must have known when it received the notice of assignment (if not before) that Orion had taken an assignment for value of the rental stream in ignorance of the terms of the supplemental agreement and that the assignment was the means by which a tripartite composite arrangement had

D   been financed. In these circumstances Crown should not have signed the acknowledgement at the end of the notice of assignment but should have sent it to Orion and made it clear that it would treat the assignment as invalid.

Mr Rimer submitted that there is no evidence that Orion acted to its detriment on the faith of any representation that Crown would not rely on the absence of written consent to the assignment. I do not agree. If the facts had been known to Orion, Orion would have had at least an arguable claim that Atlantic's failure to inform it of the terms of the

E   supplemental agreement amounted to a misrepresentation entitling it to set aside the purchase of the equipment and the hire-purchase agreement. At that time Atlantic would have been able to meet a claim for repayment of the purchase price. Moreover, faced with that claim there must be a lively possibility that Atlantic would have been able to persuade Crown to enter into a confirmatory assignment with consent.

F

The management agreement

Mr Rimer submitted that the management agreement which was signed on the same day as the lease should be read as part of the lease and as conferring options binding on a successor of Atlantic. He submitted in the alternative that the options conferred by the management agreement were binding in equity upon Orion on the footing that Orion took subject to all equities as between Crown and Atlantic which came into existence before notice of the assignment was given to Crown. He relied upon the decision of the

G   House of Lords in *Mangles v Dixon* (1852) 3 HLC 702; 10 ER 278 and of the Court of Appeal in *Roxburghe v Cox* (1881) 17 ChD 520. I can deal very shortly with those submissions. In my judgment if the management agreement is taken in its full context it is plain that it was intended and was known by Crown to be intended that the lease and the management agreement would be treated as wholly separate agreements. The bundle of rights created by the lease would bind Crown for the full term after the assignment of the benefit of the lease – in effect Crown would be bound to pay rent during the entire

H   term. The other would be binding only as between Atlantic and Crown; following exercise of the option Atlantic would take over Crown's obligations as lessee.

In my judgment therefore, the second action succeeds. On 16 March 1990 Crown returned the equipment comprised in the second lease to Atlantic's warehouse in breach of the terms of the lease and asserted that it was not liable to pay rentals due in respect of the quarter days following December 1992 (the expiry of five years from the date of the lease). Orion has accepted the conduct of Crown as amounting to a repudiation. I understand that the damages to which Orion is entitled have been agreed in principle and will be embodied in a minute to be drawn up.

Costs

I find the question of costs by no means the simplest of the difficult issues raised in this litigation. The two actions were directed to be heard together but they remain two actions. Orion has succeeded in one, Crown has succeeded in the other. It would be wrong, I think, in these circumstances to make an order which would, in effect, result in Orion recovering any part of the costs attributable to the first action. I have, I think, two alternatives: one is to make no order upon the footing that the costs of the second action, if it had been separately fought, would have been little if any different from the costs in the first action; the second is to take the simple course of ordering Crown to pay Orion's costs in the second action and Orion to pay Crown's costs in the first action, leaving it for the taxing master to perform the difficult task of evaluating the way in which costs should be apportioned between the two actions. It is tempting to take the first course and to say that the costs should lie with those who have incurred them but I think it is too short a short cut. I expressed the view in the course of argument that to tax these costs separately was a counsel of despair but I find myself, in view of the disagreement between counsel, driven to that despairing solution. I think I must order the costs of the first action to be paid by Orion and the costs of the second action to be paid by Crown. I would only say that I have no doubt that the taxing master, when he comes to deal with the apportionment of costs, will have very much in mind that in the second action (if it had been fought as a separate action) almost all the documentary evidence adduced in both actions would have been necessary and the court would have had to form a view as to the conduct of the parties in relation to the first transaction in order fully to understand and evaluate the effect of the second transaction.

(*Order accordingly*)

Clarkson v Clarkson & Ors.

Chancery Division (Bristol) and Court of Appeal (Civil Division).
His Honour Judge Weeks QC; Stuart-Smith, Hoffmann and Saville L JJ.
Judgment delivered 11 January and 26 April 1994.

Bankruptcy – Transaction at an undervalue – Trustees exercised power of appointment – Trustees became bankrupt – Whether appointment was transaction at undervalue – Whether power was property of bankrupt – Insolvency Act 1986, s. 283, 339.

This was an appeal raising the question whether the exercise of a power of appointment was a transaction at an undervalue within s. 339 of the Insolvency Act 1986.

The three director shareholders of a company each took out life insurance and agreed to hold the proceeds on trust with a power to the three of them as trustees to appoint to the family of the director taking out the policy and the other directors. The company became insolvent and its lenders called on the director shareholders as guarantors. As trustees they then executed a deed appointing the proceeds of one director's policy to his wife. The three trustees were soon afterwards made bankrupt. Their trustees in bankruptcy argued that the appointment to the wife was a 'transaction at an undervalue within the meaning of s. 339 of the Insolvency Act 1986' and therefore liable to be set aside. The District Judge agreed. The High Court reversed that decision holding that the power of appointment was not property of the bankrupt trustees and that the trustees' prior agreement to take out insurance for each other's mutual benefit was consideration for the appointment. The trustees in bankruptcy appealed.

Held, dismissing the appeal:

1. The appointment in favour of the wife was unilateral and unconditional. If it was a transaction it contained no terms as to consideration at all. It would be more natural to say that she received a gift, but she must have received it from her husband. He took out the policy and created the settlement upon which the policy was to be held. The gift did not consist in the appointment to the wife by the three trustees but in the creation of the settlement. The appointee took the property of the settlor and not that of the donee of the power. Thus, if the settlement had been made less than two years before the bankruptcy petition was presented, it would have been open to attack under s. 339.

2. The power of appointment was not property within s. 283(4). First, the power was not exercisable 'by him', that is by either trustee. It was only exercisable jointly by all three of the trustees acting together. It could not be severed and divided between them like property which was beneficially jointly owned. Second, even assuming that s. 283(4) brought the power within the meaning of property for the purposes of s. 283(1), it would be excluded by s. 283(3)(a): the powers were given to the trustees in their capacity as such and they held them in trust for all the persons interested or potentially interested under the settlement just as much as they held the fund itself.

The following cases were referred to in the judgments:

Cooper, Re (1884) 27 ChD 565.
Gilchrist, Ex parte (1886) 17 QBD 521.
Governors of St Thomas's Hospital v Richardson [1910] 1 KB 271.
Gulbenkian's Settlements, Re [1970] AC 508.
Mathieson, Re [1927] 1 Ch 283.

Miss M Maher in the High Court, and Stephen Rees Davies in the Court of Appeal (instructed by Lawrence Tucketts, Bristol) for the appellant.

M Roberts (instructed by M H Greet & Co, Bristol) for the respondent.

HIGH COURT JUDGMENT
(11 January 1994)

His Honour Judge Weeks QC: This appeal raises a rather difficult problem on the construction of s. 339 of the *Insolvency Act* 1986, and in particular its application to the exercise of a power of appointment. The question arises in the bankruptcy of three gentlemen, Mr Clarkson, Mr Dawber and Mr Smith, all of whom were directors of a property company called Property Enhancement Development Ltd, which in the 1980s was trading successfully in the property business, the directors having given a guarantee of the company's debts to the company's bankers, who were at the time Barclays.

In 1989, when on the evidence before me the company was solvent and was trading successfully, there was a meeting of the directors. There is in evidence a copy of a minute of that meeting, the validity of which is apparently not accepted by the respondent trustees in bankruptcy, but no evidence has been produced to me to suggest that the copy is inaccurate and for present purposes I will take this as an accurate version of a directors' meeting held on 23 March 1989, at which in addition to the three directors I have mentioned there was present the company accountant, Mr Bradley.

'Mr Clarkson opened the meeting and said the only item for discussion was personal insurance. Mr Bradley said he was concerned that with the increased profitability of the company the surviving directors would be left vulnerable should one die. He went on to say that the directors ought to take out a policy in order to enable surviving directors to purchase a dying director's shares in order to retain control. Each of the directors said they would not want wives involved with the business. Mr Bradley advised that the directors should be looking at £1.5m as the value of the company group and advised the directors to have life insurance policies of half a million each.

Mr Bradley then suggested that in order to protect both wives and surviving directors: (a) a policy should be taken out naming the surviving directors as beneficiaries; (b) that the directors acknowledge that the principal aim of the insurances is to protect their spouses, that they hold the benefit of any payment from the policy as trustees for the wives; (c) that agreement is sought from the spouses that they will relinquish all and any interest or ownership in the company group on payment to them of the sum assured. There was unanimous agreement to this suggestion . . .'

– and the minute, a copy of which is before me, appears to be signed by the three directors and shareholders, Mr Clarkson, Mr Dawber and Mr Smith.

They each proceeded in accordance with that agreement to take out policies with Hill Samuel Investment Services on their own lives. The one with which I am concerned is Mr Clarkson's policy, because the other two have been allowed to lapse. Mr Clarkson's policy is especially valuable because unfortunately Mr Clarkson has been diagnosed in the last two years as suffering from terminal cancer.

The policy has the commencement date of 19 June 1989, policy date of 21 June 1989, and names the grantee as David Clarkson, the life assured is David Clarkson who was born in 1946, the sum assured is half a million pounds and the premium is £175 payable monthly until the death of Mr Clarkson. Special provisions are incorporated which say that:

'this policy is issued to the grantee as trustee to be held under trust in accordance with the request signed by the grantee, a copy of which is attached and which is deemed to be incorporated in this policy.'

The request referred to was the application made and signed by Mr Clarkson on 14 April 1989 for a policy on his life for the sum of half a million pounds in which he said that he requested that:

A   'the policy to be issued in acceptance thereof shall be issued to me and the persons named in sch. 3, thereinafter called the trustees, which expression shall include the trustee or trustees for the time being hereof, to hold irrevocably upon the trusts specified overleaf.'

The additional trustees are Mr Dawber and Mr Smith named in the third schedule.

The trusts specified overleaf are so far as material:

B

'(1) The trustees shall stand possessed of the policy and the full benefit thereof (hereinafter together called the trust fund) on such trusts for the benefit of one or more exclusive of the other or others of the persons named in sch. 1 in such shares and subject to such terms and limitations as the trustees being at least two in number or a trust corporation shall from time to time in their absolute discretion by deed or deeds revocable or irrevocable having due regard to the rules against

C   perpetuity and excessive accumulation appoint, provided that no appointment shall be made on or after the second anniversary of the death of the settlor.' The settlor being Mr Clarkson himself. 'Subject as aforesaid, the trustees shall hold the trust fund and the income thereof from the date of this trust deed in trust for the person or persons whose names are set out in sch. 2 and if more than one in the shares there specified or if no shares are so specified then in equal shares absolutely.'

D

There are administrative powers to which I may have to refer later.

The policy was therefore held from the beginning subject to a power of appointment in favour of the potential beneficiaries listed in sch. 1, who include any spouse of the settlor and any child or grandchild of the settlor. The only person at present living who is within that class is the appellant today, Mrs Clarkson, the wife of David Clarkson.

E   The second paragraph of sch. 1 includes any person shown in sch. 2 below, who are the immediate beneficiaries, who are named as Mr Dawber and Mr Smith. So, subject to a power of appointment exercisable by the trustees, being not less than two in number, in favour of a class which, so far as material, has only included Mrs Clarkson, Mr Dawber and Mr Smith, the policy is held upon trust for Mr Dawber and Mr Smith in equal shares. The administrative powers include a power to remove any beneficiary from the class of potential beneficiaries, power to lend and a power vested in the settlor of

F   appointing new or additional trustees and removing trustees.

In 1990 a larger part of the company's borrowing was effectively transferred to the Bristol & West Building Society, again supported by personal guarantees from the three directors. In 1991 the company hit trouble and it soon became apparent that the company was not able to continue trading; a receiver was appointed on 24 June 1991, the directors' guarantees were called in, first by Barclays in July and later by Bristol & West in October

G   1991. During the course of 1991 the other two directors, Mr Dawber and Mr Smith, allowed their policies to lapse, but Mr Clarkson, who was by now aware of his state of health, kept his policy going out of his own income so far as he was able or it was kept going for him by members of his family, including possibly his wife.

On 22 October 1991 a revocable appointment in Hill Samuels' form D5 was obtained by Mr Clarkson from Hill Samuels and executed by him on the face of it. By the face of

H   the deed Mr Clarkson, who is described as the appointor, purports to appoint in exercise of a power of appointment conferred on him by the trust deed the whole of the trust fund to his wife, Linda Kathleen Clarkson, reserving to himself the right to revoke the appointment. The deed is signed by him on 22 October 1991 in the presence of a witness, and on the back of the form the trustees acknowledge receipt of the notice of this appointment and there are then the signatures of Mr Smith and Mr Dawber, who, together with Mr Clarkson, formed the persons who, in my judgment, were, provided

they were two in number, able to exercise the power of appointment. It seems to me
arguable, to say the least, that although the trustees did execute this appointment on the
reverse, this was not a valid appointment because it was effectively made by only Mr
Clarkson who was one of the three persons who were nominated as trustees and were
entitled to exercise the power of appointment in favour of Mrs Clarkson or the other
potential beneficiaries. I do not think I need decide that point because just over a year
later on 12 November 1992 in order to remove any doubt there was an appointment
properly executed by them all in favour of Mrs Clarkson and this time no power of
revocation was reserved.

The Bristol & West and the other creditors pressed for payment of the company's
debts and of the directors' debts under their guarantees and eventually the three directors
were made bankrupt. The petition was presented against Mr Clarkson on 21 December
1992 in the Bath County Court and against Mr Smith and Mr Dawber on 5 January
1993. The orders were made in respect of Mr Clarkson on 28 January 1993 and in respect
of Mr Dawber and Mr Smith on 9 February 1993. All three appealed against those
bankruptcy orders, but the appeals have been withdrawn.

In April 1993 Mrs Clarkson took out a summons joining as defendants her husband
and the other directors and their respective trustees in bankruptcy in order to have
determined the question as to whether either or both of the appointments in her favour
were valid, because she anticipated early receipt of the moneys and wanted to be able to
use the money in advance if she could persuade the company to split the policy and make
early payment. The three respective trustees in bankruptcy took out a summons, which
effectively is the mirror image of Mrs Clarkson's application, seeking orders that the
appointments were not valid primarily under s. 339 of the *Insolvency Act* 1986.

Both applications came before District Judge Stuart Brown on 1 November 1993 and
she made the order sought by the trustees in bankruptcy, setting aside or declaring void
the appointments in favour of Mrs Clarkson and revesting all the benefit of the policy in
the respective estates of Mr Dawber and Mr Smith so that they would pass to the trustees
in bankruptcy of those two gentlemen and become available to meet their creditors,
including the debts which they had guaranteed of the company.

The question that I have to decide is whether s. 339 of the *Insolvency Act* 1986 avoids
either or both of those appointments. For present purposes I think I need only deal with
the second appointment, that is the one made by all three trustees, because I can see no
basis upon which the early appointment which was made only by Mr Clarkson, although
countersigned on the back by the other two trustees, could be more valid that the
November 1992 appointment, and I have to decide whether that appointment made on
12 November 1992 is a transaction to which s. 339 of the 1986 Act applies.

Section 339 is in the following terms:

'*Transactions at an undervalue*

(1) Subject as follows in this section and sections 341 and 342, where an individual
is adjudged bankrupt and he has at a relevant time (defined in section 341) entered
into a transaction with any person at an undervalue, the trustee of the bankrupt's
estate may apply to the court for an order under this section.

(2) The court shall, on such an application, make such order as it thinks fit for
restoring the position to what it would have been if that individual had not entered
into that transaction.

(3) For the purposes of this section and sections 341 and 342, an individual enters
into a transaction with a person at an undervalue if–

    (a) he makes a gift to that person or he otherwise enters into a transaction with
        that person on terms that provide for him to receive no consideration,

A
      (b) he enters into a transaction with that person in consideration of marriage, or

      (c) he enters into a transaction with that person for a consideration the value of which, in money or money's worth, is significantly less than the value, in money or money's worth, of the consideration provided by the individual.'

B
There is no question that in the present case individuals have been adjudged bankrupt. They have at a relevant time executed the deed of 12 November 1992. The question is whether by doing so any of the three appointors or trustees entered into a transaction with any person at an undervalue, because it is only if an individual who has become bankrupt has entered into a transaction with any person at an undervalue that s. 339 bites.

C
I am not concerned therefore with problems of relevant time. What I am concerned with is the definition, which appears to me to be an exclusive definition, of entering into a transaction with a person at an undervalue. That is in subs. (3) which contains three subparagraphs. Subparagraph (b) is plainly not relevant in the present case, because there is no suggestion of consideration of marriage. Nor does subpara. (c), in my judgment, come into the matter, because it seems to me that this is a question of all or nothing. There is no question of partial consideration and no valuations have been adduced before me to show that any value given was significantly less than the consideration provided by the individual. So it is a question of subs. (3)(a) or nothing.

D
Subparagraph (a) provides that 'an individual enters into a transaction with a person at an undervalue if . . . he makes a gift to that person or he otherwise enters into a transaction with that person on terms that provide for him to receive no consideration . . .' I have to bear in mind also the extended definition of transaction, which one finds towards the end of the Insolvency Act in s. 436:

E
    '. . . except in so far as the context otherwise requires . . .

    "transaction" includes a gift, agreement or arrangement, and references to entering into a transaction shall be construed accordingly.'

In the present case I have the problem of three bankruptcies and all three persons who executed the deed of appointment dated 12 November 1992 have been adjudged bankrupt within the relevant time, but I have to be careful to decide which individual I am

F
considering for the purpose of s. 339(3). It is accepted by counsel for the respective trustees in bankruptcy that for this purpose Mr Clarkson's bankruptcy is not material, because he never at any stage had any beneficial interest in the relevant policy. The terms of the trust quite clearly excluded him from any possible benefit, and s. 339 is designed to deal with diminutions in a bankrupt's estate and cannot have any application to dealings by a person who happens to go bankrupt, with property which has never been his and could not by any act or event become his other than an assignment from one of the

G
existing beneficiaries. So the relevant bankruptcies I have to consider are those of Mr Dawber and Mr Smith, and I have to take them as the individuals who may or may not have entered into a transaction with a person at an undervalue.

At the other end of the alleged transaction the person with whom the transaction is said to be made is Mrs Clarkson herself, and I have to consider whether the appointment could in any sense be considered a transaction with Mrs Clarkson.

H
Going back to the wording of subs. (3)(a), I find it contains two limbs. The first limb is that a transaction with a person at an undervalue is concluded if the individual who became bankrupt makes a gift to that person, and I have to consider whether the terms or the effect of the appointment dated 12 November 1992 could be construed as a gift to Mrs Clarkson. The second limb is that a transaction at an undervalue is concluded if the individual 'otherwise enters into a transaction with', in this case, Mrs Clarkson on terms

that provide for the individual to receive no consideration. I thought at one time that
some inference could be drawn from the word 'otherwise', but in view of the extended
definition of transaction to include a gift I do not think that any necessary inference can
be drawn from the word 'otherwise', because gift is included in the definition section of
the Insolvency Act. So no emphasis can be placed on 'otherwise', which is correctly there
in any event.

What I have to do, in my judgment, is look at the position immediately after 12
November 1992 and inquire in relation to Mr Dawber and Mr Smith: have you by
making this appointment made a gift to Mrs Clarkson or have you entered into a
transaction with her on terms that provide for you to receive no consideration?

In my judgment, the answer to both those questions would be no, for two reasons. By
making this appointment the appointors were, in my judgment, exercising a power
conferred upon them by the terms of the trust deed. That is not, I think, the same as
making a gift. Nor do I think it is within the wider words of subs. (3)(a): 'enter[ing] into
a transaction with [another] person on terms that provide for [the appointor] to receive
no consideration'.

There is, in my judgment, a distinction to be drawn between an appointment under a
power which is conferred upon an appointor by the terms of a settlement and a dealing
with one's own property. That distinction was drawn in *Re Mathieson* [1927] 1 Ch 283 in
the Court of Appeal. The wording of s. 339 is very different from the wording of s. 42 of
the *Bankruptcy Act* 1914, which the Court of Appeal was considering in *Re Mathieson*. I
must be very careful of reading pre-1986 decisions to assist me in the construction of the
Insolvency Act 1986 which wrote a new chapter in the law of bankruptcy, and I have to
consider not whether the dealing in question is within s. 42 or not but within the express
words of s. 339, which is a new start. Not only is it a new start but it uses very wide words
such as 'gift' and 'transaction'. Nevertheless 'transaction', in my judgment, has
connotations of two persons involved in a dealing which are emphasised by the references
to 'transaction with any person'. An appointment seems to me to be a different matter
and not caught by the wide words of s. 339(3)(a). It may be that without the definition
section a gift would not be caught as well by parity of reasoning, but gift clearly comes in
because of the express wording of the first limb of subpara. (3)(a) and by the reference to
'gift' in the definition section. The definition section makes no reference to an
appointment, and in my judgment an appointment is not within the terms of that
subsection.

There is another reason, in my judgment, why Mr Smith and Mr Dawber, if asked in
November 1992, 'Have you made a gift to Mrs Clarkson or have you entered into a
transaction with her on terms that provide for you to receive no consideration?' would
have said, 'No', and it is this. The minute in 1989 clearly records an agreement that the
respective policies should be held upon trust for the wife of the person who took out the
policy and was to pay the premiums under it. There was, it is recorded by the minute,
'unanimous agreement' 'that the directors acknowledge that the principal aim of the
insurances is to protect their spouses' and 'that they hold the benefit of any payment
from the policy as trustees for the wives'.

From that can, I think, be deduced an agreement between the respective directors that
they would, if so required by another director, join in an appointment of the policy, in
which they would otherwise benefit because they were the director other than the director
taking out the policy, in favour of that director's wife.

The persons making the appointment therefore, other than Mr Clarkson, were not
doing so on terms that provided for them to receive no consideration. In effect they had
already had the consideration in that Mr Clarkson had agreed that if so required he
would join in an appointment with them in favour of their wives respectively of the

A policies in which Mr Clarkson would otherwise have benefited. The clear intention was that the money should go to the respective wives, and it would, in my judgment, have been monstrous for Mr Dawber or Mr Smith if asked by Mr Clarkson in November 1992 to join in an appointment of a policy under which he or his family had been paying all the premiums, to have refused to do so and said, 'No, thank you very much. We know you have been paying the premiums. We know you are in poor health and half a million is coming in very soon. We will keep the money, thank you very much, and Mrs Clarkson

B will not get an appointment in her favour.' In my judgment there already had been consideration for the other directors in the mutual agreement that the respective policy moneys should go to their respective wives. This was a commercial transaction and although Mr Dawber and Mr Smith chose to let their own policies lapse that does not, in my judgment, relieve them from any obligation to Mr Clarkson who had provided the antecedent consideration for their arrangement or undertaking or contractual obligation

C to join in an appointment in favour of Mrs Clarkson.

For those reasons, in my judgment, the appointment of November 1992 and by similar reasoning the appointment of October 1991, if it was effectively executed by the other two trustees, do not infringe s. 339 and the District Judge was wrong to make an order under that section attempting to restore the position to what it would have been if the two bankrupts had not joined in that appointment.

D I should add that I am relieved to reach this conclusion because it does seem to me that the District Judge's order raises problems as to the efficacy of any order attempting to restore the position. By restoring the position and setting aside the previous appointment one leaves open the questions of, first, whether the existing trustees (who remain the three bankrupts and are not displaced by their bankruptcy, although it is open to appoint new trustees under the terms of the Trustee Act) can make a new appointment now in favour of Mrs Clarkson. There is the further problem of whether, if

E those trustees could not make a new appointment, Mr Clarkson could, in exercise of his power to remove the trustees, appoint new trustees who would be willing to appoint to Mrs Clarkson. In either event an order restoring the position could well be nugatory.

In this context I think it is important to bear in mind s. 283, which contains the definition of the bankrupt's estate to include 'all property belonging to or vested in the bankrupt at the commencement of the bankruptcy' with the exclusion of tools of his trade, bedding etc. and property held by him on trust for any other person. Powers, it

F was authoritatively stated by Fry LJ in *Ex parte Gilchrist* (1886) 17 QBD 521 at p. 531, do not come within the first part of that definition because:

'A "power" is an individual personal capacity of the donee of the power to do something. That it may result in property becoming vested in him is immaterial; the general nature of the power does not make it property. The power of a person to appoint an estate to himself is, in my judgment, no more his "property" than

G the power to write a book or to sing a song. The exercise of any one of those three powers may result in property, but in no sense which the law recognises are they "property".'

This problem is dealt with in s. 283(4) of the 1986 Act which succeeded a corresponding provision in the 1914 Act. Subsection (4) provides that:

'References in any of this Group of Parts to property, in relation to a bankrupt,

H include references to any power exercisable by him over or in respect of property except in so far as the power is exercisable over or in respect of property not for the time being comprised in the bankrupt's estate and–

((a) is not relevant, but (b) is)

(b) cannot be so exercised for the benefit of the bankrupt;

. . .'

A

The purpose of this subsection appears to me to be to include sole powers by which the donee of the power is able to make the property his own even though that property would not otherwise be comprised in his estate. In my judgment it does not extend to joint powers, powers which are exercisable not solely by the bankrupt alone but by other persons; a fortiori it does not extend to powers which by the very terms of the trust deed can only be exercised by two persons so that the bankrupt whose estate one is considering cannot, without the concurrence of his co-appointor, make the property his own.

B

The result is that, in my judgment, the powers conferred on the trustees of the policy by the terms of the trust declaration did not vest in the trustee in bankruptcy of any of the three trustees, even though by a coincidence all three trustees have become bankrupt. The powers have, I think, remained exercisable by the trustees, and if I had decided that the disposition made by the appointment was a transaction at an undervalue which had to be restored under s. 339, I would have reached the odd result that I would have set aside the two previous appointments while still leaving the existing trustees free to go to their solicitors tomorrow and make an identical appointment in terms which, so far as I can see, could not be challenged.

C

Even if I were wrong on the construction of s. 283(4) and the vesting of the power of appointment in the trustees, it seems to me beyond argument, and indeed for present purposes I understand it is conceded, that the power of appointing new trustees remains in Mr Clarkson, so he could remove the existing trustees, appoint persons who did not suffer from any taint of bankruptcy and who could, if they thought fit, make an appointment the next day in favour of Mrs Clarkson. The result therefore in favour of the trustees in bankruptcy achieved by the District Judge's order seems to me somewhat in the nature of a Pyrrhic victory, the effect of which could be undone by the losing party within 24 hours or even less. I am fortified in my construction of s. 339 by the thought that I have not achieved a result which would appear to me to have that very odd consequence.

D

E

In the result the District Judge's order appears to me to be wrong on the construction of s. 339 for the reasons that I have given and I will allow this appeal and set aside the District Judge's order.

(Order accordingly)

F

COURT OF APPEAL JUDGMENT
(26 April 1994)

Hoffmann LJ: In 1989 Property Enhancement Development Ltd appeared to be a prosperous company. It was the height of the property boom. The three directors and shareholders valued the equity at £1.5m. But they were concerned about what might happen if one of them died. The survivors might not easily be able to find the cash to buy out his interest, so they decided that each of them would take out a policy of insurance on his life for £500,000. This case is concerned with one of those policies. It was taken out by Mr David Clarkson, and at his request issued to himself and the other two directors, Mr Peter Dawber and Mr Peter Smith, as trustees. The trusts upon which they held the property were as follows:

G

> 'The trustees shall stand possessed of the policy and the full benefit thereof and all the moneys which may become payable thereunder and the proceeds of any sale, conversion or surrender thereof and all such further property and money transferred to them (hereinafter together called "the trust fund") upon such trusts for the benefit of all or such one or more of them exclusive of the other or others of the persons named in sch. 1 in such shares and proportions and subject to such terms and limitations and with and subject to such provisions for maintenance

H

A
education or advancement or for accumulation of income or for forfeiture in the event of bankruptcy or otherwise and with such discretionary trusts and powers exercisable by such persons as the trustees being at least two in number or a trust corporation shall from time to time in their absolute discretion by deed or deeds revocable or irrevocable having due regard to the rules against perpetuities and excessive accumulations appoint PROVIDED THAT no appointment shall be made nor any power of revocation exercised on or after the second anniversary of the death of the settlor (the date of death of the survivor of them in the case of joint settlors).

B

2(a) Subject as aforesaid the trustees shall hold the trust fund and the income thereof from the date of this deed in trust for the person or persons whose names are set out in sch. 2 and if more than one in the shares there specified or if no shares are so specified then in equal shares absolutely.'

C
The only other provision I need to read is cl. 6:

'The power of appointing new or additional trustees hereof and removing trustees shall be exercisable by the settlor. After the settlor's death the power of appointing new or additional trustees shall be exercisable by the trustees hereof.'

D
The persons named as the objects of the power of appointment in sch. 1 were Mr Clarkson's spouse, widow and children or grandchildren, together with the persons named in sch. 2. The persons named in sch. 2, both as objects of the power and to take in default of appointment, were Mr Dawber and Mr Smith.

In 1990 the property boom ended, and in 1991 the company was insolvent. On 24 June 1991 it went into administrative receivership. On 15 October 1991 the company's principal lender, the Bristol & West Building Society, made a demand for payment on each of the directors under their guarantees of the company's indebtedness. On 12 June

E
1992 the three trustees executed a deed appointing the proceeds of the policy to Mr Clarkson's wife, Lynda. There was an earlier attempt at a similar appointment which was almost certainly invalid, and with which I need not be concerned.

In the course of January and February 1993 all three directors were adjudicated bankrupt. The trustees in bankruptcy of Mr Dawber and Mr Smith say that the appointment to Mrs Clarkson was a 'transaction at an undervalue within the meaning of

F
s. 339 of the *Insolvency Act* 1986'. They claim that it is therefore liable to be set aside. At first sight, a transaction at an undervalue is an odd description of the appointment. Mrs Clarkson did not acquire an interest in the policy at an undervalue. She did not give any value at all. But s. 339(3)(a) gives an extended meaning to transaction at an undervalue. It says:

'For the purposes of this section and sections 341 and 342, an individual enters

G
into a transaction with a person at an undervalue if–

(a) he makes a gift to that person or he otherwise enters into a transaction with that person on terms that provide for him to receive no consideration.'

The second part of this definition does not easily fit into the circumstances of the appointment to Mrs Clarkson. True, she gave no consideration, but this was not because of the terms of the transaction as that phrase might be ordinarily understood. The

H
appointment in her favour was unilateral and unconditional. If it was a transaction it contained no terms as to consideration at all. It would be more natural to say that Mrs Clarkson received a gift. The real question is, from whom did she receive the gift? It seems to me that she must have received it from her husband. It was he who took out the policy. He paid the premiums by deduction from his remuneration from the company. Afterwards he paid them himself and then, when he became bankrupt, his family kept them up on his behalf. Apart from that, no one has contributed a penny to the fund. It

was Mr Clarkson who created the settlement upon which the policy was to be held. If
this is right, then the gift did not consist in the appointment to Mrs Clarkson by the three
trustees. It consisted in the creation of the settlement in 1989. The appointment was
merely the exercise of a fiduciary power to select the person to whom the gift should go.
It has been for centuries a principle of the law of powers that an appointment under a
special power takes effect as if it had been written into the instrument creating the power.
The appointee takes the property of the settlor and not that of the donee of the power.
Thus, if the settlement had been made less than two years before the bankruptcy petition
was presented, it would indeed have been open to attack under s. 339 by Mr Clarkson's
trustee, but since it was made earlier and at a time when Mr Clarkson was solvent, it
cannot be set aside.

Mr Rees Davies nevertheless strenuously argued that the appointment was, if not a
gift by Mr Dawber and Mr Smith, at any rate a transaction with them on terms that Mrs
Clarkson was to give no consideration. He invited the court to give s. 339 a purposive
construction, which he said was to strike down transactions during the two year period
before bankruptcy which diminished what would otherwise have been the bankrupt's
estate. In this case, he said that the trustees could perfectly well have made an
appointment in favour of Mr Dawber and Mr Smith and there was some, although rather
inconclusive evidence, to suggest that that was what they had originally had in mind.
They were within the objects of the power, and if no appointment were made they would
take in default of appointment. So the appointment was a transaction which deprived
their creditors of the chance of getting the money.

I am quite willing to give s. 339 a purposive construction. It was intended to enable the
trustee to recover for the benefit of the creditors any property which he had given away
for nothing or at an undervalue during the relevant period as defined in s. 341. What
property did these bankrupts have at the relevant time? In the settlement they played a
triple part. First, each had individually and beneficially a vested interest in that fund in
default of appointment. Second, each was, individually and beneficially, a potential object
of the power. Third, Mr Dawber and Mr Smith and Mr Clarkson were jointly trustees
and donees of the power to appoint. The question is: are any of these interests property
which they have given away? The interests in default of appointment has been defeated
by the joint exercise of the power of appointment. But that does not mean that the
bankrupts have given it away. It was, in its nature, an interest liable to defeasance. That
is merely what has happened. Membership of the class of objects, the second interest,
was never anything more than a right to consideration as a potential appointee (see Lord
Reid's speech in *Re Gulbenkian's Settlements* [1970] AC 508). There is nothing to show
that the bankrupts did not receive such consideration. Finally, the power of appointment
itself conferred upon the bankrupts no beneficial interest in any property at all. It was a
power to deal with the fund which they held as trustees and it was vested in them in their
capacity as trustees. Mr Rees Davies said that the test for whether the bankrupts had
given away their property was whether it would, on their bankruptcy, have vested in their
trustees. That seems to me a reasonable approach. The interest in default of appointment
would have vested but this does not help because it would have remained a defeasible
interest. They might still have remained objects of the power but this also would not
make any difference because being bankrupt would not entitle them to any greater
consideration as potential appointees. What Mr Rees Davies really relied upon was the
power of appointment. This, he said, would have vested in the trustees in bankruptcy by
virtue of s. 283(4) of the *Insolvency Act* 1986.

Alternatively, he submitted that at common law it would not have been exercisable
without the consent of the trustees. This would have enabled them to produce a situation
in which the power could not be exercised and therefore the gift in default of appointment
would be bound to take effect. Section 283(4) extends the meaning of property for the

A   purposes of determining what constitutes the bankrupt's estate. Under the old law, the Court of Appeal had held in *Re Mathieson* [1927] 1 Ch 283 that the assets subject to a bankrupt's general power of appointment did not form part of his property for the purposes of s. 42 of the *Bankruptcy Act* 1914. I think that even at the time this was quite a remarkable decision. Lord St Leonards in his book on *Powers* (8th edn, 1861) said:

> 'To take a distinction between a general power and a limitation in fee is to grasp at
B   a shadow while the substance escapes.'

But the decision no longer matters because, quite plainly, s. 283(4) brings a general power into the definition of 'property'. It says that references to property, in relation to a bankrupt:

> 'include references to any power exercisable by him over or in respect of property
C   except in so far as the power is exercisable over or in respect of property not for the time being comprised in the bankrupt's estate and . . .
>
> (b) cannot be so exercised for the benefit of the bankrupt.'

Mr Rees Davies says that in this case the power could have been exercised for the benefit of the bankrupt and therefore it formed part of his estate. I think that for two reasons this is wrong. First, the power was not exercisable 'by him'; that is by either Mr Dawber or by Mr Smith. It was only exercisable jointly by all three of the trustees acting
D   together. It could not be severed and divided between them like property which is beneficially jointly owned. Second, even assuming that s. 283(4) brought the power within the meaning of 'property' for the purposes of s. 283(1), it would, in my view, be excluded by s. 283(3)(a), which says that subs. (1) does not apply to property held by the bankrupt in trust for any other person.

In this case the powers were given to the trustees in their capacity as such and, in my
E   judgment, they held them in trust for all the persons interested or potentially interested under the settlement just as much as they held the fund itself. It is true that they were not what is commonly called trust powers, in the sense of being powers that will, in default of exercise, be exercised by the court. But they were nevertheless powers exercisable by them as trustees and that, in my judgment, was sufficient to bring them within s. 283(3)(a). The concept of such a power being a part of the bankrupt's estate, which he owes a duty to his creditors not to bargain away except for adequate consideration, seems to me
F   bizarre. A trustee who accepted a personal payment in return for the exercise of such a power would be acting in breach of trust. Mr Rees Davies referred us to the decision of the Court of Appeal in *Governors of St Thomas's Hospital v Richardson* [1910] 1 KB 271, where it was decided that the legal estate in leaseholds held by a bankrupt in trust would vest in his trustee in bankruptcy in order to enable the trustee in bankruptcy to give effect to a lien upon the property which he had for expenditure for which the bankrupt
G   personally had been liable. This decision seems to me to go no further than to say that an interest held in trust will vest in the trustee in bankruptcy so far as it is necessary for the protection of an interest which the bankrupt had beneficially. That seems to me to have no application at all to the powers of appointment which are not related to any interest held by the bankrupt beneficially. The fact that two of the bankrupts were also beneficiaries in default of appointment is, in my judgment, entirely coincidental.

H   As for the common law, Mr Rees Davies was not able to refer us to any authority which said that the exercise of a fiduciary power vested in a bankrupt required the consent of his trustee. He referred us to a passage in *Farwell on Powers* and to *Re Cooper* (1884) 27 ChD 565, which decided that, when the power of a trustee to advance capital to a beneficiary in remainder is subject to the consent of the tenant for life and the tenant for life has become bankrupt, his trustee's consent is also required. This case seems to me to have nothing to do with the exercise of fiduciary powers. It concerns a right to refuse

A

consent which had been given for the protection of the beneficial interest which vests in the trustee, namely the bankrupt's life interest.

In my judgment, this is a very simple case. Mr Clarkson made a gift in settlement which is vested in his wife. The gift is unaffected by his subsequent bankruptcy more than two years later, and the fact that the trustees, who jointly exercised the power in favour of his wife became bankrupt less than two years afterwards, is, in my judgment, irrelevant. I would therefore dismiss the appeal.

B

Stuart-Smith LJ: I agree.

Saville LJ: I also agree.

(*Appeal dismissed with costs. Legal aid taxation*)

C

D

E

F

G

H

A
Re a Company No. 002081 of 1994.
Re a Company No. 002082 of 1994.

Chancery Division (Companies Court).
His Honour Judge Paul Baker QC.
Judgment delivered 29 April 1994.

B
Power of court to declare dissolution void – Striking defunct companies off register – Two companies were struck off register by registrar as defunct and dissolved – Secretary of State sought to have their dissolutions declared void to take director disqualification proceedings and commence investigation – Whether Secretary of State was 'person appearing to the court to be interested' – Whether court had jurisdiction to make consequential directions as well as declaring dissolution void – Companies Act 1985, s. 651, 653.

C
These were applications by the Secretary of State for Trade and Industry under s. 651 of the Companies Act 1985 to declare void the dissolution of two companies, and for consequential directions which differed in the two cases. The dissolutions followed the striking off of the companies from the register by the registrar of companies, the respondent, under s. 652 of the 1985 Act. The issues were (1) whether the Secretary of State could make the applications under s. 651 as a 'person appearing to the court to be interested'; (2) whether an application could be made under s. 651 where a company had been dissolved following striking off under s. 652; and (3) whether the court had power under s. 651 to give directions in respect of purported acts of the company during the period of dissolution and if so what directions should be given.

D

In one case winding-up proceedings and consequent liquidation had taken place during the period of dissolution, and the Secretary of State sought to have those proceedings validated so as to be able to take proceedings under the Company Directors Disqualification Act 1986. In the other case the Secretary of State wished to commence a confidential investigation under s. 447 of the Companies Act 1985. The registrar of companies sought formal directions to restore the companies to the register (in addition to the order declaring the dissolution void).

E

Held, acceding to the applications and giving the directions sought:

F
1. The Secretary of State, in a case where there were reasons for him to act in the regulation of companies, was a 'person appearing to the court to be interested' within s. 651, and his interest was that he needed to have the companies restored so that he could perform his statutory duties. (Re Roehampton Swimming Pool Ltd [1968] 1 WLR 1693 considered.)

2. The Secretary of State could apply under s. 651 even though the dissolution occurred through a striking off under s. 652. (Morris v Harris [1927] AC 252 considered; Re Belmont & Co Ltd [1952] Ch 10 followed.)

G
3. The words 'on such terms as the court thinks fit' in s. 651(1) allowed the court to make the directions sought. (Morris v Harris [1927] AC 252 and Re Mixhurst Ltd [1993] BCC 748 considered.)

4. The court did not have to make any direction it was asked to make; the court had to 'think fit' that the direction should be made. As a matter of discretion it would validate the liquidation. There seemed every reason to do so.

H

The following cases were referred to in the judgment:

Belmont & Co Ltd, Re [1952] Ch 10.
Mixhurst Ltd, Re [1993] BCC 748.
Morris v Harris [1927] AC 252.
Roehampton Swimming Pool Ltd, Re [1968] 1 WLR 1693.

A

Test Holdings (Clifton) Ltd, Re [1970] Ch 285.
Tyman's Ltd v Craven [1952] 2 QB 100.
Wood and Martin (Bricklaying Contractors) Ltd, Re [1971] 1 WLR 293.

AWH Charles (instructed by the Treasury Solicitor) for the Secretary of State.

JUDGMENT

His Honour Judge Paul Baker QC: These two originating summonses are applications   B
by the Secretary of State for Trade and Industry to declare void the dissolution of two
companies and for consequential directions which differ in the two cases. It has been
convenient to deal with them together. The dissolutions follow the striking off of the
companies from the register by the registrar of companies, the respondent. The registrar
was acting under s. 652 of the *Companies Act* 1985 which gives a power to the registrar
to strike off companies for failing to make returns or respond to notices.

C

The applications are brought under s. 651 of the *Companies Act* 1985. The registrar
does not oppose the applications if certain conditions are met, to which the Secretary of
State agrees and with which the court would not seek to quarrel. Accordingly the registrar
has not appeared, and I have heard argument only from counsel for the Secretary of
State, Mr Charles. As is to be expected, I have had from him an extremely thorough
presentation of the issues, for which I am grateful.

The normal power to restore a company which has been struck off as defunct under   D
s. 652 is the power to be found in s. 653 of the *Companies Act* 1985, but the Secretary of
State is not a person who can apply under s. 653. Broadly speaking applicants under that
section are confined to members and creditors, which of course he is not. So he applies
under s. 651. That is a section which is normally resorted to when the dissolution follows
completion of a liquidation and then, for example, further assets or claims come to light.
At this point I can go to the sections. I can start with s. 652, the section under which the   E
registrar acted and which gives him power to strike defunct companies off the register. I
do not read the whole of it. It is sufficient if I read only subs. (3) which deals with
dissolution. It follows provisions about having to give notices and write letters to the
company.

> 'If the registrar either receives an answer to the effect that the company is not
> carrying on business or in operation, or does not within one month after sending
> the second letter receive any answer, he may publish in the Gazette, and send to   F
> the company by post, a notice that at the expiration of 3 months from the date of
> that notice the name of the company mentioned in it will, unless cause is shown to
> the contrary, be struck off the register and the company will be dissolved.'

I have said that the normal section for people who wish to resurrect a company that
has been dissolved in that manner is to be found in s. 653, the following section. That is
headed 'Objection to striking off by person aggrieved' and it reads: G

> '(1) The following applies if a company or any member or creditor of it feels
> aggrieved by the company having been struck off the register.
>
> (2) The court, on an application by the company or the member or creditor made
> before the expiration of 20 years from publication in the Gazette of notice under
> section 652, may, if satisfied that the company was at the time of the striking off
> carrying on business or in operation, or otherwise that it is just that the company   H
> be restored to the register, order the company's name to be restored.'

Then perhaps for present purposes the third subsection is the most important:

> '(3) On an office copy of the order being delivered to the registrar of companies
> for registration the company is deemed to have continued in existence as if its name
> had not been struck off; and the court may by the order give such directions and

A   make such provisions as seem just for placing the company and all other persons in the same position (as nearly as may be) as if the company's name had not been struck off.'

Now I go to s. 651, which is the important section for the purposes of this case:

'(1) Where a company has been dissolved, the court may, on an application made for the purpose by the liquidator of the company or by any other person appearing to the court to be interested, make an order, on such terms as the court thinks fit, declaring the dissolution to have been void.

B

(2) Thereupon such proceedings may be taken as might have been taken if the company had not been dissolved.'

(3) It is the duty of the person on whose application the order was made, within 7 days after its making (or such further time as the court may allow), to deliver to the registrar of companies for registration an office copy of the order.

C

If the person fails to do so, he is liable to a fine and, for continued contravention, to a daily default fine.'

The following subsections were added by the *Companies Act* 1989.

'(4) Subject to the following provisions, an application under this section may not be made after the end of the period of two years from the date of the dissolution of the company.

D

(5) An application for the purpose of bringing proceedings against the company–

     (a) for damages in respect of personal injuries (including any sum claimed by virtue of section 1(2)(c) of the Law Reform (Miscellaneous Provisions) Act 1934 (funeral expenses)), or

E

     (b) for damages under the Fatal Accidents Act 1976 or the Damages (Scotland) Act 1976,

may be made at any time; but no order shall be made on such an application if it appears to the court that the proceedings would fail by virtue of any enactment as to the time within which proceedings must be brought.'

Then subs. (6) is material for the purposes of this case:

F

'Nothing in subsection (5) affects the power of the court on making an order under this section to direct that the period between the dissolution of the company and the making of the order shall not count for the purposes of any such enactment.'

Then subs. (7) is a definition of personal injuries which I do not think I need read and I think the rest of that amended subsection need not be read.

Those are the material statutory provisions. The following questions arise in these applications:

G

(1)   Is the Secretary of State a person who can make an application under s. 651 for the reasons that he is doing so in these cases?

(2)   Does s. 651 apply to a company that has been dissolved following a direction by the respondent, that is to say the registrar of companies, that it be struck off?

H

(3)   What directions does the court have power to give under s. 651 in respect of purported acts of the company during the period of dissolution?

The directions that are looked for here are, in one case, to validate winding-up proceedings and consequent liquidation, those proceedings having taken place during the period of dissolution. Other directions are, in both cases, formal directions to restore the companies to the register. Those latter are directions which the respondent registrar requires.

(4)   What directions should I give in the particular cases?   A

Now I turn to the facts of the cases which are very brief. I will take first of all the case of Townreach Ltd (No. 002081 of 1994). In this case the Secretary of State seeks an order so that he can be in a position to commence disqualification proceedings against the directors under s. 6 of the *Company Directors Disqualification Act* 1986. In his evidence Mr Latif, an officer of the Department of Trade and Industry, says:

'First it is the Secretary of State's case that between February 1988 and May 1992   B
Mr Christopher Argerou carried on the same business with an adequate capital through the medium of four successive limited companies. It was a so-called Phoenix operation. All those companies went into insolvent liquidation and each company failed to pay its debts due to government departments. The Secretary of State alleges that the directors adopted a policy of non-payment of debts to government departments and particulars of the Crown debts are set out below.'

There are four companies and the amounts in each case are of the order of £20,000,   C
£30,000 and £40,000. Mr Argerou has been director of three of those companies. That is the main allegation but another allegation is that the directors allowed Townreach to continue trading beyond a time when they knew or ought to have known that Townreach was unlikely to avoid insolvent liquidation and thus to the prejudice of its creditors. It is further alleged they failed to maintain adequate accounting records. So if those facts are established there is obviously a good prima facie case for disqualification proceedings.   D
But it is a prerequisite to an application under s. 6 to establish that the company has become insolvent. One does that by showing that it is in liquidation. But here the company purported to enter into a creditors' voluntary liquidation at the time when it was dissolved and it was in the course of that abortive liquidation that the liquidator reported the unfitness that I have just referred to. The de facto liquidator could make the present application, but he is unwilling to do so. The directors have been notified of the application but have not sought to intervene.   E

The basic dates in regard to this company are that on 7 April 1992 it was struck off under s. 652 and by the operation of the section, on 14 April, seven days later, it became dissolved. A couple of months later on 11 June 1992, there was the resolution for voluntary winding up. On 3 December 1992 was the liquidator's report on the unfitness of the directors and in November 1993 it was discovered on making preparations for the disqualification proceedings that the dissolution had preceded the winding up.   F

In preparation for this application there was communication between the department responsible for disqualification proceedings and the registrar of companies. As I have already mentioned the registrar stated that he would not oppose the application to restore the name to the register if certain conditions are met. These are that certain undertakings be given to the court by the applicant and for the payment of his costs. The undertakings are that:

'The applicant, the Secretary of State, will use his best endeavours to ensure that   G
all documents are filed with the registrar of companies pursuant to the Insolvency Act recording the placing of the company in voluntary liquidation and the appointment of a liquidator and seek a direction from the court that all future references to and proceedings in respect of the company shall include its number (2486190) in addition to its name.'

It is explained that the first one is required because of the relief being sought in the notice   H
of motion to validate the liquidation and the second is required because since the company has been dissolved, another company of the same name has been registered. As I have already said, those terms are acceptable to the Secretary of State.

That is that company. The other company (No. 002082) is Principle Business Machines Ltd and here the order is sought so as to enable the Secretary of State to appoint officers

A   under s. 447 of the *Companies Act* 1985 for the production of documents and explanations about the company's records. This is not a company where there has been any liquidation or purported liquidation. The dates here are 28 September 1993, when the company was struck off, and on 5 October that became valid. Here the only direction sought is for the restoration of that company's name to the register. Those are the facts in relation to the two cases.

B   The first question is whether the Secretary of State is 'any other person appearing to the court to be interested' within s. 651. Mr Charles submits that this point is a simple one of statutory construction of the ordinary words. The Secretary of State is claiming to be interested in seeking the order, so that he can properly perform his statutory duties in the regulation and supervision of companies. I am bound to say on the face of it that does seem to me a more than adequate reason for the Secretary of State to interest himself in this matter.

C   I am told by Mr Charles that an amendment of s. 653 is being considered to enable the Secretary of State in addition to members and creditors to apply under that section in the public interest, but of course I cannot take that into account in construing the section as it currently stands.

The only reason why one hesitates over this is because there has been a certain amount of authority about the meaning of 'persons interested' in this section, to which I was

D   referred. There are two cases which I need mention in this connection. *Re Roehampton Swimming Pool Ltd* [1968] 1 WLR 1693, was a decision of Megarry J in a case where after a regular dissolution had occurred – that is to say a liquidation followed by a dissolution had occurred – an infant came forward who wished to claim damages from the company. The infant and his mother were living in Germany. There were delays in issuing any proceedings until after the dissolution. The claim was for personal injuries and the limitation period was due to expire quite shortly. Because of the absence abroad

E   of the infant, the English solicitor retained by him and his mother as next friend made the application in his own name. What was held was that the 'person interested' in this section meant:

> '. . . a person having a proprietary or pecuniary interest in resuscitating the company; and since the solicitor to a proposed claimant had no such interest, he or she was not entitled to make the application.'

F   An unusual feature of this case is that the judge went into a very long dissertation about this, rejecting the application as it stood, whereupon it transpired there was a very simple answer or solution to the problem that was posed in that the solicitor had authority from his client via his mother to make the application and therefore leave was given to amend the notice of motion by substituting the name of the infant for that of the solicitor as applicant, dispense with service and order the dissolution to be avoided. So it was a very

G   simple solution to what seemed to have developed into a wide-ranging examination of persons interested in various contexts. I think all I need read is this extract from the judgment of Megarry J at p. 1698:

> 'The word "interest" is, of course, susceptible of more meanings than one; and like so much of the English language, its meaning often has to be discerned from the context. In relation to making of an order for the revival of a defunct company, it seems to me to be more probable that the word refers to a pecuniary or proprietary

H   > interest than that it embraces all matters of curiosity or concern. After all, those who are interested in companies are nearly always interested financially or in a proprietary way; the whole field is dominated by finance. I cannot conceive that Parliament intended that a man who felt a lifelong concern for dissolved companies should be free to gratify his passion by reviving them under s. 352, however deep and genuine his feelings, and whether his affections were spread among all such

A

unfortunates, or were concentrated on one favoured corporation; and I do not think that Mr Instone's argument carried him that far. What he said, when I asked him to define the interest that Mrs Dymond had, was in essence that she was interested as being the claimant's solicitor; and he did not elaborate on this concept.'

B

Now, by no stretch can the Secretary of State's interest be equated to those rather fanciful examples that the judge referred to and I would not read that case as meaning that necessarily there had to be a financial interest in the applicant before he could apply.

Then I will refer shortly to *Re Wood and Martin (Bricklaying Contractors) Ltd* [1971] 1 WLR 293, before the same judge. In this case there were facts very similar to the Townreach case in that the company had been struck off as defunct and then a purported liquidation supervened and the application here was by the liquidator or so-called liquidator. What the judge held was that:

C

'. . . "the liquidator of the company" in s. 352 [and that is the corresponding section to 651] meant normally someone who at least at one time was a duly appointed liquidator of the company and did not extend to someone who had never been a duly appointed liquidator at all but who had, without lawful authority, been carrying on the liquidation of the company; but that since there were possibilities of claims being made respectively by the applicant for work done and against him for intermeddling, albeit innocently, with property vested in the Crown as bona vacantia, the applicant could be regarded as a person appearing "to the court to be interested" within the terms of s. 352(1); that such an interest need not be firmly established or highly likely to prevail, provided it was not merely shadowy; and that, accordingly, the applicant was entitled to proceed under the section.'

D

In the Townreach case we have a liquidator who was in exactly the same position as the liquidator in *Re Wood and Martin*. He has been approached and is unwilling to make the application because there are no assets out of which his costs might be met. If he was willing to do that and the application was successful, then of course that would have achieved what the Secretary of State wished to do.

E

Those authorities have been rightly called to my attention by Mr Charles but I have to say that I do not think either of them prevents me from holding that the Secretary of State is a person interested. I am clearly of the opinion that the Secretary of State, in a case where there are reasons for him to act in the regulation of companies, is a person appearing to the court to be interested, and his interest is that he needs to have these companies restored so that he can perform his statutory duties. Indeed, it would be very odd if one public official, the registrar of companies, in carrying out his duties in regard to defectively managed companies could frustrate another public official carrying out other duties with regard to the regulation of companies.

F

Now I must address the question whether s. 651 applies to a company struck off under s. 652, or is it confined to cases of dissolution following a regular course of liquidation. That of course had not happened in either of the cases before me. The opening words of s. 651 are:

G

'Where a company has been dissolved . . .'

There is no qualification there as to the manner in which it has been dissolved. It does not have to have been dissolved in a particular way, so one would have thought: What is the problem at the heart of this matter? One of the problems is that in *Morris v Harris* [1927] AC 252, in relation to a previous incarnation of this provision, which was s. 223 of the *Companies (Consolidation) Act* 1908, Lord Blanesburgh, after having commented on the wide powers given to the court under the section that now corresponds to s. 653, said (at p. 269):

H

A   'Sect. 223, on the other hand, is confined to cases where the dissolution succeeds the complete winding up of the company's affairs and cannot take effect at all except at the instance or with the knowledge of the liquidator, the company's only executive officer. The Legislature has not seen fit to make provision for validating any intermediate acts done on behalf of such a company so dissolved.'

B   One notes the comment that the section cannot take effect except at the instance or with the knowledge of the liquidator. Certainly it does not have to be at the instance of the liquidator because the section then as now includes 'or other person interested' among those who could proceed under the section. But the main point of it is, of course, that his Lordship says that it is confined to cases where the dissolution succeeds the complete winding up of the company.

On the other hand, we have the case of *Re Belmont & Co Ltd* [1952] Ch 10, a decision of Wynn-Parry J, where, and I read from the headnote:

C   'The jurisdiction of the court under section 352(1) of the *Companies Act* 1948, to declare the dissolution of a company void, is not affected by the power of the court under s. 353(6) to restore to the Companies Register the name of a company which has been struck off under section 353. Where, therefore, the dissolution of a company was effected by striking the company's name off the register under section 353, the court has jurisdiction under section 352(1) to declare the dissolution void, and under its inherent power to order the restoration of the company's name to the register.'

D

(Section 352(3) and 353(6) of the *Companies Act* 1948 correspond to s. 651 and s. 653 respectively of the Act of 1985). I think it is right to say that the dictum of Lord Blanesburgh that I have read out was not referred to Wynn-Parry J. Nevertheless, the case is a direct authority for the proposition that the Secretary of State puts forward here that s. 651 applies in the case of all dissolutions and is not confined to one following a liquidation.

E

A case which also makes that assumption is *Re Test Holdings (Clifton) Ltd* [1970] Ch 285, another decision of Megarry J. He was concerned there with the position of the registrar in these applications and what he held was that:

F   '. . . where a company has been struck off the register under section 353, but was still carrying on business or in operation, an applicant seeking its revival under section 352(1) should be required to make the Registrar of Companies a party, as was the practice for similar applications under section 353(6), where the registrar's presence had proved advantageous . . .'

Then he deals with the registrar's costs. The registrar, of course is a party here so all I need to read for present purposes are Megarry J's observations at p. 291G where, after he had referred to the dictum in *Morris v Harris* of Lord Blanesburgh and commented that it does not seem to have been put before Wynn-Parry J in the *Re Belmont* case, he goes on as follows:

G

H   'It is thus possible to contend that *In re Belmont & Co. Ltd.* is a decision which ought not to be followed. If it is wrong, then most of the difficulties in the relationship of the two subsections disappear. However, Mr Lindsay has not urged upon me that I ought to refuse to follow the decision, partly because the case has now been relied upon in many cases. There is also the more important consideration that I think the court ought to be slow to resort to fine points of construction in order to prevent an applicant from exercising a choice which the legislature appears to have conferred upon him, particularly when the two provisions exhibit considerable variation in their scope and application. If section 352(1) was intended to be confined to cases in which the company was being

A

wound up, it would have been so easy to make this plain; and yet this was not done. True, the need for two overlapping provisions is less great than it appeared to be when *In re Belmont & Co. Ltd.* was decided. True also, there is the dictum of Lord Blanesburgh in *Morris* v. *Harris* [1927] A.C. 252. This carries high authority; yet it was uttered without this point being in issue, and is, I think, plainly obiter, whereas *In re Belmont & Co. Ltd.* is directly in point. If *In re Belmont & Co. Ltd.* had not been decided, it might have been a close question whether or not to decide the matter as it was decided in that case. But the decision is there, and on the whole I think the right course for a judge at first instance to take is to follow it.'

B

I respectfully agree with all of that. I shall be coming back to *Morris v Harris* shortly, but I certainly agree with the judge there that the dictum was obiter because in *Morris v Harris* it was a case of a dissolution following a liquidation. There was no question of a company being struck off as defunct.

C

I would also add this, that *Re Belmont & Co Ltd* was decided under the *Companies Act* 1948. The *Companies Act* 1948 has been now replaced by the Companies Acts 1985 and 1989, and without any alteration in the statute consequent on the *Belmont* decision. So I think in those circumstances one can resort to the following. Where a statute has received judicial construction in a case where it is directly in point, then the court is slow to overrule a previous decision when long acted on and more than usually so where Parliament has, since the decision, re-enacted a statute in the same terms, although that is not an absolute rule. That is a presumption and would not be applied if the decision was shown to be erroneous. There is no rule of law which prevents it being not followed, but so far from it being shown to be erroneous, it seems to me – the decision of Wynn-Parry J – to be correct.

D

Therefore I hold, in answer to the second question, that the Secretary of State can make an application under this provision even though the dissolution occurred through a striking off under s. 652.

E

The next question is whether the court can give directions under s. 651 or whether it is confined merely to declaring the dissolution to be void. This aspect really concerns Townreach more than the other company. Starting with the section, one sees in the very first subsection these words:

'. . . the court may, on an application . . . by the liquidator of the company or by any other person appearing to the court to be interested, make an order, *on such terms as the court thinks fit,* declaring the dissolution to have been void.'

F

The Secretary of State puts forward two alternative directions. The more restricted direction is on these lines:

'That the resolution for voluntary winding up of Townreach of 11 June 1992 and the voluntary winding up in consequence thereof be duly deemed to be valid and effective as they would have been had the above named company not been dissolved under s. 652 of the Companies Act at the time when such resolution was passed.'

G

One can see that if the dissolution is avoided in relation to a company where liquidation had proceeded in ignorance of the dissolution by striking off, then it would seem necessary as a practical matter to declare the resolution to wind up as if the de facto liquidation had been a regular liquidation because otherwise all sorts of practical difficulties arise in relation to what had been done under that liquidation, and undoing it, and so forth. So it would be very inconvenient if the court lacked jurisdiction to make the direction sought.

H

The alternative suggestion is of a more wide ranging term based on the orders that are given under s. 653 and such direction as 'it shall be deemed to have continued in existence

A   as if it had not been struck off', something on those lines. The argument for that would be that this company had been struck off under s. 652 and the Secretary of State is only applying under s. 651 because he cannot apply under s. 653. I am not prepared to go so far as that. It seems that it is sufficient for the Secretary of State's purposes that I make the declaration that was in the originating motion. As he is not a creditor or member but acting in a limited public interest, it does not seem necessary for me to go further.

B   Again we come back to *Morris v Harris* because there are dicta there which might suggest that I cannot make the direction, to which I must look again. The headnote in *Morris v Harris* reads this way, and it is a very brief one:

> 'An order of the court made under s. 223 of the Companies (Consolidation) Act 1908, declaring the dissolution of a company to have been void does not affect the validity of proceedings taken during the interval between the dissolution and its
C   avoidance:–

> So *held* by Viscount Dunedin, Lord Sumner and Lord Blanesburgh (Lord Shaw of Dunfermline and Lord Wrenbury dissenting).'

The question that arose was whether certain arbitration proceedings that had gone on after the occurrence of the dissolution [were valid]. This was where a dissolution had occurred following a liquidation, as I have already mentioned, but there are two
D   important distinctions on the facts that I should mention in comparing *Morris v Harris* with the cases before me. The first is that in *Morris v Harris* the order declaring the dissolution void did not in fact contain any terms or anything of that sort. It is what has been described in argument as a bare order for avoiding the dissolution. One can see what happened from Lord Wrenbury's speech on p. 263 of the report, where he said:

> 'However, on February 20, 1923, Astbury J made, under s. 223 of the Act, an order
E   declaring the dissolution "to have been void".'

Apparently Astbury J did not make any consequential directions.

The other factor that differentiates that case from the present ones is that if the arbitration proceedings had been validated, then third party rights would be affected and that might have been a reason as a matter of discretion not to make any special direction. I turn to a couple of passages in the speeches of members of the majority. Lord Sumner
F   said this at p. 258:

> 'My Lords, I think it follows that only in the rarest cases and always contrary to the contemplation of the Act is it possible for proceedings to have continued in fact during these three months when the company is moribund, and further that after dissolution, which is an event calculable by anybody from a date, of which public notice has been given, whatever is done is done at the actor's peril. The
G   Legislature would never have bestowed on the court a power to declare the dissolution void, without imposing terms, as by the section it certainly is empowered to do, if the effect of this order of avoidance might be to undo the reversion of freeholds to an original grantor or the acceleration of a reversioner's immediate title to leaseholds in the case of lands accidentally undisposed of in the winding up . . .'

H   He comments further on certain authorities and then he says:

> 'In my opinion most of the proceedings in the arbitration in this case, and, above all, the award itself, are null, for they were taken and made against a company which did not exist, and no subsequent validity has been or *could be given to them*. The respondent must therefore prove his claim afresh in proceedings, to which the appellant will be a party.' (emphasis added)

Lord Blanesburgh says at p. 268:

A

> 'It is true that a declaratory order under the section unqualified in terms does, and it was in my judgment essential, if many difficulties which readily occur to the mind were to be avoided, that such an order should have the effect of restoring to the revived company its corporate existence as from the very moment of the dissolution thereby declared "to have been void". But the expository words which follow carefully and, as I think, advisedly refrain from adding that such an order is to have the effect of restoring to the company from the same moment, not its corporate existence only, but its corporate activity also. On the contrary, these expository words import, as I think, that it is only after the order has been made – it is "thereupon" but not before – that any active consequences are to ensue.'

B

Then I think I can go to p. 269:

> 'And now is made apparent the reason for the difference in phraseology and effect between s. 223 and sub-s. 6 of s. 242.'

C

Picking up the passage I have read there:

> 'Hence the wide powers given to the Court by sub-s. 6. Sect. 223, on the other hand, is confined to cases where the dissolution succeeds the complete winding up of the company's affairs and cannot take effect at all except at the instance or with the knowledge of the liquidator, the company's only executive officer. *The Legislature has not seen fit to make provision for validating any intermediate acts done on behalf of such a company so dissolved.*' (emphasis added)

D

So those two, especially the latter parts of those dicta in those two speeches which I have emphasised, would appear to show in the opinion of their Lordships that nothing could be validated pursuant to an order under what is now s. 651.

It is apparent from what I have said that those remarks are obiter because there were no terms to be considered in the facts as presented to their Lordships in *Morris v Harris*. While of course I have to accord to them the greatest respect and consider them very seriously, nevertheless as obiter dicta they are not binding on me. In the *Belmont* case we have seen that in the same circumstances, that is to say an order being sought under what is now s. 651, a term was imposed, for example ordering the restoration of the company's name to the register. His Lordship did not confine himself to declaring the dissolution void.

E

F

I should now refer to *Tyman's Ltd v Craven* [1952] 2 QB 100, which was a case of a company being struck off the register. The application was made under the other provision. The question before the court was whether an application for a new lease under the then *Leasehold Property (Temporary Provisions) Act* 1951 was thereby validated. There was no express term about that and it was simply an order avoiding dissolution under what is now s. 653. The point was taken that the application was not valid because it was done at a time when the company was dissolved. The majority of the court held that in those circumstances and under an order made under the other section, the application for a new lease was validated without there being any special directions, so to that extent the decision is not helpful here. The dissenting judge, Jenkins LJ, differed in the construction even of the more wide-ranging provision of s. 353(6), now s. 653. The headnote I think sufficiently indicates his construction of that section:

G

H

> 'On the true construction of the section an order of the court restoring a company to the register (1) operates only to restore and preserve the original corporate status and identity of the company, and (2) may at the discretion of the court provide for the validation of acts done during dissolution, but (3) does not in the absence of any such provision validate any such acts.'

So we have here this, that if the application had been brought under s. 653, then the decision of the majority in this case was that the liquidation and all acts done under it would be ipso facto validated, but even under Jenkins LJ's judgment there was power to validate it if it was appropriate in the circumstances to do so. So it provokes the comment, well, if you could get directions under s. 653 but the particular applicant cannot bring the application under s. 653 and so it goes under s. 651, one would start off by thinking that similar terms could be imposed in the case of that application.

I think the only passage in the judgment of Jenkins LJ that I should refer to is where he comments on *Morris v Harris*. This is at p. 122. He sets out the passages that I have already read:

'It seems to me reasonably plain that their Lordships were not in these passages treating an order under section 242(6) of the Act of 1908 as having the effect of automatically validating acts done while the restored company was in a state of dissolution, but were contrasting the presence in section 242(6) of a power for the court (as Lord Sumner put it) "to replace the company and all parties affected in an 'as you were' position" with the absence of any such power in section 223(1). In view of what Lord Blanesburgh said about the possibly disastrous consequences of automatic ratification I cannot but think he would have made some comment on the automatic ratification produced by an order under section 242(6) if he had thought such an order would produce that result. Further, I think his contrast between "corporate existence" and "corporate activity" is less applicable to section 242(6) (now section 353(6)). I should add that Lord Wrenbury in his dissenting judgment uses language which by no means indicates that he would not have taken a different view on the entirely different facts of the present case.'

Those remarks are similarly obiter in regard to an application under s. 651 because this was an application under s. 653 or what was s. 653.

The final case that I have to refer to in this connection is a decision of Evans-Lombe J called *Re Mixhurst Ltd* [1993] BCC 748. What had happened here, and I read from the headnote, was an application under s. 651 for an order declaring the dissolution void:

'The applicants had issued proceedings against the company, amongst others, in July and September 1992, but thereafter discovered that the company had been dissolved in June 1992 (following a members' voluntary winding up which commenced in April 1990).'

So this was a case of a regular dissolution following an ordinary liquidation so that could only be brought under s. 651.

'The applicants sought a further order that the period between the dissolution of the company and the date of the order declaring the dissolution void should not count for the purpose of any enactment as to the time within which proceedings against the company must be brought . . .'

– and that is a 'limitation override order' as his Lordship called it. His Lordship made the declaration, declaring the dissolution to have been void, holding:

'There was no difficulty in making the declaration sought in the first part of the application. The application was made within the necessary two-year period by a potential creditor whose claim to be a creditor, on the material placed before the court, was certainly more than a shadowy claim.'

But he held that there was no jurisdiction under s. 651(1) and (2) to make a limitation override order. Nevertheless he held s. 651(6) conferred a power to make such an order in the limited circumstances contemplated by subs. (5). I have already read those sections.

I have to say that I do find, with all respect, some of the reasoning difficult to follow but I should preface this by saying that I do not quarrel at all with the result in the case. Indeed I say that the order could have been made by directions under subs. (1) and (2) of s. 651 as well as or alternatively to subs. (6). I think it is right to say that his Lordship was persuaded to that view that there was no jurisdiction by the authority of *Morris v Harris*.

In the argument to him, as he recites it, I can just pick up this point. It was submitted to him in support of making a direction under s. 651(1) and (2) that the existence of such a power – that is to say, to make the direction (at p. 752D):

'. . . was clearly assumed by the provisions of subs. (6) of s. 651 which seems to be drawn on the assumption that there is a general power in the court under the section to make orders including such orders as were made in the *Donald Kenyon* case.'

I should say at once that I would have agreed with that submission. I will come to that again, but why I am calling attention to it at this point is that the judge comments as follows (at p. 752E):

'It must be observed, however, that the provisions in subs. (6) were added by amendment by the *Companies Act* 1989 and cannot be treated as expressing the intentions of the legislature when they re-enacted the earlier provisions of the section from previous company legislation.'

With all respect, I do not approach the matter in that way. I approach it as I was invited to do by Mr Charles, that one starts off by taking the section as one finds it. One does not inquire too meticulously into the legislative history of it, certainly not if the provisions are unambiguous. That is the first point. Also, I do not see why the words even in the unamended section, the words 'on such terms as the court thinks fit' do not allow for a direction sought by the Secretary of State in this case. That is the second point. The third point relates to subs. (6), the new subsection. It will be recalled that subs. (5) had allowed the court to entertain applications to set aside a dissolution beyond the period of two years if the purpose of it was to allow claims for personal injuries to be brought against the company. That is what that subs. (5) had done, and the case before Evans-Lombe J was concerned with such a claim, but of course not the cases before me.

Having made that extension of the *Companies Act* 1985, s. 651, by subs. (5), subs. (6) says this:

'Nothing in subsection (5) affects the power of the court on making an order under this section to direct that the period between the dissolution of the company and the making of the order shall not count for the purposes of any such enactment.'

I do not read that as in some way giving extra powers to the court. It is merely making sure that nothing in subs. (5) cuts down any powers that exist already.

That has anticipated to some extent what I am coming to now. Evans-Lombe J continues his judgment with extensive citations from *Morris v Harris*, some of which I have already read here. Towards the end of his judgment occurs this paragraph (at p. 755H):

'In their speeches the House of Lords in that case seemed to be construing s. 223 as only bringing back the company for the purpose of proceedings for it or against it but commenced after the relevant declaration. The declaration did not validate anything happening during the dissolution. Further, the absence of an equivalent to subs. (6) of s. 242 from the provisions of s. 223 meant that the court had not been given any power ex post facto to validate. I interpret that as meaning that the court had no powers to make orders restoring the status quo ante the dissolution.'

A With the greatest respect I am unable to follow his Lordship on that point. It seems to me that *Morris v Harris* did not make any such decision because the order there under consideration had not contained any such directions, the validity of which their Lordships were considering. I have to differ and say that that is not the interpretation that I would put on the speeches. Then Evans-Lombe J says:

B 'It seems to me that had the facts of the present case been before Lord Blanesburgh in 1926 he plainly would have refused to make the second part of the order sought. I cannot discern anything in the differences between the new legislation and the legislation which then existed to lead me to the conclusion that Lord Blanesburgh, had he been looking at the case today, would have come to a different conclusion.'

As to that, I accept that the terms of Lord Blanesburgh's speech do indicate that possibility. But I do not have to accept that when an actual point comes before a judge for decision it is incumbent on the judge to speculate on what another judge, however
C eminent, might have done had the matter come before him. The responsibility of decision is that of the judge hearing the case. The judgment continues:

'It is, it seems to me, also significant that subs. (6) which does appear to assume a power to make limitation override orders retrospectively was added by amendment in 1989 and cannot be taken to represent the intention of the legislature in re-enacting subs. (1) and (2) in 1985. Subsection (6) by itself cannot be construed as
D itself conferring a general power to make a limitation override order. Indeed, that was not contended for. It can be construed, as it was construed in *Re Workvale Ltd* [1992] BCC 349 by Scott LJ, as conferring a power to make such an order in the limited circumstances contemplated by subs. (5).'

I have already given my reading of subs. (6), which is not positively giving a power but preserving a power that is already there. In those circumstances the power did not suddenly come to be in the section because subs. (6) was added. Subsection (6) indicated
E that any existing power was not to be taken away. I take the view that the words 'on such terms as the court thinks fit' in subs. (1) do allow the court to make the directions sought here, and for that matter a limitation override. The power is not to be found in subs. (6) ; it was preserved by subs. (6). Of course the court does not have to make any direction it is asked to make. The court has to 'think fit' that the direction should be made. As a matter of discretion it is most likely that, in the circumstances leading to *Morris v Harris*,
F if a direction to validate the arbitration proceedings had been sought, Astbury J would have refused it, or if he had granted it, the House of Lords would have reversed him.

I return to the application before me. What I am asked to do is to validate the liquidation that has been done. I hold that I have jurisdiction to do so and on a matter of discretion, there seems to me every reason to do so. What is the point of declaring this dissolution void and then having the liquidation start all over again?

G I do not overlook the necessity to consider the directors' interests. As regards that, I note three matters. First, if the liquidation had to be restarted, then that would delay for some years the start of the disqualification proceedings, if so advised, at the end of the second liquidation. It would not remove all possibility of them. Secondly, I do not regard the directors in this case as third parties in the same way as third parties who ought to be protected from having the liquidation validated. Thirdly, I am comforted by the fact that they have been given notice of these proceedings and could have come along and objected
H to them if they wished.

Therefore the consequence is that I shall accede to the application. In the case of Townreach I shall make the order sought under para. 1 of the originating motion, including a direction:

'that the resolution for voluntary winding up of the above named company dated 11 June 1992 and the voluntary winding up in consequence thereof be duly deemed

to be valid and effective as they would have been had the above named company   A
not been dissolved under s. 652 at the time such resolution was passed.'

I shall order the office copy to be delivered to the registrar. There are certain undertakings
I shall require from the Secretary of State. In the other case I shall simply declare the
dissolution void and the consequential orders for delivery of the office copies. Again
certain undertakings are required.

(Order accordingly)   B

C

D

E

F

G

H

A **Supreme Travels Ltd v Little Olympian Each-Ways Ltd & Ors.**

Chancery Division (Companies Court).

Lindsay J.

Judgment delivered 5 May 1994.

B

Unfair prejudice petition – Petitioner sought to add non-member as respondent – Width of jurisdiction to grant relief against unfair prejudice – Whether court would order relief against prospective respondent as matter of discretion – Companies Act 1985, s. 459, 461.

This was an application by which a petitioner under a s. 459 petition sought to add as a respondent a company ('OAG') which had never been a shareholder in, nor a director or manager or person responsible for the conduct of, the company whose affairs were said to have been conducted in a manner unfairly prejudicial to the interests of the petitioner. Nor
C was OAG alleged to be a wrongdoer. If the relief claimed in the amended petition were to be granted, OAG would become obliged, with others, to buy from the petitioner the petitioner's shares in the company. The issues were whether s. 459 conferred a jurisdiction so broad that such an order could be made against such a respondent, and if it did whether leave for the joinder and amendment should be granted.

Held, ruling that OAG should not be joined as a respondent:

D   1. Nothing in the authorities suggested that the words of s. 459 and s. 461 should not be given their full effect: in an appropriate case relief could be sought against a non-member other than the company itself, or against a person not involved in the acts complained of (at least if that person would be affected by the relief sought) and a person against whom no relief was in terms sought could not necessarily escape being a respondent. In point of jurisdiction the wide language of s. 459 and s. 461 was not to be cut down.

E   2. Notwithstanding that a claim could not be clearly said to be outside that wide jurisdiction, the likelihood of the court's discretion being exercised so as to lead to relief against, or relief having any material effect upon, a given respondent could be so remote that it would be an abuse of process to require that respondent to remain as such or to be added as such. This was such a case because no court would order OAG to buy the petitioner's shares, the only substantive relief sought against OAG in the amended petition.

F   The following cases were referred to in the judgment:

Aiden Shipping Co Ltd v Interbulk Ltd [1986] AC 965.
Baltic Real Estate Ltd, Re [1992] BCC 629.
Bovey Hotel Ventures Ltd, Re (unreported, 13 July 1981, Slade J).
BSB Holdings Ltd, Re [1992] BCC 915.
Company No. 5287/85, Re a (1985) 1 BCC 99,586.
Company No. 007281 of 1986, Re a (1987) 3 BCC 375.
G *Noble (R A) & Sons (Clothing) Ltd, Re* [1983] BCLC 273.

Robin Potts QC and David Mabb (instructed by Withers) for the petitioner.

Richard Snowden (instructed Taylor Joynson Garrett) for the respondents.

Charles Aldous QC and Alastair Walton (instructed by Herbert Smith) for OAG.

JUDGMENT

H **Lindsay J:** I have before me an application which, amongst other issues, raises questions as to the boundaries of s. 459 and s. 461 of the Companies Act 1985. A petitioner under a s. 459 petition seeks here to amend its petition to add a respondent and to include amongst the relief sought an order against that new respondent, Owners Abroad Group plc ('OAG'). OAG has never been a shareholder in, nor a director or manager or person responsible for the conduct of, the company whose affairs are said to have been conducted in a manner unfairly prejudicial to the interests of the petitioner. Nor is OAG alleged to be a wrongdoer. Nonetheless, if the relief claimed were to be granted, OAG would become obliged, with others, to buy from the petitioner the petitioner's shares in that company. Does s. 459 confer a jurisdiction so broad that such an order could be made against such a respondent? Even if it does, should leave for such joinder and amendment here be granted?

I shall first outline the position as it is before the amendment which is sought. On 30 August 1991, Supreme Travels Ltd, a company incorporated in Jersey ('the petitioner') presented a petition to the Companies Court under s. 459 of the *Companies Act* 1985 in the matter of Little Olympian EachWays Ltd ('the company'). The company was incorporated under the *Companies Act* 1948 and its registered office is in London. The petitioner describes itself in the petition as holding 1,017,472 preference shares in the capital of the company and as having held the same for more than the necessary six months.

The original petition was relatively short – some nine pages. It described the only shareholders of ordinary shares in the company as being Olympic Vacations Ltd ('OVL') – 51 per cent – and Mr George Michalias – 49 per cent – and said that the company and OVL were members of a group of companies known as the Olympic Holidays group, of which the ultimate holding company was said to be Star Vacations Ltd ('Star'), a company incorporated in Cyprus. The directors of the company were described as being Mr Pyliotis, Mr Michalias and Mr Christoforou, each of whom was a director of OVL. It is not necessary for me to set out, even in summary, all the matters complained of in the original petition but, in outline, one material complaint ran as follows:

(1)   on 24 November 1990 2,448,000 preference shares in the company were transferred to a company referred to as Newco, which was owned by Star and Mr Christoforou;

(2)   on 21 March 1991 at an EGM of the company it was purportedly approved that the business and goodwill of the company should be transferred to Newco in return for which Newco would take over the company's liabilities and would be obliged to pay the company £1;

(3)   that resolution was implemented on 30 April 1991;

(4)   the company was thereafter left as a shell – it ceased to trade;

(5)   the consideration given by Newco was grossly inadequate;

(6)   there were breaches of pre-emption provisions which should have operated in the petitioner's favour as a holder of existing preference shares and breaches, too, of provisions requiring notice to have been given to the petitioner of the EGM;

(7)   those and other matters led to an allegation that the affairs of the company had been conducted in a manner unfairly prejudicial to the interests of the petitioner.

The petition was intended to be served on the company itself, on OVL, on the three individuals I have mentioned – Mr Michalias, Mr Pyliotis and Mr Christoforou (referred to as 'the trio') and also on Olympic Holdings Ltd, the name assumed by Newco, but which I shall continue to call Newco.

In due course affidavits were sworn in support of and in opposition to the petition and there was a very substantial discovery. The story emerging from this mass of paper was, the petitioner began to see, a story going well beyond the bare bones of the original petition. For various reasons, counsel originally instructed by the petitioner could not continue with their case and a new team, Mr Potts QC and Mr Mabb, were instructed in their place to consider the mass of new information.

In the result, on 1 March 1994 a summons was issued by the petitioner addressed to the six persons on whom the original petition had been served (whom I shall call together

A the 'original respondents'), who appear before me by Mr Snowden. The summons asks, inter alia, that the petitioner should have leave to amend the petition by adding Star as a seventh respondent and OAG as eighth respondent. Leave is sought for a comprehensive amendment to the petition. The proposed amended petition is now a creature of some 94 pages in length. Again, I do not need to summarise all of it but the story now alleged (so far as material for immediate purposes) alleges far more complicated wrongdoings than the relatively simple sale of the company's assets to Newco for what was said to be the grossly inadequate consideration of £1 plus assumption by Newco of the company's liability as alleged in the original petition. In broadest outline the most material allegations in the amended petition (as I shall call it for convenience, although leave to amend is not yet given and is resisted) are as follows.

B

(1) The company of whom the trio were directors sold the business and goodwill of the company for a grossly inadequate consideration to Newco, a company of which the trio were directors, and the capital of which was owned by Star, a company of which the trio were shareholders.

C

(2) The company was thus reduced to a shell and the shares in it not held by the petitioner were next sold for £1 to Star.

(3) Star then sold the shares in Newco (which by then represented the value of the erstwhile business and goodwill of the company and, says the petitioner, nothing else) to OAG for a variable price likely to reach £10m.

D

The basic complaints in the original petition remain. The petitioner is left with a holding in a shell company whilst the trio and some others have shared a substantial jackpot no part of which has come to the petitioner. Leaving aside how far various heads of relief asked for need to be alternative to one another, the amended petition claims by way of relief, inter alia, that the respondents (that is to say including OAG) should buy the petitioner's preference shares in the company on described bases which I apprehend are intended to reflect the true value of the shares had there been no wrongdoing; that Newco, now a subsidiary of OAG, should account for certain benefits to the company as constructive trustee; that Newco should make certain payments to the company and that the transfer of assets from the company to Newco should be declared voidable.

E

The first question I have to decide is whether, as Mr Potts and Mr Mabb argue for the petitioner, the court has *jurisdiction* to add OAG as the eighth respondent. It is common ground OAG is not a member of the company but it is, urges Mr Potts, a person against whom relief is properly sought in the amended petition. It is, he says, also a person involved in the misdeeds alleged in the amended petition and a person affected by the relief claimed against others in the amended petition in that the position of its wholly-owned subsidiary Newco would be radically affected were the relief there claimed against Newco, or even some of it, to be granted. If I have the jurisdiction to add OAG, then the question becomes whether I should, in the exercise of the discretion conferred on me by the rules as to amendment and as to the joinder of parties, exercise it to join OAG and to allow the amendment against OAG. Mr Aldous QC and Mr Walton for OAG argue that the court does not have the necessary jurisdiction and further, even if it had, that in point of discretion the joinder and amendment so far as concerns OAG should be refused.

F

G

I shall first look at the question as to jurisdiction and, initially, shall do so without reference to the authorities that have been cited to me. The relevant sections are s. 459 and s. 461 of the 1985 Act. I shall not set out either in full. I go first to s. 461 which begins by conferring on the court by subs. (1) a power to give relief in very wide terms. If the court is satisfied that the petition under s. 459 is well founded,

H

'it may make such order as it thinks fit for giving relief in respect of the matters complained of.'

The relief does not, for example, necessarily have to compensate for or prohibit the   A
recurrence of the matters complained of. The only nexus required between relief and
complaint is that the former has to be 'in respect of' the latter.

Then s. 461(2) opens with the words:

'Without prejudice to the generality of subsection (1), the court's order may . . .'

and it goes on in para. (a)–(d) to give examples of relief within the wider generality which
is not to be prejudiced. Mr Potts argues that the two sections, s. 459 and 461, read   B
together are an example of a practice exemplified by the provisions considered in the well
known case of *Aiden Shipping Co Ltd v Interbulk* [1986] AC 965 whereby Parliament
confers an exceptionally wide jurisdiction and leaves it to the courts or to a rule-making
body or to both to find for themselves boundaries, not to the jurisdiction proper, but, by
way of the exercise of the discretion in individual cases, to the areas in which and the
manner in which, in practice, the jurisdiction would be likely, save in exceptional   C
circumstances, to lead to relief.

I do not think it profitable to determine how far *Aiden* is or is not a wholly acceptable
analogy but I do see force in Mr Potts' submission which, in my view, is supported also
by the legislative history of s. 459 and its predecessors. As to that history, a precursor of
s. 459, s. 210 of the 1948 Act, was reported on in 1960 by the Jenkins Committee as
appearing not to have produced the results expected of it, and it was given in evidence to   D
that committee that the section needed amendment if effective protection was to be given
to minorities in the circumstances in which it had been intended that it should be: see
para. 200 of the Jenkins Committee's report.

Section 210 was then superseded by s. 75 of the 1980 Act, but s. 75, which required
that the prejudice should be suffered by 'some part of the members', inevitably led to
doubts and discussion as to whether the section afforded relief in cases where the
prejudice was suffered by the whole membership. There was thus, once again, the need   E
to widen the statutory provision. Although the width of the jurisdiction conferred by
s. 459 and s. 461 is of course a matter of the construction of the language Parliament
has used, the earlier sequences of statutory provision, construction by the court, a
dawning recognition of shortcomings later followed by a statutory extension, is at least
consistent with there having been engendered in the legislature by 1985 a sense that the
thing to do was to give a very wide jurisdiction and to let the courts get on with it.   F

The broad provisions of the *Companies (Unfair Prejudice Applications) Proceedings
Rules* 1986 are examples of the same view. In relation to who is to be respondent, those
rules provide (by r. 5(a)) that on the return day:

'5 . . . the court shall give such directions as it thinks appropriate with respect to
. . .

(a) service of the petition on any person . . .'   G

– and (by r. 3(3)) for a day upon which,

'unless the court otherwise directs, the petitioner and any respondent . . . shall
attend before the registrar . . . for directions to be given in relation to the procedure
on the petition.'

The impression given both in the sections and in the rules is that the greatest possible   H
flexibility was intended by the legislature to be given to the courts. Thus s. 459 does not,
for example, require that it is by a respondent or by the respondents to the petition that
the company's affairs are being or have been conducted in the manner complained of. It
does not require that the respondents to the petition should be limited to members of the
company or to its directors or to those conducting its affairs and, of course, it is a familiar
practice that the company itself should be a respondent: see r. 4(1). I am unable to find

A   in s. 459 itself any language which points to who may be, who has to be or who cannot be respondents to a petition under its terms. Those are subjects which it does not attempt to address.

Mr Aldous and Mr Snowden argue that some restrictions in the jurisdiction have to be read in. For example, they say that there is no jurisdiction to require a person to be a respondent where no relief is claimed against him and where he is not affected by any

B   relief which is sought. A distinction needs to be drawn, says Mr Aldous, between the conduct and position of those who are in control of the company or who are members, on the one hand, and, on the other, the position and conduct of third parties – 'outsiders', as he calls them – in respect of whom the company has no cause of action and whose involvement may be no more than that, innocent of any intent to prejudice anyone and innocent also of any foresight that anyone might be prejudiced, they are, as third parties, concerned in the activity complained of as being prejudicial. That some distinctions will

C   in some cases need to be drawn is, I accept, likely enough, but I cannot find any warrant in the language of s. 459 and s. 461 for introducing them as matters of jurisdiction.

Leaving aside what the authorities I next turn to require of me, I do not feel able to decline the joinder of OAG and to refuse the proposed amendment of the petition against OAG on the ground that the petition, if so amended, would be trespassing outside the statutory jurisdiction. It may be material to add that a decision to exclude as a matter of

D   jurisdiction would have the result not only of excluding respondents, such as OAG, who wish not to be joined, but also of excluding those who, in a corresponding position, would wish to be joined as, or to continue as, respondents.

I now turn to the authorities cited to find out what guidance I am given. First in time of the cases cited to me was *Re R A Noble & Sons (Clothing) Ltd* [1983] BCLC 273 per Nourse J. It was cited by Mr Aldous only so as to lead to the citation in it at p. 290 from

E   the unreported 1981 case of Slade J, *Re Bovey Hotel Ventures Ltd*, a passage in which Slade J held, in relation to s. 75 of the 1980 Act, that the test of unfairness was an objective one; it was not necessary for the petitioner to show that those who had de facto control of the company acted in the conscious knowledge that what they were doing or omitting to do was unfair to the petitioner. Mr Aldous argues that it would be remarkable if a person, a stranger to the company, could properly find himself a respondent to a s. 459 petition without, as *Re Bovey Hotel Ventures* indicates, the least conscious

F   knowledge that he was being, or was likely to be, unfair to anyone, but simply because he was involved in some transaction which was unfairly prejudicial to the petitioner. I see the force of that but, as I have said, I cannot find any words, either in or necessarily to be implied into s. 459 and s. 461, which would aid in excluding a respondent as a matter of jurisdiction in such a case. Whilst I would not quarrel with a line of *Re Bovey Hotel Ventures*, I do not see it as restrictive of the jurisdiction conferred by s. 459.

G   The next authority was *Re a Company No. 5287/85* (1985) 1 BCC 99,586, a decision of Hoffmann J in a case where the erstwhile controlling shareholder of the company, H, sought to strike out a petition which was under s. 459 and, alternatively, for the winding up of the company. H had, it was alleged, conducted the company in breach of his fiduciary duties and in a manner unfairly prejudicial to the petitioners. Negotiations began before a petition was presented but, when it was found that H had transferred his

H   shares to an offshore company, the petitioners then issued their petition under s. 459 requiring H to account for payments of company money made without authority. The petitioners found a little later that H had left this jurisdiction and had sold the company's assets for cash. The petitioners then sought to make amendments to the petition and to include a request for an order that H and the offshore company should jointly and severally buy the petitioners' shares. Unabashed, H argued that in respect of the original relief it was only the offshore company that should have been respondent (p. 99,588).

There was no justification, he argued, for extending relief to relief against persons – the A
company itself apart – who had ceased to be members (p. 99,589), but the petitioner
could, it was argued, proceed against H by derivative shareholders' action. Hoffmann J
thought that would be inconvenient, and he went on to say:

> 'I would be reluctant to come to the conclusion that this form of duplication was
> necessary unless it was clear that the jurisdiction under s. 459 and 461 did not
> permit the whole matter to be dealt with on the petition. It seems to me that   B
> although it is true that s. 461(2) shows that the normal order under s. 461 will be
> an order against the company or another member, there is no reason why the
> words of s. 461(1) should not be given their full effect and allow the court to give
> relief in respect of a complaint that the company's affairs had been conducted in a
> manner unfairly prejudicial to the interests of members, even when this would
> involve giving relief against a respondent who is no longer a member. For that
> reason, I am not willing to strike out (H) as a party to the petition.'   C

Turning to H's opposition to the buy-out relief sought to be added by amendment and
in response to H's argument that no such order could be made against a non-member,
Hoffmann J said:

> 'Section 461(2)(d), which I have already read, provides for such an order being
> made against members of the company but says nothing about the order being
> made against a non-member. (Counsel for the petitioners), on the other hand, says   D
> that there are cases in which a person may be, for the purposes of giving relief,
> identified with a company which he controls and that it may be possible to obtain
> an order to that effect against (H) either under the broad jurisdiction of s. 461(1)
> or by identifying (H) with [the Gibraltarian company – the offshore company I
> have mentioned]. It is not necessary for me to express any view on whether that
> can be done because I do not think it would be right to strike out the paragraph   E
> seeking such relief unless I was satisfied that the possibility of obtaining it was
> perfectly hopeless. I do not feel in a position at the moment to say that and I do
> not think it would prejudice (H) very greatly if the paragraph seeking that relief
> were to remain in the petition, given that in the light of the conclusion to which I
> have already come he will remain as a respondent to the petition in respect of the
> relief sought under para. 2.'   F

It is notable that, despite his reading s. 459 and 461 together (he speaks, at p. 99,589,
of 'the jurisdiction under s. 459 and 461') Hoffmann J sees no reason why the words of
s. 461(1) should not be given their full effect. Mr Aldous can point to the judge's more
cautious approach to the buy-out jurisdiction but, even there, where he is saying:

> '. . . I do not think it would be right to strike out . . . relief unless I was satisfied
> that the possibility of obtaining it was perfectly hopeless.'   G

his words look to me more the language of a judge who considered that there might well
be jurisdiction (but one which it was urged was hopeless in point of its exercise) rather
than that of a judge who is indicating his concluded views on whether or not there was a
jurisdiction.

Mr Aldous points to the facts that H had been a controller of the company, a person
responsible for the unfair conduct alleged, had been a member of the company, was   H
personally accused of wrongdoing and could have been the object of a derivative action.
I can see that *Re a Company* thus falls well short of deciding the case before me but I
nonetheless attach some importance to the fact that Hoffmann J, upon his reading the
two sections together, had seen no reason why the words of s. 461(1) should not be given
their full effect and accordingly had permitted the addition of a claim for a buy-out
against a non-member.

A Next in time was *Re a Company No. 007281 of 1986* (1987) 3 BCC 375, a decision of Vinelott J. An investment company, 3i, which had provided working capital, held cumulative convertible participating preferred ordinary shares and cumulative redeemable preference shares in the company. The company's articles had elaborate provisions as to pre-emption rights. One of the directors was voted off the board. He found the other directors had set up a rival group of companies and had stripped the company of its assets, so he presented a petition under s. 459. 3i was a respondent to the

B petition notwithstanding that it was not said that it had taken any part in or had been concerned in any way in the unfairly prejudicial conduct. No relief was sought against it. The primary relief sought was the purchase of the petitioner's shares by the three other directors but the petition asked, alternatively, for such other relief under s. 461 as the court should think just.

Vinelott J held that as 3i was a member of the company and was affected by the relief

C sought in that an order for a buy-out by the three directors of the petitioner's shares would override 3i's pre-emption rights, it was right that it should remain a respondent.

At pp. 380–381 he said:

'A petition under s. 459 is not analogous to litigation in which the issues raised affect only those against whom allegations are made by the plaintiff. A closer analogy is an administration action, where all beneficiaries having an interest in

D the relief sought should be made parties or represented. The practice that has so far been followed in the Companies Court is to require that all members of the company whose interests would have been affected by the misconduct alleged or who would be affected by an order made by the court under the very wide powers conferred by s. 461 are to be made respondents to a petition or served with it.

In practice, this means that in the case of a small, private company every member

E ought to be joined.'

Then, a little later, still on p. 381, he said:

'In my judgment, 3i is clearly affected by the relief sought in the petition which, amongst other things, would override its rights under the pre-emption provisions. 3i also has voting control over the company in general meeting, and would be directly concerned if any order were made regulating the future conduct of the

F company pending the acquisition of the petitioner's shares.

In these circumstances I think that 3i was properly made a respondent and should not now be struck out.'

Mr Aldous is, of course, able to stress that there 3i was, first, a member of the company and, secondly, a person affected by the relief claimed. But the case does show that it is not a necessary condition of joinder that a respondent should have been involved in any

G way as a wrongdoer in the events complained of.

In *Re BSB Holdings Ltd* [1992] BCC 915 a similar problem came again before Vinelott J. The petitioner complained that the business of 'Holdings', the company in which it held shares, had been hived down to B Sky B which was at first a wholly owned subsidiary of Holdings but which later then passed into the control and ownership of the respondents in a way which was alleged unfairly to prejudice the petitioner. The petitioner sought an order that the respondents, or some of them, should transfer their shares in B

H Sky B back to Holdings or direct to the petitioner. No relief was sought against B Sky B itself, which was not a member of Holdings, and it applied that the petition should be struck out as against it.

The 3i case was cited to Vinelott J who took the view that, despite B Sky B not being a member of Holdings, it was clearly affected by the relief sought in that the order sought was that there should be a transfer and registration of its shares. The body of its

corporators would change (p. 921G–922A). But the judge added that its joinder could be   A
justified on another ground, namely that it was directly concerned in the transactions of
which complaint was made (p. 922B). It was a party, and a necessary party, to one of the
agreements which was complained of. Vinelott J held that B Sky B was properly joined
because it was an actor and played a central role in the transactions of which complaint
was made (p. 923A–B).

Finally on the authorities, in *Re Baltic Real Estate Ltd* [1992] BCC 629 Knox J had   B
before him an application in relation to a s. 459 petition of a majority (51 per cent)
shareholder in a company. The second and third respondents to the petition were the
former directors of that company who, the petitioner alleged, had committed breaches of
fiduciary duty as directors. The second and third respondents were also its former
shareholders as to 49 per cent but had held their shares only briefly before transferring
them to the fourth and fifth respondents (persons out of the jurisdiction, not served by
the time of the hearing before Knox J and in respect of whom leave to serve out was   C
needed). There were allegations that the fourth and fifth respondents, the registered
holders of the 49 per cent, were either controlled by the second and third respondents or
held the 49 per cent of the shares in the company in trust for the second and third
respondents. The petitioner sought as his principal relief an order that the second and
third respondents, alternatively the fourth and fifth respondents, should be ordered to
sell or procure the sale of the 49 per cent of the shares in the company registered in the   D
name of the fourth and fifth respondents to the petitioner at such price as the court
should think fit.

It was argued on behalf of the second and third respondents that as they were not
present members they were not proper respondents and, as they were not parties to the
relief sought either, the petition should be struck out as against them as not disclosing
any reasonable cause of action and as being an abuse of process. That argument   E
succeeded not, as I see it, because the second and third respondents were not members of
the company, but because, as Knox J put it at p. 633F:

> 'It seems to me that the proper parties to this relief are the shareholders in whom
> the shares in question are vested and with whom the court, in dealing with the
> rights of members, is primarily concerned.'

There is no discussion in the judgment of the jurisdiction under s. 459. Knox J plainly   F
took the view that the fact (as alleged) that the fourth and fifth respondents were but
trustees for the second and third respondents or were controlled by the second and third
respondents, was not, on its own, enough to justify the second and third respondents
being necessary parties. But there were some other arguments which Knox J indicated
had failed to persuade him that the second and third respondents should continue to be
respondents. First, that they were the persons against whom the breach of duty was   G
alleged and, secondly, that, under the rubric of 'such other relief as the court should think
fit', the relief eventually granted by the court might be other than the sale of shares to the
petitioner, which was the principal relief sought, and might more involve the second and
third respondents than would that sale.

That concludes a look at the authorities cited to me. Whilst I would be very willing to
follow a pattern that emerged from the earlier cases at first instance, I do not regard any   H
clear pattern as having yet emerged, and I have certainly found nothing conclusive that
suggests that the words of s. 459 and s. 461 should not be given their full effect. From the
existing authorities cited it can be seen that in an appropriate case relief can be sought
against a non-member other than the company itself, or against a person not involved in
the acts complained of (at least if that person would be affected by the relief sought) and
that a person against whom no relief is in terms sought cannot necessarily escape being a

A   respondent, whilst, on other facts, it can be right to strike out a petition, even as against those whose acts are complained of, so long as no relief is sought against such a person.

This summary suggests to me that in point of jurisdiction the wide language of s. 459 and s. 461 is not to be cut down. Nonetheless, cases may arise where, notwithstanding that the claim cannot be clearly said to be outside that wide jurisdiction, the likelihood of the court's discretion being exercised so as to lead to relief against, or relief having any material effect upon, a given respondent can be seen to be so remote that the case can B   fairly be described as 'perfectly hopeless', to use Hoffmann J's phrase, and hence that it would be abusive to require that respondent to remain as such or to be added as such. Is this such a case?

It is best first to look at the likelihood or otherwise of OAG being ordered, with the other respondents, to buy the petitioner's shares – the only substantive relief sought against OAG in the amended petition. Prima facie, when a litigant's case against a person C   is within the relevant jurisdiction he should be permitted, if he so chooses, to pursue his case against that person. Thus I framed the question at the end of the last paragraph in the way that I did, rather than by reference to O. 15, r.6, because, on the facts of this case, where no blame can be laid at the petitioner's door for not including OAG from the outset or for delay in applying to amend, it seems appropriate to look at the petitioner's position more as it would be on an application for a strike out by OAG than where the D   petitioner comes cap in hand, as it were, asking for leave to amend. However, it is also to be borne in mind that it is plainly abusive to press a person into hopeless litigation, litigation which cannot succeed. Quite apart from other vexation inherent in litigation, even a party who recovers an order for his costs against a solvent party on an indemnity basis may well be left substantially out of pocket at the end of a s. 459 petition, a type of proceeding known neither for its speed nor its economy.

E   At this point in the argument, Mr Aldous redeploys on the discretionary side of things many of the arguments used unsuccessfully (as I have held) on the jurisdiction. OAG is not and never has been a member of the company. OAG is not said to have controlled the company or its board or even to have had a nominee on the company's board. True it is that its wholly owned subsidiary, Newco, is a respondent but, as did Knox J in *Baltic Real Estate*, I see it as no reason, sufficient in itself, for the joinder of a person as a further party that an existing respondent is owned by or controlled by that person. Newco can F   respond for itself and were there a principle that shareholders in or directors or controllers of a corporate respondent could, without more, be required to be parties in addition to that corporate respondent itself, then s. 459 would indeed be oppressive.

I thus see neither OAG's ownership of Newco nor the potential effect of the petition on Newco as being reason for OAG's joinder. It is said that beyond the buy-out required of it, OAG is affected by the relief sought in that its wholly owned subsidiary Newco may G   find itself holding its assets on constructive trust for, and may be liable to account to, others, but, again, the simple answer is, as I see it, that Newco, already a party, is able fully to deal with that, and if it sufficed, without more, to require a company to be respondent that the assets of a company in which it held shares might be affected by the relief sought, that would, again, be a needlessly oppressive burden on corporations.

Mr Aldous emphasises that no substantive relief is sought against OAG in the petition H   save that it is sought that with six others (other than the company itself, and on the basis that Star is added) it should be a joint purchaser of the petitioner's shares in the company. There is no suggestion in evidence that the addition of OAG is necessary if there is to be a purchaser able to pay the price required or that the other respondents are of straw. There is nothing to suggest that a buy-out without OAG as a joint or several buyer is impracticable or impossible or that such an order against the original respondents would be worthless or nugatory. As the original respondents include persons who are alleged to

be the wrongdoers in relation to the acts complained of and who are said to have profited   A
in substantial amounts from those acts, then if they, if ordered to do so, would be able to
buy – and it is nowhere said they would not be so able – Mr Aldous urges that no court
is likely to find it necessary to join with them as a co-purchaser a party, OAG, against
whom nothing wrong is urged. It is a strong course, he says, to require a party at what is
likely to be considerable expense and against its will to become a shareholder in a
company, a shell company, and to do so when the party is not said to have done anything
wrong and where there are others who are wrongdoers and who are available as   B
alternative purchasers. So to order, Mr Aldous urges, would be remarkable,
unprecedented and unnecessary. He goes on to show that the petition contains no
allegation of any wrong done by OAG to the company; it is nowhere said the company
has a cause of action against OAG.

Against this Mr Potts took me to the provisions of the amended petition. As early as
December 1990, well before the sale of the company's assets to Newco, OAG and its   C
solicitors were involved in discussions for the grant to OAG of an option to acquire the
issued capital of Newco. Mr Potts says that from the outset a number of related steps
were planned to lead to the conclusion that was ultimately arrived at and of which the
petitioner complains and that OAG was party to the planning from that outset. He says
that OAG was involved in proposals as to a loan to the company which was made with
the intent of being lent on by the company to discharge an individual's debts and that   D
OAG was concerned in carrying through such a proposal. OAG, the amended petition
alleges, was party to an option agreement of 21 December 1990 whereunder it would be
able to acquire the capital of Newco for a price strangely expressed as 'subject to a
maximum sum of £8m or as might otherwise be agreed between Star and OAG with a
maximum of £10m and an overall minimum of £1m'.

It was, says Mr Potts and as the amended petition alleges, the intention of OAG   E
throughout in relation to the option agreement that the company would hive up its
business and goodwill to Newco in return for an indemnity and for nothing else of any
real worth and that only after that would the option be exercised by OAG. OAG knew
and approved the price paid on the hive up to Newco and was conscious of at least the
possibility of that transaction being at a substantial undervalue, as it demonstrated by
way of its solicitors pressing for and obtaining an undertaking that no steps would be
taken for at least two years to put the company into voluntary winding up. The   F
acquisition of Newco's shares by OAG was an acquisition improperly given financial
assistance by the company in breach of s. 151 of the 1985 Act, the company at the time
being a subsidiary of Newco. In these ways, says Mr Potts, as para. 107 of the amended
petition states, OAG 'was directly concerned in transactions of which complaint is made
herein'. It is in this context that Mr Potts says that the petitioner's complaint is (and I use
his words) that there is here a 'con' and that OAG is 'in it up to its neck'. However, I
think I need to be a little more analytical than that. Mr Potts' strong language is surely   G
that of, at worst, conspiracy or, at least, of OAG having knowledge – actual, imputed or
constructive knowledge – that its activities or omissions were or might represent unfair
prejudice to the petitioner or that OAG committed some other material wrongs. But no
such allegation is anywhere to be found in the petition. Such wrongs, if there were any,
under s. 151 are not said to be wrongs by OAG. It is nowhere said that what OAG
acquired was acquired for less than full market consideration, and the matters pleaded   H
suggest, if anything, that it has paid or will pay a little over the odds for what it received.
Mr Potts gave me a list of the paragraphs in the amended petition said to show OAG's
involvement in the matters complained of, and para. 107 of the amended petition gives a
similar but not identical list. I hope I have not overlooked anything material in the 94
pages of the body of the petition but I have not found any reference to anything done or
omitted by OAG being alleged to have been wrongful or unlawful or in breach of some

A   duty or obligation upon OAG. Whilst it is undoubtedly the case that OAG was, in a sense, concerned in transactions of which complaint is made, I cannot in the circumstances alleged in the amended petition see that concern as amounting to anything material. Both Mr Aldous and Mr Snowden made the valid point that if a person against whom no wrongdoing is alleged, whose involvement, such as it is, has been paid for at 100p in the pound, and who is not a member, can be required against his will to be a respondent who may be ordered to buy shares, then no trading company could feel safe

B   that it would not be expensively drawn into the internal disputes of its customers and of others with whom it might deal.

Mr Aldous next argues that all the attacks made on the hive up agreement are attacks not on anything done or omitted by OAG but by the trio and that the company and the petitioner (by way of derivative action) have full causes of action in respect thereof. The specially adjusted price which the petitioner claims should be paid for the petitioner's

C   shares is, in respect of any suggested adjustment, to be adjusted by reason of complaints against the trio, not against OAG. To require OAG to pay some special price for the petitioner's shares not only involves adjusting the price to be paid by OAG by reference to someone else's wrongs but, as OAG has paid full value already for what it has received, would involve it in paying more than once over for the very same assets, a step which, however possible against a wrongdoer, would be unprecedented against a party not said

D   to be in breach of any duty or obligation whatsoever.

None of these points put by OAG and by the original respondents is devoid of weight. I do not need to ascribe to each a separate force, but I do say that together their weight is such that, in my judgment, it can fairly be said that if the proposed amendments were allowed the petitioner would be quite unable on the amended petition to obtain the only relief, the buy-out, which it seeks against OAG.

E   Although the court *could*, if it chose, make a buy-out order against OAG of the kind which the petitioner seeks, it is on the case put in the amended petition, even if wholly true, plain and obvious, in my judgment, that no court *would* make such an order. Had OAG been a respondent from the start it could, in my view, have successfully moved to have the buy-out provisions and its role as a respondent struck out. It not yet being a respondent, it would be an abuse of process were it to be required, against its will, to be a respondent obliged to resist relief which would in practice never be granted.

F   Once that has emerged, so far as concerns the buy-out relief, the rest of the matter is readily determinable by reference to O. 15, r.6, which is made to apply by r. 2(2) of the 1986 rules. So far as material, O.15 , r.6(2) provides that the court may:

'(b) order any of the following persons to be added as a party, namely–

(i) any person who ought to have been joined as a party or whose presence before the Court is necessary to ensure that all matters in dispute in the

G   cause or matter may be effectually and completely determined and adjudicated upon, or

(ii) any person between whom and any party to the cause or matter there may exist a question or issue arising out of or relating to or connected with any relief or remedy claimed in the cause or matter which in the opinion of the Court it would be just and convenient to determine as between him and that

H   party as well as between the parties to the cause or matter.'

Once it is recognised that no buy-out relief will be ordered against it, OAG's presence is not necessary for the purpose specified in (i), nor is there any question or issue between OAG and the petitioner such that it would be just and convenient to hear that matter alongside the petition. Given, as I have already indicated, that OAG's ownership or control of Newco is, in my view, no reason to require the joinder of OAG, I see no reason

either why OAG is a person who 'ought to have been joined' within (i). Once the buy-out   A
relief falls away as a possibility, O. 15, r.6 requires, in my judgment, a conclusion that
OAG should not be joined as a respondent at all, and I so rule.

However, the summons before me raises questions other than the one that I have so
far dealt with and concerns respondents other than OAG. Subject to my first being
addressed on the costs so far and any other questions involving OAG, I shall, once OAG
has withdrawn, go on to hear the remaining issues on this summons and on the summons   B
as to security for costs later in the day.

Costs

So far as concerns the costs of OAG, I am concerned only with their costs of 28 March
and of the longer later two day hearing. The costs of OAG of and incidental to the
summons in relation to those two hearings should be paid by the petitioner, they to be
taxed and paid forthwith.   C

So far as concerns the costs of the original respondents other than the company which,
as it transpires, has taken no part, it seems to me that their costs of three occasions are in
issue: those before Mr Registrar Buckley on 22 March, those before me on 28 March,
and the later fuller hearing of two days or so. The argument has, all along, even on the
part of the original respondents, principally concerned the original respondents' wish
that OAG should not be required to be a respondent and it seems to me that the original   D
respondents were entitled to take that view, just as much as OAG was entitled to take
that view and, moreover, the original respondents have in that respect succeeded.

Mr Potts argues that they would have been before the court in any event, even if
OAG's addition had not been sought, but it seems to me that the battle would have been
then a very much simpler one and might indeed not have taken place.

I think the appropriate order for the costs of the original respondents other than the   E
company is that those costs should be taxed on a standard basis (not forthwith) and that
they should be required to be paid in any event by the petitioners to the original
respondents other than the company.

(*Order accordingly*)

────────────────   F

G

H

A
Re Little Olympian Each-Ways Ltd.

Chancery Division (Companies Court).
Lindsay J.
Judgment delivered 18 July 1994.

B
Security for costs – Unfair prejudice petition – Whether Jersey company ordinarily resident out of the jurisdiction – Rules of the Supreme Court, O. 23, r. 1(1)(a).

The Companies Court (applying the 'central management and control' test from De Beers Consolidated Mines Ltd v Howe **[1906] AC 455**) held that a non-trading company incorporated in Jersey, which was the petitioner in a s. 459 petition, was 'ordinarily resident out of the jurisdiction' for the purposes of O. 23, r. 1(1)(a) of the Rules of the Supreme Court.

C
The court found that the company had a Jersey registered office, Jersey resident shareholders, a Jersey board, and a Jersey secretary and that the board met as such and had not surrendered its powers nor had them removed but rather operated them within what it conceived to be the law of Jersey. The shareholders appeared to be nominees but it was the Jersey board which allowed the personal wishes, proposals or even instructions of others to become an activity of the Jersey company.

D
The court exercised its discretion under O. 23, r. 1(1)(a) to order security for costs. The petitioner's evidence failed to show that an award would stifle the proceedings.

The following cases were referred to in the judgment:

Adams & Ors v Cape Industries plc & Anor [1990] BCC 786; [1990] Ch 433.
Arnold & Ors v National Westminster Bank [1991] 2 AC 93.
Bowring (C T) & Co v Corsi & Partners Ltd [1994] BCC 713.
Cesena Sulphur Co Ltd v Nicholson (1876) 1 ExD 428.

E
Crozat v Brogden [1894] 2 QB 30.
De Beers Consolidated Mines Ltd v Howe [1906] AC 455.
DSQ Property Co Ltd v Lotus Cars Ltd & Ors (1986) 2 BCC 99,539; [1987] 1 WLR 127.
Farrer v Lacy Hartland & Co (1885) 28 ChD 482.
Goerz & Co v Bell [1904] 2 KB 136.
Jabbour & Anor v Custodian of Absentee Property of the State of Israel [1954] 1 WLR 139.

F
Jones v Scottish Accident Insurance Co Ltd (1886) 17 QBD 421.
Keary Developments Ltd v Tarmac Construction Ltd (unreported, 13 April 1994, CA).
Kwok Chi Leung Karl v Commissioner of Estate Duty [1988] 1 WLR 1035.
Mills v Cooper [1967] 2 QB 459.
Parkinson (Sir Lindsay) & Co Ltd v Triplan Ltd [1973] QB 609; [1973] 1 WLR 609.

G
Porzelack KG v Porzelack (UK) Ltd [1987] 1 WLR 420.
R v Barnet LBC, ex parte Shah [1983] 2 AC 309.
Swedish Central Railway Co Ltd v Thompson [1925] AC 495.
Unit Construction Co Ltd v Bullock [1960] AC 351.

Robin Potts QC and David Mabb (instructed by Withers) for the petitioner.

William Stubbs QC (instructed by Taylor Joynson Garrett) for the first, third, fourth
H
and fifth respondents.

Alastair Walton (instructed by Herbert Smith) for the second and sixth respondents.

JUDGMENT

Lindsay J: I have before me a summons dated 28 March 1994 by which some of the respondents to a s. 459 petition seek from the petitioner, Supreme Travels Ltd, a company incorporated under the laws of Jersey, security for costs.

The petition, which was presented on 30 August 1991, concerns the affairs of Little   A
Olympian Each-Ways Ltd ('the company'), a company incorporated under the
Companies Act 1948. The petitioner claims to hold 1,017,472 preference shares in the
capital of the company and to have held them for more than the requisite six months.
The respondents to the petition fall into three categories: Star Vacations Ltd,
incorporated in Cyprus, is a holding company which was added as seventh respondent in
May of this year and takes no part in the application now before me. The second group   B
is made up of the first, third, fourth and fifth respondents, comprising the company itself
and Mr Michalious, Mr Pyliotis and Mr Christoferou, three individuals who at an earlier
stage of the case were referred to as 'the trio'. This category appears by Mr Stubbs QC.
The second and sixth respondents, Olympic Vacations Ltd and Olympic Holdings Ltd,
are wholly owned subsidiaries of Owners Abroad Group and appear by Mr Walton, who
makes common cause with Mr Stubbs. The petitioner appears by Mr Potts QC with Mr
Mabb.   C

As there is a risk of confusion between the respondents to the petition (who are
applicants for security for costs) and the petitioner (who is respondent to the application
for security for costs) and because so much of the language used in the rules and in the
authorities on the subject of security for costs is couched in terms of 'plaintiff' and
'defendant', I hope I shall be forgiven for throughout calling the petitioner 'the plaintiff'
and the respondents to the petition 'the defendants'.   D

This is the second summons for security for costs in this petition. The first was a
summons dated 15 October 1991 and it led to an order made on 21 July 1992 by Mr
Registrar Buckley that the plaintiff should provide security for the defendants' costs for
the period up to but not including the first day of the trial in the sum of £55,000, by way
of a bank guarantee from the Royal Bank of Scotland. There was provision for a stay on
default but there was no default. The order of 21 July 1992, though not expressed as a
consent order, was, in the event, as I am told, not opposed by the plaintiff.   E

The summons now before me, so far as material, reads as follows:

> 'The petitioner do give security for the respondents' costs in the above matter to
> the satisfaction of the court pursuant to RSC, O. 23:
>
>   (a) on the ground that the petitioner is and at the date of presentation of the
>   petition was a company incorporated in Jersey whose registered office is PO
>   Box 75, Normandy House, Grenville Street, St Helier, Jersey, JE4 9PP,   F
>   Channel Islands;
>
>   (b) further or in the alternative, pursuant to s. 726 of the *Companies Act* 1985
>   on the ground that the petitioner will be unable to pay the respondents' costs
>   if ordered to do so;
>
>   (c) further or in the alternative, pursuant to the inherent jurisdiction of the court   G
>   and that in the meantime all further proceedings be stayed.'

So far as concerns subpara. (b) and as to s. 726(1), Mr Stubbs reserves whatever (if
any) argument is possible on this point for the Court of Appeal or higher. I am not asked
to do anything on that score but to note that reservation. I shall need to return later to
consideration of any inherent jurisdiction, but subpara. (a) of the summons invokes
O. 23, r. 1(1)(a) and it is to that that I shall first turn. The primary question under O. 23,
r. 1(1)(a) has been as to jurisdiction, but, as that is a question which does not require   H
a setting-out of the issues in the s. 459 petition, I shall leave that setting-out over until the
stage at which it becomes necessary (if it does), namely to the point at which, if I find
myself to have jurisdiction, I then move on to consider the discretion I would then have.

Going then to the Rules of the Supreme Court, O. 23, r. 1, so far as material to this
application, it reads as follows:

A   '1. Where, on the application of a defendant to an action or other proceeding in the High Court, it appears to the court–

      (a) that the plaintiff is ordinarily resident out of the jurisdiction . . .

then if, having regard to all the circumstances of the case, the Court thinks it just to do so, it may order the plaintiff to give such security for the defendant's costs of the action or other proceeding as it thinks just.'

B   It is convenient to speak of the passage down to the end of (a) as 'jurisdiction' and of the passage after the word 'then' as containing both 'discretion' and 'quantum'. Subject to a point I shall mention shortly, I shall need to divide my judgment principally into corresponding parts but, because the evidence on 'quantum' is very extensive and because, were the plaintiff to succeed on either jurisdiction or discretion, time spent on consideration of that evidence would prove to have been wasted, the issue of quantum

C   has been left as yet unargued and I have not yet even seen the evidence upon it. I shall thus deal with the heading of quantum only if the plaintiff fails and the defendants succeed on both jurisdiction and discretion. The plaintiff argues in point of jurisdiction that, whilst undeniably incorporated out of the jurisdiction, it is not, nor is it shown to be (the onus being on the defendants) 'ordinarily resident out of the jurisdiction' and hence that no order can be made against it under O. 23, r. 1(1)(a).

D   But before I return to O. 23 in more detail I should mention two arguments of the defendants which do not rely on the rule. First, it was sought to argue that because the plaintiff had had an earlier award for security of costs made against it, an order which, if not formally a consent order, was at least unopposed and because the plaintiff had not then taken the jurisdiction point it now takes, the plaintiff is, by way of issue estoppel, denied the ability to take the point now. In the course of arguing for issue estoppel Mr Stubbs came up against this stumbling block: the tense used in O. 23, r. 1(1)(a) is the

E   present tense – 'the plaintiff *is* ordinarily resident out of the jurisdiction'. If there were any 'res' which could be said to have been 'judicata' in respect of the earlier award for security, it was that the plaintiff was *then* ordinarily resident out of the jurisdiction. But whether the plaintiff was *then* so resident is now irrelevant; the question is now whether the plaintiff is *now* so resident, an issue not only not yet adjudged but which logically has no necessary relationship with the plaintiff's residence at an earlier date. Estoppel per rem judicatam cannot avail if the only res which can be described as already judicata is

F   strictly irrelevant at the subsequent occasion at which the doctrine is invoked, a subsequent occasion at which not that res but different res falls for decision.

That strict, perhaps surprisingly strict, approach is vividly illustrated in a criminal context in *Mills v Cooper* [1967] 2 QB 459 (CA). At an earlier trial the question of whether the defendant there was a gypsy on 22 December 1965 had been determined against the defendant. At a later trial the issue was whether the defendant was a gypsy on 13 March

G   1966. In context, being a gypsy meant having a nomadic life with no fixed abode and hence was something that could change from day to day. The Court of Appeal held, even on the assumption that issue estoppel could apply in criminal cases, that it could not apply to estop the defendant from arguing on the second occasion that he was not, on the second occasion, a gypsy, because that was a different issue to that decided only shortly before on the first occasion (see per Lord Parker CJ at p. 466C–E, Diplock LJ at

H   p. 470A–C. Mr Stubbs, recognising that I am bound by *Mills v Cooper* and finding himself not able to distinguish it, wishes to reserve for the Court of Appeal, should the defendants go there, an argument that *Mills v Cooper* is wrong or inapplicable. Lest the case does go further, I should say that even without *Mills v Cooper* I would not have held the plaintiff to be estopped. A plaintiff might well feel, apropos security for costs, that it would be better to accede to a relatively modest demand for security in a borderline case than to lay out time and money on disputing the jurisdiction. I would have wished not to

do anything which would be likely to make a sensible and practical approach of that kind   A
less likely to be adopted by litigants, as I believe would be the case if I were to hold that
the unopposed earlier small award lost the plaintiff the jurisdiction argument it now
urges, now that a very substantial award is sought. I would thus have been pleased to
draw from *Arnold v National Westminster Bank* [1991] 2 AC 93 the references at p. 107
to Lord Wilberforce's earlier dictum that issue estoppel is to be applied only where the
facts are such as to amount to an abuse and to Lord Upjohn's that estoppels are to be
applied so as to work justice and not injustice and that the principle of issue estoppel is   B
to be applied to the circumstances of the case with that overriding consideration in mind.
I would, in all the circumstances, have held there to have been nothing abusive here in
the plaintiff, now faced with a huge demand for security, taking a point it had not raised
when it elected not to oppose the smaller earlier one. I would have held it unjust, on the
basis of the earlier order, to bar the plaintiff from a genuine subject of litigation.

A second argument of the defendants outside O. 23 was an invocation of a suggested   C
inherent jurisdiction to award security for costs, a jurisdiction available, I think it was
suggested, in possibly two ways. It could perhaps be used to lead to an award even within
areas expressly covered by O. 23, r. 1(1)(a) despite the practice under the rule itself not
being to make an award, but, more importantly, it could lead to an award in areas not
covered by O. 23, r. 1(1)(a). Under the supposed latter form of inherent jurisdiction, I
could, for example, simply say that because the plaintiff is a foreign corporation, is   D
impecunious and, for good measure, is incorporated outside the EEC, I may, without
needing to consider where it ordinarily resides, make an order against it. The way O. 23
is framed puts immense difficulties in the way of an argument for a still-subsisting
inherent jurisdiction of such a kind but I need say nothing by way of decision on the
point because Mr Stubbs recognised that the point is better left to the Court of Appeal.
Order 23 cannot, says Mr Stubbs, be with total accuracy said in all respects to codify the
previous law and practice or to embody it. For example, all awards are now wholly   E
discretionary whereas at an earlier stage awards against plaintiffs resident out of the
jurisdiction were as of course or nearly so (see, for example, *Crozat v Brogden* [1894] 2
QB 30) and special provision was earlier made by rule for plaintiffs who founded
themselves on judgments, bills of exchange or negotiable instruments (see generally *DSQ
Property Co Ltd v Lotus Cars Ltd* (1986) 2 BCC 99,539 at pp. 99,543–99,544). But, for
all that, Mr Stubbs recognises the force of the observations in *C T Bowring & Co v Corsi
& Partners Ltd* [1994] BCC 713 (CA). There it is said, so far as concerns cases outside   F
s. 726 in which the courts used to order security in the exercise of their inherent
jurisdiction, that the position is now as formulated in the Rules of the Supreme Court
(see per Dillon LJ at p. 717B–C) and that whilst some theory of an inherent jurisdiction
may still remain, the addition of new categories of cases in which awards for security
might be made outside the present rules is now a matter not for the exercise of any
inherent jurisdiction by judges dealing with matters case by case but for the Rules   G
Committee or Parliament (see pp. 717H and 722D). In the same case, Millett LJ gave his
view that there was no inherent jurisdiction whatsoever (see pp. 729C–F and compare
(1986) 2 BCC 99,539 at p. 99,543). Given the force of the observations in *Bowring* in the
Court of Appeal, Mr Stubbs reserves to that court argument as to the existence and
invocability on the facts of this case of some remaining inherent jurisdiction.

Jurisdiction under O. 23, r. 1   H

I return, therefore, to O. 23, r. 1(1)(a). It relates, of course, both to individuals and
corporations but although, therefore, the language used is the same in both cases, it does
not follow from that that matters which may be significant as to residence in the one case
are also so in the other. In relation to an artificial construct such as a corporation, the
notion of 'residence' is applicable only by way of analogy, not even, in some respects, a

A   close one (see *Cesena Sulphur Co v Nicholson* (1876) 1 ExD 428 at p. 452; *Goerz & Co v Bell* [1904] 2 KB 136 at p. 146; *Unit Construction Co Ltd v Bullock* [1960] AC 351 at p. 368). Thus, for example, whilst there is little difficulty in seeing an individual as having two or more residences (if only, say, as between town and country), the position as to companies may be different.

B   I now turn to a number of arguments put to me on the authorities and my conclusions in relation to them. The addition of the adverb 'ordinarily' does add something of importance to the word 'resident'. It connotes a degree of continuity being required, a reference to the way in which things are usually or habitually ordered (see *R v Barnet LBC, ex parte Shah* [1983] 2 AC 309 at p. 341C–H). Whilst the added word might not have a corresponding effect in the case of an individual, as I see it, it is more difficult for a corporation to be ordinarily resident in more than one place than it would be for it merely to be resident in more than one place. Moreover, the context of O. 23, r. 1(1)(a)

C   is, at lowest, consistent with the propositus having only one ordinary residence. If that is not so one gets to the position, surely uncontemplated, that whereas a man ordinarily resident here could not have an order made against him by reason of his impecuniosity, if he also were to be ordinarily resident out of the jurisdiction then there would be jurisdiction to make an order against him. Both the word 'ordinarily' and the framework of O. 23 should incline me to a meaning for 'ordinarily resident' in this case such that,

D   other than in exceptional circumstances, I should be able to envisage only one such residence.

The test of residence or ordinary residence (or, correspondingly, being ordinarily resident) is a long established test in tax matters (see, for example, *Cesena* and *Goerz* above). Different considerations, though, might well apply to the determination of residence or ordinary residence for the purposes of the UK taxing statutes and to the

E   determination for other purposes, for example the service of a writ (see *De Beers Consolidated Mines Ltd v Howe* [1906] AC 455 at pp. 459–460 and, more generally, *Goerz* at p. 144).

Whilst different considerations might well apply to determining ordinary residence for tax and for other purposes, so far as concerns individuals the tests applied in tax cases have without any awkwardness or consciousness of injustice been adopted for other more general purposes (see *Shah* at pp. 341–342). Ordinary residence is not a term of art (see

F   *Shah* at p. 340G). This conclusion as to individuals suggests one need not be especially shy in this area about adopting the conclusion of tax cases to cases outside tax.

By the time O. 23 took effect in 1964 there had long been given to the expression 'ordinarily resident' in relation to a trading corporation and tax a meaning that required one to look for where the company's 'central control and management actually abides' (see Lord Loreburn LC in *De Beers* at p. 458, and *Unit Construction* at pp. 363, 365). In

G   the usual way one might be critical of an approach in which, whilst one seeks to find 'ordinary residence' for the purpose of some particular legislation or rule, one asks instead a different question, namely where the central control and management might abide, as such a process involves paraphrasing the enactment and then inquiring not into the enactment but into the paraphrase. However, it is here worth citing Lord Radcliffe in *Unit Construction* at p. 366:

H   'It is true that the law so declared substitutes a judicial formula for the general words of the statute, a form of limitation which one normally seeks to avoid. But, in the circumstances, I believe such a process to have been inevitable, and, in my opinion, the *De Beers* judgment, followed as it is by a number of other judgments of the highest authority which have accepted the same principle, must be treated today as if the test which it laid down was as precise and as unequivocal as a

positive statutory injunction. That means that there is no escape from Lord   A
Loreburn's words:

> "... a company resides for the purposes of income tax where its real business is carried on ... I regard that as the true rule, and the real business is carried on where the central management and control actually abides."

I do not know of any other test which has either been substituted for that of central management and control, or has been defined with sufficient precision to be   B
regarded as an acceptable alternative to it. To me, at any rate, it seems impossible to read Lord Loreburn's words without seeing that he regarded the formula he was propounding as constituting the test of residence. If the conditions he postulated were present, there was residence; if they were not, other conditions did not suffice to make up residence. And so, I think, his meaning was universally understood, not least in judgments of this House (see *American Thread Co v Joyce*;   C
New Zealand Shipping Co Ltd v Thew; *Bradbury v English Sewing Cotton Co Limited*) for the next twenty years.'

Given that there is no insuperable difficulty in adopting the meaning of ordinary residence used in tax cases, given the difficulty in formulating any alternative test and given the emphatic endorsement of Lord Loreburn's long established *De Beers* test in *Unit Construction* only a short while before O. 23 was introduced, it seems to me reasonable to import the 'central management and control' test into O. 23, r. 1(1)(a) as   D
the test intended by the Rules Committee in relation to a corporation, at all events unless I can find some clearly contrary indication appearing from either the context or from authority.

I have not understood there to be any clear indication to the contrary in the context, nor has any authority obliging or even encouraging me to employ some other meaning been shown to me.   E

Mr Walton mounted an attractive argument for an alternative to Lord Loreburn's *De Beers* test based on *Adams v Cape Industries plc* [1990] BCC 786 and leading to a conclusion based on the passage in *Adams* at p. 816B where the Court of Appeal adopted a passage from Pearson J's judgment in *F & K Jabbour v Custodian of Absentee Property* [1954] 1 WLR 139 at p. 146 as follows:

> 'A corporation resides in a country if it carries on business at a fixed place of   F
> business, and, in the case of an agency, the principle to be applied in determining whether the corporation is carrying on business at the agency is to ascertain whether the agent has authority to enter into contracts on behalf of the corporation without submitting them to the corporation for approval ...'

Whilst I shall be referring briefly to *Adams* on another point, I see the *Jabbour* and *Adams* approach as being less helpful than the *De Beers* one, chiefly because in *Adams* the Court of Appeal was concerned with the possibly more ephemeral 'presence' or   G
'residence' of a corporation and not with 'ordinary residence', with its connotation of continuity. Secondly, I prefer *De Beers* because *Adams* was concerned not with the question of whether, to English eyes, a company was in or out of the English jurisdiction but with the question of whether, to English eyes and for the purpose of enforcing in England a foreign court's order, a foreign court could properly have held a corporation to be within that foreign court's jurisdiction for the purpose of making the order against   H
it, a question which would be likely to be especially coloured by considerations of comity and reciprocity, issues which have so far played little part in questions of security for costs. So also I prefer *De Beers* to *Kwok Chi Leung Karl v Commissioner of Estate Duty* [1988] 1 WLR 1035 (PC) because what was discussed there was the situs of property and only indirectly that of a person, and the presence or residence of a corporation there spoken of had the quality that it could simultaneously be in several places (see at p. 1041)

A   and hence lacked the connotations which, if I am right above, the word 'ordinarily' and
     the general context of O. 23, r. 1(1)(a) suggests are to be present.

     Mr Stubbs, as an alternative approach to the *De Beers* test, ran another argument as
     follows. The only conceivable candidates for the ordinary residence of the plaintiff are
     Jersey and England. If one can overlook the possibility of the plaintiff having no ordinary
     residence anywhere, one can thus prove the ordinary residence to be in Jersey by proving
B   it not to be in England. On the test applicable to service here, for example *Jones v Scottish
     Accident Insurance Co Ltd* (1886) 17 QBD 421 – a test looking to a physical presence by
     an office or an authorised agent here – the plaintiff cannot be said to be resident here and
     hence must be ordinarily resident in Jersey and thus out of the jurisdiction. However,
     service on corporations is now regulated by a separate code not dependent on residence
     at all (see O. 65, r. 3) and in any event O. 23, as Mr Potts points out, conspicuously does
     not require the plaintiff to be not resident here but requires the plaintiff to be ordinarily
C   resident somewhere else. I would thus be uneasy about giving any great weight to an
     argument that depended on proving an absence of English residence rather than the
     proving of a foreign one.

     Accordingly I propose to adopt the *De Beers* test of central management and control
     but I am to remember that in applying that test to a non-trading corporation I may need,
     in the absence of features arising from the carrying on of its business, to look more than
D   otherwise would be the case to the petitioner's corporate activity as, in a different context,
     was suggested as appropriate in the Court of Appeal in *Adams* at p. 810F.

     The *De Beers* test is such that, in relation to a corporation, it is likely to lead to only
     one place of ordinary residence (see *Unit Construction* per Lord Radcliffe at pp. 367–
     368). To that extent it dovetails well with what I have seen to be the context O. 23,
     r. 1(1)(a). It is, moreover, very much a question of fact (see *De Beers* at p. 458 and *Unit
     Construction* at pp. 362–363).
E
     Where the central management and control of a company takes a shape contrary to
     that required by the company's constitution, the court is not on that account to be
     deterred from looking to the activity as it is and concluding from it as it would have done
     had it not been inconsistent with the constitution – see *Unit Construction* at p. 363,
     reversing the Court of Appeal on that point. However, it does not follow from that, as it
     seems to me, that the company's constitution is irrelevant. Where the company is
F   conducted in a manner consistent with or not inconsistent with its constitution, the
     consistency between the articles and the factual activity seem to me to buttress one
     another so as to make less susceptible to challenge a conclusion which is based on both
     of them than would be a conclusion derived from only one of them.

     So far as concerns activities on the part of companies and the provisions of their
     respective constitutions, in different cases, hardly surprisingly, different factors have been
G   given different weights. Thus weight has been given to the provision of a company's
     objects clause (*Cesena* at p. 454); to the place of incorporation (*Cesena* at pp. 444, 453);
     to where the real trade and business of the company is carried on (*Cesena* at p. 452); to
     where the books of the company are kept (*Cesena* at p. 455); to where the administrative
     work is done (*Cesena* at p. 455); to where the directors with a full power to disapprove of
     local steps and to require different ones to be taken themselves met or were resident
     (*Cesena* at p. 456); to where directors to whom the management of the company was
H   confided ordinarily met (*Goerz* at p. 148, *De Beers* at p. 459, *Swedish Central Railway Co
     Ltd v Thompson* [1925] AC 495 at p. 503); to considerations as to the physical presence of
     the company, as where it 'keeps house' (*De Beers* at p. 458); to where the chief office is
     situate or the company secretary is to be found (*Jones* at pp. 422–423).

     I now turn to the evidence. The plaintiff was incorporated in Jersey on 3 July 1984. Its
     present paid-up capital is £12 divided into 12 shares of £1 each on which £12 has been

paid. Its principal object is to be an 'investment trust company', an object which gives no   A
clue as to where it might reside. It has no premises anywhere but it does have a registered
office. Its present registered shareholders are B & C Nominees (Jersey) Ltd, B & C
Subscribers (Jersey) Ltd, B & C Trustees (Jersey) Ltd and B & C Administrators (Jersey)
Ltd, which four companies hold three ordinary shares each and all of which companies
have as their address PO Box 75, Normandy House, St Helier, Jersey. That is the address
of a Jersey firm of advocates, Bedell & Christin ('B & C'). The secretary of the plaintiff is
Circle Advisers Ltd, which has the same address as B & C. The memorandum of   B
association of the plaintiff states that its registered office will be situate in Jersey. The
present registered office is at the offices of B & C. Amongst the plaintiff's objects is the
object of procuring it to be registered or recognised in any part of the world outside the
island of Jersey but, so far as can be seen from the evidence, that power has not been
exercised. The original, as opposed to present, shareholders in the plaintiff company
appear to have been four individuals, each holding three shares, and all having the B &   C
C Jersey address as their address. The plaintiff's articles provide that a general meeting
should be held in the island of Jersey once in every calendar year; there appears to be no
express provision for general meetings to be ordinarily held outside the island. The
management of the business of the plaintiff is confided to its directors. Minutes are
required to be made by the directors, in books provided for the purpose, of all
appointments of officers made by the directors, of the names of the directors present at
each meeting of directors and of all resolutions and proceedings of all meetings of the   D
plaintiff and of the directors and of committees of directors. The articles provide that
books of account should be kept at what is referred to as 'the office' or at such other
place as the directors should think fit and should always be open to inspection of the
directors. There is good reason to believe that the original four individual shareholders
held not beneficially for themselves but in equal shares for Captain Lemos and Mr Pipilis,
both thought to be residents, then, of Greece. There is no reason to believe that either of   E
those two thereafter acquired any residence other than Greek. Captain Lemos died
intestate domiciled in Greece on 3 December 1989 and on 29 November 1990 letters of
administration of all his estate in this country was granted to his son, Christos Lemos of
London NW3. The gross value of Captain Lemos's estate in England and Wales and the
net estate were both given in the grant as £201,570.

A minute of the first meeting of the plaintiff (held in the Piraeus on 4 July 1984) has
been supplied by the plaintiff's solicitors to the defendants. It is, I think, the only minute   F
that has been disclosed, despite requests for more. It indicates that Captain Lemos and
Mr John Pipilis were appointed first directors of the plaintiff and that Captain Lemos
was chairman. Circle Advisers Ltd were then appointed secretary. At some date in 1986
Captain Lemos had bought the 1,017,472 preference shares in the company of which I
earlier spoke. Those preference shares were transferred to the plaintiff. When the share
certificate in respect of the preference shares was sent to the plaintiff in May 1986, the   G
plaintiff was given an address in the Piraeus.

On 29 January 1990 the petitioner was struck off the register in Jersey and dissolved
(the provisions of Jersey law differ from ours) but was restored on 10 June 1991. On the
same day that the plaintiff thus sprang back to life in Jersey, there was a grant of letters
of administration in the Royal Court of Jersey in respect of the personal estate of Captain
Lemos to Mr John Phillip Kendall.

So much for the past. Coming to the present, Christos Lemos, Captain Lemos's son,   H
has sworn affidavits in which he gives some further details as to the operation of the
plaintiff. He says that since reinstatement of the plaintiff to the register on 10 June 1991
he has provided and continues to provide the central management and control of the
petitioner. I attach very little weight to that assertion partly because he fails to indicate
to me what he has in mind by the expression 'central management and control' and

A   partly because he gives no concrete examples of his provision of central management and control. Mr Lemos swears that he has been in England since 1965 and has lived and worked here ever since, has a wife and two children here and has since 1981 lived at an address in NW3. I accept that he is resident here and, indeed, is ordinarily resident here. He deposes that on incorporation of the plaintiff, his father, Captain Lemos, and Mr John Pipilis were directors of the company 'and equal shareholders'. That latter part is incorrect. He says that from his knowledge of his late father's affairs he believes that Mr

B   Pipilis held his shares in the plaintiff as his father's nominee but he gives no greater explanation of why that should be so. He says that after his father's death he set about trying to establish the whereabouts, nature and extent of his father's estate and that he is a beneficiary of his father's estate, including any assets in England or Jersey. I am not told what proportion of Captain Lemos's estate is likely to fall to Mr Lemos, nor that there has been or can be any appropriation to Mr Lemos of some or all of the shares in

C   the plaintiff held for the Jersey estate. Mr Lemos's enquiries led him to ask the plaintiff's present solicitors, Withers, to investigate the position of the plaintiff. Withers in turn made enquiry of B & C and it was in that way that it was found that the plaintiff had been struck off and it was by way of B & C and Withers, at the instigation of Mr Lemos, that the plaintiff was restored to the register as I have mentioned.

     The s. 459 petition was presented, as I have mentioned, on 30 August 1991. It is Mr Lemos's evidence that, by way of new declarations of trust made by the four corporate

D   shareholders, what had been the 50 per cent of the shares in the plaintiff held beneficially for Mr Pipilis is now held on trust for a body called the Zoodotis Foundation and the other 50 per cent is declared to be held for, in effect, Mr Kendall as Captain Lemos's administrator. Mr Lemos says that the Zoodotis Foundation is a benevolent foundation which was set up by his father to hold the family assets and in particular the family home. He says that the members of the foundation are his mother, his two sisters and his father's

E   private secretary. Whether by that he means to say that the only persons who may benefit by way of the Zoodotis Foundation are those members or whether he means only that the foundation is run by those members is not clear. He goes on to say in evidence that the current position is that the directors of the plaintiff are four partners in B & C. (I think I may take it that they are all resident in Jersey.) He says that he makes strategic decisions relating to the plaintiff and 'in particular' in relation to this litigation. The use of the expression 'in particular' suggests that there are strategic decisions as to other

F   aspects of the plaintiff's affairs which he makes but what they might be is not explained. He says that his relationship with B & C and the lines of communication which operate are correctly set out in a letter of 30 June 1994 from a partner in B & C, Advocate Dart, one of the four B & C directors of the plaintiff. Mr Lemos says that the directors of the plaintiff 'take instructions from me', but as he indicates that it is Advocate Dart's letter that correctly sets out his relationship with B & C, it is to that letter that I shall principally

G   look. Indeed, to my mind that letter is the most important explanation of how the affairs of the plaintiff are conducted.

     However, before I turn to it I shall go next to the affidavit of Mr Adam Taylor of Withers, the plaintiff's solicitors, who also deposes on the subject of the plaintiff's residence. He, too, says that central management and control of the plaintiff is in the hands of Mr Lemos, but, again, that seems to me more a secondary conclusion or argument rather than the setting out of primary facts. As such I cannot attach any great

H   weight to it and I see no reason to prefer Mr Taylor's evidence to what can be gleaned from Advocate Dart's letter, as Mr Taylor's evidence is likely to be secondhand so far as it concerns how the B & C directors meet and act and react amongst themselves upon their having indicated to them Mr Lemos's wishes or instructions.

     Mr Taylor deposes that the shares in the company are the only asset of the plaintiff. Large parts of Mr Taylor's affidavit merely recycle passages from Mr Lemos's affidavit,

but he goes on to state that Mr Lemos takes all material decisions relating to these   A
proceedings and to the plaintiff generally, but, again, I prefer to go to Advocate Dart's
letter to find how decisions are taken.

Advocate Dart is a partner in B & C, advocates & notaries public of St Helier. He is,
as I have mentioned, one of the four partners in B & C who are the only directors of the
plaintiff. It is not material that I should examine the position as it might be if they or
some of them resigned and if Mr Lemos or others were appointed. Order 23, r. 1(1)(a) is   B
directed to the present, not to what will or might be. Advocate Dart's letter of 30 June
1994 shows that the plaintiff gave formal instructions to Withers to act as its solicitors
following a board meeting. Mr Potts would emphasise the word 'formal' as if some other
instructions had preceded the formal ones and had been given, presumably, by Captain
Lemos. There is no detailed evidence of either point and I would expect Withers, naturally
wishing to avoid being at personal risk as to costs, to have made clear that they would
wish to act only upon the due instructions of the board. Advocate Dart goes on to say,   C
as one would expect, that it was the plaintiff that authorised Withers to issue the petition.
It has been Advocate Dart who has inquired into the constitution of Zoodotis and who
has explained the position to that body. The plaintiff relies on Mr Lemos to fund the
litigation and that (with my emphasis) 'has meant that in practice the directors of
Supreme have *allowed* the litigation to be conducted *very much* in accordance with
instructions which Mr Lemos gives' to Withers. The word 'allowed' is particularly   D
significant, as is the fact that the instructions given by Mr Lemos are there to Withers not
to the board. Advocate Dart goes on:

> '. . . if Mr Lemos was ever to give instructions directly to us I would act in
> accordance with those instructions provided that I was satisfied that they were
> consistent with Jersey company law and with the interests of Zoodotis and the
> administrator of the Jersey estate as the persons interested in the share capital of   E
> Supreme.'

Advocate Dart seems there to distinguish between the four partner-directors
('instructions directly to us') and himself ('I would act') but, leaving that aside, it is
accepted by Mr Potts that the Jersey company law, as to consistency with which the
advocate would need to be satisfied, includes that a board must act with careful regard
to the interests of the company and to its shareholders as a whole. Finally, Advocate   F
Dart's letter mentions that following a board meeting the plaintiff opened a bank account
on which Mr Lemos is a signatory but his signature requires, if it is to be operative, the
countersignature of a director.

Mr Potts argues, rightly in my view, that I must have regard to the shadowy nature of
the plaintiff; it has no place of business; it carries on no business; it has only one asset,
the shares in the company; it has no branch office or place of business registered in   G
England and its only activity is the conduct of the s.459 petition proceeding in England.
Of course, it is implicit in any O. 23, r. 1(1)(a) case that the plaintiff is litigating in
England so that it is difficult to see that fact alone as decisive that the plaintiff is not
ordinarily resident out of the jurisdiction. But, in any event, I do not understand that
emphasis on the litigation assists the plaintiff. Given that English solicitors are likely to
be chary of acting for a company without due instructions from its board, the fact that
the plaintiff's sole activity is litigation here underlines that it was the board which resolved   H
to begin that sole activity, without which resolution it would have been most unlikely to
have been begun, and that the board can, by a simple resolution to withdraw instructions
from Withers bring the whole of its sole activity to a standstill. Mr Potts accepts that the
board has, putting it at its lowest, a power of veto in respect of anything Mr Lemos may
propose or wish to be done by the plaintiff, but, relying, he says, upon *Unit Construction,*

A   he argues that a power of veto in the board in Jersey is not the least inconsistent with central management and control being in Mr Lemos in England.

In *Unit Construction* an English parent company had four subsidiaries, one undeniably here and three incorporated and registered in Kenya. The English subsidiary made payments to the African subsidiaries and claimed to be entitled to deduct those payments for the purposes of UK income tax. It could do so only if the African subsidiaries were resident in the UK and carrying on a trade wholly or partly in the UK. The House of
B   Lords held, applying the *De Beers* 'central management and control' test, that the African subsidiaries were resident here. Mr Potts argues that the boards of the African subsidiaries had a power of veto, just as has the board of the plaintiff, but that that did not stop central management and control residing where the parent company, the real manager, was. So also, he says, the plaintiff's board's power of veto should not obscure that real management and control is truly in Mr Lemos in England. I find the parallel
C   unconvincing. In *Unit Construction* the parent company's board had formally resolved that local management in Africa had been so bad that the management of the African subsidiaries 'must be taken over by the directors of' the parent company in London (see p. 353). The late Mr Frank Heyworth Talbot QC, arguing for the appellant English subsidiary, is recorded as arguing, at p. 355:

D   'The peculiar feature of the present case is that the boards of the African subsidiaries did not function at all at the material times, even as a rubber stamp.'

Lord Radcliffe said that they never purported to function as a board of management. When a board fails to act *at all*, not even as a rubber stamp, I can see that it may be right to look through its by then wholly theoretical power of veto, but no such case is made out here. The Jersey board may generally accommodate Mr Lemos, but it meets, it gives instructions from time to time to Withers, it opens a bank account, it is kept informed of developments and, if it has acted in the past as Advocate Dart suggests it will for the
E   future, it asks itself whether the implementation of any particular proposals of Mr Lemos are consistent with the best interests of the plaintiff and its shareholders, who do not include Mr Lemos and who hold for beneficiaries who might or might not include Mr Lemos.

Mr Stubbs makes the further important distinction that in *Unit Construction* the English holding company was the sole beneficial shareholder in the African subsidiaries, which were wholly owned. Its resolution to take over the management of the African
F   subsidiaries had a constitutional force which Mr Lemos has not achieved and maybe could not achieve. Indeed, the route by which Mr Lemos could impose his will upon the Jersey board should they choose not to implement it is totally unclear and, even it if exists, would take time. There is no real analogy between the African boards in *Unit Construction* and the Jersey board of the plaintiff and, in turn, I cannot ignore the power residing in the Jersey board.

G   I shall now attempt to stand back a little in order to see the whole uncovered picture. I see a company incorporated in Jersey, with a Jersey registered office, with Jersey resident shareholders, with a Jersey board, with a Jersey secretary and with a board that meets as such and which has not surrendered its powers nor had them removed but rather which operates them within what it conceives to be the law of Jersey. It is the Jersey board alone which works the mutation by which, if it so allows or elects, Mr Lemos's personal wishes,
H   proposals or even instructions become an activity of the plaintiff itself. In my judgment, the central management and control of the plaintiff abides in Jersey; it is ordinarily resident out of the jurisdiction.

Discretion

Accordingly I turn to the discretion I have under O. 23, r. 1(1)(a). I indicated at the outset that I would at this stage, if it arrived, briefly set out the complaints in the petition.

The petition has been very substantially amended but, says Mr Potts, its basic complaints   A
remain as they have been from the start, namely that in March 1991 the business and
goodwill of the company was transferred to a company referred to as Newco, in return
for which Newco assumed the company's liabilities and paid the company £1. The
company became a shell and ceased to trade. The plaintiff says the consideration given
by Newco was grossly inadequate and that there were breaches of pre-emption provisions
which should have operated in the plaintiff's favour as a holder of preference shares in
the company. The plaintiff complains, too, of no notice having been given to it of the   B
EGM of March 1991 at which the arrangements with Newco were apparently approved.
The so-called trio, Mr Stubbs's clients, were directors of the company when it sold its
business and undertaking to Newco and were not only directors of Newco but also
shareholders in Star Vacations Ltd which owned Newco. Star Vacations Ltd sold the
shares in Newco (which by then represented the value of the erstwhile business and
goodwill of the company and, says the plaintiff, nothing else) to the public company   C
mentioned, Owners Abroad Group, for a price of some £10m. The plaintiff is left, it
alleges, with a holding of preference shares in a shell company, whilst the trio and some
others have shared in a substantial jackpot, no part of which has come to the plaintiff.
The petition will be hotly contested and will be likely to take many weeks to try but Mr
Stubbs accepts that this summary, which largely repeats an earlier judgment of mine in
May (see [1994] BCC 947), can be taken to be an adequate summary for present purposes.

    To revert to my discretion, as to the important consideration of whether an award of   D
security would or would not probably stifle the proceedings, the plaintiff's evidence is
startlingly weak. I am told there is a Lemos family shipping business and I am given a
figure for Captain Lemos's estate in England. I am told that Mr Lemos has diversified
into the financial services business, that he is a member of NASDIM and FIMBRA and
that he is the person who has principally funded the petition so far. Beyond that I know
nothing of his resources. Nor do I know the means of the Zoodotis Foundation. Mr   E
Taylor of Withers says only:

> 'However, whatever the means of Mr Lemos (who is one of the beneficiaries of the
> Jersey estate of his late father who was a shareholder in Supreme)' – I interpose
> that that is not correct – 'or anyone else, I do not believe it is safe to assume that
> an order for security for costs of the order presently being sought would not have
> the effect of stifling the petitioner's claim.'
  F

    I have been referred to the unreported transcript of *Keary Developments Ltd v Tarmac
Construction Ltd* (13 April 1994, CA) where (at p. 14 of the transcript) Peter Gibson LJ,
with whom Butler-Sloss LJ agreed, said:

> 'Before the court refuses to order security on the grounds that it would unfairly
> stifle a valid claim, the court must be satisfied that, in all the circumstances, it is
> probable that the claim would be stifled.'
  G

A little later he added:

> 'However, the court should consider not only whether the plaintiff company can
> provide security out of its own resources to continue the litigation, but also whether
> it can raise the amount needed from its directors, shareholders or other backers or
> interested persons. As this is likely to be peculiarly within the knowledge of the
> plaintiff company, it is for the plaintiff to satisfy the court that it would be
> prevented by an order for security from continuing the litigation (see *Flender Werft*   H
> *AG v Aegean Maritime* [1990] 2 Lloyd's Rep 27.'

    The plaintiff's evidence quite fails to satisfy me that an award would probably stifle its
proper claim. That conclusion draws the strength out of another of Mr Potts's
submissions, that here the impecuniosity of the plaintiff is the defendant's fault and is a
consequence of the very acts complained of in the petition. He says this argument is

A   independent of the stifle argument but, as I see it, if an award is not shown probably to stifle the action, the basic injustice, which is here of a person escaping the consequences of his wounding another by reason only of the severity of the wound, does not arise (see also *Farrer v Lacy Hartland & Co* (1885) 28 ChD 482 at p. 485 per Bowen LJ).

B   Another point that Mr Potts urges is that just as in the case of an individual resident within the jurisdiction his impecuniosity is no good ground for an award of security against him, so it should also be no ground against the plaintiff. But why should I treat the plaintiff corporation as if an individual? Of course, if it had been an English corporation within the range of s. 726(1) its impecuniosity would have grounded an award against it. I reject this argument as I have no good reason to regard the plaintiff as if resident in England or as if an individual.

C   Next Mr Potts says that an award is here being sought oppressively. He refers to some errors in computation overstating the costs said to have been spent or to be spent. But if they were errors, as opposed to deliberate, then I see no indication of oppression.

As for the merits of the petition so far as to be borne in mind at this stage, all parties have here had in mind the strictures of Sir Nicolas Browne-Wilkinson V-C in *Porzelack KG v Porzelack (UK) Ltd* [1987] 1 WLR 420 at 423E, where he says:

D   'Undoubtedly if it can clearly be demonstrated that the plaintiff is likely to succeed, in the sense that there is a very high probability of success, then that is a matter that can properly be weighed in the balance. Similarly, if it can be shown that there is a very high probability that the defendant will succeed, that is a matter that can be weighed. But for myself I deplore the attempt to go into the merits of the case, unless it can clearly be demonstrated one way or another that there is a high degree of probability of success or failure.'

E   In the circumstances I have not been taken by either side to the literally thousands of pages of evidence which I am told have already been filed in the petition, and neither side has sought to convince me of the high degree of probability of their success or of the other's failure. The merits are thus neutral so far as concerns my present task. As I have found no argument so far to bar an award of security, I turn to the most general of considerations which as *Keary* indicates (at p. 12) are as follows:

F   'The court must carry out a balancing exercise. On the one hand it must weigh the injustice to the plaintiff if prevented from pressing a proper claim by an award for security. Against that, it must weigh the injustice to the defendant if no security is ordered and at the trial the plaintiff's claim fails and the defendant finds himself unable to recover from the plaintiff the costs which have been incurred by him in his defence of the claim.'

I have also reminded myself of the broad approach described by Lord Denning MR in *Parkinson & Co v Triplan Ltd* [1973] 1 WLR 609 at p. 626E–H. Doing the best I can to

G   conduct the balance as I am required to do, I should, in my judgment, exercise my discretion by making an award of security for costs against the plaintiff. Thus, after an interval, I shall wish to hear argument on the question of quantum of the award.

(*Order accordingly*)

H

Cunliffe Engineering Ltd & Anor v English Industrial Estates Corp.

Chancery Division (Newcastle).

His Honour Judge Howarth (sitting as a judge of the High Court, Chancery Division).

Judgment delivered 7 July 1994.

Receivership – Distress for rent – Landlord levied distress on premises of tenant in receivership – Tenant had executed a chattel mortgage in favour of bank covering equipment included in distress – Whether distress was valid – Whether goods were goods of company – Whether bank had interest in tenancy by virtue of debenture – Whether company remained reputed owner of goods – Law of Distress Amendment Act 1908, s. 1, 4.

This case concerned the validity of a purported distress by a landlord of factory premises the day after the appointment of receivers to the tenant by its bankers under a debenture. The tenant had also executed a chattel mortgage in favour of the bank covering equipment described in a schedule which included all the items which were the subject of the disputed distraint.

The questions for the court were whether the bank could take advantage of s. 1 of the Law of Distress Amendment Act 1908 on the basis that the goods were the property of the bank and that the bank had no interest in the tenancy or premises; and whether the tenant was the reputed owner of the goods under s. 4 of the 1908 Act.

Held, dismissing the plaintiffs' claim to the proceeds of sale of the goods and giving judgment for the defendant landlord on its counterclaim:

1. The owner of the chattels specified in the schedule to the chattel mortgage was at all times the company and not the bank. Up to and after the appointment of the receivers, the company remained in possession of the assets, with the permission of the bank, in circumstances such that the company was the reputed owner of the assets. Therefore s. 4 of the 1908 Act was of no help to the bank.

2. Moreover, the bank had an interest in the tenancy of the premises as a result of the charge effected by the debenture. It followed that the bank did not come within s. 1(c) of the 1908 Act.

The following cases were referred to in the judgment:

ELS Ltd, Re [1994] BCC 449.
Gomba Holdings UK Ltd & Ors v Homan & Ors (1986) 2 BCC 99,102.
Gomba Holdings UK Ltd & Ors v Minories Finance Ltd & Ors (1989) 5 BCC 27.
Harris, Ex parte. Re Pulling (1872) LR 8 Ch App 48.
Johnson (B) & Co (Builders) Ltd, Re [1955] Ch 634.
Metropolitan Life Assurance Co of New Zealand Ltd v Essere Print Ltd (1990) 5 NZCLC 775.
Ratford & Anor v Northavon District Council (1986) 2 BCC 99,242.
Smart Brothers Ltd v Holt & Ors [1929] 2 KB 303.
Times Furnishing Co Ltd v Hutchings & Anor [1938] 1 KB 775.
Western Mobile Homes Ltd v Gaudet [1971] 4 WWR 398.

Matthew Caswell (instructed by Robert Muckle, Newcastle upon Tyne) for the plaintiffs.

Carolyn Walton (instructed by Wilkinson Maughan, Newcastle upon Tyne) for the landlord.

A

AGREED FACTS

1. At all relevant times the defendant was lessor and the first plaintiff was lessee of the premises known as and being No. BT 50/2 and 50/6 in the Teesside Industrial Estate, Cleveland, pursuant to leases dated 9 October 1986 and 9 May 1990 respectively.

2. By a debenture dated 19 October 1987 the first plaintiff charged its assets to the second plaintiff by way of fixed and floating charges as therein specified.

B

3. The first and second plaintiffs entered into a chattels mortgage dated 17 December 1991 in respect of the chattels described in the schedule thereto validly registered at Companies House.

4. On 12 May 1992 the second plaintiff appointed Roger Marsh and Albert Edward James of Price Waterhouse (hereinafter called 'the administrative receivers') administrative receivers and managers of the property of the first plaintiff charged by a debenture dated 19 October 1987 and made between the first plaintiff of the one part and the second plaintiff of the other part.

C

5. On 13 May 1992 Mr Storey and Mr Arrowsmith, certified bailiffs (hereinafter called 'the bailiffs') attended Unit BT 50/2 and 50/5 on Teesside Industrial Estate, Cleveland on behalf of the defendant and there met Timothy Morgan (hereinafter called 'Mr Morgan') who introduced himself as being from the administrative receivers' office.

D

6. Mr Storey told Mr Morgan that he (Mr Storey) was holding distress warrants for outstanding rent.

7. There followed a meeting at the offices of the first plaintiff between Mr Storey, Mr Arrowsmith and Mr Harrison (the then managing director of the first plaintiff) to discuss the rent demand and the warrants that the bailiffs were holding. Mr Morgan also joined the meeting.

E

8. Mr Morgan left the meeting and returned to state that the first plaintiff did not have the funds to make payment of the rent.

9. Mr Storey then said that he would execute the distress warrants for rent. He told Mr Morgan that the first plaintiff had five days in which to pay the outstanding rent, otherwise the assets would be removed and sold. Mr Morgan said that administrative receivers had been appointed; and that the majority of the assets of the first plaintiff were the subject of a chattels mortgage. Mr Morgan and Mr Harrison then produced the chattels mortgage for the bailiffs to look at. A copy was not given to the bailiffs on that occasion (a copy was subsequently faxed on 22 May 1992 to the bailiffs by Robert Muckle, solicitors for the plaintiffs).

F

10. Mr Storey stated that it was his belief that he was entitled to distrain and take walking possession of the first plaintiff's assets.

G

11. Mr Morgan said that Mr Storey was not entitled to distrain on the goods because they were the subject of a chattels mortgage to the second plaintiff.

12. The bailiffs and Mr Morgan agreed that pending further investigation and advice, Mr Morgan would sign a walking possession form.

H

13. Mr Morgan added that he needed more than the five days to complete his investigation, consult his superiors and speak to their solicitors. Mr Storey agreed to an extension to 14 days provided such was requested in writing. Mr Storey explained that such letter had to contain a statement that the receivers would not remove the assets, and would not allow them to be removed without the written authority of the bailiffs. Mr Morgan made a note of that; went away, and returned with a letter to that effect dated 13 May 1992.

14. There followed exchanges of letters between Robert Muckle, solicitors for the A plaintiffs, Mr Storey and Wilkinson Maughan, solicitors for the defendant; starting with a letter dated 20 May 1992 from Robert Muckle to Mr Storey.

15. The parties then agreed, without prejudice to their respective stances in the dispute, as follows, that is to say that:

(a)   the defendant would cause the release of the walking possession;

(b)   the sale of the assets over which the defendant distrained or purported to distrain; B

(c)   the proceeds of sale or the sum of £20,000 (whichever was the greater) be placed in a deposit account in the joint names of Robert Muckle and Wilkinson Maughan pending the resolution of the dispute regarding the said distraint, such sum to secure any liability which the first plaintiff might have in respect of the defendant's walking possession and sheriff's costs.

The said agreement was constituted by a letter dated 6 July 1992 from Robert Muckle to C Wilkinson Vaughan, and a reply thereto from the latter to the former dated 8 May 1992.

16. By an agreement dated 13 July 1992 and made between the first plaintiff acting by its joint administrative receivers of the one part and Topside Module Engineering Ltd of the other part, the former sold assets to the latter as follows:

	£
Plant and machinery	112,500.00
Motor lorry (B53 OVN)	1,700.00
Cavalier GSi (G444 BDG)	5,500.00
Cavalier 1.6L (G160 GEF)	4,000.00
Rover Montego (G351 HUP)	4,000.00
Leasehold premises	1.00
	127,701.00
VAT	19,985.17
Total	147,686.17

17. Completion of the said agreement took place on 13 July 1992.

18. On or about 15 July 1992 it was agreed that out of the proceeds of sale as aforesaid F the sum of £27,500 and no other be held in a deposit account in the joint names of their respective solicitors pending resolution of the dispute as aforesaid; and that was done.

19. The first plaintiff passed into a creditors' voluntary winding up on 3 August 1992.

The issue: whether the levying of distress by the defendant on 12 May 1992 was lawful.

JUDGMENT

His Honour Judge Howarth: This is a judgment in the case of Cunliffe Engineering Ltd and Lloyds Bank plc v Urban Regeneration Agency (formerly English Industrial Estates Corporation). This case concerns the validity of a purported distress on behalf of a landlord of factory premises which was levied by a certificated bailiff on behalf of the landlord after the occurrence of the following events, namely, first, the execution of a debenture in favour of Lloyds Bank plc, the second named plaintiff whom I will refer to H as 'the bank'. Secondly, the execution of a chattel mortgage in favour of the bank. Thirdly, the appointment by the bank of joint receivers and managers of the property charged by the debenture.

Most of the relevant facts have been agreed between the parties. They are contained in a statement of agreed facts which has been handed in. This judgment should be treated

A   as setting out those agreed facts, though I think it not necessary to actually recite them while giving this judgment.

As I have already mentioned, the defendant has changed its name more recently. It was originally sued under one name, namely English Industrial Estates Ltd. It then became known as English Industrial Estates Corporation and is now known as Urban Regeneration Agency. The necessary leave to amend the title of the proceedings to reflect these changes of name has been given, most recently by myself yesterday.

B   In addition to the agreed facts which are set out in written form, oral evidence was given to the court by Mr Morgan who, at the relevant time, was the assistant to one of the receivers (Mr James) and, in addition, oral evidence was also given by Mr Storey who was the bailiff concerned.

For legal reasons which I shall have to deal with later on, it becomes necessary for me

C   to decide to whom the machinery and chattels in question belonged and in whose possession they were at the relevant time. The relevant time is the date of the levying of the purported distress on 13 May 1992.

The question of ownership is not straightforward. This is partly because some of the facts are not clear, partly because of the documents themselves and partly because of the law.

D   I state the documents in chronological order. Firstly, a lease dated 9 October 1986 of Unit BT 50/2. That was granted by the defendant as landlord in favour of the first plaintiff, Cunliffe Engineering Ltd as tenant.

The second document is a debenture dated 19 October 1987, registered at the companies registry two days later. That is a debenture given by Cunliffe Engineering Ltd to the bank.

E   Thirdly, a lease dated 9 May 1990 of Unit BT 50/6. The parties to the lease are the same as the parties to the 1986 lease. Finally, there is a chattel mortgage dated 17 December 1991 (registered again two days later at the companies registry) between the first plaintiff and the bank.

The debenture mortgages and charges first:

> 'The freehold and leasehold property . . . of the company, both present and future,
F   including . . . all buildings and fixtures (including trade fixtures) fixed plant and machinery from time to time on any such property . . .'

–and sixthly:

> 'the undertaking and all property and assets of the company both present and future.'

G   The charge of the property first described is a fixed first charge and, as respects that part of the property first described, which was at that date vested in the company, is to constitute a charge by way of legal mortgage thereon. The charge is a floating charge on the property sixthly described. Clearly therefore, the charge on the property comprised in the lease dated 9 October 1986 (the first of the two leases) is a first fixed charge by way of legal mortgage because that property was already owned by the company at the date of the debenture. Unfortunately, in this case there is no evidence at all as to what

H   machinery and assets the company owned as at the date of the granting of the debenture on 19 October 1987.

By the chattel mortgage, the company, as beneficial owner, assigned to the bank to hold absolutely, by way of continuing security for the payment and discharge of all moneys and liabilities, all the items of equipment described in the schedule thereto. The items listed in the schedule include all the items which are the subject of the disputed

purported distraint. The chattel mortgage contains an express covenant for further   A
assurance and an express provision for reassignment in the case of redemption.

Following the execution of the debenture and of the chattel mortgage, the items in
dispute remained in the possession of the company with the consent of the bank. They
were used by the company for the purpose of carrying out work in the ordinary course
of its business as engineers. The bank at no stage made any attempt to label any of these
items as being subject to the bank's rights, whether under the debenture or under the   B
chattel mortgage.

In argument, Mr Caswell, who appeared on behalf of the plaintiff, has said that the
bank debenture and the chattel mortgage are not mutually exclusive, they are, in effect, a
belt and braces protecting the bank's claims. I accept this proposition.

Who then was the owner of the chattels in question? In form, the chattel mortgage,
which seems to be the relevant document on which the parties placed reliance, assigned   C
the chattels to the bank absolutely. Mr Caswell says on behalf of the plaintiff that this is
conclusive. In my view it is not.

I refer to Fisher and Lightwood's *Law of Mortgage* (10th edn), and I would refer in
particular to the passage which appears between pp. 6 and 8 of that work, where there is
a discussion of the pre-1926 form of mortgages of land. That form was the same as the
form used for the chattel mortgage in this case. I think I need only quote two sentences
which appear at p. 8, they are as follows: D

> 'Before 1926, when, by the usual method of freehold mortgage, the fee simple was
> vested in the mortgagee the phrase 'equity of redemption' was used to denote the
> *equitable interest* of the mortgagor. In equity the mortgagor was the owner of the
> land subject to the mortgage.'

This is but one example of equity looking to the substance and not the form. The rules
of equity have prevailed over those rules of common law, where there is any conflict, ever   E
since 1875. It follows therefore, in my view, that the owner of the chattels specified in the
schedule to the chattel mortgage was at all times the first plaintiff, Cunliffe Engineering
Ltd, and not the bank.

It would seem that this was the view of all concerned in 1992 when the assets were sold.
I refer to the agreement dated 13 July 1992. It is an agreement for sale of those assets by
the company (the first plaintiff) acting by its receivers and managers. It is not an   F
agreement for sale by the bank as mortgagee. Indeed the bank is not even a party to this
agreement. In my view, the appointment of receivers and managers under the debenture
on 12 May 1992 does not alter this conclusion in any way. The letter of appointment
does not refer to the chattel mortgage at all. There was no attempt to appoint a receiver
under that document. It was an appointment of receivers and managers under the
debenture only.

Effectively, this appointment confers all the powers of the directors of the company on   G
the joint receivers and managers. In accordance with the debenture and in accordance
with statute, joint receivers and managers have duties to the bank as well as to the
company. Clause 7c of the debenture is a common form provision that the receivers are,
at all times and for all purposes, to be deemed to be the agents of the company. Being
administrative receivers, they are also deemed to be agents of the company under the
provisions of s. 44 of the *Insolvency Act* 1986.   H

The provision in the debenture clearly binds the bank. It is its own document. If the
assets were those of the bank there would be nothing for the receivers to receive and
manage, least of all as agents for the company.

Prior to the appointment of the receivers and managers, the company was in possession
of the assets in dispute, with the consent of the bank. As mentioned above, they were

A used by the company and nobody else for carrying out the everyday engineering work of the company. It has been conceded, rightly, by Mr Caswell on behalf of the plaintiffs that the company is, as between itself and the bank, to be treated as the reputed owner of those assets prior to the appointment of the joint receivers and managers. Possession, it seems to me, is a matter of fact which cannot be altered by the contents of documents which have been signed, save in exceptional circumstances.

B It is clear from the evidence of Mr Morgan and of Mr Storey that from 12 May 1992, when the receivers were appointed, down to 13 July 1992, the date of the agreement which I have already mentioned and also the date for completion under that document, the assets remained in the possession of the company, acting and governed by its receivers and managers. The assets were used during that period to complete the company's work in progress. The bank concurred in this use. At least I infer this must be so. I am sure the receivers and managers would not have used those assets in the manner which I have just

C described unless the bank did so concur. There is certainly no evidence to the contrary.

Was the defendant as landlord entitled to distrain on the assets because of the arrears of rent, amounting I think to £25,895.84, the arrears being under both leases and that being the total sum in arrears under both of them? At common law, a landlord was entitled to distrain on the demised premises for unpaid rent and could take any goods that he found there, whether they belonged to the tenant or to a third party. This right is

D now restricted by the *Law of Distress Amendment Act* 1908. The relevant sections of that Act are s. 1 and 4. Section 1 or at least the relevant parts for the purpose of this case provide as follows:

> 'If any superior landlord shall levy, or authorise to be levied, a distress on any furniture, goods, or chattels of–
>
> . . .

E
> (c) any other person whatsoever not being a tenant of the premises or of any part thereof, and not having any beneficial interest in any tenancy of the premises or any part thereof,
>
> for arrears of rent due to such superior landlord by his immediate tenant, such under tenant, lodger, or other person aforesaid may serve such superior landlord, or the bailiff or other agent employed by him to levy such distress, with a

F
> declaration in writing made by such under tenant, lodger, or other person aforesaid, setting forth that such immediate tenant has no right of property or beneficial interest in the furniture, goods, or chattels so distrained or threatened to be distrained upon, and that such furniture, goods, or chattels are the property or in the lawful possession of such under tenant, lodger, or other person aforesaid . . .'

G I now deal with the relevant parts of s. 4 which provides that:

> 'This Act shall not apply–
>
> (1) . . . to goods in the possession, order, or disposition of such tenant by the consent and permission of the true owner under such circumstances that such tenant is the reputed owner thereof . . .'

Those are the relevant statutory provisions and they raise certain points which have to

H be decided for the purpose of this case. Essentially, there are two questions, or perhaps three questions.

(1) In view of the finding which I have made, that the assets concerned are the assets of the tenant company, can s. 1 apply at all?

(2) If I should be wrong in that conclusion, does the bank as mortgagee have a beneficial interest in the tenancy of the premises?

(3)   After the appointment of the joint receivers and managers, did the company remain   A
in possession of those assets with the permission of the bank under circumstances
such that the company was the reputed owner of the assets?

Under s. 1, the person who can serve a counter-notice must not be the tenant of the
premises. He must claim to be the owner of the assets. As I have already held, the owner
of the assets was the company and it was the tenant of the premises, so it seems to me,
for that reason, that a notice under s. 1 simply cannot be served in this case.   B

But, I go on to deal with the question of whether the bank, if the bank were to be the
owner of those assets, has any beneficial interest in the tenancy or not? No help is to be
derived in this respect from Woodfall on *Landlord and Tenant*, or at least the passage
which has been drawn to my attention, para. 9.074 simply says:

'*Persons with no beneficial interest*

The last category of person protected is that of persons who are neither tenants   C
nor have any beneficial interest in any tenancy of the premises.'

It simply states the words of the section and does not elucidate them at all. Mr Caswell
refers me to the provisions of s. 1 of the *Law of Property Act* 1925. I quote a little more
extensively from that section than Mr Caswell did. Section 1 provides that:

'(1) The only estates in land which are capable of subsisting or of being conveyed   D
or created at law are–

(a) An estate in fee simple absolute in possession;

(b) A term of years absolute.

(2) The only interests or charges in or over land which are capable of subsisting or
of being conveyed or created at law are . . .

(c) A charge by way of legal mortgage . . .   E

(3) All other estates, interests, and charges in or over land take effect as equitable
interests.

(4) The estates, interests and charges which under this section are authorised to
subsist or to be conveyed or created at law are (when subsisting or conveyed or
created at law) in this Act referred to as "legal estates," and have the same incidents
as legal estates subsisting at the commencement of this Act; and the owner of a   F
legal estate is referred to as "an estate owner" and his legal estate is referred to as
his estate.

(8) Estates, interests, and charges in or over land which are not legal estates are in
this Act referred to as "equitable interests," . . .'

I also refer to s. 30 of the same Act, a well enough known provision which comes before
the court quite regularly. Amongst the category of persons who can apply for the   G
execution of a trust for sale under the terms of that section, 'a person interested', it is well
documented and well established that this includes a mortgagee.

It seems to me to be clear that the bank had a beneficial interest in the assets as at the
date of the distress on 13 May 1992 and, in particular and more relevantly, a beneficial
interest in the tenancy of the premises, since its interest arose as a result of the charge
effected by the debenture. It follows that the bank does not come within the meaning of   H
the words 'any other person' contained in s. 1(c) of the 1908 Act.

Looking, as equity requires, to the substance as well as to the form in the manner
mentioned above, clearly shows that this must be correct in my view. 'Beneficial interest'
under s. 1(c) of the 1908 Act is not, I am satisfied, restricted to interest under trusts or
strict settlements or the like.

A   The findings which I have already made, by themselves, are quite sufficient to dispose of this claim, but I pass on to the question of reputed ownership, in any event.

I have already held on the facts that on 13 May 1992, after the appointment of the receivers and managers, the assets concerned were in the possession of the company with the permission of the bank. It has been conceded, as I already said, rightly, that prior to 12 May 1992 this possession with consent was under such circumstances that the company was the reputed owner of the assets. Did the appointment of the joint receivers

B   and managers on 12 May 1992 effect any change in this position? It is to be noted that the company, the receivers and managers (and I would assume the bank) thought that there was no change by 13 July 1992, hence the form of the agreement of that date. Certainly, the company claims to be not merely the reputed owners but the actual owners of the goods by the execution of that agreement, and the purchasers would appear to have accepted that they had every appearance of being the owners of the goods, i.e. were

C   reputed owners.

Notice of the appointment of the joint receivers and managers was given to the registrar of companies, as required by s. 405 of the *Companies Act* 1985. It does not appear from any of the documents when this notice was received by the registrar. It is clear that this would only be notice to the registrar and not be notice to the world at large. Registration under the *Companies Act* 1985 is not the same as registration under the *Land Charges*

D   *Act* 1972. Very surprisingly, the researches of counsel have been unable to unearth any reported authorities which are directly in point on this question.

There is, however, persuasive authority in the form of the writing in textbooks which is of some relevance. I refer first of all to Picarda on the *Law relating to receivers, managers and administrators* (2nd edn) at p. 186. This relates to landlords after the appointment of a receiver and I take up the quotation at p. 185 under the heading

E   'Continued occupation':

'A receiver enjoys no statutory or other right of disclaimer. However the receiver may not wish to use the leasehold property or pay rent for it, or cause the company of which he is receiver to pay rent for it. In such a case there is no compulsion on the receiver. If he does decide to make use of the leasehold premises then plainly he must pay the rent which he will treat as a legitimate outgoing either under the terms of any relevant statutory provision or under the express terms of the

F   debenture. When he decides to continue in occupation he will in practice pay any arrears in order to avoid distress.'

It is those last words of the quotation which are persuasive authority in this case.

In addition, I refer to *Kerr on receivers and administrators* (17th edn), and I refer to p. 205, the section headed 'Leaseholds'. It is as follows:

G   'The liability of the receiver appointed on behalf of equitable incumbrancers for the rent of leaseholds has already been dealt with. A receiver appointed on behalf of debenture holders is in the same position in this respect as a receiver appointed on behalf of a mortgagee by sub-demise. He is therefore under no contractual liability to pay rent under the lease to the company, though he may be in occupation; though he may be compelled to pay arrears to avoid distress.'

H   The passage goes on to deal with other matters. I would be inclined to follow the views expressed in those textbooks unless there is authority which persuades me to do otherwise.

I have had a plethora of reported cases cited to me. I do not intend to refer to all of these cases in this judgment, though I will refer to most of them. I do not intend any discourtesy to counsel by not referring to each and every case. Some of the authorities, it

seems to me, have, at best, a tenuous connection with the point which I have to decide. I   A
do however refer to some of them briefly.

The first case is the case of *Metropolitan Life Assurance Co of New Zealand Ltd v Essere Print Ltd* (1990) 5 NZCLC 775. The New Zealand legislation is different from the 1908 Act. It only allows a landlord to make distress upon the chattels of the tenant or of the person in possession of the demised premises. The bank of New Zealand had a fixed charge over a printing press on the demised premise. The tenant and occupant was the   B
defendant company in that case. It was held that both the bank of New Zealand and the tenant company, on the most favourable scenario, had a substantial equitable interest in that printing press and it was not accordingly a chattel for tenant within the meaning of the New Zealand legislation. This case supports my conclusions as to the ownership of the assets in this case and as to the bank's beneficial interest in them.

I should add that there is no evidence before me as to whether the bank had been paid in full in respect of the debt which was owed to it by the company at the date of the   C
appointment of the joint receivers and managers. Mr Morgan was unable to assist me in this regard, since he is no longer working for Price Waterhouse, the firm of chartered accountants of which the joint receivers and managers are partners.

The second case which has been referred to me is a recent decision in the case of *Re ELS Ltd* [1994] BCC 449. This relates to a local authority's rights to distrain for unpaid business rates after the crystallisation of a debenture by the appointment of an   D
administrative receiver. The legislation is different from the 1908 Act. Distraint can only be made on 'the goods of the debtor'. Crystallisation, in addition, is not relevant to this present case. The chattel mortgage is and was, from the date of its execution, a fixed charge. All that crystallisation does is convert a floating charge into a fixed charge. In the *ELS* case the judge, Ferris J, held that crystallisation of a floating charge had the effect of making goods which prior to crystallisation had been goods of ELS no longer goods of that company under the 1989 regulations governing the rights to distrain in respect of   E
unpaid business rates. It is exactly the same decision as was made in the New Zealand case and my comments about that case apply to ELS. The truth is that the charge holder had a substantial right in the goods as well as the company and, therefore, the goods were not the goods of the debtor company.

The next case to which I have been referred is *Smart Brothers Ltd v Holt & Ors* [1929] 2 KB 303. In this case a hire-purchase agreement had been determined by notice prior to   F
the landlord's attempts to distrain on the goods in question. The tenant had been the hirer of the goods under the hire-purchase agreement. This is a decision on s. 4 of the 1908 Act, prior to that section being substantially amended by the *Consumer Credit Act* 1974. The replacement provisions are now to be found in s. 4A of the 1908 Act. In its then form, s. 4 provided that the rights of 'any other person' under s. 1 did not apply to goods 'comprised in any hire purchase agreement.' It was held that since the hire-purchase agreement had been terminated by the notice, the goods were not comprised in   G
that hire-purchase agreement and the owner of the goods therefore was entitled to serve a notice under s. 1 of the 1908 Act. I simply cannot see how this case has any relevance at all to the present case.

I have been referred to the case of *Ex parte Harris. Re Pulling* (1872) LR 8 Ch App 48. The facts and law in this case have no relevance to the present case in any shape or form.

The next case is in *Re B Johnson & Co (Builders) Ltd* [1955] Ch 634. This case concerns   H
a receiver appointed by a debenture holder, where the debenture provided that the receiver was to be agent of the company. The receiver and manager was held not to be an 'officer' of the company under s. 455 of the *Companies Act* 1948 or a 'manager' under s. 333 of that Act. I fail to see how that case or the reasoning in it is in any way relevant to the present case.

A   Another case cited to me was *Gomba Holdings v Homan* (1986) 2 BCC 99,102. This case concerned a claim by a company to try to compel its receivers to supply it and its directors with information. I derive no help from this case.

Another case cited to me was *Gomba Holdings v Minories Finance* (1989) 5 BCC 27. After the conclusion of a receivership the company (the same company as in the previous case) sought to compel its former receivers and managers to deliver up certain documents to the company. Again, I derive no help from this case.

B

Another authority is *Western Mobile Homes v Gaudet* [1971] 4 WWR 398. This is a Canadian case. The Saskatchewan legislation provided that a landlord could only distrain for rent on the goods of the tenant. The tenant had executed a chattel mortgage on the mobile home, which was the goods in question in that case. The mortgagee under that mortgage had 'seized' the mobile home. I assume this was an exercise of the right of possession. It was held the landlord could still distrain on the mobile home after this seizure. This case, it seems to me, is persuasive authority to support my view that the assets in this case are assets of the company. I refer to p. 400 of the report in that case without needing to quote from it.

C

Another case referred to me was *Times Furnishing Co Ltd v Hutchings* [1938] 1 KB 775. This case was similar to the case of *Smart Brothers v Holt* except that no notice had been served by the owner of the goods determining the hire-purchase agreement prior to the landlord's distraint. The landlord was entitled to distrain because the tenant was still in possession of the goods with the permission of the owner and was the reputed owner thereof. This case strongly supports my provisional view.

D

Finally, I refer to *Ratford v Northavon District Council* (1986) 2 BCC 99,242. The question was whether the receivers and managers of a company appointed under a debenture were the rateable occupiers of the company's property. The receivers were agents for the company. This deals with the status of receivers and managers and is, I believe, of no help to me.

E

I am not constrained by authority, or at least any of those authorities which I have cited. I can therefore decide this case on principle and upon the law as I perceive it to be.

In my view, following the views of Mr Picarda and of the editors of *Kerr*, the company remained in possession of the assets, with the permission of the bank, in circumstances such that the company was the reputed owner of the assets, not merely up to 12 May 1992 but thereafter and indeed down to the making of the contract for sale in July 1992. It seems to me, therefore, for these reasons, that s. 4 of the 1908 Act is of no help to the bank.

F

For the three reasons which I have given above, it follows that the claim to the sum of £27,500 and interest which is held in a solicitors' joint account and which has been made by the plaintiff must fail and that that sum must be properly paid to the defendant landlord. The defendant landlord's counterclaim therefore succeeds and the claim is dismissed.

G

(Order accordingly)

H

Ibex Trading Co Ltd v Walton & Ors.

A

Employment Appeal Tribunal.
Morison J, Mrs M E Sunderland and G H Wright.
Judgment delivered 13 July 1994.

Administration – Redundancy – Unfair dismissal – Transfer of undertaking – Administrators dismissed employees before business was sold – Whether reason for dismissal was transfer or connected with it – Whether there was an economic reason for dismissals – Whether transferor or transferee liable for any unfair dismissal – Transfer of Undertakings (Protection of Employment) Regulations 1981 (SI 1981/1794), reg. 5, 8.

B

This was an appeal from the decision of an industrial tribunal.

The company concerned ('the transferor') went into administration in August 1991. Employees who did not agree to lower wages were dismissed in November 1991. Later in November an offer was made for the business which was sold in February 1992. The employees presented complaints to an industrial tribunal alleging that they had been unfairly dismissed and claiming relief against the transferor and transferee of the business.

C

The industrial tribunal held that the reason for the dismissals was either redundancy or 'one connected with a relevant transfer' within the meaning of reg. 8(1) of the Transfer of Undertakings (Protection of Employment) Regulations 1981. The reason was not the sale to the transferee; that had not been contemplated at that time. The dismissals were not automatically unfair because of the application of reg. 8(2): the business needed to be made attractive to a prospective purchaser, it was uneconomic and it was hoped to make it more economical and therefore saleable by reason of the redundancies. However, the dismissals were clearly unfair within the meaning of s. 57(3) of the Employment Protection (Consolidation) Act 1978.

D

The industrial tribunal went on to hold, purportedly applying Litster v Forth Dry Dock & Engineering Co Ltd [1989] ICR 341, that the employees were not employed immediately before the transfer under reg. 5(3) of the 1981 regulations. Therefore the liability for the unfair dismissals remained with the transferor and was not transferred under reg. 5.

E

The transferor appealed.

Held, dismissing the appeal:

F

1. Whilst it could be said that the employees were dismissed for a reason connected with a possible transfer of the business, on the facts they were not dismissed by reason of 'the' transfer or for a reason connected with 'the' transfer within reg. 8(1). (Harrison Bowden Ltd v Bowden [1994] ICR 186 not followed.)

2. In any event it would be difficult to say on the facts that the employees would have been employed at the date of completion but for their dismissal.

G

3. Therefore, under reg. 5(3) the employees were not employed in the undertaking immediately before the transfer and their dismissal was not for a reason falling within reg. 8(1). Accordingly, reg. 5(1) and 5(2) did not apply to make the transferee liable. (Litster v Forth Dry Dock & Engineering Co Ltd [1989] ICR 341 applied.)

4. The industrial tribunal fell into error when it moved from the premise that the business was uneconomic and the dismissals were designed to make it more economic and therefore saleable, to the conclusion that the reason for the dismissal fell within reg. 8(2). (Wheeler v Patel [1987] ICR 631 followed; Anderson v Dalkeith Engineering Ltd [1985] ICR 66 not followed.)

H

Per curiam: In the absence of express language, subject to reg. 5(4), where reg. 5(1) and 5(2) applied the transferor ceased to be the employer of those whose contracts of

A   employment were transferred; all his rights, powers, duties and liabilities in relation to the contract were transferred and everything he did prior to the transfer was to be treated as though it had been done by the transferee. The scope of reg. 5(1) and (2) could not be wider and was inconsistent with the transferor remaining liable, after the transfer, for anything connected with the employment of those to whom the regulation applied. (Allan v Stirling District Council [1994] ICR 434 not followed.)

B   The following cases were referred to in the judgment:

Allan & Ors v Stirling District Council [1994] ICR 434.
Anderson & Anor v Dalkeith Engineering Ltd [1985] ICR 66.
Gateway Hotels Ltd v Stewart & Ors [1988] IRLR 287.
Harrison Bowden Ltd v Bowden [1994] ICR 186.
Litster v Forth Dry Dock & Engineering Co Ltd & Anor [1989] ICR 341; [1990] 1 AC
C   546.
Powdrill & Anor v Watson & Anor [1994] BCC 172.
Wendelboe v LJ Music ApS (Case 19/83) [1985] ECR 457.
Wheeler v Patel & Anor [1987] ICR 631.

John Bowers (instructed by Wilde Sapte) for the transferor.

Andrew Hogarth (instructed by O H Parsons & Partners) for the employees.

D   JUDGMENT

Morison J: Background

Alpine Double Glazing were, before certain events in 1991, a well known company which sold double glazing products to the public. It was not a profitable venture. The Furniture, Timber and Allied Workers Union was a recognised union and had negotiated
E   for the company's employees rates of pay more favourable than that provided for in the national agreement. At the beginning of 1991 no wage increase was on offer and the employees voted for strike action; they were locked out but on their return to work they were paid for the time they were out but not given any wage increase.

In July 1991, Alpine's parent company decided not to continue to support it and caused it to apply for administration. On 8 August 1991 an administration order was
F   made and Mr Barry and Mr Monjack, accountants, were appointed joint administrators. Because of underlying debt and future obligations under guarantees, it was not judged sensible to seek to dispose of the shares, but rather to make an arrangement whereby the business could be transferred free of debt and commitments. The administrators sought to reduce the size of the workforce and to reduce the wages of those who remained. To this end a meeting was held which was attended by the shop stewards, a full-time official and one of the two administrators. The workforce was told by the administrator that a
G   new method of payment was being put into operation which would mean a substantial reduction in wages. He also announced the start of the 30-day consultation process, although the number of redundancies he had in mind were not disclosed.

Letters were sent to each of the employees which they were asked to sign, accepting the new lower wage arrangements. Although the letter did not say that this would be the consequence, those who refused to accept, that is 40 out of a total of 94, were dismissed
H   by reason of redundancy. The fact that the production manager calculated that he needed only to retain exactly 54 people, the precise number who had accepted the reduction, was said to be a coincidence.

The decision was implemented and the 40 refuseniks were dismissed, despite the union's suggestions that if 40 redundancies were called for it should be done on the basis of last in first out.

The dismissals were effected by letters sent on 16 October 1991 which took effect at 4   A
November 1991. On 11 November 1991 an offer to purchase the business was made, which ultimately led to a purchase of Alpine's business by a shell company which then changed its name to Alpine. The negotiations with the prospective purchaser proceeded and came to fruition when a contract was signed on 13 February 1992.

The transferor company changed its name to Ibex Trading Co Ltd and the new company, the transferee, is called Alpine (Double Glazing) Co Ltd; that company went   B
into liquidation whilst the hearings before the industrial tribunal were taking place.

To avoid any confusion arising from company name changes, throughout this judgment we shall refer to the companies as the transferor and the transferee, respectively. We shall refer to the dismissed employees as the employees.

The employees presented complaints to an industrial tribunal alleging that they had been unfairly dismissed and claimed relief against the transferor and transferee. The   C
matter came before an industrial tribunal held at Newcastle upon Tyne on 11 May 1993, a considerable time after the ITIs had been presented and after the dismissals of which complaint was being made. At that date, the transferee was still in business and, as counsel, who appeared for the employees at that time, as well as on the appeal, acknowledged, it was perceived to be to his clients' advantage that there should be a finding against the transferee so that any award they obtained would be against a solvent target. However, around the third day of the hearing the transferee went into liquidation,   D
and it became clear that the employees would be better off if their claim succeeded against the transferor, which, although in administration, had some assets; whereas it was believed that there would be no dividend from the liquidation of the transferee. As a result, the emphasis of the case changed in midstream. This sequence of events may go some way to explaining why, in certain parts of their well-reasoned decision, the industrial tribunal may have fallen into error. Further, we have had the benefit of able   E
argument and assistance from counsel, Mr John Bowers, on behalf of the transferor; whereas the transferor was not legally represented in the industrial tribunal.

The industrial tribunal decision

The reasoning behind the decision may be summarised thus:

(1)   As to the dismissals, the reason for them was either redundancy or 'one connected   F
with a relevant transfer' within the meaning of reg. 8(1) of the *Transfer of Undertakings (Protection of Employment) Regulations* 1981 ('the regulations'). 'The reason was not the sale to (the transferee). That had not been contemplated at that time.' The business needed to be made attractive to a prospective purchaser, it was uneconomic 'and it was hoped to make it more economical and therefore saleable by reason of the redundancies'.

(2)   The dismissals were not automatically unfair because of the application of   G
reg. 8(2), and the tribunal had to consider whether or not they were fair within the meaning of s. 57(3) of the *Employment Protection (Consolidation) Act* 1978.

(3)   The industrial tribunal found as facts that: there was no customary arrangement or agreed procedure relating to redundancy; the employees were never specifically told that their jobs were at risk if they refused to accept the lower wages; there was no consultation or discussion with the recognised union about the method of   H
selection; the employees were never consulted and given the chance to accept a change in their wages rather than face dismissal. Accordingly, they concluded that the dismissals were 'clearly unfair'.

(4)   The employees were not employed immediately before the transfer, within the meaning of reg. 5(3). Even if a dismissal can be connected with a relevant transfer

A within the meaning of reg. 8(1) where, as here, there was no identified purchaser and no certainty that there would ever be a sale, it would be extending the decision in *Litster v Forth Dry Dock & Engineering Co Ltd* [1989] ICR 341 too far to say that employees were employed immediately before a transfer when many months elapsed between dismissal and transfer. They noted that in *Litster* there was a gap of one hour between dismissal and transfer and there had been collusion between transferor and transferee in an attempt to avoid the impact of the regulations. The

B industrial tribunal, therefore, concluded that on a proper construction of the regulations the liability remained with the transferor and was not transferred under reg. 5.

 Shortly before the appeal was due to be heard, the employees sought from us leave to join the administrators as additional respondents, in the mistaken belief that following the decision of the Court of Appeal in *Powdrill & Anor v Watson & Anor* [1994] BCC 172

C administrators were personally liable in respect of contracts of employment which they adopted. That application was refused as being misconceived.

The appeal

 Without doing full justice to them, we summarise the main points which were argued on this appeal.

D *A. Arguments on behalf of the transferor (the appellant)*

(1) The industrial tribunal should have applied *Litster* rather than seeking to distinguish it. The House of Lords held that, in order to give effect to the purpose of the regulations and the directive, the words 'so employed immediately before the transfer' should be construed to include those persons who would have been so employed had they not been dismissed unfairly before the transfer for a reason

E connected with the transfer. Therefore, on the finding by the industrial tribunal that the employees had been dismissed in connection with a transfer, they were persons who, but for that dismissal, would have been employed immediately before the transfer on 13 February 1992. The House of Lords decision is not to be treated as applying only where there is a very short gap between the dismissal and the transfer; nor is it to be confined to those cases where there has been collusion

F between transferor and transferee to avoid the application of the regulations. In support, reliance was placed on a decision of this tribunal in *Harrison Bowden Ltd v Bowden* [1994] ICR 186 at p. 191F.

(2) The industrial tribunal gave an unduly wide meaning to the word 'economic' in reg. 8(2) where the words are:

 'Where an economic, technical or organisational reason entailing changes in the workforce of either the transferor or the transferee before or after a relevant

G transfer is the reason or principal reason for dismissing an employee . . .'

 In *Wheeler v Patel & Anor* [1987] ICR 631 the EAT chaired by Scott J refused to follow a decision of the EAT held in Scotland and presided over by Lord Macdonald (*Anderson v Dalkeith Engineering Ltd* [1985] ICR 66), and said (at p. 639F):

H 'A desire to sell a business so as to obtain in money the value of the business is an economic reason for the sale; a desire to obtain an enhanced price is an economic reason. If Lord Macdonald's view as to the scope of the phrase "economic, technical or organisational" is correct, it is difficult to think of any case falling within para. [8](1) where the reason for dismissal would not be an "economic" reason for the purposes of para. [8](2). Paragraph (1) applies where "the transfer or a reason connected with it is the reason or principal reason"

for the dismissal. The transfer is, itself, in a sense an economic reason. If the   A
case is to be taken out of para. (1) wherever the reason for the transfer is an
economic reason in the broad literal sense, it does not seem to us that any scope
will be left for para. (1). We think "economic" must be given a more restricted
than literal meaning.

. . .

The references to "technical" and to "organisational" reasons seem to us to be   B
references to reasons which relate to the conduct of the business. In our view,
the adjective, "economic", must be construed *eiusdem generis* with the
adjectives "technical" and "organisational". The "economic" reasons apt to
bring the case within para. (2) must, in our view, be reasons which relate to the
conduct of the business. If the economic reason were no more than a desire to
obtain an enhanced price, or no more than a desire to achieve a sale, it would   C
not be a reason which related to the conduct of the business. It would not, in
our judgment, be an "economic,' reason for the purposes of para. (2) . . . We
think the need to leave a sensible scope for para. (1) similarly requires a limited
meaning to be given to the adjective "economic" in para. (2).'

(See also *Gateway Hotels Ltd v Stewart & Ors* [1988] IRLR 287, a subsequent
decision of an appeal tribunal held in Scotland, which followed *Wheeler* rather
than *Anderson*.)   D

(3)   Thus, the industrial tribunal should have concluded that:

   (a)   the employees were dismissed for a reason connected with the transfer within
      the meaning of reg. 8(1) of the regulations and were deemed to have been
      unfairly dismissed;

   (b)   the reason for the dismissals did not fall within reg. 8(2) of the regulations;   E

   (c)   but for their dismissal, they would have been employed in the undertaking
      at the time of the transfer to the transferee, within the meaning of reg. 5(3),
      as interpreted by the House of Lords in *Litster* and, therefore, the liability
      for unfair dismissal was transferred to the transferee under reg. 5(2).

(4)   The decision that the dismissals were unfair was perverse or demonstrated a
misdirection.   F

B. *Arguments on behalf of the employees*

(1)   The fair result of the case is that the transferor should be liable.

(2)   The EAT should follow the decision of the EAT sitting in Scotland and presided
over by Lord Coulsfield in *Allan & Ors v Stirling District Council* [1994] ICR 434.
There, employees of the council were dismissed when, as a result of compulsory   G
competitive tendering, the work done by the employees in the council's direct
services organisation was contracted out to a third party company. The industrial
tribunal held that the dismissals were unfair under reg. 8(1) of the regulations and
that the employees would, but for their dismissal, have been employed in the
undertaking which was transferred to the third party, and, following *Litster*, they
were employees to whom reg. 5(3) applied and, thus, under reg. 5(2), responsibility
for the dismissals and for the payment of compensation fell solely upon the third   H
party. The EAT, in an interesting judgment, held that:

    '. . . it would not be right to regard reg. 5(2) as transferring to the transferee
    responsibility for a dismissal carried out entirely by the transferor and taking
    effect before, or simultaneously with, the transfer, to the exclusion of any
    liability on the transferor in the absence of an express provision to that effect.'

A   (3)   Thus, it was argued, in this case, both the transferor and transferee are liable for the unfair dismissal.

      (4)   Alternatively, the dismissals were effected before the transfer was more than a mere possibility and, therefore, reg. 5(3) did not apply and this was simply a case of unfair dismissal by the administrators on behalf of the transferor, and that liability is not passed over to the transferee.

B   The application of the regulations is seldom straightforward, as anyone who sits on industrial tribunals and in this tribunal knows. There is always a real danger, in this area, of hard cases making bad law and of points being decided beyond what is strictly necessary for the particular decision. For understandable reasons, it is sometimes tempting for parties to open up issues which do not strictly arise: whether it be people who frequently act as administrators or unions who frequently have to confront transfer situations. The circumstances in which points relating to the regulations, or the analogous

C   continuity provisions in Sch. 13 to the Act, vary. As the House of Lords pointed out in *Litster* a purposive approach to the construction of the regulations required an extended interpretation of the words of reg. 5(3): it was unsatisfactory to leave employees to whistle for their money from the transferor, who was frequently not in a position to pay. In this case, it is somewhat anomalous that the administrators of the transferor should be striving to have the liability transferred to the transferee, whereas the employees are

D   anxious to say that the transferor is liable, either solely or jointly with the transferee. Normally, one would expect each to take exactly the opposite position. In issues as to continuity, an industrial tribunal is likely to be influenced by the presumption in favour of continuity and to find a transfer of a business wherever the facts make such a finding possible.

      It is, therefore, necessary that we tread warily because of the unusual circumstances in

E   which this case comes before us.

      That said, we have not had any real difficulty in reaching our conclusions which may be summarised thus:

      (1)   Contrary to what was said in the *Harrison Bowden* case, we attach significance to the definite article in reg. 8(1) 'that employee shall be . . . as unfairly dismissed if *the* transfer or a reason connected with it is the reason or the principal reason for

F   the dismissal'. The link, in terms of time, between the dismissals and the transfers will vary considerably. In *Litster* the time difference was one hour; often it will be more. A transfer is not just a single event: it extends over a period of time culminating in a completion. However, here, the employees were dismissed before any offer had been made for the business. Whilst it could properly be said that they were dismissed for a reason connected with a possible transfer of the business, on the facts here we are not satisfied that they were dismissed by reason of *the*

G   transfer or for a reason connected with *the* transfer. A transfer was, at the stage of the dismissal, a mere twinkle in the eye and might well never have occurred. We do not say that in every case it is necessary for the prospective transferee to be identified; because sometimes one purchaser drops out at the last minute and another purchaser replaces him.

      (2)   In any event, it seems to us, on the facts, to be difficult to say, by reason of the

H   timing of the dismissal and the sale of the business, that the employees would have been employed at the date of completion but for their dismissal, and we adopt what the industrial tribunal said on this point towards the end of para. 16 of their decision.

      (3)   Therefore, adopting the interpretation of the House of Lords in *Litster*, under reg. 5(3) the employees were not employed in the undertaking immediately before

the transfer and their dismissal was not for a reason falling within reg. 8(1).   A
Accordingly, reg. 5(1) and 5(2) do not apply to make the transferee liable.

(4)   We agree with the submission that the industrial tribunal erred in their approach
to *Litster*. They took the view that they were not prepared to imply further words
into the regulations or to extend the principles enunciated there. We, for our part,
do not think that any question of implying further words is required: it is simply a
question of seeking to apply the decision as it stands. Further, we do not think that   B
industrial tribunals should seek to distinguish the case on the basis that in *Litster*
there was collusion between transferor and transferee, whereas in this case there
was none. We do not read the speeches in the House of Lords as being confined in
that way.

(5)   If, as we hold, reg. 8(1) did not apply to render the dismissals automatically unfair,
the question as to the application of reg. 8(2) does not arise. We should say,
however, that industrial tribunals would be well-advised to have regard to the   C
judgment in *Wheeler*, to which we have referred, when considering whether there
is an economic, technical or organisational reason for the dismissal. It follows,
therefore, that we are of the view that the industrial tribunal fell into error when it
moved from the premise that the business was uneconomic and the dismissals were
designed to make it more economic and therefore saleable, to the conclusion that
the reason for the dismissal fell within reg. 8(2). That was the very argument   D
adopted by Lord Macdonald in *Anderson* which may now not be regarded as a
decision to be followed.

(6)   We understood from counsel for the employees that the transferee does not have
any money and they would be content with a finding merely against the transferor.
In these circumstances the question as to whether we ourselves would be prepared
to follow *Allan* does not strictly arise for decision in this case. We understand that   E
Allan is under appeal to the Inner House. We have not heard full argument on the
question and, accordingly, our views are obiter and necessarily tentative. For our
part we would not have been prepared to follow *Allan*. Although art. 3(1) of
Council Directive No. 77/187 leaves open to a member state the power to,

> 'provide that, after the date of transfer within the meaning of article 1(i) and in
> addition to the transferee, the transferor shall continue to be liable in respect of   F
> obligations which arose from a contract of employment or an employment
> relationship'

the UK Parliament, when it introduced the regulations into our law, did not avail
itself of that opportunity. In other words, contrary to the approach of the Scottish
EAT, we would have said that, in the absence of express language, subject to
reg. 5(4), where reg. 5(1) and 5(2) apply the transferor ceases to be the employer of
those whose contracts of employment are transferred; *all* (we emphasise) his rights,   G
powers, duties and liabilities in relation to the contract are transferred and, for the
avoidance of doubt, everything he did prior to the transfer shall be treated as
though it had been done by the transferee. The scope of reg. 5(1) and (2) could not
be wider and is inconsistent, we think, with the transferor remaining liable, after
the transfer, for anything connected with the employment of those to whom the
regulation applies. The primary meaning of 'transfer' in the 1989 edition of the   H
Oxford English Dictionary is:

> 'To convey or take from one place, person, etc to another, to transmit,
> transport, to give or hand over from one to another.'

In other words, the use of the word 'transfer' in its natural and ordinary meaning
suggests a taking away from one and a handing over to another. This is more

A
consistent with the transferee taking on obligations in place of the transferor than that the transferor retains liability.

We were told by counsel that they were unaware of any academic support for the view adopted in *Allan*. Having regard to the definition of 'transferor' in the directive and the decision in *Wendelboe v LJ Music* [1985] ECR 457 we consider that the interpretation in *Allan*, namely that in the absence of express language to the contrary the transferor remains liable, is inconsistent with the directive and has

B
no support in any decision of a UK court or tribunal.

We stress, we did not have the benefit of full argument on the point.

(7) It seems to us that the argument that the industrial tribunal had wrongly approached the question of unfairness is unsustainable. It is said that they failed to refer or apply the 'band of reasonable responses' test or to recognise the purpose and effect of the administration order or to take account of the size and

C
administrative resources of the transferor. None of these points has any merit, in our view. There is no need for a tribunal to mention the 'band of reasonable responses test' merely to show that they have applied themselves to s. 57(3) correctly: we look at the substance and not form of the decision. Nor is a tribunal to be criticised for failing to mention the size and administrative resources of the employer simply for form's sake. Where such a matter is important no doubt it will be mentioned. The tribunal were fully alert to the purpose of the

D
administration order as what they said in para. 14 of their decision makes clear. This was a very plain case of unfairness, as the tribunal themselves said. We hope that there is no view going about that administrators can behave as they like to the employees of the company of which they are the agent, and use, as an excuse for unfairness, the economic circumstances of the company which brought them there in the first place. Employees are always entitled to be treated with respect, especially where their jobs may be at risk due to economic circumstances which

E
may be out of their own control to a greater or lesser extent.

(8) Accordingly, we do not need to deal with an argument raised on behalf of the employees that the industrial tribunal were perverse in concluding that there was neither an agreed procedure or customary arrangement for selection for redundancy and that these dismissals were in breach of such. Suffice it to say we considered in advance of the hearing that such an argument was likely to be as

F
hopeless as the challenge to the finding of unfairness.

It follows, therefore, that we have differed from the industrial tribunal on two matters:

(1) the application of reg. 8(1);

(2) the proper interpretation of reg. 8(2).

It was submitted to us, on behalf of the transferor, that we should remit the matter back to the industrial tribunal for it to reconsider the matter in the light of our judgment.

G
Under para. 21(1) of Sch. 11 to the Act, for the purposes of an appeal we may exercise any powers of the industrial tribunal. There has been considerable delay in this case. Further, we do not think that there would be any point in remitting the matter: the decision on unfairness was clear and obvious and we can, without injustice to either party, resolve the matter ourselves.

Accordingly, we can simply dismiss the appeal on the grounds that the employees were unfairly dismissed by the transferor who, alone, is responsible for meeting any liability.

H
It seems to us that a further hearing by the same or a differently composed industrial tribunal should be arranged as soon as is practicable so that the question of compensation can be determined, in default of agreement.

(Order accordingly)

Secretary of State for Trade and Industry v Palmer.

A

Court of Session (Inner House).
Lord Allanbridge, Lord Prosser and Lord Penrose.
Judgment delivered 13 October 1994.

Disqualifying unfit directors of insolvent companies – Making of administration order – Whether interim order was administration order for purposes of disqualification application – Whether disqualification application was out of time – Insolvency Act 1986, s. 8–11; Company Directors Disqualification Act 1986, s. 6(2), 7(2).

B

This was a reclaiming motion against the decision of the Lord Ordinary (see [1993] BCC 650) that an application by the Secretary of State under s. 6 of the Company Directors Disqualification Act 1986 made more than two years after the court made interim orders under s. 9(4) of the Insolvency Act 1986 but within two years of the making of administration orders under s. 8(3) was not out of time under s. 7(2) of the Disqualification Act.

C

Held, **refusing the reclaiming motion:**

For the purposes of s. 6(2) of the Disqualification Act no order pronounced by the court in terms of s. 9(4) or (5) of the Insolvency Act could properly be viewed as an administration order under s. 8 and nothing done ad interim could constitute an administration order or the appointment of an administrator in the sense in which those terms were used in Pt. II of the Act.

D

The following case was referred to in the opinion of the court:

Cavco Floors Ltd, Re [1990] BCC 589.

A R Dewar (instructed by the solicitor to the Secretary of State) for the Secretary of State for Trade and Industry.

E

Neil Davidson QC (instructed by Drummond Miller WS) for the respondent and reclaimer.

OPINION OF THE COURT
(Delivered by Lord Penrose)

The reclaimer was a director of two related companies Hinari Consumer Electronics Ltd and Hinari Domestic Ltd. The companies got into financial difficulties. Applications were made to the court for administration orders and for the appointment of administrators in terms of Pt. II of the *Insolvency Act* 1986. On 3 October 1989, the Lord Ordinary pronounced a first order, in common form, for intimation and service. The interlocutor proceeded to set out the following additional orders:

F

'Meantime makes an administration order *ad interim* and nominates and appoints Frank Blin and Robert John Templeton Glen . . . insolvency practitioners, to be the joint administrators *ad interim*. . . for the purposes specified in section 8(3)(a), (b) and (d) of said Act; appoints the clerk of court to give notice of this order forthwith to the said *interim* administrators; and appoints the said *interim* administrators to advertise and give notice of this order forthwith in terms of r. 2.3 of the Insolvency (Scotland) Rules 1986.'

G

On 1 November 1989 the Lord Ordinary made administration orders and appointed the same named insolvency practitioners to hold office as administrators, thereby disposing of the applications.

H

On 31 October 1991 the Secretary of State for Trade and Industry presented the present petition for an order against the reclaimer prohibiting his participation, either directly or indirectly, in the promotion, formation, or management of any company for such period

A   as the court thought proper. The petition was presented under s. 6 of the *Company Directors Disqualification Act* 1986. It was common ground between the parties that the date of insolvency relevant for the purposes of the application in terms of s. 6(2) was the date when an administration order was made in relation to each of the two companies. Section 7(2) of the Disqualification Act provides that, except with leave of the court, an application for the making of a disqualification order shall not be made after the end of the period of two years beginning with the day on which the company in question became

B   insolvent. Leave of the court was not sought for the presentation out of time of the present application.

    The reclaimer challenged the competency of the petition on the basis that the interlocutor of 3 October 1989 had made an administration order, and that the two-year period had therefore expired prior to the presentation of the petition.

C   The reclaimer's plea was debated before the Lord Ordinary on 24 June 1993. He repelled the plea, and allowed the Secretary of State's petition to proceed, see [1993] BCC 650. It is against that decision that the reclaimer has appealed.

    The argument before us followed substantially the same lines as had been debated before the Lord Ordinary. Mr Davidson made it clear that neither party challenged the competency of either of the orders of 3 October and 1 November 1989. The orders of 3

D   October 1989 bore in terms to be administration orders and were so structured as to reflect the view that they were granted in terms of s. 8 of the Act. It was the practice of the Scottish court to pronounce such orders: *Stair Encyclopaedia*, vol. 4, para. 615. The orders were generally regarded as being administration orders in terms of the Act. Procedure before the Companies Court in England was different. Different expedients were adopted there to deal with the urgent demands of situations in which accelerated disposal of the case was necessary: *Re Cavco Floors Ltd* [1990] BCC 589. But the Scottish

E   practice was established and should have effect for the purposes of the time-limits specified in the Company Directors Disqualification Act. The Lord Ordinary had erred in rejecting the argument and his interlocutor should be recalled. The Lord Ordinary was in any event in error in relying upon s. 18 in support of the disposal and he had, in certain respects, proceeded upon erroneous information. For the Secretary of State Mr Dewar contended that the Lord Ordinary had reached the correct decision and that the reclaiming motion should be refused. There could be one date only for an administration

F   order under the Insolvency Act in the case of any one company. The Act did not envisage *interim* administration orders. The only orders which could properly be so described were those pronounced on 1 November 1989.

    The issue turns on the interpretation of the provisions of the *Insolvency Act* 1986. Section 8 provides for the making of an administration order where the court is satisfied that the company is or is likely to become unable to pay its debts, in the sense of s. 123 of

G   the Act, and where the court considers that the making of an order would be likely to achieve one or more of the purposes specified in s. 8(3). Administration under s. 8 effectively provides an alternative to receivership or liquidation in circumstances in which the court can properly form the view that the making of the order would achieve one or other of the purposes set out in subs. (3). Thus the survival of the company as a going concern may be a proper purpose warranting the making of an administration order rather than leaving creditors to work out their remedies against the company in other

H   ways. Similarly the approval of a scheme of arrangement under Pt. I of the Insolvency Act or a form of composition with creditors under s. 425 of the Companies Act are purposes that may warrant the making of an order again as an alternative to leaving creditors to work out their ordinary remedies against the company. The fourth purpose, (d), the achieving of a more advantageous realisation of the companies' assets than would be effected on a winding up, is directly an alternative to liquidation. In terms of s. 11 the

making of the order leads to the dismissal of any current liquidation application and any   A
administrative receiver then in office is required to vacate that office. The exercise of the
court's jurisdiction under s. 8 may often require the balancing of competing interests in
resolving which of a number of alternatives ought to be adopted as the proper way of
dealing with the apparent insolvency of the company. Section 9 specifies the procedures
to be followed in dealing with such applications. Provision is made for notice to
prescribed classes of persons. In certain circumstances the court is obliged to dismiss an
application. Subject to these, s. 9(4) provides that: B

> '. . . on hearing a petition the court may dismiss it, or adjourn the hearing
> conditionally or unconditionally, or make an interim order or any other order that
> it thinks fit.'

Subsection (5) provides that:

> 'Without prejudice to the generality of subsection (4), an interim order under that   C
> subsection may restrict the exercise of any powers of the directors of the company
> (whether by reference to the consent of the court or of a person qualified to act as
> an insolvency practitioner in relation to the company, or otherwise).'

The powers conferred on the court at the interim stage are very wide. It is clear from
s. 9(5) that the powers of the directors of the company under its constituent documents
may be restricted generally. The court may require that those powers be exercised only   D
with the consent of the court itself or of a qualified insolvency practitioner. The structure
of the provision is such as to require positive consideration of the extent to which it is
necessary or appropriate in the particular circumstances to restrict directors' powers and
to decide on the nature and terms of the restriction to be imposed in the particular case.
In that respect the provision is in marked contrast to s. 14 which provides that the
appointment of an administrator in terms of the Act effectively supersedes the directors
and other officers of the company in the independent exercise of the powers conferred on   E
them by the memorandum and articles of association of the company where there could
be conflict with the exercise by the administrator of his statutory powers. Section 9 does
not contain any equivalent provision automatically superseding directors' powers *ad
interim*. The limitation envisaged by s. 9 requires an exercise of the court's power in the
particular circumstances of the case. As a matter of language and structure one may
compare the provisions made in s. 135 of the Insolvency Act for the appointment of a
liquidator provisionally, and in s. 138 for the appointment of an interim liquidator, all in   F
anticipation of the confirmation of appointment of an official liquidator in due course.
The absence of any similar provision in the structure of s. 8 and 9 for the appointment of
an interim administrator, in the sense that the expression 'administrator' is used in the
Act, militates against the view that the court has authority to make *ad interim* orders
which create a state of administration and, in the case of the nominee, the status of
administrator prior to the completion of the procedures stipulated by Parliament.   G

There are further reasons for the view that nothing done *ad interim* can constitute an
administration order or the appointment of an administrator in the sense in which those
terms are used in Pt. II of the Insolvency Act. As already mentioned, the making of an
administration order has an immediate impact on subsisting liquidation proceedings, and
on the exercise by any administrative receiver of his powers: s. 11. These important
provisions cut across the right of a creditor to apply to the court and to insist in an   H
application for the winding up of a creditor company which has proved incapable of
meeting the legitimate claims of that creditor. In the case of an administrative receiver
the provisions of a security writ, commonly a floating charge, providing for receivership
are effectively superseded by the exercise by the court of its power to order
administration. In an appropriate case the decision to make an administration order
must require an exercise of judgment as to which of a number of competing alternative

A forms of procedure ought to be adopted having regard to the competing interests of several classes of creditor as well as of the company, its members and its employees. Section 10 provides that during the period between the presentation of the petition and its disposal by dismissal or the making of an administration order, an administrative receiver may be appointed, and carry out his functions, and that an application for the winding up of the company may competently be made. These provisions recognise that the competition between the competing alternatives may be real and that when the court

B exercises its power in relation to the application for an administration order real and substantial choices may require to be made. If it were competent to make an administration order on an *interim* basis the consequence would appear necessarily to be that the specific rights provided in s. 10 for qualifying creditors in this respect would be defeated and that the court would risk premature election for the specific option of administration without having the opportunity to consider the alternatives that might be

C put before it. In the circumstances the language of s. 9, omitting any reference to administration *ad interim* or interim administrators, appears to be deliberately conceived. On this view no order pronounced by the court in terms of s. 9(4) or (5) could properly be viewed as an administration order under s. 8.

Having regard to the language of the Insolvency Act, while it is no doubt competent for the court to make an order which effectively provides *ad interim* for the administration of the company to be in the control of a nominee of the court, it does not follow that it is

D proper to describe the person so appointed as an administrator in the sense that that term appears in the Act, or to use in relation to the order nominating him the expression 'administration order'. Each of those expressions has a specific meaning, applicable exclusively to the stage at which the application has finally been dealt with by the court and not at any intermediate stage.

The terms of the Company Directors Disqualification Act itself lends additional

E support to this view. Section 6 of the Act applies where the company in question is insolvent. The making of an administration order is one of the events which constitutes insolvency for the purposes of the provision. It is hardly conceivable that Parliament could have contemplated that there would be two competing dates for the deemed insolvency of any given company in terms of the Insolvency Act for the purposes of the Disqualification Act. If an administration order pronounced *ad interim* were to have the characteristics of a s. 8 order, that, however, would be the inevitable consequence. If an

F order made *ad interim* were an administration order in terms of s. 8 of the Insolvency Act then, albeit *ad interim*, insolvency would follow in terms of s. 6. Section 6 would appear similarly to stipulate that the eventual making of an administration order on disposal of the application would again amount to insolvency. Such a situation cannot have been contemplated. The two provisions cannot be read together if more than one date of deemed insolvency can exist. Mr Davidson accepted that interim insolvency as such was

G not a concept readily recognised in the law.

Mr Davidson's argument relied heavily upon the terms of the interlocutor. The form adopted clearly also encouraged the author of the article in the Encyclopaedia to express the views there contained. As already mentioned the competency of the orders pronounced was not an issue before us and it would not be appropriate to express views on such a subject without debate. But it may be that some review of the practice of the

H liquidation judge is required if similar confusion is to be avoided in the future.

In the whole circumstances we are of the opinion that the Lord Ordinary clearly reached the correct conclusion in this case. We therefore refuse the reclaiming motion.

(*Order accordingly*)

Re a Debtor No. 162 of 1993.
Doorbar v Alltime Securities Ltd.

A

Chancery Division.
Knox J.
Judgment delivered 3 November 1994.

Individual voluntary arrangement – Voting rights – Whether arrangement bound　　　B
landlord for future rent – Whether arrangement had been modified to include
future rent – Whether future rent capable of being included in arrangement –
Whether chairman had agreed to put estimated minimum value on landlord's claim
for future rent – Insolvency Act 1986, s. 258, 260(2); Insolvency Rules 1986 (SI
1986/1925), r. 5.17.

This was a debtor's application to set aside a District Judge's order declaring that the　　C
debtor's voluntary arrangement did not include future rent under a lease with the respondent
landlord.

The original proposal for a voluntary arrangement did not cover future rent; the landlord
was shown as a creditor for arrears of rent in the sum of £7,430. At the date of the creditors'
meeting the landlord's claim for accrued arrears and interest was £32,911.61. The landlord
voted in that sum against the proposal. It also sought to vote for the aggregate of rent
prospectively payable until the end of the contractual term of the lease. The chairman　　D
offered to value the landlord's claim under that head at a minimum of one year's rent
(£13,830) for voting purposes. There was no agreement and no vote was cast in respect of
that claim. If the landlord's claim to future rent had been accepted and voted against the
proposal the arrangement would not have been approved. Conversely if it had been valued
at one year's rent and voted against, the proposal would still have been approved.

The landlord argued that the proposal as approved did not include any future liability for　　E
rent and that at the meeting there was no intention on the landlord's part for future rent
liability to be included save on terms that it should be allowed to vote for the whole of the
rent during the remainder of the contractual period. The District Judge found that the
original proposal did not refer to the debtor's continuing liability under the terms of the
lease and held that a future debt could not be included in the arrangement unless there was
an agreement between the debtor and the creditor that that should be so. Accordingly he　　F
granted the declaration that the future rent liability was not within the terms of the voluntary
arrangement.

The debtor appealed arguing that agreement with the landlord was not necessary, nor
was it relevant to the question whether there had been an effective modification of the
proposed voluntary arrangement.

Held, allowing the debtor's appeal:　　　　　　　　　　　　　　　　　　　　　G

1. No form of contractual agreement between the debtor and a dissenting creditor was
relevant or requisite to enable a modification not reduced to writing but understood by all
those present at or represented at a meeting which approved a voluntary arrangement to be
validly incorporated within it. It was clear that at the meeting the chairman who held proxies
for five other creditors understood that what was proposed was that the future rent payments
under the lease should be within the arrangement. The landlord's representative understood
that too, otherwise he would not have asked to be allowed to vote in respect of the total　　H
value of the rent payments until the end of the contractual term, as he accepted that he did.
In the circumstances, although the inclusion of the future payments of rent under the lease
constituted a modification within the meaning of s. 436 of the Act, and was not included
under the formal written modifications set out in the chairman's report, nevertheless it did
form part of the arrangement which was agreed to at the meeting. Contrary to the view of

A   the District Judge when he said that there was no evidence that there was a clear agreement between the debtor and his creditor, what mattered was evidence that the debtor's proposal, upon which the creditors were to vote, provided for the debt in question to be included. The evidence did satisfy that requirement.

2. Future rent under a lease was not incapable of being included in a voluntary arrangement. (Burford Midland Properties Ltd v Marley Extrusions Ltd & Ors [1994]
B   BCC 604 considered.)

3. Rule 5.17(3) of the Insolvency Rules required the chairman's agreement to put a minimum value on a debt and not an agreement upon the minimum value. What the chairman did amounted to expressing a willingness to put a minimum value on the landlord's claim. Accordingly the landlord was entitled to vote in respect of the claim for future rent and was bound by the voluntary arrangement in respect of that claim. (Re Cranley Mansions Ltd [1994] BCC 576 not followed.)
C
The following cases were referred to in the judgment:

Burford Midland Properties Ltd v Marley Extrusions Ltd & Ors [1994] BCC 604.
Cranley Mansions Ltd, Re [1994] BCC 576.
Joscelyne v Nissen & Anor [1970] 2 QB 86.

Antony Zacaroli (instructed by Isadore Goldman) for the debtor.

D   Amanda Tipples (instructed by Tinklin Springall) for the landlord.

JUDGMENT

Knox J: The application of Mr Richard Leon Doorbar ('the debtor') which is before the court is one for an order that an order of District Judge Hollis dated 5 July 1994 (whereby it was declared that the debtor's voluntary arrangement did not include future
E   rent under a lease with the respondent dated 3 April 1981 and did not affect the applicant's liability for the same) be set aside and for an order that the declaration sought in para. 1 of the respondent's amended application be refused. The respondent is Alltime Securities Ltd. Paragraph 1 of its amended application only sought the relief in fact granted by District Judge Hollis's order and is therefore the mirror image of the relief sought in this appeal.

F   The lease mentioned in the application ('the lease') forms the background to this application. It was dated 3 April 1981 and was expressed to be made between Alltime of the first part and defined as 'the landlord', Menage Graphic Production, called 'the tenant' with the usual extension so as to include the tenant's successors in title and permitted assigns of the second part, and the debtor and Christine Doorbar, then his wife, of the third part, described as 'the sureties'.

G   In fact Menage Graphic Production was a mere trade name that was used by the debtor at that time and was not a separate legal person so the debtor had a dual role in that he was, in fact, the tenant and he was one of the two persons described as 'the sureties'.

The premises were at 343 Eden Park Avenue, Beckenham in the London Borough of Bromley. The term granted was one of 20 years from 4 April 1981 and the rent reserved was £7,500 per annum reviewable every five years upwards only. The only provision in
H   the lease involving the sureties was cl. 5, which reads as follows:

'IF the tenant shall go into liquidation and the liquidator shall disclaim this lease or if the tenant shall be wound up or cease to exist (or if the tenant for the time being shall be an individual and shall become bankrupt and the trustee in bankruptcy shall disclaim this lease) and if the landlord shall within three months after such disclaimer or other event putting an end to the effect of this lease as

A

aforesaid so far as concerns the tenant by notice in writing require the surety to accept a lease of the premises for a term commensurate with the residue which if there had been no disclaimer or if this lease had continued to have had effect as aforesaid would have remained of the term hereby granted at the same rent and subject to the like covenants and conditions as are reserved by and contained in this lease (with the exception of this clause) the said new lease and the rights and liabilities thereunder to take effect as from the date of the said disclaimer or if this lease ceases to have effect as aforesaid then and in such case the surety shall pay the costs of and accept such new lease accordingly and will execute and deliver to the landlord a counterpart thereof.'

B

It is not contended that the use of the singular 'the surety', as opposed to the name given to Mr and Mrs Doorbar in the lease of 'the sureties' in the plural, is significant. In fact, that clause in the lease does not provide for any suretyship in any normally accepted sense of the word. In the light of the duplication of roles played by the debtor cl. 5 of the lease had the effect of requiring him and his wife, should he be made bankrupt and should his trustee in bankruptcy disclaim the lease, to take a fresh lease for the unexpired term and in a sense, so far as the debtor was concerned, it really amounted to a provision for undoing the effect of the trustee's disclaimer. How far this is a valid provision was not explored in argument. It would hardly seem to have been likely to have very favourable practical consequences for the landlord to have a bankrupt tenant restored as a tenant after a disclaimer, but the inclusion of his wife as tenant could obviously be a valuable right if she was a person of substance.

C

D

The debtor got into financial difficulties. Notably, he had gone into arrears on his liabilities under the lease, the rent under which was reviewed up to £13,830 per annum with effect from 29 September 1990. A statutory demand in respect of rent arrears in the sum of £7,430 was served on the debtor on behalf of Alltime on 24 April 1993 and, after an unsuccessful attempt to have it set aside, a bankruptcy petition was presented based on that statutory demand.

E

On 24 August 1993, the same day as the hearing of the bankruptcy petition, an interim order was made on the debtor's application pursuant to s. 253(1) of the *Insolvency Act* 1986.

The voluntary arrangement envisaged was circulated to creditors on 27 August 1993 and a creditors' meeting announced for 20 September 1993 to consider those proposals. The arrangement proposed included the following; in para. (1) that the voluntary arrangement should last for four years; and in para. (2) that the nominee to the arrangement should be Mr Kenneth Morton Bradshaw. I can pass over the other paragraphs until I get to (12), which reads:

F

'All future potential liabilities arising under the guarantee on property owned by Alltime Securities Ltd are to be included in the arrangement.'

G

The schedule of creditors included Alltime in a figure of £7,434 with the notation 'Bankruptcy petition issued' and a variety of other creditors, notably the Halifax Building Society which was included as a figure described as 'unquantified'. There is no other provision in the proposal for the voluntary arrangement which bears directly on any liability under the lease. There is a mention of leasehold premises, but those are different premises and have nothing to do with the property vested in Alltime.

H

As a matter of construction of that written document from which I have read extracts, and in particular of cl. 12 therein, I have no doubt but that the reference to 'future potential liabilities arising under the guarantee on property owned by Alltime' refers to liability of the debtor under cl. 5 of the lease, that is to say, to any liability which could arise if the debtor were to be made bankrupt and his trustee in bankruptcy disclaimed the lease. It does not on its true construction include the liability under the covenant in

A   the lease to pay the rent thereby reserved. Mr Zacaroli for the debtor did not contend otherwise.

At the meeting of 20 September 1993 there was an adjournment to 4 October 1993. In the meanwhile there was an exchange of correspondence between the solicitors for Alltime and Mr Bradshaw, the nominee. On 16 September 1993 the solicitors for Alltime wrote a letter to Mr Bradshaw which included the following:

B   'We would draw to your attention the total amount of our clients' claim as at 1 September 1993 is £31,482.79, not the sum of £7,434, as stated in the schedule of creditors attached to the proposed voluntary arrangement.

In addition, we take issue with the following points raised in Mr Doorbar's affidavit . . .

C   3. At para. 12 Mr Doorbar purports to include in the voluntary arrangement all future potential liabilities arising under the "Guarantee" on the property. Once again we would point out that Mr Doorbar's liability arises as tenant under the lease of the premises owned by our client. Further, as there is a continuing liability under the lease, we cannot agree to all future liabilities being included in the voluntary arrangement.

In the circumstances we are of the opinion that the proposed voluntary
D   arrangement is unrealistic, and therefore intend to oppose the arrangement.'

On 1 October the same firm of solicitors updated the figures for the accrued liability in respect of rent and interest to £32,911.61. That is merely a function of the elapse of a certain amount of time. They said:

'In addition we would like to draw your attention to para. 12 of the proposed voluntary arrangement of Mr Doorbar. This paragraph refers to the 'Guarantee'
E   on property owned by Alltime Securities Ltd. As there never has been a guarantee on property owned by our clients, we are unable to understand this paragraph.'

The reply next day from Mr Bradshaw included this:

'Our understanding of the wording of the lease is that it is in the name of Menage Graphic Production and then refers to Mr Doorbar as a surety (or guarantor).'

At that stage, before the meeting of 4 October 1993, there was nothing in my view to
F   displace the construction which I have placed upon the proposed voluntary arrangement (cl. 12) that only liability under cl. 5 of the lease was to be included in the voluntary arrangement. Mr Bradshaw did not understand that the debtor's liability to pay rent under the covenant in the lease was involved save in so far as the debtor might be a surety for another entity, Menage Graphic Production, which he does not appear to have realised was the alter ego of the debtor.

There then ensued the meeting and the evidence before the court with regard to that is
G   as follows. Mr Bradshaw in his affidavit said this in para. 4:

'I would ask the court to note that at the meeting of 4 October 1993, I invited the applicant to submit a claim for the future rent liabilities in the sum of one year's rent. I would not accept a calculation of all the future rent because there was a duty to mitigate, but I would have been prepared to accept one year's future rent. The applicant did not ask for such a sum to be included in the voting and as such
H   its vote was in the sum of £32,911.61. Even if one year's rent (in the sum of £13,830) had been admitted for the purposes of voting, the proposal would still have been approved by the requisite majority.'

That account of what happened is not effectively challenged in the affidavit later sworn by Mr Springall, the managing director of Alltime. Mr Bradshaw also made a report after the meeting on 4 October, as he was required to do. The material parts of that are

as follows. He set out who was present, that is to say himself, the debtor, Mr Springall   A
and a lady also representing Alltime. I will read the rest of the report:

'The chairman held five proxies in his favour.

Mr Bradshaw opened the meeting by producing to those present a list of
modifications which were requested by National Westminster Bank plc and
Halifax Building Society, together with details of the proxies which he held voting
in favour of the arrangement, and the indication of a vote against the arrangement   B
by Alltime Securities Ltd which had been indicated to him in a letter from
solicitors.

Mr Bradshaw was asked about cl. 12 of the proposals, and it was confirmed that it
was intended that any liabilities arising under the lease of premises should be
included in the arrangement. Mr Springall suggested that the whole of the future
rent should therefore be included, but Mr Bradshaw said that this could not be so   C
because there had to be mitigation for the likelihood of the property being re-let,
and it was therefore not possible to quantify a liquidated sum due. The only
liquidated sum due at today's date was the figure claimed in Alltime Securities
Ltd's proof of debt in the sum of £32,911.61. The most which would be accepted
for future liability at this stage would be one year's future rent.'

I need not read the next passage, but later on one finds this: D

'The modifications and the proxy details are shown on the attached sheet, and
showed that the voting was 87.34 per cent in favour.

The arrangement was then agreed with the modifications.'

If one turns over one finds the modifications are four matters which I need not read in
detail. One of them, in fact, was that the terms of the arrangement were to be extended
to five years with minimum monthly payments in year five of £500 per month, amending   E
the original provision that it was to run for four years. Then there are set out the proxies
held in favour, with the Halifax Building Society in at the sum of £203,594.13 and four
other much smaller sums for other creditors, those all totalling £226,898.77 including the
Halifax, and voting against Alltime at £32,911.61, giving a total of voting debt of
£259,810.38.

The debtor in an affidavit sworn by him confirmed Mr Bradshaw's affidavit so far as   F
the account of the meeting on 4 October is concerned. Mr Springall's affidavit does not
contain much information on the happenings at the meeting. What he does say is this:

'10. Further, in the creditors' meeting, whilst the chairman permitted all future
liabilities arising under the lease to be included in the voluntary arrangement, he
would not allow the applicant, as creditor, the value of this future liability for
voting purposes.'

The applicant, of course, is Alltime.   G

'11. The chairman only allowed the value for voting purposes in the sum of
£32,911.61 being the sum owing at the date of the meeting and consisting of arrears
of rent, interest and allowable costs for past legal actions. However, this sum was
marked as being objected to, and I verily believe that there were no grounds for
doing so.'

That objection concerned some question concerning the validity of the rent review   H
process, but that matter has not been pursued before me and is not relevant to anything
I have to decide. The only significant factual difference between Mr Springall on the one
hand and Mr Bradshaw and the debtor on the other is that Mr Springall claims that Mr
Bradshaw would not allow Alltime the value for voting purposes of the future liability
for rent under the lease. That is a very abbreviated statement of the situation as explained

A   somewhat more fully by Mr Bradshaw and corroborated by the debtor that Mr Bradshaw was prepared to accept one year's future rent as the value for future rent payments but was not prepared to accept what Mr Springall for Alltime was asking for as the appropriate value, namely all the rent at the current amount payable down to the end of the contractual term.

B   I see no reason not to accept Mr Bradshaw's version of the events as a matter of fact, and I conclude that Mr Bradshaw accepted and acted on the basis that the arrangement being proposed by the debtor was one in which the future rent liability under the lease was to be included in the arrangement and offered to Mr Springall to value it at a minimum value of one year's rent, £13,830, for voting purposes. This was rejected by Mr Springall, who appreciated perfectly well that it was proposed to include future rent liability in the arrangement and on that basis wished Alltime's debt for voting purposes to include not only the accrued liability for rent and interest up to the date of the meeting

C   at £32,911.61 but also the aggregate of rent prospectively payable until the end of the contractual term of the lease, disregarding possible upward rent reviews.

There was no agreement between Mr Springall, for Alltime, and Mr Bradshaw upon the value for voting purposes of Alltime's right to future rent, and no vote in respect of it was in fact cast. Upon the figures it is clear that if Mr Springall's proposed valuation of Alltime's right to future rent had been accepted it would have had, together with its rights

D   to accrued rent and interest, significantly over 25 per cent by value of the vote at the meeting. Conversely, if Mr Bradshaw's offer to value it at one year's rent had been acted upon it would have had significantly less than 25 per cent by value of the votes.

I turn to the relevant legislation. Section 253(1) of the 1986 Act defines a voluntary arrangement. That means:

E   'Application to the court for an interim order may be made where the debtor intends to make a proposal to his creditors for a composition in satisfaction of his debts or a scheme of arrangement of his affairs (from here on referred to, in either case, as a "voluntary arrangement").'

I need not refer to the various provisions regarding interim orders since one was made and no issue arises concerning it. Section 257 reads as follows, under the heading

F   'Summoning of creditors' meeting':

'(1) Where it has been reported to the court under section 256 that a meeting of the debtor's creditors should be summoned, the nominee (or his replacement under section 256(3)(a)) shall, unless the court otherwise directs, summon that meeting for the time, date and place proposed in his report.

G   (2) The persons to be summoned to the meeting are every creditor of the debtor of whose claim and address the person summoning the meeting is aware.'

I need not read (3), which only applies where the debtor is an undischarged bankrupt. Then s. 258, so far as relevant, provides as follows:

'(1) A creditors' meeting summoned under section 257 shall decide whether to approve the proposed voluntary arrangement.

H   (2) The meeting may approve the proposed voluntary arrangement with modifications, but shall not do so unless the debtor consents to each modification.

(3) The modifications subject to which the proposed voluntary arrangement may be approved may include one conferring the functions proposed to be conferred on the nominee on another person qualified to act as an insolvency practitioner in relation to the debtor.'

A

That, in fact, happened but nothing turns on it.

'(4) The meeting shall not approve any proposal or modification which affects the right of a secured creditor of the debtor to enforce his security, except with the concurrence of the debtor of the creditor concerned.

(5) Subject as follows, the meeting shall not approve any proposal or modification under which–

B

(a) any preferential debt of the debtor is to be paid otherwise than in priority to such of his debts as are not preferential debts, or

(b) a preferential creditor of the debtor is to be paid an amount in respect of a preferential debt that bears to that debt a smaller proportion than is borne to another preferential debt by the amount that is to be paid in respect of that other debt.

. . .

C

(6) Subject as above, the meeting shall be conducted in accordance with the rules.'

That is, of course, a reference to the Insolvency Rules. Then s. 260 reads:

'(1) This section has effect where the meeting summoned under section 257 approves the proposed voluntary arrangement (with or without modifications).

(2) The approved arrangement–

D

(a) takes effect as if made by the debtor at the meeting, and

(b) binds every person who in accordance with the rules had notice of, and was entitled to vote at, the meeting (whether or not he was present or represented at it) as if he were a party to the arrangement.'

It was not disputed that a person not entitled to vote at a meeting in respect of a debt to him is not bound as regards that debt by an approved arrangement. That is the clear effect of s. 262(b). Equally, it was not contended that where, as here, there was a creditor entitled to vote in respect of one debt he thereby was bound by an approved arrangement in respect of a different debt if he was not entitled to vote in respect of that different debt. So Alltime's entitlement to vote in respect of its accrued rents to £32,911.61 did not by itself cause the approved arrangement to bind Alltime in respect of future rent claims.

E

Section 262 makes provision for applications to be made to the court by persons entitled to vote at a creditors' meeting on the basis that the arrangement unfairly prejudices a creditor of the debtor or that there has been some material irregularity at the meeting. I am not at this stage dealing with any such question.

F

Finally in the Act I should refer to the definitions in Pt. IX which apply inter alia to Pt. VIII of the Act, which deals with individual voluntary arrangements. In s. 385(1) debt is defined in the following terms:

' "Debt", is to be construed in accordance with section 382(3).'

G

One turns to that, where one finds:

'For the purposes of references in this Group of Parts to a debt or liability, it is immaterial whether the debt or liability is present or future, whether it is certain or contingent or whether its amount is fixed or liquidated, or is capable of being ascertained by fixed rules or as a matter of opinion; and references in this Group of Parts to owing a debt have to be read accordingly.'

H

Section 383(1) contains a definition of creditor which is not effective in relation to a person involved in a voluntary arrangement. It reads as follows:

' "Creditor" –

(a) in relation to a bankrupt, means a person to whom any of the bankruptcy debts is owed . . .

A   (b) in relation to an individual to whom a bankruptcy petition relates, means a person who would be a creditor in the bankruptcy if a bankruptcy order were made on that petition.'

Paragraph (a) only refers to bankrupts and the debtor, of course, is not and has not at any material time been a bankrupt, and (b) is aimed at bankruptcy petitions which would only accidentally be a feature of an individual voluntary arrangement. Nevertheless, in

B my view the term 'creditor' needs to be understood in the light of the definition of 'debt' as a person entitled to the benefit of a debt as thus defined and therefore does, in my judgment, include a contingent creditor.

Section 436 provides that the word 'modifications' includes additions, alterations and omissions.

I turn now to the relevant Insolvency Rules. Rule 5.3(2) governs what is to be included

C in a proposal for an individual voluntary arrangement. I need only mention para. (c), which reads, in conjunction with the beginning of the subrule:

'(2) The following matters shall be stated, or otherwise dealt with, in the proposal –

. . .

D   (c) the nature and amount of the debtor's liabilities (so far as within his immediate knowledge), the manner in which they are proposed to be met, modified, postponed or otherwise dealt with by means of the arrangement . . .'

Then there are various matters that are required to be dealt with in particular, which I need not read in detail.

E Rule 5.17 is the rule that deals with entitlement to vote. That, so far as material, reads as follows:

'(1) Subject as follows, every creditor who was given notice of the creditors' meeting is entitled to vote at the meeting or any adjournment of it.

(2) In Case 1, votes are calculated according to the amount of the creditor's debt as at the date of the bankruptcy order,' – that is not relevant – 'and in Case 2,

F according to the amount of the debt as at the date of the meeting.'

Paragraph (3) is of critical importance:

'(3) A creditor shall not vote in respect of a debt for an unliquidated amount, or any debt whose value is not ascertained, except where the chairman agrees to put upon the debt an estimated minimum value for the purpose of entitlement to vote.

G (4) The chairman has power to admit or reject a creditor's claim for the purpose of his entitlement to vote, and the power is exercisable with respect to the whole or any part of the claim.

(5) The chairman's decision on entitlement to vote is subject to appeal to the court by any creditor, or by the debtor.

(6) If the chairman is in doubt whether a claim should be admitted or rejected, he

H shall mark it as objected to and allow the creditor to vote, subject to his vote being subsequently declared invalid if the objection to the claim is sustained.'

I need not read the rest of that rule.

The District Judge's decision is recorded in a note which I am told the District Judge himself took. The relevant parts are as follows. He notes the affidavits that he has read, which include the ones to which I have made reference, and then his notes read as follows:

'A primary point. Declaration under para. 1 of amended application matter of A construction of cl. 12 of the arrangement in terms of lease. Was it intended to include future rent in arrangement?'

Then he deals with the question about the identity between the debtor and the trade name that he used in the lease, and nothing turns on that. He says:

'It is also clear from correspondence that chairman did not appreciate the nature B of the debtor's liability under the terms of the lease.'

That is a reference, I take it, to Mr Bradshaw's letter (which I have read an extract from) that he wrote to Alltime's solicitors before the second meeting. Going on with the District Judge's note:

'Contents of the original proposal not clear: no reference to debtor's continuing liability under the terms of the lease: merely an implication of liability under a guarantee in cl. 12 of the arrangement. I am concerned that the extent of his C liability would not have been at all clear to other creditors.'

Then he goes into the requirements of the Insolvency Rules (r. 5.3(2)(c) of which I have read) which require details of liabilities to be given. Then he comes to what I take to be the central part of his decision, when his notes read:

'I cannot see how a future debt, particularly where the exact amount is unliquidated, can be included in a voluntary arrangement unless there is clear D agreement between the debtor and the creditor that this shall be so. There is no evidence that this is the case here.'

Accordingly he granted the declaration which he did, namely that the future rent liability was not within the terms of the voluntary arrangement.

Miss Tipples for Alltime submitted that the proposal that was presented for approval to the creditors on its true construction only included the accrued debt and not any future E liability to rent. She pointed to the fact that the schedule of creditors, which I have read extracts from, only mentioned the accrued liability and did not mention at all any future liability to rent, and that of course is right. As I have already said, I accept the submission that the original proposal did not on its true construction include amongst the liabilities which were included in the proposed arrangement future liability to rent under the lease as opposed to contingent liability under cl. 5 of the lease. There is provision for the amendment of the debtor's proposal under r. 5.3(3) of the Insolvency Rules with the F agreement in writing of the nominee at any time up to the delivery of the nominee's report to the court under s. 256, but there is no evidence that this occurred, nor was it suggested in argument that it had.

This, however, leaves the possibility of an amendment or modification at the creditors' meeting. In relation to that Miss Tipples submitted that the parties at that meeting on 4 October 1993 were not agreed, in that there was no intention on Alltime's part for future G rent liability under the lease to be included, save on terms that Alltime should be allowed to vote on the whole of the rent during the remainder of the contractual term of the lease and, as Miss Tipples put it, Alltime was not allowed to vote at all in respect of future rent liability.

As against that submission, Mr Zacaroli for the debtor submitted that agreement with a dissenting creditor, as Alltime clearly was, is not necessary, nor is it relevant to the H question whether there is an effective modification of the proposed voluntary arrangement. In answer to a suggestion which I made that perhaps the test for seeing whether a proposal with certain stated modifications should be treated as containing other modifications not included among the written modifications was whether it would be possible to satisfy the requirements that apply for written documents to be rectified, namely a continuing common intention down to the date of the written document that

A the modification thus omitted from the written modification should be included (compare *Joscelyne v Nissen & Anor* [1970] 2 QB 86), Mr Zacaroli submitted that what needed to be shown was a common understanding of what the terms of the proposed arrangement being submitted for the creditors' approval really were. So, if it was clearly understood that the proposal which the debtor was submitting for the creditors' approval included future liability for rent under the lease and the requisite majority approved the proposal with that knowledge, it would not be right to limit the voluntary arrangement to the

B written proposal and the written modifications since they did not state what all parties knew was being offered and what the assenting creditors were accepting.

I prefer this latter analysis, and in particular I do not accept that any form of contractual agreement between the debtor and a dissenting creditor is relevant or requisite to enable a modification not reduced to writing but understood by all those present at or represented at a meeting which approves a voluntary arrangement to be

C validly incorporated within it. There must, as I see it, be a power to remedy accidental omissions in preparing the documentation.

At the meeting of 4 October it is clear that Mr Bradshaw, who held proxies from five creditors other than Alltime, understood that what was proposed was that the future rent payments under the lease should be within the arrangement. It is also clear that Mr Springall from Alltime understood that too, otherwise he would not have asked to be

D allowed to vote in respect of the total value of the rent payments until the end of the contractual term, as he accepts that he did. In these circumstances it seems to me right that, although the inclusion of the future payments of rent under the lease constituted a modification within the meaning given to that word by s. 436 of the Act, as Mr Zacaroli accepted, and was not included under the formal written modifications set out in Mr Bradshaw's report, nevertheless it did form part of the arrangement which was agreed to at the meeting. None of the qualifications contained in s. 258 to the power to approve the

E proposed voluntary arrangement with modifications was infringed, the debtor consented and no secured or preferential creditor was suggested to have been affected.

My conclusion is contrary to the view that District Judge Hollis took when he said that there was no evidence that there was a clear agreement between the debtor and his creditor that this should be so. What matters is that there should be clear evidence that the debtor's proposal, upon which the creditors are to vote, provides for the debt in

F question to be included. Mr Bradshaw's evidence, in my judgment, did satisfy that requirement.

Miss Tipples' second submission was that future rent under a lease was, as a matter of law, incapable of being included in a voluntary arrangement. This submission was made on the basis of what His Honour Judge Cooke said in *Burford Midland Properties Ltd v Marley Extrusions Ltd & Ors* [1994] BCC 604. The issue there was whether the terms of

G a voluntary arrangement which had elaborate provisions defining such expressions as 'unascertained liabilities', 'ascertained liabilities' and 'liabilities' was apt to include future payments of rent under a lease. Judge Cooke was not concerned with the question of whether it was legally permissible or possible to include such payments within a voluntary arrangement, but rather whether it had in fact been done, although it is to be observed that, had it been a legal impossibility, the questions of construction debated at some

H considerable length in his judgment could have been omitted. For it to be established that it is not possible to include future payments of rent under a lease, it would in my view have to be shown that the expression in s. 253(1) 'a scheme of arrangement of his affairs' was not wide enough to comprehend the liability to make such future payments. That is not a subject addressed by Judge Cooke in the *Burford Midland Properties* case, and I derive no assistance from it on what I have to decide. No other authority was cited in favour of the proposition that it is legally impossible to include liabilities to make

future payments of rent under an existing lease in a voluntary arrangement and I do not
feel able to accept such a proposition.

The third and last issue raised is the most difficult. Miss Tipples submitted that no
value was placed upon the right to receive future payments of rent under the lease,
Alltime was not empowered to vote in respect thereof and was therefore not bound by
the voluntary arrangement in respect of that right. It was not disputed that, subject to
questions of unfair prejudice and material irregularity with which I am not dealing at this
stage, Alltime was bound by the arrangement in relation to the accrued debt of rent and
interest down to the date of the meeting. I record that Mr Zacaroli accepted that it was
desirable that this issue should be determined at this stage since it was likely it would
have to be decided in any event, and I take no time therefore in considering whether it
strictly arises on the notice of application which is before me. Miss Tipples included the
submission in her argument and naturally raised no objection to my dealing with it.

I have quoted s. 262(b) above and need not repeat it. It is common ground that a
person not entitled to vote at a meeting in respect of a liability owed to him is not bound
by a voluntary arrangement in relation to that liability. The issue therefore turns on
r. 5.17, which I have also set out. It is common ground that the relevant paragraph as
regards entitlement to vote is r. 5.17(3), which I have already read but repeat:

'A creditor shall not vote in respect of a debt for an unliquidated amount, or any
debt whose value is not ascertained, except where the chairman agrees to put upon
the debt an estimated minimum value for the purpose of entitlement to vote.'

Miss Tipples submitted that agreement was not reached between Mr Bradshaw and
Mr Springall on the minimum value to be put on Alltime's right and that therefore the
exception to the general rule that a creditor should not be entitled to vote on a debt for
an unliquidated amount or a debt of unascertained value was inapplicable and the general
rule applied, so that Alltime was not entitled to vote upon it and by the same token was
not bound in respect of it by the voluntary arrangement. Miss Tipples relied upon the
decision of Ferris J in *Re Cranley Mansions Ltd* [1994] BCC 576. I take the facts from the
headnote:

'This was an application by a creditor, "S", of Cranley Mansions Ltd ("the
company") seeking an order under s. 6 of the Insolvency Act 1986 revoking or
suspending the approval of a company voluntary arrangement in respect of the
company; alternatively, equivalent relief was sought by way of appeal under
r. 1.17(5) of the Insolvency Rules 1986.

The company held the freehold of a property containing long-leasehold flats. The
shareholders were the leaseholders including S. In 1988 the company decided to
undertake a programme of major works. S wished to carry out some alterations to
her flat. Both sets of work were carried out by the same contractors under a single
building contract. S complained of poor workmanship and refused to pay her
share of the cost. The company in turn failed to pay the contractor. The company
started legal proceedings against S who claimed damages against the company in
respect of defects. The contractor started proceedings against the company. The
actions were consolidated with S as plaintiff.

In 1993 the directors of the company realised that as a result of the building
contract and legal proceedings, the company had become insolvent. An insolvency
practitioner, 'G', devised a proposal to be put to the company's creditors for a
company voluntary arrangement under Pt. I of the Insolvency Act 1986. The
statement of affairs set out the company's unsecured creditors which included the
sum of £1 in respect of S's 'unliquidated and unascertained contingent claim'
against the company in the building proceedings.

A S's claim had been lodged in the sum of £900,000 but at the meeting G, as chairman, considered that as the value of the debt was not ascertained it was proper for him to place an estimated minimum value of £1 on the debt for voting purposes under r. 1.17(3) of the Insolvency Rules. The voluntary arrangement was approved. If S's vote against the arrangement had been valued at anything over about £1,700 the proposal would have been defeated.'

B The letters used in the headnote refer to Mrs Saigol for 'S' and Mr Goldstein for 'G', who was the chairman of the meeting. The nature of Mrs Saigol's claim against the company appears in slightly more detail at p. 580F of the report, where Ferris J said:

'Mrs Saigol's primary claim was for damages against all the defendants. The statement of claim made no attempt to apportion to particular defendants the loss and damage alleged. The main heads of loss and damage claimed were as follows:

C
 (1) loss of value of Mrs Saigol's apartment by reason of Mrs Saigol's inability to sell it or to pay the money due to Dunbar Bank, resulting in its repossession and sale by Dunbar Bank;

 (2) diminution in the value of the apartment by reason of defective building works; and

 (3) the cost of remedying the defective work to the apartment.'

D It is to be noted, of course, that this was a case which was concerned with a company voluntary arrangement and therefore with r. 1.17 of the Insolvency Rules, but there is no material difference between that rule and the rule with which I am concerned, r. 5.17, dealing with individual voluntary arrangements, and it was not suggested before me that what Ferris J said in relation to company voluntary arrangements was not equally applicable in principle to individual voluntary arrangements.

E Ferris J dealt with the question whether there was a material irregularity in the conduct of the meeting and held that there was (at p. 593) in that Mrs Saigol's vote was admitted in respect of £1 whereas she was precluded from voting by the opening words of r. 1.17(3), the exception to the general prohibition not being applicable because no estimated minimum value had been put upon her debt in accordance with the requirements of the latter part of the subrule.

F Although in that conclusion it is not in terms stated that the necessity for agreement in the process of putting an estimated minimum value on the debt was not satisfied, it is quite clear from the earlier passage in the report that this is what tipped the scale in Ferris J's view. The relevant arguments on either side are recorded at p. 591E:

'On behalf of Mrs Saigol, Miss Agnello pointed out that r. 1.17(3) imposes a prohibition upon voting by a creditor in Mrs Saigol's position unless a particular exception applies. Moreover the wording of that exception begins:

G
"except where the chairman agrees to put upon the debt an estimated minimum value . . ."

If it had been intended that the chairman should be entitled to act unilaterally the rule would surely have said:

"except where the chairman puts upon the debt an estimated minimum value . . ."

H
While the word "agrees" does not necessarily import a requirement for an offer followed by acceptance and supported by consideration, so as to give rise to a contract (cf. *Re Nuneaton Borough Association Football Club Ltd* (1989) 5 BCC 377), Miss Agnello argued that it does require an element of bilateral consensus.

Miss Stokes on behalf of the company and Mr Green on behalf of Mr Goldstein argued against this. They relied upon one of the dictionary definitions of "agree",

namely "To accede, consent to, grant". I do not think that this helps them. Both   A
"accede" and "consent to" imply a bilateral element, in that something proposed
by one party is being assented to by another. As to "grant", I find it somewhat
difficult to see how agreeing to put a value on a debt involves anything which can
be regarded as equivalent to a grant, and even a grant in the form of a voluntary
gift requires acceptance by the grantee before it is complete.'

I pass over a reference to an argument that the judge did not accept and to a case   B
which he did not find helpful, and continue at p. 592 of Ferris J's judgment:

'Both Miss Stokes and Mr Green pointed out that unless the chairman is entitled
to put a value upon the claim of a creditor which is unliquidated or unascertained
without regard to the wishes of that creditor, the utility of the statutory provisions
in respect of corporate voluntary arrangements (and, indeed, individual voluntary
arrangements and other matters to be decided at meetings governed by rules as to   C
voting equivalent to r. 1.17) would be greatly reduced. If the creditor is not entitled
to vote in respect of such a claim without a value being put upon the claim under
r. 1.17(3) or its equivalent (which is a matter to be considered in a moment) a
disaffected creditor could stultify proposals for a voluntary arrangement by the
simple expedient of failing to concur in a value being put on his claim. The
arrangement might then be approved by the requisite majorities of those entitled
to vote on it, but it would not be binding on the disaffected creditor. In most, if   D
not all, cases there will be no point in having an arrangement which is not binding
upon all creditors.

I see the force of this submission, which causes me some anxiety because my
decision is likely to affect many other cases. Nevertheless I cannot escape the fact
that the relevant words of r. 1.17(3) are "where the chairman agrees to put upon
the debt an estimated minimum value", not "where the chairman puts upon the   E
debt an estimated minimum value". Moreover I think it would be perverse to say
that the requirement imported by the word "agrees" can be satisfied by an
agreement between the chairman and someone other than the creditor, such as the
company, as was suggested in argument. In my judgment "agrees" requires some
element of bilateral concurrence between the chairman and the creditor in question.
If the creditor puts forward an estimated minimum value without prejudice to a   F
contention that his real claim is much larger and if the chairman accepts this, the
words of the rule would, in my view, clearly be satisfied notwithstanding that there
is nothing in the nature of a contract between the chairman and the creditor. The
same would be the case if the chairman took the initiative in suggesting a value
and the creditor concurred in this suggestion for the purpose of r. 1.17(3), although
not for the purpose of limiting the claim. The matter would be more difficult if the
chairman put forward a value for the purpose of r. 1.17(3) and the creditor rejected   G
this for all purposes but nevertheless insisted upon voting. The outcome would, in
my view, then depend upon an evaluation of precisely what was said and done.'

The judge at p. 593 reached the conclusion that I have already referred to. The judge
did, in my view, clearly regard some form of bilateral concurrence between the chairman
and the creditor as essential and that was a link in his reasoning. Mr Zacaroli invited me
not to follow that decision and advanced a different argument from that which appears   H
to have been advanced before Ferris J, namely that what the subrule requires is the
chairman's agreement to put a minimum value and not an agreement upon or in relation
to the minimum value. He submitted that an agreement by the chairman to put a value
was satisfied on 4 October by Mr Bradshaw's expression of willingness to put a value of
£13,830, one year's rent, upon the debt. The fact that that was not acceptable to Mr
Springall does not detract from the effect of Mr Bradshaw's willingness to put a minimum

A value. In support of that construction Mr Zacaroli pointed out that the appeal machinery in r. 5.17(5), which applies to subr. (3) just as much as to subr. (4), would be rendered effectively nugatory since it would only be if there was agreement that a minimum value could be placed upon the debt, and, if there was agreement, it is difficult to see how there could be an effective appeal. It is apparent that Ferris J himself was caused anxiety by what he took to be the inescapable requirement of bilateral concurrence between the creditor and the chairman, and I respectfully share that anxiety. I should, of course,

B normally follow what one of my brethren in this division had previously held but I am not bound to do so, and in the light of the argument addressed to me by Mr Zacaroli, which was not, so far as I could see, addressed to Ferris J, I have reached the conclusion that the only agreement that subr. 5.17(3) requires is an expressed willingness by the chairman to put an estimated minimum value on the debt in question. If the subrule is thus interpreted it avoids the undesirable result that the relevant creditor can avoid the

C consequence of being in a minority of 25 per cent or less and be bound by the 75 per cent or more majority by the simple expedient of refusing to agree any minimum value for any purpose, and it gives the appeal procedure a proper field within which to operate.

I should add that I am not suggesting that *Re Cranley Mansions* was wrongly decided, since it is clear from what Ferris J held regarding the chairman's valuation at £1, namely that it was, to say the least, deeply suspect (see p. 591) and that he, the chairman, made no real attempt to value Mrs Saigol's claim or even to arrive at a minimum value for that

D claim (see p. 590). Such conduct on the part of the chairman would, in my view, fall a long way short of agreeing to put a minimum value on the claim, because the £1 value was not a genuine exercise of his powers and should in those circumstances be disregarded.

In the case before me I am satisfied on the facts that what Mr Bradshaw did amounted to expressing a willingness to put a minimum value on Alltime's claim and on that basis

E I consider that the exception to r. 5.17(3) does apply and for those reasons I propose to allow this appeal.

(Order accordingly)

F

G

H

CASES CITED

This table lists alphabetically all cases referred to in judgments of the courts reported in British Company Cases in 1994. References are to the first page of the relevant case.

LEGISLATION FINDING LIST

The following Legislation Finding List covers all cases reported in British Company Cases 1994. References to legislative provisions are to section numbers unless otherwise stated. References are to the first page of the relevant case.

TOPICAL INDEX

References are to the first page of the relevant case.